WORLD
CIVILIZATIONS

Educational Advisory Panel

The following educators provided ongoing review during the development of prototypes and key elements of this program.

Contents

HISTORY® Partnership xviii

Reading Social Studies H2

Using This Book H6

Module 1

Uncovering the Past, 450 BC–Present 2

Reading Social Studies Specialized Vocabulary of History 4

Lesson 1 Studying History 6
Lesson 2 Studying Geography 12
Lesson 3 Studying Economics 22
Lesson 4 Studying Civics 30

Social Studies Skills Make Maps 35
Module Assessment 36

Module 2

The Stone Ages and Early Cultures,
5 million BC–5000 BC 38

Reading Social Studies Chronological Order 40

Lesson 1 The First People 42
Lesson 2 Early Human Migration 50
Lesson 3 Beginnings of Agriculture 55

Social Studies Skills Identify Central Issues 59
Module Assessment 60

Module 3

The Fertile Crescent, Mesopotamia,
and the Persian Empire, 7000–480 BC 62

Reading Social Studies Main Ideas in Social Studies 64
Lesson 1 Geography of the Fertile Crescent 66
Lesson 2 The Sumerians 72
Lesson 3 Military Empires 82
Lesson 4 The Phoenicians 87
Lesson 5 The Persian Empire 91

Social Studies Skills Interpret Physical Maps 97
Module Assessment 98

Module 4

Kingdoms of the Nile, 4500 BC–AD 400 100

Reading Social Studies Causes and Effects in History 102
Lesson 1 Geography and Early Egypt 104
Lesson 2 The Old Kingdom 110
Lesson 3 The Middle and New Kingdoms 117
Lesson 4 Egyptian Achievements 123
Lesson 5 Kush and Aksum 129

Social Studies Skills Assess Primary and Secondary Sources 137
Module Assessment 138

Module 5

🌐

Ancient India, 2500 BC–AD 500 140

Reading Social Studies Inferences about History 142

Lesson 1　Geography and Early India 144
Lesson 2　Vedic Society 149
Lesson 3　Origins of Hinduism 155
Lesson 4　Origins of Buddhism 160
Lesson 5　Indian Empires 167
Lesson 6　Indian Achievements 172

Social Studies Skills Interpret Diagrams 177
Module Assessment 178

Module 6

🌐

Ancient China, 1600 BC–AD 1 180

Reading Social Studies Summarize Historical Texts 182

Lesson 1　Geography and Early China 184
Lesson 2　The Zhou Dynasty and New Ideas 192
Lesson 3　The Qin Dynasty 200
Lesson 4　The Han Dynasty 206
Lesson 5　The Silk Road 216

Social Studies Skills Conduct Internet Research 219
Module Assessment 222

HISTORY **Multimedia Connections**
China and the Great Wall 223 MC1

Module 7

The Hebrews and Judaism, 2000 BC–AD 70 224

Reading Social Studies Facts and Opinions about the Past 226

Lesson 1 The Early Hebrews 228
Lesson 2 Jewish Beliefs and Texts 236
Lesson 3 Judaism over the Centuries 242

Social Studies Skills Identify Short- and Long-Term Effects 249
Module Assessment 250

Module 8

Ancient Greece, 2000–330 BC 252

Reading Social Studies Preview Text 254

Lesson 1 Geography and the Early Greeks 256
Lesson 2 The Glory of Athens 264
Lesson 3 Athens and Sparta 272
Lesson 4 Greek Mythology and Literature 280
Lesson 5 Greek Art, Philosophy, and Science 292

Social Studies Skills Analyze Costs and Benefits 299
Module Assessment 300

Multimedia Connections
Ancient Greece 301 MC1

Module 9

The Hellenistic World, 330–30 BC 302

Reading Social Studies
Compare and Contrast Historical Facts 304

Lesson 1 Alexander the Great 306
Lesson 2 The Hellenistic Kingdoms 311
Lesson 3 Hellenistic Achievements 316

Social Studies Skills Interpret Charts 321
Module Assessment 322

Module 10

🌐

Ancient Rome, 753 BC–AD 476 324

Reading Social Studies Create an Outline........................ 326

Lesson 1   Geography and the Rise of Rome 328
Lesson 2   The Roman Republic.......................... 336
Lesson 3   From Republic to Empire 346
Lesson 4   A Vast Empire............................... 354
Lesson 5   The Fall of Rome 364
Lesson 6   Rome's Legacy 371

Social Studies Skills Interpret Globes..................... 377
Module Assessment 378

Multimedia Connections
Rome: Engineering an Empire 379 MC1

Module 11

🌐

The Growth of Christianity, AD 1–400 380

Reading Social Studies Ask Questions 382

Lesson 1   Religion in the Roman Empire 384
Lesson 2   Origins of Christianity 388
Lesson 3   The Spread of Christianity................... 396
Lesson 4   The Early Christian World.................... 400

Social Studies Skills Continuity and Change in History 403
Module Assessment 404

Module 12

🌐

Civilizations of Eastern Europe, AD 300–1480 406

Reading Social Studies Stereotypes and Bias in History 408

Lesson 1 The Geography of Eastern Europe. 410
Lesson 2 The Byzantine Empire 415
Lesson 3 Early Russia 420

Social Studies Skills Chance, Error, and Oversight in History 425
Module Assessment 426

Module 13

🌐

The Rise of Islam, AD 550–900 428

Reading Social Studies Descriptive Text. .430

Lesson 1 Geography and Life in Arabia .432
Lesson 2 Origins of Islam 437
Lesson 3 Expansion of Islam 448
Lesson 4 Muslim Cultural Achievements 456

Social Studies Skills Interpret Timelines .463
Module Assessment 464

Module 14

🌐

Early African Civilizations, 500 BC–AD 1600 466

Reading Social Studies Organization of Facts and Information 468

Lesson 1 Geography and Early Africa 470
Lesson 2 The Empire of Ghana 480
Lesson 3 The Empires of Mali and Songhai 488
Lesson 4 Historical and Artistic Traditions of West Africa. 498
Lesson 5 Sub-Saharan Cultures. 506

Social Studies Skills Make Decisions. 511
Module Assessment 512

Module 15

🌐

Later Chinese Dynasties, 589–1644 514

Reading Social Studies Draw Conclusions about the Past 516

Lesson 1 China Reunifies 518
Lesson 2 Tang and Song Achievements 523
Lesson 3 Confucianism and Government 530
Lesson 4 The Yuan and Ming Dynasties 534
Lesson 5 China and Its Neighbors 544

Social Studies Skills Determine the Context of Statements 551
Module Assessment 552

Module 16

🌐

Japan, 550–1868 554

Reading Social Studies Main Ideas and Their Support 556

Lesson 1 Geography and Early Japan 558
Lesson 2 Art and Culture in Heian 566
Lesson 3 Growth of a Military Society 572

Social Studies Skills Solve Problems 579
Module Assessment 580

Ⓗ **Multimedia Connections**
HISTORY Japan and the Samurai Warrior 581 MC1

Module 17

Cultures of South and Southwest Asia,
1299–1857 582

Reading Social Studies Ask Questions to Make Predictions 584

Lesson 1   The Ottoman Empire 586
Lesson 2   Safavid Persia. 591
Lesson 3   Sikhism in South Asia. 595
Lesson 4   The Mughal Empire. 600

Social Studies Skills Visualize Social Studies Texts 605
Module Assessment 606

Module 18

The Early Americas, 12,000 BC–AD 1537 608

Reading Social Studies Analyze Historical Information 610

Lesson 1   Geography and Early Cultures 612
Lesson 2   The Mayas 619
Lesson 3   The Aztec Empire. 630
Lesson 4   The Inca Empire 640
Lesson 5   North American Cultures 650

Social Studies Skills Interpret Culture Maps. .657
Module Assessment 658

Multimedia Connections
HISTORY The Maya 659 MC1

Module 19

The Middle Ages, 500–1500

The Middle Ages, 500–1500 660

Reading Social Studies Evaluate Sources 662

Lesson 1   Europe after the Fall of Rome 664
Lesson 2   Feudalism, Manors, and Towns 673
Lesson 3   Popes and Kings 680
Lesson 4   The Crusades 685
Lesson 5   Christianity and Medieval Society 691
Lesson 6   Political and Social Change 698

Social Studies Skills Develop and Interpret Models 707
Module Assessment 710

Multimedia Connections
HISTORY The Crusades: The Crescent & the Cross 711 MC1

Module 20

The Renaissance, 1271–1600

The Renaissance, 1271–1600 712

Reading Social Studies Greek and Latin Word Roots 714

Lesson 1   Origins of the Renaissance 716
Lesson 2   The Italian Renaissance 722
Lesson 3   The Renaissance Beyond Italy 732

Social Studies Skills Speak and Listen 739
Module Assessment 742

Module 21

The Reformation, 1492–1650

The Reformation, 1492–1650 744

Reading Social Studies Online Research 746

Lesson 1   The Protestant Reformation 748
Lesson 2   The Catholic Reformation 755
Lesson 3   Effects of the Reformation 760

Social Studies Skills Develop Graphs 765
Module Assessment 766

Module 22

The Scientific Revolution, 1525–1725 768

Reading Social Studies Recognize Fallacies in Reasoning 770

Lesson 1 A New View of the World............................ 772
Lesson 2 Discoveries and Inventions 776
Lesson 3 Science and Society 782

Social Studies Skills Analyze Tables 789
Module Assessment 790

Module 23

The Age of Exploration, 1400–1650 792

Reading Social Studies Vocabulary Clues 794

Lesson 1 Great Voyages of Discovery........................ 796
Lesson 2 The Columbian Exchange......................... 806
Lesson 3 Origins of Capitalism 812

Social Studies Skills Identify Print Research Sources 819
Module Assessment 820

Multimedia Connections
Ponce de León 821 MC1

Module 24

Enlightenment and Revolution, 1642–1831 822

Reading Social Studies Points of View in Historical Texts 824

Lesson 1 Ideas of the Enlightenment 826
Lesson 2 New Views on Government 830
Lesson 3 The Age of Revolution........................... 837
Lesson 4 The Spread of Revolutionary Ideals 844

Social Studies Skills Accept Social Responsibility 851
Module Assessment 852

Multimedia Connections
The American Revolution........................... 853 MC1

Module 25

🌐

Industry and Imperialism, 1750–1900 854

Reading Social Studies Compare Historical Texts 856

Lesson 1 The Industrial Revolution 858
Lesson 2 Imperialism in Africa 863
Lesson 3 Europeans and Americans in Asia and the Pacific 870
Lesson 4 The Spanish-American War 876

Social Studies Skills Create and Interpret Databases 881
Module Assessment 882

Module 26

🌐

Nationalism and World War I, 1860–1941 884

Reading Social Studies Public Documents in History 886

Lesson 1 Nationalism in Europe 888
Lesson 2 World War I 891
Lesson 3 Results of the War 897
Lesson 4 The Russian Revolution 901
Lesson 5 The Great Depression 905

Social Studies Skills Use Visual Resources 911
Module Assessment 912

Multimedia Connections
HISTORY Dear Home: Letters from WW I 913 MC1

Module 27

🌐

World War II, 1922–1945 914

Reading Social Studies Information and Propaganda. 916

Lesson 1   The Rise of Dictators 918
Lesson 2   World War II 924
Lesson 3   The Holocaust 934
Lesson 4   Results of World War II 941

Social Studies Skills Construct Timelines 947
Module Assessment 948

Multimedia Connections
Memories of World War II 949 MC1

Module 28

🌐

The Cold War Years, 1945–1991 950

Reading Social Studies Set a Purpose for Reading 952

Lesson 1   The Cold War Begins 954
Lesson 2   Cold War Conflicts 961
Lesson 3   Changes in Strategy 969
Lesson 4   The Breakup of the Soviet Union 973

Social Studies Skills Use Supporting Evidence 979
Module Assessment 980

Multimedia Connections
October Fury: The Cuban Missile Crisis 981 MC1

Module 29

🌐

The Postwar World, 1945–Present 982

Reading Social Studies Review Texts 984

Lesson 1   Nationalist Movements in Asia. .986
Lesson 2   A New Asia 993
Lesson 3   Independence Movements in Africa. 1000
Lesson 4   Africa Since Independence. 1006
Lesson 5   Conflict in the Middle East. 1014
Lesson 6   Latin America Since 1945 1021

Social Studies Skills Determine the Strength of an Argument 1027
Module Assessment 1028

Module 30

🌐

Contemporary Issues, 2000–Present. 1030

Reading Social Studies Categorize 1032

Lesson 1   Human Rights. 1034
Lesson 2   Democracy in the World Today .1044
Lesson 3   Technology and Globalization .1051
Lesson 4   Protecting the Environment. 1059
Lesson 5   Global Health 1067
Lesson 6   Trade and Economic Development. 1073

Social Studies Skills Research Current Events 1081
Module Assessment 1082

References

Atlas R2

Writing Workshops R14

English and Spanish Glossary R36

Index R62

Credits and Acknowledgments R92

Available Online

Reading Like a Historian

Biographical Dictionary

Economics Handbook

Geography and Map Skills Handbook

Skillbuilder Handbook

Close-Read Screencasts

 Multimedia Connections

▶ These online lessons feature award-winning content and include short video segments, maps and visual materials, primary source documents, and more.

China and the Great Wall

Ancient Greece

Rome: Engineering an Empire

Japan and the Samurai Warrior

The Maya

The Crusades: The Crescent & the Cross

Ponce de León

The American Revolution

Dear Home: Letters from WW I

Memories of World War II

October Fury: The Cuban Missile Crisis

HISTORY

HISTORY® is the leading destination for revealing, award-winning, original non-fiction series and event-driven specials that connect history with viewers in an informative, immersive and entertaining manner across multiple platforms. HISTORY is part of A+E Networks, a global entertainment media company that includes, among others, A&E®, HISTORY®, Lifetime®, H2®, FYI™, and LMN®.

HISTORY programming greatly appeals to educators and young people who are drawn into the visual stories our documentaries tell. Our Education Department has a long-standing record in providing teachers and students with curriculum resources that bring the past to life in the classroom. Our content covers a diverse variety of subjects, including American and world history, government, economics, the natural and applied sciences, arts, literature and the humanities, health and guidance, and even pop culture.

The HISTORY website, located at **www.history.com**, is the definitive historical online source that delivers entertaining and informative content featuring broadband video, interactive timelines, maps, games, podcasts and more.

"We strive to engage, inspire and encourage the love of learning..."

Since its founding in 1995, HISTORY has demonstrated a commitment to providing the highest quality resources for educators. We develop multimedia resources for K–12 schools, two- and four-year colleges, government agencies, and other organizations by drawing on the award-winning documentary programming of A&E Television Networks. We strive to engage, inspire and encourage the love of learning by connecting with students in an informative and compelling manner. To help achieve this goal, we have formed a partnership with Houghton Mifflin Harcourt.

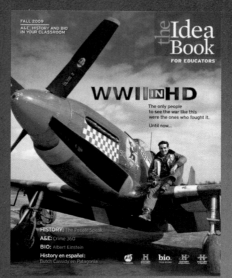
The Idea Book for Educators

Classroom resources that bring the past to life

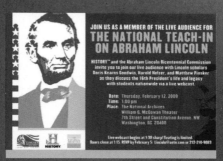
Live webcasts

HISTORY Take a Veteran to School Day

In addition to premium video-based resources, **HISTORY** has extensive offerings for teachers, parents, and students to use in the classroom and in their in-home educational activities, including:

- *The Idea Book for Educators* is a biannual teacher's magazine, featuring guides and info on the latest happenings in history education to help keep teachers on the cutting edge.

- **HISTORY Classroom (www.history.com/classroom)** is an interactive website that serves as a portal for history educators nationwide. Streaming videos on topics ranging from the Roman aqueducts to the civil rights movement connect with classroom curricula.

- **HISTORY email newsletters** feature updates and supplements to our award-winning programming relevant to the classroom with links to teaching guides and video clips on a variety of topics, special offers, and more.

- **Live webcasts** are featured each year as schools tune in via streaming video.

- **HISTORY Take a Veteran to School Day** connects veterans with young people in our schools and communities nationwide.

In addition to **Houghton Mifflin Harcourt**, our partners include the *Library of Congress*, the *Smithsonian Institution, National History Day, The Gilder Lehrman Institute of American History*, the Organization of American Historians, and many more. HISTORY video is also featured in museums throughout America and in over 70 other historic sites worldwide.

Reading Social Studies

Did you ever think you would begin reading your social studies book by reading about reading? Actually, it makes better sense than you might think. You would probably make sure you learned soccer skills and strategies before playing in a game. Similarly, you need to learn reading skills and strategies before reading your social studies book. In other words, you need to make sure you know whatever you need to know in order to read this book successfully.

Tip #1

Use the Reading Social Studies Pages

Take advantage of the two pages on reading at the beginning of every module. Those pages introduce the module themes, explain a reading skill or strategy, and identify key terms and people.

Themes

Why are themes important? They help our minds organize facts and information. For example, when we talk about baseball, we may talk about types of pitches. When we talk about movies, we may discuss animation.

Historians are no different. When they discuss history or social studies, they tend to think about some common themes: Economics, Geography, Religion, Politics, Society and Culture, and Science and Technology.

Reading Skill or Strategy

Good readers use a number of skills and strategies to make sure they understand what they are reading. These lessons will give you the tools you need to read and understand social studies.

Key Terms and People

Before you read the module, review these words and think about them. Have you heard the word before? What do you already know about the people? Then watch for these words and their meanings as you read the module.

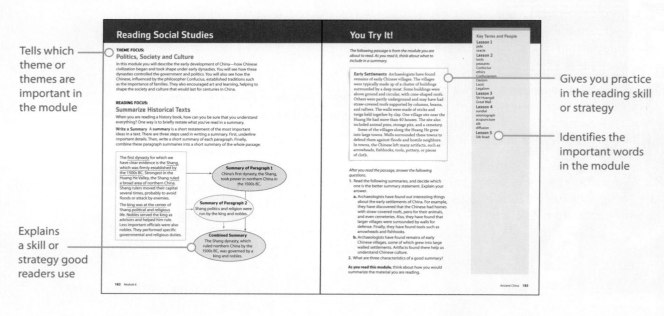

Tells which theme or themes are important in the module

Explains a skill or strategy good readers use

Gives you practice in the reading skill or strategy

Identifies the important words in the module

Tip #2

Read like a Skilled Reader

You will never get better at reading your social studies book—or any book for that matter—unless you spend some time thinking about how to be a better reader.

Skilled readers do the following.

- They preview what they are supposed to read before they actually begin reading. They look for vocabulary words, titles of lessons, information in the margin, or maps or charts they should study.

- They divide their notebook paper into two columns. They title one column "Notes from the Lesson" and the other column "Questions or Comments I Have."

- They take notes in both columns as they read.

- They read like **active readers**. The Active Reading list below shows you what that means.

- They use clues in the text to help them figure out where the text is going. The best clues are called signal words.

Chronological Order Signal Words:
first, second, third, before, after, later, next, following that, earlier, finally

Cause and Effect Signal Words:
because of, due to, as a result of, the reason for, therefore, consequently

Comparison/Contrast Signal Words:
likewise, also, as well as, similarly, on the other hand

Active Reading

Successful readers are **active readers**. These readers know that it is up to them to figure out what the text means. Here are some steps you can take to become an active, and successful, reader.

Predict what will happen next based on what has already happened. When your predictions don't match what happens in the text, reread the confusing parts.

Question what is happening as you read. Constantly ask yourself why things have happened, what things mean, and what caused certain events.

Summarize what you are reading frequently. Do not try to summarize the entire module! Read a bit and then summarize it. Then read on.

Connect what is happening in the part you're reading to what you have already read.

Clarify your understanding. Stop occasionally to ask yourself whether you are confused by anything. You may need to reread to clarify, or you may need to read further and collect more information before you can understand.

Visualize what is happening in the text. Try to see the events or places in your mind by drawing maps, making charts, or jotting down notes about what you are reading.

Tip #3

Pay Attention to Vocabulary

It is no fun to read something when you don't know what the words mean, but you can't learn new words if you use or read only the words you already know. In this book, we know we probably have used some words you don't know. But we have followed a pattern as we have used more difficult words.

Key Terms and People

At the beginning of each lesson you will find a list of key terms and people that you will need to know. Be on the lookout for those words as you read through the lesson.

> into clay tablets,
> d sent by computer.
>
> types. A **primary source** is an acc
> o took part in or witnessed the e
> legal documents, and ro

Academic Vocabulary
distribute to divide among a group of people

Academic Vocabulary

When we use a word that is important in all classes, not just social studies, we define it in the margin under the heading Academic Vocabulary. You will run into these academic words in other textbooks, so you should learn what they mean while reading this book.

Academic and Social Studies Words

As you read this social studies textbook, you will be more successful if you know or learn the meanings of the words on this page. Academic words are important in all classes, not just social studies. Social studies words are special to the study of world history and other social studies topics.

Academic Words

acquire   to get

affect   to change or influence

agreement   a decision reached by two or more people or groups

aspects   parts

authority   power, right to rule

cause   the reason something happens

classical   referring to the cultures of ancient Greece or Rome

competition   a contest between two rivals

conflict   an open clash between two opposing groups

consequences   the effects of a particular event or events

contract   a binding legal agreement

defend   to secure from danger

develop/development   1. to grow or improve; 2. the process of growing or improving

distribute   to divide among a group of people

effect   the result of an action or decision

efficient/efficiency   the quality of being efficient

establish   to set up or create

features   characteristics

function   use or purpose

ideals   ideas or goals that people try to live up to

impact   effect, result

implications   effects of a decision

influence   change or have an effect on

innovation   a new idea or way of doing something

logic/logical   1. well-thought-out idea; 2. reasoned, well thought out

motive   a reason for doing something

neutral   unbiased, not favoring either side in a conflict

opposition   the act of opposing or resisting

oppressed   treated harshly and unfairly

per capita   for each person

policy   rule, course of action

primary   main, most important

principle   basic belief, rule, or law

procedure   a series of steps taken to accomplish a task

process   a series of steps by which a task is accomplished

purpose   the reason something is done

rebel   to fight against authority

role   1. a part or function; 2. assigned behavior

strategy   a plan for fighting a battle or war

structure   the way something is set up or organized

traditional   customary, time-honored

values   ideas that people hold dear and try to live by

vary/various   1. to be different; 2. of many types

Social Studies Words

AD   refers to dates after the birth of Jesus of Nazareth

BC   refers to dates before the birth of Jesus

BCE   refers to "Before Common Era," dates before the birth of Jesus

CE   refers to "Common Era," dates after the birth of Jesus

century   a period of 100 years

civilization   the culture of a particular time or place

climate   the weather conditions in a certain area over a long period of time

culture   the knowledge, beliefs, customs, and values of a group of people

custom   a repeated practice, tradition

democracy   governmental rule by the people, usually on a majority rule principle

economy   the system in which people make and exchange goods and services

era   a period of time

geography   the study of the earth's physical and cultural features

monarchy   governmental rule by one person, a king or queen

physical features   features on the earth's surface, such as mountains and rivers

politics   government

region   an area with one or more features that make it different from surrounding areas

resources   materials found on the earth that people need and value

society   a group of people who share common traditions

trade   the exchange of goods and service

Using This Book

Studying world history will be easy for you using this textbook. Take a few minutes to become familiar with the easy-to-use structure and special features of this history book. See how this world history textbook will make history come alive for you!

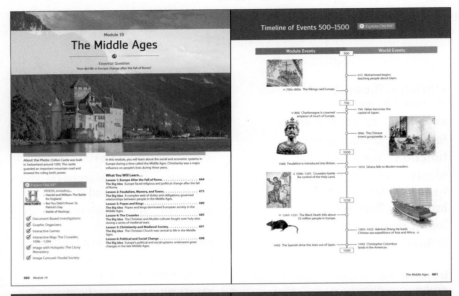

Module

Each module begins with an Essential Question and a Timeline of Events showing important dates in world history and ends with a Module Assessment.

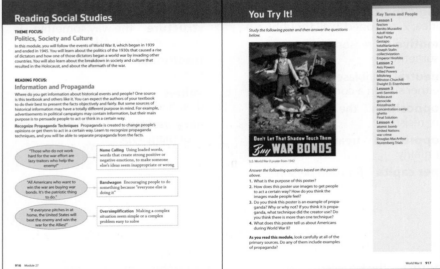

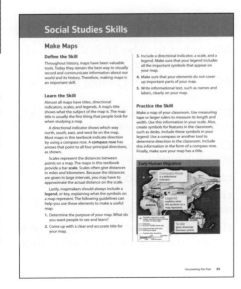

Reading Social Studies

These reading lessons teach you skills and provide opportunities for practice to help you read the textbook more successfully. There are questions in the Module Assessment to make sure you understand the reading skill.

Social Studies Skills

The Social Studies Skills lessons give you an opportunity to learn and use a skill you will most likely use again while in school. You will also be given a chance to make sure that you understand each skill by answering related questions in the Module Assessment activity.

Lesson

The lesson opener includes an overarching Big Idea statement, Main Ideas, and Key Terms and People.

If YOU were there . . . introductions

begin each lesson with a situation for you to respond to, placing you in the time period and in a situation related to the content you will be studying in the lesson.

Headings and subheadings organize

the information into manageable chunks of text that will help you learn and understand the lesson's main ideas.

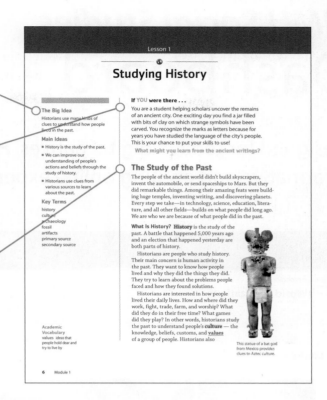

Lesson 1

Studying History

The Big Idea
Historians use many kinds of clues to understand how people lived in the past.

Main Ideas
- History is the study of the past.
- We can improve our understanding of people's actions and beliefs through the study of history.
- Historians use clues from various sources to learn about the past.

Key Terms
history
culture
archaeology
fossil
artifacts
primary source
secondary source

Academic Vocabulary
values ideas that people hold dear and try to live by

6   Module 1

If YOU were there . . .
You are a student helping scholars uncover the remains of an ancient city. One exciting day you find a jar filled with bits of clay on which strange symbols have been carved. You recognize the marks as letters because for years you have studied the language of the city's people. This is your chance to put your skills to use!

What might you learn from the ancient writings?

The Study of the Past

The people of the ancient world didn't build skyscrapers, invent the automobile, or send spaceships to Mars. But they did remarkable things. Among their amazing feats were building huge temples, inventing writing, and discovering planets. Every step we take—in technology, science, education, literature, and all other fields—builds on what people did long ago. We are who we are because of what people did in the past.

What Is History? **History** is the study of the past. A battle that happened 5,000 years ago and an election that happened yesterday are both parts of history.

Historians are people who study history. Their main concern is human activity in the past. They want to know how people lived and why they did the things they did. They try to learn about the problems people faced and how they found solutions.

Historians are interested in how people lived their daily lives. How and where did they work, fight, trade, farm, and worship? What did they do in their free time? What games did they play? In other words, historians study the past to understand people's **culture** — the knowledge, beliefs, customs, and **values** of a group of people. Historians also

This statue of a bat god from Mexico provides clues to Aztec culture.

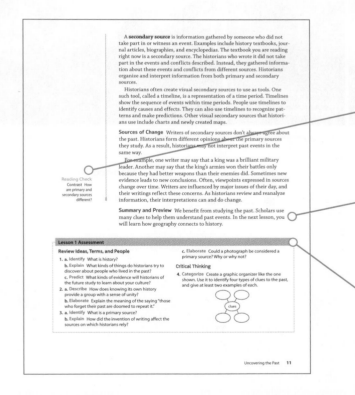

A **secondary source** is information gathered by someone who did not take part in or witness an event. Examples include history textbooks, journal articles, biographies, and encyclopedias. The textbook you are reading right now is a secondary source. The historians who wrote it did not take part in the events and conflicts described. Instead, they gathered information about these events and conflicts from different sources. Historians organize and interpret information from both primary and secondary sources.

Historians often create visual secondary sources to use as tools. One such tool, called a timeline, is a representation of a time period. Timelines show the sequence of events within time periods. People use timelines to identify causes and effects. They can also use timelines to recognize patterns and make predictions. Other visual secondary sources that historians use include charts and newly created maps.

Sources of Change Writers of secondary sources don't always agree about the past. Historians form different opinions about the primary sources they study. As a result, historians may not interpret past events in the same way.

For example, one writer may say that a king was a brilliant military leader. Another may say that the king's armies won their battles only because they had better weapons than their enemies did. Sometimes new evidence leads to new conclusions. Often, viewpoints expressed in sources change over time. Writers are influenced by major issues of their day, and their writings reflect these concerns. As historians review and reanalyze information, their interpretations can and do change.

Reading Check
Contrast How are primary and secondary sources different?

Summary and Preview We benefit from studying the past. Scholars use many clues to help them understand past events. In the next lesson, you will learn how geography connects to history.

Lesson 1 Assessment

Review Ideas, Terms, and People
1. a. Identify What is history?
   b. Explain What kinds of things do historians try to discover about people who lived in the past?
   c. Predict What kinds of evidence will historians of the future study to learn about your culture?
2. a. Describe How does knowing its own history provide a group with a sense of unity?
   b. Elaborate Explain the meaning of the saying "those who forget their past are doomed to repeat it."
3. a. Identify What is a primary source?
   b. Explain How did the invention of writing affect the sources on which historians rely?

   c. Elaborate Could a photograph be considered a primary source? Why or why not?

Critical Thinking
4. Categorize Create a graphic organizer like the one shown. Use it to identify four types of clues to the past, and give at least two examples of each.

clues

Uncovering the Past   11

Reading Check questions are at

the end of each main heading so you can test whether or not you understand what you have just studied.

Summary and Preview statements

connect what you have just studied in the lesson to what you will study in the next lesson.

Lesson Assessment boxes pro-

vide an opportunity for you to make sure you understand the main ideas of the lesson.

HMH Social Studies
Dashboard

Designed for today's digital natives, *HMH® Social Studies* offers you an informative and exciting online experience.

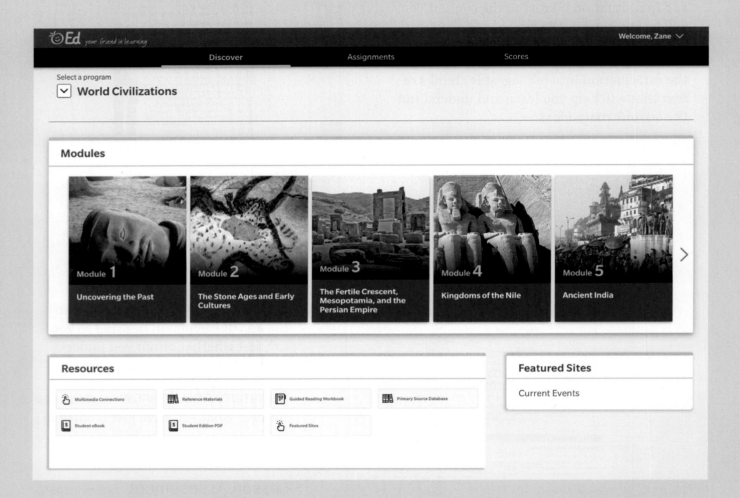

Your personalized Dashboard is organized into three main sections:

1. **Discover**—Quickly access content and search program resources

2. **Assignments**—Review your assignments and check your progress on them

3. **Scores**—Monitor your progress on the course

Explore Online ▷

to **Experience** the **Power** of
World Civilizations

Houghton Mifflin Harcourt™ is changing
the way you **experience** social studies.

By delivering an immersive experience through compelling narratives
enriched with media, we're connecting you to history through experiences that are
energizing, inspiring, and memorable. The following pages highlight
some digital tools and instructional support that will help you
approach history through active inquiry, so you can connect to the past
while becoming active and informed citizens for the future.

The Student eBook is the primary learning portal.

More than just the digital version of a textbook, the Student eBook serves as the primary learning portal for you. The narrative is supported by a wealth of multimedia and learning resources to bring history to life and give you the tools you need to succeed.

Bringing Content to Life

HISTORY® videos and Multimedia Connections bring content to life through primary source footage, dramatic storytelling, and expert testimonials.

In-Depth Understanding

Close Read Screencasts model an analytical conversation about primary sources.

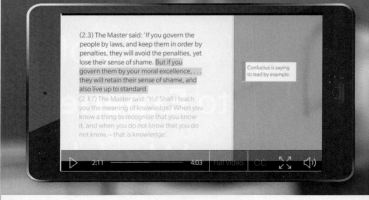

Content in a Fun Way

Interactive Features, Maps, and **Games** provide quick, entertaining activities and assessments that present important content in a fun way.

Investigate Like a Historian

Document-Based Investigations in every lesson build to end-of-module DBI performance tasks so you can examine and assess primary sources as historians do.

Full-Text Audio Support

You can listen while you read.

Skills Support

Point-of-use support is just a click away, providing instruction on critical reading and social studies skills.

Personalized Annotations

Notes encourages you to take notes while you read and allows you to customize them to your study preferences. You can easily access them to review later as you prepare for exams.

Interactive Lesson Graphic Organizers

Graphic organizers help you process, summarize, and keep track of your learning for end-of-module performance tasks.

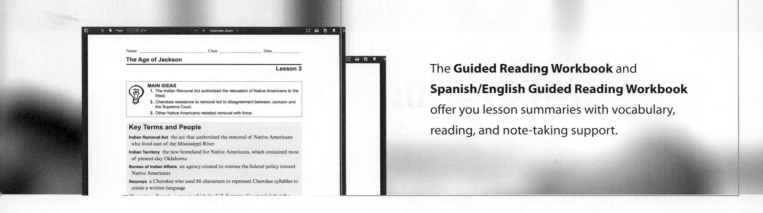

The **Guided Reading Workbook** and **Spanish/English Guided Reading Workbook** offer you lesson summaries with vocabulary, reading, and note-taking support.

Current Events features trustworthy articles on today's news that connect what you learn in class to the world around you.

No Wi-Fi®? No problem!

HMH Social Studies World Civilizations
allows you to connect to content and resources
by downloading when online and accessing when offline.

Module 1

Uncovering the Past

Essential Question

Why do scholars study the people, events, and ideas of long ago?

About the Photo: Finds like these clay warriors from China can teach us a lot about the history of ancient places.

▶ Explore ONLINE!

VIDEOS, including...
- Cult of Djedfre
- Grand Canyon
- Boom
- America Gets a Constitution
- Birth of Democracy

✓ Document-Based Investigations

✓ Graphic Organizers

✓ Interactive Games

✓ Image with Hotspots: Studying the Past

✓ Interactive Maps: California

✓ Animation: How Satellites Gather Map Data

✓ Image Carousel: Forms of Modern Currency

In this module you will learn how historians and geographers study the past in order to learn more about the present, and the role that economics and government have played throughout history.

What You Will Learn...

Lesson 1: Studying History **6**
The Big Idea Historians use many kinds of clues to understand how people lived in the past.

Lesson 2: Studying Geography **12**
The Big Idea Physical geography and human geography contribute to the study of history.

Lesson 3: Studying Economics **22**
The Big Idea Economic systems help people buy the goods and services they need.

Lesson 4: Studying Civics **30**
The Big Idea Government plays an essential role in every country.

Timeline of Events 450 BC–Present

▷ Explore ONLINE!

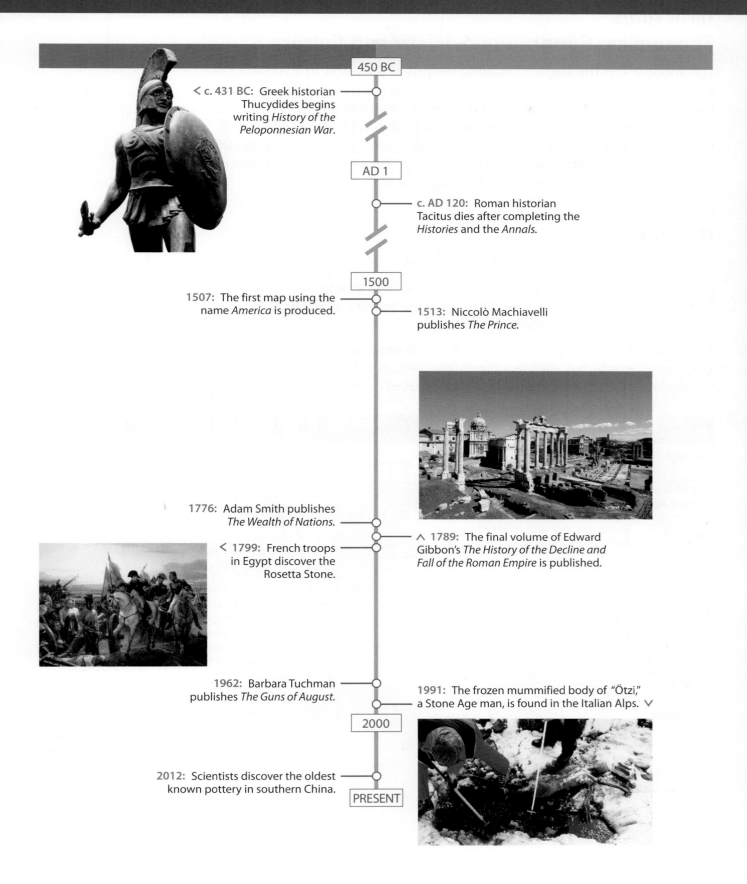

450 BC

< c. 431 BC: Greek historian Thucydides begins writing *History of the Peloponnesian War*.

AD 1

c. AD 120: Roman historian Tacitus dies after completing the *Histories* and the *Annals*.

1500

1507: The first map using the name *America* is produced.

1513: Niccolò Machiavelli publishes *The Prince*.

1776: Adam Smith publishes *The Wealth of Nations*.

∧ 1789: The final volume of Edward Gibbon's *The History of the Decline and Fall of the Roman Empire* is published.

< 1799: French troops in Egypt discover the Rosetta Stone.

1962: Barbara Tuchman publishes *The Guns of August*.

1991: The frozen mummified body of "Ötzi," a Stone Age man, is found in the Italian Alps. ∨

2000

2012: Scientists discover the oldest known known pottery in southern China.

PRESENT

Reading Social Studies

THEME FOCUS:

Economics, Geography, Society and Culture

This module sets the stage for reading the rest of the book. In it you will learn the definitions of many important terms. You will learn how studying history helps you understand the past and the present. You will also read about the study of geography and learn how the world's physical features influenced when and where civilization began. In addition, you will learn how economics and politics have influenced our lives. Finally, you will begin to think about how society and culture have interacted throughout time.

READING FOCUS:

Specialized Vocabulary of History

Have you ever done a plié at the barre or sacked the quarterback? You probably haven't if you've never studied ballet or played football. In fact, you may not even have known what those words meant.

Specialized Vocabulary *Plié, barre, sack,* and *quarterback* are specialized vocabulary words that are used in only one field. History has its own specialized vocabulary. The charts list some terms often used in the study of history.

Terms that identify periods of time	
Decade	a period of 10 years
Century	a period of 100 years
Millennium	a period of 1,000 years
Age	a long period of time marked by a single cultural feature
Epoch	a long period of time containing more than one age
Era	a long period of time marked by great events, developments, or figures
Historic	important to history
Ancient	old, or from a long time ago
Prehistoric	from a time before people recorded history

Terms used with dates	
circa or c.	a word used to show that historians are not sure of an exact date; it means "about."
BC	a term used to identify dates that occurred long ago, before the birth of Jesus Christ, the founder of Christianity; it means "before Christ." As you can see on the timeline, BC dates get smaller as time passes, so the larger the number the earlier the date.
AD	a term used to identify dates that occurred after Jesus's birth; it comes from a Latin phrase that means "in the year of our Lord." Unlike BC dates, AD dates get larger as time passes, so the larger the number, the later the date.
BCE	another way to refer to BC dates; it stands for "before the common era."
CE	another way to refer to AD dates; it stands for "common era."

You Try It!

As you read, you will find many examples of specialized vocabulary terms that historians use. Many of these terms will be highlighted in the text and defined for you as key terms. Others may not be highlighted, but they will still be defined. For some examples, read the passage. Learning these words as you come across them will help you understand what you read later in the book. For your own reference, you may wish to keep a list of important terms in your notebook.

Read the following passage, and then answer the questions below.

We must rely on a variety of sources to learn history. For information on the very first humans, we have fossil remains. A **fossil** is a part or an imprint of something that was once alive. Bones and footprints preserved in rock are examples of fossils.

As human beings learned to make things, by accident they also created more sources of information for us. They made what we call **artifacts**, objects created by and used by humans. Artifacts include coins, arrowheads, tools, toys, and pottery.

Answer these questions based on the passage you just read.

1. What is a fossil? What is an artifact? How can you tell?
2. Were you born in a BC year or an AD year?
3. Put the following dates in order: AD 2000, 3100 BC, 15 BCE, AD 476, AD 3, CE 1215.
4. If you saw that an event happened c. AD 1000, what would that mean?

As you read this module, keep a list in your notebook of specialized vocabulary words that you learn.

Key Terms

Lesson 1
history
culture
archaeology
fossil
artifacts
primary source
secondary source

Lesson 2
geography
landforms
climate
environment
region
resources

Lesson 3
economy
scarcity
profit
entrepreneur
mixed economy
trade
wealth

Lesson 4
civics
government
constitution
democracy
republic
tax

Studying History

The Big Idea

Historians use many kinds of clues to understand how people lived in the past.

Main Ideas

- History is the study of the past.

- We can improve our understanding of people's actions and beliefs through the study of history.

- Historians use clues from various sources to learn about the past.

Key Terms

history
culture
archaeology
fossil
artifacts
primary source
secondary source

Academic Vocabulary
values ideas that people hold dear and try to live by

If YOU were there . . .

You are a student helping scholars uncover the remains of an ancient city. One exciting day you find a jar filled with bits of clay on which strange symbols have been carved. You recognize the marks as letters because for years you have studied the language of the city's people. This is your chance to put your skills to use!

What might you learn from the ancient writings?

The Study of the Past

The people of the ancient world didn't build skyscrapers, invent the automobile, or send spaceships to Mars. But they did remarkable things. Among their amazing feats were building huge temples, inventing writing, and discovering planets. Every step we take—in technology, science, education, literature, and all other fields—builds on what people did long ago. We are who we are because of what people did in the past.

What Is History? **History** is the study of the past. A battle that happened 5,000 years ago and an election that happened yesterday are both parts of history.

Historians are people who study history. Their main concern is human activity in the past. They want to know how people lived and why they did the things they did. They try to learn about the problems people faced and how they found solutions.

Historians are interested in how people lived their daily lives. How and where did they work, fight, trade, farm, and worship? What did they do in their free time? What games did they play? In other words, historians study the past to understand people's **culture** — the knowledge, beliefs, customs, and **values** of a group of people. Historians also

This statue of a bat god from Mexico provides clues to Aztec culture.

examine how past cultures interacted with their natural surroundings to create cultural landscapes. Examples of cultural landscapes include farms, battlefields, and religious sites.

All historians specialize in studying a certain part, or aspect, of the past. Some focus on a specific event, while others focus on a specific group of people. Some focus on a specific time period, era, or age. Dividing the past into smaller sections helps organize history.

Historians often use a method called historical inquiry to develop our understanding of the past. They first identify a question that needs to be answered. An example of this could be, *What natural resources did a specific group of people use to make shelters?* Then historians create educated guesses called hypotheses. After testing these hypotheses, they form possible conclusions based on evidence.

What Is Archaeology? An important field that contributes much information about the past is **archaeology** (a-hr-kee-AH-luh-jee). It is the study of the past based on what people left behind. Archaeologists, or people who practice archaeology, explore places where people once lived, worked, or fought. The things that people left in these places may include jewelry, dishes, or weapons. They range from stone tools to huge buildings.

Archaeologists examine the objects they find to learn what they can tell about the past. In many cases, the objects that people left behind are the only clues we have to how they lived. In ancient Greece, for example, earthquakes forced people to leave the settlement of Akrotiri. A volcanic explosion later covered the settlement in ash. Our knowledge of Akrotiri is based on objects the people left behind, such as furniture and paintings, that were preserved by the ash.

This archaeologist uses a delicate tool to remove soil from an ancient pot.

Objects allow us to determine the dates of early human communities. There are several different methods that archaeologists use to determine these dates. In relative dating, archaeologists determine if one object is older or newer than another object. Often an older object will be found buried beneath a newer one. In absolute dating, archaeologists determine the date of an object by analyzing its material.

Archaeologists use objects to help describe events and issues from the perspectives of people living at certain times. Understanding individual and group perspectives from the past is essential when analyzing history.

Geology and History Evidence used by other scholars also helps us understand the past. People who study geology, or the science and history of the earth, are called geologists. They study subjects ranging from rocks and minerals to forces that shape the earth's surface. Like archaeologists, geologists often use relative and absolute dating to determine the age of materials.

The geology of an area shapes the lives of people living there. Therefore, analyzing geology is important when studying human history. For example, certain kinds of stone chip easily to create sharp edges. Early humans who had these kinds of stone nearby could chip them into specific shapes or make stone tools such as axes and arrowheads.

Understanding Through History

There are many reasons why people study history. Understanding the past helps us understand the world today. History can also provide us with a guide to making better decisions in the future.

Knowing Yourself History can teach you about yourself. What if you did not know your own past? You would not know which subjects you liked in school or which sports you enjoyed. You would not know what makes you proud or what mistakes not to repeat. Without your own personal history, you would not have an identity.

History is just as important for groups as it is for individuals. What would happen if countries had no record of their past? People would know nothing about how their governments came into being. They would not remember their nation's great triumphs or tragedies. History teaches us about the experiences we have been through as a people. It shapes our identity and teaches us the values that we share. By studying and preserving our history, we pass down our culture and heritage to future generations.

Knowing Others Like today, the world in the past included many cultures. History teaches about the cultures that were unlike your own. You learn about other peoples, where they lived, and what was important to them. History teaches you how cultures were similar and how they were different.

History also helps you understand why other people think the way they do. You learn about the struggles people have faced. You also learn how these struggles have affected the way people view themselves and others.

Reading Check
Compare How are the fields of history and archaeology similar?

For example, Native Americans, European settlers, enslaved Africans, and Asian immigrants all played vital roles in our country's history. But the descendants of each group have a different story to tell about their ancestors' contributions.

Learning these and other stories that make up history can help you see the viewpoints of other peoples. Therefore, historians try to avoid evaluating past events and issues based solely on today's values. Understanding the perspectives of people living at the time can help teach you to respect and understand different opinions. This knowledge helps promote tolerance. History can also help you relate more easily to people of different backgrounds. In other words, knowing about the past can help build social harmony throughout the world today.

Knowing Your World History can provide you with a better understanding of where you live. You are part of a culture that interacts with the outside world. Even events that happen in other parts of the world affect your culture. History helps you understand how today's events are shaped by the events of the past. In addition, understanding different perspectives helps you analyze contemporary issues. Current inequality problems, for instance, have roots in the past. So knowing the past helps you figure out what is happening now.

History is concerned with the entire range of human activities. It is the record of humanity's combined efforts. So while you are studying history, you can learn more about topics such as math, science, and religion. You also gain a better understanding of the social sciences, including politics and economics.

Studying the past will also help you develop mental skills. History encourages you to ask important questions. It forces you to analyze the facts you learn. Such analysis teaches you how to recognize which information is important and which is extra. This skill helps you find the main facts when studying any topic.

History also promotes good decision-making skills. A famous, often repeated saying warns us that those who forget their past are doomed to repeat it. This means that people who ignore the results of past decisions often make the same mistakes over and over again. In addition, history provides models of human character. When we read about historical figures, from famous leaders to ordinary citizens, we are often inspired. Their bravery, humility, and wisdom speak to us.

Individuals and countries both benefit from the wisdom that history can teach. Your own history may have taught you that studying for a test results in better grades. In a similar way, world history has taught that providing young people with education makes them more productive when they become adults.

Historians have been talking about the value of history for centuries. More than 2,000 years ago a great Greek historian named Polybius wrote:

> ". . . the knowledge gained from the study of true history is the best of all educations for practical life. For it is history, and history alone, which . . .will mature our judgment and prepare us to take right views. . . ."
>
> —Polybius, from *The Histories,* Book I

Reading Check
Summarize What are some benefits of studying history?

History can help us understand the world around us. For example, why do these buildings in San Francisco look the way they do? The answer is history. These buildings are in a neighborhood called Chinatown, where Chinese immigrants began settling in the 1800s.

Immigrants painted these houses bright colors like the houses in China. Chinese-style roofs and pillars were also added.

Chinese people who moved to California brought their language with them. By studying the languages spoken in a region, historians can learn who settled there.

Using Clues

We must rely on a variety of sources to learn history. For information on the very first humans, we have fossil remains. A **fossil** is a part or an imprint of something that was once alive. Bones and footprints preserved in rock are examples of fossils.

As human beings learned to make things, by accident they also created more sources of information for us. They made what we call **artifacts**, objects created by and used by humans. Artifacts include coins, arrowheads, tools, toys, and pottery. Archaeologists examine artifacts and the places where the artifacts were found to learn about the past.

Sources of Information About 5,000 years ago, people invented writing. They wrote laws, poems, speeches, battle plans, letters, contracts, and many other things. In these written sources, historians have found countless clues about how people lived. In addition, people have recorded their messages in many ways over the centuries. Historians have studied writing carved into stone pillars, stamped onto clay tablets, scribbled on turtle shells, typed with typewriters, and sent by computer.

Historical sources are of two types. A **primary source** is an account of an event created by someone who took part in or witnessed the event. Letters, diaries, artifacts, photographs, legal documents, and royal commands are all primary sources. Oral interviews and audio or video recordings of an event are also primary sources. Like historical sites, primary sources are critical to world history. They help us connect and relate to past events in personal ways. A document or artifact allows us to see things through the eyes of the person who wrote the document or made the artifact.

A **secondary source** is information gathered by someone who did not take part in or witness an event. Examples include history textbooks, journal articles, biographies, and encyclopedias. The textbook you are reading right now is a secondary source. The historians who wrote it did not take part in the events and conflicts described. Instead, they gathered information about these events and conflicts from different sources. Historians organize and interpret information from both primary and secondary sources.

Historians often create visual secondary sources to use as tools. One such tool, called a timeline, is a representation of a time period. Timelines show the sequence of events within time periods. People use timelines to identify causes and effects. They can also use timelines to recognize patterns and make predictions. Other visual secondary sources that historians use include charts and newly created maps.

Sources of Change Writers of secondary sources don't always agree about the past. Historians form different opinions about the primary sources they study. As a result, historians may not interpret past events in the same way.

For example, one writer may say that a king was a brilliant military leader. Another may say that the king's armies won their battles only because they had better weapons than their enemies did. Sometimes new evidence leads to new conclusions. Often, viewpoints expressed in sources change over time. Writers are influenced by major issues of their day, and their writings reflect these concerns. As historians review and reanalyze information, their interpretations can and do change.

Summary and Preview We benefit from studying the past. Scholars use many clues to help them understand past events. In the next lesson, you will learn how geography connects to history.

Reading Check
Contrast How are primary and secondary sources different?

Lesson 1 Assessment

Review Ideas, Terms, and People

1. a. **Identify** What is history?

    b. **Explain** What kinds of things do historians try to discover about people who lived in the past?

    c. **Predict** What kinds of evidence will historians of the future study to learn about your culture?

2. a. **Describe** How does knowing its own history provide a group with a sense of unity?

    b. **Elaborate** Explain the meaning of the saying, "Those who forget their past are doomed to repeat it."

3. a. **Identify** What is a primary source?

    b. **Explain** How did the invention of writing affect the sources on which historians rely?

    c. **Elaborate** Could a photograph be considered a primary source? Why or why not?

Critical Thinking

4. **Categorize** Create a graphic organizer like the one shown. Use it to identify four types of clues to the past, and give at least two examples of each.

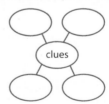

Studying Geography

The Big Idea
Physical geography and human geography contribute to the study of history.

Main Ideas
- Geography is the study of places and people.
- Studying location is important to both physical and human geography.
- Geography and history are closely connected.

Key Terms
geography
landforms
climate
environment
region
resources

If YOU were there . . .

Your parents are historians researching a city that disappeared long ago. You go with them to a library to help search for clues to the city's location and fate. While thumbing through a dusty old book, you find an ancient map stuck between two pages. Marked on the map are rivers, forests, mountains, and straight lines that look like roads. It is a map that shows the way to the lost city!

How can this map help you find the city?

Studying Places and People

When you hear about an event on the news, the first questions you ask may be, "Where did it happen?" and "Who was there?" Historians ask the same questions about events that happened in the past. That is why they need to study geography. **Geography** is the study of the earth's physical and cultural features. Physical features include mountains and rivers. Cultural features include people, cities, and countries. The characteristics of human populations are also cultural features. These characteristics are called demographics. Demographics include age, gender, and race.

Physical Geography Physical geography is the study of the earth's land and features. People who work in this field are called physical geographers.

Physical geographers organize the earth's land surface into seven large landmasses, called continents. Except for Antarctica and Australia, the continents are further organized into different countries. Earth's land surface is also organized into different regions. You'll learn about regions later in this lesson.

Physical geographers also study **landforms**, the natural features of the land's surface. Mountains, valleys, plains, and other such places are landforms. In addition, they study **climate**, the pattern of weather conditions in a certain area

Geography

Geography is the study of the earth's physical and cultural features.

Physical Geography
The study of the earth's physical features and processes, such as mountains, rivers, oceans, rainfall, and climate, including this section of California's coast

Human Geography
The study of the earth's people, such as these children in the African country of Tanzania, and their way of life, homes and cities, beliefs, and travels

over a long period of time. Climate is not the same as weather. Weather is the atmospheric conditions at a specific time and place. If you say that your city has cold winters, you are talking about climate. If you say it is below freezing and snowing today, you are talking about the weather.

Climate affects many features of an area. For example, it affects plant life. Tropical rainforests require warm air and heavy rain, whereas a dry climate can create deserts. Climate also affects landforms. For example, constant wind can wear down mountains into flat plains.

Although climate affects landforms, landforms can also affect climate. For example, the Coast Ranges in northern California are mountains parallel to the Pacific coast. As air presses against these mountains, it rises and cools. Any moisture that the air was carrying falls as rain. Meanwhile, on the opposite side of the range, the Central Valley stays dry. In this way, a mountain range creates two very different climates.

Landforms and climate are part of a place's environment. The **environment** includes all the living and nonliving things that affect life in an area. This includes the area's climate, land, water, plants, soil, animals, and other features.

Physical Processes Different types of physical processes can shape environments. One type of physical process is called weathering. Weathering is the process by which natural forces break down rocks. For example, ice and plant roots can cause rocks to crack and break. Another physical process that shapes environments is called erosion. Erosion is the movement of small pieces of rock and other loose materials from one location to another. A river that carries away sand and dirt is part of the erosion process. Both weathering and erosion change the topography, or landscape, of an area.

A third type of physical process is pollution, the introduction of harmful substances into an environment. An example of pollution is the dangerous chemicals people pour into water. This water pollution can harm plants and animals in the environment's ecosystem. An ecosystem is the relationship between living things and natural resources in an environment.

Human Geography The other branch of geography is human geography—the study of people and the places where they live. Specialists in human geography study many different things about people and their cultures. What kind of work do people do? How do they get their food? What are their homes like? What religion, or set of mutual values that help explain the world, do they practice?

Human geography also deals with how the environment affects people. For example, how do people who live near rivers protect themselves from floods? How do people who live in deserts survive? Do different environments affect the size of families? Do people in certain environments live longer? Why do some diseases spread easily in some environments but not in others? As you can see, human geographers study many interesting questions about people and this planet.

The Six Essential Elements of Geography It is useful to have a framework for studying the world and its people. One such framework is called the Six Essential Elements of Geography. You can think of these elements as windows you look through to study a place. If you looked at the same place through six different windows, you would have six different viewpoints.

The first of these elements is called the World in Spatial Terms. This refers to the locations of people, places, and environments on the earth. When you study the second element, Places and Regions, you examine how our identities are influenced by where we live. Physical Systems refer to the physical processes that shape the earth, while Human Systems refer to the patterns of human populations. When you study Environment and Society, you examine how the earth is affected by the activities of humans. The last element, the Uses of Geography, refers to how the study of geography increases our knowledge of the earth and ourselves.

Reading Check
Summarize What are the two main branches of geography?

Studying Location

Both physical and human geographers study location. Location is the exact description of where something is. Every place on the earth has a specific location, and even small differences between places can lead to major differences in how people live. By comparing locations, geographers learn more about the factors that affected each of them. For example, they may study why a town in one location grew while a town nearby got smaller.

To study various locations, geographers use maps and globes. A map is a drawing of an area. A globe is a scale model of the earth. It is useful for showing the entire earth or studying large areas of the earth's surface.

Using Globes

Interpret Maps

1. **Location** What is the absolute location of New Orleans, using longitude and latitude?

2. **Location** What is the relative location of New Orleans?

Mapping the Earth A pattern of lines circles a globe in east-west and north-south directions. This pattern is called a grid. It helps people use and interpret globes.

The east-west lines in the grid are lines of latitude. These imaginary lines measure distance north and south of the equator. The equator is an imaginary line that circles the globe halfway between the North and South Poles. The north-south lines are lines of longitude. These imaginary lines measure distance east and west of the prime meridian. The prime meridian is an imaginary line that runs through Greenwich, England.

Lines of latitude and longitude measure distance in degrees. The symbol for degree is °. Degrees are further divided into minutes. The symbol for minute is '. There are 60 minutes in a degree.

Lines of latitude range from 0°, for locations on the equator, to 90°N or 90°S, for locations at the Poles. Lines of longitude range from 0° on the prime meridian to 180° on a meridian in the mid-Pacific Ocean. Meridians west of the prime meridian to 180° are labeled with a *W*. Those east of the prime meridian to 180° are labeled with an *E*.

The intersection of these imaginary lines helps us find the absolute location of places on the earth. An absolute location is provided by a place's longitude and latitude. For instance, the absolute location of the Statue of Liberty is 40°41′N, 74°2′W. Absolute location is different from relative location. A relative location is provided by a place's relationship to other places. For example, you could say that the relative location of the Statue of Liberty is around 5.6 miles from the Empire State Building. You could also say its relative location is east of the Mississippi River.

Learning from Maps People study locations by using different types of maps. Physical maps show physical features. Political maps show cities and the boundaries of states or countries. Special-purpose maps highlight specific details, such as weather or population. Most maps have symbols to show different things. For example, large dots often stand for cities. Blue lines show where rivers flow. Most maps also include a guide to show direction.

People have been making maps for more than 4,000 years. Maps help with many activities. Planning battles, looking for new lands, and designing new city parks all require good maps. On the first day of class, you may have used a map of your school to find your classrooms.

Geographic Tools In the past, people developed maps using tools such as sextants. A sextant is an instrument with two mirrors that can help measure the distance between two visible objects, such as the horizon and the sun. By using sextants, people could determine points of latitude and longitude.

Today, people use computers and satellites to develop maps. A satellite is an object that orbits a planet. LANDSAT satellites provide images of the earth's surface. These images are then used to make highly accurate maps. The Global Positioning System, or GPS, uses satellites to show one's exact location on an electronic map. A geographic information system, or GIS, is a computer system that displays various types of information on one map. For example, a GIS can create a map showing demographic similarities and differences.

Learning About Regions Learning about regions is another key part of studying geography. A **region** is an area with one or more features that make it different from surrounding areas. These features may be physical, such as forests or grasslands. There may also be differences in climate. For example, a desert area is a type of region. Physical barriers such as mountains and rivers often form a region's boundaries. Human features can also define regions. Some regions are identified by the language that people there speak. Other regions are identified by the religion their people practice.

There are three main types of regions. A formal region is an area with clear or distinct boundaries. The United States is an example of a formal region. A functional region is an area with a central point and surrounding parts dependent on the central point. An example of a functional region is a city and its surrounding towns. The third type of region is a perceived region. This is an area in which people share common attitudes and feelings. One of the perceived regions within the United States is the Midwest.

Reading Check
Categorize What are some types of features that can identify a region?

What Geography Means

Some people think of geography as the ability to read maps or name state capitals. But as geographer Kenneth C. Davis explains, geography is much more. It is related to almost every branch of human knowledge.

Analyze Historical Sources
Why does the writer think geography is important?

"Geography doesn't simply begin and end with maps showing the location of all the countries of the world. In fact, such maps don't necessarily tell us much. No—geography poses fascinating questions about who we are and how we got to be that way, and then provides clues to the answers. It is impossible to understand history, international politics, the world economy, religions, philosophy, or 'patterns of culture' without taking geography into account."

—Kenneth C. Davis,
from *Don't Know Much About Geography*

Geography and History

Geography gives us important clues about the people who came before us and the places where they lived. Like detectives, we can piece together a great deal of information about ancient cultures by knowing where people lived and what the area was like.

Geography Affects Resources An area's geography was critical to early settlements. People could survive only in areas where they could get enough food and water. Early people settled in places that were rich in **resources**, materials found in the earth that people need and value. All through history, people have used a variety of resources to meet their basic needs.

In early times, essential resources included water, animals, fertile land, and stones for tools. Over time, people learned to use other resources, including metals such as copper, gold, and iron.

Geography Shapes Cultures Geography also influenced the early development of cultures. Early peoples, for example, developed vastly different cultures because of their environments. People who lived along rivers learned to make fishhooks and boats, while those far from rivers did not. People who lived near forests built homes from wood. In other areas, builders had to use mud or stone. Some people developed religious beliefs based on the geography of their area. For example, ancient Egyptians believed that the god Hapi controlled the Nile River.

Geography also played a role in the growth of civilizations. The world's first societies formed along rivers. Crops grown on the fertile land along these rivers fed large populations.

Some geographic features could also protect areas from invasion. A region surrounded by mountains or deserts, for example, was hard for attackers to reach.

Studying Maps

By studying and comparing maps, you can see how a place's physical and human features are related.

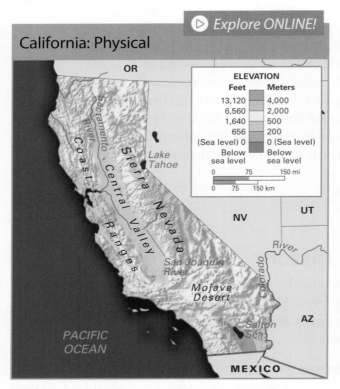

▷ Explore ONLINE!

California: Physical

1. What are some of California's main physical features? Where are the state's highest mountains?

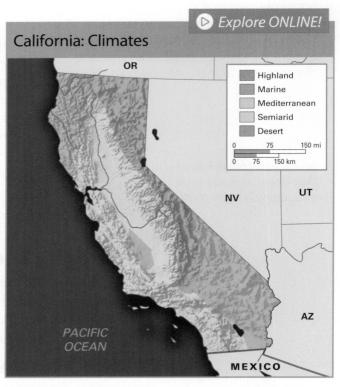

▷ Explore ONLINE!

California: Climates

2. What climates are found in California? By knowing that California is a major producer of agricultural goods, what conclusions can you draw about climate?

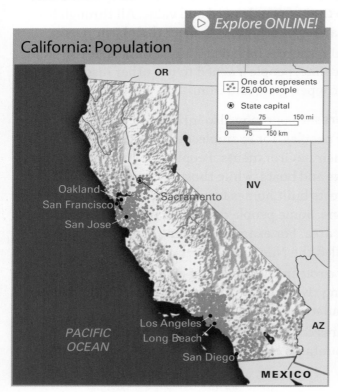

▷ Explore ONLINE!

California: Population

3. Where are California's two main population centers? Where do you think future major population centers in California will develop?

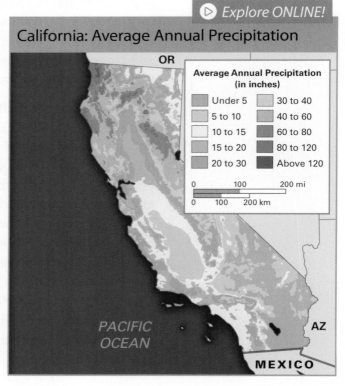

▷ Explore ONLINE!

California: Average Annual Precipitation

4. How much average annual precipitation does the Central Valley receive? How would you describe the weather along California's coast?

Geography Influences History Geography has helped shape history and has affected the growth of societies. People in areas with many natural resources could use their resources to get rich. They could build glorious cities and powerful armies. Features such as rivers also made trade easier. Many societies became rich by trading goods with other peoples.

On the other hand, geography has also caused problems. Floods, for example, have killed millions of people. Lack of rainfall has brought deadly food shortages. Storms have wrecked ships, and with them, the hopes of conquerors. In the 1200s, for example, a people known as the Mongols tried to invade Japan. However, most of the Mongol ships were destroyed by a powerful storm. Japanese history might have been very different if the storm had not occurred.

The relationship between geography and people has not been one-sided. For centuries, people have influenced their environments in positive and negative ways. People have planted millions of trees. They have created new lakes in the middle of deserts. But people have also created waste-lands where forests once grew and built dams that flooded ancient cities. This interaction between humans and their environment has been a major factor in history. It continues today.

Summary and Preview The field of geography includes physical geography and human geography. Geography has had a major influence on history. In the next lesson, you will learn how economics has also influenced history.

Reading Check
Summarize
In what ways has geography shaped human history?

Lesson 2 Assessment

Review Ideas, Terms, and People

1. a. **Define** What is geography?
   b. **Summarize** What are some of the topics included in human geography?
2. a. **Describe** Identify a region near where you live, and explain what sets it apart as a region.
   b. **Predict** How might a map of a city's landforms help an official who is planning a new city park?
3. a. **Recall** Where did early peoples tend to settle?
   b. **Compare and Contrast** How could a river be both a valuable resource and a problem for a region?

Critical Thinking

4. **Compare and Contrast** Use a chart like the one shown to compare and contrast physical and human geography.

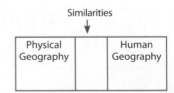

Similarities

Physical Geography		Human Geography

History and Geography

Natural Wonders of the Ancient World

Natural wonders are physical features known for their incredible beauty and size. Many natural wonders fascinate and inspire us, just as they fascinated and inspired people of the ancient world. Our world history is full of stories about these geographical features.

This map shows the location of three natural wonders of the ancient world. Study this map. What can it tell you about the natural wonders?

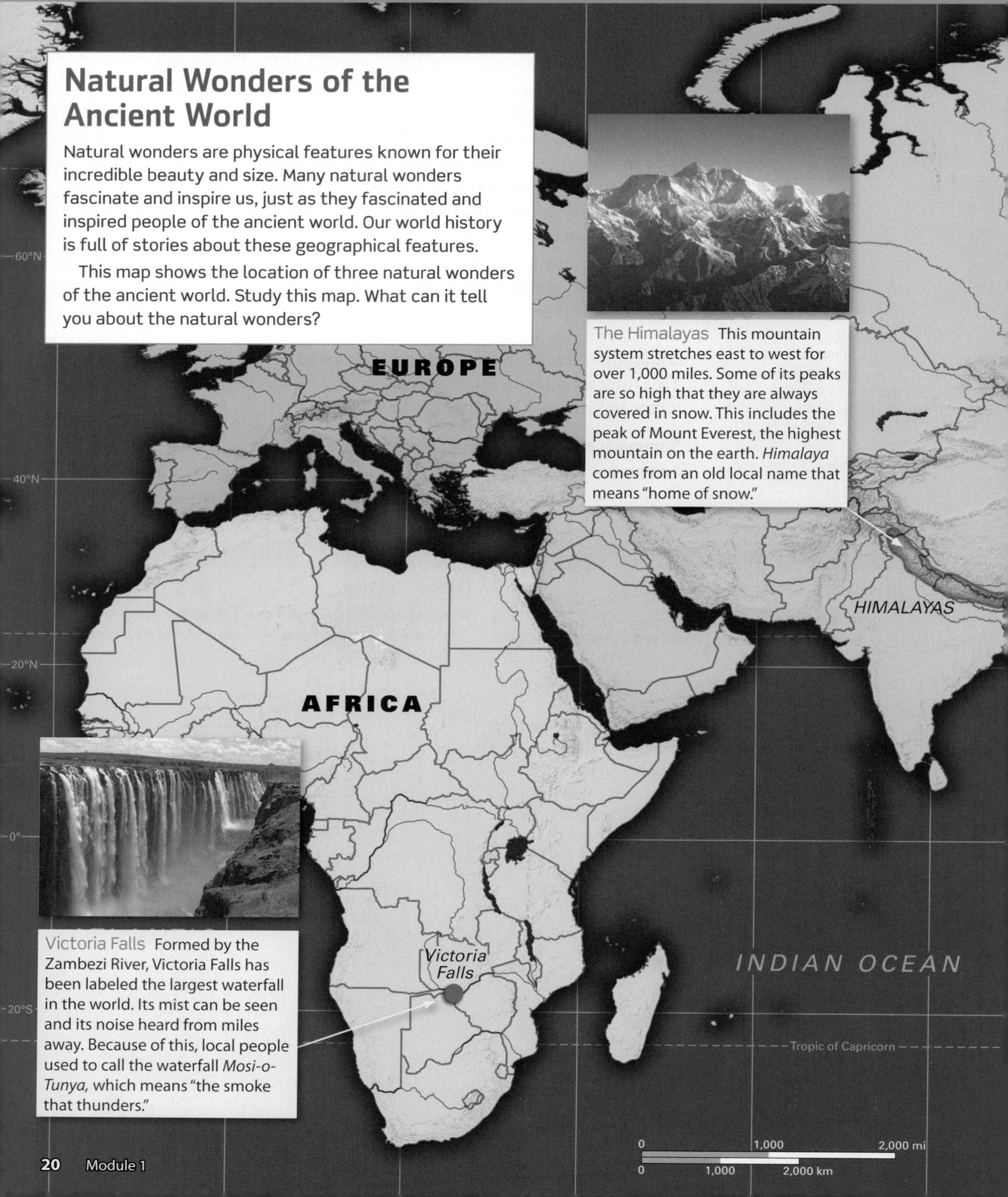

The Himalayas This mountain system stretches east to west for over 1,000 miles. Some of its peaks are so high that they are always covered in snow. This includes the peak of Mount Everest, the highest mountain on the earth. *Himalaya* comes from an old local name that means "home of snow."

EUROPE

AFRICA

HIMALAYAS

Victoria Falls Formed by the Zambezi River, Victoria Falls has been labeled the largest waterfall in the world. Its mist can be seen and its noise heard from miles away. Because of this, local people used to call the waterfall *Mosi-o-Tunya,* which means "the smoke that thunders."

Victoria Falls

INDIAN OCEAN

Tropic of Capricorn

| 0 | 1,000 | 2,000 mi |
| 0 | 1,000 | 2,000 km |

The Gobi Desert *Gobi* is a Mongolian word that means "waterless place." However, the Gobi is not your typical desert. Because of its northern location and high elevation, the Gobi is cold. The Gobi is also rockier and less sandy than many deserts. Over the years, many fossils have been discovered in the Gobi.

ASIA

GOBI DESERT

PACIFIC OCEAN

Tropic of Cancer

AUSTRALIA

60°N
40°N
20°N
Equator 0°
20°S

Interpret Maps

1. **Location** Which natural wonder of the ancient world has an absolute location of 17°55′S, 25°51′E?

2. **Draw Conclusions** How does the relative location of the Himalayas most likely affect the climate of the Gobi Desert?

Studying Economics

The Big Idea

Economic systems help people buy the goods and services they need.

Main Ideas

- The main problem in economics is scarcity.

- Businesses and countries have to make decisions about economic resources.

- Businesses and other organizations help people meet their needs and wants.

- Money is used as a medium of exchange, a store of value, and a unit of account.

- Economics helps explain events in world history.

Key Terms and People

economy
scarcity
profit
entrepreneur
mixed economy
trade
wealth

If YOU were there . . .

You want to make a sandwich but you discover that you have no bread. How can you get more? Do you have to grind wheat into flour so that you can bake a new loaf? Of course you don't. With a quick trip to the store, you can buy a loaf of bread.

How are you able to buy what you want or need?

Economic Fundamentals

Every day, people purchase goods and services from other people. Goods are products that people can consume or use, such as food or tools. Services are things that people do. For example, a tutor provides a service by helping someone learn a subject. How people get goods and services is determined by global, national, and local economies. An **economy** is a system of producing, selling, and buying goods and services. The study of economies is called economics.

Scarcity and Choice The work of economists, or people who study economics, shows that we all face one main economic problem. This problem is scarcity. **Scarcity** is when there are not enough resources to meet people's wants. People's wants are unlimited, but the resources available to satisfy wants are limited. When a resource becomes scarce, it is harder for producers to get. Products made with that resource also become more difficult to get. As a result, the prices for these items usually rise.

Scarcity affects everyone and forces us to make choices. We must decide what things we need and want. Scarcity also forces businesses to choose which goods and services to provide and how much to charge for them.

Choices lead to trade-offs. A trade-off is when you give up one thing in order to get something else. In economics, a trade-off always leads to an opportunity cost. An opportunity cost is the value of what is given up by making a trade-off. For example, suppose you want to buy a video game and a concert ticket. However, you do not have enough money for both. If you choose the game, the value of the ticket is the opportunity cost.

Supply and Demand The price of a good or service is usually determined by the laws of supply and demand. Supply is the amount of a good or service that businesses are willing and able to produce. Demand is the desire to have a good or service and the ability to pay for it.

The law of supply states that businesses are willing to produce more of a good or service at a higher price. The law of demand states that consumers will want to buy more of a good or service when its price falls. As the price of a good or service rises, consumers will want to buy less of it.

Incentives Economic activity is influenced by incentives, or benefits. For individuals and businesses, profit is a major incentive. **Profit** is the money an individual or business has left after paying expenses. The profit motive, or the desire to make a profit, is essential in many economies. If people do not want profit, they will not start businesses and people will have no way to get goods and services.

Saving money is also an incentive. Coupons, or advertisements that allow you to buy a good or service at a low price, can encourage people to buy certain products. When you use a coupon, you save money. A third type of incentive is receiving something extra. Sometimes, when people buy a certain good or service, they also receive a free good or service.

Reading Check
Summarize What is the connection between scarcity and trade-offs?

▶ Explore ONLINE!

Supply and Demand

Interpret Graphs

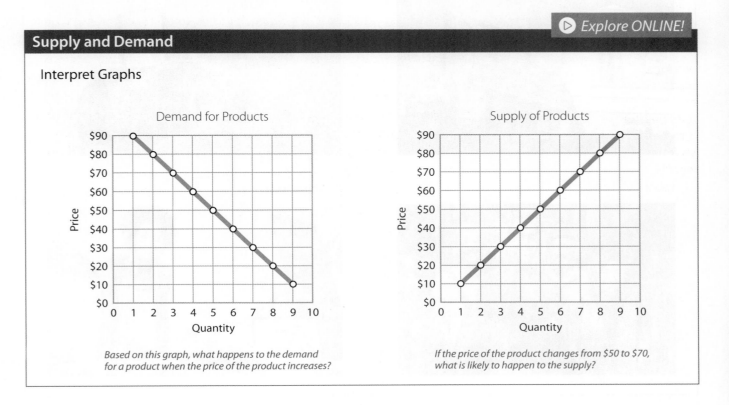

Demand for Products

Supply of Products

Based on this graph, what happens to the demand for a product when the price of the product increases?

If the price of the product changes from $50 to $70, what is likely to happen to the supply?

Systems to Organize Resources

People have to make decisions about how to spend money. Sometimes, there may be only one thing that you want. That makes your decision easy. If you want more than one thing but your funds are limited, you have to make a choice.

Businesses make similar choices about production. Their choices affect how they use economic resources called factors of production. There are four factors of production: natural resources, capital, labor, and entrepreneurs.

Factors of Production The raw materials needed to produce goods of all kinds come from natural resources, such as oceans, mines, and forests. Another important natural resource for businesses is land. Every business needs a place to locate. Companies that provide services need to be in a location easily reached by potential customers. Companies that make goods want to be in areas with transportation so they can ship their goods.

Businesses also need capital. Capital is the goods used to make other goods and services. Capital includes tools, trucks, machines, and office equipment. These items are often called capital goods to distinguish them from financial capital. Financial capital is the money used to buy the tools and equipment, or capital goods, used in production.

Factors of Production

Natural Resources

Capital

Labor

Entrepreneurs

The third factor of production is labor. Labor is the human effort, skills, and abilities to produce goods and services. Workers sell their labor in exchange for payment, called income. Many workers earn a form of income called hourly wages. Other workers, such as those who manage companies or have a great deal of responsibility, are paid salaries. Salaries are fixed earnings rather than hourly wages.

Entrepreneurs are the fourth factor of production. An **entrepreneur** is a person who organizes, manages, and assumes the risk of a business. Entrepreneurs often come up with an idea for a new product or a new way of doing business. They put up their own labor or capital and take the risks of failure. In return for taking the risks, an entrepreneur hopes to make a substantial profit.

Types of Economies Countries also have to make choices about production. A country's economic system determines how resources, goods, and services are distributed. There are three basic economic systems that countries use: traditional, command, and market economies.

In a traditional economy, economic decisions are based on how economic activity has been carried out in the past. People may grow their own food and make everything they need to survive, or they might trade with others to get things that they cannot make themselves. Many ancient civilizations, such as Sumer in the Middle East, were based on traditional economies. Today some parts of the developing world still have traditional economies.

A second type of economic system is called a command economy. In this system, the government makes all economic decisions and owns or controls all the factors of production. The government tells people what they can produce, how much of it to produce, and how much they can charge for it. Only a few countries in the world, such as North Korea and Cuba, have command economies.

The third type of economy is called a market economy. A market economy is one in which economic decisions are made by people looking out for their own best interests. A market economy is based on freedom. People are free to own or control factors of production. They can own property, start companies, and buy and sell products as they choose. Companies also need to be free to compete with one another. In a free market, competition among sellers is the main factor in setting prices. Sellers try to price their goods lower than their competition so that people will buy them. At the same time, they have to be careful not to set their prices so low that they lose money.

Today many countries have what is sometimes called a **mixed economy**. They are primarily market economies but with features of traditional and command economic systems. In these mixed economies, businesses are largely free to operate as they please. However, they must obey laws and rules set up by the government. The United States is an example of a mixed economy.

Reading Check
Contrast How are command and market economies different?

Needs and Wants

All around the world, people need certain things to survive. People cannot live without food and water, shelter, and clothing. These basic materials that people cannot live without are called needs.

In addition to their needs, there are many items that people want in order to make their lives more comfortable. These items are not necessary for survivial, but they can have great value to people. For example, you may want a television, a smart phone, or a car. You do not really need any of these things in order to live, but they can make your life easier, more comfortable, or more enjoyable. These types of items are called wants. Different people have different wants. In addition, a person's wants can change over time.

People satisfy their needs and wants by obtaining goods and services. However, the process of obtaining goods and services has changed over time. Today there are many ways that individuals receive goods and services.

Meeting Needs and Wants In the past, most people were farmers, growing what they needed to survive. Eventually, people started forming businesses, and customers bought goods and services from them. Most businesses were small. Only a few people, generally wealthy people, could afford to create large businesses. Over time, however, many businesses began to grow. Today big businesses are essential to the economy of the United States and other countries. Many of the goods and services we use every day to meet our needs and wants could not be produced by small companies. For example, producing automobiles or electricity requires large and expensive machines. Only large companies have the resources and the tools to produce these goods efficiently. The Internet is also changing the way people buy goods and services. People can often shop online. They can view goods and some services on their computers or smart phones and purchase items electronically.

As you have read, businesses sell goods and services to earn profits. However, some business organizations provide goods and services without seeking to earn profits. These organizations are known as nonprofit organizations. They include charities, scientific research associations, and groups dedicated to culture and education.

Businesses are not alone in meeting the needs of individuals. By providing assistance to unemployed workers, governments make certain that these workers can still buy goods and services. Schools provide free or low-cost food to students, and religious institutions often provide free clothing and other items to people. Families help by providing meals and clothing, while friends help by sharing or letting other friends borrow things.

Money and Trade

As you have read, the main economic problem is scarcity. Almost no country can meet all its needs without outside help. As a result, almost every country in the world engages in some international trade. **Trade** is the activity of buying, selling, or exchanging goods and services.

Countries trade because they cannot produce everything their citizens need or want. For example, the United States has to import coffee. To

Reading Check
Summarize How do businesses meet the needs of people?

import is to bring in goods or services from another country. The United States also exports products such as automobiles. To export is to send goods or services to another country. Many countries tend to specialize or concentrate on producing certain kinds of goods and services. The resources available in a country often determine the kinds of goods it produces.

Countries that specialize in production and then engage in trade with one another are interdependent. Interdependence means that peoples depend on one another for different goods and services.

The History of Trade The first type of trade system was called the barter system. Using this system, people exchanged goods and services directly for other goods and services. For example, a farmer might give another farmer wheat in exchange for cattle.

The growth of cities led to the demand for more goods and services. However, natural resources are not evenly distributed on the earth. Therefore, some civilizations had access to natural resources that other civilizations did not. This gave some civilizations a comparative advantage. People have a comparative advantage when they can produce a good more efficiently, or at a lower cost, than other people. Civilizations located near mineral resources could produce certain goods more efficiently than civilizations not located near mineral resources.

In order to get the goods and services they needed, early civilizations began trading with each other. Over time, trade routes were formed. One major trade route was known as the Silk Road. This route stretched from China to Rome. Trade along this route allowed people in Rome to obtain silk, and people in China to obtain wool and other goods.

The benefits of trade were enormous for early civilizations. Interactions along trade routes led to the exchange of languages, religions, tools, and inventions. For example, the religions of Christianity and Buddhism were introduced to China by traders traveling the Silk Road. However, trade did have drawbacks, such as the spread of disease.

Today, countries continue to experience the benefits and drawbacks of trade. These benefits include the exchange of new technologies. Drawbacks include increased competition from businesses in other countries.

Using Money As trade between early civilizations increased, problems with the barter system became clear. It was often difficult to determine or agree upon the value of goods and services. In addition, it was often hard to transport goods for bartering. Eventually, people started to use certain materials, such as silver, for money. Money has three basic functions:

- It is a medium of exchange. People can use it to purchase goods and services.
- It is a store of value. People can easily store or transport "value," and exchange it for something else when they need to.
- It is a unit of account. People can use money to measure, and agree upon, the price of a good or service.

Today every country in the world has a currency, or type of money. For example, the United States has the dollar, Mexico has the peso, and many European countries have the euro.

▶ *Explore ONLINE!*

Yen Japan

Peso Mexico

Euro Europe

Yuan China

Dollar United States

Real Brazil

Rupee India

Wealth When talking about economics, people may confuse money with wealth. **Wealth** is the value of all possessions that a person or country has. Money is just one form of wealth. Land and other valuable resources are also forms of wealth.

People and countries can possibly increase their wealth by investing money. When you invest money, you spend money in the hopes of making more. There are different ways to invest money. One popular way is to invest in stocks. Stocks represent partial ownership of a business. If the company does well, this entitles you to a share of its profits based on the amount of stock you own. You can also invest directly in starting a new business. Another way to invest money is to buy property. However, most financial investment involves some level of risk. If a business is not profitable, its stock value typically falls. Investing in property such as real estate holds a similar risk that prices will fall. Investors then lose money.

Reading Check
Generalize How has trade changed over time?

The Importance of Economics

There are different reasons why people study economics. One reason is that an understanding of economics can help us make everyday decisions about money. Another reason is that it helps explain world history. Events have affected economics, and economics have affected events. Understanding economic history can help us interpret the past. It can also help us explain the present and predict future consequences of economic decisions.

Historical Factors and Economic Growth Throughout history, various historical factors have helped increase economic growth. These include the discovery of new resources and expansion. Over the course of several centuries, Europeans explored North America and claimed territory for various European nations. The explorers brought new resources back with them, which created demand in Europe. Demand for these new resources increased trade between North America and Europe. While the trade cycle benefitted many Europeans, it also had terrible drawbacks. Europeans brought new and deadly diseases to North America, which killed millions of Native Americans. The trade cycle also led to the creation of a slave economy in North America in order to grow more resources, such as sugar. Many Africans were enslaved and brought to North America.

Increased Productivity Economic growth is also affected by productivity, a measure of how efficiently goods and services are produced. Two factors that have increased productivity are technology and education. In the late 1800s, inventor Thomas Edison made the widespread use of electricity practical and affordable. This helped increase productivity because electric power is faster and cheaper than older sources of power, such as steam. The establishment of more schools over the past few centuries has led to more educated workers. The more educated a worker is, the easier it is for him or her to learn new skills and use new technology.

Reading Check
Predict What might happen to productivity if a new source of energy is discovered?

Summary and Preview Scarcity is a problem that has affected economics throughout history. Different types of economic systems address the distribution of economic resources. In the next lesson, you will learn the role of government in the economy.

Lesson 3 Assessment

Review Ideas, Terms, and People

1. a. **Recall** What is scarcity?

   b. **Predict** According to the law of supply, will a company make a greater or smaller amount of a product when the price is low?

   c. **Describe** What are some examples of economic incentives?

2. a. **Evaluate** Which factor of production is the most important?

   b. **Describe** Why is the U.S. economy described as a mixed economy?

3. a. **Contrast** What is the difference between a need and a want?

   b. **Identify** What are some examples of nonprofit organizations?

4. a. **Analyze** What is the connection between location and comparative advantage?

   b. **Categorize** What are the three functions of money?

   c. **Explain** What is the connection between money and wealth?

5. a. **Recall** What are some factors that have helped increase economic growth?

Critical Thinking

6. **Summarize** Copy the graphic organizer. Use it and your notes to identify the four factors of production necessary for a business to be successful.

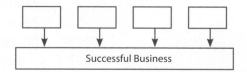

Studying Civics

The Big Idea

Government plays an essential role in every country.

Main Ideas

- A country's government affects the lives of its people.

- There have been many different forms of government throughout history.

- Governments have a role to play in the economy, including providing services and collecting taxes.

Key Terms and People

civics
government
constitution
democracy
republic
tax

If YOU were there . . .

You see a problem in your town or city that needs to be solved. How do you try to help solve this problem? Do you need to try to solve it yourself? Or is there someone in your local government who can help?

What are the roles and responsibilities of government?

Need for Governments

What is civics, and why do you study it? **Civics** is the study of citizenship and government. A citizen is a legally recognized member of a country. A **government** is the organizations and individuals who have the right to rule over a group of people.

As citizens, we are faced with many questions. Could we manage our lives without any help from our government? Who would provide basic services, such as public roads or fire departments? What are the basic purposes of government? Over time, government has grown more complex. Yet its basic purposes have remained the same.

Helping People Cooperate When people live together in a community, it is important for them to work together and avoid conflict. Government provides a way for people to unite, solve problems, and cooperate. Even in the earliest periods of human history, people relied on government to make their lives safer and easier.

Providing Services Governments provide expensive or important services to larger groups of people who might otherwise have to do without the service. For example, by establishing schools, government makes it possible for all children to receive a good education. Governments also provide police to protect lives and property, and fire departments to protect homes and businesses.

Because of government, we can travel highways that stretch from border to border. We have a system of money that makes it easy for us to buy and sell things and to know

Fire departments are one example of an important service provided by the government.

the price of these things. Trash is collected, and health laws are enforced to protect us. We can go to public libraries. Government provides these and many more services.

Providing Laws Governments also provide laws to guide and protect citizens. Today, many countries around the world are ruled according to a **constitution**, or a written plan of government. A constitution sets forth the purposes of the government and describes how the government is to be organized. Laws must be constitutional, or in agreement with the constitution, to be valid. The laws are recorded so that people can know and obey them.

Laws can also guarantee certain freedoms, including freedom of speech, the press, and religion. These freedoms have limitations, however. For example, having free speech and a free press does not mean we are free to tell lies or write false statements about another person. Each person has the right to have his or her reputation protected. Laws must always strike a balance between freedom and protecting people.

Reading Check
Summarize What are the basic purposes of government?

Forms of Government

Every country in the world has a government. However, these governments vary widely. Governments differ in the way their leaders are chosen and in the amount of power held by citizens. For example, many countries allow their citizens to vote, but some do not.

Governments generally fall into two different types: nondemocratic and democratic governments. In a country with a nondemocratic government, citizens do not have the power to rule. Other countries have democratic governments. In a **democracy**, the people either rule directly or they elect officials who act on their behalf. Each country's government has been shaped by the beliefs of its people and their history.

Ancient Government Around the world, the earliest form of government was based upon family. This form of government is known as the kinship system. In a kinship system, leaders were not elected. The oldest living male or female members of the family had the right to rule. These members of the family often made and enforced laws for the family. Individual rights mattered less than the well-being of the family.

Eventually, groups of families united to form larger communities. They did this for many reasons, including the need for common defense. Over time, this led to the formation of cities and kingdoms, and different forms of government developed. The right to rule might be passed down through a powerful family, creating a dynasty. The empires of ancient Egypt and ancient China were both ruled by dynasties. Other early civilizations were ruled by theocracies. A theocracy is a government controlled by one or more religious leaders who claim to rule on behalf of God or the gods worshipped in their country.

Democracies and Republics Several different forms of government developed among the city-states of ancient Greece. A city-state is an independent city with its own government. Some city-states were ruled by dictators. A dictator is a person who rules with complete and absolute power. Dictators often take power by force. Other city-states were ruled by oligarchies. An oligarchy is a type of dictatorship in which all power is concentrated in a small group of people.

In the ancient Greek city-state of Athens, a form of government called democracy was developed. The word *democracy* comes from an ancient Greek term meaning "rule of the people." Ancient Athens practiced what is called direct democracy. This is where all voters in a community meet in

Forms of Government

Government	Characteristics	Examples
Theocracy	Religious leaders hold power. Laws and government are based on religious teachings.	Islamic Republic of Iran, the Vatican
Direct Democracy	All eligible citizens participate in government and make laws.	Ancient Athens, Switzerland
Republic	Citizens elect an executive and representatives who participate in government and make laws.	United States, Germany, France
Monarchy	A monarch by birth governs with absolute power or shares some power with a small group.	Saudi Arabia
Constitutional Monarchy	A monarch holds limited power. An elected legislature and executive run the government.	United Kingdom, Japan
Dictatorship	A supreme leader governs with absolute power.	North Korea

one place to make laws and decide what actions to take. Historically, direct democracies have been suited only to small communities.

Around the same time that Athens developed direct democracy, Rome developed representative democracy. In this form of democracy, the people elect representatives to carry on the work of government for them. The people consent to be ruled by their elected leaders. This system of government is called a **republic**. The United States is another example of a republic. However, democracy would not last in ancient Rome. A series of dictators, including Julius Caesar, turned the Roman Republic into the Roman Empire.

Monarchies After the fall of the Roman Empire in the late 400s, European countries were ruled by monarchies. A monarch is a person, such as a king or queen, who rules over a kingdom or an empire. Under these monarchies, members of the aristocracy had much more power, money, and land than did common citizens. An aristocracy is a class of rich land owners or nobles.

In the past, many monarchies were absolute monarchies. This means the monarch had full control of the government. The power of monarchs changed over time. In 1215, members of the English aristocracy forced King John to sign the *Magna Carta,* which means "Great Charter." The Magna Carta protected certain rights for English citizens. This made England a limited monarchy, where the power of the ruler is restricted by law. In a limited monarchy, the ruler usually shares power with elected officials.

Ideas about monarchies continued to change. During the 17th and 18th centuries, philosophers such as John Locke argued that all people were born equal with the natural rights of life, liberty, and property. Locke also believed that if a government failed to protect its citizens' natural rights, they had the right to overthrow it. Locke's ideas helped inspire Americans to separate from the monarchy of Great Britain in 1776 and form an independent nation.

Reading Check
Contrast How are monarchies and democracies different?

Today most monarchies are constitutional monarchies. For example, the monarchs of Sweden and the United Kingdom serve as ceremonial heads of state and have limited powers. The real power lies elsewhere, such as with elected officials. Saudi Arabia is one of a few modern countries where the monarch still has full control.

The Role of Government in the Economy

Throughout history, governments have influenced economics because they determine how goods and services are produced and distributed. Many theocracies, dictatorships, and monarchies have had command economies. Many democracies have had market or mixed economies.

Taxes Governments also collect taxes. A **tax** is a charge people pay to a government. In return, the government provides public services and protection. Before the invention of money, governments used to collect taxes in the form of goods and services. These included livestock, grain, labor, and military service. The ancient Incans, for example, had a tax system

The *mita* system allowed Incan rulers to build grand cities such as Machu Pichu.

called the *mita* system. Citizens paid the *mita* tax by working for the government as farmers, soldiers, or builders. In return, the government would provide basic needs, such as food and clothing.

Today, governments at the national, state, and local levels may all collect taxes. Each level uses tax dollars to provide goods and services, such as national defense, public schools, police protection, and roads. These goods and services benefit individuals, businesses, and the economy. For example, you probably use a government road or sidewalk to go to school. A business might use the same road to transport goods and services. Moreover, the government likely hired a private construction firm to build this road and pays for workers to maintain it.

Trade Many governments also participate in their economies by making laws about trade. They may use trade barriers to protect jobs and industries from foreign competition. A trade barrier is a limit on the exchange of goods. One type of trade barrier is a protective tariff. Protective tariffs are taxes on imports that make foreign goods cost more. In the United States, for example, protective tariffs mean that Americans will be more likely to choose goods made in the United States. However, nearly all governments still support international trade. In fact, the U.S. government has signed trade agreements with other countries to help reduce or eliminate certain trade barriers.

Summary Government provides many things, including important services and laws. There have been many different forms of government throughout history. Governments can influence their economies by taxing citizens and controlling trade.

Reading Check
Explain How does the U.S. government influence international trade?

Lesson 4 Assessment

Review Ideas, Terms, and People

1. a. **Analyze** Why was government necessary for early human communities?
   b. **Describe** What are some services that government can provide?
   c. **Explain** What is the purpose of a **constitution**?
   d. **Identify** What is one freedom protected by U.S. laws?
2. a. **Define** What is an oligarchy?
   b. **Contrast** What is the difference between an absolute monarchy and a constitutional monarchy?
3. a. **Predict** What would happen if the U.S. government stopped collecting taxes?

Critical Thinking

4. **Categorize** Copy the graphic organizer. Fill in each box with the name of a form of government and a brief summary of that form of government.

Forms of Government	

Make Maps

Define the Skill

Throughout history, maps have been valuable tools. Today they remain the best way to visually record and communicate information about our world and its history. Therefore, making maps is an important skill.

Learn the Skill

Almost all maps have titles, directional indicators, scales, and legends. A map's title shows what the subject of the map is. The map title is usually the first thing that people look for when studying a map.

A directional indicator shows which way north, south, east, and west lie on the map. Most maps in this textbook indicate direction by using a compass rose. A **compass rose** has arrows that point to all four principal directions, as shown.

Scales represent the distances between points on a map. The maps in this textbook provide a bar **scale**. Scales often give distances in miles and kilometers. Because the distances are given in large intervals, you may have to approximate the actual distance on the scale.

Lastly, mapmakers should always include a **legend**, or key, explaining what the symbols on a map represent. The following guidelines can help you use these elements to make a useful map.

1. Determine the purpose of your map. What do you want people to see and learn?

2. Come up with a clear and accurate title for your map.

3. Include a directional indicator, a scale, and a legend. Make sure that your legend includes all the important symbols that appear on your map.

4. Make sure that your elements do not cover up important parts of your map.

5. Write informational text, such as names and labels, clearly on your map.

Practice the Skill

Make a map of your classroom. Use measuring tape or larger rulers to measure its length and width. Use this information in your scale. Also, create symbols for features in the classroom, such as desks. Include these symbols in your legend. Use a compass or another tool to determine direction in the classroom. Include this information in the form of a compass rose. Finally, make sure your map has a title.

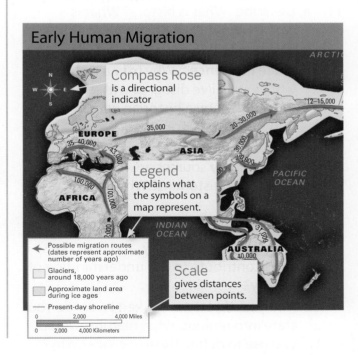

Early Human Migration

Compass Rose is a directional indicator

Legend explains what the symbols on a map represent.

Scale gives distances between points.

ARCTIC

EUROPE

ASIA

AFRICA

PACIFIC OCEAN

INDIAN OCEAN

AUSTRALIA

35,000
35–40,000
43,000
20–30,000
100,000
100,000
40,000
31,000

← Possible migration routes (dates represent approximate number of years ago)
☐ Glaciers, around 18,000 years ago
☐ Approximate land area during ice ages
— Present-day shoreline

0   2,000   4,000 Miles
0   2,000   4,000 Kilometers

Review Vocabulary, Terms, and People

*For each statement, write **T** if it is true or **F** if it is false. If the statement is false, write the correct term that would make the sentence a true statement.*

1. <u>History</u> is the study of the past based on what people left behind.
2. Knowledge, beliefs, customs, and values of a group of people are part of their <u>environment</u>.
3. A handwritten letter from a soldier to his family would be considered a <u>primary source</u>.
4. <u>Geography</u> is the study of the past, whether recent or long ago.
5. Your state probably has many different <u>landforms</u>, such as mountains, plains, and valleys.
6. Weather changes from day to day, but a location's <u>climate</u> does not change as often.
7. <u>Scarcity</u> is a major incentive for individuals and businesses.
8. The first type of <u>wealth</u> system was called the barter system.
9. <u>Civics</u> is the study of citizenship and government.
10. The United States is an example of a <u>republic</u>.

Comprehension and Critical Thinking

Lesson 1

11. a. **Describe** What is history? What is archaeology? How do the two fields work together?
    b. **Make Inferences** Why may a historian who is still alive disagree with conclusions drawn by a historian who lived a hundred years ago?
    c. **Evaluate** Do you think primary sources or secondary sources are more valuable to modern historians? Why?

Lesson 2

12. a. **Identify** What are the two main branches of geography, and how does each contribute to our understanding of history?
    b. **Analyze** If you were asked to divide your state into regions, what features would you use to define those regions? Why?
    c. **Predict** How might a long period of severe heat or cold affect the history of a city or region?

Lesson 3

13. a. **Predict** What would happen to a business if it lacked capital?
    b. **Summarize** Why do people invest money in stocks and new businesses?
    c. **Evaluate** Do you think new technologies always lead to economic growth? Why or why not?

Lesson 4

14. a. **Explain** Why are laws recorded and passed?
    b. **Contrast** How was democracy different in ancient Athens than in the Roman Republic?
    c. **Draw Conclusions** What would happen if the U.S. government removed certain protective tariffs?

Review Themes

15. Society and Culture How may a historian's description of a battle reveal information about his or her own society or culture?

16. Economics If hundreds of years from now historians study the impact of economics of our time, what may they conclude about American society? Explain your answer.

Reading Skills

17. Specialized Vocabulary of History Read the following passage in which several words have been left blank. Fill in each of the blanks with the appropriate word that you learned in this module.

> Although _____ is defined as the study of the past, it is much more. It is a key to understanding our _____, the ideas, languages, religions, and other traits that make us who we are. In the _____ left behind by ancient peoples, we can see reflections of our own material goods: plates and dishes, toys, jewelry, and work objects. These objects show us that human _____ have not changed that much.

Social Studies Skills

Make Maps *Answer the following questions about making maps.*

18. How are maps valuable?

19. What is the purpose of a compass rose?

20. How are map scales and legends used differently?

21. What would happen if someone tried reading a map that lacked a title?

Focus On Writing

22. Write Interview Questions Image that you are a writer for a history website. Write questions for an interview with a historian. What would your readers want to learn more about? Write at least ten interview questions that your readers will want answered.

Module 2

The Stone Ages and Early Cultures

Essential Question
Why was the invention of farming revolutionary?

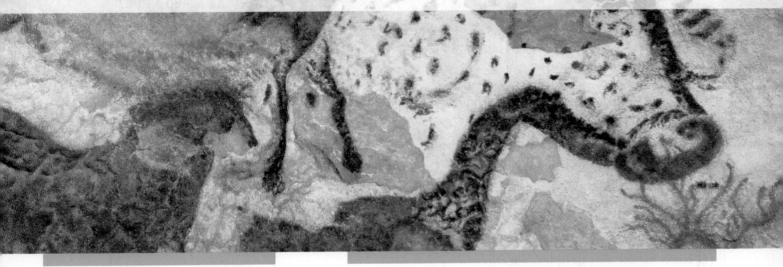

About the Photo: This cave painting in France is more than 15,000 years old.

▶ *Explore ONLINE!*

HISTORY

VIDEOS, including...
• Stone Age Weapons
• Ötzi the Iceman
• Last Rites: Death Ceremonies

☑ Document-Based Investigations

☑ Graphic Organizers

☑ Interactive Games

☑ Image Carousel: Hominids

☑ Image with Hotspots: Hunter-Gatherers

☑ Interactive Map: Early Human Migrations

☑ Image with Hotspots: An Early Farming Society

In this module, you will learn about the earliest people. You will see how they learned to make tools, hunt, gather food, and even create art.

What You Will Learn...

Lesson 1: The First People **42**
The Big Idea Prehistoric people learned to adapt to their environment, to make simple tools, to use fire, and to use language

Lesson 2: Early Human Migration **50**
The Big Idea As people migrated around the world, they learned to adapt to new environments.

Lesson 3: Beginnings of Agriculture **55**
The Big Idea The development of agriculture brought great changes to human society.

Timeline of Events 5 million BC–5000 BC

▶ Explore ONLINE!

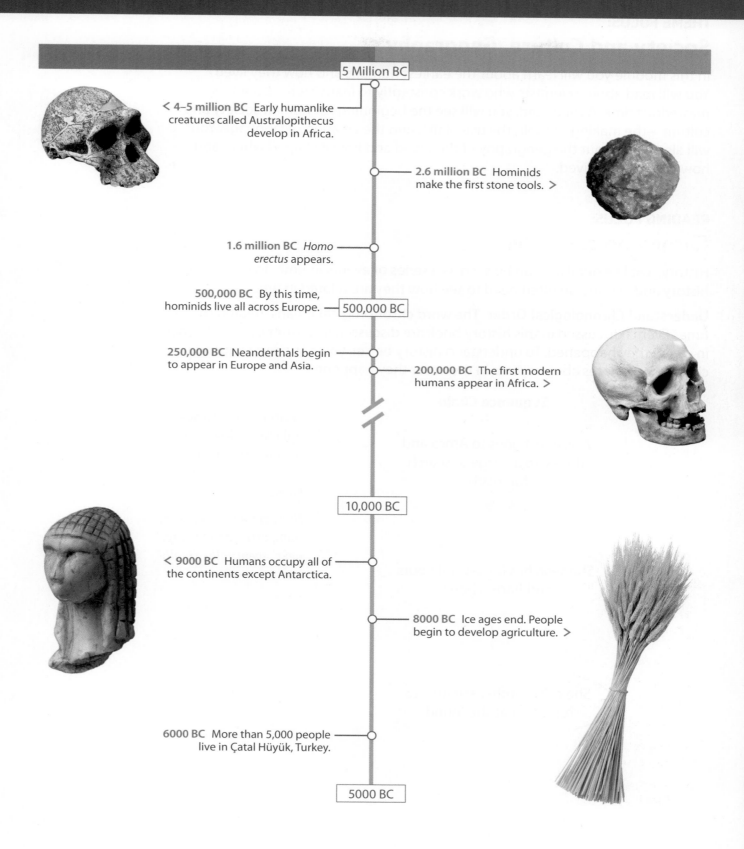

5 Million BC

< 4–5 million BC Early humanlike creatures called Australopithecus develop in Africa.

2.6 million BC Hominids make the first stone tools. >

1.6 million BC *Homo erectus* appears.

500,000 BC By this time, hominids live all across Europe.

500,000 BC

250,000 BC Neanderthals begin to appear in Europe and Asia.

200,000 BC The first modern humans appear in Africa. >

10,000 BC

< 9000 BC Humans occupy all of the continents except Antarctica.

8000 BC Ice ages end. People begin to develop agriculture. >

6000 BC More than 5,000 people live in Çatal Hüyük, Turkey.

5000 BC

Reading Social Studies

Society and Culture, Geography

In this module you will learn about the earliest humans and how they lived. You will read about scientists who work constantly to learn more about this mysterious time. As you read, you will see the beginnings of human society and culture—the making of tools, the use of fire, and the creation of language. You will also read about the geography of the world and how it shaped where and how early people lived.

READING FOCUS:
Chronological Order

History, just like our lives, can be seen as a series of events in time. To understand history and events, we often need to see how they are related in time.

Understand Chronological Order The word **chronological** means "related to time." Events discussed in this history book are discussed in **sequence**, in the order in which they happened. To understand history better, you can use a sequence chain to take notes about events in the order they happened.

Sequence Chain

A scientist goes to Africa and drives to a gorge to search for fossils.

↓

She searches for several hours and finds a bone.

↓

She calls another scientist to report what she found.

Writers sometimes signal chronological order, or sequence, by using words or phrases like these:

first, before, then, later, soon, after, before long, next, eventually, finally

You Try It!

Key Terms and People

Lesson 1
prehistory
hominid
ancestor
tool
Paleolithic Era
society
hunter-gatherers

Lesson 2
migrate
ice ages
land bridge
Mesolithic Era

Lesson 3
Neolithic Era
domestication
agriculture
megaliths

Read the following passage and then answer the questions below.

Scientists Study Remains One archaeologist who made important discoveries about prehistory was Mary Leakey. In 1959 she found bones in East Africa that were more than 1.5 million years old. She and her husband, Louis Leakey, believed that the bones belonged to an early hominid. A hominid is an early ancestor of modern-day humans. . . .

In 1974 anthropologist Donald Johanson (joh-HAN-suhn) found bones from another early ancestor. . . . Johanson named his find Lucy. Tests showed that she lived more than 3 million years ago. . . .

In 1994 anthropologist Tim White found remains of a hominid that he believes may have lived as long as 4.4 million years ago. But some scientists disagree with White's time estimate. Discoveries of ancient bones give us information about early humans and their ancestors, but not all scientists agree on the meaning of these discoveries.

Answer these questions based on the passage you just read.

1. Complete the timeline below with information about scientific discoveries from the passage you just read.

Donald Johanson
finds Lucy.

2. Each of the scientists discussed in the passage found the bones of people who lived at different times. Make another timeline that shows the order in which these people lived. What do you notice about this order compared to the order in which the bones were found?

As you read this module, look for words that indicate the order in which events occurred.

The First People

The Big Idea

Prehistoric people learned to adapt to their environment, to make simple tools, to use fire, and to use language.

Main Ideas

- Scientists study the remains of early humans to learn about prehistory.
- Hominids and early humans first appeared in East Africa millions of years ago.
- Stone Age tools grew more complex as time passed.
- Hunter-gatherer societies developed language, art, and religion.

Key Terms

prehistory
hominid
ancestor
tool
Paleolithic Era
society
hunter-gatherers

If YOU were there . . .

You live 200,000 years ago, in a time known as the Stone Age. A member of your group has offered to teach you his skill. You watch carefully as he strikes two black rocks together. A small piece flakes off. You try to copy him, but the rocks just break. Finally you learn to strike the rock just right. You have made a sharp stone knife!

How will you use your new skill?

Scientists Study Remains

Although humans have lived on the earth for more than a million years, writing was not invented until about 5,000 years ago. Historians call the time before there was writing **prehistory**. Historic time periods, on the other hand, are those for which information has been recorded with letters, words, or numbers. To study prehistory, historians rely on the work of archaeologists and anthropologists.

One archaeologist who made important discoveries about prehistory was Mary Leakey. In 1959 she found bones in East Africa that were more than 1.5 million years old. She and her husband, Louis Leakey, believed that the bones belonged to an early **hominid** (HAH-muh-nuhd). A hominid

Mary Leakey found some of the earliest ancestors of humans in Olduvai Gorge.

is an early ancestor of modern-day humans. An **ancestor** is a relative who lived in the past.

In fact, the bones belonged to an *Australopithecus* (aw-stray-loh-PI-thuh-kuhs), one of the earliest hominids. In 1974 anthropologist Donald Johanson (joh-HAN-suhn) found bones from another early ancestor. He described his discovery:

"We reluctantly headed back toward camp. . . . I glanced over my right shoulder. Light glinted off a bone. I knelt down for a closer look. . . . Everywhere we looked on the slope around us we saw more bones lying on the surface."

—Donald Johanson, from *Ancestors: In Search of Human Origins*

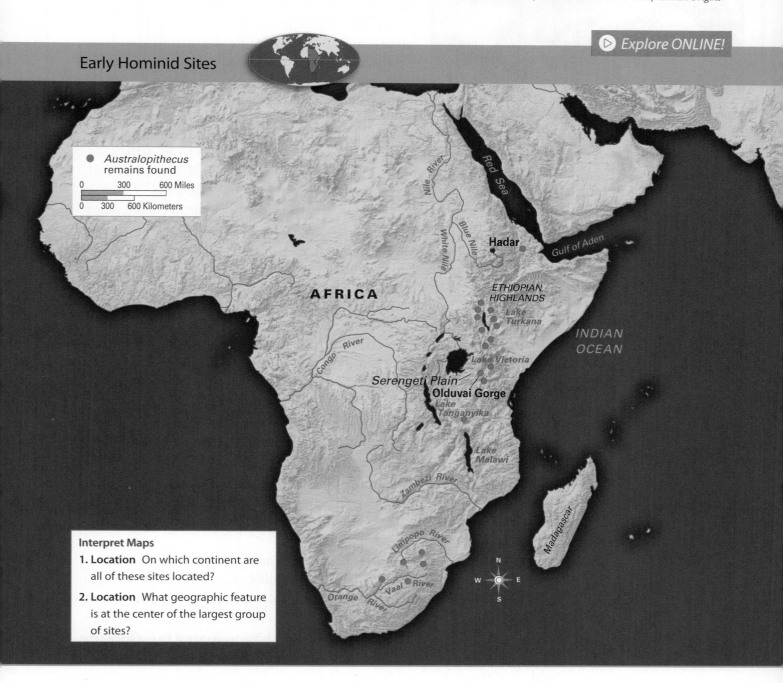

Early Hominid Sites

Explore ONLINE!

Australopithecus remains found

0   300   600 Miles
0   300   600 Kilometers

Nile River
Red Sea
White Nile
Blue Nile
Hadar
Gulf of Aden
AFRICA
ETHIOPIAN HIGHLANDS
Lake Turkana
INDIAN OCEAN
Congo River
Lake Victoria
Serengeti Plain
Olduvai Gorge
Lake Tanganyika
Lake Malawi
Zambezi River
Madagascar
Limpopo River
Vaal River
Orange River

Interpret Maps

1. **Location** On which continent are all of these sites located?

2. **Location** What geographic feature is at the center of the largest group of sites?

Donald Johanson discovered the bones of Lucy, an early hominid that lived more than 3 million years ago.

Johanson named his find Lucy. Tests showed that she lived more than 3 million years ago. Johanson could tell from her bones that she was small and had walked on two legs. The ability to walk on two legs was a key step in human development.

In 1994 anthropologist Tim White found remains of a hominid that he believes may have lived as long as 4.4 million years ago. But some scientists disagree with White's time estimate. Discoveries of ancient bones give us information about early humans and their ancestors, but not all scientists agree on the meaning of these discoveries.

Scientists have been able to study more complete remains of later hominids. In 1991 two hikers discovered the frozen body of a mummified, or preserved, Stone Age human. Also known as the Iceman, he was nicknamed Ötzi after the location in the Italian Alps where he was found. Glaciers preserved his body, clothing, and other objects for thousands of years. This has given scientists the chance to study items like a pair of leather shoes, an early version of a backpack, and an ax with a copper blade. An arrowhead was also found in Ötzi's shoulder. These objects have provided valuable information about how he lived and possibly died.

Anthropologists and archaeologists are not the only scholars who study prehistory. Linguists study the shape of the mouth and the throat to learn more about how early humans might have developed language. Geneticists use what they know about DNA to help support evidence from ancient bones and other remains. DNA is a substance that is found in the cells of a plant or animal and that carries the basic genetic information about that plant or animal. Geographers are interested in genetic information because it could tell them more about the migration routes of early humans.

Reading Check
Make Inferences
What can ancient bones and other physical evidence tell us about human ancestors?

Hominids and Early Humans

Later groups of hominids began to appear about 3 million years ago. As time passed they became more like modern humans.

In the early 1960s Louis Leakey found hominid remains that he called *Homo habilis*, or "handy man." Leakey and his son Richard believed that *Homo habilis* was more closely related to modern humans than Lucy and had a larger brain.

Scientists believe that another group of hominids appeared in Africa about 1.5 million years ago. This group is called *Homo erectus*, or "upright man." Scientists think these people walked completely upright like modern people do.

Scientists believe that *Homo erectus* knew how to control fire. Once fire was started by natural causes, such as lightning, people used it to cook food. Fire also gave them heat and protection against animals.

During the Stone Age, people used tools like these, often for processing food.

Reading Check
Contrast
How was *Homo erectus* different from *Homo habilis*?

Eventually, hominids developed characteristics of modern humans. Scientists are not sure exactly when or where the first modern humans lived. Many think that they first appeared in Africa about 200,000 years ago. Scientists call these people *Homo sapiens*, or "wise man." Every person alive today belongs to this group.

Stone Age Tools

The first humans and their ancestors lived during a long period of time called the Stone Age. To help in their studies, archaeologists divide the Stone Age into three periods based on the kinds of tools used at the time. To archaeologists, a **tool** is any handheld object that has been modified to help a person accomplish a task.

The first part of the Stone Age is called the **Paleolithic** (pay-lee-uh-LI-thik) **Era**, or Old Stone Age. It lasted until about 10,000 years ago. During this time people used stone tools.

The First Tools Scientists have found the oldest tools in Tanzania, a country in East Africa. These sharpened stones, about the size of an adult's fist, are about 2.6 million years old. Each stone had been struck with another rock to create a sharp, jagged edge along one side. This process left one unsharpened side that could be used as a handle.

Scientists think that these first tools were mostly used to process food. The sharp edge could be used to cut, chop, or scrape roots, bones, or meat. Tools like these were used for about 2 million years.

Later Tools Over time, people learned to make better tools. For example, they developed the hand ax. They often made this tool out of a mineral called flint. Flint is easy to shape, and tools made from it can be very sharp. People used hand axes to break tree limbs, to dig, and to cut animal hides.

Hominids

Four major groups of hominids appeared in Africa between 5 million and about 200,000 years ago. Each group was more advanced than the one before it and could use better tools.

Australopithecus

- Name means "southern ape"
- Appeared in Africa about 4–5 million years ago
- Stood upright and walked on two legs
- Brain was about one-third the size of modern humans

Homo habilis

- Name means "handy man"
- Appeared in Africa about 2.4 million years ago
- Used early stone tools for chopping and scraping
- Brain was about half the size of modern humans

An early Stone Age chopper

Homo erectus

- Name means "upright man"
- Appeared in Africa about 2–1.5 million years ago
- Used early stone tools like the hand ax
- Learned to control fire
- Migrated out of Africa to Asia and Europe

A hand ax

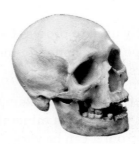

Homo sapiens

- Name means "wise man"
- Appeared in Africa about 200,000 years ago
- Migrated around the world
- Same species as modern human beings
- Learned to create fire and use a wide variety of tools
- Developed language

A flint knife

Early people were hunter-gatherers. They hunted animals and gathered wild plants to survive. Life for these hunter-gatherers was difficult and dangerous. Still, people learned how to make tools, use fire, and even create art.

Analyze Visuals
What tools are people using in this picture?

Reading Check
Summarize How did tools improve during the Old Stone Age? Give evidence from the text to support your answer.

People also learned to attach wooden handles to tools. By attaching a wooden shaft to a stone point, for example, they invented the spear. Because a spear could be thrown, hunters no longer had to stand close to animals they were hunting. As a result, people could hunt larger animals. Among the animals hunted by Stone Age people were deer, horses, bison, and elephant-like creatures called mammoths.

Hunter-Gatherer Societies

As early humans developed tools and new hunting techniques, they formed societies. A **society** is a community of people who share a common culture. These societies developed cultures with languages, religions, and art.

Society Anthropologists believe that early humans lived in small groups. In bad weather they might have taken shelter in a cave if there was one nearby. When food or water became hard to find, groups of people would have to move to new areas.

The early humans of the Stone Age were **hunter-gatherers**—people who hunt animals and gather wild plants, seeds, fruits, and nuts to survive. Hunter-gatherer societies still exist in some places today. Historians and anthropologists study them to draw conclusions about hunter-gatherers long ago.

Each person in a hunter-gatherer society did tasks to help meet the needs of the community. Anthropologists believe that most Stone Age hunters were men. They hunted in groups, sometimes chasing entire herds of animals over cliffs. This method was both more productive and safer than hunting alone.

Women in hunter-gatherer societies probably took responsibility for collecting plants to eat. They likely stayed near camps and took care of children. Children helped their communities as well. For example, scholars think children may have made noise to encourage animals, birds, or fish to move into nets or confined spaces so they could be captured. The first pets may also have appeared at this time. People kept dogs to help them hunt and for protection.

Language, Art, and Religion The most important development of early Stone Age culture was language. Scientists have many theories about why language first developed. Some think it was to make hunting in groups easier. Others think it developed as a way for people to form relationships. Still others think language made it easier for people to resolve issues like how to **distribute** food.

Language wasn't the only way early people expressed themselves. They also created art. People carved figures out of materials like stone, ivory, and bone. They carved beads for personal ornamentation. They painted and carved images of people and animals on cave walls. Scientists still

Academic Vocabulary
distribute to divide among a group of people

Link to Today

Stone Tools

Did you know that Stone Age people's tools weren't as primitive as we might think? They made knife blades and arrowheads—like the one shown—out of volcanic glass called obsidian. The obsidian blades were very sharp. In fact, they could be 100 times sharper and smoother than the steel blades used for surgery in modern hospitals.

Today some doctors are going back to using these Stone Age materials. They have found that blades made from obsidian are more precise than modern scalpels. Some doctors use obsidian blades for delicate surgery on the face because the stone tools leave "nicer-looking" scars.

Analyze Information
How do you think modern uses of obsidian blades are different from those in the Stone Age? Give evidence from the text to explain your answer.

Cave Paintings

Thousands of years ago, early people decorated cave walls with paintings like this one in Africa. No one knows for sure why people created cave paintings, but many historians think they were related to hunting.

Reading Check
Analyze Causes
What was one possible reason for the development of language?

aren't sure why people made art. They think that perhaps the cave paintings were used to teach people how to hunt. They might also have had religious meanings.

Scholars know little about the religious beliefs of early people. Archaeologists have found graves that included food and artifacts. Many think these discoveries show that human religion developed during the period.

Summary and Preview Scientists have discovered and studied the remains of hominids and early humans who lived in East Africa millions of years ago. These Stone Age people were hunter-gatherers who used fire, stone tools, and language. In the next lesson, you will learn how early humans moved out of Africa and populated the world.

Lesson 1 Assessment

Review Ideas, Terms, and People

1. **a.** Identify Who found the bones of Lucy?
   b. Explain Why do historians need archaeologists and anthropologists to study prehistory?

2. **a.** Recall What is the scientific name for modern humans?
   b. Make Inferences What might have been one advantage of walking completely upright?

3. **a.** Recall What kinds of tools did people use during the Paleolithic Era?
   b. Synthesize Design a model of a stone and wood tool you could use to help you with your chores. Describe your tool in a sentence or two.

4. **a.** Define What is a hunter-gatherer?
   b. Form Opinions In your opinion, what was the most important change brought about by the development of language? Why?

Critical Thinking

5. **Evaluate** In this lesson, you learned about advances made by prehistoric humans. Using a graphic organizer like the one shown here, rank the three advances you think are most important. Next to your organizer, write a sentence explaining why you ranked the advances in that order.

1.   2.   3.

Early Human Migration

The Big Idea

As people migrated around the world, they learned to adapt to new environments.

Main Ideas

- People moved out of Africa as the earth's climates changed.

- People adapted to new environments by making clothing and new types of tools.

Key Terms

migrate
ice ages
land bridge
Mesolithic Era

Stone age peoples often had to migrate during the ice ages to find animals to hunt.

If YOU were there . . .

Your tribe of hunter-gatherers has lived in this place for as long as anyone can remember. But now there are not enough animals to hunt. Whenever you find berries and roots, you have to share them with people from other tribes. Your leaders think it's time to find a new home in the lands far beyond the mountains. But no one has ever traveled there, and many people are afraid.

How do you feel about moving to a new home?

People Move Out of Africa

During the Old Stone Age, climate patterns around the world changed, transforming the earth's geography. In response to these changes, people began to **migrate**, or move, to new places.

The Ice Ages Most scientists believe that about 1.6 million years ago, many places around the world began to experience long periods of freezing weather. These freezing times are called the **ice ages**. The ice ages ended about 10,000 years ago.

During the ice ages, huge sheets of ice covered much of the earth's land. These ice sheets were formed from ocean water, leaving ocean levels lower than they are now. Many areas that are now underwater were dry land then. For example, a narrow body of water now separates Asia and North America. But scientists think that during the ice ages, the ocean level dropped and exposed a **land bridge**, a strip of land connecting two continents. Land bridges allowed Stone Age peoples to migrate around the world.

Settling New Lands Scientists agree that migration around the world took hundreds of thousands of years. Early hominids, the ancestors of modern humans, migrated from Africa to Asia as early as 2 million years ago. From there, they spread to Southeast Asia and Europe.

Later, humans also began to migrate around the world. Earlier hominids died out. Look at the map to see the routes of early human migration. Humans began to migrate from East Africa to southern Africa and southwestern Asia around 100,000 years ago. From there, people moved east across southern Asia. They could then migrate to Australia. Scientists are not sure exactly how the first people reached Australia. Even though ocean levels were lower then, there was always open sea between Asia and Australia.

From southwestern Asia, humans also migrated north into Europe. Geographic features such as high mountains and cold temperatures delayed migration northward into northern Asia. Eventually, however, people from both Europe and southern Asia moved into that region.

From northern Asia, people moved into North America. Scientists disagree on when and how the first people arrived in North America. Most scholars think people must have crossed a land bridge from Asia to North America. Once in North America, these people moved south, following herds of animals and settling in South America. By 9,000 BC, humans lived on all continents of the world except Antarctica.

Early humans often migrated because of climate change and the need to find new food sources. For example, scientists have discovered that large areas of Sub-Saharan Africa experienced periods of drought between 280,000

▶ Explore ONLINE!

Early Human Migration

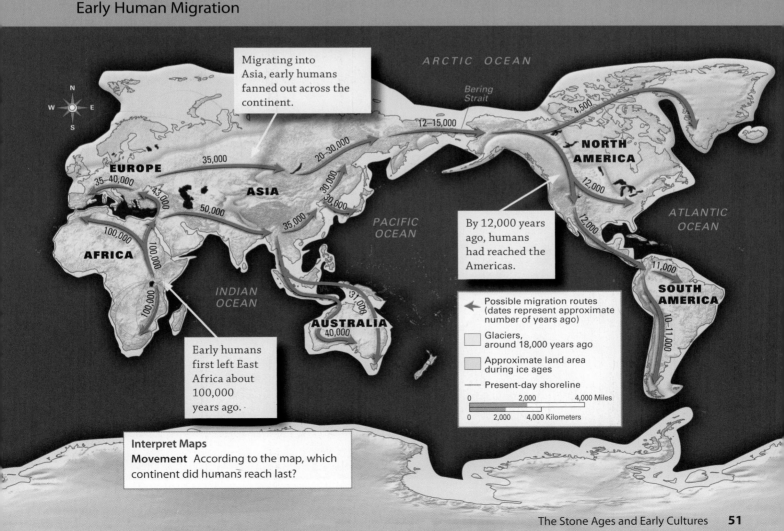

Migrating into Asia, early humans fanned out across the continent.

By 12,000 years ago, humans had reached the Americas.

Early humans first left East Africa about 100,000 years ago.

Possible migration routes (dates represent approximate number of years ago)

Glaciers, around 18,000 years ago

Approximate land area during ice ages

Present-day shoreline

0   2,000   4,000 Miles

0   2,000   4,000 Kilometers

Interpret Maps
Movement According to the map, which continent did humans reach last?

and 30,000 years ago. A drought is an extended period of time when an area receives little or no rain. The southeastern part of the African continent became warm, wet, and humid at the same time. These conditions led early people to move to the southeast, where living environments were much more favorable.

People Adapt to New Environments

As early people moved to new lands, they found environments that differed greatly from those in East Africa. Many places were much colder and had new plants and animals. Early people had to learn to adapt to these different environments.

Clothing and Shelter Although fire helped keep people warm in very cold areas, people needed more protection. To keep warm, they learned to sew animal skins together to make clothing.

In addition to clothing, people needed shelter to survive. Some took shelter in caves. When they moved to areas with no caves, they built their own shelters. One early type of human-made shelter was pit houses. They were pits in the ground with roofs of branches and leaves.

Early people also built homes above the ground. Some lived in tents made of animal skins. Others built more permanent structures of wood, stone, clay, or other materials. Even bones from large animals such as mammoths were used in building shelters.

Early people encountered new environments and colder climates as they migrated away from East Africa.

Views of Migration to the Americas

For many years scientists were fairly certain that the first Americans came from Asia, following big game through an ice-free path in the glaciers. New discoveries have challenged beliefs about the first Americans. Some scientists now are not so sure the first Americans came along an ice-free path in the glaciers.

Analyze Historical Sources
Describe the contrasting points of view in the sources.

"Doubtless it was a formidable [challenging] place, an ice-walled valley of frigid winds, fierce snows, and clinging fogs. 'Man didn't travel it on the basis of a bag lunch,' notes Dr. Morian. Yet grazing animals would have entered, and behind them would have come a rivulet [stream] of human hunters."

—Thomas Canby, from "Search for the First Americans," *National Geographic*, September 1979

"There's no reason people couldn't have come along the coast, skirting [going around] the glaciers just the way recreational kayakers do today."

—James Dixon, quoted in *National Geographic*, December 2000

New Tools and Technologies People also adapted to new environments with new types of tools. These tools were smaller and more complex than tools from the Old Stone Age. They defined the **Mesolithic** (me-zuh-LI-thik) **Era**, or the Middle Stone Age. This period began more than 10,000 years ago and lasted to about 5,000 years ago in some places.

During this time period, people found new uses for bone and stone tools. People who lived near water invented hooks and fishing spears. Other groups invented the bow and arrow.

A Mammoth House

Early people used whatever was available to make shelters. In Central Asia, where wood was scarce, some early people made their homes from mammoth bones.

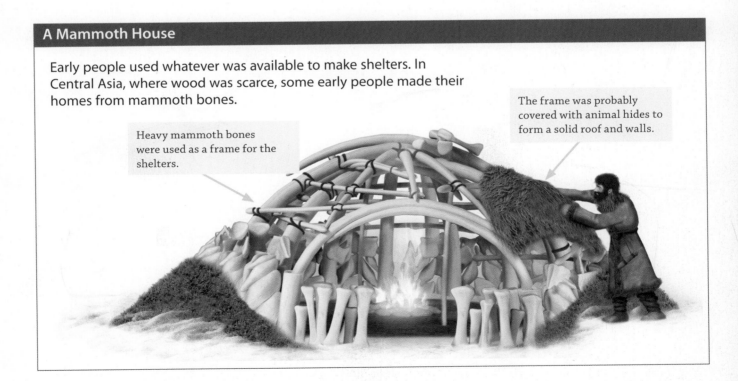

The frame was probably covered with animal hides to form a solid roof and walls.

Heavy mammoth bones were used as a frame for the shelters.

In addition to tools, people developed new technologies to improve their lives. For example, some learned to make canoes by hollowing out logs. They used the canoes to travel on rivers and lakes. People also began to make pottery. Developments like these, in addition to clothing and shelter, allowed people to adapt to new environments.

Summary and Preview Early people adapted to new environments with new kinds of clothing, shelter, and tools. In Lesson 3, you will read about how Stone Age peoples developed farming.

Lesson 2 Assessment

Review Ideas, Terms, and People

1. a. **Define** What is a **land bridge**?

   b. **Analyze** Why did it take so long for early people to reach South America?

2. a. **Recall** What did people use to make tools in the **Mesolithic Era**?

   b. **Summarize** Why did people have to learn to make clothes and build shelters?

Critical Thinking

3. **Organize Information** Create a sequence chain organizer like the one shown, and use it to show the path of human migration around the world.

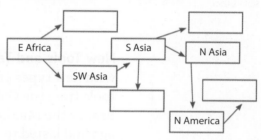

4. **Synthesize** Draw some sketches that include food, shelter, clothing, and tools to show how early communities adapted to their new environments. Include captions that describe each of your illustrations.

Beginnings of Agriculture

The Big Idea

The development of agriculture brought great changes to human society.

Main Ideas

- The first farmers learned to grow plants and raise animals in the New Stone Age.

- Farming changed societies and the way people lived.

Key Terms

Neolithic Era
domestication
agriculture
megaliths

If YOU were there . . .

As a gatherer, you know where to find the sweetest fruits. Every summer, you eat many of these fruits, dropping the seeds on the ground. One day you return to find new plants everywhere. You realize that the plants have grown from your dropped seeds.

How could this discovery change your way of life?

The First Farmers

After the Middle Stone Age came a period of time that scientists call the **Neolithic** (nee-uh-LI-thik) **Era**, or New Stone Age. It began as early as 10,000 years ago in Southwest Asia. In other places, this era began much later and lasted much longer than it did there.

During the New Stone Age, people learned to polish stones to make tools like saws and drills. People also learned how to make fire. Before, they could only use fire that had been started by natural causes such as lightning. But tools and fire weren't the only major changes that occurred during the Neolithic Era. In fact, the biggest changes came in how people produced food.

Plants After a warming trend brought an end to the ice ages, new plants began to grow in some areas. For example, wild barley and wheat plants started to spread throughout Southwest Asia. Over time, people came to depend on these wild plants for food. They began to settle where grains grew.

People soon learned that they could plant seeds themselves to grow their own crops. Historians call the shift from food gathering to food producing the Neolithic Revolution. Most experts believe that this revolution, or change, first occurred in the societies of Southwest Asia.

Eventually, people learned to change plants to make them more useful. They planted only the largest grains or the sweetest fruits. The process of changing plants or animals to make them more useful to humans is called **domestication**.

An Early Farming Society

This illustration shows the village of Çatal Hüyük in modern Turkey around 8,000 years ago. Villagers hunted, fished, and traded outside the village. They farmed wheat, barley, and peas and used simple channels to move water to the fields.

Academic Vocabulary
development
creation

The domestication of plants led to the **development** of **agriculture**, or farming. For the first time, people could produce their own food. This development changed human society forever.

Animals Learning to produce food was a major accomplishment for early people. But learning how to use animals for their own purposes was almost equally important.

Hunters didn't have to follow wild herds anymore. Instead, farmers could keep sheep or goats for milk, food, and wool. Farmers could also use large animals like cattle to carry loads or to pull large tools used in farming. Using animals to help with farming improved the chances of survival.

Reading Check
Analyze Effects
What was one effect of domestication?

Farming Changes Societies

The Neolithic Revolution brought huge changes to people's lives. With survival more certain, people could focus on activities besides finding food.

Domestication of plants enabled people to use plant fibers to make cloth. The domestication of animals made it possible to use wool from goats and sheep and skins from horses for clothes.

People also began to build permanent settlements. As they started raising crops and animals, they needed to stay in one place instead of continuing to travel in search of new food sources. Then, once people were able to control their own food production, the world's population grew. In some areas, farming communities developed into towns.

Community The village was home to about 5,000–6,000 people living in more than 1,000 houses. Houses were made of wood covered with mud. Some were built as shrines.

Analyze Visuals
Judging from the illustration, how did people enter their houses?

The village of Çatal Hüyük in modern Turkey is one of the earliest farming villages discovered.

Early Economies Two examples of Neolithic communities are Çatal Hüyük, in modern-day Turkey, and Jericho, near the Jordan River and the Dead Sea. These towns had traditional economies. In a traditional economy, people make economic decisions based on customs and beliefs passed down from generation to generation. These decisions may include which crops to plant and how they should be distributed.

In Neolithic communities like Çatal Hüyük and Jericho, people used primitive tools and methods to grow, harvest, and hunt sources of food. They created large pits for storage of food. This meant that farmers could increase their productivity by harvesting large amounts of food and storing it after harvest. Having a surplus, or an extra amount, made trade possible, since farmers had a supply of food that others might want to purchase or gain through barter. A barter system is a form of exchange where goods and services are traded for other goods and services. The people who lived in Jericho, for example, traded items like salt and grain for turquoise and gems from the Sinai region.

Religious Practices As populations of towns grew, groups of people gathered to perform religious ceremonies. Some put up megaliths. **Megaliths** are huge stones used as monuments or as the sites for religious gatherings.

Early people probably believed in gods and goddesses associated with the four elements—air, water, fire, and earth—or with animals. For example, one early European group honored a thunder god, while another

Stonehenge is a prehistoric site located in England. Some scientists believe that this circular arrangement of megaliths was connected to the practice of worshipping ancestors.

group worshipped bulls. Some scholars also believe that many prehistoric peoples prayed to their ancestors. People in some societies today still hold many of these same beliefs.

Many communities and religions have practices and structures that guide what happens when a person dies. At Çatal Hüyük, for example, flesh was removed from the body, and the bones were then bleached and buried in the floors of homes.

Government and Social Order Remains of societies can sometimes give clues about government and other social structures. At Çatal Hüyük, archaeologists have not found evidence of any government buildings or public spaces that might have been used by a group of people larger than a family. The village also does not appear to have been led by an individual. However, women seem to have been treated equally in Çatal Hüyük society. Men and women ate the same foods and did similar types of work.

Jericho, by contrast, has more evidence of an organized government. A large wall surrounded the city. Building a structure like a wall requires many people to work together under the direction of another person or group, like a government.

Summary Stone Age peoples adapted to new environments by domesticating plants and animals. These changes led to the development of religion and the growth of towns.

Reading Check
Analyze Effects
How did farming contribute to the growth of towns?

Lesson 3 Assessment

Review Ideas, Terms, and People

1. **a. Define** What is domestication of a plant or animal?

   b. Form Generalizations How did early people use domesticated animals?

2. **a. Explain** How did farming allow people to create permanent settlements?

   b. Describe What were gods and goddesses probably associated with in prehistoric religion?

   c. Summarize How did early people express their religious beliefs?

Critical Thinking

3. **Analyze** Copy the graphic organizer at right. Use it to show one cause and three effects of the development of agriculture.

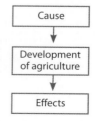

4. **Contrast** Contrast the government and social order of Çatal Hüyük and Jericho.

Social Studies Skills

Identify Central Issues

Define the Skill

Central issues are the main problems or topics that are related to an event. In world history, they usually involve political, social, economic, territorial, moral, or technological matters. The ability to identify the central issue allows you to focus on information that is most important to understanding the event.

Learn the Skill

Use these guidelines to gain a better understanding of historical events as you identify central issues.

1. Identify the subject of the information. What is the information about?

2. Determine the source of the information. Is it a primary source or a secondary source?

3. Determine the purpose of the information. Why has it been provided?

4. Find the strongest statements in the information. These are often clues to issues or ideas the writer thinks are the most central or important.

5. Think about values, concerns, and events that would have been important to the people of the times. Determine how the information might be connected to those larger issues.

Practice the Skill

Apply the guidelines to identify the central issue in the following passage. Then answer the questions.

"What distinguished [set apart] the Neolithic Era from earlier ages was people's ability to shape stone tools by polishing and grinding. This allowed people to make more specialized tools. Even more important changes took place also. The development of agriculture changed the basic way people lived. Earlier people had been wanderers, who moved from place to place in search of food. Some people began settling in permanent villages. Exactly how they learned that seeds could be planted and made to grow year after year remains a mystery. However, the shift from food gathering to food producing was possibly the most important change ever in history."

1. What is the general subject of this passage?

2. What changes distinguished the Neolithic Era from earlier periods?

3. According to the writer, what is the central issue to understand about the Neolithic Era?

4. What statements in the passage help you to determine the central issue?

Module 2 Assessment

Review Vocabulary, Terms, and People

For each group of terms below, write a sentence that shows how all the terms in the group are related.

1. prehistory
   ancestor
   hominid
2. domestication
   Neolithic Era
   agriculture
   society

3. Paleolithic Era
   tool
   hunter-gatherers
   develop
4. land bridge
   ice ages
   migrate

Comprehension and Critical Thinking

Lesson 1

5. **a. Categorize** Identify each of the following as either prehistoric or historic: Stone Age tool; map with writing on it; stone tablet engraved with pictures and symbols.

   b. Summarize What types of artifacts might scholars like linguists, geneticists, and geographers study to learn more about humans who lived during prehistory?

   c. Form Generalizations Make a statement that relates the amount of time that humans have been hunter-gatherers to the amount of time they have been farmers.

   d. Summarize Write a paragraph using information from the text to summarize how nomadic hunter-gatherers used tools, fire, weapons, and beads during the Stone Age.

Lesson 2

6. **a. Describe** What new skills did people develop to help them survive?

   b. Evaluate About 15,000 years ago, where do you think life would have been more difficult—in eastern Africa or northern Europe? Why?

Lesson 3

7. **a. Define** What is a traditional economy?

   b. Analyze Explain the impact that agriculture had on the movement and settlement of early civilizations.

   c. Draw Conclusions What do scholars believe about leadership in Çatal Hüyük? How did they come to this conclusion?

Module 2 Assessment, continued

Review Themes

8. **Society and Culture** How did the development of language change hunter-gatherer society?

9. **Geography** How did global climate change affect the migration of early people?

Reading Skills

Understand Chronological Order *Below are two lists of events. Arrange the events in each list in chronological order.*

10. *Homo sapiens* appears.
    Homo habilis appears.
    Homo erectus appears.

11. People make stone tools.
    People make metal tools.
    People attach wooden handles to tools.

Social Studies Skills

Identify Central Issues *Read the primary source passage below and then answer the question that follows.*

> "Almonds provide a striking example of bitter seeds and their change under domestication. Most wild almond seeds contain an intensely [very] bitter chemical called amygdalin, which (as was already mentioned) breaks down to yield [put out] the poison cyanide. A snack of wild almonds can kill a person foolish enough to ignore the warning of the bitter taste. Since the first stage in unconscious domestication involves gathering seeds to eat, how on earth did domestication of wild almonds ever reach that first stage?"
>
> –Jared Diamond, from *Guns, Germs, and Steel*

12. What does the author suggest is the major issue he will address in the text?

Focus On Writing

13. **Create a Storyboard** Create a storyboard that uses images to tell the story of prehistoric humans. Remember that a storyboard tells a story with simple sketches and short captions. What images will you include in each frame? How many frames will you need? How will you represent your ideas visually? After you have sketched an outline for your storyboard, begin drawing it. Be sure to include all significant adaptations and developments made by prehistoric people. If you like, you might want to draw your storyboard in the simple style of prehistoric cave paintings. As the last frame in your storyboard, write a detailed summary to conclude your story.

Module 3

The Fertile Crescent, Mesopotamia, and the Persian Empire

Essential Question

What factors helped unify early civilizations in Southwest Asia?

About the Photo: These remains of an ancient palace and temple are in Persepolis in what is now Iran.

▶ *Explore ONLINE!*

HISTORY.

VIDEOS, including...
- The Persians
- Bronze
- Persian Architecture
- Persia's Royal Road

Ⓢ Document-Based Investigations

Ⓢ Graphic Organizers

Ⓢ Interactive Games

Ⓢ Interactive Map: River Valley Civilizations

Ⓢ Image with Hotspots: The City-State of Ur

Ⓢ Image with Hotspots: Hittite Iron Making

In this module you will learn about the early civilizations in Mesopotamia and the Fertile Crescent, and about the Persian Empire.

What You Will Learn...

Lesson 1: Geography of the Fertile Crescent 66
The Big Idea The valleys of the Tigris and Euphrates Rivers were the site of the world's first civilizations.

Lesson 2: The Sumerians 72
The Big Idea The Sumerians developed the first civilization in Mesopotamia.

Lesson 3: Military Empires 82
The Big Idea After the Sumerians, many cultures ruled parts of the Fertile Crescent.

Lesson 4: The Phoenicians 87
The Big Idea The Phoenicians created a wealthy trading society along the Mediterranean Sea.

Lesson 5: The Persian Empire 91
The Big Idea Over time the Persians came to rule a great empire, which eventually brought them into conflict with the Greeks.

Timeline of Events 7000–480 BC

▶ *Explore ONLINE!*

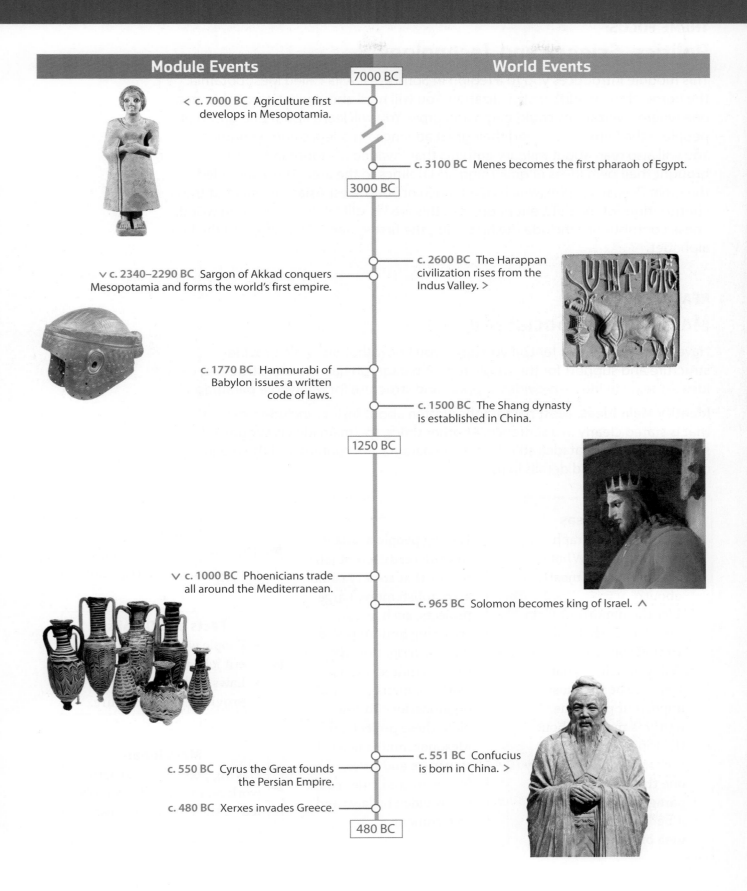

Module Events	World Events

7000 BC

< **c. 7000 BC** Agriculture first develops in Mesopotamia.

c. 3100 BC Menes becomes the first pharaoh of Egypt.

3000 BC

⌄ **c. 2340–2290 BC** Sargon of Akkad conquers Mesopotamia and forms the world's first empire.

c. 2600 BC The Harappan civilization rises from the Indus Valley. >

c. 1770 BC Hammurabi of Babylon issues a written code of laws.

c. 1500 BC The Shang dynasty is established in China.

1250 BC

⌄ **c. 1000 BC** Phoenicians trade all around the Mediterranean.

c. 965 BC Solomon becomes king of Israel. ⌃

c. 551 BC Confucius is born in China. >

c. 550 BC Cyrus the Great founds the Persian Empire.

c. 480 BC Xerxes invades Greece.

480 BC

Reading Social Studies

THEME FOCUS:
Politics, Science and Technology

This module introduces you to a region in Southwest Asia called Mesopotamia, the home of the world's first civilization. You will read about what made this area one where civilizations could begin and grow. You will learn about one group of people—the Sumerians—and their great advances in science and technology. You will also read about military empires that invaded Mesopotamia and brought their own ideas of governing and politics to the area. These included the great Persian Empire, which ruled much of Southwest Asia. The effect of the contributions of the different peoples in this area is still felt in the modern world. These contributions include the first cities, the first system of writing, and the first alphabet.

READING FOCUS:
Main Ideas in Social Studies

Have you ever set up a tent? If you have, you know that one pole provides structure and support for the whole tent. A paragraph has a similar structure. One idea—the main idea—provides support and structure for the whole paragraph.

Identify Main Ideas Most paragraphs written about history include a main idea that is stated clearly in a sentence. At other times, the main idea is suggested, not stated. However, that idea still shapes the paragraph's content and the meaning of all of the facts and details in it.

Identify Main Ideas

1. Read the paragraph. Ask yourself, "What is this paragraph mostly about?"
2. List the important facts and details that relate to that topic.
3. Ask yourself, "What seems to be the most important point the writer is making about the topic?" Or ask, "If the writer could say only one thing about this paragraph, what would it be?" **This is the main idea of the paragraph.**

Having people available to work on different jobs meant that society could accomplish more. Large projects, such as constructing buildings and digging irrigation systems, required specialized workers, managers, and organization. To complete these projects, the Mesopotamians needed structure and rules. Structure and rules could be provided by laws and government.

▶ **Topic:**
The paragraph talks about people, jobs, and structure.

+

▶ **Facts and Details:**
- People working on different jobs needed structure.
- Laws and government provided this structure.

=

▶ **Main Idea:**
Having people in a society work on many different jobs led to the creation of laws and government.

You Try It!

Read the following passage, and then answer the questions below.

The Sumerians made one of the greatest cultural advances in history. They developed cuneiform (kyoo-NEE-uh-fohrm), the world's first system of writing. But Sumerians did not have pencils, pens, or paper. Instead, they used sharp tools called styluses to make wedge-shaped symbols on clay tablets.

Earlier written communication had used pictographs, or picture symbols. Each pictograph represented an object, such as a tree or an animal. But in cuneiform, symbols could also represent syllables, or basic parts of words. As a result, Sumerian writers could combine symbols to express more complex ideas such as "joy" or "powerful."

Sumerians first used cuneiform to keep business records. A scribe, or writer, would be hired to document business transactions or keep track of the items people bought and sold. Government officials and temples also hired scribes to keep their records, including records of taxes that were collected. Becoming a scribe was a way to move up in social class.

Answer these questions based on the passage you just read.

1. Reread the first paragraph. What is its main idea?

2. What is the main idea of the third paragraph? Reread the second paragraph. Is there a sentence that expresses the main idea of the paragraph? What is that main idea? Write a sentence to express it.

3. Which of the following best expresses the main idea of the entire passage?

   a. Cuneiform had a positive effect on Sumerian society.

   b. The Sumerians invented many helpful devices.

As you read this module, find the main ideas of the paragraphs you are studying.

Key Terms and People

Lesson 1
Fertile Crescent
silt
civilization
irrigation
canals
surplus
division of labor

Lesson 2
rural
urban
city-state
Gilgamesh
Sargon
empire
polytheism
priests
social hierarchy
cuneiform
pictographs
scribe
epics
architecture
ziggurat

Lesson 3
monarch
Hammurabi
Hammurabi's Code
chariot
Nebuchadnezzar

Lesson 4
alphabet

Lesson 5
Cyrus the Great
cavalry
Darius I
Persian Wars
Xerxes I

Geography of the Fertile Crescent

The Big Idea

The valleys of the Tigris and Euphrates Rivers were the site of the world's first civilizations.

Main Ideas

- The rivers of Southwest Asia supported the growth of civilization.

- New farming techniques led to the growth of cities.

Key Terms and People

Fertile Crescent
silt
civilization
irrigation
canals
surplus
division of labor

If YOU were there . . .

You are a farmer in Southwest Asia about 6,000 years ago. You live near a slow-moving river, with many shallow lakes and marshes. The river makes the land in the valley rich and fertile, so you can grow wheat and dates. But in the spring, raging floods spill over the riverbanks, destroying your fields. In the hot summers, you are often short of water.

How can you control the waters of the river?

Rivers Support the Growth of Civilization

Early peoples settled where crops would grow. Crops usually grew well near rivers, where water was available and regular floods made the soil rich. One region in Southwest Asia was especially well suited for farming. It lay between two rivers.

The Land Between the Rivers The Tigris and Euphrates Rivers are the most important physical features of the region sometimes known as Mesopotamia (mes-uh-puh-TAY-mee-uh). *Mesopotamia* means "between the rivers" in Greek.

As you can see on the map, the region called Mesopotamia lies between Asia Minor and the Persian Gulf. The region is part of a larger area called the **Fertile Crescent**, a large arc of rich, or fertile, farmland. The Fertile Crescent extends from the Persian Gulf to the Mediterranean Sea.

In ancient times, Mesopotamia was actually made of two parts. Northern Mesopotamia was a plateau bordered on the north and the east by mountains. Southern Mesopotamia was a flat plain. The Tigris and Euphrates Rivers flowed down from the hills into this low-lying plain.

The Rise of Civilization Hunter-gatherer groups first settled in Mesopotamia more than 12,000 years ago. Over time, these people learned how to plant crops to grow their own food. Every year, floods on the Tigris and Euphrates

Rivers brought **silt**, a mixture of rich soil and tiny rocks, to the land. The fertile silt made the land ideal for farming.

The first farm settlements formed in Mesopotamia as early as 7000 BC. Farmers grew wheat, barley, and other types of grain. Livestock, birds, and fish were also good sources of food. Plentiful food led to population growth, and villages formed. Eventually, these early villages developed into the world's first civilization.

A **civilization** is an organized society within a specific area. Civilizations often include large cities in which different social classes of people live. Writing, formal education, art, and architecture are features of civilizations. In civilizations, governments are made up of leaders or family groups. The governments make decisions that help the civilization develop. These characteristics improve people's quality of life.

In an established civilization, a government makes economic decisions to help society develop. For example, as populations grow, decisions have to be made about how to effectively produce and distribute food.

Farming and Cities

Although Mesopotamia had fertile soil, farming wasn't easy there. The region received little rain. This meant that water levels in the Tigris and Euphrates Rivers depended on how much rain fell in eastern Asia Minor, where the two rivers began. When a great amount of rain fell there, water levels got very high. Flooding destroyed crops, killed livestock, and washed away homes. During a drought, a time of little or no rain,

Reading Check
Synthesize Which characteristic of a civilization do you think is most important? Why?

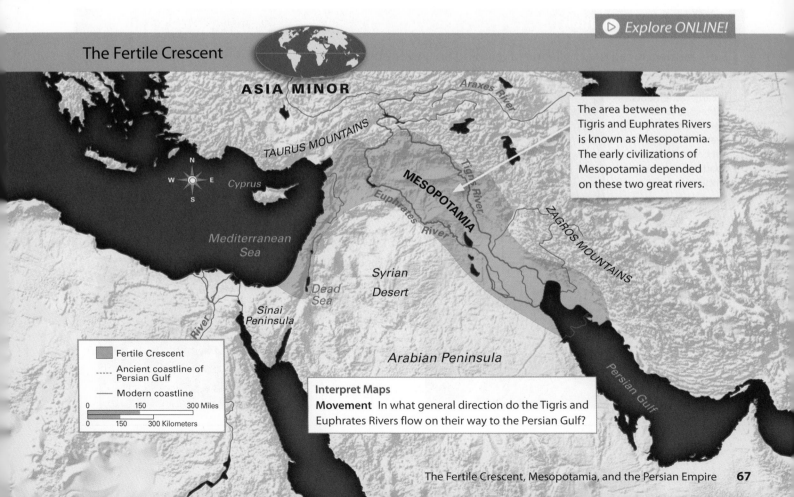

The Fertile Crescent

⊳ *Explore ONLINE!*

ASIA MINOR

Araxes River

The area between the Tigris and Euphrates Rivers is known as Mesopotamia. The early civilizations of Mesopotamia depended on these two great rivers.

TAURUS MOUNTAINS

Cyprus

Tigris River

MESOPOTAMIA

Euphrates River

ZAGROS MOUNTAINS

Mediterranean Sea

Syrian Desert

Dead Sea

Sinai Peninsula

River

Arabian Peninsula

Persian Gulf

■ Fertile Crescent
---- Ancient coastline of Persian Gulf
— Modern coastline

0   150   300 Miles
0   150   300 Kilometers

Interpret Maps
Movement In what general direction do the Tigris and Euphrates Rivers flow on their way to the Persian Gulf?

water levels became too low. Crops dried up, and there was little water for livestock. Famine could therefore result from either too much or too little rain. Farmers knew they needed a way to control the rivers' flow.

Controlling Water To solve their problems, Mesopotamians used **irrigation**, a way of supplying water to an area of land. To irrigate their land, they dug out large storage basins to hold water supplies. Then they dug **canals**, human-made waterways, that connected these basins to a network of ditches. These ditches brought water to the fields. To protect their fields from flooding, farmers constructed dams and built up the banks of the Tigris and Euphrates. This helped to control the flow of water and held back floodwaters when river levels were high.

The Mesopotamians used all the resources the rivers provided. In addition to using water for crops, they used clay from the riverbanks to create bricks for buildings. The construction of buildings and irrigation systems is an example of why early societies in Mesopotamia are considered civilizations. This construction required Mesopotamian society to be organized. Mesopotamians made good decisions to help sustain growing populations.

Irrigation systems were very important to the growth of cities. Mesopotamian kings had an obligation to construct and maintain these systems. Irrigation increased the amount of food farmers grew. In fact, farmers could produce a food **surplus**, or more than they needed. Farmers also used irrigation to water grazing areas for cattle and sheep. As a result, Mesopotamians ate a variety of foods. Fish, meat, wheat, barley, and dates were plentiful.

Irrigation and Civilization

Early farmers faced the challenge of learning how to control the flow of river water to their fields in both rainy and dry seasons.

1. Early settlements in Mesopotamia were located near rivers. Water was not controlled, and flooding was a major problem.

2. Later, people built canals to protect houses from flooding and move water to their fields.

3. With irrigation, the people of Mesopotamia were able to grow more food.

4. Food surpluses allowed some people to stop farming and concentrate on other jobs, such as making clay pots or tools.

A More Productive Society Because irrigation made farmers more productive, fewer people needed to farm. Some people became free to do other jobs. As a result, new occupations developed. For the first time, people were able to focus on other technological improvements.

Toolmakers began to make tools out of metal. This development brought an end to the Neolithic Era and the beginning of the Copper Age. Copper could be used to make arrowheads or knives.

It took special knowledge and skills to work with metal. Some people were able to devote all of their time to finding raw metal and shaping it into tools. Others focused on tasks such as weaving cloth or making pottery. An arrangement in which workers specialize in a particular task or job is called a **division of labor**. Societies with a division of labor can become more complex than ones that lack specialization.

Having people available to work on different jobs meant that society could accomplish more. Large projects, such as constructing buildings and digging irrigation systems, required specialized workers, managers, and organization. To complete these projects, the Mesopotamians needed structure and rules. Structure and rules could be provided by laws and government.

As settlements developed, they eventually became cities.

The Appearance of Cities Over time, Mesopotamian settlements grew in size and complexity. They gradually developed into cities between 4000 and 3000 BC.

Despite the growth of cities, society in Mesopotamia was still based on agriculture. Most people still worked in farming jobs. However, cities were becoming important places. People traded goods there, and cities provided places to keep surplus foods grown on farmland. Cities were the political, religious, cultural, and economic centers of civilization.

Summary and Preview Mesopotamia's rich, fertile lands supported productive farming, which led to the development of cities. In the next lesson, you will learn about some of the first city builders.

Reading Check
Analyze Causes
Why did the Mesopotamians create irrigation systems?

Lesson 1 Assessment

Review Ideas, Terms, and People

1. a. **Identify** Where was Mesopotamia?

   b. **Explain** How did the Fertile Crescent get its name?

   c. **Evaluate** What was the most important factor in making Mesopotamia's farmland fertile?

2. a. **Describe** Why did farmers need to develop a system to control their water supply?

   b. **Explain** In what ways did a division of labor contribute to the growth of Mesopotamian civilization?

   c. **Elaborate** How might running large projects prepare people for running a government?

Critical Thinking

3. **Identify Cause and Effect** Farmers who used the rivers for irrigation were part of a cause-effect chain. Use a chart like this one to show that chain.

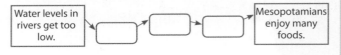

Water levels in rivers get too low. → ⬚ → ⬚ → ⬚ → Mesopotamians enjoy many foods.

History and Geography

River Valley Civilizations

All of the world's earliest civilizations had something in common—they all arose in river valleys that were perfect locations for farming. Three key factors made river valleys good for farming. First, the fields that bordered the rivers were flat, which made it easier for farmers to plant crops. Second, the soils were nourished by flood deposits and silt, which made them very fertile. Finally, the river provided the water that farmers needed for irrigation. As many societies do today, people living in Mesopotamia modified their environment to take advantage of the natural resources the rivers offered.

EUROPE

Black Sea

Caspian Sea

MESOPOTAMIA

Tigris River

Euphrates River

Mediterranean Sea

Ur

Memphis

AFRICA

EGYPT

Nile River

Red Sea

ARABIAN
PENINSULA

From Village to City With the development of agriculture, people settled into farming villages. Over time, some of these villages grew into large cities. These ancient ruins are near Memphis, Egypt.

Natural Highways River travel allowed early civilizations to trade goods and ideas. These people are traveling on the Euphrates River, one of the two main rivers of ancient Mesopotamia.

ASIA

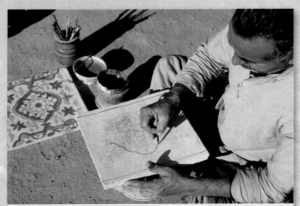

New Activities Food surpluses allowed people to pursue other activities, such as crafts, art, and writing. This tile designer lives in the Indus Valley.

Gift of the River River water was key to farming in early civilizations. This farmer is using water from the Huang He (Yellow River) in China to water her crops.

Huang He (Yellow River)

CHINA

Harappa

HIMALAYAS

Indus River

Chang Jiang (Yangzi River)

Mohenjo Daro

INDUS VALLEY

Ganges River

INDIA

Arabian Sea

Bay of Bengal

| 0 | 500 | 1,000 Miles |
| 0 | 500 | 1,000 Kilometers |

Interpret Maps

1. **Human-Environment Interaction** Why did the first civilizations all develop in river valleys?

2. **Location** Where were the four earliest river valley civilizations located?

INDIAN OCEAN

The Sumerians

The Big Idea

The Sumerians developed the first civilization in Mesopotamia.

Main Ideas

- The Sumerians created the world's first advanced society.

- Religion played a major role in Sumerian society.

- The Sumerians invented the world's first writing system.

- Technical advances and inventions changed Sumerian lives.

- Many types of art developed in Sumer.

Key Terms and People

rural
urban
city-state
Gilgamesh
Sargon
empire
polytheism
priests
social hierarchy
cuneiform
pictographs
scribe
epics
architecture
ziggurat

If YOU were there . . .

You are a crafter living in one of the cities of Sumer. Thick walls surround and protect your city, so you feel safe from the armies of other city-states. But you and your neighbors are fearful of other beings—the many gods and spirits that you believe are everywhere. They can bring illness or sandstorms or bad luck.

How might you protect yourself from gods and spirits?

An Advanced Society

In southern Mesopotamia, a people known as the Sumerians (soo-MER-ee-unz) developed the world's first civilization. No one knows where they came from or when they moved into the region. However, by 3000 BC, several hundred thousand Sumerians had settled in Mesopotamia, in a land they called Sumer (soo-muhr). There they created an advanced society.

The City-States of Sumer Most people in Sumer were farmers. They lived mainly in **rural**, or countryside, areas. The centers of Sumerian society, however, were the **urban**, or city, areas. The first cities in Sumer had about 10,000 residents. Over time, the cities grew. Historians think that by 2000 BC, some of Sumer's cities had more than 100,000 residents.

As a result, the basic political unit of Sumer combined the two areas. This unit was called a city-state. A **city-state** consisted of a city and all the countryside around it. The amount of countryside controlled by each city-state depended on its military strength. Stronger city-states controlled larger areas.

City-states in Sumer competed against one another to gain more farmland. Farmland was a resource upon which city-states depended to feed their growing populations. As a result of this competition, city-states built up strong armies to fight for control of farmland. Sumerians also built strong, thick walls around their cities for protection.

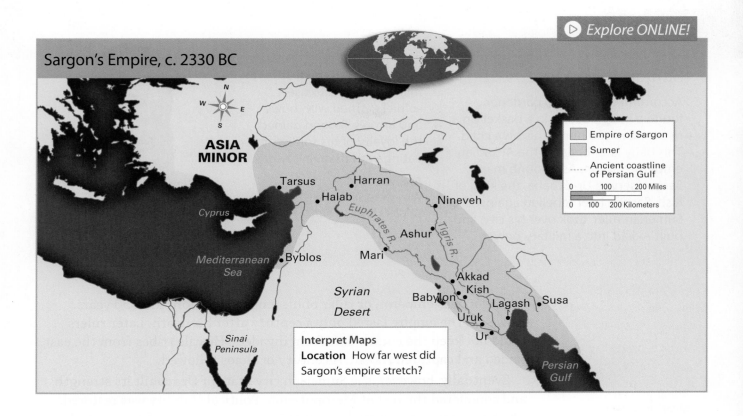

Sargon's Empire, c. 2330 BC

ASIA MINOR

Tarsus
Harran
Halab
Nineveh
Euphrates R.
Cyprus
Ashur
Tigris R.
Mediterranean Sea
Byblos
Mari
Akkad
Kish
Syrian Desert
Babylon
Lagash
Susa
Uruk
Sinai Peninsula
Ur
Persian Gulf

Empire of Sargon
Sumer
Ancient coastline of Persian Gulf
0   100   200 Miles
0 100   200 Kilometers

Interpret Maps
Location How far west did Sargon's empire stretch?

Some city-states, such as Mari on the Euphrates River, became important centers of trade. Basic building materials as well as luxury items came to Sumerian city-states along trade routes from as far away as North Africa in the west and Afghanistan in the east. Through trade, the city-states of Sumer became an important part of the region's economy.

Individual city-states gained and lost power over time. By 3500 BC, a city-state known as Kish had become quite powerful. Over the next 1,000 years, the city-states of Uruk and Ur fought for dominance. One of Uruk's kings, known as **Gilgamesh**, became a legendary figure in Sumerian literature.

Rise of the Akkadian Empire In time, another society developed along the Tigris and Euphrates. It was created by the Akkadians (uh-KAY-dee-uhns). They lived just north of Sumer, but they were not Sumerians. They even spoke a different language than the Sumerians did. In spite of their differences, however, the Akkadians and the Sumerians lived in peace for many years.

That peace was broken in the 2300s BC when a leader named **Sargon** sought to extend Akkadian territory. He built a new capital, Akkad (A-kad), on the Euphrates River, near what is now the city of Baghdad. Sargon was the first ruler to have a permanent army. He used that army to launch a series of wars against neighboring kingdoms.

Sargon's soldiers defeated all the city-states of Sumer. They also conquered northern Mesopotamia, finally bringing the entire region under his rule. With these conquests, Sargon established the world's first **empire**, or land with different territories and peoples under a single rule. The Akkadian Empire stretched from the Persian Gulf to the Mediterranean Sea.

Sargon (Ruled 2334–2279 BC)

According to legend, a gardener found a baby floating in a basket on a river and raised him as his own child. This baby later became the Akkadian emperor Sargon. As a young man, Sargon served Ur-Zababa, the king of Kish. Sargon later rebelled against the Sumerian ruler, took over his city, and built Akkad into a military power.

He was among the first military leaders to use soldiers armed with bows and arrows. Sargon gained the loyalty of his soldiers by eating with them every day.

Analyze
Why were Sargon's soldiers loyal to him?

Sargon was emperor, or ruler of his empire, for more than 50 years. However, the empire lasted only a century after his death. Later rulers could not keep the empire safe from invaders. Hostile tribes from the east raided and captured Akkad. A century of chaos followed.

Eventually, however, the Sumerian city-state of Ur rebuilt its strength and conquered the rest of Mesopotamia. Political stability was restored. The Sumerians once again became the most powerful civilization in the region.

Reading Check
Summarize How did Sargon build an empire?

Academic Vocabulary
role a part or function

Religion Shapes Society

Religion was very important in Sumerian society. In fact, it played a **role** in nearly every aspect of public and private life. In many ways, religion was the basis for all of Sumerian society.

Sumerian Religion The Sumerians practiced **polytheism**, the worship of many gods. Among the gods they worshipped were Enlil, the lord of the air, and Inanna, goddess of love and war. The sun and moon were represented by the gods Utu and Nanna. Enki was the lord of wisdom and also the god of fresh water, an important god for a people who relied so much on rivers. According to one Sumerian creation story, both Enlil and Enki were involved in the creation of humankind. Each city-state considered one god to be its special protector.

The Sumerians believed that their gods had enormous powers. Gods could bring a good harvest or a disastrous flood. They could bring illness, or they could bring good health and wealth. The Sumerians believed that success in every area of life depended on pleasing the gods. Every Sumerian had a duty to serve and to worship the gods.

Priests, people who performed religious ceremonies, had great status in Sumer. People relied on them to help gain the gods' favor. Priests interpreted the wishes of the gods and made offerings to them. These offerings were made in temples, special buildings where priests performed their religious ceremonies.

Sumerian Social Order Because of their status, priests occupied a high level in Sumer's **social hierarchy**, the division of society by rank or class. In fact, priests were just below kings. The city-states in Sumer were monarchies, each ruled by a single king or queen. The kings and queens of Sumer claimed that they had been chosen by the gods to rule.

Academic
Vocabulary
impact effect, result

Below the priests were Sumer's skilled craftspeople, merchants, and traders. Trade had a great **impact** on Sumerian society. Traders traveled to faraway places and exchanged grain for gold, silver, copper, lumber, and precious stones.

Below traders, farmers and laborers made up the large working class. Slaves were at the bottom of the social order, but their labor contributed to the Sumerian economy. Farming required many workers, and slaves were an inexpensive source of labor. Many of the slaves in Mesopotamia were foreigners who had been captured in war.

Men and Women in Sumer Sumerian men and women had different roles. In general, men held political power and made laws, while women took care of the home and children. Education was usually reserved for men, but some upper-class women were educated as well.

Reading Check
Analyze Effects
How did trade affect
Sumerian society?

Some educated women were priestesses in Sumer's temples. Some priestesses helped shape Sumerian culture. One, Enheduanna, the daughter of Sargon, wrote hymns to the goddess Inanna. She is the first known female writer in history.

The Invention of Writing

The Sumerians made one of the greatest cultural advances in history. They developed **cuneiform** (kyoo-NEE-uh-fohrm), the world's first system of writing. But Sumerians did not have pencils, pens, or paper. Instead, they used sharp tools called styluses to make wedge-shaped symbols on clay tablets.

Earlier written communication had used **pictographs**, or picture symbols. Each pictograph represented an object, such as a tree or an animal. But in cuneiform, symbols could also represent syllables, or basic parts of words. As a result, Sumerian writers could combine symbols to express more complex ideas such as "joy" or "powerful."

Sumerians first used cuneiform to keep business records. A **scribe**, or writer, would be hired to document business transactions or keep track of the items people bought and sold. Government officials and temples also

Sumerians wrote
on clay tablets
with a special tool
called a stylus.

Sumerian writing developed from early symbols called pictographs. Writers used clay tablets to record business deals. This tablet describes the number of sheep and goats.

Development of Writing				
	3300 BC	**2800 BC**	**2400 BC**	**1800 BC**
Heaven				
Grain				
Fish				
Bird				
Water				

hired scribes to keep their records, including records of taxes that were collected. Becoming a scribe was a way to move up in social class.

Sumerian students went to school to learn to read and write. But some students did not want to study. A Sumerian story tells of a father who urged his son to do his schoolwork:

"Go to school, stand before your 'school-father,' recite your assignment, open your schoolbag, write your tablet. . . . After you have finished your assignment and reported to your monitor [teacher], come to me, and do not wander about in the street."

–Sumerian essay quoted in *History Begins at Sumer*, by Samuel Noah Kramer

In time, Sumerians put their writing skills to new uses. They wrote works on history, law, grammar, and math. They also created works of literature. They wrote poems about the gods and about military victories. Some of these were **epics**, long poems that tell the stories of heroes. Later, people used some of these poems to create *The Epic of Gilgamesh*, the story of the legendary Sumerian king. These new uses of writing changed the cultural life of Sumerians and those who followed them in Mesopotamia.

Reading Check
Form Generalizations
How was cuneiform first used in Sumer?

Advances and Inventions

Writing was not the only great Sumerian invention. These early people made many other advances and discoveries.

Technical Advances Technological innovations and the use of domesticated animals improved the quality of life for many Sumerians. One of the Sumerians' most important developments was the wheel. They were the first people to build wheeled vehicles, including carts and wagons. Using the wheel, Sumerians invented a device that spins clay as a craftsperson shapes it into bowls. This device is called a potter's wheel.

The plow was another important Sumerian invention. Pulled by domesticated oxen, plows broke through the hard clay soil of Sumer to prepare it for planting.

The use of plows increased food production.

The Sumerians were among the first people in the world to build sailboats. Transporting goods along one of the great rivers on sailboats was much more efficient than using pack animals or carts with wheels.

Sumerian advances improved daily life in many ways. Sumerians built sewers under city streets. They also invented a clock that used falling water to measure time. They even produced makeup and glass jewelry.

Sumer was one of the places in the world that saw the start of the Bronze Age, when humans began making tools out of metals rather than stone. Sumerians created strong bronze tools that made it easier to construct larger cities.

Math and Sciences Another area in which Sumerians excelled was math. In fact, they developed a math system based on the number 60. Using this system, they divided a circle into 360 degrees. Dividing a year into 12 months—a factor of 60 — was another Sumerian idea. Each of the 12 months of the Sumerian calendar was 29 or 30 days long, depending on the phases of the moon. Sumerians also calculated the areas of rectangles and triangles.

Sumerian scholars studied science, too. They wrote long lists to record their study of the natural world. These lists included the names of thousands of animals, plants, and minerals.

The Sumerians also made advances in medicine. They used ingredients from animals, plants, and minerals to produce healing drugs. The Sumerians even catalogued their medical knowledge, listing treatments according to symptoms and body parts.

Reading Check
Summarize What areas of life were improved by Sumerian inventions?

The Arts of Sumer

The Sumerians' skills in the fields of art, metalwork, and **architecture**—the science of building—are well known to us. The ruins of great buildings and fine works of art have provided us with wonderful examples of the Sumerians' creativity.

Architecture Most Sumerian rulers lived in large palaces. Other rich Sumerians had two-story homes with as many as a dozen rooms. Most people, however, lived in smaller, one-story houses. These homes had six or seven rooms arranged around a small courtyard.

City centers were dominated by their temples, the largest and most impressive buildings in Sumer. A **ziggurat**, a pyramid-shaped temple tower, rose above each city. Outdoor staircases led to a platform and a shrine at the top.

The Sumerians' artistic achievements included beautiful works of gold, wood, and stone.

Cylinder seals like this one were carved into round stones and then rolled over clay to leave their mark.

This stringed musical instrument is called a lyre. It features a cow's head and is made of silver decorated with shell and stone.

This gold dagger was found in a royal tomb. The bull's head is made of gold and silver.

The Sumerians were the first people in Mesopotamia to build large temples called ziggurats.

Analyze Visuals
The head of a cow or bull is shown in some of these works. Why were cattle important to Sumerians?

The Arts Sumerian sculptors produced many fine works. Among them are the statues of gods created for temples. Many Sumerian statues are made of clay, which shows that clay was abundant in Sumer. Sumerian artists created large mosaics using clay.

Carving in stone, called relief sculpture, was popular among Sumerian artists. Artists carved scenes of important events into squares of stone, which were then mounted on the walls of a temple. They also sculpted small objects out of ivory and rare woods.

Jewelry was a popular item in Sumer. The jewelers of the region made many beautiful works out of imported gold, silver, and gems. Earrings and other items found in the region show that Sumerian jewelers knew advanced methods for putting gold pieces together. Sumerian artists also worked with other metals, such as copper and bronze, to produce different works of art.

Cylinder seals are perhaps Sumer's most famous works of art. These small objects were stone cylinders engraved with designs. They required great skill to make. When rolled over clay, the designs would leave behind their imprint. Each seal left its own distinct imprint. As a result, a person could show ownership of a container by rolling a cylinder over the container's wet clay surface. People could also use cylinder seals to "sign" documents or to decorate other clay objects.

The Sumerians also enjoyed music. Kings and temples hired musicians to play on special occasions. Sumerian musicians played reed pipes, drums, tambourines, and stringed instruments called lyres. Children learned songs in school. People sang hymns to gods and kings. Music and dance provided entertainment in marketplaces and homes.

Summary and Preview In this lesson, you learned about Sumerian city-states, religion, and society. You also learned that the Sumerians greatly enriched their society. Next you will learn about the later people who lived in Mesopotamia.

Reading Check
Make Inferences
What might historians learn from cylinder seals?

Lesson 2 Assessment

Review Ideas, Terms, and People

1. a. **Recall** What was the basic political unit of Sumer?
   b. **Explain** What evidence from the text shows that Sumer was an important part of the region's economy?
   c. **Form Opinions** How do you think Sargon's creation of an empire changed the history of Mesopotamia? Defend your answer.

2. a. **Identify** What is polytheism?
   b. **Draw Conclusions** Why do you think priests were so influential in ancient Sumerian society?
   c. **Elaborate** Why did farmers benefit by using slaves instead of hiring laborers to work on their farms?

3. a. **Identify** What is cuneiform?
   b. **Analyze** Why do you think writing is one of history's most important cultural advances?
   c. **Elaborate** What current leader would you choose to write an epic about, and why?

4. a. **Recall** What were two early uses of the wheel?

   b. **Make Inferences** Why was the invention of the plow was so important to the Sumerians?
   c. **Summarize** How did the Sumerian idea of dividing the calendar into 12 months relate to their math system?

5. a. **Make Inferences** What facts about architecture show the social hierarchy that existed in Sumerian society?

Critical Thinking

6. **Summarize** Write a summary sentence for each of the following characteristics of Sumerian society: cities, government, religion, society. Then write a sentence summarizing Sumerian civilization.

7. **Analyze Effects** In a chart like this one, list at least five Sumerian advances or achievements. Then list an effect for each Sumerian advance or achievement.

Advance/Achievement	Effect

Literature in History

A Sumerian Epic

Word Help

menacing threatening
succor help
tempest storm
felled cut down

❶ Shamash, the sun-god, supports Gilgamesh. *What human emotion seems to seize Gilgamesh here? How can you tell?*

❷ *What stops Humbaba in his tracks?*

❸ Gilgamesh tries to speak and act bravely, but he is terrified by Humbaba's evil glare.

❹ *What effect does Humbaba hope his words will have on Gilgamesh?*

About the Reading The Epic of Gilgamesh is the world's oldest epic, first recorded—carved on stone tablets—in about 2000 BC. The actual Gilgamesh, ruler of the city of Uruk, had lived about 700 years earlier. Over time, stories about this legendary king had grown and changed. In this story, Gilgamesh and his friend Enkidu seek to slay the monster Humbaba, keeper of a distant forest. In addition to his tremendous size and terrible appearance, Humbaba possesses seven splendors, or powers, one of which is fire. Gilgamesh hopes to claim these powers for himself.

As You Read Notice both the human qualities and the godly qualities of Gilgamesh.

from *The Epic of Gilgamesh*
translated by N. K. Sandars

Humbaba came from his strong house of cedar. He nodded his head and shook it, menacing Gilgamesh; and on him he fastened his eye, the eye of death. Then Gilgamesh called to Shamash and his tears were flowing, "O glorious Shamash, I have followed the road you commanded but now if you send no succor how shall I escape?" ❶ Glorious Shamash heard his prayer and he summoned the great wind, the north wind, the whirlwind, the storm and the icy wind, the tempest and the scorching wind; they came like dragons, like a scorching fire, like a serpent that freezes the heart, a destroying flood and the lightning's fork. The eight winds rose up against Humbaba, they beat against his eyes; he was gripped, unable to go forward or back. ❷ Gilgamesh shouted, "By the life of Ninsun my mother and divine Lugulbanda my father . . . my weak arms and my small weapons I have brought to this Land against you, and now I will enter your house." ❸

So he felled the first cedar and they cut the branches and laid them at the foot of the mountain. At the first stroke Humbaba blazed out, but still they advanced. They felled seven cedars and cut and bound the branches and laid them at the foot of the mountain, and seven times Humbaba loosed his glory on them. As the seventh blaze died out they reached his lair. He slapped his thigh in scorn. He approached like a noble wild bull roped on the mountain, a warrior whose elbows were bound together. The tears started to his eyes and he was pale, "Gilgamesh, let me speak. I have never known a mother, no, nor a father who reared me. I was born of the mountain, he reared me, and Enlil made me the keeper of this forest. Let me go free, Gilgamesh, and I will be your servant, you shall be my lord; all the trees of the forest that I tended on the mountain shall be yours. I will cut them down and build you a palace." . . . ❹

Word Help

execration a cursing

plunders takes by force

❺ The angry air-god Enlil curses the heroes for slaying Humbaba. He takes back the monster's powers and gives them to other creatures and elements of nature. *In your opinion, is Gilgamesh more or less heroic for slaying Humbaba and angering Enlil?*

Enkidu said, "Do not listen, Gilgamesh: this Humbaba must die. Kill Humbaba first and his servants after." But Gilgamesh said, "If we touch him the blaze and the glory of light will be put out in confusion, the glory and glamour will vanish, its rays will be quenched." Enkidu said to Gilgamesh, "Not so, my friend. First entrap the bird, and where shall the chicks run then? Afterwards we can search out the glory and the glamour, when the chicks run distracted through the grass."

Gilgamesh listened to the word of his companion, he took the ax in his hand, he drew the sword from his belt, and he struck Humbaba with a thrust of the sword to the neck, and Enkidu his comrade struck the second blow. At the third blow Humbaba fell. Then there followed confusion for this was the guardian of the forest whom they had felled to the ground. . . .

When he saw the head of Humbaba, Enlil raged at them. "Why did you do this thing? From henceforth may the fire be on your faces, may it eat the bread that you eat, may it drink where you drink." Then Enlil took again the blaze and the seven splendors that had been Humbaba's: he gave the first to the river, and he gave to the lion, to the stone of execration, to the mountain. . . . **❺**

O Gilgamesh, king and conqueror of the dreadful blaze; wild bull who plunders the mountain, who crosses the sea, glory to him.

Archaeologists think this statue from the 700s BC represents Gilgamesh.

Connect Literature to History

1. **Analyze** In Sumerian culture, the gods' powers were thought to be enormous. According to this story, what roles do gods play in people's lives?

2. **Make Inferences** Violence was common in Sumerian society. How does the character of Gilgamesh suggest that Sumerian society could be violent?

Military Empires

The Big Idea

After the Sumerians, many cultures ruled parts of the Fertile Crescent.

Main Ideas

- The Babylonians conquered Mesopotamia and created a code of law.
- Invasions of Mesopotamia changed the region's culture.

Key Terms and People

Hammurabi
monarch
Hammurabi's Code
chariot
Nebuchadnezzar

If YOU were there . . .

You are a noble in ancient Babylon, an advisor to the great king Hammurabi. One of your duties is to collect all the laws of the kingdom. They will be carved on a tall block of black stone and placed in the temple. The king asks your opinion about the punishments for certain crimes. For instance, should common people be punished more harshly than nobles?

How will you advise the king?

The Babylonians Conquer Mesopotamia

Although Ur rose to glory after the death of Sargon, repeated foreign attacks drained its strength. By 2000 BC, Ur lay in ruins. With Ur's power gone, several waves of invaders battled to gain control of Mesopotamia.

The Rise of Babylon Babylon was home to one such group. That city was located on the Euphrates River near what is today Baghdad, Iraq. Babylon had once been a Sumerian town. By 1800 BC, however, it was home to a powerful government of its own. In 1792 BC, **Hammurabi** (ham-uh-RAHB-ee) became Babylon's king. He became the city's greatest **monarch** (MAH-nark), a ruler of a kingdom or empire.

Hammurabi's Code Hammurabi was a brilliant war leader. His armies fought many battles to expand his power. Eventually, he brought all of Mesopotamia into his empire, called the Babylonian Empire, after his capital.

Hammurabi's skills were not limited to the battlefield, though. He was also an able ruler who could govern a huge empire. He oversaw many building and irrigation projects, and improved Babylon's tax collection system to help pay for them. He also brought much prosperity through increased trade. Hammurabi, however, is most famous for his code of laws.

Hammurabi's Code was a set of 282 laws that dealt with almost every part of daily life. There were laws on everything from trade, loans, and theft to marriage, injury, and murder. It contained some ideas that are still found in laws today. Specific crimes brought specific penalties. However, social class did matter. For instance, injuring a rich man brought a greater penalty than injuring a poor man.

Hammurabi's Code was important not only for how thorough it was, but also because it was written down for all to see. People all over the empire could read exactly what was against the law.

Hammurabi ruled for 42 years. During his reign, Babylon became the most important city in Mesopotamia. However, after his death, Babylonian power declined. The kings that followed faced invasions from people Hammurabi had conquered. Before long, the Babylonian Empire came to an end.

Reading Check
Analyze Effects
What was Hammurabi's most important accomplishment?

DOCUMENT-BASED INVESTIGATION   Historical Source

Hammurabi's Code

The Babylonian ruler Hammurabi is credited with putting together the earliest known written collection of laws. The code set down rules for both criminal and civil law and informed citizens what was expected of them.

196. If a man put out the eye of another man, his eye shall be put out.

197. If he break another man's bone, his bone shall be broken.

198. If he put out the eye of a freed man, or break the bone of a freed man, he shall pay one gold mina.

199. If he put out the eye of a man's slave, or break the bone of a man's slave, he shall pay one-half of its value.

221. If a physician heal the broken bone or diseased soft part of a man, the patient shall pay the physician five shekels in money.

222. If he were a freed man, he shall pay three shekels.

223. If he were a slave, his owner shall pay the physician two shekels.

—Hammurabi, from the Code of Hammurabi, translated by L. W. King

Analyze Historical Sources
How do you think Hammurabi's code of laws affected citizens of that time?

Invasions of Mesopotamia

Several other civilizations also developed in and around the Fertile Crescent. As their armies battled each other for fertile land, control of the region passed from one empire to another.

The Hittites and Kassites A people known as the Hittites built a strong kingdom in Asia Minor, in what is today Turkey. Their success came, in part, from two key military advantages they had over rivals. First, the Hittites were among the first people to master ironworking. This marked the beginning of the Iron Age, a point in history in which iron was widely used to make tools and weapons. The Hittites made the strongest weapons of the time with iron. Second, the Hittites skillfully used the **chariot**, a wheeled, horse-drawn cart used in battle. The chariots allowed Hittite soldiers to move quickly around a battlefield and fire arrows at their enemy. Using these advantages, Hittite forces captured Babylon around 1595 BC.

Hittite rule did not last long, however. Soon after taking Babylon, the Hittite king was killed by an assassin. The kingdom plunged into chaos. The Kassites, a people who lived north of Babylon, captured the city and ruled for almost 400 years.

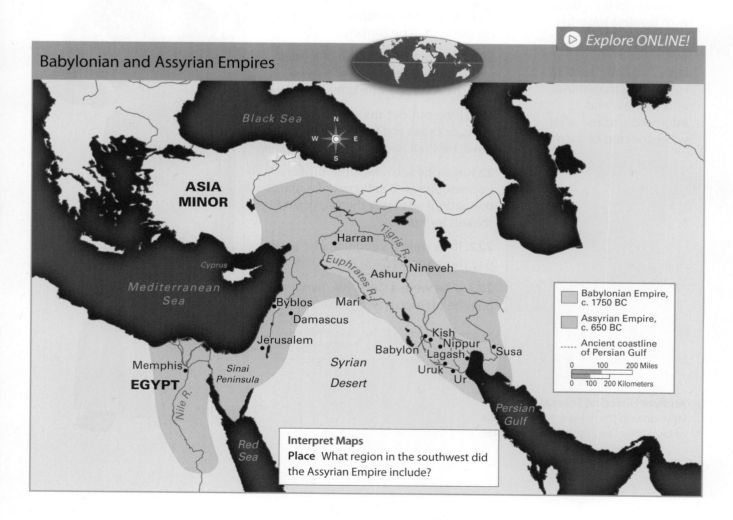

▶ Explore ONLINE!

Babylonian and Assyrian Empires

Legend:
- Babylonian Empire, c. 1750 BC
- Assyrian Empire, c. 650 BC
- ----- Ancient coastline of Persian Gulf

0 100 200 Miles
0 100 200 Kilometers

Interpret Maps
Place What region in the southwest did the Assyrian Empire include?

The Assyrians Later, in the 1200s BC, the Assyrians (uh-SIR-ee-unz) from northern Mesopotamia briefly gained control of Babylon. However, their empire was soon overrun by invaders. After this defeat, the Assyrians took about 300 years to recover their strength. Then, starting about 900 BC, they began to conquer all of the Fertile Crescent. They even took over parts of Asia Minor and Egypt.

The key to the Assyrians' success was their strong army. Like the Hittites, the Assyrians used iron weapons and chariots. The army was very well organized, and every soldier knew his role.

The Assyrians were fierce in battle. Before attacking, they spread terror by looting villages and burning crops. Anyone who still dared to resist them was killed. After conquering the Fertile Crescent, the Assyrians ruled from Nineveh (NI-nuh-vuh). They demanded heavy taxes from across the empire. Communities that resisted these demands were harshly punished.

Assyrian achievements were not just military. One king of Assyria established a huge royal library at Nineveh. It contained tens of thousands of cuneiform tablets, including legal and administrative documents as well as medical, religious, and literary texts.

The Assyrian Army

The Assyrian Army was the most powerful fighting force the world had ever seen. It conquered using weapons such as iron-tipped spears and arrows.

The Ishtar Gate led into the city of Babylon. Rebuilt by Nebuchadnezzar, the city is considered one of the greatest in the ancient world. Archeologists have found and partially reconstructed the Ishtar Gate.

Assyrian kings ruled their large empire through local leaders. Each governed a small area, collected taxes, enforced laws, and raised troops for the army. Roads were built to link distant parts of the empire. Messengers on horseback were sent to deliver orders to faraway officials.

The Chaldeans In 652 BC a series of wars broke out in the Assyrian Empire over who should rule. These wars greatly weakened the empire. Sensing this weakness, the Chaldeans (kal-DEE-unz), a group from the Syrian Desert, led other peoples in an attack on the Assyrians. In 612 BC, they destroyed Nineveh and the Assyrian Empire.

In its place, the Chaldeans set up a new empire of their own. **Nebuchadnezzar** (neb-uh-kuhd-NEZ-uhr), the most famous Chaldean king, rebuilt Babylon into a beautiful city. According to legend, his grand palace featured the famous Hanging Gardens. Trees and flowers grew on its terraces and roofs. From the ground the gardens seemed to hang in the air.

The Chaldeans admired Sumerian culture. They studied the Sumerian language and built temples to Sumerian gods.

At the same time, Babylon became a center for astronomy. Chaldeans charted the positions of the stars and kept track of economic, political, and weather events. They also created a calendar and solved complex problems of geometry.

Reading Check
Summarize List in order the peoples who ruled Mesopotamia.

Summary and Preview Many different peoples ruled in the Fertile Crescent after the Sumerians. Some made important contributions that are still valued today. In the next lesson, you will learn about a wealthy trading society that developed along the Mediterranean Sea.

Lesson 3 Assessment

Review Ideas, Terms, and People

1. **a. Identify** Where was Babylon located?
   b. Analyze What does Hammurabi's Code reveal about Babylonian society?

2. **a. Describe** What two advantages did Hittite soldiers have over their opponents?
   b. Rank Which empire discussed in this lesson do you think contributed the most to modern-day society? Why?
   c. Recall What areas did the Assyrians control by about 900 BC?
   d. Describe What did the royal library at Nineveh contain?

Critical Thinking

3. **Analyze** What was the significance of Hammurabi's Code in Babylon?

4. **Organize Information** Use a graphic organizer like the one below. List at least one advance or achievement made by each empire in this lesson.

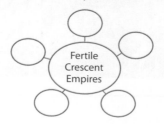

Fertile Crescent Empires

The Phoenicians

The Big Idea

The Phoenicians created a wealthy trading society along the Mediterranean Sea.

Main Ideas

- The Phoenicians built a trading society in the eastern Mediterranean region.
- The Phoenicians developed one of the world's first alphabets.

Key Term

alphabet

If YOU were there . . .

You live in the Phoenician port city of Sidon and have just agreed to be a sailor on a Phoenician trading ship. Your ship will sail from port to port on the Mediterranean Sea, delivering goods to some ports and picking up goods from others. It will be hard work, but you look forward to seeing what other places are like.

What do you think you'll see on this trading trip?

Phoenicia

At the western end of the Fertile Crescent, along the Mediterranean Sea, was a land known as Phoenicia (fi-NEE-shuh). It was not home to a great military power and was often ruled by foreign governments. Nevertheless, the Phoenicians created a wealthy trading society.

Phoenician City-States The major Phoenician city-states along the Mediterranean were established as early as 3000 BC. These included Byblos, Sidon, and Tyre. The Egyptians and Hittites each controlled the area for a time. By 1200 BC, the power of both the Egyptians and the Hittites declined.

The Phoenician cities formed a loose association of city-states, each ruled by a king. Powerful merchant families often influenced the Phoenician kings. Some city-states were also governed by a council of elders. However, the city-states generally remained independent of one another. Phoenicia lost its independence when a king of the powerful Persian Empire conquered it in 538 BC.

The Geography of Phoenicia Today the nation of Lebanon occupies most of what was once Phoenicia. Mountains border the region to the north and east. The western border is the Mediterranean.

Reading Check
Analyze Effects
What effect did geography have on the Phoenician economy?

Phoenicia had few resources. Unlike areas farther inland, Phoenicia lacked good farmland. It did have cedar trees, which provided valuable timber for trading. Even more valuable, however, was Phoenicia's location. Phoenician city-states connected Mediterranean sea routes with land routes that led deep into the Fertile Crescent. With their excellent location and limited resources, Phoenician leaders looked to the sea for a way to trade and expand their economy.

Phoenician Trade and Culture

Phoenician trading activity led to important innovations. Phoenicians made significant contributions to navigation, manufacturing, and written language.

The Expansion of Trade Motivated by a desire for trade, the people of Phoenicia became expert sailors. They built one of the world's finest harbors at the city of Tyre. Fleets of fast Phoenician trading ships sailed to ports all around the Mediterranean Sea. Most Phoenician ships had both sails for harnessing wind power and oars for rowing. Traders traveled to Egypt, Greece, Italy, Sicily, and Spain. They even passed through the Strait of Gibraltar to reach the Atlantic Ocean.

The Phoenicians founded several new colonies along their trade routes. Carthage (KAHR-thij), located on the northern coast of Africa, was the most famous of these. It later became one of the most powerful cities on the Mediterranean.

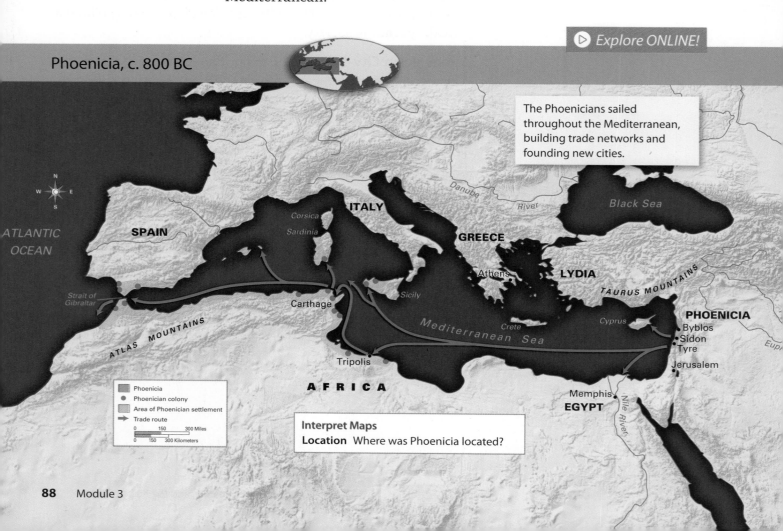

▶ Explore ONLINE!

Phoenicia, c. 800 BC

The Phoenicians sailed throughout the Mediterranean, building trade networks and founding new cities.

Legend:
- Phoenicia
- Phoenician colony
- Area of Phoenician settlement
- Trade route

0   150   300 Miles
0   150   300 Kilometers

Interpret Maps
Location Where was Phoenicia located?

Tyrian Purple

Before modern times, the process for making purple fabric was very difficult. The Phoenicians discovered how to make a rich purple dye. This dye is known as Tyrian purple because it was made in the city of Tyre. The dye's color came from an unlikely natural resource: sea snails.

Because the dye was hard to make, its supply was always low. The price of purple dye was therefore very high. Wearing purple clothing showed that a person was rich and influential. Ancient kings and emperors especially created demand for the rare and precious color. The profits earned from making and trading this valuable resource helped the Phoenician economy grow.

Synthesize
How did access to natural resources help the Phoenician economy grow?

Phoenicia grew wealthy from its trade. Besides timber, the Phoenicians traded silverwork, ivory carvings, and slaves. Beautiful glass objects also became valuable trade items after crafters invented glassblowing—the art of heating and shaping glass. In addition, the Phoenicians made purple dye from a type of shellfish. They then traded cloth dyed with this purple color. Phoenician purple fabric was very popular with rich people. Phoenicians used their goods to trade for other resources that were not readily available to them, such as ivory, gold, copper, tin, and iron.

Phoenician Culture and Achievements The Phoenicians made several important contributions to early civilization. They established trade and communication routes throughout the Mediterranean region. Different cultures throughout the region came to know one another better as they exchanged goods.

The Phoenicians' technological innovations made sea voyages safer and more efficient.

For example, Phoenician religion adopted new ideas as people interacted with surrounding civilizations. Egyptian, Hittite, Greek, and Roman traditions all shared elements with Phoenicians ones. Because of this interaction, Phoenician gods represented different elements of nature. The people worshipped them with prayer and the construction of statues.

Phoenician ships needed to sail across the wide body of the Mediterranean Sea rather than simply up and down rivers. The Phoenicians developed new navigation techniques, so ships could cross the sea safely without losing their way. They were the first sailors to use Polaris, the North Star, as the point of orientation for establishing directions at sea. Phoenician ships sailed up the coast of Europe and down the coast of Africa using the stars to ensure they were moving in the right direction.

The Phoenicians' most important achievement, however, wasn't trade or sailing skill. Earlier civilizations used pictographs or cuneiform to communicate ideas. To record their activities, however, Phoenician traders developed one of the world's first alphabets. An **alphabet** is a set of letters that can be combined to form words. The Phoenician alphabet had 22 letters. This made it easier to use writing to communicate complex ideas.

Later civilizations, including our own, benefited from Phoenician innovations like this one. In fact, the English alphabet is based on that of the Phoenicians.

Summary and Preview The Phoenicians created a trading society at the western end of the Fertile Crescent. They made important contributions that are still valued today. In the next lesson, you will learn about an empire that conquered nearly all of Asia Minor.

Reading Check
Summarize How did the Phoenicians contribute to the development of early civilizations?

Lesson 4 Assessment

Review Ideas, Terms, and People

1. **a. Identify** Who ruled Phoenician city-states?
   b. Recall What were three major city-states of Phoenicia, and when did they flourish?
   c. Analyze How did Phoenicia's lack of resources influence Phoenician leaders?
2. **a. Identify** For what trade goods were the Phoenicians known?
   b. Analyze What evidence from the text shows how Phoenicia grew wealthy?
   c. Analyze How did Phoenicia increase communication throughout the Mediterranean?
   d. Recall What star did the Phoenicians use for navigation?
   e. Contrast What is one difference between the Phoenician alphabet and the English alphabet?

Critical Thinking

3. **Evaluate** Copy the diagram, and use it to rank the significance of the Phoenician contributions to civilization in order of importance. Next to the diagram, write a sentence to explain each of your choices.

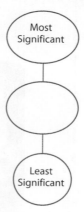

Most Significant

Least Significant

The Persian Empire

The Big Idea

Over time the Persians came to rule a great empire, which eventually brought them into conflict with the Greeks.

Main Ideas

- Persia became an empire under Cyrus the Great.
- The Persian Empire grew stronger under Darius I.
- The Persians fought Greece twice in the Persian Wars.

Key Terms and People

Cyrus the Great
cavalry
Darius I
Persian Wars
Xerxes I

If YOU were there . . .

You're a great military leader and the ruler of a great empire. You control everything in the nations you've conquered. One of your advisors urges you to force conquered people to give up their customs. He thinks they should adopt your way of life. But another advisor disagrees. Let them keep their own ways, she says, and you'll earn their loyalty.

Whose advice do you take? Why?

Persia Becomes an Empire

In the 500s BC, a new power arose to the east of the Fertile Crescent. This power was the Persian Empire. Early in their history, the Persians were an unorganized nomadic people. It took the skills of leaders like Cyrus the Great and Darius I to change that situation. Under these leaders, the Persians created a huge empire that became one of the great civilizations of the ancient world.

Cyrus the Great Early in their history, the Persians often fought other peoples of Southwest Asia. Sometimes they lost. In fact, they lost a fight to a people called the Medes (MEEDZ) and were ruled by them for about 150 years. In 550 BC, however, Cyrus II (SY-ruhs) led a Persian revolt against the Medes. His revolt was successful. Cyrus won independence for Persia and conquered the Medes. His victory marked the beginning of the Persian Empire.

Cyrus conquered much of Southwest Asia, including nearly all of Asia Minor, during his rule. Included in this region were several Greek cities that Cyrus took over. He then marched south to Mesopotamia and conquered Babylon, the most powerful city of the time. In Babylon, Cyrus found thousands of Jews enslaved in the city. Cyrus freed the Jews and allowed them to return to their homeland.

Cyrus also added land to the east to his empire. He led his army into central Asia to the Jaxartes River, which we now call the Syr Darya. When he died in about 529 BC, Cyrus ruled the largest empire the world had ever seen.

Cyrus let the people he conquered keep their own customs. He didn't force people to adopt Persian customs, and he didn't mistreat them. For example, Cyrus allowed the conquered Babylonians to keep worshipping their own gods. He hoped this would make them less likely to rebel. He was right. Few people rebelled against Cyrus, and his empire remained strong. Because of his great successes, historians call him **Cyrus the Great**.

The Persian Army Cyrus was successful in his conquests because his army was strong. It was strong because it was well organized and loyal.

At the heart of the Persian army were the Immortals, 10,000 soldiers chosen for their bravery and skill. In addition to the Immortals, the army had a powerful cavalry. A **cavalry** is a unit of soldiers who ride horses. Cyrus used his cavalry to charge the enemy and shoot at them with arrows. This strategy weakened the enemy before the Immortals attacked. Working together, the cavalry and the Immortals could defeat almost any foe.

Academic Vocabulary
strategy a plan for fighting a battle or war

Reading Check
Find Main Ideas
Who created the Persian Empire?

The Persian Empire Grows Stronger

Cyrus's son Cambyses continued to expand the Persian Empire after Cyrus died. For example, he conquered Egypt and added it to the empire. Soon afterward, though, a rebellion broke out in Persia. During this rebellion, Cambyses died. His death left Persia without a clear leader.

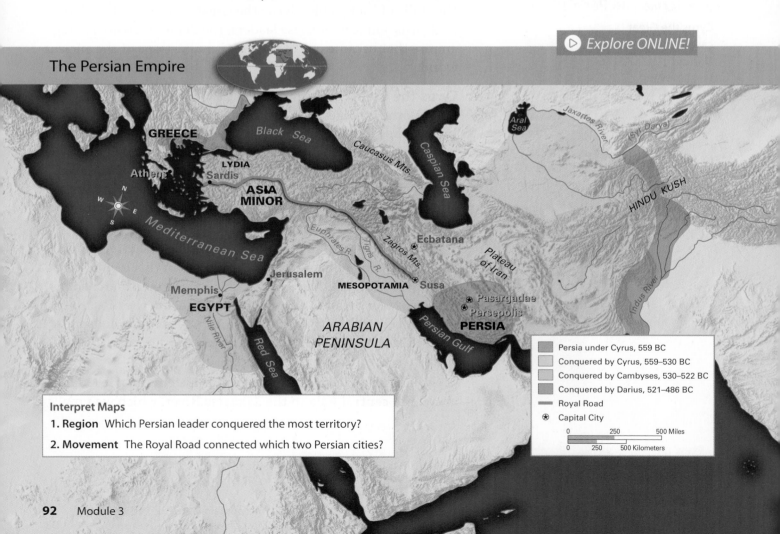

▷ Explore ONLINE!

The Persian Empire

Interpret Maps
1. **Region** Which Persian leader conquered the most territory?
2. **Movement** The Royal Road connected which two Persian cities?

Persia under Cyrus, 559 BC
Conquered by Cyrus, 559–530 BC
Conquered by Cambyses, 530–522 BC
Conquered by Darius, 521–486 BC
— Royal Road
⊛ Capital City

0   250   500 Miles
0   250   500 Kilometers

Sitting on a throne, the Emperor Darius is shown meeting with an officer of his empire.

Within four years a young prince named **Darius I** (da-RY-uhs) claimed the throne and killed all his rivals for power. Once he was securely in control, Darius worked to restore order in Persia. He also improved Persian society and expanded the empire.

Political Organization Darius organized the empire by dividing it into 20 provinces. Then he chose governors called satraps (SAY-traps) to rule the provinces for him. The satraps collected taxes for Darius, served as judges, and put down rebellions within their territories. Satraps had great power within their provinces, but Darius remained the empire's real ruler. His officials visited each province to make sure the satraps were loyal to Darius. He called himself king of kings to remind other rulers of his power.

Persian Art, Architecture, and Literature The term *classical civilization* describes civilizations that flourished long ago from the Mediterranean Sea eastward to India and China. These civilizations had advanced economies, governments, and cultures. Persia's rich classical culture included art, architecture, and literature.

For example, Darius built a new capital for the empire. It was called Persepolis. Darius wanted his capital to reflect the glory of his empire, so he filled the city with beautiful works of art. Many carvings lined the city's walls. Statues throughout the city glittered with gold, silver, and precious jewels. Darius also built an impressive palace in his new capital. Its architecture would influence building as far away as India.

The Persians were also skilled artists. Persian artists created delicate items out of gold and gems, many of them decorated with images of animals. Many of these items were used by the king and his family.

During Darius's rule a new religion arose in the Pesian Empire. This religion, which was called Zoroastrianism (zawr-uh-WAS-tree-uh-nih-zuhm), taught that there were two forces fighting for control of the universe. One force was good, and the other was evil. According to the Zoroastrian creation story, the good force created the sky, the earth, plants and animals, and the first man. At the same time, the evil force created demons, witches, and monsters.

The priests of the religion urged people to help the side of good in its struggle. This religion remained popular in Persia for many centuries, and some people still practice it today. The holy book of Zoroastrianism, the Avesta, is an important example of early Persian literature.

Persian Society Darius improved Persian society in other ways as well. For example, he standardized the currency, or the form of money used in transactions. Copper, silver, and gold coins each had their own standard worth, weight, and size. This standardization made it easier for Persians to conduct business and to trade with each other.

The Persian government encouraged trade, including by building new ports and seeking new trading partners. These policies stimulated expansion of the empire and led to great economic growth.

Darius had roads constructed to connect various parts of the empire. Royal messengers used these roads to travel quickly throughout Persia. One road, called the Royal Road, was more than 1,700 miles long. Royal messengers had specific places to receive letters and find food.

These roads helped change the way people perceived the world. Traveling great distances from one part of the empire to another became safe and secure. Good roads made it easier for peoples from different regions to interact with one another. Even Persia's enemies admired these roads and the Persian messenger system. For example, one Greek historian wrote:

> "Nothing mortal travels so fast as these Persian messengers . . . these men will not be hindered from accomplishing at their best speed the distance which they have to go, either by snow, or rain, or heat, or by the darkness of night."
>
> –Herodotus, from *History of the Persian Wars*

Reading Check
Summarize How did Darius I change Persia's political organization?

Persian Expansion Like Cyrus, Darius wanted the Persian Empire to grow. In the east, he conquered the entire Indus Valley. He also tried to expand the empire westward into Europe. However, before Darius could move very far into Europe, he had to deal with a revolt in the empire.

The Persians Fight Greece

In 499 BC, several Greek cities in Asia Minor rebelled against Persian rule. To help their fellow Greeks, a few city-states in mainland Greece sent soldiers to join the fight against the Persians.

The Persians put down the revolt, but Darius was still angry with the Greeks. Although the cities that had rebelled were in Asia, Darius was enraged that other Greeks had given them aid. He swore to take revenge on the Greeks.

The Battle of Marathon Nine years after the Greek cities rebelled, Darius invaded Greece. He and his army sailed to the plains of Marathon near Athens. This invasion began a series of wars between Persia and Greece that historians call the **Persian Wars**.

The Athenian army had only about 11,000 soldiers, while the Persians had about 15,000. However, the Greeks won the battle because they had better weapons and clever leaders.

According to legend, a messenger ran from Marathon to Athens—a distance of just over 26 miles—to bring news of the great victory. After crying out "Rejoice! We conquer!" the exhausted runner fell to the ground and died.

The Second Invasion of Greece Ten years after the Battle of Marathon, Darius's son **Xerxes I** (ZUHRK-seez) tried to conquer mainland Greece

This Greek vase shows a Persian soldier (at left) and a Greek soldier in a fight to the death.

again. In 480 BC, the Persian army set out for Greece. This time they were joined by the Persian navy.

The Greeks prepared to defend their homeland. This time Sparta, a powerful city-state in southern Greece, joined with Athens. The Spartans had the strongest army in Greece, so they went to fight the Persian army. Meanwhile, the Athenians sent their powerful navy to attack the Persian navy.

To slow the Persian army, the Spartans sent about 1,400 soldiers to Thermopylae (thuhr-MAH-puh-lee), a narrow mountain pass. The Persians had to cross through this pass to attack Greek cities. For three days, the small Greek force held off the Persian army. Then the Persians asked a traitorous Greek soldier to lead them through another pass. A large Persian force attacked the Spartans from behind. Surrounded, the brave Spartans and their allies fought to their deaths. After winning the battle, the Persians swept into Athens, attacking and burning the city.

Although the Persians won the battle in the pass, the Greeks quickly regained the upper hand. A few days after Athens was burned, the Athenians defeated the Persian navy through a clever plan. They led the larger Persian navy into the narrow straits of Salamis (SAH-luh-muhs). The Persians had so many ships that they couldn't steer well in

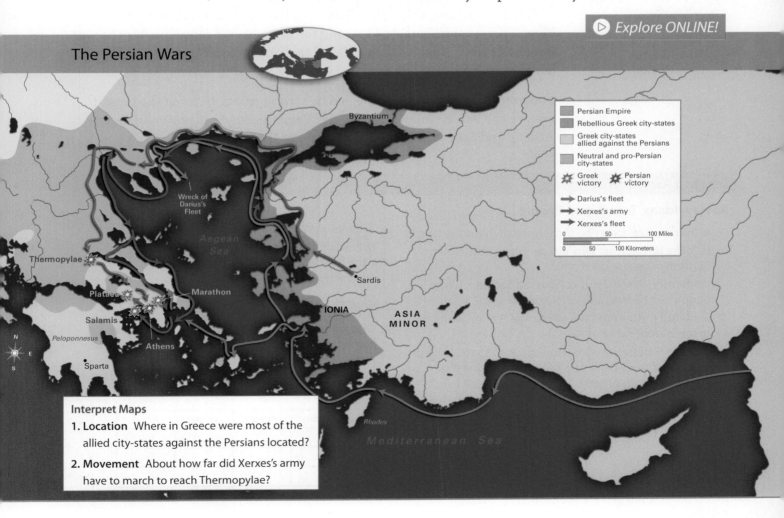

▶ Explore ONLINE!

The Persian Wars

Persian Empire
Rebellious Greek city-states
Greek city-states allied against the Persians
Neutral and pro-Persian city-states
Greek victory   Persian victory
Darius's fleet
Xerxes's army
Xerxes's fleet

0   50   100 Miles
0   50   100 Kilometers

Byzantium

Wreck of Darius's Fleet

Aegean Sea

Thermopylae

Sardis

IONIA

ASIA MINOR

Plataea

Marathon

Salamis

Peloponnesus

Athens

Sparta

Rhodes

Mediterranean Sea

Interpret Maps

1. **Location** Where in Greece were most of the allied city-states against the Persians located?

2. **Movement** About how far did Xerxes's army have to march to reach Thermopylae?

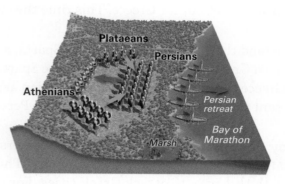

Marathon

At Marathon, the Greeks defeated a larger Persian force by luring the Persians into the middle of their forces. The Athenians then surrounded and defeated the Persians.

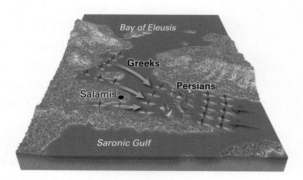

Salamis

At Salamis, the Greeks destroyed the Persian navy by attacking in a narrow strait where the Persian ships could not maneuver well.

Reading Check
Analyze Events
Why did Darius and Xerxes want to conquer Greece?

the narrow strait. As a result, the smaller Athenian boats easily sank many Persian ships. Those ships that were not destroyed soon returned home.

Soon after the Battle of Salamis, an army of soldiers from all over Greece beat the Persians at Plataea (pluh-TEE-uh). This battle ended the Persian Wars. Defeated, the Persians left Greece.

For the Persians, this defeat was humiliating, but it was not a major blow. Their empire remained strong for more than a century after the war. For the Greeks, though, the defeat of the Persians was a triumph. They had saved their homeland.

Summary The Persian Empire, led by strong rulers, became the largest empire the world had ever seen. The Persian army was powerful, but Athens and Sparta stopped its invasion of Greece.

Lesson 5 Assessment

Review Ideas, Terms, and People

1. a. **Summarize** Describe the empire of Cyrus the Great.
   b. **Make Inferences** Why did peoples conquered by Cyrus the Great seldom rebel?
   c. **Identify** When Cyrus conquered Babylon, what people did he free, and where did they go?
2. a. **Identify** How did Darius I change Persia's political organization?
   b. **Make Generalizations** How did Persia's roads help change people's perception of the world and their interaction with others?
   c. **Summarize** What were some examples of Persian architecture, art, and literature with which we associate classical civilizations?

3. a. **Explain** Why did Persia want to invade Greece?
   b. **Predict** How might the Persian Wars have ended if the Spartans had not slowed the Persians at Thermopylae?

Critical Thinking

4. **Organize Information** Using a chart like the one below, list the battles discussed in the lesson in the first column. In the other columns, identify who fought, who won, and what happened as a result of each battle.

Battle	Armies	Winner	Result

Social Studies Skills

Interpret Physical Maps

Define the Skill

A *physical* map is a map that shows the natural features and landscape, or *topography*, of an area. It shows the location and size of such features as rivers and mountain ranges. Physical maps also often show an area's *elevation*, or how high above sea level the land is. Topography and elevation often influence human activities. For example, people will live where they can find water and defend themselves. Therefore, being able to interpret a physical map can help you better understand how the history of an area unfolded.

Learn the Skill

Follow these steps to interpret a physical map.

1. Read the map's title, distance scale, and legend. These will provide basic information about the map's contents.

2. Note the colors used to show elevation. Use the legend to connect colors on the map to elevations of specific places.

3. Note the shapes of the features, such as how high a mountain range is, how far it stretches, and how long a river is. Note where each feature is in relation to others.

4. Use information from the map to draw conclusions about the effect of the region's topography on settlement and economic activities.

Practice the Skill

Use the guidelines to answer these questions about the physical map.

1. What is the elevation of the western half of the Arabian Peninsula?

2. Describe the topography of Mesopotamia. Why would settlement have occurred here before other places on the map?

3. What feature might have stopped invasions of Mesopotamia?

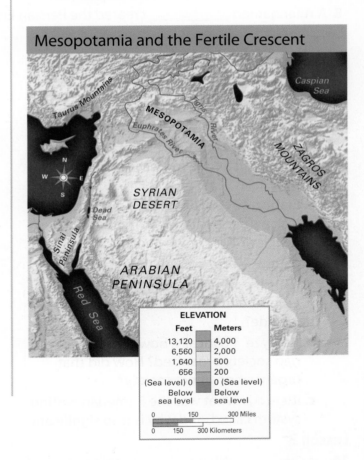

Mesopotamia and the Fertile Crescent

Module 3 Assessment

Review Vocabulary, Terms, and People

Complete each sentence by filling in the blank with the correct term or person.

1. Mesopotamian farmers built _____ to irrigate their fields.
2. While city dwellers were urban, farmers lived in _____ areas.
3. The people of Sumer practiced _____, the worship of many gods.
4. Instead of using pictographs, Sumerians developed a type of writing called _____.
5. Horse-drawn _____ gave the Hittites an advantage during battle.
6. The Babylonian king _____ is famous for his code of laws.
7. Sumerian society was organized in _____, which consisted of a city and the surrounding lands.
8. A ruler named _____ created the Persian Empire.

Comprehension and Critical Thinking

Lesson 1

9. a. Describe Where was Mesopotamia, and what does the name mean?
   b. Analyze How did Mesopotamian irrigation systems allow civilization to develop?
   c. Elaborate Do you think a division of labor is necessary for civilization to develop? Why or why not?

Lesson 2

10. a. Identify Who built the world's first empire, and what did that empire include?
    b. Analyze Politically, how was early Sumerian society organized? How did that organization affect society?
    c. Identify What was the Sumerian writing system called, and why is it so significant?

Lesson 3

11. a. Describe What technical achievement of the Hittites marks the beginning of the Iron Age?

   b. Draw Conclusions Why do you think several peoples banded together to fight the Assyrians?
   c. Evaluate Do you think Hammurabi was more effective as a ruler or as a military leader? Why?

Lesson 4

12. a. Analyze What choices did the Phoenician leaders make for their economy based on the limited resources of the area?
    b. Describe What were two important developments of the Phoenicians?
    c. Draw Conclusions How did the sail help the Phoenicians to build their economy?

Lesson 5

13. a. Identify Who were Cyrus the Great, Darius I, and Xerxes I?
    b. Analyze How did the Greeks use strategy to defeat a larger fighting force?
    c. Compare What similarities do you see between Sumerian and Persian art, architecture, and literature?

Review Themes

14. Science and Technology Which of the ancient Sumerians' technological achievements do you think has been most influential in history? Why?

15. Politics Why do you think Hammurabi is so honored for his code of laws?

Reading Skills

Identify Main Ideas *For each passage, choose the letter that corresponds to the main-idea sentence.*

16. (A) Sumerians believed that their gods had enormous powers. (B) Gods could bring a good harvest or a disastrous flood. (C) They could bring illness, or they could bring good health and wealth.

17. (A) The wheel was not the Sumerians' only great development. (B) They developed cuneiform, the world's first system of writing. (C) But Sumerians did not have pencils, pens, or paper. (D) Instead, they used sharp reeds to make wedge-shaped symbols on clay tablets.

Social Studies Skills

Interpret Physical Maps *Could you use a physical map to answer these questions? For each question, answer* yes *or* no.

18. Are there mountains or hills in a certain region?

19. What languages do people speak in that region?

20. How many people live in the region?

21. What kinds of water features such as rivers or lakes would you find there?

Focus on Writing

22. Write to Inform Write two or three paragraphs to inform readers about the significant contributions of the Mesopotamian leaders you learned about in this module. Include details about Hammurabi and Sargon. Be sure to inform readers about the main ideas of Hammurabi's Code.

Module 4

Kingdoms of the Nile

Essential Question

Why were Egyptians able to create such a long-lasting civilization?

About the Photo: The photo shows an ancient temple of Ramses II, one of Egypt's most powerful rulers.

▶ *Explore ONLINE!*

HISTORY.

VIDEOS, including...
- The Egyptian Empire Is Born
- The Sphinx of Egypt
- The Egyptian Book of the Dead

☑ Document-Based Investigations

☑ Graphic Organizers

☑ Interactive Games

☑ Animation: The Structure of a Pyramid

☑ Interactive Map: Ancient Egypt

☑ Image with Hotspots: Building the Pyramids of Giza

In this module you will learn about how the civilizations of ancient Egypt, Kush, and Aksum developed along the Nile River.

What You Will Learn...

Lesson 1: Geography and Early Egypt **104**
The Big Idea The water and fertile soils of the Nile Valley allowed a great civilization to develop in Egypt.

Lesson 2: The Old Kingdom **110**
The Big Idea Egyptian government and religion were closely connected during the Old Kingdom.

Lesson 3: The Middle and New Kingdoms **117**
The Big Idea During the Middle and New Kingdoms, order and greatness were restored in Egypt.

Lesson 4: Egyptian Achievements **123**
The Big Idea The Egyptians made lasting achievements in writing, architecture, and art.

Lesson 5: Kush and Aksum **129**
The Big Idea The kingdoms of Kush and Aksum, which arose south of Egypt, developed advanced civilizations with large trading networks.

Timeline of Events 4500 BC–AD 400

▶ Explore ONLINE!

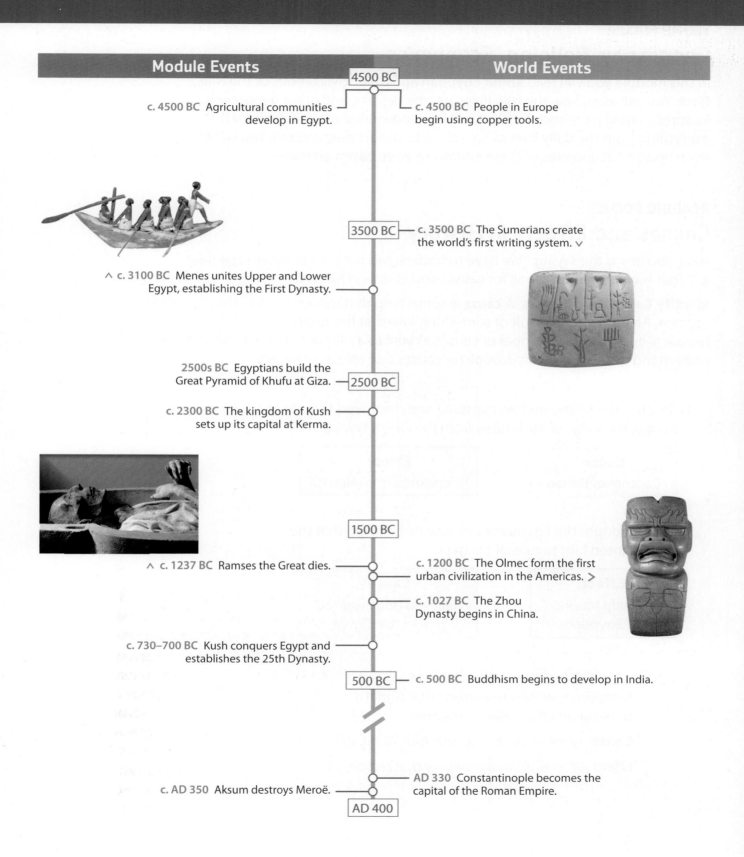

Module Events

World Events

4500 BC

c. 4500 BC Agricultural communities develop in Egypt.

c. 4500 BC People in Europe begin using copper tools.

3500 BC

c. 3500 BC The Sumerians create the world's first writing system. ∨

∧ **c. 3100 BC** Menes unites Upper and Lower Egypt, establishing the First Dynasty.

2500s BC Egyptians build the Great Pyramid of Khufu at Giza.

2500 BC

c. 2300 BC The kingdom of Kush sets up its capital at Kerma.

1500 BC

∧ **c. 1237 BC** Ramses the Great dies.

c. 1200 BC The Olmec form the first urban civilization in the Americas. >

c. 1027 BC The Zhou Dynasty begins in China.

c. 730–700 BC Kush conquers Egypt and establishes the 25th Dynasty.

500 BC

c. 500 BC Buddhism begins to develop in India.

AD 330 Constantinople becomes the capital of the Roman Empire.

c. AD 350 Aksum destroys Meroë.

AD 400

Reading Social Studies

Geography, Religion, Economics

In this module you will read about Egyptian and other civilizations of the Nile River. You will learn how the Nile River, nearby deserts, and other geographic features shaped early societies. You will learn how religious beliefs shaped everything from the daily lives of Egyptians to the art they created. You will also learn how the economies of these kingdoms were based on trade.

READING FOCUS:

Causes and Effects in History

Have you heard the saying, "We have to understand the past to avoid repeating it"? That is one reason we look for causes and effects in history.

Identify Causes and Effects A **cause** is something that makes another thing happen. An **effect** is the result of something else that has happened. Most historical events have a number of causes as well as a number of effects. You can understand history better if you look for causes and effects of events.

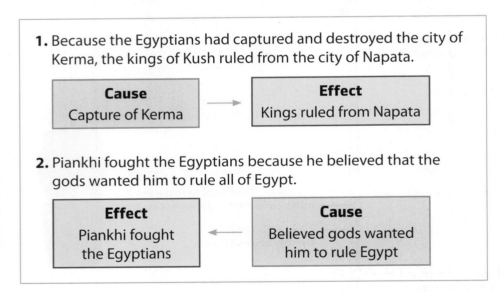

1. Because the Egyptians had captured and destroyed the city of Kerma, the kings of Kush ruled from the city of Napata.

Cause		**Effect**
Capture of Kerma	→	Kings ruled from Napata

2. Piankhi fought the Egyptians because he believed that the gods wanted him to rule all of Egypt.

Effect		**Cause**
Piankhi fought the Egyptians	←	Believed gods wanted him to rule Egypt

Sometimes writers use words that signal a cause or an effect. Here are some:

Cause—*reason, basis, because, motivated, as*

Effect—*therefore, as a result, for that reason, so*

You Try It!

As you read each of the selections below, identify which phrase or sentence describes a cause and which describes an effect.

Key Terms and People

Lesson 1
cataracts
delta
Menes
pharaoh
dynasty
Lesson 2
Old Kingdom
theocracy
Khufu
nobles
afterlife
mummies
elite
pyramids
engineering
Lesson 3
Middle Kingdom
New Kingdom
trade routes
Queen Hatshepsut
Ramses the Great
Lesson 4
hieroglyphics
papyrus
Rosetta Stone
sphinxes
obelisk
King Tutankhamen
Lesson 5
Piankhi
trade network
merchants
exports
imports
Queen Shanakhdakheto
Aksum
King Ezana

Find Causes and Effects

1. "During the mid-1000s BC the New Kingdom in Egypt was ending. As the power of Egypt's pharaohs declined, Kushite leaders regained control of Kush. Kush once again became independent."

2. "A series of inept pharaohs left Egypt open to attack."

3. "The Assyrians' iron weapons were better than the Kushites' bronze weapons. Although the Kushites were skilled archers, they could not stop the invaders.

4. "Iron ore and wood for furnaces were easily available, so the iron industry grew quickly."

Answer these questions based on the passages you just read.

1. In selection 1, is "Kush once again became independent" the cause of the Egyptians growing weaker or the effect?

2. In selection 2, what left Egypt open to attack? Is that the cause of why Egypt was easily attacked or the effect?

3. In selection 3, who is using the iron weapons, the Assyrians or the Kushites? What was the effect of using the weapons?

4. In selection 4, does the word "so" signal a cause or an effect?

As you read this module, look for words that signal causes or effects. Make a chart to keep track of these causes and effects.

Geography and Early Egypt

The Big Idea

The water and fertile soils of the Nile Valley allowed a great civilization to develop in Egypt.

Main Ideas

- Egypt was called the "gift of the Nile" because the Nile River was so important.
- Civilization developed after people began farming along the Nile.
- Strong kings unified all of Egypt.

Key Terms and People

cataracts
delta
Menes
pharaoh
dynasty

Along the banks of the Nile is a fertile river valley. Beyond the valley are hundreds of miles of desert.

If YOU were there . . .

Your family farms in the Nile Valley. Each year when the river's floodwaters spread rich soil on the land, you help your father plant barley. When you are not in the fields, you spin fine linen thread from flax you have grown. Sometimes you and your friends hunt birds in the tall grasses along the river banks.

Why do you like living in the Nile Valley?

The Gift of the Nile

Geography played a key role in the development of Egyptian civilization. The Nile River brought life to Egypt and allowed it to thrive. The river was so important to people in this region that a Greek historian named Herodotus (hi-RAHD-uh-tuhs) called Egypt the gift of the Nile. Over time, Egyptians developed technologies that helped them take advantage of the river.

Location and Physical Features The Nile is the longest river in the world. It begins in central Africa and runs north through Egypt to the Mediterranean Sea, a distance of over 4,000 miles. The civilization of ancient Egypt developed along a 750-mile stretch of the Nile.

Ancient Egypt included two regions, a southern region and a northern region. The southern region was called Upper Egypt. It was so named because it was located upriver in relation to the Nile's flow. Lower Egypt, the northern region, was located downriver. The Nile sliced through the desert of Upper Egypt. There, it created a fertile river valley about 13 miles wide. On either side lay hundreds of miles of desert.

The Nile flowed through rocky, hilly land south of Egypt. At several points, this rough terrain caused **cataracts**, or rapids, to form. The first cataract, located 720 miles south of the Mediterranean Sea, marked the southern border of Upper Egypt. Five more cataracts lay farther south. These cataracts made sailing on that portion of the Nile very difficult.

Ancient Egypt

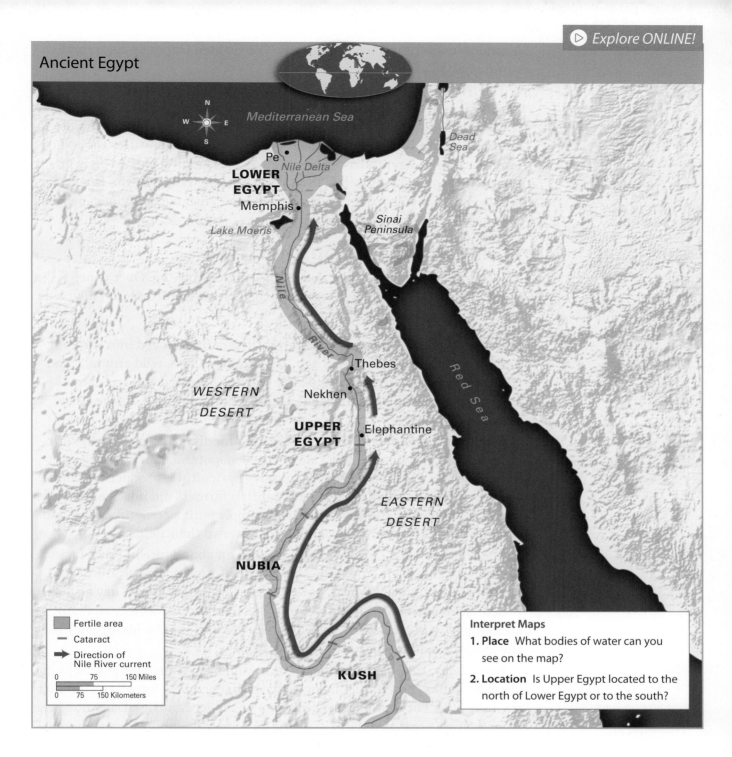

Mediterranean Sea

Dead Sea

Pe
Nile Delta
LOWER EGYPT
Memphis
Lake Moeris
Sinai Peninsula

Nile River

Red Sea

Thebes

WESTERN DESERT

Nekhen

UPPER EGYPT

Elephantine

EASTERN DESERT

NUBIA

KUSH

Fertile area
Cataract
Direction of Nile River current

0   75   150 Miles
0   75   150 Kilometers

Interpret Maps

1. **Place** What bodies of water can you see on the map?

2. **Location** Is Upper Egypt located to the north of Lower Egypt or to the south?

In Lower Egypt, the Nile divided into several branches that fanned out and flowed into the Mediterranean Sea. These branches formed a **delta**, a triangle-shaped area of land made from soil deposited by a river. In ancient times, swamps and marshes covered much of the Nile Delta. Some two-thirds of Egypt's fertile farmland was located in the Nile Delta.

The Floods of the Nile Because little rain fell in the region, most of Egypt was desert. Each year, however, rainfall far to the south of Egypt in the highlands of East Africa caused the Nile to flood. The Nile's floods were easier to predict than those of the Tigris and Euphrates rivers in

Mesopotamia. Almost every year, the Nile flooded Upper Egypt in mid-summer and Lower Egypt in the fall.

The Nile's flooding coated the land around it with a rich silt. As in Mesopotamia, the silt made the soil ideal for farming. The silt also made the land a dark color. That is why Egyptians called their country the black land. They called the dry, lifeless desert beyond the river valley the red land. Each year, Egyptians eagerly awaited the flooding of the Nile. For them, the river's floods were a life-giving miracle. This why the Nile is featured in many Egyptian myths and rituals. Without the floods, people never could have farmed in Egypt.

Reading Check
Summarize
Why was Egypt called the gift of the Nile?

Civilization Develops in Egypt

The Nile provided both water and fertile soil for farming. Over time, scattered farms grew into villages and then cities. Eventually, an Egyptian civilization developed.

Increased Food Production Hunter-gatherers first moved into the Nile Valley more than 12,000 years ago. They found plants, wild animals, and fish there to eat. In time, these people learned how to farm, and they settled along the Nile. By 4500 BC, farmers living in small villages grew wheat and barley.

Over time, however, Egyptians needed to modify their environment in order to feed growing populations. As in Mesopotamia, farmers in Egypt developed an irrigation system to improve agricultural production. Unlike farmers in Mesopotamia, however, Egyptian farmers did not need to build basins for storing water. The Egyptians simply built a series of canals and walls to direct the river's flow and carry water to their fields.

The Nile provided Egyptian farmers with an abundance of food. In addition to watering their crops, the Nile allowed farmers to raise animals. Farmers in Egypt grew wheat, barley, fruits, and vegetables. They also raised cattle and sheep. The river provided many types of fish, and hunters trapped wild geese and ducks along its banks. Like the Mesopotamians, the Egyptians enjoyed a varied diet.

Even today, the Nile continues to be a valuable resource for people living along its banks. Recent technologies have changed how Egyptians interact with the Nile. For example, construction of the Aswan High Dam along the Nile River was completed in 1970. The dam provides a significant source of electric power. This electricity has improved the standard of living for many people in the region.

Construction of the dam also has negative consequences. Farmers in Egypt still rely on the fertile lands along the Nile River to grow food. However, the dam limits the amount of silt on farmland from annual flooding. The silt from the river makes farmland more productive. Egyptians now use fertilizer on farmland to make up for the lost silt.

Two Kingdoms In addition to a stable food supply, Egypt's location offered another advantage. It had natural barriers that made it hard to invade Egypt. The desert to the west was too big and harsh to cross. To the

Farmers in ancient Egypt learned how to grow wheat and barley. This tomb painting (above) shows a couple harvesting their crop. Farmers in Egypt (right) still use the fertile lands along the Nile River to grow food.

Reading Check
Summarize
What attracted early settlers to the Nile Valley?

north, the Mediterranean Sea kept many enemies away. More desert lands and the Red Sea to the east provided protection against invasion as well. In addition, cataracts in the Nile made it difficult for invaders to sail in from the south.

Protected from invaders, the villages of Egypt grew. Wealthy farmers emerged as village leaders, and strong leaders gained control over several villages. By 3200 BC, the villages had grown, banded together, and developed into two kingdoms. One kingdom was called Lower Egypt, and the other was called Upper Egypt.

Each kingdom had its own capital city where its ruler was based. The capital of Lower Egypt was located in the northwest Nile Delta at a town called Pe. There, wearing the red crown that symbolized his authority, the king of Lower Egypt ruled. The capital city of Upper Egypt was called Nekhen. It was located on the west bank of the Nile. In this southern kingdom, the king wore a cone-shaped white crown. For centuries, Egyptians referred to their country as the two lands.

Kings Unify Egypt

According to tradition, around 3100 BC **Menes** (MEE-neez) rose to power in Upper Egypt. Some historians think Menes is a myth and that his accomplishments were really those of other ancient kings named Aha, Scorpion, or Narmer.

Menes wanted to unify Upper and Lower Egypt. His armies invaded and took control of Lower Egypt. He then married a princess from Lower Egypt to strengthen his control over the newly unified country. Menes wore both the white crown of Upper Egypt and the red crown of Lower Egypt to symbolize his leadership over the two kingdoms. Later, he combined the two crowns into a double crown. He formed one government in Egypt under a single monarchy.

Government power was more centralized in Egypt than in other places such as Sumer. In Sumer, leaders ruled over individual city-states. These city-states controlled large areas within Sumer. The government in Egypt, however, ruled over all of the cities within Egypt's borders. Many historians consider Menes to be Egypt's first **pharaoh** (FEHR-oh), the title used by the rulers of Egypt. The title *pharaoh* means "great house." The pharaoh ruled over Egypt with total control.

Egyptians believed that the pharaoh acted as a mediator between the people and the gods. This idea provided further reason to justify the pharaoh's rule. Menes founded Egypt's first **dynasty**, or series of rulers from the same family. Under dynasties, rule was generally passed from one generation to the next, which gave them significant political power. Pharaohs used this power to make laws and enforce order.

Menes built a new capital city at the southern tip of the Nile Delta. The city was later named Memphis. For centuries, Memphis was the political and cultural center of Egypt. Many government offices were located there, and the city bustled with artistic activity.

Menes combined the white crown of Upper Egypt and the red crown of Lower Egypt as a symbol of his rule of Egypt as one kingdom.

The First Dynasty lasted for about 200 years. Rulers who came after Menes also wore the double crown to symbolize their rule over Upper and Lower Egypt.

They extended Egyptian territory southward along the Nile and into Southwest Asia. Eventually, however, rivals arose to challenge the First Dynasty for power. These challengers took over Egypt and established the Second Dynasty.

Summary and Preview As you have read, ancient Egypt began in the fertile Nile River Valley. Two kingdoms developed. The two kingdoms were later united under one ruler, and Egyptian territory grew. In the next lesson, you will learn how Egypt continued to grow and change under later rulers in a period known as the Old Kingdom.

Reading Check
Make Inferences
Why do you think Menes wanted to rule over both kingdoms?

Lesson 1 Assessment

Review Ideas, Terms, and People

1. **a. Identify** Where was Lower Egypt located?

   b. Analyze Why was the Nile Delta well suited for settlement?

   c. Predict How might the Nile's cataracts have both helped and hurt Egypt?

2. **a. Describe** What foods did the Egyptians eat?

   b. Analyze What role did the Nile play in supplying Egyptians with the foods they ate?

   c. Elaborate How did the desert on both sides of the Nile help ancient Egypt?

3. **a. Identify** Who do some think was the first pharaoh of Egypt?

   b. Draw Conclusions Why did the pharaohs of the First Dynasty wear a double crown?

Critical Thinking

4. **Compare and Contrast** Draw a diagram like the one here. Use it to show the differences and similarities between Egyptian and Sumerian rulers.

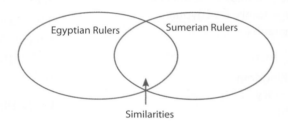

Egyptian Rulers   Sumerian Rulers

Similarities

The Old Kingdom

The Big Idea

Egyptian government and religion were closely connected during the Old Kingdom.

Main Ideas

- Life in the Old Kingdom was influenced by pharaohs, roles in society, and trade.

- Religion shaped Egyptian life.

- The pyramids were built as huge tombs for Egyptian pharaohs.

Key Terms and People

Old Kingdom
theocracy
Khufu
nobles
afterlife
mummies
elite
pyramids
engineering

If YOU were there . . .

You are a farmer in ancient Egypt. To you, the pharaoh is the god Horus as well as your ruler. You depend on his strength and wisdom. For part of the year, you are busy planting crops in your fields. But at other times of the year, you work for the pharaoh. You are helping to build a great tomb so that your pharaoh will be comfortable in the afterlife.

How do you feel about working for the pharaoh?

Life in the Old Kingdom

The First and Second Dynasties ruled Egypt for about four centuries. Around 2700 BC, though, a new dynasty rose to power in Egypt, called the Third Dynasty. Its rule began a period in Egyptian history known as the Old Kingdom.

Early Pharaohs The **Old Kingdom** was a period in Egyptian history that lasted for about 500 years, from about 2700 to 2200 BC. During this time, the Egyptians continued to develop their political system.

The system they developed was based on the belief that the pharaoh, the ruler of Egypt, was both a king and a god. It was a **theocracy**, or a government ruled by religious authorities. In a theocracy, all political authority comes from religion. Religious leaders have the power to make, approve, or enforce laws. They look to sacred texts or belief systems to justify their laws and actions. Priests and other religious leaders fill political offices. Individuals must follow religious laws carefully and may not have the right to freely choose what religion to practice.

The ancient Egyptians believed that Egypt belonged to the gods. They believed that the pharaoh had come to earth in order to manage Egypt for the rest of the gods. This is why he was chosen as a leader. The pharaoh had absolute power over all land and people in Egypt. He made laws, enforced order, and protected individual rights.

In Egypt, the pharaoh's status as both king and god came with many responsibilities such as this. People blamed him if crops did not grow well or if disease struck. They also demanded that the pharaoh make trade profitable and prevent wars.

The most famous pharaoh of the Old Kingdom was **Khufu** (KOO-foo), who ruled in the 2500s BC. Even though he is famous, we know relatively little about Khufu's life. Egyptian legend says that he was cruel, but historical records tell us that the people who worked for him were well fed. Khufu is best known for the monuments that were built to him.

Society and Trade By the end of the Old Kingdom, Egypt had about two million people. As the population grew, social classes appeared. The Egyptians believed that a well-ordered society would keep their kingdom strong. A social structure similar to what was found in Mesopotamia formed.

At the top of Egyptian society was the pharaoh. Just below him were the upper classes, which included priests and key government officials. Many of these priests and officials were **nobles**, or people from rich and powerful families.

Egyptian Society

Pharaoh
The pharaoh ruled Egypt as a god.

Nobles
Officials and priests helped run the government and temples.

Scribes and Craftspeople
Scribes wrote and craftspeople produced goods.

Farmers, Servants, and Slaves
Most Egyptians were farmers, servants, and slaves.

Analyze Visuals
Which group helped carry out religious rituals?

Next in society was the middle class. It included lesser government officials, scribes, and a few rich craftspeople.

The people in Egypt's lower class, more than 80 percent of the population, were mostly farmers. During flood season, when they could not work in the fields, farmers worked on the pharaoh's building projects. Servants and slaves also worked hard.

As society developed during the Old Kingdom, Egypt traded with some of its neighbors. The Egyptians had a comparative advantage over their trading partners. This means that Egypt had access to resources that its neighbors did not have. For example, Egyptian traders traveled south along the Nile to Nubia to **acquire** gold, copper, ivory, slaves, and stone for building. These resources were not easily available in Syria to the east.

However, Syria had wood for building. Wood was not easily available in Egypt. So Egypt traded resources such as metal and stone to Syria. In return, Syria provided Egypt with wood for building and for fire. Egypt and its neighbors benefited from trade because it gave each of them access to natural resources unavailable at home.

Egyptian society grew more complex during this time. It continued to be organized, disciplined, and highly religious.

Reading Check
Form Generalizations
How was society structured in the Old Kingdom?

Religion and Egyptian Life

Worshipping the gods was a part of daily life in Egypt. But the Egyptian focus on religion extended beyond people's lives. Many customs focused on what happened after people died.

The Gods of Egypt Like the Sumerians, the Egyptians practiced polytheism and believed the gods were very powerful. Before the First Dynasty, each village worshipped its own gods. During the Old Kingdom period, Egyptian officials expected everyone to worship the same gods, though how they worshipped the gods might differ from place to place.

The Egyptians built temples to the gods all over the kingdom. Temples collected payments from both worshippers and the government. These payments allowed the temples to grow more influential.

Compare River Valley Civilizations
Ancient Egypt and Mesopotamia
Powerful leaders were chosen by the gods.
Government managed water resources.
Social divisions existed between classes of people.
Creation myths explained the natural world.
Interpret Charts   Why was it necessary for both governments to manage water?

Over time, certain cities became centers for the worship of certain gods. As in other river valley civilizations, much of this worship was based on creation myths. Creation myths are ideas about how the world came into existence. In the city of Memphis, for example, people prayed to Ptah, who they believed created the world. Different theories about the beginning of the world developed throughout ancient Egypt. One stated that a group of eight gods called the Ogdoad were responsible. Another myth said a god named Atum rose from water to create the planet.

The Egyptians had gods for nearly everything, including the sun, the sky, and the earth. Many gods mixed human and animal forms. For example, Anubis, the god of the dead, had a human body but a jackal's head. Other major gods included

- Re, or Amon-Re, the sun god
- Osiris, the god of the underworld
- Isis, the goddess of magic
- Horus, a sky god, god of the pharaohs
- Thoth, the god of wisdom
- Geb, the earth god

Egyptian families also worshipped household gods at shrines in their homes.

Emphasis on the Afterlife Much of Egyptian religion focused on the **afterlife**, or life after death. The Egyptians believed that the afterlife was a happy place. Paintings from Egyptian tombs show the afterlife as an ideal world where all the people are young and healthy.

The Egyptian belief in the afterlife stemmed from their idea of *ka* (KAH), or a person's life force. When a person died, his or her *ka* left the body and became a spirit. The *ka* remained linked to the body and could not leave its burial site. However, it had all the same needs that the person had when he or she was living. It needed to eat, sleep, and be entertained.

To fulfill the *ka*'s needs, people filled tombs with objects for the afterlife. These objects included furniture, clothing, tools, jewelry, and weapons. Relatives of the dead were expected to bring food and beverages to their loved ones' tombs so the *ka* would not be hungry or thirsty.

Burial Practices Egyptian ideas about the afterlife shaped their burial practices. The Egyptians believed that a body had to be prepared for the afterlife before it could be placed in a tomb. This meant the body had to be preserved. If the body decayed, its spirit could not recognize it. That would break the link between the body and spirit. The *ka* would then be unable to receive the food and drink it needed.

Mummies

1. Only the god Anubis was allowed to perform the first steps in preparing a mummy.

2. The body's organs were preserved in special jars and kept next to the mummy.

3. The body was preserved as a mummy and kept in a case called a sarcophagus.

The Afterlife in Ancient Egypt

The ancient Egyptians believed that a person's soul was judged when he or she died. This papyrus shows how that judgment occurred.

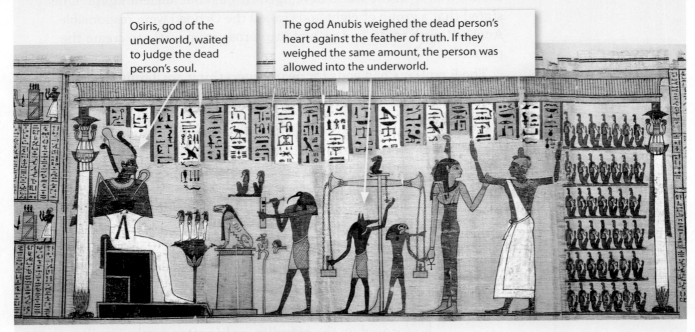

Osiris, god of the underworld, waited to judge the dead person's soul.

The god Anubis weighed the dead person's heart against the feather of truth. If they weighed the same amount, the person was allowed into the underworld.

Analyze Historical Sources Where is Osiris in this drawing?
Explain the details that help identify him as the god of the underworld.

Academic Vocabulary
method a way of doing something

To keep the *ka* from suffering, the Egyptians developed a **method** called embalming to preserve bodies and keep them from decaying. The Egyptians preserved bodies as **mummies**, specially treated bodies wrapped in cloth. Embalming preserves a dead body for many, many years. A body that was not embalmed would decay quickly in a tomb.

Embalming was a complex process that took several weeks to complete. In the first step, embalmers cut open the body and removed all the organs except for the heart. The removed organs were stored in special jars. Next, embalmers used a special substance to dry out the body and later applied some special oils. The embalmers then wrapped the dried-out body with linen cloths and bandages, often placing special charms inside the cloth wrappings. Wrapping the body was the last step in the mummy-making process. Once it was completely wrapped, a mummy was placed in a coffin.

Reading Check
Analyze Effects
How did religious beliefs affect Egyptian burial practices?

Only royalty and other members of Egypt's **elite** (AY-leet), or people of wealth and power, could afford to have mummies made. Peasant families did not need the process, however. They buried their dead in shallow graves at the edge of the desert. The hot, dry sand of the desert preserved the bodies naturally.

The Pyramids

The Egyptians believed that burial sites, especially royal tombs, were very important. As a result, they built spectacular monuments in northern Africa in which to bury their rulers. The most spectacular of all were the **pyramids**—huge, stone tombs with four triangle-shaped sides that met in a point on top. The Egyptians first built pyramids during the Old Kingdom.

Many of these huge pyramids are still standing. The largest example of this architecture is the Great Pyramid of Khufu near the town of Giza. It covers more than 13 acres at its base and stands 481 feet high. This single pyramid took thousands of workers and more than two million limestone blocks to build.

Like all the pyramids, it is an amazing reminder of Egyptian scientific contributions and **engineering**, the application of scientific knowledge for practical purposes. For example, the designers of the Great Pyramid of Khufu used a mathematical formula that is still being used millennia later.

The Egyptians applied their engineering abilities to other monuments as well. The Great Sphinx of Giza is a colossal limestone statue of a mythical creature with a lion's body and a human head. Large stones were moved over long distances to build the Sphinx.

Building the Pyramids The earliest pyramids did not have the smooth sides we usually imagine when we think of pyramids. The Egyptians began building the smooth-sided pyramids we usually see around 2700 BC. The steps of these pyramids were filled and covered with limestone. The burial chamber was deep inside the pyramid. After the pharaoh's burial, workers sealed the passages to this room with large blocks.

Historians are not sure how the Egyptians built the pyramids. What is certain is that such enormous projects required a huge labor force. As many as 100,000 workers may have been needed to build a single pyramid. The government kept records and paid the peasants for their work. Wages were paid in goods such as grain instead of money.

The Great Sphinx of Giza and the Great Pyramid of Khufu are symbols that demonstrate the importance ancient Egyptians placed on the afterlife.

For years, scholars have debated how the Egyptians moved the massive stones used to build the pyramids. Some believe that during the Nile's flooding, builders floated the stones downstream directly to the construction site. Most historians believe that workers used brick ramps and strong sleds to drag the stones up the pyramid once they reached the site.

Workers built massive pyramids as tombs for their rulers. In this illustration, men work to build the pharaoh Khafre's pyramid.

Significance of the Pyramids Burial in a pyramid demonstrated a pharaoh's importance. The size and shape of the pyramid were symbolic to ancient Egyptians. Pointing to the skies, the pyramid was an icon that symbolized the pharaoh's journey to the afterlife. The Egyptians wanted the pyramids to be spectacular because they believed that the pharaoh, as their link to the gods, controlled everyone's afterlife. Making the pharaoh's spirit happy was a way of ensuring one's own happy afterlife.

To ensure that pharaohs remained safe after their deaths, the Egyptians sometimes wrote magical spells and hymns on the pharaohs' tombs. Together, these spells and hymns are called Pyramid Texts. The first such text, addressed to Re, was carved into the pyramid of King Unas (OO-nuhs), a pharaoh of the Old Kingdom:

> "Re-Atum, this Unas comes to you,
>   A spirit indestructible . . .
>   Your son comes to you, this Unas . . .
>   May you cross the sky united in the dark,
>   May you rise in lightland, [where] you shine!"
>   —from Pyramid Text, Utterance 217

Reading Check
Summarize Why were pyramids important to the ancient Egyptians?

The builders of Unas's pyramid wanted the god to look after their leader's spirit. Even after death, their pharaoh was important to them.

Summary and Preview During the Old Kingdom, new political and social orders were created in Egypt. Religion was important, and many pyramids were built for the pharaohs. In the next lesson, you will learn about life in later periods, the Middle and New Kingdoms.

Lesson 2 Assessment

Review Ideas, Terms, and People

1. a. Recall To what does the phrase *Old Kingdom* refer?
   b. Analyze Why was the pharaoh's authority never questioned?
   c. Elaborate Why do you think pharaohs might have wanted the support of nobles?
2. a. Define What did Egyptians mean by the afterlife?
   b. Analyze Why was embalming important to Egyptians?
3. a. Describe What is engineering?

b. Elaborate What does the building of the pyramids and the Sphinx at Giza tell us about Egyptian society?

Critical Thinking

4. Organize Information Draw a pyramid like the one here. In each level, write a sentence about the corresponding social class.

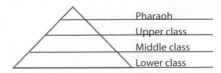

The Middle and New Kingdoms

The Big Idea

During the Middle and New Kingdoms, order and greatness were restored in Egypt.

Main Ideas

- The Middle Kingdom was a period of stable government between periods of disorder.
- The New Kingdom was the peak of Egyptian trade and military power, but its greatness did not last.
- Work and daily life were different among Egypt's social classes.

Key Terms and People

Middle Kingdom
New Kingdom
trade routes
Queen Hatshepsut
Ramses the Great

Reading Check
Summarize What caused the end of the Middle Kingdom?

If YOU were there . . .

You are a servant to Hatshepsut, the ruler of Egypt. You admire her, but some people think a woman should not rule. She calls herself king and dresses like a pharaoh—even wearing a fake beard. That was your idea! But you want to help more.

What could Hatshepsut do to show her authority?

The Middle Kingdom

At the end of the Old Kingdom, the wealth and power of the pharaohs declined. Building and maintaining pyramids cost a lot of money. Pharaohs could not collect enough taxes to keep up with their expenses. At the same time, ambitious nobles used their government positions to take power from pharaohs.

In time, nobles gained enough power to challenge the pharaohs. By about 2200 BC, the Old Kingdom had fallen. For the next 160 years, local nobles ruled much of Egypt. The kingdom had no central ruler.

Finally, around 2050 BC, a powerful pharaoh defeated his rivals, and once again all of Egypt was united. His rule began the **Middle Kingdom**, a period of order and stability which lasted to about 1750 BC. Toward the end of the Middle Kingdom, however, Egypt began to fall into disorder once more.

Around 1750 BC, a group from Southwest Asia called the Hyksos (HIK-sohs) invaded. They used horses, chariots, and advanced weapons to conquer Lower Egypt. The Hyksos ruled the region as pharaohs for 200 years.

The Egyptians eventually fought back, however. In the mid-1500s BC, Ahmose (AHM-ohs) of Thebes declared himself king and drove the Hyksos out of Egypt. Ahmose then ruled all of Egypt.

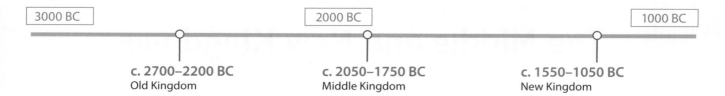

3000 BC	2000 BC	1000 BC

c. 2700–2200 BC
Old Kingdom

c. 2050–1750 BC
Middle Kingdom

c. 1550–1050 BC
New Kingdom

The New Kingdom

Ahmose's rise to power marked the beginning of Egypt's 18th Dynasty. More importantly, it was the beginning of the **New Kingdom,** the period during which Egypt reached the height of its power and glory. During the New Kingdom, which lasted from about 1550 to 1050 BC, conquest and trade brought wealth to the pharaohs.

Building an Empire After battling the Hyksos, Egypt's leaders feared future invasions. To prevent such invasions from occurring, they decided to take control of all possible invasion routes into the kingdom. In the process, these leaders turned Egypt into an empire.

Egypt's first target was the homeland of the Hyksos. After taking over that area, the army continued north and conquered Syria. Egypt took over the eastern shore of the Mediterranean and the kingdom of Kush, south of Egypt. By the 1400s BC, Egypt was the leading military power in the region. Its empire extended from the Euphrates River to southern Nubia.

Military conquests made Egypt rich. The kingdoms it conquered regularly sent treasures to their Egyptian conquerors. For example, the kingdom of Kush in Nubia south of Egypt sent annual payments of gold, leopard skins, and precious stones to the pharaohs. In addition, Assyrian, Babylonian, and Hittite kings sent expensive gifts to Egypt in an effort to maintain good relations.

— BIOGRAPHY —

Queen Hatshepsut
Ruled c. 1503–1482 BC

Hatshepsut was married to the pharaoh Thutmose II, her half-brother. He died young, leaving the throne to Thutmose III, his son by another woman. Because Thutmose III was still very young, Hatshepsut took power. Many people did not think women should rule, but Hatshepsut dressed as a man and called herself king. After she died, her stepson took back power and vandalized all the monuments she had built.

Analyze Causes
What do you think caused Hatshepsut to dress like a man?

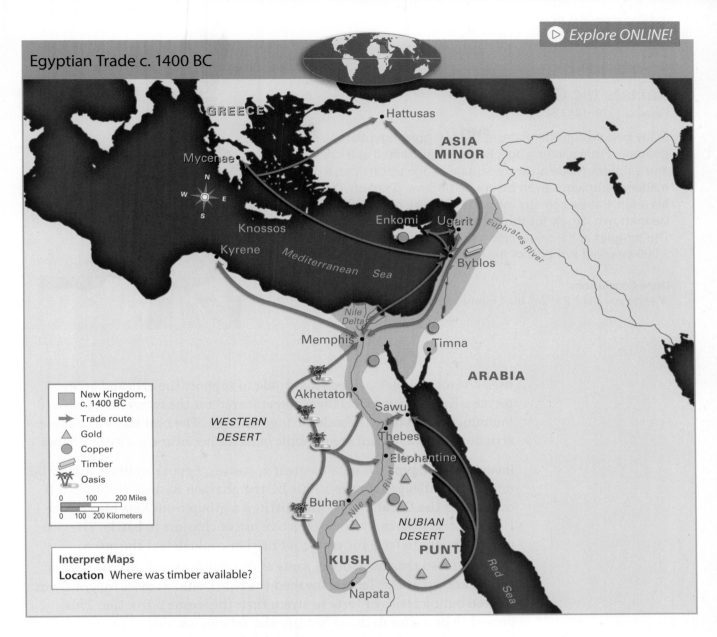

Egyptian Trade c. 1400 BC

Explore ONLINE!

Map legend:
- New Kingdom, c. 1400 BC
- Trade route
- Gold
- Copper
- Timber
- Oasis

0   100   200 Miles
0   100   200 Kilometers

Interpret Maps
Location Where was timber available?

Map labels: GREECE, Hattusas, ASIA MINOR, Mycenae, Enkomi, Ugarit, Euphrates River, Knossos, Kyrene, Mediterranean Sea, Byblos, Nile Delta, Memphis, Timna, ARABIA, WESTERN DESERT, Akhetaton, Sawu, Thebes, Elephantine, Buhen, Nubian River, NUBIAN DESERT, PUNT, KUSH, Red Sea, Napata

Growth and Effects of Trade Conquest also brought Egyptian traders into contact with more distant lands. Egypt's trade expanded along with its empire. Profitable **trade routes**, or paths followed by traders, developed. Many of the lands that Egypt took over also had valuable resources for trade. The Sinai Peninsula, for example, had large supplies of turquoise and copper.

One ruler who worked to increase Egyptian trade was **Queen Hatshepsut** (hat-SHEP-soot). She sent Egyptian traders south to trade with the kingdom of Punt on the Red Sea and north to trade with people in Asia Minor and Greece.

Hatshepsut's decision to establish these trade routes strengthened Egypt. Hatshepsut and later pharaohs

This jar probably held perfume, a valuable trade item.

Ramses the Great
Ruled c. 1279–1213 BC

Many people consider Ramses the last great Egyptian pharaoh. From a young age, Ramses was trained as a ruler and a fighter. Made an army captain at age ten, he began military campaigns even before he became pharaoh. During his reign, Ramses greatly increased the size of his kingdom. He is known largely for the massive monuments he built. The temples at Karnak, Luxor, and Abu Simbel stand as 3,000-year-old symbols of the great pharaoh's power.

Draw Conclusions
Why do you think Ramses built monuments all over Egypt?

used the money they gained from trade to support the arts and architecture. Hatshepsut especially is remembered for the many impressive monuments and temples built during her reign. The best known of these structures was a magnificent temple built for her near the city of Thebes.

Invasions of Egypt Despite its great successes, Egypt's military might did not go unchallenged. In the 1200s BC the pharaoh Ramses (RAM-seez) II, or **Ramses the Great**, fought the Hittites, a group from Asia Minor. The Hittites were known for their effective use of chariots in battle. The two powers fought fiercely for years, but neither could defeat the other.

Egypt faced threats in other parts of its empire as well. To the west, a people known as the Tehenu invaded the Nile Delta. Ramses fought them off and built a series of forts to strengthen the western frontier. This proved to be a wise decision because the Tehenu invaded again a century later. Faced with Egypt's strengthened defenses, the Tehenu were defeated once again.

Soon after Ramses the Great died, invaders called the Sea Peoples sailed into Southwest Asia. Little is known about these people. Historians are not even sure who they were. All we know is that they were strong warriors who had crushed the Hittites and destroyed cities in Southwest Asia. Only after 50 years of fighting were the Egyptians able to turn them back.

Egypt survived, but its empire in Asia was gone. Shortly after the invasions of the Hittites and the Sea Peoples, the New Kingdom came to an end. Egypt fell into a period of violence and disorder. Egypt would never regain its power.

Reading Check
Analyze Causes
What caused the growth of trade in the New Kingdom?

Work and Daily Life

Although Egyptian dynasties rose and fell, daily life for Egyptians did not change very much. But as the population grew, society became even more complex.

Egyptian scribes at work.

A complex society requires people to take on different jobs. In Egypt, these jobs were usually passed on within families. At a young age, boys started to learn their future jobs from their fathers.

Scribes Other than priests and government officials, no one in Egypt was more honored than scribes. As members of the middle class, scribes worked for the government and the temples. They kept records and accounts for the state. Scribes also wrote and copied religious and literary texts, including stories and poems. Because they were so respected, scribes did not have to pay taxes, and many became wealthy.

Artisans, Artists, and Architects Another group in society was made up of artisans whose jobs required advanced skills. Among the artisans who worked in Egypt were sculptors, builders, carpenters, jewelers, metalworkers, and leatherworkers. Most of Egypt's artisans worked for the government or for temples. They made statues, furniture, jewelry, pottery, shoes, and other items. Most artisans were paid fairly well for their work.

Architects and artists were also admired in Egypt. Architects designed the temples and royal tombs for which Egypt is famous. Talented architects could rise to become high government officials. Artists, often employed by the state or the temples, produced many different works. Artists often worked in the deep burial chambers of the pharaohs' tombs painting detailed pictures.

Merchants and Traders Although trade was important to Egypt, only a small group of Egyptians became merchants and traders. Some traveled long distances to buy and sell goods. Merchants were usually accompanied by soldiers, scribes, and laborers on their travels.

Soldiers After the wars of the Middle Kingdom, Egypt created a professional army. The military offered people a chance to rise in social status. Soldiers received land as payment and could also keep any treasure they captured in war. Those who excelled could be promoted to officer positions.

Farmers and Other Peasants As in Old Kingdom society, Egyptian farmers and other peasants were toward the bottom of Egypt's social scale. These hardworking people made up the vast majority of Egypt's population.

Farmers grew crops to support their families. Farmers depended on the Nile's regular floods to grow their crops. They used wooden hoes or plows pulled by cows to prepare the land before the flood. After the floodwaters had drained away, farmers planted seeds. They grew crops such as wheat and barley. At the end of the growing season, farmers worked together to gather the harvest.

Farmers had to give crops to the pharaoh as taxes. These taxes were intended to pay the pharaoh for using the land. Under Egyptian law, the pharaoh controlled all land in the kingdom.

All peasants, including farmers, were also subject to special duty. Under Egyptian law, the pharaoh could demand at any time that people work on projects, such as building pyramids, mining gold, or fighting in the army. The government paid the workers in grain.

Slaves The few slaves in Egyptian society were considered lower than farmers. Many slaves were convicted criminals or prisoners captured in war. Slaves worked on farms, on building projects, in workshops, and in private households. Unlike most slaves in history, however, slaves in Egypt had some legal rights. Also, in some cases, they could earn their freedom.

Family Life in Egypt Family life was important. Most families lived in their own homes. Sometimes unmarried female relatives lived with them. Men were expected to marry young and start having children.

Most Egyptian women were devoted to their homes and their families. Some, however, had jobs outside the home. A few served as priestesses, and some worked as royal officials, administrators, and artisans. Egyptian women had a number of legal rights. They could own property, make **contracts**, and divorce their husbands.

Children's lives were not as structured as adults' lives were. They played with toys such as dolls, tops, and clay animal figurines. Children also played ballgames and hunted. Most children, boys and girls, received some education. At school they learned morals, writing, math, and sports. At age 14 most boys left school to enter their father's profession. At that time, they took their place in Egypt's social structure.

Summary and Preview Pharaohs faced many challenges to their rule. After defeating the Hyksos, the kingdom expanded in land and wealth. People in Egypt worked at many different jobs. In the next lesson, you will learn about Egyptian achievements.

Servants worked for Egypt's rulers and nobles and did many jobs, like preparing food.

Academic Vocabulary
contracts binding legal agreements

Reading Check
Summarize What types of jobs existed in ancient Egypt?

Lesson 3 Assessment

Review Ideas, Terms, and People

1. **a. Define** What was the Middle Kingdom?
   b. Analyze How did Ahmose manage to become king of all Egypt?
2. **a. Identify** For what is Ramses the Great best known?
   b. Explain What did Hatshepsut do as pharaoh of Egypt?
3. **a. Identify** What job employed the most people in Egypt?
   b. Analyze What rights did Egyptian women have?
   c. Elaborate Why do you think scribes were so honored in Egyptian society?

Critical Thinking

4. **Organize Information** Draw a table like this one. Use it to identify factors in the rise and fall of Egypt's empire during the New Kingdom.

Rise	Fall

Egyptian Achievements

The Big Idea
The Egyptians made lasting achievements in writing, architecture, and art.

Main Ideas
- Egyptian writing used hieroglyphics.
- Egypt's great temples were lavishly decorated.
- Egyptian art filled tombs.

Key Terms and People
hieroglyphics
papyrus
Rosetta Stone
sphinxes
obelisk
King Tutankhamen

If YOU were there . . .

You are an artist in ancient Egypt. A noble has hired you to decorate the walls of his family tomb. You are standing inside the new tomb, studying the bare, stone walls that you will decorate. No light reaches this chamber, but your servant holds a lantern high. You've met the noble only briefly but think that he is someone who loves his family, the gods, and Egypt.

What will you include in your painting?

Egyptian Writing

If you were reading a book and saw pictures of folded cloth, a leg, a star, a bird, and a man holding a stick, would you know what it meant? You would if you were an ancient Egyptian. In the Egyptian writing system, or **hieroglyphics** (hy-ruh-GLIH-fiks), those five symbols together meant "to teach." Egyptian hieroglyphics were one of the world's first writing systems.

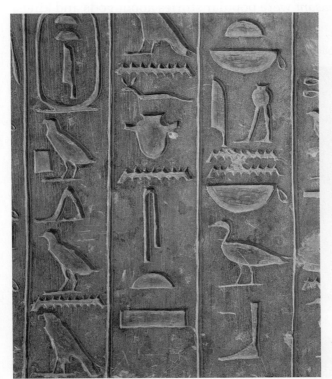

These hieroglyphics in the burial chamber of the Pyramid of Teti give us important information about Egyptian society.

Writing in Ancient Egypt The earliest known examples of Egyptian writing are from around 3300 BC. These early Egyptian writings were carved in stone or on other hard material. Later, the Egyptians learned how to make **papyrus** (puh-PY-ruhs), a long-lasting, paperlike material made from reeds. The Egyptians made papyrus by pressing layers of reeds together and pounding them into sheets. These sheets were tough and durable, yet easy to roll into scrolls. Scribes wrote on papyrus using brushes and ink.

The hieroglyphic writing system used more than 600 symbols, mostly pictures of objects. Each symbol represented one or more sounds in the Egyptian language. For example, a picture of an owl represented the same sound as our letter *M*.

Hieroglyphics could be written either horizontally or vertically. They could be written from right to left or from left to right. These options made hieroglyphics flexible to write but difficult to read. The only way to tell which way a text is written is to look at individual symbols.

The Rosetta Stone Historians and archaeologists have known about hieroglyphic writing for centuries, but for a long time they didn't know how to read it. In fact, it was not until 1799 when a lucky discovery by a French soldier gave historians the key they needed to read ancient Egyptian writing.

That key was the **Rosetta Stone**, a huge, stone slab inscribed with hieroglyphics. In addition to the hieroglyphics, the Rosetta Stone had text in Greek and a later form of Egyptian. Because the text in all three languages was the same, scholars who knew Greek were able to figure out what the hieroglyphics said.

After the soldier's discovery, the Rosetta Stone was later translated by the French historian and linguist Jean-François Champollion in the early 19th century. His world-changing discoveries helped later historians understand ancient Egypt.

Egyptian Texts Because papyrus did not decay in Egypt's dry climate, many Egyptian texts still survive. Historians today can read Egyptian government records, historical records, science texts, and medical manuals. Writing also influenced Egyptian religion and culture. It allowed Egyptians to creatively express ideas. For example, some of the world's earliest examples of literature come from ancient Egyptian culture. *The Story of Sinuhe* and *The Eloquent Peasant* were popular stories about gods and kings.

Egyptians used papyrus for written records and literature, such as this page from the *Book of the Dead*.

	Sound	Meaning
	Imn	Amon
	Tut	Image
	Ankh	Living
Translation—"Living image of Amon"		
	Heka	Ruler
	Iunu	Heliopolis
	Resy	Southern
Translation—"Ruler of Southern Heliopolis"		

Analyze Visuals
What does the symbol for ruler look like?

Egyptian hieroglyphics used picture symbols to represent sounds.

Egyptians also wrote religious texts, such as the *Book of the Dead*, which tells about the afterlife. The development of writing helped ideas such as this to be communicated from one generation to the next. Other religious texts include the *Book of Caverns*, which discussed the journey of the sun god Re. Historians have also discovered religious texts inside coffins. They were often spells or magic formulas.

Egyptian Calendar The Egyptians created two calendars. One consisted of 12 months, each of which were based on the lunar cycle. This is the time it took for the moon to revolve around the earth. Each month was 28 or 29 days long.

Another Egyptian calendar was based on the solar cycle, or the movement of the sun. It also consisted of 12 months. Each month was 30 days long with an additional 5 days at the end of the year. The solar calendar proved to be more accurate. It was the first calendar that was 365 days long.

Reading Check
Compare How is our writing system similar to hieroglyphics?

Egypt's Great Temples

In addition to their writing system, the Egyptians are famous today for their magnificent architecture of sacred spaces. You have already read about the Egyptians' most famous structures, the pyramids. But the Egyptians also built massive temples. Those that survive are among the most spectacular sites in Egypt today.

The Egyptians believed that temples were the homes of the gods. People visited the temples to worship, offer the gods gifts, and ask for favors.

Many Egyptian temples shared some similar features. Rows of stone **sphinxes**—imaginary creatures with the bodies of lions and the heads of other animals or humans—lined the path leading to the entrance. That entrance itself was a huge, thick gate. On either side of the gate might stand an **obelisk** (AH-buh-lisk), a tall, four-sided pillar that is pointed on top.

Inside, the temples were lavishly decorated. Huge columns supported the temple's roof. In many cases, these columns were covered with paintings and hieroglyphics, as were the temple walls. Statues of gods and pharaohs often stood along the walls as well. The sanctuary, the most sacred part of the building, was at the far end of the temple.

The Temple of Karnak is only one of Egypt's great temples. Others were also built by Ramses the Great at Abu Simbel and Luxor. The temple at Abu Simbel is especially known for the huge statues carved out of the sandstone cliffs at the temple's entrance. These 66-foot-tall statues show Ramses as pharaoh. Nearby are some smaller statues of his family.

Reading Check
Form Generalizations
What were some features of Egyptian temples?

Egyptian Art

One reason Egypt's temples are so popular with tourists is the art they contain. The ancient Egyptians were masterful artists. Many of their greatest works of artistic expression were created to fill the tombs of pharaohs and other nobles. The Egyptians took great care in making these items because they believed the dead could enjoy them in the afterlife.

Paintings Egyptian art was filled with lively, colorful scenes. Detailed works covered the walls of temples and tombs. Artists also painted on canvas, papyrus, pottery, plaster, and wood. Most Egyptians, however, never saw these paintings. Only kings, priests, and important people could enter temples and tombs, and even they rarely entered the tombs.

The subjects of Egyptian paintings vary widely. Some paintings show important historical events, such as the crowning of kings and the founding of temples. Others illustrate major religious rituals. Still other paintings show scenes from everyday life, such as farming or hunting. The environment in which they lived inspired Egyptian artists. Their work showed the marshes of the Nile River and the wildlife living there.

The Temple of Karnak was Egypt's largest temple. This illustration shows how Karnak's great hall may have looked during an ancient festival.

Egyptian painting has a distinctive style. People, for example, are drawn in a certain way. In Egyptian paintings, people's heads and legs are always seen from the side, but their upper bodies and shoulders are shown straight on. In addition, people do not all appear the same size. Important figures such as pharaohs appear huge in comparison to others, especially servants or conquered people. In contrast, Egyptian animals are usually drawn realistically.

Carvings and Jewelry Painting was not the only art form Egyptians practiced. The Egyptians were also skilled stoneworkers. Many tombs included huge statues and detailed carvings.

In 1922 the archaeologist Howard Carter discovered the tomb of King Tut. Although the tomb had been robbed in ancient times, it was still filled with treasures, some of which are shown here.

King Tut's tomb

Howard Carter examining King Tut's coffin in 1925

Gold mask

The back of King Tut's chair was decorated with this image of the pharaoh and his wife.

Analyze Visuals
What might archaeologists learn about ancient Egypt from these artifacts?

The Egyptians also made beautiful objects of gold and precious stones. They made jewelry for both women and men. This jewelry included necklaces, collars, and bracelets. The Egyptians also used gold to make burial items for their pharaohs.

Over the years, treasure hunters emptied many pharaohs' tombs. At least one tomb, however, was not disturbed. In 1922 some archaeologists found the tomb of **King Tutankhamen** (too-tang-KAHM-uhn), or King Tut. The tomb was filled with treasures, including boxes of jewelry, robes, a burial mask, and ivory statues. King Tut's treasures have taught us much about Egyptian burial practices and beliefs.

Summary and Preview Ancient Egyptians developed one of the best-known cultures of the ancient world. Next, you will learn about a culture that developed in the shadow of Egypt—Kush.

Reading Check
Summarize What types of artwork were contained in Egyptian tombs?

Lesson 4 Assessment

Review Ideas, Terms, and People

1. **a. Identify** What are hieroglyphics?

   b. Contrast How is hieroglyphic writing different from our writing today?

   c. Evaluate Why was finding the Rosetta Stone so important to scholars?

2. **a. Describe** What are two ways the Egyptians decorated their temples?

   b. Evaluate Why do you think pharaohs like Ramses the Great built huge temples?

3. **Recall** Why were tombs filled with art, jewelry, and other treasures?

Critical Thinking

4. **Summarize** Draw a table like the one below. In each column, list two facts about the achievements of the ancient Egyptians.

Writing	Architecture	Art

Kush and Aksum

The Big Idea

The kingdoms of Kush and Aksum, which arose south of Egypt, developed advanced civilizations with large trading networks.

Main Ideas

- The geography of early Nubia helped civilization develop there.

- Kush and Egypt traded, but they also fought.

- Later Kush became a trading power with a unique culture.

- Both internal and external factors led to the decline of Kush and Aksum.

Key Terms and People

Piankhi
trade network
merchants
exports
imports
Queen Shanakhdakheto
Aksum
King Ezana

If YOU were there . . .

You live along the Nile River, where it moves quickly through swift rapids. A few years ago, armies from the powerful kingdom of Egypt took over your country. Some Egyptians have moved here. They bring new customs, and many people are imitating them. Now your sister has a new baby and wants to give it an Egyptian name! This upsets many people in your family.

How do you feel about following Egyptian customs?

The Geography of Early Nubia

South of Egypt, a group of people settled in the region we now call Nubia. These Africans established the first great kingdom in the interior of Africa. We know this kingdom by the name the Egyptians gave it—Kush. The development of Kushite society was greatly influenced by the geography of Nubia, especially the role played by the Nile River.

The Land of Nubia Today desert covers much of Nubia, but in ancient times the region was more fertile than it is now. Rain flooded the Nile every year, providing a rich layer of silt to nearby lands. The kingdom of Kush developed in this fertile area.

Ancient Nubia was rich in minerals such as gold, copper, and stone. These resources played a major role in the area's history and contributed to its wealth.

Early Civilization in Nubia Like all early civilizations, the people of Nubia depended on agriculture for their food. Fortunately for them, the Nile's floods allowed the Nubians to plant both summer and winter crops. Among the crops they grew were wheat, barley, and other grains. Besides farmland, the banks of the Nile also provided grazing land for livestock. As a result, farming villages thrived all along the Nile by 3500 BC.

Over time some farmers grew richer than others. These farmers became village leaders. Sometime around 2000 BC, one of these leaders took control of other villages and made himself king of the region. His new kingdom was called Kush.

The kings of Kush ruled from their capital at Kerma (KAR-muh). This city was located on the Nile just south of the third cataract. Because the Nile's cataracts made parts of the river hard to pass through, they were natural barriers against invaders. For many years the cataracts kept Kush safe from the more powerful Egyptian kingdom to the north.

As time passed, Kushite society grew more complex. Besides farmers and herders, some Kushites became priests and artisans. Early Kush was influenced by cultures to the south. Later, Egypt played a greater role in Kush's history.

Reading Check
Find Main Ideas
How did geography help civilization grow in Nubia?

Kush and Egypt

Kush and Egypt were neighbors. Sometimes the neighbors lived in peace with each other and helped each other prosper. For example, Kush became a major supplier of both slaves and raw materials to Egypt. The Kushites sent materials such as gold, copper, and stone to Egypt. The slaves were forced to be domestic servants and soldiers in pharaoh's army. The

▶ Explore ONLINE!

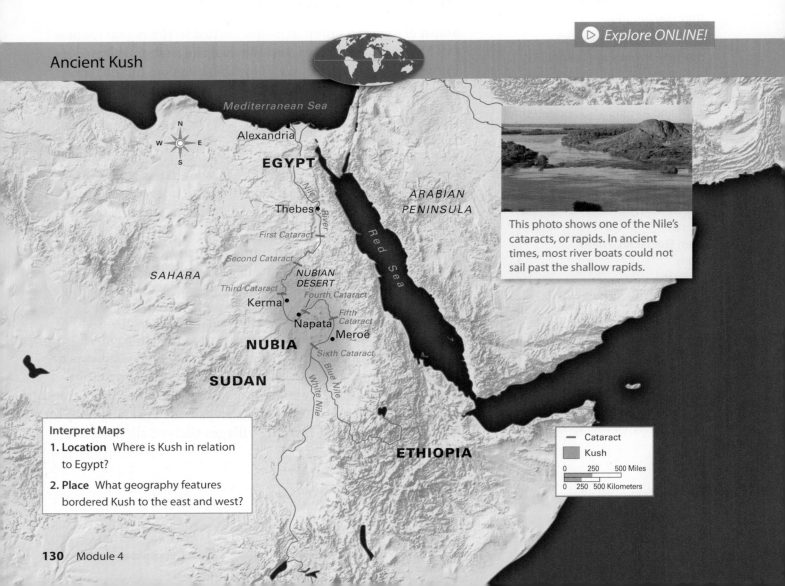

Ancient Kush

This photo shows one of the Nile's cataracts, or rapids. In ancient times, most river boats could not sail past the shallow rapids.

Interpret Maps

1. **Location** Where is Kush in relation to Egypt?

2. **Place** What geography features bordered Kush to the east and west?

The ruins of ancient Kushite pyramids stand behind those reconstructed to look the way they did when originally built.

Kushites also sent the Egyptians ebony, a type of dark, heavy wood, and ivory, the hard white material that makes up elephant tusks.

Egypt's Conquest of Kush Relations between Kush and Egypt were not always peaceful, however. As Kush grew wealthy from trade, its army grew stronger as well. Egypt's rulers soon feared that Kush would grow even more powerful and attack Egypt.

To prevent such an attack from occurring, the pharaoh Thutmose I sent an army to take control of Kush around 1500 BC. The pharaoh's army conquered all of Nubia north of the Fifth Cataract. As a result, Kush became part of Egypt.

After his army's victory, the pharaoh destroyed Kerma, the Kushite capital. Later pharaohs—including Ramses the Great—built huge temples in what had been Kushite territory.

Effects of the Conquest Kush remained an Egyptian territory for about 450 years. During that time, Egypt's influence over Kush grew tremendously. Many Egyptians settled in Kush. Egyptian became the language of the region. Many Kushites used Egyptian names and wore Egyptian-style clothing. They also adopted Egyptian religious practices.

A Change in Power During the mid-1000s BC, the New Kingdom in Egypt was ending. As the power of Egypt's pharaohs declined, Kushite leaders regained control of Kush. Kush once again became independent.

We know almost nothing about the history of the Kushites from the time they gained independence until 200 years later. Kush is not mentioned in any historical records that describe those centuries.

Piankhi (PYAN-kee)
(c. 751 BC–716 BC)

Also known as Piye, Piankhi was among Kush's most successful military leaders. A fierce warrior on the battlefield, the king was also deeply religious. Piankhi's belief that he had the support of the gods fueled his passion for war against Egypt. His courage inspired his troops on the battlefield. Piankhi loved his horses and was buried with eight of his best steeds.

Draw Conclusions
How did Piankhi's belief that he was supported by the gods affect his plans for Egypt?

The Conquest of Egypt By around 850 BC, Kush had regained its strength. It was once again as strong as it had been before it had been conquered by Egypt. Because the Egyptians had captured and destroyed the city of Kerma, the kings of Kush ruled from the city of Napata. Built by the Egyptians, Napata was on the Nile, about 100 miles southeast of Kerma.

As Kush grew stronger, Egypt was further weakened. A series of inept pharaohs left Egypt open to attack. In the 700s BC a Kushite king, Kashta, seized on Egypt's weakness and attacked it. By about 751 BC he had conquered Upper Egypt. He then established relations with Lower Egypt.

After Kashta died, his son **Piankhi** (PYAN-kee) continued to attack Egypt. The armies of Kush captured many cities, including Egypt's ancient capital. Piankhi fought the Egyptians because he believed that the gods wanted him to rule all of Egypt. By the time he died in about 716 BC, Piankhi had accomplished this task. His kingdom extended north from Napata to the Nile Delta.

The Kushite Dynasty After Piankhi died, his brother Shabaka (SHAB-uh-kuh) took control of the kingdom. Shabaka then declared himself pharaoh. This declaration began the 25th Dynasty, or the Kushite Dynasty, in Egypt.

Shabaka and later rulers of his dynasty believed that they were heirs of the great pharaohs of Egypt's past. They tried to restore old Egyptian cultural practices and renew faded traditions. Some of these practices and traditions had been abandoned during Egypt's period of weakness. For example, Shabaka was buried in a pyramid. The Egyptians had stopped building pyramids for their rulers centuries before.

The Kushite rulers of Egypt built new temples to Egyptian gods and restored old temples. They also worked to preserve Egyptian writings. As a result, Egyptian culture thrived during the 25th Dynasty.

The End of Kushite Rule in Egypt The Kushite Dynasty remained strong in Egypt for about 40 years. In the 670s BC, however, the powerful army of the Assyrians from Mesopotamia invaded Egypt. The Assyrians' iron weapons were better than the Kushites' bronze weapons. Although the Kushites were skilled archers, they could not stop the invaders. The Kushites were steadily pushed southward. In just ten years, the Assyrians had driven the Kushite forces completely out of Egypt.

Reading Check
Analyze Effects
How did internal problems in Egypt benefit Kush?

Later Kush

After losing control of Egypt, the people of Kush devoted themselves to agriculture and trade, hoping to make their country rich again. Within a few centuries, the Nubian kingdom of Kush had indeed become prosperous and powerful once more.

Kush's Iron Industry The economic center of Kush during this period was at Meroë (MER-oh-wee), the kingdom's new capital. Meroë's location on the east bank of the Nile helped Kush's economy to grow. Large deposits of gold could be found nearby, as could forests of ebony and other wood. More importantly, the area around Meroë was full of rich iron ore deposits.

In this location, the Kushites developed Africa's first iron industry. Iron ore and wood for furnaces were easily available, so the iron industry grew quickly.

The Expansion of Trade In time, Meroë became the center of a large **trade network**, a system of people in different lands who trade goods. The Kushites sent goods down the Nile to Egypt. From there, Egyptian and Greek **merchants**, or traders, carried goods to ports on the Mediterranean and Red seas and to southern Africa. These goods may have eventually reached India, and perhaps China.

Kush's **exports**—items sent out to other regions—included gold, pottery, iron tools, slaves, and ivory. Kushite merchants also traded leopard skins, ostrich feathers, and elephants. In return, the Kushites received **imports**—goods brought in from other regions—such as luxury items and inventions from Egypt, Asia, and other lands along the Mediterranean Sea. Producing and exporting goods in exchange for importing other goods encourages economic growth. In this case, acquiring new resources from other regions had a positive effect on the Kushite economy. People in Kush had access to resources they would otherwise not have had because of their trade networks.

Kushite Culture As Kushite trade grew, merchants came into contact with people from other cultures. As a result, the people of Kush combined customs from other cultures with their own unique Kushite culture.

The most obvious influence on Kushite culture and religious tradition was Egypt. Many buildings in Meroë, especially temples, resembled those in Egypt. Many people in Kush worshipped Egyptian gods and wore Egyptian clothing. Kushite rulers used the title *pharaoh* and were buried in pyramids.

Many elements of Kushite culture were not borrowed. Kushite houses and daily life were unique. One Greek geographer noted some Kushite differences.

> "The houses in the cities are formed by interweaving split pieces of palm wood or of bricks. . . . They hunt elephants, lions, and panthers. There are also serpents . . . and there are many other kinds of wild animals."
>
> —Strabo, *The Geographies*

Queens seem to have been more important in Kush than in Egypt. A few powerful queens ruled the dynasty. In addition to Egyptian gods, the people of Kush worshipped their own gods and built pyramids. They believed in the afterlife and mummified their dead, just as the Egyptians did.

The Kushites also developed their own written language, Meroitic. They made stone carvings to commemorate important buildings and events, just like in Egypt. Meroitic is similar to Egyptian hieroglyphics, but historians are not yet able to understand most of it.

▷ Explore ONLINE!

Kush's Trade Network

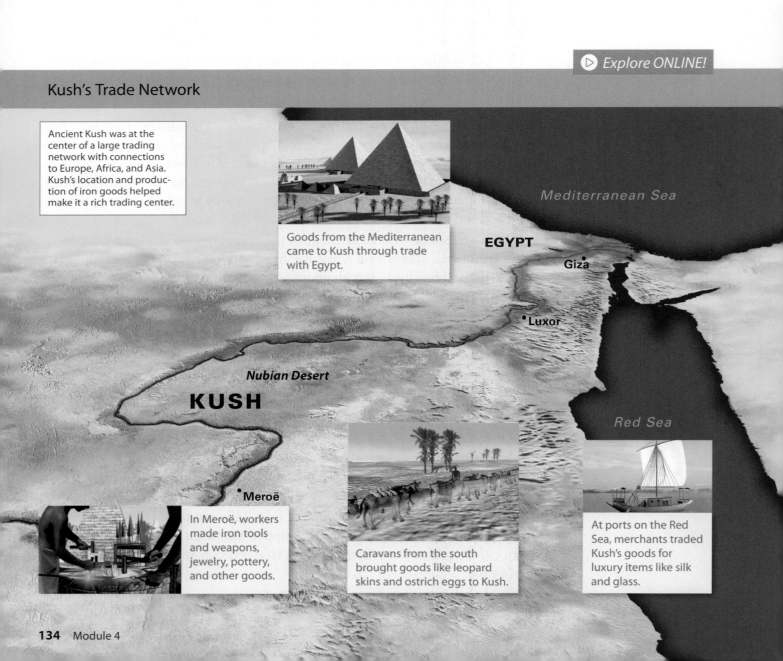

Ancient Kush was at the center of a large trading network with connections to Europe, Africa, and Asia. Kush's location and production of iron goods helped make it a rich trading center.

Goods from the Mediterranean came to Kush through trade with Egypt.

Mediterranean Sea

EGYPT

Giza

Luxor

Nubian Desert

KUSH

Red Sea

Meroë

In Meroë, workers made iron tools and weapons, jewelry, pottery, and other goods.

Caravans from the south brought goods like leopard skins and ostrich eggs to Kush.

At ports on the Red Sea, merchants traded Kush's goods for luxury items like silk and glass.

Reading Check
Contrast How do
archaeologists and
historians know
that Kushite culture
was unlike Egyptian
culture?

New Discoveries Archaeologists have uncovered evidence that helps us understand Kushite society. They study artifacts, or what people have made or used, to provide a more complete picture of Kushite society. Historians also help us learn about Kushite society and how the Kush economy functioned. By studying the written record left behind on Egyptian pottery, buildings, and other artifacts, historians have also discovered information about the people who lived in Kush. For example, artifacts and written records have helped us understand the accomplishments of Kushite rulers such as Kashta. Both historians and archaeologists help us draw conclusions about the past.

Women in Kushite Society The women of Kush were expected to be active in their society. They worked in the fields, raised children, cooked, and performed other household tasks.

Some Kushite women rose to positions of **authority**. Some served as co-rulers with their husbands or sons. A few women ruled the empire alone. Historians believe that the first woman to rule Kush was **Queen Shanakh-dakheto** (shah-nakh-dah-KEE-toh). She ruled from 170 BC to 150 BC.

The Decline of Kush

Kush gradually declined in power. A series of problems within the kingdom weakened its economy. One problem was that Kush's cattle were allowed to overgraze. When cows ate all the grass, wind blew the soil away, causing farmers to produce less food.

In addition, ironmakers used up the forests near Meroë. As wood became scarce, furnaces shut down. Kush produced fewer weapons and trade goods.

The Influence of Aksum Kush was also weakened by a loss of trade. Foreign merchants set up new trade routes that went around Kush. One such trade route bypassed Kush in favor of **Aksum** (AHK-soom), a kingdom located along the Red Sea in what is today Ethiopia and Eritrea. This location made it easy to transport goods over water, and Aksum became a major trading power in the first two centuries AD as a result.

Traders from inland Africa brought goods like gold and ivory to Aksum. From there, the items were shipped to markets as far away as India. In return for their goods, the people of Aksum received cloth, spices, and other products. Because Aksum was a thriving trade center, people from various cultures gathered there. As these people met and mingled to trade goods, they also traded ideas and beliefs.

One of the beliefs brought to Aksum by traders was Christianity. Christian teachings quickly took hold in Aksum, and many people converted. In the late AD 300s, Aksum's most famous ruler, **King Ezana** (AY-zah-nah), made Christianity the kingdom's official religion.

By the AD 300s, Kush had lost much of its wealth and military might. The king of Aksum took advantage of his former trade rival's weakness. In about AD 350 the Aksumite army destroyed Meroë and took over Kush. About two hundred years later, the Nubians also converted to Christianity. The last influences of Kush had disappeared.

Reading Check
Summarize What factors led to the decline of Kush?

The Decline of Aksum Although Aksum itself was never conquered, its major ports were taken by other peoples. As a result, the kingdom became isolated from other lands. Cut off from their allies and their trade, the people of Aksum retreated to the mountains of northern Ethiopia.

Summary The people of Kush and Aksum controlled powerful trading networks. As Kush declined, Aksum grew into an important trade center.

Lesson 5 Assessment

Review Ideas, Terms, and People

1. a. Recall On which river did Kush develop?

b. Evaluate How did Nubia's natural resources influence the early history of Kush?

2. a. Identify Who was Piankhi, and why was he important to the history of Kush?

b. Analyze What were some elements of Egyptian culture that became popular in Kush?

c. Draw Conclusions Why is the 25th Dynasty significant in the history of both Egypt and Kush?

3. a. Describe What advantages did the location of Meroë offer to the Kushites?

b. Compare How were Kushite and Egyptian cultures similar?

4. a. Identify Who conquered Kush in the AD 300s?

b. Evaluate What was the impact of new trading routes on Kush?

c. Identify What was the first kingdom in Africa to become Christian? Which ruler was responsible for its conversion?

Critical Thinking

5. Organize Information Create a table like this one. Using your notes, list an effect for each cause.

Cause	Effect
Thutmose I invades Kush.	
Power of Egyptian pharaohs declines.	
Piankhi attacks Egypt.	

Social Studies Skills

Assess Primary and Secondary Sources

Define the Skill

Primary sources in history are materials created by people who lived during the times they describe. Examples include letters, diaries, and photographs. *Secondary sources* are accounts written later by someone who was not present. They are designed to teach about or discuss a historical topic. This textbook is an example of a secondary source.

Together, primary and secondary sources can present a good picture of a historical period or event. However, they must be used carefully to make sure that the picture they present is accurate.

Learn the Skill

Here are some questions to ask to help you judge the accuracy of primary and secondary sources.

1. **What is it?** Is it a firsthand account, or is it based on information provided by others? In other words, is it primary or secondary?

2. **Who wrote it?** For a primary source, what was the author's connection to what he or she was writing about? For a secondary source, what makes the author an authority on this subject?

3. **Who is the audience?** Was the information meant for the public? Was it meant for a friend or for the writer alone? The intended audience can influence what the writer has to say.

4. **What is the purpose?** Authors of either primary or secondary sources can have reasons to exaggerate—or even lie—to suit their own goals or purposes. Look for evidence of emotion, opinion, or bias in the source. These might influence the accuracy of the account.

5. **What facts does the author use?** Why did the author use some facts or avoid others in the source? Authors will include or avoid particular facts to support their purpose.

Practice the Skill

Below are two passages about the military in ancient Egypt. Read them both, and use the guidelines to answer the questions that follow.

> "The pharaohs began . . . leading large armies out of a land that had once known only small police forces and militia. With remarkable speed the Egyptians conquered a large, profitable empire that included the rich provinces of Syria and Palestine."
>
> —C. Warren Hollister, from *Roots of the Western Tradition*

> "Let me tell you how the soldier fares . . . how he goes to Syria, and how he marches over the mountains. His bread and water are borne [carried] upon his shoulders like the load of [a donkey]; they make his neck bent as that of [a donkey], and the joints of his back are bowed [bent]. His drink is stinking water. . . . When he reaches the enemy, he is trapped like a bird, and he has no strength in his limbs."
>
> —from *Wings of the Falcon: Life and Thought of Ancient Egypt*, **translated by Joseph Kaster**

1. Which quote is a primary source, and which is a secondary source? Which do you think would be more accurate?

2. Why does the author include the fact about large armies in the first quote?

3. What is the author's purpose in the second quote? What evidence of opinion, emotion, or bias supports your answer?

Module 4 Assessment

Review Vocabulary, Terms, and People

Imagine these terms from the module are correct answers to items in a crossword puzzle. Write the clues for the answers. Then make the puzzle with some answers written down and some across.

1. cataract
2. Menes
3. pharaoh
4. nobles
5. mummy
6. elite
7. contract
8. Ramses
9. hieroglyphics
10. Tutankhamen

Comprehension and Critical Thinking

Lesson 1

11. a. **Identify** Where was most of Egypt's fertile land?
    b. **Make Inferences** Why did Memphis become a political and social center of Egypt?
    c. **Predict Effects** How might history have been different if the Nile hadn't flooded every year?

Lesson 2

12. a. **Describe** What responsibilities did pharaohs have?
    b. **Analyze** How were beliefs about the afterlife linked to items placed in tombs?
    c. **Elaborate** What challenges, in addition to moving stone blocks, do you think the pyramid builders faced?

Lesson 3

13. a. **Describe** What did a scribe do?
    b. **Analyze** What two factors contributed to Egypt's wealth during the New Kingdom?

    c. **Evaluate** Ramses the Great was a powerful pharaoh. Do you think his military successes or his building projects are more important to evaluating his greatness? Why?

Lesson 4

14. a. **Describe** For what was papyrus used?
    b. **Explain** What effect did the Rosetta Stone have on our understanding of ancient Egypt?
    c. **Elaborate** How does the Egyptian style of painting people reflect their society?

Lesson 5

15. a. **Describe** Where did the Kushite and Aksum civilizations develop?
    b. **Draw Conclusions** Why did Egypt want to gain control of Kush?
    c. **Evaluate** Why was the 25th Dynasty so important for both Kush and Egypt?

Review Themes

16. **Geography** Do you think that Egyptian society could have flourished in North Africa if the Nile had not existed? Why or why not?
17. **Religion** How did religious beliefs shape the rest of Egyptian culture?
18. **Economics** What evidence from the text shows that the ancient Egyptian economy was based on trade?

Social Studies Skills

Assess Primary and Secondary Sources *Read the following passage and answer the questions.*

> From a young age, Ramses was trained as a ruler and a fighter. Made an army captain at age ten, he began military campaigns even before he became pharaoh. During his reign, Ramses greatly increased the size of his kingdom. He is known for the massive monuments he built.

19. What facts does the author choose to include in the source?
20. What purpose does the author's use of these facts serve?

Reading Skills

Causes and Effects in History *Use the Reading Skills taught in this module to answer the questions about the reading selection below.*

> Much of Egyptian religion focused on the afterlife, or life after death. The Egyptians believed that the afterlife was a happy place. The Egyptian belief in the afterlife stemmed from their idea of *ka*, or a person's life force. When a person died, his or her *ka* left the body and became a spirit. The *ka*, however, remained linked to the body and could not leave its burial site. The *ka* had all the same needs that the person had when he or she was living. To fulfill the *ka's* needs, people filled tombs with objects for the afterlife.

21. What is the cause of the Egyptian custom of putting objects in tombs?
22. According to the passage, what is an effect of the Egyptian belief in *ka*?

Focus On Writing

23. **Write a Caption** From what you've learned about Egyptian society, create a visual representation that clearly shows the relationship between the following individuals: scribes, merchants, slaves, and the pharaoh. Write a caption that explains your visual and gives details about the relationships between the groups.

Ancient India

Essential Question

How do India's rich history and culture affect the world today?

About The Photo: This massive Hindu temple opened in New Delhi, India, in 2005. Although it is a modern temple, its builders used traditional Indian architectural styles, inspired by the designs of Indian temples built over many centuries.

▷ *Explore ONLINE!*

VIDEOS, including...
• Reincarnation
• Gandhi's Salt March
• The Dalai Lama

☑ Document-Based Investigations

☑ Graphic Organizers

☑ Interactive Games

☑ Interactive Map: India: Physical

☑ Image with Hotspots: Life in Mohenjo Daro

☑ Image Carousel: Indian Science

In this module, you will learn about the ancient civilization of India, the birthplace of two major world religions—Hinduism and Buddhism.

What You Will Learn...

Lesson 1: Geography and Ancient India 144
The Big Idea Indian civilization first developed on the Indus River.

Lesson 2: Vedic Society 149
The Big Idea Vedic society followed the decline of the Harappan civilization in the Indus Valley.

Lesson 3: Origins of Hinduism 155
The Big Idea Hinduism, the largest religion in India today, developed out of ancient Indian beliefs and practices.

Lesson 4: Origins of Buddhism 160
The Big Idea Buddhism began in India and became a major religion.

Lesson 5: Indian Empires 167
The Big Idea The Mauryas and the Guptas built great empires in India.

Lesson 6: Indian Achievements 172
The Big Idea The people of ancient India made great contributions to the arts and sciences.

Timeline of Events 2600 BC–AD 500

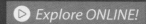 Explore ONLINE!

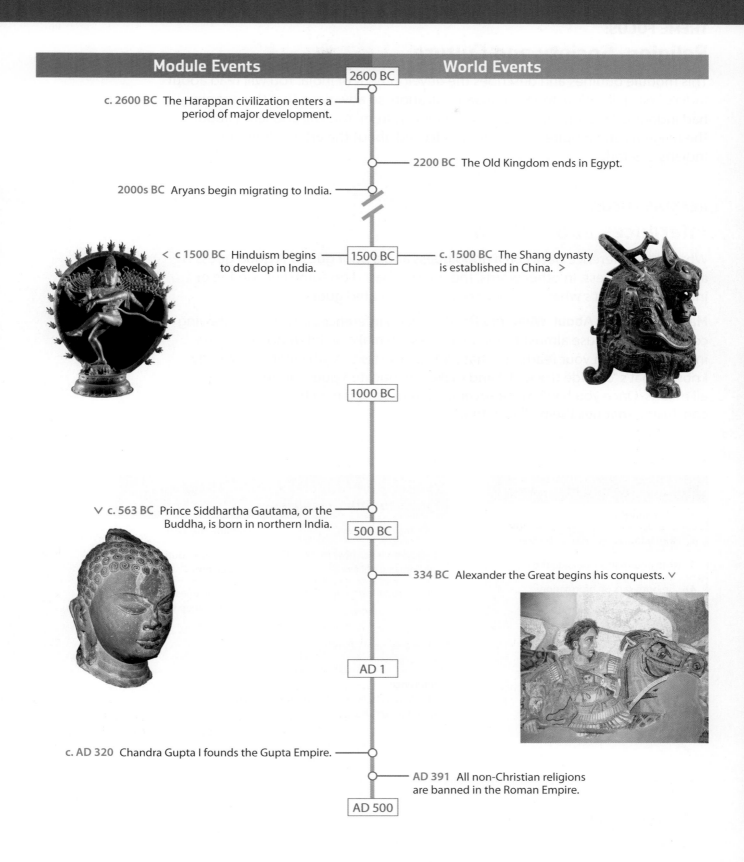

Module Events

World Events

2600 BC

c. 2600 BC The Harappan civilization enters a period of major development.

2200 BC The Old Kingdom ends in Egypt.

2000s BC Aryans begin migrating to India.

< c 1500 BC Hinduism begins to develop in India.

1500 BC

c. 1500 BC The Shang dynasty is established in China. >

1000 BC

∨ c. 563 BC Prince Siddhartha Gautama, or the Buddha, is born in northern India.

500 BC

334 BC Alexander the Great begins his conquests. ∨

AD 1

c. AD 320 Chandra Gupta I founds the Gupta Empire.

AD 391 All non-Christian religions are banned in the Roman Empire.

AD 500

Reading Social Studies

THEME FOCUS:

Religion, Society and Culture

This module outlines and describes the development of India. You will read about India's first civilization, the Harappan civilization, so advanced that the people had indoor bathrooms and their own writing system. You will also learn about the religions and empires that united India and about the art and literature that Indians created.

READING FOCUS:

Inferences about History

What's the difference between a good guess and a poor guess? A good guess is an educated guess. In other words, the guess is based on some knowledge or information. That's what an **inference** is—an educated guess.

Make Inferences About What You Read Making inferences is similar to drawing conclusions. You use almost the same process to make an inference: combine information from your reading (what's "inside the text") with what you already know (what's "outside the text") and make an educated guess about what it all means. Once you have made several inferences, you may be able to draw a conclusion that ties them all together.

Steps for Making Inferences
1. Ask a question.
2. Note information "inside the text."
3. Note information "outside the text."
4. Use both sets of information to make an educated guess, or inference.

Question: Why did Aryan priests have rules for performing sacrifices?

Inside the Text	Outside the Text
Sacred texts tell how to perform sacrifices.	Other religions have duties only priests can perform.
Priests sacrificed animals in fire.	Many ancient societies believed sacrifices helped keep the gods happy.
Sacrifices were offered to the gods.	

Inference
The Aryans believed that performing a sacrifice incorrectly might anger the gods.

You Try It!

The following passage is from the module you are about to read. Read the passage and then answer the questions that follow.

Harappan Achievements The Harappan civilization was very advanced. Most houses had bathrooms with indoor plumbing. Artisans made excellent pottery, jewelry, ivory objects, and cotton clothing from readily available resources. Cotton crops were grown in the region. Seals were often carved from soapstone, which could be found in the area. They used high-quality tools, which they also traded, and developed a system of weights and measures.

The Harappans also developed India's first writing system. However, scholars have not yet learned to read this language, so we know very little about Harappan society. We do know, however, that they traded with other regions, such as Mesopotamia. Harappan seals have been found in Mesopotamian cities. The Persian Gulf was a likely sea trade route for the Harappans.

While other river valley civilizations fell to invaders, no one is sure why Harappan civilization ended by the early 1700s BC. Perhaps invaders destroyed the cities or natural disasters, like floods, droughts, or earthquakes, caused the civilization to collapse.

Answer the following questions to make inferences about Harappan society.

1. Do you think the Harappan language was closely related to the languages spoken in India today? Consider the information in the text and things you have learned outside the text to make an inference about the Harappan language.

2. What have you just learned about Harappan achievements? Think back to other civilizations you have studied whose people made similar achievements. What allowed those civilizations to make these achievements? From this, what can you infer about earlier Harappan society?

As you read this module, use the information in the text to make inferences about Indian society.

Key Terms and People

Lesson 1
subcontinent
monsoons
seals

Lesson 2
Sanskrit
caste system

Lesson 3
Hinduism
reincarnation
karma
samskaras
Jainism
Mahavira
nonviolence
Sikhism
Guru Nanak

Lesson 4
fasting
meditation
the Buddha
Buddhism
nirvana
missionaries

Lesson 5
Chandragupta Maurya
Asoka
Chandra Gupta II

Lesson 6
metallurgy
alloys
Hindu-Arabic numerals
inoculation
astronomy

Geography and Early India

The Big Idea
Indian civilization first developed on the Indus River.

Main Ideas
- The geography of India includes high mountains, great rivers, and heavy seasonal rain.
- Harappan civilization developed along the Indus River.

Key Terms
subcontinent
monsoons
seals

If YOU were there . . .

Your people are nomadic herders in southern Asia in about 1200 BC. You live in a river valley with plenty of water and grass for your cattle. Besides looking after cattle, you spend time learning songs and myths from the village elders. They say these words hold your people's history. One day, it will be your duty to teach them to your own children.

Why is it important to pass on these words?

Geography of India

Look at a map of Asia. Do you see the large, roughly triangular landmass that juts out from the center of the southern part of the continent? That is India. It was the location of one of the world's earliest civilizations.

Landforms and Rivers India is huge. In fact, it is so big that many geographers call it a subcontinent. A **subcontinent** is a large landmass that is smaller than a continent. Subcontinents are usually separated from the rest of the continent by physical features. If you look at the physical map of India, for example, you can see that mountains largely separate the Indian subcontinent from the rest of Asia.

Among the mountains of northern India are the Himalayas, the highest mountains in the world. To the west are the Hindu Kush. Although these mountains made it hard to enter India, invaders have historically found a few paths through them. To the west of the Himalayas is a vast desert. Much of the rest of India is covered by fertile plains and rugged plateaus.

Several major rivers flow out of the Himalayas. The valley of one of them, the Indus, was the location of some of ancient India's earliest settlements. The Indus River is located in present-day Pakistan, west of India. When heavy snows in the Himalayas melted, the Indus flooded. As in Mesopotamia and Egypt, the flooding left behind a layer of fertile silt. The silt created ideal farmland for early settlers.

The Ganges River is located in the plains of the northern Indian subcontinent. The river is relatively short, but it flows through one of the most fertile and populated regions in the world. Water from the river has been used for irrigation since ancient times. Once widely used for transportation, the Ganges is still an important trade route in some areas. Today, it is also an important source of hydroelectric power.

Climate Most of India has a hot and humid climate. This climate is heavily influenced by India's **monsoons**, seasonal wind patterns that cause wet and dry seasons. In the summer, monsoon winds blow into India from the Indian Ocean, bringing heavy rains that can cause terrible floods. Some parts of India receive as much as 100 or even 200 inches of rain during this time. In the winter, winds blow down from the mountains. This forces moisture out of India and creates warm, dry winters.

Reading Check
Synthesize
How is the Ganges River important to India?

Explore ONLINE!

Physical Map of India

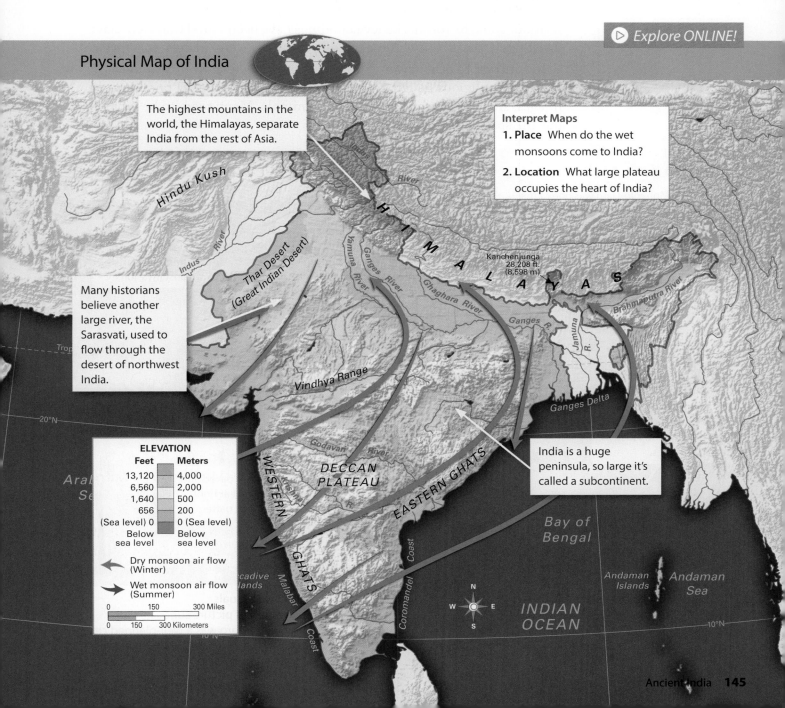

The highest mountains in the world, the Himalayas, separate India from the rest of Asia.

Interpret Maps
1. **Place** When do the wet monsoons come to India?
2. **Location** What large plateau occupies the heart of India?

Hindu Kush

Indus River

Thar Desert (Great Indian Desert)

Many historians believe another large river, the Sarasvati, used to flow through the desert of northwest India.

Yamuna River

Ganges River

Ghaghara River

H I M A L A Y A S

Kanchenjunga 28,208 ft. (8,598 m)

Ganges R.

Jamuna R.

Brahmaputra River

Ganges Delta

Vindhya Range

India is a huge peninsula, so large it's called a subcontinent.

Godavari River

ELEVATION

Feet	Meters
13,120	4,000
6,560	2,000
1,640	500
656	200
(Sea level) 0	0 (Sea level)
Below sea level	Below sea level

→ Dry monsoon air flow (Winter)
→ Wet monsoon air flow (Summer)

0   150   300 Miles
0   150   300 Kilometers

Arabian Sea

Laccadive Islands

WESTERN GHATS

Malabar Coast

DECCAN PLATEAU

Krishna R.

EASTERN GHATS

Coromandel Coast

Bay of Bengal

Andaman Islands

Andaman Sea

INDIAN OCEAN

20°N

Tropic

10°N

Harappan Civilization

Historians call India's first civilization the Harappan (huh-RA-puhn) civilization. It is the first known urban culture on the subcontinent. Hundreds of Harappan settlements have been found in northwestern India and eastern Pakistan. Most of these settlements lay along the Indus River and along the ancient course of the Sarasvati River in the desert of northwest India. Once a major river, the Sarasvati has long since disappeared.

Like other ancient societies, the Harappan civilization grew as irrigation and agriculture improved. Harappan farmers learned to control annual river floods in a way similar to the Mesopotamian model of irrigation. This allowed them to develop a farming economy. As farmers began to produce surpluses of food, towns and cities appeared in India.

With organized agriculture came organized government and the division of labor. Historians disagree on whether slavery existed in the Harappan civilization. Some historians believe buildings have been found that were slave dwellings. Others believe these buildings actually were "motels" for travelers.

In contrast to other river valley civilizations, we know little about Harappan religious beliefs. Some artifacts give clues. **Seals**, or stamped images, show pictures of humans and animals. Many seem to be religious, but the specific beliefs are unclear.

Life in Mohenjo-Daro

Mohenjo-Daro was one of the two major cities of the Harappan civilization. Located next to the Indus River in what is now Pakistan, the city probably covered one square mile. The people who lived in the city enjoyed some of the most advanced comforts of their time, including indoor plumbing.

The houses of Mohenjo-Daro had flat roofs. Many had staircases that allowed people to climb to the roof from the street.

Next to the city was a huge citadel, or fortress, to guard against invasions.

Harappan merchants used a standard set of weights to measure goods such as precious stones.

The city's streets were paved and well drained. They met at right angles, creating a grid pattern.

Analyze Visuals
What in this picture suggests that Mohenjo-Daro was a well-planned city?

India's First Cities The Harappan civilization was named after the modern city of Harappa (huh-RA-puh), Pakistan. It was near this city that ruins of the civilization were first discovered. From studying these ruins, archaeologists think that the civilization thrived between 2600 BC and 1700 BC.

Among the greatest sources of information we have about Harappan civilization are the ruins of three large cities, Harappa, Mohenjo-Daro (mo-HEN-joh DAR-oh), and Kalibangan. Harappa and Mohenjo-Daro were situated on the Indus River more than 300 miles apart, while Kalibangan was even farther away on the Sarasvati. However, the cities were remarkably similar.

All three cities were well planned. were well planned. Each stood near a towering fortress. From these fortresses, defenders could look down on the cities' brick streets, which crossed at right angles and were lined with storehouses, workshops, market stalls, and houses. In addition, both cities had many public wells.

Most of the structures were built of mud brick. Following floods, the mud deposited by the river could be shaped into bricks. Later, clay and water were mixed and placed into wooden molds. The bricks then dried in the sun or fired in a kiln.

Harappan Achievements The Harappan civilization was very advanced. Most houses had bathrooms with indoor plumbing. Artisans made excellent pottery, jewelry, ivory objects, and cotton clothing from readily available resources. Cotton crops were grown in the region. Seals were often carved from soapstone, which could be found in the area. They used

Harappan Art

Harappan people used clay pots as burial urns.

Like other ancient peoples, the Harappans made small seals like this one that were used to stamp goods.

high-quality tools, which they also traded, and developed a system of weights and measures.

The Harappans also developed India's first writing system. However, scholars have not yet learned to read this language, so we know very little about Harappan society. We do know, however, that they traded with other regions, such as Mesopotamia. Harappan seals have been found in Mesopotamian cities. The Persian Gulf was a likely sea trade route for the Harappans.

Although other river valley civilizations fell to invaders, no one is sure why Harappan civilization ended by the early 1700s BC. Perhaps invaders destroyed the cities, or perhaps natural disasters like floods, droughts, or earthquakes caused the civilization to collapse.

Summary and Preview The Harappans built an ancient civilization in the Indus Valley. In the next lesson, you will learn about a new civilization that developed in the Indus Valley—the Aryans.

Reading Check
Analyze Effects
What conclusions have historians drawn about early civilization in the Indus River Valley, and why don't they know more?

Lesson 1 Assessment

Review Ideas, Terms, and People

1. a. **Define** What are monsoons?
   b. **Contrast** How does northern India differ from the rest of the region?
   c. **Elaborate** Why is India called a subcontinent?
2. a. **Recall** Where did Harappan civilization develop?
   b. **Analyze** What is one reason that scholars do not completely understand some important parts of Harappan society?
   c. **Explain** How did Harappan artisans and merchants make use of readily available resources?

d. **Identify** What region was a trading partner for the Harappan civilization and what route did traders likely use to get there?

Critical Thinking

3. **Draw Conclusions** Draw conclusions about the effect of geography on Harappan society. Record your conclusions in a diagram like this one.

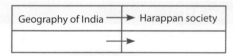

Geography of India	⟶	Harappan society
	⟶	

Vedic Society

The Big Idea

Vedic society followed the decline of the Harappan civilization in the Indus Valley.

Main Ideas

- A new civilization developed in India during the Vedic period.
- The Aryans practiced a religion known as Brahmanism.
- Indian society divided into distinct groups under the Aryans.

Key Terms

Sanskrit
caste system

If YOU were there . . .

Your family are skillful weavers who make beautiful cotton cloth. You belong to the class in society who are traders, farmers, and craftspeople. Often the raja of your town leads the warriors into battle. You admire their bravery but know you can never be one of them. To be a warrior, you must be born into that noble class. Instead, you have your own duty to carry out.

How do you feel about remaining a weaver?

The Roots of Vedic Society

Around 2000 BC, as the Harappan civilization was fading, a new society was forming in India. Much of what we know about life in this period comes from religious writings known as the Vedas (VAY-duhz). These are collections of poems, hymns, myths, and rituals that were passed down orally and later written down. Because the Vedas are our main source about this time, historians call it the Vedic (VAY-dik) period.

Disputed Origins The roots of Vedic culture are a subject of continued debate among scholars. Some historians believe that a new group of tribes arrived in the Indus River Valley around the time of the Harappan decline. They call these new arrivals the Aryans (AHR-ee-uhnz), which means "noble ones." These historians believe that the Aryans were from Central Asia and spoke an Indo-European language related to many of the modern languages of South Asia, Southwest Asia, and Europe. Over many centuries, the Aryans spread from northern India east and south into central India and the Ganges River Valley. There they established new societies.

Other historians, however, disagree with the migration theory. They strongly argue that there is no firm evidence to support the arrival of a new ethnic group in India during that time. Instead, they believe that Vedic society developed in northern India—either in Harappan cities or further east—and spread over time. These historians also argue that the term *Aryan* in the Vedas was a linguistic designation, not an ethnic one. It referred to all people who spoke one language, regardless of where they were born.

Government and Society As nomads, the Aryans took along their herds of animals as they moved. But over time, they settled in villages and began to farm. Unlike the Harappans, they did not build big cities.

The Aryan political system was also different from the Harappan system. The Aryans lived in small communities, based mostly on family ties. No single ruling authority existed. Instead, each group had its own leader, often a skilled warrior.

Aryan villages were governed by rajas (RAH-juhz). A raja was a leader who ruled a village and the land around it. Villagers farmed some of this land for the raja. They used other sections as pastures for their cows, horses, sheep, and goats.

Although many rajas were related, they didn't always get along. Sometimes rajas joined forces before fighting a common enemy. Other times, however, rajas went to war against each other. In fact, Aryan groups fought each other nearly as often as they fought outsiders. In many cases, these wars were fought over resources such as rivers and farm land. As Aryans moved from a nomadic lifestyle to an agricultural society, competition for land and water grew, causing conflict.

Aryan society at this time was highly structured. Families lived in communities called *grama*. Several of these communities made up a clan. In early Aryan society, clans assembled often for religious rituals and other activities.

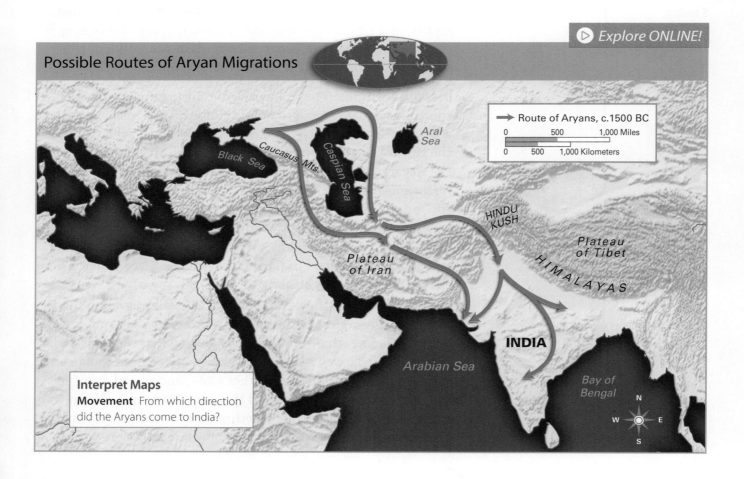

▶ *Explore ONLINE!*

Possible Routes of Aryan Migrations

Route of Aryans, c.1500 BC

0   500   1,000 Miles

0   500   1,000 Kilometers

Aral Sea

Black Sea

Caucasus Mts.

Caspian Sea

HINDU KUSH

Plateau of Tibet

Plateau of Iran

HIMALAYAS

INDIA

Arabian Sea

Bay of Bengal

Interpret Maps

Movement From which direction did the Aryans come to India?

Language Early Aryans are not known to have had a written language. Because of this, they had to memorize the poems and hymns that were important in their culture, such as the Vedas. If people had forgotten these poems and hymns, the works would have been lost forever. The fact that they were passed down for generations shows their importance to the culture and shared identity.

Aryan poems and hymns were composed in a language called **Sanskrit**, the most important language of ancient India. At first, Sanskrit was only a spoken language. Eventually, however, people figured out how to write it down so they could keep records and write down scriptures, which are the basis for Hinduism. These Sanskrit records and scriptures are a major source of information about Vedic society. Sanskrit is not widely spoken today, but it is still used in Hindu rituals. Sanskrit is also the root of many modern South Asian languages. Hindi, the most widely spoken Indian language, is based on Sanskrit.

Reading Check
Find Main Ideas
What source provides much of the information we have about the Aryans?

Early Hinduism and Vedic Religion

Religion was important during the Vedic period. Originally people's practice of religion was limited to rituals. Over time, religion took on more meaning and became part of daily life in ancient India. Many scholars call the early Hinduism of this period Vedic religion or Brahmanism because of the religion's emphasis on the Vedas and the belief in a divine reality known as Brahman.

The Vedas The Vedas were passed down orally for hundreds and in some instances thousands of years. Eventually they were written down in Sanskrit. The texts include hymns, descriptions of rituals, and philosophical and spiritual ideas about God and the soul. There are four Vedas, each containing sacred hymns and poems. The oldest of the Vedas, the *Rigveda*, was probably written around 1500 BC. It includes hymns of praise to many gods and guidance on seeking truth.

Later Vedic Texts Over the centuries, the Aryans wrote down poems and hymns in Sanskrit. In time these works were compiled into collections called Vedic texts.

One collection of Vedic texts describes religious rituals. These rituals were conducted for many reasons and often revolved around offerings of fruits, nuts, and flowers to various deities.

Rituals also frequently used the sacred fire, which represented the energy and light of the universe and the Divine. For example, the Vedas contain rituals for universal peace and the general well-being of the world.

The final group of Vedic texts are the Upanishads (oo-PAHN-ee-shads), most of which were written by about 600 BC. These writings are religious students' and teachers' reflections on the Vedas. The Upanishads had a great impact on later religious expression. Religious texts modeled after the Upanishads were written until about AD 1400. The Upanishads teach that *Brahman*, which is the force behind everything, is found in the *atman*, the soul or self of an individual. Understanding this connection is still a goal in modern Hinduism. This is seen in the following passage from *Hindu Search for Divine Reality: The Upanishads*.

> "So much for the man who desires. But as to the man who does not desire, who, not desiring, freed from desires, is satisfied in his desires, or desires the Self only, his vital spirits do not depart elsewhere, — being Brahman, he goes to Brahman."
>
> — from *Hindu Search for Divine Reality: The Upanishads*

Later Vedic Society Over the course of the later Vedic period between 800 BC and 500 BC, clan identity, or identification by family ties, changed to territorial identity, identification by area in which one lives. In some cases, chiefdoms that had been governed by rajas became kingdoms, which gave those chiefs more power. Powerful chiefs surrounded themselves with advisers and began to collect taxes.

Elaborate religious ceremonies provided more power and status to the chiefs, or kings. Vedic society had a hierarchy of priests. During rituals, sacrifices of wealth would be made from the chief to the priest. In some cases, these ceremonies allowed the priest to receive wealth from the chief and the chief to receive status and closeness to the gods. During this time, the priests and the upper class grew in importance and wealth, leading to increasing divisions in Aryan society.

Reading Check
Find Main Ideas
How did the Vedic texts influence later religious expression?

Indian Social Structure

As Aryan society became more complex, it became divided into groups. For the most part, these groups were organized by people's occupations. Rules developed about how people of different groups could interact. As time passed, these rules became stricter and became central to Indian society.

Quick Facts

The *Varnas*

Brahmins
Brahmins were India's priests, teachers, and scholars. They were seen as the highest *varna*.

Kshatriyas
Kshatriyas were rulers and warriors.

The *Varnas* According to the Vedas, there were four main *varnas*, or social divisions. These were based on temperaments that vary from person to person. In ancient Indian society, these *varnas* were

- Brahmins (BRAH-muhns), or priests, teachers, and scholars
- Kshatriyas (KSHA-tree-uhs), or rulers and warriors
- Vaisyas (VYSH-yuhs), or farmers, craftspeople, and traders
- Sudras (SOO-drahs), or workers, servants, and non-Aryans

The Vedas saw the four roles as equals, but social divisions and rankings grew over time. As Indian society developed, Brahmins came to be regarded as the highest group. Although Brahmins had a special religious role, many important Hindu writers and teachers did not belong to this *varna*.

The Caste System As time passed, Indian social order became more complex. Over hundreds of years, the four *varnas* were further divided into hundreds of subdivisions called *jatis*. Ancient texts do not explain how membership in the earliest *jatis* was determined. In time, however, some communities developed rules under which people were born into particular *jatis*. When Portuguese traders arrived in India in the 1400s, they used the term *castes* to refer to *jatis*. The term *caste* is still widely used today.

Over many centuries, the **caste system** divided Indian society into groups based on a person's birth, wealth, or occupation. In general, the caste to which a person belonged determined his or her place in society. However, in ancient Indian society, caste roles were by no means permanent. Even so, social mobility among castes became more limited over the centuries. At one time, some 3,000 castes existed in India.

Although the *varnas* had grown out of an interpretation of the *Rigveda*, caste became a social issue rather than a religious one. The caste system spread to incorporate members of other religions besides Hinduism. Many Christians and Muslims in India today, for example, belong to castes. The system eventually became an official legal entity in the late 1800s under the British, who ruled India at that time.

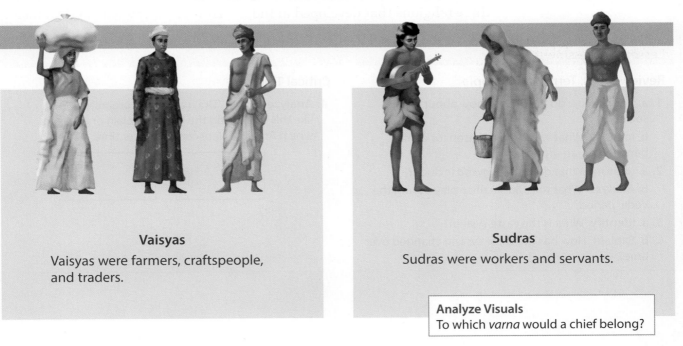

Vaisyas
Vaisyas were farmers, craftspeople, and traders.

Sudras
Sudras were workers and servants.

Analyze Visuals
To which *varna* would a chief belong?

By about AD 500, a group emerged who lived outside the caste system. They were called "untouchables" or, later, Dalits. They could hold only certain jobs, which were often unpleasant, such as removal of dead animals and other sanitation tasks. Even though caste discrimination is banned in India today, Dalits still often face obstacles.

Caste Norms As time passed, many communities within India developed rules that governed which jobs members of each caste could hold. These rules also established how members of different castes could interact. In addition, each caste developed its own norms. Norms are unwritten rules that people in a community know they are required to follow. Caste norms were passed down from generation to generation through social and cultural practices. Caste norms could be exclusive. For example, people in some communities would not marry someone from a different caste. Others might not take meals with people from another caste.

Over many centuries, caste rules have shifted repeatedly. At times they have been very restrictive, while at other times there have been looser caste divisions. Throughout history, reformers—including prominent Hindu scholars and teachers—have challenged what they viewed as social injustices in the caste system. For example, they argued against the medieval belief that only members of certain castes could reach salvation.

The Role of Women According to ancient writings, women in Vedic India were honored members of society. Those who had given birth were especially honored, because motherhood was considered sacred. In addition, many of the Vedas had been written by holy women.

Legally, women had most of the same rights as men. They could own property and receive an education. They could also perform in religious ceremonies. Over time, however, laws were passed to limit these rights.

Reading Check
Make Inferences
How did a person become a member of a caste?

Summary and Preview In this lesson, you read about the Aryan migration and the division of Indian society. In the next lesson, you will learn about three religions that developed in India—Hinduism, Jainism, and Sikhism.

Lesson 2 Assessment

Review Ideas, Terms, and People

1. **a. Recall** How do historians know about Aryan society?

   b. Identify What was a main reason for conflict between Aryan groups?

2. **a. Identify** What does the *Rigveda* include?

   b. Analyze What role did sacrifice play during the Vedic period?

3. **a. Identify** What is the caste system?

   b. Explain How has the caste system changed over time?

Critical Thinking

4. **Analyze Causes** Draw a graphic organizer like this one. Using the boxes, explain one way in which Aryan society changed over time.

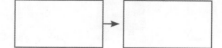

Origins of Hinduism

The Big Idea

Hinduism, the largest religion in India today, developed out of ancient Indian beliefs and practices.

Main Ideas

- Hinduism developed out of Brahmanism and influences from other cultures.

- A few groups reacted to Hinduism by breaking away to form their own religions.

Key Terms

Hinduism
reincarnation
karma
samskaras
Jainism
Mahavira
nonviolence
Sikhism
Guru Nanak

If YOU were there . . .

You are a Hindu girl who is about to have a rite of passage or *samskara*. This rite of passage will celebrate that you are becoming an adult. After this you will be allowed to light oil lamps and participate more fully in your religion. You will also receive gifts such as jewelry.

Do you look forward to becoming an adult or are you nervous?

Hinduism Develops

The Vedas, the Upanishads, and the other Vedic texts became the basis for **Hinduism**, the largest religion in India today. Over time, the ideas of these sacred texts were blended with ideas from other cultures and languages. People from Persia and other kingdoms in Central Asia, for example, brought their ideas to India. Hinduism was also influenced by religious texts written in Tamil and other South Asian languages. Since Hinduism is a blending of ideas, it does not have a single founder. It also does not have one set of teachings that all Hindus agree on. Hinduism is the third-largest religion, with about a billion followers. Many consider it to be the world's oldest major religion.

Hindu Beliefs Most Hindus believe in a single universal spirit called Brahman, which can come in many forms. While there are many deities in Hinduism, there are three who are central to many Hindu texts: Brahma the Creator, Shiva the Destroyer, and Vishnu the Preserver. These deities appear as gods and goddesses, some with both human and animal forms. Among the deities revered by many Hindus are the goddess Lakshmi and the god of wisdom, Ganesha, who is often depicted with the head of an elephant. They are popularly worshiped by Hindus across the world. However, Hindus believe that each deity is also a part of Brahman. Deities like Brahma, Shiva, and Vishnu represent different aspects of Brahman. In fact, Hindus believe that everything in the world is part of Brahman.

The god Brahma represents the creator aspect of Brahman. His four faces symbolize the four Vedas.

Shiva, the destroyer aspect of Brahman, is usually shown with four arms and three eyes. Here he is shown dancing on the back of a demon he has defeated.

Vishnu is the preserver aspect of Brahman. In his four arms, he carries a conch shell, a mace, and a discus, symbols of his power and greatness.

The Hindu creation stories are an example of how there are many different sets of teachings in Hinduism. One creation story tells that the creator built the universe just like a carpenter builds a house. Another explains that the universe was created out of the parts of a man named Purusha. He was sacrificed and the four classes of Indian society came from the parts of his body.

Life and Rebirth According to Hindu teachings, everyone has a soul, or *atman*, inside them. This soul holds the person's personality, the qualities that make an individual who he or she is. Many Hindus believe that a person's ultimate goal should be to reunite that soul with Brahman, the universal spirit.

Many Hindus believe that their souls will eventually join Brahman because the world we live in is an illusion. Brahman is the only reality. The Upanishads teach that people must try to see through the illusion of the world. Because it is hard to see through illusions, this can take several lifetimes. That is why Hindus believe that souls are born and reborn many times, each time in a new body. This process of rebirth is called **reincarnation**.

Hinduism and Society According to the traditional Hindu view of reincarnation, a person who has died is reborn in a new physical form. The type of form depends upon his or her **karma**, the effects that good or bad actions have on a person's soul. Evil actions will build bad karma. A person with bad karma will be born into a lower caste or life form.

In contrast, good actions build good karma. People with good karma will see benefits in future births. In time, good karma will bring liberation from life's worries and the cycle of rebirth. This liberation is called *moksha*. The idea of karma encourages people to behave well in society.

Hinduism teaches that each person has a *dharma,* or set of spiritual duties, to fulfill. *Dharma* is seen as Hinduism's guidelines for living a moral life and includes nonviolence, self-restraint, and honesty. Hindus are not the only group that emphasizes spiritual duty. Buddhists, Jains, and Sikhs all practice *dharma*. You will read about these other religions later.

Customs and Traditions Hindu religious practices vary widely between communities and even between individuals. Hindus are free to worship any deities they choose, or to worship none at all. Although many Hindus choose to follow family traditions, some choose to find their own paths.

Unlike some religions, Hinduism does not have a single required worship service. Worship can take place anywhere—in large temples, in small shrines, or at home. At temples, religious leaders might conduct formal ceremonies with readings from the Vedas or elaborate processions. At home, individuals might offer food, drink, or gifts to a god or goddess. He or she might also say special prayers or meditate. Meditation is silent reflection upon the world and its nature.

To help them meditate, some Hindus practice a series of physical and mental exercises called yoga. The purpose of yoga is to teach people how to focus their minds and bodies. Many Hindus believe this will aid their meditation and help them attain *moksha*.

This girl is lighting an oil lamp as part of a Hindu initiation ceremony. It signals that she is now a full participant in the Hindu faith.

Rituals and ceremonies have always been and continue to be important parts of Hinduism. **Samskaras**, which are rites of passage to prepare a person for a certain event or for their next stage in life, are still practiced today. Many rituals revolve around birth. A pellet of honey and ghee, which is clarified butter, is placed in a newborn's mouth, for example. There is also a name-giving ceremony. Often, a child is given a second, secret name. Other samskaras occur throughout childhood.

Weddings are also a time for customs and traditions. Wedding ceremonies are elaborate and filled with rituals. For example, offerings of roasted grain are thrown into a sacrificial fire. The bride and groom must also take seven steps together to symbolize their unity.

The Spread of Hinduism Hinduism spread throughout Southeast Asia. This happened largely through trade. As traders exchanged goods, they also learned about different cultures and religions. Later, Hinduism spread through colonization. Hindus were often taken to British and Dutch colonies to work as servants. They brought their religion with them to the West Indies, Fiji, and parts of Africa. Hinduism spread again in the 20th century as Indians migrated to other parts of the world, such as Great Britain, Canada, and the United States. Today, there are more than 2 million Hindus in the United States.

Reading Check
Summarize
What determined how a person -would be reborn?

Nonviolence

In modern times, nonviolence has been a powerful tool for social protest. Mohandas Gandhi led a long nonviolent struggle against British rule in India. This movement helped India win its independence in 1947. About ten years later, Martin Luther King Jr. adopted Gandhi's nonviolent methods in his struggle to win civil rights for African Americans. Then, in the 1960s, Cesar Chavez organized a campaign of nonviolence to protest the treatment of farm workers in California. These three leaders proved that people can bring about social change without using violence.

Mohandas Gandhi

Martin Luther King Jr.

Cesar Chavez

Analyze Information
How did these three leaders prove that nonviolence is a powerful tool for social change?

The Rise of Other Religions in India

Although Hinduism was widely followed in India, not everyone agreed with its beliefs. Some unsatisfied people and groups looked for new religious ideas. Two such groups were Jains (JYNZ), believers in a religion called Jainism (JY-niz-uhm), and Sikhs (SIKS), believers in Sikhism (SIK-iz-uhm).

Jainism Jainism is an ancient religion that is believed to have existed in India for thousands of years. Some people think that Jainism is older than Hinduism. Others think that it grew out of Hinduism. Jainism spread because of the teachings of a man named **Mahavira**, who is believed to have been born around 599 BC. Mahavira was an Indian prince who gave up his luxuries to become a monk. Jain teachings emphasize four basic principles: injure no life, tell the truth, do not steal, and own no property. In their efforts not to injure anyone or anything, Jains practice **nonviolence**, or the avoidance of violent actions. The Sanskrit word for this nonviolence is *ahimsa* (uh-HIM-sah), which is also an important part of Hindu philosophy.

The Jains' emphasis on nonviolence comes from their belief that everything is alive and part of the cycle of rebirth. Jains are very serious about not injuring or killing any creature—humans, animals, or even insects. Because they don't want to hurt living creatures, Jains are vegetarians. They do not eat any food that comes from animals.

Sikhism **Sikhism** has its roots in the teachings of the **Guru Nanak**, who lived in the AD 1400s. The title *guru* is Sanskrit for "teacher." While traveling, Nanak came into contact with many other religions, including Islam. In reaction to ideas of Hinduism and Islam, he preached a path that was independent from both. Over time, these teachings were explained and expanded by nine other gurus.

Sikhism, the world's fifth largest religion, is monotheistic. Sikhs believe in only one God, who has no physical form but can be sensed in the creation. For Sikhs, the ultimate goal is to be reunited with God after death. To achieve this goal, one must meditate to find spiritual enlightenment. Because they believe that achieving enlightenment may take several lifetimes, Sikhs also believe in reincarnation. Sikhism teaches that people should live truthfully and treat all people equally, regardless of gender, social class, or any other factor. The Sikh holy book, the Guru Granth Sahib, is a collection of hymns that also includes passages from Hindu and Muslim teachers.

Sikhs pray several times each day. They are expected to wear five items at all times as signs of their religion: long hair, a small comb, a steel bracelet, a sword, and a special undergarment. In addition, all Sikh men wear turbans, as do many women.

Reading Check
Find Main Ideas
What are two religions that developed out of Hinduism?

Summary and Preview In this lesson, you read about three religions that developed in India—Hinduism, Jainism, and Sikhism. In the next lesson, you will learn about another religion that began there—Buddhism.

Lesson 3 Assessment

Review Ideas, Terms, and People

1. a. **Define** What is karma?

   b. **Sequence** How did Vedic religion develop into Hinduism?

   c. **Compare and Contrast** Choose two Hindu creation stories and tell how they are similar and different.

   d. **Elaborate** How does Hinduism reinforce good behavior and social order?

2. a. **Recall** What are the four main teachings of Jainism?

   b. **Draw Conclusions** How do you think Guru Nanak's travels influenced the development of Sikhism?

Critical Thinking

3. **Summarize** Use a graphic organizer like the one below to summarize the main beliefs of Hinduism.

Gods	Life and rebirth	Karma and dharma

Origins of Buddhism

The Big Idea
Buddhism began in India and became a major religion.

Main Ideas
- Siddhartha Gautama searched for wisdom in many ways.
- The teachings of Buddhism deal with finding peace.
- Buddhism spread far from where it began in India.

Key Terms and People
fasting
meditation
the Buddha
Buddhism
nirvana
missionaries

If YOU were there . . .

You are a trader traveling in northern India in about 520 BC. As you pass through a town, you see a crowd of people sitting silently in the shade of a huge tree. A man sitting at the foot of the tree begins to speak about how one ought to live. His words are like nothing you have heard from the Hindu priests.

Will you stay to listen? Why or why not?

Siddhartha's Search for Wisdom

In the late 500s BC, a restless young man, dissatisfied with the teachings of Hinduism, began to ask his own questions about life and religious matters. In time, he found answers. These answers attracted many followers, and the young man's ideas became the foundation of a major new religion in India.

The Quest for Answers The restless young man was Siddhartha Gautama (si-DARH-tuh GAU-tuh-muh). Born around 563 BC in northern India, near the Himalayas, Siddhartha was a prince who grew up in luxury. Born a Kshatriya, a member of the warrior class, Siddhartha never had to struggle with the problems that many people of his time faced. However, Siddhartha was not satisfied. He felt that something was missing in his life.

Siddhartha looked around him and saw how hard other people had to work and how much they suffered. He saw people grieving for lost loved ones and wondered why there was so much pain in the world. As a result, Siddhartha began to ask questions about the meaning of human life.

Before Siddhartha reached age 30, he left his home and family to look for answers. He traveled to many regions in India. Wherever he traveled, he had discussions with priests and people known for their wisdom. Yet no one could give convincing answers to Siddhartha's questions.

The Buddha Finds Enlightenment Siddhartha did not give up. Instead, he became even more determined to find the answers he was seeking. For several years, he wandered in search of answers.

Siddhartha wanted to free his mind from daily concerns. For a while, he did not even wash himself. He also started **fasting**, or going without food. He devoted much of his time to **meditation**, the focusing of the mind on spiritual ideas.

According to legend, Siddhartha spent six years wandering throughout India. He eventually came to a place near the town of Gaya, close to the Ganges River. There, he sat down under a tree and meditated. After seven weeks of deep meditation, he suddenly had the answers that he had been looking for. He realized that human suffering comes from three things:

- wanting what we like but do not have
- wanting to keep what we like and already have
- not wanting what we dislike but have

Siddhartha spent seven more weeks meditating under the tree, which his followers later named the Tree of Wisdom. He then described his new ideas to five of his former companions. His followers later called this talk the First Sermon.

The Great Departure

In this painting, Prince Siddhartha leaves his palace to search for the true meaning of life, an event known as the Great Departure. Special helpers called *ganas* hold his horse's hooves so he won't awaken anyone.

Siddhartha was born into luxury. By the time of his death 80 years later, he had taught many people how to find enlightenment and happiness.

Siddhartha Gautama was about 35 years old when he found enlightenment under the tree. From that point on, he would be called **the Buddha** (BOO-duh), or the "Enlightened One." The Buddha spent the rest of his life traveling across northern India and teaching people his ideas.

Teachings of Buddhism

As he traveled, the Buddha gained many followers, especially among India's merchants and artisans. He even taught his views to a few kings. These followers were the first believers in **Buddhism**, a religion based on the teachings of the Buddha.

The Buddha was raised Hindu, and many of his teachings reflected Hindu ideas. Like Hindus, he believed that people should act morally.

Four Noble Truths At the heart of the Buddha's teachings were four guiding principles. These became known as the Four Noble Truths.

1. Suffering and unhappiness are a part of human life. No one can escape sorrow.
2. Suffering comes from our desires for pleasure and material goods. People cause their own misery because they want things they cannot have.
3. People can overcome desire and ignorance and reach **nirvana** (nir-VAH-nuh), a state of perfect peace. Reaching nirvana frees the soul from suffering and from the need for further reincarnation.
4. People can overcome ignorance and desire by following an eightfold path that leads to wisdom, enlightenment, and salvation.

The chart shows the steps in the Eightfold Path. The Buddha believed that this path was a middle way between human desires and denying oneself any pleasure. He said:

> "A life given to pleasures, devoted to pleasures and lusts: this is degrading, sensual, vulgar, ignoble, and profitless; and a life given to mortifications: this is painful, ignoble, and profitless. . . . [It is] the Middle Path which leads to insight, which leads to wisdom, which conduces to calm, to knowledge, to the Sambodhi, to Nirvana."
>
> —The Buddha, quoted in the *Mahavagga*

The Buddha believed that people should overcome their desire for material goods. They should, however, be reasonable, and not starve their bodies or cause themselves unnecessary pain.

Challenging Traditional Ideas Some of the Buddha's teachings challenged traditional Hindu ideas. For example, the Buddha told people that they did not have to follow the Vedas to achieve enlightenment. The Buddha also challenged the authority of priests. But similar to Hindu scriptures and sages, the Buddha emphasized that it was the responsibility of each individual to work for his or her own liberation. Priests could not help them. However, the

The Eightfold Path

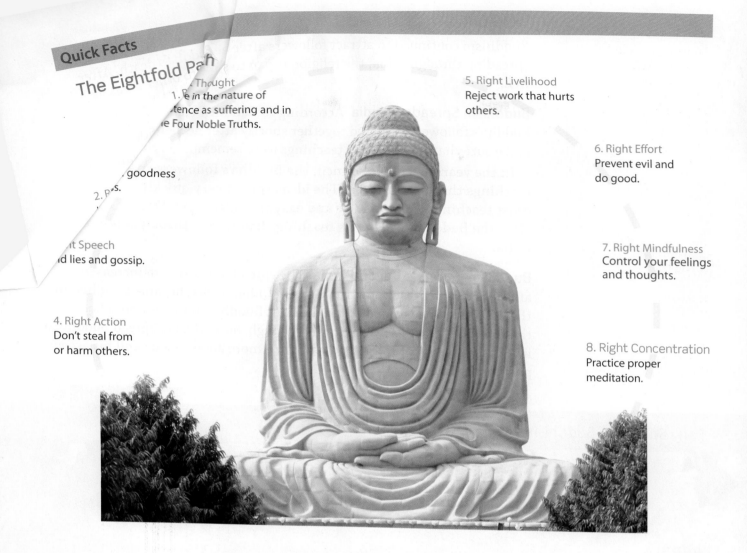

1. ... Thought
... *in the nature of* ...tence as suffering and in ...e Four Noble Truths.

...goodness

2. R...s.
...

...t Speech
...d lies and gossip.

4. Right Action
Don't steal from or harm others.

5. Right Livelihood
Reject work that hurts others.

6. Right Effort
Prevent evil and do good.

7. Right Mindfulness
Control your feelings and thoughts.

8. Right Concentration
Practice proper meditation.

Buddha did not reject the Hindu teaching of reincarnation. He taught that people who failed to reach nirvana would have to be reborn time and time again until they achieved it.

The Buddha was opposed to people needing to follow social roles in order to achieve liberation or good karma. Those who followed the Eightfold Path properly, he said, would achieve nirvana. It didn't matter what *varna* they belonged to in life as long as they lived the way they should.

The Buddha's teachings won over many people. Many of India's herdsmen, farmers, and artisans liked hearing that their lack of knowledge of sacred texts would not be a barrier to enlightenment. Buddhism made them feel that they had the power to change their lives without rituals or priests. The Buddha also gained followers among Brahmins and princes, who welcomed his ideas about avoiding extreme behavior while seeking liberation. By the time of his death around 483 BC, the Buddha's influence was spreading rapidly throughout India.

Reading Check
Compare
How did Buddha's teachings agree with Hinduism?

Buddhism Spreads

Buddhism continued to attract followers after the Buddha's death. After spreading through India, the religion began to spread to other areas as well.

Buddhism Spreads in India According to Buddhist tradition, Buddha's followers gathered together shortly after he died. The of the make sure that the Buddha's teachings were remembered correct

In the years after this council, the Buddha's followers spread h to teachings throughout India. The ideas spread very quickly, because dhist teachings were popular and easy to understand. Within 200 years after the Buddha's death, his teachings had spread throughout most of India.

Buddhism Spreads Beyond India The spread of Buddhism increased after one of the most powerful kings in India, Asoka, became Buddhist in the 200s BC. Once he converted, he built Buddhist temples and schools throughout India. More importantly, though, he worked to spread Buddhism into areas outside of India. You will learn more about Asoka and his accomplishments in the next lesson.

> ▶ *Explore ONLINE!*

Early Spread of Buddhism

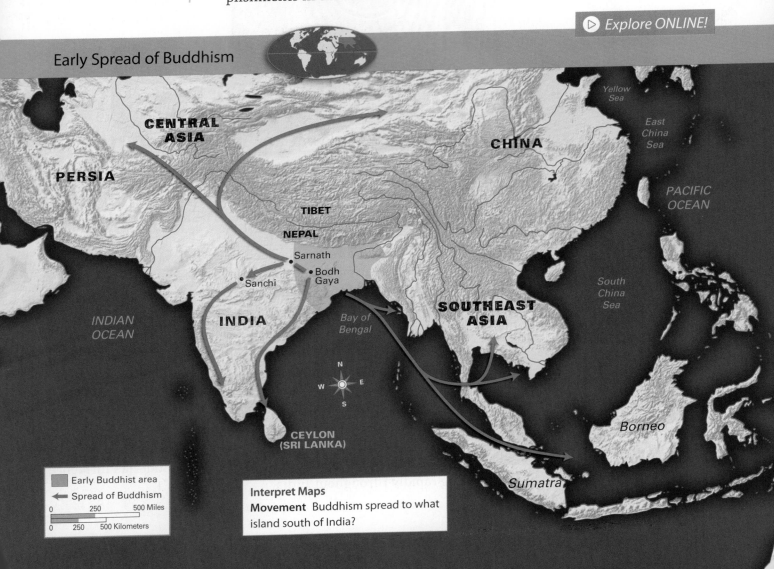

Interpret Maps
Movement Buddhism spread to what island south of India?

Legend:
- Early Buddhist area
- ← Spread of Buddhism
- 0 250 500 Miles
- 0 250 500 Kilometers

The Eightfold Path

1. Right Thought
Believe in the nature of existence as suffering and in the Four Noble Truths.

2. Right Intent
Incline toward goodness and kindness.

3. Right Speech
Avoid lies and gossip.

4. Right Action
Don't steal from or harm others.

5. Right Livelihood
Reject work that hurts others.

6. Right Effort
Prevent evil and do good.

7. Right Mindfulness
Control your feelings and thoughts.

8. Right Concentration
Practice proper meditation.

Buddha did not reject the Hindu teaching of reincarnation. He taught that people who failed to reach nirvana would have to be reborn time and time again until they achieved it.

The Buddha was opposed to people needing to follow social roles in order to achieve liberation or good karma. Those who followed the Eightfold Path properly, he said, would achieve nirvana. It didn't matter what *varna* they belonged to in life as long as they lived the way they should.

The Buddha's teachings won over many people. Many of India's herdsmen, farmers, and artisans liked hearing that their lack of knowledge of sacred texts would not be a barrier to enlightenment. Buddhism made them feel that they had the power to change their lives without rituals or priests. The Buddha also gained followers among Brahmins and princes, who welcomed his ideas about avoiding extreme behavior while seeking liberation. By the time of his death around 483 BC, the Buddha's influence was spreading rapidly throughout India.

Reading Check
Compare
How did Buddha's teachings agree with Hinduism?

Buddhism Spreads

Buddhism continued to attract followers after the Buddha's death. After spreading through India, the religion began to spread to other areas as well.

Buddhism Spreads in India According to Buddhist tradition, 500 of the Buddha's followers gathered together shortly after he died. They wanted to make sure that the Buddha's teachings were remembered correctly.

In the years after this council, the Buddha's followers spread his teachings throughout India. The ideas spread very quickly, because Buddhist teachings were popular and easy to understand. Within 200 years after the Buddha's death, his teachings had spread throughout most of India.

Buddhism Spreads Beyond India The spread of Buddhism increased after one of the most powerful kings in India, Asoka, became Buddhist in the 200s BC. Once he converted, he built Buddhist temples and schools throughout India. More importantly, though, he worked to spread Buddhism into areas outside of India. You will learn more about Asoka and his accomplishments in the next lesson.

▶ **Explore ONLINE!**

Early Spread of Buddhism

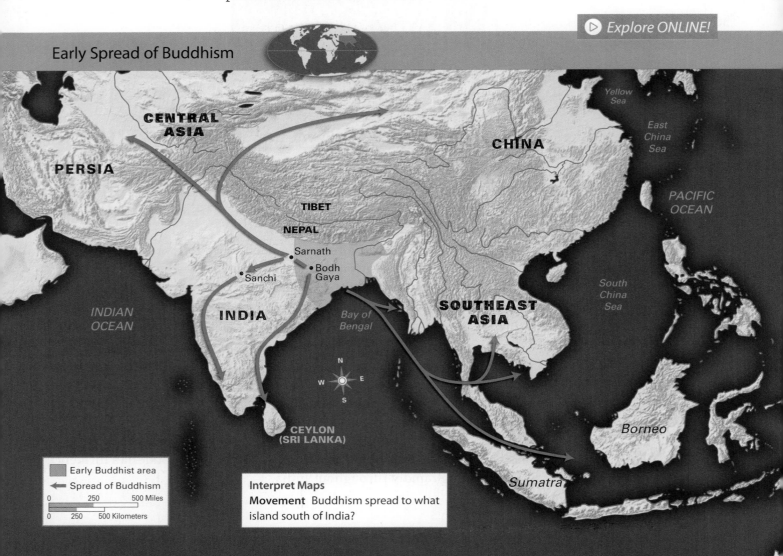

Early Buddhist area

← **Spread of Buddhism**

0   250   500 Miles

0   250   500 Kilometers

Interpret Maps
Movement Buddhism spread to what island south of India?

Young Buddhist students carry gifts in Sri Lanka, one of many places outside of India where Buddhism spread.

Asoka sent Buddhist **missionaries**, or people who work to spread their religious beliefs, to other kingdoms in Asia. One group of these missionaries sailed to the island of Sri Lanka around 251 BC. Others followed trade routes east to what is now Myanmar and to other parts of Southeast Asia. Missionaries also went north to areas near the Himalayas.

Missionaries also introduced Buddhism to lands west of India. They founded Buddhist communities in Central Asia and Persia. They even taught about Buddhism as far away as Syria and Egypt.

Buddhism continued to grow over the centuries. Eventually it spread via the Silk Road into China, then Korea and Japan. Through their work, missionaries taught Buddhism to millions of people.

A Split within Buddhism Even as Buddhism spread through Asia, however, it began to change. Not all Buddhists could agree on their beliefs and practices. Eventually, disagreements between Buddhists led to a split within the religion. Two major branches of Buddhism developed—Theravada and Mahayana.

Members of the Theravada branch tried to follow the Buddha's teachings exactly as he had stated them. Mahayana Buddhists, though, believed that other people could interpret the Buddha's teachings to help people reach nirvana. Both branches have millions of believers today, but Mahayana is by far the larger branch. These different branches have established some of their own customs and traditions. For example, in the Mahayana branch, there is less focus on nirvana and more on knowledge and the mastery of wisdom.

Traditions and Customs of Buddhism Both branches of Buddhism have some traditions and customs in common. For example, gifts play an important role in the customs of Buddhism. People can worship the Buddha by showing respect or giving gifts. Buddhists can present their gifts at shrines dedicated to the Buddha. Worshippers can also give gifts to monks. Monks are people who devote themselves to religious study and discipline.

Buddhists observe many holidays. The three main events of the Buddha's life—his birth, enlightenment, and death—are all holidays. The end of *vassa*, the rainy season, is celebrated. All Souls Day, New Year's, and Harvest Festivals are also celebrated. For some holidays, people may wear all white or new clothes, to symbolize rebirth and renewal. Or they may visit temples for special sutras, or services. One of the most important rituals in Buddhism is making a pilgrimage. These travels to holy sites are meant to aid in a person's spiritual development.

Reading Check
Summarize
How are gifts used in the customs of Buddhism?

Summary and Preview In this lesson, you read about Buddhism, one of India's major religions. You will learn about India's great empires in the next lesson.

Lesson 4 Assessment

Review Ideas, Terms, and People

1. a. **Identify** Who was the Buddha, and what does the term *Buddha* mean?

   b. **Summarize** How did Siddhartha Gautama free his mind and clarify his thinking as he searched for wisdom?

2. a. **Identify** What is nirvana?

   b. **Contrast** How are Buddhist teachings different from Hindu teachings?

   c. **Summarize** According to the Buddha in his Two Lessons, how can one gain the knowledge of the Middle Path?

   d. **Elaborate** Why do Buddhists believe that following the Eightfold Path leads to a better life?

3. a. **Describe** Into what lands did Buddhism spread?

   b. **Summarize** What role did missionaries play in spreading Buddhism?

Critical Thinking

4. **Find Main Ideas** Draw a diagram like this one. Identify and describe Buddhism's Four Noble Truths within the diagram. Write a sentence explaining how these Truths are central to Buddhism.

Indian Empires

The Big Idea

The Mauryas and the Guptas built great empires in India.

Main Ideas

- The Mauryan Empire unified most of India.
- Gupta rulers promoted Hinduism in their empire.

Key People

Chandragupta Maurya
Asoka
Chandra Gupta II

If YOU were there . . .

You are a merchant in India in about 240 BC. You travel from town to town on your donkey, carrying bolts of colorful cloth. In the heat of summer, you are grateful for the banyan trees along the road. They shelter you from the blazing sun. You stop at wells for cool drinks of water and rest houses for a break in your journey. You know these are all the work of your king, Asoka.

How do you feel about your king?

Mauryan Empire Unifies India

In the 320s BC, a military leader named **Chandragupta Maurya** (chuhn-druh-GOOP-tuh MOUR-yuh) seized control of the entire northern part of India. By doing so, he founded the Mauryan Empire. Mauryan rule lasted for about 150 years.

Mauryan Government and Economy Chandragupta Maurya ruled his empire with the help of a complex government. It included a network of spies and a huge army of some 600,000 soldiers. The army also had thousands of war elephants and thousands of chariots. In return for the army's protection, farmers paid a heavy tax to the government.

Chandragupta Maurya also introduced one currency across the empire. This single currency of copper and silver coins helped trade flourish as it made it easier for people to conduct business. Mauryan rulers also set up government systems for accounting to keep track of the empire's finances. Accountants made sure the government received taxes that were due. They also watched out for dishonest people who took money away from the empire.

Mauryan Society Mauryan society had seven occupational groups: philosophers, farmers, soldiers, herdsmen, artisans, magistrates, and councilors. The groups were considered castes since the groups were hereditary. Mauryan society also permitted slavery, although it probably was not as

Mauryan troops used war elephants in battle. As the elephants charged forward into battle, soldiers on top hurled spears at their enemies.

common as it was in other ancient societies. They did, however, expect members of lower castes to serve those of higher castes.

In 301 BC, Chandragupta decided to become a Jainist monk. To do so, he had to give up his throne. He passed the throne to his son, who continued to expand the empire. Before long, the Mauryas ruled all of northern India and much of central India as well.

Asoka Around 270 BC Chandragupta's grandson **Asoka** (uh-SOH-kuh) became king. Asoka was a strong ruler, the strongest of all the Mauryan emperors. He extended Mauryan rule over most of India. In conquering other kingdoms, Asoka made his own empire both stronger and richer.

For many years, Asoka watched his armies fight bloody battles against other peoples. A few years into his rule, however, Asoka converted to Buddhism. When he did, he swore that he would not launch any more wars of conquest.

After converting to Buddhism, Asoka had the time and resources to improve the lives of his people. He had wells dug and roads built throughout the empire. Along these roads, workers planted shade trees and built rest houses for weary travelers. Asoka also built hospitals and concentrated on

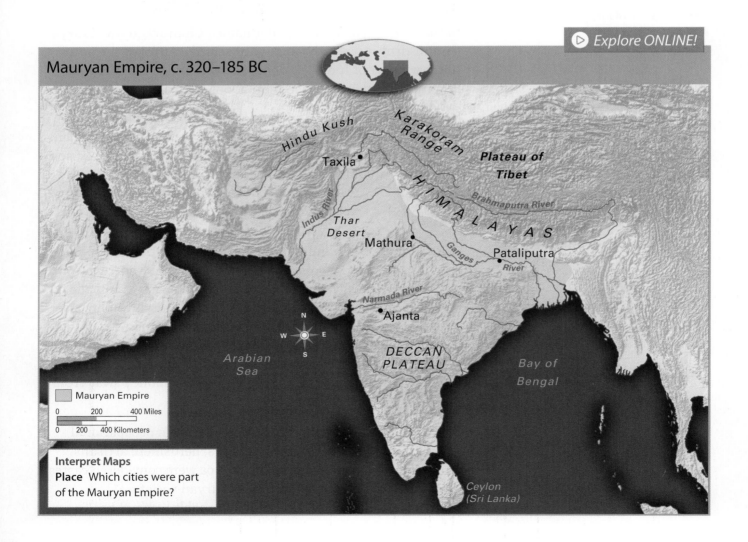

▶ *Explore ONLINE!*

Mauryan Empire, c. 320–185 BC

Interpret Maps
Place Which cities were part of the Mauryan Empire?

relieving suffering. He built universities where women as well as men could study. He also paid attention to the needs of all religious communities, not just Buddhist ones. People in Asoka's empire were well cared for and therefore the society was stable and prosperous. Asoka also encouraged the spread of Buddhism in India and the rest of Asia.

Asoka died in 233 BC, and the empire began to fall apart soon afterward. His sons fought each other for power, and invaders threatened the empire. In 184 BC the last Mauryan king was killed by one of his own generals. India divided into smaller states once again.

Reading Check
Summarize
How did Mauryan rulers work to improve the economy?

Academic Vocabulary
establish to set up or create

Gupta Rulers Promote Hinduism

After the collapse of the Mauryan Empire, India remained divided for about 500 years. During that time, Buddhism continued to prosper and spread in India, and so the popularity of Hinduism declined.

A New Hindu Empire Eventually, however, a new dynasty was **established** in India. It was the Gupta (GOOP-tuh) dynasty, which took over India around AD 320. Under the Guptas, India was once again united, and it once again became prosperous.

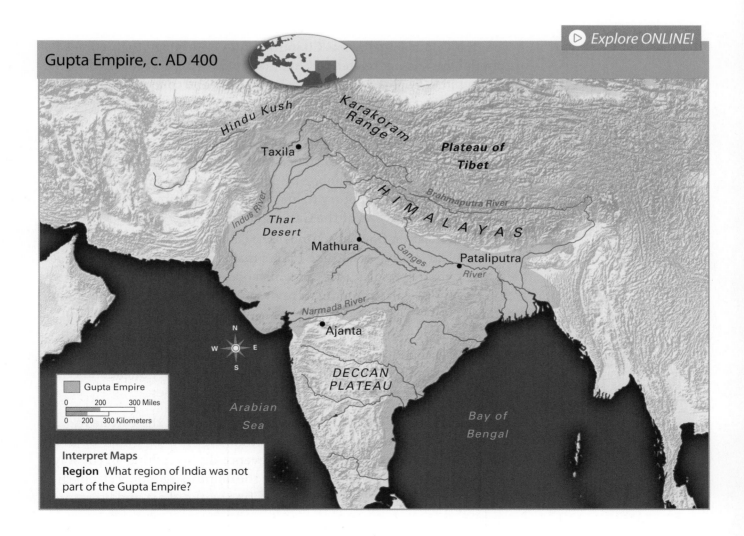

Gupta Empire, c. AD 400

▷ *Explore ONLINE!*

Interpret Maps
Region What region of India was not part of the Gupta Empire?

This painting of a palace scene was created during the Gupta period.

The first Gupta emperor was Chandra Gupta I. Although their names are similar, he was not related to Chandragupta Maurya. From his base in northern India, Chandra Gupta's armies invaded and conquered neighboring lands. Eventually he brought much of the northern part of India under his control.

Chandra Gupta was followed as emperor by his son, Samudra Gupta, a brilliant military leader. He continued his father's wars of conquest, fighting battles against many neighboring peoples. Through these wars, Samudra Gupta added more territory to his empire. By the time he died, he had taken control of nearly all of the Ganges River valley.

Indian civilization flourished under the Gupta rulers. These rulers were Hindu, so Hinduism became India's major religion. The Gupta kings built many Hindu temples, some of which became models for later Indian architecture. They also promoted a revival of Hindu writings and worship practices.

Although they were Hindus, the Gupta rulers also supported the religious beliefs of Buddhism and Jainism. They promoted Buddhist art and built Buddhist temples. They also established a university at Nalanda that became one of Asia's greatest centers for Buddhist studies.

Gupta Society In 375 Emperor **Chandra Gupta II** took the throne in India. Gupta society reached its high point during his rule. Under Chandra Gupta II, the empire continued to grow, eventually stretching all the way across northern India. At the same time, the empire's economy strengthened, and people prospered. They created fine works of art and literature.

They also made significant advances in medicine, science, and mathematics, including the numeral system. Outsiders admired the empire's wealth and beauty.

Gupta kings believed the social order of the caste system would strengthen their rule. They also thought it would keep the empire stable. As a result, the Gupta considered the caste system an important part of Indian society. *Jatis*, the occupation-based groupings, became more complex during this period.

Gupta rule remained strong in India until the late 400s. At that time the Huns, a group from Central Asia, invaded India from the northwest. Their fierce attacks drained the Gupta Empire of its power and wealth. As the Hun armies marched farther into India, the Guptas lost hope. By the middle of the 500s, Gupta rule had ended, and India had divided into small kingdoms yet again.

Summary and Preview In this lesson, you read how the Mauryas and Guptas united much of India in their empires. In the next lesson, you will learn about their many achievements.

Reading Check
Summarize
What was the Gupta dynasty's position on religion?

Lesson 5 Assessment

Review Ideas, Terms, and People

1. a. **Identify** Who created the Mauryan Empire?

   b. **Summarize** What happened after Asoka became a Buddhist?

   c. **Elaborate** Why do you think many people consider Asoka the greatest of all Mauryan rulers?

2. a. **Recall** What religion did most of the Gupta rulers belong to?

   b. **Compare and Contrast** How were the rulers Chandragupta Maurya and Chandra Gupta I alike, and how were they different?

Critical Thinking

3. **Categorize** Draw a table like this one. Fill it with information about the rulers that you read about in this lesson.

Ruler	Empire	Accomplishments

Indian Achievements

The Big Idea

The people of ancient India made great contributions to the arts and sciences.

Main Ideas

- Indian artists created great works of religious art.
- Sanskrit literature flourished during the Gupta period.
- The Indians made scientific advances in metalworking, medicine, and other sciences.

Key Terms

metallurgy
alloys
Hindu-Arabic numerals
inoculation
astronomy

If YOU were there . . .

You are a traveler in western India in the 300s. You are visiting a cave temple that is carved into a mountain cliff. Inside the cave it is cool and quiet. Huge columns rise all around you. You don't feel you're alone, for the walls and ceilings are covered with paintings. They are filled with lively scenes and figures. In the center is a large statue with calm, peaceful features.

How does this cave make you feel?

Religious Art

The Indians of the Mauryan and Gupta periods created great works of art, many of them religious. Many of their paintings and sculptures illustrated either Hindu or Buddhist teachings. Magnificent temples—both Hindu and Buddhist—were built all around India. They remain some of the most beautiful buildings in the world today.

Temples Early Hindu temples were small stone structures. They had flat roofs and contained only one or two rooms. In the Gupta period, though, temple architecture became more complex. Gupta temples were topped by huge towers and were covered with carvings of the deities worshipped inside.

Buddhist temples of the Gupta period are also impressive. Some Buddhists carved entire temples out of mountainsides. The most famous such temple is at Ajanta. Its builders filled the caves with beautiful wall paintings and sculpture.

Another type of Buddhist temple was the stupa. Stupas had domed roofs and were built to house sacred items from the life of the Buddha. Many of them were covered with detailed carvings.

Paintings and Sculpture The Gupta period also saw the creation of great works of art, both paintings and statues. Painting was a greatly respected profession, and India was home to many skilled artists. However, we don't know the names of many artists from this period. Instead, we know the names of many rich and powerful members of Gupta society who paid artists to create works of beauty and significance.

Most Indian paintings from the Gupta period are clear and colorful. Some of them show graceful Indians wearing fine jewelry and stylish clothes. Such paintings offer us a glimpse of the Indians' daily and ceremonial lives.

Artists from both of India's major religions, Hinduism and Buddhism, drew on their beliefs to create their works. As a result, many of the finest paintings of ancient India are found in temples. Hindu painters drew hundreds of gods on temple walls and entrances. Buddhists covered the walls and ceilings of temples with scenes from the life of the Buddha.

Indian sculptors also created great works. Many of their statues were made for Buddhist cave temples. In addition to the temples' intricately carved columns, sculptors carved statues of kings and the Buddha. Some of these statues tower over the cave entrances. Hindu temples also featured impressive statues of deities. In fact, the walls of some temples were completely covered with carvings and images.

Reading Check
Summarize
How did religion influence ancient Indian art?

Temple Architecture

This Hindu temple is covered with incredibly detailed carvings and decorations. Many individual sculptures are images of important Hindu deities, like the statue of Vishnu.

Indian Literature

Sanskrit was the main language of the ancient Aryans. During the Mauryan and Gupta periods, many works of Sanskrit literature were created. These works were later translated into many other languages.

Religious Epics The greatest of these Sanskrit writings are two religious epics, the *Mahabharata* (muh-HAH-BAH-ruh-tuh) and the *Ramayana* (rah-MAH-yuh-nuh). Still popular in India, the *Mahabharata* is one of the world's longest literary works. It is a story about the struggle between two families for control of a kingdom. Included within the story are many long passages about Hindu beliefs, including the importance of *dharma*. The most famous is called the *Bhagavad Gita* (BUG-uh-vuhd GEE-tah), which has influenced thinkers such as Henry David Thoreau and leaders including Mohandas Gandhi and Nelson Mandela. This passage is about how souls or spirits are eternal and compares reincarnation to changing your clothes.

> "Just as a person puts on new garments after discarding the old ones; similarly, the living entity or the individual soul acquires new bodies after casting away the old bodies."
>
> —from the *Bhagavad Gita*

The *Ramayana*, which according to Hindu tradition was written prior to the *Mahabharata*, tells about a prince named Rama. In truth, the prince was the god Vishnu in human form. He had become human so he could rid the world of demons. He also had to rescue his wife, a princess named Sita. For centuries, the characters of the *Ramayana* have been seen as models for how Indians should behave. For example, Rama is seen as the ideal ruler, and his relationship with Sita as the ideal marriage.

Other Works Writers in the Gupta period also created plays, poetry, and other types of literature. One famous writer of this time was Kalidasa (kahl-ee-DAHS-uh). His work was so brilliant that Chandra Gupta II hired him to write plays for the royal court.

Sometime before 500, Indian writers also produced a book of stories called the *Panchatantra* (PUHN-chuh-TAHN-truh). The stories in this collection were intended to teach lessons. They praise people for cleverness and quick thinking. Each story ends with a message about winning friends, losing property, waging war, or some other life event. Eventually, translations of this collection spread throughout the world. It became popular as far away as Europe.

Scientific Advances

Indian achievements were not limited to art, architecture, and literature. Indian scholars also made important advances in metalworking, math, and the sciences.

Reading Check
Summarize
What types of literature did writers of ancient India create?

Metalworking

The Indians were expert metalworkers. This gold coin shows the emperor Chandra Gupta II.

Mathematics

Indian scholars created the zero and the symbols that we use today to represent numbers. Aryabhata was an influential Indian mathematician and astronomer.

Medicine

In this modern painting, the Indian surgeon Susruta performs surgery on a patient. The ancient Indians had an advanced knowledge of medicine.

Astronomy

The Gupta made great advances in astronomy, despite their lack of modern devices such as telescopes. They used devices like this one from the 1700s to observe and map the stars.

Analyze Visuals
What are some areas of science that people studied in ancient India?

Academic Vocabulary
process a series of steps by which a task is accomplished

Metalworking The ancient Indians were pioneers of **metallurgy** (MET-uhl-uhr-jee), the science of working with metals. Their knowledge allowed them to create high-quality tools and weapons. The Indians also knew **processes** for mixing metals to create **alloys**, mixtures of two or more metals. Alloys are sometimes stronger or easier to work with than pure metals.

Metalworkers made their strongest products out of iron. Indian iron was very hard and pure. These features made the iron a valuable trade item.

During the Gupta dynasty, metalworkers built the famous Iron Pillar near Delhi. Unlike most iron, which rusts easily, this pillar is very resistant to rust. The tall column still attracts crowds of visitors. Scholars study this column even today to learn the Indians' secrets.

Mathematics and Other Sciences Gupta scholars also made advances in math and science. In fact, they were among the most advanced mathematicians of their day. They developed many elements of our modern math system. The numbers we use today are called **Hindu-Arabic numerals** because they were created by Indian scholars and brought to Europe by Arabs. The Indians were also the first people to create the zero. Although that may seem like a small thing, modern math wouldn't be possible without the zero.

The ancient Indians were also very skilled in the medical sciences. As early as the AD 100s, doctors were writing their knowledge down in textbooks. Among the skills these books describe is making medicines from plants and minerals.

Besides curing people with medicines, Indian doctors knew how to protect people against disease. The Indians practiced **inoculation** (i-nah-kyuh-LAY-shuhn), or injecting a person with a small dose of a virus to help him or her build up defenses to a disease. By fighting off this small dose, the body learns to protect itself.

For people who were injured, Indian doctors could perform surgery. Surgeons repaired broken bones, treated wounds, removed infected tonsils, reconstructed broken noses, and even reattached torn earlobes! If they could find no other cure for an illness, doctors would cast magic spells to help people recover.

Indian interest in **astronomy**, the study of stars and planets, dates back to early times as well. Indian astronomers knew of seven of the planets in our solar system. They knew that the sun was a star and that the planets revolved around it. They also knew that the earth was a sphere and that it rotated on its axis. In addition, they could predict eclipses of the sun and the moon.

Reading Check
Find Main Ideas
What were two Indian achievements in mathematics?

Summary In this lesson, you read about the great achievements in Ancient India. These scientific advances and works of literature, art, and architecture still impact how we view the world today.

Lesson 6 Assessment

Review Ideas, Terms, and People

1. **a. Describe** What did Hindu temples of the Gupta period look like?

    b. Analyze How can you tell that Indian artists were well respected?

    c. Evaluate Why do you think Hindu and Buddhist temples contained great works of art?

2. **a. Identify** What is the *Bhagavad Gita*?

    b. Explain Why were the stories of the *Panchatantra* written?

    c. Elaborate Why do you think people are still interested in ancient Sanskrit epics today?

3. **a. Define** What is metallurgy?

    b. Explain Why do we call the numbers we use today Hindu-Arabic numerals?

Critical Thinking

4. **Categorize** Draw a table like this one. Identify the scientific advances that fall into each category below.

Metallurgy	Math	Medicine	Astronomy

Interpret Diagrams

Understand the Skill

Diagrams are drawings that illustrate or explain objects or ideas. Different types of diagrams have different purposes. The ability to interpret diagrams will help you to better understand historical objects, their functions, and how they worked.

Learn the Skill

Use these guidelines to interpret a diagram:

1. Read the diagram's title or caption to find out what it represents. If a legend is present, study it as well to understand any symbols and colors in the diagram.

2. Most diagrams include labels that identify the object's parts or explain relationships between them. Study these parts and labels carefully.

3. If any written information or explanation accompanies the diagram, compare it to the drawing as you read.

This is a diagram of the Great Stupa at Sanchi in India, which is thought to contain the Buddha's remains. Like most stupas, it was shaped like a dome.

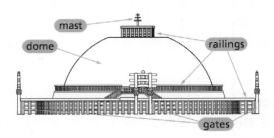

The Sanchi stupa is surrounded by a stone railing with four gates called *torenas*. About halfway up the side of the mound is a second railing next to a walkway. Worshippers move along this walkway in a clockwise direction to honor the Buddha. The stupa is topped by a cube called the *harmika*. Rising from the harmika is a mast or spire. These parts and their shapes all have religious meaning for Buddhists.

Practice the Skill

Here is another diagram of the Sanchi stupa. Interpret both diagrams to answer the questions that follow.

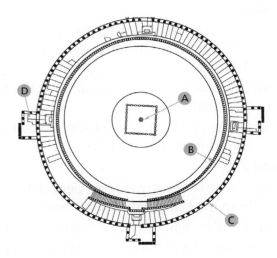

1. Which letter in this diagram labels the *torenas*?

2. What part of the stupa does the letter A label?

3. The walkway and railing are labeled by which letter?

Module 5 Assessment

Review Vocabulary, Terms, and People

Complete each sentence by filling in the blanks with the correct term or name.

1. _____ are winds that bring heavy rainfall.

2. A _____ is a division of people into groups based on birth, wealth, or occupation.

3. Hindus believe in _____, the belief that they will be reborn many times after death.

4. _____ founded the Mauryan Empire.

5. The focusing of the mind on spiritual things is called _____.

6. People who work to spread their religious beliefs are called _____.

7. People who practice _____ use only peaceful ways to achieve change.

8. _____ converted to Buddhism while he was ruler of the Mauryan Empire.

9. A mixture of metals is called an _____.

Comprehension and Critical Thinking

Lesson 1

10. a. **Describe** What caused floods on the Indus River, and what was the result of those floods?
    b. **Summarize** How do people use the Ganges River?
    c. **Elaborate** Why is the Harappan culture considered a civilization?

Lesson 2

11. a. **Contrast** How was Vedic period different from the Harappan civilization?
    b. **Identify** Who were the Brahmins, and what role did they play in Vedic society?
    c. **Analyze** How did the Upanishads influence later religious expression?
    d. **Elaborate** Discuss why conflict developed among clans in the Vedic period.

Lesson 3

12. a. **Analyze** How do Hindus believe karma affects reincarnation?
    b. **Elaborate** Hinduism has been called both a polytheistic religion—one that worships many gods—and a monotheistic religion—one that worships only one god. Why do you think this is so?

Lesson 4

13. a. **Describe** What did the Buddha say caused human suffering?
    b. **Analyze** How did Buddhism grow and change after the Buddha died?
    c. **Elaborate** Why did the Buddha's teachings about nirvana appeal to so many people?

Lesson 5

14. a. **Identify** What was Chandragupta Maurya's greatest accomplishment?
    b. **Analyze** Why did Gupta leaders believe the caste system would strengthen their rule?
    c. **Predict** How might Indian history have been different if Asoka had not become a Buddhist?

Lesson 6

15. a. **Describe** What kinds of religious art did the ancient Indians create?
    b. **Make Inferences** Why do you think religious discussions are included in the *Mahabharata*?
    c. **Evaluate** Which of the ancient Indians' achievements do you think is most impressive? Why?

Module 5 Assessment, continued

Review Themes

16. Religion What is one teaching that Buddhism and Hinduism share? What is one idea about which they differ?

17. Society and Culture How did the caste system affect the lives of most people in India?

Reading Skills

Inferences about History *Use the Reading Skills taught in this module to answer the question below.*

18. Based on what you learned about the Gupta period, what inferences can you draw about religious tolerance in ancient India? Draw a graphic organizer like this one to help you organize your thoughts.

Question:	
Inside the Text:	Outside the Text:
Inference:	

Social Studies Skills

Understand Diagrams *Use the Social Studies Skills taught in this module to answer the question below.*

19. Look back over the diagram of the Buddhist temple in the skills activity at the end of this module. Using this diagram as a guide, draw a simple diagram of your home or school. Be sure to include labels of important features on your diagram. An example has been provided for you below.

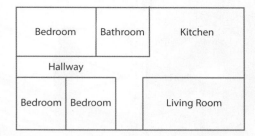

Focus On Writing

20. Make an Illustrated Poster Ancient India was a fascinating place with amazing cities and empires. It was also the birthplace of major religions. Decide how you could illustrate one aspect of Ancient Indian culture in a poster. On a large sheet of paper or poster board, write a title that identifies your subject. Then draw pictures, maps, or diagrams that illustrate it. Next to each picture, write a short caption. Each caption should be two sentences long. The first sentence should identify what the picture, map, or diagram shows. The second sentence should explain why the picture is important to the study of Indian history.

Module 6
Ancient China

Essential Question
How do the people, events, and ideas that shaped ancient China continue to influence the world?

About the Photo: China was one of the early centers of civilization. Rivers played key roles in Chinese history and the development of Chinese society.

▶ Explore ONLINE!

VIDEOS, including...
- The Great Wall of China
- Confucius: Words of Wisdom
- The Silk Road

☑ Document-Based Investigations

☑ Graphic Organizers

☑ Interactive Games

☑ Interactive Map: China: Physical

☑ Image with Hotspots: Guardians of Shi Huangdi's Tomb

☑ Image Carousel: The Great Wall

In this module, you will learn about the geography, history, and culture of ancient China, a culture that influences the world even today.

What You Will Learn...

Lesson 1: Geography and Early China **184**
The Big Idea Chinese civilization began with the Shang dynasty along the Huang He.

Lesson 2: The Zhou Dynasty **192**
The Big Idea The Zhou dynasty brought political stability and new ways to deal with political and social changes in ancient China.

Lesson 3: The Qin Dynasty **200**
The Big Idea The Qin dynasty unified China with a strong government and a system of standardization.

Lesson 4: The Han Dynasty **206**
The Big Idea The period of the Han dynasty brought new ideas about government, the arts, learning, and religion.

Lesson 5: The Silk Road **216**
The Big Idea Trade routes led to the exchange of new products and ideas among China, Rome, and other lands.

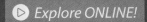
Module Events	World Events

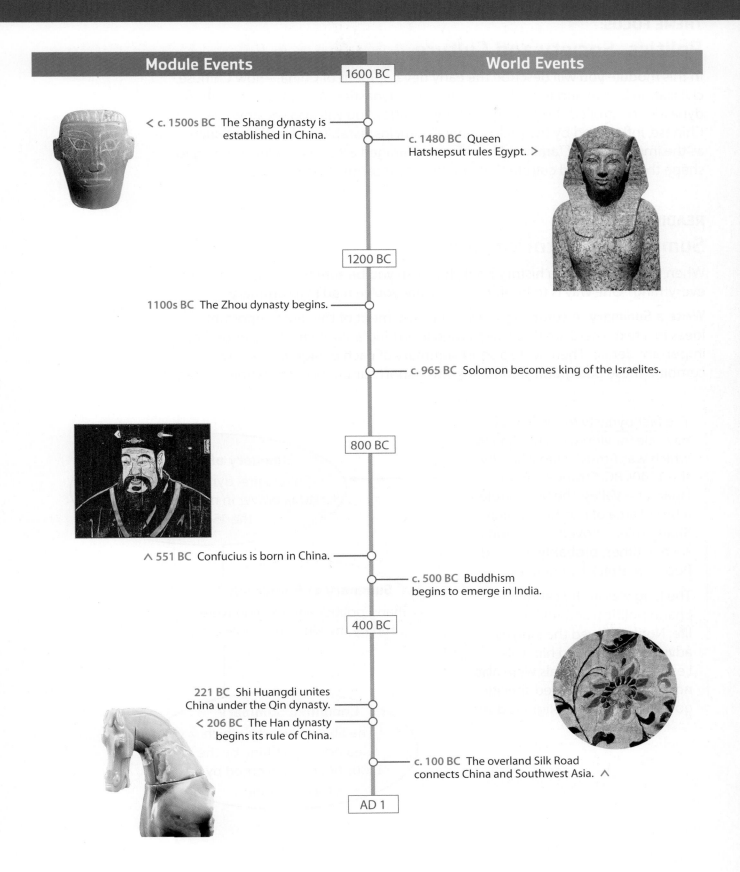

1600 BC

< c. 1500s BC The Shang dynasty is established in China.

c. 1480 BC Queen Hatshepsut rules Egypt. >

1200 BC

1100s BC The Zhou dynasty begins.

c. 965 BC Solomon becomes king of the Israelites.

800 BC

∧ 551 BC Confucius is born in China.

c. 500 BC Buddhism begins to emerge in India.

400 BC

221 BC Shi Huangdi unites China under the Qin dynasty.

< 206 BC The Han dynasty begins its rule of China.

c. 100 BC The overland Silk Road connects China and Southwest Asia. ∧

AD 1

Reading Social Studies

Politics, Society and Culture

In this module you will describe the early development of China—how Chinese civilization began and took shape under early dynasties. You will see how these dynasties controlled the government and politics. You will also see how the Chinese, influenced by the philosopher Confucius, established traditions such as the importance of families. They also encouraged art and learning, helping to shape the society and culture that would last for centuries in China.

READING FOCUS:

Summarize Historical Texts

When you are reading a history book, how can you be sure that you understand everything? One way is to briefly restate what you've read in a summary.

Write a Summary A **summary** is a short restatement of the most important ideas in a text. There are three steps used in writing a summary. First, underline important details. Then, write a short summary of each paragraph. Finally, combine these paragraph summaries into a short summary of the whole passage.

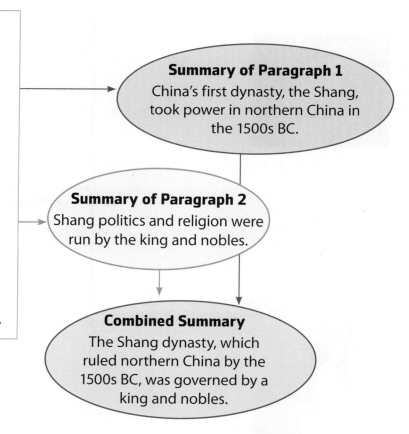

The first dynasty for which we have clear evidence is the Shang, which was firmly established by the 1500s BC. Strongest in the Huang He Valley, the Shang ruled a broad area of northern China. Shang rulers moved their capital several times, probably to avoid floods or attack by enemies.

The king was at the center of Shang political and religious life. Nobles served the king as advisors and helped him rule. Less important officials were also nobles. They performed specific governmental and religious duties.

Summary of Paragraph 1
China's first dynasty, the Shang, took power in northern China in the 1500s BC.

Summary of Paragraph 2
Shang politics and religion were run by the king and nobles.

Combined Summary
The Shang dynasty, which ruled northern China by the 1500s BC, was governed by a king and nobles.

You Try It!

The following passage is from the module you are about to read. As you read it, think about what to include in a summary.

Early Settlements Archaeologists have found remains of early Chinese villages. The villages were typically made up of a cluster of buildings surrounded by a deep moat. Some buildings were above ground and circular, with cone-shaped roofs. Others were partly underground and may have had straw-covered roofs supported by columns, beams, and rafters. The walls were made of sticks and twigs held together by clay. One village site near the Huang He had more than 40 houses. The site also included animal pens, storage pits, and a cemetery.

Some of the villages along the Huang He grew into large towns. Walls surrounded these towns to defend them against floods and hostile neighbors. In towns, the Chinese left many artifacts, such as arrowheads, fishhooks, tools, pottery, or pieces of cloth.

After you read the passage, answer the following questions.

1. Read the following summaries, and decide which one is the better summary statement. Explain your answer.

   a. Archaeologists have found out interesting things about the early settlements of China. For example, they have discovered that the Chinese had homes with straw-covered roofs, pens for their animals, and even cemeteries. Also, they have found that larger villages were surrounded by walls for defense. Finally, they have found tools such as arrowheads and fishhooks.

   b. Archaeologists have found remains of early Chinese villages, some of which grew into large walled settlements. Artifacts found there help us understand Chinese culture.

2. What are three characteristics of a good summary?

As you read this module, think about how you would summarize the material you are reading.

Key Terms and People

Lesson 1
jade
oracle

Lesson 2
lords
peasants
Confucius
ethics
Confucianism
Daoism
Laozi
Legalism

Lesson 3
Shi Huangdi
Great Wall

Lesson 4
sundial
seismograph
acupuncture
silk
diffusion

Lesson 5
Silk Road

Geography and Early China

The Big Idea

Chinese civilization began with the Shang dynasty along the Huang He.

Main Ideas

- China's physical geography made farming possible but travel and communication difficult.

- Civilization began in China along the Huang He and Chang Jiang rivers.

- China's first dynasties helped Chinese society develop and made many other achievements.

Key Terms

jade
oracle

If YOU were there . . .

You live along a broad river in China in about 1400 BC. Your grandfather is a farmer. He tells you wonderful stories about an ancient king. Long ago, this legendary hero tamed the river's raging floods. He even created new rivers. Without him, no one could farm or live in this rich land.

Why is this legend important to your family?

China's Physical Geography

Geography played a major role in the development of Chinese civilization. China has many different geographical features. Some features separated groups of people within China. Others separated China from the rest of the world.

A Vast and Varied Land China covers an area of nearly 4 million square miles, about the same size as the United States. One of the physical barriers that separates China from its neighbors is a harsh desert, the Gobi (GOH-bee). It spreads over much of China's north. East of the Gobi are low-lying plains. These plains, which cover most of eastern China, form one of the world's largest farming regions. The Pacific Ocean forms the country's eastern boundary.

More than 2,000 miles to the west, rugged mountains make up the western frontier. In the southwest the Plateau of Tibet has several mountain peaks that reach more than 26,000 feet. The southern edge of the Tibetan Plateau is bordered by the Himalayan Mountains, which are home to most of the highest mountain peaks in the world. From the plateau, smaller mountain ranges spread eastward. The most important of these ranges is the Qinling Shandi (CHIN-LING shahn-DEE). It separates northern China from southern China.

Western China's high mountains and wide deserts make travel difficult and isolate China's population centers in the east.

Ancient people lacked the easy transportation routes of today. Mountains, deserts, and oceans served as strong barriers to travel. Because of these features, ancient China remained isolated from much of the outside world. Geographical challenges also made it difficult for China's rulers to maintain control over their subjects. Trade, travel, and communication were all challenges during China's early history.

▶ Explore ONLINE!

China: Physical

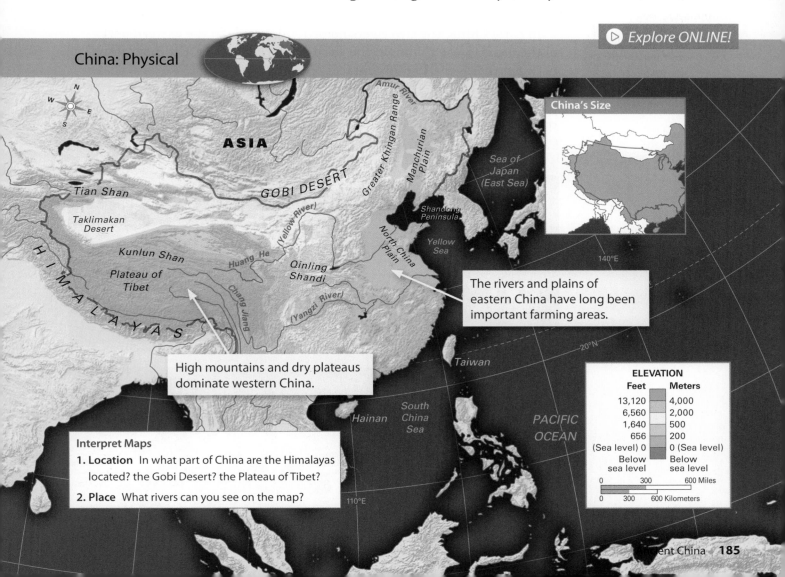

ASIA

Amur River

Greater Khingan Range

GOBI DESERT

Manchurian Plain

Tian Shan

Taklimakan Desert

Kunlun Shan

HIMALAYAS

Plateau of Tibet

Huang He (Yellow River)

Chang Jiang

(Yangzi River)

Qinling Shandi

North China Plain

Shandong Peninsula

Yellow Sea

Sea of Japan (East Sea)

China's Size

140°E

20°N

Taiwan

Hainan

South China Sea

PACIFIC OCEAN

110°E

The rivers and plains of eastern China have long been important farming areas.

High mountains and dry plateaus dominate western China.

ELEVATION

Feet	Meters
13,120	4,000
6,560	2,000
1,640	500
656	200
(Sea level) 0	0 (Sea level)
Below sea level	Below sea level

0   300   600 Miles
0   300   600 Kilometers

Interpret Maps

1. **Location** In what part of China are the Himalayas located? the Gobi Desert? the Plateau of Tibet?

2. **Place** What rivers can you see on the map?

Weather and Climate Weather and temperature patterns **vary** widely across China. In the northeast, the climate is cold and dry. Winter temperatures drop well below 0°F. Rivers there are frozen for more than half the year. In the northwest, the deserts are very dry. But on the eastern plains of China, heavy rains fall. The tropical southeast is the wettest region. Monsoons can bring 250 inches of rain each year. That's enough water to cover a two-story house!

In ancient times, weather variations were a serious concern. Archaeological evidence suggests that parts of China experienced a cooler and drier climate than usual in about 1000 BC. These changes caused droughts as rivers froze and water sources dried up.

The Rivers of China Two great rivers flow from west to east in China. The Huang He (HWAHNG HUH), or Yellow River, stretches for nearly 3,000 miles across northern China. The river often floods, and the floods leave behind layers of silt on the surrounding countryside. Because these floods can be very destructive, the river is sometimes called China's Sorrow. Over the years, millions of people have died in Huang He floods. Flooding can also ruin crops and contribute to famines.

To the south, the Chang Jiang (CHAHNG JYAHNG), or Yangzi River, cuts through central China. It flows from the mountains of Tibet to the Pacific Ocean. The Chang Jiang is the longest river in Asia.

In early China, the two rivers helped link people in the eastern part of the country with those in the west. At the same time, the mountains between the rivers limited contact.

Reading Check
Summarize How did geographical features isolate China from the rest of the world?

In northern China, the Huang He, or Yellow River, has long been the center of civilization. The silt in the river gives it a yellow look.

Archaeologists work at a Neolithic-era dig site in eastern China.

Civilization Begins

Like other ancient peoples that you have studied, people in China first settled along rivers. There they farmed and built villages. Eventually, complex civilizations with large populations developed.

The Development of Farming Farming in China started along the Huang He and Chang Jiang. The rivers' floods deposited fertile silt. These silt deposits made the land ideal for growing crops.

As early as 7000 BC, farmers grew rice in the middle of the Chang Jiang Valley. North, along the Huang He, the land was better for growing cereals such as millet and wheat.

Along with farming, the early Chinese people varied their diets in other ways. They fished and hunted with bows and arrows. They also domesticated animals such as pigs and sheep. With more sources of food, the population grew. More people needed even greater resources. Farmers had to develop better tools and ways of farming to keep up with the increased demand.

Early Settlements Archaeologists have found remains of early Chinese villages. The villages were typically made up of a cluster of buildings surrounded by a deep moat. Some buildings were above ground and circular, with cone-shaped roofs. Others were partly underground and may have had straw-covered roofs supported by columns, beams, and rafters. The walls were made of sticks and twigs held together by clay. One village site near the Huang He had more than 40 houses. The site also included animal pens, storage pits, and a cemetery.

Some of the villages along the Huang He grew into large towns. Walls surrounded these towns to defend them against floods and hostile neighbors. In towns, the Chinese left many artifacts, such as arrowheads, fishhooks, tools, pottery, or pieces of cloth.

Separate cultures developed in southern and northeastern China. These included the Sanxingdui (sahn-shing-DWAY) and Hongshan peoples. Little is known about them, however. As the major cultures along the Huang He and Chang Jiang grew, they absorbed other cultures.

Over time, Chinese culture became more advanced. After 3000 BC, people used potter's wheels to make more types of pottery. These people also learned to dig water wells. As populations grew, villages spread over larger areas in both northern and southeastern China.

Burial sites have provided information about the culture of this period. Like the Egyptians, the early Chinese filled their tombs with objects. Some tombs included containers of food, suggesting a belief in an afterlife. Some graves contained many more items than others. These differences show that a social order had developed. Often the graves of rich people held beautiful jewelry and other objects made from **jade**, a hard gemstone.

China's First Dynasties

Societies along the Huang He grew and became more complex. They eventually formed the first Chinese civilization.

The Xia Dynasty According to ancient stories, a series of kings ruled early China. Around 2200 BC, one of them, Yu the Great, is said to have founded the Xia (SHAH) dynasty.

Writers told of terrible floods during Yu's lifetime. They said that Yu dug channels to drain the water to the ocean. This labor took him more than 10 years and is said to have created the major waterways of north China.

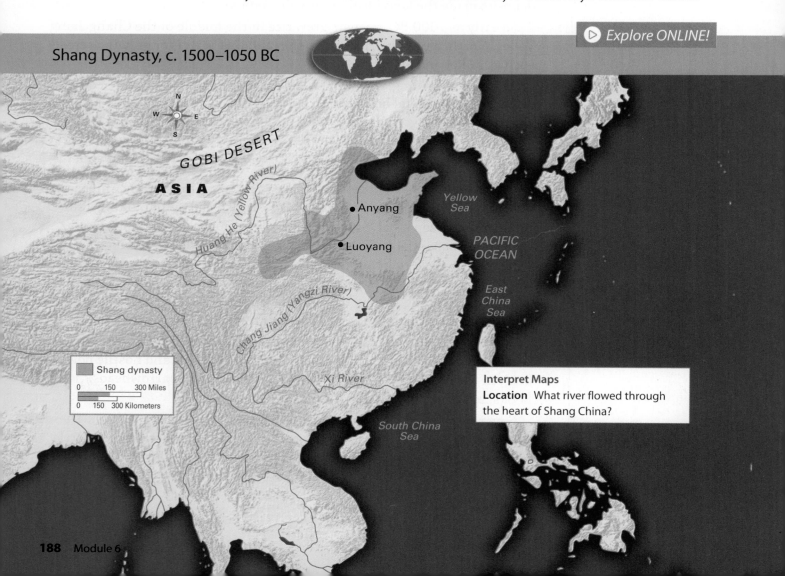

▷ Explore ONLINE!

Shang Dynasty, c. 1500–1050 BC

Shang dynasty

0   150   300 Miles
0   150   300 Kilometers

Interpret Maps
Location What river flowed through the heart of Shang China?

Archaeologists have not yet found evidence that the tales about the Xia are true. However, the stories of Xia rulers were important to the ancient Chinese because they told of kings who helped people solve problems by working together. The stories also explained the rivers and other aspects of geography that had such an impact on people's lives.

The Shang Dynasty Rules in Northern China The first dynasty for which we have clear evidence is the Shang, which was firmly established by the 1500s BC. Strongest in the Huang He Valley, the Shang ruled a broad area of northern China. Shang rulers moved their capital several times, probably to avoid floods or attack by enemies.

The king was at the center of Shang political and religious life. Nobles served the king as advisors and helped him rule. Less important officials were also nobles. They performed specific governmental and religious duties.

Shang Society The social order became more organized under the Shang. The royal family and the nobles were at the highest level. Nobles owned much land, and they passed on their power to their sons. Warrior leaders from the far regions of the empire also ranked high in society. Most people in the ruling classes lived in large homes in cities.

This bronze Shang container is shaped like a tigress.

Artisans settled outside the city walls. They lived in groups based on what they made for a living. Some artisans made weapons. Other artisans made pottery, tools, or clothing. Artisans were at a middle level of importance in Shang society.

Farmers ranked below artisans in the social order. They worked long hours but had little money. Taxes claimed much of what they earned. Slaves, who filled society's lowest rank, were an important source of labor during the Shang period.

Kinship ties were highly important in every level of society. The Shang greatly respected the relationship between one generation and the next. They also worshipped their ancestors. The king was viewed as a father figure, so past kings were also worshipped.

China's natural surroundings were another important part of religious beliefs and ceremonies. The rivers and mountains were thought to have certain powers. The Shang prayed to these powers, gave offerings of grain and millet wine, and made sacrifices.

Shang Advances The Shang made many advances. Some historians believe they may have used cowrie shells as a form of common currency. The Shang also developed China's first writing system. This system used more than 2,000 symbols to express words or ideas. Although the system has gone through changes over the years, the Chinese symbols used today are based on those of the Shang period

The development of writing allowed the Shang to leave a cultural and religious record of life during the dynasty. Shang writing has been found on thousands of cattle bones and turtle shells. Priests carved questions about the future on bones or shells, which were then heated, causing them to crack. The priests believed they could "read" these cracks to predict the future. The bones were called oracle bones because an **oracle** is a prediction. The oracle bones became part of a royal collection belonging to the Shang king.

Oracle bones were part of the system of tribute payments on which the Shang economy was based. *Tribute* is money or goods that a subject or another country is required to pay to a ruler. In the Shang system, the most valuable tribute payments were the turtle shells and cattle bones that became oracle bones. Tribute could also be in the form of humans, usually prisoners, for religious sacrifices. Or, subjects might send animals like horses to the king to honor him. Some historians believe that the Shang may also have exchanged cowrie shells as a form of common currency.

Although no literature exists today from the Shang, ceremonial inscriptions have been found. This writing used pictographs and symbols to pass down religious ideas from one generation to the next. In addition to writing, the Shang also had other achievements. Artisans made beautiful bronze containers for cooking and religious ceremonies. They also made axes, knives, and ornaments from jade. The military developed war chariots, powerful bows, and bronze body armor.

Shang astrologers also made an important contribution—a calendar system. This system had a 360-day year, with 12 months of 30 days each. Like other ancient calendars such as that of India, the Shang calendar was based on the cycles of the sun and moon. Unlike other early calendars, however, the Chinese calendar used a 60-year cycle.

Chinese Writing		
	Writing from Shang Period	**Current Chinese Writing**
Sun	☉	白
Rain	⁂	雨
Field	⊞	田
Moon	)	月

Like other early forms of writing, Chinese writing developed from pictographs—symbols that look like what they represent. Over time, the symbols became more complex and looked less like real objects. Many examples of early Chinese writing are carved into bones like this tortoise shell.

Reading Check
Contrast
What is a major
historical difference
between the Xia and
Shang dynasties?

The Shang Dynasty Falls As in other ancient civilizations, warfare with neighboring territories was common during the Shang era. For many years, the Zhou lived west of Shang territory. At times relations were peaceful, but war occasionally broke out between the two states. Zhou rulers eventually defeated the Shang and seized their territory.

Summary and Preview China is a vast land with a diverse geography. Ancient Chinese civilization developed in the fertile valleys of the Huang He and Chang Jiang. Civilization there advanced under Shang rule. People developed a social order and a writing system and made other achievements. In the next lesson, you will learn about new ideas in China during the rule of the Zhou dynasty.

Lesson 1 Assessment

Review Ideas, Terms, and People

1. **a. Identify** Name China's two major rivers.
   b. Analyze How did China's geography affect its development?

2. **a. Identify** In which river valley did China's civilization begin?
   b. Explain What made China's river valleys ideal for farming?
   c. Elaborate What do Chinese artifacts reveal about China's early civilization?

3. **a. Describe** How do historians know about the Xia dynasty?
   b. Identify What was the lowest level of Shang society?
   c. Draw Conclusions What does the use of oracle bones tell us about the early Chinese?
   d. Compare How were ancient calendars similar?

Critical Thinking

4. **Compare and Contrast** Draw a diagram like this one. Use it and your notes to compare and contrast the Xia and Shang dynasties.

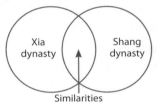

Xia dynasty   Shang dynasty

Similarities

5. **Organize Information** Draw a map to show the location of major geographic features of ancient China. Be sure to label features, including the Huang He, Chiang Jiang, Gobi Desert, Himalayas, and Plateau of Tibet.

The Zhou Dynasty and New Ideas

The Big Idea

The Zhou dynasty brought political stability and new ways to deal with political and social changes in ancient China.

Main Ideas

- The Zhou dynasty expanded China but then declined.
- Confucius offered ideas to bring order to Chinese society.
- Daoism and Legalism also gained followers.

Key Terms

lords
peasants
Confucius
ethics
Confucianism
Daoism
Laozi
Legalism

If YOU were there . . .

You are a student of the famous teacher Confucius. Like many older Chinese, he thinks that society has changed—and not for the better. He believes in old values and a strict social order. He is trying to teach you and your fellow students how to behave properly. You must respect those who are your superiors in society. You must set a good example for others.

How will these teachings affect your life?

The Zhou Dynasty

In the 1100s BC, the leaders of a people who came to be known as the Zhou (JOH) ruled over a kingdom in China. They joined with other nearby tribes and attacked and overthrew the Shang dynasty. The Zhou dynasty lasted longer than any other dynasty in Chinese history.

The Zhou Political System The Zhou kings claimed to possess the mandate of heaven, a principle similar to the European "divine right" of kings. European rulers believed they received the right to rule directly from God. The Zhou did not believe in one supreme being. They thought their right to rule came from the heavens as a whole. No one ruled without heaven's permission. In addition, Zhou rulers' power was not absolute. If a king was found to be bad, heaven would support another leader. This principle was explained thus:

> "Oh! Of old the former kings of Hsiâ [Xia] cultivated earnestly their virtue, and then there were no calamities from Heaven. The spirits of the hills and rivers likewise were all in tranquillity; and the birds and beasts, the fishes and tortoises, all enjoyed their existence according to their nature."
>
> —from "The Instructions of Î." *The Sacred Books of China: The Texts of Confucianism* in *The Sacred Books of the East,* translated by James Legge; edited by F. Max Mueller

Timeline: The Zhou Dynasty

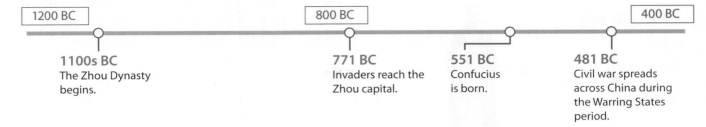

1200 BC | 800 BC | 400 BC

1100s BC
The Zhou Dynasty begins.

771 BC
Invaders reach the Zhou capital.

551 BC
Confucius is born.

481 BC
Civil war spreads across China during the Warring States period.

The Zhou came from an area west of the Shang kingdom. Early Zhou rulers used the mandate of heaven to justify their rebellion against the Shang. The Zhou believed that the Shang gave up the mandate of heaven when they did not rule in the way the Zhou thought was best. Later Zhou rulers expanded their territory to the northwest and the east. Zhou soldiers then moved south, eventually expanding their rule to the Chang Jiang.

The Zhou established a new political order. They granted land to others in return for loyalty, military support, and other services. The Zhou king was at the highest level. He granted plots of land to **lords**, or people of high rank. Lords paid taxes and provided soldiers as needed. **Peasants**, or farmers with small farms, were at the bottom of the order. Each peasant family received a small plot of land and had to farm additional land for the noble.

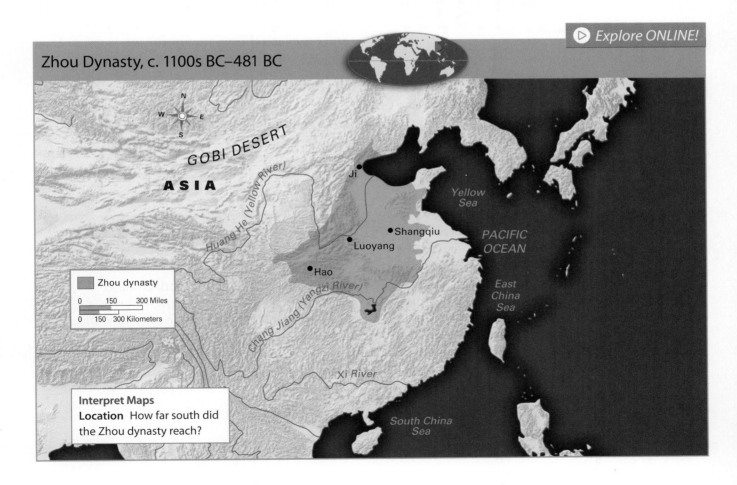

Explore ONLINE!

Zhou Dynasty, c. 1100s BC–481 BC

Interpret Maps
Location How far south did the Zhou dynasty reach?

Zhou Society

King
The king led the government and gave land to lords.

Lords and Warriors
Lords paid taxes to the king and provided warriors to protect his lands.

Peasants
Peasants farmed the nobles' land.

Academic Vocabulary
structure the way something is set up or organized

The Zhou system brought order to China. Ruling through lords helped the Zhou control distant areas and helped ensure loyalty to the king. Over time, however, the political order broke down. Lords passed their power to their sons, who were less loyal to the king. Local rulers gained power. They began to reject the authority of the Zhou kings.

The Decline of Zhou Power As the lords' loyalty to the Zhou king lessened, many refused to fight against invasions. In 771 BC, invaders reached the capital. According to legend, the king had been lighting warning fires to entertain a friend. Each time the fires were lit, the king's armies would rush to the capital gates to protect him. When the real attack came, the men thought the fires were just another joke, and no one came. The Zhou lost the battle, but the dynasty survived.

After this defeat the lords began to fight each other. By 481 BC, China had entered an era called the Warring States period, a time of many civil wars. Armies grew. Fighting became brutal and cruel as soldiers fought for territory, not honor.

Internal Problems The decline of the Zhou took place along with important changes in the Chinese family **structure**. For many centuries the family had been the foundation of life in China. Large families of several generations formed powerful groups. When these families broke apart, they lost their power. Close relatives became rivals.

Link to Economics

The Bronze and Iron Ages

China benefited from the development of technology such as bronze and iron. Early Chinese metal workers used available natural resources to form bronze goods. They created molds from local clay and then filled them with a mixture of copper and tin. Copper was used to make tools, decorative items, and other goods.

During the Warring States period, Chinese metalworking entered the Iron Age. Iron was a scarce and valuable metal in the ancient world. Many Chinese goods continued to use bronze even after Chinese metal workers began working with iron.

Analyze Information
What was copper used to make?

The Analects

The followers of Confucius placed their teacher's sayings together in a work called in Chinese the *Lun Yü* and in English *The Analects*. The word *analects* means "writings that have been collected."

Analyze Historical Sources
Summarize the qualities that Confucius valued in two or three sentences.

"(2.17) The Master said: 'Yu! Shall I teach you the meaning of knowledge? When you know a thing to recognise that you know it, and when you do not know that you do not know,— that is knowledge.'

(7.8) The Master said: 'I expound nothing to him who is not earnest, nor help out any one not anxious to express himself.'

(15.23) 'Is there any one word' asked Tzû Kung, 'which could be adopted as a lifelong rule of conduct?' The Master replied: 'Is not Sympathy the word? Do not do to others what you would not like yourself.'"

—Confucius, from *The Analects*

Reading Check
Analyze Effects
How did the Zhou's decline affect Chinese society?

Bonds of loyalty weakened even within small families, especially among the upper classes. Sons plotted against each other over inheritances. A wealthy father sometimes tried to maintain peace by dividing his land among his sons. But this created new problems. Each son could build up his wealth and then challenge his brothers. Some sons even killed their own fathers. During the Warring States period, China lacked a strong government to stop the power struggles within the ruling-class families. Chinese society fell into a period of disorder.

Confucius and Society

During the late Zhou period, thinkers came up with ideas about how to restore order to China. One such person, **Confucius** (kuhn-FYOO-shuhs), became the most influential teacher in Chinese history. Confucius is a Western form of the Chinese title of "Master Kong" or "Kongfuzi."

Confucius thought that China was overrun with rude and dishonest people. Upset by the disorder and people's lack of decency, Confucius said that the Chinese needed to return to **ethics**, or moral values. The ideas of Confucius are known as **Confucianism**.

Confucius wanted China to return to ideas and practices from a time when people knew their proper roles in society. These are basic guidelines that Confucius thought would restore family order and social harmony:

- Fathers should display high moral values to inspire their families.
- Children should respect and obey their parents.
- All family members should be loyal to each other.

Confucius's ideas about government were similar to his ideas about family:

- Moral leadership, not laws, brought order to China.
- A king should lead by example, inspiring good behavior in all of his subjects.
- The lower classes would learn from the examples of their superiors.

Confucius (551–479 BC)

Confucius, whose Chinese title is Kongfuzi, grew up in extreme poverty. Confucius was a dedicated student into his teenage years. Little is known about how he received his formal education, but he mastered many subjects, including music, mathematics, poetry, and history. He served in minor government positions, then he became a teacher. He never knew his teachings would transform Chinese life and thought.

Draw Conclusions
How do you think Confucius's government jobs helped shape his teachings?

Confucius expressed this idea when he told kings:

"Lead the people by means of government policies and regulate them through punishments, and they will be evasive and have no sense of shame. Lead them by means of virtue . . . and they will have a sense of shame and moreover have standards."

–Confucius, from *The Analects*

As Confucius traveled to many different regions, he earned the reputation of a respected teacher. He believed that when people behaved well and acted morally, they were simply carrying out what heaven expected of them. His ideas were passed down through his students and later compiled into a book called *The Analects*.

Explanations for the order of the universe became part of Confucian thought. In the *Book of Changes*, one of the five classic Confucian texts, the force behind all that exists is called taiji. Taiji is made up of two forces—the yin and the yang. Yin is associated with the passive, while yang is associated with the active. The yin and the yang must be in balance in the universe for harmony to exist.

Confucianism made its way into every aspect of life in China, including architecture, art, and stories. Traditional homes and sacred spaces such as temples were also designed according to Confucian ideology. A Chinese

Quick Facts

Main Ideas of Confucianism

- People should be respectful and loyal to their family members.
- Leaders should be kind and lead by example.
- Learning is a process that never ends.
- Heaven expects people to behave well and act morally.

home was built around a courtyard. Different areas of the home had varied levels of importance. A person's position in the family determined the rooms he or she could occupy.

Because Confucianism focuses on morality, family, society, and government, people often think of it as a philosophy or way of thinking. But it is much more. Confucianism is a unique teaching that is both philosophical and religious.

Over the centuries, Confucius's ideas about virtue, kindness, and learning became the dominant beliefs in China. Confucianism has been a guiding force in human behavior and religious understanding in China.

Reading Check
Make Inferences
What did Confucius believe about good behavior?

Daoism and Legalism

Other beliefs besides Confucianism influenced China during the Zhou period. Two in particular attracted many followers.

Daoism Daoism (DOW-ih-zum) takes its name from *Dao*, meaning "the way." **Daoism** stressed living in harmony with the Dao, the guiding force of all reality. In Daoist teachings, the Dao gave birth to the universe and all things in it. Daoism developed in part as a reaction to Confucianism. Daoists didn't agree with the idea that active, involved leaders brought social harmony. Instead, they wanted the government to stay out of people's lives.

Link to Today

Daoism Today

At the beginning of the 20th century, most followers of Daoism lived on the island of Taiwan. After 1960, however, Daoism experienced a rise in popularity and spread to countries around the world, including the United States. It is practiced by many different ethnicities, and what was once a Chinese traditional religion has been adapted to other people's own cultural practices.

Analyze Information
Where did most followers of Daoism live at the beginning of the 20th century?

Daoists believed that people should avoid interfering with nature or each other. They should be like water and simply let things flow in a natural way. For Daoists, the ideal ruler was a wise man who was in harmony with the Dao. He would govern so effortlessly that his people would not even know they were being governed.

Daoists taught that the universe is a balance of opposites: female and male, light and dark, low and high. In each case, opposing forces must be in harmony. A central figure in Daoist creation stories is that of Pan Gu, the legendary first man. He separated heaven and earth, and put the stars and planets in the universe. He then shaped Earth and its physical features.

While Confucianism focused its followers' attention on the human world, Daoists paid more attention to the natural world. Daoists regarded humans as just a part of nature, not better than any other thing. In time the Dao, as represented by nature, became so important to the Daoists that they worshipped it. Daoist temples are decorated with symbols reflecting common themes in Daoism.

Laozi (LOWD-zuh) was the most famous Daoist teacher. He taught that people should not try to gain wealth. He also thought that they should not seek power. Laozi is credited with writing the basic text of Daoism, *The Way and Its Power*. Later writers created many legends about Laozi's achievements.

Daoism spread throughout China. In later years, it also spread to other parts of Asia, including Korea and Japan. The followers of Daoism spread it during their travels on the trade routes throughout the region.

Legalism **Legalism**, the belief that people were bad by nature and needed to be controlled, contrasted with both Confucianism and Daoism. Unlike the other two beliefs, Legalism was a political philosophy without religious concerns. Instead, it dealt only with government and social control. Followers of Legalism disagreed with the moral preaching of Confucius. Legalists also rejected Daoism because it didn't stress respect for authority.

Legalists thought that society needed strict laws to keep people in line and that punishments should fit crimes. For example, they believed that citizens should be held responsible for each other's conduct. A guilty person's relatives and neighbors should also be punished. This way, everyone would obey the laws.

Unity and efficiency were also important to Legalists. They wanted appointed officials, not nobles, to run China. Legalists wanted the empire to continue to expand. Therefore, they urged the state to always be prepared for war.

BIOGRAPHY

Laozi (c. 500s or 400s BC)

Scholars have found little reliable information about Laozi's life. Some believe that his book on Daoism was actually the work of several different authors. Most ancient sources of information about Laozi are myths. For example, one legend states that when Laozi was born, he was already an old man. In Chinese *Laozi* can mean "Old Baby." Over the years, many Daoists have worshipped Laozi as a supernatural being.

Make Inferences
What do you think it meant to say Laozi was born "old"?

Han Fei Zi was the most well known of China's Legalist philosophers. He believed that an authority figure should set the laws and that subjects should follow those laws without question. He thought that people were unreliable and unable to run their own lives. Laws were put in place to prevent people from doing evil.

Confucianism, Daoism, and Legalism competed for followers. All three beliefs became popular, but the Legalists were the first to put their ideas into practice throughout China.

Summary and Preview When the Zhou dynasty crumbled, political and social chaos erupted. In response, the new teachings of Confucianism, Daoism, and Legalism emerged. In the next lesson, you will learn how the Qin dynasty applied the teachings of Legalism.

Reading Check
Contrast How did Daoism and Legalism differ in their theories about government?

Lesson 2 Assessment

Review Ideas, Terms, and People

1. **a. Identify** What is the mandate of heaven? How is it explained in the excerpt included in this lesson?

   b. Explain Describe the political order used by the Zhou kings to rule distant lands.

   c. Elaborate What happened when nobles began to reject the Zhou king's authority?

2. **a. Identify** Who was Confucius?

   b. Analyze Why did many of the teachings of Confucius focus on the family?

3. **a. Identify** Who was the most famous Daoist teacher?

   b. Summarize What were the main ideas of Daoism?

   c. Make Inferences What might be some disadvantages of Legalism?

   d. Explain Who was Han Fei Zi, and what did he believe?

   e. Identify Why did Daoism spread during ancient times?

Critical Thinking

4. **Organize Information** Draw a chart like the one here. Use it and your notes on the Zhou dynasty to list two main ideas about each set of beliefs. How are the three sets of beliefs different?

Confucianism	
Daoism	
Legalism	

The Qin Dynasty

The Big Idea

The Qin dynasty unified China with a strong government and a system of standardization.

Main Ideas

- The first Qin emperor created a strong but strict government.

- A unified China was created through Qin policies and achievements.

Key Terms and People

Shi Huangdi
Great Wall

If YOU were there . . .

You are a scholar living in China in about 210 BC. You have a large library of Chinese literature, poetry, and philosophy. The new emperor is a harsh ruler with no love for learning. He says you must burn all the books that disagree with his ideas. The idea horrifies you. But if you do not obey, the punishment may be severe.

Will you obey the order to burn your books? Why or why not?

The Qin Emperor's Strong Government

The Warring States period marked a time in China when several states battled each other for power. One state, the Qin (CHIN), built a strong army that defeated the armies of the rivaling states. Eventually, the Qin dynasty united the country under one government.

Shi Huangdi In 221 BC, the Qin king Ying Zheng succeeded in unifying China. He gave himself the title **Shi Huangdi** (SHEE hwahng-dee), which means "first emperor." Shi Huangdi followed Legalist political beliefs. He created a strong government with strict laws and harsh punishments. This was the beginning of the monarchy in China. A monarchy is a government led by a king or queen who inherits the throne by birth. An absolute monarch maintains law and order in the kingdom through total control over the government. Shi Huangdi ruled as an absolute monarch and had final say over all laws.

Shi Huangdi demanded that everyone follow his policies. He ordered the burning of all writings that did not agree with Legalism. The only other books that were saved dealt with farming, medicine, and predicting the future. Many scholars opposed the book burnings. The emperor responded to the opposition by burying 460 scholars alive.

Timeline: The Qin Dynasty

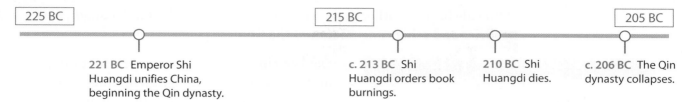

225 BC

221 BC Emperor Shi Huangdi unifies China, beginning the Qin dynasty.

215 BC

c. 213 BC Shi Huangdi orders book burnings.

210 BC Shi Huangdi dies.

205 BC

c. 206 BC The Qin dynasty collapses.

Shi Huangdi also used his armies to expand the empire. First, they occupied the lands around both of China's major rivers. Then his soldiers turned north and advanced almost to the Gobi Desert. To the south, they invaded more lands and advanced as far as the Xi River.

Shi Huangdi ensured that there would not be any future revolts in his new territories. When his soldiers conquered a city, he had them destroy its walls and take all the weapons.

China Under the Qin Shi Huangdi changed China's old political system. He claimed all the power and did not share it with the lords. He even took land away from them and forced thousands of nobles to move with their families to the capital so he could keep an eye on them. He also forced thousands of commoners to work on government building projects. Workers faced years of hardship, danger, and often, death.

To control China, Shi Huangdi divided it into districts, each with its own governor. Districts were subdivided into counties that were governed by appointed officials. This organization helped the emperor enforce his tax system. It also helped the Qin enforce a strict chain of command.

Reading Check
Summarize How did Shi Huangdi strengthen the government?

▶ Explore ONLINE!

Qin Dynasty, c. 221–206 BC

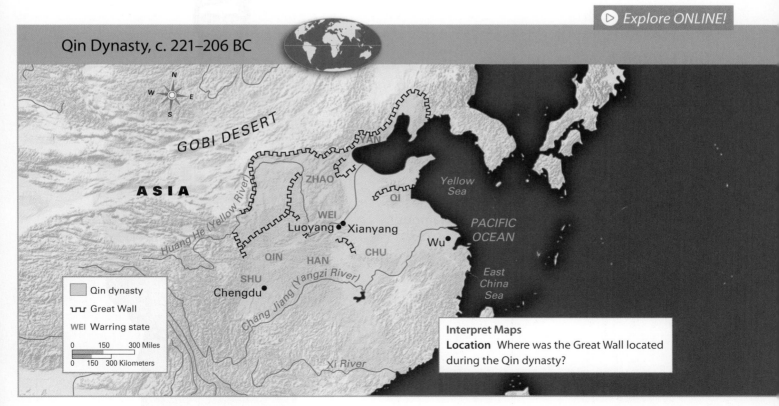

GOBI DESERT

ASIA

Huang He (Yellow River)

YAN

ZHAO

QI

Yellow Sea

WEI

Luoyang ● ● Xianyang

Wu ●

PACIFIC OCEAN

QIN HAN CHU

Chang Jiang (Yangzi River)

SHU

Chengdu ●

East China Sea

Xi River

Legend:
- Qin dynasty
- Great Wall
- **WEI** Warring state

0   150   300 Miles
0 150 300 Kilometers

Interpret Maps
Location Where was the Great Wall located during the Qin dynasty?

A Unified China

Qin rule brought other major changes to China. Under Shi Huangdi, new policies and achievements united the Chinese people.

Qin Policies As you read earlier, mountains and rivers divided China into distinct regions. Customs varied, and people in each area had their own money, writing styles, and laws. Shi Huangdi believed that all Chinese people should do things the same way, regardless of the distances and differences between them.

Early in his reign, the emperor set up a uniform system of law. Rules and punishments were to be the same in all parts of the empire. Shi Huangdi also standardized the written language. People everywhere were required to write using the same set of symbols. People from different regions could now communicate with each other in writing. This gave the Chinese a sense of shared culture and a common identity.

Next, the emperor set up a new money system. Standardized gold and copper coins became the currency used in all of China. Officials used accounting systems that kept track of agricultural resources and tax payments in order to fairly and efficiently manage resources and money. Weights and measures were also standardized. With all these changes and

——— BIOGRAPHY ———

Shi Huangdi (c. 259–210 BC)

Shi Huangdi built a new capital city at Xianyang, now called Xi'an (SHEE-AHN), in eastern China. Shi Huangdi didn't trust people. Several attempts were made on his life, and the emperor lived in fear of more attacks. He was constantly seeking new ways to protect himself and extend his life. By the time Shi Huangdi died, he didn't even trust his own advisors. Even in death, he surrounded himself with protectors: the famous terra-cotta army.

Draw Conclusions
Why do you think Shi Huangdi feared for his life?

the unified writing system, trade between different regions became much easier. The Qin government strictly enforced these new standards. Any citizen who disobeyed the laws would face severe punishment.

Qin Achievements Shi Huangdi believed that new, massive building projects would help to unify the country. Under his rule, the Chinese built a network of roads that connected the capital to every part of the empire. These roads made travel easier for everyone. Each of these new roads was the same width, 50 paces wide. This design helped the army move quickly and easily to put down revolts in distant areas. The roads also had a central lane that was sometimes reserved for the emperor. Shi Huangdi ordered that wheels on carts and wagons be the same width apart from side to side, so that the wheels would fit the width of the new roads.

China's water system was also improved. Workers built dams and canals, and used terracing to help farmers raise more crops and to control flooding. Like the new roads, the canals improved transportation throughout the country. Using the new canals and rivers together made it easier and faster to ship goods from north to south. In addition, the Qin built an irrigation system to make more good land for farming. Parts of that system are still in use today.

Shi Huangdi also wanted to protect the country from invasion. Nomads from the north were fierce warriors, and they were a real threat to China. Hoping to stop them from invading, the emperor built the **Great Wall**, a

The Great Wall has been added to and rebuilt many times since Shi Huangdi ruled China.

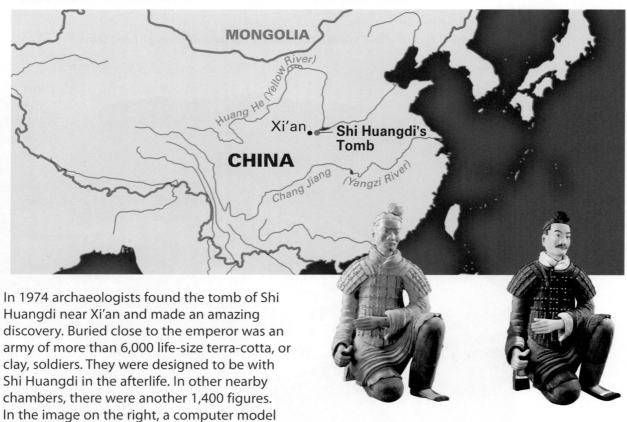

In 1974 archaeologists found the tomb of Shi Huangdi near Xi'an and made an amazing discovery. Buried close to the emperor was an army of more than 6,000 life-size terra-cotta, or clay, soldiers. They were designed to be with Shi Huangdi in the afterlife. In other nearby chambers, there were another 1,400 figures. In the image on the right, a computer model shows what a soldier may have looked like.

Analyze Visuals
Why do you think Shi Huangdi wanted his soldiers to be with him in the afterlife?

barrier across China's northern frontier. The first section of the wall had been built in the 600s BC to keep invading groups out of China. The Qin connected earlier pieces of the wall to form a long, unbroken structure. Building the wall required years of labor from hundreds of thousands of workers. Many of them died building the wall.

The Fall of the Qin Shi Huangdi's policies unified China. However, his policies also stirred resentment. Many peasants, scholars, and nobles hated his harsh ways.

Still, Shi Huangdi was powerful enough to hold the country together. When he died in 210 BC China was unified, but that didn't last. Within a few years, the government began to fall apart.

Rebel forces formed across the country. Each claimed to have received the mandate of heaven to replace the emperor. One of these groups attacked the Qin capital, and the new emperor surrendered. The palace was burned to the ground. Qin authority had disappeared. With no central government, the country fell into civil war.

Summary and Preview Qin emperor Shi Huangdi's policies and achievements unified China, but his harsh rule led to resentment. After his death, the dynasty fell apart. In the next lesson, you will learn about the Han dynasty, which came to power after the end of the Qin.

Reading Check
Summarize What massive building projects did Shi Huangdi order to unify China?

Lesson 3 Assessment

Review Ideas, Terms, and People

1. **a. Identify** What does the title Shi Huangdi mean?
   b. Explain After unifying China, why did Shi Huangdi divide the country into military districts?
   c. Contrast Which of the following acts do you think best showed how powerful Shi Huangdi was—burning books, forcing nobles to move, or forcing commoners to work on government projects? Explain your answer.

2. **a. Recall** Why was the Great Wall built?
   b. Summarize What actions did Shi Huangdi take to unify China and standardize things within the empire?
   c. Evaluate In your opinion, was Shi Huangdi a good ruler? Explain your answer.

Critical Thinking

3. **Evaluate** Using your notes and a diagram like this one, rank the effectiveness of the emperor's achievements and policies in unifying China.

Most important		Least important
1.	2.	3.

The Han Dynasty

The Big Idea

The period of the Han dynasty brought new ideas about government, the arts, learning, and religion.

Main Ideas

- The Han dynasty government was based on the ideas of Confucius.

- Family life was supported and strengthened in Han China.

- The Han made many achievements in art, literature, and learning.

- Buddhism spread to China along the trade routes from other lands.

Key Terms

sundial
seismograph
acupuncture
silk
diffusion

If YOU were there . . .

You are a young Chinese student from a poor family. Your family has worked hard to give you a good education so that you can get a government job and have a great future. Your friends laugh at you. They say that only boys from wealthy families win the good jobs. They think it is better to join the army.

Will you take the exam or join the army? Why?

Han Dynasty Government

When the Qin dynasty collapsed in 207 BC, different groups battled for power. After years of fighting, an army led by Liu Bang (lee-oo bang) won control. Liu Bang became the first emperor of the Han dynasty. This dynasty lasted for more than 400 years. The Han dynasty was a classical civilization. A classical civilization is one marked by great achievements.

The Rise of a New Dynasty Liu Bang, a peasant, was able to become emperor in large part because of the Chinese belief in the mandate of heaven. He was the first common person to become emperor. He earned people's loyalty and trust. In addition, he was well liked by both soldiers and peasants, which helped him to maintain control.

Liu Bang's rule was different from the strict Legalism of the Qin. He wanted to free people from harsh government policies. He lowered taxes for farmers and made punishments less severe. He gave large blocks of land to his supporters.

In addition to setting new policies, Liu Bang changed the way government worked. He set up a government structure that built on the foundation begun by the Qin. He also relied on educated officials to help him rule.

Wudi Creates a New Government In 140 BC Emperor Wudi (woo-dee) took the throne. He wanted to create a stronger central government. To do that, he took land from the lords, raised taxes, and placed the supply of grain under the control of the government.

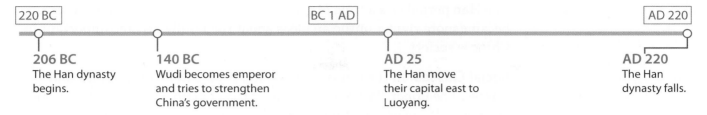

220 BC

BC 1 AD

AD 220

206 BC
The Han dynasty
begins.

140 BC
Wudi becomes emperor
and tries to strengthen
China's government.

AD 25
The Han move
their capital east to
Luoyang.

AD 220
The Han
dynasty falls.

Reading Check
Make Inferences
How was the Han
government based
on the ideas of
Confucius?

Under Wudi, Confucianism became China's official government philosophy. Government officials were expected to practice Confucianism. Wudi even began a university to teach Confucian ideas.

If a person passed an exam on Confucian teachings, he could get a good position in the government. However, not just anyone could take the test. The exams were open only to people who had been recommended for government service already. As a result, wealthy or influential families continued to control the government.

▶ Explore ONLINE!

Han Dynasty, c. 206 BC–AD 220

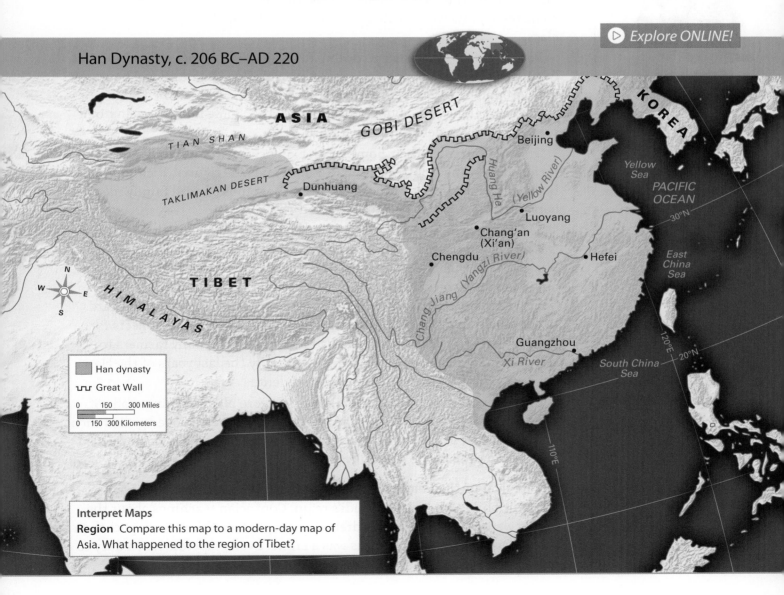

Interpret Maps

Region Compare this map to a modern-day map of Asia. What happened to the region of Tibet?

Family Life

The Han period was a time of great social change in China. Class structure became more rigid. Confucian ideas about the family became important in Chinese society.

Social Classes In the Confucian system, people were divided into four classes. The upper class was made up of the emperor, his court, and scholars who held government positions. The second class, the largest, was made up of the peasants. Next were artisans who produced items for daily life and some luxury goods. Merchants occupied the lowest class because they did not produce anything. They only bought and sold what others made. The military was not an official class in the Confucian system. Still, joining the army offered men a chance to rise in social status because the military was considered part of the government.

Lives of Rich and Poor The classes only divided people into social rank. They did not indicate wealth or power. For instance, even though peasants made up the second highest class, they were poor. On the other hand, some merchants were wealthy and powerful despite being in the lowest class.

People's lifestyles varied according to wealth. The emperor and his court lived in a large palace. Less important officials lived in multilevel houses built around courtyards. Many of these wealthy families owned large estates and employed laborers to work the land. Some families even hired private armies to defend their estates.

This Han artifact is an oil lamp held by a servant

The wealthy filled their homes with expensive decorations. These included paintings, pottery, bronze lamps, and jade figures. Rich families hired musicians for entertainment. Even the tombs of dead family members were filled with beautiful, expensive objects.

Most people in the Han dynasty, however, didn't live like the wealthy. Nearly 60 million people lived in China during the Han dynasty, and about 90 percent of them were peasants who lived in the countryside. Peasants put in long, tiring days working the land. Whether it was in the millet fields of the north or in the rice paddies of the south, the work was hard. In the winter, peasants were also forced to work on building projects for the government. Heavy taxes and bad weather forced many farmers to sell their land and work for rich landowners. By the last years of the Han dynasty, only a few farmers were independent.

Chinese peasants lived simple lives. They wore plain clothing made of fiber from a native plant. The main foods they ate were cooked grains such as barley. Most peasants lived in small villages. Their small, wood-framed houses had walls made of mud or stamped earth.

The Revival of the Family Because Confucianism was the official government philosophy during Wudi's reign, Confucian teachings about the family were also honored. Children were taught from birth to respect their elders. Disobeying one's parents was a crime. Even emperors had a duty to respect their parents.

Confucius had taught that the father was the head of the family. Within the family, the father had absolute power. The Han taught that it was a woman's duty to obey her husband, and children had to obey their father.

Han officials believed that if a family was strong and obeyed the father, then it would obey the emperor, too. Since the Han stressed strong family ties and respect for elders, some men even gained government jobs based on the respect they showed their parents.

Children were encouraged to serve their parents. They were also expected to honor dead parents with ceremonies and offerings. All family members were expected to care for family burial sites.

Chinese parents valued boys more highly than girls. This was because sons carried on the family line and took care of their parents when they were old. On the other hand, daughters became part of their husband's family. According to a Chinese proverb, "Raising daughters is like raising children for another family." Some women, however, still gained power. They could actually influence their sons' families. An older widow could even become the head of the family.

Reading Check
Analyze Causes
Why did the family take on such importance during the Han dynasty?

The Importance of Family

Honoring one's family was an important duty in Han China. In this painting, people give thanks before their family shrine. Only the men participate. The women watch from inside the house.

Han Achievements

Han rule was a time of great accomplishments. Art and literature thrived, and inventors developed many useful devices. With new inventions, productivity increased, and the empire prospered.

Art and Literature The Chinese of the Han period produced many works of art. They became experts at figure painting—a style of painting that includes portraits of people. Portraits often showed religious figures and Confucian scholars. Han artists also painted realistic scenes from everyday

Han Advancements

During the Han dynasty, the Chinese made many advances in art and learning. Some of these advances are shown here.

Science

This is a model and photograph of an ancient Chinese seismograph. When an earthquake struck, a lever inside caused a ball to drop from a dragon's mouth into a toad's mouth, indicating the direction from which the earthquake had come.

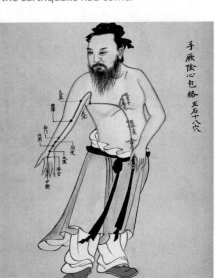

Medicine

Han doctors studied the human body and used acupuncture to heal people.

Art

This bronze horse is just one example of the beautiful objects made by Chinese artisans.

Analyze Visuals

How do these objects show the range of accomplishments in Han China?

life. Their creations covered the walls of palaces and tombs. Ceramic art made for placement in the tombs of the dead was popular during this period. Themes in art generally focused on farms, architecture, and the physical characteristics of the land.

In literature, Han China is known for its poetry. Poets developed new styles of verse, including the *fu* style, which was the most popular. *Fu* poets combined prose and poetry to create long works of literature. Another style, called *shi*, featured short lines of verse that could be sung. Han rulers hired poets known for the beauty of their verse. One famous set of works was written by Lady Wenji.

> "When I was born there was no trouble yet,
> After I was born the house of Han tottered.
> Heaven was not kind, it sent down turmoil;
> Earth was not kind, it made me come upon this era."
>
> By Cai Yan (Lady Wenji), *Eighteen Songs of a Nomad Flute*

Han writers also produced important works of history. One historian by the name of Sima Qian wrote a complete history of all the dynasties through the early Han. His format and style became the model for later historical writings.

Inventions and Advances The Han Chinese invented one item that we use every day—paper. They made it by grinding plant fibers, such as mulberry bark and hemp, into a paste. Then they let it dry in sheets. Chinese scholars produced "books" by pasting several pieces of paper together into a long sheet. Then they rolled the sheet into a scroll.

The Han also made other **innovations** in science. These included the sundial and the seismograph. A **sundial** uses the position of shadows cast by the sun to tell the time of day. The sundial was an early type of clock. A **seismograph** measures the strength of an earthquake. Han emperors were very interested in knowing about the movements of the earth. They believed that earthquakes were signs of future evil events.

Zhang Heng, the inventor of the seismograph, was a respected astronomer, mathematician, engineer, and painter during the Eastern Han Dynasty. He believed that the sun, moon, and earth moved at different rates. He used this information to explain lunar eclipses. In mathematics, he estimated the value of pi and developed the first odometer to measure a Chinese mile.

Another Han innovation, **acupuncture** (AK-yoo-punk-cher), improved medicine. Acupuncture is the practice of inserting fine needles through the skin at specific points to cure disease or relieve pain. Many Han inventions in science and medicine are still used today.

Farming and Manufacturing Many advances in manufacturing took place during the Han dynasty, and productivity increased. These changes paved the way for China to make contact with people of other cultures.

Academic Vocabulary
innovation a new idea, method, or device

By the Han period, the Chinese had become master ironworkers. They manufactured iron swords and armor. These developments made the army more powerful.

Farmers also gained from advances in iron. The iron plow and the wheelbarrow, a single-wheeled cart, increased farm output. With a wheelbarrow, a farmer could haul more than 300 pounds all by himself. With an iron plow, a farmer could till more land and raise more food.

Another item that increased in production during the Han dynasty was **silk**, a soft, light, highly valued fabric. For centuries, Chinese women had known the complicated methods needed to raise silkworms, unwind the silk threads of their cocoons, and then prepare the threads for dyeing and weaving. The Chinese were determined to keep their **procedure** for making silk a secret. Revealing these secrets was punishable by death.

During the Han period, weavers used foot-powered looms to weave silk threads into beautiful fabric. Garments made from this silk were very expensive.

Academic Vocabulary
procedure the way a task is accomplished

Reading Check
Synthesize What advances did the Chinese make during the Han period?

Silk Production

The technique for making silk was a well-kept secret in ancient China because silk was a valuable trade good in distant lands. Workers made silk from the cocoons of silkworms, just as they do today.

Buddhism Comes to China

When the Chinese people came into contact with other civilizations, they exchanged ideas along with goods. Among these ideas was a new religion. In the first century AD, Buddhism spread from India to China along trade routes.

Arrival of a New Religion Over time, the Han government became less stable. People ignored laws, and violence was common. As revolts flared up, millions of peasants went hungry. Life became violent and uncertain. Many Chinese looked to Daoism or Confucianism to find out why they had to suffer so much. They were unable to find helpful answers.

Buddhism seemed to provide more hope than the traditional Chinese beliefs did. It offered rebirth and relief from suffering, which appealed to the Chinese.

Impact on China At first, Indian Buddhists had trouble explaining their religion to the Chinese. Then they used ideas found in Daoism to help describe Buddhist beliefs. Many people grew curious about Buddhism.

Before long, Buddhism caught on in China with both the poor and the upper classes. By AD 200, Buddhist altars stood in the emperor's palace.

This giant Buddha statue in China is among the largest in the world. It was carved into a hillside and looks down over the meeting place of three rivers.

Buddhism's introduction to China is an example of **diffusion**, the spread of ideas, goods, and technology from one culture to another. Elements of Chinese culture changed in response to the new faith. For example, scholars translated Buddhist texts into Chinese. Many Chinese became Buddhist monks and nuns. Artists carved towering statues of Buddha into mountain walls.

Reading Check
Find Main Ideas
How did Chinese people learn of Buddhism?

Summary and Preview Han rulers moved away from Legalism and based their government on Confucianism. This strengthened family bonds in Han China. In addition, art and innovations thrived under Han rule. A new religion, Buddhism, arrived in China through trade. In the next lesson, you will learn about China's contact beyond its borders.

Lesson 4 Assessment

Review Ideas, Terms, and People

1. **a. Identify** On whose teachings was Han government based?

   b. Summarize How did Emperor Wudi create a strong central government?

   c. Evaluate Is an exam system best for filling government jobs? Explain.

2. **a. Describe** What was the son's role in the family?

   b. Contrast How did conditions for the wealthy differ from those of peasants?

3. **a. Identify** What device did the Chinese invent to measure earthquakes?

   b. Describe What was Zhang Heng's role in the advances made during the Han dynasty?

   c. Identify Who was Lady Wenji?

4. **Draw Conclusions** Why did people in China begin to grow curious about Buddhism?

Critical Thinking

5. **Analyze** Use your notes to complete this diagram about how Confucianism influenced Han government and family.

Government ← Confucianism → Family

Literature in History

Literature of Ancient China

Word Help

intervals periods of time

dispatched sent

envoy representative

❶ Henan (HUH-NAHN) is a region of eastern China. It is a productive agricultural region.

❷ The Xiongnu were a tribe of nomads. They lived in the north and often raided towns near China's border.

❸ *Why do you think the emperor invites Bu Shi to work for the government?*

About the Reading The *Shiji*, also called the Records of the Grand Historian, is a history that describes more than 2,000 years of Chinese culture. The author, Sima Qian (soo-MAH chee-EN), held the title Grand Historian under the Han emperor Wudi. He spent 18 years of his life writing the *Shiji*. His hard work paid off, and his history was well received. In fact, the *Shiji* was so respected that it served as the model for every later official history of China. This passage describes a man named Bu Shi, who attracted the emperor's attention through his generosity and good deeds. Eventually, the emperor invited him to live in the imperial palace.

As You Read Ask yourself why Sima Qian included Bu Shi in his history.

From *The Shiji*
by Sima Qian, translated by Burton Watson

Bu Shi was a native of Henan, where his family made a living by farming and animal raising. ❶ When his parents died, Bu Shi left home, handing over the house, the lands, and all the family wealth to his younger brother, who by this time was full grown. For his own share, he took only a hundred or so of the sheep they had been raising, which he led off into the mountains to pasture. In the course of ten years or so, Bu Shi's sheep had increased to over a thousand and he had bought his own house and fields. His younger brother in the meantime had failed completely in the management of the farm, but Bu Shi promptly handed over to him a share of his own wealth. This happened several times. Just at that time the Han was sending its generals at frequent intervals to attack the Xiongnu. ❷ Bu Shi journeyed to the capital and submitted a letter to the throne, offering to turn over half of his wealth to the district officials to help in the defense of the border. The emperor dispatched an envoy to ask if Bu Shi wanted a post in the government. ❸

"From the time I was a child," Bu Shi replied, "I have been an animal raiser. I have had no experience in government and would certainly not want such a position." . . .

Word Help

objective goal
chancellor high official
accord agreement
eccentric someone who acts strangely
populace people
tutor private teacher

❹ The Chinese people believed that their emperor was the "Son of Heaven." They thought he received his power from heavenly ancestors.

❺ The "latter" means the one mentioned last. In this case, the latter is the chancellor.

❻ *What is Bu Shi's attitude toward his wealth? How is it different from the attitude of the rich families?*

"If that is the case," said the envoy, "then what is your objective in making this offer?"

Bu Shi replied, "The Son of Heaven has set out to punish the Xiongnu. ❹ In my humble opinion, every worthy man should be willing to fight to the death to defend the borders, and every person with wealth ought to contribute to the expense. . . ."

The emperor discussed the matter with the chancellor, but the latter said, "The proposal is simply not in accord with human nature! ❺ Such eccentric people are of no use in guiding the populace, but only throw the laws into confusion. I beg Your Majesty not to accept his offer!"

For this reason the emperor put off answering Bu Shi for a long time, and finally after several years had passed, turned down the offer, whereupon Bu Shi went back to his fields and pastures. . . .

The following year a number of poor people were transferred to other regions. . . . At this point Bu Shi took two hundred thousand cash of his own and turned the sum over to the governor of Henan to assist the people who were emigrating to other regions. . . . At this time the rich families were all scrambling to hide their wealth; only Bu Shi, unlike the others, had offered to contribute to the expenses of the government. ❻ The emperor decided that Bu Shi was really a man of exceptional worth after all. . . . Because of his simple, unspoiled ways and his deep loyalty, the emperor finally appointed him grand tutor to his son Liu Hong, the king of Qi.

In this painting from the 1600s, government officials deliver a letter.

Connect Literature to History

1. **Draw Conclusions** Like many Chinese historians, Sima Qian wanted to use history to teach lessons. What lessons could the story of Bu Shi be used to teach?

2. **Analyze** The Emperor Wudi based his government on the teachings of Confucius. What elements of Confucianism can you see in this story?

The Silk Road

If YOU were there . . .

You are a trader traveling on your first trip along the Silk Road to China. The trip will be hard, through mountains, deserts, and terrible weather. You expect to make a profit from silk and are curious about China.

What do you expect to find in China?

Expansion of Trade

Chinese goods, especially silk and fine pottery, became highly valued by people in other lands. During the Han period, the value of these goods helped increase trade.

Silk Increases Trade Trade increased partly because the Han developed a powerful army that pushed the borders of the kingdom into Central Asia, Vietnam, and Korea. The army brought Chinese culture to less-developed societies. It stabilized the region, making the transport of goods over the roads safer. Trade increased when leaders in conquered lands told the Han generals that people who lived still farther west wanted silk. Emperor Wudi wanted strong Central Asian horses for his army. China's leaders saw that they could make a profit by bringing silk to Central Asia and trading the cloth for the horses. The Central Asian peoples then took the silk west and traded it for other products.

Cities Develop in Western China In 139 BC, Emperor Wudi sent one of his generals, Zhang Qian, to western lands on a diplomatic expedition to establish alliances against an enemy group. Zhang Qian was imprisoned by the enemy. He returned 13 years later with reports of great wealth and large horses in Central Asia. The emperor decided to send an army to the west to conquer new lands. As the empire grew, trade routes to the west developed. The Chinese built military bases and extended the Great Wall to protect these trade routes. Trading posts grew up along the trade routes. Farming settlements also developed with support from the government. As more people settled the region, cities developed in western China.

Reading Check
Summarize
Why did Chinese trade expand under Han rule?

Trade Along the Silk Road

Traders used a series of overland routes to take Chinese goods to distant buyers. The most famous trade route was known as the **Silk Road**. This 4,000-mile-long network of routes stretched westward from China across Asia's deserts and mountain ranges, through the Middle East, until it reached the Mediterranean Sea. By about 100 BC, an active trade had developed between China and Southwest Asia along Silk Road routes. By AD 100, the Silk Road connected Han China in the east with the Roman Empire in the west.

Goods Traded Chinese traders did not travel the entire Silk Road. Most merchants traveled only a small part of the route, selling their goods along the way. Upon reaching Central Asia, traders sold their goods to other local traders who took them the rest of the way.

Traveling the Silk Road was difficult. Groups of men and camels loaded down with goods traveled the Silk Road together for protection. Armed guards protected traders from bandits who stole cargo and water, a precious necessity. Traders also faced blizzards, desert heat, and sandstorms.

Named after the most famous item transported along it, the Silk Road was worth its many risks. Silk was so popular in Rome, for example, that China grew wealthy from that trade relationship alone. But many other

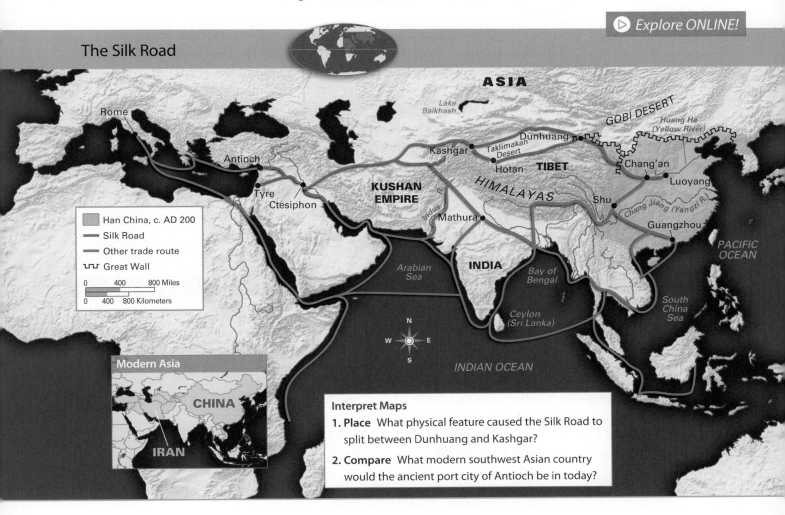

▷ Explore ONLINE!

The Silk Road

Interpret Maps

1. **Place** What physical feature caused the Silk Road to split between Dunhuang and Kashgar?

2. **Compare** What modern southwest Asian country would the ancient port city of Antioch be in today?

Cities grew along the Silk Road at secure places where the military protected traders and travelers. These ruins at Loulan in western China are evidence of a city that thrived during the Han period.

products were also traded on the routes. Spices, tools, artwork, produce, gems, precious metals, horses, and animal hides were some of the goods exchanged by traders.

Exchange of Knowledge and Technology The exchange of goods along the Silk Road helped establish a wider world economy, as goods from Europe and Africa made their way to China, and Chinese goods made their way west. Perhaps more significant, though, was the effect the Silk Road had on the exchange of knowledge and inventions. As people traveled the routes, they had to learn new languages to communicate. People from different places exchanged ideas about the arts and science.

Advanced technologies also spread across Asia by way of the Silk Road. For example, papermaking, developed by the Chinese, spread to Europe through trade. Traders also passed on the knowledge of how to irrigate farmlands.

Religion also spread along the Silk Road and other trade routes. Buddhism came from India to China by way of the new trade routes in Central Asia. Buddhist scriptures, artwork, and priests first entered China during the Han Dynasty by way of the Silk Road.

During the Han period, few foreigners ventured into China. But the trade that started with the establishment of the Silk Road brought their ideas and technology to China. In the coming centuries, the growing international trade would continue to bring merchants and others to this great Asian civilization.

Reading Check
Find Main Ideas
What was the Silk Road?

Summary Trade led to the exchange of goods and ideas between China and other regions during the years of the Han Dynasty.

Lesson 5 Assessment

Review Ideas, Terms, and People

1. **a. Identify** Which Han emperor expanded trade to the western regions of China?

   b. Summarize How did the expansion of trade affect the growth of cities ?

2. **a. Identify** Where did the Silk Road begin and end?

   b. Make Inferences How do you know silk was a valuable trade good?

   c. Identify What technologies spread along the Silk Road?

Critical Thinking

3. **Categorize** Use the chart to identify goods and ideas exchanged along the Silk Road. How did Chinese trade affect other regions ?

Into China ← Trade Along the Silk Road → Out of China

Social Studies Skills

Conduct Internet Research

Define the Skill

The Internet is a huge network of computers that are linked together. You can connect to this network from a personal computer or from a computer at a public library or school. Once connected, you can go to places called *websites*. Websites consist of one or more web pages. Each page contains information you can view on the computer screen.

Governments, businesses, individuals, and many different types of organizations such as universities, news organizations, and libraries have websites. Most library websites allow users to search their catalogs electronically. Many libraries also have databases on their websites. A *database* is a large collection of related information organized by topic.

The Internet can be a very good reference source. It allows you to gather information on almost any topic without ever having to leave your chair. However, finding the information you need can sometimes be difficult. Having the skill to use the Internet efficiently increases its usefulness.

Learn the Skill

There are millions of websites on the Internet. This can make it hard to locate specific information. The following steps will help you conduct research on the Internet.

1. **Use a search engine** A *search engine* is a website that searches other sites. Type a word or phrase related to your topic into the search engine. It will list web pages that might contain information on your topic. Clicking on an entry in this list will bring that page to your screen.

2. **Study the web page.** Read the information to see if it is useful. You can print the page on the computer's printer or take notes. If you take notes, be sure to include the page's *URL*. This is its location or "address" on the Internet. You need this as the source of the information.

3. **Use hyperlinks.** Many web pages have connections, called *hyperlinks,* to related information on the site or on other websites. Clicking on these links will take you to those pages. You can follow their links to even more pages, collecting information as you go.

4. **Return to your results list.** If the information or hyperlinks on a web page are not useful, return to the list of pages that your search engine produced and repeat the process.

The Internet is a useful tool. But remember that information on the Internet is no different from printed resources. It must be evaluated with the same care and critical thinking as other resources.

Practice the Skill

Answer the following questions to apply the guidelines to Internet research on ancient China.

1. How would you begin if you wanted information about the Qin dynasty from the Internet?

2. What words might you type into a search engine to find information about Confucianism?

3. Use a school computer to research the Great Wall of China. What kinds of pages did your search produce? Evaluate the usefulness of each type.

The Silk Road

The Silk Road was a long trade route that stretched across the heart of Asia. Along this route, an active trade developed between China and Southwest Asia by about 100 BC. By AD 100, the Silk Road connected Han China in the east with the Roman Empire in the west.

The main goods traded along the Silk Road were luxury goods—ones that were small, light, and expensive. These included silk, spices, and gold. Because such goods were small and valuable, merchants could carry them long distances and still sell them for a large profit. As a result, people in both the east and the west were able to buy luxury goods that were unavailable at home.

GAUL

SPAIN

EUROPE

Rome

ROMAN EMPIRE

Carthage

Black Sea

Byzantium

Asia Minor

GREECE

Mediterranean Sea

Antioch

Aral Sea

Caspian Sea

Merv

Ecbatana

Ctesiphon

Babylon

PERSIA

Persepolis

K

AFRICA

Alexandria

Petra

Aden

Goods from the West Roman merchants like this man grew rich from Silk Road trade. Merchants in the west traded goods like those you see here—wool, amber, and gold.

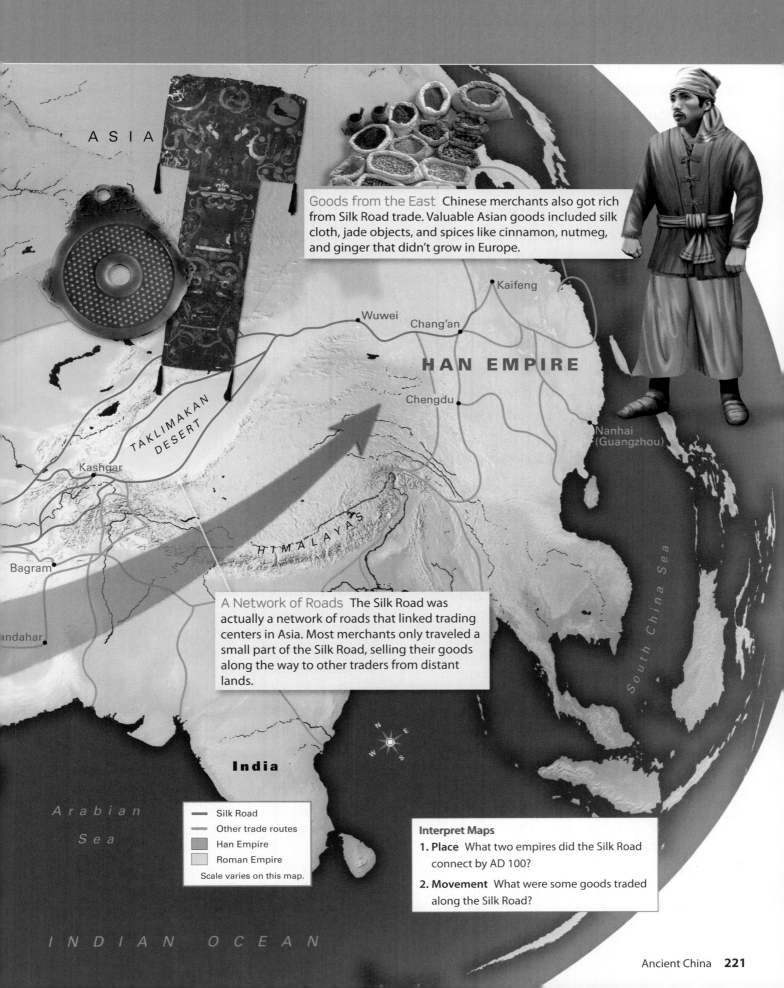

ASIA

Goods from the East Chinese merchants also got rich from Silk Road trade. Valuable Asian goods included silk cloth, jade objects, and spices like cinnamon, nutmeg, and ginger that didn't grow in Europe.

Kaifeng

Wuwei

Chang'an

HAN EMPIRE

Chengdu

Nanhai
(Guangzhou)

TAKLIMAKAN
DESERT

Kashgar

HIMALAYAS

Bagram

South China Sea

A Network of Roads The Silk Road was actually a network of roads that linked trading centers in Asia. Most merchants only traveled a small part of the Silk Road, selling their goods along the way to other traders from distant lands.

andahar

India

Arabian Sea

N
W   E
S

—	Silk Road
—	Other trade routes
▮	Han Empire
▯	Roman Empire

Scale varies on this map.

Interpret Maps

1. **Place** What two empires did the Silk Road connect by AD 100?

2. **Movement** What were some goods traded along the Silk Road?

INDIAN OCEAN

Ancient China **221**

Module 6 Assessment

Review Vocabulary, Terms, and People

Match the "I" statement with the person or thing that might have made the statement. Not all of the choices will be used.

1. "I stressed the importance of living in harmony with nature."
2. "I took a name that means 'first emperor.'"
3. "I stressed that people needed to be controlled with strict laws."
4. "I am a beautiful, hard gemstone that the Chinese made into many objects."
5. "I was built to keep invaders from attacking China."
6. "I can measure the strength of an earthquake."
7. "I am a person of high rank."
8. "I am a new idea, method, or device."
9. "I emphasized the importance of moral values and respect for the family."
10. "I am at the lowest level of Shang society."

a. jade
b. innovation
c. lord
d. oracle
e. slave
f. Confucius
g. Daoism
h. Shi Huangdi
i. seismograph
j. wheelbarrow
k. Great Wall
l. Legalism

Comprehension and Critical Thinking

Lesson 1

11. a. **Identify** In what region did the Shang dynasty develop?
    b. **Analyze** How did China's geography contribute to the country's isolation?
    c. **Evaluate** Considering the evidence, do you think the Xia dynasty was really China's first dynasty or a myth? Explain your answer.
    d. **Summarize** What typically contributed to the growth and development of ancient civilizations? What frequently caused their decline?

Lesson 2

12. a. **Identify** Which Chinese philosophy supported by Han Fei Zi encouraged strict laws and severe punishments to keep order?
    b. **Analyze** How would Confucianism benefit Chinese emperors?
    c. **Evaluate** Would you be happier under a government influenced by Legalism or by Daoism? In which type of government would there be more order? Explain your answers.
    d. **Summarize** How was the traditional practice of Daoism affected by its spread to other countries?

Lesson 3

13. a. **Describe** What were the main reasons for the fall of the Qin dynasty?
    b. **Make Inferences** Why did Shi Huangdi's armies destroy city walls and take weapons from people they conquered?
    c. **Evaluate** Shi Huangdi was a powerful ruler. Was his rule good or bad for China? Why?
    d. **Predict** Why might ancient peoples have used the cycles of the sun and moon as the basis for their calendars?

Module 6 Assessment, continued

Lesson 4

14. **a. Identify** During the Han dynasty, who belonged to the first and second social groups?

    b. Analyze What was the purpose of the exam system during Wudi's rule?

    c. Elaborate What inventions show that the Chinese studied nature?

    d. Identify Who was Zhang Heng, and what important invention did he develop?

    e. Explain Why is the Han dynasty considered a classical civilization? Give examples.

    f. Identify In what areas of manufacturing did the Han become well known?

Lesson 5

15. **a. Identify** What factors led to the growth of trade during the Han dynasty?

    b. Draw Conclusions Who do you think wore silk garments in China?

    c. Predict What might have happened if the Chinese had told foreign visitors how to make silk?

    d. Explain How did Silk Road trade affect the economies of the regions of the world involved in it?

Reading Skills

Summarize Historical Texts *Use the Reading Skills taught in this module to complete the activity below.*

16. Choose a subsection from the module. For each paragraph within that subsection, write a sentence that summarizes the paragraph's main idea. Continue with the other subsections to create a study guide.

Review Themes

17. **Politics** Why might historians differ in their views of Shi Huangdi's success as a ruler?

18. **Society and Culture** How did Confucianism affect people's roles in their family, in government, and in society?

19. **Society and Culture** Which of the major achievements of the ancient river valley civilizations do you think had the most enduring legacy? Justify your response using facts.

20. **Society and Culture** How were ancient Chinese civilizations similar to those in ancient Persia?

Social Studies Skills

Conduct Internet Research *Use the Social Studies Skill taught in this module to complete the activity below.*

21. Find a topic in the module about which you would like to know more. Use the Internet to explore your topic. Compare the sources you find to determine which seem most complete and reliable. Write a short paragraph about your results.

Focus On Writing

22. **Give an Oral Presentation** Choose a person or event, and identify why your choice is important to Chinese history. Write a brief description of what the person did or what happened during the event. Then summarize why your person or event is important to Chinese history. Give an oral presentation on your person to your class, using vivid language to create pictures in your listeners' minds. Also, use a clear but lively tone of voice.

China and the Great Wall

Today, the Great Wall of China is an impressive symbol of the Asian giant's power, genius, and endurance. It wasn't always so. For much of its history, the Chinese people saw the Great Wall as a symbol of cruelty and oppression. This is just one way in which the wall differs from what we think we know. In contrast to popular notions, the wall that draws tourists to Beijing by the millions was not built 2,000 years ago. Nor is the Great Wall a single wall. Instead, it was patched together from walls built over many centuries. And for all its grandeur, the wall failed to keep China safe from invasion.

Explore facts and fictions about the Great Wall online. You can find more information, video clips, primary sources, and activities through your online textbook.

The Great Wall of China

Watch the video to learn the history and significance of the magnificent, mysterious walls that snake across northern China.

A Land of Walls Within Walls

Watch the video to learn how the Great Wall fits within the ancient Chinese tradition of wall-building.

The Human Costs of Building

Watch the video to learn about the miseries that awaited the men who built the wall.

Twentieth-Century China

Watch the video to examine the role that the wall has played in modern Chinese history.

Module 7

The Hebrews and Judaism

Essential Question

How do the beliefs and practices of Judaism connect the ancient and modern worlds?

About the Photo: Hundreds of people pray at the Western Wall, part of the Temple complex, the holiest site in the world of Judaism. The wall was built around 19 BC.

▶ *Explore ONLINE!*

VIDEOS, including...
- Moses at Mount Sinai
- Exile of Jews
- The Dead Sea Scrolls
- The Festival of Lights
- Rosh Hashanah

☑ Document-Based Investigations

☑ Graphic Organizers

☑ Interactive Games

☑ Image with Hotspots: King Solomon's Temple

☑ Image Carousel: The Dead Sea Scrolls

☑ Interactive Maps: Jewish Migration After AD 70

In this module you will study the history and culture of the Jewish people.

What You Will Learn...

Lesson 1: The Early Hebrews 228
The Big Idea Originally desert nomads, the Israelites, descendants of the Hebrews, established a great kingdom.
Lesson 2: Jewish Beliefs and Texts 236
The Big Idea The central ideas and laws of Judaism are contained in sacred texts such as the Torah.
Lesson 3: Judaism over the Centuries 242
The Big Idea Although many Jews were forced out of Israel by the Romans, shared beliefs and customs helped Jews maintain their religion.

Timeline of Events 2000 BC–AD 70

▷ Explore ONLINE!

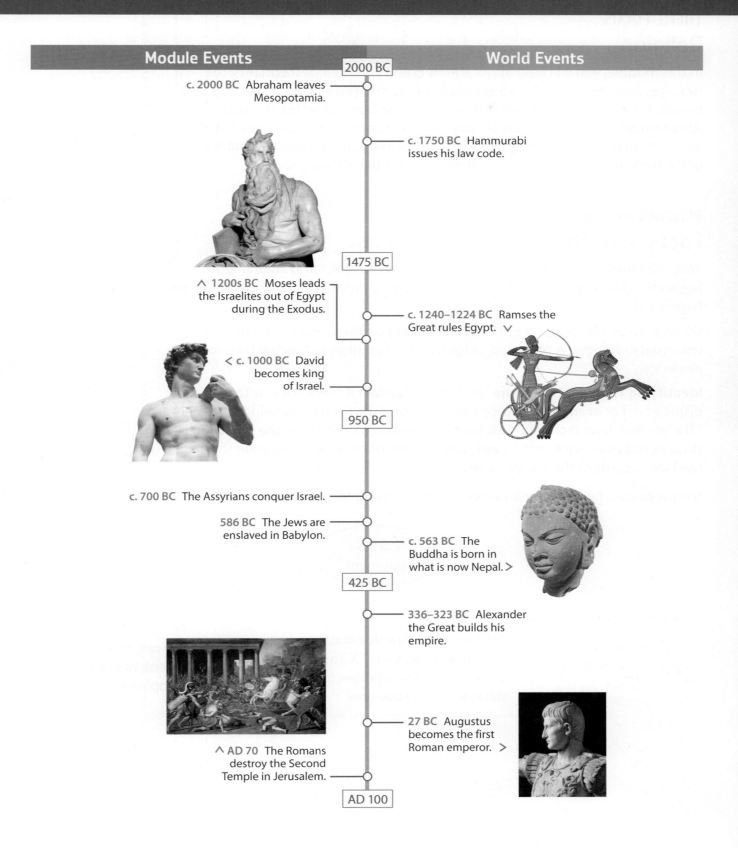

Module Events

World Events

2000 BC

c. 2000 BC Abraham leaves Mesopotamia.

c. 1750 BC Hammurabi issues his law code.

1475 BC

∧ **1200s BC** Moses leads the Israelites out of Egypt during the Exodus.

c. 1240–1224 BC Ramses the Great rules Egypt. ∨

< **c. 1000 BC** David becomes king of Israel.

950 BC

c. 700 BC The Assyrians conquer Israel.

586 BC The Jews are enslaved in Babylon.

c. 563 BC The Buddha is born in what is now Nepal. >

425 BC

336–323 BC Alexander the Great builds his empire.

27 BC Augustus becomes the first Roman emperor. >

∧ **AD 70** The Romans destroy the Second Temple in Jerusalem.

AD 100

Reading Social Studies

THEME FOCUS:
Religion

In this module, you will read about the Hebrews and their descendants, the Israelites and Jews, and the religion called Judaism. You will learn about Jewish beliefs, texts such as the Torah and the Dead Sea Scrolls, and leaders such as Abraham and Moses. As you read, pay close attention to how people's beliefs affected where and how they lived. In the process, you will discover that the lives of the early Jews revolved around their religious beliefs and practices.

READING FOCUS:
Facts and Opinions about the Past

Why is it important to know the difference between a fact and an opinion? Separating facts from opinions about historical events helps you know what really happened.

When you see the differences between fact and opinion, you can come to a reasoned judgment. A reasoned judgment is an opinion supported by good evidence.

Identifying Facts and Opinions Something is a **fact** if there is a way to prove it or disprove it. For example, research can prove or disprove the following statement: "The ancient Jews recorded their laws." But research can't prove the following statement because it is just an **opinion**, or someone's belief: "Everyone should read the records of the ancient Jews."

Use the process below to decide whether a statement is fact or opinion.

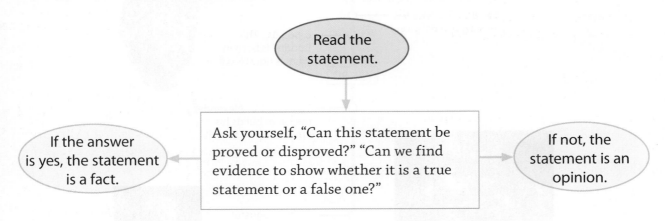

Read the statement.

Ask yourself, "Can this statement be proved or disproved?" "Can we find evidence to show whether it is a true statement or a false one?"

If the answer is yes, the statement is a fact.

If not, the statement is an opinion.

You Try It!

Lesson 1
Judaism
Abraham
Moses
Exodus
Ten Commandments
David
Solomon
Diaspora
Lesson 2
monotheism
Torah
synagogue
prophets
Talmud
Dead Sea Scrolls
Lesson 3
Zealots
rabbis
Passover
High Holy Days

The following passage tells about boys who, years ago, found what came to be called the Dead Sea Scrolls. All the statements in this passage are facts. What makes them facts and not opinions?

Scrolls Reveal Past Beliefs Until 1947 the Dead Sea Scrolls had remained hidden. In that year, young boys looking for a lost goat near the Dead Sea found a small cave. One of the boys went in to explore and found several old jars filled with moldy scrolls.

Scholars were very excited about the boy's find. Eager to find more scrolls, they began to search the desert. Over the next few decades, searchers found several more groups of scrolls.

Careful study revealed that most of the Dead Sea Scrolls were written between 100 BC and AD 50. The scrolls included prayers, commentaries, letters, and passages from the Hebrew Bible. These writings help historians learn about the lives of many Jews during this time.

Identify each of the following as a fact or an opinion. Then explain how you could use the facts you identified to make a reasoned judgement about the Dead Sea Scrolls.

1. Boys discovered the Dead Sea Scrolls in 1947.
2. The discovery of the scrolls is one of the most important discoveries ever.
3. All religious leaders should study the Dead Sea Scrolls.
4. The Dead Sea Scrolls were written between 100 BC and AD 50.

As you read this module, look for clues that will help you determine which statements are facts.

The Early Hebrews

The Big Idea

Originally desert nomads, the Israelites, descendants of the Hebrews, established a great kingdom.

Main Ideas

- Abraham led the Hebrews to Canaan and to a new religion, and Moses led the Israelites out of slavery in Egypt.

- Strong kings united the Israelites to fight off invaders.

- Invaders conquered and ruled the Israelites after their kingdom broke apart.

- Some women in Israelite society made great contributions to their history.

Key Terms and People

Judaism
Abraham
Moses
Exodus
Ten Commandments
David
Solomon
Diaspora

If YOU were there . . .

You and your family are herders, looking after large flocks of sheep. Your grandfather is the leader of your tribe. One day your grandfather says that your whole family will be moving to a new country where there is more water and food for your flocks. The trip will be long and difficult.

How do you feel about moving to a faraway land?

Abraham and Moses Lead Their People

Sometime between 2000 and 1500 BC, a new people appeared in Southwest Asia. They were the Hebrews (HEE-brooz), ancestors of the Israelites and Jews. The early Hebrews were simple herders, but they developed a culture that became a major influence on later civilizations.

Much of what is known about their early history comes from the work of archaeologists and from accounts written by Jewish scribes. These accounts describe the early history of the Jews' ancestors and the laws of **Judaism** (JOO-dee-i-zuhm), their religion. In time these accounts became the Hebrew Bible. The Hebrew Bible is largely the same as the Old Testament of the Christian Bible.

The Beginnings in Canaan and Egypt The Hebrew Bible traces the Hebrews back to a man named **Abraham**. One day, the Hebrew Bible says, God told Abraham to leave his home in Mesopotamia. He was to take his family on a long journey to the west. God promised to lead Abraham to a new land and make his descendants into a mighty nation.

Abraham left Mesopotamia and settled in Canaan (KAY-nuhn), on the Mediterranean Sea. Some of his descendants, the Israelites, lived in Canaan for many years. Later, however, some Israelites moved to Egypt, perhaps because of famine in Canaan. Mountains in the region block rainy weather. As a result, droughts can occur. Without enough water for crops, early civilizations in and surrounding Cannan could not produce enough food, which often led to famines. Once in Egypt, the Israelites lived well there, and their population grew. This growth worried Egypt's ruler, the pharaoh. He feared that the Israelites might become too powerful. To stop this from happening, the pharaoh made the Israelites slaves.

The Exodus According to the Hebrew Bible, a leader named **Moses** appeared among the Israelites in Egypt. In the 1200s BC, God told Moses to lead the Israelites out of Egypt. Moses went to the pharaoh and demanded that the Israelites be freed. The pharaoh refused. Soon afterward a series of terrible plagues, or disasters, struck Egypt.

The plagues frightened the pharaoh so much that he agreed to free the Israelites. Overjoyed with the news of their release, Moses led his people out of Egypt in a journey called the **Exodus**. To the Israelites, the release from slavery proved that God loved them and was protecting and watching over them.

The Exodus is a major event in Jewish history, but other people recognize its significance as well. Throughout history, for example, enslaved people have found hope in the story. Before the Civil War, American slaves sang about Moses to keep their hopes of freedom alive.

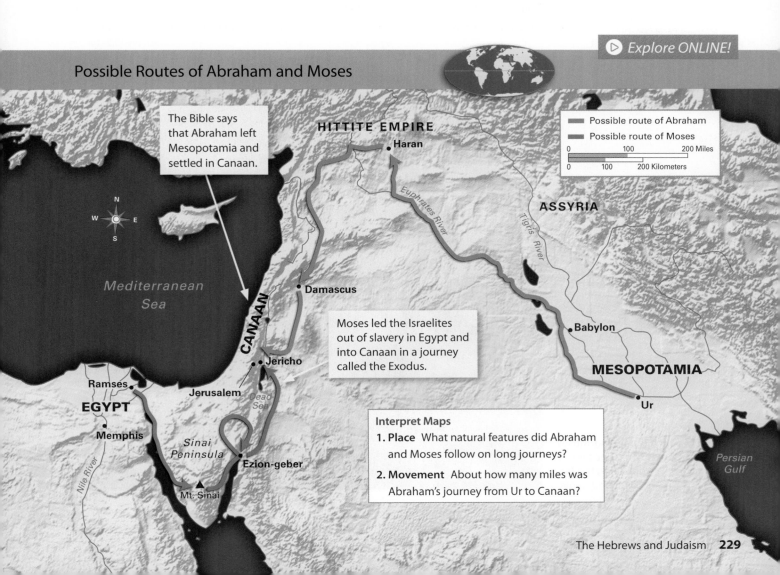

▶ Explore ONLINE!

Possible Routes of Abraham and Moses

The Bible says that Abraham left Mesopotamia and settled in Canaan.

HITTITE EMPIRE

Haran

Possible route of Abraham
Possible route of Moses

0   100   200 Miles
0   100   200 Kilometers

Euphrates River

ASSYRIA

Tigris River

Mediterranean Sea

N
W   E
S

CANAAN

Damascus

Moses led the Israelites out of slavery in Egypt and into Canaan in a journey called the Exodus.

Babylon

Jericho

MESOPOTAMIA

Ramses

Jerusalem

Dead Sea

EGYPT

Ur

Memphis

Persian Gulf

Sinai Peninsula

Ezion-geber

Nile River

Mt. Sinai

Interpret Maps

1. **Place** What natural features did Abraham and Moses follow on long journeys?

2. **Movement** About how many miles was Abraham's journey from Ur to Canaan?

For many years after their release, the Israelites traveled through the desert. When they reached a mountain called Sinai, the Hebrew Bible says, God gave Moses two stone tablets. On the tablets was written a code of moral laws known as the **Ten Commandments**:

"I the LORD am your God who brought you out of the land of Egypt, the house of bondage: You shall have no other gods besides Me.

You shall not make for yourself a sculptured image, or any likeness of what is in the heavens above, or on the earth below, or in the waters under the earth. You shall not bow down to them or serve them. For I the LORD your God am an impassioned God. . . .

You shall not swear falsely by the name of the Lord your God; for the LORD will not clear one who swears falsely by His name.

Remember the Sabbath day and keep it holy. . . .

Honor your father and your mother, that you may long endure on the land that the LORD your God is assigning to you.

You shall not murder.

You shall not commit adultery.

You shall not steal.

You shall not bear false witness against your neighbor.

You shall not covet your neighbor's house: you shall not covet your neighbor's wife, or his male or female slave, or his ox or his ass, or anything that is your neighbor's."

—Exodus 20:2–14

In this painting, Moses holds two stone tablets containing the Ten Commandments.

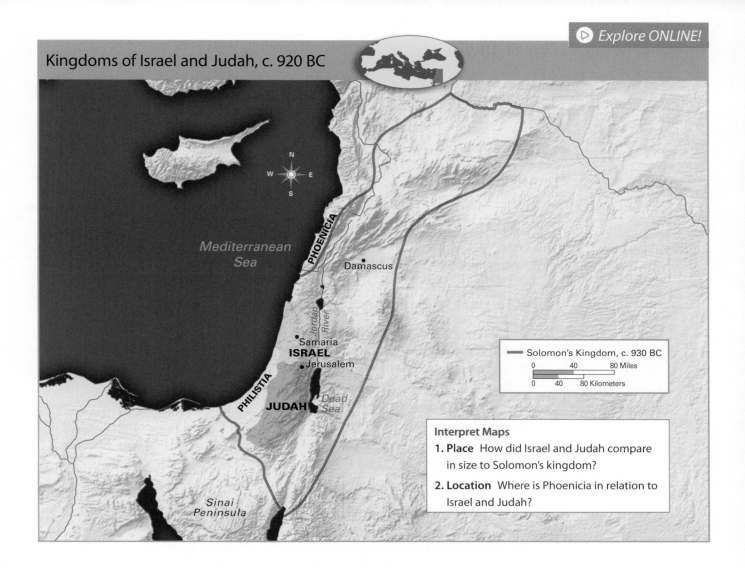

Kingdoms of Israel and Judah, c. 920 BC

Explore ONLINE!

Mediterranean
Sea

PHOENICIA

Damascus

Jordan River

Samaria
ISRAEL
Jerusalem

PHILISTIA

JUDAH   Dead
Sea

Sinai
Peninsula

Solomon's Kingdom, c. 930 BC

0   40   80 Miles

0   40   80 Kilometers

Interpret Maps

1. **Place** How did Israel and Judah compare in size to Solomon's kingdom?

2. **Location** Where is Phoenicia in relation to Israel and Judah?

By accepting the Ten Commandments, the Israelites agreed to worship only God. They also agreed to value human life, self-control, and justice. The commandments shaped the development of their society. A Jewish historian named Flavius Josephus would later use the word *theocracy* to describe the government of the Israelites. As you may recall, a theocracy is a government controlled by religious leaders.

The Return to Canaan According to the Hebrew Bible, the Israelites eventually reached Canaan, where they fought the people living there to gain control of the land. Land was an important resource for grazing and farming. Some scholars believe that having a larger population may have given the Israelites an advantage over their enemies. After they conquered Canaan and settled down, the Israelites built their own society.

In Canaan, the Israelites, divided into 12 tribes, lived in small, scattered communities. These communities had no central government. Instead, each community selected judges as leaders to enforce laws and settle disputes. Before long, though, a threat arose that called for a new kind of leadership.

Reading Check
Identify Cause and Effect
Why did Abraham leave Mesopotamia?

Timeline: Early Hebrew History

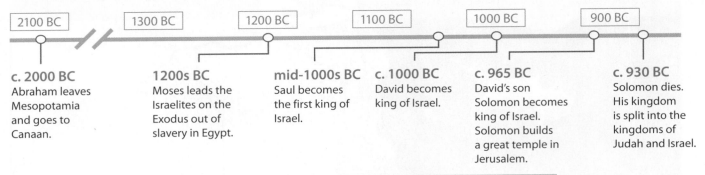

| 2100 BC | 1300 BC | 1200 BC | 1100 BC | 1000 BC | 900 BC |

c. 2000 BC
Abraham leaves Mesopotamia and goes to Canaan.

1200s BC
Moses leads the Israelites on the Exodus out of slavery in Egypt.

mid-1000s BC
Saul becomes the first king of Israel.

c. 1000 BC
David becomes king of Israel.

c. 965 BC
David's son Solomon becomes king of Israel. Solomon builds a great temple in Jerusalem.

c. 930 BC
Solomon dies. His kingdom is split into the kingdoms of Judah and Israel.

Analyze Timelines
About how many years after Abraham settled in Canaan did Saul become the first king of Israel?

Kings Unite the Israelites

The new threat to the Israelites came from the Philistines (FI-li-steenz), who lived along the Mediterranean coast. In the mid-1000s BC, the Philistines invaded the Israelites' lands.

Frightened by these powerful invaders, the Israelites banded together under a single ruler who could lead them in battle. That ruler was a man named Saul, who became the first king of Israel. Saul had some success as a military commander, but he wasn't a strong king. He never won the total support of tribal and religious leaders. They often fought against his decisions.

King David After Saul died, a man once out of favor with Saul became king. That king's name was **David**. As a young man, David had been a shepherd. The Hebrew Bible tells how David slew the Philistine giant Goliath, which brought him to the attention of the king. David was admired for his military skills and as a poet; many of the Psalms are attributed to him. For many years, David lived in the desert, gathering support from local people. When Saul died, David used this support to become king.

In this painting, a young David calms King Saul by playing music.

Solomon greets the visiting Queen of Sheba in this painting from the 1600s.

Unlike Saul, David was well loved by the Israelites. He won the full support of Israel's tribal leaders. David defeated the Philistines and fought and won wars against many other peoples of Canaan. He established the capital of Israel in Jerusalem.

King Solomon David's son **Solomon** (SAHL-uh-muhn) took the throne in about 965 BC. Like his father, Solomon was a strong king. Under Solomon's monarchy, Israel was organized into 12 districts. Each district was ruled by a governor. Not only did the governors enforce the king's laws, but they also collected taxes and provided labor for Solomon. This allowed Solomon to make great improvements within the kingdom. For example, new city walls and roads were paid for by taxes and built by slaves.

In addition, the governors provided Solomon with soldiers. Solomon expanded the kingdom and made nearby kingdoms, including Egypt and Phoenicia, his allies. Trade with these allies made Israel very rich. With these riches, Solomon built a great Temple to God in Jerusalem. This Temple became the center of the Israelites' religious life and a symbol of their faith.

Reading Check
Find Main Ideas
Why did the Israelites unite under a king?

Invaders Conquer and Rule

After Solomon's death in about 930 BC, revolts broke out over who should be king. Within a year, conflict tore Israel apart. Israel split into two kingdoms called Israel and Judah (JOO-duh). The people of Judah became known as Jews.

The two new kingdoms lasted for a few centuries. In the end, however, both were conquered. The Assyrians defeated Israel around 722 BC. The kingdom fell apart because most of its people were dispersed. Judah lasted longer, but before long it was defeated by the Chaldeans.

The Dispersal of the Jews The Chaldeans captured Jerusalem and destroyed Solomon's Temple in 586 BC. They marched thousands of Jews to their capital, Babylon, to work as slaves. The Jews called this enslavement the Babylonian Captivity. It lasted about 50 years.

Temple to God in Jerusalem

Solomon built a temple to God in Jerusalem. It was destroyed in 586 BC and rebuilt after the Persians conquered the Chaldeans.

In the 530s BC, the Persians conquered the Chaldeans and let the Jews return to Jerusalem. But many never took this opportunity to return home. Instead, some moved to other parts of the Persian Empire. Scholars call the dispersal of the Jews outside of Israel and Judah the **Diaspora** (dy-AS-pruh).

The rest of the Jews did return home to Jerusalem. There they rebuilt Solomon's Temple, which became known as the Second Temple. The Jews remained under Persian control until the 330s BC, when the Persians were conquered by invaders.

Independence and Conquest Tired of foreign rule, a Jewish family called the Maccabees (MA-kuh-beez) led a successful revolt in the 160s BC. For about 100 years, the Jews again ruled their own kingdom. Their independence, however, didn't last. In 63 BC the Jews were conquered again, this time by the Romans.

Although Jewish leaders added to the Second Temple under Roman rule, life was difficult. Heavy taxes burdened the people. The Romans were brutal masters who had no respect for the Jewish religion and way of life.

Some rulers tried to force the Jews to worship the Roman Emperor. The Roman rulers even appointed the high priests, the leaders of the Temple. This was more than the Jews could bear. They called on their people to rebel against the Romans.

Reading Check
Summarize
How did Roman rule affect Jewish society?

Women in Israelite Society

Israelite government and society were dominated by men, as were most ancient societies. Women and men had different roles. Men made most decisions, and a woman's husband was chosen by her father. However, a daughter could not be forced into marriage. A family's property was inherited by the eldest son, who provided for all children and for women without husbands.

Some Israelite and Jewish women made great contributions to their society. The Hebrew Bible describes them. Some were political and military leaders, such as Queen Esther and the judge Deborah. According to the Hebrew Bible, these women saved their people from their enemies. Other women, such as Miriam, the sister of Moses, were spiritual leaders.

Some women in the Hebrew Bible were seen as examples of how Israelite and Jewish women should behave. For example, Ruth, who left her people to care for her mother-in-law, Naomi, was seen as a model of devotion to one's family. Ruth's story is told as an example of how people should treat their family members.

Reading Check
Generalize
What was life like for most Israelite women?

Summary and Preview The history of the Jews and their ancestors began some 3,500 to 4,000 years ago. The instructions that Jews believe God gave to the early Hebrews and Israelites shaped their religion, Judaism. In the next lesson, you will learn about the main teachings of Judaism.

Lesson 1 Assessment

Review Ideas, Terms, and People

1. **a. Identify** Who was Abraham?
   b. Evaluate Why is the Exodus a significant event in Jewish history?

2. **a. Summarize** How did David and Solomon strengthen the kingdom of Israel?
   b. Compare and Contrast What did Saul, David, and Solomon have in common? How did they differ?

3. **Describe** What happened during the Babylonian Captivity?

4. **a. Describe** Who had more rights in Israelite and Jewish society, men or women?
   b. Make Inferences How did Ruth and Naomi set an example for other Israelites?

Critical Thinking

5. **Evaluate** In a chart like this one, note the contributions of the four most important people in this lesson.

Key Figure	Contribution

Jewish Beliefs and Texts

The Big Idea

The central ideas and laws of Judaism are contained in sacred texts such as the Torah.

Main Ideas

- Belief in God, commitment to education and justice, and observance of the law anchor Jewish society.

- Jewish beliefs are listed in the Torah, the Hebrew Bible, and the Commentaries.

- The Dead Sea Scrolls reveal many past Jewish beliefs.

- The ideas of Judaism have helped shape later cultures.

Key Terms and People

monotheism
Torah
synagogue
prophets
Talmud
Dead Sea Scrolls

If YOU were there . . .

You live in a small town in ancient Israel. Some people in your town treat strangers very badly. But you have been taught to be fair and kind to everyone, including strangers. One day, you tell one of your neighbors he should be kinder to strangers. He asks you why you feel that way.

How will you explain your belief in kindness?

Jewish Beliefs Anchor Their Society

Religion is the foundation upon which Jews base their whole society. In fact, much of Jewish culture is based directly on Jewish beliefs. The central concepts of Judaism are belief in God, education, justice and righteousness, and observance of religious and moral law.

Belief in One God Most importantly, Jews believe in one God. The Hebrew name for God is YHWH, which is never pronounced by Jews, because it is considered too holy. The belief in only one God is called **monotheism**. Many people believe that Judaism was the world's first monotheistic religion. It is certainly the oldest such religion that is still widely practiced today.

In the ancient world where most people worshipped many gods, the Jews' worship of only one God set them apart. This worship also shaped Jewish society and cultural expression. The Jews believed that God had guided their history through relationships with Abraham, Moses, and other leaders. Ancient Jewish art often focused on the creation of the world and the lives of these leaders.

Education Another central element of Judaism is education and study. Teaching children the basics of Judaism has always been important in Jewish society. In ancient Jewish communities, older boys—but not girls—studied with professional teachers to learn their religion. Even today, education and study are central to Jewish life.

Moses and the Golden Calf

According to the Hebrew Bible, when Moses returned from Mount Sinai, he found the Israelites worshipping a statue of a golden calf. They had become impatient waiting for Moses and wanted to worship a god they could see. Moses was furious that they were worshipping a statue instead of God. In this Italian painting from the 1600s, the Israelites are destroying the golden calf.

Justice and Righteousness Also central to Jews' religion are the ideas of justice and righteousness. To Jews, justice means kindness and fairness in dealing with other people. Everyone deserves justice, even strangers and criminals. Jews are expected to give aid to those who need it, including the poor, the sick, and orphans. Jews are also expected to be fair in business dealings.

Righteousness refers to doing what is proper. Jews are supposed to behave properly, even if others around them do not. For Jews, righteous behavior is more important than formal ceremonies.

Observance of Religious and Moral Law Observance of the law is closely related to justice and righteousness. Moral and religious laws have guided Jews through their history and continue to do so today. Jews believe that God gave them these laws to follow, and that all Jews have a moral obligation to obey them. Not even kings were above the law.

The most important Jewish laws are the Ten Commandments. The commandments, however, are only part of Jewish law. Jews believe that Moses recorded a whole system of laws that God had set down for them to obey. Named for Moses, this system is called Mosaic law.

Like the Ten Commandments, Mosaic laws guide many areas of Jews' daily lives. For example, Mosaic law governs how people pray and celebrate holidays. The laws forbid Jews to work on holidays or on the Sabbath, the seventh day of each week. The Sabbath is a day of rest because, in Jewish tradition, God created the world in six days and rested on the seventh. The Jewish Sabbath begins at sundown Friday and ends at nightfall Saturday, the seventh day of the week.

Among the Mosaic laws are rules about the foods that Jews can eat and rules that must be followed in preparing them. For example, the laws state that Jews cannot eat pork or shellfish, which are thought to be unclean. Other laws say that meat has to be killed and prepared in a way that makes it acceptable for Jews to eat. Today foods that have been so prepared are called kosher (KOH-shuhr), or "fit."

In many Jewish communities today, people still strictly follow Mosaic law. They are called Orthodox Jews. Other Jews choose not to follow many of the ancient laws. They are known as Reform Jews. A third group, the Conservative Jews, falls between the other two groups. These are the three largest groups of Jews in the world today.

Texts List Jewish Beliefs

The laws and **principles** of Judaism are described in several sacred texts, or writings. Among the main texts are the Torah, the Hebrew Bible, and the Commentaries.

Reading Check
Generalize
What are the most important beliefs of Judaism?

Academic Vocabulary
principles basic beliefs, rules, or laws

This girl is reading aloud from the Torah. The Torah is a long scroll that contains holy writings of the Jewish people.

The Torah The ancient Jews recorded most of their laws in five books. Together these books are called the **Torah**, the most sacred text of Judaism. In addition to laws, the Torah includes a history of the Jews until the death of Moses.

Readings from the Torah are central to Jewish religious services today. Nearly every **synagogue** (SI-nuh-gawg), or Jewish house of worship, has at least one Torah. Out of respect for the Torah, readers do not touch it. They use special pointers to mark their places in the text.

The Hebrew Bible The Torah is the first of three parts of a group of writings called the Hebrew Bible, or Tanakh (tah-NAHK). The second part is made up of eight books that describe the messages of Jewish prophets. **Prophets** are people who are said to receive messages from God to be taught to others.

The final part of the Hebrew Bible is 11 books of poetry, songs, stories, lessons, and history. For example, the Book of Daniel tells about a prophet named Daniel, who lived during the Babylonian Captivity. According to the book, Daniel angered the king who held the Jews as slaves. As punishment, the king had Daniel thrown into a den of lions. The story tells that Daniel's faith in God kept the lions from killing him, and he was released. Jews tell this story to show the power of faith.

Also in the final part of the Hebrew Bible are the Proverbs, short expressions of Jewish wisdom. Many of these sayings are attributed to Israelite leaders, especially King Solomon. For example, Solomon is supposed to have said, "A good name is to be chosen rather than great riches." In other words, it is better to be seen as a good person than to be rich and not respected.

The third part of the Hebrew Bible also includes the Book of Psalms. Psalms are poems or songs of praise to God. Many of these are attributed to King David. One of the most famous psalms is the Twenty-third Psalm. It includes lines often read today during times of difficulty:

"The Lord is my shepherd; I lack nothing. He makes me lie down in green pastures; He leads me to water in places of repose; He renews my life; He guides me in right paths as befits His name."

—Psalms 23:1–3

The Torah

The Torah is the most sacred of Hebrew writings. Jews believe its contents were revealed to Moses by God. The Torah plays a central role in many Jewish ceremonies, including weekly worship.

The Commentaries

The Talmud is a collection of commentaries and discussions about the Torah and the Hebrew Bible. The Talmud is a rich source of information for discussion and debate. Rabbis and religious scholars like these young men study the Talmud to learn about Jewish history and laws.

The Hebrew Bible

These beautifully decorated pages are from a Hebrew Bible. The Hebrew Bible, sometimes called the Tanakh, includes the Torah and other ancient writings.

Analyze Visuals
How does this Hebrew Bible look different from the Commentaries?

Commentaries For centuries scholars have studied the Torah and Jewish laws. Because some laws are hard to understand, the scholars write commentaries to explain them.

Many such commentaries are found in the **Talmud** (TAHL-moohd), a set of commentaries and lessons for everyday life. The writings of the Talmud were produced between AD 200 and 600. Many Jews consider them second only to the Hebrew Bible in their significance to Judaism. Talmudic writings cover various topics. For example, the architecture of some synagogues in Israel and elsewhere was determined by specific Talmudic instructions.

Reading Check
Analyze
What texts do Jews consider sacred?

Scrolls Reveal Past Beliefs

Besides the Torah, the Hebrew Bible, and the Commentaries, many other documents also explain ancient Jewish beliefs. Among the most important are the **Dead Sea Scrolls**, writings by Jews who lived about 2,000 years ago.

Until 1947 the Dead Sea Scrolls had remained hidden. In that year, young boys looking for a lost goat near the Dead Sea found a small cave. One of the boys went in to explore and found several old jars filled with moldy scrolls.

Scholars were very excited about the boy's find. Eager to find more scrolls, they began to search the desert. Over the next few decades, searchers found several more groups of scrolls.

Careful study revealed that most of the Dead Sea Scrolls were written between 100 BC and AD 50. The scrolls included prayers, commentaries, letters, and passages from the Hebrew Bible.

The Dead Sea Scrolls also show ancient beliefs about how people should behave to find favor with God:

> "Stop doing evil, learn to do good. Seek justice. . . . If you are willing and obedient, you will eat the good of the land."
>
> —The Dead Sea Scrolls

Reading Check
Find Main Ideas
What did the Dead Sea Scrolls contain?

These writings help historians learn about the lives of many Jews during this time.

Judaism and Later Cultures

For centuries, Jewish ideas have greatly influenced other cultures, especially those in Europe and the Americas. Historians call European and American cultures the Western world to distinguish them from the Asian cultures to the east of Europe.

The Dead Sea Scrolls

The Dead Sea Scrolls were found in this cave, and in similar caves, near Qumran. The hot, dry desert climate preserved the 2,000-year-old scrolls remarkably well.

Analyze Visuals
Why might historians have had trouble reading the Dead Sea Scrolls?

Because Jews lived all over the Western world, people of many cultures learned of Jewish ideas. In addition, these ideas helped shape the largest religion of Western society today, Christianity. Jesus, whose teachings are the basis of Christianity, was Jewish, and many of his teachings reflected Jewish ideas. These ideas were carried forward into Western civilization by both Jews and Christians. Judaism also influenced the development of another major religion, Islam. The first people to adopt Islam believed that they, like the Jews, were descendants of Abraham.

How are Jewish ideas reflected in our society? Many people still look to the Ten Commandments as a guide to how they should live. For example, people are expected to honor their parents, families, and neighbors and not to lie or cheat. In addition, many people do not work on weekends in honor of the Sabbath. Although not all these ideas were unique to Judaism, it was through the Jews that they entered Western culture.

Not all of the ideas adopted from Jewish teachings come from the Ten Commandments. Other Jewish ideas can also be seen in how people live today. For example, people give money or items to charities to help the poor and needy. This concept of charity is based on the teachings of Judaism and other religions.

Summary and Preview Judaism is based on the belief in and obedience to God as described in the Torah and other sacred texts. In the next lesson, you will learn how religion helped unify Jews even when they were forced out of Jerusalem.

Reading Check
Summarize
How have Jewish ideas helped shape modern laws?

Lesson 2 Assessment

Review Ideas, Terms, and People

1. a. **Define** What is monotheism?
   b. **Explain** What is the Jewish view of justice and righteousness?

2. a. **Identify** What are the main sacred texts of Judaism?
   b. **Predict** Why do you think the Commentaries are so significant to many Jews?

3. **Recall** Why do historians study the Dead Sea Scrolls?

4. **Describe** How are Jewish teachings reflected in Western society today?

Critical Thinking

5. **Find Main Ideas** Using the information in your notes, identify four basic beliefs of Judaism, and explain them in a diagram like the one shown here.

Jewish Beliefs

Judaism over the Centuries

The Big Idea

Although many Jews were forced out of Israel by the Romans, shared beliefs and customs helped Jews maintain their religion.

Main Ideas

- Revolt, defeat, and migration led to great changes in Jewish culture.

- Because Jews settled in different parts of the world, two cultural traditions formed.

- Jewish traditions and holy days celebrate the history and religion of the Jews.

Key Terms and People

Zealots
rabbis
Passover
High Holy Days

If YOU were there . . .

Foreign soldiers have taken over your homeland and are forcing you to obey their laws. So some people are urging you to stand up and fight for freedom. But your conquerors come from a huge, powerful empire. If your people revolt, you have little chance of winning.

Will you join the rebellion?
Why or why not?

Revolt, Defeat, and Migration

The teachings of Judaism helped unite the ancient Jews. After the conquest of Israel by the Romans, many events threatened to tear Jewish society apart.

One threat to Jewish society was foreign rule. By the beginning of the first century AD, many Jews in Jerusalem had grown tired of foreign rule. If they could regain their independence, these Jews thought they could re-create the kingdom of Israel.

Revolt Against Rome The most rebellious of these Jews was a group called the **Zealots** (ZE-luhts). This group didn't think that Jews should answer to anyone but God. As a result, they refused to obey Roman officials. The Zealots urged their fellow Jews to rise up against the Romans. Tensions between Jews and Romans increased. Finally, in AD 66, the Jews revolted. Led by the Zealots, they fought fiercely.

In the end, the Jews' revolt against the Romans was not successful. The revolt lasted four years and caused terrible damage. By the time the fighting ended, Jerusalem lay in ruins. The war had wrecked buildings and cost many lives. Even more devastating to the Jews was that the Romans burned the Second Temple during the last days of fighting in AD 70.

Destruction of the Second Temple

Frustrated by a century of Roman rule, many Jews rose up in armed rebellion. Led by the Zealots, they fought furiously for four years. But the experienced Roman army crushed the revolt. The Romans even destroyed the Jews' holiest site, the Second Temple in Jerusalem.

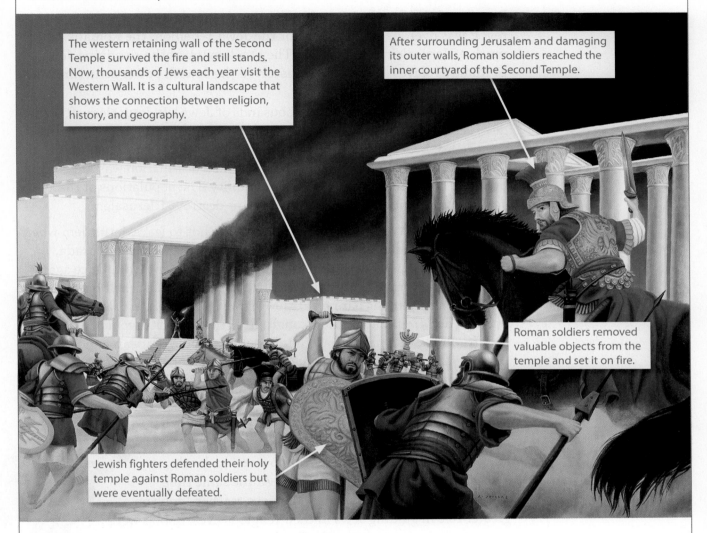

The western retaining wall of the Second Temple survived the fire and still stands. Now, thousands of Jews each year visit the Western Wall. It is a cultural landscape that shows the connection between religion, history, and geography.

After surrounding Jerusalem and damaging its outer walls, Roman soldiers reached the inner courtyard of the Second Temple.

Roman soldiers removed valuable objects from the temple and set it on fire.

Jewish fighters defended their holy temple against Roman soldiers but were eventually defeated.

Analyze Visuals
What effect do you think the burning of the Second Temple had on the Jews?

"As the flames went upward, the Jews made a great clamor [shout], such as so mighty an affliction [ordeal] required, and ran together to prevent it; and now they spared not their lives any longer, nor suffered any thing to restrain their force, since that holy house was perishing."

—Flavius Josephus, *The Wars of the Jews*

After the Temple was destroyed, most Jews lost their will to fight and surrendered. But a few refused to give up their fight. That small group of about 1,000 Zealots locked themselves in a mountain fortress called Masada (muh-SAH-duh).

Intent on smashing the revolt, the Romans sent 15,000 soldiers to capture these Zealots. However, Masada was hard to reach. The Romans had to build a huge ramp of earth and stones to get to it. For two years, the Zealots refused to surrender, as the ramp grew. Finally, as the Romans broke through Masada's walls, the Zealots took their own lives. They refused to become Roman slaves.

Results of the Revolt With the capture of Masada in AD 73, the Jewish revolt was over. As punishment for the Jews' rebellion, the Romans killed much of Jerusalem's population. They took many of the surviving Jews to Rome as slaves. The Romans dissolved the Jewish power structure and took over the city.

Besides those taken as slaves, thousands of Jews left Jerusalem after the destruction of the Second Temple. With the Temple destroyed, they didn't want to live in Jerusalem anymore. Many moved to Jewish communities in other parts of the Roman Empire. One common destination was Alexandria in Egypt, which had a large Jewish community. The populations of these Jewish communities grew after the Romans destroyed Jerusalem.

A Second Revolt Some Jews, however, chose not to leave Jerusalem when the Romans conquered it. Some 60 years after the capture of Masada, these Jews, unhappy with Roman rule, began another revolt. Once again, however, the Roman army defeated the Jews. After this rebellion in the AD 130s, the Romans banned all Jews from the city of Jerusalem. Roman officials declared that any Jew caught in or near the city would be killed. As a result, Jewish migration throughout the Mediterranean region increased. The Romans also renamed the area of Israel *Palaestina* in order to prevent Jewish claims to the land. *Palaestina* came from a term used to describe the Philistines, who had once fought the Israelites.

Migration and Discrimination For Jews not living in Jerusalem, the nature of Judaism changed. Because the Jews no longer had a single temple at which to worship, local synagogues became more important. At the same time, leaders called **rabbis** (RAB-yz), or religious teachers, took on a greater role in guiding Jews in their religious lives. Rabbis were responsible for interpreting the Torah and teaching.

This change was largely due to the actions of Yohanan ben Zaccai, a rabbi who founded a school at Yavneh, near Jerusalem. In this school, he taught people about Judaism and trained them to be rabbis. Influenced by Yohanan, rabbis' ideas shaped how Judaism was practiced for the next several centuries. Many rabbis also served as leaders of Jewish communities.

Yohanan ben Zaccai escaped from Jerusalem when it was under siege. He then founded an important school that helped Judaism survive the destruction of the Temple.

Over many centuries, Jews moved out of the Mediterranean region to other parts of the world. In many cases this movement was not voluntary. The Jews were forced to move by other religious groups who discriminated against them or were unfair to them. Jews were forced to leave their cities and find new places to live. As a result, some Jews settled in Europe and Asia, and much later, the United States.

Reading Check
Identify Cause and Effect
Why did the Romans force Jews out of Jerusalem?

Two Cultural Traditions

As you read earlier, the dispersal of Jews around the world is called the Diaspora. It began with the Babylonian Captivity in the 500s BC. After that time, Jewish communities developed all around the world.

Jews everywhere shared the basic beliefs of Judaism. For example, all Jews still believed in God and tried to obey his laws as set forth in the sacred texts. But communities in various parts of the world had different customs. As a result, the Jewish communities in different parts of the world began to develop their own languages, rituals, and cultures. These differences led to the creation of two main cultural traditions, both of which still exist today.

The Jews in Eastern Europe One of the two traditions, the Ashkenazim (ahsh-kuh-NAH-zuhm), is made up of descendants of Jews who moved to France, Germany, and Eastern Europe during the Diaspora. For the most part, these Jews had communities separate from their non-Jewish neighbors. Therefore, they developed their own customs that were

▶ Explore ONLINE!

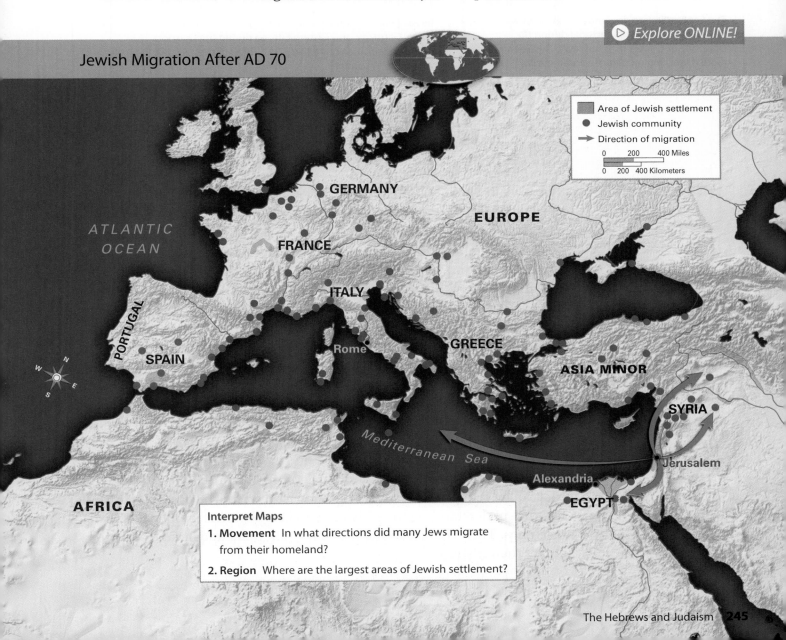

Jewish Migration After AD 70

Area of Jewish settlement
Jewish community
Direction of migration

0   200   400 Miles
0 200 400 Kilometers

ATLANTIC OCEAN

GERMANY

EUROPE

FRANCE

PORTUGAL

ITALY

SPAIN

Rome

GREECE

ASIA MINOR

SYRIA

Mediterranean Sea

Jerusalem

Alexandria

EGYPT

AFRICA

Interpret Maps

1. **Movement** In what directions did many Jews migrate from their homeland?

2. **Region** Where are the largest areas of Jewish settlement?

Jewish communities spread all over the world in the Diaspora. Many of these groups developed their own customs and traditions.

The Sephardim are descended from Jews who migrated to Spain and Portugal during the Diaspora, or dispersal, of the Jews. This Sephardic rabbi is working on part of a Torah scroll.

The Ashkenazim are descended from Jews who moved to France, Germany, and Eastern Europe during the Diaspora. These Ashkenazi Jews are carrying a Torah to their synagogue in London.

unlike those of their neighbors. As an example, they developed their own language, Yiddish. Yiddish is similar to German but is written in the Hebrew alphabet.

The Jews in Spain and Portugal Another Jewish cultural tradition developed during the Diaspora in what are now Spain and Portugal in Western Europe.

The descendants of the Jews there are called the Sephardim (suh-FAHR-duhm). They also have a language of their own—Ladino. It is a mix of Spanish, Hebrew, and Arabic. Unlike the Ashkenazim, the Sephardim mixed with the region's non-Jewish residents. As a result, Sephardic religious and cultural practices borrowed elements from other cultures. Known for their writings and their philosophies, the Sephardim produced a golden age of Jewish culture in the AD 1000s and 1100s. During this period, for example, Jewish poets wrote beautiful works in Hebrew and other languages. Jewish scholars also made great advances in mathematics, astronomy, medicine, and philosophy.

Traditions and Holy Days

Jewish culture is one of the oldest in the world. Because their roots go back so far, many Jews feel a strong connection with the past. They also feel that understanding their history will help them better follow Jewish teachings. Their traditions and holy days help them understand and celebrate their history.

Reading Check
Summarize
What are the two main Jewish cultural traditions?

Hanukkah One Jewish tradition is celebrated by Hanukkah, which falls in December. It honors the rededication of the Second Temple during the revolt of the Maccabees.

The Maccabees wanted to celebrate a great victory that had convinced their non-Jewish rulers to let them keep their religion. According to legend, though, the Maccabees didn't have enough lamp oil to perform the rededication ceremony. Miraculously, the oil they had—enough to burn for only one day—burned for eight full days.

Today Jews celebrate this event by lighting candles in a special candleholder called a menorah (muh-NOHR-uh). Its eight branches represent the eight days through which the oil burned. Many Jews also exchange gifts on each of the eight nights.

Passover More important than Hanukkah to Jews, Passover is celebrated in March or April. **Passover** is a time for Jews to remember the Exodus, the journey of the Israelites out of slavery in Egypt.

According to Jewish tradition, the Israelites left Egypt so quickly that bakers didn't have time to let their bread rise. Therefore, during Passover Jews eat only matzo, a flat, unrisen bread. They also celebrate the holy days with ceremonies and a ritual meal called a seder (SAY-duhr). During the seder, participants recall and reflect upon the events of the Exodus.

High Holy Days Ceremonies and rituals are also part of the **High Holy Days**, the two most sacred of all Jewish holy days. They take place each year in September or October. The first two days of the celebration, Rosh Hashanah (rash huh-SHAH-nuh), celebrate the beginning of a new year in the Jewish calendar.

Link to Today

A Passover Meal

Passover celebrates the Exodus, one of the most important events in Jewish history. In honor of this event from their past, Jews share a special meal called a seder. Each item in the seder symbolizes a part of the Exodus. For example, bitter herbs represent the Israelites' bitter years of slavery in Egypt. Before eating the meal, everyone reads prayers from a book called the Haggadah (huh-GAH-duh). It tells the story of the Exodus and reminds everyone present of the Jews' history. The picture shows a seder in a copy of a Haggadah from the 1300s.

Analyze Information
How does the Passover seder reflect the importance of the Exodus in Jewish history?

Reading Check
Find Main Ideas
What name is given to the two most important Jewish holy days?

On Yom Kippur (yohm ki-POOHR), which falls soon afterward, Jews ask God to forgive their sins. Jews consider Yom Kippur the holiest day of the entire year. Because it is so holy, Jews don't eat or drink anything for the entire day. Many of the ceremonies they perform for Yom Kippur date back to the days of the Second Temple. These ceremonies help many Jews feel more connected to their long past, to the days of Abraham and Moses.

Summary The Jewish culture is one of the oldest in the world. Over the course of their long history, the Jews' religion and customs have helped them maintain a sense of identity and community. This sense has helped the Jewish people endure many hardships.

Lesson 3 Assessment

Review Ideas, Terms, and People

1. a. **Recall** Who won the battle at Masada?
   b. **Evaluate** How did the defeat by the Romans affect Jewish history?
2. a. **Identify** What language developed in the Jewish communities of eastern Europe?
   b. **Contrast** How did communities of Ashkenazim differ from communities of Sephardim?
3. **Identify** What event does Passover celebrate?

Critical Thinking

4. **Evaluate** Use a graphic organizer like the one shown to describe the belief or custom that you think may have had the biggest role in strengthening Jewish society. List your reasons for choosing this belief or custom.

Major Belief or Custom

Social Studies Skills

Identify Short- and Long-Term Effects

Define the Skill

Many events of the past are the result of other events that took place earlier. When something occurs as the result of things that happened earlier, it is an effect of those things.

Some events take place soon after the things that cause them. These events are short-term effects. Long-term effects can occur decades or even hundreds of years after the events that caused them. Recognizing cause-and-effect relationships will help you better understand the connections between historical events.

Learn the Skill

Follow these steps to identify cause-and-effect connections between events.

1. Always look for what happened as a result of an action or event.

2. Short-term effects are usually fairly easy to identify. They are often closely linked to the event that caused them. Consider this sentence, for example:

   "After Solomon's death around 930 BC, revolts broke out over who should be king."

   It is clear from this information that a short-term effect of Solomon's death was political unrest. Now, consider this other passage:

   "Some Israelites . . . moved to Egypt. . . . The Israelites lived well in Egypt and their population grew. But this growing population worried Egypt's ruler, the pharaoh. He feared that the Israelites would soon become too powerful. To prevent this from happening, the pharaoh made the Israelites slaves."

   Look carefully at the information in the passage. No clue words exist. However, it shows that one effect of the Israelites' move to Egypt was the growth of their population. It takes time for a population to increase, so this was a long-term effect of the Israelites' move.

3. Long-term effects often occur well after the event that caused them. This is why you should always ask yourself why an event might have happened as you study it.

   For example, many of our modern laws are based on the Ten Commandments of the ancient Israelites. Religion is a major force in history that makes things happen.

4. The answer to *why* is often one of the major forces of history, such as religion, economics, science and technology, geography, and the meeting of peoples with different cultures. Ask yourself if one of these forces is a part of the event you are studying. If so, the event may have long-term effects.

Practice the Skill

Review the information in the module, and answer the following questions.

1. What were the short-term effects of King Solomon's rule of the Israelites? What long-term benefit resulted from his rule?

2. What was the short-term effect of the destruction of the Second Temple at Jerusalem in AD 70? What effect has that event had on the world today?

Module 7 Assessment

Review Vocabulary, Terms, and People

For each pair of terms, write a sentence that shows how the terms in the pair are related.

1. Abraham
   Judaism

2. Moses
   Exodus

3. David
   Solomon

4. Torah
   Talmud

5. Passover
   High Holy Days

6. Moses
   Ten Commandments

7. Passover
   Exodus

8. monotheism
   Judaism

9. synagogues
   rabbis

10. principles
    Torah

Comprehension and Critical Thinking

Lesson 1

11. **a. Describe** How did Abraham and Moses shape the history of the Hebrews and Israelites?

    b. Compare How was King Solomon's political system in ancient Israel similar to the Zhou political system in ancient China?

    c. Evaluate Of Esther, Deborah, Miriam, and Ruth, which do you think provided the best example of how people should treat their families? Explain your answer.

Lesson 2

12. **a. Identify** What are the basic beliefs of Judaism?

    b. Analyze What do the various sacred Jewish texts contain?

    c. Elaborate How are Jewish ideas observed in modern Western society?

Lesson 3

13. **a. Describe** What happened as a result of tensions between the Romans and the Jews?

    b. Analyze What led to the creation of the two main Jewish cultural traditions?

    c. Predict In the future, what role do you think holy days and other traditions will play in Judaism? Explain your answer.

Review Themes

14. Religion How did monotheism shape the history of the Jews?

15. Religion Do you agree or disagree with this statement: "The history of Judaism is also the history of the Hebrew and Jewish people." Why?

16. Religion How does Mosaic law affect the daily lives of Jewish people?

Reading Skills

Identify Facts and Opinions *Identify each of the following statements as a fact or an opinion.*

17. Much of what we know about Jewish history comes from the work of archaeologists.

18. Archaeologists should spend more time studying Jewish history.

19. The Exodus is one of the most fascinating events in world history.

20. Until 1947, scholars did not know about the Dead Sea Scrolls.

21. Hanukkah is a Jewish holy day that takes place every December.

Social Studies Skills

22. Identify Short- and Long-Term Effects *Identify both the short-term and long-term effects of each of the following events to fill in the chart.*

Event	Short-Term Effects	Long-Term Effects
the Exodus		
the Babylonian Captivity		
the expulsion of the Jews from Jerusalem		

Focus On Writing

23. Design a Website Imagine that you are a website designer. You have been asked to design a website that presents information about Jewish history, beliefs, values, and culture. Think about how you would organize and present this information. Then draw a rough diagram or sketch of the website's home page. Your diagram should show what text and images would appear on the home page. It should also include text in the form of menus and hot links. Be sure to label the parts of the home page, and include a title for the website.

Module 8

Ancient Greece

Essential Question

Why might historians consider ancient Greece the first Western civilization?

About the Photo: The ruins shown in this photo are from the Parthenon, a beautiful temple built to honor the Greek goddess Athena.

▶ *Explore ONLINE!*

HISTORY

VIDEOS, including...
- Origins of Western Culture
- Athens: Ancient Supercity
- Hercules: Power of the Gods

☑ Document-Based Investigations

☑ Graphic Organizers

☑ Interactive Games

☑ Interactive Map: Greek City-States and Colonies, c. 600 BC

☑ Image with Hotspots: The Parthenon

☑ Image Carousel: Government in Athens

In this module you will study Greece—home to one of the great ancient civilizations.

What You Will Learn...

Lesson 1: Geography and the Early Greeks. 256
The Big Idea Greece's geography and its nearness to the sea strongly influenced the development of trade and the growth of city-states.

Lesson 2: The Glory of Athens 264
The Big Idea The people of Athens endured war and tried many different forms of government before creating a democracy.

Lesson 3: Athens and Sparta. 272
The Big Idea The two most powerful city-states in Greece, Sparta and Athens, had very different cultures and became bitter enemies in the 400s BC.

Lesson 4: Greek Mythology and Literature. 280
The Big Idea The ancient Greeks created great myths and works of literature that influence the way we speak and write today.

Lesson 5: Greek Art, Philosophy, and Science 292
The Big Idea Ancient Greeks made lasting contributions in the arts, philosophy, and science.

Timeline of Events 2000–330 BC

▷ Explore ONLINE!

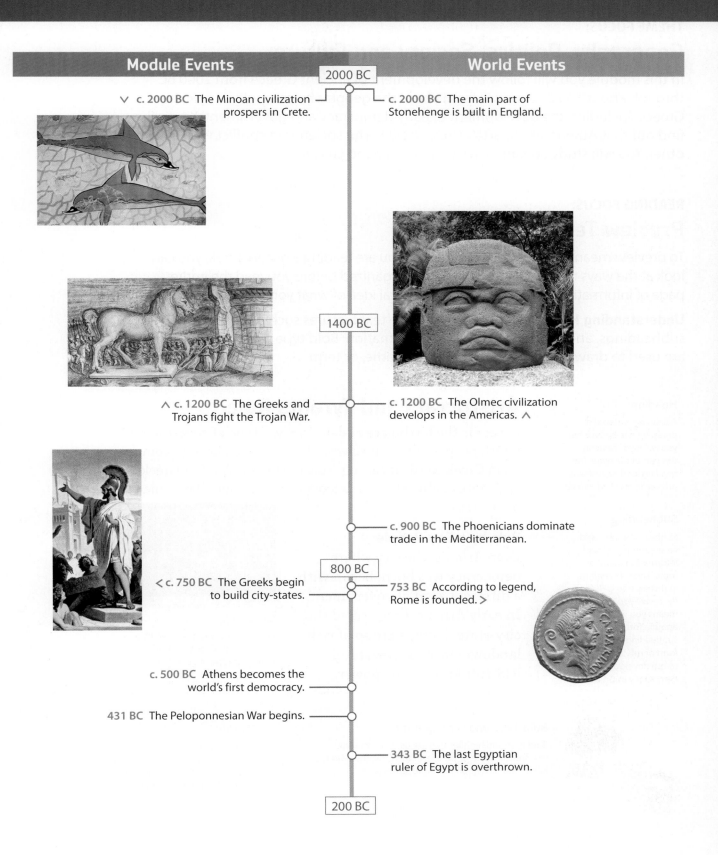

Module Events		World Events

2000 BC

∨ **c. 2000 BC** The Minoan civilization prospers in Crete.

c. 2000 BC The main part of Stonehenge is built in England.

1400 BC

∧ **c. 1200 BC** The Greeks and Trojans fight the Trojan War.

c. 1200 BC The Olmec civilization develops in the Americas. ∧

c. 900 BC The Phoenicians dominate trade in the Mediterranean.

800 BC

< **c. 750 BC** The Greeks begin to build city-states.

753 BC According to legend, Rome is founded. >

c. 500 BC Athens becomes the world's first democracy.

431 BC The Peloponnesian War begins.

343 BC The last Egyptian ruler of Egypt is overthrown.

200 BC

Reading Social Studies

Geography, Politics, Society and Culture

In this module you will follow the development of ancient Greece from 2000 BC through about 300 BC. You will learn about the geography and politics of ancient Greece, including the development of early democracy and government. You will find out that Athens and Sparta were two powerful societies in conflict with each other. You will study advances in Greek society and culture.

READING FOCUS:

Preview Text

To preview means to "look at before." When you are reading a history book, you can look at the ways that words and images are organized before you read the entire page of information. This will give you a general idea of what you will be reading.

Understanding Headings History books use text features such as headings, subheadings, and captions to organize information. Bold type and highlighting are used to draw your attention to a word, name, or term.

Heading

A heading is a word or phrase that tells you what you will read about on this part of the page. The heading for this section is *Aristocrats and Tyrants Rule*.

Subheading

Subheadings are used where there is a lot of information about a topic. The subheading in this section is *Rule By a Few People*, which means you will read about a form of rule. The subheading indicates this form of rule is related to the development of democracy in Greece.

Aristocrats and Tyrants Rule

Greece is the birthplace of democracy, a type of government in which people rule themselves. The word "democracy" comes from Greek words meaning "rule of the people." But Greek city-states didn't start as democracies, and not all became democratic.

Rule by a Few People

Even Athens, the city where democracy was born, began with a different kind of government. In early Athens, kings ruled the city-state. Later, a group of rich landowners, or aristocrats (uh-RIS-tuh-krats), took power.

Oligarchy

Early Athens was governed by a small group of aristocrats, shown here. This type of government is an oligarchy.

Bold Type and Highlighting

Bold type and highlighting are used to draw your attention to a specific word or phrase. In this case, the bold type draws your attention to a word: *aristocrats*.

Caption

Captions are words that describe images. Captions are usually over, under, or next to an image. This caption describes a painting.

You Try It!

Read the following passage and then answer the questions below.

Philosophy

The ancient Greeks worshipped gods and goddesses whose actions explained many of the mysteries of the world. But by around 500 BC a few people had begun to think about other explanations. We call these people philosophers.

Aristotle   Perhaps the greatest Greek thinker was **Aristotle** (ar-uh-STAH-tuhl), Plato's student. He taught that people should live lives of moderation, or balance. For example, people should not be greedy, but neither should they give away everything they own. Instead, people should find a balance between these two extremes.

This drawing shows how one artist imagined Plato (left), Aristotle (center), and Socrates (right) to look.

Answer these questions based on the passage you just read.

1. Identify the following text features in the passage: heading, subheading, and caption.
2. What is the purpose of the bold type and highlighting in the passage?

As you read this module, look at the ways that headings, subheadings, bold type and highlighting, and captions are used to organize information before you begin to read.

Key Terms and People

Lesson 1
polis
acropolis

Lesson 2
democracy
aristocrats
oligarchy
aristocracy
citizens
tyrant
Pericles

Lesson 3
alliance
Peloponnesian War

Lesson 4
mythology
Homer
Sappho
Aesop
fables

Lesson 5
Socrates
Plato
Aristotle
reason
Euclid
Hippocrates

Geography and the Early Greeks

The Big Idea

Greece's geography and its nearness to the sea strongly influenced the development of trade and the growth of city-states.

Main Ideas

- Geography helped shape early Greek civilization.
- Trading cultures developed in the Minoan and Mycenaean civilizations.
- The Greeks created city-states for protection and security.

Key Terms and People

polis
acropolis

Greece is a land of rugged mountains, rocky coastlines, and beautiful islands. The trees you see are olive trees. The early Greeks grew olives for food and oil.

If YOU were there . . .

You live on the rocky coast of a bright blue sea. Across the water you can see dozens of islands and points of land jutting out into the sea. Rugged mountains rise steeply behind your village. It is hard to travel across the mountains in order to visit other villages or towns. Near your home on the coast is a sheltered cove where it's easy to anchor a boat.

What could you do to make a living here?

Geography Shapes Greek Civilization

The Greeks lived on rocky, mountainous lands surrounded by water. The mainland of Greece is a peninsula, an area of land surrounded on three sides by water. But the Greek peninsula is very irregular. It's one big peninsula made up of a series of smaller peninsulas. The land and sea intertwine like your hand and fingers in a bowl of water. In addition, there are many islands. Look at the map of Greece and notice the rugged coastline.

In your mind, picture those peninsulas and islands dominated by mountains that run almost to the sea. Just a few small valleys and coastal plains provide flat land for farming and villages. Now you have an image of Greece, a land where one of the world's greatest civilizations developed.

Mountains and Settlements The Greeks lived in villages and towns separated by mountains and seas. Because mountains cover much of Greece, there are few flat areas for farmland. However, villages still thrived where people could use the landscape to their advantage. People in the mountains settled in the flat areas of the river valleys they could use for farmland. Others found flat areas along the coast.

Travel across the mountains and seas was difficult, so communities were isolated from one another. As a result, the people created their own governments and ways of life. Even though they spoke the same language, Greek communities saw themselves as separate countries.

Seas and Ships Since travel inland across the rugged mountains was so difficult, the early Greeks turned to the seas. On the south was the huge Mediterranean Sea, to the west was the Ionian (eye-OH-nee-uhn) Sea, and to the east was the Aegean (ee-JEE-uhn) Sea.

It's not surprising that the early Greeks used the sea as a source for food and as a way of trading with other communities.

The Greeks became skilled shipbuilders and sailors. Their ships sailed to Asia Minor (present-day Turkey), to Egypt, and to the islands of the Mediterranean and Aegean seas. As they traveled around these seas, they found sources of food and other products they needed. They also exchanged ideas with other cultures.

Reading Check
Draw Conclusions
How did mountains affect the location of Greek settlements?

▷ Explore ONLINE!

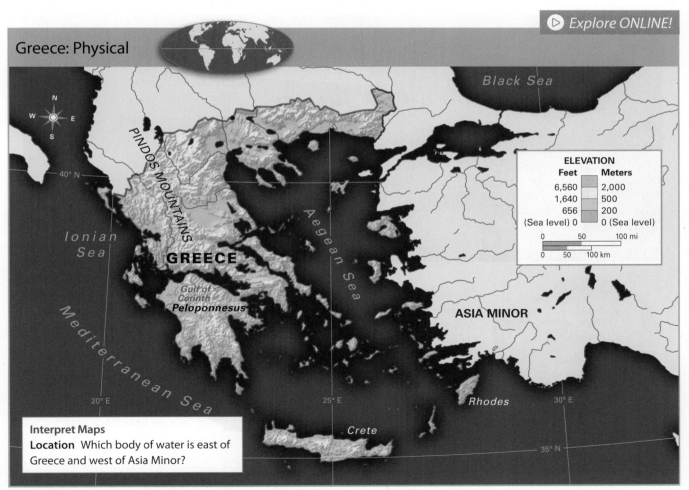

Greece: Physical

Interpret Maps
Location Which body of water is east of Greece and west of Asia Minor?

Trading Cultures Develop

Many cultures settled and developed in Greece. Two of the earliest were the Minoans (muh-NOH-uhnz) and the Mycenaeans (my-suh-NEE-uhns). By 2000 BC the Minoans had built an advanced society on the island of Crete. Crete lay south of the Aegean in the eastern Mediterranean. Later, the Mycenaeans built towns on the Greek mainland. These civilizations **influenced** the Aegean region and helped shape later cultures in Greece.

Academic Vocabulary
influence change, or have an effect on

The Minoans Because they lived on an island, the Minoans spent much of their time at sea. They were among the best shipbuilders of their time. Minoan ships carried goods such as wood, olive oil, and pottery all around the eastern Mediterranean. They traded these goods for copper, gold, silver, and jewels.

Although Crete's location was excellent for Minoan traders, its geography had its dangers. Sometime in the 1600s BC a huge volcano erupted just north of Crete. This eruption created a giant wave that flooded much of Crete. In addition, the eruption threw up huge clouds of ash, ruining crops and burying cities. This eruption may have led to the end of Minoan civilization.

Early Trading Cultures

The Minoans and Mycenaeans were expert shipbuilders and seafarers. They sailed throughout the eastern Mediterranean to trade.

The Mycenaeans

After Minoan civilization declined, the Mycenaeans became the major traders in the eastern Mediterranean. This beautiful gold mask was found in a tomb in Mycenae.

The Minoans

The Minoans traded goods like this vase decorated with an octopus. Trade made the Minoans rich enough to build magnificent buildings. These are the ruins (left) of a great palace in the Minoan city of Knossos, on the island of Crete.

Analyze Visuals
For what did the Minoans and Mycenaeans use their ships?

The Mycenaeans Although they lived in what is now Greece and influenced Greek society, historians don't consider the Minoans to be Greek. This is because the Minoans didn't speak the Greek language. The first people to speak Greek, and therefore the first to be considered Greek, were the Mycenaeans.

While the Minoans were sailing the Mediterranean, the Mycenaeans were building fortresses all over the Greek mainland. The largest and most powerful fortress was Mycenae (my-SEE-nee), after which the Mycenaeans were named.

By the mid-1400s, Minoan society had declined. That decline allowed the Mycenaeans to take over Crete and become the major traders in the eastern Mediterranean. They set up colonies in northern Greece and Italy from which they shipped goods to markets around the Mediterranean and Black Seas.

The Mycenaeans didn't think trade had to be conducted peacefully. They often attacked other kingdoms. Some historians think the Mycenaeans attacked the city of Troy, possibly starting the legendary Trojan War, which is featured in many works of literature.

Reading Check
Find Main Ideas
To what regions did Minoan and Mycenaean traders travel?

Mycenaean society began to fall apart in the 1200s BC when invaders from Europe swept into Greece. At the same time, earthquakes destroyed many cities. As Mycenaean civilization crumbled, Greece slid into a period of warfare and disorder, a period called the Dark Age.

Greeks Create City-States

The Greeks of the Dark Age left no written records. All that we know about the period comes from archaeological findings.

About 300 years after the Mycenaean civilization crumbled, the Greeks started to join together in small groups for protection and stability. Over time, these groups set up independent city-states. The Greek word for a

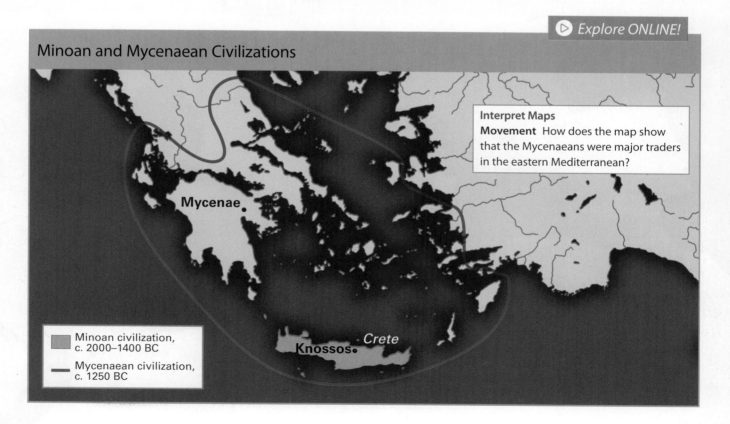

▶ *Explore ONLINE!*

Minoan and Mycenaean Civilizations

Interpret Maps
Movement How does the map show that the Mycenaeans were major traders in the eastern Mediterranean?

Mycenae

Crete

Knossos

Minoan civilization, c. 2000–1400 BC

Mycenaean civilization, c. 1250 BC

city-state is **polis** (PAH-luhs). The creation of city-states marked the beginning of what is known as Greece's classical era. During this era, the number and size of civilizations around the world began to increase. In Greece, this era saw the rise of dominant city-states.

Life in a City-State A Greek city-state was usually built around a strong fortress. This fortress often stood on top of a high hill called the **acropolis** (uh-KRAH-puh-luhs). The town around the acropolis was surrounded by walls for added protection.

Not everyone who lived in the city-state actually lived inside the city walls. Farmers, for example, usually lived near their fields outside the walls. In times of war, however, women, children, and elderly people all gathered inside the city walls for protection. As a result, they remained safe while the men of the polis formed an army to fight off its enemies.

Life in the city often focused on the marketplace, or *agora* (a-guh-ruh) in Greek. Farmers brought their crops to the market to trade for goods made by craftsmen in the town. Because it was a large open space, the market also served as a meeting place. People held both political and religious assemblies in the market. It often contained shops as well.

The city-state became the foundation of Greek civilization. Besides providing security for its people, the city gave them an identity. People thought of themselves as residents of a city, not as Greeks. Because the city-state was so central to their lives, the Greeks expected people to participate in its affairs, especially in its economy and its government.

▶ Explore ONLINE!

Greek City-States and Colonies, c. 600 BC

Interpret Maps
Location Near which geographic feature were many Greek city-states and colonies located?

Area of Greek influence

Greek city-state or colony

Trade route

0   150   300 mi
0 150 300 km

City-States and Colonization Life in Greece eventually became more settled. People no longer had to fear raiders swooping down on their cities. As a result, they were free to think about things other than defense. Some Greeks began to dream of becoming rich through trade. Others became curious about neighboring lands around the Mediterranean Sea. Some also worried about how to deal with Greece's growing population. Despite their different reasons, all these people eventually reached the same idea: the Greeks should establish colonies.

Before long, groups from city-states around Greece began to set up colonies in distant lands. Afterwards, Greek colonies became independent. In other words, each colony became a new polis. In fact, some cities that began as colonies began to create colonies of their own. This meant that Greece continued to expand. This territorial expansion increased opportunities for trade, so Greece's economy grew as well. Eventually, Greek colonies spread all around the Mediterranean and Black Seas. Many big cities around the Mediterranean today began as Greek colonies. Among them are Istanbul (is-tahn-BOOL) in Turkey, Marseille (mahr-SAY) in France, and Naples in Italy.

The sea provided early Greeks with food and a way to trade with other people.

Patterns of Trade Although the colonies were independent, they often traded with city-states in Greece. This trade was based on the supply and demand of certain goods with uniform, or agreed upon, value. For example, the colonies' location gave them access to resources that the city-states wanted. The colonies specialized in the production of metals, such as copper and iron, that were sent to mainland Greece. In return, the Greek city-states sent wine, olive oil, and other products to the colonies.

Trade made the city-states much richer. Because of their locations, some city-states became great trading centers. By 550 BC, the Greeks had become the greatest traders in the whole Aegean region. Greek ships sailed to Egypt and cities around the Black Sea.

Reading Check
Analyze Causes
Why did the Greeks develop city-states?

Summary and Preview In this lesson you learned about the creation of city-states and how they affected Greek society. In the next lesson, you will read about how the government of one city-state changed as people became more interested in how they were ruled.

Lesson 1 Assessment

Review Ideas, Terms, and People

1. **a. Summarize** What kinds of landforms are found in Greece?

   b. Synthesize How did the sea help shape early Greek society?

   c. Predict Effects How might the difficulty of mountain travel have been a benefit to the Greeks?

2. **a. Summarize** What was the first major civilization to develop in Greece?

   b. Compare How were the Minoans and Mycenaeans similar?

3. **a. Summarize** What is a polis?

   b. Draw Conclusions Why do you think the Greeks built their cities around a high acropolis?

Critical Thinking

4. **Summarize** Using your notes, write one sentence that describes Greece's geography and one sentence that describes its trade. Then write two sentences to summarize the influence of geography on trade.

| Geography | → | Trade | → | Summary |

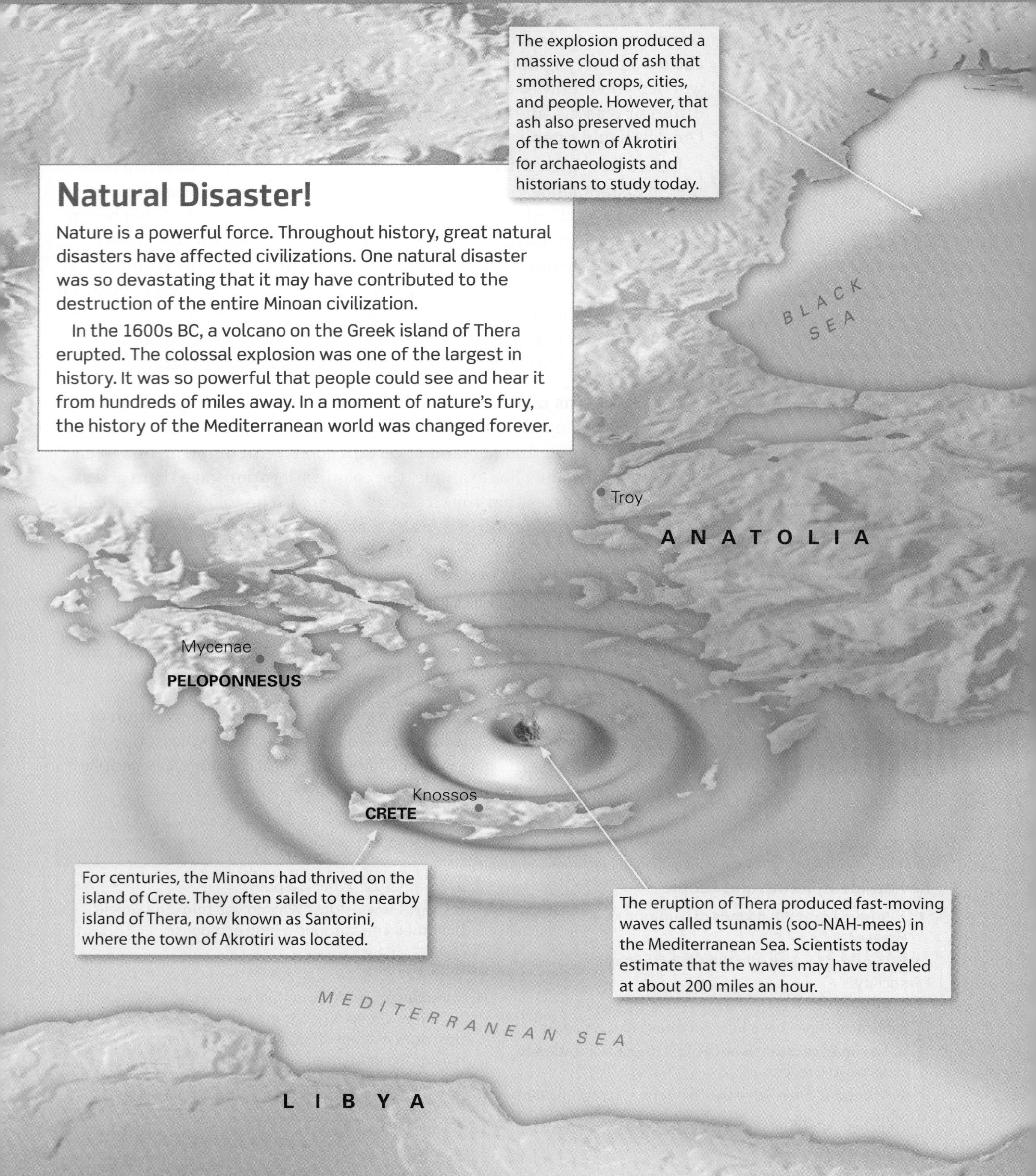

The explosion produced a massive cloud of ash that smothered crops, cities, and people. However, that ash also preserved much of the town of Akrotiri for archaeologists and historians to study today.

Natural Disaster!

Nature is a powerful force. Throughout history, great natural disasters have affected civilizations. One natural disaster was so devastating that it may have contributed to the destruction of the entire Minoan civilization.

In the 1600s BC, a volcano on the Greek island of Thera erupted. The colossal explosion was one of the largest in history. It was so powerful that people could see and hear it from hundreds of miles away. In a moment of nature's fury, the history of the Mediterranean world was changed forever.

BLACK SEA

Troy

ANATOLIA

Mycenae

PELOPONNESUS

Knossos

CRETE

For centuries, the Minoans had thrived on the island of Crete. They often sailed to the nearby island of Thera, now known as Santorini, where the town of Akrotiri was located.

The eruption of Thera produced fast-moving waves called tsunamis (soo-NAH-mees) in the Mediterranean Sea. Scientists today estimate that the waves may have traveled at about 200 miles an hour.

MEDITERRANEAN SEA

LIBYA

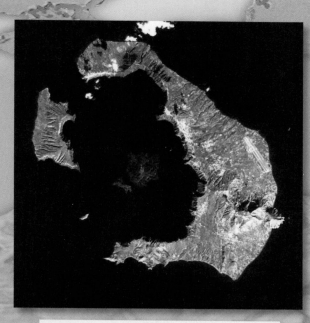

Tsunami waves and powerful earthquakes struck Akrotiri before the eruption. The huge gap on Santorini's western side and the water in the middle are evidence of the explosion more than 3,500 years ago.

CYPRUS

Aleppo

Jericho

E G Y P T

Interpret Maps

1. **Location** What direction did the ash cloud travel after the island's eruption?

2. **Human-Environment Interactions** How might the effects of the ash cloud have influenced Minoan civilization?

Three Stages of Disaster

Stage 1

Warning Signs Following a series of earthquakes, the volcano begins to shoot ash into the sky. People flee the island in fear.

Stage 2

Explosion Ash and rock are flung into the air and sweep down the volcano's sides, destroying everything in their path. Cracks through the island rock begin to form from the powerful explosions.

Stage 3

Collapse The volcano collapses and falls into the sea, creating massive waves. The powerful waves slam into Crete, flooding coastal areas.

The Glory of Athens

The Big Idea

The people of Athens endured war and tried many different forms of government before creating a democracy.

Main Ideas

- Aristocrats and tyrants ruled early Athens.
- Athens created the world's first democracy.
- Ancient democracy was different than modern democracy.

Key Terms and People

democracy
aristocrats
oligarchy
aristocracy
citizens
tyrant
Pericles

If YOU were there . . .

For many years, your city has been ruled by a small group of rich men. They have generally been good leaders. They have built new buildings and protected the city from enemies. But now a new leader wants to let all free men help run the government. It won't matter whether they are rich or poor. Some people, however, worry about giving power to ordinary people.

What do you think of this new government?

Aristocrats and Tyrants Rule

Greece is the birthplace of **democracy**, a type of government in which people rule themselves. The word *democracy* comes from Greek words meaning "rule of the people." But Greek city-states didn't start as democracies and not all became democratic.

Rule by a Few People Even Athens, the city where democracy was born, began with a different kind of government. In early Athens, kings ruled the city-state. Later, a group of rich landowners, or **aristocrats** (uh-RIS-tuh-krats), took power. A government in which only a few people have power is called an **oligarchy** (AH-luh-gar-kee).

Oligarchy

Early Athens was governed by a small group of powerful aristocrats. This type of government is called an oligarchy, which means "rule by a few."

COYPEL (Noël) 1628-1707
Solon defendant ses lois contre les Athéniens.

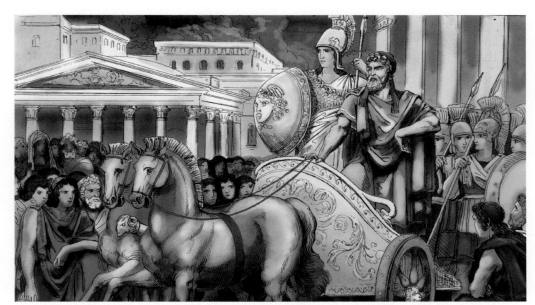

At the time, Athenian society was also known as an **aristocracy** (uh-RIS-tuh-kra-see), because only those from the highest social class had power. The aristocrats dominated Athenian society. As the richest men in town, they were the only ones who could be elected to office. These men ran the city's economy. They also served as its generals and judges. Common people had little say in the government.

In the 600s BC, a group of rebels tried to overthrow the aristocrats. They failed. Possibly as a result of their attempt, however, a man named Draco (DRAY-koh) created a new set of laws for Athens. These laws brought very harsh order to the city. For example, Draco's laws made minor crimes such as loitering punishable by death.

Many in Athens thought Draco's laws were so strict that they unfairly put limits on individual rights. In the 590s BC, a man named Solon (SOH-luhn) created a set of laws that were much less harsh and gave more rights to nonaristocrats. Under Solon's laws, all free men living in Athens became **citizens**, people who had the right to participate in government. But his efforts were not enough for the Athenians. They were ready to end the rule of the aristocracy.

The Rise of the Tyrants Because the Athenians weren't pleased with the rule of the aristocrats, they wanted a new government. In 546 BC, a noble named Peisistratus (py-SIS-truht-uhs) overthrew the oligarchy. He became the ruler of Athens. Peisistratus was called a **tyrant**, which meant he was a leader who held power through the use of force.

Today the word *tyrant* means a ruler who is harsh, but the word had a different meaning in ancient Greece. Athenian tyrants were usually good leaders. Tyrants were able to stay in power because they had strong armies and because the people supported them.

Peisistratus brought peace and prosperity to the city. He began new policies meant to unify the city. He created new festivals and built temples and monuments. During his rule, many improvements were made in Athens.

After Peisistratus died, his son took over as tyrant. Many aristocrats, however, were unhappy because their power was gone. Some of these aristocrats convinced a rival city-state to attack Athens. As a result of this invasion, the tyrants lost power and, for a short time, aristocrats returned to power in Athens.

The Use of Common Currency Greek tyrants also encouraged the development of a common currency, or unit of money, to make trade easier. Silver coins were minted and a common standard of weights and measures was established. Many people accepted the value of these coins, which made it easier to trade in the region.

Many city-states, such as Athens, minted their own coins. As Athens became more powerful, its currency did as well. Soon its coins, known as *tetradrachm,* were being used widely throughout Greece.

Corinth also minted its own coins. Corinth was an important center of trade in the region. Its location allowed the tyrants of Corinth to control trade routes on land and over water. The decision to use a common currency and Corinth's geographic location helped it become a wealthy, dominant city-state.

Reading Check
Find Main Ideas
What was a tyrant in ancient Greece?

Democracy
Around 500 BC, Athens became a democracy. *Democracy* means "rule by the people." For the first time in history, a government was based on the voices of its free citizens.

Ancient Athens was the birthplace of democracy—the system of government in which the people rule themselves. Democracy was perhaps the greatest achievement of ancient Athens. In time, it became the Greeks' greatest gift to the world. The Athenian assembly met on a hill called the Pnyx (pah-NIKS). Only free male citizens of Athens were members of the assembly with the right to vote. Women, slaves, and foreigners could not participate.

In Athenian democracy, people debated issues in the open air, and these debates were noisy affairs.

Voting was usually done by a show of hands, but sometimes assembly members wrote their votes on broken pieces of pottery.

Men spoke before the assembly to support or argue against different issues. Persuasive speakers often convinced others to pass laws they supported.

Analyze Visuals
How were the public debates in the assembly useful sources of political information for citizens?

Athens Creates Democracy

Around 500 BC, a new leader named Cleisthenes (KLYS-thuh-neez) gained power in Athens. Although he was a member of one of the most powerful families in Athens, Cleisthenes didn't want aristocrats to run the government. He thought they already had too much influence. By calling on the support of the people, Cleisthenes was able to overthrow the aristocracy once and for all. In its place, he established a completely new form of government. Under Cleisthenes' leadership, Athens developed the world's first democracy. For this reason, he is sometimes called the father of democracy.

Democracy under Cleisthenes In a democracy, the role of government is to encourage individual freedoms and to give citizens the opportunity to rule themselves. So all citizens in Athens had the right to participate in the assembly. This was a significant responsibility for citizens because this gathering created the city's laws. The assembly met outdoors on a hillside so that everyone could attend the meetings.

Citizens not only had the right to attend the assembly and vote on laws, but they also had the right to voice their opinions. In fact, the Athenians encouraged people to speak. During meetings, people stood before the crowd and gave speeches on political issues. Many wanted to hear these thoughts and debated about them. After the speeches were over, the assembly voted. Voting was usually done by a show of hands, but sometimes the Athenians used secret ballots. The creation of public assemblies established a principle known as rule of law. Rule of law means that a government and its citizens are accountable to agreed-upon law. Creating laws with public discussion helped make government accountable to the people.

The number of people who voted in the assembly changed from day to day. For major decisions, however, the assembly needed about 6,000 people to vote. But it wasn't always easy to gather that many people together in one place.

According to one Greek writer, the government sent slaves to the market to round up more citizens if necessary. In one of the writer's plays, slaves walked through the market holding a long rope between them. The rope was covered in red dye and would mark the clothing of anyone it touched. Any citizen with red dye on his clothing had to go to the assembly meeting or pay a large fine.

Because the assembly was so large, it was sometimes difficult to make decisions. The Athenians therefore selected citizens to be city officials and to serve on a smaller council. These officials decided which laws the assembly should discuss. This helped the government run more smoothly.

DOCUMENT-BASED INVESTIGATION   Historical Source

Pericles' Funeral Oration

In 430 BC, Pericles addressed the people of Athens at a funeral for soldiers who had died in battle. In his speech, Pericles tried to comfort the Athenians by reminding them of the greatness of their government.

Pericles is praising the Athenians for creating a democracy.

Athenian government was open to all free men, not just a few.

"Our form of government does not enter into rivalry with the institutions of others. We do not copy our neighbors, but are an example to them. It is true that we are called a democracy, for the administration is in the hands of the many and not of the few. . . .

There is no exclusiveness [snobbery] in our public life, and . . . we are not suspicious of one another. . . ."

—Pericles, quoted in Thucydides, *History of the Peloponnesian War*

Analyze Historical Sources
How do you think Pericles felt Athenian government compared to other cities' governments?

The Rights of Citizens

Aristotle discusses how many people were not treated equally under the law before democracy developed in Athens.

"After this event there was contention for a long time between the upper classes and the populace. Not only was the constitution at this time oligarchical in every respect, but the poorer classes, men, women, and children, were the serfs of the rich. . . . The whole country was in the hands of a few persons, and if the tenants failed to pay their rent they were liable to be hauled into slavery, and their children with them. . . . But the hardest and bitterest part of the constitution in the eyes of the masses was their state of serfdom. Not but what they were also discontented with every other feature of their lot; for, to speak generally, they had no part nor share in anything."

—Section 1, Part 2 of *The Athenian Constitution* by Aristotle; translated by Sir Frederic G. Kenyon

Analyze Historical Sources
What evidence from the text shows that some people had few rights under the Athenian constitution?

Changes in Athenian Democracy As time passed, the role of Athenian citizens expanded to include more significant powers. For example, citizens had the responsibility to serve on juries and decide court cases. Juries had anywhere from 200 to 6,000 people, though juries of about 500 people were much more common. Most juries had an odd number of members to prevent ties.

Athens remained a democracy for about 170 years. It reached its height under a brilliant elected leader named **Pericles** (PER-uh-kleez). He led the government from about 460 BC until his death in 429 BC.

Pericles encouraged the people of Athens to introduce democracy into other parts of Greece. He also championed a sense of civic duty and pride. He wanted the Athenians to be responsible for their city. Pericles believed that participating in government was just as important as defending Athens in war. To encourage more citizens to participate in government, he paid those who served in public offices or on juries. Many modern governments continue these practices today.

Greek Constitutions The Greeks created constitutions in which laws were written. A constitution is a set of beliefs and laws that are used to govern a state, nation, or organization. The philosopher Aristotle collected the constitutions of over 150 Greek city-states and wrote comments about each. One of these well-known texts is *The Athenian Constitution*. Sections of the original papyrus document still exist.

End of Democracy in Athens Eventually, the great age of Athenian democracy came to an end. In the mid-330s BC Athens was conquered by the Macedonians from north of Greece. After the conquest, Athens fell under strong Macedonian influence.

Even after being conquered by Macedonia, Athens kept its democratic government. But it was a democracy with very limited powers. The Macedonian king ruled his country like a dictator, a ruler who held all the power. No one could make any decisions without his approval.

Reading Check
Summarize Which two examples show that civic participation was important to the Athenians?

In Athens, the assembly still met to make laws, but it had to be careful not to upset the king. The Athenians didn't dare make any drastic changes to their laws without the king's consent. They weren't happy with this situation, but they feared the king's powerful army. Before long, though, the Athenians lost even this limited democracy. In the 320s BC, a new king took over Greece and ended Athenian democracy.

Ancient Democracy Differs from Modern Democracy

Like ancient Athens, the United States has a democratic government in which the people hold power. But our modern democracy is very different from the ancient Athenians' democracy.

Direct Democracy All citizens in Athens could participate directly in the government. We call this form of government a direct democracy. It is called direct democracy because each person's decision directly affects the outcome of a vote. In Athens, citizens gathered together to discuss issues and vote on them. Each person's vote counted, and the majority ruled.

They believed that citizens should also have the ability to vote, and they believed in the idea of majority rule. Greek ideals of direct democracy and rule of law influenced the founders of the United States. However, the United States was too large for direct democracy to work for the whole country. For example, it was impossible for all citizens to gather in one place for a debate. Instead, the founders of the United States set up a different kind of democracy.

Quick Facts

Democracy Then and Now

In Athenian Direct Democracy . . .

- All citizens met as a group to debate and vote directly on every issue.
- There was no separation of powers. Citizens created laws, enforced laws, and acted as judges.
- Only free male citizens could vote. Women and slaves could not vote.

In American Representative Democracy . . .

- Citizens elect representatives to debate and vote on issues for them.
- There is a separation of powers. Citizens elect some people to create laws, others to enforce laws, and others to be judges.
- Men and women who are citizens have the right to vote.

The United States Supreme Court building was designed to look similar to Greek buildings, like the Parthenon.

Representative Democracy The United States is a representative democracy, or democratic republic. In this system, citizens elect officials to represent them in the government. These elected officials then meet to make the laws that govern the nation and the decisions about how to enforce them.

In Athens, some people were treated equally and others were not. For example, women and slaves had few, if any, political rights. Similar ideas about equality existed when the U.S. Constitution was first written. Over time, however, ideas about equality and liberty in the United States changed. Citizens who are old enough are eligible to participate in the political process. The ideas about democracy and government that began in ancient Greece continue to influence democracy in the United States.

Summary and Preview In this lesson, you learned about the development and decline of democracy in Athens. You also learned how Athenian democracy influenced the government of the United States. Another city-state, Sparta, was also influential in the region. In the next lesson, you will learn what happened when Athens and Sparta became enemies.

Reading Check
Compare and Contrast How are direct democracy and representative democracy different?

Lesson 2 Assessment

Review Ideas, Terms, and People

1. **a. Contrast** How are oligarchy and tyranny different?

   b. Synthesize Describe the relationship between the power that Athens had and the way its currency was used in trade.

2. **a. Analyze** How did Pericles champion Athenian democracy?

   b. Explain How do we know that written constitutions developed in ancient Greece?

   c. Summarize How was rule of law used to govern Athens?

3. **Analyze** What type of democracy did Athens have? How did this later affect the creation of American democracy?

Critical Thinking

4. **Predict Effects** Debate as though you are discussing an issue in the Athens assembly. How might Athens be affected if women, slaves, and foreigners were allowed to vote? Present speeches about the potential effects of this decision.

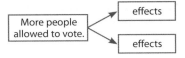

Athens and Sparta

The Big Idea

The two most powerful city-states in Greece, Sparta and Athens, had very different cultures and became bitter enemies in the 400s BC.

Main Ideas

- The Spartans built a military society to provide security and protection.
- The Athenians admired the mind and the arts in addition to physical abilities.
- Sparta and Athens fought over who should have power and influence in Greece.

Key Terms

alliance
Peloponnesian War

If YOU were there . . .

Your father, a wandering trader, has decided it is time to settle down. He offers the family a choice between two cities. In one city, everyone wants to be athletic, tough, and strong. They're good at enduring hardships and following orders. The other city is different. There, you'd be admired if you could think deeply and speak persuasively, if you knew a lot about astronomy or history, or if you sang and played beautiful music.

Which city do you choose? Why?

Spartans Build a Military Society

Spartan society was dominated by the military. According to Spartan tradition, the city's social system was created between 900 and 600 BC by a man named Lycurgus (ly-KUHR-guhs) after a slave revolt. To keep such a revolt from happening again, he increased the military's role in society. The Spartans believed that military power was the way to provide security and protection for their city. Daily life in Sparta reflected this belief.

Boys and Men in Sparta Daily life in Sparta was dominated by the army. Even the lives of children reflected this domination. When a boy was born, government officials came to look at him. If the baby was not healthy, he was taken outside of the city and left to die. Healthy boys were trained from an early age to be soldiers.

As part of their training, boys ran, jumped, swam, and threw javelins to increase their strength. They also learned to endure the hardships they would face as soldiers. For example, boys weren't given shoes or heavy clothes, even in winter. They also weren't given much food. Boys were allowed to steal food if they could, but if they were caught, they were whipped. At least one boy chose to die rather than admit to his theft.

"One youth, having stolen a fox and hidden it under his coat, allowed it to tear out his very bowels [organs] with its claws and teeth and died rather than betray his theft."

–Plutarch, from *Life of Lycurgus*

To this boy—and to most Spartan soldiers— courage and strength were more important than one's own safety.

Soldiers between the ages of 20 and 30 lived in army barracks and only occasionally visited their families. Spartan men stayed in the army until they turned 60.

The Spartans believed that the most important qualities of good soldiers were self-discipline and obedience. To reinforce self-discipline they required soldiers to live tough lives free from comforts. For example, the Spartans didn't have such luxuries as soft furniture and expensive food. They thought such comforts made people weak. Even the Spartans' enemies admired their discipline and obedience.

Quick Facts

Life in Sparta

The Spartans valued discipline, obedience, and courage above all else. Spartan men learned these values at an early age, when they were trained to be soldiers. Spartan women were also expected to be strong, athletic, and disciplined.

The Life of a Spartan Soldier

Ages 7–12: Values training Boys left home and got a basic education.

Ages 12–18: Physical training Boys developed physical skills through exercise.

Ages 18–20: Military training Men learned how to fight as part of the army.

Ages 20–30: Military service Soldiers formed the body of the Spartan army.

Age 30: Full citizenship Soldiers could participate in the assembly and move back home.

Girls and Women in Sparta Because Spartan men were often away at war, Spartan women had more rights than other Greek women. Some women owned land in Sparta and ran their households when their husbands were gone. Unlike women in other Greek cities, Spartan women didn't spend time spinning cloth or weaving. They thought of those tasks as the jobs of slaves, unsuitable for the wives and mothers of soldiers.

Spartan women also received physical training. Like the men, they learned how to run, jump, wrestle, and throw javelins. The Spartans believed this training would help women bear healthy children.

Government Sparta was officially ruled by two kings who jointly led the army. But elected officials actually had more power than the kings. These officials ran Sparta's day-to-day activities. They also handled dealings between Sparta and other city-states.

Sparta's government was set up to control the city's helots (HEL-uhts), or slaves. The helots were government-owned slaves who grew all the city's crops and did other agricultural jobs in order to feed the people. They were also used as servants and could be forced to fight during war. Their lives were miserable, and they couldn't leave their land. Although slaves greatly outnumbered Spartan citizens, fear of the Spartan army kept them from rebelling. This slave economy in Sparta helped the city-state become rich, powerful, and prosperous. Some foreigners, who lived freely, also lived in Sparta and contributed to the economy. However, they could be forced to leave at any time.

Reading Check
Summarize What was the most important element of Spartan society?

Historical Source

Xenophon's Picture of an Ideal Household

Xenophon, who studied with Socrates, wrote a story about an average day for someone in Athens.

"After this, usually I mount my horse and take a canter. I put him through his paces, suiting these, so far as possible, to those inevitable in war — in other words, I avoid neither steep slope, nor sheer incline, neither trench nor runnel, only giving my uttermost heed the while so as not to lame my horse while exercising him. When that is over, the boy gives the horse a roll, and leads him homeward, taking at the same time from the country to town whatever we may chance to need. Meanwhile I am off for home, partly walking, partly running, and having reached home I take a bath. . . ."

—from "Xenophon's Picture of an Ideal Household" in *Readings in Ancient History*, by William Sterns Davis.

Analyze Historical Sources
What evidence from the text shows that the speaker is most likely an aristocrat and a man?

Athenians Admire the Mind

Sparta's main rival in Greece was Athens. Like Sparta, Athens had been a leader in the Persian Wars and had a powerful army. But life in Athens was very different from life in Sparta. In addition to physical training, the Athenians valued education, clear thinking, and the arts.

Boys and Men in Athens From a young age, Athenian boys from rich families worked to improve both their bodies and their minds. Like Spartan boys, Athenian boys had to learn to run, jump, and fight. But this training was not as harsh or as long as the training in Sparta.

Unlike Spartan men, Athenian men didn't have to devote their whole lives to the army. All men in Athens joined the army, but for only two years. They helped defend the city between the ages of 18 and 20. Older men only had to serve in the army in times of war.

In addition to their physical training, Athenian students, unlike the Spartans, also learned other skills. They learned to read, write, and count as well as sing and play musical instruments. Boys also learned about Greek history and legend. For example, they studied the *Iliad*, the *Odyssey*, and other works of Greek literature.

DOCUMENT-BASED INVESTIGATION   Historical Source

Views of Education

Plato, an Athenian, thought that education for young boys should train both the mind and the body. Lycurgus, a Spartan lawgiver, thought education for boys should teach them how to fight.

"And what shall be their education? Can we find a better division than the traditional sort?—and this has two divisions, gymnastics for the body, and music for the soul."

—Plato from *The Republic*

"Reading and writing they gave them, just enough to serve their turn; their chief care was to make them good subjects, and to teach them to endure pain and conquer in battle."

—Plutarch from *Life of Lycurgus*

Analyze Historical Sources
How do the viewpoints of Plato and Lycurgus reflect the ideals of Athens and Sparta?

Boys from very rich families often continued their education with private tutors. These tutors taught their students about philosophy, geometry, astronomy, and other subjects. They also taught the boys how to be good public speakers. This training prepared boys for participation in the Athenian assembly.

Very few boys had the opportunity to receive this much education, however. Boys from poor families usually didn't get any education, though most of them could read and write at least a little. Most of the boys from poor families became farmers and grew food for the city's richer citizens. A few went to work with craftspeople to learn other trades.

Girls and Women in Athens Although many boys in Athens received good educations, girls didn't. In fact, girls received almost no education. Athenian men didn't think girls needed to be educated. A few girls were taught how to read and write at home by private tutors. However, most girls only learned household tasks like weaving and sewing.

Despite Athens's reputation for freedom and democracy, women there had fewer rights than women in many other city-states. Athenian women could not:

- serve in any part of the city's government, including the assembly and juries
- leave their homes, except on special occasions
- buy anything or own property
- disobey their husbands or fathers

In fact, women in Athens had almost no rights at all.

Quick Facts

Life in Athens

The Athenians valued education and the arts and believed that educated people made the best citizens.

- Boys from wealthy families were taught how to read, how to speak, and even how to think properly.
- Some boys were required to memorize long passages of plays or poems. Some had to commit both the *Iliad* and the *Odyssey* to memory.
- Very few girls, however, received educations.

Limited Rights in Athenian Society Although Athens was a democracy, Athenian rulers did not protect the rights of everyone who lived there. Athenian women did not have the same rights as in other Greek city-states. They also did not have the same rights as women in other ancient governments. For example, women in the Persian Empire were permitted to own property.

Other people also had limited rights. Athens had three classes of slaves. Slaves in the highest class could work as tutors or police officers. Next were slaves who worked as servants for families. They could sometimes buy their freedom and their masters often treated them well during festivals. The lowest level of Athenian slaves worked in nearby silver mines, where most slaves died during their work.

Foreigners in Athens were known as *metics*. Many metics were Greeks from other city-states. They were free people who worked in sanitation, maintenance, and rowing, but metics were not citizens of Athens. Therefore, they were not allowed to participate in government.

Reading Check
Draw Conclusions
Why did girls in Athens receive little education?

Sparta and Athens Fight

As you learned earlier, Sparta and Athens worked together to win the Persian Wars. The Spartans fought most of the battles on land, and the Athenians fought at sea. After the war, the powerful Athenian fleet continued to protect Greece from the Persian navy. As a result, Athens had a great influence over much of Greece.

Athenian Power After the Persian Wars ended in 480 BC, many city-states formed an **alliance**, or an agreement to work together. They wanted to punish the Persians for attacking Greece. They also agreed to help defend each other and to protect trade in the Aegean Sea. To pay for this defense, each city-state gave money to the alliance. Because the money was kept on the island of Delos, historians call the alliance the Delian League.

With its navy protecting the islands, Athens was the strongest member of the league. As a result, the Athenians began to treat other league members as their subjects. They refused to let members quit the league and forced more cities to join it. The Athenians even used the league's money to pay for buildings in Athens. Without even fighting, the Athenians made the Delian League an Athenian empire.

The Peloponnesian War The Delian League was not the only alliance in Greece. After the Persian Wars, many cities in southern Greece, including Sparta, banded together as well. This alliance was called the Peloponnesian League after the peninsula on which the cities were located.

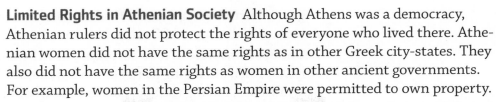

During the Peloponnesian War, sailors and soldiers rowed warships called triremes, which carried about 200 people.

The growth of Athenian power worried many cities in the Peloponnesian League. Finally, to stop the growth of Athens, Sparta declared war.

This declaration of war began the **Peloponnesian War**, a war between Athens and Sparta that threatened to tear all of Greece apart. In 431 BC the Spartan army marched north to Athens. They surrounded the city, waiting for the Athenians to come out and fight. But the Athenians stayed in the city, hoping that the Spartans would leave. Instead, the Spartans began to burn the crops in the fields around Athens. They hoped that Athens would run out of food and be forced to surrender.

The Spartans were in for a surprise. The Athenian navy escorted merchant ships to Athens, bringing plenty of food to the city. The navy also attacked Sparta's allies, forcing the Spartans to send troops to defend other Greek cities. At the same time, though, disease swept through Athens, killing thousands. For 10 years neither side could gain an advantage over the other. Eventually, they agreed to a truce. Athens kept its empire, and the Spartans went home.

A few years later, in 415 BC, Athens tried again to expand its empire. It sent its army and navy to conquer the island of Sicily. This effort failed. The entire Athenian army was defeated by Sicilian allies of Sparta and taken prisoner. Even worse, these Sicilians also destroyed most of the Athenian navy.

Taking advantage of Athens's weakness, Sparta attacked Athens, and the war started up once more. Although the Athenians fought bravely, the Spartans won. They cut off the supply of food to Athens completely. In 404 BC, the people of Athens, starving and surrounded, surrendered. The Peloponnesian War was over, and Sparta was in control.

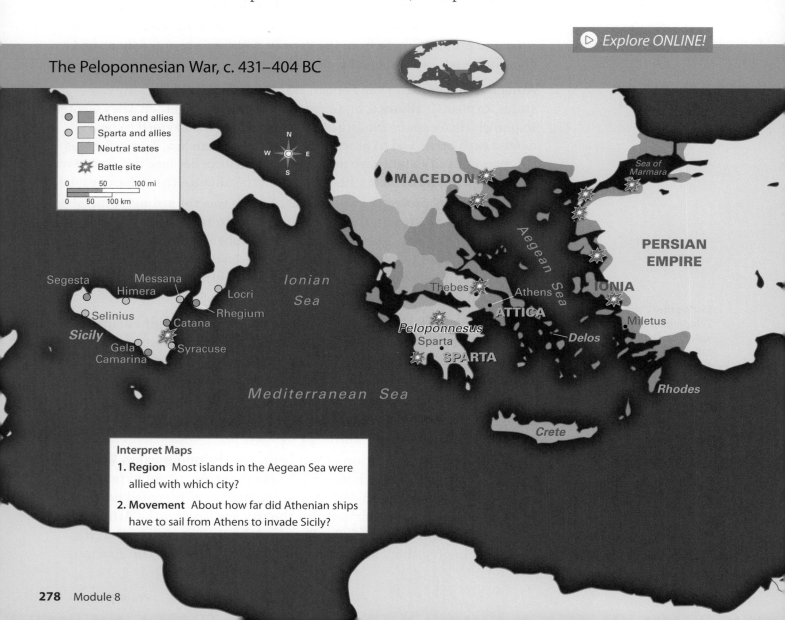

▷ Explore ONLINE!

The Peloponnesian War, c. 431–404 BC

Legend:
- Athens and allies
- Sparta and allies
- Neutral states
- ✦ Battle site

0   50   100 mi
0   50   100 km

MACEDON

Sea of Marmara

Aegean Sea

PERSIAN EMPIRE

Segesta
Messana
Himera
Locri
Selinius
Rhegium
Catana
Sicily
Gela
Syracuse
Camarina

Ionian Sea

Thebes
Athens
ATTICA
IONIA
Miletus

Peloponnesus
Sparta
Delos

SPARTA

Mediterranean Sea

Crete

Rhodes

Interpret Maps

1. **Region** Most islands in the Aegean Sea were allied with which city?

2. **Movement** About how far did Athenian ships have to sail from Athens to invade Sicily?

Reading Check
Analyze Effects
What effect did
the end of the
Peloponnesian War
have on Sparta?

Fighting Among the City-States With the defeat of Athens, Sparta became the most powerful city-state in Greece. For about 30 years, the Spartans controlled nearly all of Greece, until other city-states started to resent them. This resentment led to a period of war. Control of Greece shifted from city-state to city-state. The fighting went on for many years, which weakened Greece and left it open to attack from outside.

Summary and Preview In this lesson, you studied the similarities and differences between Athens and Sparta. You also read about conflicts among city-states for control of Greece. In the next lesson, you will learn about Greek mythology and literature.

Lesson 3 Assessment

Review Ideas, Terms, and People

1. a. Recall How long did Spartan men stay in the army?

b. Summarize How did the army affect life in Sparta?

2. a. Identify What skills did rich Athenian boys learn in school?

b. Elaborate How might the government of Athens have influenced the growth of its educational system?

3. a. Identify Which city-state won the Peloponnesian War?

b. Explain Why did many city-states form an alliance against Athens?

Critical Thinking

4. Contrast Identify the differences between the people of Athens and Sparta in the text. Create a table like this to organize the information.

People	Athens	Sparta
foreigners		
slaves		
women		

Greek Mythology and Literature

The Big Idea

The ancient Greeks created great myths and works of literature that influence the way we speak and write today.

Main Ideas

- The Greeks created myths to explain the world.

- Ancient Greek literature provides some of the world's greatest poems and stories.

- Greek literature lives on and influences our world even today.

Key Terms and People

mythology
Homer
Sappho
Aesop
fables

If YOU were there . . .

As a farmer in ancient Greece, your way of life depends on events in nature. The crops you grow need sunshine and rain, though thunder and lightning scare you. When you look up at the night sky, you wonder about the twinkling lights you see there. You know that at certain times of the year, the weather will turn cold and gray and plants will die. Then, a few months later, green plants will grow again.

How might you explain these natural events?

Myths Explain the World

The ancient Greeks believed in many gods. These gods were at the center of Greek **mythology**—a body of stories about gods and heroes that try to explain how the world works. Each story, or myth, explained natural or historical events. Greek mythology is part of the cultural landscape of Greece. A cultural landscape describes how natural resources and wildlife relate to events and people. The ancient Greeks used myths to explain natural events such as thunder or earthquakes. They explained these events as acts of the gods.

Greek Gods People in ancient Greece believed their gods caused events like volcanic eruptions to happen. They created myths to explain the gods' actions.

The most important Greek gods included:
- Zeus, king of the gods
- Hera, queen of the gods
- Poseidon, god of the sea
- Hades, god of the underworld
- Athena, goddess of wisdom
- Apollo, god of the sun
- Ares, god of war
- Aphrodite, goddess of love
- Dionysus, god of celebration
- Hermes, the messenger god

Deities, Titans, Gods, and Mythology According to Greek mythology, Gaea and Uranus were the first two deities in the world. A deity is any being that a culture believes has divine power over its people. The children and grandchildren of Gaea and Uranus were known as the Titans. The next generation of deities rebelled against the titans. Gods and Titans battled in a war known as Titanomachy, and the Titans were defeated. The young victorious deities took control of Mount Olympus and became the Olympian gods.

The Greeks saw the work of these gods in events all around them. For example, the Greeks lived in an area where volcanic eruptions were common. To explain these eruptions, they told stories about the god Hephaestus (hi-FES-tuhs), who lived underground. The fire and lava that poured out of volcanoes, the Greeks said, came from the huge fires of the god's forge. At this forge he created weapons and armor for the other gods.

The Greeks did not think the gods spent all their time creating disasters, though. They also believed the gods caused daily events. For example, they believed the goddess of agriculture, Demeter (di-MEE-tuhr), created the seasons. According to Greek myth, Demeter had a daughter who was kidnapped by another god. The desperate goddess begged the god to let her daughter go, and eventually he agreed to let her return to her mother for six months every year. During the winter, Demeter is separated from her daughter and misses her. In her grief, she doesn't let plants grow. When her daughter comes home, the goddess is happy, and summer comes to Greece. To the Greeks, this story explained why winter came every year.

To keep the gods happy, the Greeks built great temples to honor them all around Greece. In return, however, they expected the gods to give them help when they needed it. For example, many Greeks in need of advice traveled to Delphi, a city in central Greece. There they spoke to the oracle,

The actions of the gods explained natural events, such as the change of seasons and severe storms. As you can see here, the gods also possessed human qualities and emotions, to which the Greeks could relate.

a female priest of Apollo to whom they thought the god gave answers. The oracle at Delphi was so respected that Greek leaders sometimes asked her for advice about how to rule their cities.

Heroes and Mythology Not all Greek myths were about gods. Many told about the adventures of great heroes. Some of these heroes were real people, while others were not. The Greeks loved to tell the stories of heroes who had special abilities and faced terrible monsters. The people of each city had their favorite hero, usually someone from there.

The people of Athens, for example, told stories about the hero Theseus. According to legend, he traveled to Crete and killed the Minotaur, a terrible monster that was half human and half bull. People from northern Greece told myths about Jason and how he sailed across the seas in search of a great treasure, fighting enemies the whole way.

Perhaps the most famous of all Greek heroes was a man called Hercules. The myths explain how Hercules fought many monsters and performed nearly impossible tasks. For example, he fought and killed the hydra, a huge snake with nine heads and poisonous fangs. Every time Hercules cut off one of the monster's heads, two more heads grew in its place. In the end, Hercules had to burn the hydra's neck each time he cut off a head to keep a new head from growing. People from all parts of Greece enjoyed stories about Hercules and his great deeds.

Reading Check Compare and Contrast How were the Titans and the Olympian gods the same? In what ways were they different?

Link to Today

Let the Games Begin!

One way the ancient Greeks honored their gods was by holding sporting contests. The largest took place every four years at Olympia, a city in southern Greece. Held in honor of Zeus, this event was called the Olympic Games. Athletes competed in four sports. Only men could compete. The Greeks held these games every four years for more than 1,000 years, until the AD 320s.

The first modern Olympics took place in Athens in 1896. Since then, athletes from many nations have assembled in cities around the world to compete. Today the Olympics include 28 sports, and both men and women participate. They are still held every four years. In 2004, the Olympic Games were held in their birthplace, Greece.

Analyze Information
How do you think the modern Olympics honors the influence of the Greek gods?

Theseus the Hero
According to legend, Athens had to send 14 people to Crete every year to be eaten by the Minotaur, a terrible monster. But Theseus, a hero from Athens, traveled to Crete and killed the Minotaur, freeing the people of Athens from this burden.

Ancient Greek Literature

Because the Greeks loved myths and stories, it is no surprise that they created great works of literature. Early Greek writers produced long epic poems, romantic poetry, and some of the world's most famous stories.

Homer and Epic Poetry Among the earliest Greek writings are two great epic poems, the *Iliad* and the *Odyssey*, by a poet named **Homer**. Like most epics, both poems describe the deeds of great heroes. The heroes in Homer's poems fought in the Trojan War. In this war, the Mycenaean Greeks fought the Trojans, people of the city called Troy.

——— BIOGRAPHY ———

Homer 800–700s BC

Historians know nothing about Homer, but he is considered the greatest poet of the ancient world. Some don't think such a person ever lived. The ancient Greeks believed he had, and, according to ancient legend, Homer was blind and recited the *Iliad* and the *Odyssey* aloud. It wasn't until much later that the poems were written down.

Form Generalizations
Why might scholars not be sure that Homer existed?

The *Iliad* tells the story of the last years of the Trojan War. It focuses on the deeds of the Greeks, especially Achilles (uh-KIL-eez), the greatest of all Greek warriors. It describes in great detail the battles between the Greeks and their Trojan enemies.

The *Odyssey* describes the challenges the Greek hero Odysseus (oh-DI-see-uhs) faced on his way home from the war. For 10 years after the war ends, Odysseus tries to get home, but many obstacles stand in his way. He has to fight his way past terrible monsters, powerful magicians, and even angry gods.

Both the *Iliad* and the *Odyssey* are great tales of adventure. But to the Greeks Homer's epic poems were much more than just entertainment. They were central to the ancient Greek education system. People memorized long passages of the poems as part of their lessons. They admired Homer's poems and the heroes described in them as symbols of Greece's great history.

Homer's epic poems influenced later writers. They copied his writing styles and borrowed some of the stories and ideas he wrote about in his works. Homer's poems are considered some of the greatest literary works ever produced.

Lyric Poetry Other poets wrote poems that were often set to music. During a performance, the poet played a stringed instrument called a lyre while reading a poem. These poets were called lyric poets after their instrument, the lyre. Today, the words of songs are called lyrics after these ancient Greek poets.

In Homer's *Odyssey*, the half woman and half-bird Sirens sang sweet songs that made passing sailors forget everything and crash their ships. To get past the Sirens, Odysseus plugged his crew's ears with wax and had himself tied to his ship's mast.

Most poets in Greece were men, but the most famous lyric poet was a woman named **Sappho** (SAF-oh). Her poems were beautiful and emotional. Most of her poems were about love and relationships with her friends and family.

Fables Other Greeks told stories to teach people important lessons. **Aesop** (EE-sahp), for example, is famous for his fables. **Fables** are short stories that teach the reader lessons about life or give advice on how to live. Historians don't know for sure if Aesop really lived, but many ancient legends are told about him. According to one story, Aesop was a slave in about 500 BC. Another story says he was an adviser to a king. Some historians think that the fables credited to Aesop were actually written by many different people and collected together under a single name. In most of Aesop's fables, animals are the main characters. The animals talk and act like humans. One of Aesop's most famous stories is the tale of the ants and the grasshopper.

> "The Ants were spending a fine winter's day drying grain collected in the summertime. A Grasshopper, perishing [dying] with famine [hunger], passed by and earnestly [eagerly] begged for a little food. The Ants inquired [asked] of him, "Why did you not treasure up food during the summer?" He replied, "I had not leisure enough. I passed the days in singing." They then said in derision: "If you were foolish enough to sing all the summer, you must dance supperless to bed in the winter."
>
> —Aesop, from "The Ants and the Grasshopper"

The lesson in this fable is that people shouldn't waste time instead of working. Those who do, Aesop says, will be sorry.

Another popular fable by Aesop, "The Tortoise and the Hare," teaches that it is better to work slowly and carefully than to hurry and make mistakes. "The Boy Who Cried Wolf" warns readers not to play pranks on others. Since we still read these fables, you may be familiar with them.

Reading Check
Summarize Why did the Greeks tell fables?

— BIOGRAPHY —

Aesop before 400 BC

Many legends have been told about Aesop, so many in fact that most believe that this person didn't exist. Whether Aesop existed or not, many stories associated with him have been passed down from generation to generation. Today, they are generally published under one name: *Aesop's Fables.* Each of these stories offers a lesson about the choices people make in their lives.

Make Inferences
Why have *Aesop's Fables* remained popular over time?

Greek Literature Lives

The works of ancient Greek writers such as Homer, Sappho, and Aesop are still alive and popular today. In fact, Greek literature has influenced modern language, literature, and art. Did you know that some of the words you use and some of the stories you hear come from ancient Greece?

Language The Greeks modified, or changed, the Phoenician writing system to create their own alphabet. The Phoenician alphabet did not have any vowels in it, so the Greeks developed a complete alphabet with symbols that could be used as both consonants and vowels. These symbols were written in an order that followed the direction of a line. Today the Greek alphabet is the basis for most of the writing systems in the Western world.

Probably the most obvious way we see the influence of the Greeks is in our language. Many English words and expressions come from Greek mythology. For example, we call a long journey an *odyssey* after Odysseus, the wandering hero of Homer's poem. Something very large and powerful is called *titanic*. This word comes from the Titans, a group of large and powerful gods in Greek myth.

The influence of Greek stories and culture can still be seen in names. Astronomers named one of Jupiter's moons Io (EYE-oh) after a woman from Greek mythology. Sports teams also use Greek names. This college mascot is dressed like a Trojan warrior.

Many places around the world today are also named after figures from Greek myths. For example, Athens is named for Athena, the goddess of wisdom. Africa's Atlas Mountains were named after a giant from Greek mythology who held up the sky. The name of the Aegean Sea comes from Aegeus, a legendary Greek king. Europe itself was named after a figure from Greek myth, the princess Europa. Even places in space bear names from mythology. For example, Jupiter's moon Io was named after a goddess's daughter.

Greek Influence on Language

In Greek Literature and Mythology . . .	Today . . .
• Achilles was a great warrior who was killed when an arrow struck his heel.	• An "Achilles heel" is a person's weak spot.
• Hercules was the strongest man on earth who completed 12 almost-impossible tasks.	• When a person has a really hard job to do it is called a "Herculean" task.
• A fox wanted to eat some grapes, but he couldn't reach the branch they were on. So he said, "Those grapes are probably sour anyway."	• When people pretend they don't want something after they find out they can't have it, they are said to have "sour grapes."
• King Midas was granted one wish by the god Dionysus, so he wished that everything he touched turned to gold.	• A person who seems to get rich easily is said to have a "Midas touch."
• Tantalus was punished for offending the gods. He had to stand up to his chin in water and he was always thirsty, but if he tried to drink the water it went away.	• Something is "tantalizing" if you want it but it's just out of your reach.

New Forms of Writing The Greeks are known for their sculpture, painting, and architecture. As you have learned, the Greeks are also known for their literature. In fact, Greek writers created many new writing forms, including drama and history.

The Greeks created drama, or plays, as part of their religious ceremonies. Actors and singers performed scenes in honor of the gods and heroes. These plays became a popular form of entertainment, especially in Athens.

In the 400s BC, Athenian writers created many of the greatest plays of the ancient world. Some writers produced tragedies, which described the hardships faced by Greek heroes. Among the best tragedy writers were Aeschylus (ES-kuh-luhs), Sophocles (SAHF-uh-kleez), and Euripides (yoo-RI-puh-deez). Each made lasting contributions to drama.

Aeschylus changed the way plays were written. Previously, plays revealed the main idea, or climax, in an early scene. Aeschylus, however, made the audience wait for the climax until later in the play in order to add tension. He also introduced the practice of having a second actor on the stage to improve dialogue.

Sophocles made further innovations to play writing. In some of his plays, a third actor appeared on stage. This made dialogue and plot more complex. Sophocles also wanted the audience to know what would happen in a play before the characters did. This created additional tension for the audience and kept them engaged with the characters and the story. Sophocles used this technique in one of his most famous plays, *Oedipus Rex* (ED-uh-puhs REKS). In this play, he wrote about a Greek hero who mistakenly killed his own father. The audience knew this before the hero realized what he had done.

Euripides' plays showed the flaws or weaknesses of the gods' personalities. His myths focused on such dark themes as suffering or revenge. One of his best-known plays is *Medea*. This play focuses on women who have experienced injustice. Other Greek dramatists focused on comedies, which made fun of people and ideas. One famous comedy writer was Aristophanes (ar-uh-STAHF-uh-neez). He used his comedy to make serious points about war, courts of law, and famous people.

The Greeks were also among the first people to write about history. They were interested in the lessons it could teach. One of the foremost Greek historians was Herodotus (hi-ROD-uh-tuhs). He is credited as the author of a great piece of narrative writing that told the history of the Persian Wars and described the Persian Empire in detail.

Thucydides (thoo-SID-uh-deez) was also an early historian. His history of the Peloponnesian War was based, in part, on his experiences as an Athenian soldier. Even though he was from Athens, Thucydides tried to be **neutral** in his writing. He studied the war and tried to figure out what had caused it. He may have hoped the Greeks could learn from their mistakes and avoid similar wars in the future. Many later historians modeled their works after his.

Academic Vocabulary
neutral unbiased, not favoring either side in a conflict

The ancient Greek epics still influence our culture. For example, in 2014, the movie *300: The Rise of an Empire* retold the story of naval battles between the Greeks and the Persians.

Literature and the Arts Greek myths have inspired artists for centuries. Great painters and sculptors have used gods and heroes as the subjects of their works. Writers have retold ancient stories, sometimes set in modern times. Movie makers have also borrowed stories from ancient myths. Hercules, for example, has been the subject of dozens of films. These films range from early classics to a Disney cartoon.

Mythological references are also common in today's popular culture. Many sports teams have adopted the names of powerful figures from myths, like Titans or Trojans. Businesses frequently use images or symbols from mythology in their advertising. Although people no longer believe in the Greek gods, mythological ideas can still be seen all around us.

Reading Check
Summarize What evidence from the text shows that the Greeks influenced the English language?

Summary and Preview The myths, stories, and poems of ancient Greece have shaped how people today speak, read, and write. Like democracy, these myths, stories, and poems are part of ancient Greece's gift to the world. In the next lesson, you will learn more about life and culture in ancient Greece.

Lesson 4 Assessment

Review Ideas, Terms, and People

1. a. **Summarize** What is mythology?
   b. **Summarize** Why did the ancient Greeks create myths?

2. a. **Summarize** What are Homer's most famous works?
   b. **Contrast** How are fables different from myths?

3. a. **Summarize** Who is one ancient Greek playwright? Who is one ancient Greek historian?
   b. **Form Generalizations** In what areas have Greek myths influenced our culture?
   c. **Analyze** Why do you think mythological references are popular today?

d. **Evaluate** Why do you think Greek literature has been so influential throughout history?

Critical Thinking

4. **Organize Information** Using your notes and a chart like this, explain the influence of myths and literature on the world today.

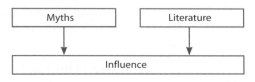

Literature in History

The Epic Poetry of Homer

Word Help

main strength
resolute determined
imploring begging

❶ *To what is Achilles being compared?*

❷ Priam, Hector's father, knows that the gods have protected and strengthened Achilles.

❸ Achilles' armor was made by the god of metalworking. *Why might the very sight of this armor make Priam afraid?*

About the Reading The *Iliad* describes one part of a ten-year war between the Greeks and the city of Troy. As the poem opens, the Greek hero Achilles (uh-KIL-eez) has left the battle to wait for help from the gods. When he learns that his best friend Patroclus is dead, however, Achilles springs back into action. In this passage, the angry Achilles sprints across the plain toward Troy—and Hector, the Trojan warrior who has killed his friend.

As You Read Look for words and actions that tell you Achilles is a hero.

From *the Iliad*
by Homer
as translated by Robert Fitzgerald

Then toward the town with might and main
he ran magnificent, like a racing chariot horse
that holds its form at full stretch on the plain. ❶
So light-footed Achilles held the pace.
And aging Priam was the first to see him
sparkling on the plain, bright as that star
in autumn rising, whose unclouded rays
shine out amid a throng of stars at dusk—
the one they call Orion's dog, most brilliant. . . . ❷
So pure and bright the bronze gear blazed
upon him as he ran. The old man gave a cry. ❸
With both his hands thrown up on high he
struck his head, then shouted, groaning,
appealing to his dear son. Unmoved, Lord
Hector stood in the gateway, resolute to
fight Achilles.

          Stretching out his hands,
old Priam said, imploring him:
            "No, Hector!
. . . don't try to hold your ground against this man,
or soon you'll meet the shock of doom. . . ."

The painting on this vase shows soldiers fighting in the Trojan War.

Word Help

travail pain
dire gorge terrible throat
spume foam or froth
maelstrom whirlpool
blanched grew pale
anguish great suffering

❶ Odysseus is the speaker. He is referring to himself and his crew. *Why might the crew be sobbing?*

❷ Three times a day, the monster Charybdis (cuh-RIB-duhs) takes in water and then spits it out.

❸ Like many Greek monsters, Scylla (SIL-uh) is part human and part animal. She has the body of a woman, six heads with snakelike necks, and twelve feet.

About the Reading The *Odyssey* takes place after the Trojan War has ended. It describes the adventures of another hero, Odysseus (oh-DIS-ee-uhs), as he makes his way home to Ithaca. His voyage is full of obstacles, including the two sea monsters described here. The idea for these monsters probably came from a strait in the Mediterranean, with a jagged cliff on one side and dangerous whirlpools on the other.

As You Read Try to picture the action in your mind.

From *the Odyssey*
by Homer
as translated by Robert Fitzgerald

> And all this time,
> in travail, sobbing, gaining on the current,
> we rowed into the strait—Scylla to port
> and on our starboard beam Charybdis, dire
> gorge of the salt sea tide. ❶ By heaven! when she
> vomited, all the sea was like a cauldron
> seething over intense fire, when the mixture
> suddenly heaves and rises.
>   The shot spume
> soared to the landside heights, and fell like rain.
> But when she swallowed the sea water down
> we saw the funnel of the maelstrom, heard
> the rock bellowing all around, and dark
> sand raged on the bottom far below. ❷
> My men all blanched against the gloom, our eyes
> were fixed upon that yawning mouth in fear
> of being devoured.
>   Then Scylla made her strike,
> whisking six of my best men from the ship.
> I happened to glance aft at ship and oarsmen
> and caught sight of their arms and legs, dangling
> high overhead. Voices came down to me
> in anguish, calling my name for the last time....❸
>   We rowed on.
> The Rocks were now behind; Charybdis, too,
> and Scylla dropped astern.

Connect Literature to History

1. **Compare** Many Greek myths were about heroes who had special abilities. What heroic abilities or traits do Achilles, Hector, and Odysseus share?

2. **Analyze** The Greeks used myths to explain the natural world. How does the *Odyssey* passage illustrate this?

Greek Art, Philosophy, and Science

The Big Idea

Ancient Greeks made lasting contributions in the arts, philosophy, and science.

Main Ideas

- The Greeks made great contributions to the arts.

- The teachings of Socrates, Plato, and Aristotle are the basis of modern philosophy.

- In science, the Greeks made key discoveries in math, medicine, and engineering.

Key Terms and People

Socrates
Plato
Aristotle
reason
Euclid
Hippocrates

If YOU were there . . .

Everyone in Athens has been talking about a philosopher and teacher named Socrates, so you decide to go and see him for yourself. You find him sitting under a tree, surrounded by his students. "Teach me about life," you say. But instead of answering, he asks you, "What is life?" You struggle to reply. He asks another question, and another. If he's such a great teacher, you wonder, shouldn't he have all the answers? Instead, all he seems to have are questions.

What do you think of Socrates?

The Arts

Among the most notable achievements of the ancient Greeks were those in the arts. These included sculptures, paintings, different types of architecture, and writings. These great works shaped Greek civilization. Many modern societies continue to hold ancient Greek art in high regard.

Statues and Paintings The ancient Greeks were master artists. Their paintings and statues have been admired for hundreds of years. Examples of these works are still displayed in museums around the world.

Greek statues are so admired because the sculptors who made them tried to make them look perfect. They wanted their statues to show how beautiful people could be. To improve

Greek sculpture is admired for its realism, natural look, and details.

their art, these sculptors carefully studied the human body, especially how it looked when it was moving. Then, using what they had learned, they carved stone and marble statues. As a result, many Greek statues look as though they could come to life at any moment.

The Greeks also made statues of various gods and goddesses for religious purposes. The Greeks considered a temple to be a god or goddess's home—the location where he or she lived. A statue was not simply an artistic expression of faith in or honor to a deity; it was the place in the temple where the god or goddess was thought to be or rest.

Greek painting is also admired for its realism and detail. For example, Greek artists painted detailed scenes on vases, pots, and other vessels using only two colors, black and red. These scenes often reflected Greece's geographic features, such as mountains and seas. These vessels often showed scenes from myths or athletic competitions as well.

The wall paintings at Akrotiri also are realistic representations of nature. Some feature different animals. Others show religious ceremonies. The paintings are one of the many reasons why Akrotiri remains a significant site for study.

Greek Architecture If you went to Greece today, you would see the ruins of many ancient buildings. Old columns still hold up parts of broken roofs, and ancient carvings decorate fallen walls. These remains give us an idea of the beauty of ancient Greek buildings.

The Greeks took great care in designing their buildings, especially their temples. Rows of tall columns surrounded the temples, making the temples look stately and inspiring. Greek designers were very careful when they measured these columns. They knew that columns standing in a long row often looked as though they curved in the middle. To prevent this optical illusion, they made their columns bulge slightly in the middle. As a result, Greek columns look perfectly straight.

Ancient Greek designers took such care because they wanted their buildings to reflect the greatness of their cities. One example is the Temple of Apollo at Delphi, which represents several Greek myths. Many ancient Greeks considered Delphi to be the center of earth.

The most impressive of all ancient Greek buildings was the Parthenon (PAHR-thuh-nahn) in Athens. The Parthenon was a beautiful temple built for the goddess Athena, whom the people of Athens considered their protector. The temple stood on the Acropolis, a fortified part of the city built on a hilltop. The Parthenon, built by Pericles, is still one of the most famous buildings in the world.

Philosophy

The ancient Greeks worshipped gods and goddesses whose actions explained many of the mysteries of the world. But by around 500 BC a few people had begun to think about other explanations. We call these people philosophers. They believed in the power of the human mind to think, explain, and understand life.

This vase features highly detailed paintings of Greek athletes.

Reading Check
Analyze Motives
Why did ancient Greek designers take such care with the design of buildings?

The Parthenon

The Parthenon was built on a hilltop in Athens. It was a center of Athenian cultural life.

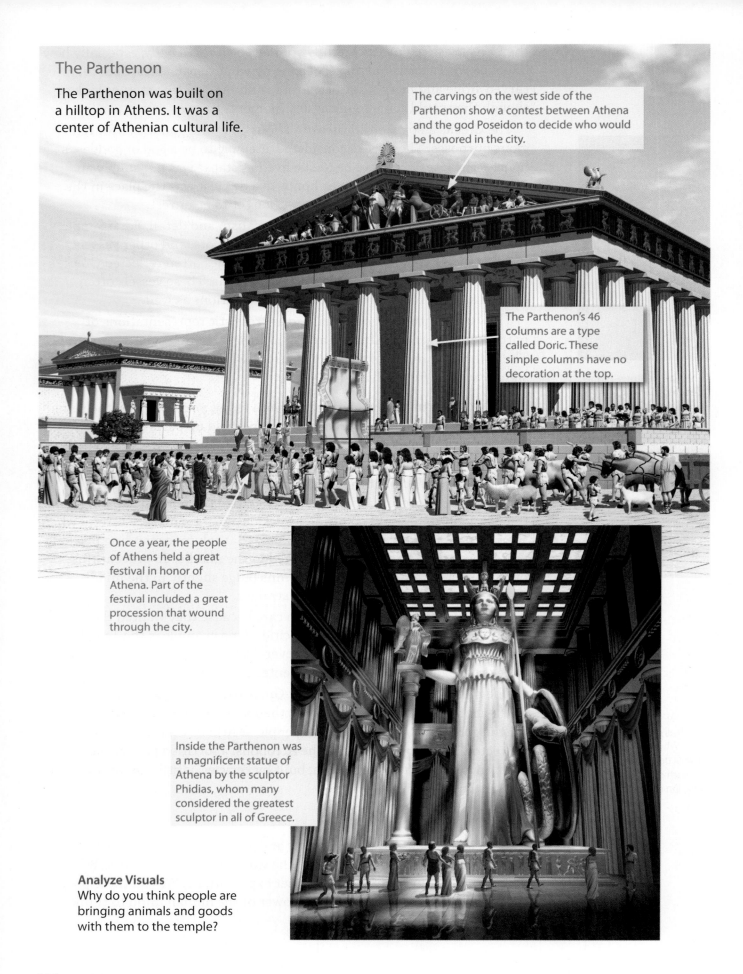

The carvings on the west side of the Parthenon show a contest between Athena and the god Poseidon to decide who would be honored in the city.

The Parthenon's 46 columns are a type called Doric. These simple columns have no decoration at the top.

Once a year, the people of Athens held a great festival in honor of Athena. Part of the festival included a great procession that wound through the city.

Inside the Parthenon was a magnificent statue of Athena by the sculptor Phidias, whom many considered the greatest sculptor in all of Greece.

Analyze Visuals
Why do you think people are bringing animals and goods with them to the temple?

Training the Body and the Mind In Greece, a gymnasium was a public place where wealthy males over the age of 18 exercised, played sports, and trained for competitions. Discussions and lectures about philosophy, literature, and music also took place at a gymnasium.

The Lyceum was the name of a specific gymnasium in Athens. Named after the "wolf god" Apollo Lyceus and located in a sacred grove, this was the place where Aristotle wrote and debated philosophy. After Aristotle left the Lyceum, the school continued to function as a place to study philosophy for centuries to come.

Socrates Among the greatest of these thinkers was a man named **Socrates** (SAHK-ruh-teez). He believed that people must never stop looking for knowledge. Socrates was a teacher as well as a thinker. Today we call his type of teaching the Socratic method.

Socrates taught by asking questions. His questions were about human qualities such as love and courage. He would ask, "What is courage?" When people answered, he challenged their answers with more questions.

Socrates wanted to make people think and question their own beliefs. But he made people angry, even frightened. They accused him of questioning the authority of the gods. For these reasons, he was arrested and condemned to death. His friends and students watched him calmly accept his death. He took the poison he was given, drank it, and died.

Plato **Plato** (PLAYT-oh) was a student of Socrates. Like Socrates, he was a teacher as well as a philosopher. Plato created a school, the Academy, to which students, philosophers, and scientists could come to discuss ideas.

Historical Source

The Death of Socrates

In 399 BC, Socrates was arrested and charged with corrupting the young people of Athens and ignoring religious traditions. He was sentenced to die by drinking poison. Socrates spent his last hours surrounded by his students. One of them, Plato, later described the event in detail.

Analyze Historical Sources
How does Socrates tell his students to act when they see him drink the poison?

Socrates himself does not protest against his sentence but willingly drinks the poison.

The students and friends who have visited Socrates, including the narrator, are much less calm than he is.

"*Then raising the cup to his lips, quite readily and cheerfully he drank off the poison. And hitherto most of us had been able to control our sorrow; but now when we saw him drinking . . . my own tears were flowing fast; so that I covered my face and wept. . . . Socrates alone retained his calmness: What is this strange outcry? he said. . . . I have been told that a man should die in peace. Be quiet then, and have patience.*"

–Plato, from *Phaedo*

Although Plato spent much of his time running the Academy, he also wrote many works. The most famous of these works is called *The Republic*. It describes Plato's idea of an ideal society. This society would be based on justice and fairness to everyone. To ensure this fairness, Plato argued, society should be run by philosophers. He thought that only they could understand what was best for everyone.

Aristotle Perhaps the greatest Greek thinker was **Aristotle** (ar-uh-STAH-tuhl), Plato's student. He taught that people should live lives of moderation, or balance. For example, people should not be greedy, but neither should they give away everything they own. Instead, people should find a balance between these two extremes.

Aristotle believed that moderation was based on **reason**, or clear and ordered thinking. He thought that people should use reason to govern their lives. In other words, people should think about their actions and how they will affect others.

Aristotle also made great advances in the field of logic, the process of making inferences. He argued that you could use facts you knew to figure out new facts. For example, if you know that Socrates lives in Athens and that Athens is in Greece, you can conclude that Socrates lives in Greece. Aristotle's ideas about logic helped inspire many later Greek scientists.

Socrates, Plato, and Aristotle thought about the world and searched for knowledge, wisdom, and truth. Between them they created the Socratic method of learning, the first book of political science, and a method of scientific reasoning. Even today, people admire their ideas. Their teachings are at the root of modern philosophy and science.

Reading Check
Make Inferences
Do you think these philosophers would have been as influential if they had lived in a different city? Why or why not?

This drawing shows how one artist imagined Plato (left), Aristotle (center), and Socrates (right) to look.

Science

Aristotle's works inspired many Greek scientists. They began to look closely at the world to see how it worked.

Mathematics Some Greeks spent their lives studying mathematics. One of these people was **Euclid** (YOO-kluhd). He was interested in geometry. Euclid is considered one of the world's greatest mathematicians. He wrote about the relationship between mathematics and other fields, including astronomy and music. But it is for geometry that he is best known. In fact, his works were so influential that the branch of geometry we study in school—the study of flat shapes and lines—is called Euclidean geometry.

BIOGRAPHY

Euclid c. 300 BC

Euclid is considered one of the world's greatest mathematicians. He lived and taught in Alexandria, Egypt, a great center of learning. Euclid's work survives in the *Elements,* a series of books about mathematical theories. Over the centuries, many scholars have read translations of the *Elements* to help them with their own work.

Draw Conclusions
Why is Euclid considered a great mathematician?

Thales (THAY-leez) was another Greek mathematician who studied geometry. He is credited with developing five theorems. Historians also believe that Thales accurately predicted a solar eclipse.

Influenced by the work of Thales, Pythagoras (puh-THAG-uh-ruhs) proved that in a right triangle, the square of the hypotenuse is equal to the sum of the squares of the other two sides. Other Greek mathematicians included a geographer who used mathematics to accurately calculate the size of the earth. Years later, in the AD 300s and 400s, a woman named Hypatia (hy-PAY-shuh) taught about mathematics and astronomy.

Medicine and Engineering Not all Greek scientists studied numbers. Some studied other areas of science, such as medicine and engineering.

Greek doctors studied the human body to understand how it worked. In trying to cure diseases and keep people healthy, Greek doctors made many discoveries.

The greatest Greek doctor was **Hippocrates** (hip-AHK-ruh-teez). He wanted to figure out what caused diseases so he could better treat them.

Reading Check
Draw Conclusions
Why do you think a
branch of geometry
is named after Euclid
and a theorem
is named after
Pythagoras?

Hippocrates is better known today, though, for his ideas about how doctors should behave.

Greek engineers also made great discoveries. Some devices they invented continue to impact the world today. For instance, farmers in many countries still use water screws to bring water to their fields. This example of early technology, which brings water from a lower level to a higher one, was invented by a Greek scientist named Archimedes (ahr-kuh-MEED-eez) in the 200s BC.

Summary Through their art, philosophy, and science, the Greeks have greatly influenced Western civilization.

Lesson 5 Assessment

Review Ideas, Terms, and People

1. a. **Summarize** What two types of drama did the Greeks invent?

b. **Summarize** Why did Greek columns bulge in the middle?

c. **Draw Conclusions** How did studying the human body help Greek artists make their statues look real?

2. a. **Analyze** How do Greek gymnasiums and the Lyceum show the importance of developing the body and the mind?

b. **Summarize** How did Socrates teach? What is this method of teaching called?

3. a. **Summarize** In what fields did Hippocrates and Thales make great achievements?

b. **Make Inferences** Why do some people call Greece the birthplace of the Western world?

Critical Thinking

4. **Summarize** Add a box to the bottom of your note-taking chart. Use it to summarize Greek contributions in the arts, philosophy, and science.

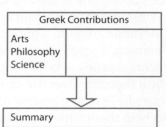

Greek Contributions

Arts
Philosophy
Science

Summary

Social Studies Skills

Analyze Costs and Benefits

Define the Skill

Everything you do has both costs and benefits connected to it. *Benefits* are what you gain from something. *Costs* are what you give up to obtain benefits. For example, if you buy a video game, the benefits of your action include the game itself and the enjoyment of playing it. The most obvious cost is what you pay for the game. However, there are also costs that do not involve money. One of these costs is the time you spend playing the game. This is a cost because you give up something else, such as doing your homework or watching a TV show, when you choose to play the game.

The ability to analyze costs and benefits is a valuable life skill as well as a useful tool in the study of history. Weighing an action's benefits against its costs can help you decide whether or not to take the action.

Learn the Skill

Analyzing the costs and benefits of historical events will help you better understand and evaluate them. Follow these guidelines to do a *cost-benefit analysis* of an action or decision in history.

1. First determine what the action or decision was trying to accomplish. This step is needed in order to determine which of its effects were benefits and which were costs.

2. Then look for the positive or successful results of the action or decision. These are its benefits.

3. Consider the negative or unsuccessful effects of the action or decision. Also think about what positive things would have happened if it had not occurred. All these things are its costs.

4. Make a chart of the costs and benefits. By comparing the list of benefits to the list of costs you can better understand the action or decision and evaluate it.

For example, you learned in Module 8 that because of Greece's geography, the early Greeks settled near the sea. A cost-benefit analysis of their dependence on the sea might produce a chart like this one.

Benefits	Costs
Used sea as a source of some food	Would have paid more attention to agriculture than they did
Didn't have to depend on Greece's poor soil for food	Had to rely on trade with other peoples for some food and other necessities
Became great shipbuilders and sailors	
Became great traders and grew rich from trade	
Settled colonies throughout the region	

Based on this chart, one might conclude that the Greeks' choice of where to settle was a good one.

Practice the Skill

In 546 BC, a noble named Peisistratus overthrew the oligarchy and ruled Athens as a tyrant. Use information from the module and the guidelines here to do a cost-benefit analysis of this action. Then write a paragraph explaining whether or not it was good for the people of Athens.

Module 8 Assessment

Review Vocabulary, Terms, and People

Unscramble each group of letters to spell a term that matches the given definition.

1. **olpsi**—a Greek city-state
2. **iciznets**—people who have the right to participate in government
3. **ntaryt**—a person who rules alone, usually through military force
4. **comdeyacr**—rule by the people
5. **bleafs**—stories that teach lessons
6. **tscyaricora**—a government of rich landowners
7. **sroena**—clear and ordered thinking
8. **nymaugmsi**—a place to exercise and play sports

Comprehension and Critical Thinking

Lesson 1

9. a. **Describe** How did geography affect the development of the Greek city-states?

    b. **Compare and Contrast** What did the Minoans and Mycenaeans have in common? How were the two civilizations different?

    c. **Elaborate** How did the concept of the polis affect the growth of Greek colonies?

Lesson 2

10. a. **Analyze** What role did Draco, Cleisthenes, and Pericles play in the history of Greek government?

    b. **Analyze** Explain the three factors that caused Corinth to become an important trade location in Greece.

    c. **Evaluate** Do you agree or disagree with this statement: "Representative democracy works better than direct democracy in large countries." Defend your answer.

Lesson 3

11. a. **Describe** What was life like for Spartan women? for Athenian women?

    b. **Compare and Contrast** How was the education of Spartan boys different from the education of Athenian boys? What did the education of both groups have in common?

    c. **Evaluate** Do you agree or disagree with this statement: "The Athenians brought the Peloponnesian War on themselves." Defend your argument.

Lesson 4

12. a. **Explain** What is a cultural landscape? How did this apply to ancient Greece?

    b. **Recall** Who were some of the main gods of Greek mythology? Who were some of the main heroes?

    c. **Analyze** What are some of the topics that appear in ancient Greek literature, such as the *Iliad* and the *Odyssey*?

Lesson 5

13. a. **Identify** What is the Parthenon? What was the Lyceum?

    b. **Compare** What did Euclid, Thales, and Pythagoras have in common?

    c. **Evaluate** Why do you think Greek accomplishments in the arts, sciences, and technology are still admired today?

Module 8 Assessment, continued

Review Themes

14. **Geography** How do you think Greek society would have been different if Greece were a landlocked country?

15. **Politics** Why was citizenship so important in Athens?

16. **Society and Culture** What evidence from the text shows cultural differences between Athens and Sparta?

Reading Skills

Preview Text *Use the Reading Skills taught in this module to complete the activities about the reading in the selection below.*

Greeks Create City-States

The Greeks of the Dark Age left no written records. All that we know about the period comes from archaeological findings.

About 300 years after the Mycenaean civilization crumbled, the Greeks started to join together in small groups for protection and stability. Over time, these groups set up independent city-states. The Greek word for a city-state is **polis** (PAH-lus). The creation of city-states marked the beginning of what is known as Greece's classical era.

Life in a City-State A Greek city was usually built around a strong fortress. This fortress often stood on top of a high hill called the **acropolis** (uh-KRAH-puh-lus).

17. Identify the following text features in the passage: heading, subheading, and bold type.

18. What is the purpose of the subheading that introduces the third paragraph?

Social Studies Skills

Analyze Costs and Benefits *Use the Social Studies Skills taught in this module to complete the activity about the chart below.*

Cleisthenes' Leadership

Costs	Benefits

19. Create a chart similar to the chart shown comparing costs and benefits of this event. Then write a sentence explaining whether or not it was good for the people of Athens.

Focus On Writing

20. **Write Your Myth** First, decide if your main character is going to be a god, a Titan, or a human who interacts with the gods and Titans. Think about the situations and decisions that your character will face, and how he or she will react to them.

    Now it's time to write your myth down. Write a paragraph of seven to eight sentences about your character. You may want to include terrible monsters or heroes with great powers. Don't forget that a myth is supposed to explain something about the world.

ANCIENT GREECE

The Acropolis of Athens symbolizes the city and represents the architectural and artistic legacy of ancient Greece. *Acropolis* means "highest city" in Greek, and there are many such sites in Greece. Historically, an acropolis provided shelter and defense against a city's enemies. The Acropolis of Athens—the best known of them all—contained temples, monuments, and artwork dedicated to the Greek gods. Archaeological evidence indicates that the Acropolis was an important place to inhabitants from much earlier eras. However, the structures that we see today on the site were largely conceived by the statesman Pericles during the Golden Age of Athens in the 5th century B.C.

Explore the Acropolis of ancient Greece and learn about the legacy of Greek civilization. You can find a wealth of information, video clips, primary sources, activities, and more through your online textbook.

HISTORY

Go online to view these and other **HISTORY**® resources.

The Persian Wars

Watch the video to find out how Athens emerged as the principal Greek city-state at the conclusion of the Persian Wars.

The Goddess Athena

Watch the video to learn how, according to Greek mythology, Athena became the protector of Athens.

The Parthenon

Watch the video to see what the Parthenon, one of the most important temples on the Acropolis, might have looked like after it was completed.

Legacy of Greece

Watch the video to analyze The School of Athens, a painting by the Italian Renaissance artist Raphael, which pays tribute to the legacy of ancient Greece in philosophy and science.

Module 9

The Hellenistic World

Essential Question

What advances did the Greeks make that still influence the world today?

About the Photo: Even after the Romans conquered the Hellenistic kingdoms, Greek influence endured. This library, built at Ephesus in the AD 100s, reflects Greek architectural designs.

In this module you will learn that Alexander the Great built a large empire and that the ancient Greeks left behind a rich legacy of art and thought.

What You Will Learn...

Lesson 1: Alexander the Great 306
The Big Idea Alexander the Great built a huge empire and helped spread Greek culture into Egypt and Asia.

Lesson 2: The Hellenistic Kingdoms 311
The Big Idea Alexander's death resulted in fighting among his generals and the division of his empire into three kingdoms.

Lesson 3: Hellenistic Achievements 316
The Big Idea The Hellenistic kingdoms had a blended, Greek-inspired culture.

▷ *Explore ONLINE!*

HISTORY.

VIDEOS, including...
- Alexander and his City
- Decisive Battles: Gaugamela
- The Lighthouse of Alexandria

☑ Document-Based Investigations

☑ Graphic Organizers

☑ Interactive Games

☑ Animation: Archimedean Screw

☑ Interactive Map: Alexander the Great's Empire, c. 323 BC

☑ Image Carousel: Hellenistic Art and Design

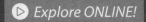
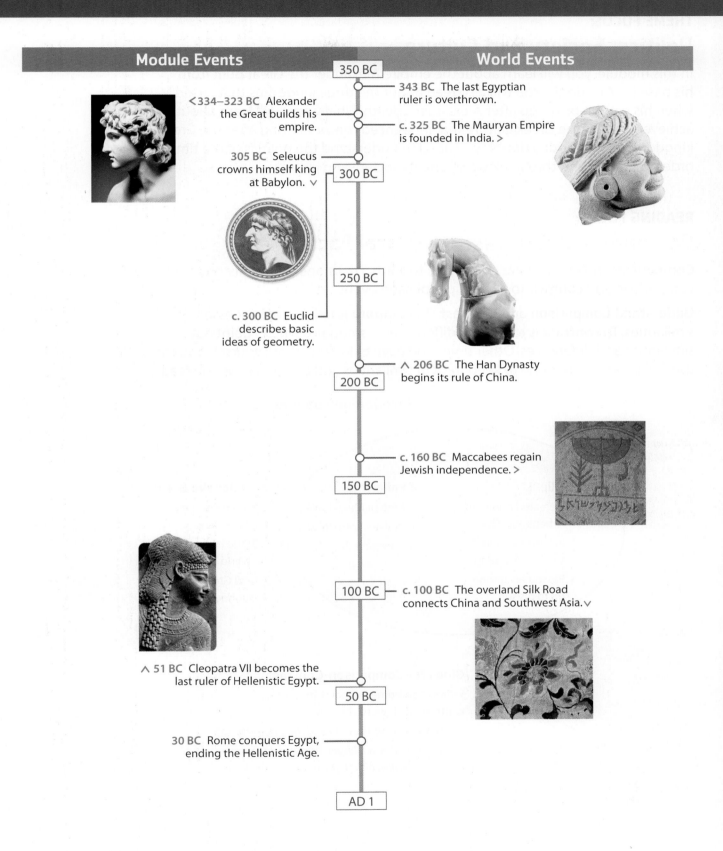

Module Events | World Events

350 BC

343 BC The last Egyptian ruler is overthrown.

<334–323 BC Alexander the Great builds his empire.

c. 325 BC The Mauryan Empire is founded in India. >

305 BC Seleucus crowns himself king at Babylon. ∨

300 BC

250 BC

c. 300 BC Euclid describes basic ideas of geometry.

∧ 206 BC The Han Dynasty begins its rule of China.

200 BC

c. 160 BC Maccabees regain Jewish independence. >

150 BC

100 BC

c. 100 BC The overland Silk Road connects China and Southwest Asia. ∨

∧ 51 BC Cleopatra VII becomes the last ruler of Hellenistic Egypt.

50 BC

30 BC Rome conquers Egypt, ending the Hellenistic Age.

AD 1

Reading Social Studies

Politics, Society and Culture

In this module, you will learn about the empire Alexander the Great built from his base in Macedonia. You will also read about the three kingdoms that lasted when his empire broke up after Alexander's death. Finally, you will learn about the achievements of the Greek culture that influenced the world long after the Greek kingdoms fell. Without a doubt, you need to understand the politics of the time in order to understand the Greek world and its society and culture.

READING FOCUS:

Compare and Contrast Historical Facts

Comparison and contrast are good ways to learn. That's one reason historians use comparison and contrast to explain people and events in history.

Understand Comparison and Contrast To **compare** is to look for likenesses, or similarities. To **contrast** is to look for differences. Sometimes writers point out similarities and differences. Other times you have to look for them yourself. You can use a diagram like this one to keep track of similarities and differences as you read.

Macedonian Leaders

Philip II
- Defeated armies of Athens and Thebes
- Improved upon the Greek phalanx
- Passed his throne on to his son

Similarities
- King of Macedonia
- Brilliant commander
- Conquered other areas

Alexander the Great
- Defeated Persians and Egyptians
- Built the largest empire the world had ever seen
- Spread Greek influence throughout his empire

Clues for Comparison-Contrast
Writers sometimes signal comparisons or contrasts with words like these:
Comparison—*similarly, like, in the same way, too*
Contrast—*however, larger, smaller, less, more, unlike, but, while, although, in contrast, instead*

You Try It!

Read the following passage and then answer the questions below.

Greek and Hellenistic Architecture and Art

Hellenistic buildings tended to be larger and more ornate than earlier Greek buildings had been. The lighthouse at Alexandria, for example, was much taller than anything the Greeks had built. Buildings were so large because they served as symbols of the rulers' power and greatness.

In addition, Hellenistic artists tried to make their works look more natural than earlier works. While many early Greek statues show people or gods in formal poses, Hellenistic sculptors liked to show their subjects in more active or natural poses. Instead of a king seated on a throne, a Hellenistic artist might choose to show a father holding a crying baby.

Answer these questions based on the passage you just read.

1. Does the word *while* introduce a comparison or a contrast?

2. Which buildings were greater in size—Hellenistic buildings or Greek buildings? What comparison or contrast signal word helped you answer this question?

3. What other comparison or contrast words do you find in the passage? How do these words or phrases help you understand the passage?

4. How are the similarities and differences organized in the passage—alternating back and forth between topics (ABAB) or first one topic and then the next (AABB)?

As you read this module, think about the organization of the ideas. Look for comparison and contrast signal words.

Key Terms and People

Lesson 1
Philip II
phalanx
Alexander the Great
Hellenistic

Lesson 2
Antigonus
Seleucus
Ptolemy
Cleopatra VII

Lesson 3
Aristarchus

Alexander the Great

The Big Idea

Alexander the Great built a huge empire and helped spread Greek culture into Egypt and Asia.

Main Ideas

- Macedonia conquered Greece in the 300s BC.
- Alexander the Great built an empire that united much of Europe, Asia, and Egypt.
- Alexander spread Greek cultural influences throughout his empire.

Key Terms and People

Philip II
phalanx
Alexander the Great
Hellenistic

If YOU were there . . .

You are a soldier in the most powerful army in the world. In just eight years, you and your fellow soldiers have conquered an enormous empire. Now your general wants to push farther into unknown lands in search of greater glory. But you're thousands of miles from home, and you haven't seen your family in years.

Do you agree to go on fighting? Why or why not?

Macedonia Conquers Greece

In 359 BC, **Philip II** became king of Macedonia. Philip spent the first year of his rule fighting off invaders who wanted to take over his kingdom. After he defeated the invaders, he was ready to launch invasions of his own.

Philip's main target was Greece. The leaders of Athens, knowing they were the target of Philip's powerful army, called for all Greeks to join together. Few people responded.

As a result, the armies of Athens and its chief ally, Thebes, were easily defeated by the Macedonians. Having witnessed this defeat, the rest of the Greeks agreed to make Philip their leader.

Philip's Military Strength Philip defeated the Greeks because he was a brilliant military leader. He borrowed and improved many of the strategies Greek armies used in battle. For example, Philip's soldiers, like the Greeks, fought as a phalanx (FAY-langks). A **phalanx** was a group of warriors who stood close together in a square. Each soldier held a spear pointed outward to fight off enemies. As soldiers in the front lines were killed, others stepped up from behind to fill their spots.

Philip improved upon the Greeks' idea. He gave his soldiers spears that were much longer than those of his opponents. This allowed his army to attack effectively in any battle. Philip also sent cavalry and archers into battle to support the phalanx.

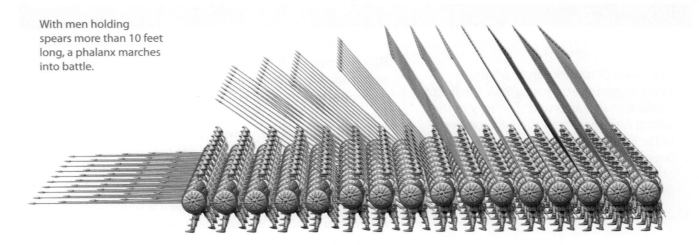

With men holding spears more than 10 feet long, a phalanx marches into battle.

Reading Check
Summarize
How was Philip II able to conquer Greece?

After conquering Greece, Philip turned his attention to Persia. He planned to march east and conquer the Persian Empire, but he never made it. He was murdered in 336 BC while celebrating his daughter's wedding. When Philip died, his throne—and his plans—passed to his son, Alexander.

Alexander Builds an Empire

When Philip died, the people in the Greek city of Thebes rebelled. They thought that the Macedonians would not have a leader strong enough to keep the kingdom together. They were wrong.

Controlling the Greeks Although he was only 20 years old, Philip's son Alexander was as strong a leader as his father had been. He immediately went south to end the revolt in Thebes.

Within a year, Alexander had destroyed Thebes and enslaved the Theban people. He used Thebes as an example to other Greeks of what would happen if they turned against him. Then, confident that the Greeks would not rebel again, he set out to build an empire.

Alexander's efforts to build an empire made him one of the greatest conquerors in history. These efforts earned him the name **Alexander the Great**.

Building a New Empire Like his father, Alexander was a brilliant commander. In 334 BC, he attacked the Persians, whose army was much larger than his own. But Alexander's troops were well trained and ready for battle. They defeated the Persians time after time.

According to legend, Alexander visited a town called Gordium in Asia Minor while he was fighting the Persians. There he heard an ancient tale about a knot tied by an ancient king. The tale said that whoever untied the knot would rule all of Asia. According to the legend, Alexander pulled out his sword and cut right through the knot. Taking this as a good sign, he and his army set out again.

After defeating the Persians near the town of Issus, Alexander went to Egypt, which was part of the Persian Empire. The Persian governor had heard of his skill in battle. He surrendered without a fight in 332 BC and crowned Alexander pharaoh.

Alexander and His Horse

In about AD 100, Plutarch, a famous Greek biographer, wrote about the life of Alexander. Plutarch told the story of the young Alexander and the wild, powerful horse Bucephalus, which no one had been able to ride. As King Philip and others watched, Alexander approached the unruly Bucephalus.

Analyze Historical Sources
Why do you think King Philip said that Macedonia didn't have room for Alexander?

"After Alexander had calmed the horse . . . he quietly cast aside his mantle and with a light spring safely bestrode [mounted] him . . . but when he saw that the horse was rid of the fear . . . he gave him his head . . . Philip and his company were speechless with anxiety at first; but when Alexander made the turn . . . and came back towards them proud and exultant, all . . . broke into loud cries, but his father . . . actually shed tears of joy, and when Alexander had dismounted, kissed him, saying: "My son, seek thee out a kingdom equal to thyself; Macedonia has not room for thee."

—Plutarch, from *Life of Alexander*, translated by Bernadotte Perrin

After a short stay in Egypt, Alexander set out again. Near the town of Gaugamela (gaw-guh-MEE-luh), he defeated the Persian army for the last time. After the battle, the Persian king fled. The king soon died, killed by one of his nobles. With the king's death, Alexander became the ruler of what had been the Persian Empire.

Marching Home Still intent on building his empire, Alexander led his army through Central Asia. In 327 BC, Alexander crossed the Indus River and wanted to push deeper into India. But his exhausted soldiers refused to go any farther. Disappointed, Alexander began the long march home.

Alexander left India in 325 BC, but he never made it back to Greece. In 323 BC, on his way back, Alexander visited the city of Babylon and became sick. He died a few days later at age 33. After he died, Alexander's body was taken to Egypt and buried in a golden coffin.

The Greek empire that Alexander built was one of the great civilizations of the ancient world. The Persian Empire was also one, and Alexander had conquered that empire. The Chinese and Indian civilizations were continuing to grow. Rome, another great ancient civilization, was still to come.

Reading Check
Find Main Ideas
What steps did Alexander take to create his empire?

Alexander on his horse Bucephalus

Spreading Greek Culture

Alexander's empire was the largest the world had ever seen. He ruled his empire as an absolute dictator—whatever he said was law. There are no individual rights under a dictatorship. At times he enforced his orders with the ultimate punishment—death. Alexander executed governors, generals, and other leaders who were dishonest or who governed poorly.

A New Culture Develops An admirer of Greek culture, Alexander worked to spread Greek influence throughout his empire by founding cities in the lands he conquered. He modeled his new cities after the cities of Greece. He named many of them Alexandria, after himself. He built temples and theaters like those in Greece. He then encouraged Greek settlers to move to the new cities. These settlers spoke Greek, which became common throughout the empire. In time, Greek art, literature, and science spread into surrounding lands.

Alexander also established standardized coins of silver and gold to be used throughout his empire. On these coins, called "Alexanders," were portraits of gods or heroes. These standard coins continued to be used in the region long after Alexander was gone.

▷ Explore ONLINE!

Alexander the Great's Empire, c. 323 BC

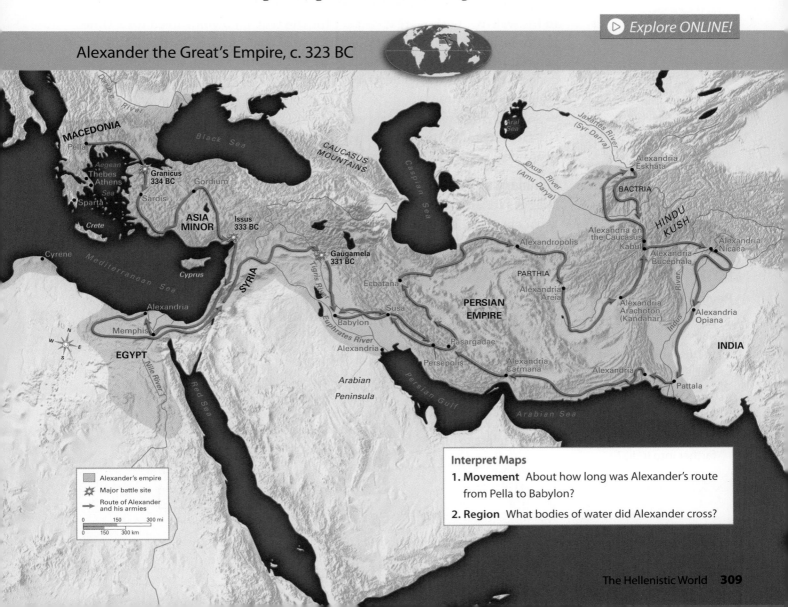

Interpret Maps

1. **Movement** About how long was Alexander's route from Pella to Babylon?

2. **Region** What bodies of water did Alexander cross?

Even as he supported the spread of Greek culture, however, Alexander encouraged conquered people to keep their own customs and traditions. As a result, a new blended culture developed in Alexander's empire. It combined elements of Persian, Egyptian, Syrian, and other cultures with Greek ideas. Because this new culture was not completely Greek, or Hellenic, historians call it **Hellenistic**, or Greek-like. It wasn't purely Greek, but it was heavily influenced by Greek ideas.

Hellenistic Literature Literature remained a popular art form during the Hellenistic period. The leading poet and dramatist of the age was Menander, who lived in Athens. Menander wrote more than 100 plays, most of which were comedies. Menander's comedies were different from those of the great Greek dramatist Aristophanes. Menander's plays often focused on romantic love and were more realistic and less satiric.

Another prominent Hellenistic poet was Callimachus, who lived in the Egyptian city of Alexandria. His poetry was polished and learned, and showed the strong connection between Greece and Hellenistic Egypt.

Writers of the Hellenistic period also crafted histories, biographies, and novels. One of the best-known Hellenistic historians was Polybius, who lived in Greece. Much like the earlier Thucydides, Polybius was neutral in his writing, with a great respect for the truth. Polybius lived for a time in Rome, and his works describe the rise of that empire. Strabo, a Greek geographer who lived later during the Hellenistic period, wrote a book called *Geography,* which describes the people and countries known to the Greeks at that time.

Some writers wrote novels with exciting or romantic plots. For example, the Hellenistic writer Longus wrote a novel about a romance between a goat herder and a shepherdess on the Greek island of Lesbos.

Summary and Preview Alexander the Great caused major political changes in Greece and the Hellenistic world. In the next lesson, you will learn about the Hellenistic kingdoms that arose after Alexander's death.

Reading Check
Analyze Effects
In what ways did Alexander help to create Hellenistic culture?

Lesson 1 Assessment

Review Ideas, Terms, and People

1. **a. Identify** What king conquered Greece in the 300s BC?

   b. Describe How did Philip improve on the Greeks' phalanx?

2. **a. Describe** What territories did Alexander the Great conquer?

   b. Synthesize Why did Alexander destroy Thebes?

   c. Recall Why did Alexander's troops refuse to march farther into India?

3. **a. Identify** What does the term *Hellenistic* mean?

   b. Compare What trait did the historian Polybius share with Thucydides?

Critical Thinking

4. **Summarize** Use a graphic organizer like this one to record details about Alexander and his empire. Then, write one sentence explaining why Alexander is an important historical figure.

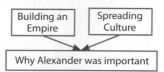

The Hellenistic Kingdoms

The Big Idea

Alexander's death resulted in fighting among his generals and the division of his empire into three kingdoms.

Main Ideas

- Three powerful generals divided Alexander's empire among themselves, establishing Hellenistic Macedonia, Hellenistic Syria, and Hellenistic Egypt.

- A uniform system of trade developed throughout the Hellenistic kingdoms, with a common language, culture, and coinage.

Key People

Antigonus
Seleucus
Ptolemy
Cleopatra VII

If YOU were there . . .

You are a Macedonian soldier in Alexander's army, stationed in Alexandria, Egypt, where you helped Alexander conquer the Egyptians. Unexpectedly, you hear that Alexander has died, far away in Asia Minor. He was a young man, with no heir to take his place. You have no idea who will take his place, though you know that several generals probably want to become the main leader. This could become dangerous. You wonder if Macedonians will begin to fight each other.

What do you think will happen now?

Three Hellenistic Kingdoms

When Alexander died, he didn't have an obvious heir to take over his kingdom, and no one knew who was in charge. The result was great confusion. Alexander's generals began to fight each other for power. In the end, three powerful generals divided the huge empire among themselves.

Hellenistic Macedonia The first of these generals was **Antigonus** (an-TIG-uh-nuhs). He became the king of Macedonia—Alexander's homeland—and part of Greece. (The rest of Greece became independent.) The Antigonid Kingdom, as it was called, was the most Greek of the three parts

Large, bustling cities could be found throughout all the Hellenistic kingdoms. The ruins of the major city of Ephesus are in modern Turkey.

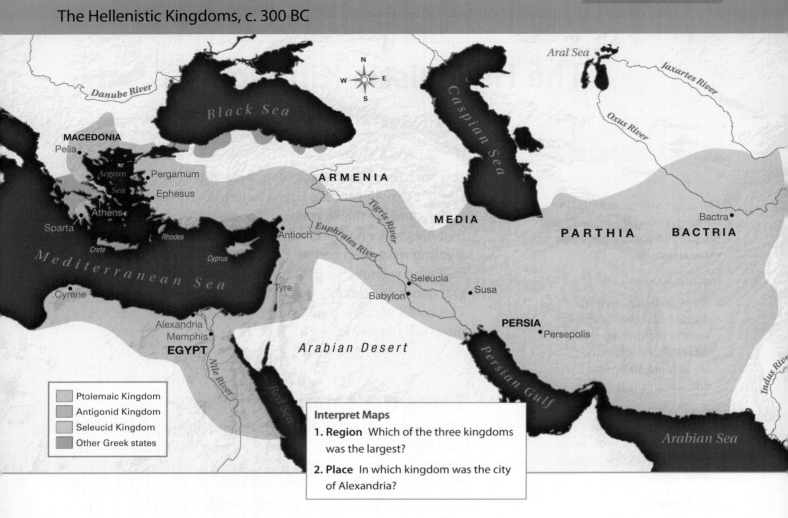

Explore ONLINE!

Interpret Maps

1. **Region** Which of the three kingdoms was the largest?

2. **Place** In which kingdom was the city of Alexandria?

Ptolemaic Kingdom
Antigonid Kingdom
Seleucid Kingdom
Other Greek states

Seleucus I

of the empire. However, it also had the weakest government. The Macedonian kings had to put down many revolts by the Greeks. Damaged by the revolts, Macedonia could not defend itself. Armies from Rome, a rising power from the Italian Peninsula, marched in and conquered Macedonia in the mid-100s BC.

Hellenistic Syria The second general to seize part of the empire was named **Seleucus** (suh-LOO-kuhs). He took control of most of Alexander's Asian conquests, including Persia. The Seleucid Kingdom, as it came to be known, was much larger than Macedonia. However, its great size proved to be a problem. The kingdom was home to many different peoples with many different customs.

After Seleucus died, his son could not keep control of the entire kingdom. The capital, Antioch, was so far away from some parts of the kingdom that people in those areas thought they could ignore the king. Large regions in the east, such as Bactria and Parthia, soon broke away from the

Cleopatra VII 69 BC–30 BC

The last ruler of Hellenistic Egypt was also the most famous. A popular subject of paintings, books, and movies, Cleopatra has become a symbol of ancient Egypt. However, Cleopatra would never have considered herself Egyptian. As a direct descendant of Ptolemy, she was Macedonian.

Cleopatra ruled Egypt jointly with her father and then with her brother. After they died, she became the sole ruler of the kingdom. When Julius Caesar, the ruler of Rome, visited Egypt, the two rulers became close allies. This alliance with Rome would eventually spell her downfall. After Caesar's death, Cleopatra allied herself with one of his aides, Marc Antony. Within a few years,

Antony became involved in a civil war in Rome, which he lost. Rather than face capture and imprisonment, both Antony and Cleopatra committed suicide. With Cleopatra's death, Egypt became a Roman territory.

Draw Conclusions Why didn't Cleopatra think of herself as Egyptian?

Ptolemy was Egypt's first Macedondonian ruler. This image shows him dressed as an Egyptian pharaoh.

Reading Check Analyze Effects Why were three kingdoms created from Alexander's empire?

kingdom. Seleucid rulers maintained control of Persia until they, too, were conquered by the Romans. In the 60s BC, the Romans marched in and took over Syria.

Hellenistic Egypt The last of Alexander's generals to become a king was **Ptolemy** (TAHL-uh-mee). He ruled Egypt, and the Ptolemaic Kingdom became the most powerful and the wealthiest of the Hellenistic kingdoms. Ptolemy took the title "pharaoh" to win the support of the Egyptian people. From the capital at Alexandria—which became one of the ancient world's greatest cities—Ptolemy and his descendants ruled over a stable and prosperous land.

The rulers of Egypt encouraged the growth of Greek culture. They built the ancient world's largest library in the city of Alexandria. Also in Alexandria, they built the Museum, a place for scholars and artists to meet. Through their efforts, Alexandria became a great center of culture and learning.

Nonetheless, Egypt eventually was drawn into conflicts with other powers, especially Rome. In the end, the Egyptian kingdom lasted longer than the other Hellenistic kingdoms. However, in 30 BC, the last Ptolemaic ruler of Egypt, **Cleopatra VII**, died, and the Romans took over Egypt. The Hellenistic kingdoms were no more.

Government and Economy

Like Alexander, the generals who divided his empire ruled without limits on their power. Rule passed down within families. In Macedonia and the Seleucid kingdom, only men could be kings. In Egypt, however, a few women became pharaohs. Cleopatra VII, perhaps the most famous and powerful woman of the ancient world, was a descendant of Ptolemy.

Hellenistic rulers surrounded themselves with advisors and officials to help their kingdoms run smoothly. These advisors were often Greek and had been raised and educated much like the rulers had. Some rulers also chose local individuals to advise them. Together, the rulers and their advisors worked to strengthen their economies. They built and repaired roads and irrigation systems, promoted manufacturing and trade, and supported the arts.

The rulers encouraged increased production of goods in the cities and on farms. The taxes on manufactured and agricultural goods made the kings wealthy. Huge cities grew up, including Antioch in the Seleucid Kingdom and Alexandria in Egypt. Most importantly, a uniform system of trade developed throughout the Hellenistic region. A form of Greek became the common language. The kingdoms continued producing the standard coins that Alexander had begun during his lifetime. Foods and manufactured goods were commonly traded items in the Hellenistic region.

Link to Economics

Booming Economies

The economies of the region grew tremendously after the generals established the Hellenistic kingdoms. The territorial expansion by Alexander had created a huge empire with new resources. Over time, the whole area was linked together by a common language and culture.

A coin used in the Hellenistic kingdoms

The kings seized much of the agricultural land in their kingdoms, and large farms meant increased agricultural production. The use of new technology, such as the iron plow, also helped increase production. Small farmers could not compete with the larger royal lands. Many independent farmers became agricultural workers. Slavery on farms decreased in the Hellenistic kingdoms because it did not cost the owners much to hire the many people looking for work. However, slave labor in manufacturing in cities remained common. Independent trade flourished throughout the kingdoms and was taxed and regulated by the royal families.

Analyze Information
How does use of the iron plow explain why small farmers became workers on larger farms?

Reading Check
Summarize
What made trade
throughout the
Hellenistic region a
uniform system of
trade?

Hellenistic civilization and the Indian and Chinese civilizations also developed trade networks. Specialized production of goods became possible because of the uniform system of trade. For example, China could send silk to the Hellenistic kingdoms, and the Hellenistic kingdoms could send other goods back to China. For two centuries after Alexander's death, the Hellenistic kingdoms prospered.

Summary and Preview In this lesson, you read about the three Hellenistic kingdoms that developed after the death of Alexander. In the next lesson, you will learn more about Hellenistic culture and achievements.

Lesson 2 Assessment

Review Ideas, Terms, and People

1. **a. Recall** What three kingdoms were created out of Alexander's empire after his death?

   b. Explain Why were these kingdoms called Hellenistic?

   c. Elaborate Why did the Seleucid Kingdom have trouble remaining united?

2. **a. Explain** How did the generals who ruled the three kingdoms make the laws for the people of the kingdoms?

   b. Identify What new technology helped increase agricultural productivity in the Hellenistic kingdoms?

   c. Summarize Where was slavery still common in the Hellenistic kingdoms?

Critical Thinking

3. **Categorize** In this lesson you learned about the development of a uniform system of trade in the Hellenistic region. Create a chart like this one to rank the reasons the system of trade became uniform throughout the region. Next to the chart, write a sentence to explain your choices.

Most Significant

1.
2.
3.

Least Significant

Hellenistic Achievements

The Big Idea

The Hellenistic kingdoms had a blended, Greek-inspired culture.

Main Ideas

- Greek-influenced culture was most noticeable in the cities, while rural areas tended to be more traditional.

- Hellenistic art and architecture demonstrated Greek influences but had their own unique touches.

Key People

Aristarchus

If YOU were there . . .

You and your family live in the large Greek city of Alexandria, Egypt. Your father was a soldier in Alexander's Macedonian army, and your mother was an Egyptian who grew up on a farm. There is a huge Greek library in the center of the city, and your children go to a school organized on a Greek model. They speak both Egyptian and Greek. You cook mostly traditional Egyptian dishes, and the clothes you wear are a mix of Greek and Egyptian.

Do you consider yourself an Egyptian or a Greek or both?

Society and Daily Life

Alexander encouraged the blending of cultures in his empire. He introduced Greek customs into the areas he conquered but did not force people to give up their own traditions. The result was a blended Hellenistic, or Greek-inspired, culture that spread into the kingdoms built by his generals. Thus, the cultural landscape of Hellenistic Egypt became a blend of Greek and traditional Egyptian.

The Greek influence was most noticeable in cities. The Greek language was used for government and official business. Many buildings in Hellenistic cities resembled those in Athens and other Greek city-states. Members of the upper classes adopted Greek philosophy and even clothing styles to feel closer to their rulers.

One excellent example of a Greek-style Hellenistic city was Alexandria, Egypt. Founded by Alexander and chosen by Ptolemy as his capital, it became one of the largest cities in the Mediterranean world.

The city was filled with splendid buildings that reflected Greek tastes and technological ability. Towering above the city was a magnificent lighthouse called the Pharos. More than 350 feet tall, the lighthouse was widely admired as one of the wonders of the ancient world. Also located in Alexandria was a huge library, the greatest collection of Greek and Hellenistic knowledge in the world.

Greek influence was less common in rural areas, particularly among the lower classes. In such areas, most people used their own native languages and kept their own religions. They built and dressed as they always had. The laws varied in some places, too. Large Greek cities, such as Alexandria, had their own Greek-influenced laws. But smaller towns and rural areas had traditional Egyptian laws that had developed over time.

As time passed, Hellenistic culture changed. One significant difference was in the treatment of women. In most Greek city-states, women had few rights. Hellenistic women, on the other hand, were less restricted. They could be educated, own property, and run businesses. However, women still had fewer rights than men.

Reading Check
Summarize
How would you describe the cultural landscape of Hellenistic Egypt?

Culture and Achievements

Like the Greeks, the people of the Hellenistic kingdoms were fascinated by architecture and art. Inspired by Greek works, they sought to create beautiful, meaningful pieces of their own. This Greek influence is obvious in Hellenistic art and architecture, but Hellenistic artists added their own touches.

For example, Hellenistic buildings tended to be larger and more ornate than earlier Greek buildings had been. The lighthouse at Alexandria, for example, was much taller than anything the Greeks had built. Buildings were so large because they served as symbols of the rulers' power and greatness.

This etching from the early 1900s shows one artist's idea of what the Lighthouse at Alexandria may have looked like. The lighthouse was destroyed before 1500.

Hellenistic rulers were great supporters of the arts. They commissioned artists to create elaborate public works such as sculptures, and collected personal luxury items like jewelry, often fashioned from gold and gems acquired through trade.

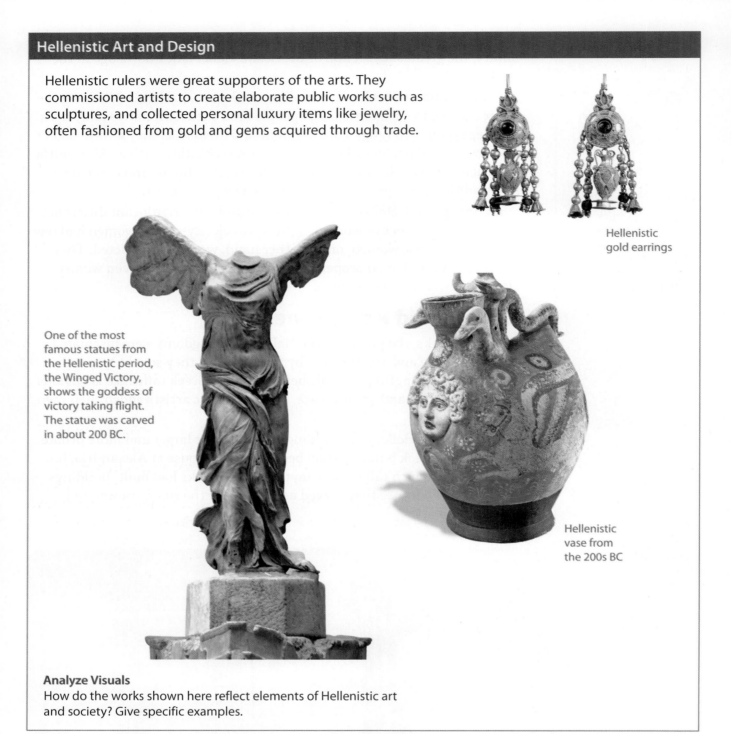

Hellenistic gold earrings

One of the most famous statues from the Hellenistic period, the Winged Victory, shows the goddess of victory taking flight. The statue was carved in about 200 BC.

Hellenistic vase from the 200s BC

Analyze Visuals
How do the works shown here reflect elements of Hellenistic art and society? Give specific examples.

In addition, Hellenistic artists tried to make their works look more natural than earlier works. While many early Greek statues show people or gods in formal poses, Hellenistic sculptors liked to show their subjects in more active or natural poses. Instead of a king seated on a throne, a Hellenistic artist might choose to show a father holding a crying baby.

The blend of the cultural landscape in Hellenistic Egypt can be seen in the artistic expression inspired by religion. People worshiped both Greek and Egyptian gods in the Ptolemaic kingdom. Artists made statues of both

Hellenistic Philosophies

Philosophy	Founder	Basic Teachings
Cynicism	Diogenes	People should live according to nature. They should ignore pleasure, wealth, and society.
Skepticism	Pyrrho	People can never know how things really are. They should just accept whatever happens to them.
Epicureanism	Epicurus	People should avoid pain and pursue pleasure. They should withdraw from public life.
Stoicism	Zeno	All people have a role to play in society. They should practice self-discipline and control their emotions.

sets of gods. Ptolemy I even had a temple built in Alexandria dedicated to the god Serapis. Serapis was a combination of a Greek god and an Egyptian god.

Another similarity between Greek and Hellenistic culture was the value placed on philosophy. Hellenistic thinkers spent much of their time thinking about how people could be happy. Some of these thinkers became very influential and formed new schools of thought. Four of these philosophies are described in the chart called "Hellenistic Philosophies."

Some Hellenistic thinkers, however, were more interested in how the physical world worked. To help them learn about the world, these thinkers turned to science. Hellenistic scientists were eager to conduct experiments that could improve their understanding of the world. As a result of these experiments, they sometimes created wondrous inventions that made

Timeline: Key Events in the Hellenistic Kingdoms

This timeline shows some key events in the history of the Hellenistic region that helped shape Hellenistic culture and society.

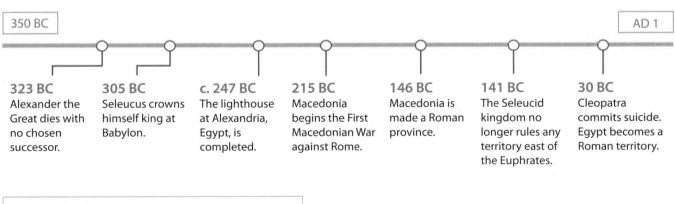

350 BC   AD 1

323 BC Alexander the Great dies with no chosen successor.

305 BC Seleucus crowns himself king at Babylon.

c. 247 BC The lighthouse at Alexandria, Egypt, is completed.

215 BC Macedonia begins the First Macedonian War against Rome.

146 BC Macedonia is made a Roman province.

141 BC The Seleucid kingdom no longer rules any territory east of the Euphrates.

30 BC Cleopatra commits suicide. Egypt becomes a Roman territory.

Analyze Timelines
When did Seleucus crown himself king at Babylon?

life easier for other people. Perhaps the greatest Hellenistic inventor was Archimedes (ahr-kuh-MEED-eez). Among his inventions was a device that helped farmers bring water uphill to their fields. He also designed a war machine that could lift a fully loaded ship out of the water.

Hellenistic scientists also made great advances in mathematics and astronomy. Around 300 BC, Euclid described the basic ideas that govern geometry. **Aristarchus** (ahr-uh-STAHR-kuhs) of Samos, an astronomer, was the first person to propose that the earth moves around the sun.

Summary In this lesson, you read about the society and daily life of the Hellenistic region and about the achievements of Hellenistic culture.

Reading Check
Synthesize
How did religion influence the art and architecture of Hellenistic Egypt?

Lesson 3 Assessment

Review Ideas, Terms, and People

1. a. **Explain** Describe the cultural landscape of Hellenistic Egypt.
   b. **Identify** How was Alexandria, Egypt, a good example of a Greek-style Hellenistic city?
   c. **Form Generalizations** How did individual rights change over time for Hellenistic women?
2. a. **Contrast** How were Hellenistic buildings different from earlier Greek buildings?
   b. **Summarize** What are the basic teachings of Stoicism?
   c. **Predict Effects** How might Archimedes' inventions have made life easier?

Critical Thinking

3. **Evaluate** In this lesson you learned about people in the Hellenistic kingdoms as well as their culture and achievements. Create a graphic organizer like this one listing how Greek culture influenced the culture of the Hellenistic kingdoms.

Language	Art	Architecture	Philosophy

Social Studies Skills

Interpret Charts

Define the Skill

Charts present information visually to make it easier to understand. Different kinds of charts serve different purposes. *Organizational charts* can show relationships among the parts of something. *Flowcharts* show steps in a process or cause-and-effect relationships. *Classification charts* group information so it can be easily compared. Tables are a type of classification chart that organize information into rows and columns for easy comparison. The ability to interpret charts helps you to analyze information and understand relationships.

Learn the Skill

Use these basic steps to interpret a chart.

1. Identify the type of chart, and read its title in order to understand its purpose and subject.

2. Note the parts of the chart. Read the headings of rows and columns to determine the categories and types of information. Note any other labels that accompany the information presented in the chart. Look for any lines that connect its parts. What do they tell you?

3. Study the chart's details. Look for relationships in the information it presents. If it is a classification chart, analyze and compare all content in the rows and columns. In flowcharts and organizational charts, read all labels and other information. Follow and analyze directional arrows or lines.

Hellenistic Kingdoms

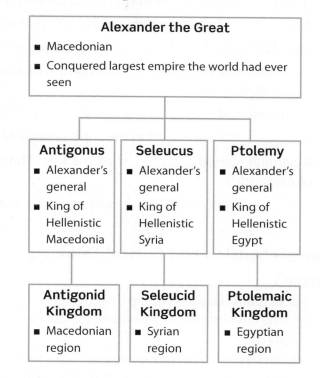

Practice the Skill

Apply the strategies given to interpret the chart, and answer the following questions.

1. What type of chart is this, and what is its purpose?

2. In what way was Alexander the Great connected to Antigonus, Seleucus, and Ptolemy?

3. Which general became king of Hellenistic Egypt?

4. What was the name of the Hellenistic kingdom in the Syrian region?

Module 9 Assessment

Review Vocabulary, Terms, and People

Complete each sentence by filling in the blank with the correct term or person.

1. A king of Macedonia named _____ easily defeated Athens and Thebes.

2. A _____ was a group of warriors who stood close together in a square.

3. The Macedonian _____ built the largest empire the world had ever seen.

4. A general named _____ took control of Alexander's Asian conquests after Alexander died.

5. A ruler named _____ was the last ruler of Hellenistic Egypt.

6. _____ is a term used to describe Greek-like culture.

7. A general named _____ took the title "Pharoah" and ruled Egypt from the capital of Alexandria.

8. _____ proposed that the earth moves around the sun.

Comprehension and Critical Thinking

Lesson 1

9. a. Explain How did Philip improve on the Greeks' idea of a phalanx for use in battle?

   b. Analyze In Plutarch's story of Alexander and Bucephalus, Philip said that his son should seek a kingdom equal to himself. What did he mean by that?

   c. Elaborate Why do you think Alexander's empire was considered one of the great civilizations of the ancient world?

Lesson 2

10. a. Identify Who ruled Hellenistic Macedonia, Hellenistic Syria, and Hellenistic Egypt after Alexander's death?

   b. Explain What were the characteristics of the uniform system of trade in the Hellenistic kingdoms?

   c. Draw Conclusions What led to the economic boom in the Hellenistic kingdoms after Alexander died?

Lesson 3

11. a. Describe How would you describe the cultural landscape of Hellenistic Egypt?

   b. Analyze How was artistic expression in Hellenistic Egypt inspired by religion?

   c. Contrast How were the Hellenistic philosophies of Epicureanism and Stoicism different?

Module 9 Assessment, continued

Review Themes

12. **Politics** How would you describe the way that Alexander governed his empire?

13. **Politics** What happened when Alexander died and left no obvious heir to take over his empire?

14. **Society and Culture** In what ways was the culture of Hellenistic Egypt a blend of two cultures?

Reading Skills

Compare and Contrast Historical Facts *Use the Reading Skills taught in this module to complete the activity below.*

15. Complete the chart to compare and contrast two powerful leaders you studied in this module, Philip II and Alexander the Great.

Compare
List two characteristics that Philip and Alexander shared.
a. _____
b. _____

Contrast	
How did Philip's and Alexander's empires differ?	
Philip	Alexander
c. _____	d. _____
What happened to their empires after they died?	
Philip	Alexander
e. _____	f. _____

Social Studies Skills

Interpret Charts *Use the Social Studies Skills taught in this module to complete the activity below.*

16. Create a chart in your notebook that identifies key Hellenistic achievements in architecture, art, and philosophy. Use details from this module.

Focus On Writing

17. **Write a Rap for a Hero** Write a rap song that tells the story of Alexander the Great, who rose from childhood in a small country to become the leader of the greatest empire the world had ever known. Include events in his life that you have read about in the module, and describe how his empire changed after he died. Make your rap rhyme in ways that make sense to you.

Module 10
Ancient Rome

Essential Question
Was Rome more successful as a republic or as an empire?

About the Photo: The Roman Forum, the ruins of which are shown above, was a public meeting place at the heart of Rome.

▶ Explore ONLINE!

VIDEOS, including...
- The Growth of Rome
- The Glory of Rome's Forum
- Carthage
- Hail Caesar!
- Deconstructing History: Pompeii
- Rome Falls

✓ Document-Based Investigations

✓ Graphic Organizers

✓ Interactive Games

✓ Image with Hotspots: The Roman Forum

✓ Interactive Map: Roman Trade Routes, AD 200

✓ Image with Hotspots: Roman Engineering

In this module you will read about the history of the Roman Republic and Roman Empire. You will learn about Rome's growth from a small city into the center of one of the most powerful civilizations of the ancient world.

What You Will Learn...

Lesson 1: Geography and the Rise of Rome 328
The Big Idea Rome's location and government helped it become a major power in the ancient world.

Lesson 2: The Roman Republic 336
The Big Idea Rome's tripartite government and written laws helped create a stable society and paved the way for expansion.

Lesson 3: From Republic to Empire. 346
The Big Idea Julius Caesar and Augustus led Rome's transition from a republic to an empire.

Lesson 4: A Vast Empire 354
The Big Idea After Augustus became emperor, the Roman Empire grew politically and economically, and life improved for the Roman people.

Lesson 5: The Fall of Rome 364
The Big Idea Problems from both inside and outside caused the Roman Empire to split and the western half to collapse.

Lesson 6: Rome's Legacy 371
The Big Idea Many features of Roman culture were copied by later civilizations and continue to influence our lives today.

Timeline of Events 753 BC–AD 476

▶ Explore ONLINE!

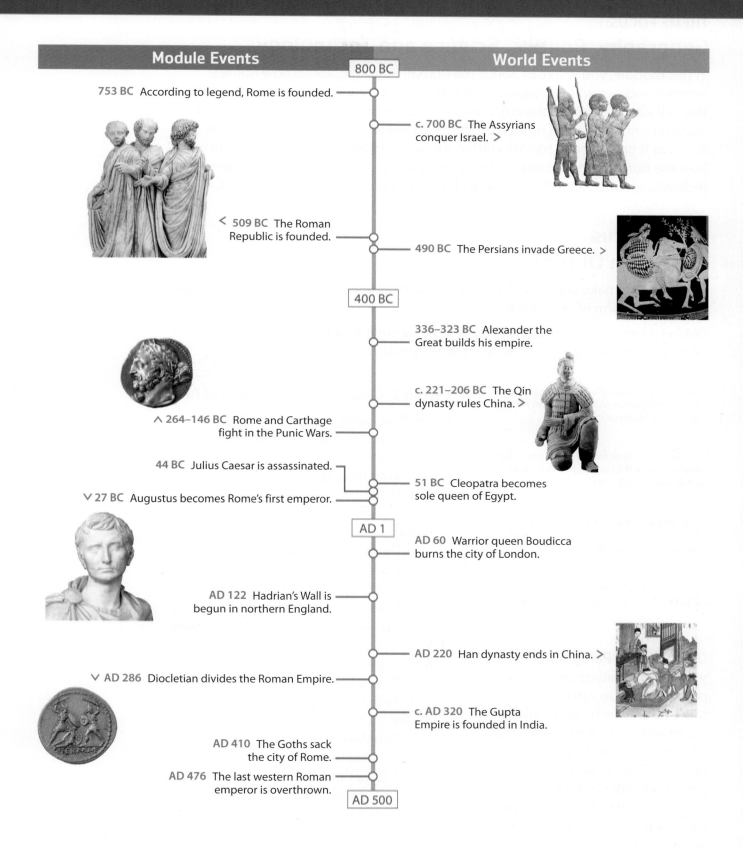

Module Events

753 BC According to legend, Rome is founded.

< 509 BC The Roman Republic is founded.

∧ 264–146 BC Rome and Carthage fight in the Punic Wars.

44 BC Julius Caesar is assassinated.

∨ 27 BC Augustus becomes Rome's first emperor.

AD 122 Hadrian's Wall is begun in northern England.

∨ AD 286 Diocletian divides the Roman Empire.

AD 410 The Goths sack the city of Rome.

AD 476 The last western Roman emperor is overthrown.

World Events

800 BC

c. 700 BC The Assyrians conquer Israel. >

490 BC The Persians invade Greece. >

400 BC

336–323 BC Alexander the Great builds his empire.

c. 221–206 BC The Qin dynasty rules China. >

51 BC Cleopatra becomes sole queen of Egypt.

AD 1

AD 60 Warrior queen Boudicca burns the city of London.

AD 220 Han dynasty ends in China. >

c. AD 320 The Gupta Empire is founded in India.

AD 500

Reading Social Studies

THEME FOCUS:

Geography, Politics, Science and Technology

In this module, you will read about the Roman Republic, about how Rome's location and geography helped it become a major power in the ancient world. You will also read about the city's politics and discover how its three-pronged government affected all of society. Then you will learn about the development of Rome as it grew from a republic into a strong and vast empire. You will read about how the Romans' many contributions to literature, language, law, and science and technology have shaped how people have lived for more than 2,000 years.

READING FOCUS:

Create an Outline

How can you make sense of all the facts and ideas in a module? One way is to take notes in the form of an outline.

Outline a Lesson Here is an example of a partial outline for Lesson 1. Notice how the writer used the lesson's heads to determine the main and supporting ideas.

The writer picked up the first heading in the lesson as the first main idea. She identified it with Roman numeral I.

The writer saw three smaller heads under the bigger head of The Geography of Italy and listed them as A, B, and C.

The writer then decided it was important to note some individual facts under B.1. That's why she added a and b.

The writer later identified two facts that supported II.A. She listed them as numbers 1 and 2.

Lesson 1, Geography and the Rise of Rome

I. The Geography of Italy
  A. Physical features—many types of features
    1. Mountain ranges
    2. Hills
    3. Rivers
  B. Impact of Geography
    1. Helped city of Rome become powerful
      a. Strategic location
      b. Access to resources
  C. Climate—warm summers, mild winters
II. Rome's Legendary Origins
  A. Aeneas
    1. Trojan hero
    2. Sailed to Italy and became ruler
  B. Romulus and Remus
    1. Twin brothers
    2. Decided to build city
      a. Romulus killed Remus
      b. City named for Romulus
  C. Rome's Early Kings

Outline a Few Paragraphs When you need to outline only a few paragraphs, you can use the same outline form. Just look for the main idea of each paragraph, and give each one a Roman numeral. Supporting ideas within the paragraph can be listed with A, B, and so forth. You can use Arabic numbers for specific details and facts.

You Try It!

Read the following passage from this module. Then fill in the blanks to complete the outline.

Growth of Territory Roman territory grew mainly in response to outside threats. In about 387 BC, a people called the Gauls attacked Rome and took over the city. The Romans had to give the Gauls a huge amount of gold to leave the city. Inspired by the Gauls' victory, many of Rome's neighboring cities also decided to attack. With some difficulty, the Romans fought off these attacks. As Rome's attackers were defeated, the Romans took over their lands. As you can see on the map, the Romans soon controlled all of the Italian Peninsula except far northern Italy.

One reason for the Roman success was the organization of the army. Soldiers were organized in legions. . . . This organization allowed the army to be very flexible.

Complete this outline based on the passage you just read.

I. Roman territory grew in response to outside threats.
   A. Gauls attacked Rome in 387 BC.
      1. Took over the city
      2. _____
   B. The Gauls' victory inspired other people to attack Rome.
      1. _____
      2. Romans took lands of defeated foes.
      3. _____

II. _____
   A. Soldiers were organized in legions.
   B. _____

As you read this module, identify the main ideas you would use in an outline of the module.

Key Terms and People

Lesson 1
Aeneas
Romulus and Remus
republic
dictators
Cincinnatus
plebeians
patricians

Lesson 2
magistrates
consuls
Roman Senate
majority rule
veto
Latin
checks and balances
Forum
legions
Punic Wars
Hannibal

Lesson 3
Gaius Marius
Lucius Cornelius Sulla
Spartacus
Cicero
orator
Julius Caesar
Pompey
Cleopatra VII
Brutus
Marc Antony
Augustus

Lesson 4
Hadrian
provinces
currency
Pax Romana

Lesson 5
Diocletian
Clovis
Attila
corruption

Lesson 6
Galen
aqueduct
Virgil
Ovid
satire
Romance languages
civil law

Geography and the Rise of Rome

The Big Idea

Rome's location and government helped it become a major power in the ancient world.

Main Ideas

- The geography of Italy made land travel difficult but helped the Romans prosper.

- Ancient historians were very interested in Rome's legendary history.

- Once subject to a monarchy, the Romans created a republic.

Key Terms and People

Aeneas
Romulus and Remus
republic
dictators
Cincinnatus
plebeians
patricians

Mountains cover much of the Italian Peninsula. These mountains are in the Alps in northern Italy.

If YOU were there . . .

You are the ruler of a group of people looking for a site to build a new city. After talking with your advisors, you have narrowed your choice to two possible sites. Both locations have plenty of water and good soil for farming, but they are otherwise very different. One is on top of a tall rocky hill overlooking a shallow river. The other is on a wide open field right next to the sea.

Which site will you choose for your city? Why?

The Geography of Italy

Rome eventually became the center of one of the greatest civilizations of the ancient world. In fact, the people of Rome conquered many of the territories you have studied in this book, including Greece, Egypt, and Asia Minor.

Italy, where Rome was built, is a peninsula in southern Europe. If you look at the map, you can see that Italy looks like a high-heeled boot sticking out into the Mediterranean Sea.

Physical Features Look at the map again to find Italy's two major mountain ranges. In the north are the Alps, Europe's highest mountains. Another range, the Apennines (A-puh-nynz), runs the length of the Italian Peninsula. This rugged land made it hard for ancient people to cross from one side of the peninsula to the other. In addition, some of Italy's mountains, such as Mount Vesuvius, are volcanic. Their eruptions could devastate Roman towns.

Not much of Italy is flat. Most of the land that isn't mountainous is covered with hills. Throughout history, people have built cities on these hills for defense. As a result, many of the ancient cities of Italy—including Rome—sat atop hills. Rome was built on seven hills.

Several rivers flow out of Italy's mountains. Because these rivers were a source of fresh water, people also built their cities near them. For example, Rome lies on the Tiber (TY-buhr) River.

Impact of Geography Rome's geography is one reason it became so powerful during ancient times. Its strategic position atop the hills, the roadblock created by the Alps, and the natural moat formed by the surrounding seas protected Rome from invasion. Resources from the land also helped the city develop economically. Building materials such as stone and marble were abundant. Artisans used local clay to create pottery and crafted other goods that they traded with other civilizations. The Mediterranean Sea provided a route for Roman traders to reach many other cities. These factors helped Rome's economy to grow and Romans to prosper. Rome's strong economy and its military advantages allowed a powerful government to form over time.

Climate Most of Italy, including the area around Rome, has warm, dry summers and mild, rainy winters. This climate is similar to that of southern California. Italy's mild climate allows people to grow a wide variety of crops. Grains, citrus fruits, grapes, and olives all grow well there. A plentiful food supply was one key factor in Rome's early growth.

Reading Check
Draw Conclusions
How did Rome's location affect its early history?

Explore ONLINE!

Italy: Physical

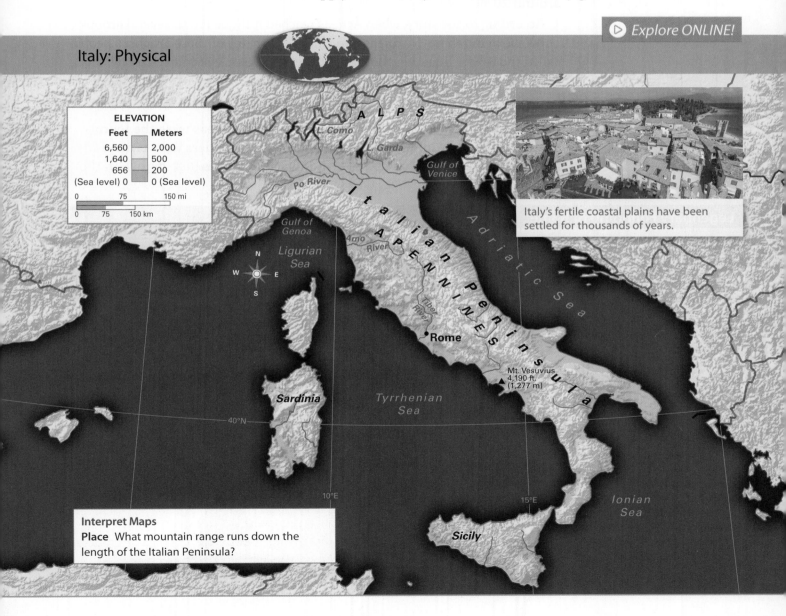

ELEVATION

Feet	Meters
6,560	2,000
1,640	500
656	200
(Sea level) 0	0 (Sea level)

0   75   150 mi
0   75   150 km

Italy's fertile coastal plains have been settled for thousands of years.

Interpret Maps
Place What mountain range runs down the length of the Italian Peninsula?

Rome's Legendary Origins

Rome's early history is wrapped in mystery. No written records exist, and we have little evidence of the city's earliest days. All we have found are ancient ruins that suggest people lived in the area of Rome as early as the 800s BC. However, we know very little about how they lived.

Would it surprise you to know that the ancient Romans were as curious about their early history as we are today? Rome's leaders wanted their city to have a glorious past that would make the Roman people proud. Imagining that glorious past, they told legends, or stories, about great heroes and kings who built the city.

Aeneas The Romans believed their history could be traced back to a great Trojan hero named **Aeneas** (i-NEE-uhs). When the Greeks destroyed Troy in the Trojan War, Aeneas fled with his followers. After a long and dangerous journey, he reached Italy. The story of this trip is told in the *Aeneid* (i-NEE-id), an epic poem written by a poet named Virgil (VUHR-juhl) around 20 BC.

According to the story, when Aeneas reached Italy, he found several groups of people living there. He formed an alliance with one of these groups, a people called the Latins. Together they fought the other people of Italy. After defeating these opponents, Aeneas married the daughter of the Latin king. Aeneas, his son Ascanius, and their descendants became prominent rulers in Italy.

Romulus and Remus Among the descendants of Aeneas were the founders of Rome. According to Roman legends, these founders were twin brothers named **Romulus** (RAHM-yuh-luhs) and **Remus** (REE-muhs). In the

Legendary Founding of Rome

Roman historians traced their city's history back to legendary figures such as Aeneas, Romulus, and Remus.

Aeneas

According to the *Aeneid*, Aeneas carried his father from the burning city of Troy and then searched for a new home for the Trojans. After traveling around the Mediterranean, Aeneas finally settled in Italy.

Romulus and Remus

The Romans believed the twins Romulus and Remus were descendants of Aeneas. In Roman legend, Romulus and Remus were rescued and raised by a wolf. Romulus later killed Remus and built the city of Rome.

story, these boys led exciting lives. When they were babies, they were put in a basket and thrown into the Tiber River. They didn't drown, though, because a wolf rescued them. The wolf cared for the boys for many years. Eventually, a shepherd found the boys and adopted them.

After they grew up, Romulus and Remus decided to build a city to mark the spot where the wolf had rescued them. While they were planning the city, Remus mocked one of his brother's ideas. In a fit of anger, Romulus killed Remus. He then built the city and named it Rome after himself.

Rome's Early Kings According to ancient historians, Romulus was the first king of Rome, taking the throne in 753 BC. Modern historians believe that Rome could have been founded 50 years before or after that date. Roman records list seven kings who ruled the city. Not all of them were Roman.

Rome's last three kings were Etruscans (i-TRUHS-kuhnz), members of a people who lived north of Rome. The Etruscans, who had been influenced by Greek colonies in Italy, lived in Italy before Rome was founded.

The Etruscan kings made great contributions to Roman society. They built huge temples and Rome's first sewer. Many historians think that the Romans learned their alphabet and numbers from the Etruscans.

The last Roman king was said to have been a cruel man who had many people killed, including his own advisors. Finally, a group of nobles rose up against him. According to tradition, he was overthrown in 509 BC. The nobles, who no longer wanted kings, created a new government.

Reading Check
Draw Conclusions
Why did early Romans want to get rid of the monarchy?

The Early Republic

The government the Romans created in 509 BC was a **republic**. In a republic, people elect leaders to govern them. Each year the Romans elected officials to rule the city. These officials had many powers but stayed in power for only one year. This system was supposed to keep any one person from becoming too powerful in the government.

But Rome was not a democracy. Nearly all the city's elected officials came from a small group of wealthy and powerful men. These wealthy and powerful Romans held all the power, and other people had little to no say in how the republic was run.

Challenges from Outside Shortly after the Romans created the republic, they found themselves at war. For about 50 years, the Romans were at war with other peoples of the region. For the most part, the Romans won these wars. But they lost several battles, and the wars destroyed many lives and much property.

During particularly difficult wars, the Romans chose **dictators**—rulers with almost absolute power—to lead the city. They were appointed during tough times because there was a greater need to enforce order. Dictators were given the power to make laws, although they were held in check by the Senate and the courts. To keep them from abusing their power, dictators could stay in power for only six months. When that time was over, the dictator gave up his power.

Cincinnatus c. 519 BC–?

Cincinnatus is the most famous dictator from the early Roman Republic. Because he wasn't eager to hold on to his power, the Romans considered Cincinnatus an ideal leader. They admired his abilities and his loyalty to the republic. The early citizens of the United States admired the same qualities in their leaders. In fact, some people called George Washington the "American Cincinnatus" when he refused to run for a third term as president. The people of the state of Ohio also honored Cincinnatus by naming one of their major cities, Cincinnati, after him.

Draw Conclusions
Why did the Romans consider Cincinnatus an ideal leader?

One of Rome's famous dictators was **Cincinnatus** (sin-suh-NAT-uhs), who gained power in 458 BC. Although he was a farmer, the Romans chose him to defend the city against a powerful enemy that had defeated a large Roman army.

Cincinnatus quickly defeated the city's enemies. Immediately, he resigned as dictator and returned to his farm, long before his six-month term had run out.

The victory by Cincinnatus did not end Rome's troubles. Rome continued to fight its neighbors on and off for many years.

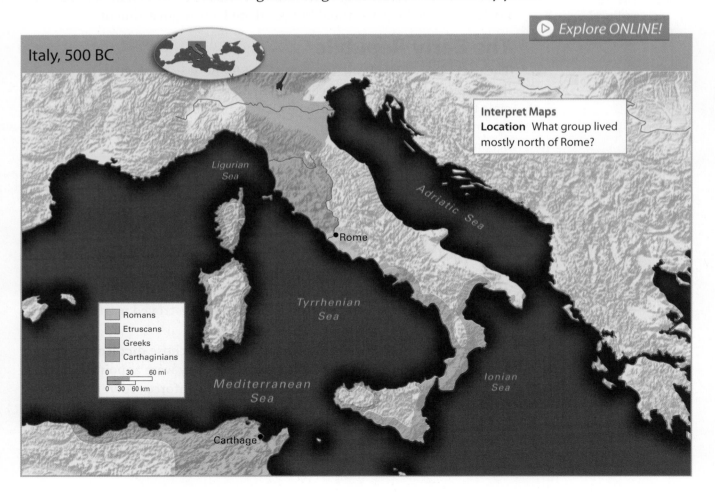

Italy, 500 BC

▶ Explore ONLINE!

Interpret Maps
Location What group lived mostly north of Rome?

Ligurian Sea

Adriatic Sea

Rome

Tyrrhenian Sea

Ionian Sea

Mediterranean Sea

Carthage

Romans
Etruscans
Greeks
Carthaginians

0   30   60 mi
0 30 60 km

Roman Society

Patricians

- Wealthy, powerful citizens
- Nobles
- Small minority of the population
- Once controlled all aspects of government
- After 218 BC, not allowed to participate in trade or commerce

Plebeians

- Common people
- Peasants, craftspeople, traders, other workers
- Majority of the population
- Gained right to participate in government
- Only Romans who could be traders, often wealthy

Challenges Within Rome Enemy armies weren't the only challenge facing Rome. Within the city, Roman society was divided into two groups. Many of Rome's **plebeians** (pli-BEE-uhnz), or common people, were calling for changes in government. They wanted more of a say in how the city was run.

Rome was run by powerful nobles called **patricians** (puh-TRI-shuhnz). Only patricians could be elected to office, so they held all political power.

The plebeians were peasants, craftspeople, traders, and other workers. Some of these plebeians, especially traders, were as rich as patricians. Even though the plebeians outnumbered the patricians, they couldn't take part in the government.

In 494 BC, the plebeians formed a council and elected their own officials, an act that frightened many patricians. They feared that Rome would fall apart if the two groups couldn't cooperate. The patricians decided that it was time to change the government.

Reading Check
Contrast How were patricians and plebeians different?

Summary and Preview Rome was founded as a city in Italy, ruled at first by kings and later by a republican government. In the next lesson, you will learn more about that government, its strengths and weaknesses, how it worked, and how it changed over time.

Lesson 1 Assessment

Review Ideas, Terms, and People

1. **a. Describe** Where is Italy located?
   b. Explain How did mountains affect life in Italy?
   c. Predict How do you think Rome's location on the Mediterranean affected its history as it began to grow into a world power?
2. **a. Identify** Which brothers supposedly founded the city of Rome?
   b. Summarize What role did Aeneas play in the founding of Rome?

3. **a. Describe** What type of government did the Romans create in 509 BC?
   b. Contrast How were patricians and plebians different?

Critical Thinking

4. **Categorize** As you review your notes, separate the legends from the historical events in Rome's founding and growth. Then use a diagram like this one to list the key legendary events.

Literature in History

A Roman Epic

Word Help

tranquilly calmly
astray off course
broached crossed
moored anchored
constraint force
gale storm

❶ Both "Teucrians" and "sons of Dardanus" are ways of referring to Trojans.

❷ Ilioneus says that the Trojans are not lost. A seamark is similar to a landmark, a feature sailors use to find their way.
How does Ilioneus address the king? Why do you think he does so?

About the Reading Virgil wrote the *Aeneid* to record the glorious story of Rome's founding and to celebrate the Rome of his day. At the center of the poem stands the hero Aeneas, survivor of the Trojan War and son of the goddess Venus. After wandering for seven years, Aeneas finally reaches southern Italy—then known as Ausonia. Here, Aeneas's friend Ilioneus leads a group of representatives to visit a nearby Latin settlement.

As You Read Try to identify each group's goals and desires.

From *the Aeneid*

by Virgil, Translated by Robert Fitzgerald

          Latinus
Called the Teucrians before him, saying
Tranquilly as they entered:
          "Sons of Dardanus—
You see, we know your city and your nation,
As all had heard you laid a westward course—
Tell me your purpose. ❶ What design or need
Has brought you through the dark blue sea so far
To our Ausonian coast? Either astray
Or driven by rough weather, such as sailors
Often endure at sea, you've broached the river,
Moored ship there. Now do not turn away
From hospitality here. Know that our Latins
Come of Saturn's race, that we are just—
Not by constraint or laws, but by our choice
And habit of our ancient god. . . ."
Latinus then fell silent, and in turn
Ilioneus began:
          "Your majesty,
Most noble son of Faunus, no rough seas
Or black gale swept us to your coast, no star
Or clouded seamark put us off our course. ❷
We journey to your city by design
And general consent, driven as we are
From realms in other days greatest by far.

Aeneas, from an Italian painting in the 1700s

progeny offspring
threshold door
oracle person who gives advice
averted turned away
immobile unmoving

❸ Ilioneus explains that the Trojans have come to Italy "by design"—both on purpose and with help from the gods.

❹ Aeneas and Dardanus, the founder of Troy, were both believed to be descendants of Jove, the king of the gods.

❺ The Romans believed that Troy's founder, Dardanus, was born in Italy. *What does Ilioneus ask the king to give the Trojans?*

❻ Virgil included this vision of Rome's great future to point out the city's greatness to his readers.

The Sun looked down on, passing on his way
From heaven's far eastern height. ❸ Our line's from Jove,
In his paternity the sons of Dardanus
Exult, and highest progeny of Jove
Include our king himself—Trojan Aeneas,
Who sent us to your threshold. . . . ❹
So long on the vast waters, now we ask
A modest settlement of the gods of home,
A strip of coast that will bring harm to no one,
Air and water, open and free to all. . . .
Our quest was for your country. Dardanus
Had birth here, and Apollo calls us back,
Directing us by solemn oracles
To Tuscan Tiber. . . . ❺ Here besides
Aeneus gives you from his richer years
These modest gifts, relics caught up and saved
From burning Troy. . . ."
        Latinus heard
Ilioneus out, his countenance averted,
Sitting immobile, all attention, eyes
Downcast but turning here and there. The embroidered
Purple and the scepter of King Priam
Moved him less in his own kingliness
Than long thoughts on the marriage of his daughter,
As he turned over in his inmost mind
Old Faunus' prophecy.
        "This is the man,"
he thought, "foretold as coming from abroad
To be my son-in-law, by fate appointed,
Called to reign here with equal authority—
The man whose heirs will be brilliant in valor
And win the mastery of the world." ❻

Connect Literature to History

1. **Analyze** Rome's leaders wanted their city to have a glorious past that would make the Roman people proud. What details in this passage would make Roman readers proud of their past?

2. **Draw Conclusions** When Aeneas reached Italy, he formed an alliance with the Latins. Think about how Virgil portrays the Latins in this passage. What words or phrases would you use to describe them? Why might such people make good allies?

The Roman Republic

The Big Idea

Rome's tripartite government and written laws helped create a stable society and paved the way for expansion.

Main Ideas

- Roman government was made up of three parts that worked together to run the city.

- Written laws helped keep order in Rome.

- Male citizens, women, children, slaves, and foreigners all played a role in Roman society.

- The late republic period saw the growth of territory and trade.

- As Rome became more powerful, it conquered land in Europe and Africa.

Key Terms

magistrates
consuls
Roman Senate
majority rule
veto
Latin
checks and balances
Forum
legions
Punic Wars
Hannibal

If YOU were there . . .

You have just been elected a government official in Rome. Your duty is to represent the plebeians, the common people. You hold office for only one year, but you have one important power—you can stop laws from being passed. Now city leaders are proposing a law that will hurt the plebeians. If you stop the new law, it will hurt your future in politics. If you let it pass, it will hurt the people you are supposed to protect.

Will you let the new law pass? Why or why not?

Roman Government

When the plebeians complained about Rome's government in the 400s BC, the city's leaders knew they had to do something. If the people stayed unhappy, they might rise up and overthrow the whole government.

To calm the angry plebeians, the patricians made some changes to Rome's government. For example, they created new offices that could be held only by plebeians. The people who held these offices protected the plebeians' rights and interests. Gradually, the distinctions between patricians and plebeians began to disappear, but that took a very long time.

As a result of the changes the patricians made, Rome developed a tripartite (try-PAHR-tyt) government, or a government with three parts. Each part had its own responsibilities and duties. To fulfill its duties, each part of the government had its own powers, rights, and privileges.

Magistrates The first part of Rome's government was made up of elected officials, or **magistrates** (MA-juh-strayts). The two most powerful magistrates in Rome were called **consuls** (KAHN-suhlz). These leaders were elected each year to run the city and lead the army. There were two consuls so that no one person would be too powerful.

Below the consuls were other magistrates. Rome had many different types of magistrates. Each was elected for one year and had his own duties and powers. Some were judges. Others managed Rome's finances or organized games and festivals.

Senate The second part of Rome's government was the Senate. The **Roman Senate** was a council of wealthy and powerful Romans that advised the city's leaders. It was originally created to advise Rome's kings. After the kings were gone, the Senate continued to meet to advise consuls.

Unlike magistrates, senators—members of the Senate—held office for life. By the time the republic was created, the Senate had 300 members. At first most senators were patricians, but as time passed many wealthy plebeians became senators as well. Because magistrates became senators after completing their terms in office, most didn't want to anger the Senate and risk their future jobs.

As time passed, the Senate became more powerful. It gained influence over magistrates and took control of the city's finances. By 200 BC the Senate had great influence in Rome's government.

Assemblies and Tribunes The third part of Rome's government, the part that protected the common people, had two branches. The first branch was

Government of the Roman Republic

Magistrates
- Consuls led the government and army, judged court cases
- Served for one year
- Had power over all citizens, including other officials

Senate
- Advised the consuls
- Served for life
- Gained control of financial affairs

Assemblies and Tribunes
- Represented the common people, approved or rejected laws, declared war, elected magistrates
- Citizens could take part in assemblies all their adult lives; tribunes served for one year
- Could veto the decisions of consuls and other magistrates

made up of assemblies. Both patricians and plebeians took part in these assemblies. Their **primary** job was to elect the magistrates who ran the city of Rome.

The second branch was made up of a group of elected officials called tribunes. Elected by the plebeians, tribunes governed by **majority rule**. Majority rule means that the group that has the most members has the power to decide what the government will do. Tribunes also had the ability to **veto** (VEE-toh), or prohibit, actions by other officials. *Veto* means "I forbid" in **Latin**, the Romans' language. This veto power made tribunes very powerful in Rome's government. To keep them from abusing their power, each tribune remained in office only one year. Only adult male citizens were permitted to vote for these leaders.

Citizenship and Civic Duty Rome's government would not have worked without the participation of the people. Over time, the rights of citizenship expanded to include more people, and more people could participate in Rome's government. For example, plebeians gained equal voting rights in the 200s BC. Citizens could attend assembly meetings and vote in elections. Voting in Rome was a complicated process, and many people were not allowed to do it, including women. Those who could, however, had a responsibility to take part in all elections. People participated in the government because they felt it was their civic duty, or their duty to the city. That civic duty included doing what they could to make sure the city prospered.

Link to Today

Do as the Romans Do

The government of the Roman Republic was one of its greatest strengths. When the founders of the United States sat down to plan our government, they copied many elements of the Roman system. Like the Romans, we elect our leaders. Our government also has three branches—the president, the Congress, and the federal court system. The powers of these branches are set forth in our Constitution, just like the Roman officials' powers were. Our government also has a system of checks and balances to prevent any one branch from becoming too strong. For example, Congress can refuse to give the president money to pay for programs. Like the Romans, Americans have a civic duty to participate in the government to help keep it as strong as it can be.

Make Inferences
Why do you think the founders of the United States borrowed ideas from Roman government?

Wealthy and powerful citizens also felt it was their duty to hold public office to help run the city. In return for their time and commitment, these citizens were respected and admired by other Romans.

The ability to vote wasn't the only benefit of citizenship. Citizens could run for office, own property, get married, and have a trial. In return, they were expected to pay taxes and serve in the military.

Checks and Balances In addition to limiting terms of office, the Romans established limited government by putting other restrictions on their leaders' power. Limited government is a system that allows the powers of the government to be restricted. They did this by giving government officials the ability to restrict the powers of other officials. For example, one consul could block the actions of the other.

Laws proposed by the Senate had to be approved by magistrates and ratified by assemblies. We call these methods to balance power **checks and balances**. Checks and balances keep any one part of a government from becoming stronger or more influential than the others.

Checks and balances made Rome's government very complicated. Sometimes quarrels arose when officials had different ideas or opinions. When officials worked together, however, Rome's government was strong and efficient, as one Roman historian noted:

"In unison [together] they are a match for any and all emergencies, the result being that it is impossible to find a constitution that is better constructed. For whenever some common external danger should come upon them and should compel [force] them to band together in counsel [thought] and in action, the power of their state becomes so great that nothing that is required is neglected [ignored]."

—Polybius, from *The Constitution of the Roman Republic*

Reading Check
Find Main Ideas
What were the three parts of the Roman government?

Written Laws Keep Order

Rome's officials believed in the rule of law, the belief that all people must follow an established set of rules. The officials were responsible for making the city's laws and making sure that people obeyed them. At first these laws weren't written down. The only people who knew all the laws were the patricians who had made them.

Many people were unhappy with this situation. They did not want to be punished for breaking laws they didn't even know existed. As a result, they began to call for Rome's laws to be written down and made accessible to everybody.

Rome's first written law code was produced in 450 BC on 12 bronze tables, or tablets. These tables were displayed in the **Forum**, Rome's public meeting place. Because of how it was displayed, this code was called the Law of the Twelve Tables. In addition to listing laws people had to follow, it listed many rights, including the right to a trial, an assurance that a person would have 30 days to pay off a debt, and guarantees regarding property.

The Law of the Twelve Tables, inscribed on 12 bronze tablets, was originally displayed in the Roman Forum for all to see.

Law of the Twelve Tables

The Law of the Twelve Tables governed many parts of Roman life. Some laws were written to protect the rights of all Romans. Others protected only the patricians. The laws listed here should give you an idea of the kinds of laws the tables included.

Analyze Historical Sources
How are these laws similar to and different from our laws today?

A Roman who did not appear before a government official when called or did not pay his debts could be arrested.

Women—even as adults—were legally considered to be children.

No one in Rome could be executed without a trial.

[from Table I] *If anyone summons a man before the magistrate, he must go. If the man summoned does not go, let the one summoning him call the bystanders to witness and then take him by force.*

[from Table III] *One who has confessed a debt, or against whom judgment has been pronounced, shall have thirty days to pay it. After that forcible seizure of his person is allowed . . . unless he pays the amount of the judgment.*

[from Table V] *Females should remain in guardianship even when they have attained their majority.*

[from Table IX] *Putting to death of any man, whosoever he might be, unconvicted is forbidden.*

—Law of the Twelve Tables, translated in *The Library of Original Sources* edited by Oliver J. Thatcher

Over time, Rome's leaders passed many new laws. They were established in a variety of ways. For example, magistrates issued proclamations called edicts, the Senate passed legislation, and plebeians enacted resolutions. Still, throughout their history, the Romans looked to the Law of the Twelve Tables as a symbol of Roman law and of their rights as Roman citizens.

Enforcing the law was the responsibility of the magistrates. However, Roman officials sometimes struggled to maintain order, since there was no police force.

Reading Check
Make Inferences
Why did many people want a written law code?

Life in Ancient Rome

The laws and government of Rome helped shape the way society functioned. The roles and responsibilities of different members of society shaped daily life in Rome. In addition to male citizens, women, children, slaves, and foreigners all played a part.

Women and Children Women were expected to run the household and take care of children. They taught their daughters homemaking skills. Despite their responsibilities, mothers did not have legal rights over children. However, Roman women did have more freedom and power than women in some later cultures because a woman could inherit money from her father when he died.

Children in Roman society shared some similarities with children today. They played games and had dolls and toys. They also owned pets like dogs and birds. However, girls sometimes married as early as age 12 and were expected to be married by the age of 16. Boys could get married later. Most children did not go to school, because they had to work to help their families. Only rich families could afford to pay a teacher.

Slaves and Foreigners Slaves played a very significant role in Rome. In fact, about 30 percent of the population was enslaved. They were treated cruelly and were often whipped and beaten. They worked in homes as servants and as laborers on farms, in factories, and in mines. They also worked for the government building roads, aqueducts, and buildings.

Foreigners enjoyed a slightly higher social standing than slaves, though neither group had legal protection. Even so, foreigners had more rights in Rome than they did in Greek city-states. They could also be granted citizenship if they adopted Roman ways.

The Roman Forum The Roman Forum, the place where the Law of the Twelve Tables was kept, was the heart of the city of Rome. It was the site of important government buildings and temples. Government and religion were only part of what made the Forum so important, though. It was also a popular meeting place for Roman citizens. People met there to shop, chat, and gossip.

The Roman Forum

The Forum was the center of life in ancient Rome. The city's most important temples and government buildings were located there, and Romans met there to talk about the issues of the day. The word *forum* means "public place."

The Temple of Jupiter stood atop the Capitoline Hill, overlooking the Forum.

Important government records were stored in the Tabularium.

The Senate met here in the curia, or Senate House.

Roman citizens often wore togas, loose-fitting garments wrapped around the body. Togas were symbols of Roman citizenship.

Analyze Visuals
What can you see in this illustration that indicates the Forum was an important place?

Public officials often addressed people from this platform.

The Forum lay in the center of Rome, between two major hills. On one side was the Palatine (PA-luh-tyn) Hill, where Rome's richest people lived. Across the forum was the Capitoline (KA-pet-uhl-yn) Hill, where Rome's grandest temples stood. Because of this location, city leaders could often be found in or near the forum, mingling with the common people. These leaders used the Forum as a speaking area, delivering speeches to the crowds.

But the Forum also had attractions for people not interested in speeches. Various shops lined the open square, and public ceremonies were commonly held there. Crowds also gathered for fights between gladiators or prisoners. These fights were a popular and violent spectator sport. Seneca, a Roman philosopher, said this about them:

"But now all the trifling is put aside and it is pure murder. The men have no defensive armor. They are exposed to blows at all points. . . ."

—Seneca, Epistle 7: On Crowds

Reading Check
Form Generalizations
How was the Forum the heart of Roman society?

Growth of Territory and Trade

After about 400 BC the Roman Republic grew quickly, both geographically and economically. Within 200 years the Roman army had conquered nearly all of Italy. Meanwhile Roman traders had begun to ship goods back and forth around the Mediterranean in search of new products and wealth.

Growth of Territory Roman territory grew mainly in response to outside threats. In about 387 BC a people called the Gauls attacked Rome and took over the city. The Romans had to give the Gauls a huge amount of gold to leave the city.

Link to Economics

Roman Banking

Rome had a large system of state and private banks. Banking helped money flow all across Roman territories, encouraging economic growth and trade. People exchanged money to pay taxes and conduct trade. Banks lent money to individuals and businesses to help them meet needs. People could also give money and valuable goods to banks for safekeeping. Special state bankers were responsible for removing old, worn coins from circulation and replacing them with newly minted one.

The Roman government developed rules for bankers. Banks had to keep records showing each transaction. This kept banks honest and served as legal proof of loans and deposits. Improvements in recordkeeping also allowed banks to send money using paper notes instead of coins, which could be stolen.

Analyze Information
In what ways is banking in the United States today similar to Roman banking?

Inspired by the Gauls' victory, many of Rome's neighboring cities also decided to attack. With some difficulty, the Romans fought off these attacks. As Rome's attackers were defeated, the Romans took over their lands. As you can see on the map, the Romans soon controlled all of the Italian Peninsula except far northern Italy.

One reason for the Roman success was the organization of the army. Soldiers were organized in **legions** (LEE-juhnz), or groups of up to 6,000 soldiers. Each legion was divided into centuries, or groups of 100 soldiers. This organization allowed the army to be very flexible. It could fight as a large group or as several small ones. This flexibility allowed the Romans to defeat most enemies.

Farming and Trade Before Rome conquered Italy, most Romans were farmers. As the republic grew, many people left their farms for Rome. In place of these small farms, wealthy Romans built large farms in the countryside. These farms were worked by slaves who grew one or two crops. The owners of the farms didn't usually live on them. Instead, they stayed in Rome or other cities and let others run the farms for them.

Roman trade also expanded as the republic grew. Rome's farmers couldn't grow enough food to support the city's increasing population, so merchants brought food from other parts of the Mediterranean. These merchants also brought metal goods and slaves to Rome. To pay for these goods, the Romans made coins out of copper, silver, and other metals. Roman coins began to appear in markets all around the Mediterranean.

Reading Check
Analyze Causes
Why did the Romans conquer their neighbors?

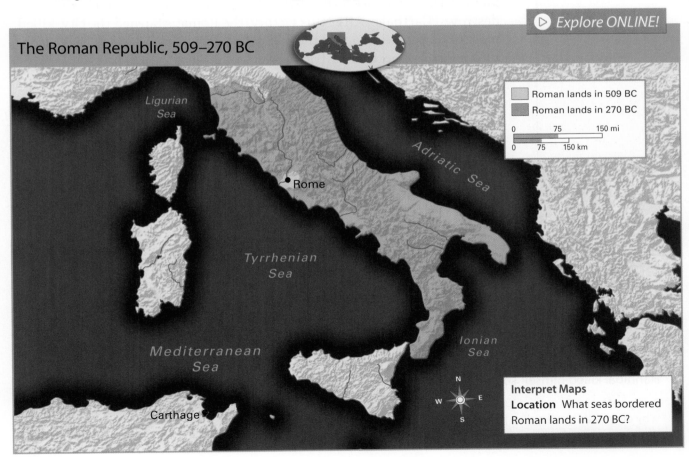

▷ *Explore ONLINE!*

The Roman Republic, 509–270 BC

Roman lands in 509 BC
Roman lands in 270 BC

0   75   150 mi
0   75   150 km

Ligurian Sea

Adriatic Sea

Rome

Tyrrhenian Sea

Ionian Sea

Mediterranean Sea

Carthage

Interpret Maps
Location What seas bordered Roman lands in 270 BC?

Rome Grows Beyond Italy

As Rome's power grew, other countries came to see the Romans as a threat to their own power and declared war on them. In the end, the Romans defeated their opponents, and Rome gained territory throughout the Mediterranean.

The Punic Wars The fiercest of the wars Rome fought were the **Punic** (PYOO-nik) **Wars**, a series of wars against Carthage, a city in northern Africa. The word *Punic* means "Phoenician" in Latin. As you might recall, the Phoenicians, who had built the city of Carthage, were an ancient civilization.

Rome and Carthage went to war three times between 264 and 146 BC. The wars began when Carthage sent its armies to Sicily, an island just southwest of Italy. In response, the Romans also sent an army to the island. Before long, war broke out between them. After almost 20 years of fighting, the Romans forced their enemies out and took control of Sicily.

In 218 BC Carthage tried to attack Rome itself. An army led by the brilliant general **Hannibal** set out for Rome. Although he forced the Romans right to the edge of defeat, Hannibal was never able to capture Rome itself. In the meantime, the Romans sent an army to attack Carthage. Hannibal rushed home to defend his city, but his troops were defeated at Zama (ZAY-muh).

By the 140s BC many senators had grown alarmed that Carthage was growing powerful again. They convinced Rome's consuls to declare war on Carthage, and once again the Romans sent an army to Africa and destroyed Carthage. After this victory, the Romans burned the city, killed most of its people, and sold the rest of the people into slavery. They also took control of northern Africa.

Later Expansion During the Punic Wars, Rome took control of Sicily, Corsica, Spain, and North Africa. As a result, Rome controlled most of the western Mediterranean region. As more land was conquered, more people were recruited to join the Roman army.

In the years that followed, Roman legions marched north and east as well. Rome went on to conquer Greece, as well as parts of Gaul and Asia.

BIOGRAPHY

Hannibal 247–183 BC

Many historians consider Hannibal to be one of the greatest generals of the ancient world. From an early age, he hated Rome. In 218 BC, he began the Second Punic War by attacking one of Rome's allies in Spain. After the war he became the leader of Carthage, but later the Romans forced him to flee the city. He went to Asia and joined with a king fighting the Romans there. The king was defeated, and Hannibal killed himself so that he wouldn't become a Roman prisoner.

Analyze Motives
Why do you think Hannibal began by attacking Rome's ally?

Rome Battles Carthage

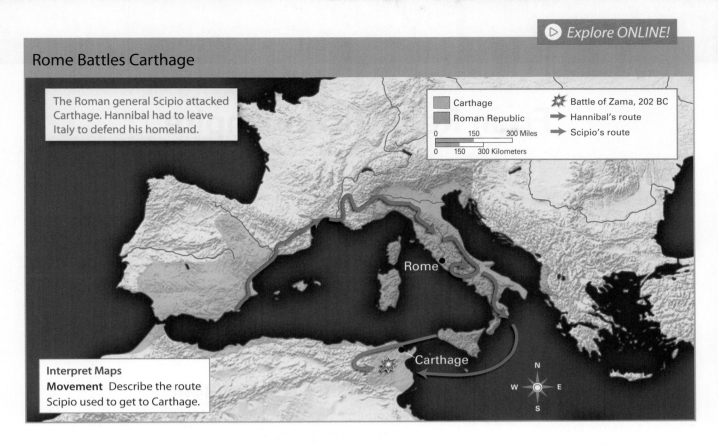

The Roman general Scipio attacked Carthage. Hannibal had to leave Italy to defend his homeland.

Legend:
- Carthage
- Roman Republic
- Battle of Zama, 202 BC
- Hannibal's route
- Scipio's route

0 150 300 Miles
0 150 300 Kilometers

Rome

Carthage

Interpret Maps
Movement Describe the route Scipio used to get to Carthage.

Reading Check
Summarize How did the Romans gain territory?

Although the Romans took over Greece, they were greatly changed by the experience. We would normally expect the victor to change the conquered country. Instead, the Romans adopted ideas about literature, art, philosophy, religion, and education from the Greeks.

Summary and Preview A republic in which citizens could vote and had rights was the basic structure of Roman government. During this period, Rome grew economically and geographically. In the next lesson, you will learn about Rome's transition from a republic to an empire.

Lesson 2 Assessment

Review Ideas, Terms, and People

1. **a. Identify** Who were the consuls?
   b. Explain Why did the Romans create a system of checks and balances?
   c. Draw Conclusions How do you think the Roman Senate gained power?

2. **a. Recall** What was Rome's first written law code called?
   b. Analyze Why did Romans want their laws written down?

3. **a. Describe** What were the responsibilities of women in Rome?

4. **a. Define** What was a Roman legion?
   b. Explain Why did the Romans decide to conquer all of Italy?
   c. Analyze How did the growth of territory help increase Roman trade?

5. **a. Recall** Who fought in the Punic Wars?
   b. Summarize What led to the beginning of the Punic Wars?
   c. Elaborate Why do you think the Romans borrowed many ideas from Greek culture?

Critical Thinking

6. **Summarize** Use this diagram to note information about the powers of the parts of Rome's government.

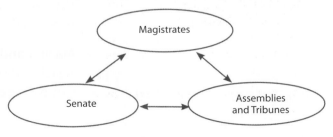

Magistrates

Senate

Assemblies and Tribunes

From Republic to Empire

The Big Idea

Julius Caesar and Augustus led Rome's transition from a republic to an empire.

Main Ideas

- Several crises struck the republic in later years.

- As Rome descended into chaos, many called for change in government.

- Julius Caesar rose to power and became the sole ruler of Rome.

- After Caesar's death, Augustus became emperor.

Key Terms and People

Gaius Marius
Lucius Cornelius Sulla
Spartacus
Cicero
orator
Julius Caesar
Pompey
Cleopatra VII
Brutus
Marc Antony
Augustus

Academic Vocabulary
purpose the reason something is done

If YOU were there . . .

You are a friend of a Roman senator. Your friend is worried about the growing power of military men in Rome's government. Some other senators want to take violent action to stop generals from taking over as dictators. Your friend wants your advice: Is violence justified to save the Roman Republic?

What advice will you give your friend?

Crises Strike the Republic

As the Romans' territory grew, problems arose in the republic. Rich citizens were getting richer, and many leaders feared that violence would erupt between rich and poor.

Tiberius and Gaius Gracchus Among the first leaders to address Rome's problems were brothers named Tiberius (ty-BIR-ee-uhs) and Gaius Gracchus (GY-uhs GRAK-uhs). Both served as tribunes.

Tiberius, who took office in 133 BC, wanted to create farms for poor Romans. The **purpose** of these farms was to keep the poor citizens happy and prevent rebellions. Tiberius wanted to create his farms on public land that wealthy citizens had illegally taken over. The public supported this idea, but the wealthy citizens opposed it. Conflict over the idea led to riots in the city, during which Tiberius was killed.

A few years later Gaius also tried to create new farms. He also began to sell food cheaply to Rome's poor citizens. Like his brother, Gaius angered many powerful Romans and was killed for his ideas.

The violent deaths of the Gracchus brothers changed Roman politics. From that time on, people saw violence as a political weapon. They often attacked leaders with whom they disagreed.

Marius and Sulla In the late 100s BC, another social change nearly led to the end of the republic. In 107 BC, the Roman army desperately needed more troops. In response, a consul

Lucius Cornelius Sulla 138–78 BC

Although the two eventually became enemies, Sulla learned much of what he knew about military affairs from Gaius Marius. He had been an assistant to Marius before he became consul. Sulla changed Rome's government forever when he became dictator, but he actually had many traditional ideas. For example, he believed the Senate should be the main ruling group in Rome, and he increased its power during his rule.

Analyze Issues
Do you think Sulla was a traditional Roman leader? Why or why not?

named **Gaius Marius** (MER-ee-uhs) encouraged poor people to join the army. Before, only people who owned property had been allowed to join. As a result of this change, thousands of poor and unemployed citizens joined Rome's army.

Because Marius was a good general, his troops were more loyal to him than they were to Rome. The army's support gave Marius great political power. Following his example, other ambitious politicians also sought their armies' support.

One such politician, **Lucius Cornelius Sulla** (LOO-shuhs kawr-NEEL-yuhs SUHL-uh), became consul in 88 BC. Sulla soon came into conflict with Marius, a conflict that led to a civil war in Rome. A civil war is a war

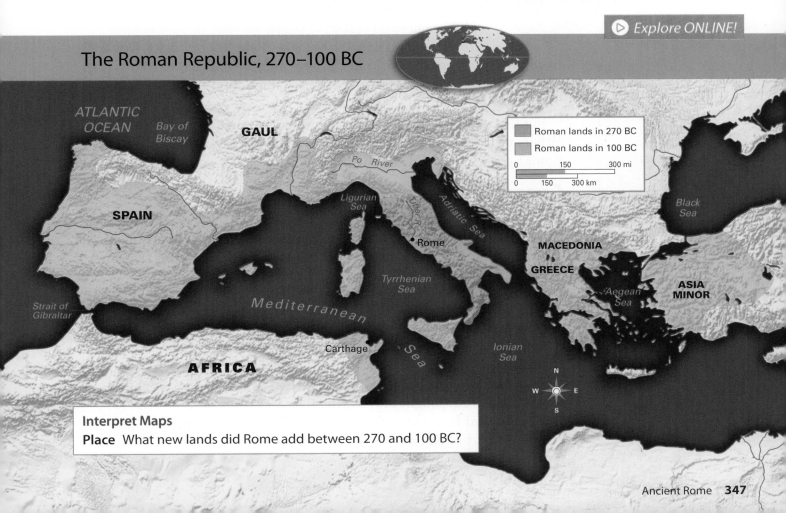

Explore ONLINE!

The Roman Republic, 270–100 BC

Roman lands in 270 BC
Roman lands in 100 BC

0   150   300 mi
0   150   300 km

ATLANTIC OCEAN
Bay of Biscay
GAUL
Po River
SPAIN
Ligurian Sea
Tiber R.
Adriatic Sea
Black Sea
Rome
MACEDONIA
GREECE
Tyrrhenian Sea
Aegean Sea
ASIA MINOR
Strait of Gibraltar
Mediterranean Sea
Carthage
Ionian Sea
AFRICA

Interpret Maps
Place What new lands did Rome add between 270 and 100 BC?

between citizens of the same country. In the end Sulla defeated Marius. He later named himself dictator and used his power to punish his enemies.

Spartacus Not long after Sulla died, another crisis arose to challenge Rome's leaders. Thousands of slaves led by a former gladiator, **Spartacus** (SPAHR-tuh-kuhs), rose up and demanded freedom. Spartacus was widely admired. The Greek historian Plutarch said he "had a great spirit and great physical strength, [and] was, much more than one would expect from his condition, most intelligent and cultured."

Spartacus and his followers defeated an army sent to stop them and took over much of southern Italy. Eventually, though, Spartacus was killed in battle. Without his leadership, the revolt fell apart. Victorious, the Romans executed 6,000 rebellious slaves as an example to others who thought about rebelling. The rebellion was over, but the republic's problems were not.

Reading Check
Contrast How did the reforms of the Gracchus brothers differ from those of Gaius Marius?

The Call for Change

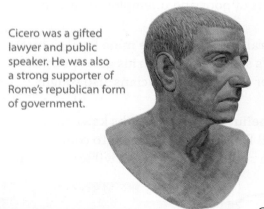

Cicero was a gifted lawyer and public speaker. He was also a strong supporter of Rome's republican form of government.

Rome in the 70s BC was a dangerous place. Politicians and generals went to war to increase their power even as political order broke down in Rome. Unemployed Romans rioted in the streets because they couldn't get enough food. All the while more and more people from all around the republic flooded into the city, further adding to the confusion.

Some Romans tried to stop the chaos in Rome's government. One such person was **Cicero** (SIS-uh-roh), a gifted philosopher and **orator**, or public speaker. In his speeches Cicero called on Romans to make Rome a better place. One way to do this, he argued, was to limit the power of generals. Cicero wanted the Romans to give more support to the Senate and to restore the checks and balances on government.

But Cicero was unsuccessful. Many Romans didn't agree with him. Others were too caught up in their own affairs to pay any attention. Rome's government did not change.

Reading Check
Summarize What did Cicero want Romans to do?

Caesar's Rise to Power

As Cicero was calling on the Romans to take power away from the generals, a new group of generals was working to take over the government. The most powerful of these generals was **Julius Caesar** (JOOL-yuhs SEE-zuhr).

Caesar the General Caesar was probably the greatest general in Roman history. Other Romans admired him for his bravery and skill in battle. At the same time, his soldiers respected him because he treated them well.

Between 58 and 50 BC, Caesar conquered nearly all of Gaul—a region that included much of modern France, Germany, and northern Italy. When he invaded Britain in 55 BC, however, he encountered a fierce fighting force. The Britons fought bravely, and Caesar was forced to retreat. He returned a year later with an additional 30,000 soldiers and this time conquered part of Britain.

He wrote a description of this conquest, describing in great detail how he defeated each of the tribes he faced. Here he describes how he defeated a group called the Menapii. Notice how he refers to himself as "Caesar."

"Caesar, having divided his forces . . . and having hastily [quickly] constructed some bridges, enters their country in three divisions, burns their houses and villages, and gets possession of a large number of cattle and men. Constrained [forced] by these circumstances the Menapii send ambassadors to him for the purpose of suing [asking] for peace."

—Julius Caesar, from *The Gallic Wars*

Caesar's military successes made him a major figure in Roman politics. In addition to being a good leader, Caesar was an excellent speaker. He won many people to his side with his speeches in the forum.

Caesar also had powerful friends. Before he went to Gaul, he made an **agreement** with two of the most powerful men in Rome, **Pompey** and Crassus. The three agreed to work together to fight against the Senate. Together, Caesar and his allies changed the course of Roman history.

Conflict with an Ally At the end of the fighting in Gaul, Caesar was one of the most powerful men in the Roman Republic. He was so powerful that even his friends were jealous and afraid of him. This jealousy and fear changed Caesar's relationship with Pompey.

In 50 BC, Pompey's allies in the Senate ordered Caesar to give up command of his armies and return to Rome. Caesar refused. He knew that Pompey was trying to take power away from him and would arrest him

Julius Caesar conquered Gaul and added it to the empire. This painting from the late 1800s shows a Frankish leader surrendering to Caesar by dropping his weapons at Caesar's feet.

In 46 BC, Julius Caesar founded the southern French town of Arles. In 2007, archaeologists and divers discovered this bust at the bottom of the Rhône River near Arles. It is believed to be the only known statue of Caesar carved during his lifetime.

if he gave up his command. As a result, Caesar led his army into Italy. In 49 BC, Caesar and his troops crossed the Rubicon River, the boundary between Gaul and Italy.

Because Roman law said that no general could enter Italy with his army, Pompey and the Senate considered Caesar's return to Italy a sign of war. Afraid that Caesar would attack him, Pompey and his allies fled Italy. They didn't think they had enough troops to defeat Caesar.

Caesar and his army chased Pompey's forces around the Mediterranean for a year. Eventually they drove Pompey into Egypt, where he was killed. There Caesar met **Cleopatra VII**, whom he made queen of Egypt. As queen, Cleopatra became his new ally.

Conflict with the Senate Finally, Caesar returned to Rome. When he got there, he forced the Senate to name him dictator for ten years. Later this term was extended, and Caesar became dictator for life.

Although Caesar wanted to improve Roman society, some people resented the way he had gained power. They feared that Caesar was trying to make himself the king of Rome. The Romans certainly didn't want a king.

The Death of Julius Caesar

Caesar was stabbed to death on March 15, 44 BC. To the Romans, March 15 was called the Ides of March, and before Caesar was killed he was warned to "beware the Ides of March."

Some Senators were especially angry with Caesar. On March 15—a date the Romans called the Ides of March—in 44 BC, a group of Senators attacked Caesar in the Senate house and stabbed him to death.

Among the attackers was a young Senator named **Brutus** (BROOT-uhs), who had been a friend and ally of Caesar's. Some Romans even believed that Brutus may have been Caesar's son but didn't know it. According to Roman historians, Caesar was shocked by Brutus's betrayal and stopped fighting against his attackers when he recognized him. Plutarch described the scene by writing, "[W]hen he saw Brutus's sword drawn, he covered his face with his robe and submitted, letting himself fall. . . ."

The military of the Roman Empire used symbols to inspire pride and to communicate on the battlefield. These were called standards, and soldiers would attach them to a staff or pole to identify their legion. The *aquila*, or eagle, which represented strength, is the best known Roman standard. It was made of gold or silver.

DOCUMENT-BASED INVESTIGATION   Historical Source

Views of Caesar

Different people held contrasting views of Julius Caesar's death. Some Senators admired Caesar and were horrified by his murder. The biographer Plutarch (PLOO-tahrk) described their reactions to the event. The historian Suetonius (swe-TOH-nee-uhs) explained that other Senators thought Caesar deserved to be killed because his actions were threatening the republic.

Analyze Historical Sources
Contrast how Plutarch and Suetonius each wrote about Caesar's death.

"So the affair began, and those who were not privy to the plot were filled with consternation [dismay] and horror at what was going on; they dared not fly, nor go to Caesar's help, nay, nor even utter a word."

—Plutarch
from *Life of Caesar*

"He abused his power and was justly slain. For not only did he accept excessive honors, such as an uninterrupted consulship, the dictatorship for life, and the censorship of public morals . . . but he also allowed honors to be bestowed on him which were too great for mortal man."

—Suetonius
from *The Lives of the Caesars, The Deified Julius*

Reading Check
Analyze Events
What were the events
that led to Caesar's
gaining power in
Rome?

Rather than becoming heroes, Caesar's murderers were forced to flee for their lives. Rome was shocked by Caesar's murder, and many people were furious about it. He had been loved by many common people, and many of these people rioted after his death. From the chaos that followed Caesar's assassination, the Senate had to act quickly to restore order.

Augustus the Emperor

Two leaders emerged to take control of Roman politics. One was Caesar's former assistant, **Marc Antony**. The other was Caesar's adopted son Octavian (ahk-TAY-veeuhn), later called **Augustus** (aw-GUHS-tuhs).

Antony and Octavian Antony and Octavian worked to punish the people who had killed Caesar. At Caesar's funeral, Antony delivered a famous speech that turned even more Romans against the killers. Shortly afterward, he and Octavian set out with an army to try to avenge Caesar's death.

Their army caught up to the killers near Philippi (FI-luh-py) in northern Greece. In 42 BC, Antony and Octavian soundly defeated their opponents. After the battle, the leaders of the plot to kill Caesar, including Brutus, killed themselves.

Octavian Becomes Emperor After the Battle of Philippi, Octavian returned to Italy while Antony went east to fight Rome's enemies. In Turkey, Antony met Cleopatra VII, the queen of Egypt, and the two fell in love. Antony divorced his wife, Octavian's sister, to be with Cleopatra. Octavian saw this divorce as an insult to his sister and to himself.

Antony's behavior led to civil war in Rome. In 31 BC, Octavian sent a fleet to attack Antony. Antony sailed out to meet it, and the two forces met just west of Greece in the Battle of Actium (AK-shee-uhm). Antony's fleet was defeated, but he escaped back to Egypt with Cleopatra. There the two committed suicide, so they wouldn't be taken prisoner by Octavian.

With Antony's death, Octavian became Rome's sole ruler. Over the next few years, he gained power. In 27 BC, Octavian announced that he was giving up all his power to the Senate, but, in reality, he kept much power. He took the title *princeps* (PRIN-seps), or first citizen. The Senate gave him a new name—*Augustus,* which means "revered one." Modern historians

---

BIOGRAPHY

Cleopatra VII 69–30 BC

Cleopatra was a devoted ally of Julius Caesar and Marc Antony, but she didn't like Octavian. After the Battle of Actium, she feared that Octavian would arrest her and take over Egypt. Rather than see Octavian running her kingdom, Cleopatra chose to commit suicide. According to tradition, she poisoned herself with the venom of a deadly snake.

Draw Conclusions
Why do you think Cleopatra feared that Octavian would take over Egypt?

Reading Check

Summarize How did the Roman Republic become an empire?

consider the naming of Augustus the end of the Roman Republic and the beginning of the Roman Empire.

Augustus made many improvements in the city of Rome. He created a fire department and a police force to protect people. He built new aqueducts and repaired old ones to increase Rome's water supply. Augustus also worked on improving and expanding Rome's road network.

Summary and Preview Julius Caesar, and later Augustus, gained power in times of crisis and made the Roman Republic into an empire. In the next lesson you'll learn what he and his successors did as the heads of that empire.

Lesson 3 Assessment

Review Ideas, Terms, and People

1. **a. Identify** Who was Spartacus?

   b. Explain How did the deaths of the Gracchus brothers change Roman politics?

2. **a. Recall** Whom did Cicero want Romans to give power to?

   b. Explain Why did some Romans call for change in their government?

3. **a. Identify** Who killed Julius Ceasar?

   b. Explain Why did many senators consider Caesar a threat?

   c. Elaborate Why do you think Caesar wanted the title of dictator for life?

4. **a. Identify** Who took over Rome after Caesar's death?

   b. Summarize How did Octavian take power from Marc Antony?

Critical Thinking

5. **Sequence** Draw a timeline like the one shown here. Use it to identify key events in Rome's change from a republic to an empire.

A Vast Empire

The Big Idea

After Augustus became emperor, the Roman Empire grew politically and economically, and life improved for the Roman people.

Main Ideas

- The Roman Empire expanded to control the entire Mediterranean world.

- Trade increased in Rome, both within the empire and with other people.

- The Pax Romana was a period of peace and prosperity in the cities and the country.

- The Romans were very religious and worshipped many gods.

Key Terms and People

Hadrian
provinces
currency
Pax Romana

If YOU were there . . .

You live in the Roman town of Londinium, in the Roman province of Britannia. Your people were conquered by the Roman army many years ago. Roman soldiers have mixed with your people, and many have settled down here. Many Britons in Londinium have adopted Roman customs. You live in a Roman-style house and eat from pottery made in Italy. Your cousins in the country live very differently, however. They still think of the Romans as invaders.

How do you like being part of the Roman Empire?

The Empire Expands

When Rome became an empire, it already controlled most of the Mediterranean world. Within about 150 years, though, the empire had grown even bigger. Augustus and the emperors who followed him pushed the boundaries of their empire, taking over huge chunks of Europe, Africa, and Asia. At its height Rome ruled one of the largest empires in all of world history.

Emperors After Augustus Augustus was the first of the five emperors who belonged to the Julio-Claudian family. None of his followers lived up to his success. Augustus named his stepson, Tiberius, to be emperor after him. Tiberius was a less skillful ruler, and his harsh policies were unpopular with the Roman people. The next emperor, Caligula, was even worse. Members of his personal guard assassinated Caligula in AD 41 after a few short years of rule. The guard declared Caligula's uncle Claudius the new emperor. After Claudius died, his adopted son Nero became emperor.

The last Julio-Claudian, Nero, seemed like a good ruler when he first came to power in AD 54. He undid some of the harsh policies of past emperors. He ended secret trials, gave more independence to the Senate, and allowed slaves to sue their masters for poor treatment.

However, Nero changed over time. He later ordered soldiers to kill his mother and his wife. When he realized he would not be punished for his behavior, he began to act very strangely. He played music in public and performed on stage, which the Roman people believed was shameful behavior for an emperor.

The people of Rome grew more uncomfortable with Nero's leadership and extravagant spending. He made many enemies and was eventually overthrown. Nero did not leave behind a successor and with no leader to rule the empire, a series of civil wars followed. However, he did have some military successes under his rule.

The Roman Military Like the Gupta Empire in ancient India, the Roman Empire expanded through military might. Rome's military was successful in part because it was well organized. They adopted a structure with different ranks that is similar to modern armies. Forces were led by high-ranking officers, who oversaw *triarii, principes,* and *hastati.* These ranks were similar to modern-day lieutenants, sergeants, and privates.

The military's tactics were also highly organized. In battle, soldiers would form several lines in an open field. The first line would rush toward the center to attack the enemy. They would fight for a period of time and then the second line would advance. The survivors from the first line would then reorganize in a line behind them, and the process would continue until the battle ended.

Reasons for Expansion Why did emperors add so much land to the empire? They had many reasons. One of these reasons was to control hostile neighbors. Some countries that shared borders with Rome were threatening Rome. To keep these countries from attacking the empire or its citizens, the Romans conquered them.

Not all of the territories the Romans conquered were political threats. Some were conquered for economic reasons. The people who lived in conquered lands were required to pay taxes. The money was used to pay for the military and for public works projects such as roads.

Many of these territories had vast supplies of gold, good farmlands, or other resources the Romans wanted. Other areas were conquered for another reason: some emperors liked a good fight.

Expanded Citizenship As the Roman Empire's territory expanded, some people in the newly conquered lands became citizens. Rome's rulers gave citizenship to the upper-class members of these places to make them loyal to the empire. Over time, citizenship was granted to all free men and women of the empire.

Citizenship had changed since the days of the Roman Republic. For example, in the Roman Empire, voting was no longer allowed and military service was not required. However, citizens were still required to pay taxes. Even though citizenship offered fewer benefits than it had during the Roman Republic, it was still considered an honor.

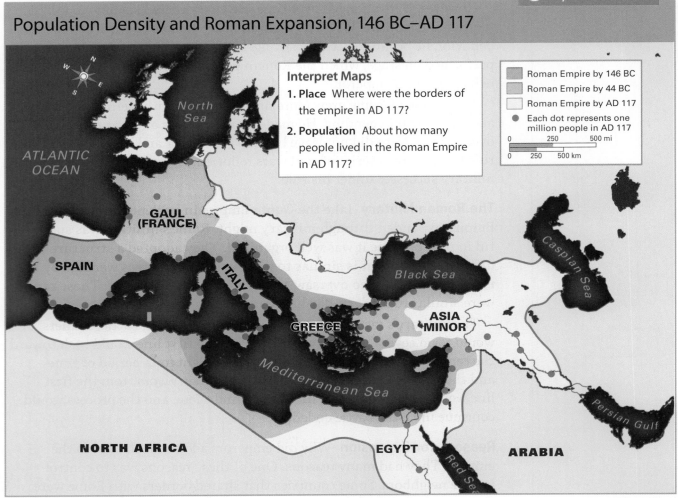

Population Density and Roman Expansion, 146 BC–AD 117

Explore ONLINE!

Interpret Maps

1. **Place** Where were the borders of the empire in AD 117?

2. **Population** About how many people lived in the Roman Empire in AD 117?

Roman Empire by 146 BC
Roman Empire by 44 BC
Roman Empire by AD 117
Each dot represents one million people in AD 117

0   250   500 mi
0   250   500 km

North Sea

ATLANTIC OCEAN

GAUL (FRANCE)

SPAIN

ITALY

Black Sea

Caspian Sea

GREECE

ASIA MINOR

Mediterranean Sea

Persian Gulf

NORTH AFRICA

EGYPT

Red Sea

ARABIA

Directions of Expansion As the map shows, the Roman Empire grew after Augustus died. By the early 100s, the Romans had taken over Gaul and much of central Europe. Its boundary in Europe was formed by the Danube River and the Rhine River.

By the time of the emperor **Hadrian**, the Romans had also conquered most of the island of Britain. The people of Britain, the Celts (KELTZ), had fought fiercely against the Roman army. Fearing attacks by barbarian invaders in the north, Hadrian built a huge wall across northern Britain. Hadrian's Wall marked the border between Roman and non-Roman territory.

In the east, the empire stretched all the way into Mesopotamia. Other Asian territories the Romans ruled included Asia Minor and the eastern coast of the Mediterranean. All of the North African coast belonged to Rome as well, so the Romans controlled everything that bordered the Mediterranean. In fact, Roman control of the Mediterranean was so great that they called it *Mare Nostrum*, or "Our Sea."

In order to effectively control such a vast amount of territory, the empire decentralized its government. It would have been nearly impossible to govern distant lands from Rome, so the Roman leaders transferred power to more local leaders. Regional governors, who had a strong understanding of what imperial leaders wanted, were put in charge.

Reading Check
Draw Conclusions
Why did Roman emperors want to expand the empire?

Trade Increases

As the empire grew, the Romans met many different peoples. In many cases, these peoples had goods that the Romans wanted. Thinking that there would be a market for these products in Rome, merchants began to travel all over the empire, as you can see on the map.

People in the city of Rome needed raw materials that they couldn't produce themselves. Many of the materials could be found, though, in Rome's **provinces**, the areas outside of Italy that the Romans controlled. Traders brought cloth, metals, and food from the provinces to the city. They also brought more exotic goods, such as spices from Asia and animals from Africa. In return, the Romans sent goods made by artisans to the provinces. These goods included jewelry, glass, and clothing.

Some Roman traders also traveled beyond the empire's borders. The Mediterranean Sea provided an easy way to reach the Middle East, Africa, and other areas in Europe. The Roman navy protected trading ships from pirate attacks. The unity of the Roman Empire led to a period of peace that allowed trade to grow around the Mediterranean and elsewhere.

Roman traders sailed as far as eastern Africa, India, and what is now Vietnam to find goods they couldn't get in the empire. Traders also used the roads that the Roman government had spent money to build. They traveled overland into Asia to meet merchants bringing goods from China on the Silk Road. Silk was especially popular in Rome. Wealthy Romans were willing to pay high prices for it.

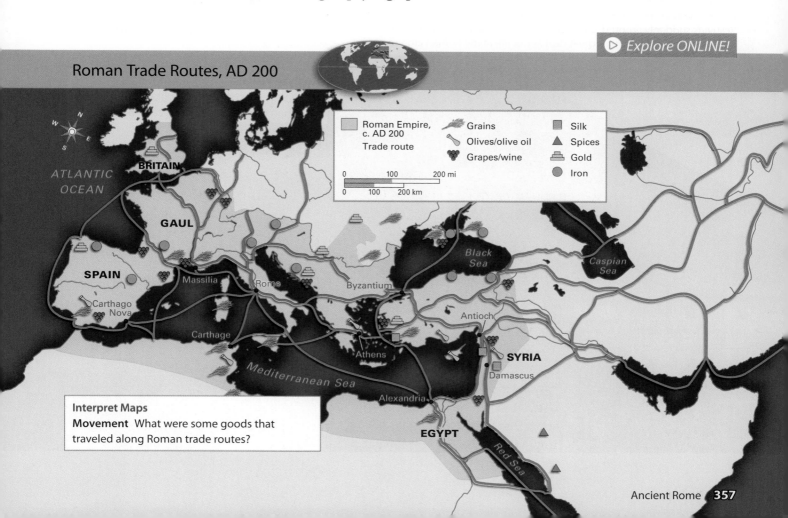

Explore ONLINE!

Roman Trade Routes, AD 200

Roman Empire, c. AD 200
Trade route
Grains
Olives/olive oil
Grapes/wine
Silk
Spices
Gold
Iron

ATLANTIC OCEAN

BRITAIN

GAUL

SPAIN

Massilia

Carthago Nova

Rome

Carthage

Byzantium

Black Sea

Caspian Sea

Athens

Antioch

SYRIA

Damascus

Mediterranean Sea

Alexandria

EGYPT

Red Sea

Interpret Maps

Movement What were some goods that traveled along Roman trade routes?

Reading Check
Form Generalizations
How did currency help
Roman trade grow?

To pay for their trade goods, Romans used **currency**, or money. They traded coins made of gold and silver for the items they wanted. These coins allowed the Romans to trade with people even if they had no items their trade partners wanted. Because the empire had established a uniform currency, everybody used the same money, which helped trade grow even more.

The Pax Romana

The first 200 years of the Roman Empire were a time of general peace and prosperity. Several characteristics, such as a stable government and an organized military, helped the empire thrive and maintain peace during these years. There were no major wars or rebellions in the empire. We call this peaceful period the **Pax Romana**, or Roman Peace. It lasted until about AD 180.

**Academic
Vocabulary**
effect the result of
an action or decision

During the Pax Romana the empire's population grew. Trade continued to increase, and many Romans became wealthy through this trade. One **effect** of these changes was an improvement in the quality of life for people living in Rome and in its provinces.

Life in Cities During the Pax Romana many Romans lived in cities scattered throughout the empire. Some of these cities, like Alexandria in Egypt, were major centers

This famous painting shows a young couple who lived in Pompeii.

Pompeii: A City Preserved
Pompeii was located at the foot of a volcano called Mount Vesuvius. In AD 79, Vesuvius suddenly erupted, and ash buried Pompeii. The well-preserved remains of Pompeii have taught us a great deal about life in the Roman Empire.

Analyze Visuals
From the ruins, does it look like Pompeii was an urban or rural area? How can you tell?

Chariot racing was the most popular sport in ancient Rome. Slaves, soldiers, senators, and emperors all loved to go to the track and watch thrilling competitions. Devoted fans cheered for their favorite teams and drivers.

of trade and had huge populations. Other cities, like Pompeii (pom-PAY) in Italy, had much smaller populations.

By far the largest city in the empire was, of course, Rome. Some historians think that Rome may have had more than a million residents at its height. Although many were wealthy, many were not, and that large population led to difficulties for the city's poorer residents. Many poor Romans lived in crowded, sometimes dangerous, apartment buildings.

Despite their poor living conditions, the people of Rome enjoyed various types of entertainment. They could go to comic plays, thrilling chariot races, or fierce gladiator fights. Those who wanted more peace and quiet could head for one of Rome's public baths. The huge bath complexes in Rome were more like spas or health clubs than bathtubs. At the bath, people could swim, soak in a hot pool, or mingle with other Romans.

Romans looking for fun could also just tour the city. Rome was filled with beautiful temples and monuments built by city leaders. The Romans were proud of their city and took great pride in how it looked.

"In great buildings as well as in other things the rest of the world has been outdone by us Romans. If, indeed, all the buildings in our City are considered . . . together in one vast mass, the united grandeur of them would lead one to imagine that we were describing another world, accumulated in a single spot."

–Pliny the Elder, from *Natural History*

Roman cities in the provinces became more like Rome after they were conquered. Their new rulers introduced Roman architecture, art, and fashion. The Romans also brought technological change, building roads and aqueducts.

Life in the Country When we think of life in the Roman Empire, we often think of a city. In truth, though, more people lived in the country than in the empire's cities. People outside the cities had a very different way of life than city dwellers did.

In rural areas, most people farmed. On their small farms, they grew just enough food for themselves and their families. People on larger farms used improved technology to increase output. They cut flat surfaces into the sides of hills to create more farmable land. This practice was called terracing. Farmers in dry regions began using irrigation, aided by aqueducts.

Many of these farmers spoke languages other than Latin. In fact, many people in the country didn't seem Roman at all. These people had kept many of their own customs and traditions when they were conquered by the Romans.

Scattered among the groups of farmers, though, were large farms and villas, or country homes, belonging to rich Romans. Many people from the cities liked to have a house outside the city. They visited these homes when they wanted a break from the city crowds.

At their villas, these wealthy Romans lived much like they did at home. They hosted huge, elaborate dinner parties where they served exotic foods. Some of the foods served at these parties sound very unusual to modern people. For example, Romans cooked and served peacocks, ostriches, jellyfish, and even mice!

These meals were often served by slaves who worked in the villas. Other slaves worked in the villa owners' fields. The sale of crops grown in these fields helped pay for the villa owners' extravagant expenses.

Reading Check
Contrast How was life different in the country than in the city?

Romans Allow Many Religions

The Romans were a very religious people. Many Roman myths were about the founding and rulers of Rome. These often connected the rulers of the past to a divine source such as a god or goddess. To celebrate their religious beliefs, the Romans held many festivals in honor of their gods. Because of the empire's huge size and diverse population, the nature of these festivals varied widely from place to place.

As you have read, the Romans were a very practical people. This practicality also extended into their religious lives. For example, the Romans worshipped *lares*, or household dieties. The Romans believed that they were the spirits of the dead who would protect houses, crossroads, and cities. They also worshipped the *penates* who were responsible for the wealth and prosperity of the Roman household. Most families had shrines in their homes dedicated to the lares and penates.

Another example of Roman practicality was in the number of gods they worshipped. The Romans didn't think that they could be sure which gods did or did not exist. To avoid offending any gods who did exist, the Romans prayed to a wide range of gods and goddesses. Many of the most popular gods in the Roman Empire were adopted from people the Romans had conquered. For example, many Romans worshipped the Olympian gods of Greece. When the Romans conquered Greece, they learned about Greek mythology. Before long, the Greek gods became the main gods of Rome as well, but with different names. Romans worshipped the Greek goddess Hera, for example, as the goddess Juno. In the same way, Roman mythology was also inspired by the gods from the Egyptians, Gauls, or Persians. The Romans had many gods, including ones whose names you might recognize: Jupiter, Mercury, Venus, Mars, Neptune, Saturn, Uranus, and Pluto.

Jupiter was the main Roman god and the god of the sky. Mars, the god of war, was the second-most important deity in Rome. The gods were very important in Roman society, and many had temples built in their honor. Roman mythology continues to influence our culture, even today. For example, our planets are named after Roman gods, and the month of June is named after Juno.

This statue of Neptune, god of the sea, is part of Rome's famous Trevi Fountain.

Reading Check
Find Main Ideas
Why did the Romans worship such a wide range of gods?

Summary and Preview The Roman Empire grew and changed during its first 200 years. In the next lesson, you will learn about the great advances made in art, engineering, and other fields.

Lesson 4 Assessment

Review Ideas, Terms, and People

1. a. Identify Which areas of the world did the Romans take over?

b. Explain Why did Hadrian build a wall in northern Britain?

c. Explain Why did a series of civil wars follow the overthrow of Nero?

2. a. Define What were provinces?

b. Summarize Why did trade increase as the Roman Empire expanded?

c. Evaluate What might have happened if there hadn't been a uniform currency?

3. a. Explain Why is the period before AD 180 called the Pax Romana?

b. Evaluate Would you prefer to have lived in a Roman city or the country? Why?

4. a. Summarize What were some of the origins of Roman gods and goddesses?

b. Identify What were some of the major Roman gods?

Critical Thinking

5. Contrast Draw two houses like these. In the house on the left, write two facts about life in a Roman city. In the house on the right, write two facts about life in the country.

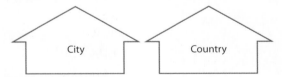

City   Country

History and Geography

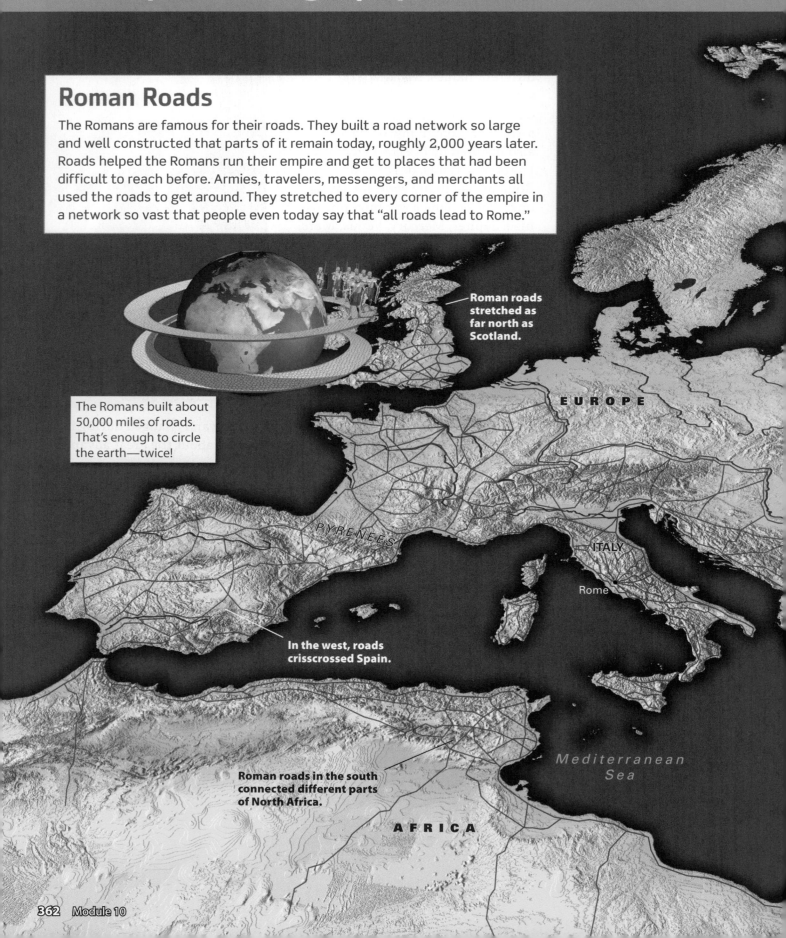

Roman Roads

The Romans are famous for their roads. They built a road network so large and well constructed that parts of it remain today, roughly 2,000 years later. Roads helped the Romans run their empire and get to places that had been difficult to reach before. Armies, travelers, messengers, and merchants all used the roads to get around. They stretched to every corner of the empire in a network so vast that people even today say that "all roads lead to Rome."

Roman roads stretched as far north as Scotland.

The Romans built about 50,000 miles of roads. That's enough to circle the earth—twice!

EUROPE

PYRENEES

ITALY

Rome

In the west, roads crisscrossed Spain.

Roman roads in the south connected different parts of North Africa.

Mediterranean Sea

AFRICA

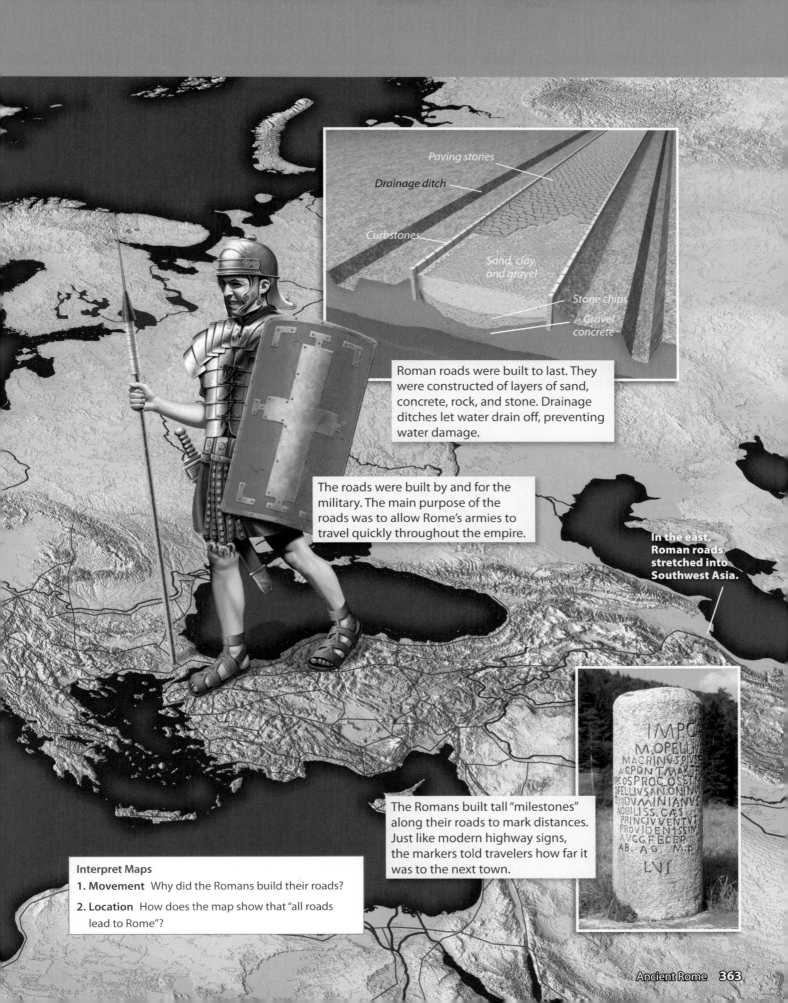

Paving stones

Drainage ditch

Curbstones

Sand, clay, and gravel

Stone chips

Gravel concrete

Roman roads were built to last. They were constructed of layers of sand, concrete, rock, and stone. Drainage ditches let water drain off, preventing water damage.

The roads were built by and for the military. The main purpose of the roads was to allow Rome's armies to travel quickly throughout the empire.

In the east, Roman roads stretched into Southwest Asia.

The Romans built tall "milestones" along their roads to mark distances. Just like modern highway signs, the markers told travelers how far it was to the next town.

Interpret Maps

1. **Movement** Why did the Romans build their roads?

2. **Location** How does the map show that "all roads lead to Rome"?

The Fall of Rome

The Big Idea

Problems from both inside and outside caused the Roman Empire to split and the western half to collapse.

Main Ideas

- Many problems threatened the Roman Empire, leading one emperor to divide it in half.

- Barbarians invaded Rome in the 300s and 400s.

- Many factors contributed to Rome's fall.

Key Terms and People

Diocletian
Clovis
Attila
corruption

If YOU were there . . .

You are a former Roman soldier who has settled on lands in Gaul. In the last few months, groups of barbarians have been raiding local towns and burning farms. The commander of the local army garrison is an old friend, but he says he is short of loyal soldiers. Many troops have been called back to Rome. You don't know when the next raid will come.

How will you defend your lands?

Problems Threaten the Empire

At its height the Roman Empire included all the land around the Mediterranean Sea. The empire in the early AD 100s stretched from Britain south to Egypt, and from the Atlantic Ocean all the way to the Persian Gulf.

But the empire did not stay that large for long. By the end of the 100s, emperors had given up some of the land the Roman army had conquered. These emperors feared that the empire had become too large to defend or govern efficiently. As later rulers discovered, these emperors were right.

Problems in the Empire Even as emperors were giving up territory, new threats to the empire were appearing. Tribes of Germanic warriors, whom the Romans called barbarians, attacked Rome's northern borders. At the same time, Persian armies invaded in the east. The Romans defended themselves for 200 years, but only at great cost.

The Romans struggled with problems within the empire as well. As frontier areas were abandoned because they were too dangerous, Germanic tribes moved in. A large army meant that there weren't enough farmers. To help produce more food, the Romans invited Germanic farmers to grow crops on Roman lands. These farmers often came from the same tribes that threatened Rome's borders. Over time, whole German communities had moved into the empire.

Timeline: Key Events in Roman History

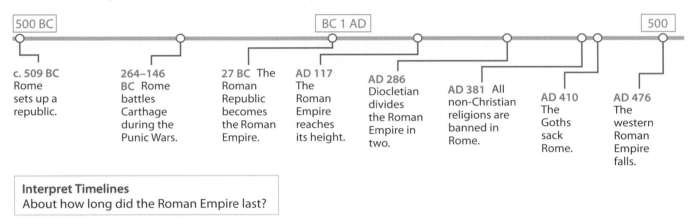

500 BC

c. 509 BC Rome sets up a republic.

264–146 BC Rome battles Carthage during the Punic Wars.

BC 1 AD

27 BC The Roman Republic becomes the Roman Empire.

AD 117 The Roman Empire reaches its height.

AD 286 Diocletian divides the Roman Empire in two.

AD 381 All non-Christian religions are banned in Rome.

AD 410 The Goths sack Rome.

500

AD 476 The western Roman Empire falls.

Interpret Timelines
About how long did the Roman Empire last?

They chose their own leaders and largely ignored the emperors, which caused problems for the Romans.

Other internal problems also threatened Rome's survival. Disease swept through the empire, killing many people. The government increased taxes to pay for the defense of the empire. Desperate, the Romans looked for a strong emperor to solve their problems.

Division of the Empire The emperor the Romans were looking for was **Diocletian** (dy-uh-KLEE-shuhn), who took power in the late 200s. Convinced that the empire was too big for one person to rule, Diocletian divided the empire. He ruled the eastern half of the empire and named a co-emperor to rule the west.

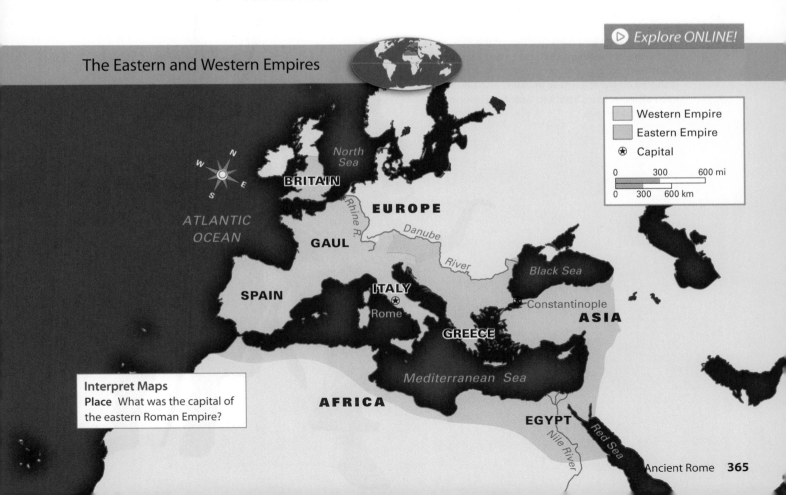

▶ *Explore ONLINE!*

The Eastern and Western Empires

Western Empire
Eastern Empire
⊛ Capital

0   300   600 mi
0 300 600 km

North Sea
BRITAIN
ATLANTIC OCEAN
EUROPE
Rhine R.
GAUL
Danube River
Black Sea
SPAIN
ITALY
Rome
Constantinople
ASIA
GREECE
Mediterranean Sea
AFRICA
EGYPT
Nile River
Red Sea

Interpret Maps
Place What was the capital of the eastern Roman Empire?

Not long after Diocletian left power, Emperor Constantine (KAHN-stuhn-teen) reunited the two halves of the Roman Empire for a short time. Constantine went on to become one of the empire's most influential leaders. In his book *Ecclesiastical History*, Eusebius of Caesaria described Constantine: "He was the kindest and mildest of emperors, and the only one of those in our day that passed all the time of his government in a manner worthy of his office."

Constantine moved the empire's capital to the east into what is now Turkey. He built a grand new capital city there. It was called Constantinople (KAHN-stant-uhn-oh-puhl), which means "the city of Constantine."

Constantinople was located on the Black Sea and was close to the Mediterranean Sea. As the doorway between Europe and Asia, it held great strategic importance, both economically and militarily. Many trade routes passed through the city, and it was difficult to attack because it was accessible by land from only one direction. Although the empire was still called the Roman Empire, Rome was no longer the real seat of power. Power had moved to the east.

Reading Check
Analyze Causes
Why did Diocletian divide the Roman Empire in two?

Barbarians Invade Rome

Not long after Constantine moved Rome's capital, German barbarians—people the Romans considered uncivilized—from the north began to raid the Roman Empire. As you have already read, barbarian tribes had settled along the empire's northern border in the 200s. For more than 100 years these tribes mostly stayed out of Roman territory. Late in the 300s, though, the barbarians began raiding deep into the heart of the empire.

The Goths and Huns were just two of the groups that invaded the Roman Empire. In this illustration, a Goth warrior is shown on the right, and a Hun is shown on the left. These invaders also battled each other, as Huns attacked Goths and fought for territory and riches.

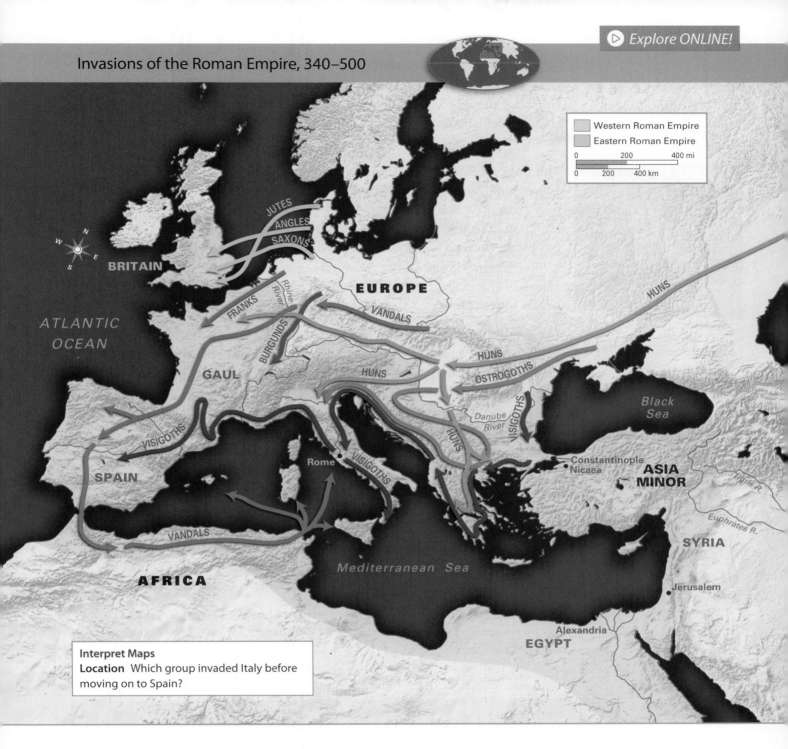

Invasions of the Roman Empire, 340–500

Explore ONLINE!

Western Roman Empire
Eastern Roman Empire

0   200   400 mi
0 200 400 km

JUTES
ANGLES
SAXONS
BRITAIN
ATLANTIC OCEAN
FRANKS
Rhine River
EUROPE
VANDALS
HUNS
BURGUNDS
GAUL
HUNS
OSTROGOTHS
VISIGOTHS
Danube River
Black Sea
VISIGOTHS
SPAIN
VANDALS
Rome
VISIGOTHS
HUNS
Constantinople
Nicaea
ASIA MINOR
Tigris R.
Euphrates R.
SYRIA
Mediterranean Sea
AFRICA
Jerusalem
Alexandria
EGYPT

Interpret Maps
Location Which group invaded Italy before moving on to Spain?

Early Invasions The source of these raids was a new group of people who moved into Europe. Called the Huns, they were fierce warriors from Central Asia.

As you can see on the map, the Huns invaded southeastern Europe. From there they launched raids on nearby kingdoms. Among the victims of these raids were several groups of people called the Goths.

The Goths could not defeat the Huns in battle. As the Huns continued to raid their territories, the Goths fled. Trapped between the Huns and Rome, they had nowhere to go but into Roman territory.

Rome's leaders were afraid that the Goths would destroy Roman land and property. To stop this destruction, the emperors fought to keep the Goths out of Roman lands. In the east, the armies were largely successful. They forced the Goths to move farther west. As a result, however, the western armies were defeated by the Goths, who moved into Roman territory.

The Sack of Rome The Romans fought desperately to keep the Goths away from Rome. They also paid the Goths not to attack them. For many years this strategy worked. In 408, however, the Romans stopped making payments. This made the Goths furious. Despite the Romans' best efforts to defend their city, the Goths sacked, or destroyed, Rome in 410.

The destruction of Rome absolutely devastated the Romans. No one had attacked their city in nearly 800 years. For the first time, many Romans began to feel afraid for the safety of their empire.

The Empire in Chaos Unfortunately for Rome, the city's fall to the Goths in 410 wasn't the end of the invasions. The Gothic victory served as an example for other barbarian groups to invade the western half of the empire.

In the early 400s, the Vandals invaded Spain. Then they crossed into northern Africa and destroyed Roman settlements there. As they passed through Roman areas, the Vandals destroyed nearly everything in their path. At about the same time, the Angles, Saxons, and Jutes invaded Britain, and the Franks invaded Gaul.

By the 480s, a Frankish king named **Clovis** had built a huge kingdom in Gaul. Clovis, a Christian, was one of the most powerful of all the German kings.

Meanwhile, the Huns, under a new leader named **Attila** (AT-uhl-uh), raided Roman territory in the east. Attila was a brilliant leader and a very scary enemy. Here is one account that describes him as terrifying.

"He was a man born into the world to shake the nations, the scourge of all lands, who in some way terrified all mankind by the dreadful rumors noised abroad concerning him."

—Jordanes, from *History of the Goths*

In 410, the Goths sacked Rome and destroyed the city. This was the beginning of the end for the Roman Empire.

The Fall of Empires		
Roman Empire	**Gupta Empire**	**Han Dynasty**
Weakened by corruption	Weakened by corruption	Weakened by corruption
Difficulty communicating over vast distances	Unable to enforce law and order over such a large area	Could not raise enough taxes to fund such a large empire and army
Political unrest	Unskilled political leaders	Internal political conflict
Fell to invaders	Fell to invaders	Fell to invaders

Attila led the Huns in raids against Constantinople, Greece, Gaul, and parts of northern Italy. But because he was told that diseases ran wild in southern Italy, he decided not to go south to Rome.

The End of the Western Empire Rome needed strong leaders to survive these constant attacks, but the emperors of the 400s were weak. As attacks on Rome's borders increased, military leaders took power away from the emperors. By the 450s military leaders ruled Rome.

Unfortunately for Rome, most of these military leaders were too busy fighting among themselves to protect the empire. Barbarian leaders took advantage of this situation and invaded Rome. In 476, a barbarian general overthrew the last emperor in Rome and named himself king of Italy. Many historians consider this event the end of the western Roman Empire.

Reading Check
Analyze Events Why did Rome fall to barbarians in the 400s?

Academic Vocabulary
cause the reason something happens

Factors in Rome's Fall

Barbarian invasions are often considered the **cause** of Rome's decline. In truth, they were only one of several causes.

One cause of Rome's decline was the vast size of the empire. In some ways, Rome had simply grown too big to govern. Communication among various parts of the empire was difficult, even in peaceful times. During times of conflict, it became even more difficult.

Political crises also contributed to the decline. By the 400s, **corruption**, the decay of people's values, had become widespread in Rome's government. Corrupt officials used threats and bribery to achieve their goals, often ignoring the needs of Roman citizens. Because of officials like these, Rome's government was no longer as efficient as it had been in the past.

In the face of this corruption, many wealthy citizens fled the city of Rome to their country estates. This action created a series of causes and effects that further weakened the empire.

Outside Rome, many landowners used slaves or serfs to work on their lands. To protect their estates and their wealth, many landowners created their own armies. Ambitious landowners used these personal armies to overthrow emperors and take power for themselves.

Quick Facts

Why Rome Fell

Problems Inside the Empire

- Large size made communication difficult.
- Corruption became common.
- Rich citizens left Rome for country estates.
- Taxes and prices rose.

Problems Outside the Empire

- Barbarians began invading the empire.

Reading Check
Find Main Ideas
How did corruption
change Roman society
in the 400s?

As wealthy citizens abandoned Rome and other cities, city life became more difficult for those who remained. Rome's population decreased, and schools closed. At the same time taxes and prices soared, leaving more and more Romans poor. By the end of the 400s, Rome was no longer the city it had once been. As it changed, the empire slowly collapsed around it.

Summary and Preview By the early 500s, Rome no longer ruled western Europe. Factors inside and outside the Roman Empire led to its decline. In the next lesson, you will learn about the accomplishments of Romans and the lasting impact of these achievements.

Lesson 5 Assessment

1. a. **Recall** Where did Constantine move Rome's capital?

   b. **Explain** Why did Diocletian divide the empire in two?

2. a. **Identify** Who was Attila?

   b. **Summarize** Why did the Goths move into the Roman Empire in the 300s?

   c. **Elaborate** Why do you think the sack of Rome was so devastating?

3. a. **Describe** What kinds of problems did Rome's size cause for its emperors?

   b. **Form Generalizations** How did corruption weaken Rome in the 400s?

Critical Thinking

4. **Draw Conclusions** Draw a word web like the one shown here. In each of the outer circles, list a factor that helped lead to the fall of the western Roman Empire. You may add more circles if needed.

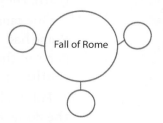

Fall of Rome

Rome's Legacy

The Big Idea

Many features of Roman culture were copied by later civilizations and continue to influence our lives today.

Main Ideas

- The Romans looked for ways to use science and engineering to improve their lives.

- Roman architecture and art were largely based on Greek ideas.

- Roman literature and language have influenced how people write and speak.

- Roman law serves as a model for modern law codes around the world.

- The Romans made important contributions to the fields of philosophy and history.

Key Terms and People

Galen
aqueducts
Virgil
Ovid
satire
Romance languages
civil law

If YOU were there . . .

You live on a farm in Gaul but are visiting your older brother in town. You are amazed by the city's beautiful temples and towers. Another surprise is the water! At home you must draw up water from a well. But here, water bubbles out of fountains all over the city. It even runs through pipes in the public baths. One day your brother introduces you to the engineer who maintains the water system.

What questions will you ask the engineer?

Roman Science and Engineering

The Romans took a practical approach to their study of science and engineering. Unlike the Greeks, who studied the world just to know about it, the Romans were more concerned with finding knowledge that they could use to improve their lives.

Science Roman scientists wanted to produce results that could benefit their society. For example, they studied the stars not just to know about them but to produce a calendar. They studied plants and animals to learn how to produce better crops and meat.

The practical Roman approach to science can also be seen in medicine. Most of the greatest doctors in the Roman Empire were Greek. One doctor in the empire was **Galen**, who lived in the AD 100s. He was a Greek surgeon who made many discoveries about the body. For example, Galen described the valves of the heart and noted differences between arteries and veins. For centuries, doctors based their ideas on Galen's teachings and writings.

Engineering The Romans' practical use of science can also be seen in their engineering. The Romans were great builders. Even today people walk along Roman roads and drive over Roman bridges built almost 2,000 years ago. How have these structures survived for so long?

The Romans developed some new building materials to help their structures last. The most important of these materials was cement. They made cement by mixing a mineral called lime with volcanic rock and ash. The resulting material dried to be very hard and watertight.

More important than the materials they used, though, were the designs the Romans had for their structures. For example, they built their roads in layers. This layered construction made the road durable. Many Roman roads have not worn down even after centuries have passed.

Another way the Romans created structures to last was by using arches. Because of its rounded shape, an arch can support much heavier weights than other shapes can. This strength has allowed arched structures such as Roman bridges to last until the present. Engineers used the same technology to invent the arch dam. Because the arch strengthens the structure, arch dams require less material than any other type of dam.

The Romans also used arches in their **aqueducts** (A-kwuh-duhkts). An aqueduct was a channel used to carry water from mountains into cities. When they crossed deep valleys, aqueducts were supported by rows of arches. The Romans' aqueducts were so well built that many still stand. Engineering helped the Romans modify their environment in ways that had not been possible before.

Roman builders also learned how to combine arches to create vaults. A vault is a set of arches that supports the roof of a building. The Romans used vaults to create huge, open areas within buildings. As a result, Roman buildings were much larger than anything that had come before.

Living conditions improved as a result of Roman inventiveness. For example, the Romans developed central heating. They designed buildings with open spaces below floors and between walls through which hot air could travel. Sanitation also improved. They invented a flush toilet and built sewer systems, making Roman cities cleaner places to live.

Reading Check
Summarize
What were two ways the Romans built strong structures?

The Roman Arch

The Romans were the first people to make wide use of the arch. A Roman aqueduct might be supported by hundreds of arches. The drawing shows how Roman engineers built their tall and strong arches. The final piece was the keystone, placed at the top to lock all the stones into place.

Analyze Visuals
How did the Romans support arches during their construction?

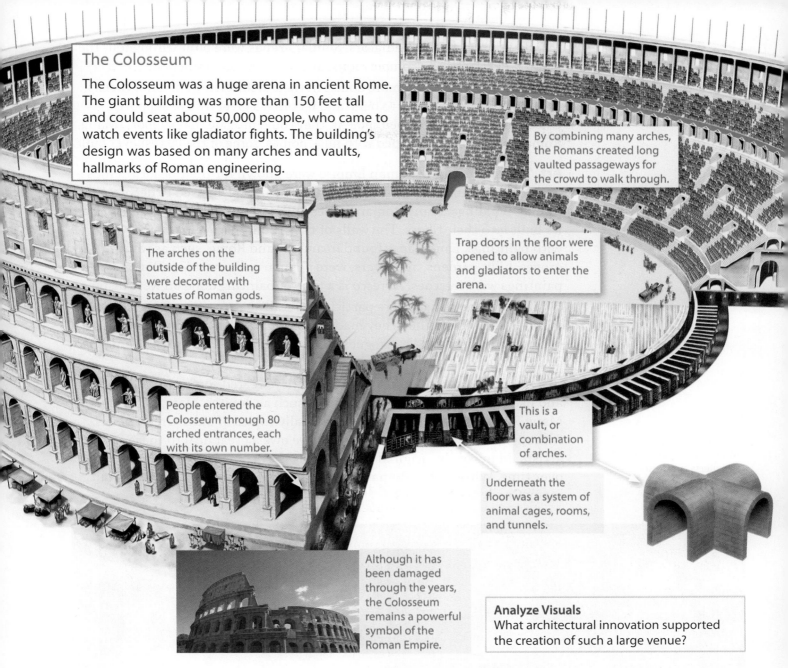

The Colosseum

The Colosseum was a huge arena in ancient Rome. The giant building was more than 150 feet tall and could seat about 50,000 people, who came to watch events like gladiator fights. The building's design was based on many arches and vaults, hallmarks of Roman engineering.

By combining many arches, the Romans created long vaulted passageways for the crowd to walk through.

The arches on the outside of the building were decorated with statues of Roman gods.

Trap doors in the floor were opened to allow animals and gladiators to enter the arena.

People entered the Colosseum through 80 arched entrances, each with its own number.

This is a vault, or combination of arches.

Underneath the floor was a system of animal cages, rooms, and tunnels.

Although it has been damaged through the years, the Colosseum remains a powerful symbol of the Roman Empire.

Analyze Visuals
What architectural innovation supported the creation of such a large venue?

Architecture and Art

The Romans weren't interested only in practicality, though. They also admired beauty. Roman appreciation for beauty can be seen in their architecture and art. People still admire their magnificent buildings, statues, and paintings.

Architecture Roman architecture was based largely on older Greek designs. Like the ancient Greeks, the Romans used columns to make their public buildings look stately and impressive. Also like the Greeks, the Romans covered many of their buildings with marble to make them more majestic.

But Roman engineering techniques allowed them to take architecture beyond what the Greeks had done. For example, the Roman vault let them build huge structures, much larger than anything the Greeks could build. One such Roman structure that used vaults was the Colosseum. It was built to hold fights between gladiators. Similar arenas were built throughout the empire. Plays, athletic competitions, and chariot races were held there.

The Romans also used more domes in their architecture than the Greeks had. Domes were difficult to build and required a great deal of support. Once the Romans developed cement, they could provide that support. Many Roman structures are topped with huge domes, some of the largest ever built.

Art The artists of the Roman Empire were known for their beautiful mosaics, paintings, and statues. Mosaics and paintings were used to decorate Roman buildings. Many Roman homes and businesses had elaborate mosaics built into their floors. The walls of these buildings were often covered with paintings. Landscapes found in and around Rome, such as woods, groves, hills, gardens, and rivers, were popular subjects. Most Roman paintings were frescoes. A fresco is a type of painting done on wet plaster.

Many Roman artists were particularly skilled at creating portraits, or pictures of people. When they made a portrait, artists tried to show their subject's personality. We can guess a great deal about individual Romans by studying their portraits.

Roman sculptors were also talented. They created some original works and used their skills to honor the gods, such as Jupiter, Mars, and Venus. Many Roman statues, however, are actually copies of older Greek works. Although their works are not original, we owe a great deal to these Roman artists. Many of the original Greek works they copied have been destroyed over time. Without the Roman copies, the world would know little about many Greek masterpieces.

Reading Check
Draw Conclusions
Why did many Roman architects and artists base their work on earlier Greek works?

A Roman Fresco

A fresco is a type of painting in which paint is applied to wet plaster and then left to dry. Roman artists painted many beautiful frescoes like this one.

Analyze Visuals
What activities can you see in this fresco?

Ovid was a Roman poet. His works were popular during his lifetime, and his collection of 250 myths titled Metamorphoses is considered to be his greatest work.

Literature and Language

Like Roman artists, Roman authors are greatly admired. In addition, the works they created and the language they used have shaped our language today.

Literature The Romans admired good writers. Many emperors encouraged authors to write. As a result, Rome was home to many of the greatest authors of the ancient world. One such author was **Virgil**, who wrote a great epic about the founding of Rome, the *Aeneid*. Another was **Ovid** (AHV-uhd), who wrote poems about Roman mythology. In his epic poem *Metamorphoses,* he wrote: "In the make-up of human beings, intelligence counts for more than our hands, and that is our true strength."

The Romans also excelled in other types of writing:
- **satire**, a style of writing that pokes fun at people or society
- history and speeches
- drama, both tragedies and comedies

Many of these works have served as models for hundreds of years and are still enjoyed today.

Language Virgil, Ovid, and other poets wrote in Latin, the language of ancient Rome. The Roman Empire was huge, and it had two official languages. In the east, some people spoke Greek. People throughout the western Roman world wrote, conducted business, and kept records in Latin. This wide use of Latin helped tie people in various parts of the empire together.

After the Roman Empire ended, Latin developed into many different languages. Together, the languages that developed from Latin are called **Romance languages**. The main Romance languages are Italian, French, Spanish, Portuguese, and Romanian. They share many elements with one another and with Latin.

Over time, Latin also influenced other languages. For example, many Latin words entered non-Romance languages, including English. Words like *et cetera, circus,* and *veto* were all originally Latin terms. Latin words are also common in scientific terms and mottoes. For example, the motto of the United States is the Latin phrase *e pluribus unum* (ee PLOOHR-uh-buhs OO-nuhm), which means "out of many, one." Many legal terms also come from Latin.

Although most people stopped speaking Latin more than 1,000 years ago, it continued to be used in education long afterward. It was widely taught in European schools until the 18th century. Latin has not disappeared completely. It is still used in scientific names and is spoken in some Roman Catholic religious services.

Reading Check
Find Main Ideas
How did Roman literature and language influence later societies?

The Beginning of Civil Law

Perhaps even more influential than Rome's artistic and literary traditions was its system of law. Roman law was enforced across much of Europe. After the empire fell apart, Roman laws continued to exist.

Over time, Roman law inspired a system called civil law. **Civil law** is a legal system based on a written code of laws, like the one created by the Romans.

Reading Check
Summarize How
are Roman legal
ideas reflected in the
modern world?

Most countries in Europe today have civil-law traditions. In the 1500s and 1600s, European explorers and colonists carried civil law around the world. As a result, some countries in Africa, Asia, and the Americas developed law codes as well.

Philosophy and History

Although the Romans were heavily influenced by Greek philosophy, they still made important contributions of their own. For example, many of the words that are often used in philosophy come from Latin, such as *morality, argument,* and *proof.* Roman leaders often used philosophy when talking to the public.

Reading Check
Summarize What
are two ways the
Greeks influenced the
Romans?

In addition to poetry and philosophy, Romans studied and wrote about their own history. Roman historians were influenced by Greek writers and documented the way the republic and empire changed over time. Livy, one of the best-known Roman historians, wrote about the founding of the city of Rome and the establishment of the Roman Empire. Others, like Caesar and Tacitus, also wrote about Roman history.

Summary You have read about just some of the contributions of Romans in the fields of science, architecture, literature, law, and philosophy. The Roman Republic and Empire made many contributions to the world and continue to influence our society.

Lesson 6 Assessment

Review Ideas, Terms, and People

1. a. **Contrast** How was the Romans' attitude toward science different from the Greeks'?

   b. **Identify** What were aqueducts used for?

2. a. **Define** What is a fresco?

   b. **Explain** What influence did Greek art have on Roman art?

3. a. **Recall** What were three forms of writing in which the Romans excelled?

   b. **Elaborate** Why did Latin develop into different languages after the fall of the Roman Empire?

4. **Identify** What type of law is based on the Roman law code?

5. **Recall** In what ways did Romans have an impact on philosophy?

Critical Thinking

6. **Compare and Contrast** Draw a chart like this one. In the first column, list two ways Greek and Roman architecture were similar. In the other, list two ways they were different.

Same	Different

Social Studies Skills

Interpret Globes

Define the Skill

A globe is a sphere on which a map of the earth is shown. Globes help us understand where countries, bodies of water, and other features are located in relationship to one another. In many ways, they are more informative than flat maps, which can be misleading because the earth is not flat. The people who make flat maps sometimes change the sizes of some places to make them fit. At other times, the shapes of places are changed. Since spheres are closer to the earth's shape, globes are the most realistic maps. Therefore, being able to interpret them is important for understanding history and geography.

Learn the Skill

Follow these guidelines to interpret a globe.

1. Start with map basics. Note the labels, legend, and scale. Like a flat map, a globe also has lines of longitude and latitude. You can use these lines to find and describe any location on the globe.

2. Study the globe as a whole. Locate features such as the North and South Poles, the equator, and the hemispheres.

3. Next, examine the location of different countries. Ask yourself how they relate to the rest of the world. Is a particular country larger or smaller than its neighbors? What bodies of water or other natural features might affect its history or culture?

4. Finally, connect the information on the globe to any written information about the subject in the text.

Practice the Skill

Use the globe pictured here and the one in your classroom to answer the following questions.

1. What are the differences between the globe and a flat map?

2. Compare a globe to a flat map. Do some places look bigger or smaller on the globe? Why do you think this is?

3. Locate the Mediterranean Sea on the globe. Using your finger, trace the trade routes Roman ships might have taken to Egypt, Greece, Turkey and Spain. Which of these journeys do you think would have been the fastest?

Module 10 Assessment

Review Vocabulary, Terms, and People

Match each numbered definition with the correct lettered vocabulary term.

1. a leader with absolute power for six months
2. the emperor who divided the empire
3. a government in which people elect leaders
4. a legal system based on a written code of laws
5. the common people of Rome
6. a channel used to carry water from mountains into cities
7. a council that advised Rome's leaders
8. the two most powerful officials in Rome
9. noble, powerful Romans
10. Roman Peace

a. republic
b. plebeians
c. dictator
d. civil law
e. Roman Senate
f. patricians
g. consuls
h. aqueduct
i. Diocletian
j. Pax Romana

Comprehension and Critical Thinking

Lesson 1

11. a. **Describe** What are two legends that describe Rome's founding? How are the two legends connected?

    b. **Compare and Contrast** What roles did the plebeians and the patricians take in the early Roman government? In what other ways were the two groups different?

    c. **Predict** How do you think Italy's geography and Rome's location would affect the spread of Rome's influence?

Lesson 2

12. a. **Describe** What were the three parts of Rome's government?

    b. **Analyze** How do checks and balances protect the rights of the people? How do written laws do the same thing?

    c. **Elaborate** What are some places in modern society that serve purposes similar to those of the Roman Forum?

Lesson 3

13. a. **Identify** What difficulties did Hannibal, Lucius Cornelius Sulla, and Spartacus cause for Rome?

    b. **Analyze** How did Roman occupations, economics, and society change during the Late Republic?

    c. **Evaluate** How did Augustus's improvements to the city of Rome strengthen his rule?

Lesson 4

14. a. **Evaluate** Why were the emperors after Augustus unpopular with the Roman people?

    b. **Compare** How did both the Roman Empire and Gupta Empire expand?

    c. **Describe** What did the Romans do to grow their wealth?

    d. **Explain** Which class of people had most government control in Rome?

Lesson 5

15. a. **Identify** Who were the Huns? Who were the Goths?

    b. **Compare and Contrast** What did Diocletian and Constantine have in common? How did their actions differ?

    c. **Evaluate** Of all the causes for the fall of the western Roman Empire, which, if any, could have been prevented? Explain your answer.

Lesson 6

16. **a. Describe** What were the main Roman achievements in architecture? In literature and language?

   b. Contrast How did the Roman attitude toward science compare to the traditional Greek attitude? What is an example of the Roman attitude?

   c. Evaluate Of all the Romans' achievements, which do you think has affected the most people? Defend your answer.

Review Themes

17. **Politics** Why did Roman magistrates hold office for only one year?

18. **Science and Technology** What Roman achievement in science or engineering do you think is most impressive? Why?

19. **Geography** How do you think Rome's location helped the Romans in their quest to conquer the entire Mediterranean region?

Reading Skills

Create an Outline *Use the Reading Skills taught in this module to answer the question below.*

20. Look back at the discussion "Crises Strike the Republic" in Lesson 3. Prepare an outline that will help clarify the people, events, and ideas of this discussion. Before you prepare your outline, decide what your major headings will be. Then choose the details that will appear below each heading. Remember that most outlines follow this basic format:

> I. Main Idea
>   A. Supporting Idea
>   B. Supporting Idea
>   1. Detail
>   2. Detail
> II. Main Idea
>   A. Supporting Idea

Social Studies Skills

Interpret Globes *Look at the globe in Social Studies Skills and the one in your classroom. Then answer the following questions.*

21. Which geographic feature do you think helped Rome become so strong?

22. Which continents are nearest to Rome? Explain how that might have influenced the direction of the empire's expansion.

Focus On Writing

23. **Write and Present a Legend** Aeneas, Romulus, and Remus are all part of Rome's founding legends. Think about the different elements of a legend, including a main character, the gods or mythological figures who helped them, the setting, and the event or topic of the legend. Then, choose a subject from this module for a legend you will create. Your subject could be a person or an event from history. Brainstorm the elements of your own legend. Then, as you write your legend, focus on exciting details that will bring the subject to life in your listeners' minds. Once you've finished writing, share your legend with the class. Try to make your legend exciting as you present it. Remember to alter the tone and volume of your voice to convey the appropriate mood.

ROME:
ENGINEERING AN EMPIRE

The Roman Empire was one of the largest and most powerful empires in ancient history. With its strong military, the Roman Empire expanded to dominate the entire Mediterranean region, including much of western Europe and northern Africa. Keys to this expansion were the engineering and construction innovations made by Roman engineers. As the empire grew and prospered,

Roman engineers made advances in city planning, road and bridge design, water and sewage systems, and many other areas.

Explore some of the incredible monuments and engineering achievements of the Roman Empire online. You can find a wealth of information, video clips, primary sources, and activities through your online textbook.

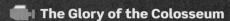

The Glory of the Colosseum

Watch the video to go inside the Colosseum, Rome's premier entertainment venue and one of the most famous buildings of the Roman Empire.

HISTORY Go online to view these and other **HISTORY**® resources.

Caesar Builds an Empire

Watch the video to learn why Julius Caesar built a bridge across the Rhine River as a demonstration of Roman power.

Growth of the Roman Empire

Explore the map to analyze the growth of one of the largest empires of the ancient world.

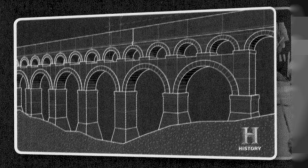

Arches, Angles, Innovations

Watch the video to learn about Roman engineering advances and the construction of aqueducts.

Module 11

The Growth of Christianity

Essential Question
How did developments within the Roman Empire affect Christianity's growth?

About the Photo: Members of one Christian church, the Roman Catholic Church, gather in Vatican City in Rome.

▶ Explore ONLINE!

VIDEOS, including...
• The Spread of Christianity

HISTORY.

☑ Document-Based Investigations

☑ Graphic Organizers

☑ Interactive Games

☑ Image with Hotspots: The Siege of Masada

☑ Image with Hotspots: The Last Supper

☑ Interactive Map: Paul's Journeys

In this module you will learn about the beginnings of Christianity in the Roman Empire.

What You Will Learn...

Lesson 1: Religion in the Roman Empire 384
The Big Idea The Roman Empire accepted many religions, but it came into conflict with Judaism.

Lesson 2: Origins of Christianity 388
The Big Idea Christianity is based on the teachings of Jesus of Nazareth.

Lesson 3: The Spread of Christianity 396
The Big Idea Christianity spread quickly after Jesus' death.

Lesson 4: The Early Christian World 400
The Big Idea Within three centuries after Jesus' death, Christianity had spread through the empire and became Rome's official religion.

Timeline of Events AD 1–400

▶ Explore ONLINE!

Module Events		World Events

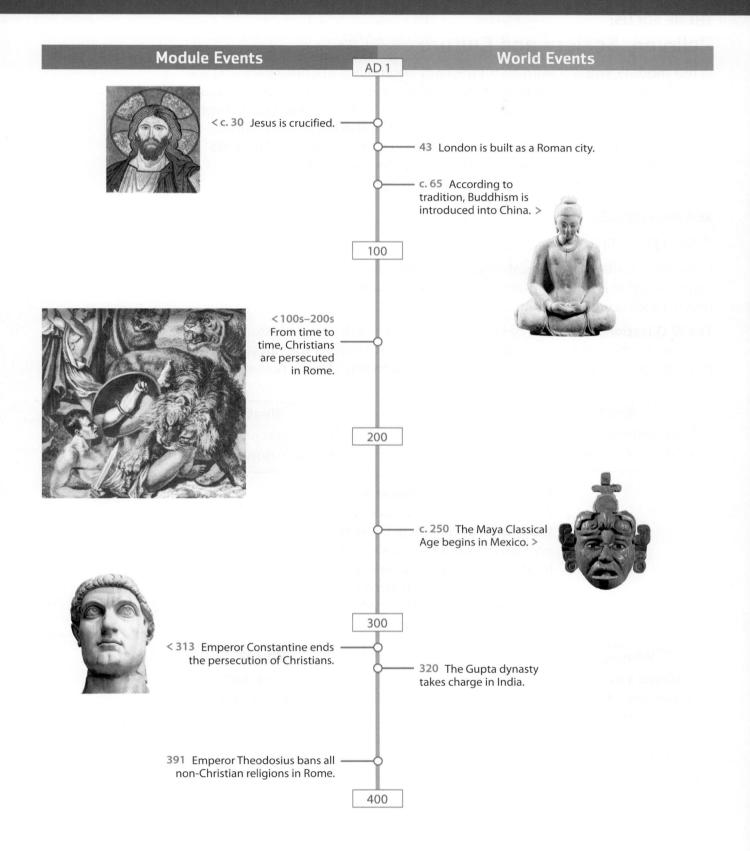

AD 1

< **c. 30** Jesus is crucified.

43 London is built as a Roman city.

c. 65 According to tradition, Buddhism is introduced into China. >

100

< **100s–200s** From time to time, Christians are persecuted in Rome.

200

c. 250 The Maya Classical Age begins in Mexico. >

300

< **313** Emperor Constantine ends the persecution of Christians.

320 The Gupta dynasty takes charge in India.

391 Emperor Theodosius bans all non-Christian religions in Rome.

400

Reading Social Studies

Religion, Society and Culture

In this module, you will learn about the early beginnings of Christianity. You will read about the life and teachings of Jesus of Nazareth and about the Apostles who spread Jesus's teachings after his death. Later in the module, you will see how Christianity spread through the Roman Empire and became its official religion. Throughout the module, you will see how the Christian religion has shaped the society and culture of many people throughout history.

READING FOCUS:

Ask Questions

If you don't understand something your teacher says in class, how do you get an explanation? You ask a question. You can use the same method to improve your understanding while reading.

The W Questions The most basic questions you can ask about a historical text are *who, what, when,* and *where*—the *W* questions. Answering these questions will help you get to the very basics of what you need to learn from a passage.

Who?
Augustine of Hippo, a Christian writer

What?
read works of classical philosophers

New Teachings and Emperors
As Christianity spread through the Roman world, Christian writers read the works of classical philosophers. One such writer was Augustine of Hippo. He lived in Hippo, a town in northern Africa, in the late 300s and early 400s.

Where?
Hippo, a town in northern Africa

When?
the late 300s and early 400s

You Try It!

Read the following passage, and then answer the questions.

Christianity Spreads Quickly in Rome Early Christians like Paul wanted to share their message about Jesus with the world. Because of their efforts, Christianity spread quickly in many Roman communities. But as it grew more popular, Christianity began to concern some Roman leaders. They looked for ways to put an end to this new religion.

Early Growth The first Christians worked to spread Jesus' teachings only among Jews. But some early Christians, including Paul, wanted to introduce Christianity to non-Jews as well.

As a result, Christianity began to spread in the Roman Empire. Within a hundred years after Jesus's death, historians estimate that thousands of Christians lived in the Roman Empire.

Answer these questions based on what you just read.

1. Who is this passage about?
2. What did they do?
3. When did they live?
4. Where did they live and work?
5. How can knowing the answers to these questions help you better understand what you've read?

As you read this module, use the *W* questions of *who, what, when,* and *where* as guides to help you clarify your understanding of the text.

Key Terms and People

Lesson 1
Christianity
Jesus of Nazareth
Messiah
John the Baptist
Lesson 2
Bible
crucifixion
Resurrection
disciples
Apostles
Lesson 3
Paul
saint
monotheism
martyrs
persecution
Lesson 4
bishops
Eucharist
pope
Augustine of Hippo
Constantine

Religion in the Roman Empire

The Big Idea

The Roman Empire accepted many religions, but it came into conflict with Judaism.

Main Ideas

- The Romans allowed many religions to be practiced in their empire.
- Jews and Romans clashed over religious and political ideas.
- The roots of Christianity had appeared in Judea by the end of the first century BC.

Key Terms and People

Christianity
Jesus of Nazareth
Messiah
John the Baptist

If YOU were there . . .

You are a Roman soldier stationed in one of the empire's many provinces. You are proud that you've helped bring Roman culture to this place far from the city of Rome. But one group of local people refuses to take part in official Roman holidays and rituals, saying it is against their beliefs. Other than that, they seem peaceful. Some soldiers think that this group is dangerous.

What will you do about this group?

Roman Ideas About Religion

Romans worshipped many gods, and many Romans were open to different religious beliefs found throughout the empire. Because of their ideas about religion, the Romans allowed people they conquered to keep their beliefs. In many cases, these beliefs also spread among nearby Romans. As time passed, the Romans built temples to the gods of these new religions, and knowledge of them spread throughout the empire.

The Romans built many temples to honor their many gods. Temples built to honor all the gods were called pantheons, and the most famous of these is the Pantheon in Rome, first built in the 20s BC. Its huge dome awes visitors even today.

Reading Check
Find Main Ideas
Why did the Romans forbid certain religions?

The only time the Romans banned a religion was when the rulers of Rome considered it a political problem. In these cases, government officials took steps to prevent problems. Sometimes they placed restrictions on when and where members of a religion could meet. One religion that some Roman leaders came to consider a political problem was Judaism.

Jews and Romans Clash

Roman leaders considered Judaism to be a potential problem for two reasons. One reason was religious, the other political. Both reasons led to conflict between the Romans and the Jews of the empire.

Religious Conflict Unlike the Romans, the Jews did not worship many gods. They believed that their God was the only god. Some Romans, though, thought the Jews were insulting Rome's gods by not praying to them.

Still, the Romans did not attempt to ban Judaism in the empire. They allowed the Jews to keep their religion and practice it as they pleased. It was not until later when political conflict arose with the Jews that the Romans decided to take action.

Political Conflict Political conflict arose because the Jews rebelled against Roman rule. Judea, the territory in which most Jews lived, had been conquered by Rome in 63 BC. Since then, many Jews had been unhappy with Roman rule. They wanted to be ruled only by Jews, not by outsiders. As a result, the Jews rebelled in the AD 60s. The rebellion was defeated, however, and the Jews were punished for their actions.

Unhappy with Roman rule, many Jews rebelled in the AD 60s but were defeated. Refusing to accept defeat, about 1,000 Jews locked themselves in a mountain fortress called Masada and held off the Romans for four years. In the end, these rebels killed themselves to avoid surrendering to the Romans.

The Roman general Titus captured Jerusalem in AD 70. To celebrate this victory, the Romans built an arch that shows Roman soldiers carrying a stolen menorah from Jerusalem's holy Second Temple.

In the early 100s the Jews rebelled once more against the Romans. Tired of putting down Jewish revolts, the emperor Hadrian banned the practice of certain Jewish rituals. He thought this ban would cause people to give up Judaism and end their desire for independence.

Hadrian was wrong. His actions made the Jews even more upset with Roman rule. Once again they rebelled. This time Hadrian decided to end the rebellions in Jerusalem once and for all.

The Roman army crushed the Jews' revolt, destroyed the Jewish capital of Jerusalem, and forced all Jews to leave the city. Then the Romans built a new city on the ruins of Jerusalem and brought settlers from other parts of the empire to live there. Jews were forbidden to enter this new city more than once a year. Forced out of their ancient city, many Jews moved into other parts of the Roman world.

Reading Check
Summarize
Why did the Romans come to consider Judaism a threat?

The Roots of Christianity

Early in the first century AD, before the Jews' first rebellion against the Romans, what would become a new religion appeared in Judea. This religion began as one of the many Jewish sects and later developed into **Christianity**. It was based on the life and teachings of the Jew **Jesus of Nazareth**. Christianity was rooted in Jewish ideas and traditions.

At the time that Jesus was born, there were several groups of Jews in Judea. The largest of these groups was very strict in how it practiced Judaism. Members of this group were particularly strict in obeying the laws of Moses. Jews believed that Moses had given them these laws to follow.

Many Jews followed the laws closely because Jewish prophets had said that a new leader would appear among the Jews. Many people thought this leader was more likely to appear if Jews were strict in their religious behavior.

According to the prophecies, the Jews' new leader would be a descendent of King David. When he came, he would restore the greatness of David's ancient kingdom, Israel. The prophets called this leader the **Messiah** (muh-SY-uh), which means "anointed" in Hebrew. In other words, the Jews believed that the Messiah would be chosen by God to lead them. However, no one knew when the Messiah would come.

Reading Check
Summarize Why were Jews waiting for the Messiah to arrive?

When the Romans took over Judea in 63 BC, many Jews thought the Messiah would soon appear. Prophets wandered throughout Judea, announcing that the Messiah was coming. The most famous of these prophets was **John the Baptist**. Inspired by the prophets' teachings, many Jews anxiously awaited the Messiah.

Summary and Preview You just read about Jewish prophecies that foretold the coming of a Messiah. In the next lesson, you'll learn what happened when a man many people believed to be that Messiah—Jesus—was born.

Lesson 1 Assessment

Review Ideas, Terms, and People

1. **a. Describe** What was the Roman attitude toward religion?
   b. Explain Why did the Romans ban some religions?
2. **a. Recall** What was a major religious difference between the Romans and the Jews?
   b. Analyze Why did the Romans destroy Jerusalem?
   c. Elaborate How do you think the spreading of Jews through the Roman world affected Jewish culture?
3. **a. Define** Who did Jews believe the Messiah was?
   b. Make Inferences How did the anticipation of the Messiah's arrival lead many Jews to follow laws strictly?

Critical Thinking

4. **Categorize** Draw a graphic organizer like the one here. Use it to identify reasons the Romans might accept or forbid a religion.

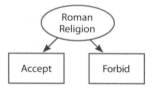

Origins of Christianity

The Big Idea

Christianity is based on the teachings of Jesus of Nazareth.

Main Ideas

- In Christian belief, Jesus was the Messiah and the son of God.
- Jesus taught about salvation, love for God, and kindness.
- Jesus' followers spread his teachings after his death.

Key Terms and People

Bible
crucifixion
Resurrection
disciples
Apostles

If YOU were there . . .

You are a fisher in Judea, bringing in the day's catch. As you reach the shore, you see a large crowd. They are listening to a man tell stories. A man in the crowd whispers to you that the speaker is a teacher with some new ideas about religion. You are eager to get your fish to the market, but you are also curious.

What might convince you to stay to listen?

The Life and Death of Jesus of Nazareth

Jesus of Nazareth, the man whom many people believe was the Jewish Messiah, lived at the beginning of the first century AD. Although Jesus was one of the most influential figures in world history, we know relatively little about his life. Most of what we know about Jesus is contained in the New Testament of the Christian **Bible**, the holy book of Christianity.

The Christian Bible is made up of two parts. The first part, the Old Testament, is largely the same as the Hebrew Bible. It tells the history and ideas of the Hebrew people. The second part, the New Testament, is an account of the life and teachings of Jesus and of the early history of Christianity.

The Birth of Jesus According to the Bible, Jesus was born in a small town called Bethlehem (BETH-li-hem) at the end of the first century BC. In fact, in our calendar system his birth marks the shift from BC to AD. Jesus' mother, Mary, was married to a carpenter named Joseph. But Christians believe God, not Joseph, was Jesus' father.

As a young man Jesus lived in the town of Nazareth and probably studied with Joseph to become a carpenter. Like many young Jewish men of the time, he also studied the laws and teachings of Judaism. By the time he was about 30, Jesus had begun to travel and teach. Stories of his teachings and actions from this time make up the beginning of the New Testament.

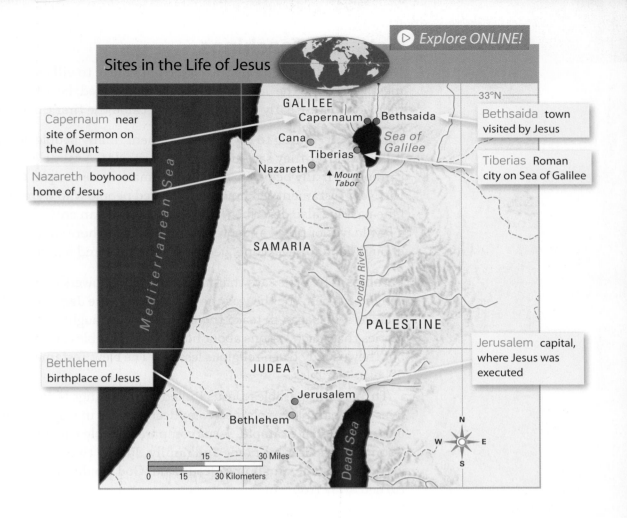

Explore ONLINE!

Sites in the Life of Jesus

Capernaum near site of Sermon on the Mount

Nazareth boyhood home of Jesus

Bethlehem birthplace of Jesus

Bethsaida town visited by Jesus

Tiberias Roman city on Sea of Galilee

Jerusalem capital, where Jesus was executed

GALILEE

Capernaum

Bethsaida

Cana

Sea of Galilee

Tiberias

Nazareth

▲ Mount Tabor

Mediterranean Sea

SAMARIA

Jordan River

PALESTINE

JUDEA

Jerusalem

Bethlehem

Dead Sea

0   15   30 Miles

0   15   30 Kilometers

N W E S

33°N

The Crucifixion As a teacher, Jesus drew many followers with his ideas. But at the same time, his teachings challenged the authority of political and religious leaders. The Roman Empire allowed the practice of many religions, except those that challenged Roman authority. According to the Christian Bible, Roman authorities arrested Jesus while he was in Jerusalem in or around AD 30.

Shortly after his arrest, Jesus was tried and executed. He was killed by **crucifixion** (kroo-suh-FIK-shuhn), a type of execution in which a person was nailed to a cross. In fact, the word *crucifixion* comes from the Latin word for "cross." After he died Jesus' followers buried him.

The Resurrection According to Christian beliefs, Jesus rose from the dead and vanished from his tomb three days after he was crucified. Christians refer to Jesus' rise from the dead as the **Resurrection** (re-suh-REK-shuhn).

Christians further believe that after the Resurrection, Jesus appeared to several groups of his **disciples** (di-SY-puhls), or followers. Jesus stayed with these disciples for the next 40 days, teaching them and giving them instructions about how to pass on his teachings. Then Jesus rose up into heaven.

Early Christians believed that the Resurrection was a sign that Jesus was the Messiah and the son of God. Some people began to call him Jesus Christ, from the Greek word for Messiah, *Christos*. It is from this word that the words *Christian* and *Christianity* eventually developed.

Reading Check
Summarize
What do Christians believe happened after Jesus died?

Acts and Teachings

During his lifetime, Jesus traveled from village to village spreading his message among the Jewish people. As he traveled, he attracted many followers. These early followers later became the first Christians.

Miracles According to the New Testament, many people became Jesus' followers after they saw him perform miracles. A miracle is an event that cannot normally be performed by a human. For example, the books of the New Testament tell how Jesus healed people who were sick or injured. One passage also describes how Jesus once fed an entire crowd with just a few loaves of bread and a few fish. Although there should not have been enough food for everyone, people ate their fill and had food to spare.

Parables The Bible says that miracles drew followers to Jesus and convinced them that he was the son of God. Once Jesus had attracted followers, he began to teach them. One way he taught was through parables, stories that teach lessons about how to live. Parables are similar to fables, but they usually teach religious lessons. The New Testament includes many of Jesus' parables.

Through his parables, Jesus linked his teachings to people's everyday lives. The parables explained complicated ideas in ways that people could understand. For example, Jesus compared people who lived sinfully to a son who had left his home and family. Just as the son's father would joyfully welcome him home, Jesus said, God would forgive sinners who turned away from sin.

Link to Today

Christian Holidays

For centuries, Christians have honored key events in Jesus' life. Some of these events inspired holidays that Christians celebrate today.

The most sacred holiday for Christians is Easter, which is celebrated each spring. The exact date changes from year to year. Easter is a celebration of the Resurrection. Christians usually celebrate Easter by attending church services. Many people also celebrate by dyeing eggs because eggs are seen as a symbol of new life.

Another major Christian holiday is Christmas. It honors Jesus' birth and is celebrated every December 25. Although no one knows on what date Jesus was actually born, Christians have celebrated Christmas in December since the 200s. Today, people celebrate with church services and the exchange of gifts. Some, like people in this picture, reenact scenes of Jesus's birth.

Analyze Information
Why do you think people celebrate events in Jesus' life?

The Last Supper

This famous painting by Italian artist Leonardo da Vinci shows Jesus and his Apostles at the Last Supper. The Last Supper was the last meal they shared before Jesus was arrested. Later, the Apostles would spread Jesus' teachings.

Jesus' Message Much of Jesus' message was rooted in older Jewish traditions. For example, he emphasized two rules that were also in the Torah: love God and love other people.

Jesus expected his followers to love all people, not just friends or family. He encouraged his followers to be generous to the poor and the sick. He told people that they should even love their enemies. The way people treated others, Jesus said, showed how much they loved God.

Another important theme in Jesus' teachings was salvation, or the rescue of people from sin. Jesus taught that people who were saved from sin would enter the Kingdom of God when they died. Many of his teachings dealt with how people could reach the kingdom.

Over the many centuries since Jesus lived, people have interpreted his teachings in different ways. As a result, many different denominations of Christians have been developed. A denomination is a group of people who hold the same beliefs. Still, despite their differences, Christians around the world share some basic beliefs about Jesus and his importance to the world.

Reading Check
Summarize Why did Jesus tell parables?

Jesus' Followers

Shortly after the Resurrection, the Bible says, Jesus' followers traveled throughout the Roman world telling about Jesus and his teachings. Among the people to pass on Jesus' teachings were 12 chosen disciples called **Apostles** (uh-PAHS-uhlz), including the writers of the Gospels (GAHS-puhlz).

The Apostles The Apostles were 12 men whom Jesus chose to receive special teaching. During Jesus' lifetime, they were among his closest followers and knew him very well. Jesus frequently sent the Apostles to spread his teachings. After the Resurrection, the Apostles continued this task.

One of the Apostles, Peter, became the leader of the group after Jesus died. Peter traveled to a few Roman cities and taught about Jesus in the Jewish communities there. Eventually he went to live in Rome, where he had much authority among Jesus' followers. In later years after the Christian Church was more organized, many people looked back to Peter as its first leader.

The Gospels Some of Jesus's disciples wrote accounts of his life and teachings. These accounts are called the Gospels. Four Gospels are found in the New Testament of the Christian Bible. They were written by men known as Matthew, Mark, Luke, and John. Both historians and religious scholars depend on the Gospels for information about Jesus' life.

The Gospels also influenced Christian beliefs. According to the Gospels, Jesus was baptized by John the Baptist. When a person is baptized, they are partially or wholly immersed in water. Those who followed Jesus also chose to be baptized. Baptism signified a person's desire to be a Christian and to be purified, or cleaned, of sin. The practice of baptism continues today.

The Gospels also influenced other Christian practices. One practice common to many Christians is known as the Eucharist. The Eucharist is also known as the Lord's Supper or Holy Communion. This practice helps Christians to remember what Jesus said and did when he was alive. The Eucharist is mentioned in several of the Gospels. According to tradition, Jesus shared his last meal with some of his disciples. He gave his disciples bread and wine. Many Christians celebrate this last meal today in a similar fashion. They eat bread and drink wine to think about the importance of Jesus to their faith.

Reading Check
Summarize What are the Gospels?

Before his death, Jesus taught the Apostles a special prayer known as the Lord's Prayer. It remains a common prayer for many Christians. Prayer continues to be an important tradition in the Christian faith.

Summary and Preview Jesus and his Apostles significantly influenced early Christian beliefs. As you will learn, Christianity soon spread beyond Judea into many parts of the Roman world.

Lesson 2 Assessment

Review Ideas, Terms, and People

1. a. Define In Christian teachings, what was the Resurrection?

   b. Elaborate Why do you think Christians use the cross as a symbol of their religion?

2. a. Identify What did Jesus mean by salvation?

   b. Explain How have differing interpretations of Jesus' teachings affected Christianity?

3. a. Recall Who were the Apostles?

Critical Thinking

4. Find the Main Idea

   Draw a graphic organizer like the one shown here. Use it to identify and describe some of Jesus' acts and teachings.

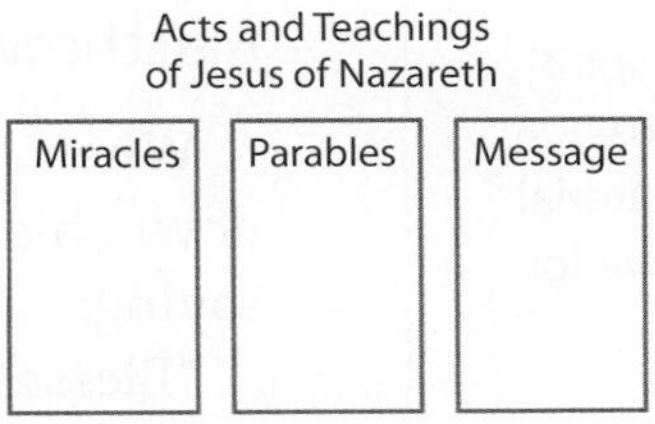

   Acts and Teachings
   of Jesus of Nazareth

Miracles	Parables	Message

Literature in History

The Teachings of Jesus

Word Help

meek enduring hardships without complaining

righteousness good living

persecute to punish someone for their beliefs

revile hate

trampled stepped on

❶ The poor in spirit are those people who give up material goods out of love for God.

❷ Here Jesus is saying that people who are punished or killed for their beliefs will be honored in heaven.

❸ Jesus compares his ideals with light. *What do you think Jesus means when he says "let your light shine before others"?*

About the Reading The Bible says that Jesus attracted many followers. One day he led his followers onto a mountainside to preach a sermon, or religious speech, called the Sermon on the Mount. Jesus taught that people who love God will be blessed when they die. The sayings that Jesus used to express this message are called the Beatitudes (bee-A-tuh-toodz), because in Latin they all begin with the word *beati*, or blessed.

As You Read Note who Jesus says are blessed.

From *The Sermon on the Mount*
Matthew 5:1–16 New Revised Standard Version

When Jesus saw the crowds, he went up the mountain; and after he sat down, his disciples came to him. Then he began to speak, and taught them, saying:

"Blessed are the poor in spirit, for theirs is the kingdom of heaven. ❶

"Blessed are those who mourn, for they will be comforted.

"Blessed are the meek, for they will inherit the earth.

"Blessed are those who hunger and thirst for righteousness, for they will be filled.

"Blessed are the merciful, for they will receive mercy.

"Blessed are the pure in heart, for they will see God.

"Blessed are the peacemakers, for they will be called children of God.

"Blessed are those who are persecuted for righteousness' sake, for theirs is the kingdom of heaven. ❷

"Blessed are you when people revile you and persecute you and utter all kinds of evil against you falsely on my account. Rejoice and be glad, for your reward is great in heaven, for in the same way they persecuted the prophets who were before you.

"You are the salt of the earth; but if salt has lost its taste, how can its saltiness be restored? It is no longer good for anything, but is thrown out and trampled under foot.

"You are the light of the world. A city built on a hill cannot be hid. No one after lighting a lamp puts it under the bushel basket, but on the lampstand, and it gives light to all in the house. In the same way, let your light shine before others, so that they may see your good works and give glory to your Father in heaven." ❸

Word Help

Levite (LEE-vyt)
a member of the
Hebrew priest class

**denarii
(di-NAR-ee-eye)**
Roman coins

① Oil and wine were
used to clean cuts and
wounds.
*What does the
Samaritan do after he
cleans the traveler's
wounds?*

② *Which person did
the man say was the
traveler's neighbor?*

About the Reading In his teaching, Jesus used many parables, or stories intended to teach lessons about how people should live. One of his most famous parables is the story of the Good Samaritan. The Samaritans were a minority group who lived in what is now northern Israel. The parable of the Good Samaritan is Jesus' response to someone who asks what Jesus means when he says to love your neighbor.

As You Read Think about the lesson Jesus is trying to teach.

From *The Parable of the Good Samaritan*
Luke 10:29–37 New Revised Standard Version

But wanting to justify himself, he asked Jesus, "And who is my neighbor?" Jesus replied, "A man was going down from Jerusalem to Jericho, and fell into the hands of robbers, who stripped him, beat him, and went away, leaving him half dead. Now by chance a priest was going down that road; and when he saw him, he passed by on the other side. So likewise a Levite, when he came to the place and saw him, passed by on the other side. But a Samaritan while traveling came near him; and when he saw him, he was moved with pity. He went to him and bandaged his wounds, having poured oil and wine on them. **①** Then he put him on his own animal, brought him to an inn, and took care of him. The next day he took out two denarii, gave them to the innkeeper, and said, 'Take care of him; and when I come back, I will repay you whatever you spend.' Which of these three, do you think, was a neighbor to the man who fell into the hands of the robbers?" He said, "The one who showed him mercy." Jesus said to him, "Go and do likewise." **②**

Connect Sacred Texts to History

1. **Analyze** Jesus taught that people who loved God and lived good lives would achieve salvation. How do the Beatitudes support this teaching?

2. **Synthesize** Jesus also told people that they should be kind to everyone, even their enemies. How is the parable of the Good Samaritan an example of this?

The Spread of Christianity

The Big Idea

Christianity spread quickly after Jesus' death.

Main Ideas

- Paul, one of Jesus' followers, spread Jesus' teachings after his death.

- Christianity spread quickly in Rome, but its growing strength worried some emperors.

Key Terms and People

Paul
saint
monotheism
martyrs
persecution

Academic Vocabulary
ideals Ideas or goals that people try to live up to

If YOU were there . . .

You live in a town in Greece in the first century AD. Near your town are two places dedicated to the ancient Greek gods—a grove of sacred trees and a temple to the god Apollo. One day, two Christians come to your town talking about their religion. They urge people to give up their old gods and follow Christian ways. Some townspeople listen eagerly. Others, however, get angry.

What do you think the townspeople will do?

Paul of Tarsus

Probably the most important figure in the spread of Christianity after Jesus' death was named **Paul** of Tarsus. He had never met Jesus, but Paul did more to spread Christian **ideals** than anyone else did. He was so influential that many people consider him an additional Apostle. After he died, Paul was named a **saint**, a person known and admired for his or her holiness.

Like most of Jesus' early followers, Paul was born Jewish. At first he didn't like Jesus' ideas, which he considered a threat to Judaism. For a time, Paul even worked to prevent the followers of Jesus from spreading their message.

According to the Bible, though, one day while Paul was traveling to Damascus he saw a blinding light and heard the voice of Jesus calling out to him. Soon afterward, Paul became a Christian.

Paul of Tarsus was an important figure in the early Christian church. Many of his letters are in the Bible today.

After his conversion, Paul traveled widely, spreading Christian teachings. He visited many of the major cities along the eastern coast of the Mediterranean on his journeys. In addition, he wrote long letters that he sent to communities throughout the Roman world. These letters helped explain and elaborate on Jesus' teachings.

In his letters, Paul wrote at length about the Resurrection and about salvation. He also mentioned ideas of the Trinity. The Trinity is a central Christian belief that God is made up of three persons—God the Father, Jesus the Son, and the

Paul's Letter to the Romans

In the late AD 50s, Paul traveled to Corinth, a city in Greece. While there he wrote a letter to the people of Rome. In this letter he told the Romans that he planned to come to their city to deliver God's message. In the meantime, he told them, they should learn to live together peacefully.

"Let love be genuine; hate what is evil, hold fast to what is good; love one another with mutual affection; outdo one another in showing honor. Do not lag in zeal, be ardent [strong] in spirit, serve the Lord. Rejoice in hope, be patient in suffering, persevere in prayer. Contribute to the needs of the saints; extend hospitality to strangers.

Bless those who persecute you; bless and do not curse them. Rejoice with those who rejoice, weep with those who weep. Live in harmony with one another; do not be haughty, but associate with the lowly; do not claim to be wiser than you are. Do not repay anyone evil for evil, but take thought for what is noble in the sight of all. If it is possible, so far as it depends on you, live peaceably with all."

—Romans 12:9–18 NRSV

Analyze Historical Sources
How did Paul's letter express Jesus' teachings?

Holy Spirit. But even though there are three persons, there is still only one God. Belief in the existence of only one god is known as **monotheism**. Monotheism is a central feature of Christianity.

Paul's teachings attracted both Jews and non-Jews to Christianity. He taught that Christians who were not Jewish didn't have to follow all the Jewish laws and customs. Although the two faiths had much in common, differences continued to develop between Christianity and Judaism.

Reading Check
Draw Conclusions
Why was Paul important to early Christianity?

Christianity Spreads Quickly in Rome

Early Christians like Paul wanted to share their message about Jesus with the world. Because of their efforts, Christianity spread quickly in many Roman communities. But as it grew more popular, Christianity began to concern some Roman leaders. They looked for ways to put an end to this new religion.

Early Growth The first Christians worked to spread Jesus' teachings only among Jews. But some early Christians, including Paul, wanted to introduce Christianity to non-Jews as well. As a result, Christianity began to spread in the Roman Empire. Historians estimate that within 100 years after Jesus' death, thousands of Christians lived in the Roman Empire.

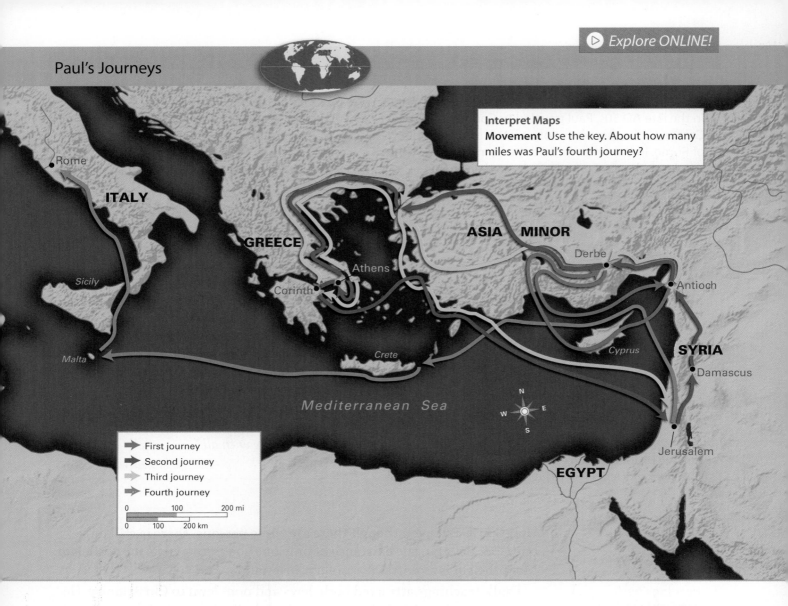

Explore ONLINE!

Interpret Maps
Movement Use the key. About how many miles was Paul's fourth journey?

First journey
Second journey
Third journey
Fourth journey

0   100   200 mi
0 100   200 km

ITALY
Rome
Sicily
Malta
GREECE
Athens
Corinth
Crete
Mediterranean Sea
ASIA MINOR
Derbe
Antioch
Cyprus
SYRIA
Damascus
Jerusalem
EGYPT

As Christianity spread, Christians began to write down parts of Jesus' message, including the Gospels. They distributed copies of the Gospels and other writings to strengthen people's faith. The written Gospels also helped to spread Christianity.

Persecution From time to time, Christians trying to spread their beliefs faced challenges from local officials. Some of these officials even arrested and killed Christians who refused to worship the Roman gods. We call such people who suffer death for their religious beliefs **martyrs** (MAHR-tuhrz). Many leaders of the early Christians—including Peter and Paul—were killed for spreading Christian teachings. Even today, Christians honor them as martyrs and saints.

Most of Rome's emperors let Christians worship as they pleased. A few emperors in the 200s and 300s, though, feared that the Christians could cause unrest in the empire. To prevent such unrest, these emperors banned Christianity. This ban led to several periods of persecution (puhr-si-KYOO-shuhn) against Christians. **Persecution** means punishing a group because of its beliefs or differences.

Timeline: Early Christianity

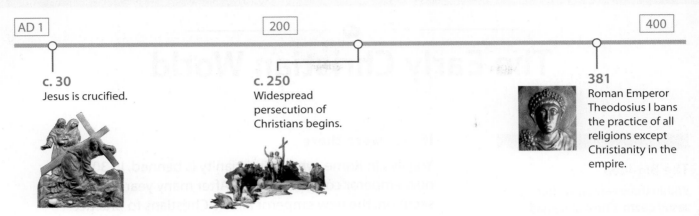

AD 1   200   400

c. 30
Jesus is crucified.

c. 250
Widespread persecution of Christians begins.

381
Roman Emperor Theodosius I bans the practice of all religions except Christianity in the empire.

Read Timelines
About how many years after Christianity began were other religions banned in Rome?

Reading Check
Analyze Causes
Why did the Romans begin persecuting Christians?

Because their religion had been banned, Christians were often forced to meet in secret. To arrange their meetings, they used secret symbols to identify people who shared their beliefs. One of the most common symbols they used was a fish. The fish became a Christian symbol because the Greek word for *fish* begins with the same letters as the Greek words for *Jesus* and *Christ*.

Summary and Preview Paul helped Christianity spread across the region. In the next lesson, you will read about how Christianity found greater acceptance in the Roman Empire.

Lesson 3 Assessment

Review Ideas, Terms, and People

1. **a. Summarize** How did Paul influence early Christianity?
   b. Describe How did Paul change the way people spread Christianity?
   c. Explain What is the Trinity?
2. **a. Elaborate** Why do you think martyrs are admired?
   b. Define What is persecution?
   c. Explain Why did the fish become a common Christian symbol?

Critical Thinking

3. **Analyze Causes** Draw a diagram like this one. In each box identify one cause of the early spread of Christianity.

Causes of Spread of Christianity

1.	2.	3.

The Early Christian World

The Big Idea

Within three centuries after Jesus' death, Christianity had spread through the empire and became Rome's official religion.

Main Ideas

- The pope influenced the growth of the early Christian Church.

- As the church grew, new leaders and ideas appeared, and Christianity's status in the empire changed.

Key Terms and People

bishops
Eucharist
pope
Augustine of Hippo
Constantine

If YOU were there . . .

You live in Rome, where Christianity is banned. In 306, a new emperor comes to power. After many years of persecution, the new emperor allows Christians to practice their religion freely.

How do you think people will react to this change?

The Church Grows

Because the early church largely had to meet in secret, it didn't have any single leader to govern it. Instead, **bishops**, or local Christian leaders, led each Christian community. Most bishops lived in cities. They helped people understand and live by Christian teachings.

One of the bishops' most important duties was leading Christians in celebrating the Eucharist (YOO-kuh-ruhst). The **Eucharist** was the central ceremony of the Christian Church. It was created to honor the last supper Jesus shared with his Apostles. During the Eucharist, Christians ate bread and drank wine in memory of Jesus' death.

By the late 100s Christians were looking to the bishops of large cities for guidance. These bishops had great influence, even over other bishops. The most honored of all the empire's bishops was the bishop of Rome, or the **pope**. The word *pope* comes from the Greek word for father. The pope was so honored in the Christian world largely because Peter, the leader of the Apostles and a key figure in the early church, had been the first bishop of Rome. Later popes were seen as his spiritual successors.

Gradually, the pope's influence grew, and many people in the West came to see him as the head of the whole Christian Church. The pope and the church offered spiritual guidance to many individuals. As the church grew, so did the influence and significance of the papacy, the office of the pope.

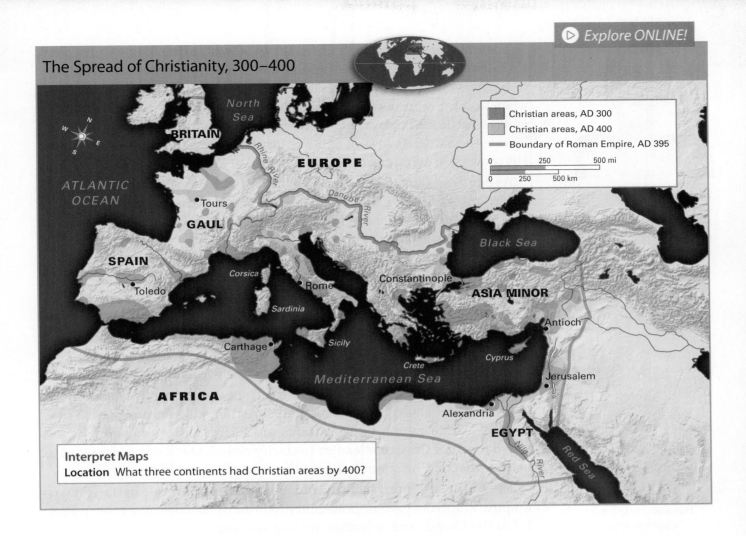

The Spread of Christianity, 300–400

Explore ONLINE!

Legend:
- Christian areas, AD 300
- Christian areas, AD 400
- Boundary of Roman Empire, AD 395

Interpret Maps
Location What three continents had Christian areas by 400?

Reading Check
Summarize Why was the pope a significant figure in the early church?

Academic Vocabulary
classical referring to the cultures of ancient Greece or Rome

In the following centuries, the Christian Church expanded to have a presence in what is now Spain, France, Italy, Greece, and Turkey. It also grew in northern Africa in what is now Tunisia. Christianity was also introduced in Ethiopia in east-central Africa in the 4th century. The Ethiopian Orthodox Church continues to influence Ethiopia's culture today.

New Teachings and Emperors

As Christianity spread through the Roman world, Christian writers read the works of **classical** philosophers. One such writer was **Augustine** (AW-guhs-teen) **of Hippo**. He lived in Hippo, a town in northern Africa, in the late 300s and early 400s. As a young man, Augustine studied the works of Plato. When he became a Christian, he applied Plato's ideas to Christian beliefs. Augustine taught that Christians should focus not on worldly goods but on God's plan for the world. His ideas helped shape Christian beliefs for hundreds of years.

At about the same time that Saint Augustine was writing, an event changed the standing of Christians in Rome. The emperor himself became a Christian.

Emperor Constantine converted to Christianity. Under his rule, Roman persecution of Christians ended.

The emperor who became a Christian was **Constantine** (KAHN-stuhn-teen). He came to power in 306 after fighting and defeating many rivals. According to legend, Constantine was preparing for battle against one of these rivals when he saw a cross in the sky. He thought that this vision meant he would win the battle if he converted to Christianity. Constantine did convert, and he won the battle. As a result of his victory he became the emperor of Rome. His conversion encouraged others to convert to Christianity as well.

As emperor, Constantine removed bans against the practice of Christianity. He also called together a council of Christian leaders from around the empire to clarify Christian teaching. Under Constantine, a close relationship existed between the church and the government. For example, the emperor appointed bishops himself and regularly met with councils of bishops to discuss matters of Christian faith.

After he converted to Christianity, Constantine came to believe that he had been successful all his life because he had God's favor. He built several great churches in the empire, including one in Jerusalem at the spot where Jesus was believed to have been buried. Throughout history Christians have considered him one of Rome's greatest emperors.

Almost 60 years after Constantine died, another emperor, Theodosius I (thee-uh-DOH-shuhs), banned all non-Christian religious practices in the Empire. Like Constantine, Theodosius was a Christian. As emperor, he called together Christian leaders to clarify church teachings. He wanted to be sure that all Christians believed the same things he did.

The Christian Church continued to play a significant role in the Roman Empire. Emperors gave responsibility to bishops, who became more powerful in the Church and in Roman society as a whole.

Reading Check
Summarize How did Constantine and Theodosius help the church develop?

Summary By the late 300s, Christianity had become one of the most influential forces in the Roman world. Its influence provided security and stability for many people throughout the Roman Empire.

Lesson 4 Assessment

Review Ideas, Terms, and People

1. **a. Define** What was the Eucharist?

   b. Explain What was the relationship between the Apostle Peter and the popes who led the Christian Church?

   c. Explain Why did the pope have influence over many other bishops?

2. **a. Identify** Who was Rome's first Christian emperor?

   b. Explain What evidence from the lesson shows that the Christian Church was a significant part of the Roman Empire?

   c. Contrast How did Constantine's policies toward Christianity differ from Theodosius's?

Critical Thinking

3. **Sequence** Draw a diagram like this one. In each box identify one step in the relationship between Christianity and the Roman Empire.

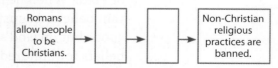

Romans allow people to be Christians. → ☐ → ☐ → Non-Christian religious practices are banned.

Social Studies Skills

Continuity and Change in History

Define the Skill

A well-known saying claims that "the more things change, the more they stay the same." Nowhere does this observation apply more than to the study of history. Any look back over the past will show many changes—nations expanding or shrinking, empires rising and falling, changes in leadership, and people on the move, to name just a few.

The reasons for change have not changed, however. The same general forces have driven the actions of people and nations across time. These forces are the "threads" that run through history and give it continuity, or connectedness. They are the "sameness" in a world of constant change.

Learn the Skill

You can find the causes of all events of the past in one or more of these major forces or themes that run throughout history.

1. **Cooperation and Conflict:** Throughout time, people and groups have worked together to achieve goals. They have also opposed others who stood in the way of their goals.

2. **Cultural Invention and Interaction:** The values and ideas expressed in peoples' art, literature, customs, and religion have enriched the world. But the spread of cultures and their contact with other cultures has also sometimes produced conflict.

3. **Geography and Environment:** Physical environment and natural resources have shaped how people live. Efforts to gain or protect land and resources have been a major cause of cooperation and conflict in history.

4. **Science and Technology:** Technology, or the development and use of tools, has helped people make better use of their environment. Science has also changed people's lives.

5. **Economic Opportunity:** From hunting and gathering to farming, manufacturing, and trade, people have tried to make the most of their resources. Hope for a better life is a main reason people have moved from one place to another.

6. **The Impact of Individuals:** Political, religious, military, business, and other leaders have been a major influence in history. The actions of many ordinary people have also shaped history.

7. **Nationalism and Imperialism:** Nationalism is the desire of a people to have their own country. Imperialism is the wish to control other peoples. Both have existed through history.

8. **Political and Social Systems:** People have always been part of groups—families, villages, nations, or religious groups, for example. The groups to which people belong affect how they relate to people around them. History is mostly the study of past interactions of people.

Practice the Skill

Check your understanding of the sources of continuity and change in history by answering the following questions.

1. How did relations between the Romans and the Jews show cultural interaction and conflict in history?

2. What are three forces of history that are illustrated by the rise and spread of Christianity?

Module 11 Assessment

Review Vocabulary, Terms, and People

Match the "I" statement with the person or thing that might have made the statement.

1. "I helped spread Christian teachings through the Mediterranean world through my journeys and letters."
2. "I died for my religious beliefs."
3. "My teachings became the foundations for Christianity."
4. "I was the first Christian emperor of Rome."
5. "I was a Christian writer who combined Plato's ideas with Christian teachings."
6. "I am an idea or goal that people try to live up to."
7. "I am the holy book of Christianity."
8. "I was the bishop of Rome who became the head of the Christian Church."
9. "I was a promised leader who was to appear among the Jews."
10. "I was one of Jesus' 12 chosen followers."

a. Messiah
b. Constantine
c. Apostle
d. Jesus of Nazareth
e. Bible
f. martyr
g. pope
h. Paul
i. Augustine of Hippo
j. ideal

Comprehension and Critical Thinking

Lesson 1

11. a. **Identify** Who were Jesus of Nazareth and John the Baptist?
    b. **Contrast** How did the Romans' attitude toward religion differ from the Jews' attitude?
    c. **Evaluate** Why might an historian say that one ancient religion, Judaism, set the scene for a new religion, Christianity?

Lesson 2

12. a. **Describe** According to the Bible, what were the crucifixion and the Resurrection? What do Christians believe the Resurrection means?
    b. **Analyze** Why do you think Jesus' teachings appealed to many people within the Roman Empire?

Lesson 3

13. a. **Evaluate** Why is Paul considered one of the most important people in the history of Christianity?
    b. **Predict** Why do you think Christianity spread despite the fact that early Christians were often persecuted?

Lesson 4

14. a. **Describe** What was the connection between the Apostle Peter and the papacy?
    b. **Compare and Contrast** What did the Roman emperors Constantine and Theodosius I have in common? How did their actions differ?

Review Themes

15. **Society and Culture** How did early Christian leaders such as Paul help separate Christianity from Judaism?

16. **Religion** How do you think the early Christian Church would have been different if Paul had not converted to Christianity?

Reading Skills

Ask Questions *Read the following passage and answer the questions that follow.*

The emperor who became a Christian was Constantine. He came to power in 306 after fighting and defeating many rivals. According to legend, Constantine was preparing for battle against one of these rivals when he saw a cross in the sky. He thought that this vision meant he would win the battle if he converted to Christianity. Constantine did convert, and he won the battle. As a result of his victory he became the emperor of Rome. His conversion encouraged others to convert to Christianity as well.

17. Who is this passage about?

18. When did he live?

19. What action did he take and what was the impact of that action?

Social Studies Skills

Understand Historical Continuity *Use the Social Studies Skills taught in this module to answer the question below.*

20. Christianity has been one of the forces that has most influenced the course of world history. Why has its influence been so great? Choose one of the following factors that help promote historical continuity. Then write a sentence explaining how that factor is related to Christianity's influence.

Cooperation and conflict	Economic opportunity
Cultural interaction	Impact of individuals
Geography and environment	Nationalism and imperialism
Science and technology	Political and social systems

Focus On Writing

21. **Write a Magazine Article** You're a writer who has been assigned to write a short magazine article about religion and early Christianity in the Roman Empire. Organize your ideas into several main ideas and supporting details about each one that you can use to write your two- to three-paragraph article. Write it in chronological order, and include a catchy title that describes the article. You might begin the article with a question or an intriguing fact to get your audience's attention.

Module 12
Civilizations of Eastern Europe

Essential Question
How might trade have changed the way eastern European society developed?

About the Photo: Geography, trade, and religious ties connected the civilizations of the Byzantine Empire and early Russia. Hagia Sophia, shown here, was one of the Byzantine Empire's most important churches.

▶ *Explore ONLINE!*

VIDEOS, including...
- Hagia Sophia
- Taming the Horse

☑ Document-Based Investigations

☑ Graphic Organizers

☑ Interactive Games

☑ Interactive Map: Early Russia, 860 – 1240

☑ Image with Hotspots: View of Constantinople

☑ Image Carousel: Russian Religious Architecture

In this module, you will learn about the development of the Byzantine Empire and Russia in eastern Europe.

What You Will Learn...

Lesson 1: The Geography of Eastern Europe 410
The Big Idea The geography of eastern Europe heavily impacted the history of the region's people.

Lesson 2: The Byzantine Empire. 415
The Big Idea The eastern Roman Empire prospered for hundreds of years after the western empire fell.

Lesson 3: Early Russia 420
The Big Idea Early Russia was influenced by different cultures and experienced frequent changes in government.

Timeline of Events 300–1480

Module Events		World Events

300

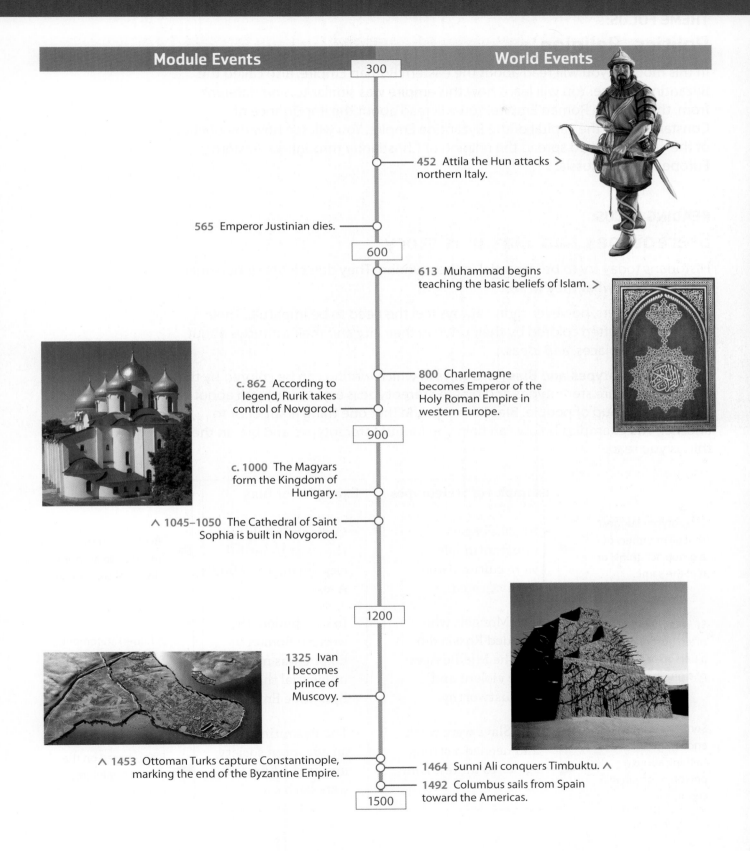

452 Attila the Hun attacks northern Italy. >

565 Emperor Justinian dies.

600

613 Muhammad begins teaching the basic beliefs of Islam. >

c. 862 According to legend, Rurik takes control of Novgorod.

800 Charlemagne becomes Emperor of the Holy Roman Empire in western Europe.

900

c. 1000 The Magyars form the Kingdom of Hungary.

∧ 1045–1050 The Cathedral of Saint Sophia is built in Novgorod.

1200

1325 Ivan I becomes prince of Muscovy.

∧ 1453 Ottoman Turks capture Constantinople, marking the end of the Byzantine Empire.

1464 Sunni Ali conquers Timbuktu. ∧

1492 Columbus sails from Spain toward the Americas.

1500

Reading Social Studies

Politics, Religion

In this module, you will read about the eastern Roman Empire, also called the Byzantine Empire. You will learn how this empire was similar to, and different from, the western Roman Empire. You will read about the importance of Constantinople, the capital of the Byzantine Empire. You will see how the politics of the empire helped spread the religion of Christianity throughout eastern Europe and into Russia.

READING FOCUS:

Stereotypes and Bias in History

Historians today try to be impartial in their writing. They don't let their personal feelings affect what they write.

Byzantine writers, however, didn't always feel the need to be impartial. Their writings were often colored by their pride in their city and their attitudes about other people, places, and ideas.

Identify Stereotypes and Bias Two ways in which writing can be colored by the author's ideas are stereotypes and bias. A **stereotype** is a generalization about a person or group of people. **Bias** is an attitude that one thing is superior to another. The examples below can help you identify stereotypes and bias in the things you read.

	Examples of Stereotypes	**Examples of Bias**	
Stereotypes suggest that all members of a group act, think, or feel the same.	• All citizens of Constantinople were cultured and sophisticated.	• Constantinople was the most beautiful city during the Middle Ages.	Bias is often the result of an author's dislike of something.
Stereotypes can often hurt or offend a person or members of a group.	• The Mongols who invaded Russia during the Middle Ages were violent and untrustworthy.	• In my opinion, the western Roman Empire was more influential than the Byzantine Empire.	A biased statement obviously favors one thing or person over another.
Some stereotypes encourage the reader to think about a person or group in a certain way.	• The Slavs were weak and needed a strong leader to unite them.	• The Byzantines had an advanced society, unlike the Rus, who were barbaric.	Bias is based on the author's opinions, not facts.

You Try It!

Read the following passage and then answer the questions below.

Justinian and Public Funds "As soon as he found himself the head of his uncle's empire, he at once did his utmost to squander [waste] the public treasure over which he now had control. For he lavished [heaped] wealth extravagantly [wastefully] upon the Huns whom from time to time came across and . . . ever afterwards, the Roman provinces were subject to constant incursions [invasions]; for these barbarians, having once tasted our wealth, could not tear themselves away. . . ."

–Procopius, from *The Secret History of the Court of Justinian*

Answer these questions about the passage you just read.

1. What word in the passage shows the author's bias toward his fellow citizens?
2. What stereotypes about the Huns does the author express? Are these stereotypes positive or negative?
3. Is the author biased toward or against Justinian? Explain.

As you read this module, look for other examples of bias or stereotypes toward or against people and places.

Key Terms and People

Lesson 1
Ural Mountains
Carpathians
Balkan Peninsula
Danube
Volga
taiga
Rus
Lesson 2
Justinian
Theodora
Byzantine Empire
mosaics
Lesson 3
Ivan III
czar
principalities
icons

The Geography of Eastern Europe

The Big Idea

The geography of eastern Europe heavily impacted the history of the region's people.

Main Ideas

- The physical geography of eastern Europe varies widely from place to place.

- The climate and vegetation of eastern Europe also vary greatly from place to place.

- The early history of eastern Europe was shaped by the movement of different groups of people into the region from other areas.

Key Terms and People

Ural Mountains
Carpathians
Balkan Peninsula
Danube
Volga
taiga
Rus

If YOU were there . . .

You are traveling on a boat down the Danube River, one of the longest rivers in Europe. As you float downstream, you pass through dozens of towns and cities. Outside the cities, the banks are lined with huge castles, soaring churches, and busy farms. From time to time, other boats pass you, some loaded with passengers and some with goods.

Why do you think the Danube is so busy?

Physical Features

Geographers and historians sometimes differ over the boundaries of what we call *eastern Europe*. As a political term, *Eastern Europe* often refers to the countries that were controlled by the Soviet Union after World War II, until the Soviet Union broke apart. Geographically speaking, however, there are few defining landforms creating a solid boundary between Europe and Asia. Most modern geographers set the boundary between Asia and eastern Europe at the **Ural Mountains**, in western Russia.

The Carpathian Mountains run through the center of eastern Europe.

Eastern Europe is a land of amazing contrasts. The northern parts of the region lie along the cold Baltic and Barents seas. In the south, however, are warm, sunny beaches along the Adriatic and Black seas. Jagged mountain peaks jut high into the sky in some places, while wildflowers dot the gently rolling hills of other parts of the region. These contrasts stem from the region's wide variety of landforms, water features, and climates.

Landforms The landforms of eastern Europe are arranged in a series of broad bands. In the north is the Northern European Plain. This large plain stretches across most of northern Europe. It then rises to form the Ural Mountains in the east. These low mountains are worn down and rounded from erosion.

South of the Northern European Plain is a low mountain range called the **Carpathians** (kahr-PAY-thee-uhnz). These rugged mountains are an extension of the Alps of west-central Europe. They stretch in a long arc

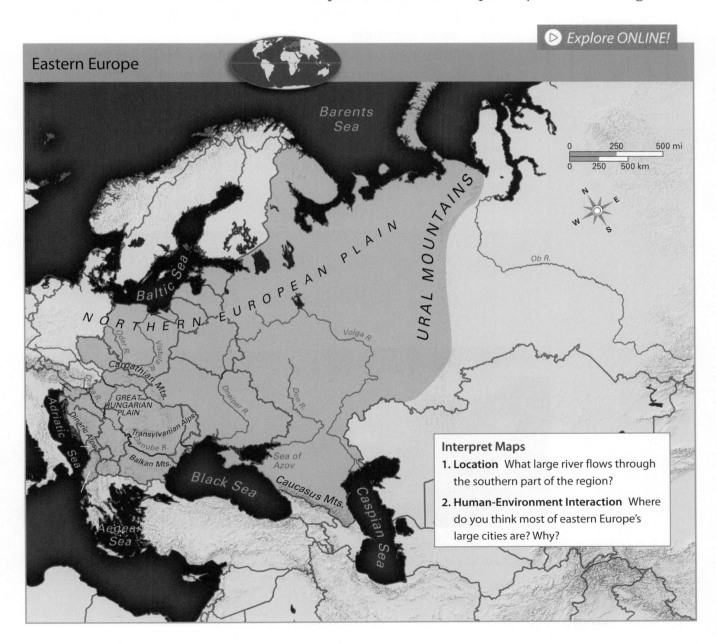

Eastern Europe

Explore ONLINE!

Barents Sea

URAL MOUNTAINS

Ob R.

Baltic Sea

NORTHERN EUROPEAN PLAIN

Oder R.

Vistula R.

Volga R.

Carpathian Mts.

Drava R.

Dnieper R.

Don R.

GREAT HUNGARIAN PLAIN

Transylvanian Alps

Dinaric Alps

Danube R.

Balkan Mts.

Adriatic Sea

Sea of Azov

Black Sea

Caucasus Mts.

Caspian Sea

Aegean Sea

0   250   500 mi
0   250   500 km

Interpret Maps

1. **Location** What large river flows through the southern part of the region?

2. **Human-Environment Interaction** Where do you think most of eastern Europe's large cities are? Why?

from the Alps to the Black Sea. East of the Black Sea lie the Caucasus (KAW-kuh-suhs) Mountains and the Caspian Sea. The Caspian Sea is the largest inland sea in the world.

South and west of the Carpathians is another plain, the Great Hungarian Plain. As its name suggests, this fertile area is located mostly within Hungary.

South of the plains are more mountains, the Dinaric (duh-NAR-ik) Alps and the Balkan Mountains. These two ranges together cover most of the **Balkan Peninsula**, one of the largest peninsulas in Europe. The Balkan Peninsula extends south into the Mediterranean Sea.

Water Features Like the rest of the continent, eastern Europe has many bodies of water that affect how people live. To the southwest is the Adriatic Sea, an important route for transportation and trade. To the east, the Black Sea and the Caspian Sea serve the same functions. In the far north is the Baltic Sea. It is another important trade route, though parts of the sea freeze over in the winter.

In addition to these seas, eastern Europe has several rivers that are vital paths for transportation and trade. The **Danube** (DAN-yoob) begins in Germany and flows east across the Great Hungarian Plain. The river winds its way through nine countries before it finally empties into the Black Sea. The longest river in Europe, the **Volga**, flows south through western Russia to the Caspian Sea. The Volga has long formed the core of Russia's river network. Canals now link the Volga to the nearby Don River and to the Baltic Sea.

Reading Check
Draw Conclusions
What two types of physical features might have affected transportation in eastern Europe?

Many rivers flow across the plains of eastern Europe. The Vistula, shown here, is one of them.

Climate and Vegetation

Like its landforms, the climates and vegetation of eastern Europe vary widely. The climates and landforms affect which plants will grow there.

Mount Kazbek is part of the Caucasus mountain range. As this photograph shows, climate in this range varies due to elevation.

Winters along the Baltic Sea are long, cold, and harsh. This northern part of eastern Europe receives less rain than other areas, but fog is common. In fact, parts of the area have as few as 30 sunny days each year. The climate encourages the growth of huge forests.

The interior plains of eastern Europe are much milder than the far north. Winters there can be very cold, but summers are generally pleasant and mild. The western parts of the plains receive much more rain than those areas farther east.

Because of this variation in climate, the plains of eastern Europe have many types of vegetation. Huge forests cover much of the north. South of these forests are open, grassy plains. In the spring, these plains are covered with colorful wildflowers.

European Russia's northern coast is a type of region called the tundra. Winters are dark and bitterly cold, and the brief summers are cool. Much of the ground is permafrost, or permanently frozen soil. Only small plants such as mosses grow. South of the tundra is a vast forest of evergreen trees called the **taiga** (TY-guh). This huge forest covers about half of Russia. South of the taiga is a flat grassland called the steppe (STEP). With rich, black soil and a warmer climate, the steppe is Russia's most important farming area. Farther south, the climate is warm and wet along the Black Sea.

Along the Adriatic Sea, the Balkan coast has a Mediterranean climate, with warm summers and mild winters. Because a Mediterranean climate does not bring much rain, the Balkan coast does not have many forests. Instead, the land there is covered by shrubs and hardy trees that do not need much water.

Reading Check
Summarize
Which regions of Russia have the mildest climates?

Eastern European Peoples

Throughout history, many different peoples ruled in eastern Europe. Each group influenced the culture and customs of the region. Trade patterns also influenced the history of eastern Europe.

The Balts The area around the Baltic Sea was settled in ancient times by many different groups. One of these groups, called the Balts, farmed the land and raised cattle. The Balts also used amber found in the area to barter for other goods. Amber is a fossilized substance from ancient plants and trees that can be used for jewelry. During the Middle Ages, some Balts were conquered by people from Germany. Other Balts were assimilated by a group of people called the Slavs. To *assimilate* means to become part of another group or culture.

The Slavs The Slavs settled in eastern Europe. Part of the lands they settled included what is now Ukraine, Slovakia, the Czech (CHEK) Republic, and western Russia. The Slavs developed towns and began trading with people from other areas. Eventually, the Slavs founded small kingdoms. As time went on and kingdoms grew larger, Slav society began to separate into different classes.

The Rus One group the Slavs most likely traded with was the **Rus** (ROOS). According to legend, the Rus were Vikings from Scandinavia. The word *Russia* probably comes from their name. In the mid-800s, a Rus leader named Rurik was invited to become the ruler of the Slavs. The Slavs had been fighting among themselves and hoped a new ruler could bring order. Rurik put an end to their fighting and took over the city now known as Novgorod, in present-day Russia, to serve as his capital. The Rus shaped the first Russian state among the Slavs.

The Magyars In the 900s, a fierce group called the Magyars swept into what is now Hungary. Some historians think that the Magyars were originally from the Ural Mountains. Around AD 1000, the Magyars formed the Kingdom of Hungary. Although they were later conquered by other countries, the Magyars continued to shape Hungarian culture. The Hungarian language is based on the language spoken by the Magyars. In fact, people in Hungary today still refer to themselves as Magyars.

The Greeks and Romans By the 600s BC, the ancient Greeks had founded colonies on the northern coast of the Black Sea. The area they settled is now part of Bulgaria and Romania. Later, the Romans conquered most of the area from the Adriatic Sea to the Danube River. When the Roman Empire divided into west and east in the late AD 300s, the Balkan Peninsula became part of the eastern empire.

Reading Check
Analyze Effects
How did the Slavs influence the region's history?

Summary and Preview The landforms of eastern Europe vary widely, as did the groups of people who lived there in the region's early history. In the next lesson, you will read about the growth of the Byzantine Empire in eastern Europe.

Lesson 1 Assessment

Review Ideas, Terms, and People

1. a. **Identify** What are the major mountain ranges of eastern Europe?

   b. **Describe** Why is the Volga River significant?

2. a. **Explain** Why are there few trees along the coast of the Balkan Peninsula?

   b. **Identify** Why is the steppe Russia's most important farming area?

3. a. **Define** Who were the Rus?

   b. **Identify** What group continues to shape the development of Hungarian culture?

Critical Thinking

4. **Form Generalizations** Draw a chart like the one here. Enter two general ideas for each topic in the chart.

Eastern Europe

Geography	
People	

The Byzantine Empire

The Big Idea

The eastern Roman Empire prospered for hundreds of years after the western empire fell.

Main Ideas

- Eastern emperors ruled from Constantinople and tried but failed to reunite the whole Roman Empire.

- The people of the eastern empire created a new society that was very different from society in the west.

- Byzantine Christianity was different from Christianity in the west.

Key Terms and People

Justinian
Theodora
Byzantine Empire
mosaics

If YOU were there . . .

You are a trader visiting Constantinople. You have traveled to many cities but have never seen anything so magnificent. The city has huge palaces and stadiums for horse races. In the city center, you enter a church and stop, speechless with amazement. Above you is a vast, gold dome lit by hundreds of candles.

How does the city make you feel about its rulers?

Emperors Rule from Constantinople

In the late 200s, the emperor Diocletian divided the Roman Empire into two parts—east and west—hoping to make the empire easier to rule. In spite of his efforts, years of invasions and economic instability eventually led to the fall of the western Roman Empire, in 476.

Even before the fall of Rome, power had begun to shift to the richer, more stable east. The people of the eastern Roman Empire considered themselves Romans, but their culture was very different from that of Rome itself.

The center of the eastern Roman Empire was the city of Constantinople. Constantinople was built on the site of an old Greek trading city called Byzantium (buh-ZAN-tee-uhm).

Constantinople was strategically located where Europe and Asia meet. As a result, the city was in a perfect location to control trade routes between the two continents.

City walls

Harbor

Forum

Hippodrome

Hagia Sophia

Imperial Palace

It lay on a peninsula near both the Black Sea and the Mediterranean Sea. Constantinople was a magnificent city filled with great buildings, palaces, and churches.

Constantinople was located in an ideal place to grow in wealth and power. First of all, the two seas protected the city from attack. The city also had a deep, natural harbor. This allowed large boats to enter the city and drop off or pick up goods and people. Finally, the city was located along major trade routes. One of these, known as the Silk Road, stretched from the Mediterranean to China. Being located on the Silk Road allowed the city to control trade between Europe and Asia.

Justinian After Rome fell in AD 476, the emperors of the eastern Roman Empire dreamed of taking it back and reuniting the old Roman Empire. For **Justinian** (juh-STIN-ee-uhn), an emperor who ruled from AD 527 to 565, reuniting the empire was a passion. He couldn't live with a Roman Empire that didn't include the city of Rome, so he sent his army to retake Italy. In the end this army conquered not only Italy but also a great deal of land around the Mediterranean. Retaking the land was expensive, however. Also, many areas of Italy were unable to pay the taxes required by Justinian's government. In the quote below, Byzantine historian Procopius takes note of how Justinian spent the money he collected. Procopius also indicates that invaders from outside the empire were a constant threat.

> "As soon as [Justinian] took over the rule from his uncle, his first measure was to spend the public money without restraint, now that he had control of it. He gave much of it to the Huns who, from time to time, entered the state; and in consequence the Roman provinces were subject to constant incursions [invasions], for these barbarians, having once tasted Roman wealth, never forgot the road that led to it."
>
> –Procopius, from the *Secret History of Procopius*, translated by Richard Atwater

In addition to reuniting the empire, Justinian's other passions were the law and the church. He ordered officials to examine all of Rome's laws and remove any out-of-date or unchristian laws. He then organized all the laws into a system called Justinian's Code. By simplifying Roman law, this code helped guarantee fair treatment for all.

Despite his achievements, Justinian made many enemies. Two groups of these enemies joined forces and tried to overthrow him in AD 532. These groups led riots in the streets and set fire to buildings. Fearing for his life, Justinian prepared to leave Constantinople.

Justinian and Theodora

Justinian was stopped from leaving by his wife, **Theodora** (thee-uh-DOHR-uh). She convinced Justinian to stay in the city. Smart and powerful, Theodora helped her husband rule effectively. With her advice, he found a way to end the riots. Justinian's soldiers killed all the rioters—some 30,000 people—and saved the emperor's throne.

The Empire After Justinian After the death of Justinian in AD 565, the eastern empire began to decline. Faced with invasions by barbarians, Persians, and Muslims, later emperors lost all the land Justinian had gained. The eastern empire remained a major power for several hundred years, but it never regained its former strength.

In the end, the strategic location and economic importance of Constantinople led to conflict with a group called the Ottoman Turks. In 1453, nearly 900 years after the death of Justinian, the Ottoman Turks captured Constantinople. With this defeat, the 1,000-year history of the eastern Roman Empire came to an end.

A New Society

In many ways Justinian was the last Roman emperor of the eastern empire. After he died, non-Roman influences took hold throughout the empire. People began to speak Greek, the language of the eastern empire, rather than Latin. Scholars studied Greek, not Roman, philosophy. Gradually, the empire lost its ties to the old Roman Empire, and a new society developed.

The people who lived in this society never stopped thinking of themselves as Romans. But modern historians have given their society a new name. They call the society that developed in the east after the west fell the **Byzantine** (BI-zuhn-teen) **Empire**, after the Greek town of Byzantium.

Reading Check
Draw Conclusions
Why did Justinian reorganize Roman law?

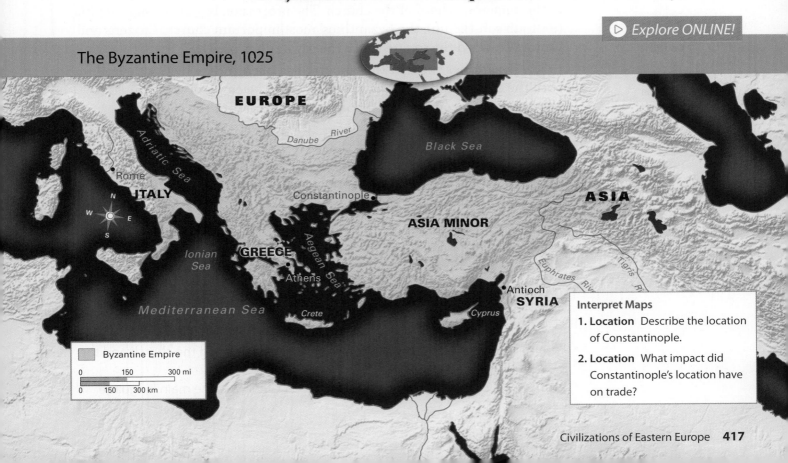

▶ Explore ONLINE!

The Byzantine Empire, 1025

EUROPE
Adriatic Sea
Danube River
Black Sea
Rome
ITALY
Constantinople
ASIA
ASIA MINOR
Ionian Sea
GREECE
Aegean Sea
Euphrates River
Tigris River
Athens
Antioch
Mediterranean Sea
SYRIA
Crete
Cyprus

Byzantine Empire
0   150   300 mi
0   150   300 km

Interpret Maps

1. **Location** Describe the location of Constantinople.

2. **Location** What impact did Constantinople's location have on trade?

The Church of St. Jason and St. Sosipater on the island of Corfu, Greece, is one of the earliest examples of the Byzantine domed church.

Outside Influence One way eastern and western Roman society differed was the Byzantines' interaction with other groups. This interaction was largely a result of trade. Because Constantinople was located along trade routes that connected Europe and Asia, it became the greatest trading city in Europe.

Merchants from all around Europe, Asia, and Africa traveled to Constantinople to trade. Not only did the Byzantine Empire grow as a commercial center, but it also grew as a unique cultural center. While the Byzantine Empire preserved some Greek and Roman learning and traditions, its society began to reflect outside influences, such as Arab and Persian elements. For example, Byzantine architecture incorporated Persian styles of decoration, and Byzantine art incorporated Arab patterns. Byzantine architecture and art went on to influence culture throughout eastern Europe.

Government During the early period of the Byzantine Empire, Greek and Roman systems of government were preserved and followed. Over time, a different form of government developed. Byzantine emperors had more power than western emperors did, and they liked to show it off. For example, people could not stand while they were in the presence of the eastern emperor. They had to crawl on their hands and knees to talk to him.

The power of an eastern emperor was greater, in part, because the emperor was considered the head of the church as well as the political ruler. In Constantinople, rulers led processions, or ceremonial walks, to show their wealth and power. The processions showed the power and importance of the emperor as head of the church. The procession began at Hagia Sophia (HAH-juh soh-FEE-uh), the Byzantines' most important church. Citizens and visitors crowded the square to see the royal rulers pass by.

The Byzantines thought the emperor had been chosen by God to lead both the empire and the church. In the west, the emperor was limited to political power. Popes and bishops were the leaders of the church.

Byzantine Christianity

Just as it was to the Romans in the west, Christianity was central to the Byzantines' lives. From the beginning, nearly everyone who lived in the Byzantine Empire was Christian.

Reading Check
Contrast
What were two ways in which eastern and western Roman society differed?

Quick Facts

The Western Roman and Byzantine Empires

In the Western Roman Empire . . .	In the Byzantine Empire . . .
• Popes and bishops led the church, and the emperor led the government.	• Emperors led the church and the government.
• Latin was the main language.	• Greek was the main language.

To show their devotion to God and the Christian Church, Byzantine artists created beautiful works of religious art. Among the grandest works were **mosaics**, pictures made with pieces of colored stone or glass. Some mosaics sparkled with gold, silver, and jewels.

Even more magnificent than the mosaics were Byzantine churches, especially Hagia Sophia. Built during Justinian's rule in the AD 530s, its huge domes rose high above Constantinople. According to legend, when Justinian saw the church he exclaimed in delight:

> "Glory to God, who has judged me worthy to complete this work! Solomon, I have surpassed thee!"
>
> –Justinian, from *The Story of the Building of the Church of Santa Sophia*

As time passed, people in the east and west began to interpret and practice some elements of Christianity differently. For example, eastern priests could get married, while priests in the west could not. Religious services were performed in Greek in the east. In the west they were held in Latin.

For hundreds of years, church leaders from the east and west worked together peacefully despite their differences. However, the differences between their ideas continued to grow. In time the differences led to divisions within the Christian Church. In the 1000s the split between east and west became official. Eastern Christians formed what became known as the Eastern Orthodox Church. As a result, eastern and western Europe were divided by religion.

Reading Check
Summarize
What led to a split in the Christian Church?

Summary and Preview The Roman Empire and the Christian Church each divided into two parts. As the Byzantine Empire grew, another empire began to develop in eastern Europe. You will read about the beginning of this empire—Russia—in the next lesson.

Lesson 2 Assessment

Review Ideas, Terms, and People

1. a. Describe Where was Constantinople located?

b. Summarize What were two of Justinian's major accomplishments?

c. Elaborate What do you think Theodora's role in the government says about women in the eastern empire?

2. a. Identify What was one major difference between the powers of emperors in the east and the west?

b. Explain How did contact with other cultures help change the Byzantine Empire?

3. a. Define What is a mosaic?

b. Form Generalizations What led to the creation of two different Christian societies in Europe?

Critical Thinking

4. Compare and Contrast Draw a Venn diagram like this one. In the left oval, describe the western Roman Empire. In the right oval, describe the eastern empire. Where the ovals overlap, list features the two had in common.

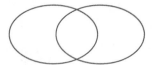

Early Russia

The Big Idea

Early Russia was influenced by different cultures and experienced frequent changes in government.

Main Ideas

- Russia was invaded by Mongol armies and later freed by Prince Ivan III.
- Trade played an important part in Russian daily life.
- Orthodox Christianity greatly influenced Russian culture.

Key Terms and People

Ivan III
czar
principalities
icons

If YOU were there . . .

You live in a small village in the Russian state of Muscovy. You hear from other villagers that the Mongol army has left Russia for Asia. Some people believe that your ruler, Prince Ivan III, will now try to unite the rest of the Russian states and form one kingdom.

Do you think it will be easy or difficult to unite the various Russian states?

Early Russian History

About the same time as Christianity began spreading throughout eastern Europe, a new power was forming there. A people called the Rus established the kingdom that would eventually be known as Russia.

As you read in Lesson 1, the Rus were Vikings, led by a man named Rurik. In the mid-800s, Rurik was invited to become the ruler of the Slavs in eastern Europe. He then took over the city now known as Novgorod to serve as his capital. After his death, his successor moved the capital south to Kiev (KEE-ehf). Kiev was closer than Novgorod to Constantinople. It was located along the Dnieper River, part of a trade route from Scandinavia to the Byzantine Empire.

Under the Rus, Kiev became the heart of a powerful state. Traders from Kiev traveled far and wide. The Kievan Rus formed alliances with many kingdoms, including the Byzantine Empire and several western European nations.

The greatest of the Kievan rulers was Yaroslav the Wise, who ruled from 1019 to 1054. As ruler, he created a new legal system for his kingdom. He built Kiev's first library and many churches. He also strengthened Russia's alliances and regained some land that previous rulers had lost in wars.

After Yaroslav's death, Kiev broke apart into many smaller states, which often fought among themselves. Then, in the mid-1200s, fierce nomads from Central Asia invaded Russia. They were the Mongols. Mongol armies destroyed Kiev in 1240. In 1243 a writer described the Mongols' nature:

"They use to fight constantly and valiantly [bravely] with javelins [spears], maces [clubs], battle-axes, and swords. But specially they are excellent archers . . . Vanquished [defeated], they ask no favor, and vanquishing, they shew [show] no compassion. . . . And suddenly diffusing [spreading] themselves over a whole province, and surprising all the people thereof unarmed, . . . they make such horrible slaughters, that the king or prince of the land invaded cannot finde [find] people sufficient enough to wage battle against them, . . ."

—quoted in *The Principal Navigations Voyages Traffiques & Discoveries of the English Nation* by Richard Hakluyt

For 200 years, Russia remained under Mongol rule. In the end, the effort to free Russia from the Mongols began not in Kiev but in Muscovy, which we now call Moscow. Like Kiev, Muscovy was the heart of a small but powerful trading state. In the 1320s, a prince of Muscovy named Ivan I began to strengthen his rule. Ivan actually worked with the Mongols to prevent rebellions. As a result, he was given additional power and the title Grand Prince. Ivan and his descendants slowly and carefully worked to increase that power even more.

Finally, in 1480, Prince **Ivan III** of Muscovy broke away from the Mongol Empire. Ivan took the title **czar** (ZAHR), which later became the title of Russian emperors. When he refused to pay taxes to the Mongols, they sent

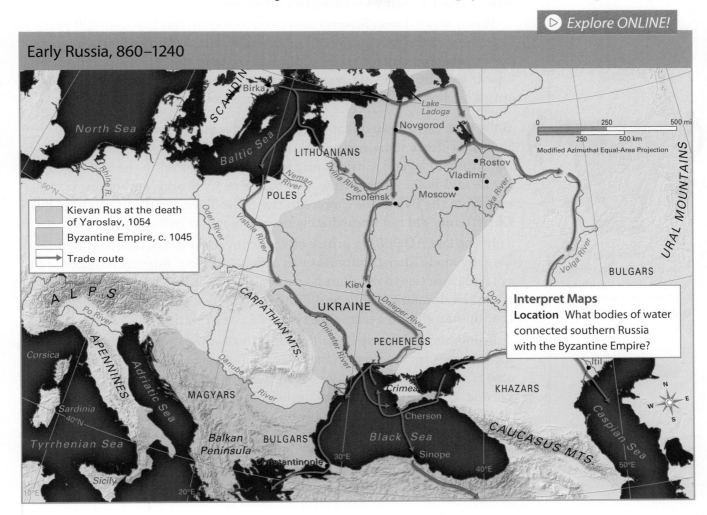

▶ Explore ONLINE!

Early Russia, 860–1240

Kievan Rus at the death of Yaroslav, 1054

Byzantine Empire, c. 1045

Trade route

Modified Azimuthal Equal-Area Projection

Interpret Maps
Location What bodies of water connected southern Russia with the Byzantine Empire?

Reading Check
Summarize
What ended Mongol
rule in Russia?

an army to force him to pay. However, Ivan would not back down. He led his own army to face the Mongols, but little fighting actually occurred. After a two-month standoff, the Mongols pulled back to Central Asia. Russia was free once again.

Russian Society and Daily Life

Early Russian culture developed from a blend of Slavic, Viking, and other cultures. By the AD 900s, Christianity was one of the most influential elements in shaping life in Russia.

Government During its early history, Russia experienced several changes in government. In the Kievan period, Russia was a cluster of **principalities**—small states ruled by princes. As grand princes, Kiev's rulers held great power, as much as any other European king of the period.

Under the Mongols, Russian princes remained in power. However, they had to swear allegiance to the Mongols. Princes also had to collect taxes for the Mongols and end any rebellions that began in their territories. For the most part, princes worked peacefully with the Mongols. Their cooperation was largely the result of the efforts of a prince from Novgorod named Alexander Nevsky. Alexander persuaded his fellow princes to work with the Mongols. Other princes listened to him in part because he defended Russia from an army invading from Sweden.

When Ivan III won Russia's independence from the Mongols 200 years later, he was the most powerful prince in Russia. With the Mongols gone, he was able to launch a series of wars to conquer the other Russian states. By the time of his death, Ivan—the first czar—had unified much of Russia into a single state. Czars ruled Russia until the early 20th century.

This Russian chalice dates from the 1000s. Its religious symbols reveal the importance of Christianity across the region by this period.

Daily Life Despite frequent changes in government, some elements of Russian culture remained constant. One such element was Christianity. According to legend, Christianity was first introduced to the Slavic peoples in the mid-800s. At that time, two brothers, Cyril and Methodius, traveled from the Byzantine Empire to teach the Slavs about Christianity. But Christianity did not immediately become popular in Russia.

In the late AD 900s, a prince of Kiev converted to Christianity. Before long, he made Christianity Russia's official religion. Russia's religious leaders had close ties to religious leaders in the Byzantine Empire. As a result, when the Roman Catholic and Eastern Orthodox churches split in 1054, the Russian church became part of the Eastern Orthodox Church.

Economic life in early Russia was mostly devoted to trade. The Russians' most important trading partner was the Byzantine Empire, but they also traded with the kingdoms of western Europe, the Slavs of northern Europe, and the Muslim areas to the south. Traders often traveled along the Volga River as part of a trade route that connected the Caspian Sea in the south with the Baltic Sea in the north. Among the most valuable trade goods from Russia were fur, wax, and honey. In addition, the Russians sold many slaves. In return they received wine, silk, art objects, spices, and other valuable goods. Trade made Russia very wealthy.

Reading Check
Analyze Causes
Why did Russia become Eastern Orthodox Christian?

Traders were respected in Kiev and other Russian cities. As a result, they ranked just below princes and nobles socially. Because of the importance of religion in Russia, clergy were also well respected. In addition to their religious duties, members of the clergy ran schools, hospitals, and other charities.

Russian Culture and Achievements

Because religion was so central to life in early Russia, most of Russia's cultural landscape reflects a religious influence. Architecture, art, and music from the period illustrate the importance of Orthodox Christianity.

The people of early Russia were master builders. They designed magnificent churches, many of which still stand today. One common feature of Russian churches was the use of multiple domes. Early churches had simple domes, but by the end of the Kievan Rus period, pointed domes had become popular. For example, the Cathedral of Saint Sophia in Novgorod features six gold and silver domes, all of which taper to points on top. Later, during the Muscovite period, domes became even more elaborate. Onion-shaped domes, which flared out from a narrow base before tapering to a point, eventually became a symbol of Russian architecture.

The interiors of Russian churches were filled with mosaics and paintings. Especially popular were **icons**, religious images painted on wood. Most icons showed saints or figures from the Bible and were meant to help people focus on their prayers. Icons could also be found in Russian homes.

From its earliest days, the Russian church embraced music as part of its celebrations. As a result, music filled Russian churches. Early church music featured entire choirs singing together in unison. Later, however, choirs began to sing in complex, beautiful harmonies.

Saint Sophia Cathedral

Built between 1045 and 1050, the Cathedral of Saint Sophia in Novgorod is a beautiful example of early Russian architecture, both inside and out.

Analyze Visuals
How does the Cathedral of Saint Sophia reflect the characteristics of Russian architecture?

The text on the scroll in this Russian icon of Mary, the mother of Jesus, is written in the Cyrillic alphabet. The Cyrillic alphabet was developed by Cyril and Methodius.

Most early Russian music and religious texts were created in a language known as Slavonic. Before the AD 800s, Slavonic could not be written down. Around that time, however, the missionaries Cyril and Methodius developed an alphabet to use with Slavonic. Cyril and Methodius were the men who introduced Christianity to eastern Europe.

The writing system Cyril and Methodius developed is called the Cyrillic (suh-RIL-ik) alphabet. This alphabet is still used to write Russian and other related languages today. The Cyrillic alphabet uses characters not familiar to most English speakers. For example, in Russian the word Russia is written **Россия** and the name *Yaroslav* is written **Ярослай**. By the time of Yaroslav the Wise, Russian scholars familiar with the Cyrillic alphabet had translated many religious texts from Greek into Slavonic.

Reading Check
Find Main Ideas
What features were common to early Russian churches?

Summary The Rus founded a Russian state and made the city of Kiev its capital. The Mongols later invaded Kiev and forced Russian princes to swear allegiance to them. Prince Ivan III eventually forced the Mongols out of Russia and unified most of Russia into a single state. Christianity became a central part of life in Russia.

Lesson 3 Assessment

Review Ideas, Terms, and People

1. a. Explain Why did the Rus move their capital from Novgorod to Kiev?

b. Identify Who was Prince Ivan III?

2. a. Form Generalizations How did Russian government change under the Mongols?

b. Identify How did Christianity spread into Russia?

3. a. Describe What were icons, and for what were they used?

b. Contrast In what major way is the Russian language different from the English language?

Critical Thinking

4. Organize Information Draw a timeline like this one. Then add four events in Russian history to your timeline.

Social Studies Skills

Chance, Error, and Oversight in History

Define the Skill

History is nothing more than what people thought and did in the past, and the people of the past were just as human as people today. Like us, they occasionally forgot or overlooked things. They made mistakes in their decisions or judgments. Unexpected things happened that they couldn't control. Sometimes, these oversights, errors, and just plain luck shaped history.

Learn the Skill

The text that follows notes several examples of the role of oversight, error, and chance in history.

1. **Oversight:** Emperor Justinian's subjects failed to appreciate his wife's importance. Theodora was a commoner, so they gave her little respect. When they launched a revolt in 532, Justinian was ready to flee. However, Theodora gave a powerful speech about the rewards of risking one's life for a great cause. Her speech inspired Justinian's supporters to attack and defeat the rebels.

2. **Error:** After the death of Yaroslav the Wise, Kiev broke apart into many smaller states, which often fought among themselves. As a result, Russian states were not unified when the Mongols invaded and were conquered.

3. **Chance:** In 1480, Prince Ivan III refused to pay taxes to the Mongols. The Mongols sent an army to force him to pay, but Ivan had organized his own army. After a standoff, the Mongols retreated to Central Asia. If the Mongols had not retreated, Ivan might have been killed in battle, and early Russia might not have been unified.

Practice the Skill

As you read in the module, the eastern Roman Empire flourished after the western Roman Empire fell. Write a paragraph to explain how chance, error, or oversight influenced the eastern Roman Empire's survival and growth.

Module 12 Assessment

Review Vocabulary, Terms, and People

Unscramble each group of letters to spell a term that matches the given definition.

1. **tsraciaanph**—mountain range in eastern Europe

2. **knepnallbaaunin**—extends south into the Mediterranean Sea

3. **lavgo**—longest river in Europe

4. **anzbtiuym**—the site of the Greek trading city on which the center of the eastern Roman Empire was built

5. **ohtradoe**—empress of the Byzantine Empire

6. **smiacso**—pictures made from pieces of colorful glass or stone

7. **njiasunti**—Byzantine emperor who tried to reunite the entire Roman Empire

8. **yppaiiitcnlr**—a small state ruled by a prince

9. **llnalvl**—the first czar of Russia

Comprehension and Critical Thinking

Lesson 1

10. **a.** Compare In what way is the Adriatic Sea similar to the Baltic Sea?

    b. Draw Conclusions Do you think more people in Russia live in the tundra or in the steppe? Why?

    c. Identify Who were the Balts and the Slavs, and how did they interact?

Lesson 2

11. **a.** Identify Who were Justinian and Theodora, and what did they accomplish?

    b. Contrast In what ways was the Byzantine Empire different from the western Roman Empire?

    c. Elaborate Do you think that Constantinople would have been an exciting place to visit in the AD 500s? Why or why not?

Lesson 3

12. **a.** Define What is a czar?

    b. Explain Why did traders in early Russia travel along the Volga River?

    c. Draw Conclusions Why might culture in western Russia have similarities with cultures in neighboring eastern European countries?

Review Themes

13. **Politics** "Justinian was an effective emperor." Do you agree with this statement? Why or why not?

14. **Religion** Do you think the split between the Roman Catholic and the Eastern Orthodox churches was avoidable? Why or why not?

Reading Skills

Stereotypes and Bias in History *Use the Reading Skills taught in this module to answer the question about the reading selection below.*

"They used to fight constantly and valiantly [bravely] with javelins [spears], maces [clubs], battle-axes, and swords. But specially they are excellent archers. . . . Vanquished [defeated], they ask no favor, and vanquishing [conquering], they show no compassion. . . . And suddenly diffusing [spreading] themselves over a whole province, and surprising all the people thereof unarmed, . . . they make such horrible slaughters, that the king or prince of the land invaded, cannot find people sufficient to wage battle against them. . . ."

—quoted in *The Principal Navigations, Voyages, Traffiques and Discoveries of the English Nation* by Richard Hakluyt

15. Is the author biased toward or against the fighting ability of the Mongols? Explain.

16. Would the author suggest that the Russians can trust the Mongols? How can you tell?

17. Overall, does this passage provide a negative or a positive stereotype of the Mongols? Explain.

Social Studies Skills

Chance, Oversight, and Error in History *Use the Social Studies Skills taught in this module to answer the questions below.*

18. How might the revolt against Justinian in 532 have been caused by an oversight on his part? What might he have done to prevent the revolt?

19. Do you consider the fighting among Russian states to be an error in judgment? Why or why not?

20. After Ivan III met the Mongol army, the Mongols retreated to Central Asia. How might history have been different if the Mongols had not retreated?

Focus on Writing

21. **Write a Poem** Write a narrative poem, or a poem that tells a story, about civilizations that developed in eastern Europe. Choose five or six events to include in your poem. In the first one or two lines, introduce the subject. Write five or six more lines, each one about an event that occurred during the history of the Byzantine Empire or early Russia. Then write one or two lines about the importance of these civilizations. Once you have finished writing, present your poem. Practice altering your voice and the rhythm of your words to make your poem more interesting to listeners.

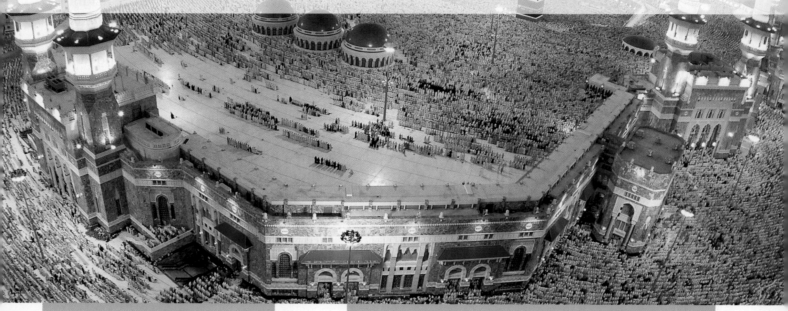

Module 13
The Rise of Islam

Essential Question
Why were Muslim leaders able to spread Islam and create an empire?

About the Photo: This photo shows thousands of people praying in Mecca, the place where Islam began. Mecca is the most sacred place in the Islamic world.

In this module you will learn about a religion called Islam and how it spread into lands outside of Arabia.

What You Will Learn...

Lesson 1: Geography and Life in Arabia. **432**
The Big Idea Life in Arabia was influenced by the harsh desert climate of the region.

Lesson 2: Origins of Islam. **437**
The Big Idea Muhammad, a merchant from Mecca, introduced a major world religion called Islam.

Lesson 3: Expansion of Islam. **448**
The Big Idea Conquest and trade led to the spread of Islam, the blending of cultures, and the growth of cities.

Lesson 4: Muslim Cultural Achievements. **456**
The Big Idea Muslim scholars and artists made contributions to science, art, and literature.

▶ *Explore ONLINE!*

HISTORY.

VIDEOS, including...
• Machines of the East

☑ Document-Based Investigations

☑ Graphic Organizers

☑ Interactive Games

☑ Image with Hotspots: Nomads and Townspeople

☑ Image Carousel: The Mosque at Medina

☑ Interactive Map: Early Muslim Conquests

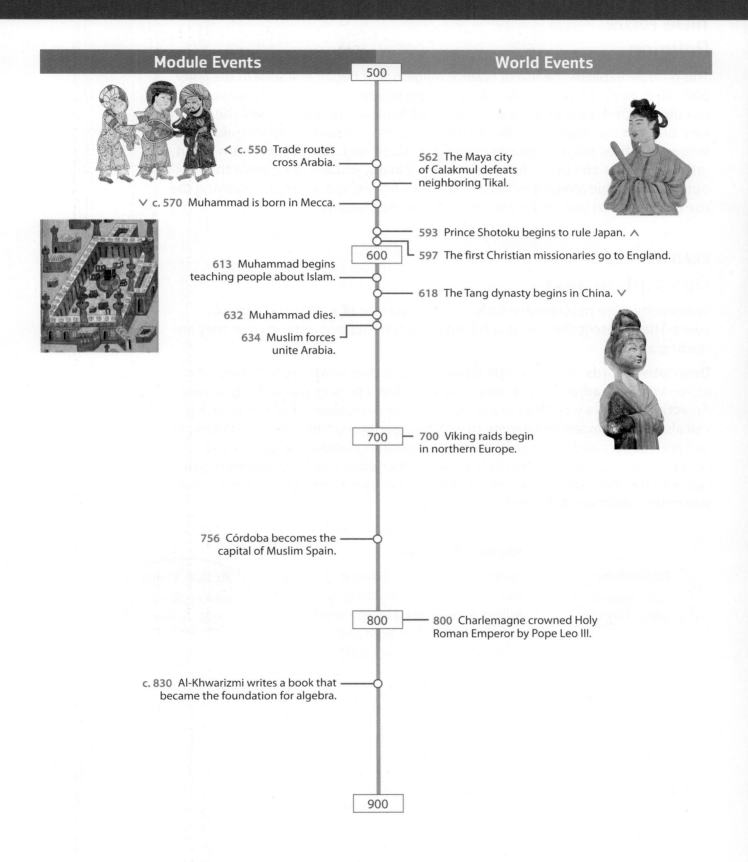

Module Events		World Events

500

< c. 550 Trade routes cross Arabia.

562 The Maya city of Calakmul defeats neighboring Tikal.

∨ c. 570 Muhammad is born in Mecca.

593 Prince Shotoku begins to rule Japan. ∧

600

597 The first Christian missionaries go to England.

613 Muhammad begins teaching people about Islam.

618 The Tang dynasty begins in China. ∨

632 Muhammad dies.

634 Muslim forces unite Arabia.

700

700 Viking raids begin in northern Europe.

756 Córdoba becomes the capital of Muslim Spain.

800

800 Charlemagne crowned Holy Roman Emperor by Pope Leo III.

c. 830 Al-Khwarizmi writes a book that became the foundation for algebra.

900

Reading Social Studies

Religion

This module explains the rise of Islam, a religion that began in Arabia in the early 600s. First, you'll learn about Arabia, including where it is and how the desert climate affected trade in the area. Then, you'll learn about Muhammad, the person who brought the religion of Islam to the Arabs. You will see how Islam guides its followers in their religious practices and their daily lives. You will also learn about great conquests and powerful Muslim rulers. Finally, you will read about the outstanding achievements of Muslim scholars, artists, and scientists. Studying the rise of Islam helps you understand the faith of the Muslims.

READING FOCUS:

Descriptive Text

Writers often use descriptive words to paint a picture of a particular place or event. These descriptive words can help readers better understand what they are reading about.

Descriptive Words The two main types of descriptive words are adjectives and action verbs. An **adjective** is a word that describes a person, place, thing, or idea. An **action verb** is a word that expresses action or movement. Descriptive words can also communicate the degree to which something is true—like the difference between *hungry* and *starving*. To better understand geographical places and historical events, pay attention to the use of descriptive words. As you read, you can use adjectives and action verbs to create a picture in your mind. This can help you better understand the text.

Adjectives
huge, sandy, large, high

Physical Features

Huge, sandy deserts cover large parts of Arabia. Sand dunes, or hills of sand shaped by the wind, can rise to 800 feet high and stretch for hundreds of miles!

Action Verbs
cover, shaped, rise, stretch

You Try It!

Read the following passage and then answer the questions below.

Arabia is one of the hottest, driest places in the world. With a blazing sun and clear skies, summer temperatures in the interior reach 100°F daily. This climate makes it hard for plants and animals to survive.

Desert plants do live in areas that get little rain. Many of them have roots that stretch deep or spread out far to collect as much water as possible. Just as plants have adapted to life in Arabia, so too have people found ways to live there.

Answer these questions based on the passage you just read.

1. What adjectives in the first sentence of the passage help describe the climate of Arabia?
2. Why do you think the writer used the action verb *reach* in the second sentence?
3. What would happen to the meaning of the fourth sentence if the adjective *little* were removed?
4. What picture is painted by the action verbs *stretch* and *spread* in the fifth sentence?

As you read this module, be on the lookout for descriptive words in the text. Use those words to form a picture in your mind and support your understanding.

Key Terms and People

Lesson 1
sand dunes
oasis
sedentary
caravan
souk

Lesson 2
Muhammad
Islam
Muslim
Qur'an
shrine
pilgrimage
mosque
jihad
Sunnah
Five Pillars of Islam

Lesson 3
Abu Bakr
caliph
tolerance

Lesson 4
Ibn Battutah
Sufism
Omar Khayyám
patrons
minaret
calligraphy

Geography and Life in Arabia

The Big Idea

Life in Arabia was influenced by the harsh desert climate of the region.

Main Ideas

- Arabia is mostly a desert land.
- Two ways of life—nomadic and sedentary—developed in the desert.

Key Terms and People

sand dunes
oasis
sedentary
caravan
souk

Academic
Vocabulary
features
characteristics

If YOU were there . . .

Your town is a crossroads for traders and herders. You have always lived in town, but sometimes you envy the freedom of the desert travelers. Your uncle, a trader, says you are old enough to join his caravan. It would mean traveling many days by camel. Your parents don't like the idea but will let you decide.

Will you join the caravan? Why or why not?

A Desert Land

The Arabian Peninsula, or Arabia, is mostly a hot and dry desert land. Scorching temperatures and a lack of water make life difficult. But in spite of the difficulty, people have lived in Arabia for thousands of years. During this time, Arabia's location, physical features, and climate have shaped life in the region.

Crossroads Location The Arabian Peninsula is located in the southwest corner of Asia. As you can see on the map, it lies near the intersection of three continents—Africa, Asia, and Europe. Trade routes linking the three continents have passed through the region for thousands of years. Geographers call Arabia a "crossroads" location.

Merchants carried goods such as spices, silk, and gold along the trade routes. Some of these trade routes were on land. Others were water routes along the coast or across the seas. Trade brought many different groups of people through Arabia. These people introduced products and ideas from around the world, influencing Arabian culture and society.

Physical Features Arabia's location has also shaped its physical <u>features</u>. It lies in a region with hot and dry air. This climate has created a band of deserts across Arabia and northern Africa.

Huge, sandy deserts cover large parts of Arabia. **Sand dunes**, or hills of sand shaped by the wind, can rise to 800 feet high and stretch for hundreds of miles! The world's largest sand desert, the Rub' al-Khali (ROOB ahl-KAH-lee), covers much of southern Arabia. Rub' al-Khali means "Empty Quarter," a name given to the desert because there is so little life there.

Arabia's deserts have a very limited amount of water. There are no permanent lakes or rivers. Water exists mainly in oases scattered across the deserts. An **oasis** is a wet, fertile area in a desert. These wet areas form where underground water bubbles to the surface. Oases have long been key stops along Arabia's overland trade routes.

Although deserts cover much of the interior of Arabia, other landforms appear along the edges of the peninsula. Mountains border the southern and western coasts, and marshy land lies near the Persian Gulf. Most of the settlement in Arabia has been in these milder coastal regions.

Desert Climate Arabia is one of the hottest, driest places in the world. With a blazing sun and clear skies, summer temperatures in the interior reach 100°F daily. This climate makes it hard for plants and animals to survive.

Desert plants do live in areas that get little rain. Many of them have roots that stretch deep or spread out far to collect as much water as possible. Just as plants have adapted to life in Arabia, so too have people found ways to live there.

Reading Check Summarize What are the main physical features of Arabia's environment?

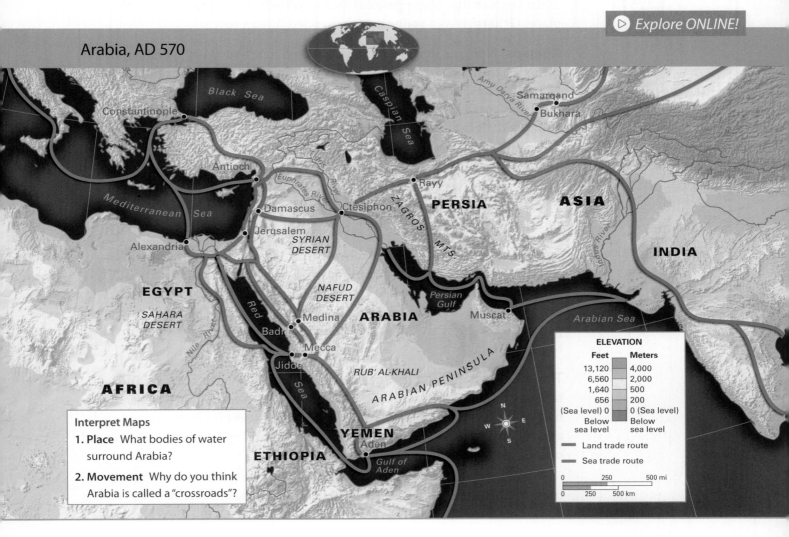

Explore ONLINE!

Arabia, AD 570

Interpret Maps

1. **Place** What bodies of water surround Arabia?

2. **Movement** Why do you think Arabia is called a "crossroads"?

Much of Arabia is covered by a vast, sandy desert.

Two Ways of Life

To live in Arabia's difficult desert environment, people developed two main ways of life. Some people lived a nomadic life, moving from place to place. Others lived a **sedentary**, or settled, life in towns.

Nomads Nomads lived in tents and raised herds of sheep, goats, and camels. The animals provided milk, meat, and skins for the nomads' tents. Nomads traveled with their herds across the desert, moving along regular routes as seasons changed, to get food and water for their animals. They depended on camels for transportation and milk.

Among the nomads, camels and tents belonged to individuals. Water and grazing land belonged to tribes. Membership in a tribe, a group of related people, was important to nomads. The tribe offered protection from desert dangers, such as violence that often took place when people competed for water and grazing land.

Townspeople While nomads moved around the desert, other people settled in oases, where they could farm. These settlements, particularly the ones in oases along trade routes, became towns. Most people in Arabia lived in towns. Merchants and craftspeople lived there and worked with people in the caravan trade. A **caravan** is a group of traders that travel together.

Trade Centers Towns became centers of trade for both nomads and townspeople. Many towns had a **souk** (SOOK)—a market or bazaar. In the market, nomads traded animal products and desert herbs for goods such as cooking supplies and clothing. Merchants sold spices, gold, leather, and other goods brought by the caravans.

Arabian towns were important stations on the trade routes linking India with Northeast Africa and the Mediterranean. Some of these towns

Nomads and Townspeople

The city of Mecca is shown here as it might have looked in the late 500s. Nomads from the desert and merchants from distant countries all came to trade at Mecca. Trade made some Meccan merchants wealthy.

Nomads traveled across Arabia, moving their animals as the seasons changed.

Towns developed near oases, where access to water allowed people to grow food.

Towns became centers of trade for both nomads and townspeople. Merchants traded goods such as leather, food, spices, and blankets.

Analyze Visuals
How can you tell which figures are nomads and which figures are townspeople?

Shopping

Did you know that the mall you go to today is similar in some ways to the souks of early Arabia? For example, souks sold clothing, home goods, and food. Often, similar products were grouped in different areas, sort of the way restaurants in a mall are often grouped together in a food court. Souks were open and busy during the day but closed at night. The larger ones were covered with a roof. People went to souks to socialize as well as to shop.

Souks weren't just the same as malls are, however. The shops in souks were smaller than most shops in modern malls, and prices were not fixed. Instead, the buyer and seller bargained to try to agree on a price.

Analyze Information
Why might people want to shop at a souk or a mall?

Reading Check
Summarize What two ways of life were common in Arabia?

were located on overland trade routes. Camel caravans carried goods on these routes. Other towns were ports located on the Arabian coasts. Ships sailed to and from these ports carrying goods from as far away as India. Trade brought Arabs into contact with people and ideas from around the world.

Summary and Preview The geography of Arabia encouraged trade and influenced the development of nomadic and sedentary lifestyles. In the next lesson, you will read about a religion that began to influence many people in Arabia.

Lesson 1 Assessment

Review Ideas, Terms, and People

1. **a. Define** What is an oasis?

   b. Explain How has Arabia's "crossroads" location affected its culture and society?

   c. Elaborate How might modern developments have changed trade routes through Arabia since the 500s?

2. **a. Identify** Where were nomads and townspeople likely to interact?

   b. Make Generalizations Why did towns often develop near oases?

   c. Elaborate What are some possible reasons nomads chose to live in the desert?

Critical Thinking

3. **Compare and Contrast** Draw a graphic organizer like this one. Use it to show some differences and similarities between nomadic and sedentary lifestyles in Arabia

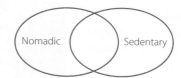

Nomadic   Sedentary

Origins of Islam

The Big Idea

Muhammad, a merchant from Mecca, introduced a major world religion called Islam.

Main Ideas

- Muhammad became a prophet and introduced a religion called Islam in Arabia.

- Muhammad's teachings had similarities to Judaism and Christianity, but they also presented new ideas.

- Islam spread in Arabia after being rejected at first.

- The Qur'an is the holy book of Islam.

- Along with the Qur'an, the Sunnah guides Muslims' lives.

- Islamic law is based on the Qur'an and the Sunnah.

Key Terms and People

Muhammad
Islam
Muslim
Qur'an
shrine
pilgrimage
mosque
jihad
Sunnah
Five Pillars of Islam

If YOU were there . . .

You live in a town in Arabia, in a large family of wealthy merchants. Your family's house is larger than most others in the town. You have beautiful clothes and many servants to wait on you. Many townspeople are poor, but you have always taken such differences for granted. Now you hear that some people are saying the rich should give money to the poor.

How might your family react to this idea?

Muhammad Becomes a Prophet

A man named **Muhammad** brought a different religion to the people of Arabia. Historians don't know much about Muhammad. What they do know comes from religious writings.

Muhammad's Early Life Muhammad was born into an important family in Mecca around 570. Muhammad's early life was not easy. His father, a merchant, died before he was born; and his mother died later, when he was six.

With his parents gone, Muhammad was first raised by his grandfather and later by his uncle. As a child, he traveled with his uncle's caravans, visiting places such as Syria and Jerusalem. Once he was grown, he managed a caravan business owned by a wealthy woman named Khadijah (ka-DEE-jah). Eventually, at age 25, Muhammad married Khadijah.

The caravan trade made Mecca a rich city. But most of the wealth belonged to just a few people. Poor people had hard lives. Traditionally, wealthy people in Mecca had helped the poor. But as Muhammad was growing up, many rich merchants began to ignore the poor and keep their wealth for themselves.

A Message for Muhammad Concerned about the changing values in Mecca, Muhammad often went by himself to the hills outside the city to pray and meditate. One day, when he was about 40 years old, Muhammad went to meditate in a cave. Then, according to Islamic teachings, something happened that changed his life forever. An angel appeared and spoke to Muhammad, telling him to "Recite! Recite!" Confused at first, Muhammad asked what he should recite. The angel answered:

> "Recite in the name of your Lord who created, created man from clots of blood! Recite! Your Lord is the Most Bountiful One, who by the pen taught man what he did not know."
>
> –From *The Koran*, translated by N. J. Dawood

Muslims believe that God had spoken to Muhammad through the angel and had made him a prophet, a person who tells of messages from God. At first Muhammad was afraid and didn't tell anyone except his wife about the voice in the cave. A few years later, in 613, Muhammad began to tell other people about the messages.

The messages Muhammad received form the basis of the religion called **Islam**. The word *Islam* means "to submit to God." A follower of Islam is called a **Muslim**. Muslims believe that Muhammad continued receiving messages from God for the rest of his life. These messages were collected in the **Qur'an** (kuh-RAN), the holy book of Islam.

Reading Check Summarize How did Muhammad bring Islam to Arabia?

Timeline: Three Religions Begin

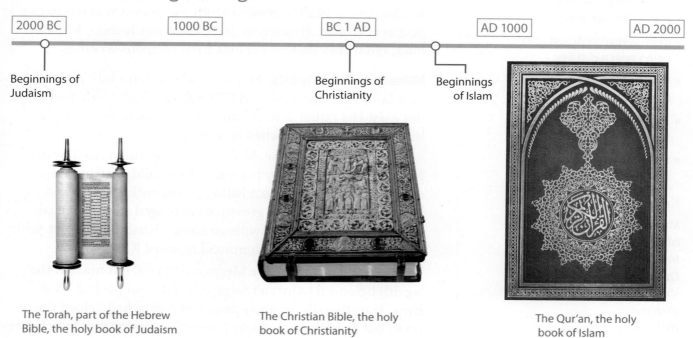

| 2000 BC | 1000 BC | BC 1 AD | AD 1000 | AD 2000 |

Beginnings of Judaism

Beginnings of Christianity

Beginnings of Islam

The Torah, part of the Hebrew Bible, the holy book of Judaism

The Christian Bible, the holy book of Christianity

The Qur'an, the holy book of Islam

Three Religions

The three main monotheistic religions in the world are Judaism, Christianity, and Islam. Each religion has its own particular beliefs and practices. Yet they also have important similarities. For example, all three began in the same part of the world—Southwest Asia. Also, all three religions teach similar ideas about kindness to fellow people and belief in one God.

Analyze Timelines
About how long after the beginnings of Christianity were the beginnings of Islam?

Muhammad's Teachings

Not all of Muhammad's early teachings were new. In fact, some were much like the teachings of Judaism and Christianity. But Muhammad's teachings challenged and upset the people of Arabia. These teachings brought changes to many aspects of life in Arabia.

A Belief in One God Muhammad taught that there was only one God, Allah, which means "the God" in Arabic. In that way, Islam is like Judaism and Christianity. It is a monotheistic religion, a religion based on a belief in one God. Although people of all three religions believe in one God, their beliefs about God are not all the same.

Jews, Christians, and Muslims also recognize many of the same prophets. Muhammad taught that prophets such as Abraham, Moses, and Jesus had lived in earlier times. Unlike Christians, Muslims do not believe Jesus was the son of God, but they do believe many stories about his life. Muhammad told stories about these prophets similar to the stories in the Torah and the Christian Bible. Muhammad respected Jews and Christians as "people of the Book" because their holy books taught many of the same ideas that Muhammad taught.

A Challenge to Old Ideas Some of Muhammad's teachings would have seemed familiar to Jews and Christians, but they were new to most Arabs. For example, most people in Arabia believed in many different gods, a belief system called polytheism.

Before Muhammad told them to believe in one God, Arabs worshipped many gods and goddesses at shrines. A **shrine** is a place at which people worship a saint or a god. A very important shrine, the Kaaba (KAH-buh), was in Mecca. People traveled there every year on a **pilgrimage**, a journey to a sacred place.

— BIOGRAPHY —

Fatimah c. 605—633

Muhammad's daughter Fatimah holds a place of honor in the Islamic religion. Stories describe Fatimah as a loyal daughter who cared for her father and suffered hunger and other hardships with him as he preached. Fatimah can also be linked, through her husband, Ali, to the origin of the split between Sunni and Shia Muslims. Members of the Shia branch of Islam believe that Muhammad wanted Ali to be the next leader of Islam. Those who did not believe that Ali was the rightful leader formed the Sunni branch of Islam.

Explain
Why does Fatimah hold a place of honor in Islam?

Several of Muhammad's teachings upset many Arabs. First, they didn't like being told to stop worshipping their gods and goddesses. Second, Muhammad's new religion seemed like a threat to people who made money from the yearly pilgrimages to the Kaaba. Mecca's powerful merchant leaders thought they would lose business if people didn't worship their gods at the Kaaba.

Another of Muhammad's teachings also worried Mecca's wealthy merchants. Muhammad said that everyone who believed in Allah would become part of a community in which rich and poor would be equal. But the merchants wanted to be richer and more powerful than the poor people, not equal to them.

Muhammad also taught that people should give money to help the poor. However, many wealthy merchants didn't want to help the poor. Instead, they wanted to keep all of their money. Because many of the people in Mecca didn't want to hear what Muhammad had to say, they rejected his teachings.

Reading Check
Compare How were Islamic teachings like the teachings of Judaism and Christianity?

Islam Spreads in Arabia

At first Muhammad did not have many followers. Mecca's merchants refused to believe in a single God and rejected the idea of equality. They even made Muhammad leave Mecca for a while. Eventually, however, Muhammad's teachings began to take root.

Academic Vocabulary
influence change, or have an effect on

From Mecca to Medina Slowly, more people began to listen to Muhammad's ideas. But as Islam began to **influence** people, the rulers of Mecca became more and more worried. They began to threaten Muhammad and his small group of followers with violence. They even planned to kill Muhammad. As a result, Muhammad had to look for support outside of Mecca.

A group of people from a city north of Mecca invited Muhammad to live in their city. As the threats from Mecca's leaders got worse, Muhammad accepted the invitation. In 622 he and many of his followers, including his daughter Fatimah, left Mecca and went to Medina (muh-DEE-nuh). Named after Muhammad, Medina means "the Prophet's city" in Arabic, the language of the Arabs. Muhammad's departure from Mecca became known in Muslim history as the hegira (hi-JY-ruh), or journey.

Timeline: Beginnings of Islam

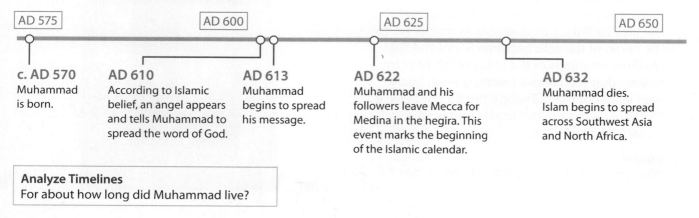

AD 575   AD 600   AD 625   AD 650

c. AD 570 Muhammad is born.

AD 610 According to Islamic belief, an angel appears and tells Muhammad to spread the word of God.

AD 613 Muhammad begins to spread his message.

AD 622 Muhammad and his followers leave Mecca for Medina in the hegira. This event marks the beginning of the Islamic calendar.

AD 632 Muhammad dies. Islam begins to spread across Southwest Asia and North Africa.

Analyze Timelines
For about how long did Muhammad live?

From Medina to the Rest of Arabia Muhammad's arrival in Medina holds an important place in Islamic history. There he became both a spiritual and a political leader. His house became the first **mosque** (MAHSK), or building for Muslim prayer. The year of the hegira, 622, became so important to the development of Islam that Muslims made it the first year in the Islamic calendar.

According to Islamic belief, in Medina Muhammad reported new revelations about rules for Muslim government, society and worship. For example, God told Muhammad that Muslims should face Mecca when they pray. Before, Muslims faced Jerusalem like Christians and Jews did. Muslims recognized the importance of Mecca as the home of the Kaaba. They believe the Kaaba was built by Abraham and was dedicated to the worship of one God.

As the Muslim community in Medina grew stronger, other Arab tribes in the region began to accept Islam. Geography played a part in this political development, since Muhammad's ideas were especially popular among poorer people who lived in areas with little fertile soil. Even as Islam spread, conflict with the Meccans increased. In 630, after several years of fighting, the people of Mecca gave in. They welcomed Muhammad back to the city and accepted Islam as their religion.

In Mecca Muhammad and his followers destroyed the statues of the gods and goddesses in the Kaaba. Soon most of the Arabian tribes accepted Muhammad as their spiritual leader and became Muslims.

Muhammad died in 632 at his home in Medina. Although he didn't live long after Mecca became Muslim, the beliefs he preached would live on and spread widely, thanks in part to a book known as the Qur'an.

Reading Check
Summarize How did Islam spread in Arabia?

▶ *Explore ONLINE!*

Islam in Arabia, AD 632

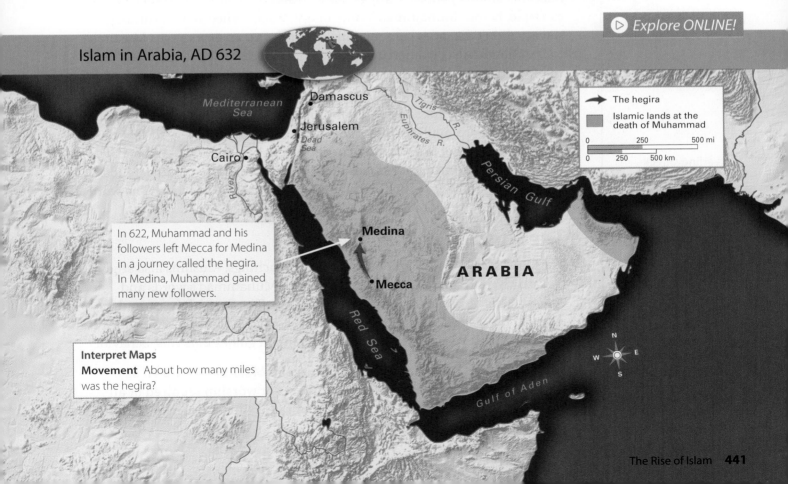

The hegira

Islamic lands at the death of Muhammad

0   250   500 mi
0   250   500 km

Mediterranean Sea

Damascus

Jerusalem
Dead Sea

Cairo

Tigris R.

Euphrates R.

Persian Gulf

Medina

ARABIA

Mecca

Nile River

Red Sea

Gulf of Aden

In 622, Muhammad and his followers left Mecca for Medina in a journey called the hegira. In Medina, Muhammad gained many new followers.

Interpret Maps
Movement About how many miles was the hegira?

The Qur'an

During Muhammad's life, his followers memorized his messages from God along with his words and deeds. After Muhammad's death, they collected his teachings and wrote them down to form the book known as the Qur'an. Muslims consider the Qur'an to be the exact word of God as it was told to Muhammad.

Beliefs The central teaching in the Qur'an is that there is only one God—Allah—and that Muhammad is his prophet. The Qur'an says people must obey Allah's commands. Muslims learned of these commands from Muhammad.

Islam teaches that the world had a definite beginning and will end one day. Muhammad said that on the final day God will judge all people. Those who have obeyed his orders will be granted life in paradise. According to the Qur'an, paradise is a beautiful garden full of fine food and drink. People who have not obeyed God, however, will suffer.

Guidelines for Behavior Like holy books of other religions, the Qur'an describes acts of worship, guidelines for moral behavior, and rules for social life. Muslims look to the Qur'an for guidance in their daily lives. For example, the Qur'an describes how to prepare for worship. Muslims must wash themselves before praying, so they will be pure before Allah. The Qur'an also says what Muslims shouldn't eat or drink. Muslims aren't allowed to eat pork or drink alcohol.

In addition to guidelines for individual behavior, the Qur'an describes relations among people. Many of these ideas changed Arabian society. For example, before Muhammad's time many Arabs owned slaves. Although slavery didn't disappear among Muslims, the Qur'an encourages Muslims to free slaves. Also, women in Arabia had few rights. The Qur'an describes rights of women, including rights to own property, earn money, and get an education. However, most Muslim women still had fewer rights than men.

Another important subject in the Qur'an has to do with **jihad** (ji-HAHD), which means "to make an effort, or to struggle." Jihad refers to the inner struggle people go through in their effort to obey God and behave according to Islamic ways. Jihad can also mean the struggle to defend the Muslim community, or, historically, to convert people to Islam. The word has also been translated as "holy war."

Reading Check
Analyze Causes
Why is the Qur'an important to Muslims?

The Sunnah

The Qur'an is not the only source of Islamic teachings. Muslims also study the hadith (huh-DEETH), the written record of Muhammad's words and actions. This record is the basis for the Sunnah. The **Sunnah** (SOOH-nuh) refers to the way Muhammad lived, which provides a model for the duties and the way of life expected of Muslims. The Sunnah guides Muslims' behavior.

The Five Pillars of Islam The first duties of a Muslim are known as the **Five Pillars of Islam**, which are five acts of worship required of all Muslims. The first pillar is a statement of faith. At least once in their lives,

Sources of Islamic Beliefs

Qur'an

Holy book that includes all the messages Muhammad received from God

Sunnah

Muhammad's example for the duties and way of life expected of Muslims

Shariah

Islamic law, based on interpretations of the Qur'an and Sunnah

Muslims must state their faith by saying, "There is no god but God, and Muhammad is his prophet." Muslims say this when they accept Islam. They also say it in their daily prayers.

The second pillar of Islam is daily prayer. Muslims must pray five times a day: before sunrise, at midday, in late afternoon, right after sunset, and before going to bed. At each of these times, a call goes out from a mosque, inviting Muslims to come pray. Muslims try to pray together at a mosque. They believe prayer is proof that someone has accepted Allah.

The third pillar of Islam is a yearly donation to charity. Muslims must pay part of their wealth to a religious official. This money is used to help the poor, build mosques, or pay debts. Helping and caring for others is important in Islam.

The fourth pillar is fasting—going without food and drink. Muslims fast daily during the holy month of Ramadan (RAH-muh-dahn). The Qur'an says Allah began his revelations to Muhammad in the month of Ramadan. During Ramadan, most Muslims will not eat or drink anything

The Five Pillars of Islam

Saying "There is no god but God, and Muhammad is his prophet"

Praying five times a day

Giving to the poor and needy

Fasting during the holy month of Ramadan

Traveling to Mecca at least once on a hajj

Analyze Visuals
Which of the five pillars shows how Muslims are supposed to treat other people?

The Qur'an plays a central role in the lives of many Muslims. Children study and memorize verses from the Qur'an at home, at Islamic schools, and in mosques. Muslims who memorize the entire book are respected as "Keepers" of the Qur'an.

between dawn and sunset. Muslims believe fasting is a way to show that God is more important than one's own body. Fasting also reminds Muslims of people in the world who struggle to get enough food.

The fifth pillar of Islam is the hajj (HAJ), a pilgrimage to Mecca. All Muslims must travel to Mecca at least once in their lives if they can. The Kaaba, in Mecca, is Islam's most sacred place.

The Sunnah and Daily Life In addition to the five pillars, the Sunnah has other examples of Muhammad's actions and teachings. These form the basis for rules about how to treat others. According to Muhammad's example, people should treat guests with generosity.

The Sunnah also provides rules for how followers of Islam should treat one another :

"Do not envy one another; do not inflate prices one to another; do not hate one another; do not turn away from one another; and do not undercut one another, but be you, O servants of Allah, brothers."
—Hadith #35

Reading Check
Form Generalizations
What do Muslims learn from the Sunnah?

In addition to describing personal relations, the Sunnah provides guidelines for relations in business and government. For example, one Sunnah rule says that it is bad to owe someone money. Another rule says that people should obey their leaders.

Islamic Law

The Qur'an and the Sunnah are important guides for how Muslims should live. They also form the basis of Islamic law, or Shariah (shuh-REE-uh). Shariah is a system based on Islamic sources and human reason that judges the rightness of actions an individual or community might take. These actions fall on a scale ranging from required to accepted to disapproved to forbidden. Islamic law makes no distinction between religious beliefs and daily life, so Islam affects all aspects of Muslims' lives.

Shariah sets rewards for good behavior and punishments for crimes. It also describes limits of authority. It was the basis for law in Muslim countries until modern times. Most Muslim countries today blend Islamic law with Western legal systems like we have in the United States.

Islamic law is not found in one book. Instead, it is a set of opinions and writings that have changed over the centuries. Different ideas about Islamic law are found in different Muslim regions.

Summary and Preview You have just read about Muhammad's life, about some of his teachings, and about the main Islamic beliefs. Inspired by the life of Muhammad, many people in Arabia accepted Islam and became Muslims. In the next lesson you will learn more about Muslim culture and the spread of Islam from Arabia to other lands.

Reading Check
Find Main Ideas
What is the purpose of Islamic law?

Lesson 2 Assessment

Review Ideas, Terms, and People

1. a. **Recall** When did Muhammad begin teaching people about Islam?
   b. **Explain** According to Islamic belief, what was the source of Islamic teachings and how did Muhammad receive them?

2. a. **Identify** What is one key Islamic belief about God?
   b. **Compare** In what ways are Islamic beliefs similar to those of Judaism and Christianity?

3. a. **Recall** Where was the first mosque?
   b. **Explain** Why did Muhammad go to Medina?
   c. **Describe** What role did geography play in the acceptance of Islam in Arabia?

4. a. **Recall** What is the central teaching of the Qur'an?
   b. **Explain** How does the Qur'an help Muslims obey God?

5. a. **Recall** What are the Five Pillars of Islam?
   b. **Make Generalizations** Why do Muslims fast during Ramadan?

6. a. **Identify** What is Islamic law called?
   b. **Make Inferences** How is Islamic law different from law in the United States?
   c. **Elaborate** What is a possible reason that opinions and writings about Islamic law have changed over the centuries?

Critical Thinking

7. **Sequence** Draw a timeline. Use it to identify key dates in Muhammad's life.

Sacred Texts of Islam

Word Help

compassionate caring
merciful kind
articulate clear and understandable
adoration praise
transgress violate
jinn (plural) or **jinnee** (singular) a type of spirit
abide last
beseech beg

❶ Palms, grain, and herbs are among the small number of plants that grow in the Arabian desert.

❷ Jinn are spirits that appear in many Arabic tales. In English, the word is also spelled *djinn* or *genies.*

❸ "The two easts" and "the two wests" refer to the different locations where the sun appears to rise and set in summer and winter. The "two oceans" are fresh water and salt water. *What is the Qur'an saying in this passage?*

About the Reading The Qur'an (or Koran), the holy book of Islam, is divided into 114 chapters called suras (SUR-uhs). The suras vary widely in length. In general, the longest suras are at the beginning of the Qur'an, and the shortest are at the end. Each sura opens with the same phrase, translated here as "In the Name of Allah, the Compassionate, the Merciful."

As You Read Look for words and phrases that are repeated within the text. Think about the reasons for this repetition.

from *The Koran*
translated by N. J. Dawood
The Merciful Sura 55:1–55

> In the Name of Allah, the Compassionate, the Merciful
> It is the Merciful who has taught the Qur'an.
> He created man and taught him articulate speech. The sun and the moon pursue their ordered course. The plants and the trees bow down in adoration.
> He raised the heaven on high and set the balance of all things, that you might not transgress it. Give just weight and full measure.
> He laid the earth for His creatures, with all its fruits and blossom-bearing palm, chaff-covered grain and scented herbs. Which of your Lord's blessings would you deny? ❶
> He created man from potter's clay and the jinn from smokeless fire. Which of your Lord's blessings would you deny? ❷
> The Lord of the two easts is He, and the Lord of the two wests. Which of your Lord's blessings would you deny? ❸
> He has let loose the two oceans: they meet one another. Yet between them stands a barrier which they cannot overrun. Which of your Lord's blessings would you deny?
> Pearls and corals come from both. Which of your Lord's blessings would you deny?
> His are the ships that sail like banners upon the ocean. Which of your Lord's blessings would you deny?
> All who live on earth are doomed to die. But the face of your Lord will abide for ever, in all its majesty and glory. Which of your Lord's blessings would you deny?
> All who dwell in heaven and earth beseech Him. Each day some new task employs Him. Which of your Lord's blessings would you deny?
> Mankind and jinn, We shall surely find the time to judge you! Which of your Lord's blessings would you deny?

Mankind and jinn, if you have power to penetrate the confines of heaven and earth, then penetrate them! But this you shall not do except with Our own authority. Which of your Lord's blessings would you deny?

Flames of fire shall be lashed at you, and molten brass. There shall be none to help you. Which of your Lord's blessings would you deny?

When the sky splits asunder and reddens like a rose or stainéd leather (which of your Lord's blessings would you deny?), on that day neither man nor jinnee shall be asked about his sins. Which of your Lord's blessings would you deny?

The wrongdoers shall be known by their looks; they shall be seized by their forelocks and their feet. Which of your Lord's blessings would you deny? ④

That is the Hell which the sinners deny. They shall wander between fire and water fiercely seething. Which of your Lord's blessings would you deny?

⑤ But for those that fear the majesty of their Lord there are two gardens (which of your Lord's blessings would you deny?) planted with shady trees. Which of your Lord's blessings would you deny?

Each is watered by a flowing spring. Which of your Lord's blessings would you deny?

Each bears every kind of fruit in pairs. Which of your Lord's blessings would you deny?

They shall recline on couches lined with thick brocade, and within their reach will hang the fruits of both gardens. Which of your Lord's blessings would you deny?

Muslims read about Allah in the Qur'an.

Connect Sacred Texts to History

1. **Analyze** Muslims believe that Allah created the world. What words and phrases in this passage illustrate that belief?

2. **Analyze** The first Muslims lived in an area that was mostly desert. How does this passage reflect the early Muslims' desert location?

Expansion of Islam

The Big Idea
Conquest and trade led to the spread of Islam, the blending of cultures, and the growth of cities.

Main Ideas
- Muslim armies conquered many lands into which Islam slowly spread.
- Trade helped Islam spread into new areas.
- A mix of cultures was one result of Islam's spread.
- Islamic influence encouraged the growth of cities.

Key Terms and People
Abu Bakr
caliph
tolerance

If YOU were there . . .

You are a farmer living in a village on the coast of India. For centuries, your people have raised cotton and spun its fibers into a soft fabric. One day, a ship arrives in the harbor, bringing traders from far away. They bring interesting goods you have never seen before. They also bring new ideas.

What ideas might you learn from the traders?

Muslim Armies Conquer Many Lands

After Muhammad's death, many of the Muslim leaders chose **Abu Bakr** (uh-boo BAK-uhr), one of Muhammad's first converts, to be the next leader of Islam. He was the first **caliph** (KAY-luhf), a title that Muslims use for the highest leader of Islam. In Arabic, the word *caliph* means "successor." As Muhammad's successors, the caliphs had to follow the prophet's example. This meant ruling according to the Qur'an. Unlike Muhammad, however, early caliphs were not religious leaders.

Although not a religious leader, Abu Bakr was a political and military leader. Under his rule, the Muslims began a series of wars in which they conquered many lands outside of Arabia.

Beginnings of an Empire Abu Bakr directed a series of battles against Arab tribes that did not follow Muhammad's teachings. By his death in 634, he had made Arabia a unified Muslim state.

With Arabia united, Muslim leaders turned their attention elsewhere. Their armies won many stunning victories. They defeated armies of the Persian and Byzantine empires, which were weak from years of fighting.

When the Muslims conquered lands, they made treaties with any non-Muslims there. These treaties listed rules that conquered people—often Jews and Christians—had to follow. For example, some non-Muslims could not build places of worship in Muslim cities or dress like Muslims. In return, the Muslims would not attack them. One such treaty was the Pact of Umar, named after the second caliph. It was written in about 637, after Muslims conquered Syria.

During this period, differences between groups of Muslims solidified into what became the Shia-Sunni split. Shias believed that caliphs should be descended from Muhammad's family, specifically, Ali, the husband of Fatimah, his daughter. Sunnis believed that the faithful or religious leaders should elect caliphs. One prominent incident in the history of the Shia-Sunni split was the killing of Hussein, grandson of Muhammad. He represented the hopes of the Shia Muslim branch. Today, most of the Muslims across the world are Sunni. Shia Muslims live mostly in Iran, Iraq, Pakistan, and India.

Growth of the Empire Many early caliphs came from the Umayyad (oom-EYE-yuhd) family. The Umayyads moved their capital from Medina to Damascus and continued to expand the empire. They took over lands in Central Asia and in northern India. The Umayyads also gained control of trade in the eastern Mediterranean and conquered part of North Africa.

In the late 600s, battles with the Berbers slowed the growth of Muslim rule in North Africa. The Berbers are the native people of North Africa. After years of fighting, many Berbers converted to Islam. Following their conversion, they joined the Arabs in efforts to spread Islam.

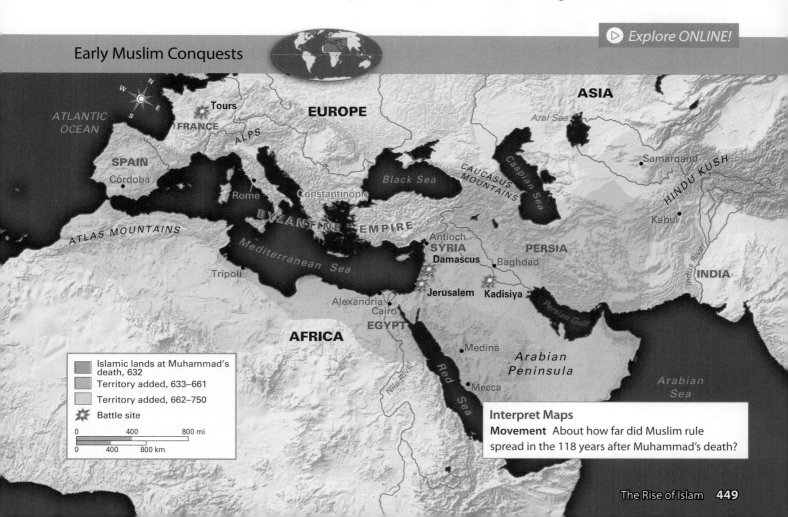

Early Muslim Conquests

Explore ONLINE!

Islamic lands at Muhammad's death, 632

Territory added, 633–661

Territory added, 662–750

Battle site

Interpret Maps
Movement About how far did Muslim rule spread in the 118 years after Muhammad's death?

Next, the Muslims tried to expand their empire into Europe. A combined Arab and Berber army invaded Spain in 711 and quickly conquered it. The army moved on into what is now France, but it was stopped by a Christian army near the city of Tours (TOOR). Despite this defeat, Muslims called Moors continued to rule parts of Spain for the next 700 years.

In continuing the expansion, a new dynasty, the Abbasids (uh-BAS-idz), came to power in 750. The Abbasids reorganized the government to make it easier to rule such a large region. In addition to reorganizing, the philosophy of government also changed. Some scholars consider the government of the Abbasids to be a theocracy. Unlike the Umayyads, the Abbasids claimed to rule by divine right, on behalf of Allah.

Reading Check
Form Generalizations
What role did armies play in spreading Islam?

Trade Helps Islam Spread

Islam gradually spread through areas the Muslims conquered. At the same time trade helped spread Islam into other areas as well. Arabia's crossroads location gave Muslim merchants easy access to South Asia and Africa. After the fall of the Roman Empire, trade between the Arab world and Europe had decreased. As the Islamic faith expanded, trade between the two regions increased once again.

A far-reaching trade network brought wealth and new knowledge to the Muslim world and helped spread Islam. In this drawing, an Arab trader prepares perfume, a valuable trade good.

Merchants and the Spread of Islam Along with their trade goods, Arab merchants took Islamic beliefs to new lands. For example, merchants introduced Islam into India. Although many Indian kingdoms remained Hindu, coastal trading cities soon had large Muslim communities. In Africa, societies often reflected both African and Muslim culture. For example, Arabic influenced local African languages. Also, many African leaders converted to Islam. Between 1200 and 1600, Muslim traders carried Islam as far east as what are now Malaysia and Indonesia. Even today, Islam is a major influence on life there.

Products and Inventions In addition to helping spread Islam, trade brought new products to Muslim lands and made many people rich. First, new products and inventions created by other peoples made their way to the Muslim world. For example, Arabs learned from the Chinese how to make paper and use gunpowder. New crops such as cotton, rice, and oranges arrived from India, China, and Southeast Asia. Second, traders made money on trade between regions.

In addition to trade with Asia, African trade was important to Muslim merchants. Many merchants set up businesses next to African market towns. They wanted slaves and also African products such as ivory and cloves. In return they offered fine white pottery called porcelain from China, cloth goods from India, and iron from Southwest Asia and Europe. Arab traders even traveled south across the Sahara, the world's largest desert, to get gold. In exchange, they brought the Africans salt, which was scarce south of the desert.

Reading Check
Find Main Ideas
How did trade affect the spread of Islam?

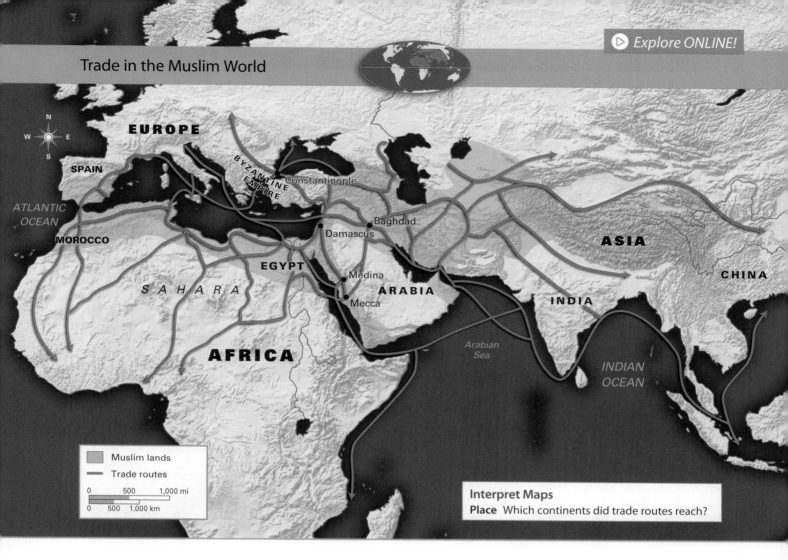

Explore ONLINE!

Interpret Maps
Place Which continents did trade routes reach?

Muslim lands

Trade routes

0   500   1,000 mi
0   500   1,000 km

A Mix of Cultures

As Islam spread through trade, warfare, and treaties, Arabs came in contact with people who had different beliefs and lifestyles than they did.

Muslims generally practiced religious **tolerance**, or acceptance, with regard to people they conquered. In other words, the Muslims did not ban all religions other than Islam in their lands. Jews and Christians in particular kept many of their rights, since they shared some beliefs with Muslims.

Although Jews and Christians were allowed to practice their own religions, they had to pay a special tax. They also had to follow the rules of the treaties governing conquered peoples.

Many people conquered by the Arabs converted to Islam. Along with Islamic beliefs, these people often adopted other parts of Arabic culture. For example, many people started speaking Arabic. The Arabs also adopted some of the customs of the people they conquered. For example, they copied a Persian form of bureaucracy in their government.

As Islam spread, language and religion helped unify the many groups that became part of the Islamic world. Cultural blending changed Islam from a mostly Arab religion into a religion of many different cultures.

Reading Check
Draw Conclusions
Did Muslim tolerance encourage or limit the spread of Islam?

Córdoba, Spain, was a great center of Islamic learning. In fact, in the early 900s, its inhabitants were some of the richest and most educated in Europe.

A Center of Learning

This map of the world was created by the Muslim geographer al-Idrisi in the 1100s. Al-Idrisi studied in Córdoba and used many different sources, including sailors' stories, to make this map.

Analyze Visuals

How do the Great Mosque and al-Idrisi's map suggest that Córdoba was a center of culture and learning?

The Great Mosque

Córdoba's Great Mosque is famous for its beautiful marble columns and red and white arches. The mosque was just one of the many impressive buildings constructed in Córdoba.

The Growth of Cities

The growing cities of the Muslim world reflected this blending of cultures. Trade had brought people, products, and ideas together. It had also created wealth, which supported great cultural **development** in cities such as Baghdad in what is now Iraq and Córdoba (KAWR-doh-bah) in Spain.

Academic Vocabulary
development the process of growing or improving

Baghdad Baghdad became the capital of the Islamic Empire in 762. Located near both land and water transportation routes, it was a major trading center. In addition to trade, farming contributed to a strong economy. Dates and grains grew well in the fertile soil. Trade and farming made Baghdad one of the world's richest cities in the 700s and early 800s.

The center of Baghdad was known as the "round city," because three round walls surrounded it. Within the walls was the caliph's palace, which took up one-third of the city. Outside the walls were houses and souks for the city's huge population.

Caliphs at Baghdad supported science and the arts. For example, they built a hospital and an observatory. They also built a library that was used as a university and housed Arabic translations of many ancient Greek works. Because Baghdad was a center of culture and learning, many artists and writers went there. Artists decorated the city's public buildings, while writers wrote literature that remains popular today.

Córdoba Córdoba, too, became a great Muslim city. In 756, Muslims chose it to be the capital of what is now Spain. Like Baghdad, Córdoba had a strong economy based on agriculture and trade. It was also located along a large river that served as a trade route. Córdoba exported textiles and jewelry, which were valued throughout Europe.

By the early 900s, Córdoba was the largest and most advanced city in Europe. It had mansions and mosques, busy markets and shops, and aqueducts. It also had public water and lighting systems.

Córdoba was a great center of learning. Men and women from across the Muslim world and Europe came to study at the university there. They studied Greek and Roman scientific writings and translated them into Arabic. In addition, they studied writings produced in the Muslim world and translated them from Arabic to Latin. As a result, Arabic writings on such subjects as mathematics, medicine, astronomy, geography, and history could be studied throughout Europe.

Córdoba was also a center of Jewish culture. Many Jews held key jobs in the government. Jewish poets, philosophers, and scientists made great contributions to Córdoba's cultural growth.

Reading Check
Compare What did Baghdad and Córdoba have in common?

Summary and Preview Through wars and treaties, Muslim territory grew tremendously, and Islam spread through this territory. In the next lesson, you will learn about some other achievements of the Islamic world.

Lesson 3 Assessment

Review Ideas, Terms, and People

1. a. **Define** What is a caliph?
   b. **Sequence** To what regions, and in what general order, had Islam spread by 750?
2. a. **Recall** What were three places Islam spread to through trade?
   b. **Explain** How did trade spread Islam?
3. **Identify** What helped unify the groups that became part of the Islamic world?
4. a. **Identify** What were two important cities in the Islamic world?

b. **Analyze** How did life in Córdoba show a mix of cultures?

c. **Evaluate** Do you think tolerance is a good or bad policy for governing people? Why?

Critical Thinking

5. **Analyze Effects** Draw a graphic organizer like this one. Use it to identify two ways Arab traders affected the Islamic world.

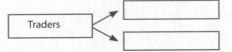

History and Geography

The Hajj

Every year, as many as 2 million Muslims make a religious journey, or pilgrimage, to Mecca, Saudi Arabia. This journey, called the hajj, is one of the Five Pillars of Islam—all Muslims are expected to make the journey at least once in their lifetime if they can.

Mecca is the place where Muhammad lived and taught more than 1,300 years ago. As a result, it is the holiest city in Islam. The pilgrims who travel to Mecca each year serve as a living reminder of the connection between history and geography.

Europe and the Americas Many countries in Europe and the Americas have a Muslim population. These pilgrims are from Germany.

On the Road to Mecca

- Before entering Mecca, pilgrims undergo a ritual cleansing and put on special white garments.
- At Mecca, guides help pilgrims through religious rituals.
- One important ritual is the "Standing," on Mount Arafat, near Mecca. Pilgrims stand for hours, praying, at a place where Muhammad is said to have given his last sermon.
- Pilgrims then participate in a three-day ritual of "Stoning," in which they throw pebbles at three pillars.
- Finally, pilgrims complete their journey by returning to the Grand Mosque in Mecca, where a great feast is held.

Africa Pilgrims also come from Africa. These pilgrims are from Nigeria, just one of the African countries that is home to a large Muslim population.

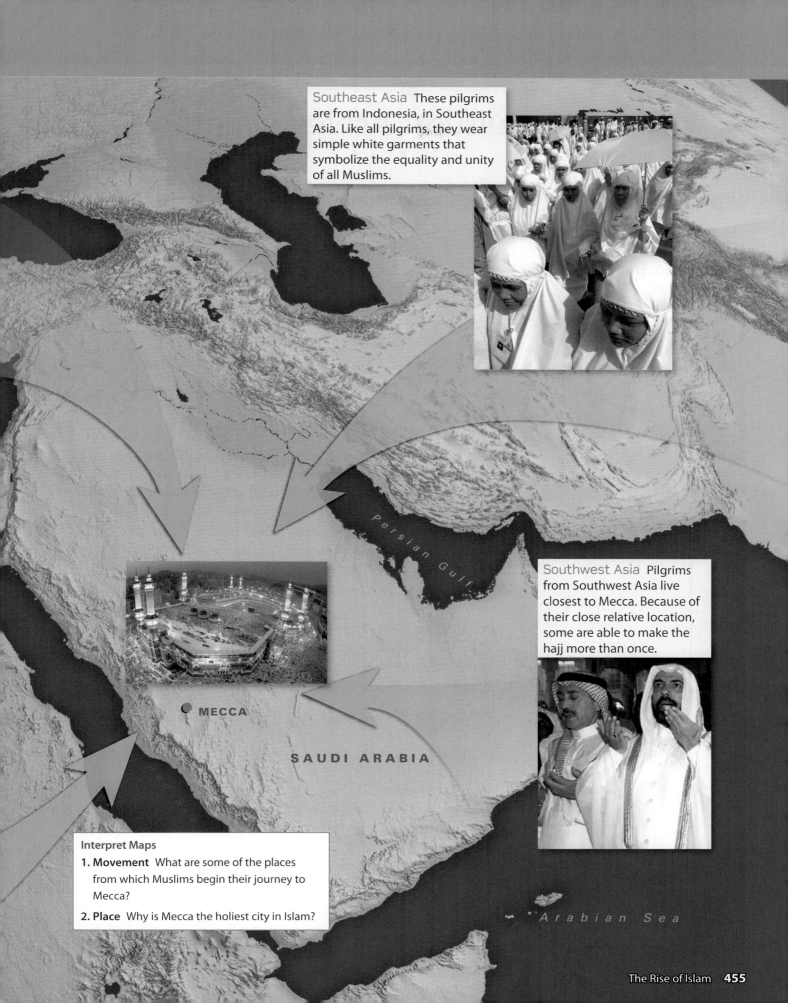

Southeast Asia These pilgrims are from Indonesia, in Southeast Asia. Like all pilgrims, they wear simple white garments that symbolize the equality and unity of all Muslims.

Persian Gulf

Southwest Asia Pilgrims from Southwest Asia live closest to Mecca. Because of their close relative location, some are able to make the hajj more than once.

● **MECCA**

SAUDI ARABIA

Arabian Sea

Interpret Maps

1. **Movement** What are some of the places from which Muslims begin their journey to Mecca?

2. **Place** Why is Mecca the holiest city in Islam?

Muslim Cultural Achievements

If YOU were there...

You are a servant in the court of a powerful ruler. Your life at court is comfortable, though not one of luxury. Now the ruler is sending your master to explore unknown lands and distant kingdoms in Africa. The dangerous journey will take him across oceans and deserts. He can take only a few servants with him. He has not ordered you to come but has given you a choice.

Will you join your master's expedition or stay home? Why?

Science and Philosophy

The empires of the Islamic world contributed to the achievements of Islamic culture. Muslim scholars made advances in astronomy, geography, math, and science. Scholars at Baghdad and Córdoba translated many ancient writings on these subjects into Arabic.

Having a common language helped scholars throughout the Islamic world share what they learned, even though many scholars came from different cultures and spoke other languages.

In addition, the Islamic world helped preserve education and learning in the Mediterranean area after the fall of the Roman Empire. Advances in science and technology were eventually introduced into western Europe by the Muslim conquest of Spain.

Astronomy Many cities in the Muslim world had observatories where people could study astronomy—the sun, moon, and stars. Scientists studied astronomy to better understand time and clockmaking. Muslim scientists also improved the astrolabe, which the Greeks had invented to chart the position of the stars. Arab scholars used the astrolabe to figure out their location on the earth. This helped Muslims know what direction to turn so they could face Mecca for their prayers. The astrolabe became an important contribution to

Geography

Muslim travelers collected much information about the world, some of which was used to make this map. New and better maps led to even more travel and a greater understanding of the world's geography.

The Astrolabe

Muslim scientists used astrolabes like this one to figure out their location, direction, and even the time of day. Although the Greeks invented the astrolabe, Muslim scholars greatly improved it.

Astronomy

Muslim scientists made remarkable advances in astronomy. This observatory was built in the 1700s in Delhi, the capital of Mughal India.

the exploration of the seas. In fact, this technological advancement helped Muslim explorers spread Islam to different parts of the globe. As a result, the size of the Islamic world increased.

Geography Studying astronomy also helped Muslims explore the world. As people learned to use the stars to calculate time and location, merchants and explorers began to travel widely. For example, **Ibn Battutah** traveled to Africa, India, China, and Spain in the 1320s. To help travelers on their way, Muslim geographers made more accurate maps than were available before. They also developed better ways of calculating distances.

During the mid-1100s, a Muslim geographer named al-Idrisi (uhl-i-DREE-see) collected information from Arab travelers. He was writing a geography book and wanted it to be very accurate. When al-Idrisi had a question about where a mountain, river, or coastline was, he sent trained geographers to figure out its exact location. Using the information the

Travels in Asia and Africa

Ibn Battutah wrote detailed descriptions of his pilgrimage to Mecca. In this passage, he talks about crossing the desert from Syria to Medina.

Analyze Historical Sources
What parts of Ibn Battutah's description would be useful to a mapmaker?

> "The caravan then sets out from Tabuk and pushes on speedily night and day, for fear of this wilderness. Halfway through is the valley of al-Ukhaidir. . . . One year the pilgrims suffered severe distress in this place, by reason of the samoom-wind which blows [there], their water supplies dried up and the price of drink of water rose to a thousand dinars, but both seller and buyer perished. The story of this is inscribed on one of the rocks in the valley."
>
> —Ibn Battutah, from *The Travels*

geographers brought back, al-Idrisi made some important discoveries. For example, he proved that land did not go all the way around the Indian Ocean, as many people thought.

Math Muslim scholars also made advances in mathematics. In the 800s they combined the Indian number system, including the use of zero, with the Greek science of mathematics. The Muslim mathematician al-Khwarizmi (al-KWAHR-iz-mee) then used these new ideas to write a math textbook on what he called *al-jabr*, or "algebra." It laid the foundation for the modern algebra that students around the world learn today. When the book was brought to Europe in the 1500s, Europeans called the new numbers "Arabic" numerals.

Medicine Muslims made many advances in other sciences, but their greatest scientific achievements may have come in medicine. They studied Greek and Indian medicine, adding to this knowledge with discoveries of their own.

As early as the 800s, Muslim doctors in Baghdad began to improve medicine. As they studied, Muslim doctors
- created tests for doctors to pass before they could treat people
- made encyclopedias of drugs with descriptions of each drug's effects
- wrote descriptions of diseases
- started the first pharmacy school to teach people how to make medicines

The first Muslim public hospital was built in Baghdad. In that hospital, a doctor named Ar-Razi discovered how to diagnose and treat the deadly disease smallpox. Another doctor, Ibn-Sina, who was known in the West as Avicenna (av-uh-SEN-uh), wrote a medical encyclopedia. This encyclopedia, which was translated into Latin and used throughout Europe until the 1600s, is one of the most famous books in the history of medicine.

Medicine

Muslim doctors made medicines from plants like this mandrake plant, which was used to treat pain and illnesses. Muslim doctors developed better ways to prevent, diagnose, and treat many diseases.

$$2x + 4$$

Philosophy

Muslim philosophy led to the development of Sufism. Sufis celebrated their love of God through music and dance. These dancers whirl in circles as they dance with joy.

Math

Muslim mathematicians combined Indian and Greek ideas with their own to dramatically increase human knowledge of mathematics. The fact that we call our numbers today "Arabic" numerals is a reminder of this contribution.

Philosophy Many Muslim doctors and scientists also studied the ancient Greek philosophy of reason and rational thought. Other Muslims developed a new philosophy. Worried about the growing interest in worldly things, they focused on spiritual issues. Many of them lived a simple life of devotion to God.

The focus on spiritual issues led to a movement called Sufism (SOO-fi-zuhm). People who practice Sufism are called Sufis (SOO-feez). **Sufism** teaches that people can find God's love by having a personal relationship with God. They focus on loving God and call him their Beloved. Sufism had a strong impact on Islam.

Reading Check
Analyze Events In your opinion, what was the most important advance in science and learning in the Muslim world?

Literature and the Arts

The blending of traditional Islam and the cultures of conquered peoples produced fresh approaches to art, architecture, and writing. As a result, literature and the arts flourished in the Islamic world.

Omar Khayyám was a Persian mathematician, astronomer, and poet. Now, he is best known for his poetry.

Literature Two forms of literature were popular in the Muslim world— poetry and short stories. Poetry was influenced by Sufism. Some Sufis wrote poems about their loyalty to God. Through their poetry, the mystical ideas of Sufism spread among other Muslims. One of the most famous Sufi poets was **Omar Khayyám** (OH-mahr ky-AHM). In a book of poems known as *The Rubáiyát*, Khayyám wrote about faith, hope, and other emotions. Some of his poems express deep sadness or despair. Others, like this one, describe lighter, happier scenes.

> "A Book of Verses underneath the bough,
> A Jug of Wine, a Loaf of Bread—and Thou,
> Beside me singing in the Wilderness—
> Oh, Wilderness were Paradise enow [enough]."

— Omar Khayyám, from *The Rubáiyát*, translated by Edward FitzGerald

Muslims also enjoyed reading short stories. One famous collection of short stories is *The Thousand and One Nights*. It includes stories about legendary heroes and characters. A European compiler later added short stories that were not part of the medieval Arabic collection. Among these were some of the most famous, such as "Sinbad the Sailor," "Aladdin," and "Ali Baba and the 40 Thieves." Many of these tales came from India, Egypt, and other lands that had become part of the Muslim world. Another popular collection was *The Book of Golden Meadows*, by a writer from Baghdad called al-Masudi (mas-OW-dee). It contained historical stories about the caliphs. Some of these stories were humorous, while others were more serious.

Historical Source

The Book of Golden Meadows

Al-Masudi, a writer from Baghdad, wrote stories about caliphs. This story about Haroun Al Rashid illustrates the caliph's greatness. Al-Masudi includes details that show why Al Rashid was a good leader.

"*Haroun Al Rashid became Caliph in the year A.D. 786, and he ranks among the Caliphs who have been most distinguished by eloquence, learning, and generosity. . . . His daily prayers exceeded the number fixed by the law, and he used to perform the pilgrimage on foot, an act which no previous Caliph had done. When he went on pilgrimage he took with him a hundred learned men and their sons, and when he did not perform it himself he sent three hundred substitutes, whom he appareled richly, and whose expenses he defrayed with generosity.*"

—Al-Masudi,
from *The Book of Golden Meadows*

Analyze Historical Sources
What are two of the examples al-Masudi gives that show Al Rashid was a good caliph?

The Blue Mosque in Istanbul was built in the early 1600s for an Ottoman sultan. It upset many people at the time it was built because they thought its six minarets—instead of the usual four—were an attempt to make it as great as the mosque in Mecca.

Calligraphy is an important feature of Islamic art.

The most sacred part of a mosque is the mihrab, the niche that points the way to Mecca.

The mosque gets its name from its beautiful blue Iznik tiles.

Architecture Architecture was one of the most important Muslim art forms. Most people would say that the greatest architectural achievements of the Muslim empires were mosques. Like the great medieval cathedrals in Europe, mosques honored God and inspired religious followers.

The first mosques were simple. They were built to look like the courtyard of Muhammad's house in Medina where he had led the community in prayer. As the Muslim world grew richer, rulers became great **patrons**, or sponsors, of architecture. They used their wealth to pay for elaborately decorated mosques.

The main part of a mosque is a huge hall where people gather to pray. Many mosques have a dome and a **minaret**, or narrow tower from which Muslims are called to prayer. Some mosques, such as the Blue Mosque in

Istanbul, have many domes and minarets. Great mosques were built in major cities such as Mecca, Cairo, Baghdad, and Córdoba.

In addition to the mosques, Muslim architects built palaces, market-places, and libraries. These buildings have complicated domes and arches, colored bricks, and decorated tiles. Many also feature colorful mosaics that create repeating geometric patterns. Muslim architecture is known for these features.

Art Although Muslim buildings are often elaborately decorated with art, most of this art does not show any animals or humans. Muslims think only Allah can create humans and animals or their images. As a result, most Muslim artists didn't include people or animals in their works.

Because they couldn't represent people or animals in paintings, Muslim artists turned **calligraphy**, or decorative writing, into an art form. They used calligraphy to make sayings from the Qur'an into great works of art that they could use to decorate mosques and other buildings. They also painted decorative writing on tiles, wove it into carpets, and hammered it into finely decorated steel sword blades. Muslim art and literature show the influence of Islamic beliefs and practices. They also reflect the regional traditions of the places Muslims conquered. This mix of Islam with cultures from Asia, Africa, and Europe gave literature and the arts a unique style and character.

Summary As Islam spread through Europe and Asia, powerful new empires developed. These empires blended Islamic traditions with the traditions of conquered peoples. The result was a new kind of Islamic culture, unified by a common language and religion, but not specifically Arab in character.

Reading Check

Form Generalizations
What two architectural elements were usually part of a mosque?

Lesson 4 Assessment

Review Ideas, Terms, and People

1. a. Identify Who traveled to India, Africa, China, and Spain and contributed his knowledge to the study of geography?

b. Explain How did Muslim scholars help preserve learning from the ancient world?

c. Rank In your opinion, what was the most important Muslim scientific achievement? Why?

2. a. Describe What function do minarets play in mosques?

b. Summarize What did patrons do for art and architecture in the Muslim world?

c. Make Inferences What is the connection between Islamic belief and calligraphy?

d. Summarize How did Muslim artists create art without showing humans or animals?

Critical Thinking

3. Categorize Draw a graphic organizer like this one. In the second column, identify one important achievement or development Muslims made in each category listed in the first column.

Category	Achievement or Development
Astronomy	*Improved astrolabe*
Geography	
Math	
Medicine	
Philosophy	

Social Studies Skills

Interpret Timelines

Define the Skill

Timelines are visual summaries of what happened when. They show events in chronological order—that is, the sequence in which events occurred. Timelines also illustrate how long after one event another event took place. They help you to see relationships between events and to remember important dates.

A timeline covers a span of years. Some timelines cover a great number of years or centuries. Other timelines, such as the one here, cover much shorter periods of time. Timelines can be horizontal or vertical. Whichever direction they run, timelines should always be read from the earliest date to the latest date.

Learn the Skill

Follow these steps to interpret a timeline.

1. *Determine the timeline's framework.* Note the range of years covered and the intervals of time into which it is divided.

2. *Study the order of events on the timeline.* Note the length of time between events.

3. *Supply missing information.* Think about the people, places, and other events associated with each item on the timeline.

4. *Note relationships.* Ask yourself how an event relates to earlier or later events on the timeline. Look for cause-and-effect relationships and long-term developments.

Practice the Skill

Study the timeline about Muhammad and the early spread of Islam. Use it to answer the following questions.

1. What is the framework of this timeline?

2. How long was it before Muhammad told many people in Mecca about the messages?

3. For how long did Muhammad spread his teachings in Mecca before going to Medina?

4. What event or events led to warfare between Mecca and Medina?

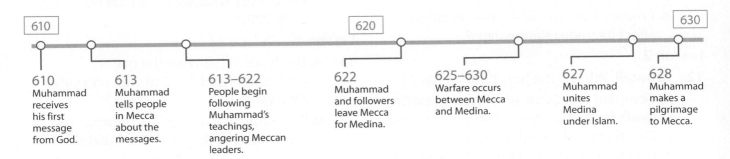

| 610 | 620 | 630 |

610 Muhammad receives his first message from God.

613 Muhammad tells people in Mecca about the messages.

613–622 People begin following Muhammad's teachings, angering Meccan leaders.

622 Muhammad and followers leave Mecca for Medina.

625–630 Warfare occurs between Mecca and Medina.

627 Muhammad unites Medina under Islam.

628 Muhammad makes a pilgrimage to Mecca.

Module 13 Assessment

Review Vocabulary, Terms, and People

*For each statement, write **T** if it is true and **F** if it is false. If the statement is false, write the correct term that would make the sentence a true statement.*

1. Muslims gather to pray at a <u>souk</u>.
2. Traders often traveled in <u>caravans</u> to take their goods to markets.
3. A(n) <u>Islam</u> is a person who submits to God and follows the teachings of Muhammad.
4. According to Islamic belief, God's messages to Muhammad during his lifetime make up the <u>Sunnah</u>.
5. Some people might worship gods or saints at a <u>shrine</u>.
6. A hill of sand shaped by the wind is called a(n) <u>oasis</u>.
7. <u>Jihad</u> is a journey to a sacred place.
8. Abu Bakr was the first <u>caliph</u>.
9. <u>Calligraphy</u> teaches that people can find God's love by having a personal relationship with God.
10. Many mosques have a dome and a <u>minaret</u>.

Comprehension and Critical Thinking

Lesson 1

11. **a. Describe** What are some important characteristics of the Arabian Peninsula's physical geography?
    b. Contrast What are the two main ways of life that developed in Arabia? How are they different?
    c. Predict How would Arabia's location affect its trade relationships?

Lesson 2

12. **a. Recall** What is the holy book of Islam?
    b. Compare and Contrast How did Muhammad's teachings compare to Judaism and Christianity? How did they contrast with common beliefs of Arabs at the time?
    c. Elaborate Why is 622 an important year in Islamic history?
    d. Define What is the hajj?
    e. Analyze How are the Qur'an and the Sunnah connected to Shariah?
    f. Elaborate How do the Five Pillars of Islam affect Muslims' daily lives?

Lesson 3

13. **a. Identify** Who was Abu Bakr, and what did he do?
    b. Draw Conclusions How did trade affect the Arab world?
    c. Elaborate What was Baghdad like in the early 800s? What was Córdoba like in the early 900s?

Lesson 4

14. **a. Describe** What were the major contributions of Ibn Battutah and Omar Khayyám?
    b. Compare In studying astronomy, how were Muslims similar to the Greeks?
    c. Contrast In what major way was Muslim art different from ancient Egyptian art?
    d. Predict Of all the accomplishments of Muslim scholars and artists, which do you think would have the most lasting impact on people around the world?

Module 13 Assessment, continued

Review Themes

15. Religion In what ways did Islam change life in Arabia?

16. Religion What teachings or beliefs does Islam share with Judaism and Christianity?

Reading Skills

Descriptive Text *Use the Reading Skills taught in this module to answer the following questions about using descriptive words when writing.*

17. List action verbs that could be used to describe Muhammad's trip to Mecca.

18. What adjectives could be used to describe Islamic art?

19. Write a sentence about the geography of Arabia using the two main types of descriptive words.

Social Studies Skills

Interpret Timelines *Use the Social Studies Skills taught in this module to answer the question below.*

20. Draw a timeline like the one shown. Use it to show relationships among the people and events listed from Lesson 2. Include any dates you may know on your timeline.

550   650

a. Mecca's merchants reject Muhammad's teachings.

b. Muhammad dies in Medina.

c. Muhammad begins to tell other people about the messages from God.

d. The people of Mecca welcome Muhammad back to their city.

e. Muhammad is born in Mecca.

f. Muhammad tells his wife Khadijah about the voice in the cave.

g. Muhammad and some followers are forced to leave Mecca for Medina.

h. The people of Medina accept Islam.

i. Muhammad hears a voice in a cave.

Focus On Writing

21. Write an "I Am" Poem Write an "I Am" poem about one person—real or imaginary—from this period of Muslim history. You might choose an actual person, such as Omar Khayyám, or an imaginary person, such as a Muslim merchant. Read over the text carefully to find details about the person, and then fill in information with your imagination. Choose descriptive language, including adjectives and action verbs, to help create a picture in your reader's mind. Your poem should be six lines long. The lines should begin, "I am . . .""I believe . . .""I see . . .""I feel . . .""I want . . ." and "I am . . ."

Early African Civilizations

🌐

Essential Question
What was more important for the development of African societies, trade or warfare?

About the Photo: This photo shows women in front of a mosque in the city of Djenné, in the modern country of Mali.

In this module, you will read about the geography, early cultures, and great empires of Africa. You will also learn about the ways religion, trade, and natural resources all influenced how early African civilizations developed.

▶ Explore ONLINE!

VIDEOS, including...
• The Sahara

HISTORY

✅ Document-Based Investigations

✅ Graphic Organizers

✅ Interactive Games

✅ Interactive Map: Early African Empires

✅ Image with Hotspots: Timbuktu

✅ Image Carousel: Crossing the Sahara

What You Will Learn...

Lesson 1: Geography of Early Africa **470**
The Big Idea Natural resources, trade, family ties, religion, and iron technology all contributed to the growth of West African societies.

Lesson 2: The Empire of Ghana **480**
The Big Idea The rulers of Ghana built an empire by controlling the salt and gold trade.

Lesson 3: The Empires of Mali and Songhai **488**
The Big Idea The wealthy and powerful Mali Empire ruled West Africa after the fall of Ghana, and the Songhai Empire strengthened Islam in the region.

Lesson 4: Historical and Artistic Traditions of West Africa **498**
The Big Idea Because the people of West Africa did not have a written language, their culture has been passed down through oral history, writings by other people, and the arts.

Lesson 5: Sub-Saharan Cultures. **506**
The Big Idea The movement and interaction of cultures and peoples created unique ways of life in sub-Saharan Africa.

Timeline of Events 500 BC–AD 1600

▶ Explore ONLINE!

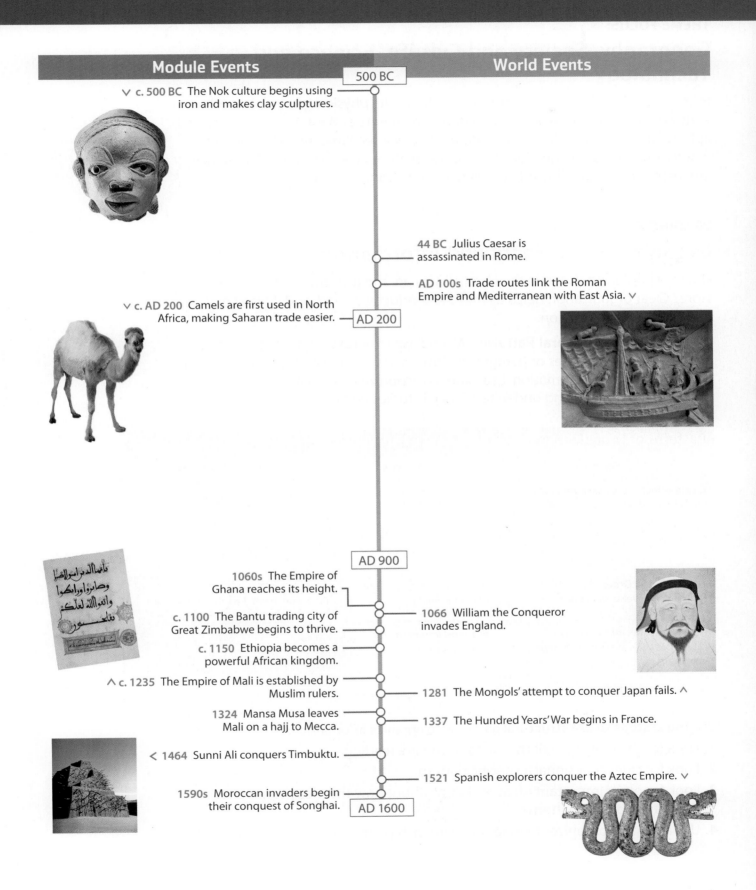

Module Events

World Events

500 BC

∨ **c. 500 BC** The Nok culture begins using iron and makes clay sculptures.

44 BC Julius Caesar is assassinated in Rome.

AD 100s Trade routes link the Roman Empire and Mediterranean with East Asia. ∨

∨ **c. AD 200** Camels are first used in North Africa, making Saharan trade easier.

AD 200

AD 900

1060s The Empire of Ghana reaches its height.

1066 William the Conqueror invades England.

c. 1100 The Bantu trading city of Great Zimbabwe begins to thrive.

c. 1150 Ethiopia becomes a powerful African kingdom.

∧ **c. 1235** The Empire of Mali is established by Muslim rulers.

1281 The Mongols' attempt to conquer Japan fails. ∧

1324 Mansa Musa leaves Mali on a hajj to Mecca.

1337 The Hundred Years' War begins in France.

< **1464** Sunni Ali conquers Timbuktu.

1521 Spanish explorers conquer the Aztec Empire. ∨

1590s Moroccan invaders begin their conquest of Songhai.

AD 1600

Reading Social Studies

THEME FOCUS:

Geography, Society and Culture, Science and Technology

In this module, you will read about West Africa—its physical geography and early cultures. You will learn about different elements of West African society and culture, such as oral traditions and dance. You will see West Africa is a land of many resources and varied features. Some resources were the basis for science and technology that allowed people to create strong tools and weapons.

READING FOCUS:

Organization of Facts and Information

How are books organized in the library? How are the groceries organized in the store? Clear organization helps us find the product we need, and it also helps us find facts and information.

Understanding Structural Patterns Writers use structural patterns to organize information in sentences or paragraphs. What's a structural pattern? It's simply a way of organizing information. Learning to recognize those patterns will make it easier for you to read and understand social studies texts.

Patterns of Organization		
Pattern	**Clue Words**	**Graphic Organizer**
Cause-effect shows how one thing leads to another.	*as a result, because, therefore, this led to*	Cause → Effect, Effect, Effect
Chronological Order shows the sequence of events or actions.	*after, before, first, then, not long after, finally*	First → Next → Next → Last
Listing presents information in categories such as size, location or importance.	*also, most important, for example, in fact*	Category • Fact • Fact • Fact

Use these steps to use structural patterns to organize information:

1. Look for the main idea of the passage you are reading.
2. Look for clues that signal a specific pattern.
3. Look for other important ideas and think about how the ideas connect. Is there any obvious pattern?
4. Use a graphic organizer to map the relationships among the facts and details.

You Try It!

Read the following passage and then answer the questions below.

Recognize Structural Patterns

A. "Living in present day Nigeria, the Nok made iron farm tools. One iron tool, the hoe, allowed farmers to clear the land more quickly and easily than they could do with earlier tools. As a result, they could grow more food."

B. "Thousands of years ago, West Africa had a damp climate. About 5,000 years ago the climate changed, though, and the area became drier. As more land became desert, people had to leave areas where they could no longer survive. People who had once lived freely began to live closer together. Over time, they settled in villages."

C. "Four different regions make up the area surrounding the Niger River. . . . The northern band across West Africa is the southern part of the Sahara. . . . The next band is the semiarid Sahel (sah-HEL), a strip of land that divides the desert from wetter areas. . . . Farther south is a band of savannah, or open grassland. . . . The fourth band gets heavy rain."

Answer these questions based on the passage you just read.

1. What structural pattern did the writer use to organize the information in passage A? How can you tell?

2. What structural pattern did the writer use to organize the information in passage B? How can you tell?

3. What structural pattern did the writer use to organize the information in passage C? How can you tell?

As you read this module, think about the organization of the ideas. Look for signal words, and ask yourself why the author has arranged the text in the way he or she did.

Key Terms and People

Lesson 1
rifts
sub-Saharan Africa
Sahel
savannah
rain forests
kinship system
extended family
patrilineal
matrilineal
animism

Lesson 2
silent barter
income
Tunka Manin

Lesson 3
Sundiata
Mansa Musa
Sunni Ali
Askia the Great

Lesson 4
oral history
griots
proverbs
kente

Lesson 5
Ethiopia
Coptic Christianity
Bantu
Great Zimbabwe
Swahili

Geography and Early Africa

The Big Idea

Natural resources, trade, family ties, religion, and iron technology all contributed to the growth of West African societies.

Main Ideas

- The landforms, water, climate, and plant life affected history in West Africa.

- West Africa's resources included farmland, gold, and salt.

- Family and religion influenced daily life in early West African society.

- Iron technology changed life in West Africa.

Key Terms and People

rifts
sub-Saharan Africa
Sahel
savannah
rain forests
kinship system
extended family
patrilineal
matrilineal
animism

If YOU were there . . .

You and your family are farmers in West Africa in about 400 BC. The Niger River is not too far away from where you live. The river is full of life—birds, fish, and crocodiles. You use its water to grow crops and raise cattle. Farming is hard work. You use a sharp, wooden stick to dig the soil and put seeds in the ground. One day, you are given farm tools made of a dark metal you've never seen before. These fine tools are so strong you can't break them! They have clean, sharp edges.

Why is this a good place to live? How will these new tools change your life?

Landforms, Water, Climate, and Plant Life

Africa is a big place. In fact, it is the second-largest continent on earth. Only Asia is bigger. An immense desert, the Sahara, stretches across most of North Africa. Along the northwestern edge of the Sahara are the Atlas Mountains. At the opposite edge of the continent, in the southeast, the Drakensberg Mountains rise. In eastern Africa, mountains extend alongside great rifts. These **rifts** are long, deep valleys formed by the movement of Earth's crust. From all these mountains the land dips into plateaus and wide, low plains.

The plains of **sub-Saharan Africa**, or Africa south of the Sahara, are crossed by mighty rivers. Among the main rivers are the Congo, the Zambezi, and the Niger. Along the Niger River in West Africa great civilizations arose. The role this river played in the development of civilizations is one example of the way the physical geography of West Africa affected history there.

West Africa's Great River The Niger River was a source of water, food, and transportation, which allowed many people to live in the area.

Along the Niger's middle section is a low-lying area of lakes and marshes. This watery region is called the inland delta. Although it looks much like the area where a river flows into the sea, it is hundreds of miles from the coast. Many animals and birds find food and shelter in the area. Among them are crocodiles, geese, and hippopotamus. Fish are also plentiful.

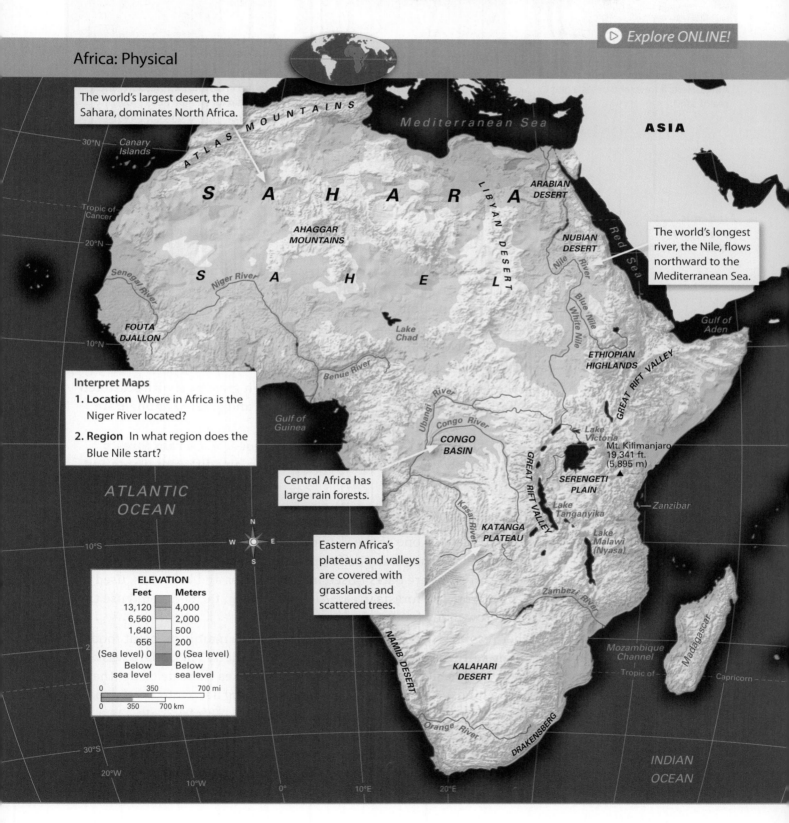

▶ Explore ONLINE!

Africa: Physical

The world's largest desert, the Sahara, dominates North Africa.

ATLAS MOUNTAINS

Mediterranean Sea

ASIA

Canary Islands

30°N

Tropic of Cancer

S A H A R A

LIBYAN DESERT

ARABIAN DESERT

The world's longest river, the Nile, flows northward to the Mediterranean Sea.

20°N

AHAGGAR MOUNTAINS

NUBIAN DESERT

Nile

Red Sea

Senegal River

Niger River

S A H E L

Nile River

Blue Nile

Gulf of Aden

10°N

FOUTA DJALLON

Lake Chad

White Nile

ETHIOPIAN HIGHLANDS

GREAT RIFT VALLEY

Benue River

Interpret Maps

1. Location Where in Africa is the Niger River located?

2. Region In what region does the Blue Nile start?

Ubangi River

Congo River

CONGO BASIN

Gulf of Guinea

Central Africa has large rain forests.

Lake Victoria

Mt. Kilimanjaro 19,341 ft. (5,895 m) ▲

GREAT RIFT VALLEY

SERENGETI PLAIN

Zanzibar

ATLANTIC OCEAN

Kasai River

Eastern Africa's plateaus and valleys are covered with grasslands and scattered trees.

KATANGA PLATEAU

Lake Tanganyika

Lake Malawi (Nyasa)

10°S

N
W   E
S

Zambezi River

Mozambique Channel

Madagascar

ELEVATION

Feet	Meters
13,120	4,000
6,560	2,000
1,640	500
656	200
(Sea level) 0	0 (Sea level)
Below sea level	Below sea level

NAMIB DESERT

KALAHARI DESERT

Tropic of Capricorn

INDIAN OCEAN

0   350   700 mi
0   350   700 km

Orange River

DRAKENSBERG

30°S

20°W

10°W

0°

10°E

20°E

Desert

The huge Sahara covers most of North Africa. Here, a traveler crosses a giant sea of sand.

Savannah

Much of Africa is covered by grasslands called savannah. Scattered across the savannah are clumps of trees like these acacia trees.

Rain Forest

Thick rain forests like this one are found in central and western Africa. The rain forests' tall trees provide homes for many different animals.

Academic Vocabulary
impact effect, result

West Africa's Climates and Plants Four different climate regions make up the area surrounding the Niger River. These regions, which run from east to west, are like broad bands or stripes across West Africa. The entire area is warm, but rainfall varies from north to south. The amount of rainfall each region gets has an **impact** on what vegetation, or plant life, exists there.

The northern band across West Africa is the southern part of the Sahara. This huge expanse of sand and gravel is the world's largest desert. Temperatures can climb above 120°F. Rain is very rare.

The next band is the semiarid **Sahel** (sah-HEL), a strip of land that divides the desert from wetter areas. Although the Sahel is fairly dry, it has enough vegetation to support hardy grazing animals.

Farther south is a band of **savannah**, or open grassland with scattered trees. Tall grasses and shrubs also grow there, and grazing animals are common.

Reading Check
Summarize What are West Africa's four climate and vegetation regions?

The fourth band gets heavy rain. Near the equator are **rain forests**, or moist, densely wooded areas. They contain many different plants and animals.

West Africa's Resources

Academic Vocabulary
traditional customary, time-honored

West Africa's land is one of the region's resources. With its many climates, the land could produce many different crops. Among the **traditional** West African crops are dates raised in desert oases and kola nuts, used for medicines, from the forests' trees. Along the Niger, farmers could use the water to grow many food crops.

Other resources were minerals. People who live mainly on plant foods, like many early Africans, must add salt to their diets. The Sahara was a source of this precious mineral. When ancient lakes there dried up, they left salt behind. Workers mined the salt by digging deep into the earth.

Reading Check
Find Main Ideas What are some of West Africa's major resources?

Gold was another mineral resource of West Africa. Although gold is soft and therefore useless for tools or weapons, it makes beautiful jewelry and coins. Gold came from the southern forests. Miners kept the exact locations of the gold mines a secret. To this day, no one knows exactly where the mines were located, but gold became a valuable trade good.

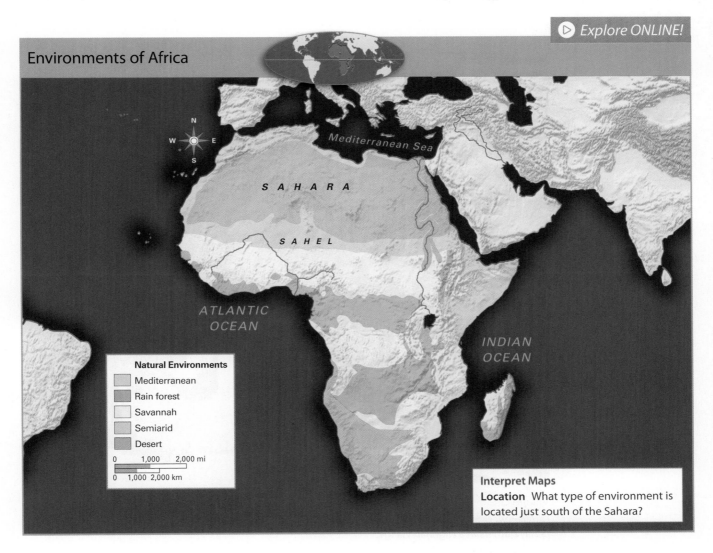

▷ Explore ONLINE!

Natural Environments

- Mediterranean
- Rain forest
- Savannah
- Semiarid
- Desert

0   1,000   2,000 mi
0   1,000 2,000 km

Interpret Maps
Location What type of environment is located just south of the Sahara?

Families, Religion, and Daily Life

Thousands of years ago, West Africa had a damp climate. About 5,000 years ago the climate changed, though, and the area became drier. As more land became desert, people had to leave areas where they could no longer survive. People who had once roamed freely began to live closer together. Over time, they settled in villages. At the heart of village life was the family.

Families, Villages, and Loyalties Historians today look at traditional African communities to learn about how life was lived long ago. They believe that such communities have a social organization similar to that of early communities in West Africa and other parts of the world.

The main way people organized themselves was by living in larger groups of relatives. This is called a kinship system. A **kinship system** is a system of social organization based on family ties. These family ties are used for production and group decision-making.

Village Life
Families were an important part of West African village society. Here a family gathers in a Nigerian village.

The kinship system started with an **extended family**, which included a father, mother, children, and close relatives. Extended families lived with other people related to them in villages. People in villages were parts of larger clans. A clan is a large group of people who are related to each other.

African societies could also include another type of group—age-sets. In age-sets, men who had been born within the same two or three years formed special bonds. Men in the same age-set had a duty to help each other. Women, too, sometimes formed age-sets.

In some West African villages, the older people, or elders, of the village were the leaders and made the decisions. Other groups had a chief who was descended from the founder of the clan. The chief relied on a council of important people who advised him. The council also helped him make laws for the community.

In most of these societies, leadership was hereditary, meaning that it was passed down from a relative. Some societies were **patrilineal**. Leadership passed from fathers or grandfathers to sons, grandsons, or

Village Society

Families

Families were the basic group of village society.

Extended Families

Extended families included grandparents, aunts, uncles, cousins, and their families.

Village Chiefs

Extended families often had a male leader who served as a village chief.

Council of Elders

Sometimes, village chiefs formed a council of elders that led the village. Sometimes a village would just be run by a council of elders.

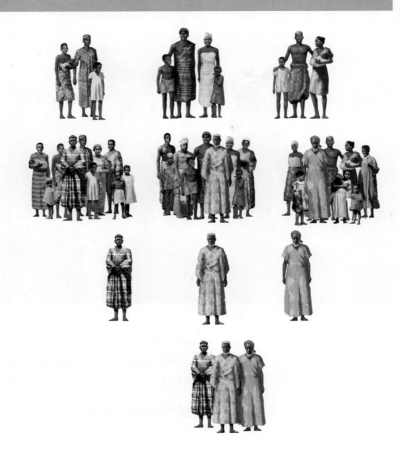

nephews. By contrast, others were **matrilineal**. Even though men still served as leaders, leadership passed down through the mother's family. For example, in matrilineal societies a new leader might be the son of the old leader's daughter.

Members of families, villages, and clans were expected to be loyal to one another. Loyalty to family and age-sets helped people work together and maintained order in the community. It seems that there was not the same concept of individual rights in these communities that we have today.

Social Roles Everyone in a community had specific duties. The men hunted and farmed. Among the crops that men tended were millet and sorghum. These hardy grains grew well in the savannah in spite of the poor soil there. After being harvested, the grain could be made into a thick paste or ground into flour to make bread. Cattle could eat the grain. Farmers also raised goats and sheep.

Like the men, West African women worked very hard. They farmed, collected firewood, ground grain, and carried water. Women also cared for children. Even the very young and the very old had their own tasks. For example, the elders, or old people, taught the family's traditions to younger generations. Through songs, dances, and stories, elders passed on the

This photo shows West African villagers performing a traditional dance learned from their elders.

community's history and values. Among the values that children learned was the need for hard work. Children began working beside older family members as soon as they were able.

Religion and Culture Another central feature of village life was religion. Some religious practices were similar from village to village. A traditional belief showed the importance of families. Many West Africans believed that the unseen spirits of their ancestors stayed nearby. To honor these spirits, families marked places as sacred spaces by putting specially carved statues there. Family members gathered in these places to share news and problems with the ancestors. Families also offered food to the ancestors' spirits. Through these practices they hoped to keep the spirits happy. In return, they believed, these spirits would protect the village from harm.

Another common West African belief had to do with nature. We call it **animism**—the belief that bodies of water, animals, trees, and other natural objects have spirits. Animism reflected West Africans' dependence on the natural world for survival.

This Nok terra cotta (ceramic clay) sculpture depicts human heads, a common feature of Nok artistry .

Reading Check
Form Generalizations
What role did families play in traditional West African culture?

Technology and Change

As time passed, the people of West Africa developed advanced and diverse cultures. Changes in technology helped some early communities grow.

Sometime around 500 BC West Africans made a discovery that would change their region forever. They found that they could heat certain kinds of rock to get a hard metal. This metal was iron. By heating the iron again, they could shape it into useful things. Stronger than other metals, iron was good for making tools.

One of the earliest peoples to use this new technology was the Nok. Living in what is now Nigeria, the Nok made iron farm tools. One iron tool, the hoe, allowed farmers to clear the land more quickly and easily than they could with earlier tools. As a result, they could grow more food. The Nok also used iron tips for arrows and spears. Iron weapons provided a better defense against invaders and helped in hunting. As better-equipped farmers, hunters, and warriors, the Nok gained power. They also became known for fine sculptures of animals and human heads they made from clay.

Iron tools also provided another benefit. They helped West Africans live in places where they couldn't live before. Iron blades allowed people to cut down trees to clear land for farms. Because they had more places to live and more farms for growing food, the population of West Africa grew.

Summary and Preview Families and religion were central to early West African cultures. The physical geography of the continent also impacted people's lives. When West Africans developed iron technology, communities grew. In the next lesson, you will read about the West African empires based on the trade of gold and salt.

Reading Check
Find Main Ideas
How did technology change life in West Africa?

Lesson 1 Assessment

Review Ideas, Terms, and People

1. **a. Define** What is a savannah?

   b. Contrast How might living in the Sahel be different from living in a rain forest?

   c. Evaluate In which African climate region would you most like to live? Why?

2. **a. Identify** What were two of early West Africa's important mineral resources?

   b. Explain How were these resources related to West Africa's physical geography?

   c. Elaborate Why do you think miners kept the location of the gold mines a secret?

3. **a. Identify** What are two groups to which a person in early West Africa may have owed loyalty?

   b. Analyze How did animism reflect what was important to early West African peoples?

4. **a. Describe** How did the use of iron change farming?

   b. Make Inferences What evidence do you think historians have for how the Nok people lived?

Critical Thinking

5. **Summarize** Create a chart like this one. Use it to describe the characteristics of West Africa's four climate regions.

Climate region	Characteristics

History and Geography

Crossing the Sahara

Crossing the Sahara has never been easy. Bigger than the entire continent of Australia, the Sahara is one of the hottest, driest, and most barren places on earth. Yet for centuries, people have crossed the Sahara's gravel-covered plains and vast seas of sand. Long ago, West Africans crossed the desert regularly to carry on a rich trade.

Salt, used to preserve and flavor food, was available in the Sahara. Traders from the north took salt south. Camel caravans carried huge slabs of salt weighing hundreds of pounds.

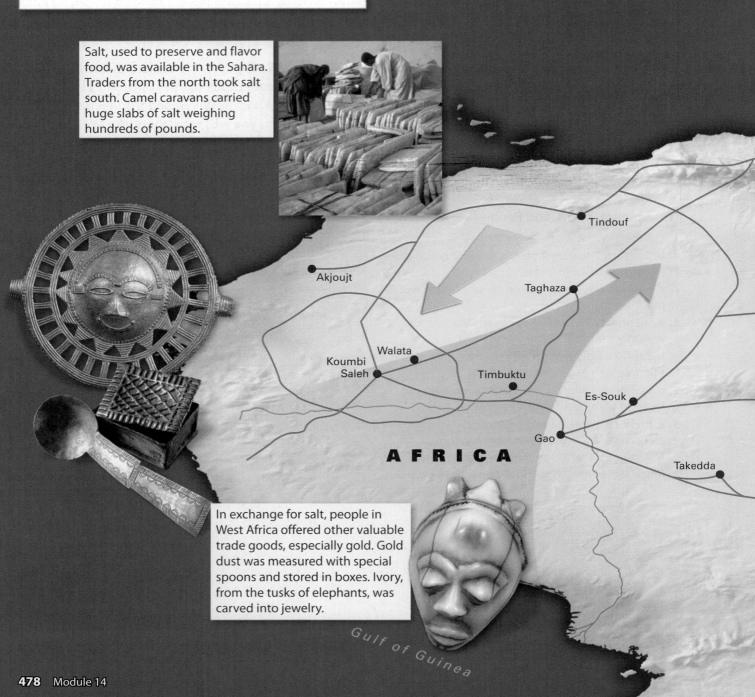

Akjoujt

Tindouf

Taghaza

Walata

Koumbi
Saleh

Timbuktu

Es-Souk

Gao

AFRICA

Takedda

In exchange for salt, people in West Africa offered other valuable trade goods, especially gold. Gold dust was measured with special spoons and stored in boxes. Ivory, from the tusks of elephants, was carved into jewelry.

Gulf of Guinea

ATLANTIC OCEAN

EUROPE

Some goods that were traded across the Sahara, like silk and spices, came all the way from Asia along the Silk Road. These luxury items were traded for West African goods like gold and ivory.

MEDITERRANEAN SEA

Ghadames

Ghat

Zawilah

S A H A R A

Bilma

Daima

| | Trade route |
| ● | Settlement |

Scale varies on this map.

RED SEA

A Difficult Journey

Temperature Temperatures soared to well over 100°F during the day and below freezing at night. Dying of heat or cold was a real danger.

Water Most areas of the Sahara gets less than 1 inch of rain per year. Travelers had to bring lots of water or they could die of thirst.

Distance The Sahara is huge, and the trade routes were not well marked. Travelers could easily get lost.

Bandits Valuable trade goods were a tempting target for bandits. For protection, merchants traveled in caravans.

Interpret Maps

1. **Movement** What were some goods traded across the Sahara?

2. **Human-Environment Interaction** Why was salt a valued trade good?

The Empire of Ghana

The Big Idea

The rulers of Ghana built an empire by controlling the salt and gold trade.

Main Ideas

- Ghana grew as larger populations settled on desert trade routes.

- Ghana controlled trade and became wealthy.

- Through its control of trade, Ghana built an empire.

- Ghana's decline was caused by attacking invaders, overgrazing, and the loss of trade.

Key Terms and People

silent barter
income
Tunka Manin

Carving of a human head from Ghana

If YOU were there . . .

You are a trader, traveling in a caravan from the north into West Africa around AD 1000. The caravan carries many goods, but the most precious is salt. Salt is so valuable that people trade gold for it! You have never met the mysterious men who trade you the gold. You wish you could talk to them to find out where they get it.

Why do you think the traders are so secretive?

An Empire at the Desert's Edge

For hundreds of years, trade routes crisscrossed West Africa. For most of that time, West Africans did not profit much from the Saharan trade because the routes were run by Berbers from northern Africa. Eventually, that situation changed. Ghana (GAH-nuh), an empire in West Africa, gained control of the valuable routes. As a result, Ghana became a powerful state.

Desert Trade For a long time, West Africans had ventured into the desert for trade. However, those early travelers could only make short trips from oasis to oasis. Their horses couldn't go far without water.

In the AD 200s, the situation changed. At about that time, Romans started to use camels to carry goods throughout northern Africa. These long-legged animals could store water and energy in their bodies for long periods of time. They could also carry heavy loads.

With camels, people could cross the Sahara in two months. Traders formed caravans to make the trip. A North African people called the Berbers used their knowledge of the desert to lead the caravans. Even with camels and the Berbers' skills, crossing the Sahara was dangerous. Supplies could run out, thieves could attack, and caravans could lose their way.

Ghana's Beginnings The empire of Ghana lay between the Niger and Senegal rivers. This location was north and west of the location of the modern nation that bears the name Ghana. As the people of West Africa grew more food, communities had more than they needed to survive. West Africans began to trade the area's resources with buyers who lived thousands of miles away.

Archaeology provides some clues to Ghana's early history, but we do not know much about its earliest days. Historians think the first people in Ghana were farmers. Sometime after 300 these farmers, the Soninke (soh-NING-kee), were threatened by nomadic herders. The herders wanted to take the farmers' water and pastures. For protection, groups of Soninke families began to band together. This banding together was the beginning of Ghana.

Once they banded together, the people of Ghana grew in strength. They learned how to work with iron and used iron tools to farm the land along the Niger River. They also herded cattle for meat and milk. Because these farmers and herders could produce plenty of food, the population of Ghana increased. Towns and villages grew.

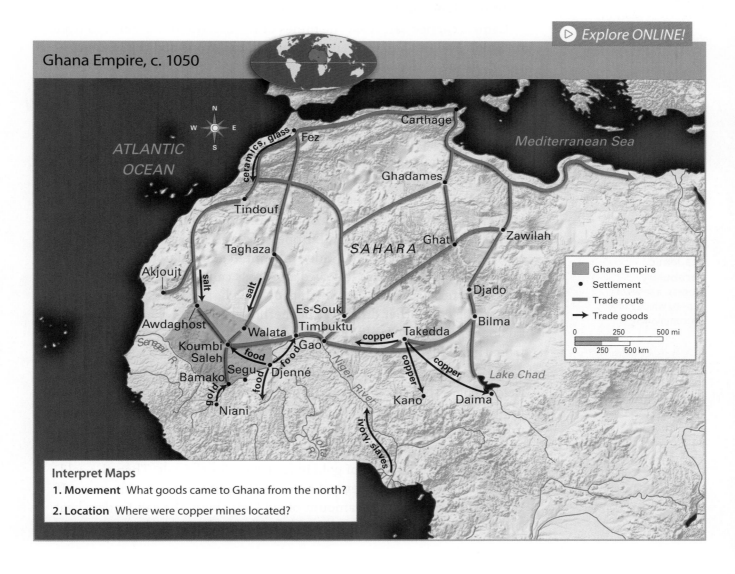

▶ Explore ONLINE!

Ghana Empire, c. 1050

ATLANTIC OCEAN

Mediterranean Sea

Carthage

Fez

ceramics, glass

Ghadames

Tindouf

Ghat

Zawilah

SAHARA

Taghaza

salt

salt

Akjoujt

Djado

Es-Souk

Bilma

Awdaghost

Walata

Timbuktu

copper

Takedda

Koumbi Saleh

Gao

food

food

Senegal R.

Segu

Djenné

Niger River

copper

copper

Bamako

gold

food

Kano

Daima

Lake Chad

Niani

Volta R.

ivory, slaves

Legend:
- Ghana Empire
- • Settlement
- — Trade route
- → Trade goods

0   250   500 mi
0   250   500 km

Interpret Maps

1. **Movement** What goods came to Ghana from the north?

2. **Location** Where were copper mines located?

Early African Civilizations **481**

Reading Check
Analyze Effects
How did camels change Saharan trade?

Besides farm tools, iron was also useful for making weapons. Other armies in the area had weapons made of bone, wood, and stone. These were no match for the iron spear points and blades used by Ghana's army.

As with other early societies, as the towns and villages grew, people in Ghana began to specialize in types of labor. Some people became blacksmiths, others were gold miners, while still others were farmers or traders.

Trade in Ghana and West Africa

Ghana lay between the vast Sahara Desert and deep forests. In this location, they were in a good position to trade in the region's most valuable resources—gold and salt.

Gold and Salt Gold came from the south, from mines near the Gulf of Guinea and along the Niger. Salt came from the Sahara in the north.

West Africa's gold and salt trade became a source of great wealth. People wanted gold for its beauty. But they needed salt in their diets to survive. Salt, which could be used to preserve food, also made bland food tasty. These qualities made salt very valuable. In fact, Africans sometimes cut up slabs of salt and used the pieces as money.

Camels carried salt from the mines of the Sahara to the south to trade for gold. Traders then took the gold north, to Europe and the Islamic world. Along with gold and salt, traders carried cloth, copper, silver, and other items. They also bought and sold human beings as slaves.

Slavery was part of Ghana's society and the other West African empires that followed it. Over more than 1,000 years, the trans-Saharan slave trade affected at least 10 million enslaved men, women, and children. Slave traders moved people from West and East Africa to places in North Africa, the Middle East, and India. These slaves and their descendants became part of the royal households and armies of these regions' rulers.

Scarcity drove the trade in gold and salt. South of the Sahara, salt was scarce. In northern Africa and Europe, gold was scarce. People had to make trade-offs to get what they needed or wanted and did not have. In Ghana, this exchange sometimes followed a **process** called silent barter. **Silent barter** is a process in which people exchange goods without ever contacting each other directly. The method made sure that the traders did business peacefully. It also kept the exact location of the gold mines secret from the salt traders.

In the silent barter process, salt traders went to a riverbank near gold fields. There they left slabs of salt in rows and beat a drum to tell the gold miners that trading had begun. Then the salt traders moved back several miles from the riverbank.

Soon afterward, the gold miners arrived by boat. They left what they considered a fair amount of gold in exchange for the salt. Then the gold miners also moved back several miles so the salt traders could return. If they were happy with the amount of gold left there, the salt traders beat the drum again, took the gold, and left. The gold miners then returned and

Academic Vocabulary
process a series of steps by which a task is accomplished

Gold and Salt

Ghana's rulers got rich by controlling the trade in salt and gold. Salt came from the north in large slabs like the ones shown here. Gold, like the woman is wearing in the photo, came from the south.

picked up their salt. Trading continued until both sides were happy with the exchange.

Growth of Trade As the trade in gold and salt increased, Ghana's rulers gained power. Over time, their military strength grew as well. With their armies, they began to take control of this trade from the merchants who had once controlled it. Merchants from the north and south met to exchange goods in Ghana. As a result of their control of trade routes, the rulers of Ghana became wealthy.

Additional sources of wealth and trade were developed to add to Ghana's wealth. Wheat was grown and came from the north. Sheep and cattle were raised, and honey was produced. These items came from the south. Local products, including leather and cloth, were also traded for wealth. Among the prized special local products were tassels made from golden thread.

As trade increased, Ghana's capital grew. The largest city in West Africa, Koumbi Saleh (KOOM-bee SAHL-uh) was an oasis for travelers. These travelers could find all the region's goods for sale in its markets. As a result, Koumbi Saleh gained a reputation as a great trading center.

Influence of Islam The Soninke name for the empire was Wagadou. Today it is usually called its Arabic name, Ghana, which was the name Muslim traders gave the empire. The name is not the only way Islam influenced Ghana. Muslim traders had a large influence on the society. The written language, currency, architecture, and business practices were all influenced by Islamic culture. Muslims also became government officials and treasurers.

Trade in West Africa

For centuries, West Africans have traded goods in markets like this one. At these regional markets, people could get local goods like food and clothing, as well as more valuable goods from far away.

Reading Check
Form Generalizations
How did trade help Ghana develop?

Some historians believe that Islamic beliefs about slavery influenced the growth of the slave trade in Ghana. The Qur'an, the Muslim holy book, recognizes slavery as a condition that exists. The text encourages the kind treatment of slaves and states that it is a humane act for an owner to free a slave. Islam forbids Muslims from enslaving other Muslims. However, any non-Muslim who lived outside of Muslim territory was someone who could become a slave. Traders began to see profit in the slave trade. An Arab geographer described an area along a trans-Saharan trade route as "chiefly remarkable for black slaves. . . ." The slave trade continued to play a significant role in Ghana's growing economy.

Ghana Builds an Empire

By 800, Ghana was firmly in control of West Africa's trade routes. Nearly all trade between northern and southern Africa passed through Ghana. Traders were protected by Ghana's army, which kept trade routes free from bandits. As a result, trade became safer. Knowing they would be protected, traders were not scared to travel to Ghana. Trade increased, and Ghana's influence grew as well.

Taxes and Gold With so many traders passing through their lands, Ghana's rulers looked for ways to make money from them. One way they raised money was by forcing traders to pay taxes. Every trader who entered

Ghana had to pay a special tax on the goods carried. Then the trader had to pay another tax on any goods taken away when leaving.

Traders were not the only people who had to pay taxes. The people of Ghana also had to pay taxes. In addition, Ghana conquered many small neighboring tribes and then forced them to pay tribute. Rulers used the money from taxes and tribute to support Ghana's growing army.

Traders from Ghana exchanged goods made from gold at centralized marketplaces.

Not all of Ghana's wealth came from taxes and tribute. Ghana's rich mines produced huge amounts of gold. Some of this gold was carried by traders to lands as far away as England, but not all of Ghana's gold was traded. Ghana's kings kept huge stores of gold for themselves. In fact, all the gold produced in Ghana was officially the property of the king. Taxes, tributes, and gold were all forms of **income** for Ghana.

Knowing that rare materials are worth far more than common ones, the rulers banned anyone else in Ghana from owning gold nuggets. Common people could own only gold dust, which they used as money. By limiting who could own gold nuggets, Ghana's leaders increased the metal's economic value. When only a small number of people have access to something, that item becomes more valuable. Gold dust did not have as much value because everyone was allowed to have it. This decision to restrict gold ownership also ensured that the king was richer than his subjects.

Expansion of the Empire Ghana's kings used their great wealth to build a powerful army. With this army the kings of Ghana conquered many of their neighbors. Many of these conquered areas were centers of trade. Taking over these areas made Ghana's kings even richer.

Ghana's kings didn't think that they could rule all the territory they conquered by themselves. Their empire was quite large, and travel and communication in West Africa could be difficult. To keep order in their empire, they allowed conquered kings to retain much of their power. These kings acted as governors of their territories, answering only to the king.

The empire of Ghana reached its peak under **Tunka Manin** (TOOHN-kah MAH-nin). All we know about this king comes from the writings of a Muslim geographer who wrote about Ghana. From this geographer, we know that Tunka Manin was the nephew of the previous king, a man named Basi. Kingship and property in Ghana did not pass from father to son but from uncle to nephew. Only the king's sister's son could inherit the throne.

Once he became king, Tunka Manin surrounded himself with finery and many luxuries. He had a splendid court where he displayed the vast wealth of the empire. A Spanish writer noted the court's luxuries.

"The king adorns himself . . . round his neck and his forearms, and he puts on a high cap decorated with gold and wrapped in a turban of fine cotton. Behind the king stand ten pages holding shields and swords decorated with gold."

–al-Bakri, from *The Book of Routes and Kingdoms*

Reading Check
Analyze Causes
How did the rulers of Ghana make sure that gold nuggets were worth more than gold dust?

Overgrazing

Too many animals grazing in one area can lead to problems, such as the loss of farmland that occurred in West Africa.

1 Animals are allowed to graze in areas with lots of grass.

2 With too many animals grazing, however, the grass disappears, leaving the soil exposed to the wind.

3 The wind blows the soil away, turning what was once grassland into desert.

Ghana's Decline

In the mid-1000s, Ghana was rich and powerful, but by the end of the 1200s, the empire had collapsed. Three major factors contributed to its end.

Invasion The first factor that helped bring about Ghana's end was invasion. A Muslim group called the Almoravids (al-moh-RAH-vidz) attacked Ghana in the 1060s in an effort to force its leaders to convert to Islam.

The people of Ghana fought hard against the Almoravid army. For 14 years they kept the invaders at bay. In the end, however, the Almoravids won. They destroyed the city of Koumbi Saleh.

The Almoravids didn't control Ghana for long, but they certainly weakened the empire. They cut off many trade routes through Ghana and formed new trading partnerships with Muslim leaders instead. Without this trade, Ghana could no longer support its empire.

Overgrazing A second factor in Ghana's decline was a result of the Almoravid conquest. When the Almoravids moved into Ghana, they brought herds of animals with them. These animals ate all the grass in many pastures, leaving the soil exposed to hot desert winds. These winds blew away the soil, leaving the land worthless for farming or herding. Unable to grow crops, many farmers had to leave in search of new homes.

Internal Rebellion A third factor also helped bring about the decline of Ghana's empire. In about 1200, the people of a country that Ghana had conquered rose up in rebellion. Within a few years the rebels had taken over the entire empire of Ghana.

Once in control, however, the rebels found that they could not keep order in Ghana. Weakened, Ghana was attacked and defeated by one of its neighbors. The empire fell apart.

Summary and Preview The empire of Ghana in West Africa grew rich and powerful through its control of trade routes. The empire lasted for centuries, but eventually Ghana fell. In the next lesson, you will learn that it was replaced by two new empires, the Mali and Songhai.

Reading Check
Analyze Causes
Why did Ghana decline in the 1000s?

Lesson 2 Assessment

Review Ideas, Terms, and People

1. a. Identify What animal made trade across the Sahara easier?

   b. Summarize In what directions did the main trade items of West Africa move?

2. a. Identify What were the two most valuable resources traded in Ghana?

   b. Explain How did the silent barter system work?

3. a. Identify Who was Tunka Manin?

   b. Form Generalizations What did Ghana's kings do with the income they raised from taxes?

   c. Elaborate Why did the rulers of Ghana not want everyone to have gold?

4. a. Identify What group invaded Ghana in the late 1000s?

   b. Summarize How did overgrazing help cause the fall of Ghana?

Critical Thinking

5. Organize Information Draw a diagram like the one shown here. Use it to identify factors that helped Ghana's trade grow and those that led to its decline.

The Empires of Mali and Songhai

The Big Idea
The wealthy and powerful Mali Empire ruled West Africa after the fall of Ghana, and the Songhai Empire strengthened Islam in the region.

Main Ideas
- A ruler named Sundiata made Mali into an empire.
- Mali reached its height under the ruler Mansa Musa.
- Mali fell to invaders in the late 1400s.
- Songhai regained power from Mali.
- Askia the Great ruled Songhai as an Islamic empire.
- Songhai fell to Moroccan invaders, ending the great era of West African empires.

Key People
Sundiata
Mansa Musa
Sunni Ali
Askia the Great

If YOU were there . . .

You are a farmer in the Niger River Valley in about 1500. You're making your first visit to the great city of Timbuktu. You stare around you at the buildings with their tall towers. In the streets you hear people talking in many different languages. Some are telling old stories about the wealthy Mali ruler Mansa Musa and his pilgrimage to Mecca. Others must be students from other countries who have come to study in the universities here. From the tower of a mosque, you hear the call to prayer.

How does the great city make you feel?

Sundiata Makes Mali an Empire

Like Ghana, Mali (MAH-lee) lay along the upper Niger River. This area's fertile soil helped Mali grow. In addition, Mali's location on the Niger allowed its people to control trade on the river. Through this control of trade, the empire became rich and powerful. According to legend, Mali's rise to power began under a ruler named **Sundiata** (soohn-JAHT-ah).

Beginnings of the Empire Because written records about Mali are scarce, the details of its rise to power are unclear. Many legends about this period exist, though. According to these legends, Sundiata, Mali's first strong leader, was both a mighty warrior and a magician. According to the legends, he had to overcome great hardships before he could build his empire.

Sundiata was the son of a previous king of Mali. When he was a boy, however, Mali was conquered by a powerful king who treated the people of Mali badly. Sundiata grew up hating the king. When he reached adulthood, Sundiata built a huge army and won his country's independence. Then he set about conquering many nearby kingdoms, including Ghana.

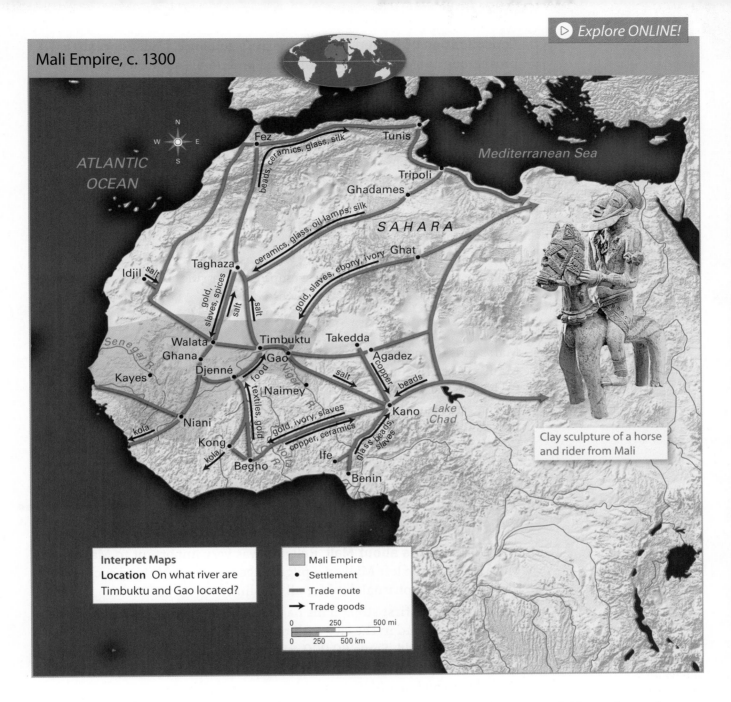

Mali Empire, c. 1300

ATLANTIC OCEAN

Mediterranean Sea

SAHARA

beads, ceramics, glass, silk

ceramics, glass, oil lamps, silk

gold, slaves, ebony, ivory

gold, slaves, spices

salt

salt

salt

food

textiles, gold

gold, ivory, slaves

copper, ceramics

glass beads, slaves

copper

beads

kola

kola

kola

Fez
Tunis
Tripoli
Ghadames
Ghat
Taghaza
Idjil
Walata
Ghana
Timbuktu
Takedda
Agadez
Gao
Djenné
Naimey
Kayes
Kano
Lake Chad
Niani
Kong
Begho
Ife
Benin
Senegal R.
Niger R.
Volta R.

Clay sculpture of a horse and rider from Mali

Interpret Maps
Location On what river are Timbuktu and Gao located?

☐ Mali Empire
• Settlement
▬ Trade route
→ Trade goods

0   250   500 mi
0   250   500 km

Improvements in Mali After Sundiata had conquered Ghana, he took over the salt and gold trades. He also worked to improve agriculture in Mali. Sundiata had new farmlands cleared for beans, onions, rice, and other crops. He even introduced a new crop to Mali—cotton. People used cotton to make clothing that was comfortable in the warm climate. Realizing its value, they also sold cotton to other people.

To help feed the people of his new empire, legend says that Sundiata put some soldiers to work in the fields. Once Mali's enemies had been defeated, the soldiers didn't need to fight, so they worked alongside slaves on large farms. Using conquered people as slaves was a common practice in Mali as it was in Ghana.

Consolidation of Power Under Sundiata's guidance, Mali grew into a prosperous kingdom. To keep order and protect his authority, Sundiata took power away from local leaders. These local leaders had borne the title *mansa* (MAHN-sah), a title Sundiata now took for himself.

Mansas had both political and religious roles in society. By taking on the religious authority of the *mansas*, Sundiata gained even more power in Mali.

The religious role of the *mansa* grew out of traditional Malian beliefs. According to these beliefs, the people's ancestors had made an agreement with the spirits of the land. The spirits would make sure that the land provided plenty of food. By keeping in touch with their ancestors, the people could contact these spirits.

Sundiata died in 1255. His son, who was the next ruler of Mali, also took the title of *mansa*, as did the empire's later rulers. Unlike Sundiata, though, most of these later rulers were Muslims.

Reading Check
Analyze Motives
What steps did Sundiata take to turn Mali into an empire?

Mansa Musa

Mansa Musa

Mali's most famous ruler was a Muslim king named **Mansa Musa** (MAHN-sah moo-SAH). Under his skillful leadership, Mali reached the height of its wealth, power, and fame in the 1300s. Because of Mansa Musa's influence, Islam spread through a large part of West Africa.

Mansa Musa ruled Mali for about 25 years. During that time, his army captured many trade cities, including Timbuktu (tim-buhk-TOO), Gao (GOW), and Djenné (je-NAY). These cities became part of Mali's empire.

The World Learns about Mali Religion was very important to Mansa Musa. In 1324, he left Mali on a pilgrimage to Mecca. Making such a journey, or hajj, is a spiritual duty for all Muslims.

Mansa Musa's first stop on his hajj was Cairo, Egypt. According to one account, he arrived in the city with nearly 100 camels, each loaded with 300 pounds of gold. Some 60,000 men traveled with him, along with his wives, servants, and slaves. About 10 years later, a historian spoke to an official who had met him.

> "[H]e did me extreme honour and treated me with the greatest courtesy. He addressed me, however, only through an interpreter despite his perfect ability to speak in the Arabic tongue. Then he forwarded [sent] to the royal treasury many loads of unworked native gold and other valuables. . . . He left no court emir nor holder of a royal office without the gift of a load of gold. The Cairenes [people of Cairo] made incalculable [uncountable] profits out of him."
> —Ibn Fadl Allah al-Umari, from "The Kingdom of Mali and What Appertains to It" in *Corpus of Early Arabic Sources for West African History*

This historian says that Mansa Musa gave away so much gold that it was no longer rare in Egypt! As a result, gold's value dropped steeply.

Through his journey, Mansa Musa introduced the empire of Mali to the world. Before he came to power, only a few people outside of West Africa had ever heard of Mali, even though it was one of the world's largest empires. Mansa Musa made such a great impression on people, though, that Mali became famous throughout Africa, Asia, and Europe.

Learning and Religion in Mali Mansa Musa supported education. In his first years as ruler, he sent scholars to study in Morocco. These scholars later set up schools in Mali for studying the Qur'an. Timbuktu became famous for its schools.

Mansa Musa wanted Muslims to be able to read the Qur'an. Therefore, he stressed the importance of learning to read and write the Arabic language. Arabic became the main language not only for religious study but also for government and trade.

Mansa Musa wanted to spread Islam in West Africa. To encourage this spread, he hired architects from other Muslim countries to build mosques throughout his empire. Elaborate mosques were built in Timbuktu, Djenné, and other cities.

Mansa Musa hoped that people would accept Islam as he had, but he did not want to force people to convert. He allowed animism to continue to be practiced in his empire along with Islam. Some historians believe that even the rulers of ancient Mali after Mansa Musa never completely gave up their belief in animism. Still, during Mansa Musa's reign Islam became very popular in Mali. Following their king's example, many people from Mali went to Mecca. In turn, Muslims from Asia, Egypt, and other parts of Africa visited Mali. These journeys between regions helped create more trade and made Mali even richer.

Reading Check
Analyze Events
How did Mansa Musa spread Islam?

This Spanish map from the 1300s shows Mansa Musa sitting on his throne.

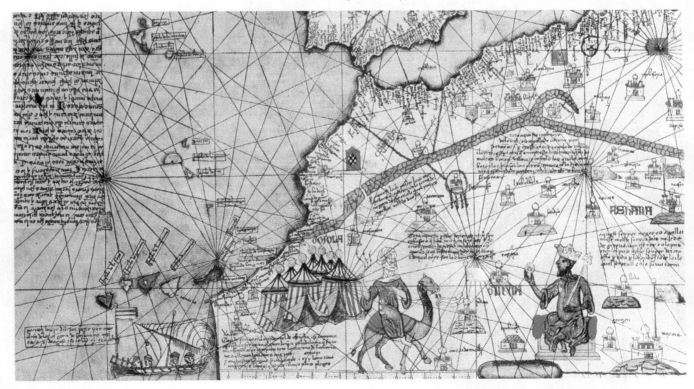

Timbuktu

Timbuktu became a major trading city at the height of Mali's power under Mansa Musa. Traders came to Timbuktu from the north and south to trade for salt, gold, metals, shells, and many other goods.

Mansa Musa and later rulers built several large mosques in the city, which became a center of Islamic learning.

Winter floods allowed boats to reach Timbuktu from the Niger River.

Timbuktu's walls and buildings were mostly built with bricks made of dried mud. Heavy rains could soften the bricks and destroy buildings.

At crowded market stalls, people traded for goods like sugar, kola nuts, and glass beads.

Camel caravans from the north brought such goods as salt, cloth, books, and slaves to trade at Timbuktu.

Analyze Visuals
How did traders from the north bring their goods to Timbuktu?

The Fall of Mali

Mali's success depended on strong leaders. Unfortunately, some of Mali's leaders were not strong. Their poor leadership weakened the empire.

When Mansa Musa died, his son Maghan (MAH-gan) took the throne. Unlike his father, however, Maghan was a weak ruler. When raiders poured into Mali, he couldn't stop them. The raiders set fire to Timbuktu's great schools and mosques. Mali never fully recovered from this terrible blow. Weakened, the empire gradually declined.

One reason the empire declined was its size. The empire had become so large that the government could no longer control it. Parts of the empire began to break away. For example, the city of Gao declared its independence in the 1400s.

Invaders also helped weaken the empire. In 1431, the Tuareg (TWAH-reg), nomads from the Sahara, attacked and seized Timbuktu. Soon afterward, the kingdom of Takrur (TAHK-roohr) in northern Mali declared its independence. Gradually, the people living at the edges of Mali's empire broke away. By 1500, nearly all of the lands the empire had once ruled were lost. Only a small area of Mali remained.

Reading Check
Analyze Effects
How did Mali's growth eventually weaken the empire?

The Songhai Build an Empire

Even as the empire of Mali was reaching its height, a rival power was growing in the area. That rival was the Songhai (SAHNG-hy) kingdom. From their capital at Gao, the Songhai participated in the same trade that had made Ghana and Mali so rich.

By the 1300s, the Songhai had become rich and powerful enough to draw the attention of Mali's rulers. Mansa Musa sent his army to conquer the Songhai and make their lands part of his empire. As you have already seen, Gao became one of the most important cities in all of Mali.

The Birth of the Empire Songhai did not remain part of Mali's empire for long. As Mali's government grew weaker, the people of Songhai rose up against it and regained their freedom.

Even before they were conquered by Mali, the leaders of the Songhai had become Muslims. As such, they shared a common religion with many of the Berbers who crossed the Sahara to trade in West Africa. Because of this shared religion, the Berbers were willing to trade with the Songhai, who began to grow richer.

Growth and Conquest As the Songhai grew richer from trans-Saharan trade, they expanded their territory. Gradually, they built an empire.

Songhai's growth was largely the work of one man, **Sunni Ali** (SOOH-nee ah-LEE), who became the ruler of Songhai in 1464. Before Ali took over, the Songhai state had been disorganized and poorly run. As ruler, he worked constantly to unify, strengthen, and enlarge it.

Much of the land that Sunni Ali added to his empire had been part of Mali. For example, he conquered the wealthy trade cities of Timbuktu and Djenné. In 1468, the rulers of Mali asked Sunni Ali to help fight off Tuareg

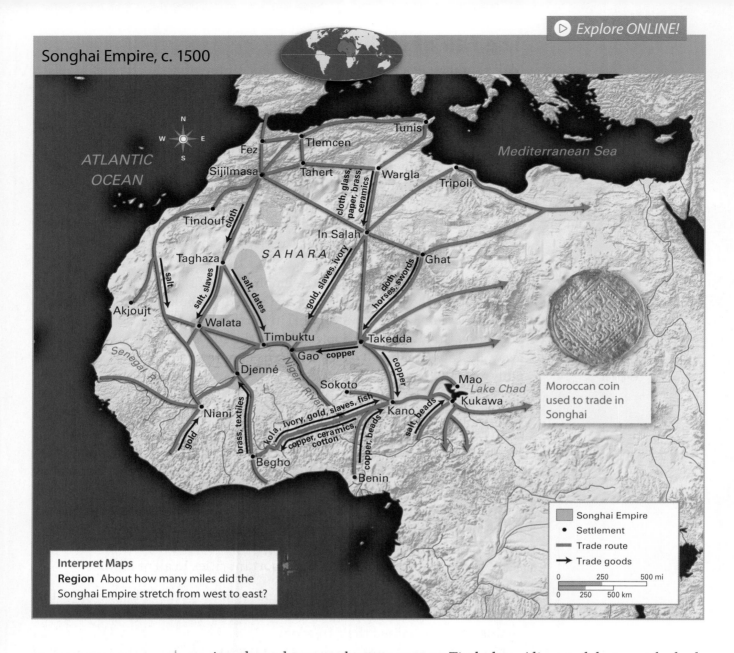

Songhai Empire, c. 1500

ATLANTIC OCEAN

N W E S

Fez
Tlemcen
Tunis
Mediterranean Sea
Sijilmasa
Tahert
Wargla
Tripoli

cloth, glass, paper, brass, ceramics

Tindouf
cloth
In Salah
Ghat

SAHARA

Taghaza
salt
salt, slaves
salt, dates
gold, slaves, ivory
cloth, horses, swords

Akjoujt
Walata
Timbuktu
Takedda
Gao copper
copper

Senegal R.
Djenné
Niger River
Sokoto

Mao
Lake Chad
Kukawa

Niani
brass, textiles
kola, ivory, gold, slaves, fish
copper, ceramics, cotton
Kano
salt, beads
copper, beads

gold

Begho
Benin

Moroccan coin used to trade in Songhai

Songhai Empire
Settlement
Trade route
Trade goods

0   250   500 mi
0   250   500 km

Interpret Maps
Region About how many miles did the Songhai Empire stretch from west to east?

invaders who were about to capture Timbuktu. Ali agreed, but once he had driven off the invaders he decided to keep the city for himself. From there he launched attacks against Djenné, which he finally captured five years later.

As king, Sunni Ali encouraged all people in his empire to work together. To build peace between religions, he participated in both Muslim and local religions. As a result, he brought peace and stability to Songhai.

Reading Check
Find Main Ideas
What did Sunni Ali achieve as ruler of the Songhai?

Askia the Great

Sunni Ali died in 1492. He was followed as king by his son, Sunni Baru, who was not a Muslim. However, most of the people of the empire's towns were. They were afraid that if Sunni Baru didn't support Islam they would lose power in the empire, and trade with other Muslim lands would suffer. As a result, they rebelled against Sunni Baru.

The Songhai kingdom prospered during Askia's reign.

The leader of the people's rebellion was a general named Muhammad Ture (moo-HAH-muhd too-RAY). After overthrowing Sunni Baru, he took the title *askia,* a title of high military rank. This man became the ruler of Songhai when he was nearly 50 years old. And he ruled for about 35 years. History now calls him **Askia the Great**.

Religion and Education Like Mansa Musa, the famous ruler of Mali, Askia the Great took his Muslim faith very seriously. After he defeated Sunni Baru, Askia made a pilgrimage to Mecca, just as Mansa Musa had 200 years earlier.

Also like Mansa Musa, Askia worked to support education. Under his rule, the city of Timbuktu flourished once again. The great city contained universities, schools, libraries, and mosques. Especially famous was the University of Sankore (san-KOH-rah). People arrived there from all over West Africa to study mathematics, science, medicine, grammar, and law. In the early 1500s, a Muslim traveler and scholar called Leo Africanus wrote this about Timbuktu.

"Here are great store of [many] doctors, judges, priests, and other
learned men, that are bountifully maintained at the kings cost
and charges. And hither are brought diuers manuscripts or written
bookes out of Barbarie [North Africa] which are sold for more
money than any other merchandize."

—Leo Africanus, from *History and Description of Africa*

The city of Djenné was another place of learning and scholarly study, especially in medicine. Doctors there discovered that mosquitoes spread malaria. They even performed surgery on the human eye.

The people of Songhai depended on the Niger River for many things. It was an important transportation route and provided fertile lands and a source of water for farming. People continue to depend on the river today.

Trade and Government Timbuktu and Djenné were centers of learning, but they were also trading centers. Merchants from distant lands came to these cities and to Gao. Most of Songhai's traders were Muslim, and as they gained influence in the empire so did Islam. Askia the Great, himself a devout Muslim, encouraged the growth in Islamic influence. Many of the laws he made were similar to those of Muslim nations across the Sahara.

To help maintain order, Askia set up five provinces within Songhai. He removed local leaders and appointed new governors who were loyal to him. One such governor ran the empire when Askia was away on pilgrimage to Mecca. When Askia returned, he brought even more Muslim influence into his government.

Askia also created special departments to oversee certain tasks. These departments worked much like government offices do today. He created a standing professional army, the first in West Africa.

Reading Check
Draw Conclusions
What do you think was Askia's greatest accomplishment?

Songhai Falls to Morocco

When he was in his 80s, Askia went blind. His son Musa forced him to leave the throne. Askia was sent to live on an island. He lived there for nine years until another of his sons brought him back to the capital, where he died. His tomb is still one of the most honored places in all of West Africa.

After Askia the Great lost power in 1528, other *askias* ruled Songhai. The empire did not survive for long, though. Areas along the empire's borders started to nibble away at Songhai's power.

The Moroccan Invasion One of Songhai's northern neighbors, Morocco, wanted to control the Saharan salt mines. To get those mines, Moroccan troops invaded Songhai. With them they brought a terrible new weapon—the arquebus (AHR-kwih-buhs). The arquebus was an early form of a gun.

The Moroccans wanted control of the salt mines because they needed money. Not long before the fight over the mines, Morocco had defended itself against huge invading armies from Portugal and Spain. The Moroccans had eventually defeated the Europeans, but the defense had nearly ruined Morocco financially. Knowing of Songhai's wealth, the Moroccan ruler decided to attack Songhai for its rich deposits of salt and gold.

The Moroccan army set out for the heart of Songhai in 1591. Not all of the troops were Moroccan, though. About half were actually Spanish

Timeline: West African Empires

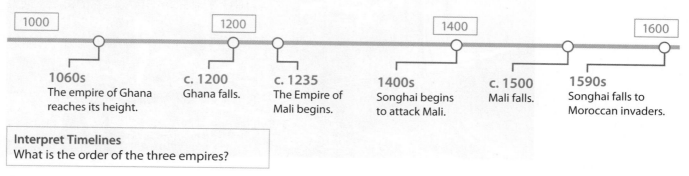

| 1000 | 1200 | 1400 | 1600 |

1060s
The empire of Ghana reaches its height.

c. 1200
Ghana falls.

c. 1235
The Empire of Mali begins.

1400s
Songhai begins to attack Mali.

c. 1500
Mali falls.

1590s
Songhai falls to Moroccan invaders.

Interpret Timelines
What is the order of the three empires?

and Portuguese war prisoners. These prisoners had agreed to fight against Songhai rather than face more time in prison. Well trained and disciplined, these soldiers carried **various** weapons, including the deadly new guns. The Moroccans even dragged a few small cannons across the desert with them.

**Academic
Vocabulary
various** of many
types

The Destruction of Songhai The Moroccans' guns and cannons brought disaster to Songhai. The swords, spears, and bows carried by Songhai's warriors were no match for firearms.

The Moroccans attacked Timbuktu and Gao, looting and taking over both cities. The Moroccans didn't push farther into Songhai, but the damage was done. Songhai never recovered from the loss of these cities and the income they produced.

Changes in trade patterns completed Songhai's fall. Overland trade declined as port cities north and south of the old empire became more important. For example, people who lived south of Songhai began to trade along the Atlantic coast. European traders preferred to sail to Atlantic ports than to deal with Muslim traders. Slowly, the period of great West African empires came to an end.

**Reading Check
Make Inferences**
What do you think happened to the people of West Africa after the empire of Songhai was defeated?

Summary and Preview The empires of Mali and Songhai were known for their wealth, culture, learning, and effective leaders like Mansa Musa and Askia the Great. In the next lesson, you will study the historical and artistic traditions of West Africa.

Lesson 3 Assessment

Review Ideas, Terms, and People

1. a. **Identify** Who was Sundiata?
   b. **Explain** How did Sundiata turn Mali into an empire?
2. a. **Identify** What became the main language of government, trade, and Islamic scholarship in West Africa?
   b. **Summarize** How did Mansa Musa's journey change people's perceptions of Mali?
   c. **Elaborate** How did Islam help turn Mali into a center of learning?
3. a. **Identify** What group invaded Mali in 1431?
   b. **Explain** How did Mali's size lead to its fall?
4. a. **Identify** In what part of West Africa did Songhai begin?
   b. **Summarize** What did Sunni Ali accomplish?

5. a. **Identify** What religion gained influence in Songhai under Askia the Great?
   b. **Analyze** How did contact with other cultures change Songhai's government?
6. a. **Identify** Which group of people invaded the Songhai Empire in the 1590s?
   b. **Predict Effects** How might West Africa's history have been different if the invaders who conquered Songhai had not had firearms?

Critical Thinking

7. **Organize Information** Draw three boxes. In them, list three major accomplishments of Sundiata, Mansa Musa, and Askia the Great.

Sundiata	Mansa Musa	Askia the Great

Historical and Artistic Traditions of West Africa

The Big Idea

Because the people of West Africa did not have a written language, their culture has been passed down through oral history, writings by other people, and the arts.

Main Ideas

- Storytellers helped maintain the oral history of the cultures of West Africa.

- Visitors to West Africa from other lands wrote histories and descriptions of what they saw there.

- Traditionally, West Africans have valued the arts.

Key Terms

oral history
griots
proverbs
kente

If YOU were there . . .

You are the youngest and smallest in your family. People often tease you about not being very strong. In the evenings, when work is done, the people of your village gather to listen to storytellers. One of your favorites is about the hero Sundiata. As a boy he was small and weak, but he grew to be a great warrior and hero.

How does the story of Sundiata make you feel?

Storytellers Maintain Oral History

Although cities like Timbuktu and Djenné were known for their universities and libraries, writing was never very common in West Africa. In fact, none of the major early civilizations of West Africa developed a written language. Arabic was the only written language they used. Many Muslim traders, government officials, and religious leaders could read and write Arabic.

The lack of a written language does not mean that the people of West Africa didn't know their history, though. They passed along information through oral histories. An **oral history** is a spoken record of past events. The task of remembering West Africa's history was entrusted to storytellers.

The Griots West African storytellers were called **griots** (GREE-ohz). They were highly respected in their communities because the people of West Africa were very interested in the deeds of their ancestors. Griots helped keep this history alive for each new generation.

The griots' stories were entertaining as well as informative. They told of past events and of the deeds of people's ancestors. For example, some stories explained the rise and fall of the West African empires. Some griots made their stories more lively by acting out events from the past like scenes in a play.

Oral Traditions

West African storytellers called griots had the job of remembering and passing on their people's history. In this photo, everyone wears their best clothes and gathers around a griot to listen.

In addition to stories, the griots recited **proverbs**, or short sayings of wisdom or truth. They used proverbs to teach lessons to the people. For example, one West African proverb warns, "Talking doesn't fill the basket in the farm." This proverb reminds people that they must work to accomplish things. They can't just talk about what they want to do. Another proverb advises, "A hippopotamus can be made invisible in dark water." It warns people to remain alert. Just as it can be hard to see animals in a deep pool, people don't always see the problems they will face.

In order to recite their stories and proverbs, the griots memorized hundreds of names and events. Through this memorization process the griots passed on West African history from generation to generation. However, some griots confused names and events in their heads. When this happened, specific facts about some historical events became distorted. Still, the griots' stories tell us a great deal about life in the West African empires.

West African Epics Some of the griot poems are epics—long poems about kingdoms and heroes. Many of these epic poems are collected in the *Dausi* (DAW-zee) and the *Sundiata*.

The *Dausi* tells the history of Ghana. Intertwined with historical events, though, are myths and legends. For example, one story is about a terrifying seven-headed snake god named Bida. This god promised that Ghana would prosper if the people sacrificed a young woman to him every year. One year a mighty warrior killed Bida. But as the god died, he cursed Ghana. The griots say that it was this curse that caused the empire of Ghana to fall.

Like the *Dausi*, the *Sundiata* is about the history of an empire, Mali. It is the story of Sundiata, Mali's legendary first ruler. According to the epic, when Sundiata was still a boy, a conqueror captured Mali and killed Sundiata's father and 11 brothers. He didn't kill Sundiata because the boy was sick and didn't seem like a threat. However, Sundiata grew up to be an expert hunter and warrior. Eventually he overthrew the conqueror and became king.

Reading Check
Draw Conclusions
Why were oral traditions important in West Africa?

Visitors Write Histories

The people of West Africa left no written histories of their own. Visitors to West Africa from other parts of the world, however, did write about the region. Much of what we know about early West Africa comes from the writings of travelers and scholars from Muslim lands such as Spain and Arabia.

One of the first people to write about West Africa was an Arab scholar named al-Masudi (ahl-mah-SOO-dee). He visited the region in the 900s. In his writings, al-Masudi described the geography, customs, history, and scientific achievements of West Africa.

About 100 years later, another writer, Abu Ubayd al-Bakri, wrote about West Africa. He lived in Córdoba, Spain, where he met many people who had been to West Africa. Based on the stories these people told him, al-Bakri wrote about life in West African kingdoms.

More famous than either of these two writers was Ibn Battutah, a tireless traveler who described most of the Muslim world. From 1353 to 1354, Ibn Battutah traveled through West Africa. His account of this journey describes the political and cultural lives of West Africans in great detail.

DOCUMENT-BASED INVESTIGATION   Historical Source

A Description of Mali

In the 1300s, Ibn Battutah traveled through much of Asia and Africa. This passage describes the people of Mali, one of the places he visited in Africa.

Analyze Historical Sources
Why may Ibn Battutah have been particularly interested in security within Mali?

> "[They] possess some admirable qualities. They are seldom unjust, and have a greater abhorrence [hatred] of injustice than any other people. Their sultan [ruler] shows no mercy to anyone who is guilty of the least act of it. There is complete security in their country. Neither traveler nor inhabitant in it has anything to fear from robbers or men of violence. . . . They are careful to observe the hours of prayer, and assiduous [careful] in attending them in congregations [gatherings], and in bringing up their children to them."
>
> —Ibn Battutah, from *Travels in Asia and Africa 1325–1354*

Reading Check
Form Generalizations
Why were the written histories of West Africa written by people from other lands?

The last of the major Muslim visitors to West Africa was a young man called Leo Africanus (LEE-oh af-ri-KAY-nuhs), or Leo the African. Born in what is now Spain, Leo traveled through northern and western Africa on missions for the government. On his way home, however, pirates captured Leo and brought him to Rome as a prisoner. Although he was freed, he stayed in Rome for many years. There he wrote a description of what he had seen in Africa. Because Leo lived and wrote in Europe, for a long time his work was the only source about life in Africa available to Europeans.

West Africans Value Arts

Like most peoples, West Africans valued the arts. The art they produced took many forms. Common West African art forms included sculpture, mask making, cloth making, music, and dance.

Sculpture Of all the visual art forms, the sculpture of West Africa is probably the best known. West Africans made ornate statues and carvings out of wood, brass, clay, ivory, stone, and other materials.

Most statues from West Africa are of people—often the sculptor's ancestors. In most cases, these statues were made for religious rituals, to ask for the ancestors' blessings. Sculptors made other statues as gifts for the gods. These sculptures were kept in holy places. They were never meant to be seen by people.

Link to Today

Music From Mali to the United States

Did you know that the music you listen to today may have begun with the griots? From the 1600s to the 1800s, many people from West Africa were brought to America as slaves. In America, these enslaved people continued to sing the way they had in Africa. They also continued to play traditional instruments such as the *kora* played by Senegalese musician Soriba Kouyaté, the son of a griot (right). Over time, this music developed into a style called the blues, made popular by such artists as Buddy Guy. Some newer musicians, like Gary Clark, Jr., and Rhiannon Giddens, continue to make blues music. Over time, the blues shaped other styles of music, including jazz , rock, and hip-hop. So, the next time you hear a popular song, listen for its ancient African roots!

Analyze Information
How did West African music affect modern American music?

Because their statues were often used in religious rituals, many African artists were deeply respected. People thought artists had been blessed by the gods.

Long after the decline of Ghana, Mali, and Songhai, West African art is still admired. Museums around the world today display African art. In addition, African sculpture helped inspire some European artists of the 1900s, including Henri Matisse and Pablo Picasso.

Masks and Clothing In addition to statues, the artists of West Africa carved elaborate masks. Made of wood, these masks bore the faces of animals such as hyenas, lions, monkeys, and antelopes. Artists often painted the masks after carving them. People wore these masks during rituals as they danced around fires. The way firelight reflected off the masks made them look fierce and lifelike.

Many African societies were also famous for the cloth they wove. The most famous of these cloths is called kente (ken-TAY). **Kente** is a hand-woven, brightly colored fabric. The cloth was woven in narrow strips that were then sewn together. Kings and queens in West Africa wore garments made of kente for special occasions.

Like West African music and dance, many West African crafts have been handed down for generations. This woman in the modern nation of Ghana is weaving traditional baskets.

Music and Dance In many West African societies, music and dance were as important as the visual arts. Singing and dancing were great forms of entertainment, but they also helped people honor their history and were central to many celebrations. For example, music was played when a ruler entered a room.

Dance has long been a central part of African society. Many West African cultures used dance to celebrate specific events or ceremonies. For example, they may have performed one dance for weddings and another for funerals. In some parts of West Africa, people still perform dances similar to those performed hundreds of years ago.

Summary and Preview The societies of West Africa never developed written languages, but their histories and cultures have been passed on through traditions and customs. In the next lesson, you will read about the cultures of the African peoples who lived in southern Africa.

Reading Check
Summarize
Summarize how traditions were preserved in West Africa.

Lesson 4 Assessment

Review Ideas, Terms, and People

1. a. **Summarize** What is oral history?
   b. **Form Generalizations** Why were griots and their stories important in West African society?
   c. **Evaluate** Why may an oral history provide different information than a written account?
2. a. **Identify** Name one writer who wrote about West Africa.
   b. **Make Inferences** How do you think these writers' views of West Africa may have differed from the views of West Africans?

3. **Identify** What were two forms of visual art popular in West Africa?

Critical Thinking

4. **Categorize** Create a chart like the one here. Use it to describe the *Dausi* and the *Sundiata*.

Great Epics of West Africa	
Dausi	Sundiata

Literature in History

African Oral Traditions

Word Help

rampart a protective bank or wall
colossal gigantic
provisions supplies
assailants attackers

❶ *Soumaoro* is another name for Sumanguru. Noumounkeba is one of his assistants.

❷ *Sogolon* Djata is another name for Sundiata. *Imagine that you are one of Sundiata's warriors. How do you feel as you look down on the city of Sosso?*

❸ A *sofa* is a warrior.

❹ The Mandingoes were the people of Mali.

About the Reading For almost 900 years, West African griots have been telling the story of Sundiata, king and founder of the Mali Empire. Like other ancient epics, this one is a blend of history and legend. Some parts of the story are based on fact—such as Sundiata's defeat of the tyrant-king Sumanguru, which took place in about 1235. Other elements, though, were added over time for dramatic effect. In the following episode, for example, an almost superhuman Sundiata swoops down upon Sumanguru's capital city, Sosso, vowing to destroy it in a single morning.

As You Read Imagine the sequence of events.

From *Sundiata*

by D. T. Niane, as told by Djeli Mamoudou Kouyaté, translated by G. D. Pickett

Sosso was a magnificent city. In the open plain her triple rampart with awe-inspiring towers reached into the sky. The city comprised a hundred and eighty-eight fortresses and the palace of Soumaoro loomed above the whole city like a gigantic tower. Sosso had but one gate; colossal and made of iron, the work of the sons of fire. Noumounkeba ❶ hoped to tie Sundiata down outside of Sosso, for he had enough provisions to hold out for a year.

The sun was beginning to set when Sogolon Djata appeared before Sosso the Magnificent. ❷ From the top of a hill, Djata and his general staff gazed upon the fearsome city of the sorcerer-king. The army encamped in the plain opposite the great gate of the city and fires were lit in the camp. Djata resolved to take Sosso in the course of a morning. . . .

At daybreak the towers of the ramparts were black with sofas. ❸ Others were positioned on the ramparts themselves. They were the archers. The Mandingoes were masters in the art of storming a town. ❹ In the front line Sundiata placed the sofas of Mali, while those who held the ladders were in the second line protected by the shields of the spearmen. The main body of the army was to attack the city gate. When all was ready, Djata gave the order to attack. The drums resounded, the horns blared and like a tide the Mandingo front line moved off, giving mighty shouts. With their shields raised above their heads the Mandingoes advanced up to the foot of the wall, then the Sossos began to rain large stones down on the assailants. From the rear, the bowmen of Wagadou shot arrows at the ramparts. The attack spread and the town was assaulted at all points. . . . On one knee the

surmounting rising above

razing tearing down

⑤ Fakoli, Soumaoro's nephew, had rebelled against his uncle.

⑥ Manding Bory is Sundiata's half-brother and best friend.

archers fired flaming arrows over the ramparts. Within the walls the thatched huts took fire and the smoke swirled up. The ladders stood against the curtain wall and the first Mandingo sofas were already at the top. Seized by panic through seeing the town on fire, the Sossos hesitated a moment. The huge tower surmounting the gate surrendered, for Fakoli's smiths had made themselves the masters of it. ⑤ They got into the city where the screams of women and children brought the Sossos' panic to a head. They opened the gates to the main body of the army.

Then began the massacre. Women and children in the midst of fleeing Sossos implored mercy of the victors. Djata and his cavalry were now in front of the awesome tower palace of Soumaoro. Noumounkeba, conscious that he was lost, came out to fight. With his sword held aloft he bore down on Djata, but the latter dodged him and, catching hold of the Sosso's braced arm, forced him to his knees whilst the sword dropped to the ground. He did not kill him but delivered him into the hands of Manding Bory. . . . ⑥

Just as he had wished, Sundiata had taken Sosso in the course of a morning. When everything was outside of the town and all that there was to take had been taken out, Sundiata gave the order to complete its destruction. The last houses were set fire to and prisoners were employed in the razing of the walls. Thus, as Djata intended, Sosso was destroyed to its very foundations.

This blanket was woven by the Fulani people of modern Mali, the descendants of Sumanguru and his subjects.

Connect Literature to History

1. **Analyze Motives** West African epics sometimes included both elements of truth and fictional embellishments. Which details in this excerpt sound like they could be true? Which were probably invented later? What makes you think that?

2. **Make Inferences** Griots had to commit to memory hundreds of events in order to tell their stories. They would sometimes act stories out like plays. If you were a griot, how might you bring the action in this excerpt to life?

Sub-Saharan Cultures

The Big Idea

The movement and interaction of cultures and peoples created unique ways of life in sub-Saharan Africa.

Main Ideas

- African customs blended with Christian religious beliefs to create a new form of Christianity in Ethiopia.

- Some historians think the migration of the Bantu caused one of the most significant cultural transformations in African history.

- Sub-Saharan Africans and Muslim merchants, among others, traded precious metals and cattle.

Key Terms and People

Ethiopia
Coptic Christianity
Bantu
Great Zimbabwe
Swahili

If YOU were there . . .

You are a traveler passing through the kingdom of Ethiopia. As you approach a town, you see a huge crowd gathered around what appears to be a hole in the ground. Walking closer, you see that there is a building in the hole. The entire building has been carved out of the rock on which you are standing. Never in your travels have you seen anything like this.

What do you think of this new building style?

The Ethiopian Kingdom

At the same time that Ghana was declining and Mali was rising to take its place, another great kingdom existed on the other side of the continent. In East Africa, the descendants of the people of Aksum, who had fled to the mountains, formed a new kingdom, Ethiopia. By about 1150, **Ethiopia** had become one of Africa's most powerful kingdoms.

The most famous of Ethiopia's rulers was King Lalibela, who ruled in the 1200s. He is famous for the 11 Christian churches he built, many of which still stand. The churches of Lalibela were carved into solid rock, many of them set into the ground. Worshippers had to walk down long flights of steps to get to them. Impressive feats of engineering, these churches also show the Ethiopians' devotion to Christianity. This devotion to Christianity set the Ethiopians apart from their neighbors, most of whom were Muslim.

Shared beliefs helped unify Ethiopians, but their isolation from other Christians led to some changes in their beliefs. Over time, some local African customs blended with Christian teachings. This resulted in a new form of Christianity in Africa called **Coptic Christianity**. The name *Coptic* comes from an Arabic word for "Egyptian." Most Christians who live in North Africa today—including many Ethiopians—belong to Coptic churches.

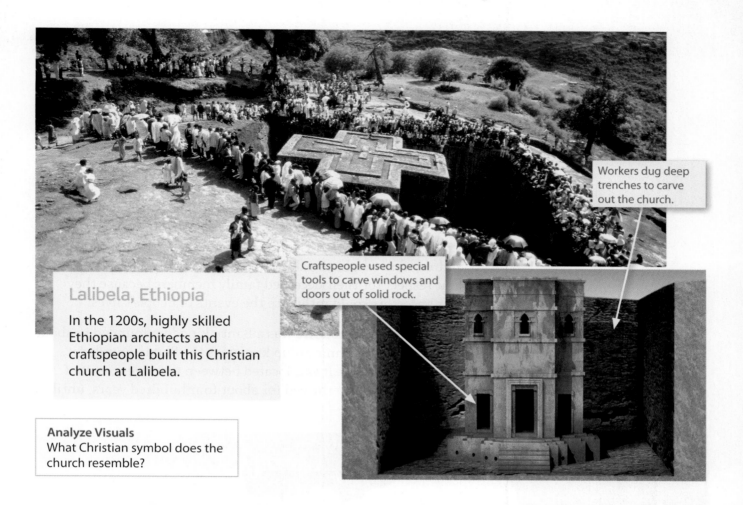

Lalibela, Ethiopia

In the 1200s, highly skilled Ethiopian architects and craftspeople built this Christian church at Lalibela.

Workers dug deep trenches to carve out the church.

Craftspeople used special tools to carve windows and doors out of solid rock.

Analyze Visuals
What Christian symbol does the church resemble?

Reading Check
Analyze Events
How did Christianity take hold in parts of Africa?

Although most people in Ethiopia were Christian, not everyone was. For example, a Jewish group known as the Beta Israel lived there. Although some Christian rulers tried to force the Beta Israel to give up their religion and adopt Christianity, they were not successful. Ethiopia's Jewish population remained active for centuries.

The Bantu Migration and Great Zimbabwe

Historians use the name **Bantu** as a way to discuss 400 different ethnic groups that come from the eastern, central, and southern regions of Africa. The word *bantu* means "people" in many of the native languages that these groups spoke.

The Bantu Migration Between 5,000 and 2,000 years ago, the Bantu people began spreading out from parts of West Africa. This movement of people is sometimes called the Bantu Expansion or the Bantu Migration. Some historians think the migration of the Bantu caused one of the most significant cultural transformations in the history of Africa.

No one is certain why the Bantu migrated. There are probably a few reasons. Some experts believe people left their homes because the Sahara was drying out and becoming a desert. Others think population growth and new crops, like the banana, led people to search for new land. Most Bantu were farmers or herders who raised large groups of cattle. They made and used iron tools. They needed pasture areas where they could raise animals and fields where they could grow crops like millet, beans, rice, and melons. The Bantu were migrating into regions where the people were hunter-gatherers. These people could not hold back the Bantu. By about AD 300, Bantu had conquered and settled much of Africa south of the Sahara.

No matter what the location, chiefs usually led the Bantu. These chiefs had great political power in their communities. They were thought to be greater than the common people. The chiefs did not have total power, however.

Bantu society had strong social structures. The old were also considered to be of higher standing than the young. Men were socially above women, and the rich were over the poor. Kinship systems were strong in Bantu society. Children were taught to value family and community. The Bantu also had great respect for their deceased family members because they believed their ancestors could influence the events of people's lives.

Great Zimbabwe **Great Zimbabwe** was a Bantu kingdom founded in about the year 1000. The Bantu ethnic group known as the Shona founded it. Zimbabwe was a trading city. It was located between two rivers, east of the Kalahari Desert. The city thrived for about four hundred years, until

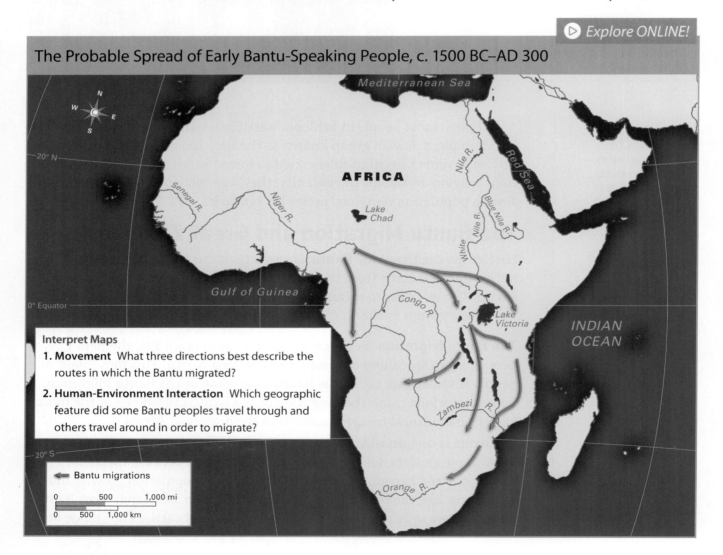

▶ Explore ONLINE!

The Probable Spread of Early Bantu-Speaking People, c. 1500 BC–AD 300

Interpret Maps

1. **Movement** What three directions best describe the routes in which the Bantu migrated?

2. **Human-Environment Interaction** Which geographic feature did some Bantu peoples travel through and others travel around in order to migrate?

Bantu migrations

0   500   1,000 mi

0   500   1,000 km

The ruins of Great Zimbabwe include the Conical Tower and Circular Wall, shown here.

Reading Check
Analyze Causes
What do historians believe caused the Bantu Migration?

the 15th century. Not much is known about the people who lived in Great Zimbabwe or of other aspects of their society. No written records exist about the kingdom of Great Zimbabwe. However, archeologists have found three important sets of ruins. These ruins appear to be the remains of granite buildings or structures. The name *Zimbabwe* comes from a Shona term that means "stone houses."

Archeologists think that a structure known as the Hill Complex was a temple or served some religious purpose. It sits in the oldest part of the city on a steep, raised hill. Another set of ruins is known as the Great Enclosure. It is the largest ancient structure in sub-Saharan Africa. Some researchers believe the Great Enclosure might have been constructed to separate the royal families from the rest of the community. This would mean that Great Zimbabwe had both a social structure and a political structure for governing the city. The last set of ruins is called the Valley Complex. Many experts believe that this is where average citizens lived.

Some historians disagree with these theories about the ruins. They believe that each set of ruins was built one after the other when new rulers took power. According to this theory, each structure was the place where a particular ruler lived.

Sub-Saharan Trade

The people who lived south of the Sahara traded across long distances. This trade helped many people to prosper. Trade also helped change the cultures of the sub-Saharan region.

Cattle, Crops, and Metals Throughout the Bantu Migration, people were involved in trade. For example, the Bantu had become skilled at working with iron. This led to the development of iron tools that they used for farming, but iron also became an important trade item. The Bantu traded iron tips for weapons with the hunter-gatherers in exchange for plants used for medicine or wild game the hunter-gatherers had killed.

Copper was another metal important to sub-Saharan trade. There was high demand for it in coastal **Swahili** (swah-HEE-lee) markets. The term *Swahili* refers to the blended African-Arab culture that had become common in East Africa. A steady supply of copper came from the head of the Congo and Zambezi rivers to eastern Africa. Places like Kilwa and Lamu, in what later would become Kenya, prospered because of the copper trade. These cities became thriving markets.

Great Zimabwe was also a trading city. Archeologists have found Chinese pottery, a Persian bowl, and an Arabic coin from the city of Kilwa in the ruins of Great Zimbabwe. Some archeologists also believe that Great Zimbabwe was built on top of a gold mine and that it was an important part of the gold trade. Others say evidence from the site does not support this claim.

East African Trade and Islamic Influence East Africa was heavily influenced by its involvement with trade. While Islam came to North Africa through conquest, the religion's arrival in East Africa was less violent.

Located on the Indian Ocean, East Africa had been a destination for traders from Asia for centuries. Among these traders were Muslims from India, Persia, and Arabia. They came to Africa in search of African goods and new markets for products from their homelands.

One of the goods that Muslims discovered in Africa was coffee. An Ethiopian tribe called the Galla ground up coffee beans, added animal fat, and formed the mixture into balls. The Galla ate this food during trips. Other Ethiopian tribes ate porridge or drank a wine made from coffee beans. Coffee became popular in the Islamic word because it was considered to be both a powerful medicine and a religious potion that could help keep people awake during prayer.

Muslim traders searching for coffee and other African goods settled down in many coastal trading cities like Mogadishu, Mombasa, Kilwa, and Sofala. Trade was easy and profitable in these locations. As a result of the traders' presence, the cities developed large Muslim communities. Africans, Arabs, and Persians lived near one another and worked together. One result of this closeness was the spread of Islam through East Africa. People at all levels of society, from workers to rulers, adopted Islam. As a result, mosques appeared in cities and towns throughout the region.

The contact between cultures also led to other changes in East Africa. For example, the architecture of the region changed. People began to build houses that mixed traditional materials, such as coral and mangrove trees, with Arab designs, such as arched windows and carved doors.

As the cultures grew closer, their speech began to reflect their new relationship. Some Africans, who spoke mostly Bantu languages, adopted many Arabic and Persian words. In time, the languages blended into the new language of Swahili. The name *Uganda* comes from a Swahili term.

Reading Check
Summarize
How did Islam change African society?

Summary In this lesson, you learned about people in East Africa and the great migration of Bantu people into southern Africa.

Lesson 5 Assessment

Review Ideas, Terms, and People

1. **a. Analyze** What led to the creation of Coptic Christianity in Africa?

   b. Describe Why did Christianity serve as a unifying factor for the people of Ethiopia?

2. **a. Summarize** How did the Bantu influence the way people lived in southern Africa?

   b. Form Opinions Which theory do you agree with about the purpose of the ruins at Great Zimbabwe?

3. **a. Define** What does *Swahili* mean?

   b. Contrast How did the arrival of Islam in North Africa differ from its arrival in East Africa?

c. Predict Effects How might life in East Africa have been different if the people there had not accepted the presence of Muslim traders?

Critical Thinking

4. **Analyze** Use the graphic organizer to examine how the arrival of Christianity and Islam in Africa influenced local culture and led to changes in the two religions.

Social Studies Skills

Make Decisions

Define the Skill

Making a decision can be a complicated and difficult skill to learn. However, it is an important skill that people use in most areas of daily life. Making a decision involves knowing and understanding options, predicting what might happen with each option, selecting an option, and acting based on that option.

Learn the Skill

In this module, you learned about the silent barter process. Salt traders and gold miners had to make decisions when they were doing business. Both groups had to think about things like amounts of gold and salt. They also had to decide if and when those amounts made them happy. The salt traders and the gold miners had to consider their options to help them make a decision.

1. *Know and understand the options.* An option is a choice. Understanding the options means that you are aware of what these choices can help you do (or not do).

2. *Think about what might happen.* Each option has a consequence. Options and consequences are like causes and effects. An option will cause you to do (or not do) an action. The effect is the consequence of doing (or not doing) the action. Consequences can be positive or negative.

3. *Pick an option.* This is the step where you are making the decision.

4. *Do (or don't do) an action based on the choice that you picked.*

Practice the Skill

Imagine you are one of the rulers of Ghana. Expanding the empire means making it grow larger. One of the ways to do that is to send your army into nearby areas. Since you are in charge of the army, you have several decisions to make before you can tell your people what to do (or not do). Create a plan of action using the following questions. Think about the options that you have and the consequences of each option. After that, make a decision about how to handle your army and defend the decision that you make.

1. Do you have enough people to send away from Ghana, or do you only have enough to protect the empire? Can the entire army be sent away, or do some soldiers have to remain at home?

2. What kind of weapons do your people have to defend themselves? Do they have enough weapons to fight safely? What happens if any of your people are injured or captured?

3. If your army finds and conquers another people, will you demand that they pay a tribute to Ghana? What will the tribute be and how much of it will you ask for as payment?

Module 14 Assessment

Review Vocabulary, Terms, and People

Imagine that these terms and people from the module are correct answers to items in a crossword puzzle. Write the clues for the answers. Then make the puzzle with some answers written down and some across.

1. silent barter
2. kinship system
3. Swahili
4. Mansa Musa
5. animism
6. Askia the Great
7. oral history
8. griots
9. proverbs
10. kente
11. Ethiopia
12. Sahel

Comprehension and Critical Thinking

Lesson 1

13. a. **Identify** Along what river did great civilizations develop in early West Africa?
    b. **Analyze** How does Africa's climate affect vegetation?
    c. **Identify** What are the two main purposes of age-sets?

Lesson 2

14. a. **Identify** What were the two major trade goods that made Ghana rich? Where did they come from?
    b. **Summarize** How did Ghana's rulers use taxes and tributes to generate income? What is income?
    c. **Evaluate** Who do you think was more responsible for the collapse of Ghana, the people of Ghana or outsiders? Why?

Lesson 3

15. a. **Describe** How did Islam influence society in Mali and Songhai?
    b. **Elaborate** How did Mali's growth and power help lead to its downfall?
    c. **Evaluate** Which do you think played more of a role in Songhai's society, warriors or traders? Why?

Lesson 4

16. a. **Describe** Who were the griots? What role did they play in West African society?
    b. **Make Inferences** Why do you think music and dance were so important in West African society?
    c. **Evaluate** Which do you think is a more reliable source about life in the Mali Empire—a story told by a modern griot or an account written by a Muslim scholar who had spoken to travelers from Mali? Defend your answer.

Lesson 5

17. **a. Contrast** How did Coptic Christianity set Ethiopians apart from the rest of Africa?

    b. Explain Why is Great Zimbabwe a significant site in Africa?

    c. Draw Conclusions Why were coastal cities like Kilwa among the first to be influenced by Islam?

Review Themes

18. **Geography** How did the location of the West African empires affect their success at trade?

19. **Society and Culture** How do oral traditions reflect the culture of West African civilizations?

20. **Science and Technology** What evidence in the text shows that West African civilizations benefited from technological innovation?

Reading Skills

Organization of Facts and Information *Use the Reading Skills taught in this module to answer the questions about the reading selection below.*

> "Other resources were minerals. People who live mainly on plant foods, like many early Africans, must add salt to their diets. The Sahara was a source of this precious mineral. Gold was another mineral resource of West Africa. Although gold is soft and therefore useless for tools or weapons, it makes beautiful jewelry and coins."

21. What structural pattern did the writer use to organize the information in the passage?

22. What signal words helped you determine the structural pattern of the information?

Social Studies Skills

Make Decisions *Use the Social Studies Skill taught in this module to answer the question about the chart below.*

23. Imagine you are a member of an extended family of West Africa. Consider the tasks and responsibilities of each family member, and then decide what role you will play— mother, father, elder, teenager, or young child. Then imagine a challenge that your family must face, such as a dangerous wild animal, crop failure, or loss of hunting grounds. With a partner, discuss how your family will face the problem by using decision-making and planning skills. Then, on your own, write 4–5 sentences explaining the problem and how you and your partner decided to deal with it. You may want to use a chart like this one to help you organize your thoughts.

Problem	Possible Action (Option)	Result (Consequence)

Focus On Writing

24. **Write a Journal Entry** Choose an imaginary character who might have lived during the time period covered by this module. You might choose, for example, a Berber caravan leader, a member of the Bantu who raises cattle in sub-Saharan Africa, or a woman or man living in Ghana, Mali, or Songhai. Then match that person with a specific place. Finally, write five to six sentences as your journal entry. Include details on what the character sees, feels, and does on a typical day.

Module 15
Later Chinese Dynasties

Essential Question

Which dynasty in Chinese history would you most like to have lived in and why?

About the Photo: The magnificent Forbidden City, shown in this photo, was built in the 1400s as a royal palace. Today it is a museum.

> ▶ *Explore ONLINE!*

HISTORY.

VIDEOS, including...
- Confucius: Words of Wisdom
- Song Inventions

✓ Document-Based Investigations

✓ Graphic Organizers

✓ Interactive Games

✓ Interactive Map: Chinese Dynasties, 589–1279

✓ Image with Hotspots: The Forbidden City

✓ Image Carousel: Early Korean Culture

In this module you will learn about Chinese history from the 500s, with the fall of the Han dynasty, to the 1600s.

What You Will Learn...

Lesson 1: China Reunifies. **518**
The Big Idea Rulers of the Sui, Tang, and Song dynasties reunited China after the Period of Disunion.

Lesson 2: Tang and Song Achievements **523**
The Big Idea The eras of the Tang and Song dynasties were periods of economic, cultural, and technological accomplishments.

Lesson 3: Confucianism and Government **530**
The Big Idea Confucian thought influenced the Song government.

Lesson 4: The Yuan and Ming Dynasties. **534**
The Big Idea The Chinese were ruled by foreigners during the Yuan dynasty, but they threw off Mongol rule and prospered during the Ming dynasty.

Lesson 5: China and Its Neighbors **506**
The Big Idea China had a major influence on the region's other civilizations.

Timeline of Events 589–1644 ▶ *Explore ONLINE!*

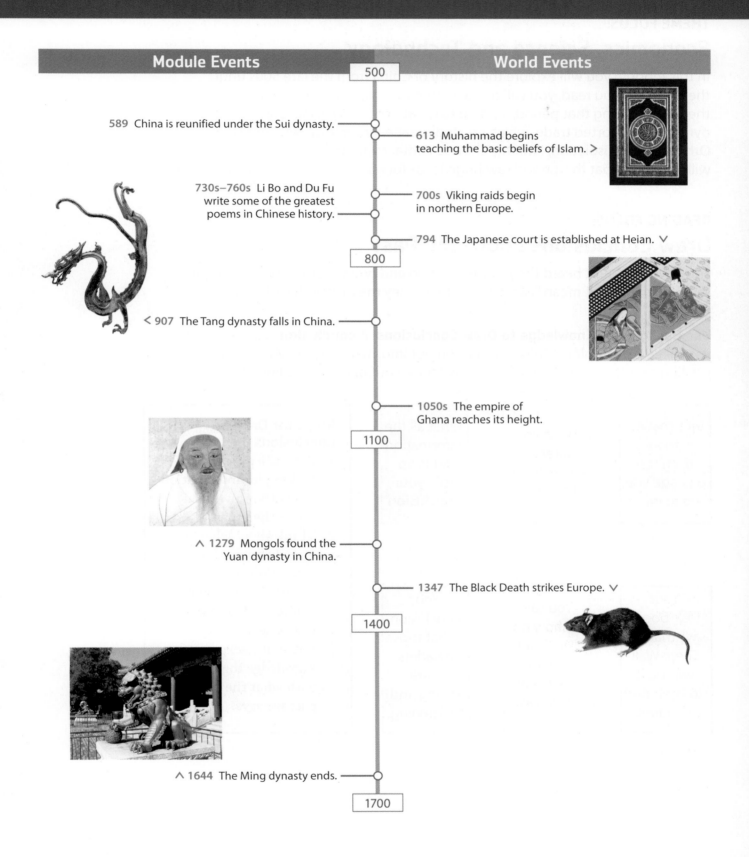

Module Events		World Events

500

589 China is reunified under the Sui dynasty.

613 Muhammad begins teaching the basic beliefs of Islam. >

730s–760s Li Bo and Du Fu write some of the greatest poems in Chinese history.

700s Viking raids begin in northern Europe.

794 The Japanese court is established at Heian. ∨

800

< **907** The Tang dynasty falls in China.

1050s The empire of Ghana reaches its height.

1100

∧ **1279** Mongols found the Yuan dynasty in China.

1347 The Black Death strikes Europe. ∨

1400

∧ **1644** The Ming dynasty ends.

1700

Reading Social Studies

THEME FOCUS:

Economics, Science and Technology

In this module you will explore the history of China from the late 500s until the 1600s. As you read, you will discover that many different dynasties ruled the region during that period, leading to great political change. Some of those dynasties supported trade, which created great economic growth and stability. Others favored isolation, limiting Chinese contact with the rest of the world. You will also learn that this period saw huge leaps forward in science and technology.

READING FOCUS:

Draw Conclusions about the Past

You have no doubt heard the phrase "put two and two together." When people say that, they don't mean "two + two = four." They mean "put the information together."

Use Background Knowledge to Draw Conclusions A **conclusion** is a judgment you make by combining information. You put information from what you are reading together with what you already know, your background knowledge.

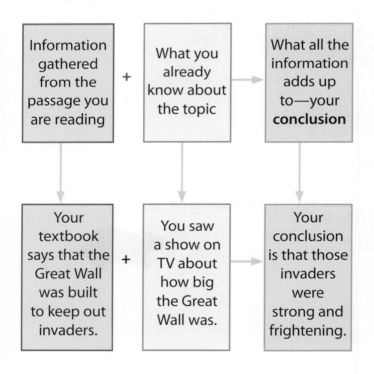

Steps for Drawing Conclusions
1. Read the passage, looking for information the author gives you about the topic.
2. Think about what you already know about the topic. Consider things you've studied, books you've read, or movies you've seen.
3. Put your background knowledge together with what the passage says.

You Try It!

Read the following passage and then answer the questions below.

Advances in Agriculture Early Chinese civilization was based on agriculture. Over thousands of years, the Chinese had become expert farmers. In the north, farmers grew wheat, barley, and other grains. In the warmer and wetter south, they grew rice.

During the Song dynasty, though, Chinese farming reached new heights. The improvement was largely due to new irrigation techniques. For example, some farmers dug underground wells. A new irrigation device, the dragon backbone pump, allowed one person to do the work of several. With this light and portable pump, a farmer could scoop up water and pour it into an irrigation canal. Using these new techniques, farmers created elaborate irrigation systems.

Answer these questions based on the passage you just read.

1. Think back on what you've learned about irrigation systems in other societies. What do you think irrigation was like in China before the Song dynasty?

2. What effect do you think this improved irrigation had on Chinese society? Why do you think this?

3. Based on this passage, what kinds of conditions do you think rice needs to grow? What conditions do you think wheat needs?

4. Which crop was most likely grown near the Great Wall—wheat or rice? Why do you think so?

As you read this module, think about what you already know about China, and draw conclusions to fill gaps in what you are reading.

Key Terms and People

Lesson 1
Period of Disunion
Grand Canal
Empress Wu

Lesson 2
porcelain
celadon
woodblock printing
gunpowder
compass

Lesson 3
bureaucracy
civil service
scholar-official

Lesson 4
Genghis Khan
Kublai Khan
Zheng He
isolationism

Lesson 5
cultural diffusion
Trung sisters

China Reunifies

The Big Idea

Rulers of the Sui, Tang, and Song dynasties reunited China after the Period of Disunion.

Main Ideas

- The Period of Disunion was a time of war and disorder that followed the end of the Han dynasty.

- China was reunified under the Sui, Tang, and Song dynasties.

- The Age of Buddhism saw major religious changes in China.

Key Terms and People

Period of Disunion
Grand Canal
Empress Wu

If YOU were there . . .

You are a peasant in China in the year AD 264. Your grandfather often speaks of a time when all of China was united, but all you have known is warfare among rulers. A man passing through your village speaks of even more conflict in other areas.

Why might you want China to have just one ruler?

The Period of Disunion

When the Han dynasty collapsed, China split into several rival kingdoms, each ruled by military leaders. Historians sometimes call the time of disorder that followed the collapse of the Han the **Period of Disunion**. It lasted from AD 220 to 589.

Although war was common during the Period of Disunion, peaceful developments also took place at the same time. During this period, nomadic peoples settled in northern China. Some Chinese people adopted the nomads' culture, while the invaders adopted some Chinese practices. For example, one former nomadic ruler ordered his people to adopt Chinese names, speak Chinese, and dress like the Chinese. Thus, the cultures of the invaders and the traditional Chinese mixed.

A similar cultural blending took place in southern China. Many northern Chinese, unwilling to live under the rule of the nomadic invaders, fled to southern China. There, northern Chinese culture mixed with the more southern cultures.

As a result of this mixing, Chinese culture changed. New types of art and music developed. New foods and clothing styles became popular. The new culture spread over a wider geographic area than ever before, and more people became identified as Chinese.

Reading Check
Find Main Ideas
How did Chinese culture change during the Period of Disunion?

The Sui, Tang, and Song

Finally, after centuries of political confusion and cultural change, China was reunified. For about 700 years, it remained unified under a series of powerful dynasties.

The Sui Dynasty The man who finally ended the Period of Disunion was a northern ruler named Yang Jian (YANG jee-EN). In 589, he conquered the south, unified China, and created the Sui (SWAY) dynasty.

The Sui dynasty didn't last long, only from 589 to 618. During that time, though, its leaders restored order to China and began the **Grand Canal**, a canal linking northern and southern China.

The Tang Dynasty A new dynasty arose in China in 618 when a former Sui official overthrew the old government. This dynasty, the Tang, ruled for nearly 300 years. China grew under the Tang dynasty to include much of eastern Asia and large parts of Central Asia.

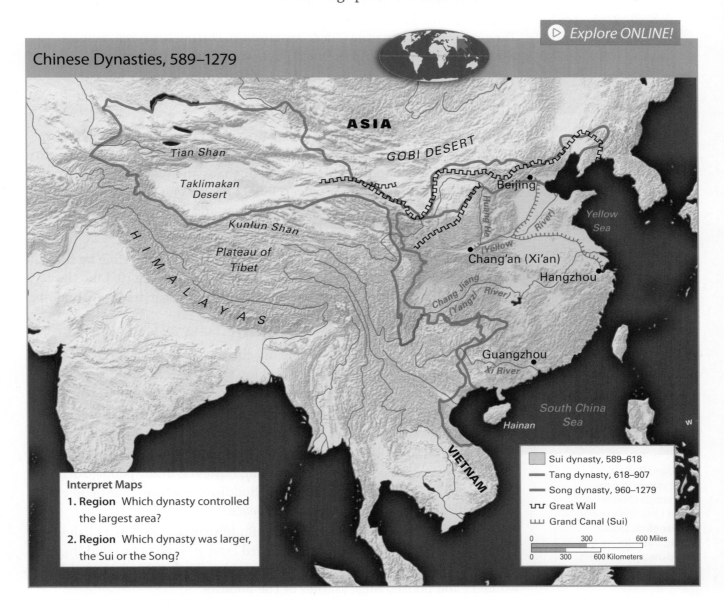

Explore ONLINE!

Chinese Dynasties, 589–1279

ASIA
Tian Shan
GOBI DESERT
Taklimakan Desert
Beijing
Kunlun Shan
Yellow Sea
Huang He (Yellow River)
Plateau of Tibet
Chang'an (Xi'an)
HIMALAYAS
Hangzhou
Chang Jiang (Yangzi River)
Guangzhou
Xi River
South China Sea
Hainan
VIETNAM

Interpret Maps

1. **Region** Which dynasty controlled the largest area?

2. **Region** Which dynasty was larger, the Sui or the Song?

Sui dynasty, 589–618
Tang dynasty, 618–907
Song dynasty, 960–1279
Great Wall
Grand Canal (Sui)

0   300   600 Miles
0   300   600 Kilometers

Empress Wu c. 625–705

Married to a sickly emperor, Empress Wu became the virtual ruler of China in 655. After her husband died, Wu decided her sons were not worthy of ruling. She kept power for herself and ruled with an iron fist. Those who threatened her power risked death.

Unlike many earlier rulers, she chose advisors based on their abilities rather than their ranks. Although she was not well liked, Wu was respected for bringing stability and prosperity to China.

Draw Conclusions
Why do you think Empress Wu was never very popular?

Historians view the Tang dynasty as a golden age of Chinese civilization. One of its greatest rulers was Taizong (TY-tzoong). He conquered many lands, reformed the military, and created a code of laws. Another brilliant Tang ruler was Xuanzong (SHOO-AN-tzoong). During his reign, culture flourished. Many of China's finest poets wrote during this period.

The Tang dynasty also included the only woman to rule China—**Empress Wu**. Her methods were sometimes vicious, but she was intelligent and talented.

In the 800s, rebellions broke out against the Tang rulers. The dynasty finally fell apart into a number of kingdoms in 907. After the Tang dynasty fell, China entered another brief period of chaos and disorder, with separate kingdoms competing for power. In fact, China was so divided during this period that it is known as Five Dynasties and Ten Kingdoms. The disorder lasted only 53 years, though, from 907 to 960.

The Song Dynasty In 960, China was again reunified, this time by the Song dynasty. The Song ruled for about 300 years, until 1279. Like the Tang, the period of the Song dynasty was a time of great accomplishments.

Reading Check
Summarize When was China reunified? When did the Tang dynasty fall?

The Age of Buddhism

While China was experiencing changes in its government, another major change was taking place in Chinese culture. A new religion was spreading quickly throughout the vast land.

Buddhism, one of the world's major religions, originated in India about 500 BC. Buddhism first came to China during the Han dynasty. But for some time, there were few Buddhists in China.

During the troubled Period of Disunion, however, many people turned to Buddhism. They took comfort in the Buddhist teaching that people can escape suffering and achieve a state of peace.

By the end of the Period of Disunion, Buddhism was well established in China. As a result, wealthy people donated land and money to Buddhist temples, which arose across the land. Some temples were architectural wonders and housed huge statues of the Buddha.

The Grand Buddha statue was added to the spiritual complex at Mount Ling-Shang while the Xiangfu Buddhist temple, built during the Tang dynasty, was being rebuilt.

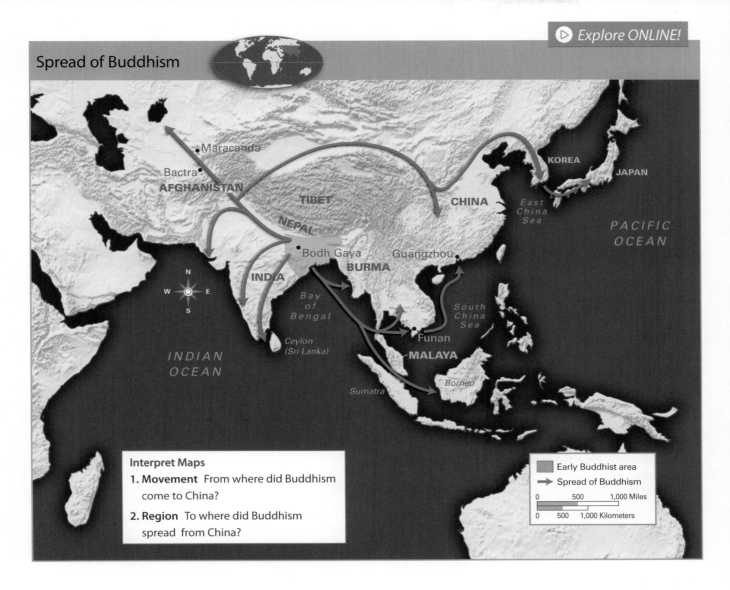

Spead of Buddhism

▶ Explore ONLINE!

Maracanda

Bactra
AFGHANISTAN

TIBET

NEPAL

Bodh Gaya

INDIA

Bay of Bengal

Ceylon (Sri Lanka)

INDIAN OCEAN

CHINA

East China Sea

KOREA

JAPAN

PACIFIC OCEAN

Guangzhou

BURMA

South China Sea

Funan

MALAYA

Sumatra

Borneo

Interpret Maps

1. **Movement** From where did Buddhism come to China?

2. **Region** To where did Buddhism spread from China?

Early Buddhist area

→ Spread of Buddhism

0   500   1,000 Miles
0   500   1,000 Kilometers

Buddhism continued to influence life in China after the country was reunified. In fact, during the Sui and Tang dynasties, Buddhism grew and spread. Chinese missionaries, people who travel to spread their religion, introduced Buddhism to Japan, Korea, and other Asian lands.

Buddhism influenced many aspects of Chinese culture, including art, literature, and architecture. In fact, so important was Buddhism in China that the period from about 400 to about 845 can be called the Age of Buddhism.

This golden age of Buddhism came to an end when a Tang emperor launched a campaign against the religion. He burned many Buddhist texts, took lands from and destroyed Buddhist temples, and turned others into schools.

The emperor's actions weakened the influence of Buddhism in China, but they did not destroy it completely.

Quick Facts

Reasons for Buddhism's Spread

- Buddhist missionaries spread the religion.
- People took comfort from Buddhist teachings during the Period of Disunion.

Reading Check
Analyze Causes
Why did Buddhism
spread more easily
during the Period of
Disunion?

Buddhism continued to play a key role in Chinese society for centuries. As it had during the early Tang period, it continued to shape Chinese art and literature. But even as it influenced life in China, Buddhism changed. People began to blend elements of Buddhism with elements of other philosophies, especially Confucianism and Daoism, to create a new way of thinking.

Summary and Preview From the disorder that followed the fall of the Han dynasty, new dynasties arose to restore order in China. You will read about their many advances in the next lesson.

Lesson 1 Assessment

Review Ideas, Terms, and People

1. a. Define What was the Period of Disunion?

   b. Explain How did Chinese culture change during the Period of Disunion?

2. a. Identify Who was Empress Wu? What did she do?

   b. Recall What important event occurred in 907 in China?

3. a. Identify When was the Age of Buddhism?

   b. Explain Why did people turn to Buddhism during the Period of Disunion?

   c. Elaborate How did Buddhism influence Chinese culture?

Critical Thinking

4. Organize Information Draw a timeline like this one. Place the lesson's main events and their dates on the timeline.

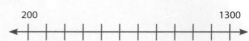

200   1300

Tang and Song Achievements

The Big Idea

The eras of the Tang and Song dynasties were periods of economic, cultural, and technological accomplishments.

Main Ideas

- Advances in agriculture led to increased trade and population growth.

- Cities and trade grew during the Tang and Song dynasties.

- The Tang and Song dynasties produced fine arts and inventions.

Key Terms and People

porcelain
celadon
woodblock printing
gunpowder
compass

If YOU were there . . .

It is the year 1270. You are a rich merchant in a Chinese city of about a million people. The city around you fills your senses. You see people in colorful clothes among beautiful buildings. Glittering objects lure you into busy shops. You hear people talking—discussing business, gossiping, laughing at jokes. You smell delicious food cooking at a restaurant down the street.

How do you feel about your city?

Advances in Agriculture

Early Chinese civilization was based on agriculture. Over thousands of years, the Chinese had become expert farmers. In the north, farmers grew wheat, barley, and other grains. In the warmer and wetter south, they grew rice.

During the Song dynasty, though, Chinese farming reached new heights. The improvement was largely due to new irrigation techniques. For example, some farmers dug underground wells. A new irrigation device, the dragon backbone pump, allowed one person to do the work of several. With this light and portable pump, a farmer could scoop up water and pour it into an irrigation canal. Using these new techniques, farmers created elaborate irrigation systems.

Under the Song, the amount of land under cultivation increased. Lands along the Chang Jiang that had been wild now became farmland. Farms also became more productive, thanks to the discovery of a new type of rice. Because it grew and ripened quickly, this rice enabled farmers to grow two or even three crops in the time it used to take to grow just one.

Chinese farmers also learned to grow new crops, such as cotton, efficiently. Workers processed cotton fiber to make clothes and other goods. The production of tea, which had been grown in China for centuries, also increased.

Rice has long been a vital crop in southern China, where the warm, wet climate is perfect for rice growing.

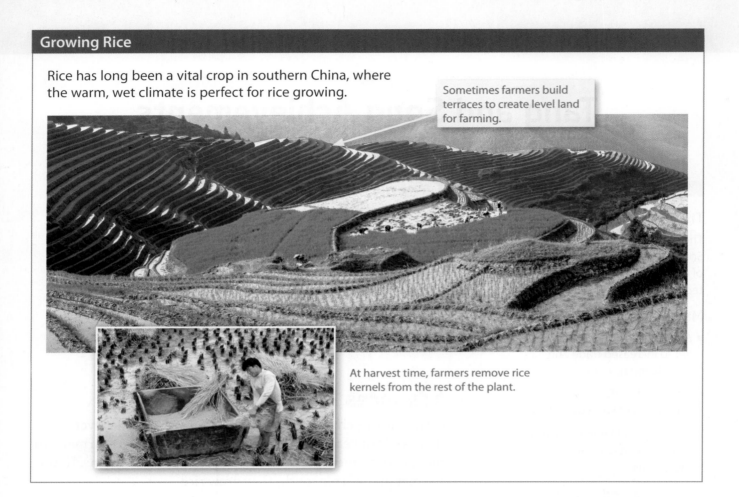

Sometimes farmers build terraces to create level land for farming.

At harvest time, farmers remove rice kernels from the rest of the plant.

Reading Check
Analyze Effects
How did agricultural advances affect population growth and the Chinese government?

Agricultural surpluses helped pay taxes to the government. Merchants also traded food crops. As a result, food was abundant not just in the countryside but also in the cities. Because food was plentiful, China's population grew quickly. During the Tang dynasty, the population had been about 60 million. During the Song dynasty, the farmers of China fed a country of nearly 100 million people. At the time, China was the largest country in the world.

Cities and Trade

Throughout the Tang and Song dynasties, much of the food grown on China's farms flowed into the growing cities and towns. China's cities were crowded, busy places. Shopkeepers, government officials, doctors, artisans, entertainers, religious leaders, and artists made them lively places as well.

City Life China's capital and the largest city of the Tang dynasty was Chang'an (chahng-AHN), a bustling trade center. With a population of more than a million, it was by far the largest city in the world at the time.

Chang'an, like other trading cities, had a mix of people from many cultures—China, Korea, Persia, Arabia, and Europe. It was also known as a religious and philosophical center, not just for Buddhists and Daoists but for Asian Christians as well.

China's Grand Canal is the world's longest human-made waterway. It was begun during the Sui dynasty largely to transport rice and other foods from the south to feed China's cities and armies in the north.

Cities continued to grow under the Song. Several cities, including the Song capital, Kaifeng (KY-fuhng), had about a million people. A dozen more cities had populations close to half a million.

Trade in China and Beyond Trade grew along with Chinese cities. This trade, combined with China's agricultural base, made China richer than ever before. Much trade took place within China itself. Traders used the country's rivers to transport goods on barges and ships.

The Grand Canal was a series of waterways that linked major cities. The canal carried a huge amount of trade goods, especially farm products. Construction on the canal had begun during the Sui dynasty. During the Tang dynasty, it was improved and expanded. The Grand Canal allowed the Chinese to move goods and crops from distant agricultural areas into cities.

The Chinese also carried on trade with other lands and peoples. During the Tang dynasty, most foreign trade was over land routes leading west to India and Southwest Asia, though Chinese traders also went to Korea and Japan in the east. The Chinese exported many goods, including tea, rice, spices, and jade. Nomadic tribes to the north of China adopted the habit of drinking tea, and the Chinese exported tea to them in exchange for horses. However, one export was especially important—silk. So valuable was silk

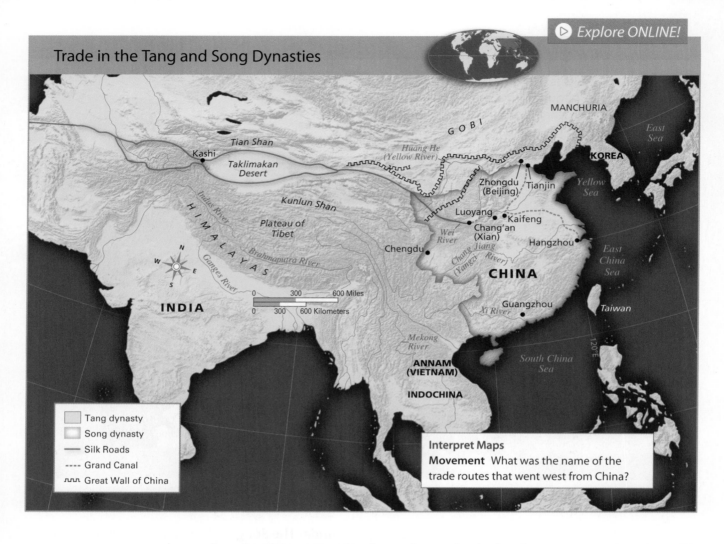

Explore ONLINE!

Legend:
- Tang dynasty
- Song dynasty
- Silk Roads
- Grand Canal
- Great Wall of China

Interpret Maps
Movement What was the name of the trade routes that went west from China?

that the Chinese tried to keep the method of making it secret. In exchange for their exports, the Chinese imported different foods and plants, wool, glass, gold, and silver.

During the Song dynasty, maritime trade, or sea trade, became more important. China opened its Pacific ports to foreign traders. The largest seaport during the Song dynasty was Quanzhou, on China's southeast coast. From there, large Chinese ships carried goods to Japan, other parts of Asia, and down the coast of Africa. During this time, the Chinese also developed another valuable product—a thin, beautiful type of pottery called **porcelain**.

All of this trade helped create a strong economy. As a result, merchants became important in Chinese society. Also because of the growth of trade, the Song created the world's first system of paper money in the 900s.

Reading Check
Summarize How far did China's trade routes extend?

Arts and Inventions

While China grew rich economically, its cultural riches also increased. In literature, art, and science, China made huge advances.

Artists and Poets The artists and writers of the Tang dynasty were some of China's greatest. Wu Daozi (DOW-tzee) painted murals that celebrated Buddhism and nature. Li Bo and Du Fu wrote poems that readers still enjoy for their beauty. Also noted for its literature, the Song period produced Li Qingzhao (ching-ZHOW), perhaps China's greatest female poet. She once said that the purpose of her poetry was to capture a single moment in time.

Artists of both the Tang and Song dynasties made exquisite objects in clay. Tang figurines of horses clearly show the animals' strength. Song artists made porcelain items covered in a pale green glaze called **celadon** (SEL-uh-duhn).

Important Inventions The Tang and Song dynasties produced some of the most remarkable—and most important—inventions in human history. Some of these inventions influenced events around the world.

According to legend, a man named Cai Lun invented paper in the year 105 during the Han dynasty. A later Tang invention built on Cai Lun's achievement—**woodblock printing**, a form of printing in which an entire page is carved into a block of wood. The printer applies ink to

---

Quick Facts

Chinese Inventions

Paper
Invented during the Han dynasty around 105, paper was one of the greatest of all Chinese inventions. It gave the Chinese a cheap and easy way of keeping records and also made printing possible.

Woodblock printing
The Chinese invented printing during the Tang dynasty, centuries before it was known in Europe. Printers could copy drawings or texts quickly, much faster than they could be copied by hand.

Movable type
Inventors of the Song dynasty created movable type, which made printing much faster. Carved characters could be rearranged and reused to print many different messages.

Paper money
The world's first paper money was invented by the Song. Lighter and easier to handle than coins, paper money helped the Chinese manage their growing wealth.

Porcelain
Porcelain was first made during the Tang dynasty, but it wasn't perfected for many centuries. Chinese artists were famous for their work with this fragile material.

Gunpowder
Invented during the late Tang or early Song dynasty, gunpowder was used to make fireworks and signals. The Chinese did not generally use it as a weapon.

Magnetic compass
Invented no later than the Han period, the compass was greatly improved by the Tang. The new compass allowed sailors and merchants to travel vast distances.

The Paper Trail

The dollar bill in your pocket may be crisp and new, but paper money has been around a long time. Paper money was printed for the first time in China in the AD 900s and was in use for about 700 years, through the Ming dynasty, when the bill shown here was printed. However, so much money was printed that it lost value. The Chinese stopped using paper money for centuries. Its use caught on in Europe, though, and eventually became common. Most countries now issue paper money.

Analyze Information
What is an advantage of paper money?

the block and presses paper against the block to create a printed page. The world's first known printed book was printed in this way in China in 868.

Another invention of the Tang dynasty was gunpowder. **Gunpowder** is a mixture of powders used in guns and explosives. It was originally used only in fireworks, but it was later used to make small bombs and rockets. Eventually, gunpowder was used to make explosives, firearms, and cannons. Gunpowder dramatically altered how wars were fought and, in doing so, changed the course of human history. Mongol armies later carried gunpowder to Europe when they conquered much of Asia and parts of eastern Europe.

One of the most useful achievements of Tang China was the perfection of the magnetic **compass**. This instrument, which uses the earth's magnetic field to show direction, revolutionized travel. A compass made it possible to find direction more accurately than ever before. The perfection of the compass had far-reaching effects. Explorers the world over used the compass to travel vast distances. The navigators of trading ships and warships also came to rely on the compass. Thus, the compass has been a key factor in some of the most important sailing voyages in history.

The Song dynasty also produced many important inventions. Under the Song, the Chinese invented movable type. Movable type is a set of letters or characters that is used to print books. Unlike the blocks used in block printing, movable type can be rearranged and reused to create new lines of text and different pages. The ability to print books more quickly and easily made them much less expensive. Lower prices led to an increased demand for books and contributed greatly to the spread of literacy in the region. Movable type probably made its way to Europe a few hundred years later when the Mongols established trade routes between China and the West.

The Song dynasty also introduced the concept of paper money. People were used to buying goods and services with bulky coins made of metals such as bronze, gold, and silver. Paper money was far lighter and easier to use. As trade increased and many people in China grew rich, paper money became more popular.

Reading Check
Find Main Ideas
What were some important inventions of the Tang and Song dynasties?

Summary and Preview The Tang and Song dynasties were periods of great advancement. Many great artists and writers lived during these periods. Tang and Song inventions also had dramatic effects on world history. In the next lesson, you will learn about the philosophy and government of the Song dynasty.

Lesson 2 Assessment

Review Ideas, Terms, and People

1. a. **Recall** What advances in farming occurred during the Song dynasty?

   b. **Explain** How did agricultural advancements affect China's population?

2. a. **Describe** What were the capital cities of Tang and Song China like?

   b. **Draw Conclusions** How did geography affect trade in China?

   c. **Recall** What did the Chinese trade with the northern nomadic tribes to get good horses?

3. a. **Identify** Who was Li Bo?

   b. **Draw Conclusions** How might the inventions of paper money and woodblock printing have been linked?

   c. **Form Opinions** Which Tang or Song invention do you think was most important? Defend your answer.

Critical Thinking

4. **Categorize** Copy the chart. Fill in each category with information about the Tang and Song dynasties.

	Tang dynasty	Song dynasty
Agriculture		
Cities		
Trade		
Art		
Inventions		

Confucianism and Government

The Big Idea
Confucian thought influenced the Song government.

Main Ideas
- Confucianism underwent changes and influenced Chinese government.
- Scholar-officials ran China's government during the Song dynasty.

Key Terms and People
bureaucracy
civil service
scholar-official

Academic Vocabulary
function work or perform

If YOU were there . . .

You are a student in China in 1184. Night has fallen, but you cannot sleep. Tomorrow you have a test. You know it will be the most important test of your entire life. You have studied for it—not for days or weeks or even months, but for *years*. As you toss and turn, you think about how your entire life will be determined by how well you do on this one test.

How could a single test be so important?

Development of Confucianism

The leading philosophy in China, Confucianism, is based on the teachings of Confucius. He lived more than 1,500 years before the Song dynasty. His ideas, though, had a dramatic effect on the Song system of government.

Confucian Ideas Confucius's teachings focused on ethics, or proper behavior, for individuals and governments. He said that people should conduct their lives according to two basic principles. These principles were *ren*, or concern for others, and *li*, or appropriate behavior. Confucius argued that society would **function** best if everyone followed *ren* and *li*.

Confucius thought that everyone had a proper role to play in society. Order was maintained when people knew their place and behaved appropriately. For example, Confucius said that young people should obey their elders and that subjects should obey their rulers.

Early Confucianism After his death, Confucius's ideas were spread by his followers, but they were not widely accepted. In fact, the Qin dynasty officially suppressed Confucian ideas and teachings. By the time of the Han dynasty, Confucianism had again come into favor, and Confucianism became the official state philosophy.

In addition to ethics, Confucianism stressed the importance of education. This painting, created during the Song period, shows earlier Confucian scholars during the Period of Disunion sorting scrolls containing classic Confucian texts.

During the Period of Disunion, which followed the Han dynasty, Confucianism was overshadowed by Buddhism as the major tradition in China. You may recall that many Chinese people turned to Buddhism for comfort during these troubled times. In doing so, they largely turned away from Confucian ideas and outlooks.

Later, during the Sui and early Tang dynasties, Buddhism was very influential. Unlike Confucianism, which stressed ethical behavior, Buddhism stressed a more spiritual outlook that promised escape from suffering. As Buddhism became more popular in China, Confucianism lost some of its influence.

Neo-Confucianism Late in the Tang dynasty, many Chinese historians and scholars again became interested in the teachings of Confucius. Their interest was sparked by their desire to improve Chinese government and society.

During and after the Song dynasty, a new philosophy called Neo-Confucianism developed. The term *neo* means "new." Based on Confucianism, Neo-Confucianism was similar to the older philosophy in that it taught proper behavior. However, it also emphasized spiritual matters. For example, Neo-Confucian scholars discussed such issues as what made human beings do bad things even if their basic nature was good. Central to the philosophy of Neo-Confucianism was kinship, or the family. Each person should put the interests of the family above his or her interests. This dedication to the family brought peace and order to society.

Neo-Confucianism became much more influential under the Song. Later, its influence grew even more. In fact, the ideas of Neo-Confucianism became official government teachings after the Song dynasty.

Reading Check
Contrast How did Neo-Confucianism differ from early Confucianism?

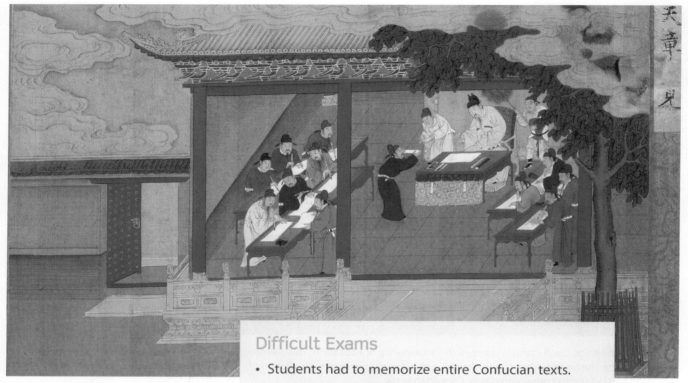

Civil Service Exams

This painting from the 1600s shows civil servants writing essays for China's emperor. Difficult exams ensured that government officials were chosen for ability—not because of wealth or family connections.

Difficult Exams

- Students had to memorize entire Confucian texts.
- To pass the most difficult tests, students might study for more than 20 years!
- Some exams lasted up to 72 hours, and students were locked in private rooms while taking them.
- Some dishonest students cheated by copying Confucius's works on the inside of their clothes, paying bribes to the test graders, or paying someone else to take the test for them.
- To prevent cheating, exam halls were often locked and guarded.

Civil Service Examinations

The Song dynasty took another major step that affected China for centuries. Song rulers improved the system by which people went to work for the government. These workers formed a large **bureaucracy**, or a body of unelected government officials. They joined the bureaucracy by passing civil service examinations. **Civil service** means service as a government official.

To become a civil servant, a person had to pass a series of written examinations. The examinations tested students' knowledge of Confucianism and related ideas. Because the tests were so difficult, students spent years preparing for them. Only a very small fraction of the people who took the tests would reach the top level and be appointed to a position in the government. However, candidates for the civil service examinations had a good reason to study hard. Passing the tests meant life as a **scholar-official**—an educated member of the government.

Scholar-officials were elite members of society. They performed many important jobs in the government and were widely admired for their knowledge and ethics. Their benefits included considerable respect and reduced penalties for breaking the law. Many also became wealthy from gifts given by people seeking their aid.

The civil service examination system helped ensure that talented, intelligent people became scholar-officials. It was a major factor in the stability of the Song government.

Reading Check
Analyze Events
How did the Song dynasty change China's government?

Summary and Preview During the Song period, Confucian ideas helped shape China's government. In the next lesson, you will read about the two dynasties that followed the Song—the Yuan and the Ming.

First rising to prominence under the Song, scholar-officials remained important in China for centuries. The illustration of the scholar-officials shown here offers an impression of what they may have looked like.

Lesson 3 Assessment

Review Ideas, Terms, and People

1. **a. Identify** What two principles did Confucius believe people should follow?

   b. Explain What was Neo-Confucianism?

   c. Recall What aspect of Neo-Confucianism brought order to society?

2. **a. Define** What was a scholar-official?

   b. Explain Why would people want to become scholar-officials?

   c. Evaluate Do you think civil service examinations were a good way to choose government officials? Why or why not?

Critical Thinking

3. **Organize Information** In a graphic organizer like this one, explain the relationship between Confucianism and Neo-Confucianism, and Neo-Confucianism and government bureaucracy.

The Yuan and Ming Dynasties

The Big Idea

The Chinese were ruled by foreigners during the Yuan dynasty, but they threw off Mongol rule and prospered during the Ming dynasty.

Main Ideas

- The Mongol Empire included China, and the Mongols ruled China as the Yuan dynasty.

- The Ming dynasty was a time of stability and prosperity.

- China under the Ming saw great changes in its government and relations with other countries.

Key Terms and People

Genghis Khan
Kublai Khan
Zheng He
isolationism

If YOU were there . . .

You are a farmer in northern China in 1212. As you pull weeds from a wheat field, you hear a sound like thunder. Looking toward the sound, you see hundreds—no, *thousands*—of armed horsemen on the horizon, riding straight toward you. You are frozen with fear. Only one thought fills your mind—the dreaded Mongols are coming.

What can you do to save yourself?

The Mongol Empire

Among the nomadic peoples who attacked the Chinese were the Mongols. For centuries, the Mongols had lived as separate tribes in the vast plains north of China. Then in 1206, a powerful leader, or khan, united them. His name was Temüjin. When he became leader, though, he was given a new title: "Universal Ruler," or **Genghis Khan** (GENG-guhs KAHN).

The Mongol Conquest Genghis Khan organized the Mongols into a powerful army and led them on bloody expeditions of conquest. The brutality of the Mongol attacks terrorized people throughout much of Asia and eastern Europe. Genghis Khan and his army killed all of the men, women, and children in countless cities and villages. Within 20 years, he ruled a large part of Asia.

Genghis Khan then turned his attention to China. He first led his armies into northern China in 1211. They fought their way south, wrecking whole towns and ruining farmland. By the time of Genghis Khan's death in 1227, all of northern China was under Mongol control. His empire also included almost all of Central Asia, to the borders of European Russia.

The Mongol conquests did not end with Genghis Khan's death, though. His sons and grandsons continued to raid lands all over Asia and eastern Europe. The destruction the Mongols left behind was terrible.

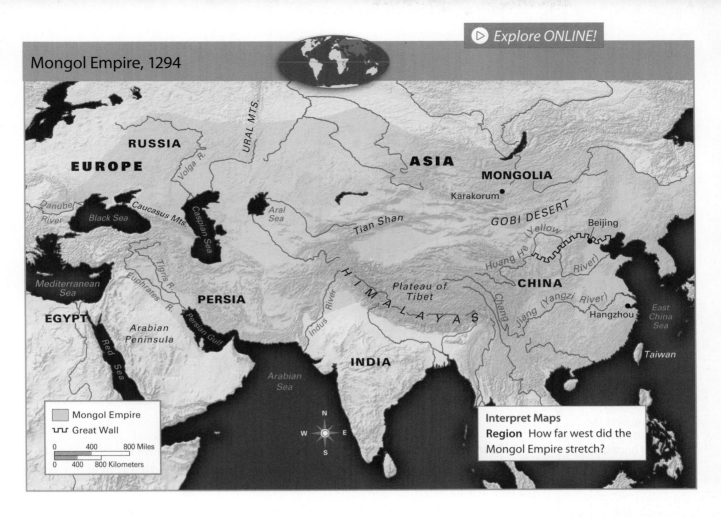

Mongol Empire, 1294

▶ Explore ONLINE!

RUSSIA
EUROPE
ASIA
MONGOLIA
Karakorum
Danube River
Volga R.
Caucasus Mts.
Black Sea
Aral Sea
Caspian Sea
URAL MTS.
GOBI DESERT
Beijing
Yellow
Huang He
(River)
Tian Shan
Mediterranean Sea
Tigris R.
Euphrates R.
Plateau of Tibet
CHINA
EGYPT
PERSIA
Persian Gulf
Indus River
HIMALAYAS
Chang Jiang (Yangzi River)
Hangzhou
East China Sea
Arabian Peninsula
Red Sea
INDIA
Arabian Sea
Taiwan

Mongol Empire
Great Wall

0   400   800 Miles
0   400   800 Kilometers

N W E S

Interpret Maps
Region How far west did the Mongol Empire stretch?

In 1260, Genghis Khan's grandson **Kublai Khan** (KOO-bluh KAHN) became ruler of the Mongol Empire. He completed the conquest of China and in 1279 declared himself emperor of China. The lands he ruled made up one of the largest empires in world history—it stretched from the Pacific Ocean to eastern Europe. Kublai Khan unified all of China under his rule. This began the Yuan dynasty, a period that some people also call the Mongol Ascendancy. For the first time in its long history, foreigners ruled all of China.

---- BIOGRAPHY ----

Kublai Khan 1215–1294

Kublai came from Mongolia but spent much of his life in China. His capital, Dadu, was near the modern city of Beijing. He completed the conquest of China that Genghis Khan had begun and ruled China as the emperor of the Yuan dynasty.

The lands Kublai Khan ruled made up one of the largest empires in world history, stretching from the Pacific Ocean to eastern

Europe. As China's ruler, Kublai Khan welcomed foreign visitors, including the Italian merchant Marco Polo and the Arab historian Ibn Battutah. The stories these two men told helped create interest in China and its products among Westerners.

Form Generalizations
How did Kublai Khan's actions help change people's views of China?

This painting from the 1200s shows Kublai Khan hunting on horseback.

Life in Yuan China Kublai Khan and the Mongol rulers he led belonged to a different ethnic group from the Chinese. They spoke a different language, worshipped different gods, wore different clothing, and had different customs. The Chinese resented being ruled by these foreigners, whom they saw as rude and uncivilized.

However, Kublai Khan did not force the Chinese to accept Mongol ways of life. Some Mongols even adopted aspects of the Chinese culture, such as Confucianism. Still, the Mongols made sure to keep control of the Chinese. They prohibited Confucian scholars from gaining too much power in the government, for example. The Mongols also placed heavy taxes on the Chinese.

Much of the tax money the Mongols collected went to pay for vast public-works projects. These projects required the labor of many Chinese people. The Yuan extended the Grand Canal and built new roads and palaces. Workers also improved the roads that were part of China's postal system. In addition, the Yuan emperors built a new capital, Dadu, near modern Beijing.

Mongol soldiers were sent throughout China to keep the peace as well as to keep a close watch on the Chinese. The soldiers' presence kept overland trade routes safe for merchants. Sea trade between China, India, and Southeast Asia continued, too. The Mongol emperors also welcomed foreign traders at Chinese ports. Some of these traders received special privileges.

Part of what we know about life in the Yuan dynasty comes from one such trader, an Italian merchant named Marco Polo. Between 1271 and 1295 Polo traveled in and around China. He was highly respected by the

A Chinese City

In this passage, Marco Polo describes his visit to Hangzhou (HAHNG-JOH), a city in southeastern China.

"Inside the city there is a Lake . . . and all round it are erected [built] beautiful palaces and mansions, of the richest and most exquisite [finest] structure that you can imagine. . . . In the middle of the Lake are two Islands, on each of which stands a rich, beautiful and spacious edifice [building], furnished in such style as to seem fit for the palace of an Emperor. And when any one of the citizens desired to hold a marriage feast, or to give any other entertainment, it used to be done at one of these palaces. And everything would be found there ready to order, such as silver plates, trenchers [platters], and dishes, napkins and table-cloths, and whatever else was needful. The King made this provision for the gratification [enjoyment] of his people, and the place was open to every one who desired to give an entertainment."

—Marco Polo, from *The Story of Marco Polo*

Analyze Historical Sources
From this description, what impression might Europeans have had of Hangzhou?

Mongols and even served in Kublai Khan's court. When Polo returned to Europe, he wrote of his travels. Polo's descriptions of China fascinated many Europeans. His book sparked much European interest in China.

The End of the Yuan Dynasty Despite their vast empire, the Mongols were not content with their lands. They decided to invade Japan. A Mongol army sailed to Japan in 1274 and again in 1281. The campaigns, however, were disastrous. Violent storms and fierce defenders destroyed most of the Mongol force.

The failed campaigns against Japan weakened the Mongol military. The huge, expensive public-works projects had already weakened the economy. These weaknesses, combined with Chinese resentment, made China ripe for rebellion.

In the 1300s, many Chinese groups rebelled against the Yuan dynasty. In 1368, a former monk named Zhu Yuanzhang (JOO yoo-ahn-JAHNG) took charge of a rebel army. He led this army in a final victory over the Mongols. China was once again ruled by the Chinese.

Reading Check
Find Main Ideas
How did the Mongols come to rule China, and what part of the world outside of China did they dominate?

The Ming Dynasty

After Zhu Yuanzhang's army defeated the Mongols, he became emperor of China. The Ming dynasty that he founded ruled China from 1368 to 1644—nearly 300 years. Ming China proved to be one of the most stable and prosperous times in Chinese history. The Ming expanded China's fame overseas and sponsored extensive building projects across China.

Great Sea Voyages During the Ming dynasty, the Chinese improved their ships and their sailing skills. The greatest sailor of the period was **Zheng He** (juhng HUH). Between 1405 and 1433, he led seven grand voyages to places around Asia. Zheng He's fleets were huge. One included more than 60 ships and 25,000 sailors. Some of the ships were gigantic too, perhaps more than 300 feet long. That is longer than a football field!

In the course of his voyages, Zheng He sailed his fleet throughout the Indian Ocean. He sailed as far west as the Persian Gulf and the eastern-most coast of Africa.

The Voyages of Zheng He

Zheng He's ocean voyages were remarkable. Some of his ships, like the one shown here, were among the largest in the world at the time.

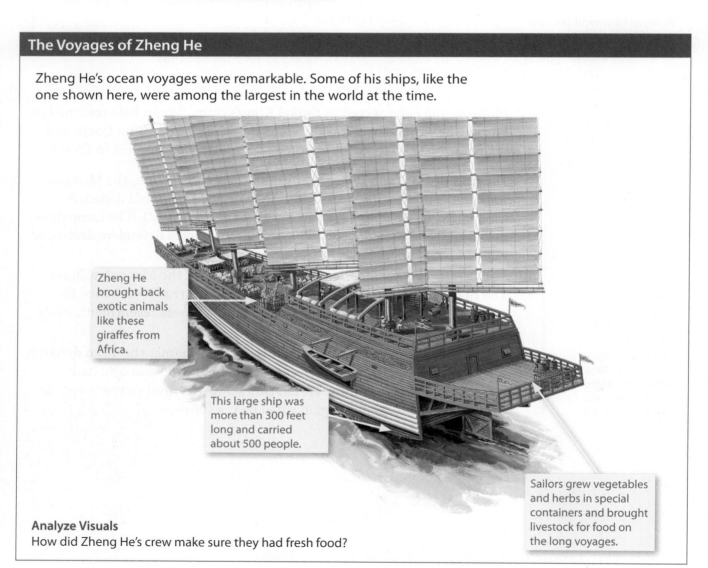

Zheng He brought back exotic animals like these giraffes from Africa.

This large ship was more than 300 feet long and carried about 500 people.

Sailors grew vegetables and herbs in special containers and brought livestock for food on the long voyages.

Analyze Visuals
How did Zheng He's crew make sure they had fresh food?

Everywhere his ships landed, Zheng He presented leaders with beautiful gifts from China. He boasted about his country and encouraged foreign leaders to send gifts to China's emperor. From one voyage, Zheng He returned to China with representatives of some 30 nations, sent by their leaders to honor the emperor. He also brought goods and stories back to China.

Zheng He's voyages rank among the most impressive in the history of seafaring. Although they did not lead to the creation of new trade routes or the exploration of new lands, they served as a clear sign of China's power.

Great Building Projects The Ming were also known for their grand building projects. Many of these projects were designed to impress both the Chinese people and their enemies to the north.

In Beijing, for example, Ming emperors built the Forbidden City. This amazing palace complex included hundreds of imperial residences, temples, and other government buildings. Within the buildings were some

The Forbidden City

The Forbidden City is not actually a city. It's a huge complex of almost 1,000 buildings in the heart of China's capital. The Forbidden City was built for the emperor, his family, his court, and his servants, and ordinary people were forbidden from entering.

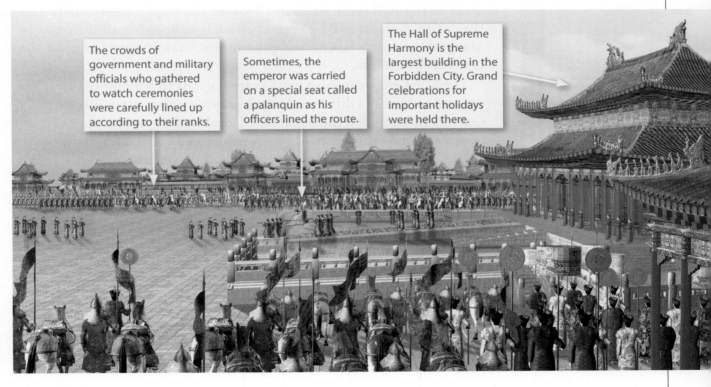

The crowds of government and military officials who gathered to watch ceremonies were carefully lined up according to their ranks.

Sometimes, the emperor was carried on a special seat called a palanquin as his officers lined the route.

The Hall of Supreme Harmony is the largest building in the Forbidden City. Grand celebrations for important holidays were held there.

Analyze Visuals
How did the Forbidden City show the power and importance of the emperor?

9,000 rooms. The name *Forbidden City* came to be used because the common people were not even allowed to enter the complex. For centuries, this city within a city was a symbol of China's glory.

Ming rulers also directed the restoration of the famous Great Wall of China. Large numbers of soldiers and peasants worked to rebuild collapsed portions of walls, connect existing walls, and build new ones. The result was a construction feat unmatched in history. The wall was more than 2,000 miles long. It could reach from San Diego to New York City! The wall was about 25 feet high and, at the top, 12 feet wide. Protected by the wall—and the soldiers who stood guard along it—the Chinese people felt safe from invasions by the northern tribes.

Reading Check
Form Generalizations
In what ways did the Ming dynasty strengthen China?

China Under the Ming

Chinese society began to change under the Ming emperors. Having expelled the Mongols, the Ming emperors worked to eliminate all foreign influences from Chinese society. This decision had significant <u>consequences</u>. As a result, China's government and relations with other countries changed dramatically.

Academic Vocabulary
consequences
effects of a particular event or events

Ming Government When the Ming took over China, they adopted many Tang and Song government programs. However, the Ming emperors were much more powerful than the Tang and Song emperors had been. They abolished the offices of some officials, such as the position of prime minister, and took a larger role in running the government. They punished anyone who challenged their authority.

Despite their personal power, though, the Ming emperors did not disband the civil service system. Because the emperor personally oversaw the entire government, he needed officials to keep his affairs organized. Many of these officials passed government examinations to enter the civil service system.

The Ming emperors also used examinations to appoint censors. The censors served in a different branch of government than other officials. Censors investigated the behavior of local leaders and judged the quality of schools and other institutions. Censors had existed for many years in China, but under the Ming emperors their power and influence grew.

The Chinese government continued to function in a similar manner long after the Ming dynasty. In fact, the basic governmental structure of strong emperors and government officials continued until the early 1900s.

Relations with Other Countries In the 1430s, a new Ming emperor made Zheng He return to China and dismantle his fleet. At the same time, the emperor banned trade. China entered a period of isolationism. **Isolationism** is a policy of avoiding contact with other countries.

Reading Check
Analyze Effects
How did isolationism
affect China?

Isolationism had great consequences for China. In 1644, the Ming dynasty was overthrown. By the late 1800s, the Western world had made huge leaps in technological progress. Westerners were then able to gain influence in Chinese affairs. Partly because of its isolation and lack of progress, China was too weak to stop them.

Summary and Preview Under the Yuan and Ming dynasties, Chinese society changed. Eventually, the Ming began a policy of isolationism. In the next lesson, you will read about China's influence on its neighbors.

Lesson 4 Assessment

Review Ideas, Terms, and People

1. a. Identify Who was Genghis Khan?

   b. Explain How did the Mongols gain control of China?

   c. Evaluate Judge this statement: "The Mongols should never have tried to invade Japan."

2. a. Identify Who was Zheng He, and what did he do?

   b. Analyze How might residents of Beijing have felt about the Forbidden City?

   c. Predict Effects How might the Great Wall have both helped and hurt China?

3. a. Define What is isolationism?

   b. Explain How did the Ming change China?

   c. Evaluate What are the advantages and disadvantages of isolationism?

Critical Thinking

4. Compare and Contrast Draw a diagram like this one. Use your notes to see how the Yuan and Ming dynasties were alike and different.

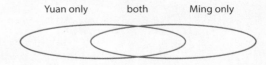

Yuan only   both   Ming only

The Great Wall

The Great Wall of China is one of the longest structures ever built. It stretches for many miles across China's northern lands. Along the way, the Great Wall crosses mountains, deserts, plains, and valleys.

Why did the Chinese build such a gigantic wall? The answer is for defense. For centuries, the people of China had been attacked by nomadic horsemen from Mongolia and other lands to the north. The Great Wall was built to keep these invaders—and their horses—out.

Standing Guard Watchtowers allowed soldiers to see invaders in the distance. During battles, watchtowers could be used as fortresses.

Great Facts about the Great Wall

- Parts of the Great Wall have been built and rebuilt for more than 2,000 years. Most of the wall that stands today was built during the Ming dynasty (1368–1644).

- The Great Wall was also used for communication. Soldiers marched along the wall, and guards used smoke signals and torches to send messages along it.

- Many people died building the Great Wall. Some historians estimate that as many as 8 million people died working on the wall over the years.

Built to Last Workers used the best materials available locally to build the wall. Some parts are built of compacted dirt, some are built of stone blocks, and others are built of brick and rubble.

Interpret Maps

1. **Movement** Why was the Great Wall built?

2. **Region** From what area to the north of China did many invaders come?

China and Its Neighbors

The Big Idea

China had a major influence on the region's other civilizations.

Main Ideas

- Ideas and philosophies central to life in China spread to other nearby states and took root.

- The Koryo dynasty of Korea adopted several elements of Chinese culture, including the civil service system.

- Under Chinese rule, the Vietnamese absorbed many features of Chinese civilization.

Key Terms and People

cultural diffusion
Trung sisters

If YOU were there . . .

You are a public official in Vietnam in the 900s. You speak Vietnamese at home, but you use the Chinese language at work, where you wear Chinese-style clothing. Your religion is Buddhism, not a traditional Vietnamese belief system. All your life, you've lived under Chinese rule. Now you hear that a rebellion against China has begun.

Why might you want Vietnam to be free from China?

Neighbors to the North, East, and South

By the time of the Sui dynasty, China was the largest and most powerful state in East Asia. During the Sui and the dynasties that followed, China became a major influence on the region's other civilizations. At various times, the Chinese even conquered and ruled parts of the region, such as Southeast Asia, forcing people to adopt Chinese ways of life. In other cases, the influence was more gradual and indirect. Ideas and philosophies central to life in China spread into other nearby regions and took root. Many of these ideas were carried by Chinese traders, who traveled widely throughout Asia. The spread of cultural traits from one region to another, such as from China to its neighbors, is called **cultural diffusion**.

One region that was heavily influenced by China early in its history was Korea. As you can see on the map, Korea is located on a peninsula just northeast of China. Because the two nations are so close, there has been contact between them for centuries. Several times, the Chinese attempted to invade and conquer Korea, but they were usually unsuccessful. Still, traders and missionaries carried elements of Chinese culture, such as Buddhism, into Korea.

Just east of Korea are the islands of Japan. Like Korea, Japan was heavily influenced by Chinese culture. Early in Japan's history, Chinese missionaries—many of whom traveled through Korea—introduced Buddhism to the islands. In addition, several early rulers of Japan were great admirers of Chinese culture. They invited Chinese officials and scholars to come to Japan and share their ideas. Later, you will learn more about China's influence on Japan.

The region south and east of China was located between the two most advanced civilizations of early Asia—China and India. Throughout most of Southeast Asia, Indian culture was a much greater influence than was Chinese culture. In the kingdom of Vietnam, however, the opposite was true. The Vietnamese embraced many elements of Chinese culture, which helped to shape life there for centuries.

Reading Check
Analyze Causes
Why did China become a major influence on the region's other civilizations?

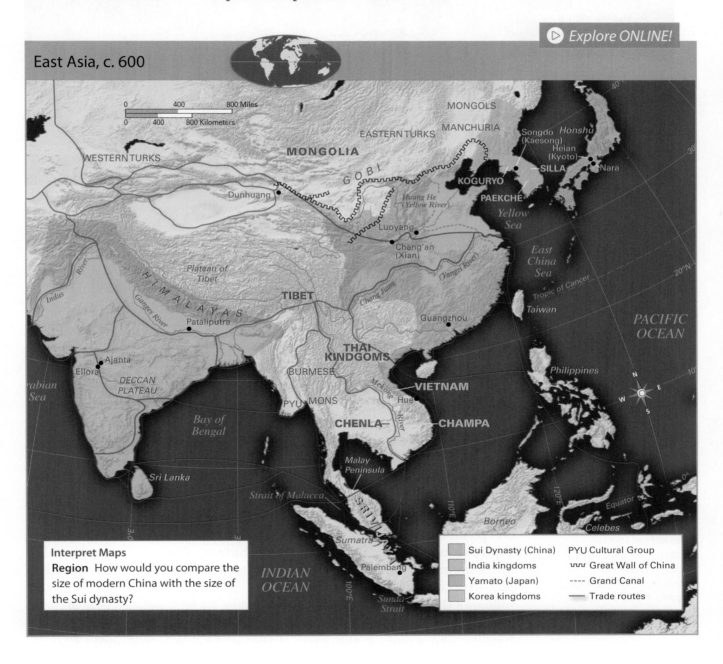

Explore ONLINE!

East Asia, c. 600

Interpret Maps
Region How would you compare the size of modern China with the size of the Sui dynasty?

Legend:
- Sui Dynasty (China)
- India kingdoms
- Yamato (Japan)
- Korea kingdoms
- PYU Cultural Group
- Great Wall of China
- Grand Canal
- Trade routes

China's long influence in East Asia is reflected in the architecture of neighboring states. Changdeokgung Palace in Seoul was the home of many of Korea's rulers. Its horizontal design and curved roof suggest early Chinese influence.

This Korean statue from the 700s shows Buddha holding a pose. Buddhism spread rapidly in Korea and was synthesized with local Shamanism.

Chinese Influence in Korea

In the 100s BC, a kingdom called Choson ruled much of what is now Korea. However, China soon came to influence life in the Korean peninsula. In 108 BC, China's Han dynasty conquered Choson and colonized part of Korea. During this period, the Koreans adopted Chinese writing. They also copied China's political systems and farming methods. Eventually, Chinese missionaries introduced Buddhism to Korea.

After the Han dynasty declined, Korea broke away from Chinese control. Three rival kingdoms rose to power in Korea. By 668, the rulers of one of these kingdoms, Silla (SHIH-lah), allied with China's Tang dynasty. With Chinese assistance, Silla conquered the other two Korean kingdoms. Then the Silla drove the Chinese out of Korea. By about 680, the Silla ruled all of Korea.

Although they were independent, Silla's rulers wanted to maintain trading ties with the larger and more powerful China. This trade helped maintain peace and good feelings between the two countries. Under Silla rule, the Koreans embraced many aspects of Chinese culture. For example, Silla rulers promoted Buddhism. They also formed a strong government modeled after the Tang bureaucracy.

Eventually, the Silla kingdom grew weaker. By 935, rebels had overthrown the Silla and formed a new dynasty, the Koryo dynasty. This dynasty, whose name is the origin of the word *Korea*, lasted until 1392.

Early Korean Culture

During the Silla and Koryo periods, the people of Korea made great advances in art and technology. Korean culture reflected a combination of Chinese influence and native ideas.

This celadon kettle from the Koryo period is shaped like a tortoise.

Koryo artists were gifted metalworkers. This bell was used to call people to religious ceremonies.

Goldsmiths made delicate golden crowns for Silla rulers. Such crowns may have never been worn. Instead, they were created as burial objects.

Buddhism was a major influence on life in the Silla period. These golden religious texts were found in a Silla tomb.

Analyze Visuals
What elements of the kettle above reflect Chinese influence?

Like earlier rulers, the Koryo adopted several elements of Chinese culture. For example, they created a civil service system similar to the one in China. At the same time, they did not want Korea to turn into another China. They urged the Korean people to maintain elements of their traditional culture, such as religion. As a result, Korean religion during the Koryo period blended elements of Chinese Buddhism with traditional Korean beliefs in nature spirits.

Also during the Koryo period, Korean culture thrived. Artisans created beautiful pottery covered with a celadon glaze. Korean printers invented metal movable type—an improvement over the earlier Chinese wooden type. With this invention, they printed thousands of Buddhist texts.

Buddhism was introduced to Vietnam from India and China before AD 300 and quickly became a major influence on life in the country. Temples and shrines like this one near the ancient capital of Hoa Lu can still be found throughout the country.

Reading Check
Summarize
What cultural features did Koreans adopt from the Chinese?

In the 1200s, the Mongol rulers of China invaded and conquered Korea. The Mongols were harsh and unpopular rulers. Finally, in the 1380s, a young Korean general forced the Mongols out of Korea. He then defeated all his rivals and ended the Koryo dynasty, uniting Korea as he took power for himself. He named his new dynasty Choson, in honor of Korea's first kingdom.

Vietnam Seeks Independence

Like Korea, Vietnam was invaded by the Chinese early in its history. In 111 BC armies from the Han dynasty conquered the kingdom of Nam Viet in what is now northern Vietnam. The Chinese called the conquered region Annam, and they ruled it for about 800 years.

Timeline: Key Events in China, Korea, and Vietnam

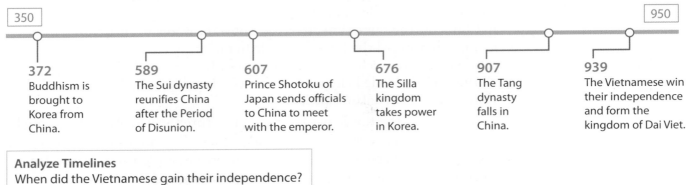

350

372 Buddhism is brought to Korea from China.

589 The Sui dynasty reunifies China after the Period of Disunion.

607 Prince Shotoku of Japan sends officials to China to meet with the emperor.

676 The Silla kingdom takes power in Korea.

907 The Tang dynasty falls in China.

939 The Vietnamese win their independence and form the kingdom of Dai Viet.

950

Analyze Timelines
When did the Vietnamese gain their independence?

Ly Dai Hanh was one of the first rulers of the kingdom of Dai Viet. During his reign, the Vietnamese held off an attack by the Chinese and expanded their kingdom to the south.

Under Chinese rule, the Vietnamese absorbed many features of Chinese civilization. Chinese rulers forced them to adopt the Chinese language and clothing styles. The Chinese imposed their own system of government on Vietnam, including a bureaucracy headed by Chinese governors. The Chinese also introduced Confucianism, Daoism, and Buddhism. Buddhist art and architecture became common in Vietnam. Despite the many ways in which China influenced Vietnam, though, the Vietnamese were determined to maintain much of their own culture. For example, they continued to worship nature spirits alongside other belief systems.

Hoping to regain their independence, the Vietnamese sometimes rebelled when Chinese rule grew weak. One of the most famous rebellions took place in AD 39. In that year, two sisters raised an army and briefly drove the Chinese out of Vietnam. However, the Chinese soon regained control of the country. Although they were unsuccessful, the **Trung sisters** are regarded as heroes in Vietnam today.

The fall of China's Tang dynasty in the early 900s allowed the Vietnamese to finally win their independence. In 939, they established the independent kingdom of Dai Viet. For about 60 years, fighting within Vietnam caused chaos.

In 1009, however, the first of a series of strong rulers took power in Dai Viet. These rulers belonged to the Ly dynasty. Ly rulers created a civil service system in Dai Viet similar to the one in China. They also created a standing army that kept their country safe from invasion by China and allowed them to expand southward. In more peaceful pursuits, they built canals and roads, and improved the country's farming practices. They also established Dai Viet's first university and supported art and literature. During the Ly dynasty, Chinese literature was popular in Vietnam.

Reading Check
Summarize
What did the Trung sisters do to become heroes to the Vietnamese?

The Ly dynasty lasted until 1225, when it was replaced by the Tran dynasty. Many great works of Vietnamese literature date from the Tran period. During the reign of the Tran, the Mongol rulers of China attempted to invade Vietnam. They were unsuccessful, however, and Vietnam remained free. The Tran remained in power until 1400, when the Chinese once again took control of Vietnam.

Summary China, the most powerful state in East Asia, had a major influence on the region's other civilizations, including Korea, Vietnam, and Japan.

Lesson 5 Assessment

Review Ideas, Terms, and People

1. **a. Identify** Where is Korea located?

   b. Explain In which Southeast Asian kingdom was Chinese influence the strongest?

2. **a. Identify** What were two important Korean inventions?

   b. Describe How did Korean culture remain distinct from Chinese culture?

3. **a. Explain** What elements of Chinese culture were adopted in Vietnam?

   b. Explain How did Vietnam become an independent kingdom?

Critical Thinking

4. **Compare and Contrast** Draw a chart like the one here. Using your notes, list two similarities and two differences between Chinese and Korean cultures.

Similarities	Differences
1. 2.	1. 2.

Social Studies Skills

Determine the Context of Statements

Define the Skill

A *context* is the circumstances under which something happens. *Historical context* includes values, beliefs, conditions, and practices that were common in the past. At times, some of these were quite different from what they are today. To truly understand a historical statement or event, you have to take its context into account. It is not right to judge what people in history did or said based on present-day values alone. To be fair, you must also consider the historical context of the statement or event.

Learn the Skill

To better understand something a historical figure said or wrote, use the following guidelines to determine the context of the statement.

1. Identify the speaker or writer, the date, and the topic and main idea of the statement.

2. Determine the speaker's or writer's attitude and point of view about the topic.

3. Review what you know about beliefs, conditions, or practices related to the topic that were common at the time. Find out more about the times in which the statement was made, if you need to.

4. Decide how well the statement reflects the values, attitudes, and practices of people living at that time. Then, determine how well it reflects values, attitudes, and practices related to the topic today.

Applying these guidelines will give you a better understanding of Chinese scholars. You read in this module that scholar-officials were elite members of Chinese society. However, becoming a scholar-official meant having to pass a series of difficult written examinations. Students spent years studying for the exams so they could pass them and become civil servants. How well they did determined their careers and place in Chinese society. The ninth-century Chinese writer Bai Xingjian describes his character's experience when passing examinations:

> "He went in for the examination and passed at the first attempt. His reputation spread rapidly through the examination rooms, and even older men, when they saw the compositions, were filled with admiration and respect, and sought his friendship."

By modern standards, the reaction to a student passing an exam may seem extreme. But think about the times in which Bai Xingjian wrote his story. Positions in the government were based on merit, and doing well on the exams meant that the student might have an important role in Chinese government. When the historical context is considered, the admiration and respect the student gained makes sense.

Practice the Skill

Read the following passage by Bai Juyi, a Chinese poet from the Tang Dynasty. Then answer the questions to determine its context and better understand it.

> "For ten years I never left my books; I went up . . . and won unmerited praise. My high place I do not prize; the joy of my parents will first make me proud."

1. Why does Bai Juyi value his parents' joy more than his own accomplishment?

2. How might the values of Chinese society during this time cause him to feel this way?

Module 15 Assessment

Review Vocabulary, Terms, and People

Match the words or names with their definitions or descriptions.

1. ruthless but effective Tang dynasty ruler
2. porcelain made with a pale-green glaze
3. leader who united the Mongols and began invasion of China
4. body of unelected government officials
5. thin, beautiful pottery
6. device that indicates direction
7. policy of avoiding contact with other countries
8. founder of the Yuan dynasty
9. mixture of powders used in explosives
10. commanded huge fleets of ships
11. educated government worker
12. heroes who drove the Chinese out of Vietnam

a. Kublai Khan
b. celadon
c. scholar-official
d. Empress Wu
e. bureaucracy
f. Zheng He
g. compass
h. porcelain
i. Genghis Khan
j. isolationism
k. Trung sisters
l. gunpowder

Comprehension and Critical Thinking

Lesson 1

13. **a. Identify** What period did China enter after the Han dynasty collapsed? What dynasty brought an end to this period?

    b. Analyze Why is the Tang dynasty considered a golden age of Chinese civilization?

    c. Predict Effects How might Chinese culture have been different in the Tang and Song dynasties if Buddhism had not been introduced to China?

Lesson 2

14. **a. Describe** What did Wu Daozi, Li Bo, Du Fu, and Li Qingzhao contribute to Chinese culture?

    b. Analyze What led to the growth of cities in China? What were China's cities like during the Tang and Song dynasties?

    c. Evaluate Which Chinese invention has had a greater effect on world history, the magnetic compass or gunpowder? Why?

Lesson 3

15. **a. Define** What is Confucianism? How did it change during and after the Song dynasty?

    b. Make Inferences Why do you think the civil service examination system was created?

    c. Elaborate Why were China's civil service examinations so difficult?

Lesson 4

16. **a. Describe** How did the Mongols create their huge empire? What areas were included in it?

    b. Draw Conclusions How did Marco Polo and Zheng He help shape ideas about China?

    c. Elaborate Why do you think the Ming emperors spent so much time and money rebuilding and enlarging the Great Wall?

Module 15 Assessment, continued

Lesson 5

17. a. Identify What are three East Asian civilizations on which China had a major influence?

b. Make Inferences Why did the Koreans unify after the Mongols invaded?

c. Elaborate In what way did the Vietnamese try to maintain their own culture while under Chinese rule?

Review Themes

18. Science and Technology How did Chinese inventions alter the course of world history?

19. Economics How did the strong agricultural and trading economy of the Tang and Song eras affect China?

Reading Skills

Draw Conclusions About the Past *Use the Reading Skill taught in this module to answer the question about the reading selection below.*

> The Ming ruled China from 1368 to 1644.
> Zhu Yuanzhang was a Ming emperor.
> The Great Wall was rebuilt by the Ming.

20. Read the statements about the Ming dynasty. For each conclusion that follows, decide whether the statements provide sufficient evidence to justify the conclusion.

  a. The Great Wall is located in China.

  b. Zhu Yuanzhang was a good emperor.

  c. Zhu Yuanzhang ruled sometime between 1368 and 1644.

  d. Zhu Yuanzhang rebuilt the Great Wall.

Social Studies Skills

Determine the Context of Statements *Use the Social Studies Skills taught in this module to answer the question about the reading selection below.*

> "That year it happened that the Emperor had decreed a special examination for the selection of candidates of unusual merit from all parts of the Empire. The young man competed, and came out top in the 'censorial essay.' He was offered the post of Army Inspector at Chengdu."
>
> —Bai Xingjian, *The Story of Miss Li*

21. Do you think that Bai Xingjian's statement accurately describes China at this time? Why or why not?

Focus On Writing

22. Write a Magazine Article Now that you have read about later Chinese dynasties, write a magazine article about three achievements or inventions that struck you as interesting. You may want to use the Internet to search for more information on your choices. Open with a sentence that states your main idea. Include three or four sentences about each achievement or invention you have chosen. These sentences should describe the achievement or invention and explain why it was so important. End your article with a sentence or two summarizing China's importance to the world.

Module 16

Japan

Essential Question

How did periods of isolation followed by contact with other cultures influence the development of Japanese society?

About the Photo: Mount Fuji is a snow-covered volcano that has long been a symbol of Japan.

In this module you will learn about the geography and history of early Japan.

What You Will Learn...

Lesson 1: Geography and Early Japan **558**
The Big Idea Japan's early societies were both isolated from and influenced by China and Korea.

Lesson 2: Art and Culture in Heian **566**
The Big Idea Japanese culture experienced a golden age during the Heian period of the 800s to the 1100s.

Lesson 3: Growth of a Military Society **572**
The Big Idea Japan developed a military society led by generals called shoguns.

Timeline of Events 550–1868

▶ Explore ONLINE!

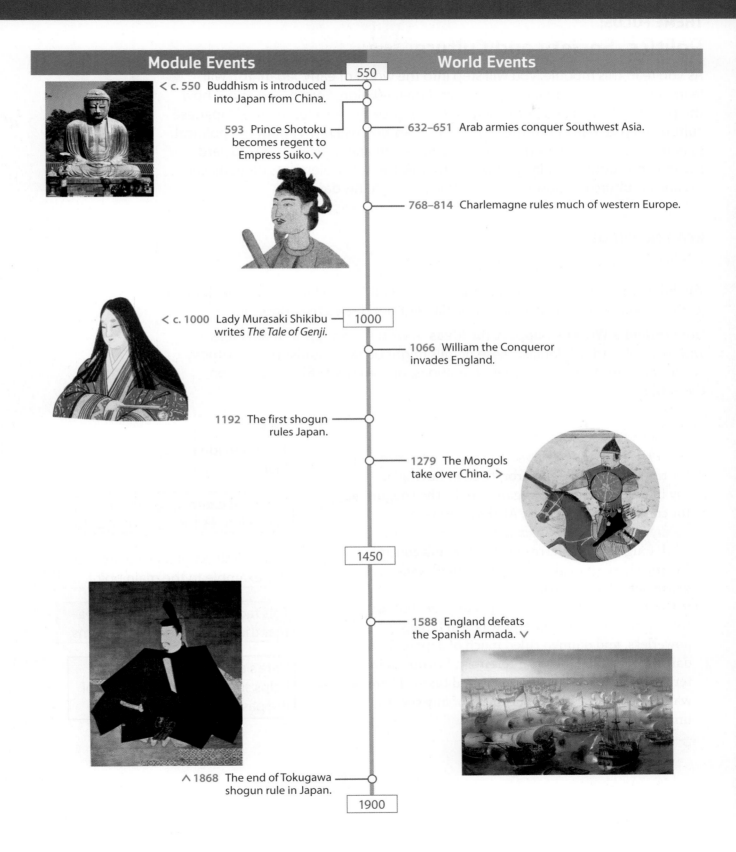

Module Events

c. 550 Buddhism is introduced into Japan from China.

593 Prince Shotoku becomes regent to Empress Suiko. ∨

c. 1000 Lady Murasaki Shikibu writes *The Tale of Genji.*

1192 The first shogun rules Japan.

∧ **1868** The end of Tokugawa shogun rule in Japan.

World Events

632–651 Arab armies conquer Southwest Asia.

768–814 Charlemagne rules much of western Europe.

1066 William the Conqueror invades England.

1279 The Mongols take over China. ＞

1588 England defeats the Spanish Armada. ∨

550

1000

1450

1900

Reading Social Studies

THEME FOCUS:
Politics, Society and Culture

As you read this module, you will step into the world of early Japan. You will learn about the first Japanese people and their religion, Shinto, and about how the people of China and Korea began to influence the development of Japanese culture. As you read about the history of Japan, you will learn about the political systems the Japanese used to govern their nation and their attitudes toward society and culture. Finally, you will learn how the social elements of medieval Japanese culture continue to affect life in Japan to this day.

READING FOCUS:
Main Ideas and Their Support

You know that if you take the legs from under a table it will fall flat on the floor. In just the same way, a main idea will fall flat without details to support it.

Understand a Writer's Support for Ideas A writer can support main ideas with several kinds of details. These details might be facts, statistics, eyewitness accounts, brief stories, examples, definitions, or comments from experts on the subject.

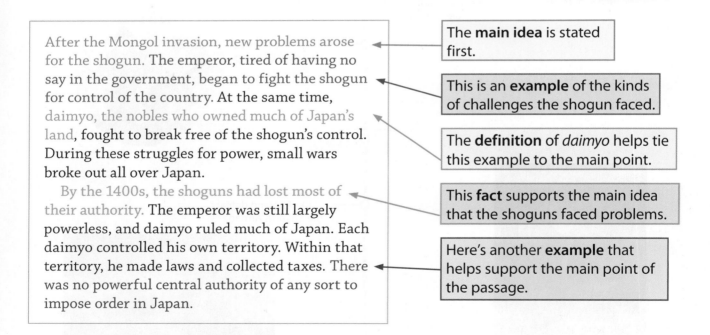

After the Mongol invasion, new problems arose for the shogun. The emperor, tired of having no say in the government, began to fight the shogun for control of the country. At the same time, daimyo, the nobles who owned much of Japan's land, fought to break free of the shogun's control. During these struggles for power, small wars broke out all over Japan.

By the 1400s, the shoguns had lost most of their authority. The emperor was still largely powerless, and daimyo ruled much of Japan. Each daimyo controlled his own territory. Within that territory, he made laws and collected taxes. There was no powerful central authority of any sort to impose order in Japan.

The **main idea** is stated first.

This is an **example** of the kinds of challenges the shogun faced.

The **definition** of *daimyo* helps tie this example to the main point.

This **fact** supports the main idea that the shoguns faced problems.

Here's another **example** that helps support the main point of the passage.

You Try It!

Read the following passage and then answer the questions below.

> **Samurai** The word *samurai* comes from the Japanese word for "servant." Every samurai, from the weakest soldier to the most powerful warrior, was supposed to serve his lord. Because all lords in Japan were supposed to serve the emperor, all samurai were required to be loyal to him.
>
> An army of samurai was expensive to support. Few lords could afford to buy armor and weapons for their warriors. As a result, lords paid their samurai with land and food.

Answer these questions based on the passage you just read.

1. Which sentence best states the main idea of the passage?
   a. Samurai were supposed to serve their lords.
   b. Samurai were paid with land and food.
   c. Few lords could afford to buy armor and weapons for their warriors.

2. Which of the following is not a detail that supports the main idea of the passage?
   a. An army of samurai was expensive to support.
   b. Every samurai was supposed to serve his lord.
   c. In Japan at this time, there were more than 10,000 samurai.

3. Which of the following methods of supporting a main idea does the author use in this passage?
   a. statistics
   b. eyewitness account
   c. facts

As you read this module, identify the main idea of a section or paragraph and note its supporting details in order to help you understand what you are reading.

Key Terms and People

Lesson 1
clans
Shinto
Prince Shotoku
regent

Lesson 2
court
Lady Murasaki Shikibu
Zen

Lesson 3
daimyo
samurai
figurehead
shogun
Bushido

Geography and Early Japan

The Big Idea

Japan's early societies were both isolated from and influenced by China and Korea.

Main Ideas

- Geography shaped life in Japan.

- Early Japanese society was organized in clans, which came to be ruled by an emperor.

- Japan learned about language, society, and government from China and Korea.

- During the Nara period, Buddhism became the official religion of Japan.

Key Terms and People

clans
Shinto
Prince Shotoku
regent

If YOU were there . . .

You live in a small farming village on one of the islands of Japan. You're very happy with your life. The sea is nearby and food is plentiful. You have a large, extended family to protect and take care of you. Your grandmother says that life in your village has not changed for hundreds of years, and that is good. But now you have heard that some people from across the sea are coming to your village. They are bringing new ideas and new ways of doing things.

How do you feel about these changes?

Geography Shapes Life in Japan

The islands of Japan are really just the tops of undersea mountains and volcanoes, sticking up from the ocean. Mountains cover nearly all of Japan. Only about 20 percent of the land is flat. Because it is difficult to live and farm on mountain slopes, most Japanese people have always lived in those flat areas, the coastal plains.

In addition to the mountains and the lack of flat land, the nearness of the sea shaped the lives of Japanese people. Their homes were never far from the sea. Naturally, they turned to the sea for food. They learned to prepare all kinds

Mountains cover most of the land in Japan. The tallest mountain in Japan, Mount Fuji, is an active volcano. Its last major eruption was in 1707.

of seafood, from eel to shark to octopus to seaweed. As a result, seafood has been a key part of the Japanese diet for thousands of years.

The islands' location affected the Japanese people in another way as well. Because they lived on islands, the Japanese were separated from the other people of Asia. This separation allowed the Japanese to develop their own culture. For example, they created a religion and a social **structure** very different from those in other parts of Asia. This separation has always been an important part of Japanese society.

Japan isn't totally isolated, however. Look at the map to find Korea and China. As you can see, neither country is very far from the Japanese islands. Korea is only about 100 miles from Japan. China is about 400 miles away. Those short distances allowed the older Korean and Chinese cultures to influence the new culture of Japan.

Academic Vocabulary
structure the way something is set up or organized

Reading Check
Summarize
What is Japan's geography like?

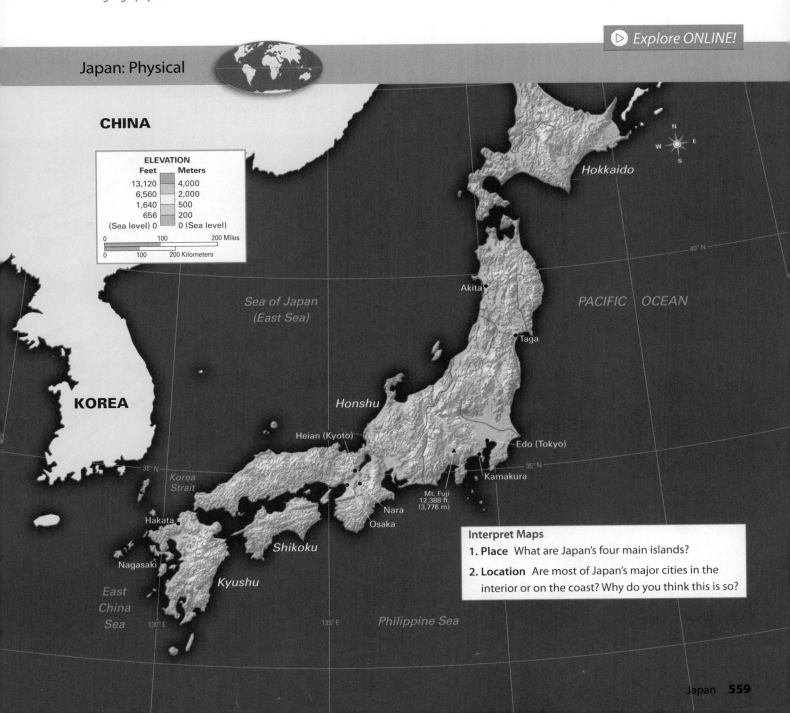

▷ *Explore ONLINE!*

Japan: Physical

ELEVATION
Feet	Meters
13,120	4,000
6,560	2,000
1,640	500
656	200
(Sea level) 0	0 (Sea level)

CHINA

KOREA

Hokkaido

Sea of Japan
(East Sea)

PACIFIC OCEAN

40° N

Akita

Taga

Honshu

Heian (Kyoto)

Edo (Tokyo)

35° N — 35° N

Kamakura

Korea
Strait

Mt. Fuji
12,388 ft.
(3,776 m)

Nara

Osaka

Hakata

Shikoku

Nagasaki

Kyushu

East
China
Sea

130° E   135° E   Philippine Sea

Interpret Maps

1. **Place** What are Japan's four main islands?

2. **Location** Are most of Japan's major cities in the interior or on the coast? Why do you think this is so?

Early Japanese Society

Korea and China played a major part in shaping Japanese society, but not at first. Early Japan was home to two different cultures, neither of which had any contact with the rest of Asia.

The Ainu One culture that developed in Japan was the Ainu (EYE-noo). Historians aren't sure exactly when or how the Ainu moved to Japan. Some people think they came from what is now Siberia in eastern Russia. Wherever they came from, the Ainu spoke a language unlike any other language in eastern Asia. They also looked different from the other people of Japan.

Over time, the Ainu began to fight with other people for land. They lost most of these fights, and so they lost their land as well. Eventually the Ainu were driven back onto a single island, Hokkaido. Over time, the Ainu culture almost disappeared. Many people gave up the Ainu language and adopted new customs.

A Shinto Shrine

Visitors to a Shinto shrine gather near a gate called a torii (TOR-ee). The torii marks the boundary of a shrine or other sacred Shinto site. Over time, the torii has become a symbol of Shinto, Japan's ancient religion.

Analyze Visuals
What elements of nature can you see in this painting?

The First Japanese The people who lived south of the Ainu eventually became the Japanese. They lived mostly in small farming villages. These villages were ruled by powerful **clans**, or extended families. Other people in the village, including farmers and workers, had to obey and respect members of these clans.

At the head of each clan was a chief. In addition to his political power, each chief also had religious duties. The Japanese believed that their clan chiefs were descended from nature spirits called *kami* (KAH-mee). Clan chiefs led their clans in rituals that honored their *kami* ancestors.

Over time, these rituals became a central part of the traditional religion of Japan, **Shinto**. According to Shinto teachings, everything in nature— the sun, the moon, trees, waterfalls, and animals—has *kami*. Shintoists believe that some *kami* help people live and keep them from harm. People build shrines to *kami* and perform ceremonies in which they ask the *kami* to bless them.

The First Emperors The clans of early Japan weren't all equal. Some clans were larger and more powerful than others. In time a few of these powerful clans built up armies and set out to conquer their neighbors.

One clan that gained power in this way lived in the Yamato region, the western part of Japan's largest island, Honshu. In addition to military might, the Yamato rulers claimed to have a glorious family history. They believed they were descended from the most powerful of all *kami*, the goddess of the sun.

By the 500s the Yamato rulers had extended their control over much of Honshu. Although they didn't control the whole country, the leaders of the Yamato clan began to call themselves the emperors of all Japan.

Reading Check
Synthesize How did emperors take power in Japan?

Japan Learns from China and Korea

Cultures from mainland Asia had very little influence on early Japanese society. Occasionally, officials from China, Korea, or other parts of Asia visited Japan. For the most part, however, these visits didn't have a great impact on the Japanese way of life.

By the mid-500s, though, some Japanese leaders thought that Japan could learn a great deal from other cultures. In particular, they wanted to learn more about the cultures of China and Korea.

To learn what they wanted to know, the rulers of Japan decided to send representatives to China and Korea to gather information about their cultures. They also invited people from China and Korea to move to Japan. The emperors hoped that these people could teach the Japanese new ways of working and thinking.

Changes in Language One of the first things the Japanese learned from China was language. The early Japanese didn't have a written language. Therefore, many learned to write in Chinese. They continued to speak in Japanese, however, which is very different from Chinese. It wasn't until about 200 years later that people devised a way of writing in Japanese. They used Chinese characters to represent the sounds used in Japanese.

As Japan's contact with China increased, some Japanese people—especially rich and well-educated people—began to write in the Chinese language. Japanese writers used Chinese for their poems and stories. One of the first histories of Japan, written in the 700s, is in Chinese. For many years Chinese was even the official language of Japan's government.

Changes in Trade Trade with Korea helped Japan's economy grow. The Japanese sailed across the Yellow Sea to Korean port towns such as Naju. There, they traded for iron tools, such as the hoe and spade. These tools helped improve Japanese agriculture by enabling farmers to move soil and dig irrigation canals.

The Japanese also traded with Korea for Chinese goods. Bronze mirrors made in China were used in Japanese burial tombs, for example. In the same way, Japanese raw materials, such as silk, went through Korea before ultimately ending up in China.

Quick Facts

Influences from China and Korea

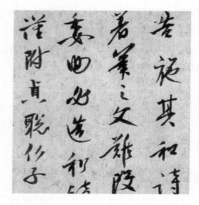

Language

The earliest Japanese writing used Chinese characters.

Philosophy

The ideas of the Chinese philosopher Confucius helped shape Japanese culture and family life.

Religion

Buddhism came to Japan from Korea.

Changes in Religion and Philosophy One of the people most influential in bringing Chinese ideas to Japan was **Prince Shotoku** (shoh-TOH-koo). He served from 593 to 621 as regent (REE-juhnt) for his aunt, the empress. A **regent** is a person who rules a country for someone who is unable to rule alone.

All his life, Prince Shotoku admired Chinese culture. As regent, Shotoku saw a chance for Japan to adopt more Chinese ideas. He sent scholars to China to learn all they could about Chinese society.

The ideas these scholars brought back changed Japanese society. For example, they taught the Japanese about Confucianism.

Prince Shotoku c. 573–621

Prince Shotoku was one of Japan's greatest leaders. He helped rule Japan when he was only 20 years old. For many centuries, people have admired him. Legends have developed about his wisdom. According to one early biography, Shotoku was able to talk as soon as he was born and never made a wrong decision.

Draw Conclusions
Why do you think legends developed around Prince Shotoku?

Among other things, Confucianism outlined how families should behave. Confucius taught that fathers should rule their families. He believed that wives should obey their husbands, children should obey their parents, and younger brothers should obey older brothers. Families in China lived according to these rules. As Confucian ideas spread through Japan, the Japanese began to live by them as well.

More important than these social changes, though, were the vast religious changes Shotoku made in Japan. He was a Buddhist, and he wanted to spread Buddhism throughout his country. Buddhism wasn't new to Japan. Korean visitors had introduced the religion to Japan about 50 years earlier. But it was not very popular. Most people preferred to keep their traditional religion, Shinto.

Prince Shotoku ordered beautiful Buddhist temples to be built, such as the Horyuji Temple in Nara, Japan. Prince Shotoku's efforts changed many people's minds about Buddhism in Japan.

Shotoku worked to change people's minds about Buddhism. He built a grand Buddhist temple that still stands today. He also wrote commentaries on Buddhist teachings. Largely because of his efforts, Buddhism became very popular, especially among Japanese nobles.

Changes in Government Shotoku also wanted to change Japan's government to be more like China's. He especially wanted Japan's emperors to have more power, like China's emperors did.

Afraid that they would lose power to the emperor, many clan leaders opposed Shotoku's government plans. As a result, Japan's emperors gained little power.

Reading Check
Summarize What aspects of Chinese society did Shotoku bring to Japan?

The Nara Period

Yamato rulers had set up capitals on their personal estates. When a new ruler came into power, the capital moved. Eventually, the Japanese followed the Chinese practice of setting up a permanent capital. In 710, Nara became Japan's permanent governing city. The next 84 years would be known as the Nara Period.

Japanese leaders chose Nara as the permanent capital in part because of its favorable geography and landscape. Another reason was that Buddhist temples already had been built there. Buddhism officially became the country's religion during the Nara Period. The first ruler in the new capital was Empress Gemmi (GEM-me). She took the throne as a regent after the death of her son.

A statue of the Buddha in Horyuji Temple in Nara, Japan. The spread of Buddhism changed many areas of Japanese culture during the Nara period.

Reading Check
Summarize
Why was Nara
chosen as Japan's
permanent capital?

Nara grew rapidly, and the government built a network of roads to remote areas. This helped the emperor collect taxes. Government officials also minted coins for the first time. However, few people used them.

Most common people in Nara society were either slaves or free farmers. However, noble families grew in wealth and influence during this period.

Summary and Preview In this lesson, you learned how early Japan grew and developed. In the next lesson, you'll see how Japan's emperors encouraged nobles to create great works of art and literature.

Lesson 1 Assessment

Review Ideas, Terms, and People

1. a. Recall What types of landforms cover most of Japan?

b. Explain How did Japan's location both separate it from and tie it to China and Korea?

2. a. Define What is Shinto?

b. Summarize How did the Yamato rulers gain power?

3. a. Explain How did Prince Shotoku help spread Buddhism in Japan?

b. Draw Conclusions What do you think was the most important idea the Japanese borrowed from China or Korea? Why?

4. a. Recall Before Nara became the capital, how did the Japanese choose governing towns?

b. Explain How did the Japanese government benefit from the construction of roads?

Critical Thinking

5. Categorize Draw a diagram like this one. Using your notes on Japan's culture, list in the arrow ideas that the Japanese borrowed from other people, and list in the circle ideas that developed within Japan.

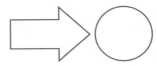

Art and Culture in Heian

The Big Idea

Japanese culture experienced a golden age during the Heian period of the 800s to the 1100s.

Main Ideas

- Japanese nobles created great art in their court at Heian.
- Buddhism changed in Japan during the Heian period.

Key Terms and People

court
Lady Murasaki Shikibu
Zen

Japanese writing could be an art form in itself. This album made in the shape of a fan is covered in text and pictures.

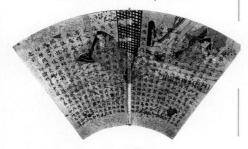

If YOU were there . . .

You are a noble who serves the empress of Japan and lives in the capital city. While walking in the garden one day, she gives you a small book with blank pages. When you ask her why, she says the book is a diary for you to write in. She tells you that nobles, both men and women, keep diaries to record their lives.

What will you write in your new diary?

Japanese Nobles Create Great Art

In 794 the emperor and empress of Japan moved to Heian (HAY-ahn), a city now called Kyoto. The nobles who followed Japan's emperor to Heian wanted to win his favor by living close to him. In Heian, these nobles created an imperial **court**, a group of nobles who live near and serve or advise a ruler.

Members of the noble court had little to do with the common people of Heian. They lived apart from poorer citizens and seldom left the city. These nobles enjoyed their lives of ease and privilege. In fact, their lives were so easy and so removed from the rest of Japan that many nobles called themselves "dwellers among the clouds."

The nobles of this court loved beauty and elegance. Because of this love, many nobles were great supporters of the arts. As a result, the court at Heian became a great center of culture and learning. In fact, the period between 794 and 1185 was a golden age of the arts in Japan.

Fashion The nobles' love of beauty began with their own appearances. They had magnificent wardrobes full of silk robes and gold jewelry. Nobles loved elaborate outfits. For example, women wore gowns made of 12 layers of silk cleverly cut and folded to show off many layers at once.

To complete their outfits, nobles often carried delicate decorative fans. These fans were painted with flowers, trees, and birds. Many nobles also attached flowers and long silk cords to their fans.

Literature In addition to how they looked, Japanese nobles took great care with how they spoke and wrote. Writing was very popular among the nobles, especially among the women. Many women wrote diaries and journals about their lives at court. In their diaries, these women carefully chose their words to make their writing beautiful.

Unlike men, who usually wrote in Chinese, noble women wrote in the Japanese language. As a result, many of the greatest works of early Japanese literature were written by women.

One of the greatest writers in early Japanese history was **Lady Murasaki Shikibu** (moohr-ah-SAHK-ee shee-KEE-boo). Around 1000, she wrote *The Tale of Genji*. Many historians consider this book to be the world's first full-length novel. Many readers also consider it one of the best.

The Tale of Genji is the story of a prince named Genji and his long quest for love. During his search he meets women from many different social classes.

Many people consider *The Tale of Genji* one of Japan's greatest novels. The characters it describes are very colorful and seem real. In addition, Lady Murasaki's writing is clear and simple but graceful at the same time. She describes court life in Japan with great detail.

Most early Japanese prose was written by women, but both men and women wrote poetry. Nobles loved to read and write poems. Some nobles held parties at which they took turns writing poetry and reading their poems aloud to one another.

A favorite theme in Japanese painting was *The Tale of Genji*. In this illustration of a scene from the novel, Genji's son is reading a letter as his wife approaches.

Poems from this time usually had only five lines. They followed a specific structure that outlined how many syllables each line could include. Most were about love or nature, but some described everyday events. People also kept diaries describing everyday life. This is from Lady Murasaki's diary, describing another noble woman:

"Lady Koshosho, all noble and charming. She is like a weeping willow tree at budding time. Her style is very elegant and we all envy her manners."

— Lady Murasaki Shikibu, from *The Diary of Lady Murasaki Shikibu*, in *Anthology of Japanese Literature* edited by Donald Keene

Visual Art Besides literature, Japan's nobles also loved the visual arts. The most popular art forms of the period were paintings, calligraphy, and architecture.

In their paintings, the nobles of Heian liked bright, bold colors. They also liked paintings that illustrated stories. In fact, many of the greatest paintings from this period illustrate scenes from literature, such as *The Tale of Genji*. Other paintings show scenes from nature or from court life. Many artists painted on doors and furniture rather than on paper.

Another popular form of art in Heian was calligraphy, or decorative writing. Calligraphers spent hours carefully copying poems. They wanted the poems to look as beautiful as they sounded.

The Buddha was a popular subject for statues in the Heian period.

Architecture The nobles of Heian worked to make their city beautiful. They greatly admired Chinese architecture and modeled Heian after the Chinese capital, Chang'an. They copied Chinese building styles, especially in the many temples they built. These styles featured buildings with wooden frames that curved slightly upward at the ends. The wooden frames were often left unpainted to look more natural. Thatched roofs also added to the natural feel.

For other buildings, the nobles liked simple, airy designs. Most buildings were made of wood with tiled roofs and large, open spaces inside. To add to the beauty of these buildings, the nobles surrounded them with elegant gardens and ponds. Similar gardens are still popular in Japan.

Performing Arts The performing arts were also popular in Japan during the Heian period. The roots of later Japanese drama can be traced back to this time. People often gathered to watch performances by musicians, jugglers, and acrobats. These performances were wild and fun. Especially popular were the plays in which actors skillfully mimicked other people.

In later centuries, these types of performances developed into a more serious form of drama called Noh. Created in the 1300s, Noh plays combine music, speaking, and dance. These plays often tell about great heroes or figures from Japan's past.

Reading Check
Summarize What forms of art were popular in the Heian period?

	Zen	Shintoism
	Began in China	Began in Japan
	Founded c. AD 500	Founded c. 500 BC
	Belief in no gods	Belief in many gods
	Human wisdom through self-discipline and meditation	Humans part of nature and basically good
	Belief in nirvana	Belief in ancestor spirits
	Suffering caused by lack of harmony	Suffering a natural part of life

Many Zen gardens like this one include raked gravel shaped to look like water and small boulders arranged like mountains.

Buddhism Changes

Religion became something of an art form in Heian. The nobles' religion reflected their love of elaborate rituals. Most of the common people in Japan, though equally religious, didn't have the time or money for these ceremonies. As a result, different forms of Buddhism developed in Japan.

One new form of Buddhism was very popular with Japan's common people. It was called Pure Land Buddhism and didn't require any special rituals. Instead, Pure Land Buddhists chanted the Buddha's name over and over to achieve an enlightened state.

In the 1100s, another popular new form of Buddhism called **Zen** arrived from China. Zen Buddhists believed that neither faith nor good behavior led to wisdom. Instead, people seeking wisdom should practice self-discipline and meditation, or quiet thinking. These ideas appealed to many Japanese, especially warriors. As these warriors gained more influence in Japan, so did Zen Buddhism.

Reading Check
Find Main Ideas
How did Buddhism change in Japan?

Summary and Preview At Heian, Japan's emperors presided over an elegant court. In the next lesson, you'll learn what happened when emperors and the court lost power and prestige.

Lesson 2 Assessment

Reviewing Ideas, Terms, and People

1. **a. Recall** Where did Japan's court move in the late 700s?

   b. Form Generalizations Why are the 800s to the 1100s considered a golden age for Japanese literature and art?

   c. Evaluate Do you think women in Heian had more rights and freedoms than women in other societies? Why or why not?

2. **a. Identify** What new form of Buddhism developed in Japan?

   b. Compare and Contrast How was religion among Japan's nobles different from religion among the common people?

   c. Elaborate Why do you think Pure Land Buddhism was popular with common people?

Critical Thinking

3. **Categorize** Draw a Japanese fan like the one shown here. List two contributions the Japanese made in each category shown on the fan.

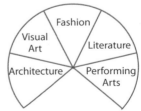

Literature in History

Literature of Early Japan

Word Help

fête festival

preliminary in preparation for

verdure greenery, especially related to plants

eminently remarkably

Kariobinga in Buddhist belief, a sacred bird with a beautiful voice

personage an important person

❶ *What kind of modern-day American event might be compared to the emperor's visit?*

❷ *What does the attendance by the nobility tell you about this event?*

About the Reading *The Tale of Genji* was written by Lady Murasaki Shikibu at the height of Japan's golden age. This thousand-page novel traces the life and adventures—especially in love—of a noble known as "the shining Genji." Although Genji is the favorite son of the emperor, his mother is only a commoner, so Genji cannot inherit the throne. Instead, it passes first to his half-brother Suzaku (soo-ZAH-koo) and then to Genji's own son. Here, the emperor attends a gathering called the Maple Festival, at which Genji performs.

As You Read Look for details that describe the lives of Japanese nobles.

From *The Tale of Genji*
by Lady Murasaki Shikibu
translated by Suyematz Kenchio

The Royal visit to the Suzak-in was arranged to take place toward the middle of October, and was anticipated to be a grand affair. Ladies were not expected to take part in it, and they all regretted their not being able to be present.

The Emperor, therefore, wished to let his favourite, the Princess Wistaria, above others, have the opportunity of witnessing a rehearsal that would represent the coming *fête*, and ordered a preliminary concert to be performed at the Court, in which Genji danced the "Blue Main Waves," with To-no-Chiujio for his partner. They stood and danced together, forming a most pleasing contrast—one, so to speak, like a bright flower; the other, an everlasting verdure beside it. The rays of the setting sun shone over their heads, and the tones of the music rose higher and higher in measure to their steps. The movements both of head and foot were eminently graceful; as well, also, was the song of Genji, which was sung at the end of his dance, so that some of the people remarked that the sound of the holy bird, Kariobinga, might even be like this. And so the rehearsal ended.

When the day of the *fête* came, all the Royal Princes, including the Heir-apparent, and all personages of State, were present at the scene. On the lake, "the music boat," filled with selected musicians, floated about, as usual on such occasions; and in the grounds, the bands, which were divided into

Yemon-no-Kami master of ceremonies, a court official

harmony a pleasing combination

knoll a small hill

Sadaishio a court official

foliage leaves

Shosammi a title of high honor

Shoshii a title of honor, somewhat below Shosammi in rank

③ *What is the symbolism of the sunlight softening during Genji's performance?*

④ *What do the new titles given to Genji and To-no-Chiujio suggest about Japanese views of the arts in this period?*

two divisions on the right and left, under the direction of two Ministers and two Yemon-no-Kami, played. With this music different dances, including Chinese and Korean, were performed, one after another, by various dancers. As the performance went on, the high winds rustled against the tall fir-trees, as though Divine strains of music had broken forth on high in harmony with them. The tune of the bands became quick and thrilling, as different coloured leaves whirled about overhead.

Then, at length, the hero of the "Blue Main Waves" made his appearance, to the delight of the suddenly-startled spectators, from the midst of a knoll in the grounds, covered with maple leaves. The twigs of maple which crowned his head, became thinned as he danced, and a Sadaishio, plucking a bunch of chrysanthemums from in front of the Royal stand, replaced the lessened maple leaves. The sun was by this time descending, and the sky had become less glaring, while the face of Nature seemed as if it were smiling on the scene. Genji danced with unusual skill and energy. All the pages and attendants, who were severely stationed here under the side of the rock, there under the shade of the foliage, were quite impressed with the effects of the performance.

After Genji, a little prince, the child of the Niogo of Shokoden, danced the "Autumn Gales," with a success next to that of Genji. Then, the principal interest of the day being over, as these dances were finished, the *fête* ended. This very evening Genji was invested with the title of Shosammi, and To-no-Chiujio with that of Shoshii. Many other persons also received promotion in rank according to their merits.

A portrait of Lady Murasaki Shikibu, author of *The Tale of Genji*

Connect Literature to History

1. **Summarize** Japanese nobles enjoyed the arts. Based on this passage, what specific arts did Japanese nobles enjoy?

2. **Form Generalizations** The nobles enjoyed their lives of privilege. What details suggest that Japanese nobles lived lives of luxury?

3. **Form Generalizations** After reading this passage, what is your overall impression of Japanese court life?

Growth of a Military Society

The Big Idea

Japan developed a military society led by generals called shoguns.

Main Ideas

- Samurai and shoguns took over Japan as emperors lost influence.
- Samurai warriors lived honorably.
- Order broke down when the power of the shoguns was challenged by invaders and rebellions.
- Strong leaders took over and reunified Japan.

Key Terms and People

daimyo
samurai
figurehead
shogun
Bushido

If YOU were there . . .

You are a Japanese warrior, proud of your fighting skills. For many years you've been honored by most of society, but you face an awful dilemma. When you became a warrior, you swore to protect and fight for both your lord and your emperor. Now your lord has gone to war against the emperor, and both sides have called for you to join them.

How will you decide whom to fight for?

Samurai and Shoguns Take Over Japan

By the late 1100s, Heian was the great center of Japanese art and literature. But in the rest of Japan, life was very different. Powerful nobles fought each other over land. Rebels fought against imperial officials. This fighting destroyed land, which made it difficult for peasants to grow food. Some poor people became bandits or thieves. Meanwhile, Japan's rulers were so focused on courtly life, they didn't notice the many problems growing in their country.

The Rise of the Samurai With the emperor distracted by life in his court, Japan's large landowners, or **daimyo** (DY-mee-oh), decided that they needed to protect their own lands. They hired **samurai** (SA-muh-ry), or trained professional warriors, to defend them and their property. The samurai wore light armor and fought with swords and bows. Most samurai came from noble families and inherited their positions from their fathers.

The word *samurai* comes from the Japanese word for "servant." Every samurai, from the weakest soldier to the most powerful warrior, was supposed to serve his lord. Because all lords in Japan were supposed to serve the emperor, all samurai were required to be loyal to him.

An army of samurai was expensive to support. Few lords could afford to buy armor and weapons for their warriors. As a result, lords paid their samurai with land or food.

Only the most powerful samurai got land for their service. Most of these powerful samurai didn't live on the land they received, but they did profit from it. Every year, the peasant farmers who worked on the land gave the samurai money or food. Samurai who received no land were given food—usually rice—as payment.

Shoguns Rule Japan Many of the nobles outside Heian were unhappy with the way Japan's government was being run. Frustrated, these nobles wanted a change of leadership. Eventually, a few very strong noble clans decided to try to take power for themselves.

Two of these powerful clans went to war with each other in the 1150s. For almost 30 years, the two clans fought. Their fighting was terrible, destroying land and property and tearing families apart. In the end, the Minamoto clan won. Because he had a very powerful army, and because the emperor was still busy in Heian, the leader of the Minamoto clan was the most powerful man in Japan. He decided to take over the country.

He didn't, however, want to get rid of the emperor. He kept the emperor as a **figurehead**, a person who appears to rule even though real power rests with someone else. As a samurai, the Minamoto leader was supposed to be loyal to the emperor, but he decided to rule in the emperor's place. In 1192, he took the title **shogun**, a general who ruled Japan in the emperor's name. When he died, he passed his title and power on to one of his children. For about the next 700 years, a shogun would rule in Japan.

Reading Check
Synthesize How did the shogun rise to power in Japan?

Quick Facts

Samurai Society

Emperor

The emperor was a figurehead for the powerful shogun.

Shogun

A powerful military leader, the shogun ruled in the emperor's name.

Daimyo and Samurai

Daimyo were powerful lords who often led armies of samurai. Samurai warriors served the shogun and daimyo.

Peasants

Most Japanese were poor peasants who had no power.

Analyze Visuals
Who was the most powerful person in Japan's samurai society?

The samurai were bold, highly trained warriors. They followed a strict code of behavior called Bushido, or "the way of the warrior."

Samurai were often called on to fight, like in this scene. They were expected to serve with honor and loyalty in battle.

The samurai in this scene is writing a poem on a cherry tree. Writing poetry helped train the samurai to concentrate.

Samurai wore armor and special helmets. Many carried two swords.

Analyze Visuals
What equipment did samurai have to protect themselves?

Samurai Live Honorably

Under the shogun, who were military rulers, samurai warriors became more central to Japanese society. As a result, samurai enjoyed many social privileges. Common people had to treat the samurai with respect. Anyone who showed disrespect to a samurai could be killed.

At the same time, tradition placed restrictions on samurai. For example, they couldn't attend certain types of entertainment, such as theater, which were considered beneath them. They also couldn't take part in trade or commerce.

Bushido More importantly, all samurai had to follow a strict code of rules that taught them how to behave. The samurai code of rules was known as **Bushido** (BOOH-shi-doh). This name means "the way of the warrior." Both men and women from samurai families had to follow Bushido rules.

Bushido required samurai to be brave and honorable fighters. Both men and women of samurai families learned how to fight, though only men went to war. Women learned to fight so they could protect their homes from robbers.

Samurai were expected to live simple, disciplined lives. They believed that self-discipline made them better warriors. To improve their discipline, many samurai participated in peaceful rituals that required great concentration. Some created intricate flower arrangements or grew miniature bonsai trees. Others held elaborate tea ceremonies. Many samurai also adopted Zen Buddhism, which stressed self-discipline and meditation.

More than anything else, Bushido required a samurai to be loyal to his lord. Each samurai had to obey his master's orders without hesitation, even if it caused the samurai or his family to suffer. One samurai expressed his duties in this way:

"If one were to say in a word what the condition of being a samurai is, its basis lies first in seriously devoting one's body and soul to his master."

—Yamamoto Tsunetomo, from *Hagakure*

Obeying his lord was important to the samurai's sense of honor. Honor was the most important thing in a samurai's life. If he did anything to lose honor, a samurai was expected to commit suicide rather than live with his shame. Such shame might be caused by disobeying an order, losing a fight, or failing to protect his lord.

Link to Today

Modern Samurai

Although the samurai class disappeared from Japan at the end of the 1800s, samurai images and values live on. Fierce samurai appear on posters, in advertisements and movies, and in video games, challenging foes with their sharp swords and deadly skills. Many people study the same martial arts, such as sword fighting, that the samurai practiced. In addition, the loyalty that samurai felt toward their lords is still a key part of Japanese society. Many Japanese feel that same loyalty toward other groups—their families, companies, or favorite sports teams. Samurai values such as hard work, honor, and sacrifice have also become deeply rooted in Japanese society.

Analyze Information
How are Japan's samurai values still alive today?

Reading Check
Find Main Ideas
What customs did samurai follow?

Academic Vocabulary
values ideas that people hold dear and try to live by

Bushido and Modern Japan Although it was created as a code for warriors, Bushido influenced much of Japanese society. Even today, many Japanese feel a connection to the samurai. For example, the samurai's dedication and discipline are still greatly admired in Japan. <u>Values</u> such as loyalty and honor, the central ideas of the samurai code, remain very important in modern Japan.

Order Breaks Down

For about a century, the shoguns kept order in Japan. Supported by the samurai, the shoguns were able to put down challenges to their authority. Eventually, however, more serious challenges arose that brought this order to an end.

Foreign Invasion One of the greatest challenges to the shoguns was an invasion by the Mongols from China. China's emperor, Kublai Khan, sent an army to conquer the islands in 1274. Faced with invasion, the shogun sent troops to fight the Mongols. In addition, Japan's warring nobles put aside their differences to fight the enemy. The Japanese warriors were

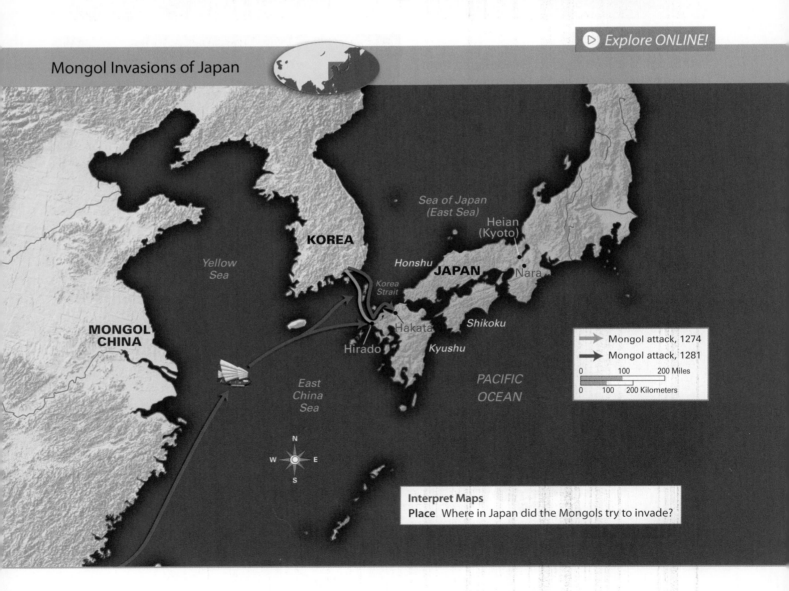

▶ **Explore ONLINE!**

Mongol Invasions of Japan

Mongol attack, 1274
Mongol attack, 1281

Interpret Maps
Place Where in Japan did the Mongols try to invade?

aided by a great storm. The storm sank many Mongol ships and forced the Mongols to flee.

In 1281, the Mongols invaded again. This time they sent two huge armies and threatened to overwhelm the Japanese warriors. For weeks, the two armies were locked in deadly combat.

Once again, though, the weather helped the Japanese. A huge storm swept over Japan, sinking most of the Mongol fleet. Many Mongol soldiers drowned, and many more returned to China. The grateful Japanese called the storm that had saved them the *kamikaze* (kah-mi-KAH-zee), or "divine wind." They believed the gods had sent the storm to save Japan.

But many nobles were left unhappy by the war. They didn't think the shogun gave them enough credit for their part in the fighting. Many came to resent the shogun's power over them.

Internal Rebellion After the Mongol invasion, new problems arose for the shogun. The emperor, tired of having no say in the government, began to fight the shogun for control of the country. At the same time daimyo, the nobles who owned much of Japan's land, fought to break free of the shogun's control. During these struggles for power, small wars broke out all over Japan.

By the 1400s, the shoguns had lost most of their authority. The emperor was still largely powerless, and daimyo ruled much of Japan. Each daimyo controlled his own territory. Within that territory, he made laws and collected taxes. There was no powerful central authority of any sort to impose order in Japan.

Reading Check
Summarize What challenges appeared to the shogun's authority?

Strong Leaders Take Over

Soon new leaders rose to power. They began as local rulers, but these men wanted more power. In the 1500s, each fought to unify all of Japan under his control.

Unification The first such leader was Oda Nobunaga (OHD-ah noh-booh-NAH-gah). Oda gave his soldiers guns that had been brought to Japan by Portuguese traders. This was the first time guns had been used in Japan. With these new weapons, Oda easily defeated his opponents.

After Oda died, other leaders continued his efforts to unify Japan. By 1600, one of them, Tokugawa Ieyasu (toh-koohg-AH-wuhee E-yahs-ooh), had conquered his enemies. In 1603, Japan's emperor made Tokugawa shogun. From his capital at Edo (AY-doh)—now Tokyo—Tokugawa ruled all of Japan.

Tokugawa's rise to power began the Tokugawa shogunate (SHOH-guhn-uht), or rule by shoguns of the Tokugawa family. Early in this period, which lasted until 1868, Japan traded with other countries and let Christian missionaries live in Japan.

Isolation Not all of the shoguns who followed Tokugawa liked this contact with the world, though. Some feared that Japan would become too much

Reading Check
Draw Conclusions
How did Japan change
in the Tokugawa
shogunate?

like Europe, and the shoguns would lose their power. To prevent such a thing from happening, in the 1630s the ruling shogun closed off Japan from the rest of the world.

Japan's rulers also banned guns. They feared that peasants with guns could defeat their samurai armies. The combination of isolation from the world and limited technology helped extend the samurai period in Japan until the 1800s, far longer than it might have otherwise lasted.

Summary By the 1100s, the growing power of shoguns, daimyo, and samurai had turned Japan into a military society.

Lesson 3 Assessment

Review Ideas, Terms, and People

1. **a. Recall** What was the relationship between samurai and daimyo?

   b. Elaborate Why do you think the first shogun wanted to keep the emperor as a figurehead?

2. **a. Define** What was Bushido?

   b. Explain Why did samurai take up pursuits like flower arranging?

3. **a. Identify** Who invaded Japan in the 1270s and 1280s?

   b. Summarize How did the daimyo help weaken the shoguns?

4. **Identify** What strong leaders worked to unify Japan in the late 1500s?

Critical Thinking

5. **Analyze** Draw a word web. In the center, write a sentence that describes the samurai. Using your notes about life in a military society, write one of the samurai's jobs, duties, or privileges in each outer circle.

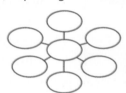

Social Studies Skills

Solve Problems

Define the Skill

Problem solving is a process for finding good solutions to difficult situations. It involves asking questions, identifying and evaluating information, comparing and contrasting, and making judgments. It is useful in studying history because it helps you better understand problems a person or group faced in the past and how they dealt with those issues.

The ability to understand and evaluate how people solved problems in the past also can help in solving similar problems today. The skill can be applied to many other kinds of difficulties besides historical ones. It is a method for thinking through almost any situation.

Learn the Skill

Using the following steps will help you better understand and solve problems.

1. **Identify the problem.** Ask questions of yourself and others. This first step helps you to be sure you know exactly what the situation is. It also helps you understand why it is a problem.

2. **Gather information.** Ask other questions and do research to learn more about the problem. For example, what is its history? What caused the problem? What contributes to it?

3. **List the options.** From the information you have gathered, identify possible options for solving the problem. It will be easier to find a good solution if you have several options.

4. **Evaluate the options.** Weigh each option you are considering. Think of the advantages it has as a solution. Then think of its potential disadvantages. It may help you compare your options if you make a list of advantages and disadvantages for each possible solution.

5. **Choose and apply a solution.** After comparing the advantages and disadvantages of each possible solution, choose the one that seems best and apply it.

6. **Evaluate the solution.** Once the solution has been tried, evaluate how effective it is in solving the problem. This step will tell you if the solution was a good one, or if you should try another of the options instead. It will also help you know what to do in the future if you happen to face the same problem again.

Practice the Skill

Read again the "If YOU were there" in Lesson 3. Imagine that you are the warrior with this problem. You can apply the steps for solving problems to help you decide what to do. Review the information in the lesson about the samurai and this time period in Japan's history. Then, in the role of the samurai warrior, answer the questions.

1. What is the specific problem that you face? Why is it a problem?

2. What events led to your problem? What circumstances and conditions have contributed to it?

3. What options can you think of to solve your problem? List the advantages and disadvantages of each.

4. Which of your options seems to be the best solution for your problem? Explain why. How will you know if it is a good solution?

Review Vocabulary, Terms, and People

Unscramble each group of letters to spell a term that matches the given definition.

1. etrgne—a person who rules in someone else's name
2. misaaru—a Japanese warrior
3. aclsn—large, extended families
4. elauvs—ideas that people hold dear
5. uctro—a group of nobles who surround a ruler
6. nguosh—a great Japanese general who ruled instead of the emperor
7. enz—a form of Japanese Buddhism
8. osnith—a nature religion that began in Japan
9. odmiya—Japanese lords who gave land to samurai
10. kosouth—prince who introduced many Chinese ideas to Japan
11. rctusrteu—the way something is set up

Comprehension and Critical Thinking

Lesson 1

12. a. **Identify** Who was Prince Shotoku, and what did he do?
    b. **Compare and Contrast** Why was Japan isolated from China and Korea? How did China and Korea still affect Japan?
    c. **Predict Effects** How would Japan's physical geography affect the development of Japanese government and society?

Lesson 2

13. a. **Recall** Why is Murasaki Shikibu a major figure in the history of Japanese culture?
    b. **Analyze** What made the period between the 800s and the 1100s a golden age of the arts in Japan?
    c. **Evaluate** Would you like to have been a member of the imperial court at Heian? Why or why not?

Lesson 3

14. a. **Define** What was the Tokugawa shogunate?
    b. **Analyze** How did Japan develop into a military society? What groups made up that society?
    c. **Elaborate** What was daily life like for the samurai?

Module 16 Assessment, continued

Review Themes

15. **Politics** How did Prince Shotoku try to change the political system in Japan?

16. **Society and Culture** What new technology did Japan's rulers ban, starting in the 1630s? Why?

17. **Society and Culture** How did Bushido affect modern Japanese culture?

Reading Skills

Main Ideas and Their Support *Use the Reading Skills taught in this module to answer the questions about the reading selection below.*

One of the people most influential in bringing Chinese ideas to Japan was Prince Shotoku. He served from 593 to 621 as regent for his aunt, the empress. A regent is a person who rules a country for someone who is unable to rule alone.

All his life, Prince Shotoku admired Chinese culture. As regent, Shotoku saw a chance for Japan to adopt more Chinese ideas. He sent scholars to China to learn more about Chinese society.

18. Explain in your own words the main idea of this passage.

19. Which other method might the author have used to make the explanation more informative and interesting? What would this method have contributed to the passage's meaning?

20. What is a definition the author gives in this passage? How does it help support the main idea?

Social Studies Skills

Solve Problems *Use the Social Studies Skills taught in this module to solve the problem described below.*

21. Imagine that you are a samurai warrior who has been called upon to help fight the Mongol invasion. You are stationed in a small village that is directly in the path of the Mongol army. Some people in the village want to stay and fight the Mongols, but you know they will be killed if they try to fight. The town's leaders want your opinion about what they should do. Write down one or two ideas you might suggest for how to save the people of the village. For each idea, make notes about what consequences your proposed action may have.

Focus On Writing

22. **Create a Travel Brochure** Create a travel brochure that describes Japan's historic attractions from the time period covered by this module. Keep your writing brief—remember that you have to get your audience's attention with just a few words. To help get their attention, draw or find pictures to illustrate your travel brochure.

Japan and the Samurai Warrior

For over a thousand years, the samurai—an elite warrior class—were a powerful force in Japanese society. The way of life of the samurai lords and warriors was, in many ways, like those of the medieval lords and knights of Europe. The great samurai warlords ruled large territories and relied on the fighting skills of their fierce samurai warriors to battle their enemies. But samurai warriors were more than just soldiers. Samurai were expected to embrace beauty and culture, and many were skilled artists. They also had a strict personal code that valued personal honor above all things—even life itself.

Explore the fascinating world of the samurai warrior online. You can find a wealth of information, video clips, primary sources, activities, and more through your online textbook.

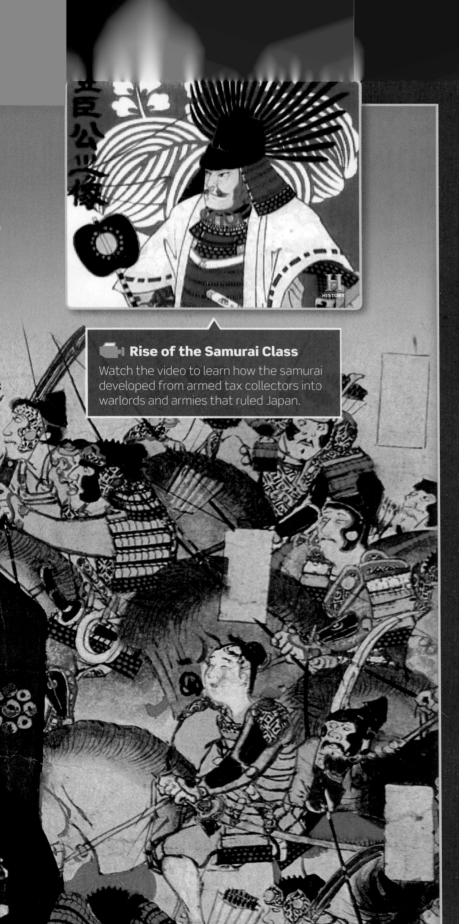

Rise of the Samurai Class

Watch the video to learn how the samurai developed from armed tax collectors into warlords and armies that ruled Japan.

A New Way of Life in Japan

Watch the video to learn how peace and isolation took hold in Japan and changed the role of the samurai in society.

> *" I have no eyes;*
> *I make the Flash of Lightning my Eyes.*
> *I have no ears; I make Sensibility my Ears.*
> *I have no limbs;*
> *I make Promptitude my Limbs.*
> *I have no laws;*
> *I make Self-Protection my Laws. "*

A Code for Samurai Living

Read the document to learn about the strict but lyrical code of the samurai warrior

Death of the Samurai Class

Watch the video to see how the end of Japan's isolation from the outside world signaled the beginning of the end of the samurai class.

Cultures of South and Southwest Asia

Essential Question

How do politics, economics, and religion relate to the rise and fall of cultures in South and Southwest Asia?

About the Photo: In this photo, Sikhs share a meal sitting together on the ground. This practice signifies a strong belief in social equality.

▶ *Explore ONLINE!*

VIDEOS, including...
• The Mughals of South Asia: Taj Mahal

☑ Document-Based Investigations

☑ Graphic Organizers

☑ Interactive Games

☑ Compare Images: Byzantine Influences on Ottoman Architecture

☑ Interactive Map: The Safavid Empire

☑ Interactive Map: Mughal Empire

In this module, you will learn about the great Islamic Empires of South and Southwest Asia.

What You Will Learn...

Lesson 1: The Ottoman Empire 586
The Big Idea After the early spread of Islam, the Ottoman Empire controlled parts of Europe, Asia, and Africa.

Lesson 2: Safavid Persia 591
The Big Idea The Safavid Empire took over Persia in the early 1500s, blending Persian and Islamic traditions.

Lesson 3: Sikhism in South Asia 595
The Big Idea Sikhism originated in the Punjab region of India and has grown to include nearly 25 million followers around the world.

Lesson 4: The Mughal Empire 600
The Big Idea The Mughal Empire was the last great empire in India before British rule.

Timeline of Events 1299–1857

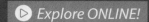 Explore ONLINE!

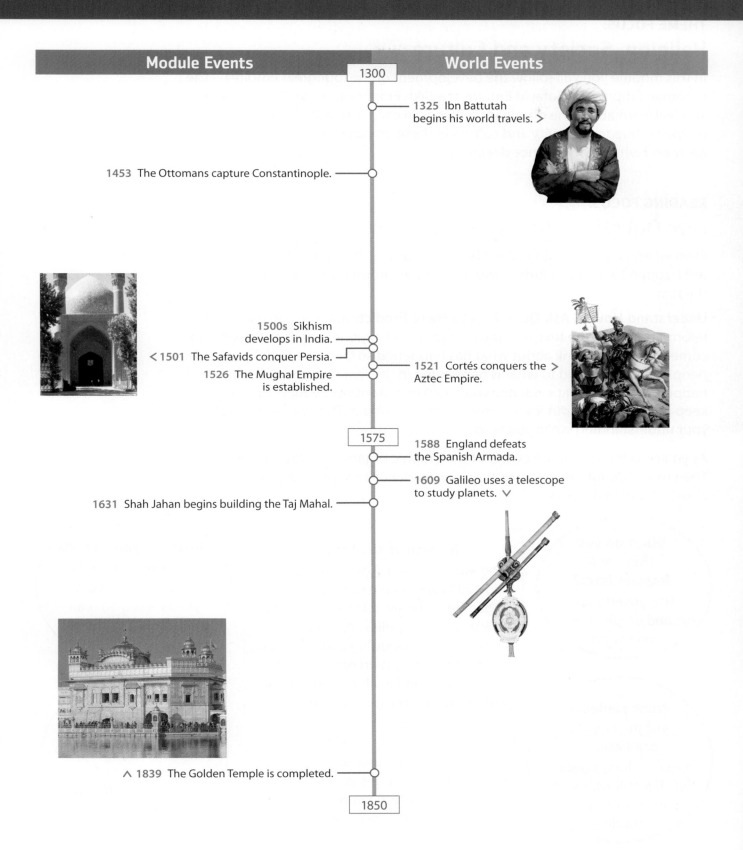

Module Events		World Events

1300

1325 Ibn Battutah begins his world travels. >

1453 The Ottomans capture Constantinople.

1500s Sikhism develops in India.

< **1501** The Safavids conquer Persia.

1526 The Mughal Empire is established.

1521 Cortés conquers the > Aztec Empire.

1575

1588 England defeats the Spanish Armada.

1609 Galileo uses a telescope to study planets. ∨

1631 Shah Jahan begins building the Taj Mahal.

∧ **1839** The Golden Temple is completed.

1850

Reading Social Studies

Religion, Society and Culture

In this module you will follow the development of the four great empires—the Ottoman Empire, the Safavid Empire, the Sikh Empire, and the Mughal Empire. You will learn about the dominant religions in each. You will also learn how religion influenced society and culture in these empires. You will learn how they grew and why their influence declined.

READING FOCUS:
Ask Questions to Make Predictions

Even when you are reading about history, you can make predictions about what will happen to help you better understand the information and dig deeper into the text.

Understand How to Ask Questions to Make Predictions You can use information from the text, images, and your own experiences to anticipate what comes next. First, think about what has happened so far in the text. Then ask how people might respond to what is happening in the text. Ask yourself what might happen next and what evidence you could use to support your position. Then, keep reading to find out if your prediction was correct. This will help you to adjust your understanding while you read.

As you read the text in the center of the graphic organizer, make a prediction. Then read through the ovals, noting how evidence to support a prediction is clearly found in the text.

What do you think will happen next?
The government and empire will be strong.

Growth of the Empire
[The Mughal Empire] grew in the mid-1500s under an emperor named Akbar. He . . . began a tolerant religious policy. . . . Akbar believed that no single religion, including Islam, had all the answers. He got rid of the tax on non-Muslims and invited Hindus to be part of the Mughal government.

How can you confirm your predictions?
To find out if your prediction is accurate, read further in the text.

What evidence supports your prediction?
Akbar included people of all religions, which may encourage less conflict.

It is okay if some of your predictions are not accurate. Revising your predictions helps you to learn.

Does your prediction need to be revised?
Revise your prediction if something different happened.

You Try It!

Read the following passage and then answer the questions below.

In the 1600s, Mughal emperors expanded the empire to control almost all of India. This period of expansion was not a peaceful time. In the late 1600s, a new emperor, Aurangzeb, changed the tolerant religious policies Akbar had established. The new emperor ordered people to obey strict religious laws and destroyed Hindu temples throughout India. He also persecuted non-Muslims and made them pay a special tax.

Answer these questions based on the passage you just read.

1. What do you predict will happen next?
2. What evidence supports your prediction?
3. How can you confirm your prediction?
4. What should you do if your prediction isn't correct?

As you read this module, make predictions about what will happen next.

Key Terms and People

Lesson 1
Janissaries
Mehmed II
sultan
Suleyman I
harem
Lesson 2
Shia
Sunni
Lesson 3
langar
gurdwara
Lesson 4
Babur
Akbar

The Ottoman Empire

The Big Idea

After the early spread of Islam, the Ottoman Empire controlled parts of Europe, Asia, and Africa.

Main Ideas

- The Ottoman Empire covered a large area in eastern Europe and was a large commercial center.

- Ottoman society produced lasting scientific and cultural contributions.

Key Terms and People

Janissaries
Mehmed II
sultan
Suleyman I
harem

If YOU were there . . .

You are one of several advisors to the leader of a great empire. His armies have conquered many lands and peoples. But the ruler wants to be known for something other than his military conquests. He wants to be remembered as a wise ruler who united the empire. How can he do this? Some of his advisors tell him to rule strictly. Others urge him to be tolerant of the different peoples in the empire. Now it is your turn.

What advice will you give the ruler?

The Rise of the Ottoman Empire

Centuries after the early Arab Muslim conquests, Muslims ruled several powerful empires containing various peoples. Rulers and military leaders in Persian empires spoke Persian, Turkish leaders spoke Turkish, while Arabic continued as a language of religion and scholarship. One of these empires was the Ottoman Empire, which controlled much of Europe, Asia, and Africa. Built through conquest, the Ottoman Empire was a political and cultural force.

Growth of the Empire In the mid-1200s, Muslim Turkish warriors known as Ottomans began to take land from the Christian Byzantine Empire. As the map shows, they eventually ruled lands from eastern Europe to North Africa and Arabia.

The key to the empire's expansion was the Ottoman army. The Ottomans trained Christian boys from conquered towns to be soldiers. These slave soldiers, called **Janissaries**, converted to Islam and became fierce fighters. Besides these slave troops, the Ottomans were aided by new gunpowder weapons—especially cannons.

In 1453, Ottomans led by **Mehmed II** used huge cannons to conquer Constantinople. With the city's capture, Mehmed defeated the Byzantine Empire. He became known as "the Conqueror." Mehmed made Constantinople, which the Ottomans called Istanbul, his new capital. He also turned the Byzantines' great church, Hagia Sophia, into a mosque.

Mehmed II 1432–1481

Mehmed II ruled the Ottoman Empire from 1451 to 1481. During this time he greatly improved the new capital, Istanbul. He repaired damage caused by fighting and built palaces and mosques. He also built a huge, covered bazaar. He encouraged people from the far reaches of the empire to move to the city.

Make Inferences
What facts show that Mehmed II was a successful ruler?

Istanbul continued to grow as a commercial and cultural center. Mehmed II lowered taxes to attract merchants and artisans to the city. This encouraged industry and trade. The Ottoman Empire as a whole flourished along trade routes throughout the Mediterranean region. The Ottomans controlled much of the Mediterranean coast as well as ports along major inland rivers such as the Danube.

A later **sultan**, or Ottoman ruler, continued Mehmed's conquests. He expanded the empire to the east through the rest of Anatolia, another name for Asia Minor. His armies also conquered Syria and Egypt. Soon afterward, the holy cities of Mecca and Medina accepted Ottoman rule as well. These triumphs made the Ottoman Empire a major world power.

▶ *Explore ONLINE!*

Growth of the Ottoman Empire

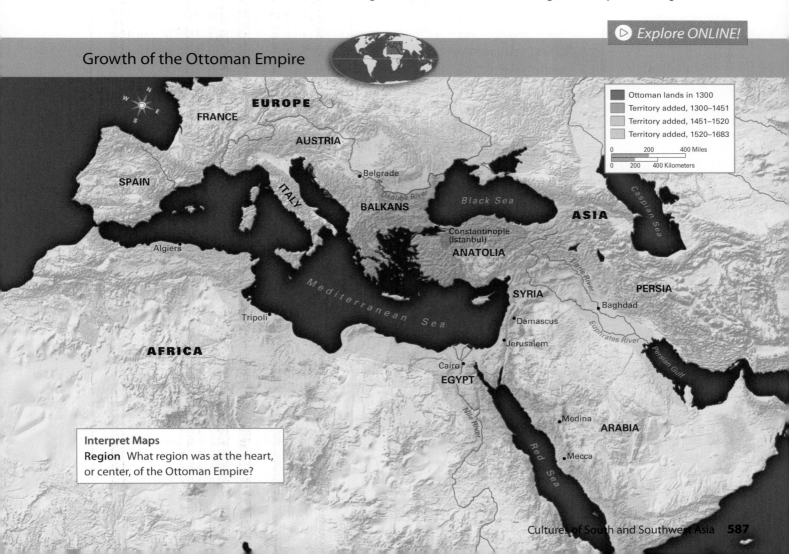

Ottoman lands in 1300
Territory added, 1300–1451
Territory added, 1451–1520
Territory added, 1520–1683

0   200   400 Miles
0   200   400 Kilometers

EUROPE
FRANCE
AUSTRIA
SPAIN
ITALY
Belgrade
Danube River
BALKANS
Black Sea
ASIA
Algiers
Constantinople (Istanbul)
ANATOLIA
Caspian Sea
Mediterranean Sea
SYRIA
PERSIA
Tripoli
Damascus
Tigris River
Baghdad
AFRICA
Jerusalem
Euphrates River
Cairo
Persian Gulf
EGYPT
Nile River
Medina
ARABIA
Red Sea
Mecca

Interpret Maps
Region What region was at the heart, or center, of the Ottoman Empire?

The Ottoman Empire reached its height under **Suleyman I** (soo-lay-MAHN), "the Magnificent." During Suleyman's rule, from 1520 to 1566, the Ottomans took control of the eastern Mediterranean and pushed farther into Europe, areas they would control until the early 1900s.

Also during Suleyman's rule, the Ottoman Empire reached its cultural peak. Muslim poets wrote beautiful works, and architects worked to turn Istanbul from a Byzantine city into a Muslim one.

Ottoman Government and Society The sultan issued laws and made all major decisions in the empire. Most Ottoman law was based on Shariah, or Islamic law, but sultans also made laws of their own.

Ottoman society was divided into two classes. Judges and other people who advised the sultan on legal and military matters were part of the ruling class. Members of the ruling class had to be loyal to the sultan, practice Islam, and understand Ottoman customs.

People who didn't fit these requirements made up the other class. Many of them were Christians or Jews from lands the Ottomans had conquered. Christians and Jews formed religious communities, or millets, within the empire. Each millet had its own leaders and religious laws.

Ottoman society limited the freedom that women enjoyed, especially women in the ruling class. These women usually had to live apart from men in an area of a household called a **harem**. By separating women from men, harems kept women out of public life. However, wealthy women could still own property or businesses. Some women used their money to build schools, mosques, and hospitals.

Reading Check
Find Main Ideas
How did the Ottomans gain land for their empire?

Scientific and Cultural Advances

One of the strengths of the Ottoman Empire was its vast trade network around the Mediterranean. However, Ottoman society is also well known for its many scientific and cultural advancements. This was a time of great discoveries. New technology enabled people to learn more about the world than ever before.

This illustration shows Taqi-al-Din and other scholars in the Istanbul Observatory.

Taqi al-Din and the Istanbul Observatory

The Ottoman Empire is known for its many scientific innovations. Taqi al-Din was an Ottoman astronomer and mathematician. He founded the Istanbul Observatory in order to learn more about stars and planets. There, he and others made significant advancements in astronomy and mathematics. Taqi al-Din also wrote many books on astronomy and other scientific topics, such as medicine and physics. He also studied

The Mosque of Suleyman shows the influence of Byzantine and Ottoman cultures.

mechanical-automatic clocks and was the first astronomer to use this type of clock to help make his astronomical observations.

Arts and Architecture The Ottoman Empire controlled large areas of land on different continents. Therefore, people from many different cultures lived under Ottoman rule. We can see elements of these different cultures in different forms of art and architecture.

Ottoman architecture was influenced in part by previous building in the region. For example, the Hagia Sophia was originally a Byzantine church built in the fourth and fifth centuries. The Ottomans converted the church to a mosque. Other mosques built during the Ottoman Empire, such as the Mosque of Suleyman, have many features in common with the Hagia Sophia. For example, both buildings feature large domes.

Elements of Ottoman architecture have other features in common with different regions. For example, the designs of exteriors, windows, and gates of Ottoman mosques have features found in Italian buildings. Evidence of Ottoman architecture is also seen in other regions, such as North Africa and the Balkans.

Metalwork, wood inlaid with ivory, carpets, and textiles were popular in Istanbul and other centers of the empire. In turn, these ornamental objects had great influence on European decorative arts at the time.

Literature and poetry were also very popular. Yunus Emre introduced a form of mythical poetry in the Turkish part of the empire. Many later poets imitated his style. Numerous poets lived in Istanbul, making it a cultural center. Different forms of theater were also popular throughout the empire, including mime shows and comedies.

Summary and Preview In this lesson you learned about the growth of the Ottoman Empire and its influence. Next, you'll learn about the Ottomans' neighbors to the east in Persia.

Reading Check
Synthesize
What architectural evidence shows interaction between the Ottomans and other cultures?

Lesson 1 Assessment

Review Ideas, Terms, and People

1. a. Summarize Who were the Janissaries?

   b. Draw Conclusions In what ways was the Ottoman society tolerant and in what ways was it not?

   c. Form Generalizations What was life like for women in Ottoman society?

2. a. Summarize In what areas of science did Taqi al-Din make advancements?

   b. Draw Conclusions In what ways did Ottoman arts and culture influence other cultures?

Critical Thinking

3. Analyze The Ottoman Empire was an enormous and powerful commercial center. In the graphic organizer below, list reasons the empire was able to grow commercially and remain powerful.

Reasons for Growth and Expansion of Ottoman Empire
1.
2.
3.

Safavid Persia

The Big Idea

The Safavid Empire took over Persia in the early 1500s, blending Persian and Islamic traditions.

Main Ideas

- The Safavid Empire blended Persian cultural traditions with Shia Islam.
- The Safavids supported trade networks throughout the region.

Key Terms and People

Shia
Sunni

If YOU were there . . .

You are a Sunni living in Persia when it is conquered by the Safavid leader Esma'il. Soon he will make Shiism the official religion of the empire. Many Sunnis like yourself disagree with some aspects of Shiism.

How do you feel? What will you do?

The Safavid Empire

As the Ottoman Empire reached its height, a group of Persian Muslims known as the Safavids (sah-FAH-vuhds) was gaining power to the east. Before long the Safavids came into conflict with the Ottomans and other Muslims.

Religious Conflict

The conflict came from an old disagreement among Muslims about who should be caliph. In the mid-600s, Islam split into two groups. The two groups were the Shia (SHEE-ah) and the Sunni (SOO-nee). Both groups of Muslims have much in common.

Daily prayer is a religious observance Shia and Sunni Muslims share.

For example, they both believe in daily prayer, and they both fast in the daytime during the holy month of Ramadan. However, they had different ideas about a caliph.

A caliph is someone who leads all Muslims. He is seen as the successor to Muhammad. The **Shia** were Muslims who thought that only members of Muhammad's family could become caliphs. On the other hand, the **Sunni** didn't think caliphs had to be related to Muhammad as long as they were good Muslims and strong leaders. Over time, religious differences developed between the two groups as well.

Growth of the Empire

The Safavid Empire began in 1501 when the Safavid leader Esma'il (is-mah-EEL) conquered Persia. He took the ancient Persian title of shah, or king.

As shah, Esma'il made Shiism—the beliefs of the Shia—the official religion of the empire. This act worried Esma'il's advisors because most people in the empire were Sunnis. But Esma'il said:

> "God and the Immaculate Imams [pure religious leaders] are with me . . . and I fear no one. By God's help, if the people utter one word of protest, I will draw the sword and leave not one of them alive."
>
> —Esma'il, quoted in *A Literary History of Persia, Volume 4* by Edward G. Browne

Esma'il dreamed of conquering other Muslim territories and converting all Muslims to Shiism. He battled the Uzbeks to the north, but he suffered a crushing defeat by the Ottomans, who were Sunni. Esma'il died in 1524, and the next leaders struggled to keep the empire together.

In 1588, the greatest Safavid leader, 'Abbas, became shah. He strengthened the military and gave his soldiers modern gunpowder weapons. Copying the Ottomans, 'Abbas trained foreign slave boys to be soldiers. Under 'Abbas's rule, the Safavids defeated the Uzbeks and took back land that had been lost to the Ottomans. 'Abbas also made great contributions to the Safavid culture and economy.

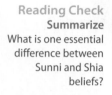

Reading Check
Summarize
What is one essential difference between Sunni and Shia beliefs?

Safavid Culture and Economy

The Safavids blended Persian and Muslim traditions. They built beautiful mosques in their capital, Esfahan (es-fah-HAHN). People admired the colorful tiles and large dome of the Shah Mosque, built for 'Abbas. Esfahan was considered one of the world's most magnificent cities in the 1600s.

Traditional Safavid architecture included vaulted ceilings and beautiful colored tiles.

Popular scenes in woven textiles included pastimes like hunting, falconry, and reading poetry in gardens.

One description of the city says it had 162 mosques, 1,802 commercial buildings, and 283 baths. Many buildings had domes decorated in colored tiles. Other forms of art included rugs and objects made in silver, gold, and enamel. Painting and drawing were popular, as was poetry. For example, Esma'il wrote Turkish mystical verses of poetry. Interestingly, his enemy at the time, the sultan of Turkey, wrote lyric poems in Persian.

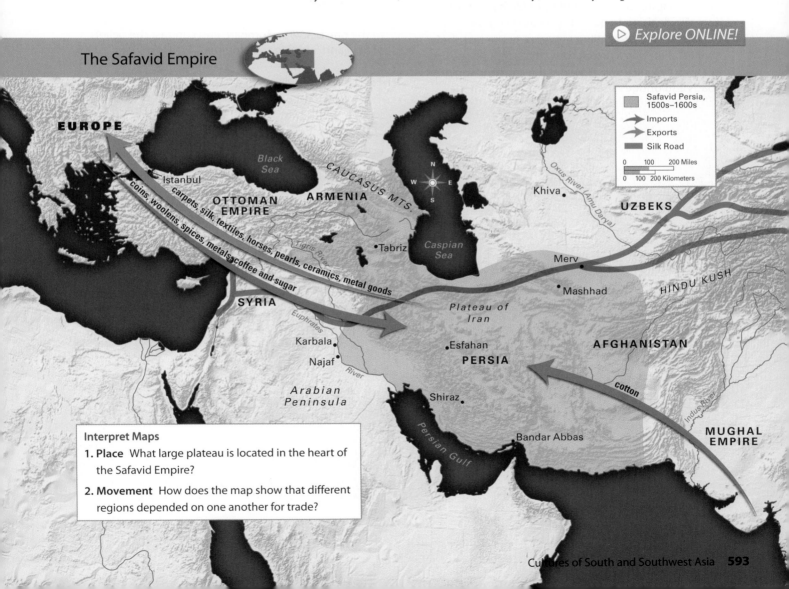

The Safavid Empire

▶ Explore ONLINE!

Interpret Maps

1. **Place** What large plateau is located in the heart of the Safavid Empire?

2. **Movement** How does the map show that different regions depended on one another for trade?

Reading Check
Summarize
How did the Safavids
strengthen trade
networks between
Persia and Europe?

Safavid culture played a role in the empire's economy because 'Abbas encouraged the manufacturing of traditional products. Handwoven carpets became a major export. Other textiles, such as silk and velvet, were made in large workshops and also sold to other peoples. In addition, the Safavids were admired for their skills in making ceramics and metal goods, especially goods made from steel.

The Safavids also built roads and bridges to encourage trade throughout the region. As a result, merchants came from as far away as Europe to trade for Safavid goods. Such trade brought wealth to the Safavid Empire and helped **establish** it as a major Islamic civilization. It lasted until the mid-1700s.

Summary and Preview In this lesson, you learned how the Safavid Empire affected Persia and about its relationship with other regions. Next, you'll look at another group of people farther to the east, the Sikhs.

Lesson 2 Assessment

Review Ideas, Terms, and People

1. a. **Recall** When did the Safavid Empire begin?

   b. **Form Opinions** How might people have reacted to Esma'il's decision to make the Safavid Empire Shia?

2. a. **Make Inferences** What evidence in the text shows that Esfahan was a prosperous city?

   b. **Draw Conclusions** How did the construction of roads and bridges strengthen the Safavid Empire?

Critical Thinking

3. **Compare and Contrast** In this lesson, you learned about the beginnings of the Safavid Empire and the role religion played. Create a graphic organizer similar to the one below to compare and contrast the beliefs of Shia and Sunni in the empire.

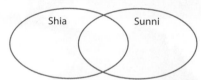

Shia   Sunni

Sikhism in South Asia

The Big Idea

Sikhism originated in the Punjab region of India and has grown to include nearly 25 million followers around the world.

Main Ideas

- Sikhs believe in equality and generally reject the caste system.
- Sikhs have responded to historical and modern-day challenges.

Key Terms

langar
gurdwara

If YOU were there . . .

You hear a guru, or teacher, speaking in public. He is a Sikh, and he believes that all people should be treated equally. He talks about a community of Sikhs near you who embrace this principle.

Would you have been curious to learn more about Sikhism?

Sikh Religious Philosophies

Sikhism (SIK-iz-uhm) began in the Punjab in the late 15th century and people who follow the religion are known as Sikhs (SIKS). Sikhism was started by Guru Nanak, who actually grew up as a Hindu. While Guru Nanak was raised Hindu, Sikhs do not consider their religion a branch of Hinduism.

The Origin of Sikhism In the Punjabi language, the word *sikh* means "learner." People who joined the Sikh community looked for spiritual guidance. In Punjabi, Sikhism is called Gurmat, which means "the way of the Guru." Guru Nanak, who lived from 1469 to 1539, was the first guru. Nanak opposed some elements of Indian culture during his time, including the caste system. He thought people from different social classes should be treated equally. Many people were attracted to Nanak's ideas about equality. After he died, nine other gurus followed Nanak. The essential beliefs of Sikhism are found in the teachings of all ten of these gurus.

Sikh Beliefs Sikhs believe that each of these gurus was inhabited by a single spirit. Each time a guru died, this spirit, or eternal Guru, transferred itself to the next human guru. The tenth guru, Guru Gobind Singh, died in 1708. Sikhs believe that at that time, the spirit transferred itself to the sacred scripture of the Sikhs. This scripture is called Guru Granth Sahib. It contains the actual words spoken by the Sikh gurus, which Sikhs believe to be the word of Waheguru, or God.

In this photo, a Sikh is wearing traditional dress and demonstrating a traditional Indian martial art called *gatka*.

Sikhs believe there is only one God and that God does not have a form or gender. They also believe that everyone has equal access to God and that everyone is equal before God. Living honestly and caring for others is important to Sikhs. Like Hindus, Sikhs believe that humans cycle through life, death, and reincarnation. They also believe in karma.

Sikh Religious Practices Sikhs do not agree with most aspects of the caste system. They believe in equality between social classes. You can see this equality in the kitchens at their places of worship. In the **langar**, or kitchen, food is served without charge. Everyone must sit together on the floor. This practice came about as a protest against the caste system. Sitting together on the floor, with no person seated in a favored position, is a symbol of social equality.

However, some aspects of the caste system are voluntarily observed in two areas of some Sikh societies—marriage and **gurdwaras**, or places of worship. While not required, some Sikhs may choose to marry someone of their own caste. Some castes have also created gurdwaras.

Sikhism is based on a need to understand and experience God. It is a goal to eventually become one with God. To achieve this, Sikh philosophy refers to three duties: to pray, to work, and to give. This means keeping God in mind at all times through prayer and meditation, earning an honest living, and giving to others. One way to keep God in mind is to wear certain articles that signify faith. These articles include uncut hair, a sword, a metal bracelet, and a wooden comb.

Sikhs also believe there are five vices that make people self-centered, which they try to avoid. The five vices are lust, greed, attachment to worldly things, anger, and pride. Sikhs believe that avoiding these vices will help in attaining spiritual liberation.

Reading Check
Draw Conclusions
What effects has Sikhism's rejection of the caste system had on its society?

Sikh History

Many Sikhs lived in the Punjab region of India. In the 1600s, Sikhs occasionally came into conflict with the ruling Mughal Empire. The Mughals controlled much of what is now India, Pakistan, and Bangladesh. There were uprisings over unfair taxes and other mistreatment. When Sikhs gathered to protest, the Mughals often sent war elephants to stop them. As a result of these harsh policies, violent revolts occurred throughout the region in the 1600s and 1700s.

Articles of Faith	
Kesh	uncut hair covered by a distinctive turban, which represents spirituality
Kirpan	a religious sword, which represents readiness to protect the weak and fight against injustice
Kara	a metal bracelet, which reminds people to do good deeds in their daily activities
Kanga	a wooden comb, which represents cleanliness
Kachera	cotton undergarments, which represent self-discipline

Interpret Charts
Why do you think many Sikhs wear these articles on a daily basis?

Sikh Power in the Punjab Region Over time, however, the Mughal Empire began to weaken, and Sikh resistance to Mughal rule intensified. After conflict with the Mughals to the east and the Afghans to the west, Sikhs controlled much of the Punjab in the late 1700s. In 1799, a man named Ranjit Singh declared himself maharaja, or ruler, of the Punjab. This was the beginning of the Sikh Empire.

The Golden Temple in Amritsar, India, is an important religious site for Sikhs. Anyone is welcome, regardless of the person's religion, caste, or race.

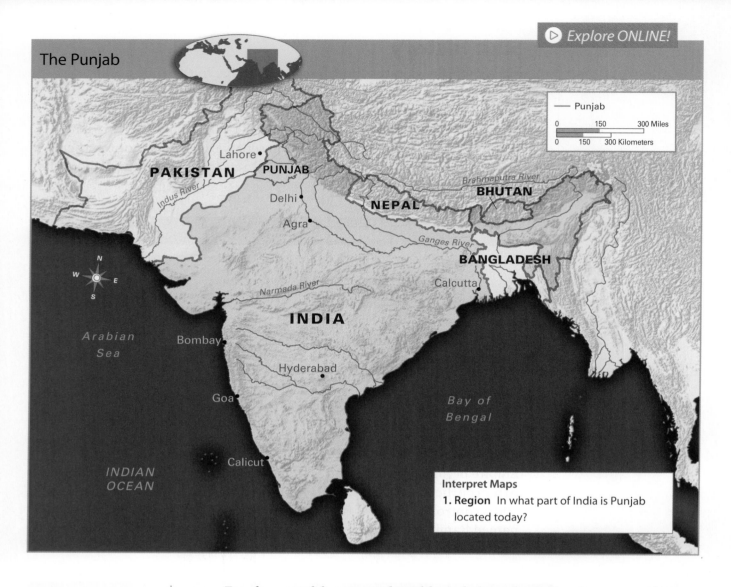

Explore ONLINE!

Punjab

0   150   300 Miles
0   150   300 Kilometers

Interpret Maps
1. **Region** In what part of India is Punjab located today?

For the next fifty years, the Sikhs ruled much of what is now northwestern India and eastern Pakistan. It was during this time that a gurdwara in northwestern India was rebuilt using marble and gold. This was a symbol of Sikh power. It became known as the Golden Temple. Ranjit Singh was a strong ruler, and the Sikh Empire thrived for many years. However, the Sikh Empire began to weaken when he died in 1839. After conflict with the British, the Punjab became a part of British India in 1849.

Sikhs Migrate Across the World There are nearly 25 million Sikhs worldwide today. Most live in India, with the largest number still in the Punjab. After the decline of the Sikh Empire, though, some Sikhs moved to other parts of the Indian subcontinent. Many of these migrants were traders who moved in search of new markets for their goods. When the British took control of India in 1858, they recruited Sikhs to serve as soldiers. Sikh soldiers were posted in the British colonies of Malaya and Hong Kong. This encouraged Sikh migration to other parts of the world.

Sikh migration expanded in the 20th century to different regions in Asia, Australia, and North America. The west coast of North America provided opportunities for jobs, and the first Sikhs began arriving there in 1903.

Reading Check
Analyze Motives
Why have many Sikhs
left India?

Globalization presents both struggles and opportunities to Sikhs living outside India. Because of their distinctive dress, Sikhs remain a visible minority in their adopted homelands. In response to economic challenges, many Sikhs migrated to the United Kingdom and North America after World War II. They arrived in search of educational and employment opportunities. In the United States and Canada, there are now large Sikh communities consisting of thousands of people.

Summary and Preview In this lesson you learned about the beliefs of Sikhism and how it began. You also learned about the Sikh Empire and why many Sikhs have migrated from India to other parts of the world. In the next lesson, you will learn about the Mughal Empire in India.

Lesson 3 Assessment

Review Ideas, Terms, and People

1. a. **Summarize** How did Sikhism begin, and how has it been passed down through generations?

   b. **Recall** What are the three duties referred to in Sikh philosophy?

   c. **Summarize** What do the Sikhs believe will happen if they avoid the five vices?

   d. **Form Opinions** What is your opinion of the duties and vices described in Sikh philosophy? Explain.

2. a. **Analyze** Why did Sikhs first leave India?

   b. **Summarize** What drew Sikhs to other countries after World War II?

Critical Thinking

3. **Compare and Contrast** In this lesson you learned about how Sikhism is similar to and different from Hinduism. Create a graphic organizer similar to the one below to note these differences and similarities.

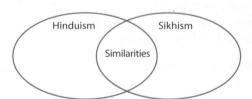

Hinduism · Similarities · Sikhism

The Mughal Empire

The Big Idea

The Mughal Empire was the last great empire in India before British rule.

Main Ideas

- Akbar was able to unify the Mughal Empire through his tolerant religious and political policies.

- Many cultures blended together to create a society unique to the Mughal Empire.

Key Terms and People

Babur
Akbar

If YOU were there . . .

You are a Hindu who is part of the government of the Mughal Empire. It is the late 1600s, and you enjoy a peaceful life filled with great culture and religious tolerance. But your emperor dies, and the new emperor changes many of the policies that make it possible for you to be part of society. You are soon pushed out of the government, and your Hindu temple is destroyed.

How do you react to this change?

The History of the Mughal Empire

East of the Safavid Empire, in India, lay the Mughal (MOO-guhl) Empire. Like the Ottomans, the Mughals united a large and diverse empire. They left a cultural heritage known for poetry and architecture.

Growth of the Empire The Mughals were Turkish Muslims from Central Asia. The founder of the Mughal Empire was called **Babur** (BAH-boohr), or "tiger." He tried for years to make an empire in Central Asia. When he didn't succeed there, he decided to build an empire in northern India instead. There Babur established the Mughal Empire in 1526.

The empire grew in the mid-1500s under an emperor named **Akbar**. He conquered many new lands and worked to make the Mughal government stronger. The central government itself was reformed to be more responsive to its citizens' needs. It consisted of four different departments that oversaw fifteen different provinces in the empire.

In this painting, Akbar leaves his palace on a hunting trip.

Akbar also began a tolerant religious policy. Although he was raised Muslim, Akbar believed that no single religion, including Islam, had all the answers. He got rid of the tax on non-Muslims and invited Hindus to be part of the Mughal government. Akbar appointed many Hindus to government posts. Akbar's tolerant policies helped unify the empire.

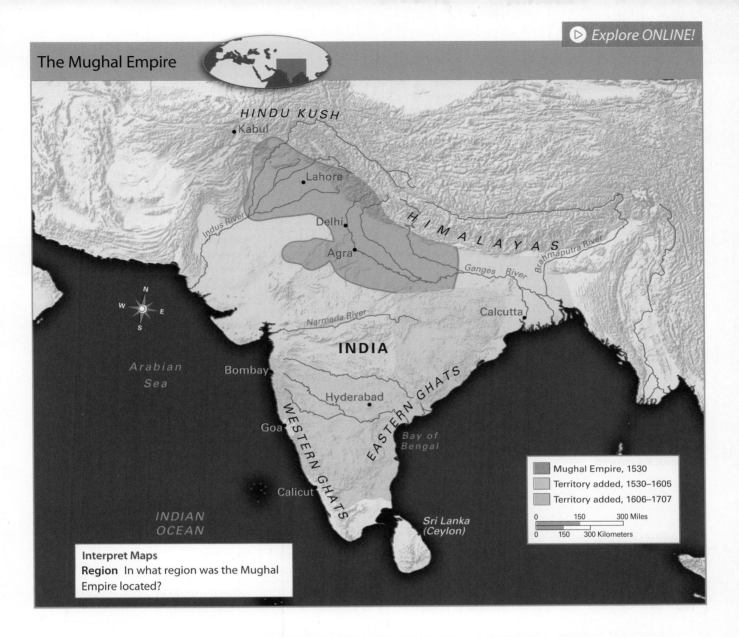

Explore ONLINE!

HINDU KUSH
• Kabul

• Lahore

Indus River

Delhi •

HIMALAYAS

Agra •

Ganges River

Brahmaputra River

Narmada River

Calcutta •

INDIA

Arabian Sea

Bombay •

Hyderabad •

EASTERN GHATS

WESTERN GHATS

Goa •

Bay of Bengal

Calicut •

INDIAN OCEAN

Sri Lanka (Ceylon)

▉	Mughal Empire, 1530
▨	Territory added, 1530–1605
▨	Territory added, 1606–1707

0   150   300 Miles
0   150   300 Kilometers

Interpret Maps
Region In what region was the Mughal Empire located?

In the 1600s, Mughal emperors expanded the empire to control almost all of India. Look at the map to see how it grew. This period of expansion was not a peaceful time. In the late 1600s, a new emperor, Aurangzeb, changed the tolerant religious policies Akbar had established. The new emperor ordered people to obey strict religious laws and destroyed Hindu temples throughout India in order to spread Islam. He also persecuted non-Muslims and made them pay a special tax. Violent revolts occurred throughout the empire in the 1600s as a result of these harsh decisions.

The Mughal Empire grew quickly because of its location along trade routes. In time, it became a commercial center that produced quality textiles. Other goods were traded as well, and the Mughals were soon at the center of trade routes that stretched across Asia. Like other empires that existed before it, the Mughal Empire was influential for many reasons. In fact, the Mughal Empire had several characteristics in common with these other empires.

A Comparison of Empires

Beginning and End Dates	Greece c.1200–323 BC	Rome 27 BC–AD 476	Han Dynasty China 202 BC–AD 220	Mughal Empire India AD 1526–1857
Reason for Growth	Grew out of the ruins of Mycenaean civilization and different city-states and kingdoms through colonization	Replaced republic	Replaced rival kingdoms	Grew as Mughal leaders conquered parts of modern-day India
Type of Government	Decentralized government of largely independent city-states	Centralized, bureaucratic government	Centralized, bureaucratic government	Centralized government with provincial governments
Notable Accomplishments	Built great military structures, beginnings of democracy	Built roads and defensive walls	Built roads and defensive walls	Built great architectural monuments
Conquered Peoples	Conquered many diverse peoples on three continents. (Africa, Asia, Europe)	Conquered many diverse peoples in regions of three continents	Conquered many diverse peoples in regions bordering China	Conquered many peoples on the Indian subcontinent
Largest Boundaries	Encompassed southern Europe, northern Africa, as well as east to India	Covered 3.4 million square miles and a population of 55 million	Covered 1.5 million square miles and a population of 60 million	Covered almost the entire subcontinent of India
Common Language	Adopted Greek as a common language, but did not replace other languages	Adopted Latin, which did not replace other written languages	Adopted Chinese, which became common written language	Created Urdu from Arabic, Hindi, and a Persian language
Fall	Fell apart, eventually yielding to Rome	Fell apart, never restored	Fell apart, restored by Tang Dynasty in 618	Fell apart, replaced by British rule

Interpret Charts

How were the empires similar? How were they different?

Decline of the Empire Aurangzeb's political and religious intolerance was the beginning of the end of the Mughal Empire. He did not allow Hindus to have their own customs, as previous emperors had. Aurangzeb ruled that the entire empire should be under Islamic law. These decisions were unpopular with many Hindus. The many revolts that resulted took their toll, and the quality of the Mughal government began to decline. As a result, the economy also did poorly. The Mughal Empire soon fell apart. When Aurangzeb died in 1707, his authority was disputed throughout the empire. By the mid-1700s, the empire was reduced to only a small area around Delhi.

During this time, the British continued to trade with the Mughals. However, the British began to assert greater control over political and economic life in India. Great Britain began to replace Indian leaders with British officials. Many Indians resented this control.

In 1857, a mutiny against British rule began in different cities throughout India. The British military was better equipped than the Indians. The British had many weapons, such as rifles and cannons, that were fired with gunpowder. This gave them a significant advantage over Indian troops who were not as well equipped. The mutiny was suppressed the following year. The last Mughal shah, Bahādur Shah II, was forced to leave the country. The British government then took formal control of India.

Cultural Achievements

A conflict of cultures led to the end of the Mughal Empire. For much of the empire's history, however, Muslims and Hindus lived together peacefully. For example, Muslim and Hindu scholars made significant advances in astronomy based on Islamic and Hindu traditions. One Mughal ruler, Humayun, even built a personal observatory to better see the movement of the stars.

Reading Check
Analyze Causes
How was Akbar able to build a strong empire and government?

The Taj Mahal, built by the Mughal emperor Shah Jahan, still stands in Agra, India.

Many Muslims embraced different forms of Hindu culture, such as literature and festivals. Persians and Indians lived and worked in the same communities. As a result, elements of their cultures, such as language, blended together. This created a culture unique to the Mughal Empire.

For example, during Akbar's rule, the Persian language and Persian clothing styles were popular. At the same time, Akbar supported the translation of ancient Sanskrit literature into Persian. He also encouraged the blending of Persian, Islamic, and Hindu architectural styles in new buildings throughout his capital. Akbar even borrowed elements of cultures from distant lands. When Christian missionaries brought European paintings to India, Akbar was impressed by their style. He had artists in his empire adopt the realistic style of this European art into their own works. The Mughals also reformed education for the region's children.

The Mughal Empire is known for its monumental architecture—particularly the Taj Mahal. The Taj Mahal is a dazzling tomb built between 1631 and 1647 by Akbar's grandson Shah Jahan for his wife. He brought workers and materials from all over India and Central Asia to build the Taj Mahal. The buildings of the palace include a main gateway and a mosque. Gardens with pathways and fountains add beauty to the palace grounds. Many of the monuments the Mughals built have become symbols of India today.

Reading Check
Summarize
What cultures blended in the Mughal Empire to create a distinct culture?

Summary The Mughals built great empires and continued the spread of Islam.

Lesson 4 Assessment

Review Ideas, Terms, and People

1. a. Summarize Where was the Mughal Empire located?

b. Contrast How did Akbar's religious policy in the mid-1500s differ from the religious policy of Aurangzeb?

c. Analyze How did Aurangzeb's policies ultimately affect the Mughal Empire?

d. Analyze What role did the British play in the decline of the Mughal Empire?

2. a. Summarize What role did Akbar play in the blended culture in the Mughal Empire?

b. Draw Conclusions How did the Mughal Empire play a large role in trade in Asia?

c. Analyze Why was the Taj Mahal built?

Critical Thinking

3. Compare and Contrast Draw the graphic organizer below. Use it to compare and contrast different characteristics of the Ottoman, Safavid, and Mughal empires.

	Ottoman	Safavid	Mughal
Leaders			
Location			
Religious policy			

Social Studies Skills

Visualize Social Studies Texts

Define the Skill

One of the best ways to comprehend a text is to visualize what you are reading. This means learning to create a picture in your mind from the details of the text.

Learn the Skill

Follow these steps to visualize as you read.

1. As you read the text, look for words that help you picture characters, places, descriptions, and processes.

2. As you read, visualize what is happening in the text. Think about the setting, the time period, and the event. Notice any descriptive details that will help you form a mental image in your mind. If a lot of action is described, create a movie in your mind.

3. Use additional resources to help you visualize. For example, if a description includes information about particular locations, use a map to help you visualize how those locations are related and influence the event.

Practice the Skill

Read the following text. Visualize what you are reading as you read it.

1. Write a description of what you visualized as you went.

2. Were there any words or phrases that helped you picture the passage?

"Sikhs do not agree with most aspects of the Hindu caste system. They believe in equality between social classes. You can see this equality in the kitchens at their places of worship. In the langar, or kitchen, food is served without charge. Everyone must sit in a straight line. This practice came about as a protest against the caste system. Sitting in a straight line, with no person ahead or behind someone else, is a symbol of social equality."

Module 17 Assessment

Review Vocabulary, Terms, and People

For each group of terms below, write the letter of the term that does not relate to the others. Then write a sentence that explains how the other two terms are related.

1. a. Janissaries
   b. Mehmed II
   c. Suleyman I
2. a. Shia
   b. sultan
   c. Sunni
3. a. langar
   b. gurdwara
   c. harem
4. a. Babur
   b. Akbar
   c. Janissaries

Comprehension and Critical Thinking

Lesson 1

5. a. **Identify** Who were Mehmed II and Suleyman I?
   b. **Summarize** Describe the location and size of the Ottoman Empire.
   c. **Evaluate** What geographical factors contributed to the Ottoman Empire's success as a commercial center?

Lesson 2

6. a. **Identify** Who was 'Abbas?
   b. **Analyze** What role did 'Abbas play in the culture and economy of the Safavid Empire?
   c. **Make Inferences** What evidence shows that the Safavids were a significant Islamic civilization?

Lesson 3

7. a. **Identify** Who was Guru Nanak?
   b. **Explain** Why does Sikhism generally not follow the Hindu caste system?
   c. **Analyze** How did the British influence Sikh migration from India?

Lesson 4

8. a. **Identify** Who was Akbar?
   b. **Analyze** How did the issue of religious tolerance both help the empire to grow and lead to its demise?
   c. **Form Opinions** Which of the four empires, Ottoman, Safavid, Sikh, or Mughal seems to have been the most successful? On what do you base your answer?

Module 17 Assessment, continued

Review Themes

9. **Society and Culture** Do you agree or disagree with this statement: "Muslim leaders from the Ottoman, Safavid, and Mughal Empires were tolerant of those they conquered." Defend your answer.

10. **Religion** How did a religious division affect the Safavid Empire?

11. **Society and Culture** What contributions to science and technology are associated with the Ottoman Empire?

Reading Skills

Ask Questions to Make Predictions *Use the Reading Skills taught in this module to answer the questions about the reading selection below.*

From the time the British set foot in India, there was a general belief that they wanted to westernize Indians. Many Indians wanted to keep their traditional ways. This is why many Indian soldiers were not happy with the new Enfield rifle. To load the rifle, Indian soldiers had to bite off the ends of the cartridges. This didn't seem so difficult, but there was a rumor that the grease used on the cartridges was a mix of pigs' and cows' lard. Muslims do not eat pork and Hindus do not eat either animal for religious reasons. Whether the rumor was true or not, a young [Indian] soldier . . . walked into a British military garrison. He had had enough.

12. What is most likely to occur next?

13. What evidence from the text supports your prediction?

Social Studies Skills

Visualize Social Studies Texts *Use the Social Studies Skills taught in this module to answer the question about the reading selection below.*

The Mughal Empire is known for its monumental architecture—particularly the Taj Mahal. The Taj Mahal is a dazzling tomb built between 1631 and 1647 by Akbar's grandson Shah Jahan for his wife. He brought workers and materials from all over India and Central Asia to build the Taj Mahal. The buildings of the palace include a main gateway and a mosque. Gardens with pathways and fountains add beauty to the palace grounds. Many of the monuments the Mughals built have become symbols of India today.

14. Write a description of what you visualized as you read the selection.

Focus On Writing

15. **Create a Brochure** What facts about the Mughal Empire do you think made it a good place to live for its citizens? Create a one-page brochure that outlines these facts. Your brochure should include a title, four reasons why Hindus and Muslims would have liked living in the Mughal Empire, and at least one hand-drawn picture with a caption.

The Early Americas

Essential Question

How did geography and climate impact the way American civilizations developed?

About the Photo: This photo shows the ruins of a great Maya temple in Tikal, Guatemala. More than 1,500 years ago, the Mayas built large cities in their American homeland.

In this module, you will learn about the development of civilization in the Americas.

What You Will Learn...

Lesson 1: Geography and Early Cultures **612**
The Big Idea The landforms and climate of the Americas affected farming and the development of early cultures.

Lesson 2: The Mayas **619**
The Big Idea The Maya civilization was characterized by great cities, trade, and achievements in art, science, and technology.

Lesson 3: The Aztecs **630**
The Big Idea The Aztecs developed complex social, religious, artistic, and scientific systems in their empire in central Mexico.

Lesson 4: The Inca Empire **640**
The Big Idea The Incas built a huge empire in South America and made many great achievements in architecture, art, and oral literature.

Lesson 5: North American Cultures. **650**
The Big Idea Varied environments and available resources shaped the cultures of North American native peoples over thousands of years.

▶ Explore ONLINE!

VIDEOS, including...
- The Ancient Civilizations of Mexico
- Corn: The Super Product that Changed the World
- Studying Glyphs
- Tracking Time
- What Happened to the Aztecs?
- Machu Picchu
- Rise of the Incas

✓ Document-Based Investigations

✓ Graphic Organizers

✓ Interactive Games

✓ Image with Hotspots: Tenochtitlán

✓ Compare Images: Spanish Conquistador and Inca Warrior

✓ Image Carousel: Mound Builders

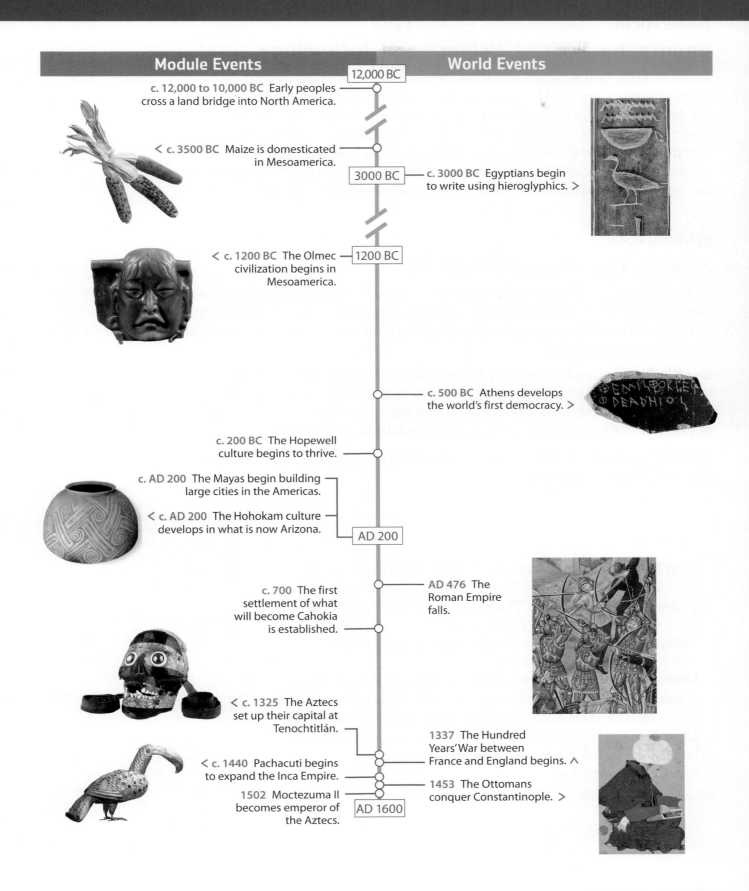

Module Events

12,000 BC

c. 12,000 to 10,000 BC Early peoples cross a land bridge into North America.

< **c. 3500 BC** Maize is domesticated in Mesoamerica.

3000 BC

< **c. 1200 BC** The Olmec civilization begins in Mesoamerica.

1200 BC

c. 200 BC The Hopewell culture begins to thrive.

c. AD 200 The Mayas begin building large cities in the Americas.

< **c. AD 200** The Hohokam culture develops in what is now Arizona.

AD 200

c. 700 The first settlement of what will become Cahokia is established.

< **c. 1325** The Aztecs set up their capital at Tenochtitlán.

< **c. 1440** Pachacuti begins to expand the Inca Empire.

1502 Moctezuma II becomes emperor of the Aztecs.

AD 1600

World Events

c. 3000 BC Egyptians begin to write using hieroglyphics. >

c. 500 BC Athens develops the world's first democracy. >

AD 476 The Roman Empire falls.

1337 The Hundred Years' War between France and England begins. ∧

1453 The Ottomans conquer Constantinople. >

Reading Social Studies

THEME FOCUS:

Geography, Politics, Science and Technology

In this module, you will read about the development of civilizations in Mesoamerica, a region that includes parts of Mexico and Central America; in the Andes, which are in South America; and in North America. As you read about these civilizations, you will learn about the politics and government that developed in different empires, and you will see how the geography and resources of the areas affected their way of life. You will also learn that these ancient civilizations made advancements in science and technology.

READING FOCUS:

Analyze Historical Information

History books are full of information. As you read, you are confronted with names, dates, places, terms, and descriptions on every page. Because you're faced with so much information, you don't want to have to deal with unimportant or untrue material in a history book.

Identify Relevant and Essential Information Information in a history book should be relevant, or related to the topic you're studying. It should also be essential, or necessary to understanding that topic. Anything that is not relevant or essential distracts from the important material you are studying.

The passage below contains some irrelevant and nonessential information, so that you can learn to identify it.

The Mayas

Who They Were The Maya (MY-ah) civilization developed in Mesoamerica. Early Mayas lived in the lowlands of this region beginning about 1000 BC. Thick forests covered most of the land, so the Mayas had to clear wooded areas for farmland. Today, there are many farms in the region that grow corn.

Communication The Mayas also developed a writing system. It was similar to Egyptian hieroglyphics. Symbols represented both objects and sounds. The Mayas created records, especially about the achievements of their kings, by carving symbols into large stone tablets. Today, most people use computers to record information.

The first sentence of the paragraph expresses the main idea. Anything that doesn't support this idea is not essential.

The last sentence does not support the main idea and is not essential.

This paragraph discusses Maya communication. Any other topics are irrelevant.

The use of computers has nothing to do with Maya communication. This sentence is irrelevant.

You Try It!

The following passage has some sentences that aren't relevant or essential to understanding the topic. Read the passage and identify those sentences.

The Maya Way of Life

Religion The Mayas worshipped many gods related to different aspects of their daily life. The most important god was the creator. This god would take many different forms. Other gods included a sun god, moon goddess, and maize god. One of the most important Aztec gods was the rain god. The Mayas believed their kings communicated with the gods.

Social Structure Most Mayas belonged to the lower classes as farming families. Farming families today aren't always as large as they once were. A portion of the crops grown were given as tribute to the ruler, the local lord, and other members of the ruling class. *Tribute* is a payment to a more powerful ruler or country. A *tribute* can also be a statement that shows respect. Most modern kings don't require tribute.

After you read the passage, answer the following questions.

1. Which sentence in the first paragraph is irrelevant to the topic? How can you tell?
2. Which three sentences in the second paragraph are not essential to learning about the Mayas? Do those sentences belong in this passage?

As you read this module, notice how the writers have left out information that is not essential or relevant to what you are reading.

Key Terms and People

Lesson 1
Mesoamerica
maize

Lesson 2
obsidian
Pacal
observatories
Popol Vuh

Lesson 3
causeways
codex
conquistadors
Hernán Cortés
Moctezuma II

Lesson 4
Pachacuti
Quechua
llamas
Atahualpa
Francisco Pizarro

Lesson 5
adobe
potlatch
wampum
Iroquois Confederacy

Geography and Early Cultures

The Big Idea

The landforms and climate of the Americas affected farming and the development of early cultures.

Main Ideas

- The geography of the Americas is varied, with a wide range of landforms.
- The first people to arrive in the Americas were hunter-gatherers.
- The development of farming led to early settlements in the Americas.

Key Terms

Mesoamerica
maize

If YOU were there . . .

You are a hunter-gatherer in North America. All of your life you have been moving south, following herds of animals. This year you have found a place where the climate is warmer and there are more kinds of plants to eat. Some people say this would be a good place to stay and make a permanent home. But others think you need to keep moving.

Do you think your people should keep going or settle down in this new place? Why?

Geography of the Americas

Two continents—North America and South America—make up the region we call the Americas. These two continents have a wide range of landforms and climates. Early peoples had to adapt to the varied environments as they spread throughout the region.

The northern continent, North America, has high mountains. These include the Rocky Mountains and the Appalachian Mountains. North America also has desert plateaus, grassy plains, and forests. The Mississippi River and its tributaries run through much of the central part of the continent. Look at a physical map to find the location of some of these physical features. In the northern part of the continent, the climate is cold and icy. Temperatures get warmer toward the south.

In the southern part of North America lies Mesoamerica. **Mesoamerica** is a region that includes the southern part of what is now Mexico and parts of the northern countries of Central America. Steamy rain forests cover some of this region. In some places, volcanoes rise above the forest. Their activity over the years has made the surrounding soil very fertile. Fertile mountain valleys, rivers, and a warm climate make Mesoamerica good for farming. In fact, the first farmers in the Americas domesticated plants in Mesoamerica.

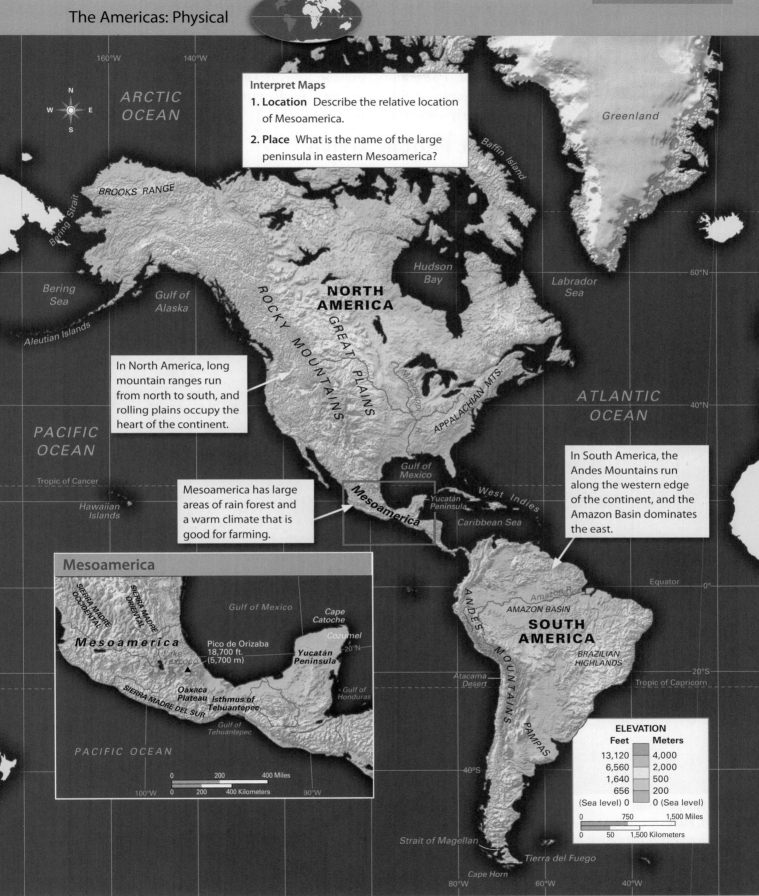

Explore ONLINE!

Interpret Maps

1. **Location** Describe the relative location of Mesoamerica.

2. **Place** What is the name of the large peninsula in eastern Mesoamerica?

ARCTIC OCEAN

Greenland

BROOKS RANGE

Baffin Island

Bering Strait

Bering Sea

Gulf of Alaska

Aleutian Islands

Hudson Bay

NORTH AMERICA

Labrador Sea

60°N

ROCKY MOUNTAINS

GREAT PLAINS

MISSISSIPPI R.

APPALACHIAN MTS.

ATLANTIC OCEAN

40°N

In North America, long mountain ranges run from north to south, and rolling plains occupy the heart of the continent.

PACIFIC OCEAN

Tropic of Cancer

Hawaiian Islands

Gulf of Mexico

Mesoamerica

Yucatán Peninsula

West Indies

Caribbean Sea

Mesoamerica has large areas of rain forest and a warm climate that is good for farming.

In South America, the Andes Mountains run along the western edge of the continent, and the Amazon Basin dominates the east.

Equator 0°

Amazon R.

ANDES MOUNTAINS

AMAZON BASIN

SOUTH AMERICA

BRAZILIAN HIGHLANDS

Atacama Desert

Tropic of Capricorn

20°S

PAMPAS

40°S

Strait of Magellan

Tierra del Fuego

Cape Horn

80°W   60°W   40°W

Mesoamerica

SIERRA MADRE OCCIDENTAL

SIERRA MADRE ORIENTAL

Mesoamerica

Gulf of Mexico

Cape Catoche

Cozumel

Pico de Orizaba 18,700 ft. (5,700 m)

Lake Texcoco

Yucatán Peninsula

20°N

SIERRA MADRE DEL SUR

Oaxaca Plateau

Isthmus of Tehuantepec

Gulf of Honduras

Gulf of Tehuantepec

PACIFIC OCEAN

0   200   400 Miles

0   200   400 Kilometers

100°W   90°W

ELEVATION

Feet	Meters
13,120	4,000
6,560	2,000
1,640	500
656	200
(Sea level) 0	0 (Sea level)

0   750   1,500 Miles

0   50   1,500 Kilometers

Reading Check
Compare What kinds of landforms and climates do North and South America have in common?

Like North America, South America has many different kinds of landforms. The towering Andes Mountains run along the western side of the continent. A narrow desert runs along the edge of rich fishing waters in the Pacific Ocean. East of the Andes lies the Amazon region—a huge, hot rain forest. The mighty Amazon River drains this region. As you will see, the geography of the Americas played an important role in the development of early societies there.

The First People Arrive

Scholars are not sure when the first people arrived in the Americas. Archaeologists, who study ancient civilizations, have uncovered sites throughout the Americas, from Washington state to Chile, containing early human remains. Most of these sites date back 10,000 to 14,000

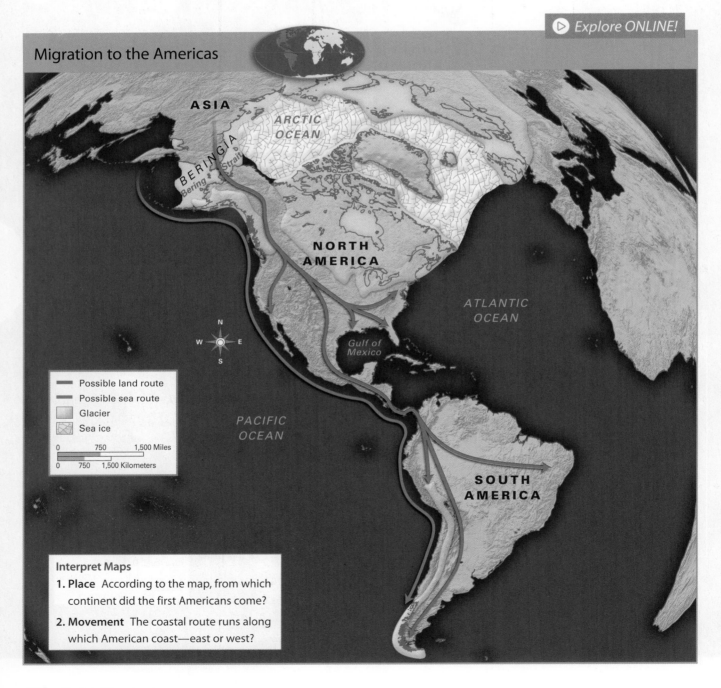

Explore ONLINE!

Migration to the Americas

Legend:
- Possible land route
- Possible sea route
- Glacier
- Sea ice

0 750 1,500 Miles
0 750 1,500 Kilometers

Interpret Maps

1. **Place** According to the map, from which continent did the first Americans come?

2. **Movement** The coastal route runs along which American coast—east or west?

years, but a few show signs of being much older. Some sites have been dated to 20,000 years ago. Scholars have suggested that humans may have reached the Americas even earlier than that. One archaeologist working in South Carolina, for example, thinks people lived in the region nearly 50,000 years ago, though other scholars dispute his findings. No one knows how these first Americans arrived in the region. Some scientists believe that they may have arrived in the Americas by boat, sailing along the coasts.

Most scientists agree that more early people reached the Americas between 12,000 and 15,000 years ago, during a worldwide ice age. The world's temperature dropped dramatically, and vast amounts of seawater turned to ice. This lowered the sea level enough that a strip of land was exposed between Asia and North America. People traveled across this strip and, over centuries, spread through North and South America.

Regardless of how they arrived, the first people to arrive in the Americas were hunter-gatherers. They hunted herds of large animals that wandered the land. These animals, including bison and huge woolly mammoths, provided the main food source. Early people also gathered fruits, nuts, and wild grains to eat. Early people didn't settle in one place very long because they were always looking for food.

Eventually, some early people began to settle down. They formed small settlements on the coasts of North and South America, where they fished and gathered food. As populations grew, people started to experiment with seeds.

Reading Check
Make Inferences
How do you think the geography of the Americas affected early peoples' search for food?

A man sits on a stack of maize in Mexico City. In the early Americas, maize was most widely grown among large urban populations.

Farming and Settlement

From their experiments with seeds, people eventually learned to farm. Farming allowed people to stop following animal herds and settle permanently in one place.

First Farming Settlements The first permanent farming settlements in the Americas appeared in Mesoamerica. This region had rich soils, warm temperatures, and plenty of rain. By 3500 BC, people in Mesoamerica were growing **maize** (MAYZ), or corn. Later, they learned to grow beans and squash. By growing these foods, settlements could support larger populations. More advanced societies grew, and people began to focus on activities such as building, trade, art, and organized religion. Eventually, settlements developed into towns and cities.

The Olmecs Around 1200 BC, the Olmecs (OHL-meks) settled in the lowlands along the Gulf of Mexico in what are today the

Views of Writing

Scientists have discovered an Olmec roller used for printing symbols. It may be evidence of the earliest writing system in the Americas. Some people don't believe the Olmecs had a written language. Scientists disagree on what defines a written language. Some think written language must include symbols that stand for sounds—not just for images.

Other scientists think a system of symbols is a form of written communication. The symbols do not have to represent sound or spoken language. These scientists think written communication is the same thing as written language.

Analyze Historical Sources
Which author believes that visual symbols can represent written language? Which part of the quotation makes this point?

"Even if you have symbols—like a light-bulb in a cartoon—that's not writing."

—archaeologist David Grove,
University of Florida, Gainesville

"We're not arguing that we have phonetics [sounds]. . . . But we say we do have logographs [symbols representing words], and we're arguing that the Maya copied this. We have a system here that goes back to the Olmec."

—anthropologist Mary E. D. Pohl,
Florida State University

southern Mexico states of Veracruz and Tabasco. They formed the first urban civilization in Mesoamerica. This region's climate is hot and humid. Abundant rainfall and rich, fertile soil made this a perfect area for the Olmecs to grow maize.

Most Olmecs lived in small villages, but some lived in larger towns. These towns were religious and government centers with temples and plazas. Impressive sculptures and buildings mark the Olmecs as the first complex civilization in the Americas. They built the first pyramids in the Americas. They also made sculptures of huge stone heads. Each head probably represented a different Olmec ruler. Other sculptures, such as jaguars, probably represented Olmec gods.

Another factor that marks the Olmec as a civilization is a system of writing. Scientists recently found an Olmec artifact with symbols on it. Researchers believe that the symbols may have been the first writing system in the Americas. The Olmecs may have also had a calendar.

The Olmec civilization also had a large trading network. Villages traded with each other and with other peoples farther away. The Olmecs may have even established a string of trading colonies along the Pacific coast. Through trade, the Olmecs got valuable goods, such as the stones they used for building and sculpture.

Olmec civilization ended around 400 BC. By then trade had spread Olmec influence across Mesoamerica. Later peoples were able to build on their achievements. Some also followed Olmec traditions.

Farming and the Growth of Other Civilizations Early civilizations also developed in other parts of the Americas. As in Mesoamerica, people in North and South America formed civilizations after they domesticated plants and learned how to farm.

About the time Mesoamericans started growing maize, South Americans in the Andes started growing potatoes. Later, maize farming spread south into the Andes from Mesoamerica. By about 2000 BC, South Americans were growing maize and beans as well as potatoes.

A number of small civilizations developed in South America, but the first major civilization began in the Andes. It is known as the Chavín (chah-VEEN) culture, and it lasted from about 900 to 200 BC. Its city was a major religious and trading center. The Chavín culture is known for its woven textiles, carved stone monuments, and pottery shaped like animals and humans.

Several hundred years after farming began in South America, maize farming also spread north from Mesoamerica. People began growing maize in what is now the southwestern United States. The dry climate made farming difficult there, so people learned to choose fertile soils and use

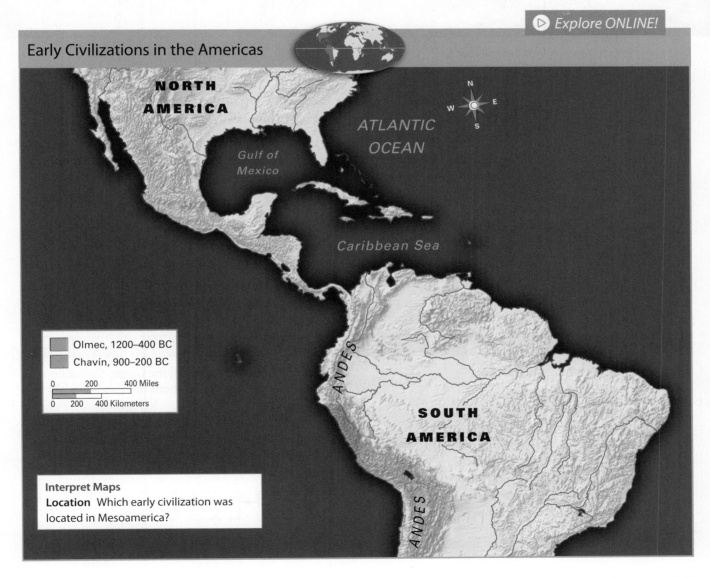

Explore ONLINE!

Early Civilizations in the Americas

NORTH AMERICA

ATLANTIC OCEAN

Gulf of Mexico

Caribbean Sea

ANDES

SOUTH AMERICA

ANDES

Olmec, 1200–400 BC

Chavín, 900–200 BC

0   200   400 Miles
0   200   400 Kilometers

Interpret Maps
Location Which early civilization was located in Mesoamerica?

By learning to farm, the people of the Americas no longer had to rely on hunting and gathering.

Reading Check
Find Main Ideas
How did farming influence settlement patterns in the Americas?

river water to irrigate their crops. Eventually, maize became an important crop to people in the region. It was the main food of people in hundreds of small villages.

The development of farming was important in the growth of civilizations all over the Americas. As with other peoples you have studied, a steady food supply led to population growth. Farming also encouraged people to establish permanent villages and cities.

Summary and Preview You have learned that geography affected settlement and farming in the Americas. Early civilizations, such as the Olmec and the Chavín, developed there. In the next lesson, you will learn about a later civilization influenced by the Olmecs—the Mayas.

Lesson 1 Assessment

Review Ideas, Terms, and People

1. a. **Recall** Where is Mesoamerica?

   b. **Explain** In what ways is the geography of Mesoamerica good for agriculture?

2. a. **Identify** What landform do most scientists think early people crossed to reach America?

   b. **Make Inferences** Why do you think scientists aren't sure how the first people came to the Americas?

3. a. **Identify** What was the first crop domesticated in Mesoamerica?

   b. **Predict Effects** How might the Olmec civilization have influenced later civilizations in Mesoamerica?

Critical Thinking

4. **Analyze Effects** Draw the graphic organizer. Use it to show how the development of maize farming laid the foundation for cultural advances.

The Mayas

The Big Idea

The Maya civilization was characterized by great cities, trade, and achievements in art, science, and technology.

Main Ideas

- Geography affected early Maya civilization.

- The Maya Classic Age was characterized by great cities, trade, and warfare.

- A complex class structure shaped roles in Maya society.

- The Mayas worshipped many gods and believed their kings communicated with them.

- The Maya culture made great achievements in art, science, math, and writing.

- Maya civilization declined, and historians have several theories for why.

Key Terms and People

obsidian
Pacal
observatories
Popol Vuh

Reading Check
Find Main Ideas
What were two ways in which the early Mayas relied on their physical environment?

If YOU were there . . .

You live in a village in the lowlands of Mesoamerica. Your family members have always been weavers, and now your aunts are teaching you to weave cloth from the cotton grown by nearby farmers. Traders from other areas often pass through your village. They tell wonderful stories about strange animals and sights they see in their travels. After talking to the traders who buy your cloth, you begin to think about becoming a trader, too.

Why might you want to become a trader?

Geography Affects Early Mayas

The Maya (MY-ah) civilization developed in Mesoamerica. Early Mayas lived in the lowlands of this region beginning about 1000 BC. Thick forests covered most of the land, so the Mayas had to clear wooded areas for farmland. Like earlier Mesoamericans, the Mayas grew maize and other crops.

Although the thick forests made farming hard, they provided valuable resources. Forest animals such as deer and monkeys were a source of food. In addition, trees and other plants made good building materials. For example, the Mayas used wood poles and vines, along with mud, to build their houses.

The early Mayas lived in small villages. Eventually, these villages started trading with one another. They traded goods such as cloth and **obsidian**, a sharp, glasslike volcanic rock that came from different parts of Mesoamerica. As trade helped support larger populations, villages grew. By about AD 200, the Mayas were building large cities in the Americas.

Obsidian, valued for its sharp edges and considered sacred by the Mayas, was mined in the mountains and traded throughout the Maya world.

Maya Classic Age

The Maya civilization reached its height between about AD 250 and 900. Historians call this period the Classic Age. During the Classic Age, Maya civilization spread to the Yucatán Peninsula and included more than 40 cities of 5,000 to 50,000 people each.

Trade Maya cities in the highlands traded with those in the lowlands. In this way, people all over Maya territory got things that they didn't have nearby.

Different goods were available in different areas of Mesoamerica during the Classic Age. For example, the warm lowlands were

Jade was mined in the mountains and traded to lowland cities.

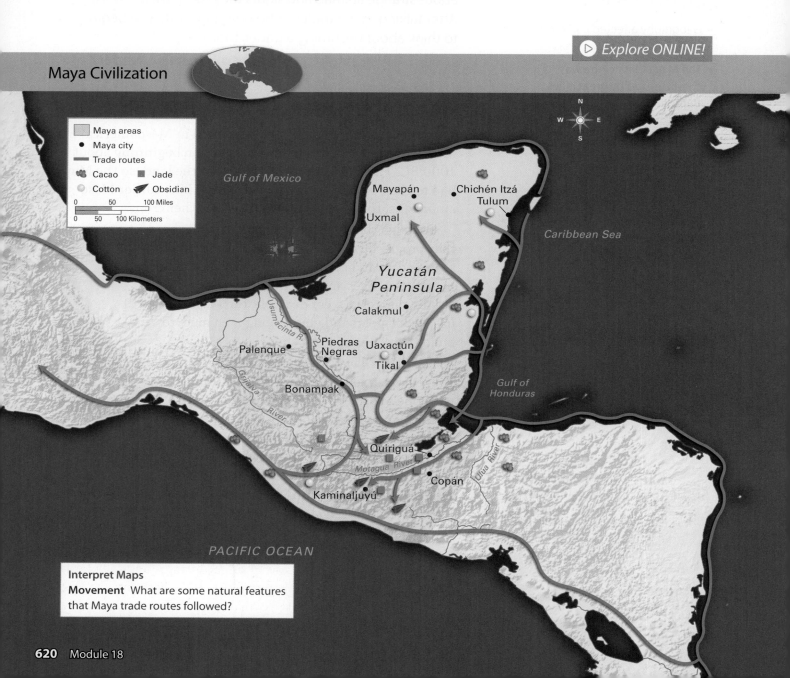

Maya Civilization

Explore ONLINE!

Maya areas
● **Maya city**
— **Trade routes**
🌰 **Cacao** ▪ **Jade**
○ **Cotton** ⟤ **Obsidian**

0 50 100 Miles
0 50 100 Kilometers

Gulf of Mexico

Mayapán

Chichén Itzá
Tulum

Uxmal

Caribbean Sea

Yucatán Peninsula

Calakmul

Usumacinta R.

Piedras
Negras   Uaxactún

Palenque

Tikal

Grijalva River

Bonampak

Gulf of Honduras

Quiriguá

Motagua River

Copán

Ulúa River

Kaminaljuyú

PACIFIC OCEAN

Interpret Maps
Movement What are some natural features that Maya trade routes followed?

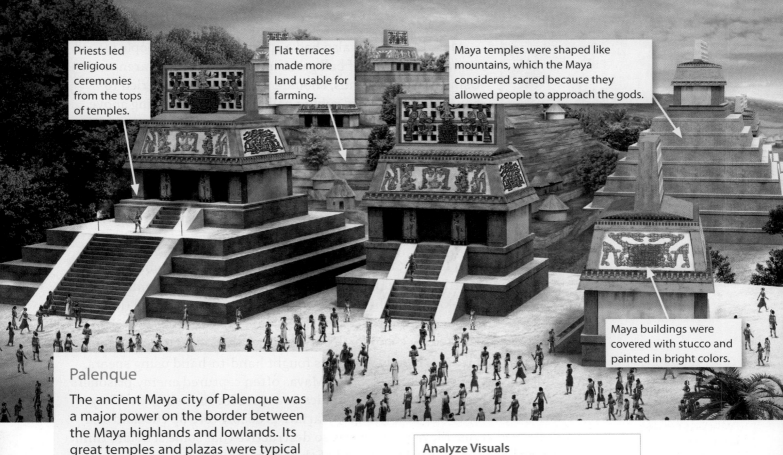

Priests led religious ceremonies from the tops of temples.

Flat terraces made more land usable for farming.

Maya temples were shaped like mountains, which the Maya considered sacred because they allowed people to approach the gods.

Maya buildings were covered with stucco and painted in bright colors.

Palenque

The ancient Maya city of Palenque was a major power on the border between the Maya highlands and lowlands. Its great temples and plazas were typical of the Classic Age of Maya civilization.

Analyze Visuals
In what ways might Palenque's setting have helped the city? In what ways might it have hurt the city?

good for growing cotton, rubber trees, and cacao (kah-KOW) beans, the source of chocolate. Cacao beans had great value. Chocolate was known as the food of rulers and of the gods. The Mayas even used cacao beans as currency.

Lowland crops didn't grow well in the cool highlands. Instead, the highlands had valuable stones such as jade and obsidian. People carried these and other products along Maya trade routes.

Cities Maya cities had many grand buildings, including large stone pyramids, temples, and palaces. Maya artists decorated temples and palaces with carvings and colorful paintings. Some of these buildings honored local Maya kings. For example, in the city of Palenque (pah-LENG-kay), a temple honored the king **Pacal** (pah-KAHL). Pacal had the temple built to record his achievements as a ruler. He became king of the Maya city of Palenque when he was just 12 years old. As king, Pacal led many important community events, such as religious dances and public meetings. When he died, he was buried at the bottom of the pyramid-shaped Temple of the Inscriptions.

In addition to temples and palaces, the Mayas built structures to improve city life. Builders paved large plazas for public gatherings, and they built canals to control the flow of water through their cities. Farmers shaped nearby hillsides into flat terraces so they could grow crops on them.

Tikal was one of the most powerful Maya cities. More than 60,000 people lived there, and its central plaza featured impressive structures.

Reading Check
Summarize
What were two ways Maya cities interacted with each other?

Most Maya cities also had a special ball court. People played or watched a type of ball game in these large stone arenas. Using only their heads, shoulders, or hips, players tried to bounce a heavy, hard rubber ball through a stone ring above their heads. Players weren't allowed to use their hands or feet. The winners were awarded jewels and clothing. The losers were sometimes killed. This ball game was one that the Mayas had picked up from Olmec traditions.

The Maya cities were really city-states. Each city-state had its own government and its own king. No single ruler united the many cities into one empire.

Warfare Among Cities Conflicts between cities often led to fighting. Maya cities usually battled each other to gain power and land. For example, the city of Tikal (tee-KAHL) fought many battles with its rival Calakmul (kah-lahk-MOOL). Both cities wanted to control a smaller city that lay between them. Power shifted back and forth between the two larger cities for years.

Maya warfare was bloody. Warriors fought hand-to-hand using spears, flint knives, and wooden clubs. The Mayas often captured enemy prisoners and killed them in religious ceremonies as a sacrifice to their gods. They burned enemy towns and villages. Warfare probably tore up the land and destroyed crops. Maya warfare was so destructive that some scholars think it may have contributed to the end of the Maya civilization.

Roles in Maya Society

Maya society had a complex class structure that affected people's social, political, and economic roles. As you might expect, life for the upper social classes differed greatly from life for the lower classes.

Upper Class The upper class of Maya society included different groups of people. The king held the highest position in society. The Mayas believed their rulers were related to the gods. For this reason, rulers were often involved in religious ceremonies. They also led battles. As the richest people in Maya society, rulers had beautiful clothing and jewelry. Kings wore huge feather headdresses and capes of cotton, jaguar skins, and feathers.

Each of the major city-states, or political units, had its own ruling elite that held all political, religious, and economic power. Members of the upper class controlled trade and served as governors, military commanders, scholars, and administrators. A class of lower-level elite served as military officers, engineers, administrators, and merchants.

Priests were also part of the upper class. Priests were usually born into their role in Maya society. They led religious ceremonies. They were also the most educated people. Priests used their knowledge of astronomy and math to plan the best times for religious ceremonies.

Professional warriors fought battles against other Maya cities. In battle, these warriors wore animal headdresses, jade jewelry, and jaguar-skin capes. They painted their bodies red and black.

A Maya King and His Court

The king and his court were the center of Maya government and religious life. This vase painting shows a Maya king relaxing with some of his servants. Kings enjoyed all the luxuries of Maya life, such as music, fine clothing and food, and even chocolate.

The king is gazing at this mirror, which the Mayas believed held magical powers.

A bodyguard stands behind the king.

The fly whisk in the king's hand is a symbol of authority.

These vases held a chocolate drink, a favorite of Maya nobles.

Analyze Visuals
What about the king indicates he is an important person?

Merchants directed trade among the cities and organized the distribution of goods. They also supervised the people who carried goods between cities. Together, the members of the upper class controlled the politics, religion, and economy in Maya society.

Lower Classes Most Mayas belonged to the lower classes as farming families. They worked a noble's land and farmed a small plot for themselves. A portion of the crops grown were given as tribute to the ruler, the local lord, and other members of the ruling class. *Tribute* is a payment to a more powerful ruler or country. Crops were not the only form of tribute required. If lower-class Mayas made goods for trade, they had to give some of the goods as tribute. They also had to work to build temples, palaces, and roads.

Mayas in the lower classes lived in small houses outside the cities. Girls learned from their mothers how to cook, make yarn, and weave. Women cared for children and taught them skills and moral values at home. Most children also helped the family by working in the fields or in the home.

Men crafted household tools such as knives. They had to provide food for their family, so they also spent a lot of time hunting and farming. They kept small home gardens and worked together to farm larger fields.

Reading Check
Analyze Causes
How might one become a slave in Maya society?

Academic
Vocabulary
aspects parts

Reading Check
Form Generalizations
Why did the Mayas want to please their gods?

If captured in battle, a lower-class man usually became a slave. Orphans, slaves' children, and people who owed money also became slaves. Slaves had to carry trade goods between cities. They also served upper-class Mayas by working as farmers or household servants.

Although the lower class supported the upper class with food and labor, the upper class also helped the lower class. For example, upper-class Mayas led the religious ceremonies that were part of daily life for all Mayas.

Religious Traditions

The Mayas worshipped many gods related to different **aspects** of their daily life. The most important god was the creator. This god would take many different forms. Other gods included a sun god, moon goddess, and maize god. The Mayas believed their kings communicated with the gods.

According to Maya beliefs, the gods could be helpful or harmful, so people tried to please the gods to get their help. The Mayas believed their gods needed blood to prevent disasters or the end of the world. All people offered blood to the gods by piercing their tongue or skin. The Mayas sometimes held special ceremonies to give blood at events such as births, weddings, and funerals.

On special occasions the Mayas believed they needed extra amounts of blood. On these occasions they made human sacrifices to their gods. They usually used prisoners captured in battle for this ritual. A priest would offer human hearts to stone carvings of gods, usually at a temple.

This photo shows the observatory at the Maya city of Chichén Itzá.

Cultural Achievements

The Mayas' many artistic and architectural skills are reflected in their sculpture and in their temples. Maya achievements also included discoveries in science and math, as well as developments in writing.

Art and Architecture Some of the best-known Maya art is their sculpture and their jade and gold jewelry. They carved stone sculptures of kings or gods for their cities.

Maya cities showed the talent of their architects and builders. The Mayas built cities without using metal tools. They didn't even have wheeled vehicles to carry supplies. Instead, workers used obsidian tools to cut limestone into blocks. Then, to move the giant blocks, workers rolled them over logs and lifted them with ropes. It took many workers to build Maya cities, perhaps the most recognizable Maya achievement.

Science and Math Maya achievements in science and math were just as important as their achievements in art and architecture. The Mayas built **observatories**, or buildings to study astronomy, so their priests could study the stars. Maya astronomers figured out that a year is about 365 days long. They also learned about the cycles of the moon and how to predict eclipses.

Partly based on their discoveries in astronomy, the Mayas developed calendars. They had a religious calendar to plan religious events. The Mayas used a different calendar for agriculture. It had symbols for different months tied to farming activities such as planting or harvesting. These activities matched changes in the seasons. The Maya calendar was more accurate than the calendar used in Europe at that time.

To go along with their calendars, the Mayas created a number system that included some new concepts in math. For example, the Mayas were among the first people with a symbol for zero. The Mayas used their number system to record important dates in their history.

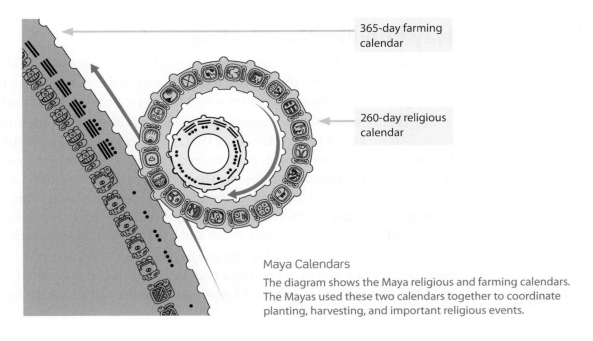

365-day farming calendar

260-day religious calendar

Maya Calendars

The diagram shows the Maya religious and farming calendars. The Mayas used these two calendars together to coordinate planting, harvesting, and important religious events.

Writing and Oral Traditions The Mayas also developed a writing system. It was similar to Egyptian hieroglyphics. Symbols represented both objects and sounds. The Mayas created records, especially about the achievements of their kings, by carving symbols into large stone tablets. They also wrote in bark-paper books.

Stories and poetry were passed down orally from one generation to the next. After the Spanish arrived, Maya legends and history were written in a book called the *Popol Vuh* (poh-pohl VOO). This book provides valuable information about the Mayas.

Reading Check
Find Main Ideas
What activities did the Maya calendar regulate?

Historical Source

A Maya Carving

This carving comes from the palace at Yaxchilán (yahsh-chee-LAHN). The Mayas recorded historical events on carvings like this one. Historians can now translate most Maya writing. They study the pictures and writings to learn about events in Maya history.

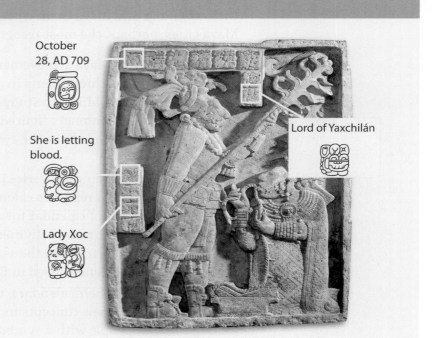

October 28, AD 709

She is letting blood.

Lady Xoc

Lord of Yaxchilán

Analyze Historical Sources
Who are the people in this carving?

Maya Civilization Declines

Maya civilization began to collapse in the 900s. People stopped building temples and other structures. They left the cities and moved back to the countryside. Historians aren't sure why, but they do have some theories.

One theory says that increased warfare brought about the end of the Maya Classic Age. A related theory is that, as cities grew, perhaps the Mayas could not grow enough food to feed everyone. Growing the same crops year after year might have left the soil too weak for farming. As a result, competition between cities for land may have increased. This competition could have led to even more warfare than before. Increased warfare would have destroyed more crops and made farming more difficult.

Another possible cause of the decline of Maya civilization is the demands Maya kings made on their people. Kings forced people to build huge temples or farm for them. Maybe people didn't want to work for

Academic Vocabulary
rebel to fight against authority

Reading Check
Make Inferences
Why do you think scientists aren't sure what caused the end of the Classic Age of Maya civilization?

the kings. They might have **rebelled** or left the cities because of these demands. Some historians also think climate might have played a role in the collapse of Maya civilization. Scientists have learned that the region suffered from droughts for about 150 years. These droughts took place about the time the Mayas moved away from their cities. A drier climate and droughts would have made it hard to grow enough food to feed everyone in the cities.

Most researchers agree that there was probably no single event that caused the end of the Classic Age. More likely, a mix of several factors led to the decline of the Maya civilization.

Summary and Preview You have learned that the Mayas built a great civilization with a complex social structure, but it collapsed for what were probably several reasons. The Mayas left behind many records of their society and history. In the next lesson, you will learn about another great empire that developed in the Americas—the Aztecs.

Lesson 2 Assessment

Review Ideas, Terms, and People

1. **a. Recall** What resources did the Mayas get from the forest?
   b. Make Inferences How might the Mayas have used obsidian?
2. **a. Identify** Who was an important king of Palenque?
   b. Make Generalizations Why did Maya cities fight each other?
3. **a. Identify** Who were members of the upper class in Maya society?
   b. Explain In what ways did lower-class Mayas support upper-class Mayas?
4. **a. Describe** What did the Mayas do to try to please their gods?
   b. Explain Why did the Mayas practice human sacrifice?
5. **a. Recall** What did the Mayas study in observatories?
   b. Draw Conclusions What do you think was the most impressive Maya achievement?

6. **a. Describe** What happened to Maya civilization in the 900s?
   b. Analyze In what way did warfare, drought, and the growth of cities possibly affect Maya civilization?
   c. Elaborate What might scientists study to find out about the end of Maya civilization?

Critical Thinking

7. **Synthesize** Draw a diagram like the one here. Use it to identify some major achievements of the Mayas.

Literature in History

Maya Literature

Word Help

invoked called on
venerate respect greatly
conferred discussed
aimlessly without purpose

❶ Why do the gods wish to make human beings?

❷ What do the gods use to make the body? What happens to it?

About the Reading *In the language of the Mayas,* Popol Vuh *means "Council Book." This work contains both the myths and the history of a group of Mayas. It was first used by Maya kings and lords to help them govern their people. Today, the* Popol Vuh *helps modern readers understand how the Mayas lived and what they believed. The following myth, for example, tells us how the gods tried to create people several times before they eventually succeeded.*

As You Read Pay close attention to the behavior of the creator-gods.

From *The Book of the People: Popol Vuh*
translated by Delia Goetz and Sylvanus Griswold Morley

For this reason another attempt had to be made to create and make men by the Creator, the Maker, and the Forefathers.

"Let us try again! Already dawn draws near: Let us make him who shall nourish and sustain us! ❶ What shall we do to be invoked, in order to be remembered on earth? We have already tried with our first creations, our first creatures; but we could not make them praise and venerate us. So, then, let us try to make obedient, respectful beings who will nourish and sustain us." Thus they spoke.

Then was the creation and the formation. Of earth, of mud, they made [man's] flesh. But they saw that it was not good. It melted away, it was soft, did not move, had no strength, it fell down, it was limp, it could not move its head, its face fell to one side, its sight was blurred, it could not look behind. At first it spoke, but had no mind. Quickly it soaked in the water and could not stand. ❷

And the Creator and the Maker said: "Let us try again because our creatures will not be able to walk nor multiply. Let us consider this," they said.

Then they broke up and destroyed their work and their creation. And they said: "What shall we do to perfect it, in order that our worshipers, our invokers, will be successful?"

Thus they spoke when they conferred again: "Let us say again to Xpiyacoc, Xmucané, Hunahpú-Vuch, Hunahpú-Utiú: 'Cast your lot again. Try to create again.'". . .

And instantly the figures were made of wood. They looked like men, talked like men, and populated the surface of the earth.

They existed and multiplied; they had daughters, they had sons, these wooden figures; but they did not have souls, nor minds, they did not remember their Creator, their Maker; they walked on all fours, aimlessly.

Word Help

annihilated destroyed

deluged flooded

resin a gooey substance that comes from trees

gouged made a hole

❸ The Heart of Heaven is the father-god of the Mayas.

❹ *In your own words, explain what happened to the creatures.*

❺ *This myth explains the origin, or beginning, of what animal?*

Monkeys were common subjects in Maya carvings.

They no longer remembered the Heart of Heaven ❸ and therefore they fell out of favor. It was merely a trial, an attempt at man. At first they spoke, but their face was without expression; their feet and hands had no strength; they had no blood, nor substance, nor moisture, nor flesh; their cheeks were dry, their feet and hands were dry, and their flesh was yellow.

Therefore, they no longer thought of their Creator nor their Maker, nor of those who made them and cared for them.

These were the first men who existed in great numbers on the face of the earth.

Immediately the wooden figures were annihilated, destroyed, broken up, and killed.

A flood was brought about by the Heart of Heaven; a great flood was formed which fell on the heads of the wooden creatures. . . .

But those that they had made, that they had created, did not think, did not speak with their Creator, their Maker. And for this reason they were killed, they were deluged. A heavy resin fell from the sky. The one called Xecotco-vach came and gouged out their eyes; Camalotz came and cut off their heads; Cotzbalam came and devoured their flesh. Tucumbalam came, too, and broke and mangled their bones and their nerves, and ground and crumbled their bones. . . . ❹

So was the ruin of the men who had been created and formed, the men made to be destroyed and annihilated; the mouths and faces of all of them were mangled.

And it is said that their descendants are the monkeys which now live in the forests; these are all that remain of them because their flesh was made only of wood by the Creator and the Maker.

❺ And therefore the monkey looks like man, and is an example of a generation of men which were created and made but were only wooden figures.

Connect Literature to History

1. **Evaluate** According to Maya beliefs, the gods could be helpful or harmful, so people tried to please the gods to get their help. Are the gods in this myth helpful or harmful? Explain your answer.

2. **Analyze** By studying Maya records, archaeologists are learning about the achievements of the Mayas. What have you learned about the Mayas by reading this "record" of their life and society?

The Aztec Empire

The Big Idea

The Aztecs developed complex social, religious, artistic, and scientific systems in their empire in central Mexico.

Main Ideas

- The Aztecs built an empire through warfare and trade, and created an impressive capital city in Mesoamerica.
- Aztec society was divided by social roles and by class.
- Aztec religion required human sacrifice for keeping the gods happy.
- The Aztecs had many achievements in science, art, and language.
- Hernán Cortés conquered the Aztec Empire.

Key Terms and People

causeways
codex
conquistadors
Hernán Cortés
Moctezuma II

If YOU were there . . .

You live in a village in southeast Mexico that is ruled by the powerful Aztec Empire. Each year your village must send many baskets of corn to the emperor. You have to dig gold for him, too. One day some strangers arrive by sea. They tell you they want to overthrow the emperor. They ask for your help.

Should you help the strangers? Why or why not?

The Aztecs Build an Empire

The first Aztecs were farmers from northern Mexico. In about the 1100s, they migrated south. When they arrived in central Mexico, they found that other tribes had taken all the good farmland. All that was left for the Aztecs was a swampy island in the middle of Lake Texcoco (tays-KOH-koh). To survive, the Aztecs hired themselves out as skilled fighters.

War, Tribute, and Trade War was a key factor in the Aztecs' rise to power. The fierce Aztec warriors conquered many towns. In addition, the Aztecs sometimes made alliances, or partnerships, to build their empire. For example, in the late 1420s the Aztecs formed a secret alliance with two other cities on Lake Texcoco. With their allies' help, they defeated the other towns around the lake.

The Aztecs made people they conquered pay tribute with goods such as cotton, gold, or food. This system was the basis of the Aztec economy.

The Aztecs also controlled a huge trade network. Goods were exchanged for items such as cacao, tiny gold nuggets, beautiful feathers, or even cloth or tin, rather than for a standard currency. Most towns in the empire had a market where local farmers and artisans brought their goods to trade. One enormous market near the capital drew buyers and sellers from all over the Aztec Empire. Merchants carried luxury goods such as gems and rare foods to sell there. Because these merchants dealt with people in many parts of the empire, the emperors used them as spies. These spy merchants reported trouble building in the empire.

War, tribute, and trade made the Aztecs rich. As they grew rich, they grew even stronger and conquered more people. By the early 1500s, they ruled the most powerful state in Mesoamerica.

Geographical Challenges Nowhere was the Aztec Empire's power and wealth more visible than in its capital, Tenochtitlán (tay-NAWCH-teet-LAHN). To build this amazing city, the Aztecs had to overcome many geographical challenges.

The city's island location made travel and trade difficult. To make it easier to get to and from their city, the Aztecs built three wide **causeways**—raised roads across water or wet ground—to connect the island to the shore. The causeways were made of rocks covered with dirt. The Aztecs also built a stone aqueduct, or channel, to bring fresh water to the city because the water surrounding it was undrinkable.

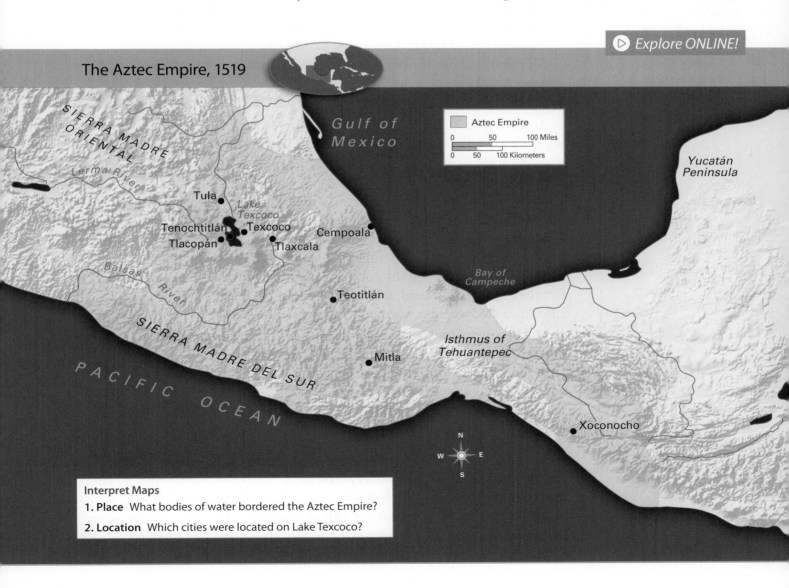

Explore ONLINE!

The Aztec Empire, 1519

Interpret Maps

1. **Place** What bodies of water bordered the Aztec Empire?

2. **Location** Which cities were located on Lake Texcoco?

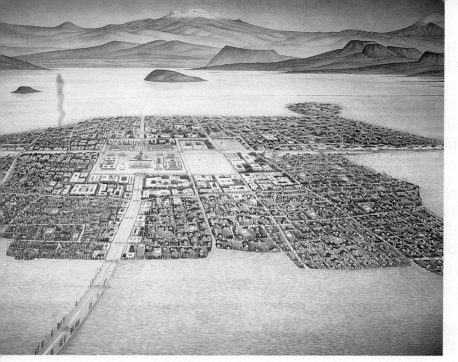

The Aztecs' magnificent capital, Tenochtitlán, was built on an island in Lake Texcoco.

Reading Check
Find Main Ideas
What was one key factor in the Aztecs' rise to power?

Geography also posed agricultural challenges. People who lived in the mountains had to deal with cold weather and little rain. People who lived at lower elevations faced a dry season and a rainy season. In Tenochtitlán, there wasn't even any land to farm on. Farmers had to build "floating gardens," or *chinampas*, by putting soil on rafts in Lake Texcoco.

Through the Aztecs' efforts, Tenochtitlán became the greatest city in the Americas. It had huge temples, a busy market, clean streets, and a magnificent palace. The first Europeans in the city were stunned by what they saw.

"We were amazed . . . on account of the great towers and cues [temples] and buildings rising from the water, and all built of masonry. . . . I do not know how to describe it, seeing things as we did that had never been heard of or seen before, not even dreamed about."

–Bernal Díaz del Castillo, from *The True History of the Conquest of New Spain*

At its height, Tenochtitlán was one of the world's largest cities, with somewhere between 200,000 and 400,000 people.

Aztec Society

People in Aztec society had clearly defined roles. These roles, along with social class, determined how Aztec men and women lived. Marriages were generally arranged by parents or other relatives. Married couples lived in their own homes or with relatives. Often, families lived in organized groups called *calpullis* (kahl-POOH-yees). A *calpulli* was a community of families that shared land, schools, and a temple. Each *calpulli* elected a leader who took orders from the king.

Mothers were in charge of teaching their daughters the skills they would need to maintain a household in later life. Fathers undertook the education of their sons, teaching them the skills and values they would need as adults. Older children might also be sent to school.

Kings and Nobles The king was the most important member of the Aztec society. The king lived in a great palace that had gardens, a zoo, and an aviary, or large enclosure, full of beautiful birds. Some 3,000 servants attended to the king's every need. Of these servants, 300

Kings
Aztec kings ruled the empire and lived in luxury.

did nothing but tend to the animals in the zoo. Three hundred additional servants tended to the birds in the aviary! Other servants fed and entertained the emperor.

The king was in charge of law, trade and tribute, and warfare. These were huge responsibilities, and the king couldn't have managed them without people to help. These people, including tax collectors and judges, were Aztec nobles. Noble positions were passed down from fathers to their sons. Young nobles went to special schools to learn the responsibilities of government officials, military leaders, or priests.

Priests and Warriors Just below the king and his nobles were priests and warriors. Priests had great influence and many duties, including

- keeping calendars and deciding when to plant crops or perform ceremonies
- passing down Aztec history and stories to keep traditions alive
- performing various religious ceremonies, including human sacrifice

Aztec warriors also had many duties. They fought fiercely to capture victims for religious sacrifices. Partly because they played this role in religious life, warriors had many privileges and were highly respected. Warriors were also respected for the wealth they brought to the empire. They fought to conquer new lands and people, bringing more tribute and trade goods to enrich the Aztec civilization.

Warriors

Warriors fought to conquer other peoples and capture victims for sacrifice.

DOCUMENT-BASED INVESTIGATION   Historical Source

An Aztec Festival

The Aztecs often used the occasion of the crowning of a new king to remind the leaders of their conquered territories just who the true masters were. An observer in Tenochtitlán recalled one such event.

Analyze Historical Sources
Do you think Fray Diego Durán admired the Aztecs? Why or why not?

"The intentions of these Mexicans [Aztecs] in preparing a festival . . . was to make known their king, and to ensure that their enemies . . . should be terrorized and filled with fear; and that they should know, by the . . . wealth of jewels and other presents, given away at the ceremonies, how great was the abundance of Mexico, its valor and its excellence. Finally, all was based on ostentation [extravagance] and vain glory, with the object of being feared, as the owners of all the riches of the earth and of its finest provinces. To this end they ordered these feasts and ceremonies so splendidly."

—Fray Diego Durán, from *Historia de Las Indias de Nueva España e Islas de la Tierra Firme*

Merchants and Artisans Not really members of the upper class, merchants and artisans fell just below priests and warriors in Aztec society. Merchants gathered goods from all over Mesoamerica and sold them in the main market. By controlling trade in the empire, they became very rich. Many used their wealth to build large, impressive houses and to send their sons to special schools.

Artisans
Skilled artisans made a wide variety of goods that people needed.

Like merchants, most artisans were also rich and important. They made goods such as beautiful feather headdresses and gold jewelry, which they sold at high prices. Many of the richest artisans lived in Tenochtitlán. Other artisans, who lived outside the capital and made items for everyday use, lived more like the lower class. Artisans from other tribes often sent crafts to the Aztecs as tribute.

Farmers and Slaves Farmers and slaves were in the lower class of Aztec society. However, some of these people could improve their lives and positions by becoming warriors in the army. They could also study at special schools.

Most of the empire's people were farmers who grew maize, beans, and a few other crops. Farmers did not own their land, and they were very poor. They had to pay so much in tribute that they often found it tough to survive. Farmers lived outside Tenochtitlán in huts made of sticks and mud, and wore rough capes.

The poor could decide to become what were called pawns. In Aztec society, pawns were people who sold themselves to rich families to work for a certain amount of time. Pawns' rights were protected by Aztec law.

No one in the Aztec Empire suffered as much as slaves did. Some people were forced into slavery for not paying their debts. A debtor might choose to sell himself or his children into slavery to pay the debt owed. Other people were enslaved as a punishment for committing certain crimes or for failing to pay tribute. Most slaves were people captured in battle. Captives were frequently sacrificed to the gods.

Aztec slaves had the right to marry and to have children. Their children were not born into slavery. Slaves could also buy their own freedom. Slave owners could not sell their slaves, and when a slave owner died, his or her slaves were often freed.

Aztec Religion

The Aztecs believed gods ruled all parts of life. Their gods' powers could be seen in nature, such as in trees or storms, and in great people, such as kings or ancestors.

Like other Mesoamericans, the Aztecs always tried to please their gods. They believed sacrifice was necessary to keep the gods strong and the world safe.

Farmers
Most Aztecs were farmers who lived in simple huts.

Reading Check
Summarize
What groups of people were in the upper class in Aztec society?

The Aztecs worshipped hundreds of gods. Two of the most important were Tlaloc and Huitzilopochtli, who are shown here.

Huitzilopochtli was the Aztec god of war. The Aztecs believed he made the sun rise. The eyes of this statue of Huitzilopochtli are made of shell and obsidian.

Tlaloc was the Aztec god of rain. The Aztecs believed he made the rain fall. A mask of Tlaloc decorates this vessel.

Aztecs made their greatest number of sacrifices to the war god Huitzilopochtli (wee-tsee-loh-POHSHT-lee) and the rain god Tlaloc (TLAH-lohk). The Aztecs believed the former made the sun rise every day, and the latter made the rain fall. Without them, their crops would die, and they would have no food.

To prevent this, Aztec priests led bloody ceremonies on the top of the Great Temple in Tenochtitlán. These priests cut themselves to give their blood to the gods.

Priests also sacrificed human victims to their gods. Many of the victims for these sacrifices were warriors from other tribes who had been captured in battle. Priests would sacrifice these victims to "feed" their gods human hearts and blood, which they thought would make the gods strong. Aztec priests sacrificed as many as 10,000 victims a year in religious ceremonies.

Reading Check
Find Main Ideas
Why was human sacrifice part of Aztec religion?

Science, Art, and Language

The Aztecs valued learning and art. Aztec scientific achievements, artistic traditions, and language contributed to their culture.

Achievements in Math and Science The Aztecs made several advances in science and mathematics. Many of these they accomplished by building on the achievements of the peoples they conquered. The Aztec system of

Aztec artists were very skilled. They created detailed and brightly colored items such as the ones you see here. Many were used in religious ceremonies.

This mask represented the god Quetzalcoatl. It is made of turquoise, shell, and wood.

This modern drawing shows the Aztec calendar with brightly painted colors.

tribute and their large trading network allowed them to learn skills from people all over the empire. For example, they learned how to build their *chinampas* from neighboring tribes.

The Aztecs created a numbering system that allowed them to keep track of land holdings and measurements. Historians have also found evidence that the Aztecs used multiplication, division, and the basic features of geometry. They also studied astronomy and created a calendar much like the Maya one. The calendar helped the Aztecs choose the best days for ceremonies, for battles, or for planting and harvesting crops. The Aztecs also knew many different uses for plants. For example, they knew of more than 100 plants that could be used as medicines.

Artistic Traditions The Aztecs also had a rich artistic tradition that included architecture, sculpture, and jewelry. Both the architecture and the sculpture made use of stone. Workers built bridges and lined canals with stone. Carpenters and stonecutters built huge pyramid-shaped stone temples. Hundreds of these temples stood in Tenochtitlán.

Talented Aztec artisans used turquoise mosaics to decorate knife handles and masks. Artisans also used gold and colorful feathers to make jewelry. Aztec women wove cloth from cotton and other fibers, and embroidered it with colorful designs.

Writing and Literature The Aztecs had a complex writing system. They kept written historical records. The records were written down in books made up of separate pages. Another name for this type of ancient book is a **codex** (KOH-deks). Many of the pages of Aztec books were made of bark or animal skins.

In addition to their written records, the Aztecs had a strong oral tradition. They considered fine speeches very important, and they also enjoyed riddles. Knowing the answers to riddles showed that one had paid attention in school.

Stories about ancestors and gods formed another part of the Aztec oral tradition. The Aztecs told these stories to their children, passing them down from one generation to the next. After the Spanish conquered the Aztec Empire, these stories were written down. Much of what historians know about the Aztecs they learned from these written stories.

Reading Check
Summarize
What was one purpose of the Aztec oral tradition?

Cortés Conquers the Aztecs

In the late 1400s, Spanish explorers and soldiers arrived in the Americas. The soldiers, or **conquistadors** (kahn-kees-tuh-DOHRS), came to explore new lands, search for gold, and spread their Catholic religion.

Cortés and Moctezuma A small group of conquistadors led by **Hernán Cortés** (er-NAHN kohr-TAYS) reached Mexico in 1519. The group was looking for gold. Hearing of the conquistadors' arrival, the Aztec emperor, **Moctezuma II** (MAWK-tay-SOO-mah), believed Cortés to be a god. According to an Aztec legend, the god Quetzalcoatl (ket-suhl-kuh-WAH-tuhl) was to return to Mexico in 1519. Cortés resembled the god's description from the legend.

Academic Vocabulary
motive reason for doing something

Thinking that the god had returned, Moctezuma sent Cortés gifts, including gold. With getting more gold as his **motive**, Cortés marched to the Aztec capital. When he got there, Moctezuma welcomed him, but Cortés took the emperor prisoner.

Enraged, the Aztecs attacked and drove the Spanish out. In the confusion Moctezuma was killed. Cortés and his men came back, though, with many native peoples as allies. In 1521, they conquered Tenochtitlán.

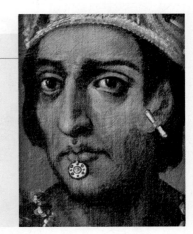

--- BIOGRAPHY ---

Moctezuma II 1466–1520

Moctezuma II ruled the Aztec Empire at its height, but he also contributed to its downfall. The tribute he demanded from neighboring tribes made the Aztecs unpopular. In addition, his belief that Cortés was Quetzalcoatl allowed Cortés to capture him and eventually conquer the empire.

Summarize
How did Moctezuma II contribute to the downfall of the Aztec Empire?

Malintzin c. 1501–1550

Malintzin played a major role in the Spanish conquest of the Aztec Empire. She was from a noble Aztec family but was sold into slavery as a child. While enslaved, Malintzin learned the Maya language, in addition to her first language spoken by the Aztecs. After she was given to Cortés, Malintzin's knowledge of languages helped him make deals with the Aztecs' enemies. She became Cortés's companion and interpreter.

However, because Malintzin helped the Spanish defeat the native Aztecs, today many Mexicans consider her a traitor. Some Mexicans use the word *malinchista* to describe someone who betrays his or her own people.

Make Inferences
Why do you think Malintzin helped the Spanish rather than the Aztecs?

Causes of the Defeat of the Aztecs How did a few conquistadors defeat a powerful empire? Four factors were vital in the Spanish victory: alliances, weapons and horses, geography, and disease.

First, alliances in the region helped the Spanish forces. One important ally was an Aztec woman named Malintzin (mah-LINT-suhn), also known as Malinche. She was a guide and interpreter for Cortés. With her help, he made alliances with tribes who did not like losing battles and paying tribute to the Aztecs. The allies gave the Spaniards supplies, information, and warriors to help defeat the Aztecs.

The Spaniards also had better weapons. The Aztecs couldn't match their armor, cannons, or swords. In addition to these weapons, the Spaniards brought horses to Mexico. The Aztecs had never seen horses and at first were terrified of them.

The third factor, geography, gave the Spanish another advantage. They blocked Tenochtitlán's causeways, bridges, and waterways. This cut off drinking water and supplies. Thousands of Aztecs died from starvation.

In this drawing, Cortés, shown seated in a chair, makes a treaty with the Aztecs. Malintzin is standing by his side interpreting.

Reading Check
Summarize
What four factors helped the Spanish defeat the Aztecs?

The final factor in the Spanish success was disease. Unknowingly, the Spanish had brought deadly diseases such as smallpox to the Americas. These new diseases swept through Aztec communities. Many Aztecs became very weak or died from the diseases.

Together, these four factors gave the Spanish forces a tremendous advantage and weakened the Aztecs. When the Spanish conquered Tenochtitlán, the Aztec Empire came to an end.

Summary and Preview The Aztecs established a great capital city and built a powerful empire in central Mexico. They valued learning and art and made many scientific achievements. A few hundred years later, their empire ended in defeat by Spanish conquistadors. In the next lesson, you will learn about another empire of the Americas—the Inca Empire—and the vast area that it included.

Lesson 3 Assessment

Review Ideas, Terms, and People

1. **a. Define** What is a causeway? Where did the Aztecs build causeways?
   b. Explain How did the Aztecs adapt to their island location?
   c. Elaborate How might Tenochtitlán's location have been both a benefit and a hindrance to the Aztecs?

2. **a. Describe** How was it decided when the Aztecs should plant crops or hold ceremonies?
   b. Evaluate Who do you think had the most difficult social role in Aztec society? Why?

3. **a. Identify** What did the Aztecs feed their gods?
   b. Explain Why did the Aztecs think human sacrifice was important?

4. **a. Identify** What might you find in an Aztec codex?
   b. Make Inferences Why do you think the Aztecs used so much stone in their art and building?
   c. Explain What primary sources can historians use to find out about the lives of the Aztecs?

5. **a. Identify** Who was the ruler of the Aztecs when Cortés and the conquistadors arrived in Mexico?
   b. Form Generalizations How and why did allies help Cortés conquer the Aztec Empire?
   c. Evaluate Did Moctezuma make good decisions as the Aztec leader?

Critical Thinking

6. **Categorize** Copy the graphic organizer. Write the names of the different social groups in Aztec society in each of the empty boxes.

King

Slaves

The Inca Empire

The Big Idea

The Incas built a huge empire in South America and made many great achievements in architecture, art, and oral literature.

Main Ideas

- The rise of the Inca Empire was due to conquest and the achievements of the Inca people.

- For the Incas, position in society affected daily life.

- The Incas made great achievements in building, art, and in oral literature.

- Pizarro conquered the Incas and took control of the region.

Key Terms and People

Pachacuti
Quechua
llamas
Atahualpa
Francisco Pizarro

If YOU were there . . .

You live in the Andes Mountains, where you raise llamas. You weave their wool into warm cloth. Last year, soldiers from the powerful Inca Empire took over your village and took your leaders away. Now you have new leaders—and they have totally different rules! They say you must all learn to speak a new language and send much of your woven cloth to the Inca ruler.

How do you feel about living in the Inca Empire?

The Rise of the Inca Empire

The Aztecs arose in Mesoamerica, in what is now Mexico. In South America another great empire arose. That empire belonged to the Incas. However, South America was the home of several civilizations before the Incas built their empire. These civilizations provided a foundation for the Incas. The Incas borrowed from the scientific and cultural achievements, such as farming techniques and craft-making skills, of these cultures.

Pre-Inca Civilizations Around 900 BC, complex civilizations began to develop in what is now Peru. These included the Chavín (chah-VEEN) culture in the highlands, and the Nazca, Moche (MOH-chay), and Chimú (chee-MOO) cultures on the coast.

Each of these cultures learned to adapt to its environment. In doing so, each made scientific advances. For example, in the steep mountains, people made terraces for farming. On the coast they developed irrigation systems, so they could farm in the desert. As a result, farming could support large populations both in the highlands and on the coast.

These early cultures also built some of South America's first cities. In these cities people developed crafts such as textiles, pottery, and gold jewelry. Because the cities were also religious centers, religious symbols frequently appeared in the crafts. The influence of these early civilizations set the stage for the Inca civilization.

The Early Incas The Incas began as a small tribe in the Andes. Their capital was Cuzco (KOOS-koh). In the mid-1400s, a ruler named **Pachacuti** (pah-chah-KOO-tee) led the Incas to expand their territory. He gained territory through agreements with other tribes or through conquest.

Later Inca leaders continued to expand their territory. By the early 1500s, the Inca Empire was huge. It stretched from what is now northern Ecuador to central Chile and included coastal deserts, snowy mountains, fertile valleys, and thick forests. At its center, in modern-day Peru, are three distinct climate regions. The west coast of Peru, which borders the Pacific Ocean, is extremely dry. Towering mountains to the east block

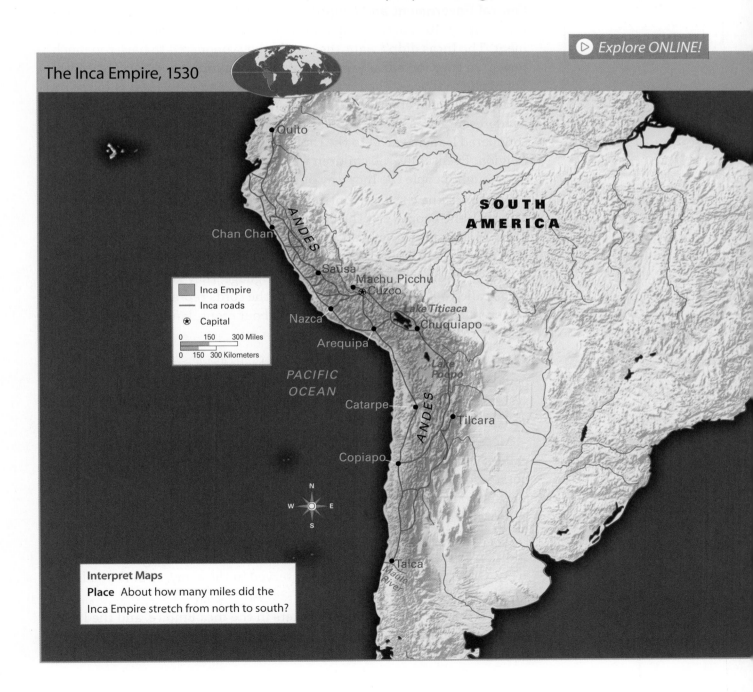

The Inca Empire, 1530

▶ *Explore ONLINE!*

Interpret Maps
Place About how many miles did the Inca Empire stretch from north to south?

The Incas lived in a region that included high plains and mountains.

moisture flowing in from the hot and humid Amazon rain forest. This coastal region is mostly desert that does not support agriculture. However, nutrient-rich waters along the coast support an abundant fish population. Fishing was an important part of Inca life and trade.

Inland from the coast lie the massive Andes Mountains. At lower elevations, temperatures are fairly mild, but the higher elevations are cold. Terraced agriculture is possible at lower elevations. Numerous rivers cascade down the Andes to rich farmlands at lower elevations. Lake Titicaca is the highest navigable lake in the world at 12,500 feet above sea level. The land around it is also a productive agricultural region. In areas where rivers do not flow year-round, the Inca built irrigation systems.

Central Government and Language About 12 million people lived in the Inca Empire. To rule this empire, the Incas formed a strong central government. The Incas didn't want the people they conquered to have too much power, so they forced large groups of people in conquered areas to move out of their villages. The Incas often brought conquered leaders to the capital to teach them about Inca culture, so they could return to their regions as representatives of the empire. The Incas also made the children of conquered leaders travel to the capital to learn about Inca government and religion. Eventually, the children went back to rule their villages, where they taught people the Inca way of life.

The Incas knew that to control their empire they had to communicate with the people. But the people spoke many different languages. To unify their empire, the Incas established an official language, **Quechua** (KE-choo-wah). All official business had to be done in that language.

Although the Incas had no written language, they kept records with cords called *quipus* (KEE-poos). Knots in the cords represented numbers. Different colors stood for information about crops, land, and other important topics.

Economy The Inca government also controlled the economy. Instead of paying taxes, Incas had to "pay" their government in labor. This labor tax system was called the *mita* (MEE-tah). Under the *mita*, the government told each household what work to do.

Most Incas were farmers. They grew crops such as maize and peanuts in valleys where the climate was warm. In the cooler mountains, they grew potatoes. In the highest mountains, people raised animals such as **llamas** (LAH-mahz), animals that are related to camels but native to South America, for meat and wool.

As part of the *mita*, farmers worked on government-owned farms in addition to their own farms. Villagers produced cloth and grain for the army. Other Incas worked in mines, served in the army, or built roads to pay their labor tax.

There were no merchants or markets in the Inca Empire, and the Inca had no currency. Instead, government officials **distributed** goods collected through the *mita*. Leftover goods were stored for emergencies.

Academic Vocabulary
distribute to divide among a group of people

Reading Check
Summarize
How did the Incas control government and language?

Early American Societies

Olmec	Maya	Aztec	Inca
• worshipped many gods and influenced later religions	• worshipped many gods	• worshipped many gods	• worshipped many gods
• developed first urban civilization in Mesoamerica	• built grand buildings	• built one of the world's largest cities	• built stone structures without using mortar
• created large-scale sculpture	• created sophisticated calendar	• created highly layered society	• used advanced terrace agriculture
• may have developed first writing with symbols in the Americas	• used hieroglyphics	• used advanced writing and mathematical systems	• selectively bred plants
• built large trade network	• studied astronomy and understood the 365-day year	• built large trade network	• created central government and language
	• used writing and number system, including zero		• used the *mita*, a labor tax system
	• built large trade network		• built advanced system of roads

Interpret Charts
Which cultures contributed to the development of written language?

Society and Daily Life

Inca society had two main social classes—an upper class and a lower class. The Incas from Cuzco made up the upper class. As they conquered new lands, the conquered people became Inca subjects and joined the lower class.

Daily Life for the Upper Class The king, priests, and government officials made up the Inca upper class. Most noblemen worked for the government as local government officials or administrators. They could also enter politics—positions were often passed down from father to son.

Women from noble families had similar household duties as women of the lower classes. They spent their time at home spinning, weaving, cooking, cleaning, and running the household. They made the family's clothing and cared for the children. Inca women could own land and herds and inherit both from relatives.

Sons of upper-class families went to school in Cuzco. They studied Quechua, religion, history, and law to prepare for lives as government or religious officials.

Upper-class families had many privileges. They lived in stone houses in Cuzco and wore the best clothes. They didn't have to pay the labor tax, and they often had servants. Still, as part of the Inca government, they had a duty to make sure that people in the empire had what they needed.

Daily Life for the Lower Class Most Incas were farmers, artisans, or servants. There were no slaves in Inca society. Lower-class men and women farmed on government lands, served in the army, worked in mines, and built roads.

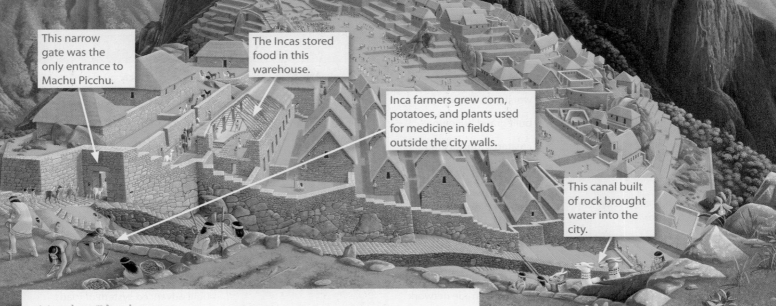

> This narrow gate was the only entrance to Machu Picchu.

> The Incas stored food in this warehouse.

> Inca farmers grew corn, potatoes, and plants used for medicine in fields outside the city walls.

> This canal built of rock brought water into the city.

Machu Picchu

Machu Picchu was a royal retreat for the Inca rulers. Built amid sacred mountain peaks, the city is an amazing engineering accomplishment. Its massive stone walls, steep staircases, and level fields were built so well that many remain today, more than 500 years later.

Parents taught their children the skills they would need as adults, so most children didn't go to school. Girls learned household skills from their mothers. Boys learned from their fathers to work the fields, care for animals, or master a craft. Some carefully chosen young girls did go to school to learn weaving, cooking, and religion. Then they were sent to serve the king or work in the temple in Cuzco.

Lower-class Incas lived outside Cuzco in small houses. By law they had to wear plain clothes. Also, they couldn't own more goods than they needed.

Religion The Inca Empire had an official religion. When the Incas conquered new territories, they taught it to the conquered peoples. But the people could still worship their own gods, too. As a result, the many groups of people who made up the empire worshipped many different gods.

The sun god was important to Inca religion. As the sun set earlier each day in the winter, at Machu Picchu priests performed a ceremony to tie down the sun and keep it from disappearing completely. The Incas believed their kings were related to the sun god. As a result, the Incas thought their kings never really died.

In fact, priests brought mummies of former kings to many ceremonies. People gave these royal mummies food and gifts. Some Inca rulers even asked them for advice.

Inca ceremonies often included sacrifice. But unlike the Mayas and the Aztecs, the Incas rarely sacrificed humans. They usually sacrificed llamas, cloth, or food.

Incas outside Cuzco worshipped their gods at local sacred places. The Incas believed certain mountaintops, rocks, and springs held magical powers. Incas performed sacrifices at these places as well as at the temple in Cuzco.

Reading Check
Contrast
How was daily life different for upper- and lower-class Incas?

Building, Art, and Oral Literature

The Incas had strong traditions of building, art, and storytelling. Many of their creations still exist today.

Building The Incas are known for their massive buildings and forts made of huge, stone blocks. Workers cut the blocks so precisely that they didn't have to use mortar to hold them together. Inca masonry, or stonework, was of such high quality that even today it is nearly impossible to fit a knife blade between the stones. In fact, many Inca buildings in Cuzco are still being used.

As the Incas gained wealth and power, they began to build a vast network of roads. They constructed two roads running north and south. The coastal road ran about 2,250 miles along the Pacific. An inland route hugged the lower reaches of the Andes Mountains. The rugged terrain challenged the Incas to innovate. They built rock tunnels through Andean foothills. They made strong ropes out of vines to support suspension bridges over rivers and deep valleys. Numerous side roads were connected to the main "highways."

Only government officials and the military were allowed to use the roads. As the network of roads expanded, it made the movement of armies more efficient. The roads connected all parts of the empire and gave the Incas easier access to neighboring regions they sought to conquer.

Inca arts included beautiful textiles and gold and silver objects. Although many gold and silver objects have been lost, some Inca textiles have survived for hundreds of years.

Art The Incas produced works of art as well. Artisans made gold and silver jewelry and offerings to the gods. They even created a life-sized field of corn out of gold and silver in a temple courtyard. Each cob, leaf, and stalk was individually crafted. The Incas also made some of the best textiles in the Americas. Archaeologists have found brightly colored Inca textiles that are still in excellent condition.

Oral Literature While archaeologists have found many Inca artifacts, there are no written records about the empire. Instead, Incas passed down stories and songs orally. Incas sang about daily life and military victories. Official "memorizers" learned long poems about Inca legends and history.

Later, after the conquistadors came, some Incas learned how to speak and write in Spanish. They wrote about Inca legends and history. We know about the Incas from these records and from the stories that survive in the songs, dances, and religious practices of people in the region today.

Reading Check
Make Inferences
How might the Inca road system have helped strengthen the empire?

Pizarro Conquers the Incas

A civil war began in the Inca Empire around 1530. After the Inca ruler died, his two sons, **Atahualpa** (ah-tah-WAHL-pah) and Huáscar (WAHS-kahr), fought to become the new ruler. Atahualpa won the war, but fierce fighting had weakened the Inca army.

The Capture of the King On his way to be crowned, Atahualpa got news that a group of Spaniards had come to Peru. They were conquistadors led by **Francisco Pizarro**. Stories about the Spaniards amazed Atahualpa. One Inca reported:

> "They and their horses were supposed to nourish [feed] themselves on gold and silver. . . . Above all, it was said that all day and all night the Spaniards talked to their books and papers. . . . They were all dressed alike and talked together like brothers and ate at the same table."

–Anonymous Inca, quoted in *Letter to a King* by Huamán Poma

Spaniard Francisco Pizarro kidnapped the Inca leader Atahualpa to defeat the Incas. This painting from the 1800s shows Pizarro leading the attack on the Inca ruler.

After he had heard of the Spaniards' arrival, Atahualpa agreed to meet Pizarro. At that meeting, the Spaniards told Atahualpa to convert to Christianity. When he refused, they attacked. They captured Atahualpa and killed thousands of Inca soldiers.

Spanish Control To win his freedom, Atahualpa asked his people to fill a room with gold and silver for Pizarro. The people rushed to bring jewelry, statues, and other objects. Melted down, the precious metals may have totaled 24 tons. However, the Spaniards killed Atahualpa anyway. Some Incas fought the Spaniards, but in 1537 the Spaniards defeated the last of the Incas and gained control over the entire region.

The fall of the Inca Empire was similar to the fall of the Aztec Empire.
- Both empires had internal problems when the Spanish arrived.
- Cortés and Pizarro captured the leaders of each empire.
- Guns and horses gave the Spanish a great military advantage.
- Disease weakened native peoples.

After defeating both the Aztecs and Incas, the Spanish ruled their lands for around 300 years.

Reading Check
Analyze Causes
What events led to the end of the Inca Empire?

Summary and Preview The Inca Empire's strong central government helped it control a huge area. But it could not survive the challenge posed by the Spanish. In the next lesson, you will learn about the development of Native American civilizations to the north.

Lesson 4 Assessment

Review Ideas, Terms, and People

1. a. Identify What were two things the central Inca government controlled?

b. Explain How did pre-Inca civilizations adapt to their environment?

c. Evaluate Do you think the *mita* system was a good government policy? Why or why not?

2. a. Identify Who were members of the Inca upper class?

b. Explain How were Inca government and religion related?

c. Elaborate Why do you think Inca law outlined what clothes people of various classes could wear?

3. a. Describe What was impressive about Inca masonry?

b. Draw Conclusions Were Inca oral traditions successful in preserving information? Why or why not?

c. Make Inferences Why do you think the Incas wanted to connect all parts of their empire with roads?

4. a. Recall When did the Spanish gain full control over the entire Inca region?

b. Compare How was the end of the Inca Empire similar to the end of the Aztec Empire?

c. Predict What might have happened if Atahualpa had told Pizarro he accepted Christianity?

Critical Thinking

5. Organize Information Draw a timeline like this one. Use it to identify three key dates and events in the history of the Inca Empire.

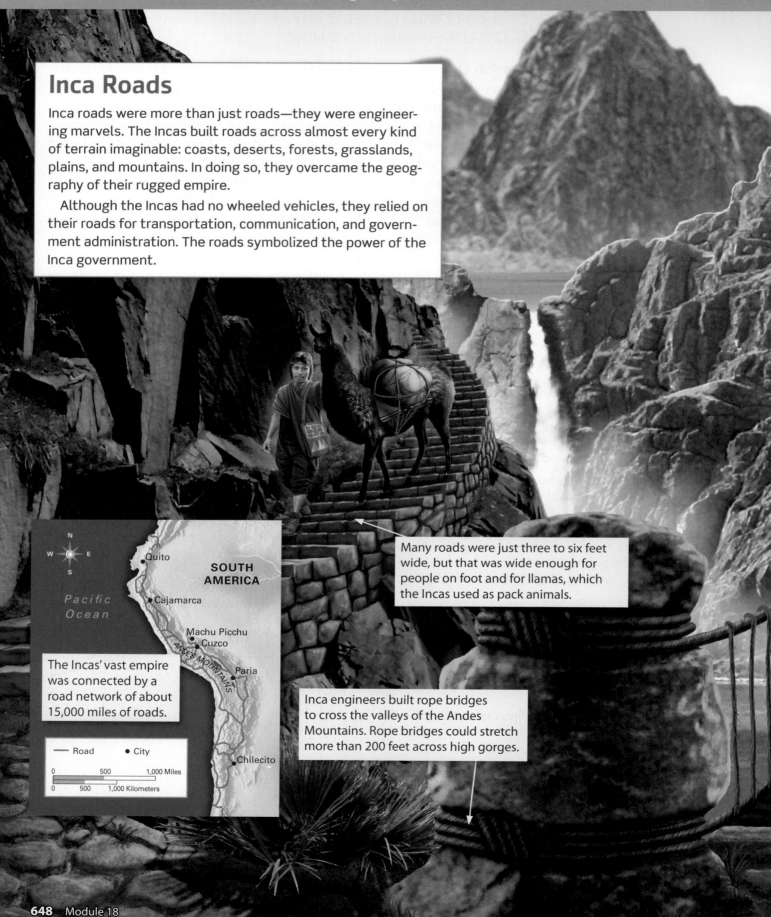

Inca Roads

Inca roads were more than just roads—they were engineering marvels. The Incas built roads across almost every kind of terrain imaginable: coasts, deserts, forests, grasslands, plains, and mountains. In doing so, they overcame the geography of their rugged empire.

Although the Incas had no wheeled vehicles, they relied on their roads for transportation, communication, and government administration. The roads symbolized the power of the Inca government.

Many roads were just three to six feet wide, but that was wide enough for people on foot and for llamas, which the Incas used as pack animals.

The Incas' vast empire was connected by a road network of about 15,000 miles of roads.

Inca engineers built rope bridges to cross the valleys of the Andes Mountains. Rope bridges could stretch more than 200 feet across high gorges.

SOUTH AMERICA

Pacific Ocean

Quito

Cajamarca

Machu Picchu
Cuzco

ANDES MOUNTAINS

Paria

Chilecito

Road • City

0   500   1,000 Miles
0   500   1,000 Kilometers

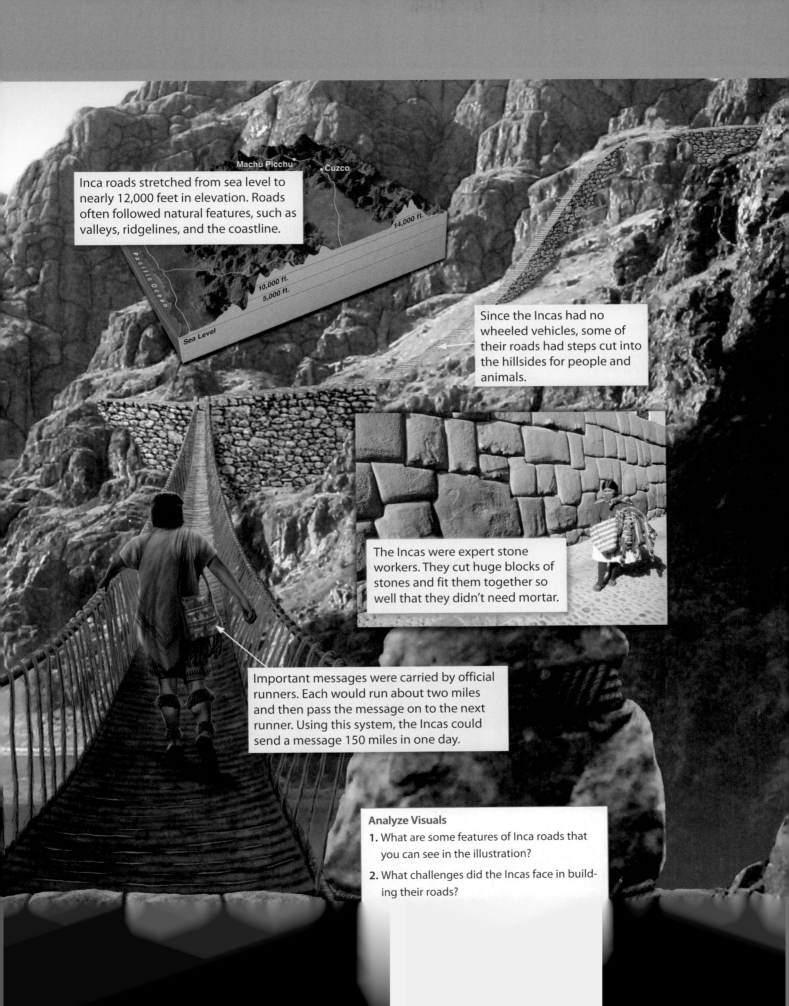

Inca roads stretched from sea level to nearly 12,000 feet in elevation. Roads often followed natural features, such as valleys, ridgelines, and the coastline.

Machu Picchu • Cuzco

14,000 ft.

10,000 ft.

5,000 ft.

Sea Level

Pacific Ocean

Since the Incas had no wheeled vehicles, some of their roads had steps cut into the hillsides for people and animals.

The Incas were expert stone workers. They cut huge blocks of stones and fit them together so well that they didn't need mortar.

Important messages were carried by official runners. Each would run about two miles and then pass the message on to the next runner. Using this system, the Incas could send a message 150 miles in one day.

Analyze Visuals

1. What are some features of Inca roads that you can see in the illustration?

2. What challenges did the Incas face in building their roads?

North American Cultures

The Big Idea

Varied environments and available resources shaped the cultures of North American native peoples over thousands of years.

Main Ideas

- The earliest North American cultures developed in the Southwest and eastern woodlands.
- North America's diverse geographical features led to the development of varied cultures.

Key Terms and People

adobe
potlatch
wampum
Iroquois Confederacy

If YOU were there . . .

You are a member of the Tlingit people in northwest North America. You are hosting a feast and have invited your entire community. In addition to feeding your guests seal and salmon, you will follow your traditions by giving them special gifts. Many guests will receive a gift of food, but you want to give your most honored guest something valuable. You have blankets, tools, and a canoe.

What will you give your most important guest?

The Earliest North American Cultures

The civilizations of the Maya, Aztec, and Inca were among the most advanced in the Americas. They were not, however, the only civilizations to develop in the hemisphere. Farther north, in what are now the United States and Canada, thousands of smaller societies developed and thrived.

Southwestern Cultures The southwestern United States is largely a desert region. The cultures that developed there had to adapt to a harsh, dry environment.

Many Anasazi pueblos were built into cliffs for safety. Often, ladders were needed to reach the buildings. The ladders could be removed, keeping invaders from reaching the dwellings.

For example, the Anasazi, or Ancestral Pueblo, thrived between around AD 1 and 1300. To survive in the desert, they built irrigation canals to bring water to their fields and villages. They also dug homes called pit houses into the ground. These pit houses had roofs made of a clay called **adobe**. In addition to pit houses, the Anasazi developed a new form of architecture called pueblo. Pueblo structures were several stories tall and had many rooms, like modern apartment buildings.

Although the Anasazi lived in the area for many centuries, after 1300 they began to abandon their villages. Historians are not sure why. Perhaps drought, disease, or attacks caused them to leave the area. Despite this decline, many descendants of the Anasazi, called the Hopi and the Pueblo, still live in the Southwest.

The Mound Builders Farther east, in the woodlands along the Mississippi and Ohio rivers, a different culture developed. These river systems were hugely important to these culture groups. The Mississippi River, for example, provided peoples in the region with abundant fish, fertile land, and access to transportation routes.

The societies that grew up in the region became known for the huge earthen mounds they built. Together they are called the mound-building cultures. An early mound-building culture was the Hopewell, who lived from 200 BC to AD 500. The Hopewell built their mounds as burial sites. In addition to bodies, many of these mounds contain items such as pottery and metal ornaments. Some ornaments came from as far away as the Rocky Mountains in the west and the Gulf of Mexico and Atlantic Ocean in the east. Hopewell artifacts have also been found in these locations. For this reason, scholars believe that the Hopewell peoples developed extensive trading routes that followed the Mississippi River and its tributaries.

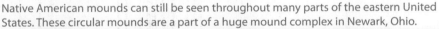

Native American mounds can still be seen throughout many parts of the eastern United States. These circular mounds are a part of a huge mound complex in Newark, Ohio.

Explore ONLINE!

Interpret Maps

1. Region Which cultural group settled throughout the Arctic and Subarctic region?

2. Region In which region did the Seminole live? The Apache?

Arctic and Subarctic
Eastern Woodlands
Great Plains
Desert West
Far West

0   150   300 Miles
0   150   300 Kilometers

Projection: Azimuthal Equal-Area

Inuit

Ingalik

Inuit

Aleut

Saschutkenne

Inuit

Tlingit

Beaver

Hudson Bay

Inuit

Naskapi

Beothuk

Haida

Swampy Cree

Montagnais

Micmac

NORTH AMERICA

Nootka

Columbia

Blackfoot

Plains Cree

Algonquian

Pequot
Mohegan
Narraganset
Mohawk
Iroquois

Chinook

Walla Walla

Nez Percé

Crow

ROCKY MOUNTAINS

Great Lakes

Modoc

Northern Paiute

Cheyenne

Teton Sioux

Omaha

PACIFIC OCEAN

Northern Shoshone

Shawnee

Powhatan

ATLANTIC OCEAN

Miwok

Western Shoshone

Osage

Cherokee

Ute

Chickasaw

Chumash

Hopi (Pueblo)

Apache

Kiowa

Navajo

Zuni

Comanche

Creek

Mohave

Wichita

Choctaw

Seminole

Apache

Caddo

Tarahumara

Gulf of Mexico

N
W   E
S

Yaqui

MESOAMERICA

Caribbean Sea

Reading Check
Summarize
How did varied environments influence the lives of early North American peoples?

Artifacts like this copper crow made by the Hopewell help archaeologists learn about early Native American culture.

After the Hopewell declined, another group called the Mississippian culture arose. The Mississippians were more advanced than the Hopewell. They built some of the earliest cities in North America. Their largest city, Cahokia, in what is now Illinois, was home to some 30,000 people. Like the Hopewell, the Mississippians were mound builders. Cahokia alone had more than 100 mounds, which are believed to have been built for religious ceremonies.

Later Cultures

By the time Europeans arrived in the 1500s, thousands of Native American groups lived in North America. Like the Anasazi, Hopewell, and Mississippians, these groups were shaped by their environments. As a result, distinct cultures developed in the various regions of North America.

Northwestern Cultures The Arctic lands of the far north are among the harshest regions of North America. They are covered in ice for a large part of the year. Yet the region was home to several cultures, among them the Inuit. Living in northern Alaska and Canada, the Inuit built igloos and hide tents for shelter. They fished and hunted large animals and used dogs for many tasks, such as hunting and pulling sleds.

Farther south, in the Pacific Northwest, civilizations such as the Haida lived among towering trees and survived on the region's plentiful animals and plants. Many people of the Northwest depended on fish, especially salmon, for food. Some cultures of this area carved images of totems, or animal spirits, on tall wooden poles. Totem poles held great religious significance.

Northwestern peoples also held ceremonies, dances, and events known as **potlatches**. During a potlatch, a host prepared a feast for one or more members of the group. The host gave valuable gifts to honored guests. Potlatches and other events were used for trading, socializing, and improving relations within the community or with a neighboring community.

Native American groups in different regions developed very different cultures. The totem pole is a re-creation of a traditional style on Vancouver Island, Canada.

This image of Plains Indians hunting buffalo was painted on hide—most likely buffalo hide. Buffalo were central to the culture and survival of Plains Indians.

Plains Cultures Many cultures lived on the Great Plains of North America. Most of the people who lived in this vast, largely treeless region were nomadic hunters. They used bows and other weapons to hunt the plains' plentiful animals, especially buffalo. Besides food, the buffalo provided other essentials of life. For example, people used buffalo hides to build teepees for shelter.

Eastern Cultures A variety of cultures developed in eastern North America. Groups like the Cherokee, Creek, and Seminole lived in the Southeast in villages governed by councils. People farmed, hunted, gathered plants, and fished. Many used **wampum**, or strings of beads, as currency.

Native peoples of the Northeast lived among seemingly endless forests, which blanketed the land east of the Mississippi River. Many Northeastern peoples built homes and other structures with wood. They were good

Timeline: Key Events in North America

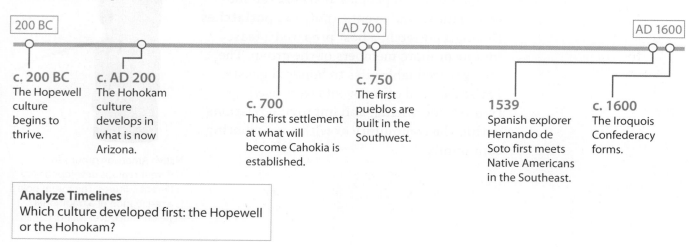

| 200 BC | | | AD 700 | | | AD 1600 |

c. 200 BC
The Hopewell culture begins to thrive.

c. AD 200
The Hohokam culture develops in what is now Arizona.

c. 700
The first settlement at what will become Cahokia is established.

c. 750
The first pueblos are built in the Southwest.

1539
Spanish explorer Hernando de Soto first meets Native Americans in the Southeast.

c. 1600
The Iroquois Confederacy forms.

Analyze Timelines
Which culture developed first: the Hopewell or the Hohokam?

Making Economic Decisions

Even people living in small communities must decide how to answer the basic economic questions of what goods and services to produce and how and for whom to produce them. Native Americans typically worked together to decide the answers to these questions. Chiefs and tribal council members usually talked about how to find and use resources together. They considered the needs and opinions of the entire tribe. Then, they made decisions that were based on the good of the group. For Native Americans, the well-being of the entire group was all-important.

This point of view also influenced Native American decisions about trade and land use. Native Americans often saw trade as a form of gift-giving or sharing. They also believed land belonged to the entire tribe instead of just one person or family. Iroquois land, for example, was owned by the community. Every few years, the Iroquois Clan Mothers Council decided how the community's land would be shared among its people. They based their decisions on the makeup of the population. They also considered how clans had used their lands in the past.

Analyze Information
What effect did gift-giving have on the culture of Native American culture groups?

hunters who relied on game, such as deer, for food. They also grew crops such as maize, beans, and squash. Northeastern cultures included those of the **Iroquois** (IR-uh-kwoy) **Confederacy**. This group was an alliance of five peoples—the Cayuga, Mohawk, Oneida, Onondaga, and Seneca. They called themselves "the people of the longhouse" after the houses they built.

Together, the five peoples of the Iroquois Confederacy waged war against and made peace with non-Iroquois peoples. Combining their strength made the Iroquois one of the most powerful Native American peoples in North America.

Iroquois longhouses were made of wooden poles and bark. Large longhouses could shelter up to a dozen families through a hard winter.

Northeastern native peoples had governments similar to those of many Native American cultures. Most groups had a chief, whose title and power were often inherited. A council that included the chief and as many as 50 other respected members of the group made important decisions.

Family and social life was typically based on the clan. A clan was a small group of people who worked together and considered themselves relatives, even if there was no blood relation. In some groups, such as the Delaware, children were part of their mother's clan. In others, such as the Algonquian, children were members of the father's clan. Every clan was responsible for the well-being of all its members.

Summary Native American peoples adapted to their physical environment. They developed cultures based on the geography and environment in which they settled.

Reading Check
Draw Conclusions
What is one way the Plains cultures differed from those of the Northwest and the East?

Lesson 5 Assessment

Review Ideas, Terms, and People

1. a. Identify What enabled the early Anasazi peoples of the Southwest to grow crops?

   b. Evaluate What was the main purpose of early North Americans' mound-building?

2. a. Summarize How did the Plains people use the buffalo?

   b. Identify In which regions of North America did Native Americans rely most heavily on forests and timber?

   c. Describe What is a potlatch?

Critical Thinking

3. Evaluate What method did many Native American tribes use to make important decisions? What are the positive and potentially negative aspects of this form of decision making?

4. Compare How did Native American peoples living in different regions use the resources in their environment? Create a comparison chart to show each region, its resources, and how these resources were used by native peoples there.

Region	Resources	How Resources Were Used
Northwestern		
Plains		
Eastern		

Social Studies Skills

Interpret Culture Maps

Define the Skill

A culture map is a special type of political map. As you may recall, political maps show human features of an area, such as boundaries, settlements, and roads. The human features on a culture map are cultural features, such as languages spoken, major religions, or groups of people. Culture maps are one of several different types of political maps that historians often use. The ability to interpret them is an important skill for understanding history.

Learn the Skill

The guidelines for interpreting a culture map are similar to those for understanding any map.

1. Use map basics. Read the title to identify the subject. Note the labels, legend, and scale. Pay particular attention to special symbols for cultural features. Be sure you understand what these symbols represent.

2. Study the map as a whole. Note the location of the cultural symbols and features. Ask yourself how they relate to the rest of the map.

3. Connect the information on the map to any written information on the subject.

Practice the Skill

Apply the guidelines to the map here. Use them to answer the questions.

1. What makes this map a culture map?

2. Where did the Aztecs live?

3. What people lived to the north of the Aztecs?

4. What other peoples lived in the Lake Texcoco area?

5. What was the main culture in the city of Texcoco?

6. How does this map help you better understand the Aztec Empire?

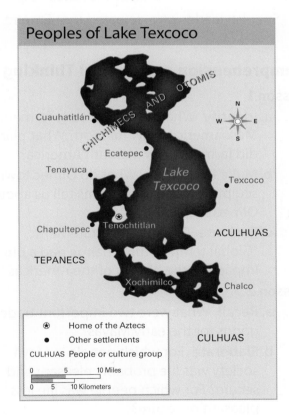

Peoples of Lake Texcoco

Module 18 Assessment

Review Vocabulary, Terms, and People

Match each numbered definition with the correct lettered vocabulary term.

1. book that contains Maya legends and history
2. type of ancient book
3. leader who expanded Inca Empire
4. raised paths across water or wet ground
5. Spanish leader who defeated Aztec Empire
6. Spanish soldiers who came to the Americas to explore new lands, search for gold, and spread their religion
7. sharp, glasslike volcanic rock
8. Inca leader captured by the Spanish
9. region that includes the southern part of what is now Mexico and parts of the northern countries of Central America
10. Aztec leader at the fall of the Aztec Empire
11. Spanish leader who defeated Inca Empire

a. codex
b. obsidian
c. Moctezuma II
d. Pachacuti
e. causeways
f. *Popul Vuh*
g. Francisco Pizarro
h. conquistadors
i. Hernán Cortés
j. Mesoamerica
k. Atahualpa

Comprehension and Critical Thinking

Lesson 1

12. a. **Identify** What plants did early farmers in Mesoamerica grow for food? What plants did farmers grow in South America?
    b. **Make Inferences** What do Olmec towns, sculptures, and other items tell us about Olmec society?
    c. **Evaluate** Evaluate this statement: "Global temperature change had a big impact on the history of the Americas."

Lesson 2

13. a. **Recall** What were two important trade goods for the early Mayas?
    b. **Elaborate** For which people in Maya society was life probably pleasant and secure? For which people was life less pleasant or secure?
    c. **Analyze** Why did the Maya civilization decline?

Lesson 3

14. a. **Describe** What was Tenochtitlán like? Where was it located?
    b. **Elaborate** How did Aztec art and architecture make use of natural materials?
    c. **Draw Conclusions** What factor do you think played the biggest role in the Aztecs' defeat? Defend your answer.

Lesson 4

15. a. **Recall** Who was Pachacuti, and what did he accomplish?
    b. **Predict** What might have happened if Atahualpa and Huáscar had settled their argument peacefully?
    c. **Compare and Contrast** In what ways were the economies of the Mayas, Aztecs, and Incas similar in terms of the common person's responsibilities to the rulers of the empire? In what ways did this system differ among the three empires?

Module 18 Assessment, continued

Lesson 5

16. **a. Explain** How did the Southwestern peoples adapt to their environment?

    b. Summarize Why do scholars believe that the Hopewell developed extensive trade networks?

    c. Analyze What was the purpose of potlatches?

Review Themes

17. **Science and Technology** "The Mayas were clever and talented because they built their cities without the help of metal tools or wheeled vehicles." Do you agree with that statement? Why or why not?

18. **Politics** What were the similarities between the rise of the Aztec Empire and the rise of the Inca Empire?

19. **Science and Technology** What methods did Aztec and Inca builders develop to overcome geographical challenges?

20. **Geography** What evidence from the text shows how early peoples in the Americas adapted to their physical environments?

Reading Skills

Analyze Information *Use the Reading Skills taught in this module to determine relevant and irrelevant information. In each of the following passages, one underlined selection is irrelevant, nonessential to the meaning of the sentence, or cannot be verified as true. Identify the irrelevant, nonessential, or unverifiable selection in each sentence.*

21. Pacal was greatly honored by the Mayas. He was very tall. The Mayas built a great temple to record his achievements.

22. Ball games were popular in Maya cities. Players could not use their hands or feet to touch the ball. The Mayas would not enjoy modern basketball very much.

23. Chocolate was valuable in Maya society. Only rulers and gods could have chocolate. Today, many people enjoy chocolate every day.

24. The Mayas developed an accurate calendar system. They knew that a year had 365 days. The ancient Romans also had a calendar. The Maya calendar used symbols to represent months.

25. Mesoamerica is largely covered by rain forests. Many kinds of plants and animals live in rain forests. The people of Mesoamerica probably liked to watch monkeys playing in the trees.

Social Studies Skills

Understand Culture Maps *Use the Social Studies Skills taught in this module to answer the question about maps in the module.*

26. Look in the module at the map of the Aztec empire. Why do you think the Aztec Empire didn't include all the land from Tula to Xoconocho?

27. Look in the module at the map of the Inca empire. How would physical features have affected the Inca rulers' ability to rule their empire?

Focus on Writing

28. **Write a Travel Guide** Travel guides often feature exciting descriptions of tours. Use what you have learned in the module to write such a description for a historical tour of the ancient Americas. Your tour should have at least five stops. Choose sites from the oldest civilizations to the Inca cities. For each site, write several sentences about the people who lived there. You might tell how they came to live there or how an object there played a part in their lives. Most travel guides show lots of pictures. What pictures would you choose to go with what you've written? Include them in your guide.

THE Mayas

The Mayas developed one of the most advanced civilizations in the Americas, but their story is shrouded in mystery. Around AD 250, the Mayas began to build great cities in southern Mexico and Central America. They developed a writing system, practiced astronomy, and built magnificent palaces and pyramids with little more than stone tools. Around AD 900, however, the Mayas abandoned their cities, leaving their monuments to be reclaimed by the jungle and, for a time, forgotten.

Explore some of the incredible monuments and cultural achievements of the ancient Mayas online. You can find a wealth of information, video clips, primary sources, activities, and more through your online textbook.

"Thus let it be done! Let the emptiness be filled! Let the water recede and make a void, let the earth appear and become solid; let it be done . . . "Earth!" they said, and instantly it was made."

The Popol Vuh
Read the document to learn how the Maya believed the world was created.

Destroying the Maya Past
Watch the video to learn how the actions of one Spanish missionary nearly destroyed the written record of the Maya world.

Finding the City of Palenque
Watch the video to learn about the great Maya city of Palenque and the European discovery of the site in the eighteenth century.

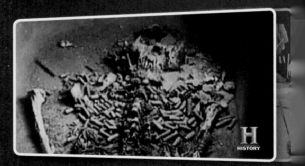

Pakal's Tomb
Watch the video to explore how the discovery of the tomb of a great king helped archaeologists piece together the Maya past.

The Middle Ages

Essential Question

How did life in Europe change after the fall of Rome?

About the Photo: Chillon Castle was built in Switzerland around 1005. The castle guarded an important mountain road and showed the ruling lord's power.

In this module, you will learn about the social and economic systems in Europe during a time called the Middle Ages. Christianity was a major influence on people's lives during these years.

What You Will Learn...

Lesson 1: Europe After the Fall of Rome **664**
The Big Idea Europe faced religious and political change after the fall of Rome.

Lesson 2: Feudalism, Manors, and Towns **673**
The Big Idea A complex web of duties and obligations governed relationships between people in the Middle Ages.

Lesson 3: Popes and Kings **680**
The Big Idea Popes and kings dominated European society in the Middle Ages.

Lesson 4: The Crusades **685**
The Big Idea The Christian and Muslim cultures fought over holy sites during a series of medieval wars.

Lesson 5: Christianity and Medieval Society **691**
The Big Idea The Christian Church was central to life in the Middle Ages.

Lesson 6: Political and Social Change **698**
The Big Idea Europe's political and social systems underwent great changes in the late Middle Ages.

▶ *Explore ONLINE!*

HISTORY

VIDEOS, including...
- Harold and William: The Battle for England
- Bet You Didn't Know: St. Patrick's Day
- Battle of Hastings

✓ Document-Based Investigations

✓ Graphic Organizers

✓ Interactive Games

✓ Interactive Map: The Crusades, 1096 – 1204

✓ Image with Hotspots: The Cluny Monastery

✓ Image Carousel: Feudal Society

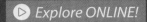
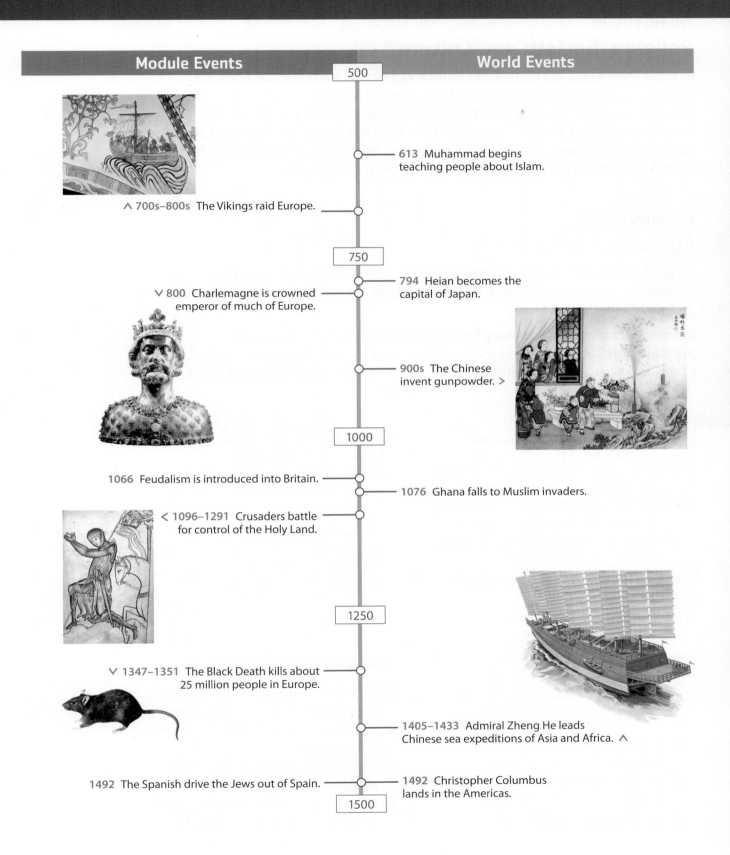

Module Events	500	World Events

∧ 700s–800s The Vikings raid Europe.

613 Muhammad begins teaching people about Islam.

750

∨ 800 Charlemagne is crowned emperor of much of Europe.

794 Heian becomes the capital of Japan.

900s The Chinese invent gunpowder. >

1000

1066 Feudalism is introduced into Britain.

1076 Ghana falls to Muslim invaders.

< 1096–1291 Crusaders battle for control of the Holy Land.

1250

∨ 1347–1351 The Black Death kills about 25 million people in Europe.

1405–1433 Admiral Zheng He leads Chinese sea expeditions of Asia and Africa. ∧

1492 The Spanish drive the Jews out of Spain.

1492 Christopher Columbus lands in the Americas.

1500

Reading Social Studies

THEME FOCUS:

Religion, Society and Culture

In this module you will read about Europe during the early Middle Ages. You will learn how the geography of the land affected growth and trade and see how the Christian religion spread throughout northern Europe during this time. You will learn about the invaders who tried to conquer the land and see how the feudal system developed. As you read, you will understand how this feudal system shaped the entire society and culture of Europe.

READING FOCUS:

Evaluate Sources

As you have already learned, historians study both primary and secondary sources to learn about the past. By studying both types, they can get a better picture of what life was like.

Assess Primary and Secondary Sources However, not all sources are accurate or reliable. You need to be careful when you read historical sources. Checklists like these can help you judge which sources are reliable and worth using in your research.

Checklist for Primary Sources

✔ Who is the author? Does he or she seem trustworthy?

✔ Was the author actually present for the event described in the source?

✔ How soon after the event occurred was the source written?

✔ Can the information be verified in other sources?

Historians in the past were not always careful about what they put in their books. Some included rumors, gossip, or hearsay.

The more time that passed between the event and the writing, the greater the chance of errors or distortion in the description.

Not everyone who writes about history is a good historian. Try to use sources by qualified writers.

Good historians will always tell you where they got their information. If information isn't documented, you can't always trust that it is true or accurate.

Checklist for Secondary Sources

✔ Who is the author? What are his or her credentials or qualifications?

✔ Where did the author get his or her information?

✔ Is the information in the source properly documented?

✔ Has the author drawn valid conclusions from his or her sources?

You Try It!

Read the following passage and then answer the questions below.

> "Lord, make me an instrument of your peace. Where there is hatred, let me sow love; where there is injury, pardon; where there is doubt, faith; where there is despair, hope; where there is darkness, light; and where there is sadness, joy."
>
> —Francis of Assisi, from *The Prayer of Saint Francis*

Answer these questions based on the passage you just read.

1. The passage you have just read is from a prayer credited to Francis of Assisi, a friar who lived in the late 1100s and early 1200s. If a historian wanted to study what religious people who lived at that time believed, would this be a good source to use? Why or why not?

2. Where else might a historian look to verify the information found in this source?

3. Would this be a good source to study to learn what friars believe today? Why or why not?

As you read this module, look at the primary sources included in the module. Why do you think these sources were chosen to be included?

Key Terms and People

Lesson 1
Eurasia
Middle Ages
medieval
Patrick
monks
monasteries
Benedict
Charlemagne

Lesson 2
knights
vassal
feudalism
William the Conqueror
manor
serfs
Eleanor of Aquitaine

Lesson 3
excommunicate
Pope Gregory VII
Emperor Henry IV

Lesson 4
Crusades
Holy Land
Pope Urban II
King Richard I
Saladin

Lesson 5
clergy
religious order
Francis of Assisi
friars
Thomas Aquinas
natural law

Lesson 6
Magna Carta
Parliament
Hundred Years' War
Joan of Arc
Black Death
heresy
Reconquista
King Ferdinand
Queen Isabella
Spanish Inquisition

Europe After the Fall of Rome

The Big Idea

Europe faced religious and political change after the fall of Rome.

Main Ideas

- Geography has shaped life in Europe, including where and how people live.

- Christianity spread to northern Europe through the work of missionaries and monks.

- The Franks, led by Charlemagne, created a huge Christian empire and brought together scholars from around Europe.

- Invaders threatened much of Europe in the 700s and 800s.

Key Terms and People

Eurasia
Middle Ages
medieval
Patrick
monks
monasteries
Benedict
Charlemagne

If YOU were there . . .

You're returning to your village in northern Europe after a hard day working in the fields. But as you reach the top of a hill, you smell smoke. Alarmed, you break into a run. Finally, your village comes into sight, and your fears are realized. Your village is on fire! In the distance, you can see sails moving away on the river.

What do you think has happened to your village?

Geography Shapes Life in Europe

Europe is a small continent, but it is very diverse. Many different landforms, water features, and climates can be found there.

Although we call Europe a continent, it is actually part of **Eurasia**, the large landmass that includes both Europe and Asia. Geographers consider the Ural Mountains to be the boundary between the two continents.

Landforms and Waterways Looking at a map of Europe, you can see that different parts of Europe have very different features. In other words, Europe's topography varies widely from place to place. For example, while mountain ranges cover much of southern Europe, plains make up most of northern Europe.

These plains are part of the vast Northern European Plain. This is the location of most of Europe's rivers. Many of these rivers begin with melting snow in the southern mountains and flow out across the plain northward to the sea.

Even farther north from the Northern European Plain, the land starts to rise again to form rugged hills and low mountains. You can see these hills and mountains in the northern part of the British Isles and in Scandinavia, Europe's largest peninsula. Scandinavia is only one of Europe's many peninsulas. These peninsulas give Europe a very long, jagged coastline.

ARCTIC OCEAN

ASIA

SCANDINAVIAN PENINSULA

Iceland

Norwegian Sea

URAL MOUNTAINS

N. Dvina River

British Isles

PENNINES

North Sea

Gulf of Bothnia

Baltic Sea

NORTHERN EUROPEAN PLAIN

Kama River

ATLANTIC OCEAN

English Channel

Paris

Seine River

Rhine River

Elbe River

Oder River

Vistula River

Don River

Dnieper River

Volga River

Ural River

Mont Blanc 15,781 ft. (4,810 m)

A L P S

Danube River

Rhône River

Po River

CARPATHIAN MTS.

Dnestr River

Mt. Elbrus 18,510 ft. (5,642 m)

Caspian Sea

Bay of Biscay

PYRENEES

Ebro River

CAUCASUS MTS.

Black Sea

ITALIAN PENINSULA

Adriatic Sea

BALKAN PENINSULA

ASIA

IBERIAN PENINSULA

Corsica

Sardinia

Balearic Islands

Tyrrhenian Sea

Aegean Sea

Strait of Gibraltar

Sicily

Crete

Mediterranean Sea

ELEVATION

Feet		Meters
13,120		4,000
6,560		2,000
1,640		500
656		200
(Sea level) 0		0 (Sea level)
Below sea level		Below sea level

Ice cap

0   250   500 Miles

0   250   500 Kilometers

Interpret Maps

1. **Region** What four peninsulas do you see labeled?

2. **Movement** How might the Alps have affected the movement of peoples?

Climate and Vegetation Like its landforms, Europe's climates and vegetation vary widely from region to region. For example, southern Europe is largely warm and sunny. As a result, shrubs and trees that don't need a lot of water are common there.

Most of northwestern Europe, in contrast, has a mild and cooler, wetter climate. One reason for this mild climate is the North Atlantic Drift. This is an ocean current that brings warm water to northwestern Europe. Cold winds from the north and northeast can bring freezing weather in winter.

Southern Europe As in other parts of the world, geography has affected history in Europe. It influenced where and how people lived. In southern Europe, most people lived on coastal plains or in river valleys where the land was flat enough to farm. People grew crops like grapes and olives that could survive the region's dry summers. In the mountains where the land was steep or rocky, people raised sheep and goats.

Because southern Europe had many peninsulas, people there lived relatively close to the sea. As a result, many became traders and seafarers.

Northern Europe Most people in northern Europe lived farther from the sea. They still had access to the sea, however, through northern Europe's rivers. Because rivers were an easy method of transportation, towns grew up along them. Rivers also provided protection. The city of Paris, France, for example, was built on an island in a river to make the city hard for raiders to reach. London, England, was built along the Thames (TEMZ) River. This river became an important trade and transportation route. Its location helped London grow.

In the fields around cities, farmers grew all sorts of crops. These fields were excellent farmlands, but the flat land also made an easy route for invaders to follow. No mountains blocked people's access to northern Europe, and as a result, the region was frequently invaded. These invasions changed Europe in many ways.

Reading Check
Contrast How did geography influence where people lived in Europe?

Geography and Living

Farmers have long grown olives and other hardy crops in the drier, warmer areas along the Mediterranean in southern Europe.

Many people in cold, snowy Scandinavia have settled on the coasts, looking to the sea and lands beyond for the resources they need.

Cities have grown along rivers such as the Rhine in Germany. Rivers have been routes for moving people and goods.

Christianity Spreads to Northern Europe

As the Roman Empire fell, various groups from the north and east moved into former Roman lands. As they moved in, these groups created their own states. The rulers of these states, usually powerful warlords, began to call themselves kings. These kings often fought among themselves. As a result, by the early 500s Europe was divided into many small kingdoms.

The creation of these kingdoms marked the beginning of the **Middle Ages**, a period that lasted from about 500 to about 1500. We call this time the "middle" ages because it falls between ancient times and modern times. Another name for the Middle Ages is the **medieval** (mee-DEE-vuhl) period, from the Latin words for "middle age."

At the beginning of the Middle Ages, many of the kingdoms of northern Europe were not Christian. Christianity was common only in places that had been part of the Roman Empire, such as Italy and Spain. As time passed, however, Christianity slowly spread farther north. This spread was largely through the efforts of two groups of Christians—missionaries and monks.

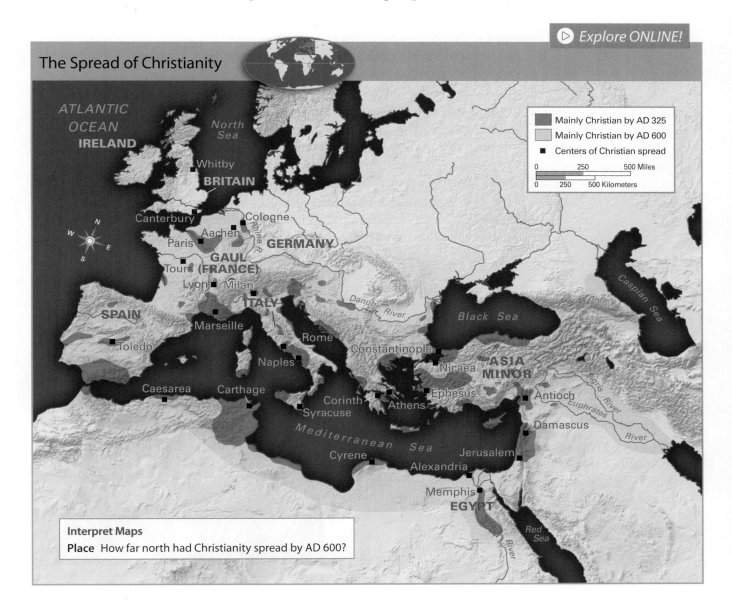

▷ Explore ONLINE!

The Spread of Christianity

Legend:
- Mainly Christian by AD 325
- Mainly Christian by AD 600
- ■ Centers of Christian spread

0   250   500 Miles
0   250   500 Kilometers

Interpret Maps

Place How far north had Christianity spread by AD 600?

Missionaries Perhaps the most powerful force that helped spread Christianity into northern Europe was the pope. Over the years, many popes sent missionaries to teach people in northern kingdoms about Christianity. Missionaries are people who try to convert others to a particular religion. Some missionaries traveled great distances to spread Christianity to new lands.

One of the first places to which popes sent missionaries was Britain. These missionaries traveled all over the island, and eventually most people in Britain became Christian. From Britain, other missionaries carried Christianity into areas that are now France and Germany.

Not all missionaries, though, were sent by the pope. In fact, one of the first missionaries to travel to northern Europe was **Patrick**, who took it upon himself to teach people about Christianity. In the mid-400s, Patrick traveled from Britain to Ireland to convert the people there.

Unlike most missionaries, Patrick traveled alone. Although he faced resistance to his teachings, he eventually converted many Irish people to Christianity.

Monks While missionaries traveled to spread Christian teachings, men called monks were equally dedicated to their faith. **Monks** were religious men who lived apart from society in isolated communities. In these communities, monks spent their time in prayer, work, and meditation.

Communities of monks, or **monasteries**, were built all over Europe in the Middle Ages. Life in a monastery was strictly organized. The monks had to follow rules that were intended to help them live as good Christians. These rules outlined the day-to-day affairs of the monastery, including how monks should dress and what they should eat.

Most European monasteries followed a set of rules created in the early 500s by an Italian monk named **Benedict**. His code was called the Benedictine Rule, and those who followed it were called Benedictine

BIOGRAPHY

Patrick AD 400s

Patrick was a monk who helped convert the Irish to Christianity. As a teenager, Patrick was kidnapped in Britain and taken to Ireland, where he was forced to work as a shepherd. After six years, he escaped. But later he returned to Ireland to spread Christianity.

According to legend, he won favor with the Irish by driving all of the snakes in Ireland into the sea. After Patrick died, he was declared a saint by the people of Ireland.

Form Generalizations
Why did Patrick return to Ireland after his escape?

monks. But not all monks in Europe were Benedictines. Different groups of monks created their own rules. For example, monks in Ireland were very different from monks in France or Germany.

Even though they lived apart from society, monks had a big influence on Europe. Monks performed many services, both inside and outside the monasteries. Monasteries sometimes provided basic services, such as health care, that were unavailable to many members of their communities. The poor and needy would arrive at a monastery, and the monks would give them aid.

In addition to giving aid to people in their communities, monks
- ran schools and copied books for those who couldn't read or write
- collected and saved ancient writings from Greece and Rome
- served as scribes and advisors to local rulers

Monks also helped spread Christian teachings into new areas. Many monasteries were built in remote locations where Christians had never traveled before. People living near the monasteries learned about Christianity from the monks.

Reading Check
Summarize How did missionaries and monks help spread Christianity into new areas?

The Franks Build an Empire

As Christianity was spreading into northern Europe, political changes were also taking place. In the 480s, a powerful Germanic tribe called the Franks conquered Gaul, the region we now call France. Under a ruler named Clovis, this Germanic tribe became Christian and created one of the strongest kingdoms in Europe.

As strong as the Franks were under Clovis, though, they had yet to reach their greatest power. That power would not come until the late 700s, when a leader named **Charlemagne** (SHAHR-luh-mayn) appeared. Charlemagne was a brilliant warrior and a strong king, and he led the Franks in building a huge empire.

— BIOGRAPHY —

Charlemagne 742–814

Charlemagne, or Charles the Great, ruled most of what is now France and Germany. Through his wars of conquest, Charlemagne united many of the tribes of central and western Europe into a single empire.

While Europe was still reeling from the collapse of Rome, Charlemagne brought people together. He helped Europeans realize that they shared common bonds, such as Christianity. He helped people see themselves as Europeans, not members of tribes.

Draw Conclusions
How did efforts to help people see their common bonds affect later European society?

This painting shows Charlemagne being crowned by the pope in AD 800.

To build this empire, Charlemagne spent much of his time at war. He led his armies into battle against many neighboring kingdoms and conquered them. By the time he was finished, Charlemagne's empire included all of what is now France. It also stretched into modern Germany, Austria, Italy, and northern Spain.

Charlemagne, a Christian king, had conquered parts of the former Roman Empire. For that reason, on Christmas Day in 800, Pope Leo III crowned Charlemagne Emperor of the Romans. This title symbolized a return to the greatness of the Roman Empire.

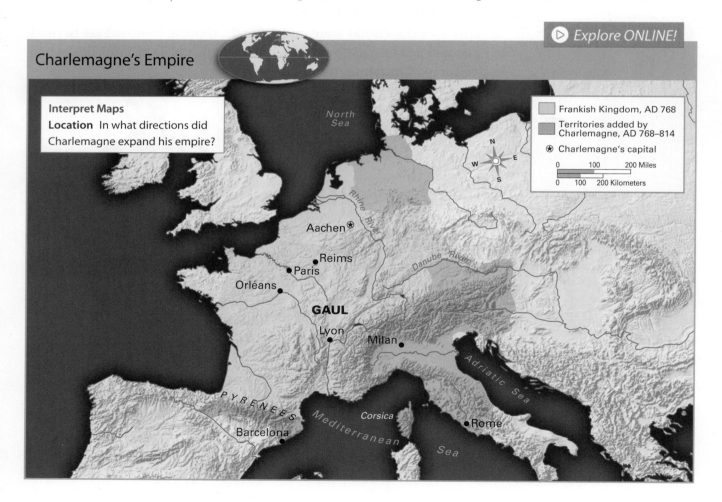

Charlemagne's Empire

▷ *Explore ONLINE!*

Interpret Maps

Location In what directions did Charlemagne expand his empire?

Frankish Kingdom, AD 768

Territories added by Charlemagne, AD 768–814

⊛ Charlemagne's capital

0   100   200 Miles
0   100   200 Kilometers

North Sea

Rhine River

Aachen ⊛

Reims

Paris

Orléans

Danube River

GAUL

Lyon

Milan

Adriatic Sea

PYRENEES

Corsica

Mediterranean Sea

Rome

Barcelona

Charlemagne didn't spend all of his energy on warfare, however. A great admirer of education, he built schools across Europe. He also brought scholars to teach in his capital at Aachen (AH-kuhn), now in western Germany. Among these scholars were some of the greatest religious scholars and teachers of the Middle Ages. Their teachings helped shape religious and social life in Europe for centuries.

Reading Check
Find Main Ideas
What were Charlemagne's major accomplishments?

Invaders Threaten Europe

Even while Charlemagne was building his empire, though, new threats appeared in Europe. Invaders began to attack settlements all over the continent. Muslim armies poured into southern France and northern Italy. Fierce warriors called the Magyars swept into Europe from the east, attacking towns and destroying fields. From Scandinavia came perhaps the most frightening invaders of all, the Vikings.

The Vikings raided Britain, Ireland, and other parts of western Europe. They looted towns and monasteries and took prisoners to sell into slavery.

▷ *Explore ONLINE!*

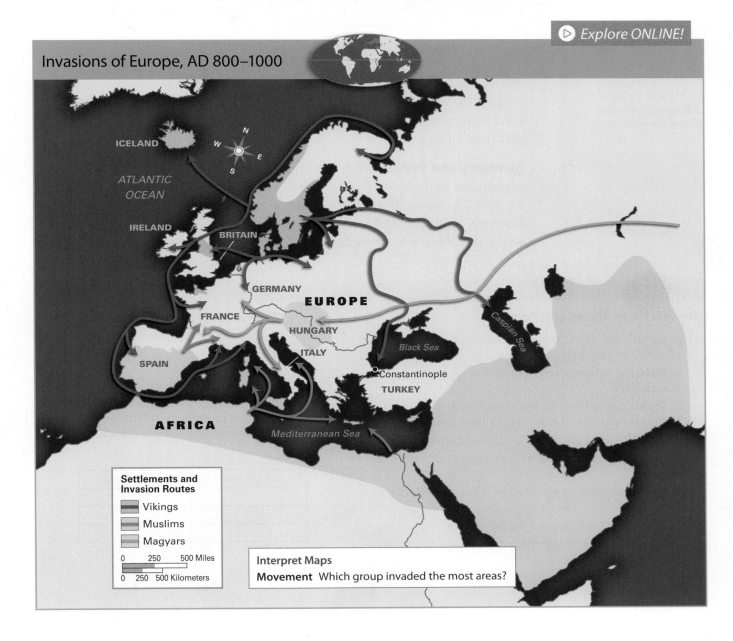

Invasions of Europe, AD 800–1000

Settlements and Invasion Routes
- Vikings
- Muslims
- Magyars

0   250   500 Miles
0   250   500 Kilometers

Interpret Maps
Movement Which group invaded the most areas?

Vikings used their versatile ships to invade much of Europe.

Reading Check
Find Main Ideas
What groups invaded Europe in the 700s and 800s?

Their attacks were swift and savage, and Europeans lived in terror of Viking raids.

Because Vikings could sail their ships up rivers, their raids weren't limited to coastal areas. The Vikings also reached inland cities and attacked cities in the Iberian and Italian peninsulas.

Summary and Preview You have just read about the role Europe's geography played in its history. After the fall of Rome, northern Europe gradually became Christian. But Europe could still be a dangerous place. Europe's flat land made it easy for other people to invade. In the next lesson, you will learn about ways people tried to protect themselves from invaders.

Lesson 1 Assessment

Review Ideas, Terms, and People

1. **a. Summarize** How do Europe's landforms and climates vary by region?

   b. Describe Where do most people in southern Europe live?

   c. Draw Conclusions Do you think Europe's major farming regions are in the north or the south? Why?

2. **a. Describe** How are monks and monasteries related?

   b. Explain Why did missionaries travel to northern Europe?

   c. Elaborate Why do you think monks followed such strict rules?

3. **a. Recall** What is Charlemagne famous for?

   b. Evaluate What do you think Charlemagne's greatest accomplishment was? Why?

4. **a. Identify** What areas of Europe did the Vikings raid?

   b. Form Generalizations Why were people in Europe so frightened of Viking raids?

Critical Thinking

5. **Analyze** Using your notes, determine which events brought unity to Europe and which brought division or disruption. Write your answers in a diagram like this one.

Brought Unity	Brought Division

Feudalism, Manors, and Towns

The Big Idea

A complex web of duties and obligations governed relationships between people in the Middle Ages.

Main Ideas

- Feudalism governed how knights and nobles dealt with one another.
- Feudalism spread through much of Europe.
- The manor system dominated Europe's economy.
- Towns and trade grew and helped end the feudal system.

Key Terms and People

knights
vassal
feudalism
William the Conqueror
manor
serfs
Eleanor of Aquitaine

If YOU were there . . .

You are a peasant in the Middle Ages, living on the land of a noble. Although you and your family work very hard for many hours of the day, much of the food you grow goes to the noble and his family. Your house is very small, and it has a dirt floor. Your parents are tired and weak, and you wish you could do something to improve their lives.

Is there any way you could change your life?

Feudalism Governs Knights and Nobles

When the Vikings, Magyars, and Muslims began their raids in the 800s, the Frankish kings were unable to defend their empire. Their army was too slow to defend against the lightning-fast attacks of their enemies. Because nobles couldn't depend on protection from their kings, they had to defend their own lands. As a result, the power of nobles grew, and kings became less powerful. In fact, some nobles became as powerful as the kings themselves. Although these nobles remained loyal to the king, they ruled their lands as independent territories. Kingdoms like France, for example, were unified in name only.

Knights and Land To defend their lands, nobles needed soldiers. The best soldiers were **knights**, warriors who fought on horseback. However, knights needed weapons, armor, and horses. This equipment was expensive, and few people had money in the early Middle Ages.

As a result, nobles gave knights fiefs (FEEFS), or parcels of land, instead of money for their military service. A noble who gave land to a knight in this way was called a lord.

Feudal Society

Kings and Queens

Kings and queens were the greatest lords and ladies of Europe, and all nobles and knights were their vassals.

Nobles

Nobles were vassals of kings and queens. Many were also lords of lower-ranking nobles and knights.

Knights

Knights served their noble lords in exchange for land.

Peasants

Peasants owned no land, so they were not part of the feudal system. But many peasants worked on land owned by nobles or knights.

Analyze Visuals
How could a noble be both a lord and a vassal?

In return for the land, a knight promised to support the noble in battle or in other matters. A knight who promised to support a lord in exchange for land was called a **vassal**. The vassal swore that he would always remain loyal to his lord. Historians call this system of promises that governed the relationships between lords and vassals **feudalism** (FYOO-duh-lih-zuhm).

A Lord's Duties The ties between lords and vassals were the heart of feudalism. Each group had certain responsibilities toward the other. A lord had to send help to his vassals if an enemy attacked. In addition, he had to be fair toward his vassals. He couldn't cheat them or punish them for no reason. If a lord failed to do what he was supposed to, his vassals could break all ties with him.

To defend their lands, many lords built castles. A castle is a large building with strong walls that can easily be defended against attacks. Early castles didn't look like the towering structures we see in movies and storybooks. Those great castles were built much later in the Middle Ages. Most early castles were made of wood, not stone. Nevertheless, these castles provided security in times of war.

Reading Check
Analyze Causes
What led to the creation of feudalism?

A Vassal's Duties When a lord went to war, he called on his vassals to fight with him. But fighting wasn't a vassal's only duty. For example, vassals had to give their lords money on special occasions, such as when a lord's son became a knight or when his daughter married. A vassal also had to give his lord food and shelter if he came to visit. If a vassal gained enough land, he could become a lord. In this way a person might be both a lord and a vassal. A knight could also accept fiefs from two different lords and become a vassal to both. Feudal obligations could become complicated.

Feudalism Spreads

Feudalism was created by the Franks. Before long the system began to spread into other kingdoms. In the 1000s, Frankish knights introduced feudalism into northern Italy, Spain, and Germany. Feudalism then spread into eastern Europe.

Feudalism also reached Britain in the 1000s. It was brought there by a French noble named William, who was the duke of Normandy, a region of northern France. In 1066, he decided to conquer England. This conquest of England became known as the Norman Invasion.

William and his knights sailed into England. Soon, they defeated the English king near the town of Hastings. After winning the Battle of Hastings, William declared himself the new king of England. He became known as **William the Conqueror**.

The impact of the Battle of Hastings and William's reign was enormous. Britain and northern France united politically. The British people were now ruled by a foreign government. French became the language of the government. As a result, French words entered the British vocabulary. To reward his knights for their part in the victory, William gave them large estates of land in his new country. This was the beginning of feudalism in England.

This photograph shows a statue of William the Conqueror, the duke of Normandy who conquered England and made himself king.

After he came to power, William needed money to fund his army. He created a survey of his new kingdom to see what taxes he could collect. This survey became known as the Domesday Book. Today, it gives historians a better understanding of England during the Middle Ages.

The Manor System

When a knight received a fief from his lord, he needed a way to farm it. Knights were fighters who didn't have time to work in the fields. At the same time, peasants, or small farmers, needed to grow food to live. Very few peasants, however, owned any land.

As a result, a new economic system developed. Under this system, knights allowed peasants to farm land on their large estates. In return, the peasants had to give the knights food or other payment.

The large estate owned by a knight or lord was called a **manor**. In general, each manor included a large house or castle, pastures, fields, and forests. It also had a village where the peasants who worked on the manor lived.

Reading Check
Summarize How did feudalism spread to England?

Life on a Manor

Manors were large estates that developed in Europe during the Middle Ages. Many manors were largely self-sufficient, producing most of the food and goods they needed. This picture shows what a manor in Britain might have looked like.

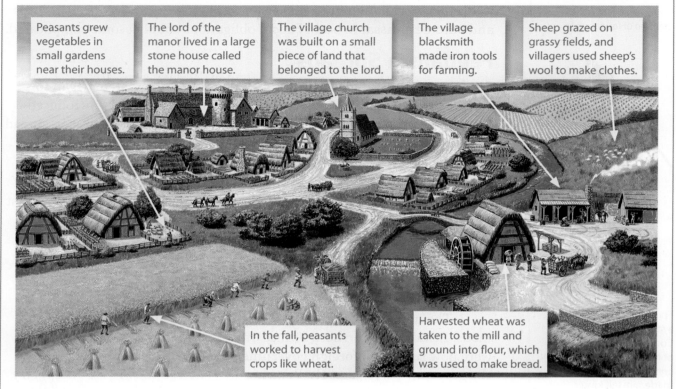

Peasants grew vegetables in small gardens near their houses.

The lord of the manor lived in a large stone house called the manor house.

The village church was built on a small piece of land that belonged to the lord.

The village blacksmith made iron tools for farming.

Sheep grazed on grassy fields, and villagers used sheep's wool to make clothes.

In the fall, peasants worked to harvest crops like wheat.

Harvested wheat was taken to the mill and ground into flour, which was used to make bread.

Analyze Visuals
What goods can you see being produced on this manor?

Peasants, Serfs, and Other Workers Most medieval lords kept about one-fourth to one-third of their land for their own use. The rest of the land was divided among peasants and **serfs**—workers who were tied to the land on which they lived.

Although they weren't slaves, serfs weren't allowed to leave their land without the lord's permission. Serfs spent much of their time working in their lord's fields. In return for this work, they got a small piece of land to farm for themselves. They also received their lord's protection against outlaws and raiders.

The lives of serfs and peasants weren't easy. Farm labor was hard, and they often worked in the fields late into the night. Men did most of the farming. Women made clothing, cooked, grew vegetables, and gathered firewood. Even children worked, tending sheep and chickens.

Most manors, in addition to peasants and serfs, had several skilled workers. These workers traded their goods and services to the peasants in exchange for food. Lords wanted the people who lived on the manor to produce everything they needed, including food and clothing.

Manor Lords The lord of a manor controlled everything that happened on his lands. His word was law. The lord resolved any disputes that arose on the manor and punished people who misbehaved. He also collected taxes from the people who lived on his manor.

As you would expect, manor lords and ladies lived more comfortably than other people on the manor. They had servants and large houses. Still, their lives weren't easy. Lords who survived diseases faced the possibility of being killed in war.

Women in the Middle Ages Regardless of their social class, women in the Middle Ages had fewer rights than men. Women generally had to obey the wishes of their fathers or husbands. But women still had important **roles** in society. As you have read, peasant women worked to support their families. Noblewomen also had duties. They ran manor households and supervised servants. Women governed manors when their husbands went to war. Some noblewomen, like the French woman **Eleanor of Aquitaine**, had great political power. Other women who wanted power and influence joined the most powerful of institutions, the Christian Church.

Academic Vocabulary
role assigned behavior

Reading Check
Contrast How were the lives of nobles and peasants different?

BIOGRAPHY

Eleanor of Aquitaine
c. 1122–1204

Eleanor of Aquitaine was one of the most powerful people of the Middle Ages. She ruled Aquitaine, a region in southwestern France, as the king's vassal. In 1137, Eleanor became queen of France when she married King Louis VII. Later, she divorced Louis and became queen of England by marrying King Henry II of England. Even while she was queen of England, she spent much of her time ruling her own territory. Eleanor had many children, and two of her sons later became kings of England.

Draw Conclusions
Why do you think Eleanor had more power than other women in the Middle Ages?

Towns and Trade Grow

In the Middle Ages, most people lived on manors or on small farms, not in towns. As a result, most towns were small. After about 1000, however, this situation began to change. A process called urbanization began to take place. More people began to live in certain areas. As a result, some towns became big cities. At the same time, new towns appeared.

What led to the growth of medieval towns? For one thing, Europe's population increased, partly because more food was available. New technology helped farmers produce larger harvests than ever before. Among these improvements was a heavier plow. With this plow farmers could dig deeper into the soil, helping their plants grow better. Another new device, the horse collar, allowed farmers to plow fields using horses. In times past, farmers had used oxen, which were strong but slow. With horses, farmers could tend larger fields, grow more food, and feed more people.

Towns also grew because trade increased. As Europe's population grew, so did trade. Trade routes spread all across Europe. Merchants also brought goods from Asia and Africa to sell in markets in Europe. The chance to make money in trade led many people to leave their farms and move to cities, causing cities to grow even larger.

In time, the growth of trade led to the decline of feudalism. Knights began to demand money for their services instead of land. At the same time, serfs and peasants left their manors for towns, slowly weakening the manor system.

The resulting growth of towns had several effects in medieval Europe. Workers began to focus on making or selling particular types of goods. This process is known as labor specialization. Over time, groups of specialized workers formed associations called guilds. For example, a town might

Medieval Market

In the Middle Ages, some towns held large trade fairs each year. This illustration shows a bishop blessing a trade fair in France.

Reading Check
Analyze Causes
Why did towns and
trade grow in the
Middle Ages?

have a baker's guild and a blacksmith's guild. The guild system helped address changes in the economy. Often they dictated pricing for products and set standards for quality. Guilds also influenced town government to benefit the interests of their members.

Summary and Preview In this lesson, you learned about European feudalism and the social and economic relationships it created among people. In the next lesson, you will learn how European society changed after feudalism disappeared in the later Middle Ages. One major change was the growing importance of religion.

Lesson 2 Assessment

Review Ideas, Terms, and People

1. a. Define What was a knight?

b. Explain Why did vassals have to serve lords?

c. Elaborate Do you think knights or lords benefited more from feudalism? Why?

2. a. Explain How did William the Conqueror help spread feudalism?

b. Identify What was the Domesday Book?

3. a. Describe What was a typical manor like?

b. Elaborate How do you think most serfs felt about the manor system?

4. a. Recall What led to the growth of Europe's population in the Middle Ages?

b. Draw Conclusions Why do you think many peasants left their farms for cities?

Critical Thinking

5. Analyze Draw a flow chart like this one. Then in each box, list the duties and obligations that each group had toward the other.

Popes and Kings

The Big Idea

Popes and kings dominated European society in the Middle Ages.

Main Ideas

- Popes and kings ruled Europe as spiritual and political leaders.

- Popes fought for power, leading to a permanent split within the church.

- Kings and popes clashed over some issues.

Key Terms and People

excommunicate
Pope Gregory VII
Emperor Henry IV

Rome was the center of western Christianity because it was where the pope lived.

If YOU were there . . .

You are one of the children of the king of France. One day your father announces that he wants to make an alliance with a powerful noble family. To seal the alliance, he has arranged for you to marry one of his new ally's children. Your father wants you to be happy and asks what you think of the idea. You know the alliance will make your father's rule more secure, but it means leaving home to marry a stranger.

What will you say to your father?

Popes and Kings Rule Europe

In the early Middle Ages, great nobles and their knights held a great deal of power. As time passed, though, this power began to shift. More and more, power came into the hands of two types of leaders, popes and kings. Popes had great spiritual power, and kings had political power. Together, popes and kings controlled most of European society.

The Power of the Popes In the Middle Ages, the pope was the head of the Christian Church in western Europe. Since nearly everyone in the Middle Ages belonged to this church, the pope had great power. People saw the pope as God's representative on Earth. They looked to him for guidance about how to live and pray.

Because the pope was seen as God's representative, it was his duty to decide what the church would teach. From time to time, a pope would write a letter called a bull to explain a religious teaching or outline a church policy. In addition, the pope decided when someone was acting against the church.

If the pope felt someone was working against the church, he could punish the person in many ways. For serious offenses, the pope or other bishops could choose to **excommunicate**, or cast out from the church, the offender.

This punishment was deeply feared because Christians believed that a person who died while excommunicated would not get into heaven.

In addition to spiritual power, many popes had great political power. After the Roman Empire collapsed, many people in Italy looked to the pope as their leader. As a result, some popes began to live like royalty. They became rich and built huge palaces. At the same time, they came into conflict with Europe's other political leaders, kings.

The Power of Kings Europe in 1000 was divided into many small states. Most of these states were ruled by kings, some of whom had little real power. In a few places, though, kings had begun to take firm control of their countries. Look at the map to find England, France, and the Holy Roman Empire. At this time, Europe's most powerful kings ruled those three countries.

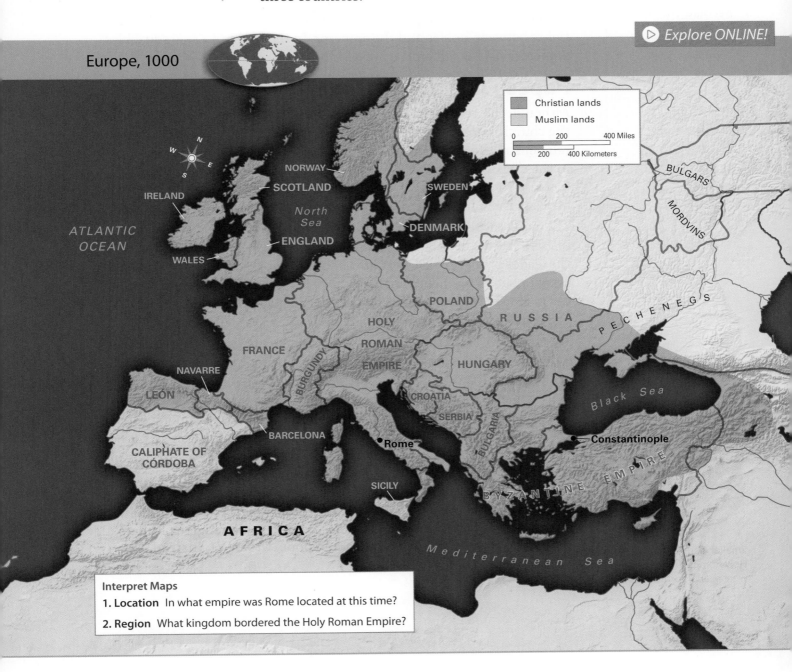

▶ Explore ONLINE!

Europe, 1000

Christian lands

Muslim lands

0   200   400 Miles
0   200   400 Kilometers

NORWAY
SCOTLAND
IRELAND
North Sea
SWEDEN
DENMARK
ATLANTIC OCEAN
ENGLAND
WALES
POLAND
RUSSIA
BULGARS
MORDVINS
HOLY ROMAN EMPIRE
PECHENEGS
FRANCE
BURGUNDY
HUNGARY
NAVARRE
CROATIA
Black Sea
LEÓN
SERBIA
BULGARIA
BARCELONA
• Rome
• Constantinople
CALIPHATE OF CÓRDOBA
BYZANTINE EMPIRE
SICILY

AFRICA

Mediterranean Sea

Interpret Maps

1. **Location** In what empire was Rome located at this time?

2. **Region** What kingdom bordered the Holy Roman Empire?

In England and France, kings inherited their thrones from their fathers. At times, nobles rebelled against the kings, but the kings usually reestablished order fairly quickly. They maintained this order through alliances as well as warfare.

The Holy Roman Empire In the Holy Roman Empire, however, the situation was different. This empire grew out of what had been Charlemagne's empire. As you read earlier, Charlemagne built his empire in the 700s with the pope's approval.

In the mid-900s, another emperor took the throne with the approval of the pope. Because the empire was approved by the pope and people saw it as a rebirth of the Roman Empire, it became known as the Holy Roman Empire.

Holy Roman emperors didn't inherit their crowns. Instead, they were elected by the empire's nobles. Sometimes, these elections led to fights between nobles and the emperor. In the worst of these squabbles, emperors had to call on the pope for help.

Reading Check
Contrast How did the powers of popes and kings differ?

Popes Fight for Power

Although the people of western Europe considered the pope the head of the church, people in eastern Europe disagreed. There, bishops controlled religious matters with little or no guidance from the pope. Beginning in the mid-1000s, however, a series of clever and able popes sought to increase their **authority** over eastern bishops. They believed all religious officials should answer to the pope.

Academic Vocabulary
authority power, right to rule

Among those who believed this was Pope Leo IX, who became pope in 1049. He argued that because the first pope, Saint Peter, had been the leader of the whole Christian Church, later popes should be as well. Despite Leo's arguments, many bishops in eastern Europe, most notably the bishop of Constantinople, wouldn't recognize his authority. In 1054, Leo decided to excommunicate that bishop.

Leo's decision created a permanent split within the church. Christians who agreed with the bishop of Constantinople formed the Orthodox Church. Those who supported Leo's authority became known as Roman Catholics. This event became known as the "Great Schism." A schism is a split or division among people. With their support, the pope became head of the Roman Catholic Church and one of the most powerful figures in western Europe.

Another schism occurred in the late 1300s and early 1400s. In 1309, the pope moved from Rome to Avignon, France. Roman Catholic popes remained there for about 70 years. Eventually, the pope returned to Rome. However, some religious leaders did not agree with the new Roman pope, Urban VI. Instead, they

Smaller German states made up the Holy Roman Empire. The emperors were seen as protectors of the pope.

Reading Check
Form Generalizations
How did Leo IX try
to increase popes'
authority?

elected their own pope, Clement VII, who ruled from France. Starting in 1378, some Roman Catholics obeyed the pope in Rome. Others obeyed the pope in France. This schism was finally resolved by the Roman Catholic Church in 1417. The pope was to remain in Rome.

Kings and Popes Clash

As popes worked to increase their power, they often came into conflict with kings. For example, kings thought they should be able to select bishops in their countries. Popes, on the other hand, argued that only they could choose religious officials.

In 1073, a new pope came to power in Rome. His name was **Pope Gregory VII**. Trouble arose when Gregory disapproved of a bishop chosen by the Holy Roman **Emperor Henry IV**. Angry because the pope questioned his authority, Henry convinced Germany's bishops that they should remove Gregory as pope. In response, the pope excommunicated Henry. He called on the empire's nobles to overthrow Henry.

Desperate to stay in power, Henry went to Italy to ask the pope for forgiveness. Gregory refused to see him. For three days Henry stood barefoot in the snow outside the castle where Pope Gregory was staying. Eventually, Gregory accepted Henry's apology and allowed the emperor back into the church. Gregory had proven himself more powerful than the emperor, at least for that moment.

DOCUMENT-BASED INVESTIGATION   Historical Source

Views of Power

Pope Gregory VII thought popes should have the power to choose bishops. He believed popes—not kings—got their power from God.

Emperor Henry IV thought popes had too much power. He argued that kings should choose bishops because God had chosen the king.

Analyze Historical Sources
What words indicate Pope Gregory's view that the church has more power than monarchs do?

"Who does not know that kings and princes derive their origin from men ignorant of God who raised themselves above their fellows by . . . every kind of crime? . . . Does anyone doubt that the priests of Christ are to be considered as fathers and masters of kings and princes and of all believers?"

—Pope Gregory VII,
from a letter to the Bishop of Metz, 1081,
in *Readings in Medieval History*,
edited by Patrick Geary

"Our Lord, Jesus Christ, has called us to kingship, but has not called you to the priesthood. . . . You who have not been called by God have taught that our bishops who have been called by God are to be [rejected]. . . ."

—Emperor Henry IV,
from a letter to Pope Gregory VII, 1076,
in *Readings in Medieval History*,
edited by Patrick Geary

Reading Check
Analyze Causes
What caused Gregory and Henry's power struggle?

The fight over the right to choose bishops continued even after Henry and Gregory died. In 1122, a new pope and emperor reached a compromise. They decided that church officials would choose all bishops and abbots. The bishops and abbots, however, would still have to obey the emperor.

This compromise did not end all conflict. Kings and popes continued to fight for power throughout the Middle Ages, changing lives all over Europe.

Summary and Preview In this lesson you read about the powers of popes and kings. In many cases, these powers led to conflict between the two. In the next lesson, though, you will read about popes and kings working together against a common enemy.

Lesson 3 Assessment

Review Ideas, Terms, and People

1. a. **Describe** What was the pope's role in the Roman Catholic Church?

   b. **Draw Conclusions** How did cooperation with the pope help kings like Charlemagne and the early Holy Roman Emperors?

2. **Explain** Why did Pope Leo IX excommunicate the bishop of Constantinople?

3. a. **Identify** With whom did Pope Gregory VII clash?

   b. **Explain** Why do you think the pope made Emperor Henry IV wait for three days before forgiving him?

Critical Thinking

4. **Compare** Draw a diagram like the one shown here. Use it and your notes to compare the power of popes with the power of kings.

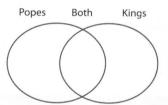

The Crusades

The Big Idea

The Christian and Muslim cultures fought over holy sites during a series of medieval wars.

Main Ideas

- The pope called on Crusaders to invade the Holy Land.

- Despite some initial success, the later Crusades failed.

- The Crusades changed Europe forever.

Key Terms and People

Crusades
Holy Land
Pope Urban II
King Richard I
Saladin

If YOU were there . . .

You belong to a noble family that has produced many great knights. One day your uncle, the head of the family, tells you that the pope has called on warriors to defend holy places in a faraway land. Your uncle is too old to fight, so it falls on you to answer the pope's call to war. The journey will be long and dangerous. Still, you will see new places and possibly win glory for your family.

How do you feel about joining this war?

Crusaders Invade the Holy Land

The **Crusades** were a long series of wars between Christians and Muslims in Southwest Asia. They were fought over control of Palestine, a region of Southwest Asia. Europeans called Palestine the **Holy Land** because it was the region where Jesus had lived, preached, and died.

Causes of the Crusades For many years, Palestine had been in the hands of Muslims. In general, the Muslims did not bother Christians who visited the region. In the

The Holy Land was the scene of many bloody battles during the Crusades, like the one near the city of Antioch, shown in this medieval painting.

These reenactors show what Crusaders may have worn in battle.

1000s, though, a group of Turkish Muslims entered the area and captured the city of Jerusalem. Pilgrims returning to Europe said that these Turks had attacked them in the Holy Land, which was no longer safe for Christians.

Before long, the Turks began to raid the Byzantine Empire. The Byzantine emperor, fearing an attack on Constantinople, asked **Pope Urban II** of the Roman Catholic Church for help. Although the Byzantines were Orthodox Catholics and not Roman Catholic, the pope agreed to the request.

The Call to Arms Pope Urban called on Christians from all over Europe to retake the Holy Land from the Muslim Turks. He challenged Europe's kings and nobles to quit fighting among themselves and fight together against the Turks. In response, people joined the pope's army by the thousands.

Crusaders from all over Europe flocked to France to prepare for their long journey. They sewed crosses onto their clothing to show that they were fighting for God. In fact, the word *crusade* comes from the Latin for "marked with a cross." As they marched off to war, the Crusaders yelled their rallying cry, "God wills it!"

Why would people leave home to fight in a distant land? Some just hoped to save their souls or to do what they thought God wanted. They thought that God would look favorably on them for fighting his enemies, as one French abbot noted:

"What a glory to return in victory from such a battle! . . . [I]f they are blessed who die in the Lord, how much more are they who die for the Lord!"
—Saint Bernard of Clairvaux, from *In Praise of the New Knighthood*

Other Crusaders wanted land and treasure. Still others were looking for something to do. Adventure called to them.

The First Crusade About 5,000 Crusaders left Europe for the Holy Land in 1096. Some of the first ones to set out were peasants, not soldiers. On their way to the Holy Land, these peasant Crusaders attacked Jews in Germany. They blamed the Jews for Jesus' death.

Turkish troops killed most of these untrained, poorly equipped peasants before they even reached the Holy Land.

The nobles and knights fared better. When they reached Jerusalem in 1099, they found the Muslim army disorganized and unready to fight. After about a month of fighting, the Crusaders took Jerusalem.

After the Europeans took Jerusalem, they set up four small kingdoms in the Holy Land. The rulers of these kingdoms created lord and vassal systems like they had known at home. They also began to trade with people back in Europe.

Reading Check **Summarize** What did the First Crusade accomplish?

Richard I 1157–1199

Called "Lion Heart" for his courage, Richard I was a skilled soldier and a great general. He did not succeed in taking Jerusalem during the Third Crusade, but he earned the respect of Muslims and Christians alike. Since his death, he has become the hero of countless stories and legends.

Draw Conclusions
Why do you think both Muslims and Christians respected Richard I?

Later Crusades Fail

The kingdoms the Christians created in the Holy Land didn't last, though. Within 50 years the Muslims had started taking land back from the Christians. In response, the Europeans launched more Crusades.

The Second and Third Crusades French and German kings set off in 1147 to retake land from the Muslims. This Second Crusade was a terrible failure. Poor planning and heavy losses on the journey to the Holy Land led to the Christians' total defeat. Ashamed, the Crusaders returned to Europe in less than a year.

The Third Crusade began after the Muslims retook Jerusalem in 1189. The rulers of England, France, and the Holy Roman Empire led their armies to the Holy Land to fight for Jerusalem, but problems soon arose. The German king died, and the French king left. Only **King Richard I** of England stayed in the Holy Land.

King Richard's main opponent in the Third Crusade was **Saladin**, the leader of the Muslim forces. Known as "Saladin the Great," he was a brilliant leader. Even Crusaders respected his kindness toward fallen enemies. In turn, the Muslims admired Richard's bravery.

For months, Richard and Saladin fought and negotiated. Richard captured a few towns and won protection for Christian pilgrims. In the end, however, he returned home with Jerusalem still in Muslim hands.

Saladin 1137–1193

Saladin is often called one of the greatest generals of the Middle Ages. The Muslim leader successfully held Jerusalem against Richard I in the Third Crusade. Saladin's people considered their leader a wise ruler. Crusaders respected his sometimes kind treatment of fallen enemies. Many Christians saw him as a model of knightly chivalry.

Compare
What did Saladin have in common with Richard I?

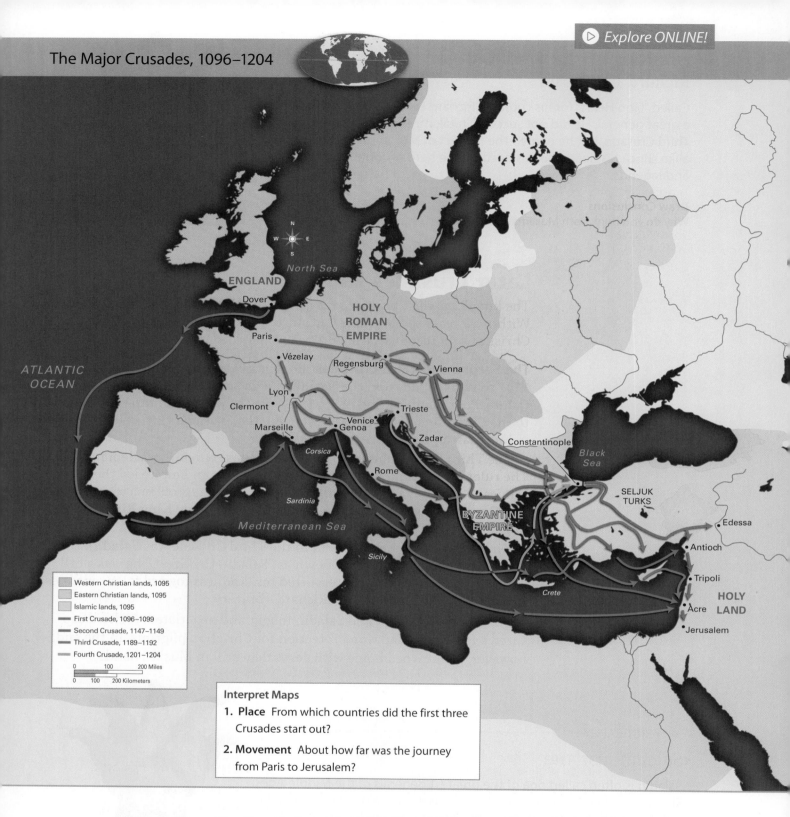

The Major Crusades, 1096–1204

ENGLAND

Dover

ATLANTIC OCEAN

North Sea

HOLY ROMAN EMPIRE

Paris

Vézelay

Regensburg

Vienna

Lyon

Clermont

Trieste

Marseille

Venice

Genoa

Zadar

Constantinople

Black Sea

Corsica

Rome

SELJUK TURKS

Sardinia

Mediterranean Sea

BYZANTINE EMPIRE

Edessa

Sicily

Crete

Antioch

Tripoli

Acre

HOLY LAND

Jerusalem

Western Christian lands, 1095
Eastern Christian lands, 1095
Islamic lands, 1095
First Crusade, 1096–1099
Second Crusade, 1147–1149
Third Crusade, 1189–1192
Fourth Crusade, 1201–1204

0   100   200 Miles
0   100   200 Kilometers

Interpret Maps

1. **Place** From which countries did the first three Crusades start out?

2. **Movement** About how far was the journey from Paris to Jerusalem?

The Fourth Crusade In 1201, French knights arrived in Venice ready to sail to the Holy Land to begin a Fourth Crusade. However, the knights didn't have money to pay for the voyage. For payment, the Venetians asked the knights to conquer Zara, a rival trade city. The knights agreed. Later they also attacked Constantinople and carried off many treasures. The city that had been threatened by Muslims before the Crusades was sacked by Christians!

The End of the Crusades Other Crusades followed, but none were successful. By 1291, the Muslim armies had taken back all of the Holy Land, and the Crusades had ended. Why did the Crusades fail? There were many reasons.

- Crusaders had to travel huge distances just to reach the war. Many died along the way.
- Crusaders weren't prepared to fight in Palestine's desert climate.
- The Christians were outnumbered by their well-led and organized Muslim foes.
- Christian leaders fought among themselves and planned poorly.

Whatever the reasons for their failure, the Crusades ended just as they had begun so many years before, with the Holy Land under Muslim control.

Reading Check
Analyze Causes
How did geography limit the success of the Crusades?

Crusades Change Europe

Although the Crusades failed, they changed Europe forever. More trade routes between Europe and Asia were established. Europeans who went to the Holy Land learned about products such as apricots, rice, and cotton cloth. Crusaders also brought ideas of Muslim thinkers back with them. In both these ways, Islamic achievements in math, science, and other subjects were introduced to Europe.

Politics in Europe also changed. Some kings increased their power because many nobles and knights had died in the Holy Land. These kings seized lands that were left without clear owners. During the later Crusades, kings also gained influence at the popes' expense. The popes had wanted the church to be in charge of all the Crusades. Instead, rulers and nobles took control. The use of gunpowder to make explosives during the Crusades also had political effects. European rulers used gunpowder to develop new weapons. Countries later used those weapons to fight each other and conquer new territory.

The Crusades had lasting effects on relations among peoples as well. Because some Crusaders had attacked Jews, many Jews distrusted Christians. In addition, tension between the Byzantines and western Christians increased, especially after Crusaders attacked Constantinople.

Quick Facts

The Crusades

Causes

- Turks take control of the Holy Land in 1071.
- Turks threaten Constantinople in the 1090s.
- Byzantine emperor asks pope for help.

Effects

- Trade between Europe and Asia increases.
- Kings become more powerful.
- Christian-Muslim and Christian-Jewish tensions increase.

Reading Check
Find Main Ideas
What were some
results of the
Crusades?

The greatest changes occurred with Christian and Muslim relationships. Each group learned about the other's religion and culture. Sometimes this led to mutual respect. In general, though, the Crusaders saw Muslims as unbelievers who threatened innocent Christians. Most Muslims viewed the Crusaders as vicious invaders. Some historians think the distrust that began during the Crusades still affects Christian and Muslim relationships today.

Summary and Preview In this lesson, you learned how religious beliefs led to a series of wars. In the next lesson, you will learn about the role of religion in most people's daily lives in the Middle Ages.

Lesson 4 Assessment

Review Ideas, Terms, and People

1. a. **Recall** What did Pope Urban II ask Christians to do?

   b. **Elaborate** Why do you think so many people were willing to go on a Crusade?

2. a. **Identify** In which Crusade did Saladin and King Richard I fight?

   b. **Analyze** Which Crusade do you think was the least successful? Why?

3. a. **Identify** What new products were introduced to Europe after the Crusades?

   b. **Draw Conclusions** Why did the Crusades change relationships between Christians and other groups?

Critical Thinking

4. **Compare and Contrast** Draw a diagram like the one here. Use it and your notes to compare and contrast Europe before and after the Crusades.

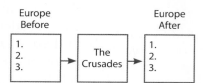

Christianity and Medieval Society

The Big Idea

The Christian Church was central to life in the Middle Ages.

Main Ideas

- The Christian Church shaped both society and politics in medieval Europe.
- Orders of monks and friars did not like the church's political nature.
- Church leaders helped build the first universities in Europe.
- The church influenced the arts in medieval Europe.

Key Terms and People

clergy
religious order
Francis of Assisi
friars
Thomas Aquinas
natural law

If YOU were there . . .

You are a stone carver, apprenticed to a master builder. The bishop has hired your master to design a huge new church. He wants the church to inspire and impress worshippers with the glory of God. Your master has entrusted you with the decoration of the outside of the church. You are excited by the challenge.

What kind of art will you create for the church?

The Church Shapes Society and Politics

Nearly everyone who lived in Europe during the Middle Ages was Christian. In fact, Christianity was central to every part of life. Church officials, called **clergy**, and their teachings were very influential in European culture and politics.

The Church and Society In the Middle Ages, life revolved around the local church. Markets, festivals, and religious ceremonies all took place there.

For some people, however, the local church was not enough. They wanted to see important religious sites—the places where Jesus lived, where holy men and women died, and where miracles happened. The church encouraged these people to go on pilgrimages, journeys to religious locations. Among the most popular destinations were Jerusalem, Rome, and Compostela, in northwestern Spain. Each of these cities had churches that Christians wanted to visit.

Another popular pilgrimage destination was Canterbury, near London in England. Hundreds of visitors went to the cathedral in Canterbury each year. One such visit is the basis for one of the greatest books of the Middle Ages, *The Canterbury Tales* by Geoffrey Chaucer (CHAW-suhr).

The Church and Politics The church also gained political power during the Middle Ages. Many people left land to the church when they died. In fact, the church was one of the largest landholders in Europe. Eventually, the church divided this land into fiefs. In this way, it became a feudal lord.

Of all the clergy, bishops and abbots were most involved in political matters. They often advised local rulers. Some clergy got so involved with politics that they spent little time dealing with religious affairs.

Reading Check
Synthesize In what ways were clergy members important political figures?

Monks and Friars

Some people were unhappy with the political nature of the church. They thought the clergy should focus only on spiritual matters. These people feared that the church had become obsessed with wealth and power.

The Monks of Cluny Among those unhappy with the church were a group of French monks. In the early 900s they started a monastery in the town of Cluny (KLOO-nee). The monks of Cluny followed a strict schedule of prayers and religious services. They paid little attention to the world, concerning themselves only with religious matters.

The changes at Cluny led to the creation of a religious order, the Cluniac monks. A **religious order** is a group of people who dedicate their lives to religion and follow common rules. Across Europe, people saw Cluny as an example of how monks should live. They built new monasteries and tried to live like the Cluniacs.

The towers of old Christian churches still rise above many European towns and cities. Christianity became a strong influence on European life in the Middle Ages.

The Cluny Monastery

The great monastery at Cluny, France, is shown here as it appeared in the 1100s. Together the buildings made up something like a small town. At one point, more than 300 monks lived there.

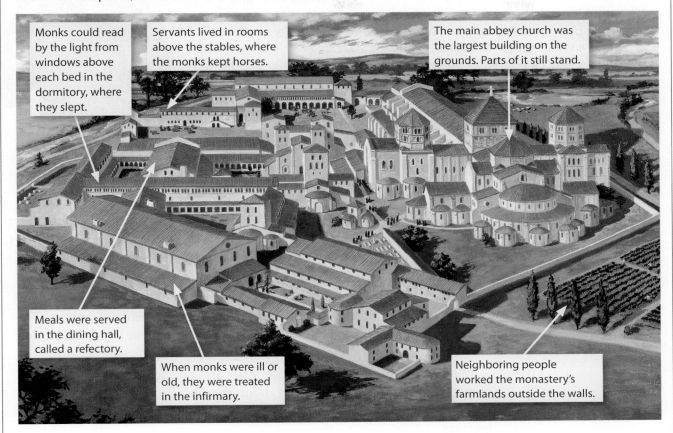

Monks could read by the light from windows above each bed in the dormitory, where they slept.

Servants lived in rooms above the stables, where the monks kept horses.

The main abbey church was the largest building on the grounds. Parts of it still stand.

Meals were served in the dining hall, called a refectory.

When monks were ill or old, they were treated in the infirmary.

Neighboring people worked the monastery's farmlands outside the walls.

Analyze Visuals
How does this illustration show the wealth of the church?

Other New Orders By the 1100s, though, some monks thought that even Cluny's rules weren't strict enough. They created new orders with even stricter rules. Some took vows of silence and stopped speaking to each other. Others lived in tiny rooms and left them only to go to church services.

Men were not the only ones to create and join religious orders. Women were allowed to join these kinds of orders as well. Communities of nuns called convents appeared across Europe. Like monks, these nuns lived according to a strict set of rules. The nuns of each convent prayed and worked together under the watchful eyes of an abbess, the convent's leader.

Although monks and nuns lived apart from other people, they did a great deal for society. For example, they collected and stored texts that explained Christian teachings. Monks spent hours copying these documents, and they sent copies to monasteries across Europe.

Francis of Assisi c. 1182–1226

Born in Assisi, Italy, Francis was the son of a wealthy merchant. As a young man, however, Francis gave all his money and possessions away and left his father's house. He lived a simple life, preaching and tending to people who were poor or ill. Francis considered everyone his brother or sister, including animals. He encouraged people to take care of animals just as they would take care of other people. Within a few years other people had begun to copy his lifestyle. In 1210, they became the first members of the Franciscan Order.

Form Generalizations
How do you think Francis's generosity and compassion might inspire Christians to follow the church's teachings?

The Friars Not everyone who joined a religious order wanted to live apart from society. Some wanted to live in cities and spread Christian teachings. As a result, two new religious orders were begun in the early 1200s.

These orders were the Dominicans and the Franciscans, named for their founders, Dominic de Guzmán and **Francis of Assisi**. Because they didn't live in monasteries, members of these orders were not monks. They were **friars**, people who belonged to religious orders but lived and worked among the general public.

Friars lived simply, wearing plain robes and no shoes. Like monks, they owned no property. They roamed about, preaching and begging for food. For that reason, friars were also called mendicants, from a Latin word for beggars.

The main goal of the friars was to teach people how to live good Christian lives. They taught people about generosity and kindness. A prayer credited to Francis illustrates what the friars hoped to do.

"Lord, make me an instrument of your peace. Where there is hatred, let me sow love; where there is injury, pardon; where there is doubt, faith; where there is despair, hope; where there is darkness, light; and where there is sadness, joy."

—Francis of Assisi, from *The Prayer of Saint Francis*

Reading Check
Summarize Why did people create new religious orders?

Universities Are Built

While some people were drawing away from the world in monasteries and convents, others were looking for ways to learn more about it. In time, their search for knowledge led to the creation of Europe's first universities.

Some of the earliest universities were created by the church. The church's goal was to teach people about religion. In order to do this, church universities also collected and preserved religious texts. Other universities were created by groups of students who went searching for teachers who could tell them about the world.

Most teachers in these universities were members of the clergy. Besides religion, schools taught law, medicine, astronomy, and other courses. All

School Days

Did you know that many customs that schools and universities follow today began in the Middle Ages? For example, medieval teachers taught groups of students instead of individuals. Classes ran according to a fixed schedule, and students had to take tests. Many students participated in sports such as races and ball games after classes. At graduation, students dressed up in caps and gowns. Medieval universities were not exactly the same as universities are now, however. Medieval students entered the university at age 14, and only boys could attend.

Analyze Information
Why do you think some customs followed by universities in the Middle Ages have lasted until today?

classes were taught in Latin. Although few people spoke Latin, it was the language of scholars and the church. As a result, these universities helped preserve the Latin language during the Middle Ages.

As people began to study new subjects, some of them developed new ideas about the world. In particular, they wondered how human reason and Christian faith were related. In the past, people had believed that some things could be proven with reason, but other things had to be taken on faith. Some people in universities, though, began to wonder if the two ideas could work together.

One such person was the Dominican philosopher **Thomas Aquinas** (uh-KWY-nuhs). Thomas was a teacher at the University of Paris. He argued that rational thought could be used to support Christian beliefs. For example, he wrote an argument to prove the existence of God.

— BIOGRAPHY —

Thomas Aquinas 1225–1274

Although he was born in Italy, Thomas Aquinas lived most of his life in France. As a student and then a teacher at the University of Paris, Thomas spent most of his time in study. He wrote a book, called the *Summa Theologica*, in which he argued that science and religion were related.

Although some people did not like Thomas's ideas, most considered him the greatest thinker of the Middle Ages. Later teachers modeled their lessons after his ideas.

Form Generalizations
Why might people believe someone is a great thinker even if they disagree with his or her ideas?

Reading Check
Summarize How did universities help create new ideas?

Thomas also believed that God had created a law that governed how the world operated. He called it **natural law**. If people could study and learn more about this law, he argued, they could learn to live the way God wanted.

The Church and the Arts

In addition to politics and education, the church was also a strong influence on art and architecture. Throughout the Middle Ages, religious feeling inspired artists and architects to create beautiful works of art.

Religious Architecture Many of Europe's churches were remarkable works of art. The grandest of these churches were cathedrals, large churches in which bishops led religious services. Beginning in the 1100s, Europeans built their cathedrals using a dramatic new style called Gothic architecture.

Gothic Architecture

One of the most beautiful of all Gothic cathedrals is in Chartres (SHAHRT), near Paris, France. At 112 feet high, it is about as tall as a 10-story building.

Flying buttresses support heavy walls.

Huge stained glass windows called rose windows are found in many Gothic cathedrals.

Pointed arches support the high ceilings.

Analyze Visuals
What would it have been like to travel from a small farm and see this cathedral for the first time?

This illuminated manuscript is from a 15th-century book of hours. The illustrations were an important part of the text and one reason for the book's popularity.

Gothic cathedrals were not only places to pray but also symbols of people's faith. As a result, they were towering works of great majesty and glory. The walls often rose up hundreds of feet, and the ceilings seemed to reach to heaven. Huge stained glass windows let sunlight pour in, filling the churches with dazzling colors. Many of these amazing churches still exist, and people still worship in them.

Religious Art Medieval churches were also filled with beautiful objects created to show respect for God. Ornate paintings and tapestries covered the walls and ceilings. Even the clothing priests wore during religious services was attractive. Their robes were often highly decorated, sometimes with threads made of gold.

Many of the books used during religious ceremonies were beautiful objects. Monks had copied these books carefully. They also decorated them using bright colors to adorn the first letters and the borders of each page. Some monks added thin sheets of silver and gold to the pages. Because the pages seem to glow, we use the word *illuminated* to describe them.

Reading Check
Synthesize How were medieval art and religion related?

Summary and Preview Besides its religious role, the church played important roles in politics, education, and the arts. The church changed as time passed. In the next lesson, you will learn about other changes that took place in Europe at the same time. These changes created new political systems around the continent.

Lesson 5 Assessment

Review Ideas, Terms, and People

1. a. **Recall** What are church officials called?
   b. **Explain** Why did people go on pilgrimages?
2. a. **Identify** What new monastery founded in France in the 900s served as an example to people around Europe?
   b. **Contrast** How were friars different from monks?
3. **Analyze** How did Thomas Aquinas think reason and faith could work together?
4. a. **Identify** What new style of religious architecture developed in Europe in the 1100s?
   b. **Elaborate** Why do you think so much of the art created in the Middle Ages was religious?

Critical Thinking

5. **Categorize** Draw a chart like this one. Using your notes, decide which of the church's roles were political, which were intellectual, and which were artistic. List each role in the appropriate column of your chart.

The Church in the Middle Ages		
Political	Intellectual	Artistic

Political and Social Change

The Big Idea

Europe's political and social systems underwent great changes in the late Middle Ages.

Main Ideas

- Magna Carta caused changes in England's government and legal system.

- The Hundred Years' War led to political changes in England and France.

- The Black Death led to social changes.

- The church reacted to challengers by punishing people who opposed its teachings.

- Christians fought Moors in Spain and Portugal in an effort to drive Muslims out of Europe.

- Jews faced discrimination across Europe in the Middle Ages.

Key Terms and People

Magna Carta
Parliament
Hundred Years' War
Joan of Arc
Black Death
heresy
Reconquista
King Ferdinand
Queen Isabella
Spanish Inquisition

If YOU were there . . .

You are a baron, one of England's great nobles, living in northern Britain. Winter is approaching, and it looks like it will be very cold soon. To prepare for the winter, you send some of your servants to a forest on your land to gather firewood. When they return, though, they don't have much wood. The king has chopped down many of the trees in your forest to build a new castle. Dismayed, you send a messenger to ask the king to pay a fair price for the wood, but he refuses.

How can you get the king to respect your rights?

Magna Carta Causes Change in England

In 1215, a group of nobles decided to force the king to respect their rights. In the middle of a field called Runnymede near London, they made King John approve a document they had written. This document listing rights that the king could not ignore was called **Magna Carta**. Its name is a Latin phrase meaning "Great Charter."

The Effects of Magna Carta Magna Carta changed the feudal system in England. To begin with, it required the king to honor certain rights. Among these rights was habeas corpus (HAY-bee-uhs KOHR-puhs), a Latin phrase meaning "you have the body." The right of habeas corpus meant that people could not be kept in jail without a reason. They had to be charged with a crime and convicted at a jury trial before they could be sent to prison. Before, kings could arrest people for no reason at all.

Magna Carta

Magna Carta

Magna Carta was one of the first documents to protect the rights of the people. Magna Carta was so influential that the British still consider it part of their constitution. Some of its ideas are also in the U.S. Constitution. Included in Magna Carta were 63 demands that English nobles made King John agree to follow. A few of these demands are listed here.

Demand 31 defended people's right to own any property, not just wood.

Magna Carta guaranteed that everyone had the right to a fair trial.

Analyze Historical Sources
In what ways do you think the ideas listed here influenced modern democracy?

"We have also granted to all freemen of our kingdom, for us and our heirs forever, all the underwritten liberties. . . .

(9) Neither we nor our bailiffs shall seize any land or rent for any debt, so long as the chattels [belongings] of the debtor are sufficient to repay the debt. . . .

(30) No sheriff or bailiff of ours, or other person, shall take the horses or carts of any freeman for transport duty, against the will of the said freeman.

(31) Neither we nor our bailiffs shall take, for our castles or for any other work of ours, wood which is not ours, against the will of the owner of that wood.

(38) No bailiff for the future shall, upon his own unsupported complaint, put any one to his 'law,' [on trial] without credible [believable] witnesses brought for this purpose."

—from *Magna Carta*

More importantly, Magna Carta required that everyone—even the king—had to obey the law. This idea that everyone must follow the law is known as the rule of law. It became one of the basic principles of English government.

Changes After Magna Carta Magna Carta inspired the English to find more ways to limit the king's power. A council of nobles was created to advise the king. In time, the council developed into **Parliament** (PAHR-luh-muhnt), the highest law-making body in the United Kingdom today. Over the years, membership in Parliament was opened to knights and town leaders. By the late Middle Ages, kings could do little without Parliament's support.

The English continued to work to secure and protect their rights. To ensure that everyone was treated fairly, people demanded that judges be free of royal control. Many people believed judges chosen by the king would always side with him. Eventually, in the late 1600s, the king agreed to free the courts of his control. This creation of an independent judicial system was a key step in the development of democracy in England.

Reading Check
Summarize How did Magna Carta and Parliament limit the king's power?

Timeline: Beginnings of Democracy in England

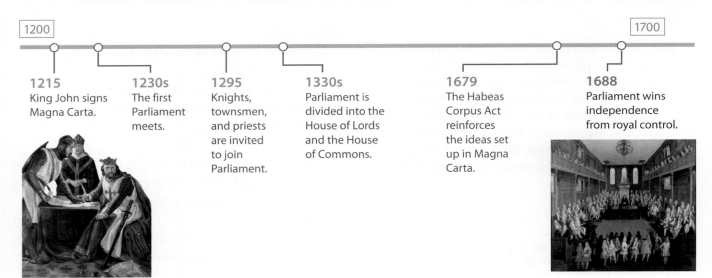

1200

1215
King John signs Magna Carta.

1230s
The first Parliament meets.

1295
Knights, townsmen, and priests are invited to join Parliament.

1330s
Parliament is divided into the House of Lords and the House of Commons.

1679
The Habeas Corpus Act reinforces the ideas set up in Magna Carta.

1688
Parliament wins independence from royal control.

1700

The Hundred Years' War

Although Magna Carta changed England's government, it had no effect outside of that country. Kings in other parts of Europe continued to rule as they always had. Eventually, however, these kings also had to face great political changes.

The Course of the War One of the countries in which political change occurred was France. In 1328 the king of France died with no sons, and two men claimed his throne. One was French. The other was the king of England. In the end, the French man became king.

This did not sit well with the English king, and a few years later he invaded France. This invasion began a long conflict between England and France that came to be called the **Hundred Years' War**.

At first the English armies did well, winning most of the battles. After nearly 100 years of fighting, however, a teenage peasant girl, **Joan of Arc**,

In this scene, French teenager Joan of Arc carries a religious flag as she leads an army into battle during the Hundred Years' War.

rallied the French troops. Although the English eventually captured and killed Joan, it was too late. The French drove the English from their country in 1453.

Results of the War The Hundred Years' War changed the governments of both England and France. In England, Parliament's power grew because the king needed Parliament's approval to raise money to pay for the costly war. As Parliament gained more influence, the king lost power.

In France, on the other hand, the king's power grew. During the war, the king had become popular with his nobles. Fighting the English had created a bond between them. As a result, the nobles supported the king after the war as well.

The Hundred Years' War also changed how European armies fought. During the conflict, armies used cannons and other large weapons powered by gunpowder. These weapons became known as artillery. Artillery would have political effects as well. Countries could now fight wars and expand territory faster and less expensively.

Reading Check
Contrast How did the governments of England and France change after the war?

The Black Death

While the English and French fought the Hundred Years' War, an even greater crisis arose. This crisis was the **Black Death**, a deadly plague that swept through Europe between 1347 and 1351.

The plague originally came from central and eastern Asia. Unknowingly, traders brought rats carrying the disease to Mediterranean ports in 1347. From there it quickly swept throughout much of Europe. Fleas that feasted on the blood of infected rats passed on the plague to people.

Link to Today

Disease Prevention

Over the centuries, people have had different ideas about how humans are infected by disease. People often used to think that demons or evil spirits caused diseases. This explanation is still believed by some people around the world. Modern scientists discovered that microscopic germs and viruses cause diseases.

The bubonic plague is now fairly rare, but cases are still reported in Asia, Africa, and South America. Doctors treat plague victims with antibiotics. Governments use pesticides to control the insects that spread the disease.

Today, we understand that inoculations can prevent people from getting specific types of diseases. They are an important part of modern medicine that medieval doctors did not have. Children now usually get inoculations to prevent diseases.

Analyze Information
Why is the bubonic plague fairly rare today?

The Black Death was not caused by one disease but by several different forms of plague. One form called bubonic plague (byoo-BAH-nik PLAYG) could be identified by swellings called buboes that appeared on victims' bodies. Another even deadlier form could spread through the air and kill people in less than a day.

The Black Death killed so many people that many were buried quickly without priests or ceremonies. In some villages nearly everyone died or fled as neighbors fell ill. In England alone, about 1,000 villages were abandoned.

The plague killed millions of people in Europe and millions more around the world. Some historians think Europe lost about a third of its population—perhaps 25 million people. This huge drop in population caused sweeping changes in Europe.

In most places, the manor system fell apart completely. There weren't enough people left to work in the fields. Those peasants and serfs who had survived the plague found their skills in high demand. Suddenly, they could demand wages for their labor. Once they had money, many fled their manors completely, moving instead to Europe's growing cities. The Black Death had a religious impact as well. Many church leaders were killed, while others stopped performing services. Ordinary people began to seek for answers and solutions elsewhere. The power of the church began to decline.

Reading Check
Analyze Effects
What effects did bubonic plague have in Europe?

The Church Reacts to Challengers

By around 1100, some Christians had begun to question church teachings. They felt that the clergy focused more on money and land than on God. Others didn't agree with the church's ideas. They began to preach their own ideas about religion.

Religious ideas that oppose accepted church teachings are called **heresy** (HER-uh-see). People who hold such ideas are called heretics. Church officials sent priests and friars throughout Europe to find possible heretics. Most of these priests and friars tried to be fair. A few tortured people until they confessed to heresy, even if they were innocent. Most people found guilty in these trials were fined or put in prison. Others were killed.

In the early 1200s, Pope Innocent III decided that heresy was too great a threat to ignore. He called a crusade against heretics in southern France. With this call, the pope encouraged the king of France and his knights to rid their country of heretics. The result was a bloody war that lasted about 20 years. The war destroyed towns and cost thousands of people their lives.

Reading Check
Find Main Ideas
How did church leaders try to fight heresy?

Christians Fight the Moors

France was not the only place where Christians fought people they saw as the church's enemies. In Spain and Portugal, armed Christian warriors fought to drive the Muslim Moors out of their lands.

The Weakening of Muslim Control By the late 900s, the once powerful Muslim government of Spain had begun to weaken. Political and religious leaders fought each other for power. Various ethnic groups also fought each other.

In 1002, the Muslim government fell apart completely. Caught up in fighting among themselves, Muslim leaders were too busy to guard against the Christian kingdoms of northern Spain.

The Fight Against the Moors For centuries, the kingdoms of northern Spain had been small and weak. But as the Moors' power declined, these little Christian kingdoms seized the opportunity to attack. Slowly, they

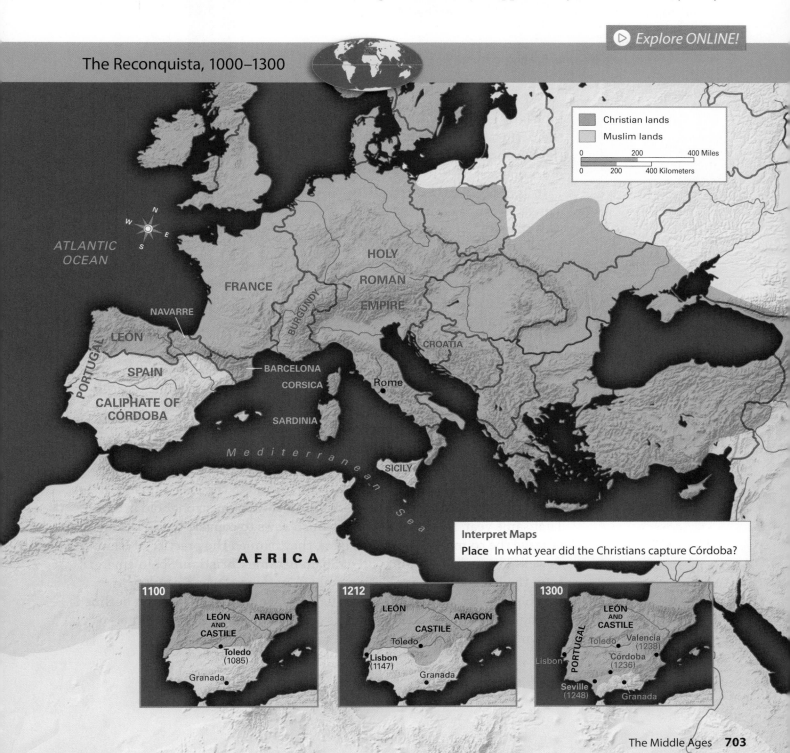

Explore ONLINE!

The Reconquista, 1000–1300

Christian lands
Muslim lands

0   200   400 Miles
0   200   400 Kilometers

ATLANTIC
OCEAN

FRANCE

HOLY
ROMAN
EMPIRE

NAVARRE

BURGUNDY

CROATIA

LEÓN

PORTUGAL

SPAIN

BARCELONA
CORSICA

Rome

CALIPHATE OF
CÓRDOBA

SARDINIA

Mediterranean Sea

SICILY

Interpret Maps
Place In what year did the Christians capture Córdoba?

AFRICA

1100
LEÓN
AND
CASTILE   ARAGON
Toledo
(1085)
Granada

1212
LEÓN
CASTILE   ARAGON
Toledo
Lisbon
(1147)   Granada

1300
LEÓN
AND
CASTILE
PORTUGAL   Toledo   Valencia
(1238)
Lisbon   Córdoba
(1236)
Seville
(1248)   Granada

Queen Isabella 1451–1504

Although she is considered one of the greatest monarchs in Spanish history, Isabella was never the queen of Spain. She was the queen of Castile and León, but she had no official power in her husband's kingdom, Aragon. In practice, however, the two ruled both kingdoms together. In addition to her role in the Reconquista, Isabella made great contributions to Spanish society. She encouraged Christianity and education and supported many artists. She also helped pay for the transatlantic voyages of Christopher Columbus, during which he reached America.

Form Generalizations
How did Isabella help promote Spanish culture?

took land away from the Moors. They called their efforts to retake Spain from the Moors the **Reconquista** (reh-kahn-KEES-tuh), or reconquest.

In 1085, Castile (ka-STEEL), the largest of the Spanish kingdoms, won a great victory against the Moors. The Castilian victory inspired other Christian kingdoms to fight the Moors. The kingdoms of Aragon and Portugal soon joined the fight.

The Christian armies won victory after victory. By the 1250s, the victorious Christian armies had nearly pushed the Moors completely out of Europe. The only territory still under Muslim control was a small kingdom called Granada (grah-NAH-dah).

The Rise of Portugal and Spain As a result of their victories, both Portugal and Spain grew more powerful than before. Portugal, once a part of Castile, broke free and declared its independence. Meanwhile, Castile and Aragon decided to unite.

In 1469, Ferdinand, the prince of Aragon, married Isabella, a Castilian princess. Ten years later, they became king and queen of their countries. Together, they ruled all of Spain as **King Ferdinand** and **Queen Isabella**.

Ferdinand and Isabella finally brought an end to the Reconquista. In 1492 their army conquered Granada, the last Muslim stronghold in Spain. That same year, they required all Spanish Jews to convert to Christianity or leave the country. A few years later, they banned the practice of Islam as well. Through this **policy**, all of Spain became Christian. Spain emerged after the Reconquista as a nation-state. A nation-state is a country in which people share a common language and culture. As feudalism declined throughout Europe, other monarchs consolidated their power. More nation-states began to emerge.

Acamedic
Vocabulary
policy rule, course
of action

The painting shows accused heretics, in the pointed hats, before the Spanish Inquisition. The Spanish artist Francisco Goya painted it in the early 1800s.

Analyze Visuals
How did the artist show what the accused heretics were feeling?

Reading Check
Summarize What was the purpose of the Spanish Inquisition?

The Spanish Inquisition Ferdinand and Isabella wanted only Christians in their kingdom. To ensure that Christianity alone was practiced, they created the **Spanish Inquisition**, an organization of priests that looked for and punished anyone in Spain suspected of secretly practicing their old religion. Later, the Inquisition spread to Portugal as well.

The Spanish and Portuguese Inquisitions were ruthless in seeking heretics, Muslims, and Jews. People found guilty of heresy were sentenced in public ceremonies. Many of those found guilty were killed. They were often burned to death. In total, the Spanish sentenced about 2,000 people to die. Almost 1,400 more were put to death by the Portuguese Inquisition.

Jews Face Discrimination

Heretics and Muslims were not the only groups punished for their beliefs in the Middle Ages. European Jews also suffered. This suffering was caused by Christians who believed that the Jews had been responsible for the death of Jesus. These Christians thought Jews should be punished.

You have already read about how Jews were killed during the Crusades. You have also read that Jews were forced to leave their homes in Spain. Similar things happened all over Europe. Rulers, supported by the church, forced Jews to leave their countries. For example, in 1290, the king of England arrested all English Jews and forced them to leave the country. The same thing happened in France in 1306 and again in 1394.

In the Holy Roman Empire, frightened people blamed Jews for the arrival of the Black Death. Many Jews had to flee their homes to escape angry mobs. Because the Jews were not Christian, many Europeans didn't want them in their towns.

Summary Magna Carta, the Hundred Years' War, and the Black Death changed European society. Religion also shaped how people thought, what they did, and where they lived. In some places religion led to wars and punishment for those who didn't agree with the Catholic Church.

Reading Check
Summarize How were Jews discriminated against in the Middle Ages?

Lesson 6 Assessment

Review Ideas, Terms, and People

1. **a. Identify** What document did English nobles hope would limit the king's power?

   b. Explain How was the creation of Parliament a step toward the creation of democracy in England?

2. **a. Identify** Who rallied the French troops during the Hundred Years' War?

   b. Elaborate The Hundred Years' War caused much more damage in France than in England. Why do you think this was the case?

3. **a. Explain** How did the Black Death contribute to the decline of the manor system?

   b. Elaborate Why do you think the Black Death was able to spread so quickly through Europe?

4. **Describe** What is heresy?

5. **a. Identify** Who did Spanish Christians try to drive out of their lands?

   b. Explain What was the purpose of the Spanish Inquisition?

   c. Evaluate How might Spanish history have been different if the Spanish had not defeated the Moors?

6. **Summarize** How did kings and other rulers punish Jews in the Middle Ages?

Critical Thinking

7. **Evaluate** Copy the diagram. Use it to rank the significance of the effects of Magna Carta, the Black Death, and the Reconquista. Next to the diagram, write a sentence to explain your choices.

Most Significant	Least Significant
1.	1.
2.	2.
3.	3.

Social Studies Skills

Develop and Interpret Models

Define the Skill

Models are three-dimensional representations of people, places, or objects. There are two main types of models. *Life-size models* are the same size as the things that they represent. *Scale models* are considerably smaller than the person, place, or object they represent.

When learning about history, students often build models. The ability to develop and interpret models will help you better understand a historical person, place, or object.

Learn the Skill

Use these basic steps to develop and interpret a model.

1. Determine what historical person, place, or object you want your model to represent.

2. Find pictures, maps, or illustrations of your subject. You will use these as visual aids.

3. Collect the materials that you will use to make your model.

4. Use your visual aids to guide you as you make your model.

5. Use your model to help answer questions you might have about your subject.

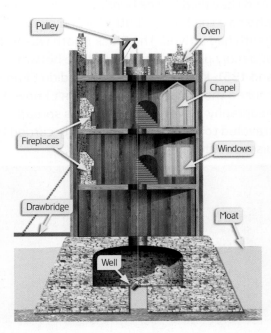

An Early Castle

Pulley · Oven · Chapel · Fireplaces · Windows · Drawbridge · Moat · Well

Practice the Skill

Study the diagram of a model, and then answer the questions below.

1. What is this a model of?

2. How could you build a model of this? What materials would you need?

3. What important features should be included in your model?

4. What are two questions your model could help you answer?

History and Geography

The Black Death

"And they died by the hundreds," wrote one man who saw the horror, "both day and night." The Black Death had arrived. The Black Death was a series of deadly plagues that hit Europe between 1347 and 1351, killing millions. People didn't know what caused the plague. They also didn't know that geography played a key role in its spread—as people traveled to trade, they unwittingly carried the disease with them to new places.

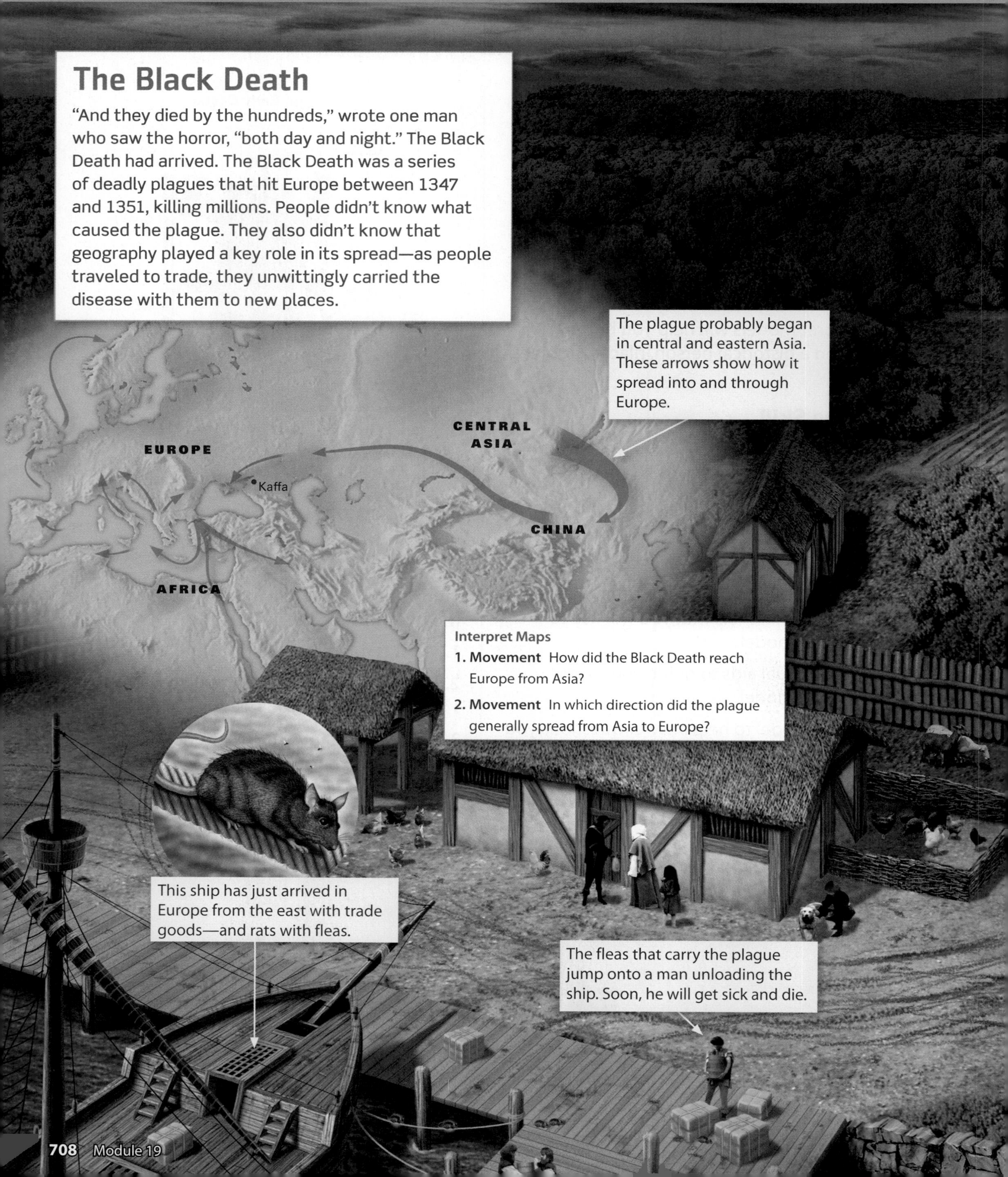

The plague probably began in central and eastern Asia. These arrows show how it spread into and through Europe.

EUROPE

CENTRAL ASIA

• Kaffa

CHINA

AFRICA

Interpret Maps

1. **Movement** How did the Black Death reach Europe from Asia?

2. **Movement** In which direction did the plague generally spread from Asia to Europe?

This ship has just arrived in Europe from the east with trade goods—and rats with fleas.

The fleas that carry the plague jump onto a man unloading the ship. Soon, he will get sick and die.

The plague is so terrifying that many people think it's the end of the world. They leave town for the country, spreading the Black Death even farther.

People dig mass graves to bury the dead. But often so many victims are infected that there is no one left to bury them.

So many people die so quickly that special carts are sent through the streets to gather the bodies.

The garbage and dirty conditions in the town provide food and a home for the rats, allowing the disease to spread even more.

Module 19 Assessment

Review Vocabulary, Terms, and People

Match the words with their definitions.

1. excommunicate
2. Charlemagne
3. serfs
4. Crusades
5. clergy
6. heresy
7. Thomas Aquinas
8. Magna Carta
9. Spanish Inquisition

a. church officials
b. punished non-Christians in Spain
c. religious ideas that oppose church teachings
d. an English document limiting the king's powers
e. cast out from the church
f. thought faith and reason could be used together
g. conquered parts of the former Roman Empire
h. wars fought to regain the Holy Land
i. spent much of their time working in their lord's fields

Comprehension and Critical Thinking

Lesson 1

10. a. **Analyze** How have rivers and seas influenced life in Europe?
    b. **Compare** In what way was the empire of the Franks under Charlemagne like the Roman Empire?
    c. **Elaborate** How do you think the building of new monasteries helped spread Christianity?

Lesson 2

11. a. **Describe** What were women's lives like during the Middle Ages?
    b. **Analyze** How did knights and lords try to make their manors self-sufficient?
    c. **Elaborate** How was feudalism related to medieval Europe's economic system?

Lesson 3

12. a. **Describe** What was the relationship between Charlemagne and the pope like?
    b. **Contrast** How did the opinions about power differ between popes like Gregory VII and kings like Henry IV?
    c. **Evaluate** Do you think conflict with kings strengthened or weakened medieval popes? Why?

Lesson 4

13. a. **Identify** What was the main goal of the Crusades?
    b. **Draw Conclusions** Why do you think the Crusades changed the relationships between Christians and other groups?
    c. **Evaluate** Which Crusade do you think was most successful? Which was least successful? Why?

Lesson 5

14. a. **Describe** How did Christianity shape art and education in the Middle Ages?
    b. **Analyze** Why was Christianity so influential in so many areas of medieval life?
    c. **Elaborate** How were the changes that took place in the medieval church related to its growing power and wealth?

Lesson 6

15. a. **Describe** What was the Black Death, and how did it affect Europe?
    b. **Make Inferences** Why do some people consider Magna Carta the beginning of democracy in England?
    c. **Identify** What were the results of the Reconquista?

Review Themes

16. **Society and Culture** Do you think religion or government had more influence on medieval societies? Why?

17. **Religion** In what ways did the Crusades demonstrate the power of the church in Europe?

Reading Skills 🏛

Evaluate Sources *Use the Reading Skills taught in this module to answer the question about the reading selection. The following passages are taken from the writings of historians in the 800s about the life of Charlemagne.*

> "I consider that it would be foolish for me to write about Charlemagne's birth and childhood . . . for nothing is set down in writing about this and nobody can be found still alive who claims to have any personal knowledge of these matters. I have therefore decided to leave out what is not really known."
>
> —Einhard, from *Two Lives of Charlemagne*, translated by Lewis Thorpe
>
> "When I was a child, he was already a very old man. He brought me up and used to tell me about these events. I was a poor pupil, and I often ran away, but in the end he forced me to listen."
>
> —Notker, from *Two Lives of Charlemagne*, translated by Lewis Thorpe

18. Are these passages primary or secondary sources?

19. Which historian do you think would be the most credible, or believable?

Social Studies Skills

Develop and Interpret Models *Use the Social Studies Skills taught in this module to answer the questions about the model below.*

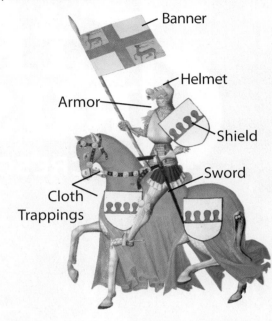

20. Which parts of a knight's outfit were used for protection? Which might help him be recognized in battle?

21. What did a knight use as a weapon?

22. Why might a knight carry a banner?

Focus On Writing

23. **Write a Want Ad** "Wanted: Brave and Loyal Knights." Write an advertisement for a job that might have been available during the time period covered by this module. Start your ad by explaining why you need knights to help you. Then write a description of the type of people who will be suitable for the job and how they will be expected to behave. Be sure to mention in your ad what knights will receive in exchange for their service.

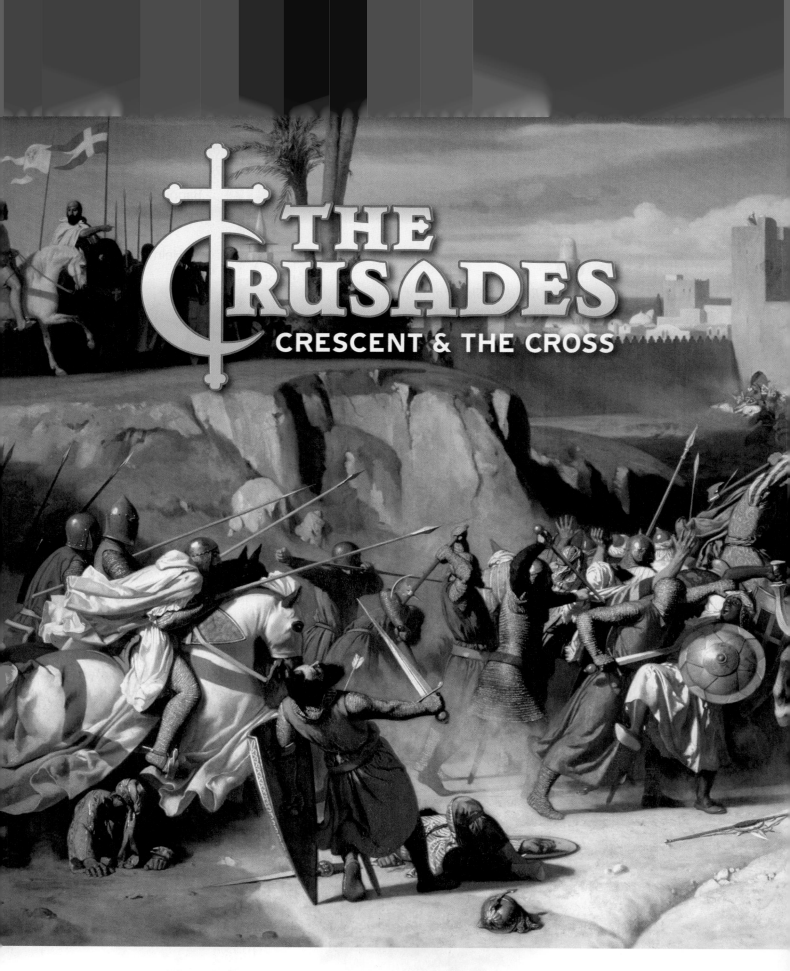

THE CRUSADES
CRESCENT & THE CROSS

Fought over nearly two centuries, the Crusades were a violent struggle between soldiers of two religions. In a series of nine wars, European Christians battled Turkish and Arabic Muslims for control of the city of Jerusalem and the surrounding areas, considered sacred by both religions. Thousands died in the fighting—both soldiers and civilians—and whole cities were destroyed. The brutality of the Crusades created strong feelings of resentment between Christians and Muslims. This resentment lingered for centuries after the wars themselves had ended.

Explore the causes, events, and results of the Crusades online. You can find a wealth of information, video clips, primary sources, activities, and more through your online textbook.

Siege of Jerusalem
Watch the video to learn how the Christian army captured Jerusalem from the Turks in 1099.

The First Four Crusades
Explore the map to see the different routes followed by Crusaders from Europe to the Holy Land.

Defeat of the Crusaders
Watch the video to understand how Muslim leaders rallied after the Second Crusade to drive Christians out of the Holy Land.

Module 20

The Renaissance

Essential Question
Why do Renaissance ideas affect people's lives today?

About the Photo: Venice is an island city crisscrossed with canals, so its "streets" are actually waterways.

 Explore ONLINE!

VIDEOS, including...
- Italy's Rebirth
- Brunelleschi's Dome
- The Printing Press

HISTORY

☑ Document-Based Investigations

☑ Graphic Organizers

☑ Interactive Games

☑ Interactive Map: Major Trading Centers in Renaissance Italy

☑ Image with Hotspots: The Printing Press

☑ Image with Hotpots: The Globe Theater

In this module, you will learn how the Renaissance changed life in Europe. The Renaissance began in Italy's great trading cities like Venice.

What You Will Learn...

Lesson 1: Origins of the Renaissance **716**
The Big Idea The growth of wealthy trading cities in Italy led to a new era called the Renaissance.

Lesson 2: The Italian Renaissance. **722**
The Big Idea New ways of thinking created a rebirth of the arts and learning in Italy.

Lesson 3: The Renaissance beyond Italy **732**
The Big Idea The Renaissance spread far beyond Italy and changed in the process.

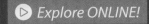 Explore ONLINE!

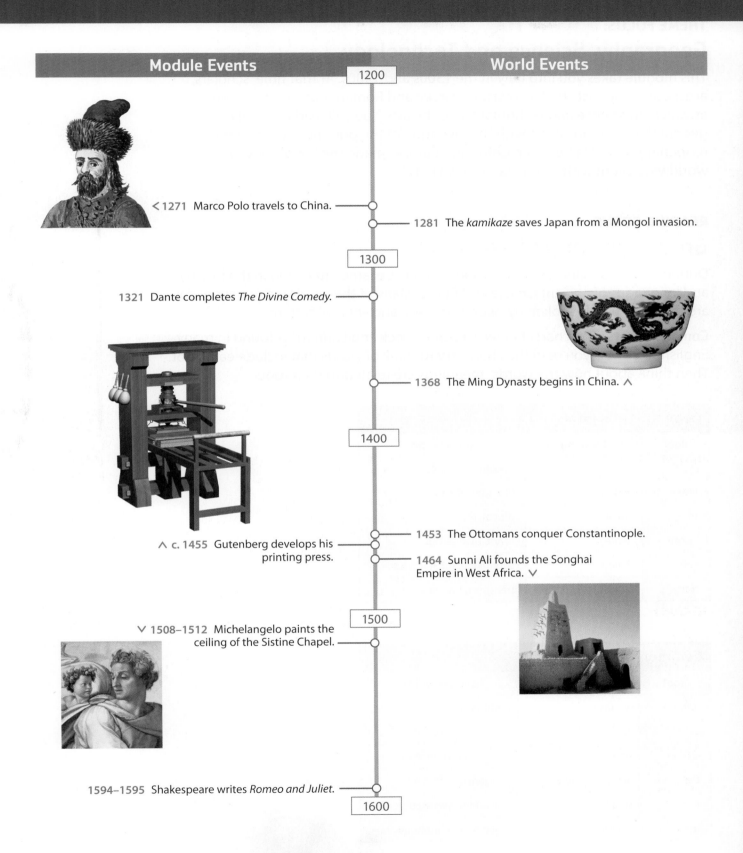

Module Events		World Events

1200

< **1271** Marco Polo travels to China.

1281 The *kamikaze* saves Japan from a Mongol invasion.

1300

1321 Dante completes *The Divine Comedy*.

1368 The Ming Dynasty begins in China. ∧

1400

∧ **c. 1455** Gutenberg develops his printing press.

1453 The Ottomans conquer Constantinople.

1464 Sunni Ali founds the Songhai Empire in West Africa. ∨

1500

∨ **1508–1512** Michelangelo paints the ceiling of the Sistine Chapel.

1594–1595 Shakespeare writes *Romeo and Juliet*.

1600

Reading Social Studies

THEME FOCUS:

Geography, Science and Technology

This module takes you into Italy in the 1300s and 1400s. At that time, scholars, artists, and scientists built on classical Greek and Roman roots to make new advances in science and technology and the arts. You will read how Italy's geographic location, along with the invention of the printing press and the reopening of routes between China and Europe, made the Renaissance a worldwide event with effects far beyond Italy.

READING FOCUS:

Greek and Latin Word Roots

During the Renaissance, scientists and scholars became interested in the history and languages of ancient Greece and Rome. Many of the words we use every day are based on words spoken by people in these ancient civilizations.

Common Roots The charts below list some Greek and Latin roots found in many English words. As you read the charts, try to think of words that include each root. Then think about how the words' meanings are related to their roots.

Common Latin Roots		
Root	**Meaning**	**Sample words**
-aud-	hear	audience, audible
liter-	writing	literature, literary
re-	again	repeat, redo
-script-	write	script, manuscript
sub-	below	submarine, substandard
trans-	across	transport, translate

Common Greek Roots		
Root	**Meaning**	**Sample words**
anti-	against	antifreeze, antiwar
astr-	star	asteroid, astronaut
-chron-	time	chronicle, chronology
dia-	across, between	diagonal, diameter
micr-	small	microfilm, microscope
-phono-	sound	telephone, symphony

You Try It!

Read the following sentences from the module and then answer the questions below.

> 1. In their luggage these scholars carried rare, precious works of <u>literature</u>.
> 2. Among the ideas that Italian scholars wanted to <u>revive</u> were subjects that the Greeks and Romans had studied.
> 3. Later <u>astronomers</u> built on all of these discoveries to lay the foundation for modern astronomy.
> 4. Although the Catholic Church fought strenuously against it, the Bible was eventually <u>translated</u> and printed.
> 5. Also, straight lines, such as on floor tiles, appear <u>diagonal</u>.

Answer the questions about the underlined words. Use the Common Roots charts for help.

1. Which of the underlined words has a root word that means "writing"? How does knowing the root word help you figure out what the word means?
2. What does the root word *astr-* mean? How does that help you figure out the meaning of *astronomers*?
3. In the second sentence, what do you think *revive* means? How could this be related to the root *re-*?
4. What's the root word in *translation?* What does *translation* mean? How is that definition related to the meaning of the root word?
5. What does the word *diagonal* mean? How is that meaning related to the meaning of *dia-*?
6. How many more words can you think of that use the roots in the charts on the previous page? Make a list and share it with your classmates.

As you read this module, be on the lookout for words with Greek and Latin root words like those listed in the chart. Use the chart to help you figure out what words mean.

Lesson 1
Marco Polo
interest
Cosimo de' Medici
Renaissance

Lesson 2
humanism
Dante Alighieri
Niccolo Machiavelli
Petrarch
perspective
Michelangelo
Leonardo da Vinci

Lesson 3
Johann Gutenberg
Christian humanism
Desiderius Erasmus
Albrecht Dürer
Miguel de Cervantes
William Shakespeare

Origins of the Renaissance

The Big Idea

The growth of wealthy trading cities in Italy led to a new era called the Renaissance.

Main Ideas

- European trade with Asia increased in the 1300s.

- Trade cities in Italy grew wealthy and competed against each other.

- As Florence became a center for arts and learning, the Renaissance began.

Key Terms and People

Marco Polo
interest
Cosimo de' Medici
Renaissance

If YOU were there . . .

You are a historian living in Florence, Italy, in the late 1300s. In your writing you describe the wonders of your city. But the place was very different only about 50 years before. At that time, the Black Death was sweeping through the city. In fact, your own grandfather was killed by the terrible disease. Some 50,000 of the city's other citizens also died from plague. Now, though, Florence is known for its beauty, art, and learning.

How did your city change so quickly?

Trade with Asia

It seems strange that the Black Death could have had any positive results, but that is what happened. You may remember that workers who survived this plague that killed approximately 25 million people in the 1300s could charge more money for their labor. In addition, the disease didn't damage farmland, buildings, ships, machines, or gold. People who survived could use these things to raise more food or make new products. They did just that. Europe's economy began to grow again.

As more goods became available, prices went down. People could buy more of the things they wanted. Trade increased, and new products appeared in the markets. Some of these goods came from India, China, and other lands to the east. How did these items move thousands of miles over high mountains and wide deserts? To learn more, we need to go back in time.

The Silk Road Reopens The Chinese and Romans did business together from about AD 1 to 200. Products moved east and west along the Silk Road. This caravan route started in China and ended at the Mediterranean Sea.

When the Roman Empire and the Han dynasty fell, soldiers no longer protected travelers between Europe and Asia. As a result, use of the Silk Road declined. Then in the 1200s

The Polo family as pictured on a map from the 1300s.

the Mongols took over China. They once again made the roads safer for travelers and traders. Among these traders were a remarkable man from Venice named **Marco Polo** and his family.

Marco Polo's Journeys Look at the map to follow the route of the Polo family's trip. Part of the journey was along the old Silk Road. When the Polos arrived in China, they met with the Mongol emperor Kublai Khan. He invited them to stay in his court and even made Marco Polo a government official.

The Polos saw many amazing things in China. For example, the Chinese used paper money in addition to the coins that Europeans used. The Polos were also fascinated by an unusual fuel source, which Marco Polo later described.

"Throughout this province there is found a sort of black stone, which they dig out of the mountains, where it runs in veins. When lighted, it burns like charcoal, and retains the fire much better than wood."

–Marco Polo, from *The Travels of Marco Polo the Venetian*

This is the first known description of coal by a European.

▶ Explore ONLINE!

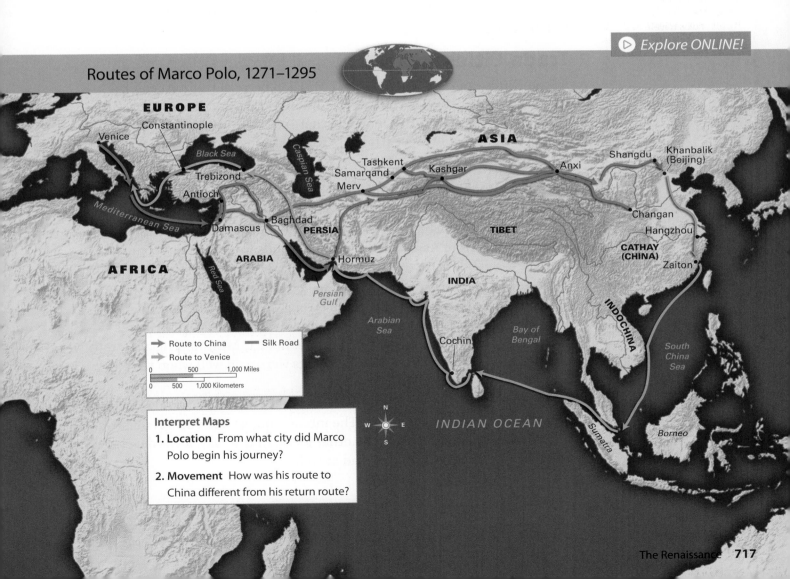

Routes of Marco Polo, 1271–1295

Interpret Maps

1. **Location** From what city did Marco Polo begin his journey?

2. **Movement** How was his route to China different from his return route?

Marco Polo 1254–1324

Marco Polo was one of the greatest travelers in history. He went from Europe to China and spent 20 years living, working, and traveling in Asia. When he returned to Venice, his friends and family didn't even recognize him. They thought he had been dead for many years.

Draw Conclusions
Why might Marco Polo's friends and family have thought he had been dead for many years?

Reading Check
Find Main Ideas
What ancient trade route did the Polos travel?

While his father and uncle stayed in China, Marco Polo visited India and Southeast Asia. He traveled as a messenger for the Mongol emperor. Marco Polo spent 20 years living and traveling in Asia.

Eventually, the Polos returned to Italy. There, a writer helped Marco Polo record his journey. At the time, many people didn't believe Polo's stories. Some people thought he had never set foot in China! Over the years his reputation grew, however. Polo's description made many Europeans curious about Asia. As their curiosity grew, people began to demand goods from Asia. Trade between Asia and Europe increased. Italian merchants organized much of this trade.

Trade Cities in Italy

By the 1300s, four northern Italian cities had become trading centers—Florence, Genoa (JEN-uh-wuh), Milan (muh-LAHN), and Venice. These cities bustled with activity. Shoppers there could buy beautiful things from Asia. Residents could meet strangers from faraway places and hear many languages on the streets.

Ports and Manufacturing Centers Italian cities played very important roles in trade. One role was as ports on the Mediterranean Sea. Venice and Genoa were Italy's main port cities. Merchant ships brought spices and other luxuries from Asia into the cities' harbors. From there, merchants shipped the goods across Europe.

Cities like Venice were well positioned on some trade routes between Asia and Europe. Muslim traders had strong ties with Venetian rulers and merchants. These traders acted as middlemen to help move spices and other goods between Asia and Europe. In fact, Muslim officials often traveled to Venice, and Venetian diplomats were paid well when they traveled to the Middle East.

However, more than goods were exchanged. People from many cultures interacted on these trade routes. The interaction between different cultures naturally exposed people to other ideas. In this way, ideas developed after the Middle Ages would spread as well.

Milan
This castle in Milan was built in the mid-1400s. It shows the wealth and power of Italy's trading cities.

Genoa
Genoa is on the Mediterranean. This location enabled Genoa to become rich through overseas trade.

Venice
Venice is an island city. Like Genoa, Venice grew rich from its overseas trade.

Florence
Florence was a banking and trade center. The city's wealthy leaders beautified the city with impressive buildings and art.

Another role of Italian cities was as manufacturing centers. Cities specialized in certain crafts. Venice produced glass. Workers in Milan made weapons and silk. Florence was a center for weaving wool into cloth. All of this economic activity put more money in merchants' pockets. Some Italian merchant families became incredibly wealthy. Eventually, this wealth would help make Italy the focus of European culture. How did this happen?

Separate States and Rival Rulers In the 1300s, Italy was not a single country. Instead, it was made up of independent states. These states had different forms of government. For example, Venice was a republic, while the pope ruled the Papal States as a monarchy.

In most big Italian cities, a single rich merchant family controlled the government. This type of government was called a *signoria* (seen-yohr-EE-uh). The head of the family, the *signore* (seen-YOHR-ay), ruled the city. Under the *signori*, trade grew in Italy. In fact, the *signori* competed against one another to see whose city could grow richest from trade. They also competed for fame. Each one wanted to be known as powerful, wise, and devoted to his city.

Florence

In the 1300s, trade goods from Asia poured into Europe. Many of those items came through Italian ports. As a result, the merchant families in these cities made money. As the families grew rich and powerful, they wanted everyone to see what their money could buy. Although these factors affected most big Italian cities, one city—Florence—stands out as an example of trade and wealth at this time.

The Medici Family Although Florence's wealth began with the wool trade, banking increased that wealth. Bankers in Florence kept money for merchants from all over Europe. The bankers made money by charging interest. **Interest** is a fee that borrowers pay for the use of someone else's money. This fee is usually a certain percentage of the loan.

The greatest bankers in Florence were the Medici (MED-i-chee) family. In the early 1400s they were Florence's richest family, and by 1434 **Cosimo de' Medici** (KOH-zee-moh day MED-i-chee) ruled the city.

As ruler, Cosimo de' Medici wanted Florence to be the most beautiful city in the world. He hired artists to decorate his palace. He also paid architects to redesign many of Florence's buildings.

Florence

A market buzzes with activity in this scene showing what Florence may have looked like in the late 1300s.

Analyze Visuals
What can you see in this illustration that shows the wealth of Florence?

Merchants traded goods from Europe and Asia in the city's markets.

Cloth was a major trade good in Florence.

Bankers kept detailed records of their investments.

Cosimo de' Medici also valued education. After all, his banks needed workers who could read, write, and understand math. To improve education, he also built libraries and collected books.

During the time that the Medici family held power, Florence became the center of Italian art, literature, and culture. In other Italian cities, rich families tried to outdo the Medicis—and each other—in their support of the arts and learning.

Beginning of the Renaissance This love of art and education was a key feature of a time we call the **Renaissance** (REN-uh-sahns). The word *Renaissance* means "rebirth" and refers to the period that followed Europe's Middle Ages.

What was being "reborn"? Interest in Greek and Roman writings was revived. Also new was an emphasis on people as individuals. These ideas were very different from the ideas of the Middle Ages.

Summary and Preview Changes in Italy led to the beginning of an era called the Renaissance. In the next lesson, you'll learn about the Italian Renaissance—its ideas, people, and arts.

Reading Check
Find Main Ideas
How did Florence help begin the Renaissance?

Lesson 1 Assessment

Review Ideas, Terms, and People

1. a. **Recall** What road did Marco Polo travel to Asia?

   b. **Summarize** How did the Polos affect trade with Asia?

2. a. **Identify** What were the four major trade cities of Italy?

   b. **Analyze** How were these cities important economically?

3. a. **Analyze** How did charging interest lead to the rise of the Medici family and the city-state of Florence?

   b. **Draw Conclusions** What is one reason why education was important to Cosimo de' Medici?

Critical Thinking

4. **Organize Information** Draw a graphic organizer like this one. Use it to describe the results of increased trade with Asia.

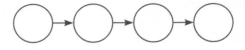

The Italian Renaissance

The Big Idea

New ways of thinking created a rebirth of the arts and learning in Italy.

Main Ideas

- During the Italian Renaissance, people found new ways to see the world.
- Italian writers contributed great works of literature.
- Italian art and artists were among the finest in the world.
- Science and education made advances during this time.

Key Terms and People

humanism
Dante Alighieri
Niccolo Machiavelli
Petrarch
perspective
Michelangelo
Leonardo da Vinci

If YOU were there . . .

You are an apprentice working in the studio of a famous painter. You admire him but think some of his ideas are old-fashioned. Most of the time, your job is to paint the background of the master's pictures. Now, though, you have finished a painting of your own. You are proud of it and want the world to know who made it. But the master says an artist should never put his name on a painting.

Will you sign your painting?

New Ways to See the World

During the Middle Ages, most people in Europe had devoted themselves entirely to Christianity. People looked to the church for answers to problems in their lives, and most of Europe's brilliant and influential thinkers were church figures.

By the late 1300s, however, scholars had begun to study subjects besides religion. They studied history, literature, public speaking, and art, subjects that emphasized the actions and abilities of humans. Together, these subjects are called the humanities. The study of the humanities led to a new way of thinking and learning known as **humanism**.

Humanism and Religion The humanists of the Renaissance were no less religious than people had been before. Like the people of the Middle Ages, they were devout Christians. At the same time, however, people in the Renaissance were interested in ideas besides religion. Medieval thought had mainly focused on Christian beliefs and teachings. Humanists liked to study ancient Greek and Roman writings. They wanted to learn more about ideas like ethics and responsibility, so they could lead honorable and successful lives. Followers of humanism were interested in the positive qualities that make us human.

People's newfound interest in the humanities led them to respect those who could write, create, or speak well. As a result, talented writers and artists won great fame and honor. This too was a great change from the Middle Ages, when most people had worked only to glorify God.

Rediscovering the Past The popularity of the humanities was due in large part to a new interest in ancient history. During the 1300s, Turks had conquered much of the Byzantine Empire. Scholars seeking to escape the Turks fled to Italy. In their luggage they carried rare, precious works of literature.

Many of the works these scholars brought to Italy were ancient **classical** writings, such as works by Greek thinkers. You may remember some of their names—Plato and Thucydides, for example. Europeans had thought many of these ancient writings had been lost. Excited by the return of these great works, scholars then went looking for ancient texts in Latin. They discovered many Latin texts in monasteries, where the monks had preserved works by Roman writers. As Italian scholars read the ancient texts, they rediscovered the glories of Greece and Rome. As a result, they longed for a renewal of classical culture.

Among the ideas that Italian scholars wanted to revive were subjects that the Greeks and Romans had studied. These subjects included grammar, speaking, poetry, history, and the Greek and Latin languages—the humanities.

Academic Vocabulary
classical referring to the cultures of ancient Greece and Rome

Rebirth of Classical Ideas

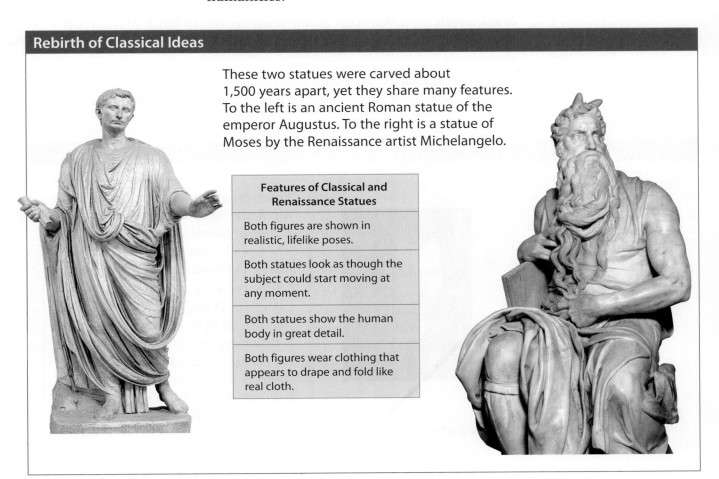

These two statues were carved about 1,500 years apart, yet they share many features. To the left is an ancient Roman statue of the emperor Augustus. To the right is a statue of Moses by the Renaissance artist Michelangelo.

Features of Classical and Renaissance Statues

Both figures are shown in realistic, lifelike poses.

Both statues look as though the subject could start moving at any moment.

Both statues show the human body in great detail.

Both figures wear clothing that appears to drape and fold like real cloth.

Reading Check
Summarize
What sources inspired Renaissance artists and scholars?

Other ancient sources of inspiration for Renaissance artists and architects were all around. Roman ruins still stood in Italy. Fine classical statues were on display, and more were being found every day. Throughout the Renaissance, Italian artists studied these ancient statues. They tried to make their own works look like the works of the Romans and Greeks. In fact, some artists wanted their works to look ancient so badly that they buried their statues in the ground to make them look older!

Italian Writers

Many Italian writers contributed great works of literature to the Renaissance. The earliest was the politician and poet named **Dante Alighieri** (DAHN-tay ahl-eeg-YEH-ree), or simply Dante. Before Dante, most medieval authors had written in Latin, the language of the church. But Dante wrote in Italian, which was the common language of the people. By using Italian, Dante showed that he considered the people's language to be as good as Latin. Later writers continued to use common languages in their works of literature.

Dante's major work was *The Divine Comedy*. It describes an imaginary journey he took through the afterlife. On this journey, Dante meets people from his past as well as great figures from history. In fact, the Roman poet Virgil is one of the guides on the journey. In the course of his writing, Dante described many of the problems he saw in Italian society.

A later Italian writer was also a politician. His name was **Niccolo Machiavelli** (neek-koh-LOH mahk-yah-VEL-lee). In 1513, Machiavelli wrote a short book called *The Prince*. It gave leaders advice on how they should rule.

Machiavelli didn't care about theories or what *should* work. In his writings, he argued that rulers had to focus on the "here and now," not

---

DOCUMENT-BASED INVESTIGATION Historical Source

The Prince

In *The Prince,* Machiavelli offers advice for rulers on how to stay in power. In this famous passage, he explains why in his view it is better for rulers to be feared than to be loved.

"From this arises the question whether it is better to be loved more than feared, or feared more than loved. The reply is, that one ought to be both feared and loved, but as it is difficult for the two to go together, it is much safer to be feared than loved, if one of the two has to be wanting. . . . for love is held by a chain of obligation which, men being selfish, is broken whenever it serves their purpose; but fear is maintained by a dread of punishment which never fails."

–Niccolo Machiavelli, from *The Prince*

Analyze Historical Sources
Do you think that Machiavelli gave good advice in this passage? Why or why not?

theories, to be successful. He was only interested in what really happened in both war and peace. For example, Machiavelli thought that sometimes rulers had to be ruthless to keep order. However, one of his later works seemed to support a republican government in which citizens elect their leaders and representatives. This idea became popular in Florence. Machiavelli's writings serve as a good example of how interest in human behavior affected Renaissance politics and society.

An Italian poet known as **Petrarch** (PEH-trahrk) also had a lot to say about human behavior. He believed that God set humans at the center of that world. Petrarch explored classical thought and Christian teachings. He thought both concepts were connected and could exist together. Some historians believe that humanism would not have developed without Petrarch's ideas.

Reading Check
Draw Conclusions
How did Dante, Machiavelli, and Petrarch reflect the ideas of the Renaissance?

Italian Art and Music

During the Renaissance, Italian artists and composers created some of the most beautiful artistry in the world. Rich families and church leaders hired artists to create these works. New techniques made their work come alive.

New Methods for a New Era Renaissance ideas about the value of human life are reflected in the art of the time. Artists showed people more realistically than medieval artists had done. Renaissance artists studied the human body and drew what they saw. However, because artists often used classical statues as their guides, many of the human beings they drew were as perfect as Greek gods.

Artists also used a new discovery—**perspective**, a method of showing a three-dimensional scene on a flat surface so that it looks real. Perspective uses various techniques. For example, people in the background are smaller than those in front. Also, straight lines, such as on floor tiles, appear diagonal. Colors could also show distance. So mountains in the background of a picture are a hazy blue.

Titian's works reflect a variety of subject matter and include portraits, landscapes, and religious scenes. He painted the portrait *Violante*, shown here, in about 1515.

Great Works In the work of the greatest Italian artists, the people shown are clearly individuals. In this way, the art reflects the Renaissance idea of the value of human beings. For example, the figures in the painting by the artist Raphael have clear personalities.

Sandro Botticelli (bot-ti-CHEL-lee), a painter from Florence, also showed respect for people. Many of his paintings show scenes from Roman myths. But he painted everyone—whether ancient gods, saints, angels, or farmers—in fine detail.

The work of Titian reflects interest in the past. Like Botticelli, he often painted scenes from classical myths. For Venice's churches, though, Titian painted colorful scenes from Christian teachings.

Renaissance ideas also influenced music, which was an important part of religious life. New types of music were composed, or written, for the

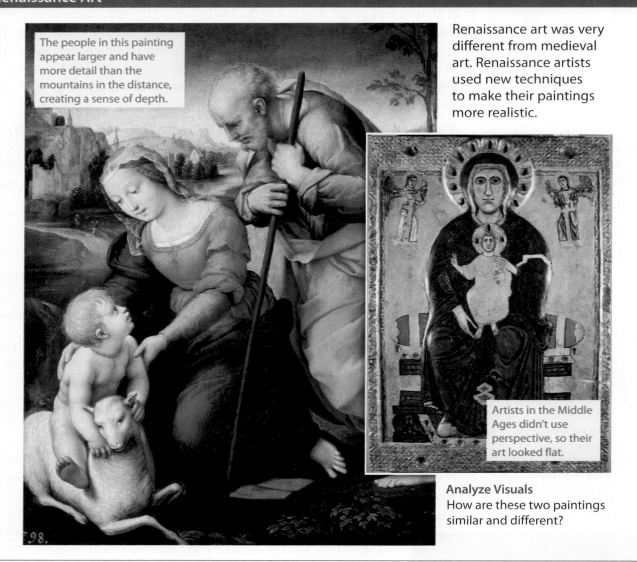

The people in this painting appear larger and have more detail than the mountains in the distance, creating a sense of depth.

Renaissance art was very different from medieval art. Renaissance artists used new techniques to make their paintings more realistic.

Artists in the Middle Ages didn't use perspective, so their art looked flat.

Analyze Visuals
How are these two paintings similar and different?

Church during this time. Giovanni da Palestrina composed many works of church music. Palestrina's pieces were designed for use in a Catholic mass. Some pieces allowed listeners to hear different melodies at the same time.

Italian music also influenced composers in other European nations. Thomas Tallis composed music for the Church of England. His music was similar to Palestrina's in that both used different melodies simultaneously.

The Master Michelangelo Of all the Italian Renaissance artists, two stand above the rest. Each is what we call a Renaissance person—someone who can do practically anything well.

One of the greatest Italian artists was **Michelangelo** (mee-kay-LAHN-jay-loh). He had many talents. Michelangelo designed buildings, wrote poetry, carved sculptures, and painted magnificent pictures. Perhaps his most famous work is a painting that covers the ceiling of the Sistine Chapel in the Vatican. The muscular human figures in this immense painting remind the viewer of Greek or Roman statues.

This painting by Michelangelo decorates part of the ceiling of the Sistine Chapel in Rome.

Michelangelo's amazing work on the ceiling of the Sistine Chapel is not one large painting—it is actually a collection of smaller paintings on plaster panels. These panels show religious imagery from the Bible. For example, some figures represent God and Adam. Another scene shows Noah escaping the epic flood.

Michelangelo also sculpted the *David*. This towering marble statue of the Biblical hero now stands in a museum in Florence. Other artists had shown David in victory over Goliath, but Michelangelo chose to sculpt David before the battle occurs. David appears to be focused, and his muscles are tense. The slingshot with which David beat Goliath is difficult to notice because David carries it over his left shoulder.

Michelangelo created some of the most famous works of art in world history for the Roman Catholic Church. Church officials hired him to decorate churches with his brilliant statues and paintings.

The Genius of Leonardo da Vinci The true genius of the Renaissance was **Leonardo da Vinci**. In fact, some call him the greatest genius that has ever lived. Leonardo was a sculptor, painter, architect, inventor, and engineer. He was even a town planner and map maker.

Like Michelangelo and many artists during the Renaissance, Leonardo created works with religious themes. One of the works Leonardo is known for is *The Last Supper*. *The Last Supper* is a painting that shows Jesus eating a meal with his apostles.

Leonardo da Vinci's work included many nonreligious subjects as well. Both nature and technology fascinated Leonardo. Detailed drawings of plants, animals, and machines fill his sketchbooks. To make his art more real, Leonardo studied anatomy, or the structure of human bodies. He dissected corpses to see how bones and muscles worked. Yet Leonardo's paintings also show human emotions, which was common during the Renaissance. For example, people who see his *Mona Lisa* can't help wondering what made the lady smile. Some think this smile was Leonardo da Vinci's way of showing the harmony between humanity and the painting's natural background.

Leonardo da Vinci's quest to learn more about anatomy benefited more than just his art. He left an illustrated set of unpublished papers that show what he had learned about the human body. For example, Leonardo found that the heart, not the liver, controlled the flow of blood through the body. He also described medical conditions, including one he called "hardening of the arteries" and another called cirrhosis, a disease of the liver. Leonardo's observations led to further advancements in anatomy and medicine.

Science and Education

There were many advances in fields of science during the Italian Renaissance. One reason for these advances was Europeans could read works by ancient Greek and Roman scientists and build on those ideas.

Islamic scholars had preserved many of these texts through prior centuries. The texts were translated from the original Greek and Latin into Arabic. Italian achievements were in part due to the previous efforts of Islamic scholars in what is now southern Spain. From approximately AD 1000 to 1200, Islamic, Christian, and Jewish scholars in Spain worked closely together to make new discoveries and to translate texts from Arabic into other languages. These scholars of different faiths worked together in a state of peaceful coexistence.

Scholars in Italy and other parts of Europe then had the opportunity to read Greek and Roman texts on many scientific subjects. After reading these works, Italian Renaissance scholars went on to make their own scientific advances.

Mathematics Some scholars thought mathematics could help them understand the universe. They studied ancient math texts and built upon

Reading Check
Summarize
Who were some of the great artists of the Italian Renaissance?

Leonardo da Vinci's Accomplishments

Leonardo was born in Vinci, a small town near Florence. He showed artistic talent at a young age. But no one could know that Leonardo would become one of the great geniuses of history.

Art

Leonardo was one of the great artists of the Renaissance. His *Mona Lisa* is one of the most famous paintings in the world.

Anatomy Studies

This page from one of Leonardo's notebooks shows how he studied the human body.

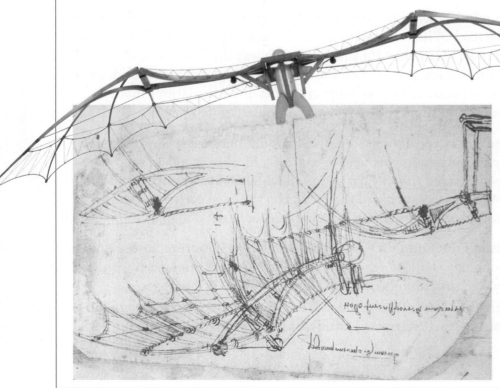

Inventions

A notebook page shows Leonardo's sketch of a wing. He sketched many ideas for machines that would let people fly. Above is a model of one of his ideas.

Analyze Visuals

How do these illustrations show that Leonardo was more than just an artist?

the ideas in them. Mathematicians from the Muslim world helped to develop algebra. They also worked with measuring in degrees and creating tables for advanced math like trigonometry. All of this study led to the creation of symbols we still use in math today. For example, scholars created symbols for the square root ($\sqrt{}$) and for positive (+) and negative (−) numbers. In turn, Italian scholars used these mathematical ideas to make other scientific advancements.

Engineering and Architecture Advances in math led to advances in other fields of science. For example, engineers and architects used new mathematical formulas to strengthen buildings.

One Renaissance architect who used these new ideas was Filippo Brunelleschi (broo-nayl-LAYS-kee). He designed a huge dome for a cathedral in Florence. But Brunelleschi ran into a problem. The dome that he wanted to build was so big that it would be too heavy for the cathedral's walls to support. To solve the problem, he built the dome out of two thin, light layers instead of one thick, heavy one.

Astronomy and Cartography Renaissance scientists also wanted to know more about the sky and what was in it. They studied astronomy to learn about the sun, stars, and planets.

In the Middle Ages, scientists had thought that the sun and stars revolved around the earth. They thought that the earth was the center of the universe. But Renaissance scientists learned that the earth moves around the sun. Astronomers in Spain theorized about other solar systems with planets that might exist in the universe. Later, Italian astronomers during the Renaissance built on all of these discoveries to lay the foundations for modern astronomy.

Some scholars were less interested in the stars and more curious about the earth itself. They wanted to know the exact size and shape of the earth and its lands. Many thought that the Earth was flat. However, scholars in Spain wrote almanacs based on the idea that the planet was round. Other European scholars later used measurements and calculations made by merchants and sailors to create better, more accurate maps.

Medicine Leonardo da Vinci studied anatomy, but his ideas were based on prior advances in medicine. For example, Muslim scholars, such as Avicenna, changed the way questions about medicine were investigated. These Muslim scholars based their ideas on the even earlier work of Aristotle and other Greek and Roman philosophers.

Changes in Education In time, these changes in literature, art, science, and technology would spread beyond Italy. For these changes to spread, however, required changes in education.

During the Middle Ages, students had concentrated on religious subjects. During the Renaissance, students learned about the humanities

Academic
Vocabulary
affect to change
or influence

Reading Check
Make Inferences
How do you think
Renaissance ideas
would change as
they spread to other
countries?

as well. History was one subject that received more attention. Petrarch wrote about the importance of knowing history.

> "O inglorious age! that scorns antiquity, its mother, to whom it owes every noble art. . . . What can be said in defense of men of education who ought not to be ignorant of antiquity [ancient times] and yet are plunged in . . . darkness and delusion?"
>
> —Francesco Petrarch, from a 1366 letter to Boccaccio

Petrarch's ideas would **affect** education for many years to come. Education and new ways of spreading information would take the Renaissance far beyond Italy.

Summary and Preview A great rebirth of art, literature, and learning began in Italy in the late 1300s. In the next lesson, you will learn about how Renaissance ideas changed as they spread across Europe.

Lesson 2 Assessment

Review Ideas, Terms, and People

1. a. Identify What are some basic ideas of humanism?

   b. Summarize How did ancient texts and statues affect Renaissance scholars?

2. a. Recall What set Dante apart from earlier Italian writers?

   b. Draw Conclusions Why may a historian call Niccolo Machiavelli "the first modern Italian"?

3. a. Identify What are three techniques for showing perspective?

   b. Summarize What are some characteristics of the Sistine Chapel and the *David*?

   c. Summarize What features help you to identify the painting *Mona Lisa* as a Renaissance work of art?

   d. Evaluate Which artist would you rather have met in real life—Michelangelo or Leonardo da Vinci? What is the reason for your choice?

4. a. Categorize Name one Renaissance achievement in each of these five categories: mathematics, architecture, astronomy, cartography, and medicine.

   b. Summarize How did the choice of school subjects change during the Renaissance?

Critical Thinking

5. Organize Information Draw a graphic organizer like the one shown here. Use it to show the societies involved in the transmission of knowledge from the ancient Greeks to the Renaissance.

The Renaissance Beyond Italy

The Big Idea

The Renaissance spread far beyond Italy and changed in the process.

Main Ideas

- Paper, printing, and new universities led to the spread of new ideas.

- The ideas of the Northern Renaissance differed from those of the Italian Renaissance.

- Literature beyond Italy also thrived in the Renaissance.

Key Terms and People

Johann Gutenberg
Christian humanism
Desiderius Erasmus
Albrecht Dürer
Miguel de Cervantes
William Shakespeare

If YOU were there . . .

You are a student from Holland, studying law at the university in Bologna, Italy. Life in Renaissance Italy is so exciting! You've met artists and writers and learned so much about art and literature. You can hardly wait to tell people at home about everything you've learned. But now a lawyer in Bologna has offered you a chance to stay and work in Italy.

Will you stay in Italy or return to Holland?

Spread of New Ideas

Travelers and artists helped spread the Renaissance throughout Europe. But the development of printing was a giant step in spreading ideas. For the first time ever, thousands of people could read books and share ideas about them.

Paper and Printing By the late 700s, papermaking had spread from China to the Middle East. From there it came to Europe. European factories were making paper by the 1300s. Because it was cheaper and easier to prepare, paper soon replaced the animal skins on which people had written before.

Then in the mid-1400s a German man, **Johann Gutenberg** (GOOT-uhn-berk), developed a printing press that used movable type. That is, each letter was a separate piece. A worker could fit letters into a frame, spread ink on the letters, and press a sheet of paper against the letters. In this way, an entire page was printed at once. Then the worker could rearrange letters in the frame to create a new page. How much faster printing was than writing!

The letters used in movable type are arranged in a frame to make a page. The letters can later be reused for different pages.

Timeline: Printing in Europe

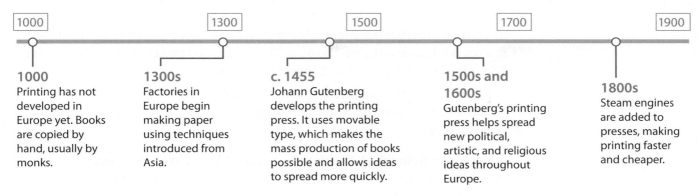

1000 1300 1500 1700 1900

1000
Printing has not developed in Europe yet. Books are copied by hand, usually by monks.

1300s
Factories in Europe begin making paper using techniques introduced from Asia.

c. 1455
Johann Gutenberg develops the printing press. It uses movable type, which makes the mass production of books possible and allows ideas to spread more quickly.

1500s and 1600s
Gutenberg's printing press helps spread new political, artistic, and religious ideas throughout Europe.

1800s
Steam engines are added to presses, making printing faster and cheaper.

> **Interpret Timelines**
> From where was papermaking introduced into Europe?

The first printed book was a Bible printed in the Latin language in about 1455. Soon, some thinkers began to call for the Bible to be translated into common languages. Although the Catholic Church fought strenuously against it, the Bible was eventually translated and printed. Church leaders objected on the grounds that some wording was not accurate. They also did not want people to interpret the Bible on their own without guidance from the Church.

In spite of the Church's objections, Bibles were suddenly available to more people. Because the Bible was available to read, more people learned to read. Then, they wanted more education.

Before the invention of the printing press, books were usually copied by hand, as shown in this illustration.

New Universities Students from around Europe traveled to Italy to study at Italian universities. By the early 1500s, most of the teachers in these universities were humanists. Students from northern Europe who studied with these teachers took Renaissance ideas back with them to their home countries.

Over time, many of the new scholars became teachers in Europe's universities. In addition, new universities opened in France, Germany, and the Netherlands. Because these schools were set up by humanists, Renaissance ideas about the value of people spread throughout Europe.

Although only men could attend universities, women also helped spread these ideas. Many noble families educated their daughters at home. They encouraged young women to study classical literature, philosophy, and the arts. Some educated women became powerful political figures. They married nobles from around Europe and encouraged the spread of Renaissance ideas in their husbands' lands.

Reading Check
Analyze Causes
How did travel and marriage spread Renaissance ideas?

The Northern Renaissance

As humanism spread, scholars in northern Europe became more interested in history. Northern scholars, however, focused not on Greece and Rome but on the history of Christianity. The resulting combination of humanist and religious ideas is called **Christian humanism**.

Many northern scholars felt that the church was corrupt and no longer true to the spirit of Jesus' teachings anymore. They began to call for church reform.

A Northern Scholar A Dutch priest named **Desiderius Erasmus** (des-i-DEER-ee-uhs i-RAZ-mus) was the most important of these scholars. Erasmus believed in the idea that humans had free will. They could choose the path in their lives that would lead them to salvation when they died. However, this did not mean that people could reach salvation without God's help. Humans had the power to decide how they wanted to live, but they still needed God.

In 1509, Erasmus published a book, *The Praise of Folly*, in which he criticized corrupt clergy. He also wanted to get rid of some church rituals that he considered meaningless. Instead of rituals, he emphasized devotion to God and the teachings of Jesus.

Northern Renaissance Art Northern Europeans also changed some Renaissance ideas about art. For one thing, the humans in northern paintings don't look like Greek gods. Instead, they are realistic, with physical flaws.

Northern artists embraced realism in another way, too. They painted objects, from rocks to flowers, so clearly that the objects don't look like they were painted at all. They almost appear to be the real thing, glued to the painting.

Historical Source

The Praise of Folly

Erasmus disagreed with some of the practices of the Catholic Church, including Church officials' desire for money. Folly is the narrator in his text. Her name is also a word that means "behavior that lacks good sense or judgment." Erasmus is criticizing the greed of some friars. The word *frier* can be used as another name for a monk.

Analyze Historical Sources
How would you summarize the relationship between monks and merchants?

> "But the most foolish and basest of all others are our merchants . . . who though they lie by no allowance, swear and forswear, steal, cozen, and cheat, yet shuffle themselves into the first rank, and all because they have Gold Rings on their Fingers. Nor are they without their flattering Friers that admire them and give 'em openly the title of Honorable, in hopes, no doubt to get some small snip of 't themselves."
>
> —from *The Praise of Folly* by Desiderius Erasmus

Biblical scenes and classical myths were the traditional subjects of Italian Renaissance art. In contrast, northern artists painted scenes of daily life. For example, consider the painting of hunters returning home. It was painted by Pieter Brueghel (BROY-guhl) the Elder, an artist from what is now Belgium. Some of Brueghel's other paintings show people working in fields, dancing, or eating. His son, called Brueghel the Younger, later used his father's ideas in his own works.

Albrecht Dürer (AWL-brekt DYUR-uhr) was a famous northern artist from Germany. Like Italian artists, Dürer studied anatomy so he could paint people more realistically. Like his fellow northerners, Dürer showed objects in great detail. A lover of nature, Dürer even drew a patch of weeds so clearly that today scientists can identify the plant species.

Northern Renaissance Art

Northern Renaissance artists often painted realistic scenes from daily life, like *Return of the Hunters,* painted by Pieter Brueghel in 1565. Albrecht Dürer created *The Four Horsemen of the Apocalypse,* shown here, in 1597 and 1598. It is a woodcut—a print made from a detailed carving in a block of wood.

Analyze Visuals
What scenes of daily life can you see in Brueghel's painting?

Dürer created religious paintings for churches. But he is most famous for his prints. A print is a work of art reproduced from an original. First, Dürer carved the image into either a metal sheet or a wooden block. Then he covered the image with ink and pressed a sheet of paper down onto it. The image transferred to the paper. Dürer sold his prints at fairs and markets.

Among other great artists of the Northern Renaissance were two portrait painters—Hans Holbein (HAWL-byn) and Jan van Eyck (yahn van YK). Holbein grew up in Switzerland but moved to England. There he painted a portrait of King Henry VIII. Among Jan van Eyck's works are many religious scenes. Van Eyck worked in oil paints, a new invention. The colors in his paintings seem to glow from within.

Reading Check
Summarize
Who were some major artists of the Northern Renaissance?

Don Quixote

In one of the most famous scenes from *Don Quixote*, the confused knight tilts, or charges, at a windmill that he believes to be a fierce giant. Because of this scene, we still use the phrase "tilting at windmills" to describe someone attempting a foolish or impossible task.

Analyze Visuals
How does this scene mock medieval ideas of bravery and knighthood?

Literature Beyond Italy

Writers in other countries besides Italy also included Renaissance ideas in their works. Many were inspired by how different life had become since the Middle Ages.

In Spain, **Miguel de Cervantes** (mee-GEL day ser-VAHN-tays) wrote *Don Quixote* (kee-HOH-tay). In this book, written in Spanish, Cervantes poked fun at romantic tales of the Middle Ages. His main character is an old man who decides to become a knight, a decision that Cervantes mocks.

> "In fine, having quite lost his wits, he fell into one of the strangest conceits that ever entered into the head of any madman; which was, that he thought it expedient and necessary, as well as for the advancement of his own reputation, as for the public good, that he should commence knight-errant, and wander through the world with his horse and arms, in quest of adventures."
>
> —Miguel de Cervantes, from *Don Quixote*, translated by Charles Jarvis

Like many writers of his day, Cervantes thought his own time was much better than the Middle Ages.

In France, too, writers poked fun at the ideas of the Middle Ages. The greatest of these French Renaissance writers was François Rabelais (franswah RAB-uh-lay). Like many Renaissance figures, Rabelais was a person of many trades. In addition to being a writer, he was a doctor and a priest. But it is for his writing that he is best known. Rabelais wrote a series of novels about characters named Gargantua and Pantagruel. Through his characters' actions, Rabelais mocks the values of the Middle Ages as well as events that had happened to him in his own life.

Readers around the world consider **William Shakespeare** the greatest writer in the English language. Although he also wrote poems, Shakespeare is most famous for his plays. Shakespeare wrote more than

---

William Shakespeare
1564–1616

Many people consider William Shakespeare the greatest playwright of all time. His plays are still hugely popular around the world. Shakespeare was such an important writer that he even influenced the English language. He invented common phrases such as *fair play* and common words such as *lonely*. In fact, Shakespeare is probably responsible for more than 2,000 English words.

Make Inferences
How do you think Shakespeare invented new words and phrases?

The Globe Theater was home to most of William Shakespeare's plays. The Globe playwrights were often involved in the production of their plays. Shakespeare also acted in some of them.

30 comedies, tragedies, and histories. London audiences of the late 1500s and early 1600s packed the theatre to see them. Ever since, people have enjoyed the beauty of Shakespeare's language and his understanding of humanity. The following passage reflects the Renaissance idea that each human being is important. Shakespeare compares people to the actors in a play who should be watched with great interest.

> "All the world's a stage, And all the men and women merely players: They have their exits and their entrances; And one man in his time plays many parts, His acts being seven ages."
>
> –William Shakespeare, from *As You Like It*, Act 2, Scene 7

The works of Cervantes, Rabelais, and Shakespeare have been translated into dozens of languages. Through these translations, their Renaissance spirit lives on.

Summary The making of paper, the printing press, and new universities helped spread the Renaissance beyond Italy into lands where its ideas changed.

Reading Check
Compare How does the choice of language used by Cervantes and Shakespeare compare to that of Italian writers?

Lesson 3 Assessment

Review Ideas, Terms, and People

1. a. Identify What two inventions helped spread the Renaissance beyond Italy?

b. Explain How did Johann Gutenberg's machine work?

2. a. Summarize How did Erasmus define free will?

b. Describe What was Erasmus's position on church rituals?

c. Contrast How did Christian humanism differ from the earlier form of humanism that developed in Italy?

d. Synthesize What is the connection between humanism and painting people working in the fields?

3. a. Compare What is one thing that Miguel de Cervantes and William Shakespeare had in common with Dante?

b. Draw Conclusions Why have Shakespeare's works remained popular around the world for centuries?

Critical Thinking

4. Summarize Copy the chart below to describe the works of Northern Renaissance artists. Add rows as needed.

Artist	Artist's Work

Social Studies Skills

Speak and Listen

Define the Skill

The topics you study in social studies are all important, but these topics are also terrific for having a discussion. Discussions help you learn to speak and listen to others. They are also a way to practice using vocabulary words.

Learn the Skill

Follow these steps to have a discussion about a social studies topic.

1. Pronounce new or unfamiliar words and names slowly and clearly. Try to use specific vocabulary and names instead of words like "thing" or "person."

2. Listen for information that helps you to understand definitions. A speaker might say, "Many artists during the Renaissance created works with religious themes. *The Last Supper* is a painting that shows Jesus eating a meal." The second sentence helps to define *religious theme* in context. Ask clarifying questions if you are confused.

3. Show that you are listening by giving a response or asking for more information. For example, the response "What other parts of *The Last Supper* show a religious theme?" repeats important information. It also asks a question that tells the speaker and others that this listener has been paying attention to the discussion and wants to know more.

4. Allow one speaker to finish talking before another person speaks. It is difficult for listeners to pay attention to more than one speaker at the same time, and it is not polite to interrupt.

5. Write down the main ideas that you hear during the discussion. Include at least one supporting detail for each. This shows that you are actively listening, and the notes will help you respond to others with appropriate points.

6. Support other people's opinions with facts, or, if you disagree, do so politely using facts and logic.

Practice the Skill

Have a discussion with four to five people about a topic from the module. You will answer questions based on this discussion in the Module Assessment.

Possible questions about which you may have a discussion include:

- Were Leonardo da Vinci's contributions to arts or sciences more important?

- How has Johann Gutenberg affected your life?

1. Speak clearly. Think about how you will say specific names or terms that could be used in the discussion. Examples are names like *Johann Gutenberg* or terms like *perspective*.

2. Use words that you have read, like *anatomy, printing press,* and *movable type,* but do not just tell their definitions.

3. Write down main ideas and supporting points as you listen to others speaking.

4. Participate by responding to at least one comment that someone else says during the discussion. If possible, repeat a part of the comment in your response or ask the speaker a question.

5. Have a polite discussion.

Renaissance Literature

Word Help

envious jealous
entreat beg
bestrides mounts
wherefore why

❶ Romeo compares Juliet to the sun and claims that even the moon will be jealous of her beauty. *To what else does he compare her in this speech?*

❷ Juliet is not asking where Romeo is. She is asking why he is Romeo, her family's enemy.

About the Reading Shakespeare's plays spotlight an enormous range of human experiences—including love, loss, and everything in between. Even though *Romeo and Juliet* ends in disaster, its message is a hopeful one. Its main characters, two teenaged members of warring families, meet at a party and fall instantly in love. In this scene, which takes place later that evening, a troubled Romeo spies Juliet on her balcony.

As You Read Notice the words Romeo uses to describe Juliet's beauty.

from *Romeo and Juliet*
by William Shakespeare

     Rom. But soft! what light through yonder window breaks?
It is the east, and Juliet is the sun. ❶
Arise, fair sun, and kill the envious moon,
Who is already sick and pale with grief,
That thou, her maid, art far more fair than she. . . .
Two of the fairest stars in all the heaven,
Having some business, do entreat her eyes
To twinkle in their spheres till they return.
What if her eyes were there, they in her head?
The brightness of her cheek would shame those stars,
As daylight doth a lamp; her eyes in heaven
Would through the airy region stream so bright
That birds would sing and think it were not night.
See, how she leans her cheek upon her hand!
O that I were a glove upon that hand,
That I might touch that cheek!
     Jul.   Ay me!
     Rom.   She speaks:
O, speak again, bright angel! for thou art
As glorious to this night, being o'er my head,
As is a winged messenger of heaven
Unto the white-upturned wond'ring eyes
Of mortals that fall back to gaze on him
When he bestrides the lazy puffing clouds
And sails upon the bosom of the air.
     Jul. O Romeo, Romeo! wherefore art thou Romeo? ❷
Deny thy father and refuse thy name;
Or, if thou wilt not, be but sworn my love,
And I'll no longer be a Capulet.

doff remove

counsel secret thoughts

❸ Juliet says that she could be with Romeo if he were from a different family. *What does she ask him to do?*

Rom. [*Aside.*] Shall I hear more, or shall I speak at this?

 Jul. 'Tis but thy name that is my enemy;
Thou art thyself, though not a Montague.
What's Montague? it is nor hand nor foot,
Nor arm, nor face, nor any other part
Belonging to a man. O, be some other name!
What's in a name? That which we call a rose
By any other word would smell as sweet;
So Romeo would, were he not Romeo call'd,
Retain that dear perfection which he owes
Without that title. Romeo, doff thy name,
And for that name, which is no part of thee
Take all myself. ❸

  Rom.   I take thee at thy word:
Call me but love, and I'll be new baptiz'd;
Henceforth I never will be Romeo.

  Jul. What man art thou that thus bescreen'd in night
So stumblest on my counsel?
Rom.   By a name
I know not how to tell thee who I am:
My name, dear saint, is hateful to myself,
Because it is an enemy to thee;
Had I it written, I would tear the word.

  Jul. My ears have not yet drunk a hundred words
Of that tongue's utterance, yet I know the sound:
Art thou not Romeo, and a Montague?

  Rom. Neither, fair saint, if either thee dislike.

A painting of Romeo and Juliet from the 1800s

Connect Literature to History

1. **Evaluate** Renaissance humanists believed that people can achieve great goals if they are willing to work hard. How do the characters of Romeo and Juliet reflect this humanist idea?

2. **Analyze** Medieval writings often focused on religious topics. But the Renaissance humanists believed that people could write about many different subjects without discussing religion. Based on this passage, what new topic did some humanist writers explore?

Module 20 Assessment

Review Vocabulary, Terms, and People

Match the "I" statement with the person or thing that might have made the statement.

1. "I wrote many comedies, tragedies, and histories in which I examined human emotions."

2. "I am a group of ideas about the value of people and their achievements."

3. "I traveled the Silk Road to China."

4. "I was a rich banker in Florence who paid for great works of art."

5. "I wrote a political book called *The Prince*."

6. "I became famous for printed pictures that I sold at markets and fairs."

7. "I painted the ceiling of the Sistine Chapel."

8. "I thought that the church should give up practices that don't help people."

9. "I wrote *Don Quixote*."

10. "I filled my notebooks with drawings of plants, animals, and machines."

a. Cosimo de' Medici
b. Leonardo da Vinci
c. Desiderius Erasmus
d. Miguel de Cervantes
e. humanism
f. Albrecht Dürer
g. Marco Polo
h. Niccolo Machiavelli
i. William Shakespeare
j. Michelangelo

Comprehension and Critical Thinking

Lesson 1

11. a. **Identify** Who was Marco Polo, and how did he affect trade?
    b. **Compare** How were the four great trading cities of northern Italy similar?
    c. **Draw Conclusions** Why was Florence an important city during the early Renaissance?

Lesson 2

12. a. **Describe** What contributions did Dante Alighieri and Niccolo Machiavelli make to the Renaissance?
    b. **Compare** What are some characteristics that Michelangelo and Leonardo da Vinci shared?
    c. **Elaborate** A historian has said that the Renaissance "created something new from something old." What does this statement mean?

Lesson 3

13. a. **Recall** What were two main ways that the Renaissance spread beyond Italy?
    b. **Contrast** How was Northern European art different from Italian art?
    c. **Evaluate** William Shakespeare is often called the greatest writer in the English language. Why is this so?

Review Themes

14. **Geography** How did the location of Italy's port cities help them develop trade networks?

15. **Science and Technology** How did the development of the printing press change daily life for many Europeans?

Reading Skills

Greek and Latin Roots *Use the Reading Skills taught in this module to answer the following questions about the Greek and Latin roots of words from this module.*

16. Based on the definition of *perspective*, what do you think the Latin root *spec-* means? Hint: Think about other words that use this root, such as *spectator* and *spectacles*.
    a. to feel
    b. to see
    c. to hear
    d. to understand

17. The prefix *per-* in perspective means "through." Based on this meaning, what do you think the word *permeate* means?
    a. to spread through
    b. to dissolve in
    c. to disappear from
    d. to climb over

Social Studies Skills

Speak and Listen
Use the Social Studies Skills taught in this module to answer the questions about the group discussion you had. Discuss the questions with your group.

18. Make a list of the vocabulary words that were used in the discussion. Were any words used more than once? Based on the list, does the group think every person spoke during the discussion? Why does the group feel this way?

19. Estimate how many responses were given during the discussion and how many questions were asked. Do group members think they showed that they listened to the speakers? Would they agree or disagree that the discussion was polite to both speakers and listeners? Why does the group feel this way?

Focus on Writing

20. **Summarize a Discussion** Now that you have had a discussion, summarize your discussion in one paragraph. Be sure to include a main idea and supporting points you heard during the discussion. Include a topic sentence in your paragraph. This sentence should take a position on the discussion question that is supported by the ideas in the paragraph. Use vocabulary from the module.

Module 21
The Reformation

🌐

Essential Question
How can different ideas about religion lead to conflict?

About the Photo: The Protestant Reformation began in the town of Wittenberg, Germany. In this photo, churchgoers there celebrate Reformation Day services.

Explore ONLINE!

VIDEOS, including...
- Martin Luther Sparks a Revolution

HISTORY.

☑ Document-Based Investigations

☑ Graphic Organizers

☑ Interactive Games

☑ Compare Images: German Woodcuts

☑ Image with Hotpots: The Surrender of Granada

☑ Interactive Map: Spread of Catholicism, 1400s–1700s

In this module, you will learn about the reformations of the Catholic Church in Europe. You will also learn about the effects of these reformations.

What You Will Learn...

Lesson 1: The Protestant Reformation. **748**
The Big Idea Dissatisfied with the Roman Catholic Church, religious reformers broke away to form their own churches.

Lesson 2: The Catholic Reformation **755**
The Big Idea Catholic leaders worked to reform the Catholic Church and spread Catholic teachings.

Lesson 3: Effects of the Reformation. **760**
The Big Idea The Reformation changed religion in Europe and led to political and cultural conflicts.

Timeline of Events 1492–1650

▶ Explore ONLINE!

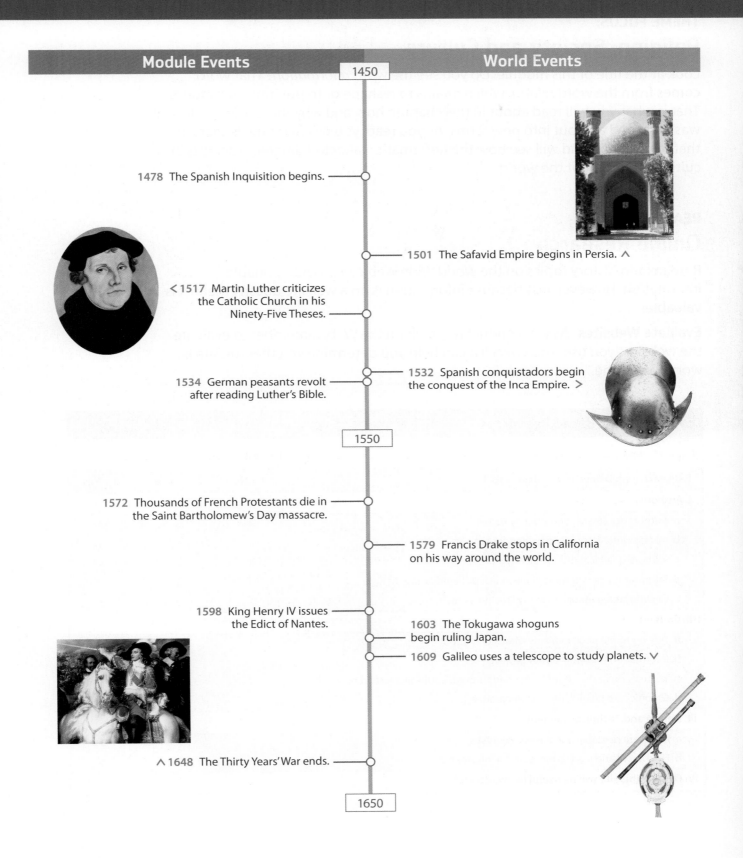

Module Events

World Events

1450

1478 The Spanish Inquisition begins.

1501 The Safavid Empire begins in Persia. ∧

< 1517 Martin Luther criticizes the Catholic Church in his Ninety-Five Theses.

1534 German peasants revolt after reading Luther's Bible.

1532 Spanish conquistadors begin the conquest of the Inca Empire. >

1550

1572 Thousands of French Protestants die in the Saint Bartholomew's Day massacre.

1579 Francis Drake stops in California on his way around the world.

1598 King Henry IV issues the Edict of Nantes.

1603 The Tokugawa shoguns begin ruling Japan.

1609 Galileo uses a telescope to study planets. ∨

∧ 1648 The Thirty Years' War ends.

1650

The Reformation **745**

Reading Social Studies

THEME FOCUS:

Religion, Society and Culture

Look at the title of this module. Do you see the word *reformation*? That word comes from the word *reform*, which means to reshape or to put into a new form. That is what you will read about in this chapter: how and why the Catholic religion was reshaped and put into new forms. As you read, you will meet the leaders of that reformation and will see how the Reformation affected different societies and cultures throughout the world.

READING FOCUS:

Online Research

Researching history topics on the World Wide Web can provide valuable information. However, just because information is on a website doesn't mean it is valuable!

Evaluate Websites As you conduct research on the Web, remember to evaluate the websites you use. This checklist can help you determine whether the site is worth your time.

Evaluate Web-Based Resources			
Name of site: _____ URL: _____ Date of access: _____			
Rate each item below on a scale of 1 to 3	1 = No	2 = Some	3 = Yes
I. Authority			
a. Authors are clearly identified by name.	1	2	3
b. Contact information is provided for authors.	1	2	3
c. Authors' qualifications are clearly stated.	1	2	3
d. Information on when the site was last updated is easy to find.	1	2	3
e. Copyrighted material is clearly labeled as such.	1	2	3
II. Content			
a. Title on home page explains what site is about.	1	2	3
b. Information is useful to your project.	1	2	3
c. Information at site could be verified through additional research.	1	2	3
d. Graphics are helpful, not just decorative.	1	2	3
III. Design and Technical Elements			
a. Pages are readable and easy to navigate.	1	2	3
b. Links work and lead to more useful information.	1	2	3
IV. Overall, this site will be useful in my research.	1	2	3

You Try It!

Key Terms and People

Lesson 1
Reformation
indulgences
purgatory
Martin Luther
Protestants
John Calvin
King Henry VIII

Lesson 2
Catholic Reformation
Ignatius of Loyola
Jesuits
Francis Xavier

Lesson 3
Huguenots
Edict of Nantes
Thirty Years' War
congregation
federalism

Imagine that the text below is the home page for a website about Martin Luther, one of the figures you will learn about in this module. Read the following text and then answer the questions below.

Dr. Smith's Martin Luther Page
by Professor John Smith, Ph.D.

"Here I stand; I can do no other. God help me!"
—Martin Luther

Welcome to my website about Martin Luther, one of the most important individuals in the entire history of Christianity. I've been teaching about Luther for nearly 30 years, and in that time I've learned a great deal about the man.

For a biography of Martin Luther, click here.

For information about his teachings, click here.

To read Luther's writings in Latin, German, or English, click the appropriate link.

For photos of important sites in Luther's life, click here.

For links to other professors' sites and to the American Lutheran church, click here.

Page last updated: October 31, 2016

Answer these questions based on the passage you just read.

1. Who is the author of the site? Does the author seem qualified to create a website about Martin Luther?
2. What information about Luther is contained on the site? Do you think that information could be useful? Why or why not?
3. To what other sites does this page link? What might this tell you about the site?
4. What other information is included on the page?
5. Overall, do you think this site could be useful for history students?

As you read this module, think about topics that might be interesting to research further online. How could you judge the quality of the sites you found if you did more research?

The Protestant Reformation

The Big Idea

Dissatisfied with the Roman Catholic Church, religious reformers broke away to form their own churches.

Main Ideas

- The Catholic Church faced challengers who were upset with the behavior of Catholic clergy and with church practices.

- Martin Luther urged reform in the Catholic Church, but he eventually broke away from the church.

- Other reformers built on the ideas of early reformers to create their own churches.

Key Terms and People

Reformation
indulgences
purgatory
Martin Luther
Protestants
John Calvin
King Henry VIII

This is the pope's palace in Avignon as it looks today.

If YOU were there . . .

You live in a town in Germany in the 1500s. The Catholic Church has a lot of influence there. Often, church officials clash with local nobles over political issues. The church also makes the nobles pay taxes. Lately, a local priest has been criticizing the way many church leaders act. He wants to make changes.

How do you think the nobles will respond to him?

The Catholic Church Faces Challengers

By the late Renaissance, some people had begun to complain about problems in the Catholic Church. They called on church leaders to erase corruption and to focus on religion. Eventually, their calls led to a reform movement of Western Christianity called the **Reformation** (re-fuhr-MAY-shuhn).

Unpopular Church Practices The reformers who wanted to change and improve the church had many complaints. They criticized the behavior of priests, bishops, and popes, as well as church practices. One church practice that brought criticism was called lay investiture. In this practice, kings, rather than church leaders or the people of the church, would "invest," or appoint, bishops and other high-ranking church officials. The church finally ended lay investiture in the 1100s.

Two problems involving the pope also lessened people's confidence in the church. In 1309, the pope moved from Rome to Avignon in southern France at the invitation of the French king. The Avignon papacy, sometimes called the French papacy, lasted almost 70 years. When the pope returned to Rome in 1377, a group of powerful church bishops in France elected another official to be pope. For a few years, there were as many as three popes who claimed to be the church's leader. This period of rival popes, called the Great Schism, lasted until 1417.

Some reformers also believed that priests and bishops weren't very religious anymore. They claimed that many priests didn't even know basic church teachings. Others thought that the pope was too involved in politics, neglecting his religious duties. These people found it difficult to see the pope as their spiritual leader.

The Wealth of the Church Other reformers had no problems with the clergy, but they thought the church had grown too rich. During the Middle Ages, the Roman Catholic Church had become one of the richest institutions in Europe. The church used a number of methods to raise money. It had been able to stay rich because it didn't have to pay any taxes.

One common method the church used to raise money was the sale of **indulgences**, a relaxation of penalties for sins people had committed. Another method was the practice of simony, or the selling of church positions or other benefits the church could offer. For instance, a wealthy man might pay for a friend to become a bishop of the church.

According to the church, some indulgences reduced the punishment that a person would receive for sins in purgatory. In Catholic teachings, **purgatory** was a place where souls went before they went to heaven. In purgatory, the souls were punished for the sins that they had committed in life. Once they had paid for these sins, the souls went to heaven. The idea that people could reduce the time that their souls would spend in purgatory by paying for indulgences enraged many Christians. They thought the church was letting people buy their way into heaven.

German Woodcuts

Many German reformers used woodcut illustrations to spread their ideas among people who couldn't read. The woodcuts here focus on a key complaint against the church: the selling of indulgences as a means of forgiving people's sins. They attack the pope by comparing him unfavorably to Jesus.

Analyze Historical Sources
How does the artist's comparison show an opinion about the pope?

The pope sells indulgences in a church. He isn't removing money from a holy place but is having it brought in.

Jesus drives moneylenders out of the temple. He taught that money didn't belong in a holy place.

The Call for Reform The unpopular practices of the church weakened its influence in many people's lives. By the early 1500s, scholars in northern Europe were calling for reforms.

One of the first people to seek reforms in the church was the Dutch priest and writer Desiderius Erasmus. Erasmus thought that the church's problems were caused by lazy clergy. He complained that church officials ignored their duties and led easy lives.

> "If there be any thing that requires their pains, they leave that . . . but if there be any thing of Honour or Pleasure, they take that to themselves. . . . Scarce any kind of men live more voluptuously [luxuriously] or with less trouble."
>
> —Desiderius Erasmus, from *The Praise of Folly*

Reading Check
Analyze Issues
What were some complaints that people had with the church?

Erasmus wanted to reform the church from within. His ideas, though, inspired later reformers who chose to break from the church completely.

Martin Luther Urges Reform

On October 31, 1517, a priest named **Martin Luther** added his voice to the call for reform. He nailed a list of complaints about the church to the door of a church in Wittenberg (VIT-uhn-berk) in the German state of Saxony. Luther's list is called the Ninety-Five Theses (THEE-seez). Thanks to the newly invented printing press, copies of Luther's complaints spread to neighboring German states.

The Ninety-Five Theses criticized the church and many of its practices, especially the sale of indulgences. The Theses also outlined many of Luther's own beliefs. For example, he didn't think people needed to do charity work or give money to the church. According to Luther, as long as people believed in God and lived by the Bible, their souls would be saved.

A Break from the Church Luther's complaints angered many German bishops. They sent a copy of the Ninety-Five Theses to Pope Leo X, who also became outraged by Luther's actions. He called Luther a heretic and

When Martin Luther nailed his Ninety-Five Theses to a church door in Wittenberg, Germany, the Reformation began. Soon, others unhappy with church practices also began to criticize the church.

Luther's Ninety-Five Theses

In Wittenberg, nailing documents to the church door was a common way of sharing ideas with the community. The Ninety-Five Theses Martin Luther posted, however, created far more debate than other such documents. The items listed here, selected from Luther's list, argued against the sale of indulgences.

Luther thought that only God—not the pope—could grant forgiveness.

Luther thought buying indulgences was useless.

Analyze Historical Sources
Why did Martin Luther argue against the sale of indulgences?

(5) *The pope will not, and cannot, remit [forgive] other punishments than those which he has imposed by his own decree [ruling] or according to the canons [laws].*

(21) *Therefore, those preachers of indulgences err [make a mistake] who say that, by the pope's indulgence, a man may be exempt from all punishments, and be saved.*

(30) *Nobody is sure of having repented [been sorry] sincerely enough; much less can he be sure of having received perfect remission [lessening] of sins.*

(43) *Christians should be taught that he who gives to the poor, or lends to a needy man, does better than buying indulgences.*

(52) *It is a vain and false thing to hope to be saved through indulgences, though the commissary [seller]—nay, the pope himself— was to pledge his own soul therefore.*

—Martin Luther, from the Ninety-Five Theses

excommunicated him. In addition, Germany's ruler, the Holy Roman Emperor, ordered Luther to appear before a diet, or council of nobles and church officials, in the German city of Worms (VOHRMS).

Although many of the nobles who attended the council supported Luther, the emperor did not. He declared Luther an outlaw and ordered him to leave the empire. But one noble secretly supported Luther. He got Luther out of Worms and to a castle, where he helped Luther hide from the emperor. Luther remained in hiding for more than a year.

Luther's ideas eventually led to a split in the Roman Catholic Church. Those who sided with Luther and protested against the church became known as **Protestants** (PRAH-tuhs-tuhnts). Those Protestants who also followed Luther's teachings were known as Lutherans.

Luther's Teachings Luther thought people could have a direct relationship with God. They didn't need priests to talk to God for them. This idea is called the priesthood of all believers.

The priesthood of all believers challenged the traditional structure of the church. To Luther, this was a benefit. People's beliefs shouldn't be based on traditions, he argued, but on the Bible, which Christians believe

Martin Luther 1483–1546

Martin Luther is credited with starting the Reformation, but he never wanted to leave the Catholic Church. He just wanted to correct what he saw as the church's mistakes and to bring the church more in line with God's word. As you have read, he vigorously opposed the sale of indulgences. After he was excommunicated, Luther began to depart more and more from church teachings. For example, although the

Roman Catholic Church didn't let priests get married, Luther married a former nun in 1525. Still, as an old man Luther regretted that his actions had caused a split in the church.

Analyze Effects
How did Luther's actions affect the Catholic Church?

contains the word of God. He thought that people should live as the Bible, not priests or the pope, instructed. Luther also disagreed with the common idea that people gained salvation, or being saved from sin or evil, by doing good works to please God. Instead, he believed that God offered forgiveness and salvation to the faithful.

To help people understand how God wanted them to live, Luther translated the Bible's New Testament into German, his native language. For the first time, many Europeans who didn't know Greek or Latin could read the Bible for themselves. In addition to translating the Bible, Luther wrote pamphlets, essays, and songs about his ideas, many of them in German.

Many German nobles liked Luther's ideas. They particularly supported Luther's position that the clergy should not interfere with politics. Because these nobles allowed the people who lived on their lands to become Lutheran, the Lutheran Church soon became the dominant church in most of northern Germany.

Reading Check
Summarize What were Martin Luther's main religious teachings?

Other Reformers

Even before Luther died in 1546, other reformers across Europe had begun to follow his example. Some of them also broke away from the Catholic Church to form churches of their own.

William Tyndale Another important reformer was William Tyndale (TIN-duhl), an English professor. Like Luther, he thought that everyone should be able to read and interpret the Bible. This belief went against the teachings of the Catholic Church, in which only clergy could interpret the Bible.

Tyndale decided to translate the Bible into English. This upset the English clergy, who tried to arrest him. Tyndale fled the country and continued his translation. He sent copies of his Bible back to England. Tyndale's work angered Catholic authorities, who had him executed.

Modern Reformers

During the Reformation, the actions of single individuals had major effects on European society. In modern times, other individuals have made similar calls for social change.

In the 1960s, Cesar Chavez organized a strike of farm workers in California and demanded fair treatment for workers. Also in the 1960s, Dr. Martin Luther King Jr. worked to gain equal rights for African Americans. Even today, people work to fight injustice around the world. For example, Aung San Suu Kyi began fighting to bring democracy to Myanmar in the 1980s. She spent 15 years under house arrest for her actions. In 2015, her party, the National League for Democracy (NLD), won Myanmar's first openly contested election in 25 years. In 2016, NLD candidate Htin Kyaw was chosen to serve as president.

Analyze Information
How have people like Cesar Chavez, Martin Luther King Jr., and Aung San Suu Kyi continued the traditions of protest and reform?

John Calvin A more influential reformer than Tyndale was **John Calvin**. One of Calvin's main teachings was predestination, the idea that God knew who would be saved even before they were born. Nothing people did during their lives would change God's plan. However, Calvin also taught that it was important to live a good life and obey God's laws. He strongly believed that closely following the word of God, as contained in the Scriptures, or writings in the Bible, would be the best way to confront the evils in the world.

In 1541, the people of Geneva, Switzerland, made Calvin their religious and political leader. He and his followers, called Calvinists, passed laws to make people live according to Calvin's teachings. Calvin's followers believed that people were generally sinful. For this reason, they banned many forms

--- BIOGRAPHY ---

John Calvin 1509–1564

Calvin was probably the most influential figure of the Reformation after Luther. Through his writings and preaching, Calvin spread basic Reformation ideas, such as the right of the common people to make church policy. Unlike many other religious leaders, Calvin didn't think that the pursuit of profits would keep businesspeople from being saved. This idea would eventually help lead to the growth of capitalism.

Make Inferences
Why might Calvin's ideas have been popular with businesspeople?

In 1534 King Henry VIII of England broke away from the Catholic Church and founded the Anglican Church.

of entertainment. These included playing cards and dancing. They thought these activities distracted people from religion. Calvin hoped to make Geneva an example of a good Christian city for the rest of the world.

Henry VIII In England the major figure of the Reformation was **King Henry VIII**. Because he had no sons and his wife couldn't have any more children, Henry asked the pope to officially end his marriage. Henry wanted to get married again so that he could have a son to whom he could leave his throne.

The pope refused Henry's request. Furious, Henry decided that he didn't want to obey the pope. In 1534, he declared himself the head of a new church, called the Church of England, or the Anglican Church.

Unlike Luther and Calvin, Henry made his break from the Catholic Church for personal reasons rather than religious ones. As a result, he didn't change many church practices. Many rituals and beliefs of the Church of England stayed very much like those of the Catholic Church. Henry's break from the church, however, opened the door for other Protestant beliefs to take hold in England.

Summary and Preview The religious landscape of Europe changed dramatically in the 1500s. The Catholic Church now had many rivals. In the next lesson, you will learn how Catholic leaders made some changes in their religion to keep their influence in Europe.

Reading Check
Compare
How were Tyndale's and Calvin's ideas similar to Luther's?

Lesson 1 Assessment

Review Ideas, Terms, and People

1. **Recall** What were five complaints people had about the Roman Catholic Church in the early 1500s?

2. **a. Identify** What was Martin Luther's list of complaints about the Roman Catholic Church called?

   b. Contrast How did Luther's ideas about interpreting the Bible differ from Catholics' ideas?

   c. Explain How did Luther think a person achieved salvation?

3. **a. Describe** What did King Henry VIII do that makes him a Reformation figure?

   b. Summarize What did John Calvin believe would be the best way to confront the evil in the world?

   c. Predict Effects How might William Tyndale's life have been different if he had lived after Henry VIII broke away from the Catholic Church?

Critical Thinking

4. **Compare and Contrast** Draw a Venn diagram like the one here. Use it to compare and contrast Luther's and Calvin's ideas about reforming the church.

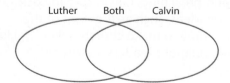

Luther   Both   Calvin

The Catholic Reformation

The Big Idea

Catholic leaders worked to reform the Catholic Church and spread Catholic teachings.

Main Ideas

- The influence of the church created a Catholic culture in Spain.

- Catholic reforms emerged in response to the Reformation.

- Missionaries worked to spread Catholic teachings.

Key Terms and People

Catholic Reformation
Ignatius of Loyola
Jesuits
Francis Xavier

If YOU were there . . .

You live in a small port city in Portugal in the 1500s. Your parents are fishers, but you have always dreamed of seeing more of the world. One day you learn that several missionaries are planning to set sail for India and Japan. Every sailor knows that the voyage will be long and dangerous. The people in those countries may welcome the missionaries—or attack them. As a result, the ship's captain is paying well for new crew members.

Will you join the crew of the missionaries' ship?

Catholic Culture in Spain

The effort to reform the Catholic Church from within is called the **Catholic Reformation**, or the Counter-Reformation. Through the late 1500s and 1600s, Catholic Reformation leaders worked to strengthen the Catholic Church and to stop the spread of Protestantism in Europe.

Many of the leaders of the Catholic Reformation came from southern Europe, especially from Spain. Spain's rulers, nobles, and clergy were used to defending the Catholic Church. They had been fighting to make Catholicism the only religion in their kingdom for hundreds of years.

The Growth of Roman Catholic Spain For centuries the region we now call Spain had been home to three religions. In many areas Christians, Muslims, and Jews all lived and worked together. Because they cooperated and didn't fight against each other, people of all three religions prospered.

They made some important advancements in art, literature, philosophy, mathematics, and science. This was referred to as the Golden Age.

Eventually, the Roman Catholic rulers decided to force the Muslims and Jews out of Spain. For hundreds of years religious wars tore up the Spanish countryside. Finally,

In 1492, Granada, the last Muslim stronghold in Spain, fell. This painting from the 1800s shows Granada's Muslim ruler surrendering to Spain's Catholic leaders.

in 1492 the king and queen of Spain defeated the last of the Spanish Muslims. They ordered all Muslims and Jews to convert to Catholicism or leave their kingdom.

The Spanish Inquisition To enforce their decision, the Spanish monarchs ordered the Spanish Inquisition to find any Muslims or Jews left in Spain. The Spanish Inquisition was a Roman Catholic Church organization charged with punishing people whose religious beliefs did not adhere to those of the church. The Inquisition was ruthless in carrying out this duty. Its members hunted down and punished converted Muslims and Jews who were suspected of keeping their old beliefs.

After a time the Inquisition began to turn its attention to Christians as well as Muslims and Jews. Catholic officials wanted to be sure that everyone in Spain belonged to the Catholic Church. They ordered the Inquisition to seek out Christians, such as Protestants, whose ideas differed from the church's.

Once the Inquisition had punished all Muslims, Jews, and Protestants, the Catholic Church in Spain had no opposition. By the late 1400s and 1500s, the Spanish church was very strong. As a result, the ideas of the Reformation did not become as popular in Spain as they did elsewhere. In fact, the Spanish clergy were among the first to fight back against the Protestant Reformation.

Reading Check
Summarize
How did the Roman Catholic Church in Spain gain power?

Catholic Reforms

By the mid-1500s, Catholic leaders in Europe were responding to Protestants' criticisms in many ways. Some reformers created new religious orders. Others tried to change church policy. Still others tried to stop the spread of Protestant teachings in Catholic areas.

New Religious Orders Catholic reformers created many new religious orders in southern Europe in the 1500s. These orders had different rules and customs. But they all shared one important goal—they wanted to win back support for the Catholic Church from people who had turned away.

Catholic Reformers

To combat the spread of Protestantism, some Catholics created new religious orders to teach young people about Catholic ideas.

Ignatius founded the Society of Jesus, or the Jesuits. His goal was to teach young men about Catholic ideas in the hope that they would reject Protestant ones.

Angela Merici founded the Ursuline Order. Her goal was to teach young women about official Catholic teachings and to give aid to people in need.

The first new order was founded in 1534 by a Spanish noble, **Ignatius** (ig-NAY-shuhs) **of Loyola**. This new order was the Society of Jesus, or the Jesuits. The **Jesuits** were a religious order created to serve the pope and the church. Ignatius came from a noble Spanish family and became a knight as a young man. In 1521, he was wounded in battle and had a lengthy recovery period. During that time he became very religious. When he founded the Jesuits, Ignatius used his military experience. He led the group as superior general and insisted that his followers be well-trained, like soldiers. He thought this would make them better able to fight against the spread of Protestantism.

One of the Jesuits' goals was to teach people about Catholic ideas. They hoped that a strong Catholic education would turn people against Protestant ideas.

Another order was created in 1535 in Italy by Angela Merici (may-REE-chee). Called the Ursuline Order, it was created to teach girls rather than boys. Like the Jesuits, the Ursulines thought Catholic education was the key to strengthening the Catholic Church and limiting the impact of Protestant teachings.

The Council of Trent The new religious orders were one response to reform, but many Catholic leaders thought that more change was needed. They decided to call together a council of church leaders. Held in Trent, Italy, this council was called the Council of Trent. At this meeting, clergy from across Europe came together to discuss, debate, and eventually reform Catholic teachings.

Results of the Council of Trent

- The selling of indulgences is banned.
- Bishops must live in the areas they oversee.
- The ideas of Luther, Calvin, and other Reformation leaders are rejected.

The Council of Trent met between 1545 and 1563 to clarify church teachings that had been criticized by Protestants. The council played a key role in restoring Europeans' faith in the Catholic Church.

The Council of Trent actually met three times between 1545 and 1563. The decisions made in these meetings led to major reforms in the Roman Catholic Church. The council restated the importance of the clergy in interpreting the Bible, but it created new rules that clergy had to follow. For example, the council ordered bishops to actually live in the areas they oversaw. Before this decision, some bishops had lived far from the churches they ran.

The Council of Trent endorsed Catholic teachings and instituted reforms in Catholic practice. From this point on, there was a clear distinction between Catholic and Protestant beliefs and practices.

The Fight Against Protestants Some Catholic Reformation leaders wanted to be more direct in their fight against Protestants. They thought Protestants were heretics who should be punished.

To lead the fight against Protestants, the pope created religious courts to punish any Protestants found in Italy. He also issued a list of books considered dangerous for people to read, including many by Protestant leaders. People reading books on this list could be excommunicated.

Missionaries Spread Catholic Teachings

Rather than change the church, many Catholics decided to dedicate their lives to helping it grow. They became missionaries. Their goal was to take Catholic teachings to people around the world. Many also hoped to win Protestants back to the Catholic Church.

Missionary work was not a new idea. Christians had been sending missionaries into non-Christian areas for hundreds of years. As early as the mid-1200s a group of Catholic missionaries had traveled as far as China. During the Catholic Reformation, however, Catholic missionary activity increased greatly. Some Protestant groups also sent out missionaries during this time, but they were generally outnumbered by Catholic missionaries.

Reading Check
Find Main Ideas
What were the goals of Catholic Reformation leaders?

The Spread of Catholicism

Catholic missionaries spread Catholicism around the world.

Catholic priests from Europe set up missions in the Americas like this one in California.

Jesuit missionaries brought Catholicism to parts of India.

This painting shows a Japanese man who converted to Christianity.

Many of the new Catholic missionaries were Jesuits. Jesuit priests went to Africa and Asia to teach people about the Catholic Church. In addition, some Jesuits traveled with explorers to America to convert the native peoples there.

Probably the most important missionary of the period was the Jesuit priest **Francis Xavier** (ZYAV-yuhr). He traveled throughout Asia in the mid-1500s, bringing Catholicism to parts of India and Japan. As a result, some people in those regions became Catholics.

Around the world Catholic missionaries baptized millions of people. Through their efforts the effects of the Catholic Reformation reached far beyond Europe.

Reading Check
Find Main Ideas
What were the goals of Catholic missionaries?

Summary and Preview Catholic leaders responded to the Reformation by making changes and gaining new followers. In the next lesson, you will see what happened when Catholics and Protestants began to interact.

Lesson 2 Assessment

Review Ideas, Terms, and People

1. a. **Define** What was the Catholic Reformation?
   b. **Explain** Why was the Catholic Church stronger in Spain than in many other parts of Europe?
2. a. **Identify** What religious order did Ignatius of Loyola create?
   b. **Summarize** How did the Catholic Church try to fight the spread of Protestant ideas?
   c. **Evaluate** Which do you think was a better way to reform the Catholic Church, new religious orders or the Council of Trent? Why?

3. **Recall** Where did Catholic missionaries travel?

Critical Thinking

4. **Organize Information** Draw a graphic organizer like the one below. In the first box, write the main cause of the Catholic Reformation. In the third box, list three effects of church reform.

Cause → Catholic Reformation → Effects

Effects of the Reformation

The Big Idea

The Reformation changed religion in Europe and led to political and cultural conflicts.

Main Ideas

- Religious division occurred within Europe and the Americas.
- Religious wars broke out between Protestants and Catholics.
- Social changes were a result of the Reformation.

Key Terms and People

Huguenots
Edict of Nantes
Thirty Years' War
congregation
federalism

If YOU were there . . .

You live in central Europe in the 1600s. As far back as you can remember, the countryside has been at war over religion. There have been riots and bloodshed. People have even been killed in the streets of your town. Now your parents have had enough of the fighting. They have decided to move the whole family to one of the American colonies, far across the ocean.

How do you feel about moving to America?

Religious Division

At the beginning of the 1500s, nearly all of Europe was Catholic. As you can see on the map, however, that situation had changed dramatically 100 years later. By 1600, nearly all of southern Europe was still Catholic. But the majority of people in northern Europe had become Protestant.

Division Within Europe In many European countries, such as Spain, nearly everyone shared the same religion. In Spain, most people were Catholic. In northern countries such as England, Scotland, Norway, and Sweden, most people were Protestant. In the Holy Roman Empire, each prince chose the religion for his territory. As a result, the empire became a patchwork of small kingdoms, some Catholic and some Protestant. Keeping peace between kingdoms with different religions was often a difficult task.

Division in the Americas When explorers and missionaries set out from Europe for other parts of the world, they took their religions with them. In this way, the distribution of religions in Europe shaped religious patterns around the world. For example, some parts of the Americas were settled by people from Catholic countries such as Spain, France, and Portugal. These areas, including parts of

Reading Check
Find Main Ideas
Which areas of Europe stayed Catholic after the Reformation?

Canada and most of Mexico, Central America, and South America, became Catholic. In contrast, places settled by Protestants from England and other countries—including the 13 colonies that became the United States—became mostly Protestant.

Religious Wars

Violence and disagreements about religion often went hand in hand. During the Reformation, this violence was sometimes tied to political concerns. For example, German peasants rebelled against their rulers in 1534 after reading Luther's Bible. It says that all people are equal, and the peasants wanted equal rights. They began a revolt that was soon defeated. In most places, though, religious concerns between Catholics and Protestants, not politics, led to conflicts and violence.

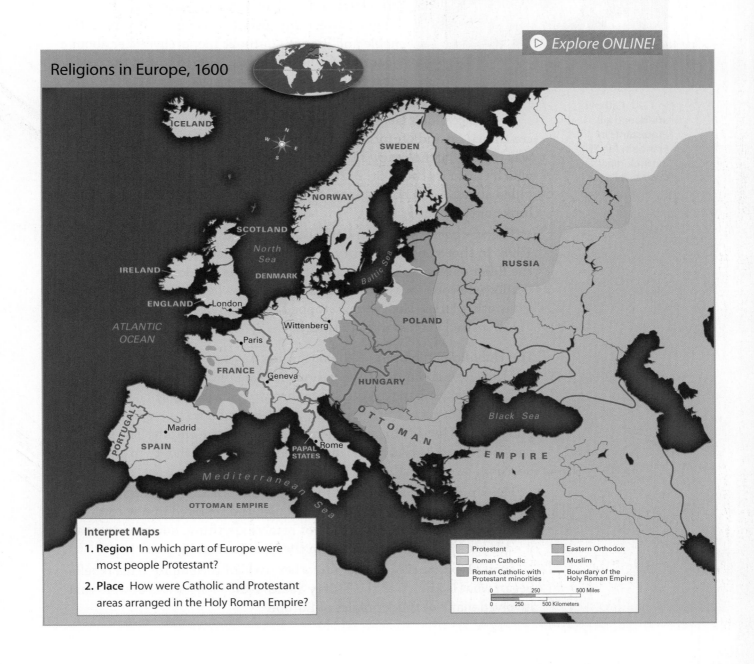

Explore ONLINE!

Religions in Europe, 1600

Interpret Maps

1. **Region** In which part of Europe were most people Protestant?

2. **Place** How were Catholic and Protestant areas arranged in the Holy Roman Empire?

Legend:
- Protestant
- Roman Catholic
- Roman Catholic with Protestant minorities
- Eastern Orthodox
- Muslim
- Boundary of the Holy Roman Empire

0   250   500 Miles
0   250   500 Kilometers

In 1572, Catholics attack and kill Protestants in France in the St. Bartholomew's Day Massacre.

France Although most people in France remained Catholic, some became Protestants. French Protestants were called **Huguenots** (HYOO-guh-nahts). A series of conflicts between Catholics and Huguenots led to years of war. The conflicts began when the French king, who was Catholic, decided to get rid of all the Protestants in France. To accomplish this, he banned all Protestant religions in France and punished or exiled any Protestants he found.

The king's efforts to eliminate Protestants increased tensions, but violence didn't break out until 1562. In that year a Catholic noble attacked and killed a group of Protestants in northwestern France. The attack infuriated Protestants throughout France. Angry Protestants rose up in arms against both the noble and France's Catholic monarchy. After about a year of fighting, both sides agreed to end the conflict. As a gesture of peace, the king allowed Protestants to remain in France, but only in certain towns.

The peace didn't last long, though. Fighting soon resumed, and the war continued on and off for almost 20 years. The worst incident of the war was the St. Bartholomew's Day Massacre. It took place on August 24, 1572, which Catholics called St. Bartholomew's Day. In one night, Catholic rioters killed about 3,000 Protestants in Paris. In the days that followed, riots broke out all over France.

The war between French Catholics and Protestants finally ended in 1598. In that year King Henry IV—who was raised a Protestant—issued the **Edict of Nantes** (NAHNT), granting religious freedom in most of France. It allowed Protestants to live and worship anywhere except in Paris and a few other cities. Henry's law stopped the war, but resentment between Catholics and Protestants continued.

The Holy Roman Empire Religious wars caused even more destruction in the Holy Roman Empire than in France. Major violence there broke out in 1618 when unhappy Protestants threw two Catholic officials out of a window in the city of Prague (PRAHG). Their action was a response to a new policy issued by the king of Bohemia—a part of the empire. The king had decided to make everyone in his kingdom become Catholic. To enforce his decision, he closed all Protestant churches in Bohemia.

The king's decision upset many Protestants. In Prague, unhappy Protestants overthrew their Catholic ruler and replaced him with a Protestant one. Their action did not resolve anything, however. Instead, it added to the religious conflict in the Holy Roman Empire.

Their revolt quickly spread into other parts of the empire. This rebellion began what is known as the **Thirty Years' War**, a long series of wars that involved many of the countries of Europe.

The Thirty Years' War took place in Europe from 1618 to 1648, with fierce fighting between Catholics and Protestants.

The war quickly became too much for the Holy Roman Emperor to handle. He sought help from other Catholic countries, including Spain. As the fighting grew worse, the Protestants also looked for help. Some of their allies weren't even Protestant. For example, the Catholic king of France agreed to help them because he didn't like the Holy Roman Emperor.

Although it began as a religious conflict, the Thirty Years' War grew beyond religious issues. Countries fought each other over political rivalries, for control of territory, and about trade rights.

After 30 years of fighting, Europe's rulers were ready for the war to end. This was especially true in the German states of the Holy Roman Empire, where most of the fighting had taken place. In 1648 Europe's leaders worked out a peace agreement.

Reading Check
Analyze Effects
How did Europe change after the Thirty Years' War?

The agreement they created, the Treaty of Westphalia, allowed rulers to determine whether their countries would be Catholic or Protestant. The treaty also introduced political changes in Europe. One important change affected the Holy Roman Empire. The states of Germany became independent, with no single ruler over them, and the Holy Roman Empire no longer existed.

Social Changes

The religious changes of the Reformation and the political turmoil that followed set other changes in motion. People began to question the role of government and the role of science in their lives. The influence of the Roman Catholic Church declined. In many European countries, the Catholic Church was just one of many churches.

This painting from the 1600s shows a Protestant church in France. Members of a congregation like this one elected leaders and made their own rules. The rise of self-government was one result of the Reformation.

Self-Government Before the Reformation, most Europeans had no voice in governing the Catholic Church. They simply followed the teachings of their priests and bishops.

Many Protestant churches didn't have priests, bishops, or other clergy. Instead, each **congregation**, or church assembly, made its own rules and elected leaders to make decisions for them. People began to think that their own ideas, not just the ideas of the clergy, were important.

Some Results of the Reformation

- Religious conflicts spread across Europe.
- Church leaders reform the Catholic Church.
- Missionaries spread Catholicism around the world.
- Northern Europe becomes largely Protestant.
- Local Protestant churches practice self-government.

Reading Check
Summarize
How did the Reformation change European society?

Once people began to govern their churches, they also began to want political power. In some places congregations began to rule their towns, not just their churches. In Scotland, England, and some English colonies in America, congregations met to decide how their towns would be run. These town meetings were an early form of self-government, in which people rule themselves.

As time passed, some congregations gained more power. Their decisions came to affect more aspects of people's lives or to control events in larger areas. The power of these congregations didn't replace national governments, but national rulers began to share some power with local governments. The sharing of power between local governments and a strong central government is called **federalism**.

New Views of the World Once people began to think that their own ideas were important, they began to ask more questions. They wanted to know more about the natural physical world around them. In addition, more and more people refused to accept information about the world based on someone else's authority. They didn't care if the person was a writer from ancient Greece or a religious leader. The desire to investigate, to figure things out on their own, led people to turn increasingly to science.

Summary The Reformation caused great changes in Europe, and not just in religion. It also paved the way for the growth of science.

Lesson 3 Assessment

Review Ideas, Terms, and People

1. a. **Recall** Where did more Protestants live, in northern or southern Europe?

   b. **Evaluate** Why do you think the Catholic Church had more influence in one part of Europe than in another?

2. a. **Identify** Where did the Thirty Years' War begin?

   b. **Explain** What started the wars of religion in France?

3. a. **Identify** How did the influence of the Catholic Church change as a result of the Reformation?

   b. **Analyze** How did the Reformation lead to the growth of federalism?

Critical Thinking

4. **Analyze** Draw a series of boxes like the ones shown here. In the first box, identify the cause of religious conflict in Europe. In the last box, list two effects of that conflict.

Social Studies Skills

Develop Graphs

Define the Skill

Graphs are drawings that display data in a clear, visual form. There are three main types of graphs. *Line graphs* show changes over time. *Bar graphs* compare quantities within a category or illustrate changes over time. *Circle graphs*, also called *pie graphs*, show the parts that make up a whole of something. Each piece of the circle shows what proportion that part is of the whole.

Graphs let you see relationships more quickly and easily than tables or written explanations do. The ability to develop graphs will help you to better understand and represent statistical information in history.

Learn the Skill

Use these guidelines to develop a bar graph that presents data in a visual form.

1. Draw two lines in an L-shape to make the borders of the bar graph. The up-and-down line is the *vertical axis*. The left-to-right line is the *horizontal axis*.

2. Label both the horizontal axis and the vertical axis. For example, the vertical axis of the graph on this page is labeled "Percentage of population." The horizontal axis is labeled "Country."

3. Create a scale on the vertical axis that would include all the data collected. For example, the scale used on the vertical axis of the graph on this page is 0–100 percent. The scale is in increments of 10 percent. Draw horizontal lines for each number on your vertical axis. Make sure to evenly space the lines.

4. Divide the horizontal axis into the number of bars you need to represent all your data. For example, the bar graph on this page includes places for six bars, two for each of the three countries.

5. Choose colors for the bars, and create a key that explains what the colors represent. For example, the bar graph below uses blue to represent Catholics and red to represent Protestants/Other Christians.

6. Add a title for the graph that clearly tells what the graph shows.

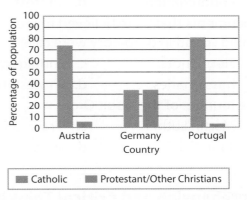

Percentage of Catholics and Other Christians Today

Practice the Skill

The Reformation brought changes to Christianity in Europe. The effects of these changes can still be seen there today. Make a bar graph similar to the one above, using the data below for Poland, Switzerland, and Denmark.

1. Poland: 87 percent Catholic and 1 percent Protestant/Other Christian

2. Switzerland: 38 percent Catholic and 27 percent Protestant/Other Christian

3. Denmark: 1 percent Catholic and 80 percent Protestant/Other Christian

Module 21 Assessment

Review Vocabulary, Terms, and People

Choose the letter of the answer that best completes each sentence.

1. The movement to reform the Roman Catholic Church that created many new religions was the
   - **a.** Council of Trent.
   - **b.** Thirty Years' War.
   - **c.** Catholic Reformation.
   - **d.** Protestant Reformation.

2. The man who began the Reformation by nailing complaints about the church to a church door was
   - **a.** Martin Luther.
   - **b.** John Calvin.
   - **c.** Francis Xavier.
   - **d.** King Henry VIII.

3. People who disagreed with and broke away from the Catholic Church during the Reformation were called
   - **a.** indulgences.
   - **b.** congregations.
   - **c.** Jesuits.
   - **d.** Protestants.

4. Documents that were believed to reduce the time a person's soul would spend in purgatory were called
   - **a.** Huguenots.
   - **b.** missionaries.
   - **c.** indulgences.
   - **d.** Protestants.

5. The founder of the Jesuit Order was
   - **a.** Martin Luther.
   - **b.** John Calvin.
   - **c.** Francis Xavier.
   - **d.** Ignatius of Loyola.

Comprehension and Critical Thinking

Lesson 1

6. **a. Describe** What were some of the complaints that people had about the Catholic Church in the 1500s?

   b. Analyze How did Martin Luther's teachings affect the beliefs of many people in northern Europe?

   c. Predict Effects How did William Tyndale and King Henry VIII affect people's lives for hundreds of years to come?

Lesson 2

7. **a. Identify** Who were Ignatius of Loyola, Angela Merici, and Francis Xavier?

   b. Analyze Why was Spain a leader in the Catholic Reformation?

   c. Evaluate Why might a historian say that the Protestant Reformation actually helped spread Catholicism around the world?

Lesson 3

8. **a. Recall** By the 1600s, which parts of Europe were mostly Catholic? Which parts were mostly Protestant?

   b. Compare and Contrast How were the wars in France and the Holy Roman Empire similar? How were they different?

   c. Elaborate How did the Reformation affect other aspects of daily life in Europe and the English colonies in America?

Module 21 Assessment, continued

Review Themes

9. **Society and Culture** What were two nonreligious effects of the Reformation?

10. **Religion** Do you think the Reformation increased or decreased most people's interest in religion? Why?

Reading Skills

Online Research *Use the Reading Skills taught in this module to complete the following activity. Each question below lists two types of websites you could use to answer the question. Decide which website is likely to be a more valuable and reliable source of information.*

11. What happened to Martin Luther after he nailed his Ninety-Five Theses to the church door?

   a. a movie studio website for a movie about Martin Luther's life

   b. an online encyclopedia

12. What happened during the Thirty Years' War?

   a. a website with an excerpt from a book by a university professor about the war

   b. a museum website for an exhibit about the Holy Roman Empire

Social Studies Skills

Develop Graphs *Use the Social Studies Skills taught in this module to answer the question below.*

13. What kind of graph (line, bar, or circle) would you create to show how the number of Protestants in the Netherlands rose and fell during the 1600s? Explain your answer.

Focus On Writing

14. **Write and Design a Book Jacket** You work at a publishing company. You've been asked to design a book jacket for a book about the Reformation. What main ideas and details should you include in a summary on the back of the jacket? What might you title the book? What image might you pick for the front of the jacket? Write 7–8 sentences about the Reformation for the back of the book jacket. Include enough detail to hook your readers and make them want to read the book. Once you've completed the summary, think of a catchy title and an image for the front cover.

Module 22

The Scientific Revolution

Essential Question

How did the scientific advances of the 16th to 18th centuries change society?

About the Photo: Powerful telescopes such as this one are used by astronomers to study the skies.

▶ *Explore ONLINE!*

VIDEOS, including...
- Issac Newton: The Gravity of Genius
- Newton's Laws
- The Telescope

☑ Document-Based Investigations

☑ Graphic Organizers

☑ Interactive Games

☑ Image with Hotspots: Ptolemy's Map

☑ Animation: Models of the Solar System

☑ Image with Hotspots: The Monk and the Mathematician

In this module, you will learn about the discoveries and inventions of the Scientific Revolution. The Scientific Revolution laid the foundations for modern science.

What You Will Learn...

Lesson 1: A New View of the World 772
The Big Idea Europeans drew on earlier ideas to develop a new way of gaining knowledge about the natural world.

Lesson 2: Discoveries and Inventions 776
The Big Idea During the Scientific Revolution, new ideas and inventions changed the nature of knowledge.

Lesson 3: Science and Society 782
The Big Idea The Scientific Revolution led to the establishment of science as a method of learning, new ideas about government, and conflict with religious authorities.

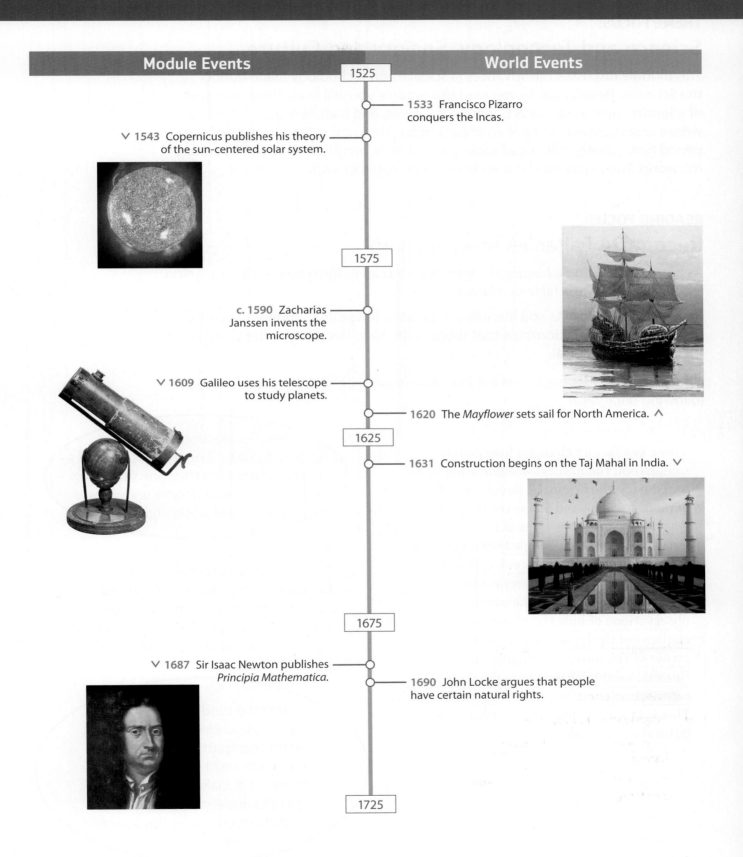

Module Events		World Events

1525

1533 Francisco Pizarro conquers the Incas.

∨ **1543** Copernicus publishes his theory of the sun-centered solar system.

1575

c. **1590** Zacharias Janssen invents the microscope.

∨ **1609** Galileo uses his telescope to study planets.

1620 The *Mayflower* sets sail for North America. ∧

1625

1631 Construction begins on the Taj Mahal in India. ∨

1675

∨ **1687** Sir Isaac Newton publishes *Principia Mathematica*.

1690 John Locke argues that people have certain natural rights.

1725

Reading Social Studies

THEME FOCUS:

Science and Technology, Society and Culture

This module discusses the advances in science and technology made during the Scientific Revolution. As you read this module you will learn about the work of scientists such as Nicolaus Copernicus, Galileo, and Isaac Newton—scientists whose ideas continue to have an impact today. They and other scientists of this period have greatly influenced society and culture, not just in Europe but around the world. Think how much different our lives would be without science!

READING FOCUS:

Recognize Fallacies in Reasoning

As part of evaluating a historical argument, you can judge whether the reasoning is sound. A fallacy is a false or mistaken idea.

Recognize Fallacies As you identify a main idea, judge its soundness. Look for cause-and-effect relationships that support the idea. Decide whether you think the argument is logical.

Notice how a reader explained the logical reasoning behind the main idea in the following paragraph.

Three key factors changed how people understood the natural world leading up to and during the Scientific Revolution. First, explorers discovered a new continent that was not on the maps created by ancient Greek philosophers. <u>People began questioning the accuracy of Greek authorities.</u> Second, astronomers' observations changed how people understood the universe. <u>Their observations of how the planets moved challenged the belief that the earth was the center of the universe.</u> Finally, <u>new inventions allowed scientists to make more accurate observations and conduct experiments.</u> This led to more discoveries about how the natural world works.

> People questioned previous knowledge based on the discovery of a new continent. This supports the main idea that the way people understood the natural world changed.

> If observations challenged how people previously understood the universe, it would make sense that the way people understood the natural world changed.

> Here's the third reason why the way people understood the natural world changed: inventions led to more accurate knowledge about the world. It makes sense that how people understood the natural world changed during the Scientific Revolution.

You Try It!

Galileo's ideas about the universe conflicted with those of the Church.

↓

Galileo was not a devout Catholic.

Tycho Brahe established an observatory and carefully recorded his observations of the stars

↓

because he wanted to keep accurate astronomical records.

Sir Isaac Newton, one of the greatest scientists in history, was English.

↓

Therefore, all scientists are from England.

1. Is the first conclusion a fallacy of reason? What reasonable conclusions can you draw from the statement?
2. Do you think the second conclusion is logical or illogical? What makes you think so?
3. Is the third conclusion reasonable? Why or why not?

As you read this module, notice how the authors use logical reasoning to support their main ideas.

Key Terms and People

Lesson 1
Scientific Revolution
science
theories
Ptolemy
rationalists
alchemy
Lesson 2
Nicolaus Copernicus
Tycho Brahe
Johannes Kepler
Galileo Galilei
Sir Isaac Newton
barometer
Lesson 3
Francis Bacon
René Descartes
scientific method
hypothesis

A New View of the World

The Big Idea

Europeans drew on earlier ideas to develop a new way of gaining knowledge about the natural world.

Main Ideas

- The Scientific Revolution marked the birth of modern science.
- The roots of the Scientific Revolution can be traced to ancient Greece, the Muslim world, and Europe.

Key Terms and People

Scientific Revolution
science
theories
Ptolemy
rationalists
alchemy

If YOU were there . . .

You are a student in Germany in the early 1500s. You love to watch the changing phases of the moon and draw the star patterns at different times of the year. You've asked your teachers many questions: Why does the moon hang in the sky? Why do the stars move? But their answers don't seem convincing to you.

How can you find the answers to your questions?

The Birth of Modern Science

During the 1500s and 1600s, a handful of brilliant individuals laid the foundations for science as we know it today. Some historians consider the development of modern science the most important event in the intellectual history of humankind.

A Revolution in Thinking The series of events that led to the birth of modern science is called the **Scientific Revolution**. It occurred between about 1540 and 1700. Why would the birth of science be called a "revolution"? The answer is that science was a radical new idea. It was a completely different way of looking at the world.

Before the Scientific Revolution, most educated people who studied the world took guidance from the explanations given by such authorities as ancient Greek writers and Catholic Church officials. After the Scientific Revolution, educated people placed more importance on what they observed and less on what they were told. They gained knowledge by observing the world around them and developing logical explanations for what they saw.

Understanding Science Science is a particular way of gaining knowledge about the world. In fact, the word *science* comes from a Latin word meaning "knowledge" or "understanding."

Science starts with observation. Scientists observe, or look at, the world. By observing the world, they can identify facts about it. A famous scientist once said, "Science is built up with facts, as a house is with stones. But a collection of facts is no more a science than a pile of stones is a house."

So scientists do more than identify facts. They use logic to explain the facts they have observed. The explanations scientists develop based on these facts are called **theories**.

Theories are not accepted on faith. They must be tested to see if they are true. Scientists design experiments to test their theories. If the experiments keep showing that the theory makes sense, the theory is kept. If the experiments do not support the theory, scientists try a new theory. In this way, scientists learn more about the world.

As you can see, scientific knowledge is based on observations, facts, and logical ideas, or theories, about them. Before the Scientific Revolution, this method of gaining knowledge was uncommon.

Reading Check
Find Main Ideas
What was the Scientific Revolution?

Roots of the Revolution

Some of the main ideas of science had been expressed long before the Scientific Revolution. In fact, some of the basic ideas of science are ancient.

Greek Thinkers Many Greek thinkers expressed ideas that today we would call scientific. The great philosopher Aristotle, for example, wrote about astronomy, geography, and many other fields. But his greatest contribution to science was the idea that people should observe the world carefully and draw **logical** conclusions about what they see.

Academic Vocabulary
logical reasoned, well thought out

Greek Thinkers

The ancient Greeks developed theories about how the world worked that influenced later scientific thinkers. This famous painting from the early 1500s by the Italian artist Raphael shows some influential Greek thinkers.

Philosophers like Plato and Aristotle used reason and logic to understand the world.

Pythagoras studied numbers and believed that things could be predicted and measured.

Euclid discovered basic mathematical laws that helped explain the natural world.

Greek Ideas

- Importance of observation, logic, and rational thought
- Basic theories about astronomy, geography, and mathematics

Scholars of Three Faiths

- Muslim preservation and study of ancient texts
- Jewish study of Greek ideas and religion
- Christian study of Greek ideas and religion

Renaissance Humanism

- Emphasis on Greek and Roman ideas
- Focus on the importance of education and learning

Knowledge of Exploration

- Better understanding of the true size and shape of the world
- Increase in knowledge
- Development of new technologies

The use of observation and logic, as you have just read, is important in gaining scientific knowledge.

Another Greek thinker was **Ptolemy** (TAHL-uh-mee), an ancient astronomer. He studied the skies, recorded his observations, and offered theories to explain what he saw. Ptolemy was also a geographer who made the best maps of his time. His maps were based on observations of the real world.

Aristotle, Ptolemy, and other Greek thinkers were **rationalists**, people who look at the world in a rational, or reasonable and logical, way. During the Renaissance, Europeans studied the works of Greek rationalists. As a result, they began to view the world in a rational way. They began to think like scientists.

Religion's Role in Promoting Knowledge European scholars could study ancient Greek writings because of the work of others. Muslim scholars translated Greek writings into Arabic. They studied them for centuries and added their own new ideas. Later, the Arabic versions were translated into

Latin, which was read in Europe. This work preserved ancient knowledge and spread interest in science to Europe.

Other religious scholars also played a role in preserving Greek ideas. The Jewish scholar Maimonides (my-MAHN-uh-deez) studied and wrote about Aristotle, trying to unite his work with Jewish ideas. The Christian scholar Thomas Aquinas tried to unite the work of Aristotle with Christian ideas. Other Christian scholars studied Greek ideas in Europe's universities.

The Catholic Church encouraged learning, as well. It helped pay for scientific research and sent priests to study at universities. The Church supported the teaching of math and science.

Developments in Europe The Scientific Revolution was not just the result of European scholars studying ancient Greek writings. Developments in Europe also helped bring about the Scientific Revolution.

One development that helped lead to the Scientific Revolution was the growth of humanism during the Renaissance. Humanist artists and writers spent much of their time studying the natural world. This interest in the natural world carried forward into the Scientific Revolution.

Another development was a growing interest in alchemy (AL-kuh-mee). **Alchemy** was a forerunner of chemistry. Alchemists experimented with various natural substances. They were best known for trying to change other metals into gold. Although they failed at that, alchemists succeeded in using experiments to learn more about how nature worked.

All of these developments—the interest in ancient Greek writings, the growth of humanism, the experiments of alchemists—came together in the early 1500s to bring about the Scientific Revolution.

Summary and Preview The Scientific Revolution was the birth of modern science. Greek, Muslim, and European thought all contributed to its beginning. In the next lesson, you will read about specific events of the Scientific Revolution.

Reading Check
Analyze Effects
How did Greek rationalism help lead to the Scientific Revolution?

Lesson 1 Assessment

Review Ideas, Terms, and People

1. a. Define What is science?

   b. Explain Why was the Scientific Revolution important in world history?

   c. Elaborate What might cause scientists to reject a theory?

2. a. Identify Who was Ptolemy?

   b. Analyze What qualities did Greek rationalists have?

   c. Elaborate Why might alchemists have thought they could turn other metals into gold?

Critical Thinking

3. Identify Cause and Effect Draw a graphic organizer like the one here. In the boxes to the left, identify four causes of the Scientific Revolution.

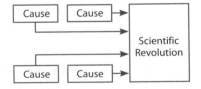

Discoveries and Inventions

The Big Idea

During the Scientific Revolution, new ideas and inventions changed the nature of knowledge.

Main Ideas

- The discovery of the Americas led scholars to doubt ancient Greek ideas.

- Advances in astronomy were key events of the Scientific Revolution.

- Sir Isaac Newton developed laws that explained much of the natural world.

- New inventions helped scientists study the natural world.

Key Terms and People

Nicolaus Copernicus
Tycho Brahe
Johannes Kepler
Galileo Galilei
Sir Isaac Newton
barometer

Reading Check
Analyze Effects
How did the European discovery of America affect the Scientific Revolution?

If YOU were there . . .

You are an innkeeper in Spain in 1498. Many of the guests who stay at your inn are sailors. Today they are telling stories about a vast new land filled with strange peoples, plants, and animals. No one had ever thought such a land really existed before.

How does this news change your view of the world?

Discovery Leads to Doubt

During the Renaissance, European scholars eagerly read and studied the works of Greek rationalists. Ancient scholars including Aristotle, Ptolemy, and Plato were viewed as authorities.

Then an event took place that caused Europeans to doubt some of what the Greeks had said. In 1492, Christopher Columbus sailed west across the Atlantic Ocean in hopes of reaching Asia. As a guide, he took the map of the world that Ptolemy had created. Columbus never reached Asia because he ran into North America instead. Within a few years, voyages of exploration made it clear that there was an entire continent that Europeans hadn't even known existed. This discovery stunned Europeans.

This continent was not on Ptolemy's map. Ptolemy was wrong. Observation of the real world had disproved the teachings of an ancient authority. Soon, European scholars began to question the accuracy of other Greek authorities. More and more, observations the Europeans made did not fit with what the authorities had described. These observations that conflicted with the Greek scholars' writings helped lead to the Scientific Revolution.

Advances in Astronomy

In 1543, an astronomer published a book that contradicted what a Greek authority had written. Many historians think the publication of this book marks the beginning of the Scientific Revolution.

Changing Views of the Universe

The diagram shows the sun at the center of the universe.
Before Copernicus, most people believed that the sun
revolved around Earth, as in this drawing.

Nicolaus Copernicus The book thought to have marked the beginning of the Scientific Revolution was written by a Polish astronomer, **Nicolaus Copernicus** (kuh-PUHR-ni-kuhs). His 1543 book was called *On the Revolution of the Celestial Spheres.*

Copernicus was familiar with Ptolemy's theories and writings. Ptolemy had written that Earth was the center of the universe and that the sun and other planets orbited, or circled around, Earth. For 1,400 years, people accepted this belief as fact.

As Copernicus studied the movements of the planets, however, what Ptolemy stated made less and less sense to him. If the planets were indeed orbiting Earth, they would have to be moving in very complex patterns.

So Copernicus tried a different explanation for what he observed in the sky. Copernicus asked, What if the planets actually orbited the sun? Suddenly, complex patterns weren't necessary to make sense of what Copernicus observed. Instead, simple circular orbits would account for the planets' movements.

What Copernicus had done was practice science. Instead of trying to make his observations fit an old idea, he came up with a different idea—a

—————— BIOGRAPHY ——————

Nicolaus Copernicus 1473–1543

Nicolaus Copernicus realized that sharing his revolutionary ideas about the universe could be dangerous. He feared persecution or even death at the hands of Church leaders. He was also worried that the scientific community would reject his theories. Eventually, he was persuaded to publish his theories, and the "Copernican system" became a landmark discovery of the Scientific Revolution.

Evaluate
If you were Nicolaus Copernicus, would you have published your theories? Why or why not?

different theory—to explain what he observed. Copernicus never proved his theory, but the Scientific Revolution had begun.

Brahe and Kepler Another important astronomer of the Scientific Revolution was **Tycho Brahe** (TYOO-koh BRAH-huh). Brahe, who was Danish, spent most of his life observing the stars. In the late 1500s, he charted the positions of more than 750 of them.

What Brahe did, however, was less important than *how* he did it. Brahe emphasized the importance of careful observation and detailed, accurate records. Careful recording of information is necessary so that other scientists can use what has previously been learned. In this way, Brahe made an important contribution to modern science.

Brahe was assisted by the German astronomer **Johannes Kepler**. Later, Kepler tried to map the orbits of the planets. But Kepler ran into a problem. According to his observations, the planet Mars did not move in a circle as he expected it to.

Kepler knew that Copernicus had stated that the orbits of the planets were circular. But Kepler's observations showed that Copernicus was mistaken. In 1609, Kepler wrote that Mars—and all other planets— moved in elliptical, or oval, orbits instead of circular ones. Here was a new theory that fit the observed facts. Kepler's work helped prove Copernicus's theory that the planets orbit the sun. In fact, Kepler became one of the first scientists to speak out in support of Copernicus.

Kepler continued to study the planets for the rest of his life. His basic ideas about the planets' movements are still accepted by scientists today.

Galileo Galilei **Galileo Galilei** (gal-uh-LEE-oh gal-uh-LAY) was one of the most important scientists of the Scientific Revolution. He was the first person to study the sky with a telescope. With his telescope, Galileo discovered craters and mountains on the moon. He also discovered that moons orbit Jupiter.

Galileo was interested in more than astronomy, however. He also was interested in such things as how falling objects behave. Today, we use the term *mechanics* for the study of objects and motion.

Galileo's biggest contribution to the development of science was the way he learned about mechanics.

Kepler's Discoveries

- Planets orbit the sun in elliptical, not circular, orbits.
- Planets move faster when they are closer to the sun.
- The human eye sees images reversed, like a camera.

Kepler demonstrated that planets move in elliptical orbits.

Galileo studied the sky and performed experiments to learn about motion mechanics.

Galileo Discovers Moons of Jupiter

In 1610, Galileo (1564–1642) wrote a book about his discovery of four moons that orbit Jupiter. At that time, many people believed that humans were at the center of the universe. Galileo's discovery challenged this belief. After explaining how he determined that the moons revolved around Jupiter, he explained its importance.

Galileo points out that his discovery should help convince people who believe Earth orbits the sun, but not that the moon orbits Earth.

Galileo argues that his observation proves it's possible for the moon to revolve around Earth while Earth also orbits the sun.

Analyze Historical Sources
Why did Galileo believe this discovery helped prove that Earth orbited the sun?

"We have a notable and splendid argument to remove the scruples [doubts] of those who can tolerate [believe] the revolution of the planets round the Sun in the Copernican system, yet are so disturbed by the motion of one Moon about the Earth, while both accomplish an orbit of a year's length about the Sun, that they consider that this theory of the constitution of the universe must be upset as impossible; for now we have not one planet only revolving about another, while both traverse [follow] a vast orbit about the Sun, but our sense of sight presents to us four satellites [stars] circling about Jupiter, like the Moon about the Earth, while the whole system travels over a mighty orbit about the Sun in the space of twelve years."

—Galileo Galilei, in *The Sidereal Messenger of Galileo Galilei and a Part of the Preface to Kepler's Dioptrics*, translated by E.S. Carlos

Reading Check
Summarize What were two major achievements in astronomy?

Instead of just observing things in nature, he set up experiments to test what he observed. Galileo was the first scientist to routinely use experiments to test his theories. For this, he is remembered as the father of experimental science.

Sir Isaac Newton

The high point of the Scientific Revolution was marked by the publication of a remarkable book. This book, published in 1687, was *Principia Mathematica*. Its author was the English scientist **Sir Isaac Newton**. Newton was one of the greatest and most influential scientists who ever lived.

Newton studied and simplified the work of earlier scientists. In doing so, he
- reviewed everything scientists had been learning
- coupled it with his own observations and ideas
- synthesized his observations with others' to formulate theories
- identified four laws that described how the physical world worked

One of Newton's laws is called the law of gravity. You may know that gravity is the force that attracts objects to each other. It's the force that makes a dropped apple fall to the ground and that keeps the planets in orbit around the sun.

Sir Isaac Newton 1642–1727

Sir Isaac Newton was interested in learning about the nature of light, so he conducted a series of experiments. In Newton's time, most people assumed that light was white. Newton proved, however, that light is actually made up of all of the colors of the rainbow. His research on light became the basis for his invention of the reflecting telescope— the type of telescope found in most large observatories today.

Summarize
What did Newton prove about the nature of light?

Newton's discoveries explained how the force of gravity pulls the moon toward Earth, keeping it in orbit around our planet.

Newton's three other laws are called the laws of motion. They describe how objects move in space. You may have heard of one of them, which he explained in *Principia Mathematica*: "For every action there is an equal and opposite reaction."

Newton proposed that the universe was like a huge machine. Within this machine, all objects follow the laws he identified. In short, Newton explained how the physical world worked—and he was correct. Newton's laws became the foundation of nearly all scientific study until the 1900s.

His discoveries were remarkable, but he did not make them by himself. Newton learned from other scientists and built upon their knowledge. In his correspondence with another scientist, he wrote, "If I have seen further, it is by standing on the shoulders of giants."

Newton also invented calculus, an advanced form of mathematics that scientists use to solve complex problems. For this, and for his laws of motion, Newton is remembered as a great scientist.

Reading Check
Summarize
What do Newton's laws describe?

New Inventions

During the Scientific Revolution, scientists invented new and better instruments. These helped them study the natural world.

Around 1590, a Dutch lens maker named Zacharias Janssen invented a simple microscope. The first person to use

This early microscope was made around 1675. The lens is protected by cardboard and leather and slides up and down.

a microscope as a scientific instrument, though, was the Dutch scientist Antoni van Leeuwenhoek (LAY-ven-hook) in the mid-1600s. Examining a drop of pond water with his microscope, he saw tiny plants and animals not visible to the naked eye.

In 1593, Galileo invented the thermometer. Thermometers are used to measure temperature. About 50 years later, an Italian doctor developed a more accurate model than Galileo's.

The telescope was probably invented by a Dutch lens maker in 1608. The next year, Galileo built a much-improved telescope that he used to make his important astronomical discoveries.

In 1643, the Italian scientist Evangelista Torricelli invented the **barometer**. A barometer is a scientific instrument that measures air pressure. Barometers are used to help forecast the weather.

These instruments—the microscope, the thermometer, the telescope, and the barometer—are very common today. In fact, you have probably used at least one of them yourself. But when they were invented, they were dramatic advances in technology. They gave scientists the tools they needed to make more accurate observations of the world and to conduct experiments. They were the tools of the Scientific Revolution.

Summary and Preview The work of Copernicus, Brahe, Kepler, Galileo, and Newton was central to the Scientific Revolution. In the next lesson, you will learn more about the effects of these scientists' accomplishments on society then and now.

Reading Check
Compare
How are the microscope and the telescope similar?

Lesson 2 Assessment

Reviewing Ideas, Terms, and People

1. a. Recall What event caused Europeans to doubt the ideas of ancient Greek authorities?
   b. Explain How did the doubting of Greek authorities help usher in the Scientific Revolution?
2. a. Identify Who was Galileo?
   b. Summarize How did Copernicus and Kepler change people's view of the universe?
3. a. Identify For what laws is Isaac Newton most famous?
   b. Evaluate Why do you think Newton is considered the greatest figure of the Scientific Revolution?

4. Define What is a barometer?

Critical Thinking

5. Compare and Contrast Draw a diagram like the one below. Describe each individual's view of how the universe is organized.

Scientist	Ptolemy	Copernicus	Kepler
View			

Science and Society

The Big Idea

The Scientific Revolution led to the establishment of science as a method of learning, new ideas about government, and conflict with religious authorities.

Main Ideas

- The ideas of Francis Bacon and René Descartes helped clarify the scientific method.

- Science influenced new ideas about government.

- As scientists developed a better understanding of the human body, medical treatments also changed.

- Science and religion developed a sometimes uneasy relationship.

Key Terms and People

Francis Bacon
René Descartes
scientific method
hypothesis

If YOU were there . . .

You are a scientist conducting an experiment about falling objects. You stand at the base of a tall tower, watching as two of your assistants drop balls from the top. The balls are the same size, but one is made of iron and one of wood. The iron ball is much heavier, so you think that it will hit the ground first. But to your surprise, the two balls appear to hit the ground at the same time! You begin to think that all items will fall at the same speed.

How could you test your new idea?

Bacon, Descartes, and the Scientific Method

The Scientific Revolution led to a dramatic change in the way people learned about the world. The new, scientific way of gaining knowledge had far-reaching effects. In fact, the Scientific Revolution still affects us today.

The first effect of the Scientific Revolution was the establishment of science as the most effective way to learn about the natural world. Two individuals played a leading role in gaining this acceptance of science.

Francis Bacon Francis Bacon was an English philosopher who had read the works of the great scientists of the Scientific Revolution. He was extremely impressed with what he read. He noted how these scientists, using observations, facts, experiments, and theories, were revealing the truth about how nature worked.

Bacon argued that science should be pursued in a systematic fashion. He even tried to get the king of England to provide money for scientific research. If science were pursued consistently and logically, Bacon wrote, then human knowledge would continually advance over the years. In 1605, Bacon published his ideas in a book titled *The Advancement of Learning*.

Science in School

If you have performed an experiment in science class, then you've seen the scientific method at work. Here, students are performing an experiment to learn about falling objects.

Students and scientists still use the scientific method because it helps them rationally solve problems. They conduct experiments to test their hypotheses. If their experiments don't produce the results they expect, they change their hypotheses and start over. Only after getting the same results time after time do scientists consider their findings conclusive.

Analyze Information
How does the scientific method help scientists solve problems?

René Descartes Another thinker who made great contributions to the establishment of science was the French philosopher **René Descartes** (ruh-NAY day-CART).

Descartes believed that nothing should be accepted as true if it isn't proven to be true. This differed from the belief that most European scholars had been supporting for generations. They believed knowledge begins with faith; Descartes said it begins with doubt.

Descartes didn't just mean that observations and experiments were needed for this proof. These things, he said, took place in the material world, and people might be tricked by their senses. Instead, Descartes emphasized that people must use clear thinking and reason to establish proof.

The Scientific Method Today scientists use a **procedure** called the scientific method when doing their research. The **scientific method** is a step-by-step method for performing experiments and other scientific research.

The scientific method combines Bacon's idea of a systematic scientific process, Descartes's insistence on proof and clear reasoning, and the work of other scientists. Using the scientific method, scientists have learned more about the universe in the few hundred years since the Scientific Revolution than in all of the thousands of years that came before. Because of this, the basics of the scientific method—observation and experimentation—are considered the main **principles** of modern science.

Academic Vocabulary
procedure a series of steps taken to accomplish a task

Academic Vocabulary
principles basic beliefs, rules, or laws

The Scientific Method

The ideas of Bacon and Descartes led to the scientific method—a method for gathering and testing ideas about the world.

Francis Bacon (1561–1626)

- Scientists should observe the world and gather data, or information, about it.
- Scientists can conduct experiments to gather data.
- Scientists can develop theories to explain their data and then test them through more experiments.

René Descartes (1596–1650)

- Doubt everything until it can be proven with reason.
- The natural world operates like a machine and follows basic physical laws.
- Individual existence is the one acceptable truth. "I think, therefore I am."

There are six basic steps in the scientific method:

1. Stating the problem. The problem is often a question that begins with *why*. For example, Copernicus's problem today would be stated, "Why do the planets move as they do?"
2. Gathering information. This can involve reading what other scientists have written and making observations.
3. Forming a hypothesis. A **hypothesis** is a solution that the scientist proposes to solve the problem.
4. Testing the hypothesis by performing experiments.
5. Recording and analyzing data gathered from the experiments.
6. Drawing conclusions from the data collected.

After scientists have concluded their experiments, they typically publish their results. This sharing of ideas is very important for two reasons.

First, publishing results lets other scientists try to reproduce the experiments. By reproducing experiments, scientists can determine whether the results are the same. If they are, they can be reasonably sure that the results are accurate. If not, a new hypothesis can be formed and tested.

Second, publishing results spreads scientific knowledge. This opens up the exchange of ideas. Sir Isaac Newton did not just publish his work, but also exchanged many letters with other scientists.

Reading Check
Summarize What are the steps in the scientific method?

Science and Government

Some of the most important effects of the Scientific Revolution had nothing to do with science at all. When philosophers began applying scientific thought to other areas of human life, they came up with some startling new ideas.

The Power of Reason By the end of the Scientific Revolution, one thing had become clear to many European thinkers: human reason, or logical thought, was a powerful tool. After all, scientists using reason had made many discoveries about the universe in a relatively short time.

Since reason proved to be a way to learn some of nature's great secrets, might reason also be used to solve the problems facing people? Philosophers decided to use reason when they considered society's problems like poverty and war, or what type of government is best.

This use of reason to consider the problems of society led philosophers to look at the world in a new way. They thought they could use reason to determine how to improve society.

Democratic Ideas One way in which scientists thought they could improve society was by changing its government. Scientists' use of reason and logic during the Scientific Revolution helped pave the way for the beginnings of democratic thought in Europe.

As scientists like Sir Isaac Newton studied the world, they discovered laws that governed nature. In time, some scientists began to think there must be laws that governed human behavior as well. Once people learned

Quick Facts

Rationalism and Democracy

Scientists believed that the world operated according to a set of natural laws that people could study and understand.

Political thinkers believed that natural laws could also explain the behavior of people. They wanted to use their understanding of human behavior to improve society.

These beliefs led people to call for personal freedom, individual rights, and equality—basic ideas of democracy.

what these laws were, the scientists argued, they could improve their lives and their societies.

But the idea that people's lives were governed by laws had a deeper meaning as well. If all people were governed by the same laws, then it stood to reason that all people must be equal. This idea of the equality of all people was a fundamental step in the development of democratic ideas in Europe.

Advances in Medicine

Before the Scientific Revolution, doctors approached medical treatment very differently from how they do today. Their understanding of the human body was not based on scientific observations. They believed health depended on keeping the body in balance. So, for example, if a patient had a cold, a doctor might place hot cups on the skin to restore the balance.

During the Scientific Revolution, the field of medicine changed thanks to the scientific method. People began to question the accepted wisdom about medicine and the human body. William Harvey was one physician who realized there was much to learn.

Harvey conducted experiments to learn how the human circulatory system worked. He asked many questions and concluded that previous beliefs about the circulatory system were wrong. Because of Harvey's discoveries and others, doctors changed the way they treated patients.

The Scientific Revolution also led to other medical discoveries. Van Leeuwenhoek's innovative use of the microscope allowed scientists to see things inside the human body that had not been visible before. They were also able to use microscopes to analyze cells.

Science and Religion

The Roman Catholic Church was a powerful force in Europe during the time of the Scientific Revolution. The birth and growth of science led to conflicts between scientists and the Church.

Reason for Conflict There were two related parts to the conflict between science and the Church. The first was that the new science was putting forth ideas that contradicted Church teachings. For example, Copernicus's idea that Earth orbited the sun contradicted the Church teaching that Earth was at the center of the universe.

A second part of the conflict was related to the first. When people contradicted the Church's teachings, they weakened the Church. Church officials were afraid that questioning even one Church teaching might lead to more and more questions about the Church. People might even start to doubt key elements of the faith. Church officials feared this would undermine the Church's influence.

The Trial of Galileo The conflict between science and the Church was illustrated by a trial. Galileo published a book that supported the view that the planets orbit the sun. For this, he was put on trial by the

Inquisition, a Church court that investigated people who questioned Church authority.

Catholic officials insisted that Galileo publicly reject his findings and accept Catholic teachings that Earth was the center of the universe and did not move. Under threat of torture, Galileo agreed. Still, legend has it that as Galileo left his trial, he muttered, "And yet it does move."

Although he is remembered for opposing this Church teaching, Galileo was a devout Catholic. He believed that experimentation was a search for an understanding of God's creation.

Knowledge and Belief Many of the scientists you have been reading about held views similar to Galileo's. For the scientists of the Scientific Revolution, science and traditional religious beliefs could exist at the same time.

Nicolaus Copernicus served as a Church official. Sir Isaac Newton saw a close connection between science and religion. For example, Newton believed that all forces in nature were actions directed by God.

Bacon, too, was a religious man. He wrote that knowledge "is a rich storehouse for the glory of the Creator." Unlike Newton, Bacon stressed the separation of reason and faith. He argued that religious leaders shouldn't

Science and Religion

The painting above shows Galileo defending himself before Church officials. Still, Galileo and other scientists were deeply religious, like the Italian monk and mathematician in the painting at right.

try to explain scientific matters. In turn, he said that scientific thinkers shouldn't try to interpret religious matters.

Despite the conflicts, science developed rapidly after the Scientific Revolution. Scientists made—and continue to make—countless discoveries. Scientific knowledge has changed human life dramatically and touches your life every day. Therefore, the Scientific Revolution ranks as one of the most influential events in history.

Summary The scientific method became the standard method for all scientific study. New philosophies based on scientific thinking would later influence government. However, scientific teachings would sometimes conflict with religious teachings.

Lesson 3 Assessment

Reviewing Ideas, Terms, and People

1. a. **Define** What is the scientific method?
   b. **Explain** Why did Francis Bacon want the king to fund scientific research?

2. a. **Identify** What type of government began to develop using ideas from the Scientific Revolution?
   b. **Draw Conclusions** Why did political philosophers begin to make greater use of reason in their work?

3. a. **Explain** How did doctors practice medicine before the Scientific Revolution?
   b. **Draw Conclusions** Why did doctors change the way they practiced medicine?

4. a. **Recall** Why did the Inquisition put Galileo on trial?
   b. **Summarize** What caused conflict between science and the Roman Catholic Church?

Critical Thinking

5. **Understand Cause and Effect** Copy the diagram. Identify effects of the Scientific Revolution. Add as many arrows and circles as you need.

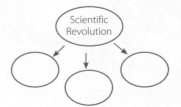

Social Studies Skills

Analyze Tables

Define the Skill

Like graphs, tables present numerical data. The data are usually listed side by side for easy reference and comparison. A table is especially useful for organizing several different categories of data. Since the data in each row or column are related, you can easily compare numbers and see relationships.

Learn the Skill

Follow these guidelines to read and analyze a table.

1. Read the table's title to determine its subject. All the data presented in the table will be related in some way to this subject.

2. Identify the data. Note the headings and labels of the table's columns and rows. This will tell you how the data are organized. A table may also contain notes in parentheses. These explain the units in which the data should be read.

3. Study the information. Note the numbers in each row and column. Read across rows and down columns.

4. Use critical thinking skills to compare and contrast numbers, identify cause-and-effect relationships, and note statistical trends. Form hypotheses and draw conclusions.

Practice the Skill

The table below provides information on planets in the solar system. Interpret the table to answer the following questions.

1. Which planets were unknown to Kepler, Galileo, and other scientists of the 1500s and 1600s?

2. What relationship does the table show between the length of a planet's year and its distance from the sun?

3. Why do you think Neptune remained undiscovered for so long?

Planets of the Solar System					
Planet	When discovered	Diameter (in miles)	Minimum distance from Earth (in millions of miles)	Distance from Sun (in millions of miles)	Length of year (in Earth years)
Mercury	ancient times	3,024	57	36	0.24
Venus	ancient times	7,504	26	67	0.62
Earth	————	7,909	————	93	1.00
Mars	ancient times	4,212	49	141	1.88
Jupiter	ancient times	88,534	390	482	11.86
Saturn	ancient times	74,400	792	885	29.46
Uranus	1781	32,488	1,687	1,780	84.01
Neptune	1846	31,279	2,695	2,788	164.80

Review Vocabulary, Terms, and People

Complete each sentence by filling in the blank with the correct term from the module.

1. In science, a logical explanation for observed facts is called a(n) _____.

2. Greek _____ used logic and reason to explain what they observed in nature.

3. The first scientist to argue that the planets orbited the sun was _____.

4. _____ put forth important theories in his book *Principia Mathematica*.

5. The _____ is a set of steps that scientists follow.

6. One important invention of the Scientific Revolution was the _____, an instrument that measures air pressure.

7. _____ believed that nothing should be accepted as true if it isn't proven to be true.

Comprehension and Critical Thinking

Lesson 1

8.
  a. **Recall** When did the Scientific Revolution occur?

  b. **Analyze** How did Muslim scholars contribute to the Scientific Revolution?

  c. **Evaluate** Do you agree or disagree with the statement that the Scientific Revolution was the single most important event in the intellectual history of humankind? Why?

Lesson 2

9.
  a. **Describe** What was Nicolaus Copernicus's theory about the planets and the sun?

  b. **Compare and Contrast** How were Copernicus's and Kepler's theories about the movement of the planets similar? How were they different?

  c. **Elaborate** Choose one invention from the Scientific Revolution and explain how it affects your life.

Lesson 3

10.
  a. **Describe** How did the Scientific Revolution help inspire democratic ideas?

  b. **Analyze** Why did many scientists believe science and religion could exist at the same time?

  c. **Elaborate** What did Sir Isaac Newton mean when he wrote, "If I have seen further it is by standing on the shoulders of Giants"?

Module 22 Assessment, continued

Review Themes

11. **Science and Technology** How do you know Earth orbits the sun? Did you gain that knowledge using methods similar to those used before or during the Scientific Revolution? Explain your answer.

12. **Society and Culture** How did the birth of science lead to the growth of democratic ideas?

Reading Skills

Recognize Logical Fallacies in Reasoning *Use the Reading Skills taught in the module to answer the questions about the reading selection below.*

> During the Scientific Revolution, scientists invented new and better instruments. In 1593, Galileo invented the thermometer. The telescope was probably invented by a Dutch lens maker in 1608. In 1609, Galileo built a much-improved telescope and made important astronomical discoveries. In 1643, the Italian scientist Evangelista Torricelli invented the barometer, a scientific instrument that measures air pressure.

13. Which of the following is an example of a false conclusion drawn from the selection above?
    a. New inventions helped scientists better observe and understand the natural world.
    b. The most important instruments ever were invented during the Scientific Revolution.
    c. During the sixteenth and seventeenth centuries, scientists invented new instruments.
    d. Though he did not invent the telescope, Galileo greatly improved it.

Social Studies Skills

Analyze Tables *Use the Social Studies Skills taught in this module to answer the questions about the table below. The table shows data collected during Hurricane Frances in 2004. Scientists measure the strength of a hurricane on a scale from 1 to 5, with 5 being the strongest.*

Date and time	Wind speed (mph)	Air pressure (mb)	Strength
9/1 12:00 noon	120	937	4
9/2 12:00 noon	125	939	4
9/3 12:00 noon	110	957	3
9/4 12:00 noon	90	960	2
9/5 11:00 am	80	963	1

14. What happened to the air pressure as the hurricane got weaker?

15. On which days did the air pressure of the hurricane measure 950 mb or greater?

Focus On Speaking

16. **Give a Speech** Prepare a speech to defend Galileo. Begin with an introduction. Then present your main points in support of his discoveries, supporting your points with reasons or evidence. Try to anticipate the other side's points, and address them in your speech. End your speech with a conclusion.

Write sentences describing each of your points. These notes will help you remember what you want to say in your speech. When you give your speech, be sure to make eye contact with your audience, use a pleasant tone of voice, and speak with confidence.

Module 23

The Age of Exploration

🌐

Essential Question

What were the impacts of the Age of Exploration?

About the Photo: This photo shows a replica of one of the ships Christopher Columbus used to sail to the Americas in 1492.

▶ *Explore ONLINE!*

HISTORY

VIDEOS, including...
- Christopher Columbus
- Who Discovered America?
- African Slave Trade

☑ Document-Based Investigations

☑ Graphic Organizers

☑ Interactive Games

☑ Image with Hotspots: The Wreck of the Spanish Armada

☑ Image with Hotspots: New Ideas Come to the Americas

☑ Interactive Map: World Trade Patterns, 1500–1800

In this module you will learn how European explorers first discovered the true size and shape of the world.

What You Will Learn...

Lesson 1: Great Voyages of Discovery 796
The Big Idea European explorers made discoveries that brought knowledge, wealth, and influence to their countries.

Lesson 2: The Columbian Exchange 806
The Big Idea The exchange of plants, animals, ideas, and technology between the Old World and the New World brought many changes all over the world.

Lesson 3: Origins of Capitalism 812
The Big Idea Changes in international trading and marketing patterns influenced the development of a new economic system called capitalism.

Timeline of Events 1400–1650

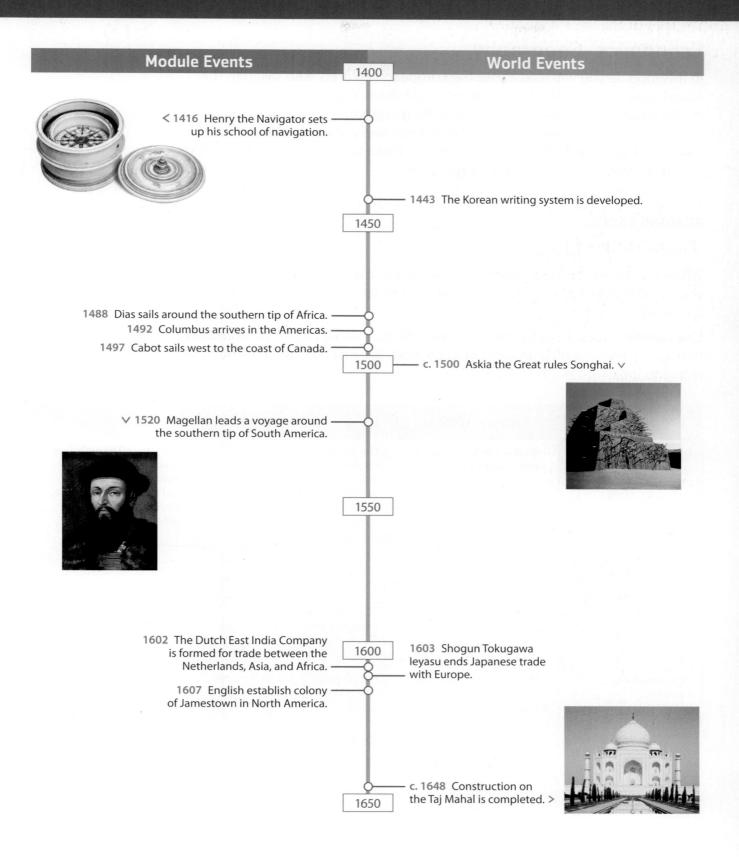

Module Events

World Events

1400

< **1416** Henry the Navigator sets up his school of navigation.

1443 The Korean writing system is developed.

1450

1488 Dias sails around the southern tip of Africa.

1492 Columbus arrives in the Americas.

1497 Cabot sails west to the coast of Canada.

1500

c. **1500** Askia the Great rules Songhai. ∨

∨ **1520** Magellan leads a voyage around the southern tip of South America.

1550

1602 The Dutch East India Company is formed for trade between the Netherlands, Asia, and Africa.

1600

1603 Shogun Tokugawa Ieyasu ends Japanese trade with Europe.

1607 English establish colony of Jamestown in North America.

c. **1648** Construction on the Taj Mahal is completed. >

1650

Reading Social Studies

Economics, Geography

In this module you will read about the European explorers who sailed to the Americas and the routes they followed to get there. You will learn how their explorations helped people understand the geography of the world. You will also learn how their explorations led to the discovery of new products and the creation of worldwide trade patterns. In time these patterns laid the foundation for a new economic system called capitalism.

READING FOCUS:

Vocabulary Clues

When you are reading your history textbook, you may often come across a word you do not know. If that word isn't listed as a key term, how do you find out what it means?

Use Context Clues *Context* means "surroundings." Authors often include clues to the meaning of a difficult word in its context. You just have to know how and where to look.

Clue	How It Works	Example	Explanation
Direct Definition	Includes a definition in the same or nearby sentence	One major trading pattern involved *the exchange of raw materials, manufactured products, and slaves among Europe, Africa, and the Americas.* This particular trade network became known as the triangular trade.	The phrase "the exchange of raw materials, manufactured products, and slaves among Europe, Africa, and the Americas" defines triangular trade.
Restatement	Uses different words to say the same thing	These innovations encouraged, or *pushed*, sailors to explore new places.	The word *pushed* is another way to say encouraged.
Comparisons or Contrasts	Compares or contrasts the unfamiliar word with a familiar word or phrase	*Harsh treatment*, like forced work and disease, killed many American Indians.	The word *like* indicates that "harsh treatment" is similar to bad treatment.

You Try It!

The following sentences are from this module. Each uses a definition or restatement clue to explain unfamiliar words. See if you can use the context to figure out the meanings of the words in italics.

---

1. People needed *depositories*, or places to securely deposit their money.
2. A new social group, the *middle class*, began to grow. Those in the middle class had less money than rulers in the upper class but more money than workers in the lower class.
3. By replacing oars on the ship's sides with a *rudder* at the back of the ship, the Portuguese also improved the steering of ships.

Answer the questions about the sentences you read.

1. In example 1, what does the word *depositories* mean? What context clues did you use to figure that out?

2. In example 2, where did you find the meaning of *middle class*? What does this phrase mean?

3. In example 3, what does the word *rudder* mean? What context clues did you use to figure that out?

As you read this module, look for context clues that can help you figure out the meanings of unfamiliar words or terms.

Key Terms and People

Lesson 1
Henry the Navigator
Vasco da Gama
Christopher Columbus
Ferdinand Magellan
circumnavigate
Francis Drake
Spanish Armada

Lesson 2
Columbian Exchange
plantations
Bartolomé de Las Casas
racism

Lesson 3
mercantilism
balance of trade
cottage industry
atlas
capitalism
market economy

Great Voyages of Discovery

The Big Idea

European explorers made discoveries that brought knowledge, wealth, and influence to their countries.

Main Ideas

- Europeans had the desire and opportunity to explore.
- Portuguese and Spanish explorations led to discoveries of new trade routes, lands, and people.
- English and French explorers found land in North America.
- A new European worldview developed because of the discoveries.

Key Terms and People

Henry the Navigator
Vasco da Gama
Christopher Columbus
Ferdinand Magellan
circumnavigate
Francis Drake
Spanish Armada

If YOU were there . . .

Your uncle is a Portuguese ship captain who has just come back from a long sea voyage. He shows you a map of the new lands he has seen. He tells wonderful stories about strange plants and animals. You are studying to become a carpenter, but you wonder if you might like to be an explorer like your uncle instead.

How would you decide which career to choose?

Desire and Opportunity to Explore

An interest in discovery and exploration grew in Europe in the 1400s. Improvements in navigational tools, cartography, and shipbuilding allowed European sailors to go farther than they ever had before. These innovations encouraged, or pushed, sailors to explore new places. We can think of these innovations as push factors, because they provided the opportunity to explore the oceans.

Some Europeans also had a desire to explore the oceans and other new places. We can think of these reasons to explore as pull factors, because they drew explorers toward new land and experiences.

Reasons to Explore Why did people set off to explore the world in the fifteenth century? First, they wanted resources, such as Asian spices. Italy and Egypt controlled the trade routes to Asia, charging very high prices for spices. In fact, pepper cost more than gold. Many countries wanted to find a route to Asia so they could get spices without having to buy from Italian or Egyptian traders.

Religion was another pull factor that gave explorers reason to set sail. European Christians wanted to convert more people to their religion to counteract the spread of Islam in Europe, Africa, and Asia.

Simple curiosity was also an important pull factor, or motivation for exploration. Many people read stories of Marco Polo's travels and other explorers' adventures. They learned about new lands and creatures, and they became curious about the world.

Advances in Technology Whatever their reasons for exploring, Europeans wouldn't have gotten very far without advances in technology. One obstacle to exploration was the vast distances across the Atlantic Ocean. Sailors started using the astrolabe and the compass to find routes they could follow to reach faraway places and return safely home. Another tool, called a sextant, helped sailors locate their position at sea. A type of clock called an hourglass showed how fast a ship sailed. More accurate maps allowed sailors to sail from one port to another without having to stay right along the coast. Before these advances, most sailors avoided the open sea out of fear they might not find their way back to land. These innovations were push factors that encouraged sailors to go farther than they ever had before.

Other advances, mainly by the Portuguese, came in shipbuilding. They began building ships called caravels (KER-uh-velz). Caravels used

The Caravel

A special type of ship called the caravel became the workhorse of many European explorers. Though small, caravels were sturdy. They could sail across huge oceans and up small rivers. Caravels featured important advances in sailing technology.

Triangular sails enabled the caravel to sail into the wind.

The smooth, rounded hull handled high seas well.

The large center rudder made quick turns possible.

Analyze Visuals
What features made the caravel an excellent sailing ship?

triangular sails that, unlike traditional square sails, allowed ships to sail against the wind. By replacing oars on the ship's sides with a rudder at the back of the ship, the Portuguese also improved the steering of ships. The new ships helped Portuguese sailors take the lead in exploring.

Portuguese and Spanish Explorations

A man who never went on any sea voyages was responsible for much of Portugal's success on the seas. Known as Prince **Henry the Navigator**, he built an observatory and a navigation school to teach sailors how to find their way. He also paid people to sail on voyages of exploration. Spanish sailors later followed the Portuguese example of exploration around the world.

Africa Even with new technology, travel on the open sea remained dangerous and scary. One person described what happened to sailors on a voyage south.

> "Those which survived could hardly be recognized as human. They had lost flesh and hair, the nails had gone from hands and feet. . . . They spoke of heat so incredible that it was a marvel that ships and crews were not burnt."
>
> –Anonymous sailor, quoted in Edward McNall Burns et al., *World Civilizations*

In spite of the dangers, Portuguese explorers sailed south on their new ships. They set up successful trading posts along the way in various places. These include the present-day African nations of Sierra Leone and Ghana.

In 1488, a ship led by Bartolomeu Dias succeeded in sailing around the southern tip of Africa. The crew, tired and afraid of the raging seas, forced Dias to turn back. However, they had found a way around Africa. **Vasco da Gama** sailed around Africa and landed on the west coast of India in 1498. A sea route to Asia had been found.

A "New World" Imagination, daring, and a few mistakes enabled Portuguese and Spanish sailors to discover the Americas. They thought these lands were a "new world."

An Italian sailor thought he could reach Asia by sailing west across the Atlantic. That sailor, **Christopher Columbus**, told his idea to the Spanish monarchs, Ferdinand and Isabella. He promised them great riches, new territory, and Catholic converts. It took Columbus several years to convince the king and queen, but Isabella eventually agreed to pay for his journey.

In August, 1492, Columbus set sail with 88 men and three small ships, the *Niña*, the *Pinta*, and the *Santa María*. On October 12, 1492, he and his tired crew landed on a small island in the Bahamas. What was Columbus's mistake? He didn't realize another continent lay in front of him, and he believed he had reached Asia. At that time Europeans called Asia the Indies, so Columbus called the people who lived on the island Indians.

Columbus's crew of 88 men varied greatly in age and skills. Some of them were as young as 12 including Diego Bermúdez who sailed on the *Santa María*.

Columbus Describes America

After his first trip to the New World, Columbus wrote a letter to the king and queen of Spain describing what he found. In his letter, he tried to convince the monarchs that it was worth making other voyages to the New World.

Columbus used very positive language to describe the New World.

Spanish explorers had hoped to find gold, as well as spices, on their voyages.

"Española is a wonder. Its mountains and plains, and meadows, and fields, are so beautiful and rich for planting and sowing, and rearing cattle of all kinds, and for building towns and villages. The harbors on the coast, and the number and size and wholesomeness of the rivers, most of them bearing gold, surpass anything that would be believed by one who had not seen them."

—Christopher Columbus, from *Selected Letters of Christopher Columbus*, translated by R. H. Major

Analyze Historical Sources
Why do you think Columbus was so impressed with the features of the New World?

Columbus made three more journeys to America during his lifetime. He also established the first Spanish settler colony in the Americas and encouraged others to come in his letters to Spain. This first settler colony, called La Isabela, was located in the present-day Dominican Republic. Spanish colonists forced American Indians to work for them. The Spanish also took gold and other resources from the region.

Columbus never realized that he had found a land unknown to Europeans. He died still believing that he had reached Asia.

Another mistake enabled Portuguese explorer Pedro Cabral to discover South America. He tried to sail around Africa, but he sailed too far west, landing on the coast of what is now Brazil. In 1520, **Ferdinand Magellan** (muh-JEHL-uhn) led a voyage around the southern tip of South America. A Portuguese navigator sailing for Spain, Magellan daringly continued sailing into the Pacific even though his ships were dangerously low on food and fresh water. Although Magellan was killed before he made it back to Spain, the voyage he directed became the first to **circumnavigate**, or go all the way around, the globe.

Conquest of America When Spanish explorers arrived in America in the early 1500s, the Aztec Empire in Mexico and the Inca Empire in Peru were at the height of their power. Their buildings and the riches of their cities impressed the conquistadors. The Spanish saw these empires as good sources of gold and silver. Spanish missionaries also saw a purpose in conquering the region. They wanted to convert the native peoples to Christianity.

Spanish explorers led by Cortés and Pizarro soon conquered the Aztecs and Incas. The Spanish had better weapons that used gunpowder. These guns helped the Spanish to quickly defeat native peoples and establish colonies. The Spanish also brought new diseases such as smallpox. Diseases killed possibly more than three-quarters of the native peoples, who had no immunity to the diseases.

▶ *Explore ONLINE!*

European Exploration, 1487–1580

PORTUGAL
➡ Dias 1487-1488
➡ Da Gama 1497-1498
➡ Cabral 1500-1501

SPAIN
➡ Columbus 1492-1493
➡ Magellan 1519-1522

FRANCE
➡ Cartier 1534-1535

ENGLAND
➡ Drake 1577-1580
➡ Cabot 1497-1498

0   1,000   2,000 Miles
0   1,000   2,000 Kilometers

Interpret Maps

1. **Location** What continent did all of these explorers come from?

2. **Movement** Which explorers' expeditions went all the way around the world?

Reading Check
Find Main Ideas
Why did Europeans
call the Americas a
"new world"?

Another explorer, Vasco Núñez de Balboa, founded a Spanish settler colony in present-day Colombia. Balboa later crossed the Isthmus of Panama, searching for gold. As a result, he became the first European to see the eastern Pacific Ocean. The Spanish soon ruled large parts of North and South America.

Europeans in America

Like Spain and Portugal, the countries of England, France, and the Netherlands wanted to find a route to Asia to get spices. After Spain and Portugal explored and gained control of the southern routes, these three nations looked for a waterway through North America.

Exploring New Lands In 1497, John Cabot, an Italian sailing for England, sailed west to the coast of Canada. Like Columbus, Cabot mistakenly thought he had reached Asia. In 1535, French explorer Jacques Cartier (zhahk kahr-TYAY) sailed up the Saint Lawrence River into Canada. Years later, English sailor **Francis Drake** sailed along North America's western coast. Drake searched for the Northwest Passage. This is an Arctic sea route connecting the Atlantic to the Pacific. Another English sailor, Henry Hudson, searched for the Northwest Passage. Hudson sailed on behalf of England and the Netherlands. These explorers failed to find a route to Asia. However, they did claim land in North America for England, France, and the Netherlands.

During the early 1600s, the French established settler colonies in present-day Canada. One of these was Port-Royal, founded in 1605. Unlike Spanish settlers, the French at Port-Royal did not enslave American Indians. In fact, the French became their allies. Port-Royal and other colonies grew as settlers sold animal furs to Europeans.

In 1607, England established Jamestown, a settler colony in present-day Virginia. Like the French, the English at Jamestown did not enslave American Indians. Instead, they traded with them. Sometimes, though, war broke out between the two groups. Eventually, Jamestown's economy became based on exporting tobacco to the Old World.

In 1613, Dutch sailor Adriaen Block explored parts of North America's eastern coast. This voyage led to the establishment of the Dutch settler colony of New Netherland. Its capital, New Amsterdam, was located near the Hudson River and the Atlantic Ocean. The city soon became a center for trade. New Amsterdam was later conquered by the English and renamed New York.

Competing for Land and Wealth Besides looking for a route to Asia, England hoped to find riches and resources in the New World. But Spain controlled the gold and silver of the former Aztec and Inca empires. The English queen, Elizabeth I, sent Francis Drake to the Americas. His mission was to steal gold and silver from Spanish ships called galleons. Drake became a rich and famous pirate. He and other English pirates became known as "sea dogs."

Defeat of the Spanish Armada The Spanish were furious with the English for these raids. In 1588, Spain sent 130 ships to attack England. This fleet, called the **Spanish Armada**, was part of Spain's large, experienced navy. But the English, with their faster ships and better guns, defeated the Armada. Returning from battle, more Spanish ships were lost in storms at sea. Fewer than half the Spanish ships ever returned to Spain.

The defeat of the Spanish Armada saved England from invasion. It also meant Spain no longer ruled the seas, and it allowed England to emerge as a world power in the following years. This era is known as the Elizabethan Age, named after the English queen.

Reading Check
Form Generalizations
Why did France and England send explorers to North America?

The Wreck of the Spanish Armada

A series of battles in the English Channel had weakened the Armada. Then, when the English launched fireships at the enemy, some of the Spanish sailors cut their anchor lines so they could escape. It was a fateful decision, because some Spanish ships were wrecked by storms in the North Atlantic.

Rebels closed the Dutch harbor where Spanish ships were waiting to launch a second force against England.

The Spanish sailors were already suffering from overcrowding, hunger, and disease by the time they encountered the English.

The English set fire to ships rigged so that their cannons would fire automatically.

Analyze Visuals
What tactics did the English use against the Armada?

A New European Worldview

The voyages of discovery changed the way Europeans thought of the world and their place in it. The explorations brought new knowledge about geography and proved some old beliefs wrong. For example, Europeans learned that ships didn't burn up crossing the equator and that the Americas were a separate landmass from Asia. Geographers made more accurate maps that reflected this new knowledge.

Improved mapmaking also helped shape a new European worldview. For the first time Europeans could see maps of the whole world. They saw new lands and possible trade routes. By controlling the trade routes and the resources in the new lands, they might gain great wealth. Voyages of discovery brought the beginning of a new period in which Europeans would spread their influence around the world.

Summary and Preview European explorers sailed on voyages of discovery in the 1400s and 1500s. They found wealth, converts for Christianity, and new continents. In the next lesson, you will read about the effects these discoveries had on Europe, Africa, the Americas, and Asia.

Reading Check
Find Main Ideas
How did cartography influence the development of a new European worldview?

Lesson 1 Assessment

Review Ideas, Terms, and People

1. **a. Summarize** What were two improvements in shipbuilding that allowed the Portuguese to establish trading posts in Africa?

   b. Analyze Why were spices so expensive in Europe?

2. **a. Summarize** Who directed the first voyage to circumnavigate the globe?

   b. Form Opinions What might have happened if Christopher Columbus had decided to look to the east to find a route to Asia?

3. **a. Contrast** How were early French settler colonies different from early Spanish settler colonies?

   b. Analyze Why were the settlements of Port-Royal, Jamestown, and New Amsterdam successful?

   c. Draw Conclusions How did the defeat of the Spanish Armada shift power in Europe?

4. **Summarize** In what ways did the European worldview change in the 1400s and 1500s?

Critical Thinking

5. **Organize Information** Draw a chart like the one here. Use it to tell what each explorer discovered. Add rows as necessary.

Explorer	Discovery

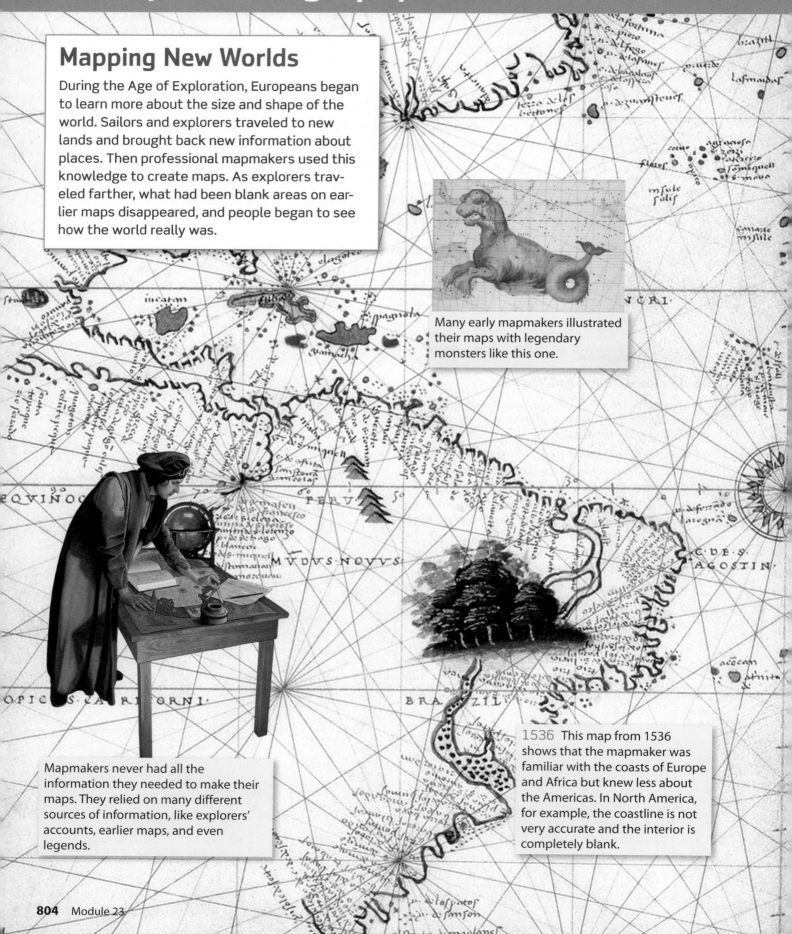

Mapping New Worlds

During the Age of Exploration, Europeans began to learn more about the size and shape of the world. Sailors and explorers traveled to new lands and brought back new information about places. Then professional mapmakers used this knowledge to create maps. As explorers traveled farther, what had been blank areas on earlier maps disappeared, and people began to see how the world really was.

Many early mapmakers illustrated their maps with legendary monsters like this one.

Mapmakers never had all the information they needed to make their maps. They relied on many different sources of information, like explorers' accounts, earlier maps, and even legends.

1536 This map from 1536 shows that the mapmaker was familiar with the coasts of Europe and Africa but knew less about the Americas. In North America, for example, the coastline is not very accurate and the interior is completely blank.

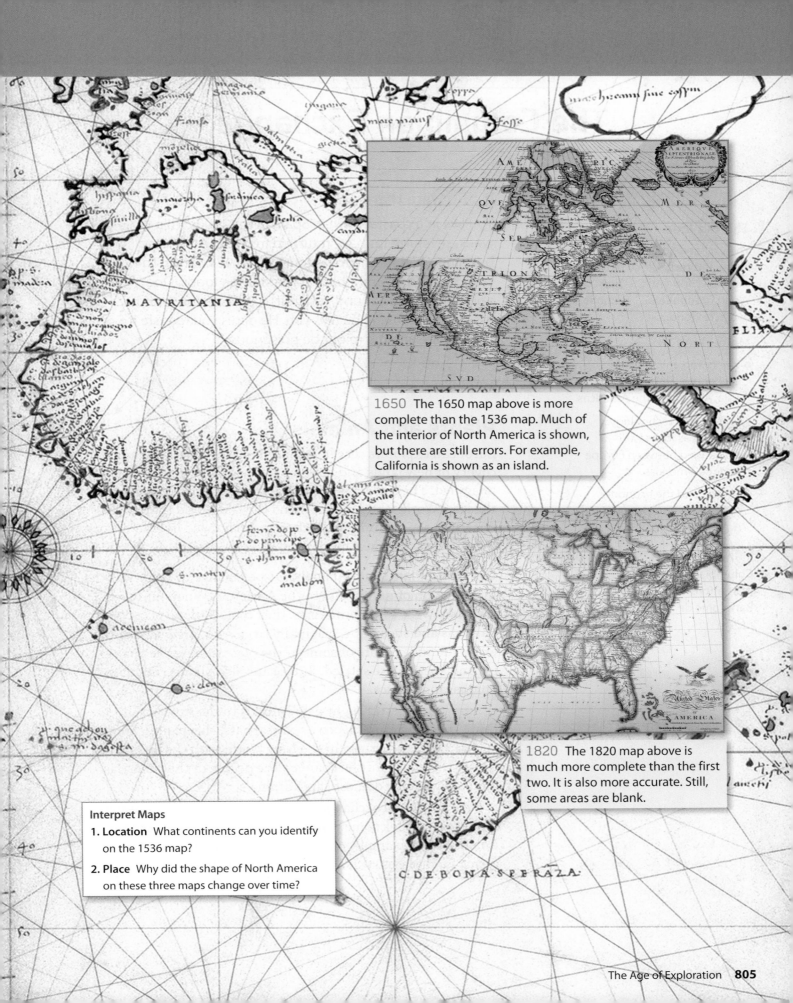

1650 The 1650 map above is more complete than the 1536 map. Much of the interior of North America is shown, but there are still errors. For example, California is shown as an island.

1820 The 1820 map above is much more complete than the first two. It is also more accurate. Still, some areas are blank.

Interpret Maps

1. **Location** What continents can you identify on the 1536 map?

2. **Place** Why did the shape of North America on these three maps change over time?

The Columbian Exchange

The Big Idea

The exchange of plants, animals, ideas, and technology between the Old World and the New World brought many changes all over the world.

Main Ideas

- Plants and animals were exchanged among Europe, Asia, Africa, and the Americas.

- Culture and technology changed as ideas were exchanged between Europe and the Americas.

- Society and the economy changed in Europe and the Americas.

Key Terms and People

Columbian Exchange
plantations
Bartolomé de las Casas
racism

If YOU were there . . .

You live in a coastal town in Spain in the 1500s. This week, several ships have returned from the Americas, bringing silver for the royal court. But that's not all. The crew has also brought back some strange foods. One sailor offers you a round, red fruit. Natives in the Americas call it a "tomatl," he tells you. He dares you to taste it, but you are afraid it might be poisonous.

**Will you taste the tomato?
Why or why not?**

Plants and Animals

European explorers set out to find routes to Asia, but their discovery of new lands and new peoples had an effect they never imagined. The exchange of plants, animals, and ideas between the New World (the Americas) and the Old World (Europe) is known as the **Columbian Exchange**. It changed lives in Europe, Asia, Africa, and the Americas.

Old World Plants and Animals One exchange to occur was the introduction of new plants to the Americas. When European explorers went to the Americas, they took seeds to plant crops. Bananas and sugarcane, originally from Asia, grew well in the warm, humid climate of some of the places where the Spanish and Portuguese settled. Europeans also planted oranges, onions, and lettuce.

Europeans also brought new animals to the Americas. Domesticated animals such as cows, goats, sheep, pigs, horses, and chickens all arrived in the New World with the Spanish. Before the arrival of the Spanish, the people of the Americas didn't have many domesticated animals.

Even accidental exchanges occurred sometimes. Europeans unknowingly took some plants, animals, and diseases to the Americas. For example, rats hid on ships, and explorers carried germs for diseases such as measles and smallpox.

The Columbian Exchange

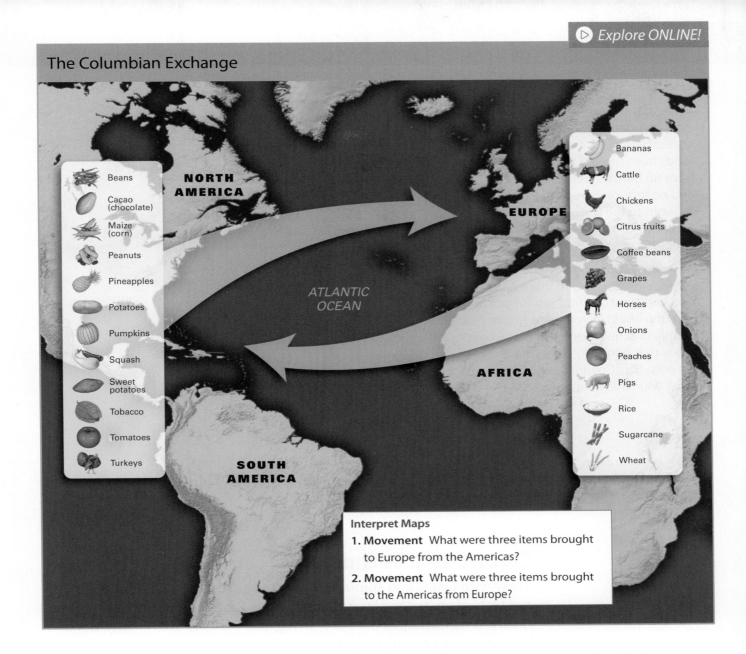

▶ Explore ONLINE!

NORTH AMERICA

Beans
Cacao (chocolate)
Maize (corn)
Peanuts
Pineapples
Potatoes
Pumpkins
Squash
Sweet potatoes
Tobacco
Tomatoes
Turkeys

EUROPE

Bananas
Cattle
Chickens
Citrus fruits
Coffee beans
Grapes
Horses
Onions
Peaches
Pigs
Rice
Sugarcane
Wheat

ATLANTIC OCEAN

AFRICA

SOUTH AMERICA

Interpret Maps

1. **Movement** What were three items brought to Europe from the Americas?

2. **Movement** What were three items brought to the Americas from Europe?

New World Plants and Animals While Europeans introduced plants and animals to the New World, they also found plants and animals there they had never seen before. They took samples back to Europe as well as to Africa and Asia. This exchange of plants changed the eating habits of people around the world. For example, Europeans hadn't tried tomatoes until explorers brought them from the Americas. Now they are a **primary** ingredient in Italian food. Europeans also took back potatoes, beans, squash, avocados, pineapples, tobacco, and chili peppers. Even chocolate came from the Americas.

Europeans also carried New World products to other parts of the world. In this way, the Columbian Exchange affected Africa and Asia. Many plants from the Americas also grew well in West Africa and Asia. Sweet potatoes, peanuts, and tomatoes became staples in African cooking. American fruits such as pineapple became popular in India. In China, peanuts and maize became major crops.

Academic Vocabulary
primary main, most important

Reading Check
Analyze Causes
What caused the Columbian Exchange?

Effects of the Columbian Exchange

Many of the foods you eat today didn't exist in America before 1492. Think of a cheeseburger, for example. Without foods from the Old World, you would have no bun, no patty, no cheese, and no lettuce. European explorers brought to the New World wheat for bread, cattle for beef and cheese, and lettuce.

They also brought many other vegetables, grains, and fruits. Now, of course, you can find foods from all over the world in your local grocery store. People in other countries also can get foods that originally were found only in America. The Columbian Exchange affects what you have for dinner nearly every day.

Old World
- Bread
- Beef
- Cheese
- Lettuce

New World
- Corn
- Potato
- Tomato

Analyze Information
How does the Columbian Exchange affect one of your favorite dinners?

Culture and Technology

Along with plants and animals, Europeans introduced their ideas, culture, and technology to the places they explored. People in Asia, Africa, and the Americas all learned new ways of living and working. This change would have enormous social and economic effects.

Religion and Language Some of the biggest cultural changes Europeans brought to places they conquered were in religion and language. Christians set out to convert people to their religion. Missionaries went to Asia and Africa, and they also worked to convert American Indians to Christianity. In some places, their religion blended with native traditions to create new kinds of religious practices.

In addition to spreading Christianity, missionaries ran schools. They taught their European languages such as Spanish, Portuguese, and Dutch, the language of the Netherlands.

Technology Changes Europe and the Americas Besides religion and language, Europeans introduced new technologies. They took guns and steel to parts of Africa. In the Americas, they introduced guns and steel, as well as ways to use the wheel.

Europeans brought new ideas and technologies when they settled new lands. This illustration shows a scene in what is now New Mexico.

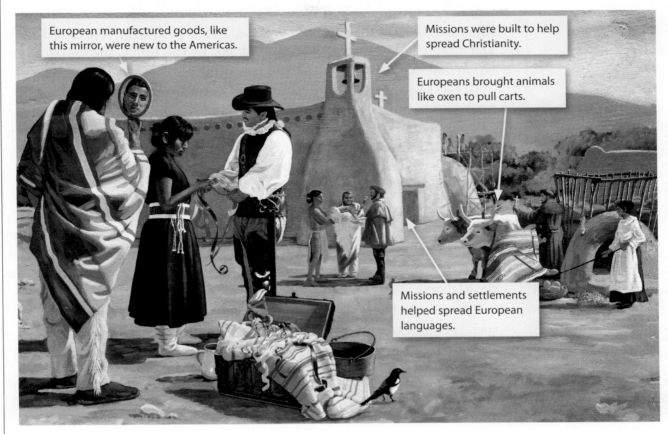

European manufactured goods, like this mirror, were new to the Americas.

Missions were built to help spread Christianity.

Europeans brought animals like oxen to pull carts.

Missions and settlements helped spread European languages.

Analyze Visuals
What evidence of technology do you see?

Europeans also introduced the idea of using animals as technology. They brought horses, which were good for transportation and for carrying heavy loads. Oxen could be used to plow fields. People also learned to make candles from cow fat.

European ideas also changed industries in the Americas. For example, animals were used to carry silver from mines. The introduction of sheep and sugarcane also created new industries. People began to make new kinds of textiles and to grow sugarcane on **plantations**, or large farms. Meanwhile, rubber trees from the Americas were introduced to Africa and Asia. People began growing these trees on plantations. This led to the development of the rubber industry in Africa and Asia.

Reading Check
Summarize How did European culture change life in the Americas?

Society and the Economy

As industries changed in some places, Europeans increased trade with Asia and the Americas. This change had huge social and economic effects, especially in Africa and the Americas.

Treatment of American Indians Plantations and mines made money for Portugal and Spain. They also made some colonists in the Americas rich. But plantation agriculture and mining brought poor treatment of American Indians.

It took a lot of workers to run a plantation, so Spanish colonists forced American Indians to work on their land. Harsh treatment, like forced work and disease, killed many American Indians. By the 1600s, the Indian population had shrunk by more than 80 percent in some areas.

Some clergy in the Americas protested the terrible treatment of American Indians. A priest named **Bartolomé de las Casas** said that the Spanish should try to convert American Indians to Christianity by showing them love, gentleness, and kindness. The Spanish monarchs agreed, creating laws about the proper treatment of American Indians. However, the colonists did not always follow the laws.

Slavery and Society Since forced labor and disease killed so many American Indians, Las Casas and others suggested using enslaved Africans as workers. Africans had already developed immunities to European diseases. Soon, thousands of Africans were being shipped to the Americas as slave labor.

The mix of Africans, Europeans, and American Indians shaped the social order of the Americas. Europeans held the highest position in society. American Indians, Africans, and those of mixed background held the lowest positions. This social order was based on conquest and racism.

Quick Facts

Effects of Exploration

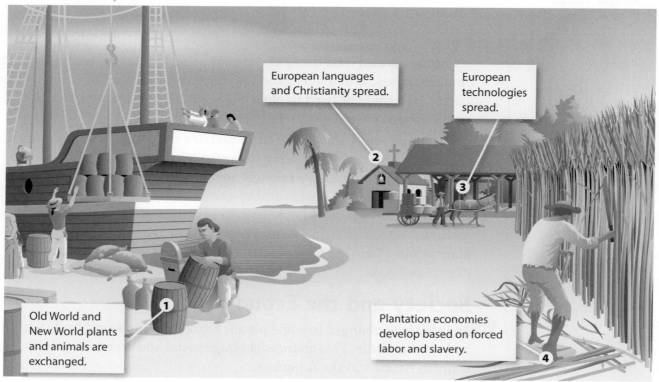

European languages and Christianity spread.

European technologies spread.

Old World and New World plants and animals are exchanged.

Plantation economies develop based on forced labor and slavery.

Racism is the belief that some people are better than others because of racial traits, such as skin color. Both Africans and Indians had darker skin than Europeans did.

Plantation agriculture and the use of slave labor continued in the Americas until the late 1800s. It continued to play a major role in the economies and societies of many countries of the Americas, Africa, and Europe for many years.

Reading Check
Analyze Effects
How did the slave trade affect life in the Americas?

Summary and Preview The voyages of discovery led to the Columbian Exchange. The Columbian Exchange brought new plants and animals, as well as social and economic changes, to Europe, Africa, Asia, and the Americas. In the next lesson, you will read about more economic changes that developed in Europe.

Lesson 2 Assessment

Review Ideas, Terms, and People

1. a. **Identify** Where did peanuts and maize become important crops?

   b. **Make Inferences** Why was the exchange of plants and animals between the Old World and the New World called the Columbian Exchange?

2. a. **Summarize** What were two technologies that Europeans introduced to the Americas?

   b. **Form Generalizations** How did contact with Europeans change life in the New World?

3. a. **Define** What is racism?

   b. **Synthesize** How was plantation agriculture related to racism in the Americas?

   c. **Draw Conclusions** Judge whether the ideas of Bartolomé de las Casas brought positive or negative changes to life in the Americas.

Critical Thinking

4. **Summarize** Draw a diagram like the one here. Use it to show at least one each of the plants, animals, cultural traits, and technologies that were exchanged between the Old World and the New World. You may draw more arrows if you need more.

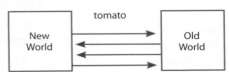

Origins of Capitalism

The Big Idea

Changes in international trading and marketing patterns influenced the development of a new economic system called capitalism.

Main Ideas

- A new economic system called mercantilism emerged.
- New trading patterns developed in the 1600s and 1700s.
- Power in Europe shifted as a result of new trade routes, banking, and increased manufacturing.
- Market economies changed business in Europe.

Key Terms and People

mercantilism
balance of trade
cottage industry
atlas
capitalism
market economy

Academic Vocabulary
acquire to get

If YOU were there . . .

You are a merchant in Holland in the early 1700s. Your friends tell you about an exciting new business plan. Each of you will spend money on a ship that is sailing to the Indies to trade for spices. If the voyage is successful, you will all share in the money that it makes. But of course, there is always the danger that the ship will sink or be lost. Then you would lose everything.

Will you take a chance on this trading business?

A New Economy

The exchange of products between European countries and their colonies changed economic relations around the world. European countries saw their colonies as a way to get rich.

This new view of the colonies was part of an economic system called **mercantilism**—a system in which a government controls all economic activity in a country and its colonies to make the government stronger and richer. In the 1500s, a country's strength was measured by how much gold and silver it had. Under mercantilism, then, governments did everything they could to get more of these precious metals. Mercantilism was the main economic policy in Europe between 1500 and 1800.

To stay rich, European countries tried to export more goods than they imported. The relationship of goods imported to goods exported is known as a country's **balance of trade**. The colonies played a key role in this balance of trade. Believing that colonies existed to help the ruling country, Europeans didn't let colonies trade with other countries. They didn't want their colonies' money going to other nations.

European countries used their colonies to **acquire** raw materials such as wood, furs, cotton, and dyes. This way they didn't have to buy raw materials from competing countries. In addition, they didn't allow their colonies to manufacture goods. That way they could take raw materials from their colonies and sell manufactured goods back to them. Manufactured goods were more valuable than raw materials were, so the colonies were good for the European countries' balance of trade.

Trade also created markets for manufactured goods. As a result, manufacturing in Europe—especially cottage industries— increased. **Cottage industry** was a system in which family members worked in their homes to make part of a product. A businessperson gave each family the materials it needed. The businessperson made money by selling the final product.

Reading Check
Analyze Issues Was mercantilism a good or bad policy for Europe? Why?

New Trading Patterns

Mercantilism created new trading patterns around the world. In the 1600s and 1700s, trade routes connected Europe, Africa, Asia, and the Americas. Many of these routes, which were established by explorers, linked European countries with their colonies. One major trading pattern

▷ *Explore ONLINE!*

World Trade Patterns, 1500–1800

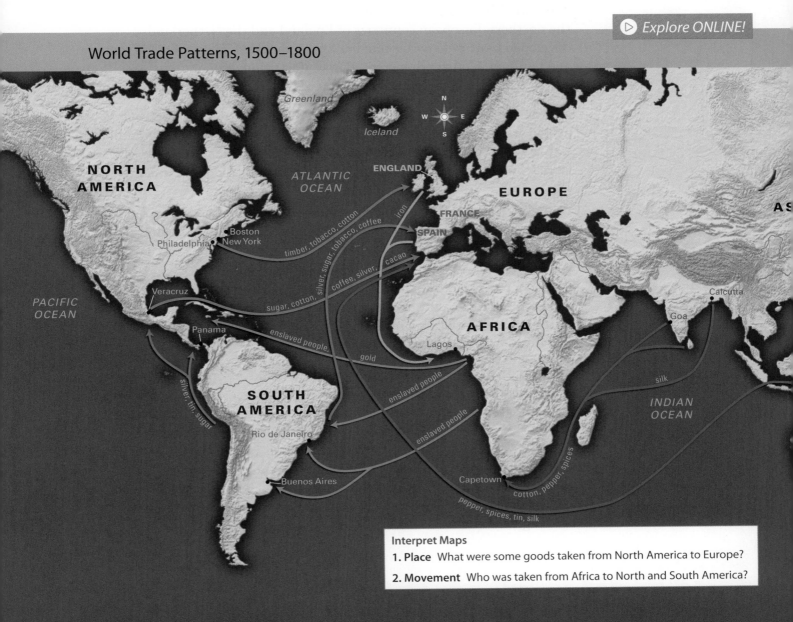

Interpret Maps

1. Place What were some goods taken from North America to Europe?

2. Movement Who was taken from Africa to North and South America?

involved the exchange of raw materials, manufactured products, and enslaved Africans among Europe, Africa, and the Americas. This particular trade network became known as the triangular trade.

The Atlantic slave trade was a major part of this trade network. The Portuguese, Dutch, and English all were active in the slave trade.

Slavery had been practiced in many places, including Africa, long before Europeans came. But the Atlantic slave trade was different in its size and its process. European traders crammed enslaved Africans on ships for the long voyage to the Americas. They chained people together, often without enough food or water. People got sick, and many died.

Between the late 1500s and early 1800s, Europeans shipped millions of enslaved Africans to colonies in the New World. Most of these people were sent to South America and the Caribbean.

Reading Check
Make Inferences
Why do you think trade among Europe, Africa, and the Americas was called the triangular trade?

Power Shifts in Europe

Mercantilism was successful in Spain and Portugal, both of which had many wealthy colonies. But while they relied on their colonies for wealth, the northern European countries of England and the Netherlands developed new trade routes and banking industries. The new trade routes and banking, along with increased manufacturing, brought more wealth to England and the Netherlands and shifted the economic power in Europe.

Northern European Trade Routes A book published in the late 1500s helped traders to find new wealth around the world. That important book was the first **atlas**, or collection of maps. Improved maps, made possible largely by the discoveries of explorers, encouraged traders to find new sources of wealth around the world.

England benefited from increased trade. New trading posts in India and China, along with trade in North American colonies, gave England access to huge markets and many resources.

The Netherlands also became a great trading power. Dutch merchants formed a company to trade directly with Asia. This company was the only one with the right to trade between the Netherlands, Asia, and Africa. The Dutch soon controlled many islands in East Asia, along with trading posts in India, Japan, and southern Africa.

Banking Increased trade created a need for banks. People needed depositories, or places to securely deposit their money. They also needed places where they could receive loans. Realizing this, the Dutch set up a bank. Jews were partly responsible for the growth of banking in the Netherlands. They migrated to the Netherlands in the late 1500s to escape religious persecution in other European countries. Because the Dutch government limited the work Jews could do, and because the Christian Church didn't allow Christians to lend money, many Jews entered the banking business.

Reading Check
Analyze Effects Why did power shift from Spain and Portugal to England and the Netherlands in the 1600s?

The Jews were so successful that English rulers invited them to England to help improve business there as well.

Banking improved business by making it easier for merchants to know they were receiving money of the proper value. This proper value is called just price. Banks also loaned money to people who wanted to start new businesses. In doing so, banks contributed to economic growth.

Market Economies

Trade routes led to increased exchange between Europe and Africa, Asia, and the Americas. The resulting economic growth and new wealth changed business in Europe. It also changed European society. A new social group, the middle class, began to grow. Those in the middle class had less money than rulers in the upper class but more money than workers in the lower class. Many in the middle class were businesspeople. Because more people had wealth, they started buying more manufactured goods. The demand for goods increased.

There were several reasons for the increased demand for manufactured goods. First, Europe's population was growing— especially in the cities. More people meant a need for more goods. Second, farmers were growing food at lower costs. With lower expenses, people had more money to spend on manufactured goods. A third reason for increased demand was the addition of colonies, which had to get their manufactured goods from Europe.

As the demand for goods rose, businesspeople realized they could make money by developing new businesses and better ways to make manufactured goods. This is called entrepreneurship. Entrepreneurs wanted to

---

Quick Facts

Supply and Demand

Market economies are based on the idea of supply and demand. This idea holds that people will produce goods that other people want. In Europe, market economies developed as populations grew and the world economy developed.

Population grew in Europe. With more people, there was a greater demand for goods.

Since people wanted more goods, companies worked to make, or supply, more goods.

Finally, the supply of goods met people's demand for goods.

create new businesses to increase the supply, or amount of goods offered, to meet the demand. This new way of doing business can be considered the beginning of a new economic system called capitalism. **Capitalism** is an economic system in which individuals and private businesses run most industries. Competition among these businesses affects how much goods cost.

The population growth of empires and cities naturally increased the size of markets as well. Markets are places where goods and services are sold and purchased. Competition among different businesses is most successful in a market economy. In a **market economy**, individuals decide what goods and services they will buy. As a result, businesses help meet the needs of individuals by supplying goods and services. The government does not decide what people can buy or sell. A market economy works on a balance between supply and demand. If there is a great demand for a product, a seller will increase the supply in order to make more money.

The ability of individuals to control how they make and spend money is a benefit of a market economy and capitalism. In the 1800s, capitalism would become the basis for most economic systems in the Western world.

Summary Discoveries and exchanges of goods and ideas around the world brought many changes, including new economic policies, such as mercantilism and capitalism.

Reading Check
Summarize What is a market economy?

Lesson 3 Assessment

Review Ideas, Terms, and People

1. **a. Summarize** What was cottage industry?
   b. Draw Conclusions How were colonies important to a country with the economic policy of mercantilism?
   c. Form Opinions Was mercantilism a good policy for Europe's colonies? Why or why not?

2. **Summarize** What countries were active in the slave trade?

3. **Analyze** Why did power shift to northern Europe?

4. **a. Summarize** In what kind of economic system do individuals and private businesses run most industries?
   b. Analyze How do supply and demand work in a market economy?

Critical Thinking

5. **Organize Information** Draw a diagram like the one here. Use it to show three other factors that contributed to the development of capitalism in Europe.

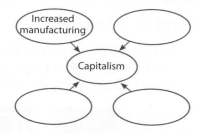

Literature in History

A Portrayal of Life in the 1600s

Word Help

inclined likely

apprentices people who work for or train under a master craftsman

❶ A major canal connected Delft to the cities of Rotterdam and The Hague. *What tells you that the canal was a central part of Griet's life?*

❷ Griet claims that she is a realist—that she saw things "as they were." *What does this tell you about the description of the city that follows?*

❸ *What details in this paragraph and the next suggest that Delft had a thriving economy?*

About the Reading The 1999 novel *Girl with a Pearl Earring* is a work of historical fiction. It is set in the bustling city of Delft, in the Netherlands, during the 1660s. At this time, the Netherlands was one of the wealthiest, most powerful nations in the world. Nevertheless, many Dutch commoners struggled to pay high taxes. The main character of this novel is the teenage daughter of one such commoner. To help support her family, Griet works as a maid to the family of a middle-class artist. The artist, Johannes Vermeer, was one of the greatest Dutch painters of his time.

As You Read Picture the city of Delft in your mind.

From *Girl with a Pearl Earring*
by Tracy Chevalier (1962–)

I had walked along that street all my life, but had never been so aware that my back was to my home. When I reached the end and turned out of sight of my family, though, it became a little easier to walk steadily and look around me. The morning was still cool, the sky a flat grey-white pulled close over Delft like a sheet, the summer sun not yet high enough to burn it away. The canal I walked along was a mirror of white light tinged with green. As the sun grew brighter the canal would darken to the color of moss.

Frans, Agnes, and I used to sit along that canal and throw things in ❶—pebbles, sticks, once a broken tile—and imagine what they might touch on the bottom—not fish, but creatures from our imagination, with many eyes, scales, hands and fins. Frans thought up the most interesting monsters. Agnes was the most frightened. I always stopped the game, too inclined to see things as they were ❷ to be able to think up things that were not.

❸ There were a few boats on the canal, moving towards Market Square. It was not market day, however, when the canal was so full you couldn't see the water. One boat was carrying river fish for the stalls at Jeronymous Bridge. Another sat low on the water, loaded with bricks. The man poling the boat called out a greeting to me. I merely nodded and lowered my head so that the edge of my cap hid my face.

I crossed a bridge over the canal and turned into the open space of Market Square, even then busy with people criss-crossing it on their way to some task—buying meat at the Meat Hall, or bread at the baker's, taking wood to be weighed at the Weigh House. Children ran errands for their parents, apprentices for their masters, maids for their households. Horses and carts clattered across the stones. To my right

Word Help

gilded overlaid with a thin layer of gold

keystones the top center stones in an arch

4 Most people in the Netherlands were Protestant. *How does Griet's description of Delft reflect the effects of the Reformation?*

was the Town Hall, with its gilded front and white marble faces gazing down from the keystones above the windows. To my left was the New Church, where I had been baptized sixteen years before. Its tall, narrow tower made me think of a stone birdcage. Father had taken us up it once. I would never forget the sight of Delft spread below us, each narrow brick house and steep red roof and green waterway and city gate marked forever in my mind, tiny and yet distinct. I asked my father then if every Dutch city looked like that, but he did not know. He had never visited any other city, not even The Hague, two hours away on foot.

I walked to the center of the square. There the stones had been laid to form an eight-pointed star set inside a circle. Each point aimed towards a different part of Delft. I thought of it as the very center of the town, and as the center of my life. Frans and Agnes and I had played in that star since we were old enough to run to the market. In our favorite game, one of us chose a point and one of us named a thing—a stork, a church, a wheelbarrow, a flower—and we ran in that direction looking for that thing. We had explored most of Delft that way.

One point, however, we had never followed. I had never gone to Papists' Corner, where the Catholics lived. The house where I was to work was just ten minutes from home, the time it took a pot of water to boil, but I had never passed by it.

4 I knew no Catholics. There were not so many in Delft, and none in our street or in the shops we used. It was not that we avoided them, but they kept to themselves.

Girl with a Pearl Earring (1665), by Johannes Vermeer

Connect Literature to History

1. **Analyze** New trade routes and banking, along with increased manufacturing, brought wealth to England and the Netherlands. What details in this excerpt point to economic success of the Netherlands?

2. **Develop Historical Perspective** The Netherlands became a great trading power. What geographical feature of Delft—and, more broadly, the Netherlands—helped its merchants to succeed in trade?

Social Studies Skills

Identify Print Research Sources

Define the Skill

You are not old enough to remember a time when the Internet did not exist. Since the Internet is now part of most people's lives, this has changed the way information is presented. Print sources are called such because they are printed on paper.

A research source is a set of facts or information about a topic. It is different from a story. Research sources can be standard text, but they can also be visuals like charts, graphs, tables, and photographs. Research sources often end with something like a bibliography or a brief caption. This tells you about the information the author used to write the source. A book about Portuguese ships, a magazine article about plants in Europe, and a paper map of North America are all examples of print research sources.

Learn the Skill

Follow these steps to identify print research sources.

1. Identify the print source. It may be a book, a magazine, a map, or another source printed on paper.

2. Does the source tell a set of facts or information about a topic?

3. Is the source a visual like a chart, graph, table, or photograph? If the source is long, are there any visuals in it?

4. Look at the end of the source. Do you see anything that tells you about the information the author used to write the source?

Practice the Skill

Read the following examples. Explain why each one is or is not a print research source.

1. a book that includes a 1500s map of North America

2. a biography of Vasco da Gama posted on a website

3. an illustration of an American Indian family in a newspaper

4. a magazine article about the Columbian Exchange

Module 23 Assessment

Review Vocabulary, Terms, and People

*For each statement, write **T** if it is true and **F** if it is false. If the statement is false, write the correct term that would make the sentence a true statement.*

1. Christopher Columbus led the first voyage to circumnavigate the globe.

2. The Spanish created large farms called plantations in the Americas.

3. The Columbian Exchange refers to the exchange of plants, animals, and ideas between the Old World and the New World.

4. An economic system in which the government controls all aspects of a country's economy to make it stronger is called capitalism.

5. In 1588, an English navy destroyed a fleet of Spanish ships called the balance of trade.

6. An atlas is a collection of maps.

7. The first person to reach India by sailing around Africa was Bartolomé de las Casas.

Comprehension and Critical Thinking

Lesson 1

8. a. **Recall** What did these people achieve: Vasco da Gama, Christopher Columbus, and Ferdinand Magellan?

    b. **Draw Conclusions** How did the astrolabe, the compass, and better maps affect travel by sea?

    c. **Predict** How might European history have been different if the Spanish Armada had defeated the English forces?

Lesson 2

9. a. **Identify** Name three plants and three animals that Europeans brought to the Americas. Name five plants that explorers took back to Europe from the Americas.

    b. **Compare and Contrast** What were some positive results of the Columbian Exchange? What were some negative results?

    c. **Elaborate** How did diseases from Europe affect America—both in the short term and in the long term?

Lesson 3

10. a. **Identify** Which countries became more wealthy and powerful by developing new trade routes and banking industries?

     b. **Analyze** How did mercantilism eventually lead to the development of capitalism?

     c. **Predict** How might the law of supply and demand affect an individual seller? How might it affect a buyer?

Module 23 Assessment, continued

Review Themes

11. **Geography** How did improvements in technology help improve understanding of the world's geography?

12. **Economics** What led to the shift from mercantilism to capitalism?

Reading Skills

Vocabulary Clues *Use the Reading Skills taught in this module to answer the question about the reading selection below.*

> European countries didn't allow their colonies to manufacture goods. That way they could take raw materials from their colonies and sell manufactured goods back to them.

13. According to the reading selection above, what is the best definition of *manufactured goods*?

   a. materials found in nature, such as wood, furs, cotton, and dyes

   b. products European countries made from raw materials, such as clothing and furniture

   c. products made by colonists for European countries

   d. materials taken from European countries to create new products

Social Studies Skills

Identify Print Research Sources *Use the Social Studies Skills taught in this module to explain why each of the following is or is not a print research source.*

14. a copy of a letter from Columbus describing his discoveries in the "new world"

15. a digital collection of original maps created by European map makers in the 1500s

16. a magazine article describing how capitalism developed in Europe

17. a television documentary that explains how caravels were built in the 1500s

Focus On Speaking

18. **Create an Informative Report** A teacher has asked you to create an informative report for fifth-graders. The report should be about changes around the world during the Age of Exploration. Think back on what you've learned about the Age of Exploration. Plan the report that you will give to younger students. Focus on the new ideas and technologies that shaped the world during this time. Include information about plants, animals, and economic systems during the Age of Exploration.

   Make notes on five to six note cards to help you remember what you want to say in your report. Also, design a chart, graph, or other visual aid that will help in your presentation.

   When you give your report, keep your audience in mind while you speak. Simplify or explain any vocabulary that a younger student might not understand. Speak slowly and clearly so the students can understand what you are saying.

Ponce de León

The Spanish conquistador Juan Ponce de León was the first European to set foot on land that later became part of the United States. Ponce de León first sailed to the Americas with Christopher Columbus on his second voyage in 1493. Once in the Caribbean region, he helped conquer what is now Puerto Rico and was named ruler of the island. According to legend, Ponce de León learned about a Fountain of Youth, whose waters could make old people young again. He may have been searching for this fountain when, in 1513, he made landfall on the coast of what today is the southeastern United States. He named the area Florida and claimed it for Spain.

Explore important events in the life of Ponce de León online. You can find a wealth of information, video clips, primary sources, activities, and more through your online textbook.

Caribbean Island Encounters
Watch the video to learn about the first encounters between Spanish explorers and the people of the Caribbean.

Claiming Florida for Spain
Watch the video to learn about Ponce de León's first landing on the coast of what is now Florida.

Ponce de León's 1513 Route
Study the map to learn about the region of the Americas that Ponce de León explored in 1513.

Module 24
Enlightenment and Revolution

Essential Question
Why did Enlightenment principles influence radical changes in governments around the world?

About the Photo: This photo shows a reenactment of the American Revolution. American revolutionaries were inspired by Enlightenment ideas.

▷ *Explore ONLINE!*

VIDEOS, including...
- Global Impact of the American Revolution
- History Alive: Thomas Jefferson
- The Declaration of Independence
- The French Revolution

✓ Document-Based Investigations

✓ Graphic Organizers

✓ Interactive Games

✓ Image Carousel: European Monarchs

✓ Image with Hotspots: Stamp Act Protest

✓ Image with Hotspots: Signers of the Declaration of Independence

In this module you will learn how ideas of the Enlightenment led to revolutions around the world.

What You Will Learn...

Lesson 1: Ideas of the Enlightenment 826
The Big Idea Enlightenment thinkers built on ideas from earlier movements to emphasize the importance of reason.

Lesson 2: New Views on Government 830
The Big Idea Enlightenment ideas influenced the growth of democratic governments in Europe and the Americas.

Lesson 3: The Age of Revolution 837
The Big Idea Revolutions changed the governments of Britain, the American colonies, and France.

Lesson 4: The Spread of Revolutionary Ideals 844
The Big Idea Napoleon's quest to rule Europe was eventually thwarted, but not before the ideals of the French Revolution spread throughout the continent and Latin America.

Timeline of Events 1642–1831

▶ Explore ONLINE!

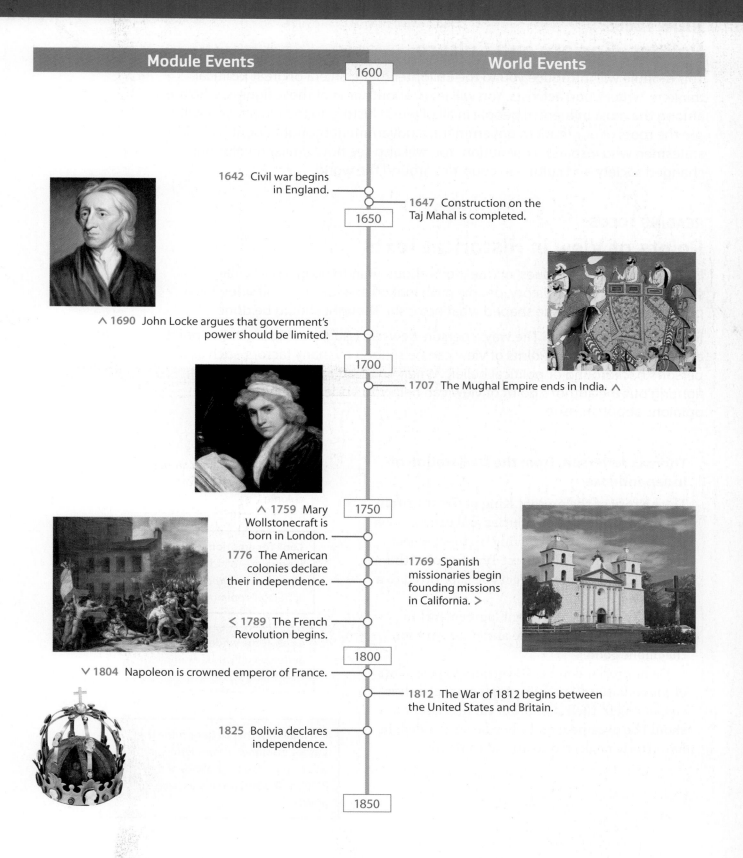

Module Events

World Events

1600

1642 Civil war begins in England.

1647 Construction on the Taj Mahal is completed.

1650

∧ **1690** John Locke argues that government's power should be limited.

1700

1707 The Mughal Empire ends in India. ∧

∧ **1759** Mary Wollstonecraft is born in London.

1750

1769 Spanish missionaries begin founding missions in California. ⟩

1776 The American colonies declare their independence.

< **1789** The French Revolution begins.

1800

∨ **1804** Napoleon is crowned emperor of France.

1812 The War of 1812 begins between the United States and Britain.

1825 Bolivia declares independence.

1850

Reading Social Studies

THEME FOCUS:

Politics, Society and Culture

This module will introduce you to the Enlightenment, an era of great political thinkers, writers, and activists. You will learn about some of these figures, who are among the most influential people in all of world history. In their ideas, you will see the roots of our modern government, a government brought about by bold statesmen who inspired a revolution. You will also see how similar revolutions changed society and culture in countries around the world.

READING FOCUS:

Points of View in Historical Texts

History is made up of issues, or questions about what to do in a particular situation. Throughout history, people have looked at issues from all sides. Each person's view of the issue shaped what he or she thought should be done.

Identify Points of View The way a person views an issue is called his or her point of view, or perspective. Points of view can be shaped by many factors, such as a person's background or political beliefs. When you read a historical document, figuring out the author's point of view can help you understand his or her opinions about an issue.

Thomas Jefferson, from the Declaration of Independence

The history of the present King of Great Britain is a history of repeated injuries and usurpations [seizures of power], all having in direct object the establishment of a direct Tyranny over these States. To prove this, let Facts be submitted to a candid world.

He has refused his Assent [agreement] to Laws, the most wholesome and necessary for the public good.

He has forbidden his Governors to pass Laws of immediate and pressing importance, unless suspended in their operation till his Assent should be obtained; and when so suspended, he has utterly neglected to attend to them.

Consider the author's background—Jefferson was a leader in the American colonies.

Look for emotional language—Words like *injuries* and *usurpations* make Jefferson's opinion clear.

Look at the evidence—Jefferson only uses examples of the king's flaws.

Put it all together to determine the author's point of view—Jefferson was opposed to the policies of the English king and wanted a change in government.

You Try It!

Read the following passage from this module. Then answer the questions that follow.

Rousseau French thinker Jean-Jacques Rousseau (roo-SOH) criticized divine right. He believed in popular sovereignty—the idea that governments should express the will of the people. In *The Social Contract*, published in 1762, Rousseau declared, "Man is born free, but he is everywhere in chains." According to Rousseau, citizens submit to the authority of government to protect their own interests, entering into a "social contract." This contract gives the government the power to make and enforce laws as long as it serves the people. The government should give up that power if it is not serving the people.

Think about the passage you have just read, and then answer the questions.

1. What do you think was Rousseau's point of view about France's government?
2. What words or phrases in this passage helped you identify his point of view?
3. How did Rousseau's own beliefs and ideas affect his point of view?
4. Do you think Rousseau's point of view was similar to or different from that of the king of France?
5. Who do you think would be more likely to share Rousseau's point of view, a wealthy French noble or a colonist planning a rebellion? Why do you think so?

As you read this module, try to determine the points of view of the various figures you are studying.

Key Terms and People

Lesson 1
Enlightenment
Voltaire
salon
Mary Wollstonecraft

Lesson 2
unlimited government
limited government
John Locke
natural rights
majority rule
Charles-Louis Montesquieu
Jean-Jacques Rousseau
popular sovereignty

Lesson 3
English Bill of Rights
rule of law
Declaration of Independence
Declaration of the Rights of Man and of the Citizen

Lesson 4
Napoleon Bonaparte
coup d'état
Klemens von Metternich
conservatism
liberalism
Simón Bolívar

Ideas of the Enlightenment

The Big Idea

Enlightenment thinkers built on ideas from earlier movements to emphasize the importance of reason.

Main Ideas

- The Enlightenment was also called the Age of Reason.

- The Enlightenment's roots can be traced back to earlier ideas.

- New ideas came mainly from French and British thinkers.

Key Terms and People

Enlightenment
Voltaire
salon
Mary Wollstonecraft

Reading Check
Find Main Ideas
How did the Enlightenment thinkers explain the world?

If YOU were there . . .

You are a student in the early 1700s. It seems your teacher can pass or fail whomever he wants. You think the teacher should make his decisions about grades based on what a student has learned. You come up with a new idea—testing students so they can prove what they know. You think this idea will improve your grades as well as relations in your school.

Will you challenge the teacher's authority?

The Age of Reason

Discoveries made during the Scientific Revolution and on the voyages of discovery led to changes in Europe. A number of scholars were beginning to challenge long-held beliefs about science, religion, and government.

These new scholars relied on reason, or logical thought, instead of religious teachings to explain how the world worked. They believed human reason could be used to achieve three great goals—knowledge, freedom, and happiness—and that achieving these goals would improve society. The use of reason in guiding people's thoughts about philosophy, society, and politics defined a time period called the **Enlightenment**. Because of its emphasis on the use of reason, the Enlightenment was also known as the Age of Reason.

The Enlightenment's Roots

The main ideas of the Enlightenment had their roots in other eras. Enlightenment thinkers looked back to the Greeks, the Romans, and the history of Christianity. The Renaissance, Reformation, and Scientific Revolution also provided ideas.

Greek and Roman Philosophers Enlightenment thinkers used ideas about the natural world from the ancient Greeks and Romans. Greek philosophers had observed an order and regularity in the natural world. Aristotle, for example, taught that people could use logic to discover new truths. Building on Greek ideas, Roman thinkers developed the concept of natural law, the idea that a law governed how the world operated.

With Greek and Roman beliefs as guidelines, Enlightenment thinkers began studying the world in a new way. They applied these beliefs not just to the natural world but also to the human world of society and government.

Christianity The history of Christianity in Europe provides other clues about ideas that emerged in the Enlightenment. One religious thinker, Thomas Aquinas, had taught in the Middle Ages that faith paired with reason could explain the world. Although it owed a great deal to Aquinas, the Enlightenment was mostly a secular, or nonreligious, movement. Enlightenment thinkers disagreed with the church's claims to authority and its intolerance toward non-Christian beliefs.

The Renaissance and Reformation Other reactions to the Christian Church in Europe also influenced the ideas of the Enlightenment. For example, some Renaissance thinkers used Greek and Roman ideas to raise questions about established religious beliefs. These Renaissance thinkers were known as humanists.

Although most humanists were religious, they focused on human value and achievement rather than on the glory of God. Renaissance humanists believed people could improve their world by studying it and changing it. These ideas contributed to the Enlightenment idea of progress—the belief that humans were capable of improving their world.

Some Reformation ideas also reappeared during the Enlightenment. Like Martin Luther and other reformers, Enlightenment scholars questioned church authority. They found that religious beliefs didn't always fit in with what they learned from their logical study of the world.

Quick Facts

Ideas of the Enlightenment

The Enlightenment is also called the Age of Reason because reason, or logical thought, is a basic part of all Enlightenment ideas.

- The ability to reason is what makes humans unique.
- Reason can be used to solve problems and improve people's lives.
- Reason can free people from ignorance, superstition, and unfair government.
- The natural world is governed by laws that can be discovered through reason.
- Like the natural world, human behavior is governed by natural laws.
- Governments should reflect natural laws and encourage education and debate.

The use of reason advanced science and technology, which in turn influenced the Enlightenment. Here, the Italian scientist Alessandro Volta explains a new invention, the battery.

Reading Check
Find Main Ideas
What ideas influenced the Enlightenment?

The Scientific Revolution The Scientific Revolution also influenced Enlightenment thinkers. Through experiments, scientists like Newton and Galileo had discovered that the world did not work exactly the way the church explained it. Using scientific methods of study, scientists discovered laws that governed the natural world. Enlightenment thinkers took the idea of natural laws one step further. They believed that natural laws must also govern human society and government.

New Ideas

Enlightenment thinkers borrowed ideas from history to develop a new worldview. They believed the use of reason could improve society. To achieve this progress, they had to share their ideas with others.

French Philosophers French philosophers popularized many Enlightenment ideas. One philosopher, **Voltaire** (vohl-TAYR), mocked government and religion in his writings. Instead of trusting God to improve human happiness, Voltaire believed humans could improve their own existence.

BIOGRAPHY

Voltaire 1694–1778

Voltaire is the pen name of the French philosopher and author François-Marie Arouet. He used his wit, intelligence, and sense of justice to poke fun at religious intolerance. Voltaire's skill and bold ideas made him a popular writer. In his writings he argued that the purpose of life is the pursuit of human happiness through progress in science and the arts.

Make Inferences
Why did Voltaire poke fun at religious intolerance?

Having gotten in trouble for some of his writings, Voltaire also spoke out against censorship—removal of information considered harmful. He argued, "I [may] disapprove of what you say, but I will defend to the death your right to say it." His statement emphasized the Enlightenment goal of freedom of thought.

Enlightenment thinkers made an effort to share their thoughts with the public. Philosopher Denis Diderot (dee-DROH) edited a book called the *Encyclopedia*. This book included articles by more than 100 experts on science, technology, and history. The French king and the pope both banned the *Encyclopedia*.

In spite of censorship, Enlightenment ideas spread. One important place for the exchange of ideas was the **salon**, a social gathering held to discuss ideas. Women often hosted the salons. Most Enlightenment thinkers did not view women as equal to men. However, in hosting salons women could influence opinions.

British Writers Women and men also began to publish their ideas in books, pamphlets, and newspaper articles. British writer **Mary Wollstonecraft**, for example, argued that women should have the same rights as men.

Enlightenment thinkers even applied their ideas of freedom and progress to economics. British writer Adam Smith believed economics was governed by natural laws. He argued that governments should not try to control the economy and that economic growth came when individuals were free to make their own choices. Like many Enlightenment thinkers, his ideas would have a lasting effect.

Summary and Preview Scholars during the Enlightenment drew on ideas from previous eras. They proposed ideas about the importance of reason and progress. In the next lesson, you will learn how the Enlightenment changed ideas about government.

Reading Check
Summarize
How did Enlightenment thinkers spread their ideas?

Lesson 1 Assessment

Review Ideas, Terms, and People

1. **a. Define** What was the Enlightenment?

   b. Explain What was the main goal of most Enlightenment thinkers?

2. **a. Define** What does it mean to say that the Enlightenment was a secular movement?

   b. Explain What was the connection between the discoveries of the Scientific Revolution and the Enlightenment?

   c. Elaborate How did the idea of natural law contribute to the Enlightenment?

3. **a. Describe** How did Voltaire feel about censorship?

   b. Explain What did Adam Smith contribute to Enlightenment ideas?

Critical Thinking

4. **Summarize** Draw a chart like this one. Use it to summarize the sources of Enlightenment ideas.

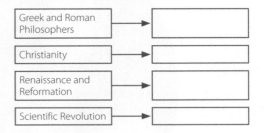

Greek and Roman Philosophers	→	
Christianity	→	
Renaissance and Reformation	→	
Scientific Revolution	→	

New Views on Government

The Big Idea

Enlightenment ideas influenced the growth of democratic governments in Europe and the Americas.

Main Ideas

- The Enlightenment influenced some monarchies.

- Enlightenment thinkers helped the growth of democratic ideas.

- In the Americas, the Enlightenment inspired a struggle for independence.

Key Terms and People

unlimited government
limited government
John Locke
natural rights
majority rule
Charles-Louis Montesquieu
Jean-Jacques Rousseau
popular sovereignty

If YOU were there . . .

You are in a coffee house, discussing everything from politics to religion with friends. It is 1770. Suddenly, someone next to you questions the king's right to rule. Other people begin to agree with that person. As you listen to their logic, you wonder about other ways to run a government.

Would you support a government that didn't include a king or queen? Why or why not?

Enlightenment Influence on Monarchies

In the 1600s and 1700s, kings, queens, and emperors ruled Europe. Many of these monarchs believed that they ruled through divine right. That is, they thought that God had given them an unlimited right to rule as they chose. An **unlimited government** is one in which one person or group of people holds all power with no restrictions. An unlimited government can also be called an authoritarian state. This type of state is one in which power is centralized and the people have few, if any, freedoms. **Limited government** is one that is not all-powerful. It is checked by laws and institutions representing the will of the people.

Unlimited Government in France King Louis XIV, who ruled France from 1643 to 1715, was an absolute monarch who saw himself as the entire government. He declared, *"L'état, c'est moi!"* or "I am the state." Louis XIV established a totalitarian state. A totalitarian state has absolute control not only over government but also over every aspect of culture, from the arts and literature to science and commerce. Censorship was common. Any artist or writer who criticized the monarchy was punished.

Although absolute monarchs like Louis XIV held all governmental power, other groups in society also had privileges. In France, the nobles paid few taxes and held the highest

King Louis XIV ruled France as an absolute monarch.

positions in the army. The French clergy paid no taxes at all. Most of the French people, the commoners, were poor, paid high taxes, and had no role in their government.

Enlightened Despotism The spread of Enlightenment ideas pushed some absolute monarchs to change how they ruled. They applied Enlightenment ideas to government. These rulers became known as enlightened despots. A despot is a ruler with absolute power. The enlightened despots tried to make life better for the commoners. They thought they could make their countries stronger if the commoners were happier. Frederick II of Prussia was one such ruler. He approved reforms in law and education.

Empress Catherine the Great of Russia was another enlightened despot. For most of its history, Russia had an unlimited government whose tsar ruled with an iron fist. Catherine the Great ruled Russia from 1762 to 1796. A German, Catherine became czarina through marriage to a

Empress Catherine the Great of Russia

Explore ONLINE!

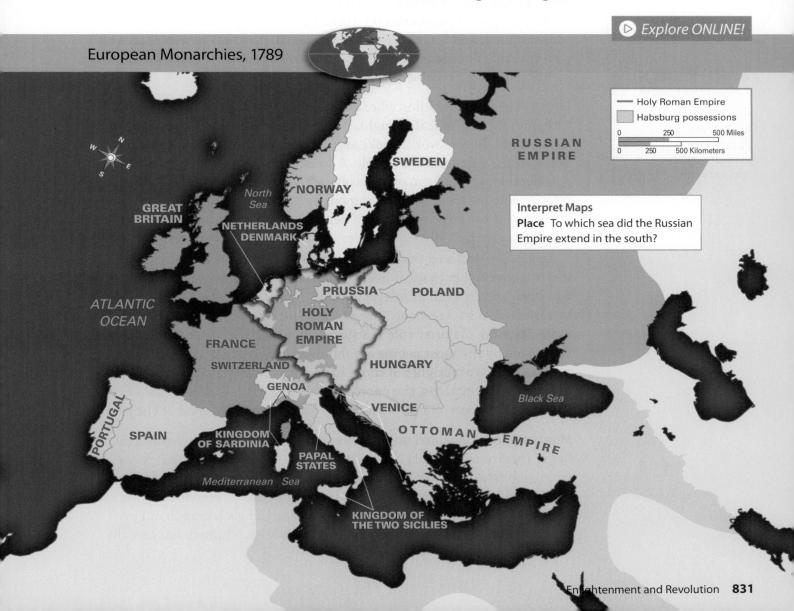

European Monarchies, 1789

Holy Roman Empire

Habsburg possessions

0   250   500 Miles
0   250   500 Kilometers

Interpret Maps
Place To which sea did the Russian Empire extend in the south?

RUSSIAN EMPIRE

SWEDEN

NORWAY

North Sea

GREAT BRITAIN

NETHERLANDS
DENMARK

PRUSSIA   POLAND

ATLANTIC OCEAN

HOLY ROMAN EMPIRE

FRANCE

SWITZERLAND

HUNGARY

GENOA

VENICE

Black Sea

PORTUGAL

SPAIN

KINGDOM OF SARDINIA

PAPAL STATES

OTTOMAN   EMPIRE

Mediterranean Sea

KINGDOM OF THE TWO SICILIES

Russian prince. Catherine became inspired by Enlightenment ideals during her rule and tried to put in place reforms. She promoted education for all by expanding the number of state-run schools in Russia. She reformed Russia's legal system according to Enlightenment principles.

Part of the reform gave "equal protection" to all Russians. Many Russians believed that Russian serfs would now be freed and provided protection under the law. Serfs were workers legally tied to a lord's land. Serfs made up the majority of the population in Russia, but Catherine needed support from the Russian nobility to maintain power. The nobility opposed freedom for the serfs. Ultimately, serfdom expanded under Catherine's rule.

Even though Catherine the Great and other enlightened despots made some improvements to their countries, many Enlightenment thinkers criticized these reform efforts. These thinkers began looking for bigger changes. They began to consider the need for democracy.

Reading Check
Contrast
How do rule by divine right and rule by an enlightened despot differ?

Democratic Ideas

Some Enlightenment thinkers challenged only the idea of rule by divine right. Others went further. They developed some completely new ideas about how governments should work. Three of these thinkers—Locke, Montesquieu, and Rousseau—tried to identify the best possible form of government. The ideas of these Enlightenment thinkers contributed to the creation of modern democracy.

Locke The English philosopher **John Locke** had a major influence on Enlightenment political thought. In 1690, he published *Two Treatises of Government*. In this work, Locke argued for government as a **contract** between the ruler and the people. A constitution, or written plan for government, is one form of this contract. A constitution defines the relationship between the government and its citizens, outlines the structure of the government, and describes the government's powers. Because a contract binds both sides, it limits the ruler's power.

Academic Vocabulary
contract a binding legal agreement

Locke also declared that all people had certain **natural rights**, which included the rights to life, liberty, and property. He thought that no person was born with special privileges. According to Locke, this equality should be reflected in government. The government's decisions should reflect **majority rule**. Majority rule is a system in which the ideas and decisions supported by the most people are followed. A government also had to protect the natural rights of those in the minority. If it didn't protect the rights of all its citizens, the people had the right to change rulers. Locke thought that government existed only for the common good of the people.

Montesquieu Charles-Louis Montesquieu (mohn-te-SKYOO) was a member of the French nobility. He built on Locke's ideas in *The Spirit of the Laws*, published in 1748. Montesquieu claimed that a government should be divided into separate branches to protect people's freedom. In this idea, known as the separation of powers, the powers of each branch of government are limited by the others. In addition, each branch has certain

Separation of Powers

When Charles-Louis Montesquieu published *The Spirit of the Laws* in 1748, it was immediately viewed by many as one of the most important political writings of the period. Montesquieu used England's government as a model for his discussion of the separation of powers, the most well-known chapter of the work. The concept later became the model for the U.S. Constitution.

Montesquieu believed that for a government to effectively protect citizens' liberty, governmental powers must be separated into three distinct branches.

If the powers to execute the law and interpret the law were granted to the same branch, then citizens would be unprotected against government oppression.

Analyze Historical Sources
What might happen if the same branch of government held both legislative and judicial power?

"When the legislative and executive powers are united in the same person, or in the same body of magistracy, there can be no liberty; because apprehensions [fear] may arise, lest the same monarch or senate should enact tyrannical laws, to execute them in a tyrannical manner.

Again, there is no liberty, if the power of judging be not separated from the legislative and executive. Were it joined with the legislative, the life and liberty of the subject would be exposed to arbitrary [random] control, for the judge would be then the legislator. Were it joined to the executive power, the judge might behave with violence and oppression."

— Charles-Louis Montesquieu from *The Spirit of the Laws*

powers that the others don't have. As a result, the separate branches must share power. None of the individual branches can control the government completely.

Rousseau French thinker **Jean-Jacques Rousseau** (roo-SOH) criticized divine right. He believed in **popular sovereignty** (SAHV-ruhn-tee)—that governments should express the will of the people. In *The Social Contract*, published in 1762, Rousseau said, "Man is born free, but he is everywhere in chains." He believed citizens submit to the authority of government to protect their own interests, entering into a "social contract." This contract gives the government the power to make and enforce laws if it serves the people. The government gives up its power if it is not serving the people.

Reading Check
Synthesize
What idea appears in the works of both Locke and Rousseau?

The Enlightenment in the Americas

The ideas of these three philosophers spread throughout Europe and then to the British colonists living in North America. Enlightenment ideas would have a big effect on the history of the Americas.

The British colonists already knew basic ideas about participation in government. Because they were British citizens, the colonists were familiar with Parliament and its control over the British monarch. When the

The ideas of Locke, Montesquieu, and Rousseau contributed to the creation of modern democracy.

John Locke
1632–1704

- Government's power is limited.
- People have natural rights, such as life, liberty, and property.

Charles-Louis Montesquieu
1689–1755

- The powers of government should be divided into separate branches.

Jean-Jacques Rousseau
1712–1778

- Governments should express the will of the people.
- People enter into a social contract with their government, giving it the right to create and enforce laws.

Analyze Visuals
Who believed in the separation of government powers?

British government began to chip away at what the colonists saw as their rights, the colonists were outraged. Many believed that they needed to fight back.

British Policy in North America To learn more about this struggle, we must go back to the founding of the colonies. Other countries besides Britain settled and controlled land in North America. One of them was France.

In North America, the French and British had many disagreements. These conflicts led to war. Even though the British eventually defeated the French, years of fighting cost Britain a lot of money.

The British government created new taxes in the colonies to pay its war debt. One tax added to the cost of molasses. Another tax, called the Stamp Act, required colonists to pay a tax on newspapers, some legal documents, and other printed materials. People in England didn't have to pay these taxes. As a result, the colonists thought the taxes were unfair. The colonists wanted to be treated as British citizens because they were subject to British laws. They wanted the same rights as people in England.

King George III ruled Great Britain when the Stamp Act was passed.

Economists of the Enlightenment

New ideas about economic freedom also became important during the Enlightenment, largely in response to the principles of mercantilism. Mercantilism was the dominant economic system in Europe from the 1500s to the 1800s. It was based on creating wealth through strict government regulations on trade.

Enlightenment thinkers supported free trade and greater economic freedom. English philosopher John Locke's theory of the social contract stated that people willingly gave up some of their freedoms to government in return for protection of their liberty and property. Laws that violated these protections, such as those restricting free trade, were unjust. Charles-Louis Montesquieu, a French Enlightenment philosopher, also called for the expansion of trade among nations as a way to achieve greater wealth and peace for all.

Economist Adam Smith took the ideas of the Enlightenment and formally applied them to economics. Smith rejected mercantilism and government control of the economy. He also rejected monopolies, or the control of a particular good or service by one person or business. He maintained that they prevented the natural competition that takes place when people have the freedom to produce, sell, and buy as they choose. Adam Smith's ideas formed the basis of capitalism, an economic system in which a country's trade and industry are controlled by private owners rather than by the state. The freedom to engage with and compete in the market and the freedom to trade openly with others in the market were key Enlightenment ideas that endure today.

Analyze Information
How did Adam Smith apply Enlightenment principles to economics?

Colonists' Views Many colonial leaders were familiar with the ideas of the Enlightenment. Two leaders in particular—Benjamin Franklin and Thomas Jefferson—applied those ideas to the colonists' complaints.

In 1766, philosopher and scientist Benjamin Franklin went to London. There he addressed the House of Commons in Parliament. He argued that the British government had no right to tax the colonists because they had no representation in Parliament. His argument against "taxation without representation" inspired riots against taxes in the colonies. The riots persuaded the British government to get rid of the Stamp Act.

Thomas Jefferson was a farmer, scientist, and scholar. He had been influenced by the Scientific Revolution. John Locke was another source of inspiration. In keeping with Locke's ideas, Jefferson believed that Britain had no right to govern or impose taxes on the colonies. He supported the idea of independence for the colonies. Jefferson also supported the separation of religious and political power. In this way, he reflected the Enlightenment's secular attitudes.

Timeline: The Enlightenment Reaches America

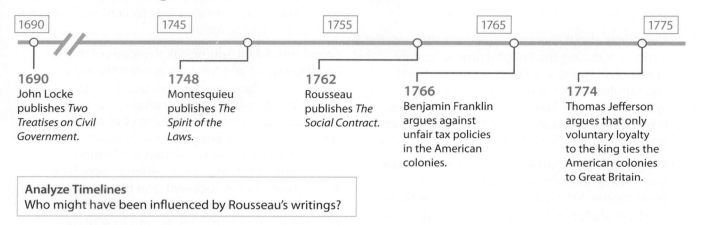

1690
John Locke publishes *Two Treatises on Civil Government.*

1748
Montesquieu publishes *The Spirit of the Laws.*

1762
Rousseau publishes *The Social Contract.*

1766
Benjamin Franklin argues against unfair tax policies in the American colonies.

1774
Thomas Jefferson argues that only voluntary loyalty to the king ties the American colonies to Great Britain.

Analyze Timelines
Who might have been influenced by Rousseau's writings?

Reading Check
Find Main Ideas
Why did some colonists want to be independent of Britain?

Jefferson would later become president of the United States. His philosophies and achievements, based on Enlightenment ideas, helped to establish the democratic government and the rights we enjoy today in the United States.

Summary and Preview In the 1600s and 1700s, some European monarchs thought they had a divine right to rule. As Enlightenment thinkers proposed new ways of thinking, people questioned the monarchs' powers. Democratic ideas spread. In the next lesson, you will learn how these ideas changed governments in England, France, and the Americas.

Lesson 2 Assessment

Review Ideas, Terms, and People

1. a. Define Describe the difference between limited and unlimited government.
   b. Explain What did enlightened despots try to do?
2. a. Define What are natural rights?
   b. Explain What did Locke believe was the purpose of government?
   c. Elaborate Why would the separation of powers protect people's freedoms?
3. a. Describe What role did Benjamin Franklin play in the American colonists' disagreement with the British government?

   b. Elaborate Why do you think many Americans consider Thomas Jefferson a hero?

Critical Thinking

4. Analyze Effects Draw a graphic organizer like the one shown. Use it to describe the effect of the British government's policies on its North American colonies.

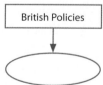

British Policies

The Age of Revolution

The Big Idea

Revolutions changed the governments of Britain, the American colonies, and France.

Main Ideas

- Revolution and reform changed the government of England.

- Enlightenment ideas led to democracy in North America.

- The French Revolution caused major changes in France's government.

Key Terms and People

English Bill of Rights
rule of law
Declaration of Independence
Declaration of the Rights of Man and of the Citizen

If YOU were there . . .

You live near Boston, Massachusetts. British soldiers have moved in and taken over your house. They say that the law allows them to take whatever they need. But your father doesn't want the soldiers living in your house and eating your food. What can he do to fight the king's laws?

Should your father disobey the king? Why or why not?

Revolution and Reform in England

Enlightenment ideas inspired commoners to oppose monarchies that ruled without concern for the people's needs. However, the monarchs wouldn't give up their privileges. In England, Parliament forced the monarchy to change.

Trouble with Parliament For many years, the English Parliament and the English monarchy had had an uneasy relationship. Parliament demanded that its rights and powers be respected. However, the monarchy stood for rule by divine right. The relationship between English monarchs and Parliament got worse.

The conflict led to a civil war in 1642. Representatives of Parliament led by Oliver Cromwell took over the country. The king, Charles I, was charged with various crimes and beheaded in 1649. Cromwell became a dictator. The years of his rule were troubled and violent.

By 1660, many English people were tired of turmoil and wanted to restore the monarchy. They invited the dead king's son to return and rule England as Charles II. They made Charles promise to allow Parliament to keep the powers it had won in the civil war. These powers included the right to approve new taxes. Parliament was able to work with Charles II during most of his rule. However, when Charles died and his brother James became king, the trouble began again.

In this painting, King John signs the Magna Carta. The English Bill of Rights drew on the ideas in the Magna Carta.

James II, an unpopular Catholic, tried to promote his religious beliefs in England, a Protestant country. As a result, Parliament invited the Protestant William of Orange, James's son-in-law, to invade England. When William and his wife, Mary, arrived in England in 1688, James and his family fled to France.

New Rights for the English People Parliament offered the throne to William and Mary on one condition. They had to accept the **English Bill of Rights**, a document that listed rights for Parliament and the English people. This document, approved in 1689, drew on the principles of Magna Carta, which limited a ruler's power and recognized some rights for the people.

Magna Carta had been in place for hundreds of years, but the monarchs had not honored it. William and Mary agreed to honor Magna Carta. They also agreed that Parliament could pass laws and raise taxes. As a result, the monarchs ruled according to laws passed by Parliament. William and Mary's agreement to accept the Bill of Rights ensured that Britain would have a limited government. The monarchs, like everyone else, were subject to the laws of the land. This principle is known as the **rule of law**.

Democracy in America

Although the power of the monarchs was limited in England, some people in North America were not satisfied. Colonists there grew increasingly unhappy with both the king and Parliament.

A New Country Some colonists disliked the laws and taxes that the British government had put in place. In addition, colonists were used to ruling themselves through their own assemblies, or congresses. They also believed that a faraway king and parliament could not understand life in America.

Many colonists protested British laws they thought were unfair. As conflict continued, colonial leaders met to resolve the crisis. At this meeting, called the First Continental Congress, the delegates decided to resist the British. Not all colonists wanted independence, but they did want to have fair laws and to feel safe. They created militias, or groups of armed men, to protect themselves from the British troops stationed in the colonies.

The American Revolution began in April 1775 when a militia exchanged fire with British troops. In 1776, the colonial leaders gathered again. At that meeting, Thomas Jefferson wrote the **Declaration of Independence**, a document declaring the colonies' independence from British rule. Like Magna Carta, the Declaration stated people's rights to certain liberties.

Reading Check
Analyze Events
What events led to the creation of the English Bill of Rights?

George Washington led the colonial army to victory over the British in the American Revolution. In this 1851 copy of a famous painting, Washington is shown leading his troops across the Delaware River to attack British forces.

The Declaration begins with a sentence that also expresses Enlightenment **ideals**:

> "We hold these truths to be self-evident, that all men are created equal, that they are endowed by their Creator with certain unalienable Rights, that among these are Life, Liberty and the Pursuit of Happiness."
>
> –from the Declaration of Independence

In this passage, the word *unalienable* means "cannot be taken away." This wording shows the influence of John Locke's ideas about natural rights. In addition, the Declaration of Independence said that people unhappy with their government had the right to change it. This statement builds on the ideas of Rousseau as well as Locke.

The Declaration of Independence was signed by representatives from all of the colonies. A new nation—the United States of America—was born.

A New Government In 1783, the British government finally agreed to end the fighting and recognize the United States. American leaders then met to form a new government. They wrote a set of rules called the Articles of Confederation. Under the Articles, the central government was weak. The Americans were afraid that a strong central government would

Signers of the U.S. Declaration of Independence

An Unwritten Constitution

A constitution is a set of laws for how a country's government operates. Many people might think all constitutions are a single written document. The U.S. Constitution, for example, is made up of a single document and its amendments, or changes that have been added over time to the original. Great Britain, however, has what has become known as an "unwritten constitution." Rather than operating according to rules set forth in one written document, Great Britain has a collection of documents, court decisions, laws, and traditions that has developed as its constitution over time. The English Bill of Rights is a key part of what has become known as Great Britain's "unwritten constitution."

Analyze Information
How is Great Britain's "unwritten constitution" different from the U.S. Constitution?

The English Bill of Rights guaranteed free speech for members of Parliament.

be too much like a monarchy. However, over time, the weak government didn't serve the needs of the people. A new plan for the American government was needed.

Virginia farmer James Madison was a main author of the new plan—the Constitution. This document reflected the ideas of Montesquieu, who had proposed the separation of powers in 1748. In keeping with Montesquieu's idea, the Constitution divided power among three branches.

- The legislative branch, called Congress, would make laws.
- The executive branch, headed by the president, would enforce laws.
- The judicial branch, or court system, would interpret laws.

The Constitution did not address the rights of women or slaves, and men without land couldn't vote. It did, however, guarantee the rights of most citizens.

Locke's idea of the social contract was included in statements ensuring that the government existed to serve the common good of the people. In addition, some states approved the Constitution only on the condition that a Bill of Rights was added. This document—the first ten amendments to the Constitution—further guaranteed the individual rights and liberties of the new nation's citizens.

Reading Check
Find Main Ideas
How were ideas of Enlightenment thinkers reflected in the American Revolution and the new American government?

The French Revolution

As the Americans fought for and created a new nation, the French people paid close attention to the events. They were inspired by the Americans to fight for their own rights.

Documents of Democracy

The growth of modern democracy was greatly influenced by several key documents.

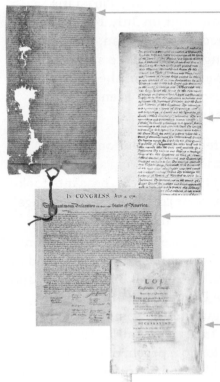

Magna Carta (1215)

- Limited the power of the monarchy
- Identified people's rights to property
- Established people's right to trial by a jury

The English Bill of Rights (1689)

- Outlawed cruel and unusual punishment
- Guaranteed free speech for members of Parliament

The U.S. Declaration of Independence (1776)

- Declared that people have natural rights that governments must protect
- Argued that people have the right to replace their government

The French Declaration of the Rights of Man and of the Citizen (1789)

- Stated that the French government received its power from the people
- Strengthened individual rights and equality

An Unfair Society The French king ruled over a society split into three groups called estates. The clergy were members of the First Estate and enjoyed many privileges. Nobles made up the Second Estate. They held important positions in the military, the government, and the courts.

Most French people belonged to the Third Estate. Included were peasants, craftworkers, and shopkeepers. The Third Estate paid the highest taxes but had few rights. Many members of the Third Estate were poor and hungry. They thought that the king didn't understand their problems. While the common people starved, King Louis XVI had fancy parties. The queen, Marie-Antoinette, also had little regard for commoners. She spent huge amounts of money on clothes.

Meanwhile, the government was badly in debt. Louis XVI wanted to raise money by taxing the rich. To do so, in 1789 he called together members of the three estates.

The meeting did not go smoothly. Some members of the Third Estate were familiar with Enlightenment ideas. These members demanded a real voice in the meeting's decisions. Eventually, the Third Estate members

During the French Revolution, about 6,000 women marched to the palace at Versailles to demand bread from the king.

formed a separate group called the National Assembly. This group demanded that the king accept a constitution limiting his powers.

Louis XVI refused to agree to the demands, angering many Parisians. Violence broke out on July 14, 1789. A mob stormed a Paris prison, the Bastille. After forcing the guards to surrender, the mob used guns from the building to free the prisoners. The French Revolution had begun.

Revolution and Change After the Bastille fell, the revolution spread to the countryside. Peasants there were afraid that the king and nobles would crush the revolution. In events called the Great Fear, peasants took revenge on their noble landlords for years of poor treatment. In their rage and fear, the peasants burned country houses and monasteries.

Other leaders of the revolution were taking peaceful steps. The National Assembly wrote a list of rights. It included some of the same ideas found in the writings of Enlightenment philosophers, the English Bill of Rights, and the Declaration of Independence. Called the **Declaration of the Rights of Man and of the Citizen**, this document guaranteed some freedoms for citizens and distributed the payment of taxes more fairly. Among the rights the Declaration supported were freedom of speech, of the press, and of religion. It also guaranteed that men could take part in the government.

Louis XVI was forced to accept the new laws, but new laws did not satisfy the revolution's leaders. In 1792, they ended the monarchy and created a republic. The next year, the leaders put Louis XVI on trial and executed him.

The French Declaration of the Rights of Man and of the Citizen stated that the French government received its power from the people.

Impact of the French Revolution

Thomas Paine was a supporter of the American Revolution. He also supported the cause of the French Revolution. He gave this speech right after the end of the French monarchy.

"It is no longer the paltry [small] *cause of kings, or of this, or of that individual, that calls France and her armies into action. It is the great cause of ALL. It is the establishment of a new era, that shall blot despotism from the earth, and fix, on the lasting principles of peace and citizenship, the great Republic of Man. . . ."*

—Thomas Paine, "Address to the People of France"

Analyze Historical Sources
What do you think Thomas Paine envisioned the "new era" to be?

Facing unrest, in 1793 the new French government began to order trials of anyone who questioned its rule. In the period that followed, called the Reign of Terror, thousands of people were executed with the guillotine. This machine beheaded victims quickly with a heavy blade. The Reign of Terror ended when one of its main leaders, Maximilien Robespierre, was himself executed in July 1794.

Although the Reign of Terror was a grim chapter in the story of the French Revolution, the revolution wasn't a failure. Eventually, France created a democratic government. Enlightenment ideas about freedom were powerful. Once they took hold, they would not go away. Many Europeans and Americans enjoy freedoms today thanks to Enlightenment ideas.

Reading Check
Summarize
What is the Declaration of the Rights of Man and of the Citizen?

Summary and Preview Questions about divine right led to struggles between the English monarchy and Parliament. Enlightenment ideas inspired the American Revolution and led to democracy in the United States. The French also formed a republic. Next, you will learn how Enlightenment ideas continued to influence world events.

Lesson 3 Assessment

Review Ideas, Terms, and People

1. **a. Summarize** What caused the conflict between the English monarchy and Parliament?

   b. Compare What was the connection between Magna Carta and the English Bill of Rights?

2. **a. Identify** What basic rights were listed in the Declaration of Independence?

   b. Explain How were Montesquieu's ideas reflected in the U.S. Constitution?

3. **a. Describe** How was French society organized before the French Revolution?

   b. Compare What did the Great Fear and the Reign of Terror have in common?

Critical Thinking

4. **Organize Information** Draw a graphic organizer like the one shown. Use it to describe the steps of the French Revolution.

The Spread of Revolutionary Ideals

The Big Idea

Napoleon's quest to rule Europe was eventually thwarted, but not before the ideals of the French Revolution spread throughout the continent and Latin America.

Main Ideas

- During the Napoleonic Era, Napoleon conquered vast territories in Europe and spread reforms across the continent.

- At the Congress of Vienna, European leaders tried to restore the old monarchies and ensure peace.

- Inspired by revolutionary ideals in Europe, Latin American colonies began to win their independence.

Key Terms and People

Napoleon Bonaparte
coup d'état
Klemens von Metternich
conservatism
liberalism
Simón Bolívar

If YOU were there . . .

You are living in Paris in 1799. You have complained for years about the weak, corrupt government officials who rule your country. Just days ago, however, a popular general led an overthrow of the government. His supporters say he is strong and patriotic.

Will you support this new leader?

The Napoleonic Era

After the French Revolution, a young general named **Napoleon Bonaparte** became a hero in France. He defeated rebels at home and foreign armies that threatened the new republic. Before long, Napoleon seized political power and made France into a great empire that dominated Europe.

The Rise of an Emperor By the late 1790s, the French had had enough of the violence. They wanted order and strong leaders, not the weak politicians who were running the country. In 1799, Napoleon took part in a **coup d'état** (koo day-TAH), the forceful overthrow of a government. Napoleon took the top position in the new government of France. Then in 1804, with his popularity soaring, he crowned himself emperor.

Napoleon was a remarkable military leader and showed his abilities as he began to take over the rest of Europe. He had learned the value of artillery as a young officer. He grouped his cannons on the battlefield to maximize their effect. Napoleon also stressed mobility. He quickly moved his troops into place to surround the enemy. Under his command and using these techniques, the French army won a series of dazzling victories against Austria, Prussia, and Russia. French troops conquered many countries and forced others to become allies of France. By 1810, Napoleon was the master of Europe. His empire stretched across most of the continent.

Between 1805 and 1808, Napoleon's armies defeated the armies of Austria, Prussia, and Russia. As a result, these countries were forced to become allies of France. This painting shows Napoleon during his victory against the Russian army at the Battle of Friedland in 1807.

Napoleon wanted an efficient government, and he created one. He put in place a system of public education. He made taxes fairer. He also created the Bank of France as a central financial institution. Perhaps most significantly, he issued a set of laws, called the Napoleonic Code, for his empire. The code reflected many of the ideals of the French Revolution. All men were equal before the law. All received the same civil rights, including trial by jury. All could practice religion freely.

With these reforms, Napoleon brought new liberties to the people of the French Empire. Yet his legal code denied rights to women. In addition, Napoleon did not allow fair elections. He restricted freedom of the press. Napoleon also tolerated no **opposition** to his rule, and he harshly punished those hostile to him.

Academic Vocabulary
opposition the act of opposing or resisting

The Defeat of Napoleon Great Britain was the one enemy Napoleon could not defeat. In 1805, the British navy destroyed the French fleet at the Battle of Trafalgar, off the coast of Spain. In response, Napoleon ordered all nations in Europe to stop trading with Great Britain.

When Russia ignored this order, Napoleon invaded with a force of 600,000 men. The decision was a disaster for the French. Smart Russian tactics and harsh winter weather forced the French into a bloody retreat.

With Napoleon's army weakened, Austria, Great Britain, Prussia, and Russia joined forces to defeat the French. These allies captured Paris in March 1814. In April they forced Napoleon to give up power and leave France. A year later, he returned and raised a new army. The British and Prussians, however, dealt Napoleon his final defeat at the Battle of Waterloo in Belgium in June 1815. The allies then sent Napoleon away to a small island in the Atlantic. He died there six years later.

Reading Check
Summarize
What changes did Napoleon bring to Europe?

The Congress of Vienna

Napoleon was driven from France in 1814. European leaders met in Vienna to draw up a peace settlement. They aimed to restore stability after many years of war.

Redrawing the Map Countries across Europe sent representatives to the Congress of Vienna. But the leaders of powerful Austria, Britain, Prussia, and Russia made all the important decisions.

Prince **Klemens von Metternich** (MEH-tuhr-nik) of Austria led the meetings. At first the congress offered generous peace terms to France. But after Napoleon returned in 1815, the diplomats were not so lenient.

> Explore ONLINE!

Europe after the Congress of Vienna, 1815

Napoleonic Empire, 1812

Boundary of the German Confederation

Interpret Maps

1. **Region** How many Italian states resulted from the Congress of Vienna's reshaping of territories?

2. **Location** How might France's location have contributed to Napoleon's rise and fall?

Following the Battle of Waterloo, they sent an army to take control of France. France had to give back the territory it had conquered. The French also had to pay 700 million francs to rebuild Europe. In addition, diplomats added and subtracted territory to reshape the kingdoms along France's borders. They did this to try to balance the strength of the different countries in Europe. After Napoleon, the diplomats wanted to make sure that no single European power could ever again threaten the rest of the continent.

Containing the French Revolution Metternich and the other leaders at the Congress of Vienna opposed the ideals of the French Revolution. They instead promoted **conservatism**, a movement to preserve the old social order and governments. The diplomats at Vienna wanted to return Europe to the way it was before the French Revolution.

The Congress of Vienna restored the old European monarchies. Royal families returned to power in Spain, Portugal, and the Italian states. In France, Louis XVIII took the throne, putting the Bourbon family back in power. The new king, however, did have to accept a constitution that left some of the reforms of the French Revolution in place.

Despite Metternich's efforts, the ideals of democratic revolution did not die. **Liberalism**, a movement for individual rights and liberties, gained strength in the following decades. In the 1820s, liberal uprisings erupted in Spain, Portugal, and a number of Italian states. But conservative forces rallied to preserve the old order. The dreams of liberals would have to wait.

Reading Check
Analyze Motives
What did the diplomats at the Congress of Vienna fear?

Latin American Independence

The ideals of the Enlightenment and the French Revolution also inspired uprisings across the Atlantic. European powers had ruled Latin America for 300 years. The people living in these colonies now wanted to control their own affairs. In the 1800s, they launched a series of revolts to throw off European rule.

Haiti, a Caribbean island under French rule, was the first colony in Latin America to gain independence. In the 1790s, Toussaint Louverture (too-SAN loo-vehr-TOOR), a freed slave, led a rebellion of the island's African slaves. Although Napoleon sent an army to retake the island, Haitian fighters defeated the French troops. In 1804, Haiti declared its independence.

Revolution in South America The movement for freedom quickly spread to the continent of South America. Here, the ideas of Locke, Montesquieu, and Rousseau had been widely discussed among the educated elite in Latin American cities. Many had begun to question Latin America's colonial status and to desire independence. The Spanish government had adopted a more liberal constitution in 1812, but it still denied colonists representation in the Spanish government and maintained rigid control over the colonies. Latin American colonists were angry at their continued lack of political and economic power.

Simón Bolívar

Simón Bolívar was born in Caracas, Venezuela. At the time of his birth, European powers governed Latin America. As a teenager, Bolívar moved to Spain to finish his education. He spent much of his adult life in South America, where he lived mostly in Venezuela and Colombia. He led independence movements in Bolivia, Colombia, Ecuador, and Venezuela, and he also helped liberate Upper Peru. The people there named their new nation Bolivia, in his honor. He later worked to build unity among Latin America's new countries and to establish the new nations as constitutional republics. Rebellions and unrest, however, defeated these efforts.

Summarize
What is Simón Bolívar known for?

Bolívar and Independence The revolutionary leaders **Simón Bolívar** (see-MOHN boh-LEE-vahr) and José de San Martín led independence movements across the continent. Bolívar condemned the Spanish rulers:

> "They have committed every manner of crime, reducing the Republic of Venezuela to the most frightful desolation [state of ruin]. Justice therefore demands vengeance, and necessity compels us to exact [get] it. Let the monsters who infest Colombian soil, who have drenched it in blood, be cast out forever."
> —Simón Bolívar, from *Proclamation to the People of Venezuela*

Bolívar's successes inspired other revolutionaries to fight for liberation. Independence movements flared up across Latin America. One by one, the colonies threw off European rule. Neither Spain nor Portugal could hold onto their New World empires. By 1831 a dozen Latin American nations had won their freedom.

Mexican Independence In 1810, Father Miguel Hidalgo, a priest who served a poor Mexican parish in Dolores, called his parish by ringing the bells atop the church. Instead of leading the people in prayer, Hidalgo issued what came to be known as *el grito de Dolores*—the cry of Dolores. Hidalgo urged the people of his parish to fight for rights and for economic justice for the poor. He demanded racial equality and the redistribution of land to the poor in Mexico. He also demanded independence from Spain.

Hidalgo was eventually caught and executed for his rebellion and his radical ideas about the poor. Another priest, José Morelos, took up the cause for Mexican independence. Morelos led many followers in the fight for four years, until he also was caught and executed in 1815. In 1821, Mexico finally gained its independence.

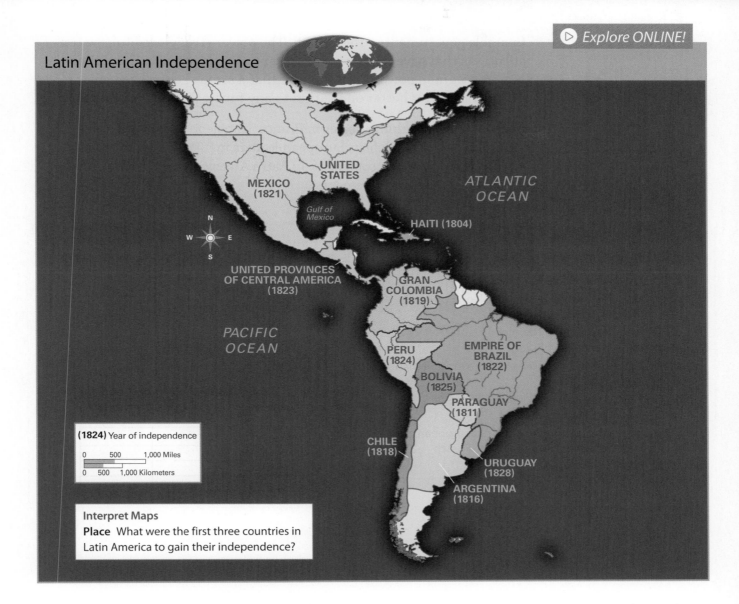

Latin American Independence

ATLANTIC OCEAN

PACIFIC OCEAN

UNITED STATES

MEXICO (1821)

Gulf of Mexico

HAITI (1804)

UNITED PROVINCES OF CENTRAL AMERICA (1823)

GRAN COLOMBIA (1819)

PERU (1824)

EMPIRE OF BRAZIL (1822)

BOLIVIA (1825)

PARAGUAY (1811)

CHILE (1818)

URUGUAY (1828)

ARGENTINA (1816)

(1824) Year of independence

0   500   1,000 Miles
0   500   1,000 Kilometers

Interpret Maps
Place What were the first three countries in Latin America to gain their independence?

Explore ONLINE!

Creating Constitutional Government Latin American republics looked to the United States, France, and Great Britain when they created their new governments. They adopted Enlightenment principles and used the U.S. Constitution as the basis for their own founding documents. The first Latin American constitutions, enacted in Chile and Venezuela (1811–1812), set up representative governments that guaranteed the rights and liberties of citizens. These first constitutions did not sufficiently separate the powers of government, however, and created a weak executive branch.

By about 1815, Latin American nations began to move away from truly liberal Enlightenment principles. **Conflict** between conservatives, who wanted the wealthy to control government at any cost, and liberals, who favored democracy, created turmoil. It was hard for inexperienced new leaders to rule under these conditions. Throughout the region,

Academic Vocabulary
conflict an open clash between two opposing groups

Reading Check
Find Main Ideas
Name three key leaders
in the movement
for Latin American
independence.

unstable governments rose and fell. The power struggle led to new constitutions that gave more power to a centralized authority. The elites not only wanted power, they thought that a strong centralized government would offer better opposition to any future Spanish interference.

Summary After gaining power in France, Napoleon conquered much of Europe. After his defeat, European leaders met in Vienna to try to restore stability to the continent. In Latin America, revolutionary ideals led to independence movements.

Lesson 4 Assessment

Review Ideas, Terms, and People

1. **a. Describe** What is a coup d'état?

   b. Explain What events led to Napoleon Bonaparte being forced to leave France in 1814?

   c. Evaluate How did the Napoleonic Code reflect the ideals of the French Revolution?

2. **a. Recall** Which four countries had the most influence at the Congress of Vienna?

   b. Contrast What is the difference between conservatism and liberalism?

   c. Evaluate Why do you think the old European monarchies opposed the ideals of the French Revolution?

3. **a. Recall** What was the first colony in Latin America to gain independence?

   b. Identify Who initially led the movement for Mexican independence?

   c. Draw Conclusions How did independence affect the new Latin American countries?

Critical Thinking

4. **Categorize** Identify two achievements and one failure of each leader. Use a chart like this one.

Leader	Achievements	Failure
Napoleon Bonaparte		
Klemens von Metternich		
Simon Bolívar		

Social Studies Skills

Accept Social Responsibility

Define the Skill

A *society* is an organized group of people who share a common set of activities, traditions, and goals. You are part of many societies— your school, community, and nation are just three. Every society's strength depends on the support and contributions of its members. *Social responsibility* is the obligation that every person has to the societies of which he or she is a member.

Learn the Skill

As a part of your school, community, and nation, you have obligations to the people around you. The most obvious is to do nothing to harm your society. You also have a duty to take part in it. At the very least, this means exercising the rights and responsibilities of membership. These include being informed about issues in your society.

Another level of social responsibility is support of change to benefit society. This level of involvement goes beyond being informed about issues to trying to do something about them. If you take this important step, here are some points to consider.

1. Few efforts to change society have everyone's support. Some people will want things to stay the same. They may treat you badly if you work for change. You must be prepared for this possibility.

2. Sometimes, efforts to improve things involve opposing laws or rules that need to be changed. No matter how just your cause is, if you break laws or rules, you must be willing to accept the consequences of your behavior.

3. Remember that violence is never an acceptable method for change. People who use force in seeking change are not behaving in a socially responsible manner, even if their cause is good.

This module was filled with the stories of socially responsible people. Many of them devoted their lives to changing society for the better. The revolutionary leader Simon Bolívar spent much of his life struggling for Latin American independence from Spain and to establish these new nations as constitutional republics.

Practice the Skill

Imagine you live in Latin America during the 1800s. You believe the Spanish government is oppressive and you want your colony to become an independent constitutional republic. But you know not everyone thinks the same way you do about a new government. Some people might report your thoughts or actions to the authorities. You might be imprisoned.

1. Would reading the ideas of Locke, Montesquieu, and Rousseau benefit society? Explain why or why not.

2. Are you willing to risk imprisonment for speaking out against the oppression of the Spanish government? Why or why not?

3. Would participating in the movements led by Simon Bolívar and other revolutionaries be a socially responsible thing to do? Explain why or why not.

Module 24 Assessment

Review Vocabulary, Terms, and People

Match the words or names with their definitions or descriptions.

1. British writer who argued that women should have the same rights as men
2. defeated rebels and foreign armies to make France into a great empire
3. a period also known as the Age of Reason
4. proposed the separation of powers
5. document that William and Mary had to sign before they could rule
6. spoke out against censorship
7. the idea that governments should express the will of the people
8. included life, liberty, and property in Locke's view
9. led revolutionary movements in Latin America in order to replace colonial rule with liberalism
10. argued against divine right in *Two Treatises on Civil Government*

a. Enlightenment
b. English Bill of Rights
c. Voltaire
d. John Locke
e. natural rights
f. popular sovereignty
g. Mary Wollstonecraft
h. Charles-Louis Montesquieu
i. Napoleon Bonaparte
j. Simon Bolívar

Comprehension and Critical Thinking

Lesson 1

11. **a. Identify** What three goals did Enlightenment thinkers believe the use of reason could achieve?
    b. Compare How was the influence of Greek and Roman ideas similar to the influence of the Scientific Revolution on the Enlightenment?
    c. Elaborate Voltaire and others have argued against censorship. Is censorship ever acceptable? Explain your answer.

Lesson 2

12. **a. Identify** Who were two important leaders in the American colonies?
    b. Compare and Contrast What ideas did Locke and Rousseau share? How did these ideas differ from most monarchs' ideas about government?
    c. Elaborate Do you think things would have happened the same way or differently in the colonies if colonial leaders had not been familiar with Enlightenment ideas? Explain your answer.

Lesson 3

13. **a. Identify** What event started the French Revolution?
    b. Analyze What basic ideas are found in both the English Bill of Rights and Magna Carta?
    c. Elaborate The way people interpret the U.S. Constitution has changed over the years. What do you think is a reason for this change?

Lesson 4

14. **a. Identify** List the four countries that controlled all the important decisions made at the Congress of Vienna.
    b. Analyze How were Napoleon's forces weakened and then defeated?
    c. Elaborate Describe the problems that faced South American nations after they threw off colonial rule.

Review Themes

15. **Politics** How did the English Bill of Rights and the Declaration of the Rights of Man and of the Citizen change the power of monarchs?

16. **Society and Culture** How would daily life have changed for a peasant after the French Revolution?

Reading Skills **21ST CENTURY**

Understand Points of View *Use the Reading Skills taught in this module and the passage below to answer the questions that follow.*

> "From whatever side we approach our principle, we reach the same conclusion, that the social compact sets up among the citizens an equality of such a kind, that they all bind themselves to observe the same conditions and should therefore all enjoy the same rights."
>
> —Jean-Jacques Rousseau, from *The Social Contract*

17. What is Rousseau's point of view about rights?

18. Who might disagree with Rousseau?

Social Studies Skills

Accept Social Responsibility *Use the Social Studies Skills taught in this module to answer the question below.*

19. Fill in the chart to answer whether each action is socially responsible, and give your reason for your conclusion.

Action	Is this socially responsible?	Why or why not?
Teach someone to read		
Throw litter on the sidewalk		
Cut in front of someone in line		
Vote		

Focus On Writing

20. **Write a Persuasive Article** Write an article on the ideas and benefits of the Enlightenment. In three to four sentences, introduce the ideas of the Enlightenment. In the next paragraph, discuss what you believe are the benefits of these ideas to society and government. Be sure you include your strongest argument about the benefits first. Then support your argument with your weaker points, and address any possible objections to your arguments. Conclude with a summary of your main points and a call to action—what you want readers of your article to do or think.

THE *American* REVOLUTION

The American Revolution led to the formation of the United States of America in 1776. Beginning in the 1760s, tensions grew between American colonists and their British rulers when Britain started passing a series of new laws and taxes for the colonies. With no representation in the British government, however, colonists had no say in these laws, which led to growing discontent. After fighting broke out in 1775, colonial leaders met to decide what to do. They approved the Declaration of Independence, announcing that the American colonies were free from British rule. In reality, however, freedom would not come until after years of fighting.

Explore some of the people and events of the American Revolution online. You can find a wealth of information, video clips, primary sources, activities, and more through your online textbook.

> "I know not what course others may take; but as for me, give me liberty or give me death!"
>
> —Patrick Henry

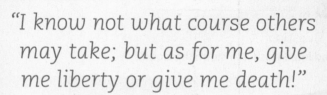

 "Give Me Liberty or Give Me Death!"
Read an excerpt from Patrick Henry's famous speech, which urged the colonists to fight against the British.

Seeds of Revolution
Watch the video to learn about colonial discontent in the years before the Revolutionary War.

Independence!
Watch the video to learn about the origins of the Declaration of Independence.

Victory!
Watch the video to learn how the American colonists won the Revolutionary War.

Industry and Imperialism

Essential Question

How did the Industrial Revolution and imperialism transform the world?

About the Photo: The steam engine revolutionized transportation and manufacturing. In this photo, a steam engine pulls an early passenger train.

▶ *Explore ONLINE!*

VIDEOS, including...
- The Spanish-American War
- Andrew Carnegie: The Prince of Steel
- Suez Canal

☑ Document-Based Investigations

☑ Graphic Organizers

☑ Interactive Games

☑ Animation: How the Panama Canal Works

☑ Interactive Map: The Spanish-American War

☑ Image with Hotspots: New York City in the Late 1800s

In this module, you will learn about a period of big changes that affected much of the world. Change came from the Industrial Revolution, war, and new political philosophies.

What You Will Learn...

Lesson 1: The Industrial Revolution 858
The Big Idea The Industrial Revolution created an economy based on factory-made goods, bringing sweeping changes to Europe and America.

Lesson 2: Imperialism in Africa 863
The Big Idea In the late 1800s, Europeans once again created colonies in Africa and became involved in Africa politics and economics.

Lesson 3: Europeans and Americans in Asia and the Pacific 870
The Big Idea In the 1700s and 1800s, Europeans and Americans swept into Asia and the Pacific and forced many political and economic changes.

Lesson 4: The Spanish-American War 876
The Big Idea Spain lost territory and the United States expanded into new parts of the world as a result of the Spanish-American War.

Timeline of Events 1750–1900

▶ *Explore ONLINE!*

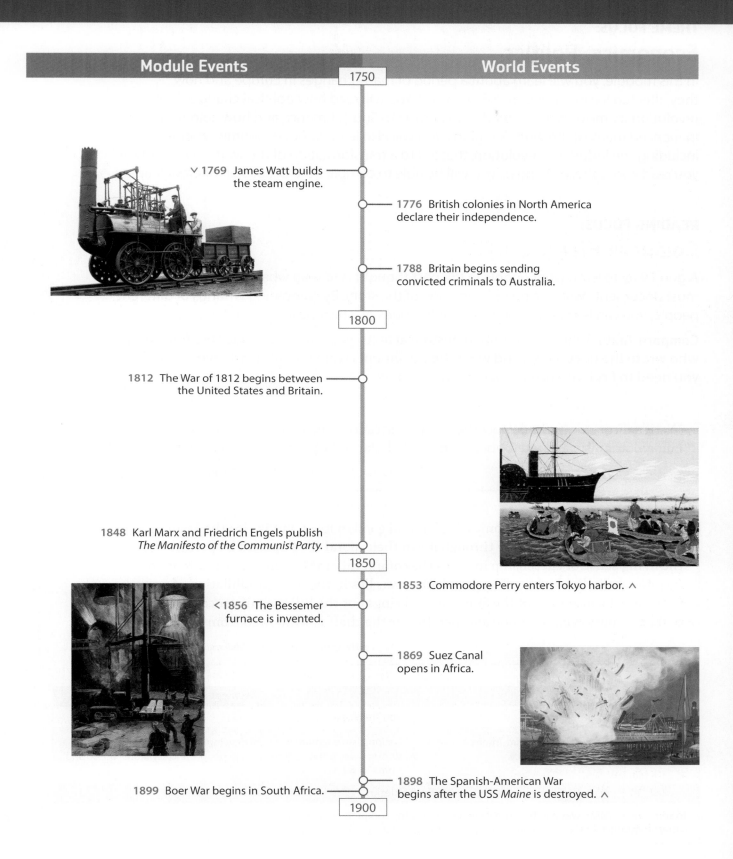

Module Events		World Events
	1750	
∨ **1769** James Watt builds the steam engine.		
		1776 British colonies in North America declare their independence.
		1788 Britain begins sending convicted criminals to Australia.
	1800	
1812 The War of 1812 begins between the United States and Britain.		
1848 Karl Marx and Friedrich Engels publish *The Manifesto of the Communist Party.*		
	1850	
		1853 Commodore Perry enters Tokyo harbor. ∧
<**1856** The Bessemer furnace is invented.		
		1869 Suez Canal opens in Africa.
		1898 The Spanish-American War begins after the USS *Maine* is destroyed. ∧
1899 Boer War begins in South Africa.		
	1900	

Reading Social Studies

THEME FOCUS:

Economics, Politics

In this module, you will learn about a period of many changes in Europe and how they affected life in other parts of the world. You will read how political changes like revolutionary movements spread from Europe to South America and how colonial policies influenced many of the world's regions. You will also learn about economic changes, including the Industrial Revolution, that led to a transformation of the world's economy. As you read about these changes, you will be able to compare the actions of different leaders.

READING FOCUS:

Compare Historical Texts

A good way to learn what people in the past thought is to read what they wrote. However, most documents will tell you only one side of the story. By comparing writings of different people, you can learn a great deal about the sides of a historical issue or debate.

Compare Texts When you compare historical texts, you should consider the following: who wrote the documents and what the documents were meant to achieve. To do this, you need to find the writer's main point or points.

> "Nationalism . . . attacks democracy, . . . fights socialism and undermines pacifism, humanitarianism and internationalism. . . . It declares the programme of liberalism finished."
>
> —Alfredo Rocco, *What Is Nationalism and What Do the Nationalists Want?* 1914

> "The State, therefore, is not only a high moral good in itself, but is also the assurance for the people's endurance. Only through it can their moral development be perfected, for the living sense of citizenship inspires the community in the same way as a sense of duty inspires the individual. . . . The grandeur of war lies in the utter annihilation of puny man in the great conception of the State, and it brings out the full magnificence of the sacrifice of fellow-countrymen for one another. In war the chaff is winnowed from the wheat."
>
> —Heinrich von Treitschke, *Politics*, vol. 1, pp. 54, 66–67

Document 1	Document 2
Rocco	Von Treitschke
Nationalism is opposed to liberalism, international cooperation, peace, and democracy.	Nationalism encourages moral development, a sense of duty, and, through war, brings out the best in people and separates the strong from the weak.
Both Sides of the Issue	
To some, nationalism was bad because it created unhealthy competition and led to war. Others thought it was good because it created a stronger state and better citizens.	

You Try It!

Read the following passages, and then answer the questions.

> "If Bonaparte was a conqueror, he conquered the grand conspiracy of kings against the abstract right of the human race to be free. . . . If he was ambitious his greatness was not founded on the . . . surrender of the rights of human nature."
>
> —William Hazlitt, *Political Essays, with Sketches of Public Characters,* 1819

> "There are only two alternatives: to take the chains of slavery or to fight for freedom. Bonaparte tyrannizes our independence by the most violent means: fire and death. . . . Are we going to allow Napoleon's eagles to come and seize our homes, outrage our families, despoil our GOD of his holy vessels, as they have just done in Portugal?"
>
> —Proclamation at La Coruña, 1808

Answer these questions based on the passages you just read.

1. What is the main point Hazlitt makes in his passage?
2. What is the main point made in the second passage?
3. How can a comparison of these two passages help you understand the issues that shaped people's attitudes toward the French emperor?

As you read this module, think about the kinds of historical documents that needed to be compared in order to write the module.

Key Terms and People

Lesson 1
factory system
laissez-faire
socialism
Karl Marx

Lesson 2
entrepreneurs
imperialism
Suez Canal
Berlin Conference
Boers

Lesson 3
British East India Company
Raj
Guangzhou
spheres of influence
Boxer Rebellion
Aborigines
Maori

Lesson 4
Emilio Aguinaldo
José Martí
yellow journalism
Anti-Imperialist League
Platt Amendment

The Industrial Revolution

The Big Idea

The Industrial Revolution created an economy based on factory-made goods, bringing sweeping changes to Europe and America.

Main Ideas

- During the Industrial Revolution, new machines and methods dramatically changed the way goods were produced.

- Industrialization and the factory system brought a new way of life to Europe and America.

Key Terms and People

factory system
laissez-faire
socialism
Karl Marx

If YOU were there . . .

For years your father has woven cloth to make a living. But new machines can now weave cloth much faster than people can, and your father has lost his job. Many people you know are moving to the city to work in factories. Everyone has heard, though, that factory work is exhausting, is dangerous, and pays poorly.

What do you think your father should do?

New Machines and Methods

In the 1700s and 1800s, new inventions completely changed the way people worked. At the same time, scientific discoveries led to key advances in health.

New Inventions Starting in the early 1700s, a series of inventions completely changed the way goods were made. In this time, called the Industrial Revolution, machines in factories began to perform the work that before had been done by hand at home or in small shops. This period of industrialization began in Great Britain but soon spread.

The textile, or cloth-weaving, industry was the first to change. Inventions like the flying shuttle, spinning jenny, and cotton gin combined to greatly increase cotton production and speed up the weaving process. As a result, Great Britain's textile industry grew rapidly.

In 1769, James Watt developed an efficient steam engine that could power the new factory machines. Since iron was used to make steam-powered machines, demand for iron grew. In 1856, Henry Bessemer developed a way to cheaply convert iron into steel. Because steel was stronger than iron, the steel industry grew as well.

Another factor that contributed to the Industrial Revolution was the development of interchangeable parts. "Interchangeable" means "identical." Inventors began creating machines that produced interchangeable parts. These parts were then used to make a large number of other devices. That meant production of these devices grew quicker and less expensive. This gave rise to mass production, or manufacturing goods in large numbers.

New inventions also improved transportation and communication. Steamships made river travel faster. Steam-powered trains replaced slow animal-drawn carts. In addition, a new device called the telegraph made it possible to quickly send messages over long distances. As a result, the telegraph allowed people to communicate over vast distances. This, in turn, helped different cultures assimilate, or become similar to one another. Another invention, called the radio, would also increase this cultural exchange and assimilation.

The Factory System Before industrialization, each good had been individually made by hand. You can imagine what a slow process this was. Industrialization shifted production to a factory system. In the **factory system**, machines rapidly produce large quantities of goods in factories.

Advances in transportation improved the efficiency of the factory system. Trains and steamships could bring raw materials to the factories and carry finished goods away. Products could then be shipped quickly to faraway markets.

Key Inventions

New inventions in the 1700s and 1800s changed the way goods were made.

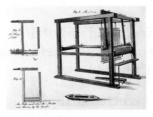

1733 Flying Shuttle

John Kay's invention sped up weaving so much that weavers outpaced their supply of thread.

1764 Spinning Jenny

James Hargreaves's invention made thread fast enough to keep up with the flying shuttle.

1856 Bessemer Furnace

The Bessemer furnace made steel from molten iron.

1769 Steam Engine

First used in factories, the steam engine later powered locomotives and ships.

1793 Cotton Gin

Eli Whitney's device efficiently cleaned cotton, helping U.S. growers meet British demand.

Analyze Visuals
How do you think these inventions made life easier for people?

The new industries that sprang up during this period needed money to operate. Bankers, merchants, and rich landowners provided capital, money to invest in activities that produce more money. Because they, not the government, were funding industrialization, capitalists wanted government to stay out of business matters. They wanted **laissez-faire** (leh-say-FAR), a "let things be" attitude on the part of government toward industry. Governments agreed and placed very few regulations on business.

Industrialization spread to the United States by the early 1800s. By the century's end, industrialization had spread to a number of countries in western Europe.

Scientific Advances The Industrial Age was also a time of increased scientific research. In medicine, Edward Jenner developed a treatment to prevent smallpox—one of the deadliest diseases of the time. Louis Pasteur discovered that germs cause disease, and he developed ways to kill them. These discoveries improved the health of millions and saved many lives.

In chemistry and physics, scientists made important discoveries about the structure of atoms, the small particles that make up everything in the universe. A husband and wife team, Marie and Pierre Curie, discovered two new elements. They named these elements radium and polonium. In 1911, Marie Curie won the Nobel Prize for Chemistry for her work. Major breakthroughs were also made in the fields of geology and psychology, the study of the mind.

Reading Check
Summarize How did new inventions promote industrialization?

A New Way of Life

The Industrial Revolution changed the work experience and way of life for millions of people in Europe and America. New immigrants and a new middle class would bring changes to cities all over the world.

New Immigrants Industrialization could not have occurred so rapidly without immigrants. Many Europeans left home and moved to Britain, France, Germany, and the United States. There were several push-pull factors for this movement. One push factor was increased population growth in countries such as Ireland. This led to a scarcity of resources and jobs. Another was the development of new transportation technologies, such as trains and steamships. These technologies made immigration easier and less expensive. Pull factors included resources, such as land to farm, and new employment opportunities in factories.

Governments also played a role in this population movement. During this time, the United States wanted to increase its agriculture production. To achieve this, it gave away government-owned land to farmers. This attracted many new immigrants to the United States.

The Workers During the 1800s, machines began to do much of the work once done by weavers, artisans, and farm workers. As a result, many people had no way to support themselves. Unemployed workers moved from farms to the cities and took jobs in the new factories. As a result, cities quickly grew.

With industrialization, more and more people went to work in factories to produce goods such as textiles. Although factory jobs were difficult and dangerous, they provided a living.

The rapid growth of cities led to social, economic, and political problems. Factory workers faced difficult conditions. Working long days on the machines was tiring and dangerous. Wages were poor. Women and children had to work too, but for lower pay than men. Many workers believed they were politically powerless and that they lacked government representation.

In addition, industrial cities were harsh places to live in. Factories polluted the air. Housing was crowded and poorly built. Garbage filled the streets. Crime became a part of daily life in many areas.

Reform Because of these problems, some reformers wanted to replace the capitalist system. In its place, they promoted **socialism**, a social system in which businesses are either owned by the workers or controlled by the government. Socialists hoped that ending private ownership of industries would stop the poor treatment of workers. German philosopher **Karl Marx** called for workers to unite in a revolution to bring down the capitalist system.

Romanticism and Realism

During the 1800s, two major artistic movements emerged: romanticism and realism. Romantic artists rebelled against the changes brought by the Industrial Revolution. They focused on beauty and nature and tried to show life as they thought it should be. Realists, on the other hand, attempted to show life as it actually was. They often dealt with the social and economic effects of the Industrial Revolution.

Analyze Visuals
Identify which artwork is an example of the realist style and which artwork is an example of the romantic style. Explain why you think this.

During this time, many workers joined together in voluntary labor associations called unions. A union spoke for all the workers in a particular trade. Unions bargained for better working conditions and higher pay. If factory owners refused these demands, union members could strike, or refuse to work. The establishment of unions became known as the labor movement. This movement underwent slow, painful growth in both Britain and the United States.

Eventually, reformers and unions forced political leaders to take action on working conditions. New laws reformed some of the worst abuses of industrialization. For example, the United States banned child labor and set maximum working hours. This and other reforms improved the workplace.

Over time, the reform movement spread. Many reformers in Britain and the United States fought for abolition—the end of slavery. Britain abolished slavery in 1833. In the United States, slavery ended in 1865, after the American Civil War. Women who fought for abolition later fought for women's suffrage, or right to vote. Reformers also fought for something called temperance. The temperance movement worked to limit alcohol consumption. They believed this would improve the lives of many people. Still other reformers worked to establish free public education. In western Europe, free public schooling became available in the late 1800s.

A Growing Middle Class Some people benefited more than others from the changes of the 1800s. The middle class grew to include factory managers, merchants, clerks, engineers, doctors, and other well-educated professionals. People in the middle class earned good incomes and could afford comfortable lives. This gave them time to help solve social issues.

The middle and upper classes also had time to read, visit museums, and attend plays and concerts. Two major trends in the arts competed for their attention. Romanticism stressed beauty, nature, emotions, and simpler times. Realism tried to show everyday life as it really was.

Summary and Preview New inventions shifted the production of goods to factories. As a result, work experiences changed, cities grew, and the middle class expanded. Next, you will learn about imperialism and its effects in Africa.

Reading Check
Find Main Ideas
What changes did industrialization bring about?

Lesson 1 Assessment

Review Ideas, Terms, and People

1. a. **Describe** What were some transportation and communication advances during the Industrial Revolution?

   b. **Contrast** How did work under the factory system differ from work done at home or in small shops?

2. a. **Recall** What led to the rapid growth of cities?

   b. **Contrast** What is the main difference between capitalism and socialism?

   c. **Summarize** Which social issues did reformers work to solve in the 1800s?

Critical Thinking

3. **Sequence** Using your notes, complete a diagram like this one. In the boxes, explain how each change in society led to the one that follows.

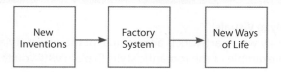

New Inventions → Factory System → New Ways of Life

Imperialism in Africa

The Big Idea

In the late 1800s, Europeans once again created colonies in Africa and became involved in African politics and economics.

Main Ideas

- The search for raw materials led to a new wave of European involvement in Africa.
- The Scramble for Africa was a race by Europeans to form colonies there.
- Some Africans resisted rule by Europeans.

Key Terms and People

entrepreneurs
imperialism
Suez Canal
Berlin Conference
Boers

If YOU lived there . . .

You are the chief of an African tribe in 1890. For many years, your people have been at war with a tribe that lives in the next valley. One day, however, a warrior from that tribe delivers a message to you. His chief has been approached by soldiers with strange clothes and weapons. They say that both tribes are now part of a colony that belongs to a place called England. The other chief wants to know how you will deal with these strangers.

How will you respond to the other chief?

New Involvement in Africa

When Europeans first arrived in Africa in the 1400s, they hoped to get rich through trade. For centuries, controlling the trade of rare products from distant lands had been the surest road to wealth in Europe. The merchants who brought spices, silks, and other goods from Asia had been among the richest people on the continent.

With the beginning of the Industrial Revolution in the 1700s, however, a new road to riches emerged. Europeans found that they could become rich by building factories and making products that other people wanted, such as cheap cloth, tools, or steel. In order to make products, business owners needed raw materials. However, Europe did not have sufficient resources to supply all the factories that were opening. Where were these resources to come from?

The Quest for Raw Materials By the 1880s, Europeans decided that the best way to get resources was to create new colonies. They wanted these colonies to be located in places that had abundant resources not available in Europe.

One such place was Africa. Since the slave trade had ended in the early 1800s, few Europeans had paid much attention to Africa. Unless they could make a huge fortune in Africa, most people did not care what happened there.

Ivory traders collected elephant tusks in Africa for export to Europe.

As factory owners looked for new sources of raw materials, though, some people took another look at Africa. For the first time, they noticed its huge open spaces and its mineral wealth.

Once again, Europeans rushed to Africa to establish colonies. Most of these new colonists who headed to Africa in the 1800s were **entrepreneurs**, or independent businesspeople. In Africa they built mines, plantations, and trade routes with the dream of growing rich.

Cultural Interference Although they were in Africa to get rich, the European entrepreneurs who moved there frequently became involved in local affairs. Often, they became involved because they thought their ideas about government and culture were better than native African ways. As a result, they often tried to impose their own ideas on the local people. This sort of attempt to dominate a country's government, trade, or culture is called **imperialism**.

European imperialists justified their behavior by claiming that they were improving the lives of Africans. In fact, many Europeans saw it as their duty to introduce their customs and **values** to what they saw as a backward land. They forced Africans to assimilate, or adopt, many elements of European culture. As a result, thousands of Africans became Christian and learned to speak European languages.

Imperialism had other effects on the lives of Africans. During the early 1900s, several famines occurred across the continent. Often, these famines began because of a lack of rain. However, the production of cash crops in African colonies made the famines worse. Instead of growing food

Academic Vocabulary
values ideas that people hold dear and try to live by

Diamond Mining

Among the resources that caught the eye of European entrepreneurs in Africa were diamonds. First discovered in South Africa in 1867, diamonds were extremely profitable. South Africa soon became the world's leading diamond producer. Nearly all of that production was done by one company, the De Beers Consolidated Mine Company, owned by English business leader Cecil Rhodes. De Beers mines, like the one shown here at Kimberley, poured the gems into the world market.

South Africa is still one of the world's leading diamond producers, and De Beers is one of the leading companies. By controlling the supply of diamonds available to the public, the company can command higher prices for its gems.

Analyze Information
How can a company control the supply of a product?

for Africans, many plantations produced raw materials for Europeans. This led to food shortages. Thousands of Africans died as a result.

One firm believer in imperialism was English business owner Cecil Rhodes. He believed that British culture was superior to all others and that it was his duty to share it with the people of Africa. To that end, he planned to build a long railroad between Britain's colonies in Egypt and South Africa. He thought this railroad would bring what he saw as the benefits of British civilization to all Africans. However, his railroad was never completed.

Government Involvement Although the early imperialists in Africa were entrepreneurs, national governments soon became involved as well. Their involvement was largely the result of rivalries between countries. Each country wanted to control more land and more colonies than its rivals did. As a result, countries tried to create as many colonies as they could and to block others from creating colonies.

For example, France began to form colonies in West Africa in the late 1800s. Seeing this, the British hurried to the area to form colonies of their own. Before long, Germany and Italy also sought to control land in West Africa. They did not want to be seen as less powerful than either France or Britain.

The English government also got involved in Africa for other reasons. The British wanted to protect the **Suez Canal**, a waterway built in Egypt in the 1860s to connect the Mediterranean and Red Seas. The building of the canal had been funded by the Suez Canal Company. At first, this company consisted of French and Egyptian investors. Later, the British government

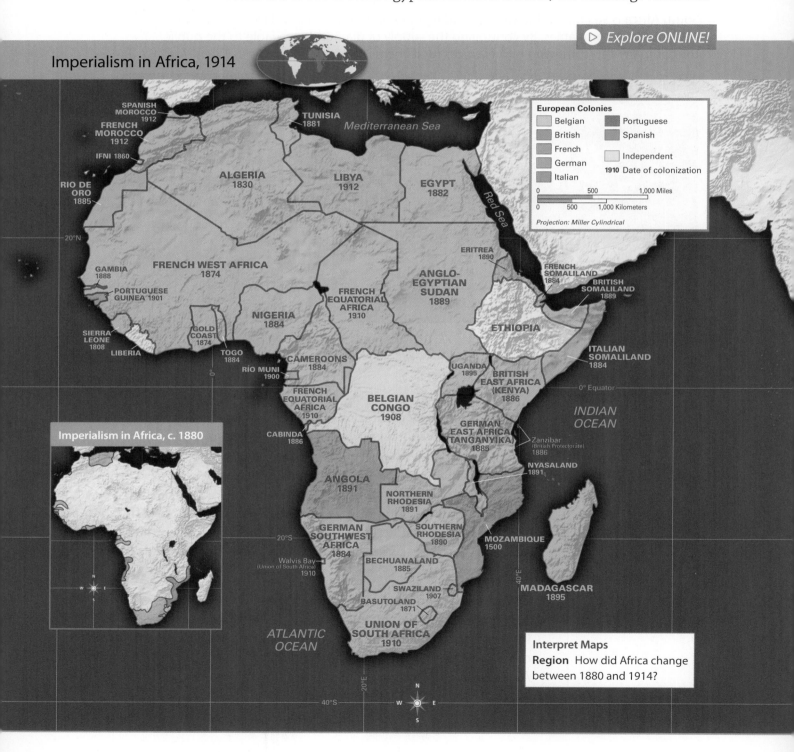

▶ *Explore ONLINE!*

Imperialism in Africa, 1914

European Colonies

Belgian	Portuguese
British	Spanish
French	
German	Independent
Italian	

1910 Date of colonization

0 — 500 — 1,000 Miles
0 — 500 — 1,000 Kilometers

Projection: Miller Cylindrical

SPANISH MOROCCO 1912
FRENCH MOROCCO 1912
IFNI 1860
RIO DE ORO 1885
TUNISIA 1881
Mediterranean Sea
ALGERIA 1830
LIBYA 1912
EGYPT 1882
Red Sea
GAMBIA 1888
FRENCH WEST AFRICA 1874
ERITREA 1890
FRENCH SOMALILAND 1884
BRITISH SOMALILAND 1889
PORTUGUESE GUINEA 1901
ANGLO-EGYPTIAN SUDAN 1889
FRENCH EQUATORIAL AFRICA 1910
NIGERIA 1884
SIERRA LEONE 1808
LIBERIA
GOLD COAST 1874
TOGO 1884
RÍO MUNI 1900
CAMEROONS 1884
ETHIOPIA
ITALIAN SOMALILAND 1884
FRENCH EQUATORIAL AFRICA 1910
BELGIAN CONGO 1908
UGANDA 1895
BRITISH EAST AFRICA (KENYA) 1886
0° Equator
CABINDA 1886
GERMAN EAST AFRICA TANGANYIKA 1885
Zanzibar (British Protectorate) 1886
INDIAN OCEAN
ANGOLA 1891
NORTHERN RHODESIA 1891
NYASALAND 1891
GERMAN SOUTHWEST AFRICA 1884
SOUTHERN RHODESIA 1890
MOZAMBIQUE 1500
Walvis Bay (Union of South Africa) 1910
BECHUANALAND 1885
SWAZILAND 1907
BASUTOLAND 1871
MADAGASCAR 1895
UNION OF SOUTH AFRICA 1910
ATLANTIC OCEAN

Imperialism in Africa, c. 1880

Interpret Maps
Region How did Africa change between 1880 and 1914?

Reading Check
Analyze Motives
What were three reasons Europeans went to Africa?

became a main investor. The British used the canal as a fast route to their colonies in India. This led to increased trade between Britain and Asia. In the 1880s, however, instability in Egypt's government made the British fear they would lose access to the canal. As a result, the British moved into Egypt and took partial control of the country to protect their shipping routes.

The Scramble for Africa

Desperate to have more power in Africa than their rivals, European countries rushed to claim as much land there as they could. Historians refer to this rush to claim land as the Scramble for Africa. The Europeans moved so quickly to snap up land that by 1914 most of Africa had been made into European colonies. Only Ethiopia and Liberia remained independent.

The Berlin Conference For many years, Europeans competed aggressively for land in Africa. Conflicts sometimes arose when many countries tried to claim the same area. To prevent these conflicts from developing into wars, Europe's leaders agreed to devise a plan to maintain order in Africa. They hoped this meeting would settle disputes and prevent future conflicts.

The meeting these European leaders held was called the **Berlin Conference**. Begun in 1884, it led to the division of Africa among various European powers. The conference left Africa a patchwork of European colonies.

When they were dividing Africa among themselves, Europe's leaders paid little attention to the people who lived there. As a result, the boundaries they drew for their colonies often divided kingdoms, clans, and families.

Separating people with common backgrounds was bad, but so was forcing people to live together who did not want to. Some European colonies grouped together peoples with different customs, languages, and religions. This forced contact between peoples often led to conflict and war. In time, the Europeans' disregard for Africans led to significant problems for Europeans and Africans alike.

The Boer War The Berlin Conference was intended to prevent conflicts over African territory, but it was not completely successful. In the late 1890s, war broke out in South Africa between British and Dutch settlers. Each group had claimed the land and wanted to drive the other out.

Dutch farmers called **Boers** had arrived in South Africa in the 1600s. There they had established two independent republics. For about 200 years, the Boers lived mainly as farmers. During that time they met with little interference from other Europeans.

Things changed in the 1800s, though. In 1886, gold was discovered near the Orange River in South Africa. Suddenly, the land on which the Boers had been living became highly desirable.

Among those who wanted to control South Africa after gold was discovered were the British. In 1899, the British tried to make the Boers' land part of the British Empire. The Boers resisted, and war broke out between the two groups.

The Boers did not think they could defeat the British in a regular war. The British had a much larger army than they did, especially once the British brought in troops from their various colonies. In addition, the British troops had much better weapons than the Boers had.

Instead, the Boers decided to wage a guerrilla war, one based on sneak attacks and ambushes. Through these tactics, the Boers quickly defeated several British forces and gained an advantage in the war.

However, these guerrilla tactics angered the British. To punish the Boers, they began attacking and burning Boer farms. They captured thousands of Boer women and children, imprisoning them in concentration camps. More than 20,000 women and children died in these camps, mostly from disease. In the end, the British defeated the Boers. As a result, South Africa became a British colony.

Reading Check
Analyze Effects
What were the results of the Berlin Conference?

African Resistance

The Europeans thought the Berlin Conference and the Boer War would put an end to conflict in Africa. Once again, however, they had overlooked the African people. For centuries, many Africans had fought against the slave trade. Now they fought against being ruled by Europeans. They refused to peacefully give up their own cultures and adopt European ways.

As a result, the Europeans who entered African territory often met with resistance from local rulers and peoples. Europeans were able to end most of these rebellions quickly with their superior weapons. However, two well-organized peoples, the Zulu and the Ethiopians, caused more problems for the Europeans.

Battle of Adwa

This painting of the Battle of Adwa was created years after the battle. The battle kept Ethiopia from becoming an Italian colony and is still celebrated today.

Analyze Visuals
Why might Ethiopians celebrate their victory at Adwa?

Cetshwayo, king of the Zulu nation, led his army to resist imperial control. Although Zulu resistance was fierce, the British defeated them in 1879.

Zulu Resistance
One of the most famous groups to resist the Europeans was the Zulu of southern Africa. In the early 1800s, a Zulu leader named Shaka had brought various tribes together into a single nation. This nation was so strong that the Europeans were hesitant to enter Zulu territory.

After Shaka's death, however, the Zulu nation weakened. Even without Shaka's leadership, the fierce Zulu army successfully fought off the British for more than 50 years. In the end, however, the superior weapons of the British helped them defeat the Zulu. Their lands were made into a new British colony.

Ethiopian Resistance
Although most resistance to European imperialism was ended, one kingdom managed to remain free from European control. That kingdom was Ethiopia. It is the only country in Africa never to have been a European colony. Its success in fighting the Europeans was due largely to the efforts of one man, Emperor Menelik II.

Menelik had seen that the strength of European armies was based on their modern weapons. He therefore decided that he would create an equally powerful army with equally modern weapons bought from Europe. As a result, when the Italians invaded Ethiopia in 1895, the Ethiopian army was able to defeat the invaders. This victory in the Battle of Adwa is celebrated as a high point in Ethiopian history.

Summary and Preview
In the 1800s, Europeans divided Africa into dozens of colonies. In the next lesson, you will learn how the arrival of Europeans and Americans in Asia lead to major culture changes.

Reading Check
Draw Conclusions
Why did many Africans resist European imperialism?

Lesson 2 Assessment

Review Ideas, Terms, and Places

1. a. **Describe** What role did entrepreneurs play in European imperialism in Africa?

   b. **Explain** Why did European governments want to form colonies in Africa?

2. a. **Summarize** What happened at the Berlin Conference?

   b. **Predict** What problems do you think the Berlin Conference caused in Africa after the Europeans left?

3. a. **Identify** Which African country never became a colony?

   b. **Make Inferences** Why did most African resistance fail?

Critical Thinking

4. **Identify** Use your notes and the diagram to the right to identify the causes and effects of European imperialism in Africa.

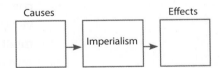

Causes   Imperialism   Effects

Europeans and Americans in Asia and the Pacific

The Big Idea

In the 1700s and 1800s, Europeans and Americans swept into Asia and the Pacific and forced many political and economic changes.

Main Ideas

- The British made India into a colony in the 1700s and 1800s.

- European countries used force to make China open its ports to trade.

- Led by the United States, the West began to trade in Japan.

- Britain colonized and allowed self-rule in Australia and New Zealand.

Key Terms

British East India Company
Raj
Guangzhou
spheres of influence
Boxer Rebellion
Aborigines
Maori

If YOU were there . . .

You are an Indian merchant, a dealer in cotton and silk cloths. You have just finished a long journey to the city of Kolkata with a shipment of your finest bolts of cloth to be sent to Great Britain. You are hoping that this shipment will make you enough money to last for several months. As you approach the docks in Kolkata, however, a British official stops you. He tells you that you will not be allowed to send your cloth to Britain anymore, because importing cloth hurts British companies.

How does this new policy affect you?

The British in India

As early as the days of the Roman Empire, Europeans had been fascinated by Asia. Traders had traveled back and forth between the two continents for centuries along the Silk Road, carrying precious goods in either direction. However, the journey along the Silk Road was long and dangerous, and few people dared it.

In the late 1200s, centuries after Rome fell, the Italian merchant Marco Polo traveled to China. When he returned home, Polo published an account of his journey, which soon became a bestseller. Still, few Europeans even dreamed of going to Asia.

Finally, in the 1400s Portuguese explorers successfully sailed to India for the first time. Other Europeans followed. Ambitious merchants built trading posts all along the Asian coast from India to China. However, Europeans seldom ventured very far inland. Their presence in Asia was limited mostly to the coast. That situation changed after the British moved into India.

British East India Company The people who changed the nature of European activity in Asia were British merchants. In the late 1700s, members of the **British East India Company**, a company created to control trade between Britain, India, and East Asia, arrived in India.

Although they had arrived to trade, the British soon became involved in Indian politics. At the time, India was ruled by the Mughal Empire. In the 1700s, that empire began to fall apart. One reason for this was a massive famine that struck India. Thousands of people died. As the Mughals lost control, the British took over. The East India Company brought in its own army to take control. Before long, the company controlled nearly all of India.

Academic Vocabulary
policy rule, course of action

The Raj Many Indians were not happy with the British East India Company's **policies**. In 1857, a rebellion broke out. The rebellion was led by sepoys, Indian soldiers who fought in the British army.

The fighting was brutal and lasted more than two years. Rebel sepoys killed British officers, women, and children. The British burned villages they suspected of supporting the rebellion.

As a result of the rebellion, the government took control of India from the East India Company and began to rule India directly. The period of British control in India is called the **Raj** (RAHZH), from the Hindi word for "rule."

During the Raj most officials who served in the Indian government were British, not Indian. These British officials considered themselves superior to the Indian people they governed. Most of them lived in separate neighborhoods and belonged to exclusive clubs. They had little contact with the common people.

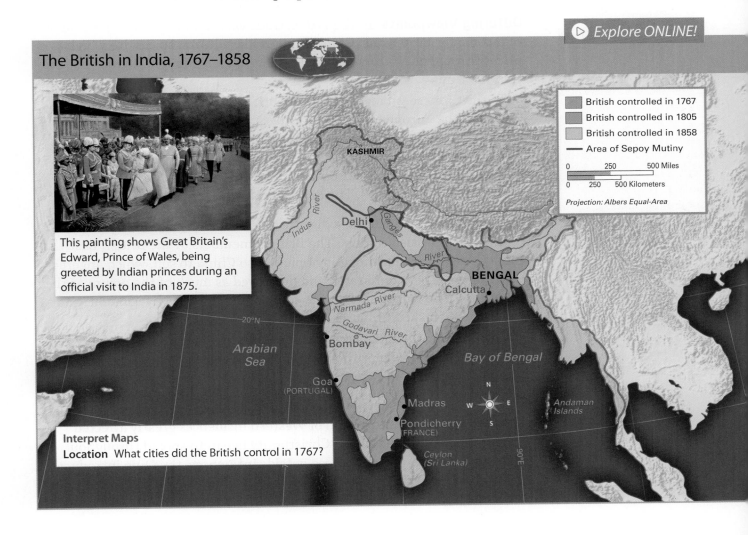

Explore ONLINE!

The British in India, 1767–1858

This painting shows Great Britain's Edward, Prince of Wales, being greeted by Indian princes during an official visit to India in 1875.

British controlled in 1767
British controlled in 1805
British controlled in 1858
Area of Sepoy Mutiny

0   250   500 Miles
0   250   500 Kilometers

Projection: Albers Equal-Area

KASHMIR

Indus River

Delhi

Ganges River

BENGAL

Calcutta

Narmada River

20°N

Godavari River

Arabian Sea

Bombay

Bay of Bengal

Goa
(PORTUGAL)

Madras

Pondicherry
(FRANCE)

Andaman Islands

90°E

Ceylon
(Sri Lanka)

Interpret Maps
Location What cities did the British control in 1767?

Changes in India Most of the British officials in India believed they were improving the lives of the Indian people by ruling them. They introduced a new Western education system and forced Indians to learn the English language. They also banned some Indian customs. At the same time, they invited Christian missionaries to teach their religious beliefs. This led to the spread of Christianity in India.

Many Indian people disagreed with these officials. They did not think their lives were better under the British. They wanted a chance to participate in government and resented having to give up their culture. Some Indians began to protest the presence of the British. They staged protests and boycotted British goods.

In the end, these protests had little effect on the situation in India. The British considered India too profitable a colony to give up. India was a major source of the raw materials, such as cotton, tea, and indigo, used in British industries. It was also a prime market for British goods. India became part of a global trade pattern between Asia and Europe.

Reading Check
Analyze Effects
How did life in India change after the British took over the government?

Europeans in China

While India was falling under the control of the British, similar events were happening in China. As in India, Europeans moved to increase their influence in—and their control over—China.

Differing Viewpoints In the 1700s, trade with China was a major source of income for Europeans. Chinese goods like silk and spices drew high prices throughout Europe. As a result, Europeans thought it vital that the trade continue.

To the Chinese, though, the trade with Europe was not as significant. They saw the Europeans as just another trading partner. In fact, China's rulers saw Europeans—and everyone else living outside of China—as barbarians. They did not want these barbarians living in their country. As a result, they allowed European traders to live in only a single city, **Guangzhou** (GWANG-JOH). The British knew the city as Canton.

Forcing the Issue In 1839, a dispute arose between the Qing government of China and British traders. The British, members of the British East India Company, were smuggling opium into China to sell, which angered the Chinese. They confiscated and destroyed as much of the opium as they could find. The British merchants complained to their government, and the British attacked China.

The British navy quickly captured the city of Shanghai. They forced the Chinese to open five more ports to European traders. China was divided into many **spheres of influence**, or areas over which other countries had economic power. Like India, China was now part of a global trade pattern.

Changes in China The growth of Western influences greatly affected Chinese society. For example, Christianity began to spread throughout the country. In response to these outside influences, the Qing introduced many changes to their culture. They thought that Western knowledge and technology was what had allowed the British to defeat them. As a result,

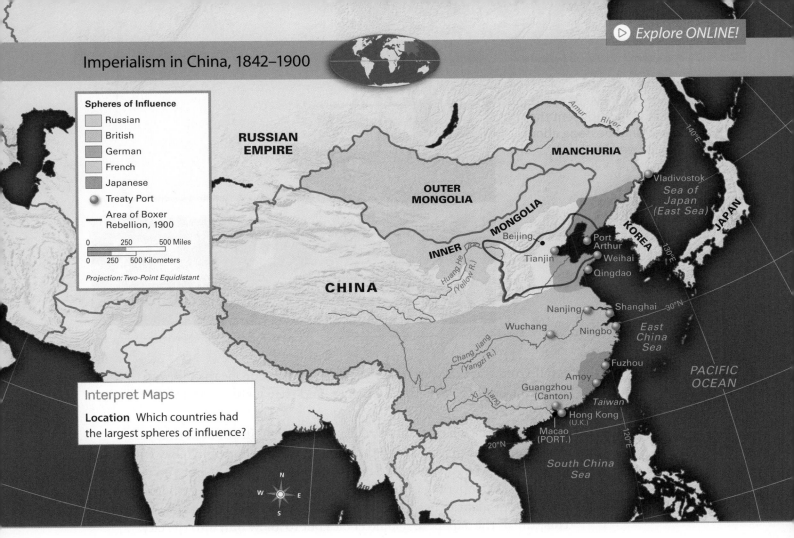

Imperialism in China, 1842–1900

▶ Explore ONLINE!

Spheres of Influence

- Russian
- British
- German
- French
- Japanese
- Treaty Port
- Area of Boxer Rebellion, 1900

0   250   500 Miles
0   250   500 Kilometers

Projection: Two-Point Equidistant

RUSSIAN EMPIRE

MANCHURIA

OUTER MONGOLIA

INNER MONGOLIA

CHINA

Beijing

Tianjin

Port Arthur

Weihai

Qingdao

Vladivostok

Sea of Japan (East Sea)

JAPAN

KOREA

Nanjing

Shanghai

Wuchang

Ningbo

East China Sea

Huang He (Yellow R.)

Chang Jiang (Yangzi R.)

Fuzhou

Amoy

Guangzhou (Canton)

Taiwan

Xi Jiang

Hong Kong (U.K.)

Macao (PORT.)

South China Sea

PACIFIC OCEAN

Amur River

30°N

20°N

140°E

130°E

120°E

Interpret Maps

Location Which countries had the largest spheres of influence?

China's leaders tried to introduce Western knowledge and languages to China. They also built Western weapons and ships.

These new weapons were tested in 1894 when China went to war with Japan. Despite their new weapons, though, China lost. The loss left China weak, and Western powers were quick to take advantage. They hurried to increase their influence in China. Americans worried that European nations would shut out American traders. To prevent this, the United States declared the Open Door Policy. This proposed that China's "doors" be open to merchants of all nations. Britain and other European nations agreed.

The Chinese were humiliated by this increased Western control. Some began planning action against the Europeans and Americans. In 1899, they began the **Boxer Rebellion**, an attempt to drive all the Westerners out of China. The Western powers easily put down the rebellion and accused the Chinese government of supporting it. The failed rebellion left China even more humiliated than before.

The West in Japan

Before the 1400s, contact between Europe and India and China had been rare but not unknown. In contrast, the Europeans had almost no knowledge of Japan at all. Unlike India and China, Japan had been able to isolate

Reading Check
Analyze Events
What led to the Boxer Rebellion?

This print shows the arrival of Matthew Perry in Tokyo Bay in 1853. Perry's hulking warships sent the Japanese a strong message about U.S. military power.

Analyze Visuals
How do the Japanese boats compare with the American ship?

itself from the West for many years. The only Europeans allowed to the islands were a few Dutch merchants, and they were restricted to the city of Nagasaki.

Japan's isolation came to a drastic end, though, in 1853. In that year, American naval commander Matthew Perry sailed into Tokyo Bay with a fleet of warships. The Japanese told him to sail on to Nagasaki, but Perry refused. He insisted on opening trade directly with Tokyo. He had been authorized by the U.S. president to use force if necessary to open Tokyo to trade. Faced with this threat, the Japanese had no choice but to allow him into the city.

Like the Chinese had before, the Japanese found their forced acceptance of the West humiliating. Yet Japan's new emperor, Mutsuhito (moot-soo-HEE-toh), decided the best plan was to modernize. He supported following the Western path of industrialization. Mutsuhito chose the name *Meiji* (MAY-gee) for his reign, which means "enlightened rule." During the Meiji era, the Japanese studied Western military tactics. They also copied Western economic practices. By the early 20th century, the Japanese economy had become modern.

Reading Check
Contrast How did Japan's response to the West differ from China's?

Australia and New Zealand

In the 1700s, Britain claimed land in Oceania. This is an area of islands in the Pacific, near Southeast Asia. The British had thought that Australia was uninhabited. In fact, Australia was sparsely populated by native people called the **Aborigines** (ab-uh-RIG-uh-nees). Aborigines are the longest ongoing culture in the world.

In 1788, Britain began colonizing Australia with convicted criminals. After they served their sentences, the newly freed prisoners could buy land and settle. Free British settlers eventually joined the former convicts. To encourage immigration, the government offered settlers cheap land. The population grew steadily in the early 1800s. Then it skyrocketed after gold was discovered in 1851.

European settlement of New Zealand grew more slowly. This was because Britain did not claim ownership of New Zealand. Rather, it recognized the land rights of the **Maori** (MAH-aw-ree). The Maori had settled in New Zealand between AD 950 and 1300. The arrival of more British settlers stirred conflicts over land. Responding to settlers' pleas, the British decided to annex New Zealand in 1839. In a treaty signed in 1840, the Maori accepted British rule. In exchange, Britain recognized Maori land rights.

Self-Government The colonists in Australia and New Zealand wanted to rule themselves. Yet they also wanted to remain in the British Empire. During the 1850s, the colonies in both Australia and New Zealand became self-governing. The people of Australia pioneered a number of political reforms. For example, the secret ballot was first used in Australia in the 1850s. In 1893, New Zealand became the first nation to give women full voting rights.

Status of Native Peoples Native peoples and other non-Europeans were excluded from democracy and prosperity. Diseases brought by the Europeans killed Aborigines and Maori. As Australian settlement grew, the colonists displaced or killed many Aborigines.

In New Zealand, tensions between settlers and Maori continued to grow. Between 1845 and 1872, the colonial government fought the Maori in several wars. The Maori were reduced by disease and outgunned by British weapons. Eventually, they were driven into a remote part of the country.

Summary and Preview The arrival of Europeans and Americans in Asia and the Pacific led to major changes in society. In the next lesson, you will learn about a conflict between the United States and Spain.

Reading Check
Contrast
How did the colonial settlement of Australia and New Zealand differ?

Lesson 3 Assessment

Review Ideas, Terms, and Places

1. **a. Define** What was the Raj?
   b. Sequence What led the British government to take control of India?
   c. Elaborate How do you think Indians felt about the attitude of British officials?

2. **a. Identify** Which country was the first to force its way into China?
   b. Identify What led to the Boxer Rebellion?

3. **a. Describe** How did the Americans force the Japanese to trade with them?
   b. Summarize What effect did the Americans' arrival have on Japan?

4. **a. Recall** What political reforms did people in Australia and New Zealand pioneer?
   b. Explain Why were the Maori driven to a remote part of New Zealand?

Critical Thinking

5. **Organize Information** Using your notes, complete the graphic organizer with details about Asian and Pacific civilizations. In the left box, describe the civilizations before Europeans arrived. In the right box, tell how they changed afterward.

India:
China:
Japan:
Australia:
New Zealand:
→ Europeans Arrive →
India:
China:
Japan:
Australia:
New Zealand:

The Spanish-American War

The Big Idea

Spain lost territory and the United States expanded into new parts of the world as a result of the Spanish-American War.

Main Ideas

- Many people living in Spain's colonies in both the Caribbean and the Pacific wanted independence.

- In 1898, the United States went to war with Spain in the Spanish-American War.

- The United States gained territories in the Caribbean and Pacific.

Key Terms and People

Emilio Aguinaldo
José Martí
yellow journalism
Anti-Imperialist League
Platt Amendment

If YOU were there . . .

You live in Spain in 1898. Newspaper headlines are screaming about the start of war in Cuba. Your father tells you that Cuba is one of Spain's last colonies in the Americas. Eager for independence, some Cubans are revolting against Spanish rule. Many Americans are sympathizing with Cuba's fight for independence.

Do you think Spain should enter a war against the United States over Cuba?

Spain's Colonies in the Caribbean and the Pacific

By the end of the 1800s, Spain's global empire had become smaller. In the Caribbean, Spain still controlled Puerto Rico and Cuba. In the Pacific Ocean, it controlled the Philippines and Guam.

Early Conflicts Spain's control of its colonies was weakening. In the Philippines, an educated middle class had developed. Many middle class Filipinos wanted independence. In 1896, revolution broke out across the islands.

One of the leaders of this rebellion was **Emilio Aguinaldo**. The following year, Spain and the rebels reached an agreement. Aguinaldo and other revolutionaries would leave the Philippines. In return, Spain promised to reform the colony's government. Yet many on both sides thought future conflict was unavoidable. Aguinaldo, exiled in Hong Kong, purchased weapons, while Spain failed to pursue reform.

In 1868, Cuba began a ten-year war for independence against Spain. In 1878, with the island in ruins, the Cubans gave up the fight. But some Cubans continued to seek independence from Spain. One of these was **José Martí**. He was only 15 when he first began speaking out for Cuban independence. In 1871, the Spanish government punished Martí by banishing him from Cuba. Martí remained in exile for about 20 years. He continued his career as a writer

and a revolutionary. In 1895, Martí returned to launch a second war for Cuban independence. Martí was killed early in the fighting, but the Cubans battled on.

American Interest The revolutions in the Philippines and Cuba were of interest to the United States. In 1890, an American named Alfred Thayer Mahan published an influential book. It was titled *The Influence of Sea Power upon History, 1660–1783.* Mahan claimed that a modernized navy would help make the United States an imperial power. Mahan also wrote that the United States should protect its trade. He argued that it should seize islands, including the Philippines and Cuba. Many Americans agreed with Mahan's ideas. American businesses had invested money in sugarcane plantations on Cuba. This meant that the United States had an economic interest in the country.

Meanwhile, newspapers in the United States were printing sensational news stories in order to attract readers. Often, the facts in these stories were exaggerated. This technique is called **yellow journalism**. The Spanish had forced many Cuban civilians into concentration camps. News stories about Spanish brutality in Cuba angered many Americans. They were convinced that the U.S. military should support the Cuban rebels.

War Erupts

Despite growing support for military action in Cuba, President Grover Cleveland did not want the United States to get involved. In 1896, William McKinley was elected president. McKinley was a supporter of Cuban independence.

The United States sent a battleship, the USS *Maine,* to Havana Harbor. Its mission was to protect U.S. citizens. It was also to protect U.S. economic interests in Cuba. On February 15, the *Maine* exploded and sank, with a loss of 266 men. The cause of the explosion was unclear. However, the American press immediately blamed Spain. "Remember the *Maine*!" became a rallying cry for angry Americans.

Shortly afterwards, U.S. newspapers published a letter written by a Spanish official. The letter insulted McKinley, calling him "weak." This made many Americans angry. President McKinley asked Congress for funds to prepare for war. Congress approved the money. On April 10, the Spanish governor of Cuba suspended fighting in Cuba. But it was too late. Congress declared that Cuba was independent and demanded that Spain leave the island. In response, Spain declared war on the United States.

The next day, Congress passed, and McKinley signed, a declaration of war against Spain.

War in the Philippines As soon as the Spanish-American War began, American warships raced to the Philippines. On May 1, they entered Manila Bay and destroyed the Spanish fleet there. The Americans sank or captured 10 ships. On the Spanish side there were 381 killed or wounded, but no Americans lives were lost.

Rebel leader Emilio Aguinaldo had also returned to the Philippines. In June, Filipinos declared their independence from Spain. On August 13, Americans took control of the Philippine capital, Manila. They were aided by Aguinaldo and other Filipino rebels. The Americans had defeated the Spanish.

War in the Caribbean In contrast to the navy, the U.S. Army was unprepared for war. At the start of the conflict, the entire U.S. Army had only 28,000 soldiers. New volunteers quickly raised that figure to more than 280,000. However, the army did not have enough rifles or bullets for all of these new soldiers. It did not even have appropriate clothing for the troops. Many soldiers received warm woolen uniforms to wear in Cuba's tropical summer heat.

U.S. troops landed in Cuba on June 22, 1898. The American forces were aided by Cuban rebels. The main U.S. force won several battles and then attacked and captured San Juan Hill. The Spanish fleet tried to leave Santiago Bay. In the battle that followed, every Spanish ship was destroyed. The capital city, Santiago, surrendered two weeks later. After their victory in Cuba, U.S. troops invaded Spanish-held Puerto Rico. The Spanish there surrendered with little resistance. Spain signed a cease-fire agreement on August 12, 1898.

Reading Check
Compare How was fighting in the Pacific and the Caribbean similar?

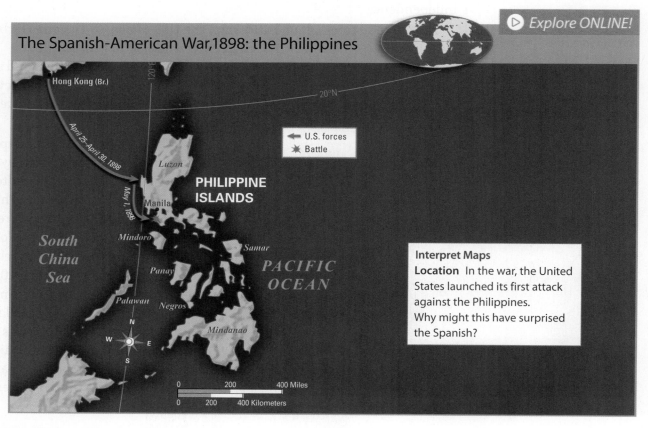

The Spanish-American War, 1898: the Philippines

Explore ONLINE!

Hong Kong (Br.)

20°N

120°E

April 25–April 30, 1898

Luzon

PHILIPPINE ISLANDS

May 1, 1898

Manila

← U.S. forces
✳ Battle

South China Sea

Mindoro

Samar

Panay

PACIFIC OCEAN

Palawan

Negros

Mindanao

0 200 400 Miles
0 200 400 Kilometers

Interpret Maps
Location In the war, the United States launched its first attack against the Philippines. Why might this have surprised the Spanish?

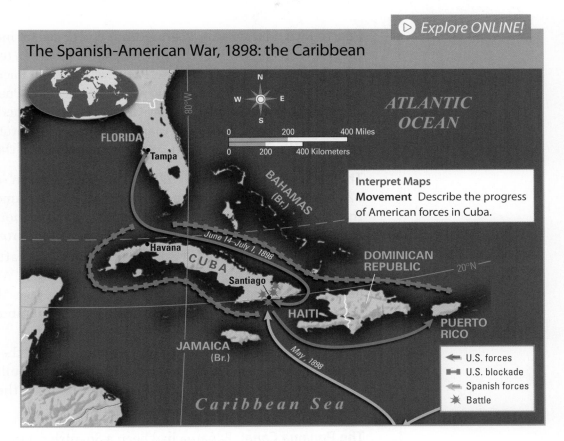

The Spanish-American War, 1898: the Caribbean

Explore ONLINE!

June 14–July 1, 1898

May, 1898

Interpret Maps
Movement Describe the progress of American forces in Cuba.

ATLANTIC OCEAN

FLORIDA

Tampa

BAHAMAS (Br.)

Havana

CUBA

Santiago

HAITI

DOMINICAN REPUBLIC

20°N

PUERTO RICO

JAMAICA (Br.)

Caribbean Sea

← U.S. forces
⊢■⊣ U.S. blockade
← Spanish forces
✳ Battle

The United States Gains Territories

A peace treaty between Spain and the United States was signed in 1899. It placed Cuba, Guam, Puerto Rico, and the Philippines under U.S. control. The United States was now a world power.

In reaction, some Americans formed the **Anti-Imperialist League**. This group opposed the treaty and the creation of an American colonial empire. They argued that the treaty threatened democracy because the people in those territories did not have self-government.

Cuba The United States had said that it would not annex Cuba. However, McKinley wanted to create stability and increase U.S. economic activity there. Therefore, he decided that the United States should occupy Cuba after all. He set up a military government and appointed a governor.

The United States also oversaw the writing of a Cuban constitution. The document included the **Platt Amendment**. This limited Cuba's right to make treaties. It also allowed the United States to intervene in Cuban affairs. Cuba was now required to sell or lease land to the United States. The Cubans reluctantly accepted the amendment, and U.S. troops withdrew. This amendment remained in force until 1934. The U.S. government stayed actively involved in Cuban affairs until the early 1960s.

Guam After the peace treaty was signed, Guam was governed by U.S. naval officers until 1950. That year, the United States declared Guam a U.S. territory. Decades later, Guam began taking steps toward self-rule. Today, it remains a commonwealth of the United States. This means that it has political and economic connections to the United States.

U.S. President William McKinley authorized the U.S. military to occupy Cuba. The United States then set up a military government there.

Puerto Rico Like Cubans, Puerto Ricans had hoped for independence after the war. Instead, the U.S. government made the island a territory. A debate over the new territory soon arose. People who lived in Puerto Rico were not considered U.S. citizens. A law passed in 1917 gave Puerto Ricans U.S. citizenship. However, another 30 years passed before Puerto Ricans could elect their own governor. Today, the island has its own constitution and elected officials. Like Guam, Puerto Rico is a commonwealth of the United States.

The Philippines Spain surrendered the Philippines in return for a $20 million payment from the United States. Many Americans believed that the islands were important for military and economic reasons. Annexing the islands would keep European nations from seizing them.

Filipinos had expected to gain their independence after the war. After all, they had helped U.S. forces capture Manila. When this did not happen, rebels led by Emilio Aguinaldo started a guerrilla war against the American forces. Hundreds of thousands of Filipinos died before the conflict ended in 1902.

After that, the United States promised to prepare the Philippine people for self-rule. To achieve this goal, the United States built roads, railroads, and hospitals. It also set up school systems. In 1946, the United States granted full independence to the Philippines.

The Panama Canal Panama had been a Spanish colony, and later it was part of Colombia. But in 1903, with support from the United States, Panama declared its independence. It also signed a treaty that gave the United States the right to a strip of land at the narrowest point of the country. Here, construction began on the Panama Canal, which was completed in 1914. The Panama Canal allowed ships to cross between the Atlantic and Pacific Oceans without having to sail all the way around South America. The United States held the so-called "canal zone" as its territory until December 31, 1999. That is when the canal zone and the canal were returned to the government of Panama.

Reading Check
Summarize
What areas did the United States control as a result of the war?

Summary The United States fought a war with Spain. Afterward, it gained new territories in the Pacific and Caribbean regions.

Lesson 4 Assessment

Review Ideas, Terms, and People

1. **a. Identify** Who was Emilio Aguinaldo?

   b. Analyze How did yellow journalism affect U.S. support for military action in Cuba?

2. **a. Recall** Where did the first U.S. victory in the war occur?

   b. Explain Why was "Remember the !" an American rallying cry?

3. **a. Draw Conclusions** How was the Spanish-American War a reflection of U.S. imperialism?

   b. Analyze Why did some Americans oppose the annexation of the Philippines?

Critical Thinking

4. **Organize Information** Draw a diagram like this one. Use it to show causes and effects of the Spanish-American War.

Causes	Effects

Social Studies Skills

Create and Interpret Databases

Define the Skill

A *database* is an organized collection of data, or information. Databases help people find and retrieve information on a specific topic quickly and easily. Learning how to interpret a database will help you learn how to create one.

Learn the Skill

Follow these steps to create and interpret databases.

1. **Determine the order of presentation of information.** For example, will you list items from largest to smallest? from oldest to newest?

2. **Identify the entries included under each heading.** Databases focus on specific topics or subjects.

3. **Ask yourself what kinds of data to include.** Your choice of data will provide the column headings.

Practice the Skill

Analyze the database. Then answer the following questions.

1. What is the title of the database?

2. What is the order of presentation of information?

3. What conclusions can you draw from the information in the database?

American Casualties During the Spanish-American War			
Type of Soldier	Killed in Action	Died of Disease	Died in Accident
Officers	18	119	4
Enlisted Men	190	3,729	97

Source:
http://www.history.army.mil/documents/spanam/ws-stat.htm

4. Create a database for major battles of the Spanish-American War. Provide information on the dates and locations of important battles. In addition, provide the significance of the outcome of each battle. Use information presented in the module to find the data. Use Internet resources to find additional information. Follow a chart format similar to the one above for your database.

Module 25 Assessment

Review Vocabulary, Terms, and Places

Complete each sentence by filling in the blank with the correct term or person.

1. One philosopher who wanted workers to unite in a revolution was _____.

2. A(n) _____ rapidly produces large quantities of goods.

3. Built in the 1860s, the _____helped increase trade between Britain and Asia.

4. The _____ divided Africa among European nations.

5. The period of British control in India is called the _____.

6. The _____ occurred in China in the late 1800s.

7. After the Spanish-American War, the _____ limited Cuba's self-rule.

8. _____ fought for Cuba's independence.

Comprehension and Critical Thinking

Lesson 1

9. a. **Recall** How did production methods change during the Industrial Revolution?

    b. **Draw Conclusions** Why did capitalists prefer laissez-faire policies toward industry?

    c. **Evaluate** What was it like to live in an industrial city in the mid-1800s?

Lesson 2

10. a. **Define** What is imperialism, and what led to European imperialism in Africa?

    b. **Sequence** What led to the Boer War?

    c. **Elaborate** Why do you think few groups were successful in resisting European imperialism?

Lesson 3

11 a. **Explain** Why were many Indians unhappy with the Raj?

    b. **Elaborate** Why did Europeans want to take over parts of China?

    c. **Describe** What changes occurred in Japan after Americans arrived there?

Lesson 4

12. a. **Describe** What events led the United States to declare war on Spain?

    b. **Analyze** How did the United States benefit from the Spanish-American War?

    c. **Predict** How might foreign countries view the actions of the United States in the Spanish-American War?

Review Themes

13. Economics How did advances in transportation affect the factory system?

14. Politics What impact did Europe's colonial boundaries in Africa have?

Reading Skills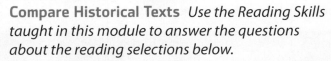

Compare Historical Texts *Use the Reading Skills taught in this module to answer the questions about the reading selections below.*

The first selection was written by an English reformer named Annie Besant. She wrote it in support of workers striking at a match factory. The second selection is an answer from a worker at the factory.

Born in slums, driven to work while still children, undersized because under-fed, oppressed because helpless, flung aside as soon as worked out, who cares if they die or go on to the streets . . . ? Girls are used to carry boxes on their heads until the hair is rubbed off and the young heads are bald at fifteen years of age. Country clergymen with shares in Bryant & May's draw down on your knee your fifteen year old daughter; pass your hand tenderly over the silky clustering curls, rejoice in the dainty beauty of the thick, shiny tresses.
—*The Link,* 23rd June, 1888

Dear Lady, they have been trying to get the poor girls to say that it is all lies that has been printed, and trying to make us sign papers that it is all lies; dear lady, no one knows what it is we have put up with, and we will not sign them. We all thank you very much for the kindness you have shown to us. My dear lady, we hope you will not get into any trouble on our behalf, as what you have spoken is quite true.
— *The Link,* 4 July, 1888

15. To whom does Annie Besant address her letter, and why?

16. Who is "they" that the worker refers to in her letter? What do "they" want the girls to do?

Social Studies Skills

Create and Interpret Databases *Use the Social Studies Skills taught in this module and the database you created to answer the questions below.*

17. What battle occurred on May 1, 1898?

18. What was the significance of the Battle of San Juan Hill?

Focus On Writing

19. Conduct an Interview With a partner, role-play a journalist interviewing a Spanish politician in 1899. First, review information about the end of the Spanish-American War. Then conduct your interview, having your partner take on the role of the politician.

Nationalism and World War I

Essential Question

How did new political and economic ideas influence global problems in the early 1900s?

About the Photo: This photo shows British soldiers using a trench during a battle in Belgium in World War I.

▶ *Explore ONLINE!*

HISTORY.

VIDEOS, including...

- The Paris Peace Conference Falls Apart
- Trench Warfare
- World War I Tech
- The League of Nations
- The Romanovs
- FDR's New Deal: The Tennessee Valley Authority Act

☑ Document-Based Investigations

☑ Graphic Organizers

☑ Interactive Games

☑ Image with Hotspots: Trench Warfare

☑ Image with Hotspots: Submarine Warfare

☑ Interactive Map: Russian Revolution and the Civil War, 1905–1922

In this module, you will learn about a period of changes in Europe that affected much of the world. Change came from revolutionary movements, world war, new political philosophies, and economic crisis.

What You Will Learn...

Lesson 1: Nationalism in Europe 888
The Big Idea Nationalism led to the creation of powerful nation-states that competed with one another to build large empires throughout the world.

Lesson 2: World War I 891
The Big Idea World War I, fought from 1914 to 1918, caused terrible destruction and changed Europe forever.

Lesson 3: Results of the War 897
The Big Idea There were many political, economic, and cultural changes in Europe after World War I.

Lesson 4: The Russian Revolution. 901
The Big Idea The Russian Revolution resulted in the world's first communist state.

Lesson 5: The Great Depression 905
The Big Idea The Great Depression was an economic event that affected the entire world.

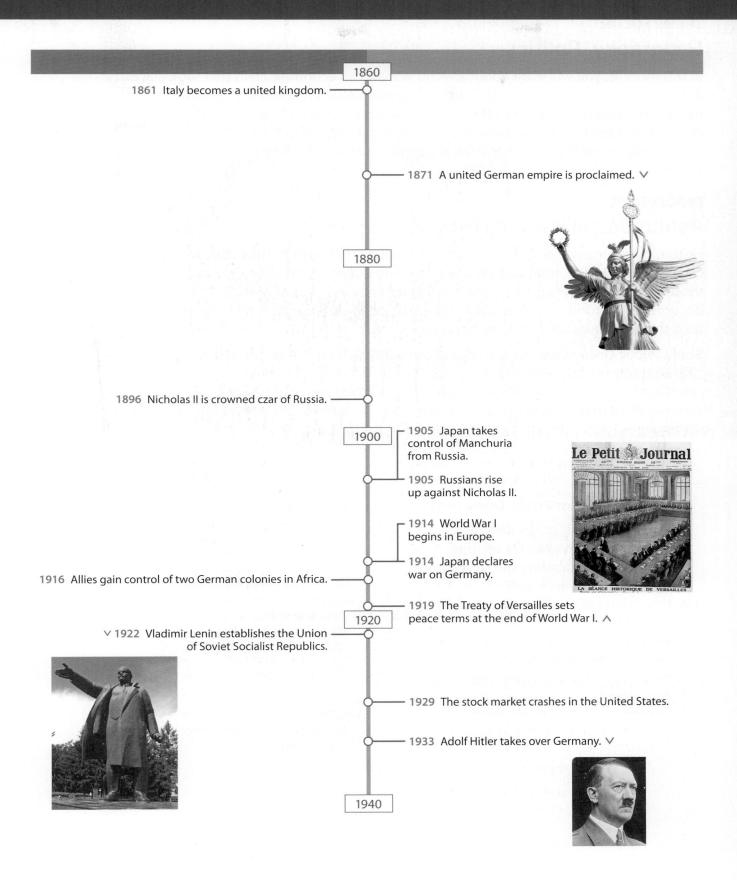

1860

1861 Italy becomes a united kingdom.

1871 A united German empire is proclaimed. ∨

1880

1896 Nicholas II is crowned czar of Russia.

1900

1905 Japan takes control of Manchuria from Russia.

1905 Russians rise up against Nicholas II.

1914 World War I begins in Europe.

1914 Japan declares war on Germany.

1916 Allies gain control of two German colonies in Africa.

1919 The Treaty of Versailles sets peace terms at the end of World War I. ∧

Le Petit Journal

LA SÉANCE HISTORIQUE DE VERSAILLES

1920

∨ **1922** Vladimir Lenin establishes the Union of Soviet Socialist Republics.

1929 The stock market crashes in the United States.

1933 Adolf Hitler takes over Germany. ∨

1940

Reading Social Studies

THEME FOCUS:

Geography, Politics

In this module, you will learn about a world war and an economic crisis that took place at the beginning of the twentieth century. You will also learn about the spread of nationalism before the war and the many challenges facing Europe after the war was over. You will see how throughout the world, geography and politics were intertwined as they influenced the way people lived during this time in history.

READING FOCUS:

Public Documents in History

Historians use many types of documents to learn about the past. These documents can often be divided into two types—private and public. Private documents are those written for a person's own use, such as letters, journals, or notebooks. Public documents, by contrast, are available for everyone to read and examine. They include such things as laws, tax codes, and treaties.

Study Public Documents Studying public documents from the past can tell us a great deal about the politics and society of a particular time. However, public documents can often be confusing or difficult to understand. When you read such a document, you may want to use a list of questions like this to be sure you understand what you're reading.

Question Sheet for Public Documents

1. What is the topic of the document?
2. Do I understand what I'm reading?
3. Is there any vocabulary in the document that I do not understand?
4. What parts of the document should I re-read?
5. What are the main ideas and details of the document?
6. What have I learned from reading this document?

You can often figure out the topic of a public document from the title and introduction.

Public documents often use unfamiliar words or use familiar words in unfamiliar ways. For example, the document on the next page uses the word *revive*. Do you know what the word means in this context? If not, you should look it up.

Many public documents deal with several issues and will therefore have several main ideas.

You Try It!

The passage below is from a speech by President Franklin Roosevelt given when many people were out of work during the Great Depression. Read the passage and then answer the questions that follow.

President Franklin Roosevelt's Inaugural Address, March 4, 1933 This great Nation will endure as it has endured, will revive and will prosper. So, first of all, let me assert my firm belief that the only thing we have to fear is fear itself. . . .

Our greatest primary task to is put people to work. This is no unsolvable problem if we face it wisely and courageously. It can be accomplished by direct recruiting by the Government itself, treating the task as we would treat the emergency of a war, but at the same time, through this employment, accomplishing greatly needed projects to stimulate and reorganize the use of our natural resources.

Answer these questions based on the passage you just read.

1. What is this document about?
2. What was the main idea of this document? What supporting details were included?
3. Are there any other words in this passage with which you are unfamiliar? How might not knowing those words keep you from understanding the passage?

As you read this module, think about why public documents need to have so many details.

Key Terms and People

Lesson 1
nationalism
nation-states
Giuseppe Garibaldi
Otto von Bismarck

Lesson 2
militarism
genocide

Lesson 3
Treaty of Versailles
League of Nations
reparations

Lesson 4
Nicholas II
Karl Marx
Marxism
Vladimir Lenin
communism

Lesson 5
Great Depression
stocks
Franklin Delano Roosevelt
New Deal

Nationalism in Europe

The Big Idea

Nationalism led to the creation of powerful nation-states that competed with one another to build large empires throughout the world.

Main Ideas

- Nationalism sparked independence movements in Europe.
- Newly created states in Europe sought to expand their influence and created larger nation-states.

Key Terms and People

nationalism
nation-states
Giuseppe Garibaldi
Otto von Bismarck

If YOU were there . . .

You and everyone you know are Italian. You are all proud of the language, culture, and history you share. But you live in a part of Italy that is ruled by Austria. Recently you have heard of a movement to unite all Italians into one kingdom to be ruled by Italians.

Will you support such an effort?

Nationalist Uprisings

Nationalism is devotion and loyalty to one's country. It typically develops among people who share a common language and religion and who believe that they share a common history or culture. Nationalism was a powerful force in the 1800s. It fueled the independence movements in Latin America. It also led a number of groups in Europe to create their own nations. As these new nations emerged, the map of Europe once again changed.

In the early 1800s, many peoples conquered by Napoleon resented French domination. They wanted to rule themselves. They also wanted to unite with others who shared their language, beliefs, and customs. Nationalists supported the idea of independent **nation-states**, self-governing countries made up of people with a common cultural background.

After Napoleon's defeat, growing feelings of nationalism led various groups in Europe to rebel against foreign control. While some succeeded, others did not. Greece, for example, won its independence from the Ottoman Empire in 1829. But a wave of revolutions in 1848 all failed. Hungarian and Czech (CHEK) nationalists in the Austrian Empire were defeated. Italians and Germans also failed in their efforts to form their own countries. They would succeed, however, in later years.

Reading Check
Analyze Causes
How did Napoleon's French Empire lead to nationalism in Europe?

New Countries Are Formed

In the latter half of the 1800s, feelings of nationalism continued to grow. German-speaking peoples came together under strong leaders, and many Italians supported efforts to live in a united Italy.

The Unification of Italy In the early 1800s, what is now Italy was divided into separate states. An Italian king ruled Sardinia in the north, but Austria ruled other northern states. The Bourbon family ruled Sicily in the south, and the pope controlled the area around Rome.

As nationalism grew, more and more Italians embraced the idea of unifying as one country. Nationalist efforts repeatedly failed, however, until Camillo di Cavour (kuh-VOOR) became prime minister of Sardinia. Cavour modernized Sardinia's army, formed shrewd alliances, and fought a war that drove the Austrians from the north. The other Italian states in the region then united with Sardinia in 1860.

That same year, **Giuseppe Garibaldi** gathered more than 1,000 passionate followers and overthrew the government in Sicily. A few months later, Garibaldi and Cavour joined their lands together. In 1861, Italy became a united kingdom. Ten years later, Rome became its capital.

German Unification Like the Italians, German-speaking peoples were divided into many separate states in the mid-1800s. But the spirit of nationalism had been growing among Germans since the days of Napoleon. As Italy unified, German nationalism became even stronger.

Prussia was the largest of the German states. Austria was its closest rival. In the 1860s, the Prussian prime minister, **Otto von Bismarck**, devised a plan to create a unified Germany under Prussian domination.

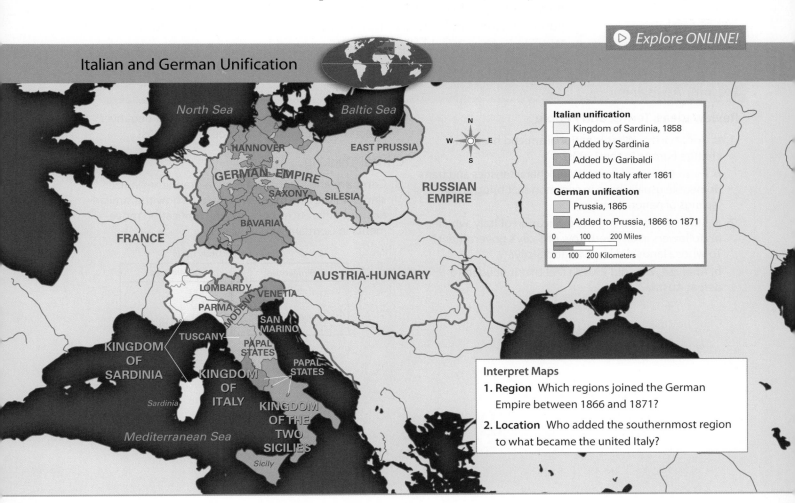

▷ *Explore ONLINE!*

Italian and German Unification

Italian unification
- Kingdom of Sardinia, 1858
- Added by Sardinia
- Added by Garibaldi
- Added to Italy after 1861

German unification
- Prussia, 1865
- Added to Prussia, 1866 to 1871

0   100   200 Miles
0   100   200 Kilometers

Interpret Maps

1. **Region** Which regions joined the German Empire between 1866 and 1871?

2. **Location** Who added the southernmost region to what became the united Italy?

Bismarck built a strong army and won wars against Denmark and Austria. Prussia's victories gave it more territory and secured its leadership of the northern German states.

Bismarck's next step was to wage war against France. Moved by nationalism, the southern German states sided with Prussia. They won a quick victory and agreed to unite permanently. Bismarck's plan had worked. The German Empire was proclaimed in January 1871. King Wilhelm of Prussia became emperor, ruling over all the German states except Austria.

Germany then concentrated on building its economic and military strength. It also joined other European powers in the fierce **competition** for colonies. European imperialism, or control of a region or country by another country, strengthened during this time. Europeans desperately needed raw materials for their factories. They turned to other continents to find them.

Academic Vocabulary
competition
a contest between two rivals

Reading Check
Summarize
Why was Prussia able to rule over most of the German states?

Otto von Bismarck played an important role in changing the government of the German-speaking people. Using force, he united the German states into one nation.

Summary and Preview The growth of nationalism led to independence movements and the unification of Italy and Germany. In the next lesson, you will learn about how nationalism was one factor that led to "the Great War" known as World War I.

Lesson 1 Assessment

Review Ideas, Terms, and People

1. a. Summarize What is nationalism and how did it change Europe in the 1800s?
   b. Form Generalizations What characteristics and traits do people usually have in common that bring about feelings of nationalism?

2. a. Summarize During the unification of Italy, who led his followers in an overthrow of Sicily's government? To whose lands did he then add Sicily?
   b. Analyze Why did Prussia feel that it needed to defeat Austria?

   c. Analyze What do you think were some negative effects of nationalism in Europe in the 1800s?

Critical Thinking

3. Compare and Contrast Create a graphic organizer similar to the one here, and use it to show the similarities and differences between the unification movements in Germany and Italy.

   Germany and Italy Unify

Similarities	Differences

World War I

The Big Idea

World War I, fought from 1914 to 1918, caused terrible destruction and changed Europe forever.

Main Ideas

- The onset of World War I can be traced to nationalism, imperialism, and the buildup of military forces in Europe.

- World War I was notable for new forms of warfare and fighting on several continents.

- The Allies' victory over the Central Powers came soon after the United States entered the war.

Key Terms and People

militarism
genocide

If YOU were there . . .

On a summer day in 1914, you're visiting the capital of your province. Suddenly, you hear angry voices and shouting in the streets. You run toward the noise and are told that a Serbian nationalist has just killed the heir to the Austria-Hungarian throne. You're upset and worried about what this might mean for your future.

How do you think Austria-Hungary will react?

The Onset of War

In the summer of 1914, war broke out in Europe. Many nations from around the world soon joined in the fighting. A number of factors led to this global conflict, which became known as World War I.

Underlying Causes By the 1900s, nationalism had created rivalries throughout Europe. People were willing to go to war to prove the superiority of their nations. At the same time, some groups that wanted to form their own nation-states were still ruled by others. For example, people in the Balkan Peninsula in southeastern Europe wanted independence from Austria-Hungary. They started nationalist movements that created tensions in the Balkans.

Imperialism added to Europe's problems. As you may recall, industrial nations competed fiercely for colonies. Many people believed that if their country had an empire, it was a great power. Also, European powers depended on raw materials from the colonies to fuel their industries. The race to grab overseas territories led to several crises that nearly resulted in war.

Another underlying cause of World War I was **militarism**. Militarism is the idea that a country should use a strong military to defend its interests. In the mid-1800s, Otto von Bismarck used the Prussian army to unite Germany. In the early 1900s, other European nations began to build large armies.

They spent heavily on modern weapons. These countries used their armies both to show strength and to threaten their enemies.

The rising nationalism, tense rivalries, and militarism caused European nations to fear each other. They began to make new alliances to protect themselves. Members of the same alliance promised to **defend** each other if any were attacked.

The alliance system would split Europe into two sides. The Central Powers, or Triple Alliance, consisted of Austria-Hungary, Italy, and Germany. Against them stood the Allies, or Triple Entente: Great Britain, France, and Russia.

Academic Vocabulary
defend to keep secure from danger

The assassination of Archduke Francis Ferdinand and his wife sparked the beginning of World War I.

▶ *Explore ONLINE!*

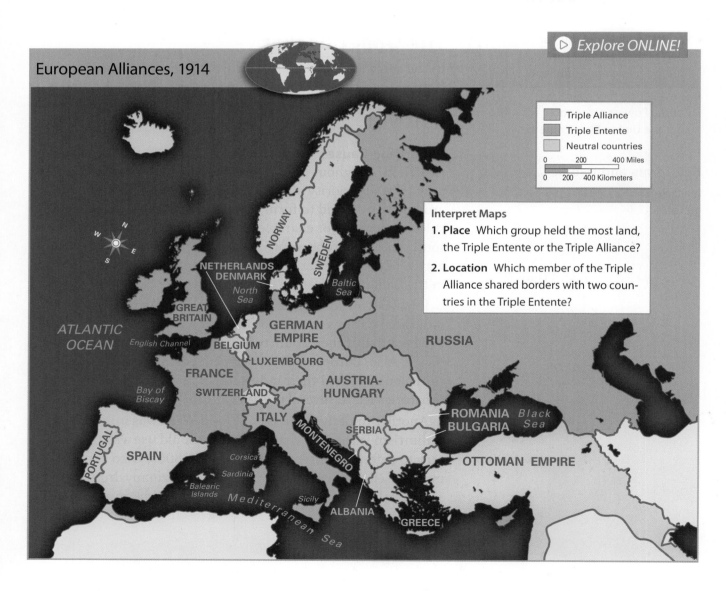

European Alliances, 1914

Legend:
- Triple Alliance
- Triple Entente
- Neutral countries

0   200   400 Miles
0   200   400 Kilometers

Interpret Maps
1. **Place** Which group held the most land, the Triple Entente or the Triple Alliance?
2. **Location** Which member of the Triple Alliance shared borders with two countries in the Triple Entente?

NORWAY
SWEDEN
NETHERLANDS
DENMARK
Baltic Sea
North Sea
GREAT BRITAIN
GERMAN EMPIRE
RUSSIA
ATLANTIC OCEAN
English Channel
BELGIUM
LUXEMBOURG
FRANCE
AUSTRIA-HUNGARY
Bay of Biscay
SWITZERLAND
ITALY
MONTENEGRO
SERBIA
ROMANIA
BULGARIA
Black Sea
PORTUGAL
SPAIN
Corsica
Sardinia
Balearic Islands
Mediterranean Sea
Sicily
ALBANIA
GREECE
OTTOMAN EMPIRE

Reading Check
Summarize
What were the main causes of World War I?

The Spark for War In 1914, Europe was on the brink of war. Tension boiled between Austria-Hungary and Serbia over a part of Austria-Hungary that the Serbs badly wanted. Then, on June 28, a Serbian nationalist killed Archduke Francis Ferdinand, the heir to the Austro-Hungarian throne, and his wife. Seeking revenge, Austria-Hungary declared war on Serbia. In time, other countries from around the globe joined in the fight.

The Great War Escalates

Germany struck the first blow of what became known as the Great War. It sent a large army into Belgium and France. But French and British troops stopped the Germans near Paris. In the Battle of Marne, Allied troops were able to push back advancing German soldiers.

Trench and Naval Warfare Both sides then dug miles of trenches, deep ditches from which the soldiers defended their positions. Generals repeatedly ordered their men to charge enemy lines. But new, deadly machine guns cut down soldiers as they tried to move forward. This cost millions of lives. Both sides also resorted to chemical warfare in the form of poison gas. Gas masks were introduced to attempt to avoid this danger.

Neither side could advance, resulting in a bloody stalemate that lasted over three years. Soldiers on both sides of the fight faced miserable conditions in the trenches. Mud, poor sanitation, and rats plagued the fighters.

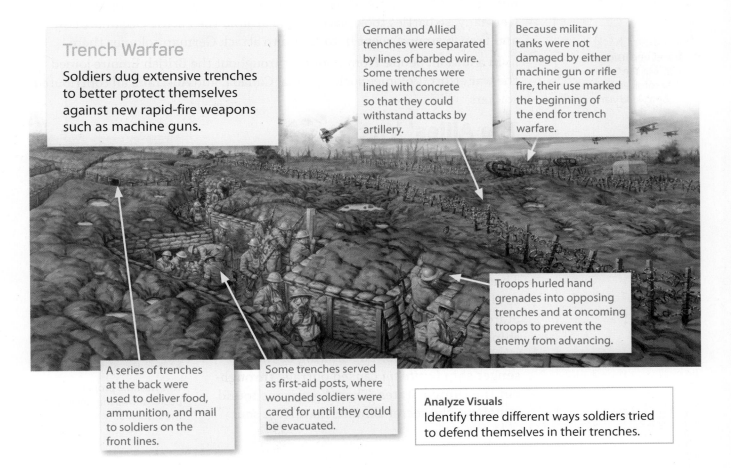

Trench Warfare

Soldiers dug extensive trenches to better protect themselves against new rapid-fire weapons such as machine guns.

German and Allied trenches were separated by lines of barbed wire. Some trenches were lined with concrete so that they could withstand attacks by artillery.

Because military tanks were not damaged by either machine gun or rifle fire, their use marked the beginning of the end for trench warfare.

Troops hurled hand grenades into opposing trenches and at oncoming troops to prevent the enemy from advancing.

A series of trenches at the back were used to deliver food, ammunition, and mail to soldiers on the front lines.

Some trenches served as first-aid posts, where wounded soldiers were cared for until they could be evacuated.

Analyze Visuals
Identify three different ways soldiers tried to defend themselves in their trenches.

Meanwhile, German leaders decided to use another kind of warfare. Naval warfare, or battle at sea, became a part of war. Germany had a powerful new weapon, the submarine. To stop the English from receiving food and supplies, German submarines began to sink ships headed for Britain.

The Gallipoli Campaign Toward the end of 1914, the Central Powers gained a new partner, the Ottoman Empire. The Ottomans controlled a strategic waterway called the Dardanelles. The Allies wanted to continue to use the Dardanelles to ship supplies to Russia. To do this, they needed to destroy the forts that lined the Dardanelles. Landing on the nearby Gallipoli Peninsula, the Allies waged a lengthy battle. Finally, after months of fighting, the Allies decided to give up their fight for control of the area.

Armenian Genocide Prior to the war, relations between the Turks and the Armenians in the Ottoman Empire had been uneasy for years. Religious and economic differences between the two groups increased tensions. As World War I began, some Armenians fought for Russia rather than for the Ottoman Empire. As a result, the Ottoman government decided to expel or execute the Armenians living within its borders. They began to commit genocide in 1915. **Genocide** is a deliberate killing of a large group of people. Many Armenians were killed, and many others left their homes.

Fighting in Other Parts of the World Battles took place not only in Europe but also in Africa and Asia as well. Japan joined the Allies to fight against Germany, so battles took place on and around the Pacific Ocean. British and French troops swept in to Africa to attack German colonies there.

In addition, people from colonies throughout the British Empire joined the war effort. Colonies such as India, Canada, and Australia all contributed soldiers.

Reading Check
Draw Conclusions
Why was the Great War considered to be a world war?

The Allies' Victory

Soldiers on both side were weary of war. Then the long-hoped-for arrival of additional troops from across the Atlantic helped turn the tide for the Allies.

The United States Joins the War The United States had vowed to stay neutral in the war. That changed when German submarines began to sink ships headed for Britain. The United States warned Germany not to attack unarmed ships. Germany ignored these warnings, angering Americans. The sinking of the passenger ship *Lusitania* caused outrage throughout the United States. Then Americans found out about the secret Zimmerman Note sent

This wartime propaganda poster shows the sinking of the *Lusitania*.

by the German government to Mexico. In the note, Germany asked Mexico to attack the United States. In return, Mexico would gain American territory if Germany won the war. Americans were ready to commit to fighting. The United States joined the Allies in April 1917.

Help from American soldiers and medics gave the Allies a fresh advantage. Soon afterward, though, the exhausted Russians pulled out of the war. The remaining Allies continued the fight.

Wartime Innovations The ability to communicate is vital during war. The telegraph was already being used to send messages over long distances. However, changing technology influenced the way soldiers communicated in World War I. Military pilots in planes could speak with radio operators on the ground. Telephones were used on the front lines.

Technological innovations also improved the medical care soldiers received. Blood transfusions were considered too dangerous in wartime conditions, but British and American medics improved the safety of transfusions. Infections from injuries were another concern. Although antibiotics had not yet been invented, new techniques to decrease the chance of infection were developed. All of these innovations helped save lives.

Soldiers Killed in World War I	
Central Powers	
Germany	1,773,700
Austria-Hungary	1,200,000
Ottoman Empire	320,000
Total for Central Powers	3,386,200
Allies	
Russia	1,700,000
France	1,357,800
British Empire	908,371
Italy	650,000
United States	116,516
Total for Allies	5,142,631
Grand Total	8,528,831

Interpret Charts
How many more soldiers did Germany lose than did France?

In addition, new warfare technology introduced during the war changed the face of battle. Tanks, or armored vehicles, and the newly developed airplanes helped both the Allies and the Central Powers win many battles but brought about many deaths.

The Allies Triumph Germany realized that the entry of American troops would shift the balance of power to the Allies. The Germans decided to act quickly and stage a new attack on France. At first, the German plan succeeded as they advanced toward Paris. Then Allied soldiers along with fresh American troops stopped the Germans and pushed them out of France. Germany's allies also suffered defeats in 1918. By November the Central Powers had collapsed. The war was finally over, after years of fighting and enormous loss of life. The Allies had won the war, but issues related to the war had to be settled. Allied leaders met to discuss peace plans that would become The Treaty of Versailles.

Summary and Preview The Allies won World War I after over four years of fighting across the globe, on land and sea. In the next lesson, you will learn about the results of the war and how peace meant that some European countries had to pay a heavy cost.

Reading Check
Draw Conclusions
How did the United States affect the outcome of the war?

Lesson 2 Assessment

Review Ideas, Terms, and People

1. a. **Recall** Why did Austria-Hungary declare war on Serbia?

   b. **Analyze** What conditions made Europe ripe for war in 1914?

2. a. **Summarize** How did the use of trenches affect the war?

   b. **Explain** How did the entry of the Ottoman Empire affect the Allies?

   c. **Define** What is the meaning of the term genocide, and how did it relate to World War I?

   d. **Identify** On which continents was World War I fought?

3. a. **Explain** Why did the United States join the Allies?

   b. **Make Inferences** Why do you think French and British soldiers were happy when American troops arrived?

Critical Thinking

4. **Summarize** Use a chart like the one below to summarize how each item relates to World War I.

Item	Details
Telegraph	
Radio	
Telephone	

Results of the War

The Big Idea

There were many political, economic, and cultural changes in Europe after World War I.

Main Ideas

- The League of Nations was formed, but it had mixed success.
- The Treaty of Versailles changed the map of Europe.
- Resentment and economic problems developed in Germany after World War I.

Key Terms and People

Treaty of Versailles
League of Nations
reparations

President Wilson, pictured here, discussed the League of Nations in his "Fourteen Points" address to Congress in 1918.

If YOU were there . . .

You are a member of the Allied delegation at the signing of the Treaty of Versailles. Germany has lost World War I. The Allies tell Germany that it has to pay a lot of money in damages. French delegates think this is an excellent idea because they want to punish Germany. Many Germans believe their nation is being treated unfairly.

Do you agree with the terms of the treaty?

League of Nations

After the war, leaders of the Allies met at Versailles (ver-SY), near Paris, to discuss the terms of peace that would be included in the **Treaty of Versailles**. U.S. president Woodrow Wilson proposed a plan intended to promote democracy and prevent future wars. One of his ideas was to create the **League of Nations**, an organization in which countries would try to solve their problems peacefully. President Wilson hoped that the League could protect the territory and independence of the countries that joined. He wanted the group to have an assembly to make rules and an international court to enforce them. He thought that the League of Nations would be able to maintain peace using the combined economic and military power of member nations.

However, the League of Nations did not accomplish what Wilson hoped. The United States did not join the League because some members of Congress were not in favor of doing so. They were concerned that the United States government would lose some freedom to make its own decisions. They also did not want to become involved in European politics. President Wilson was unable to change the minds of members of Congress.

In all, 42 countries, including France and the United Kingdom, joined, but the League of Nations did not function effectively. In the 1930s, Japan invaded China, and then Italy invaded Ethiopia. In neither case was the League of

Reading Check
Identify Problems
Why was the League of Nations not effective?

Nations allowed to take part in settling the dispute. In addition, Germany began to gather military resources, which was expressly prohibited in the Treaty of Versailles. The League of Nations could do little to address the actions. After all, it did not have the support of the United States, one of the strongest nations of the world. Also, it had no means of using military force if necessary to stop acts of aggression. The League of Nations was unable to stop these events from occurring.

New National Borders

Wilson also believed that nationalities should rule themselves. Acting on this view, the Allies redrew the map of Europe. These border changes were part of the terms of the Treaty of Versailles and other treaties with defeated nations.

The treaties took land from Russia and Germany. Austria-Hungary was broken into two separate countries. Seven new countries were created. Estonia, Latvia, and Lithuania came from areas previously controlled by Germany. Czechoslovakia and Yugoslavia were created from what was once part of Austria-Hungary. Russia gave up territory to create Finland, and the borders of Poland were redrawn as well. Some nations like Denmark and Romania grew in size. Others, like Bulgaria, decreased in size. A small piece of what remained of the Ottoman Empire became the nation of Turkey.

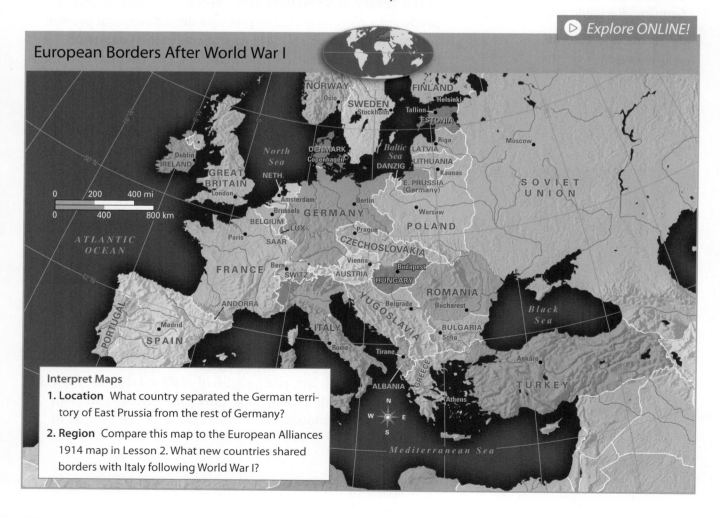

▶ *Explore ONLINE!*

European Borders After World War I

Interpret Maps

1. **Location** What country separated the German territory of East Prussia from the rest of Germany?

2. **Region** Compare this map to the European Alliances 1914 map in Lesson 2. What new countries shared borders with Italy following World War I?

The Treaty of Versailles was signed near Paris, France, in 1919.

During the war, large populations moved across Europe. Many people fled from the fighting when they could. For example, large numbers of Jews fled into Russia during the war or settled into Poland after World War I. People were also driven toward Austria-Hungary during the conflict.

The movement of people and the creation of new nations created tension in Europe. Many ethnic groups who had not lived together before were now in the same country. For example, there was tension between Russians and Jews who had migrated into Russia to avoid the war.

Reading Check
Analyze Motives
Why did the Allies create new countries in Europe?

Economic Penalties

The Allies also forced Germany to accept blame for starting the war. Germany had to slash the size of its army and reduce its navy's number of ships. The nation was also forced to give up its colonies and pay for war damages. These payments were known as **reparations**. Germany thought the payments were unfair, but other countries disagreed. The French

---

DOCUMENT-BASED INVESTIGATION   Historical Source

The War-Guilt Clause

Known as the war-guilt clause, this part of the Treaty of Versailles places blame for World War I on Germany. Many Germans resented these words.

Analyze Historical Sources
Why might Germans be upset with the words in the war-guilt clause?

"The Allied and Associated Governments affirm and Germany accepts the responsibility of Germany and her Allies for causing all the loss and damage to which the Allied and Associated Governments and their nationals have been subjected as a consequence of the war imposed upon them by the aggression of Germany and her Allies. . . ."

—Article 231, Part VIII, Section 1 of Peace Treaty of Versailles

believed that Germany was a threat to Europe. France demanded high payments so that Germany could not become powerful again.

Germany had other economic problems as well. It had borrowed money to pay for weapons and other war expenses. The reparations made it impossible to pay all the debts it owed. Many people disliked the Treaty of Versailles, and many Germans thought the economic effects of the Treaty were too harsh. Not all nationalities got their own nation. Some countries resented losing land. So, instead of leading to lasting peace, the treaty set the stage for further conflict.

Summary and Preview European nations looked very different after World War I. New countries were carved out of the land of defeated nations. Conflict within Russia would soon affect millions of people. Next you will explore what happened when revolution came to that nation.

Reading Check
Analyze Issues Why were many people unhappy with the Treaty of Versailles?

Lesson 3 Assessment

Review Ideas, Terms, and People

1. **a. Recall** What U.S. president argued in favor of the League of Nations?

   b. Evaluate Why was the president unable to convince the United States to join the League of Nations?

2. **a. Describe** What effect did the Treaty of Versailles have on borders in Europe?

   b. Explain What were the effects of people moving from place to place?

3. **a. Describe** How was Germany punished for its role in World War I?

   b. Analyze How did this punishment affect Germany's economy?

   c. Evaluate Was the Treaty of Versailles successful?

Critical Thinking

4. **Categorize** Fill in this chart about European geography after World War I. Identify with an X the nation from which each new nation in the left column was created.

	Austria-Hungary	Germany	Russia
Estonia			
Latvia			
Lithuania			
Czechoslovakia			
Yugoslavia			
Finland			
Poland			

The Russian Revolution

The Big Idea

The Russian Revolution resulted in the world's first communist state.

Main Ideas

- Population growth, wars, and limited agricultural production caused unrest in Russia.

- Communism is a political system in which the government controls much of the economy.

- The Soviet Union was formed after revolution and civil war in Russia.

Key Terms and People

Nicholas II
Karl Marx
Marxism
Vladimir Lenin
communism

If YOU were there . . .

It is a cold January day in 1905. You are a Russian peasant who lives near Czar Nicholas II's Winter Palace. People have been upset at the czar for awhile. Now word has spread that something awful has happened. The czar's guards have shot people who were peacefully protesting outside the palace. You wonder why Czar Nicholas would have given such an order.

Do you trust Czar Nicholas II to be a good leader now?

Russia Faces Challenges

Tensions between the Russian people and their government led to violent revolutions in the early 1900s. Problems and anger had been growing in Russia for decades. Food shortages and heavy loss of life were two main reasons Russians turned against the government.

Difficulties with Agriculture In the 1800s, some Russians lived in cities, but most lived in rural areas. Many people in rural areas made a living as farmers. They were able to grow enough food to feed local communities. Then Russia's population doubled in the last half of the 1800s. In addition, the Russian government wanted to sell crops to other countries. With those additional demands, farmers struggled to produce enough food. There were food shortages throughout the country, and eventually a famine caused half a million people to starve in 1891.

War with Japan In the early 1900s, Russia fought with Japan over control of Manchuria in east Asia. Japan wanted Russian troops to leave the area. Russia refused because it wanted to protect its railroads in the region. During the war that followed, Japan had better technology and skilled commanders. Japanese forces controlled the sea routes in the region and destroyed a Russian naval fleet. As a result, Russia lost the war and when it ended, gave land to Japan.

Massacre and Revolution in 1905 As war with Japan was ending, social unrest boiled over in Russia. At the time, Russia's form of government was a monarchy. Its ruler, the czar, held much of the power of government and often treated the people harshly. Different groups had been protesting against the government for years. Now people added the humiliation of defeat and further loss of life to their complaints against the government. The Russian people were ready for another form of government that granted them more rights. Above all, they wanted the right to elect a legislature to represent them in government. In January, a workers' group decided to march to the Winter Palace in St. Petersburg to demonstrate for reform. Guards at the Winter Palace shot at the protestors in what became known as the Bloody Sunday Massacre. Hundreds were killed or wounded.

People were outraged at the government because of its role in the massacre. A wave of strikes and riots swept over the nation and into distant corners of the Russian Empire. In the far east, soldiers helped workers gain control of the Trans-Siberian Railroad, which linked western Russia to the Pacific Ocean. The newly built railroad had become a vital part of Russian trade.

The angry Russian people demanded political reform and representation. In response, the Russian czar (ZAR), or emperor, **Nicholas II**, appointed a prime minister. He also promised to create a legislature and a constitution.

Not everyone agreed with what the czar offered. Those who wanted complete revolution in Russia were unsatisfied. Czar Nicholas II regained some control of his nation, but it did not last for long.

Reading Check
Analyze Causes
Why did Russia experience a famine in 1891?

New Ideas About Government

Czar Nicholas II was still the leader of Russia, but the strikes and riots showed that his authority was weakening. In response to the problems, new political groups formed. Russian czars had ruled the country for hundreds of years, but these groups had different ideas about how the Russian government should function.

Czar Nicholas II is shown here with the rest of his family in a portrait from 1914.

Marxism **Karl Marx** was a newspaper editor from Prussia. He wrote extensively on the rights of the working class. Many workers in Europe were underpaid and had few rights under their employers. Marx believed workers should have more rights. He wrote that the struggle of these **oppressed** working classes is the basis for social change. Karl Marx's ideas are known as **Marxism**.

Academic Vocabulary
oppressed treated unfairly

The ideas of Karl Marx, pictured above, influenced a new form of government in Russia.

Some political groups in Russia believed in Marx's ideas. They saw that many Russian workers and peasants were struggling. They thought that these struggles could be the basis for social and political change in Russia.

Communism One of these groups was known as the Bolsheviks. The Bolsheviks were led by **Vladimir Lenin**. Lenin agreed with much of what Marx had written. However, Marx stressed that once voting rights were extended to workers, they would be able to gain control of governments peacefully. In contrast, Lenin thought violent revolution was the best way to achieve the change he wanted to see in Russia. Lenin believed in communism. **Communism** is an economic and political system in which there is no privately owned property. The government controls the economy and production of goods.

Lenin and the Bolsheviks continued to encourage protest and revolution against the Russian government. Such actions eventually allowed them to gain control of the Communist Party.

Reading Check
Contrast How did the ideas of Karl Marx and Vladimir Lenin differ?

The Soviet Union

Russia continued to experience social and political tension. Political revolutions and a civil war would soon consume Russia. When the conflict was over, Vladimir Lenin would lead a form of government the world had never seen before.

Images of Vladimir Lenin could be seen throughout the Soviet Union. Here he appears on a stamp.

The 1917 Revolution The czar promised more political representation for the people in the Russian government. In actuality, the czar gave the people little representation in government. More people called for the czar to be overthrown. In the early months of 1917, protesters were once again on the streets of Petrograd. Food was in short supply, and they were demanding that the government provide them with bread. Many people felt that the government was not responsive to their needs. Clashes broke out between the army and the protesters, but days later, the army actually joined the people. Czar Nicholas was forced to give up power once and for all.

The legislature the czar had created in the days following the 1905 Revolution became a new government, but it could not keep order. Uprisings swept across Russia. Lenin and the Bolsheviks, supporters of communism, grew in strength. In November 1917, they overthrew the new government. A civil war began in Russia.

Civil War and a New Nation Lenin and the Bolsheviks had gained some political control of Russia. They attempted to use this power to bring peace to the Russian people and avoid a civil war. Russia's economy had suffered greatly because of the country's participation in World War I. To remove Russia from the war, Lenin's government signed a treaty with the Central Powers of Germany and its allies. The terms of the treaty required Russia to give up some of its territory, including Ukraine and Poland. This loss of territory angered some Russians who were determined to end Bolshevik rule.

The Allied powers refused to acknowledge Lenin's government and supported its opponents. The Bolsheviks controlled only a portion of the Russian military, and some Russian soldiers fought against the Bolsheviks. Known as the Whites, they received money and some additional troops from the Allies. Lenin's communist forces were called the Reds.

The civil war between the Reds and Whites lasted for several years. The Reds prevailed in 1922. Russia was renamed the Union of Soviet Socialist Republics, or the Soviet Union. A new communist nation was born with Lenin as its leader.

Reading Check
Analyze Motives
Why did Russia decide to stop fighting in World War I?

Summary and Preview Russia faced many challenges in the early 1900s. These challenges led to revolution and a change in government. More challenges lay ahead for the new Soviet Union and for the rest of the world. In the next lesson, you will study how economic collapse led to worldwide economic depression.

Lesson 4 Assessment

Review Ideas, Terms, and People

1. a. **Analyze** How did Russia's agricultural difficulties affect its people?
   b. **Summarize** Why did Russia lose the war with Japan?
2. a. **Describe** What did Karl Marx believe would be the basis for social change?
   b. **Define** What is communism?
3. a. **Analyze** Why was the Russian government overthrown in 1917?
   b. **Summarize** Why did a civil war begin in Russia?

Critical Thinking

4. **Analyze** Create a graphic organizer similar to the one below to identify the results of each event discussed in the lesson.

Event	Result
1905 Revolution	
1917 Revolution	
Civil War	

The Great Depression

The Big Idea

The Great Depression was an economic event that affected the entire world.

Main Ideas

- The stock market crash of 1929 and bank failures led to the Great Depression.

- The Great Depression challenged people and nations around the world.

- Nations responded to the Great Depression in different ways.

Key Terms and People

Great Depression
stocks
Franklin Delano Roosevelt
New Deal

If YOU were there . . .

The country is facing hard times. Many people lost all the money they had invested in the stock market. Many businesses have closed. Today, your father lost his job. He tells your family that money will be tight. You want to help your family get through these hard times.

What will you do to help your family?

Causes of the Great Depression

The United States emerged from World War I as a leading economic power. Factories ran at full power as they produced products to be sold around the world. Americans themselves purchased new products such as washing machines, refrigerators, vacuum cleaners, and radios. Doing without during the lean war years made Americans want to buy all the latest consumer goods. To quickly gain everything they wanted, some people bought on credit. They put some money down and promised to pay the rest later, with interest.

Economies around the world grew slower following the war but appeared to become stronger as time passed. European nations were starting to recover from the costs of World War I. Nations touched by war began ramping up peacetime production. World trade increased as well. People on the various continents made profits by exporting goods to other lands. Unfortunately, this time of prosperity came to an end.

The **Great Depression** was an economic collapse that occurred in the late 1920s and continued well into the 1930s. During this time, the value of money fell significantly, and unemployment rose throughout the world. Many people lost their jobs and were unable to purchase what they needed. There are many explanations for why the Great Depression occurred. One reason is the decline in value of stock markets.

Stock Market Crash As businesses boomed in the United States, many Americans had dreams of striking it rich.

Anyone with money to spare, or ways to borrow money, invested in company stock. **Stocks** represent pieces of a company. They can gain or lose value based on how well the company does in business. The stock market is the system in which stocks, or pieces of companies, are bought, sold, or traded.

Toward the end of 1929, people began to buy less. Some Americans already had all the products they needed while others had reached their credit limit. Businesses suffered because of the drop in consumer spending. Unemployment rose and the production of goods fell. People panicked because they thought company stocks would drop. They quickly began selling off stock.

In October 1929, stocks lost more than 75 percent of their value in just a few days. This caused the stock market to crash. The day when stock prices fell the most is known as Black Tuesday. Billions of dollars vanished, and many people lost all the money they had invested. Americans and people around the world would soon face economic hard times. Many would lose their jobs, their savings, and their homes.

Why did stocks lose their value so quickly? Investors, people who do business on the stock market, buy and sell stocks in the hope of making big profits. Often, investors speculate, or guess, what the price of a stock will be before they buy or sell. This practice can be risky if a stock's price falls when investors thought it would rise. This means they would lose money. Investors in the 1920s took enormous risks without thinking about possible consequences.

In the United States, companies had stockpiles of unsold goods. To cut back on expenses, they laid off many workers. In spite of this, investors thought that the value of companies would continue to rise. However, their stocks were not worth as much as people thought. The rush to invest in the 1920s caused the price of stocks to soar well beyond what the shares were really worth. In some cases, businesses used unfair practices to convince Americans to invest in them. Some people also used dishonest practices to make more money for themselves. Many investors had borrowed money to buy stocks. When panic set in, investors who had borrowed had to sell their stocks at low prices to pay back their loans. In this case, many investors lost everything.

Bank Failures Bank failures also contributed to the Great Depression. During the good times, Americans had taken out loans to make large purchases, such as automobiles. Banks were eager to loan them money. They did not question whether people had the means to pay back the loans. The banks charged a low amount of interest to encourage people to borrow more money. However, many people borrowed too much and were unable to continue making payments when they lost their jobs. With less money coming in, some banks could no longer make loans to companies. This caused even higher unemployment and even less repayment of loans. Some banks had no money and were forced to close their doors. The failure of the banks caused many Americans to lose all their savings. They had no way to recover the money they had lost.

Reading Check
Analyze Events
What factors led to the Great Depression?

Effects of the Great Depression

The Great Depression affected countries around the world. However, it was initially more devastating in the United States than other countries. One reason that explains this difference is that the drop in production was more severe in the United States. American consumers had stopped spending money on goods and services that businesses produced. When people did not buy things, industries made fewer products and needed fewer employees. Also, the closing of banks stripped Americans of their savings.

Without jobs or savings, many people could not make payments on their loans and lost their homes. Homeless, many people lived in their cars or moved to large tent cities called Shantytowns. Many Americans went hungry. Charities began to offer free food to those in need. Long lines formed as hungry people waited their turn for bread or soup.

The rest of the world was also affected by similar economic issues. Americans could no longer invest money overseas. Without the addition of American money, foreign economies suffered. Like in the United States, many businesses and factories went out of business. People around the world had no way of earning a living.

The Great Depression affected nations throughout the world differently in the 1930s. In some countries, the effects of high unemployment and failed businesses and banks lasted a short while. In other countries, those problems continued for longer periods of time.

Many people lost their jobs during the Great Depression. These people are lined up outside a soup kitchen waiting for a meal.

Many European countries lost money from stocks because of World War I. The German government tried to solve their financial problems by printing more paper money after World War I. Other European countries did the same, and the value of their currency fell when the Depression began.

However, economic problems were not as severe in some of these European countries as they were in other places. For example, countries in the Nordic region did not suffer economic collapse in the 1930s. In fact, they continued to produce and export goods during this time. Their early decision to make their economy less based on gold helped them succeed while others suffered.

Countries on other continents suffered as well. The countries of Latin America no longer could depend on the United States as a major trading partner. Their economies suffered because they could not sell products to the United States or other nations. Japan, too, lost valuable trading partners and couldn't export as much as they had before. The Japanese people faced high unemployment and rising prices. Throughout Africa, sellers of raw materials such as cotton found fewer buyers.

Reading Check
Analyze Effects
How did financial woes in the United States affect countries around the world?

Responses to the Great Depression

Because the Great Depression was felt across the world, there was not a simple solution to fix it. Each nation tried its own methods. Consider the results in the United States, Great Britain, and Germany. The American and British plans used tough actions to bring an end to the trouble. The German plan would have significant consequences later in history.

America's New Deal Voters were convinced that newly elected President **Franklin Delano Roosevelt** could restore the American economy. Roosevelt immediately went to work to do just that. His solution involved creating a group of government programs that historians call the **New Deal**. The New Deal refers to the federal government's efforts to reform business practices and to stimulate the economy. Two major goals of the New Deal were to

The federal government provided opportunities for employment, such as this construction project, through the Public Works Administration in the 1930s.

create jobs and offer financial help to those who needed it. Some people worked on construction projects and in national forests. Others helped bring electricity to seven states through the Tennessee Valley Authority (TVA). They prevented floods in those areas as well. New Deal programs gave money to farmers and helped people pay the mortgages on their houses. These programs were designed to encourage people to spend more money.

The New Deal also changed some policies to encourage people to use banks again and to prevent problems in the future. Bank deposits were federally insured. This meant the government would protect the money in banks. Customers would no longer lose their money if a bank failed. An agency called the Securities and Exchange Commission (SEC) was formed. The SEC regulates the stock market to prevent the sort of dishonest practices that led to a collapse in stock prices in 1929.

Spending Cuts in Great Britain Like the Nordic countries, Great Britain decided to stop basing its money on gold. It also pursued different economic policies to combat the effects of the Great Depression. Unlike the United States, Great Britain chose not to increase spending on programs to reduce unemployment and restore people's buying powering. Instead, the British government decreased spending and investment. This policy is called retrenchment. Wages and spending were kept low. People did receive some money if they were unemployed, but the amount was quite small. There were no public works projects like the New Deal provided in the United States. The people of Britain were encouraged to make do with what they had. Slowly, the economy made some progress. The prospect of

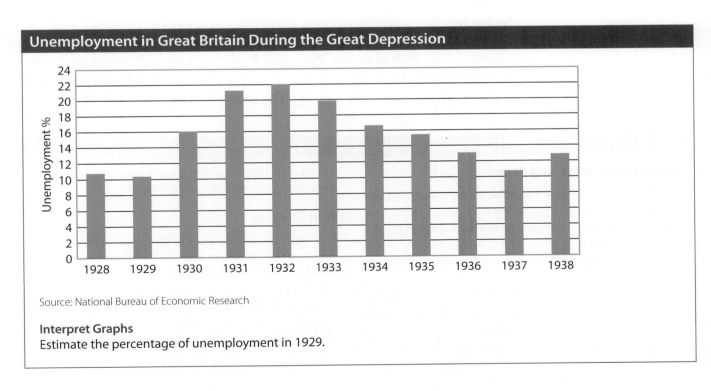

Unemployment in Great Britain During the Great Depression

Source: National Bureau of Economic Research

Interpret Graphs
Estimate the percentage of unemployment in 1929.

an approaching war served to push economic challenges out of the minds of the British people.

The German Economy Economic conditions in Germany were challenging in the 1920s. It had borrowed money to pay for weapons and other war expenses. On top of that, the Treaty of Versailles had required Germany to pay reparations. Meeting this requirement made it impossible to pay all the debts it owed. Other countries refused to lend money to the Germans. The German government decided to print more money. Prices rose quickly, and the extra money was almost worthless. People carried money in wheelbarrows when they went shopping. Many people were hungry, and over a quarter of the nation's population was unemployed.

It was in this tense climate that Adolf Hitler and his Nazi Party began their rise to power. Many Germans remained angry about the Treaty of Versailles. Hitler thought that Germany should refuse to pay reparations and build its military again. Both of these acts were violations of the treaty. Yet they appealed to the German people who desperately wanted to find ways to improve their economy. They, too, were angry that they had to pay reparations. They saw Hitler as a strong leader who could end Germany's economic problems.

When Hitler was appointed the German leader in 1933, the government spent money on public works projects such as the highway system. Farmers began to prosper again. The German economy improved over time. Yet, Hitler ruled ruthlessly. Germany had become a dictatorship. Unlike in the United States and Britain, a desire for prosperity would bring an end to democracy.

Summary The world faced great economic challenges during the Great Depression. Some nations recovered from the Depression faster than others. In the United States, President Franklin Roosevelt introduced and promoted New Deal economic policies. In Germany, Adolf Hitler promised that his strong leadership would bring economic change.

Reading Check
Identify Problems
What were conditions like in Germany when Adolf Hitler began to rise to power?

Lesson 5 Assessment

Review Ideas, Terms, and People

1. a. **Summarize** What issues affected the value of stocks before the stock market crashed?

   b. **Make Inferences** What role did banks play in the Great Depression?

2. a. **Analyze** How were Americans affected by the Great Depression?

   b. **Make Inferences** Why did trade suffer in the 1930s?

3. a. **Recall** What were two major goals of the New Deal?

   b. **Draw Conclusions** How did the New Deal encourage people to use banks again?

   c. **Develop Historical Perspective** Why did some Germans support Hitler in the 1930s?

Critical Thinking

4. **Contrast** Use a table like this one to show how the British and American governments differed in their response to the Great Depression.

Great Britain	United States

Social Studies Skills

Use Visual Resources

Define the Skill

A major part of history is understanding the events and ideas of the past. Visual resources are often good sources of information about the past. Visual resources include paintings, drawings, cartoons, posters, and photographs. The symbols and images in these resources tell us about the ideas and values of a time period. They often provide different information and points of view than do written documents.

Learn the Skill

Visual resources can have special purposes. For example, the top poster was produced by the U.S. government to inspire patriotism and encourage support for the war effort. It uses symbols and images to suggest that all Americans can contribute to the war effort.

Reducing the demand for manufactured canned food was an important part of the war effort. This poster encourages Americans to can fruits and vegetables. The pictures show vegetables in glass jars.

The poster also shows the German Kaiser in a jar. He cannot reach his sword, which is outside the jar. He is helpless. This suggests that, by canning fruits and vegetables, Americans can help defeat the German leader.

Practice the Skill

Study the World War I poster to the right. Like the first poster, it was produced by the U.S. government to encourage support for the war effort. Write a paragraph describing the poster. Your paragraph should include the specific purpose of the poster, the symbols it uses, and whether it conveys its message effectively. You can use the text above as a model.

Module 26 Assessment

Review Vocabulary, Terms, and People

Match each "I" statement with the person or thing that could have made the statement. Not all of the choices will be used.

1. I am a system in which the government owns all businesses and controls the economy.
2. I was the prime minister who helped unify Italy.
3. I was the leader of the Bolsheviks in Russia.
4. I believed that oppressed working classes could bring about social change.
5. I led the Nazi movement in Germany.
6. I am devotion and loyalty to one's country.
7. I was the American president who created the New Deal.
8. I was the American president who promoted the League of Nations.
9. I am the deliberate killing of a large group of people.
10. I represent a piece of a company that gains or loses value.

a. Vladimir Lenin
b. Franklin Roosevelt
c. Camillo di Cavour
d. genocide
e. Adolf Hitler
f. stock
g. Karl Marx
h. communism
i. Otto von Bismarck
j. nationalism
k. Woodrow Wilson
l. speculation

Comprehension and Critical Thinking

Lesson 1

11. a. **Analyze** How did nationalism change the map of Europe?
    b. **Draw Conclusions** How were Camillo di Cavour and Giuseppe Garibaldi able to unify Italy?
    c. **Describe** What series of events transformed a number of separate German states into a unified imperialist power?

Lesson 2

12. a. **Describe** Why was Austria-Hungary having problems with people who lived in the Balkans?
    b. **Explain** What is militarism? How did it affect Europe before World War I?
    c. **Identify Problems** Why were machine guns a problem in trench warfare?

Lesson 3

13. a. **Analyze** Why did some members of Congress not want the United States to join the League of Nations?
    b. **Summarize** What effect did population migration have on Europe after World War I?
    c. **Analyze** Why did the Treaty of Versailles ask Germany to pay reparations after the war?

Lesson 4

14. a. **Evaluate** Why did the Russian people force Czar Nicholas II out of power?
    b. **Make Inferences** Why did Marx's ideas appeal to many revolutionary groups in Russia?
    c. **Contrast** During the Russian civil war, what differences existed between the Reds and the Whites?

Module 26 Assessment, continued

Lesson 5

15. **a.** Analyze Why did many banks fail during the Great Depression?

   b. Summarize How did the U.S. government try to decrease unemployment during the Great Depression?

   c. Analyze From what you have read in the text, why do you think Adolf Hitler was against paying reparations to other countries?

Review Themes

16. **Geography** How did nationalism contribute to tensions in Europe before the outbreak of World War I?

17. **Politics** What evidence from the module shows that, after World War I, France was still concerned about Germany?

Reading Skills

Public Documents in History *Use the Reading Skill taught in this module to answer the question below.*

18. Read the list of documents. Then classify each document listed as either a public or private document.

   a. the letters of Franklin Delano Roosevelt

   b. the Treaty of Versailles

   c. Vladimir Lenin's diary

   d. Austria-Hungary's declaration of war against Serbia

   e. newspaper articles about the 1929 stock market crash

Social Studies Skills

Use Visual Resources *Use the Social Studies Skills taught in this module to answer the question below.*

19. What parts of the U.S. war effort are shown in this poster?

Focus On Writing

20. **Write a Cover Story** Consider the people and events you have learned about from your study of this module. Choose the person or event that you think would make the strongest cover story for a magazine. Then write a short article about your subject. Include important facts about the subject. Be sure to present your information so your audience recognizes why your person or event was important enough to be the subject of a magazine cover story.

Dear home: LETTERS FROM WWI

When U.S. troops arrived in Europe in 1917 to fight in World War I, the war had been dragging on for nearly three years. The American soldiers suddenly found themselves in the midst of chaos. Each day, they faced the threats of machine-gun fire, poison gas, and aerial attacks. Still, the arrival of American reinforcements had sparked a new zeal among the Allies, who believed the new forces could finally turn the tide in their favor. The letters soldiers wrote to their families back home reveal the many emotions they felt on the battlefield: confusion about their surroundings, fear for their own safety, concern for friends and loved ones, and hope that the war would soon be over.

Explore World War I online through the eyes of the soldiers who fought in it. You can find a wealth of information, video clips, primary sources, activities, and more through your online textbook.

"I have been on every front in France. You can't imagine how torn up this country really is. Every where there are wire entanglements and trenches and dugouts. Even out of the war zone there are entanglements and dugouts to protect the civilians from air raids."

—Corp. Albert Smith, U.S. soldier

Letter from France
Read the document to learn about one soldier's observations of wartime life.

Over There
Watch the video to learn about the experiences of American soldiers on the way to Europe and upon their arrival.

War on the Western Front
Watch the video to hear one soldier's vivid account of battle and its aftermath.

Surrender!
Watch the video to experience soldiers' reactions to the news that the war was finally over.

Module 27

World War II

Essential Question

For what reasons do people start and fight wars, such as World War II?

About the Photo: U.S. Marines raise the American flag on Iwo Jima, an island in the Pacific, during World War II.

In this module, you will read about the events before, during, and after World War II. You will also learn about the Holocaust.

What You Will Learn...

Lesson 1: The Rise of Dictators **918**
The Big Idea After World War I, dictators rose to power in several countries around the world.

Lesson 2: World War II **924**
The Big Idea The Allied Powers fought the Axis Powers in World War II.

Lesson 3: The Holocaust. **934**
The Big Idea The Nazis murdered millions of Jews and other people during the time that has become known as the Holocaust.

Lesson 4: Results of World War II **941**
The Big Idea Much of Europe and Japan were devastated by World War II.

▶ *Explore ONLINE!*

HISTORY

VIDEOS, including...
- The Attack on Pearl Harbor
- Emperor Hirohito
- The Desert War
- D-Day

☑ Document-Based Investigations

☑ Graphic Organizers

☑ Interactive Games

☑ Interactive Map: The War in the Pacific, 1942 – 1945

☑ Image with Hotspots: London Blitz

☑ Image Carousel: Leaders of War

▶ *Explore ONLINE!*

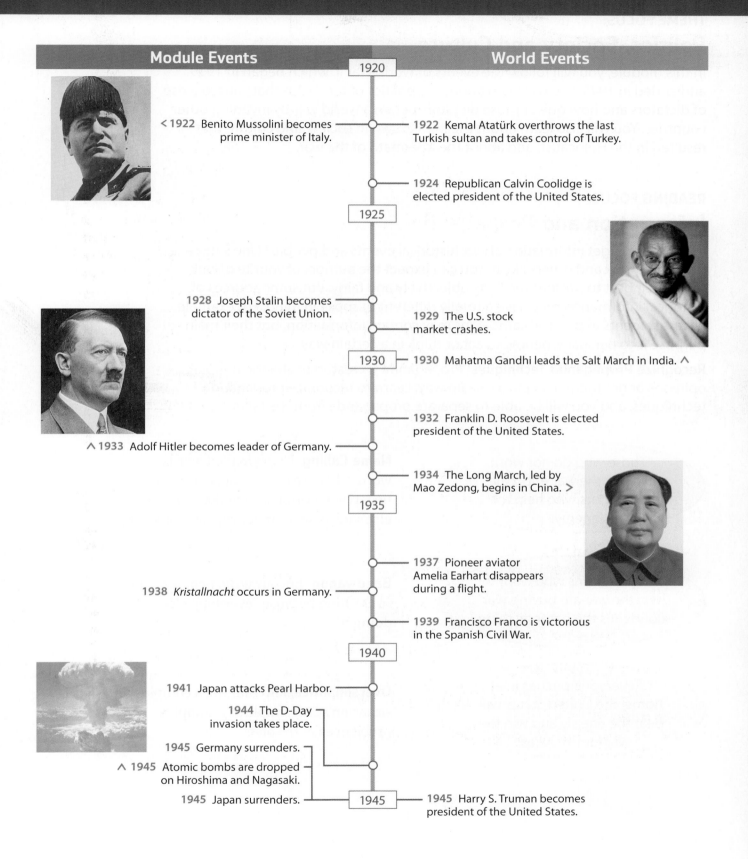

Module Events		World Events

1920

< **1922** Benito Mussolini becomes prime minister of Italy.

1922 Kemal Atatürk overthrows the last Turkish sultan and takes control of Turkey.

1924 Republican Calvin Coolidge is elected president of the United States.

1925

1928 Joseph Stalin becomes dictator of the Soviet Union.

1929 The U.S. stock market crashes.

1930

1930 Mahatma Gandhi leads the Salt March in India. ∧

1932 Franklin D. Roosevelt is elected president of the United States.

∧ **1933** Adolf Hitler becomes leader of Germany.

1934 The Long March, led by Mao Zedong, begins in China. >

1935

1937 Pioneer aviator Amelia Earhart disappears during a flight.

1938 *Kristallnacht* occurs in Germany.

1939 Francisco Franco is victorious in the Spanish Civil War.

1940

1941 Japan attacks Pearl Harbor.

1944 The D-Day invasion takes place.

1945 Germany surrenders.

∧ **1945** Atomic bombs are dropped on Hiroshima and Nagasaki.

1945 Japan surrenders.

1945

1945 Harry S. Truman becomes president of the United States.

Reading Social Studies

Politics, Society and Culture

In this module, you will follow the events of World War II, which began in 1939 and ended in 1945. You will learn about the politics of the 1930s that caused a rise of dictators and how one of those dictators began a world war by invading other countries. You will also learn about the breakdown in society and culture that resulted in the Holocaust, and about the aftermath of the war.

READING FOCUS:

Information and Propaganda

Where do you get information about historical events and people? One source is this textbook and others like it. You can expect the authors of your textbook to do their best to present the facts objectively and fairly. But some sources of historical information may have a totally different purpose in mind. For example, advertisements in political campaigns may contain information, but their main purpose is to persuade people to act or think in a certain way.

Recognize Propaganda Techniques Propaganda is created to change people's opinions or get them to act in a certain way. Learn to recognize propaganda techniques, and you will be able to separate propaganda from the facts.

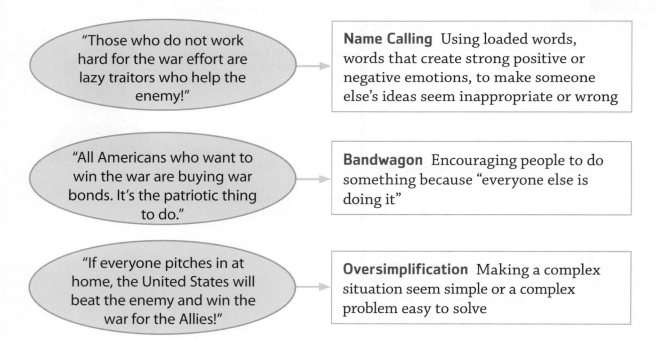

"Those who do not work hard for the war effort are lazy traitors who help the enemy!"

Name Calling Using loaded words, words that create strong positive or negative emotions, to make someone else's ideas seem inappropriate or wrong

"All Americans who want to win the war are buying war bonds. It's the patriotic thing to do."

Bandwagon Encouraging people to do something because "everyone else is doing it"

"If everyone pitches in at home, the United States will beat the enemy and win the war for the Allies!"

Oversimplification Making a complex situation seem simple or a complex problem easy to solve

You Try It!

Study the following poster and then answer the questions below.

Don't Let That Shadow Touch Them
Buy WAR BONDS

U.S. World War II poster from 1942

Answer the following questions based on the poster above.

1. What is the purpose of this poster?
2. How does this poster use images to get people to act a certain way? How do you think the images made people feel?
3. Do you think this poster is an example of propaganda? Why or why not? If you think it is propaganda, what technique did the creator use? Do you think there is more than one technique?
4. What does this poster tell us about Americans during World War II?

As you read this module, look carefully at all of the primary sources. Do any of them include examples of propaganda?

Key Terms and People

Lesson 1
fascism
Benito Mussolini
Adolf Hitler
Nazi Party
Gestapo
totalitarianism
Joseph Stalin
collectivization
Emperor Hirohito

Lesson 2
Axis Powers
Allied Powers
blitzkrieg
Winston Churchill
Dwight D. Eisenhower

Lesson 3
anti-Semitism
Holocaust
genocide
Kristallnacht
concentration camp
ghetto
Final Solution

Lesson 4
atomic bomb
United Nations
war crime
Douglas MacArthur
Nuremberg Trials

The Rise of Dictators

The Big Idea

After World War I, dictators rose to power in several countries around the world.

Main Ideas

- The devastation of World War I and economic hardship pushed many Europeans to look for stronger leadership.

- After Vladimir Lenin's death, totalitarian dictator Joseph Stalin took control of the communist Soviet Union.

- Beginning in the early 1900s, intensely nationalistic military leaders played an increasingly dominant role in the Japanese government.

Key Terms and People

fascism
Benito Mussolini
Adolf Hitler
Nazi Party
Gestapo
totalitarianism
Joseph Stalin
collectivization
Emperor Hirohito

If YOU were there . . .

You live in Germany in 1933, and a strong leader has just taken over the government. He gives powerful speeches promising a better life for Germans. But he also speaks out harshly against Jews and other groups living in Germany, and he has arrested political opponents. Although some of your classmates are excited by these speeches, others are worried about the future.

What would you say to your classmates?

Fascism in Europe

The years following World War I were difficult for many Europeans. Countries involved in the war suffered from physical destruction, heavy debt, and high unemployment. In addition, the Great Depression began in 1929 with the U.S. stock market crash and spread around the world, causing more suffering. Some people looked to strong leaders and fascist governments to turn their countries around. **Fascism** (FA-shih-zuhm) is a political system that places the interests of the nation above those of the people. It is characterized by extreme nationalism and military buildup.

Mussolini's Italy After World War I, Italy was plagued by economic troubles, strikes, and riots. A king and a democratically elected legislature governed the country, but many wanted stronger leadership. **Benito Mussolini** (moo-suh-LEE-nee), a veteran of the war, seemed to promise the stability that Italy lacked. In 1919, Mussolini founded the Fascist Party. Three years later, he organized a rebellion against the Italian government. An army of his followers surrounded Rome, Italy's capital, in October 1922. They brought down the government. Mussolini took power as prime minister.

At first, Mussolini followed existing government procedures. But within a few years, he abolished other political parties and ended elections. He ruled Italy through both strict government control and the power of his personality.

Benito Mussolini addresses a crowd at a political rally.

Mussolini was an electrifying speaker who attracted many followers. By 1925, Mussolini had become a dictator. The Fascist Party was Italy's only political party. It controlled nearly every aspect of Italians' lives. There was no freedom of speech. The Fascists controlled all newspapers and other news outlets.

Mussolini dreamed of creating an empire and restoring Italy to greatness. One way he aimed to achieve these goals was through the conquest of other countries. In 1935, the Italian army invaded Ethiopia, a country in east Africa, south of Egypt. The Italians used poison gas against the Ethiopians. Within a year, Italy had colonized Ethiopia. The League of Nations condemned the conquest, but it had little power. British and French governments also condemned Italy's actions. The hostility from western democracies caused Mussolini to draw closer to other European countries ruled by dictators, including Germany.

Germany and the Rise of Hitler Germans also suffered from the effects of World War I and the Great Depression. The Treaty of Versailles, which ended World War I, was hard on Germany. The treaty stripped Germany of territory and forced it to make reparations, or payments for the injuries it had caused during the war. The conditions of the treaty weakened the country's economy. Many Germans fell on hard times. They resented the difficulties caused by Germany's defeat and the harsh treaty. One of those frustrated by the conditions was German army veteran **Adolf Hitler**.

In 1919, Hitler joined a small German political party that he renamed the **Nazi** (NAHT-see) **Party**. He quickly became its leader. He was a strong speaker. During the 1920s, Hitler and the Nazis attracted many followers.

Hitler believed that Germans were a "master race" of people, superior to all others. He blamed other groups for Germany's problems. In particular, he blamed Jews, whom he thought were an evil and inferior "race" that

Children cheer at a Nazi rally. Beginning in 1939, membership in Hitler's youth programs was required.

lived off other races. In addition, Hitler wanted to expand the territory of Germany, especially to the east, where others of German heritage lived. Hitler's ideas became the basis of the Nazi Party.

The Nazi Party's popularity increased as the Depression wore on because the party promised a better life for Germans. In the 1932 national elections, the Nazis won more seats in the national legislature than did any other party. Hitler was one of those elected. Early the next year, Adolf Hitler was named chancellor of Germany, or the head of the national legislature. Within a few months, he had assumed total control as a dictator. He declared the Nazi Party to be the only legal party in Germany.

In the following years, Hitler eliminated communists, democrats, and Jews from government jobs and from universities. He also banned all trade unions except for Nazi workers' groups. He ordered the execution of leaders with whom he disagreed. He created a political secret police called the **Gestapo** (guh-STAH-poh) to investigate and put down any political opposition. These actions are characteristic of a totalitarian government.

BIOGRAPHY

Adolf Hitler 1889–1945

Born in Austria, Adolf Hitler moved to Germany in 1913 and then served in the German army during World War I. After the war, he became head of the Nazi Party. In 1924, while in prison for attempting to overthrow the government, Hitler wrote *Mein Kampf* ("My Struggle"), in which he told the story of his life and described his political ideas. The Nazi Party did well in a national election in 1932.

In 1933, Hitler became the German chancellor. Later that year, Hitler seized all power. His aggressive actions as Germany's leader led to the start of World War II.

Summarize
Why was Hitler imprisoned?

Totalitarianism is a system in which the government controls all areas of people's lives. There are no individual freedoms. A dictator or small group of rulers holds all of the power, and dissent, or disagreement, is not tolerated.

One of Hitler's first objectives was to remake Germany into a world power. Building up the German military was central to that goal. Hitler greatly expanded the army, and he created a new air force. Hitler's aim was to expand German territory. He knew that expansion meant war.

Reading Check
Summarize
Why did fascism develop in Europe?

Stalin's Soviet Union

In addition to condemning Jews and other groups, Hitler frequently spoke out against communists. He viewed them as a threat to Germany and the German race. One of the targets of Hitler's hatred was the Soviet Union.

The Russian Revolution had taken place in 1917, as World War I was ending. Bolshevik leader Vladimir Lenin, a founder of the Russian Communist Party, became the first head of the new Communist government of the Soviet Union. Lenin was a powerful leader who crushed all opposition. When he died in 1924, there was a fierce struggle to succeed Lenin. **Joseph Stalin** won that struggle and became Soviet dictator for the next 25 years.

Stalin was a brutal dictator who ruled by terror. There were no individual rights or freedoms for the Soviet people. During the 1930s, he consolidated power by having his rivals executed. Stalin also executed many military leaders, Communist party bosses, and industrial managers. Tens of millions of people lost their lives under his rule.

Stalin also imprisoned millions in a system of labor camps across the Soviet Union known as the Gulag. Political prisoners were arrested and sent to the Gulag, where they could be starved or executed for refusing to work.

Early in his rule, Stalin decided that the Soviet Union would never catch up with the world's advanced nations by gradually increasing industrial and agricultural output. Beginning in 1928, he instituted a series of Five-Year Plans for economic growth. The goals of the plans were increased

Russian prisoners were often used as slave labor. Here, prisoners work on the White Sea–Baltic Canal in 1932.

heavy industry, agricultural reform, and military buildup. To increase farmers' output, Stalin established a policy of **collectivization**. Peasants were forced to give up their private farms and become part of large, group-based farms. Many peasants resisted, especially the ones who owned larger farms. Stalin enforced the policy through executions and mass arrests.

Stalin's Five-Year Plans came at a terrible cost to the people. Collectivization led to mass famines. Millions of peasants died as a result. By 1937, however, Stalin had successfully industrialized the country. The Soviet military had also become one of the strongest in the world.

Reading Check
Summarize
What was the outcome of Stalin's Five-Year Plans?

Military Dominance in Japan

Although Japan never had one single dictator like those in Europe, a group of military leaders slowly gained complete control over the government during the early 1900s. Japanese aggression toward other countries in Asia began after it was victorious in the Sino-Japanese War in 1895. As a result of the conflict, Japan gained greater influence over Korea and took control of Taiwan and other territories. In 1904, the Japanese launched a war against Russia to prevent Russian influence over Korea and Manchuria (now part of northeastern China). After a year of fighting, the Japanese were victorious in the Russo-Japanese War.

Japanese military leaders were intensely nationalistic. They wanted to expand Japan through conquest. **Emperor Hirohito** took the throne of Japan in 1926. In theory, he had control over both Japan's government and its military. But Hirohito could not control the military extremists.

In 1931, Japanese troops stationed in Manchuria and Korea took over all of Manchuria and set up a Japanese-dominated government in the region. Japan's civilian government in Tokyo had lost control over Japan's army. By the mid-1930s, most of the important government positions, including prime minister, were filled by military officers.

Japanese soldiers celebrate the capture of Nanjing, China, in 1937.

In 1937, the Japanese military moved into China and took over most of the Chinese coast. Major Chinese cities were also occupied. When the Japanese army seized the Chinese city of Nanjing, Japanese soldiers destroyed more than a third of the city's buildings and massacred tens of thousands of Chinese. Japan now dominated most of the Asian territory near Japan.

Summary and Preview In this lesson, you read about the rise of dictators around the world in the 1920s and 1930s. In the next lesson, you will learn about how these dictators' aggressive actions led to war.

Lesson 1 Assessment

Review Ideas, Terms, and People

1. a. **Analyze** What caused the rise of totalitarian governments in Europe in the 1920s and 1930s?

   b. **Elaborate** What characteristics did the leaders of fascist governments share?

   c. **Recall** What African country did Italy invade in the 1930s, and why?

2. a. **Draw Conclusions** Why might many Soviets have feared Joseph Stalin?

   b. **Summarize** What were the goals of Stalin's Five-Year Plans?

   c. **Analyze** Why do you think collectivization resulted in the deaths of millions of peasants?

3. a. **Analyze** How extensive was Japanese empire building by 1937?

   b. **Summarize** What role did the emperor play in the Japanese government by the 1930s?

Critical Thinking

4. **Categorize** In this lesson, you learned about the governments of four countries in the 1930s. Create a table like the one below, and use your notes to categorize the leader and the party or organization that ruled each country.

Country	Leader	Party or Organization
Italy		
Soviet Union		
Japan		
Germany		

World War II

The Big Idea
The Allied Powers fought the Axis Powers in World War II.

Main Ideas
- The war in Europe began with Germany's invasion of Poland, and the war in the Pacific began with Japan's attack on Pearl Harbor.
- The Germans controlled much of Europe before the Allies invaded on D-Day.
- The Japanese controlled much of Asia and the Pacific until the Allies defeated Japanese naval forces at the Battle of Midway.

Key Terms and People
Axis Powers
Allied Powers
blitzkrieg
Winston Churchill
Dwight D. Eisenhower

If YOU were there . . .

In December 1941, you are spending a quiet Sunday listening to the radio. Suddenly, the radio broadcast is interrupted by an announcer's voice. You are shocked by what you hear. Japan has just launched a massive air raid on the U.S. Navy at Pearl Harbor, Hawaii. You are saddened and angered by the attack.

What do you think the U.S. response should be?

The War Begins

After taking control of the government in 1933, Adolf Hitler sought to expand German territory and unite all people of German heritage. He aligned himself with Italy and Japan in 1936, forming what became known as the **Axis Powers**. In 1938, Germany took over Austria, a neighboring country whose population spoke German. Then Hitler looked east for more land. A section of Czechoslovakia called the Sudetenland was home to a population of Germans. Hitler said they were being treated poorly. He announced that Germany would take over the Sudetenland.

Other countries in Europe hoped to avoid war. British Prime Minister Neville Chamberlain helped fashion an agreement between Germany and several European countries allowing Germany to take over the Sudetenland. In exchange, Hitler agreed to end Germany's expansion. Hitler had no intention of sticking to the agreement.

In early 1939, Germany took over the rest of Czechoslovakia, as well as some other areas east of Germany. To ensure that the Soviet Union would not oppose Germany's further expansion, Hitler made an agreement with Soviet leader Joseph Stalin that the two countries wouldn't invade each other. This agreement assured Hitler that no other country could stop his expansion. In the fall of 1939, Germany invaded Poland. In response, Great Britain and France declared war on Germany as the **Allied Powers**. World War II had begun.

German soldiers invade Poland in September 1939.

Germany's "Lightning War" World War II was a new kind of war. Tanks and trucks allowed armies to move quickly. Bombers flew long distances to strike enemy targets. With these tactics, Germany quickly defeated Poland in what the Germans called a **blitzkrieg**, or "lightning war."

Hitler's forces soon overran other European countries, too. Within a few months, Germany had defeated Norway, Denmark, Belgium, the Netherlands, and France. Only the English Channel prevented the Germany military from moving on to Great Britain.

British forces in Europe retreated to the English Channel and made it across the water to England before the German advance could catch them. Prime Minister **Winston Churchill** rallied his country in a speech to the British Parliament:

> "We shall go on to the end. We shall fight in France, we shall fight on the seas and oceans, we shall fight with growing confidence and growing strength in the air, we shall defend our island, whatever the cost may be. We shall fight on the beaches, we shall fight on the landing grounds, we shall fight in the fields and in the streets, we shall fight in the hills; we shall never surrender. . . ."
>
> —British Prime Minister Winston Churchill, from a speech to the British Parliament on June 4, 1940

BIOGRAPHY

Winston Churchill 1874–1965

Winston Churchill served as prime minister of Great Britain twice, from 1940 to 1945 and from 1951 to 1954. He was born in England to a British father and an American mother. After serving in the British Army, Churchill was elected to Parliament. He held many jobs in the national government. His warnings about the rise of Hitler in Germany helped lead to his becoming prime minister in 1940. During the war, Churchill inspired the British people with many well-known speeches and helped lead the Allies to victory.

Make Inferences
Why was Winston Churchill an effective leader during the war?

Because he couldn't send tanks to Great Britain, Hitler decided to attack from the air. The German air force began bombing British ports, factories, and airports in the summer of 1940. The Battle of Britain lasted for months. British fighter planes fought back, destroying German bombers. Hitler finally decided he was not able to force Great Britain to surrender. He turned the German air force toward the Soviet Union for an invasion.

The Attack on Pearl Harbor As the war widened in Europe, the United States declared it would remain neutral. U.S. leaders wanted to maintain the country's isolationist policy. Isolationism is avoiding becoming involved in other nations' affairs. U.S. leaders hoped to remain neutral in Asia as well, but Japanese aggression had many worried. The Japanese had invaded Manchuria, China, and Indochina (now Vietnam). U.S. diplomats demanded Japan leave the areas it had taken over, but the United States was not prepared to go to war with Japan over its actions.

The American attitude toward war with Japan changed on December 7, 1941. On that morning, Japanese fighter planes and bombers attacked the U.S. naval base at Pearl Harbor, Hawaii. The attack came as a complete surprise to Americans. Most of the American planes at the base never

DOCUMENT-BASED INVESTIGATION   Historical Source

The Attack on Pearl Harbor

The day after the attack on Pearl Harbor, President Franklin D. Roosevelt asked Congress to declare war on Japan.

Analyze Historical Sources
What was the central idea of Roosevelt's speech?

"*Yesterday, December 7, 1941—a date which will live in infamy—the United States of America was suddenly and deliberately attacked by naval and air forces of the Empire of Japan. . . .*

As commander in chief of the Army and Navy I have directed that all measures be taken for our defense. But always will our whole nation remember the character of the onslaught [attack] against us.

No matter how long it may take us to overcome this premeditated [planned] invasion, the American people, in their righteous [moral] might, will win through to absolute victory. . . .

Hostilities exist . . . our people, our territory, and our interests are in grave danger.

With confidence in our armed forces—with the unbounded determination of our people—we will gain the inevitable [unavoidable] triumph—so help us God."

—U.S. President Franklin D. Roosevelt

Leaders of War

Allies

Winston Churchill
Prime Minister of Great Britain

Franklin Roosevelt
President of the United States

Joseph Stalin
Premier of the Soviet Union

Axis Powers

Adolf Hitler
Chancellor of Germany

Benito Mussolini
Prime Minister of Italy

Hideki Tojo
Prime Minister of Japan

Reading Check
Summarize
What events began the wars in Europe and in the Pacific?

even had a chance to take off before they were destroyed. In less than two hours, more than 2,000 American soldiers were killed, and most of the Pearl Harbor fleet was destroyed.

The next day, the U.S. Congress declared war on Japan and joined the Allied Powers. Within days of the U.S. declaration of war against Japan, Germany and Italy declared war on the United States. All the major countries of the world were now at war.

Final Years of the War in Europe

The German military's lightning-quick attacks won the Axis Powers much of Europe at the beginning of the war. After defeating France and other countries in Western Europe in 1940, Germany turned east. In 1941, Hitler's troops invaded the Soviet Union—in spite of the agreement Hitler had made with Stalin. The German military was successful in its advance until late that year, when winter set in. German troops were not well outfitted for the worst Russian winter in years. They also faced strong Soviet resistance. Then, from July 1942 to February 1943, Soviet and German troops fought in the Battle of Stalingrad.

Stalingrad was a major Soviet industrial city. Some 800,000 Axis troops and as many as 1.1 million Soviet troops were missing, dead, wounded, or captured during the fighting. After the successful defense of Stalingrad, the Soviet army began pushing the Germans back.

In 1942, the British air force began flying missions over Germany to drop bombs on German industries. American bombers soon joined them. For three years, the Allies bombed German targets, causing massive damage.

Allied forces also attacked German positions in North Africa. By the spring of 1943, the Allies had defeated Axis troops in Africa. From Africa, the Allies turned their attention to an invasion of Italy. In the fall of 1943, American and other Allied forces defeated the Italian military to take most of Italy.

The D-Day Invasion In late 1943, President Roosevelt, Prime Minister Churchill, and Soviet leader Stalin met to discuss the war. Stalin urged the Allies to invade Europe from the west so that the German military would have to turn away from fighting the Soviets. Roosevelt and Churchill agreed. They made plans to mount a massive invasion in 1944.

The leader in charge of planning the Allied invasion was U.S. general **Dwight D. Eisenhower**, the Supreme Allied Commander. The date was set for June 6, 1944, known as D-Day. On that day, Allied forces would mount a surprise attack on the beaches of Normandy, a region of France.

The D-Day Invasion

The Allies planned to launch a massive attack on occupied France on June 6, 1944. The seaborne attack began on the beaches of Normandy, France.

Allied forces landed on six beaches in Normandy. This beach was named Omaha Beach. The U.S. Army landed here.

This is one of the thousands of landing craft used in the invasion. It was specially built to carry soldiers and equipment onto the beach.

The U.S. soldiers who landed on Omaha Beach faced stiff resistance from German forces. The Americans suffered more than 2,000 casualties here.

Analyze Visuals
In what ways does the photograph show the conditions faced by Allied troops during D-Day?

On the morning of D-Day, the largest seaborne invasion in history began on the Normandy beaches. The Allied force included 500 naval ships, 3,000 landing craft, and 13,000 aircraft. More than 156,000 Allied troops crossed the English Channel to land on the beaches. Americans made up about half the force. German forces were waiting. A tremendous battle raged.

Improved communication systems helped the Allies to coordinate all the forces involved in the D-Day invasion. Newly developed radio technology allowed military leaders to keep in touch with forces advancing through German lines and into the French interior.

Allied forces fought their way into France, and the Germans retreated. It took almost two months, but on August 26, 1944, Allied forces entered Paris, the capital of France. Paris was liberated, but more fighting lay ahead.

Although many Allied soldiers died in the D-Day invasion and the months of fighting afterward, advances in medicine helped save many of the injured. Before the war, scientist Alexander Fleming had discovered penicillin, but this first antibiotic wasn't used extensively until the need for it grew during World War II. Penicillin proved very effective in preventing deadly infections in many of the soldiers who had been wounded.

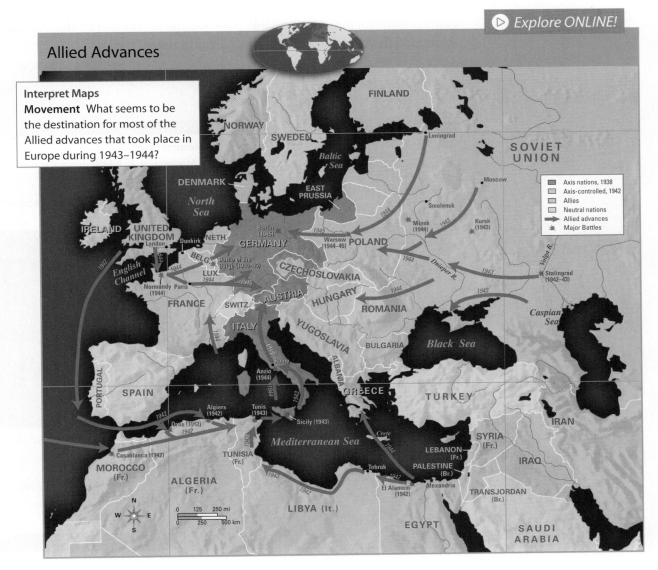

▶ Explore ONLINE!

Allied Advances

Interpret Maps
Movement What seems to be the destination for most of the Allied advances that took place in Europe during 1943–1944?

Legend:
- Axis nations, 1938
- Axis-controlled, 1942
- Allies
- Neutral nations
- → Allied advances
- ✳ Major Battles

Closing In on Germany In the fall of 1944, U.S. troops crossed into German-occupied Belgium. But the German military wasn't finished. Late in the year, German forces pushed the Allies back in Belgium and northern France. This became known as the Battle of the Bulge. The Allies eventually won this battle. By early 1945, Allied troops had entered Germany.

In the east, Soviet forces were also winning battles against the German military. By early 1945, the Soviets had liberated Poland and captured Hungary. By April 1945, the Soviets had surrounded the German capital, Berlin. The end of Nazi Germany was near.

Reading Check
Summarize
What happened on D-Day during World War II?

War in Asia and the Pacific

For the first several months after Pearl Harbor, Japan essentially ruled the Pacific. The surprise attack on Pearl Harbor had left the U.S. Navy weakened. As a result, there was nothing to stop Japan's well-prepared navy.

Early Stages of the War By 1942 the Allies decided that Japan was a major threat. Before then they had focused most of their efforts on the war in Europe. Now, however, they turned their eyes to the war in the Pacific as well.

By mid-1942, Japan controlled much of East Asia. The Japanese military quickly took Guam and Wake Island, and then captured Hong Kong, Singapore, and Burma. Also in 1942, the Japanese conquered the Philippine Islands, defeating the U.S. Army stationed there.

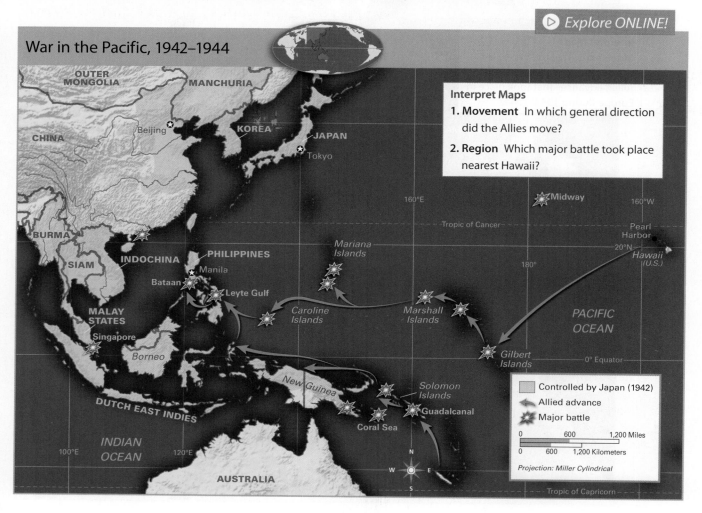

War in the Pacific, 1942–1944

▷ Explore ONLINE!

Interpret Maps
1. **Movement** In which general direction did the Allies move?
2. **Region** Which major battle took place nearest Hawaii?

Controlled by Japan (1942)
Allied advance
Major battle

0   600   1,200 Miles
0   600   1,200 Kilometers

Projection: Miller Cylindrical

The Japanese treated people in the lands they captured very harshly. When they captured the Philippines, they took more than 70,000 prisoners. They then forced these prisoners to march 60 miles to a brutal prison camp. More than 600 Americans and 10,000 Filipinos died.

Turning Point The first challenge to the Japanese came in mid-1942. First, the U.S. Navy stopped the Japanese at the Battle of the Coral Sea. Japanese naval forces then moved on to try to take Midway Island, northwest of the Hawaiian Islands. The Battle of Midway was mostly fought by airplanes launched from aircraft carriers. At Midway, American bombers sank four Japanese carriers, badly damaging the Japanese forces. This victory marked a turning point in the war. From then on, the Allies were on the offensive.

After the Battle of Midway, the Allies began attacking Japanese targets. The Allies' main strategy in the Pacific was called "island hopping." The Allies attacked only the most strategically important islands instead of each Japanese-held island. They used these captured targets as bases to launch attacks. In this way, the Allied forces worked their way closer to Japan.

Closing In on Japan By fall 1944, the Allies were in position to retake the Philippines. At the Battle of Leyte Gulf, U.S. forces crippled the Japanese fleet. This allowed the Allies to invade the Philippines and gave U.S. forces control of the Pacific. Allied forces also regained control of Burma in Southeast Asia.

Once Allied forces were secure in the Philippines and other islands in the region, heavy bombing of Japan itself began. The capture of the island of Iwo Jima in 1945 provided a perfect base for American B-29 bombers to raid Tokyo and other Japanese targets. The defeat of Japan was near.

Summary and Preview In this lesson, you learned about how World War II began and its battles. In the next lesson, you will learn about the Holocaust.

Reading Check
Analyze Effects
Why was it important that the Allies won the Battle of Midway?

Lesson 2 Assessment

Review Ideas, Terms, and People

1. **a. Summarize** What did the German military do in a blitzkrieg attack?

   b. Recall What happened to the American fleet at Pearl Harbor in December 1941?

2. **a. Explain** Why did Stalin want the Allies to invade Europe from the west?

   b. Recall Who was in charge of planning the D-Day invasion?

   c. Make Inferences Why was radio technology important in the D-Day invasion?

3. **a. Explain** Why was the Japanese military able to rule the Pacific in the early stages of the war?

   b. Recall What was the Battle of Midway?

   c. Make Inferences Why was it important that Allied forces captured the island of Iwo Jima in 1945?

Critical Thinking

4. **Organize Information** Create a timeline similar to the one below. Above the timeline, add at least three events that occurred in Europe. Below the timeline, add at least three events that occurred in Asia and the Pacific.

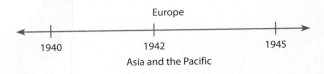

Europe

1940   1942   1945

Asia and the Pacific

Battles on Land, in the Air, and at Sea

World War II was a truly global conflict that involved countries from nearly every part of the world. During the war, battles were fought in Europe, the Soviet Union, the Middle East, Africa, Asia, and islands of the Pacific. An important factor in the fighting was the use of newly developed tanks, planes, and ships. These advanced war machines could cover much more territory than ever before. They played major roles in the deadly battles waged on land, in the air, and at sea.

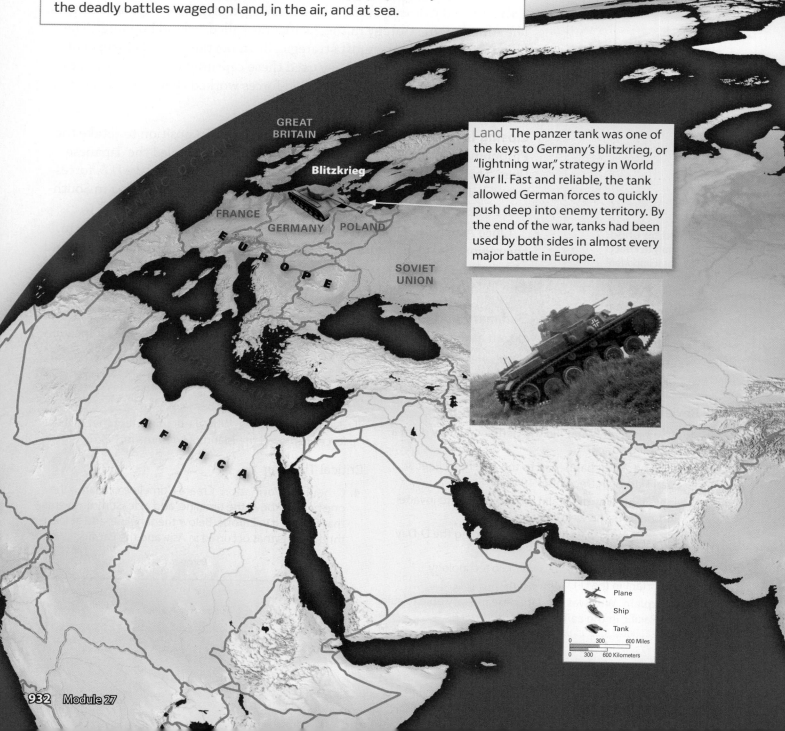

GREAT BRITAIN

Blitzkrieg

FRANCE

EUROPE

GERMANY   POLAND

SOVIET UNION

AFRICA

Land The panzer tank was one of the keys to Germany's blitzkrieg, or "lightning war," strategy in World War II. Fast and reliable, the tank allowed German forces to quickly push deep into enemy territory. By the end of the war, tanks had been used by both sides in almost every major battle in Europe.

Plane

Ship

Tank

0   300   600 Miles
0   300   600 Kilometers

Air The American B-29 bomber plane could fly almost 6,000 miles without refueling, which gave it the ability to strike targets far from its base. This is one reason the B-29 was used to drop the atomic bombs on the Japanese cities of Hiroshima and Nagasaki near the end of the war. The United States used the B-29 and other bombers to help win the war in both Europe and the Pacific.

Atomic Bombs

Sea In June 1942, several of the Japanese ships shown here took part in the Battle of Midway. In this battle, the U.S. Navy defeated the Japanese attackers and destroyed battleships and four aircraft carriers, making the United States the strongest naval power in the Pacific.

Battle of Midway

Interpret Maps

1. **Place** Based on Japan's geography, why do you think having a strong navy and air force was particularly important for this country during the war?

2. **Movement** Why was the B-29 bomber plane's ability to fly such a long distance without refueling important?

The Holocaust

The Big Idea

The Nazis murdered millions of Jews and other people during the time that has become known as the Holocaust.

Main Ideas

- The Nazis launched a campaign to terrorize and kill European Jews and other groups shortly after Hitler gained power.

- The Final Solution was the Nazi plan to ship Jews to extermination camps in Poland.

- Allied armies liberated the Nazi camps in 1944 and 1945.

Key Terms and People

anti-Semitism
Holocaust
genocide
Kristallnacht
concentration camp
ghetto
Final Solution

If YOU were there . . .

You're a U.S. Army officer making your way into Germany near the end of World War II. You and your soldiers come to a group of buildings surrounded by barbed wire. You're stunned by what you see. There are men who looked starved walking toward you, many with rags for clothes. You assume they're prisoners, held by the German army. It is horrifying to see how they have been treated.

What is this place, and how can you help these people?

Nazi Anti-Semitism

Jews had been part of the population of Europe for many centuries. During some periods of history, they faced intense discrimination. For example, during the Spanish Inquisition, many Jews were forced to leave Spain because they were not Christian. Hostility toward Jewish people and discrimination against them is called **anti-Semitism**.

Adolf Hitler and the Nazis had other reasons for their anti-Semitism. Hitler believed that different races of people had traits such as higher intelligence and other characteristics. He thought that Germans, which he called the "Aryan" race, were a master race, superior to all others.

When the Nazis took control of the German government in 1933, they almost immediately took action against German Jews. Hitler banned Jews from government employment. He limited the number of Jewish children in schools. Life began to grow increasingly difficult for German Jews.

During World War II, the Nazis launched a plan to eliminate Jews and other groups from Germany and occupied areas. The **Holocaust** was the systematic, government-sponsored murder of millions of Jewish men, women, and children by the Nazis and their collaborators during World War II. Six million Jews died in this **genocide**. Genocide is

Two German Jewish families gather for a picture before the war. Only two members of this group survived the Holocaust.

the deliberate destruction of a racial, political, or cultural group of people. Millions of other people, including Slavs, persons with disabilities, and Roma, or gypsies, were killed, too.

Nuremberg Laws In 1935, the Nazis passed two laws that increased legal anti-Semitism in Germany. These became known as the Nuremberg Laws because they had originally been proposed at a Nazi rally in Nuremberg, Germany. The first of these laws declared that only people of German blood could be citizens of Germany. Jews became subjects of the government, not citizens. The law also defined who was a Jew and who was a German. Even Jews who had converted to Christianity were defined as Jewish because Nazis believed Jews were a race, not members of a religion.

The second of the Nuremberg laws prohibited marriage between Jews and other Germans. The Nazis did not want the mixing of "races" because that would corrupt the purity of the German "race."

The Nuremberg laws made clear to Jews living in Germany that anti-Semitism under the Nazis would become more extreme over time. Many Jews tried to move to other countries, such as the United States, Palestine, and other European nations. But those countries typically had severe limitations on immigration. Most Jews found they had nowhere to go.

Kristallnacht On November 9, 1938, the Nazis carried out violent attacks against Jews throughout Germany, Austria, and German-controlled Czechoslovakia. This wave of violence became known as **Kristallnacht**, or the "Night of Broken Glass," because of the many shattered windows of Jewish businesses, homes, and synagogues. The Nazis claimed that the attacks were an unplanned outburst by the German people, but in reality, the violence was initiated by Nazi officials.

On November 9 and 10, Nazi groups smashed the windows and looted the goods of about 7,500 Jewish-owned businesses. They destroyed more than 1,000 synagogues, often burning them to the ground. They also wrecked many Jewish cemeteries.

Shown here is a view of Dachau's moat, fence, barracks, and guard tower.

Concentration Camps During the violence of *Kristallnacht*, the Nazis arrested about 30,000 Jewish men and sent them to prisons known as concentration camps. A **concentration camp** is a type of prison camp where political prisoners and other enemies of the state are confined. The Nazis had built Germany's first concentration camp near Dachau, Germany, in 1933. There, and in many other concentration camps spread throughout Germany, the Nazis imprisoned not only Jews but also others they thought of as "undesirables." These victims included communists, Christian ministers who opposed the Nazis, Jehovah's Witnesses, homosexuals, and the Roma, or gypsies.

The *Schutzstaffel*, or SS, was in charge of both Germany's police forces and the concentration camps. The SS-run concentration camps treated prisoners brutally. Prisoners could not appeal to courts or other authorities. Beginning in 1938, prisoners were often forced to do hard labor. Many concentration camp prisoners died from abuse and starvation. The SS also executed many prisoners. By the end of the war, the Nazis had imprisoned millions of Jews and others in Germany's extensive system of concentration camps.

Reading Check
Find Main Ideas
How was the anti-Semitism of the Nazis different from the anti-Semitism of the Spanish Inquisition?

The Final Solution

With the invasion of other countries in the late 1930s, Germany gained control over many more Jews. For example, about 10 percent of the population of Poland was Jewish. In 1940, the Nazis decided to separate the Polish Jews from everyone else by establishing areas called ghettos in cities and towns. A **ghetto** was a district in which Jews were isolated. Ghettos were usually enclosed by walls, fences, and gates. The Germans established about 400 ghettos in Poland and many more in occupied areas of the Soviet Union.

The Warsaw ghetto was the largest in Poland. Hundreds of thousands of Jews were packed into a tiny area of the city. Jews were shipped into the Warsaw ghetto and other ghettos from around Poland and from other

The Nazis forced Jews to live in isolated districts called ghettos. Here, young Jewish men are carted away from the Warsaw ghetto in 1941.

countries in Europe. Jews suffered terribly in these restricted areas. Food was scarce. Diseases spread rapidly in the crowded, enclosed areas. Many people in the ghettos died of starvation or disease. Eventually, the Nazis emptied the ghettos by shipping Jews to concentration camps. They also killed hundreds of thousands of Jews and others with mobile killing units that entered occupied areas along with the troops.

Death Camps Mobile killing units and concentration camps were not efficient enough for the Nazis, however. In early 1942 at a conference near Berlin, Nazi leaders decided on the **Final Solution** to the "problem" of the Jews. The plan was to ship Jews from throughout Europe to killing centers in Poland.

To carry out the Final Solution, the Nazis built extermination camps, or death camps, in Poland. Extermination camps were located at Chelmno, Treblinka, Belzec, and Sobibor. The Nazis built the camps on railroad lines so that Jews could easily be packed into cattle cars and shipped to the camps. At the extermination camps, the Nazis used special chambers to kill Jews with poison gas. From the gas chambers, the bodies were taken to cremation buildings, where they were burned.

The largest extermination camp was built at Auschwitz-Birkenau, also in Poland. As many as 6,000 Jews were executed there each day. When a crowded railroad car pulled in, people stepped off the train. They were then put through a "selection" process. Some, especially the young and healthy, would be selected to go to work camps, where they were forced into slave labor. Most were selected for immediate death. In the extermination camps, the Nazis murdered almost 2.7 million Jews in just a few years.

DOCUMENT-BASED INVESTIGATION **Historical Source**

Survival in Auschwitz

Primo Levi, an Italian chemist, was sent to Auschwitz in February 1944. In the following passage, he describes how the vast majority of Jewish prisoners were doomed upon arrival even if they weren't immediately selected for the gas chambers.

"On their entry into the camp, through basic incapacity [inability], or by misfortune, or through some banal [commonplace] incident, they are overcome before they can adapt themselves; they are beaten by time, they do not begin to learn German, to disentangle the infernal [very bad] knot of laws and prohibitions until their body is already in decay, and nothing can save them from selections or from death by exhaustion. Their life is short, but their number is endless. . . . One hesitates to call them living: one hesitates to call their death death, in the face of which they have no fear, as they are too tired to understand."

—Primo Levi, from *Survival in Auschwitz*

Analyze Historical Sources
What does the author say are the two alternatives for new prisoners coming to the camp?

Those who were not immediately killed faced terrible conditions. They worked as slave laborers, without adequate food or good shelter. Many died from starvation or disease.

Resistance to the Nazis Some Jews resisted the Nazis' Final Solution. They were able to escape the ghettos and camps and live in bands in the forests or mountains. There was also resistance in the ghettos. The Warsaw Ghetto Uprising in 1943 was the most significant ghetto rebellion against the Germans. The Germans had been shipping thousands of Jews out of the Warsaw ghetto to Treblinka, an extermination camp. In desperation, a group of Jewish fighters, armed with pistols and a few rifles, attacked the Germans and forced them to leave the ghetto. The Nazis had the advantage in weapons and soldiers, however. The Germans ended the uprising within a few weeks and destroyed the ghetto in the process of searching for those who led the resistance.

Some Jews went into hiding to escape the Nazis. One of those was Anne Frank, a teenager in the Netherlands who for two years hid with her family from the German occupation. The Nazis eventually captured the Frank family. Anne died from disease at a concentration camp in Germany. We know about her story today because of the diary she kept while in hiding.

BIOGRAPHY

Anne Frank 1929–1945

Anne Frank was a Jewish teenager living in Frankfurt, Germany, when Hitler came to power. When the Nazis' treatment of German Jews became too much to bear, Anne and her family moved to Amsterdam. Soon afterward, however, Nazis began rounding up Jews there. So, the Franks were forced to hide in a friend's home.

Anne could bring only a few items with her. She brought pictures of movie stars, books, and a diary her parents had given her on her thirteenth birthday. During this time, Anne wrote in her diary. Her diary became an important record of the Franks' years in hiding.

For two years, the Franks lived in constant fear of being caught by the Nazis. On August 4, 1944, they were discovered. For the next seven months, Anne and her family were moved from one concentration camp to another. Her mother died at Auschwitz, in Poland. Anne and her sister were moved to Bergen-Belsen in Germany, where they died of disease in March 1945. Anne Frank's father was the only family member to survive the war. Later, he published her diary.

Make Inferences
Why do you think Anne Frank's diary became an important record of this time period?

Reading Check
Summarize
What was the Nazis'
Final Solution to the
"problem" of the Jews?

A few people went out of their way to help Jews escape the Nazis. In 1944, for example, Swedish diplomat Raoul Wallenberg helped save many Hungarian Jews from death at the hands of the Germans. Most Jews, though, had few means to resist the Final Solution.

Aftermath of the Holocaust

As the Allied forces advanced toward Germany in 1944 and 1945, SS authorities in charge of the concentration camps began transferring prisoners to locations within Germany. They didn't want surviving Jews to tell about what had happened to them during the war. Prisoners were forced to march toward Germany on foot. Many died from starvation, disease, exposure to the weather, and exhaustion. The SS guards also shot hundreds of prisoners who could not keep up. These forced movements came to be known as "death marches" by the prisoners. The marches continued into the last weeks of the war.

Freedom for Prisoners During the summer of 1944, the Soviet army liberated some of the extermination camps in Poland. When the soldiers entered Auschwitz in early 1945, they found several thousand starving prisoners as well as evidence of the mass murder that had occurred there.

American forces liberated concentration camps in Germany. At Buchenwald, they freed more than 20,000 prisoners. There and at other camps, the Allied soldiers found piles of dead bodies and other evidence of the Nazis' cruelty and horror.

The Founding of Israel The Nazis killed some 6 million Jews during the Holocaust—around two-thirds of the Jews in Europe and about one-third of the Jews in the world. After the war was over, many Jews feared returning to their homes because of anti-Semitism. Tens of thousands of Holocaust survivors lived in camps for displaced persons run by the Allied

Survivors of the
Buchenwald concentration
camp, soon after they were
liberated

Reading Check
Make Inferences
Why did the Jewish survivors of the Holocaust fear returning home?

armies that occupied Germany. In 1948, the country of Israel was founded in a part of Palestine. More than 100,000 European Jews moved to Israel in the next few years. The United States also changed its laws to allow Jews and other displaced persons to enter. Other European Jews moved to Canada, South America, and other parts of the world.

Summary and Preview During World War II, the Nazis attempted to exterminate the Jewish people. Over six million Jews died in the Holocaust. In the next lesson, you will read about the end of World War II.

Lesson 3 Assessment

Review Ideas, Terms, and People

1. a. Recall What is genocide?

b. Analyze How did German Jews' status change after the Nazis passed the Nuremberg laws?

c. Summarize What happened to the Jews on *Kristallnacht*?

2. a. Recall What was the Warsaw ghetto?

b. Analyze Why do you think the German army did not immediately kill the young and healthy prisoners?

3. a. Summarize Why did many people die on the Nazi death marches?

b. Recall When were Jews able to move to Israel?

Critical Thinking

4. Organize Information Draw a diagram like this. Use the information in the lesson to put the events in the correct order.

Death Marches

Kristallnacht

Final Solution

Nuremberg Laws

Results of World War II

The Big Idea

Much of Europe and Japan were devastated by World War II.

Main Ideas

- World War II ended in 1945 with the defeat of the Axis Powers by the Allies.

- After the war, Japan adopted a new constitution that lessened the influence of the military and established a democratically elected legislature.

- Europe was divided into communist-controlled Eastern Europe and democratic Western Europe after the war ended.

Key Terms and People

atomic bomb
United Nations
war crime
Douglas MacArthur
Nuremberg Trials

If YOU were there . . .

You are a soldier in the U.S. Army stationed on a Pacific island during World War II. You have been through terrible battles, and you've seen friends die. You know that soon you may become part of an Allied force that will invade Japan. Such an invasion will take many lives, maybe your own. Then you hear that U.S. planes have dropped powerful bombs—atomic bombs—on two Japanese cities, killing many thousands of Japanese. You think maybe now the Japanese will surrender.

How do you feel about the devastating bombs that were dropped on Japan?

War Ends

World War II came to an end in 1945, first in Europe and then in Asia. The costs of the war were tremendous. Many lives were lost. Most of the countries involved in the fighting lay in ruins.

Victory in Europe In early 1945, Allied armies increased the air attack on Germany, with planes dropping bombs on many German targets. Some cities, such as Dresden, were almost completely leveled, killing tens of thousands. At the same time, the Soviet army entered Germany from the east. British, American, and Canadian armies entered from the west.

The German army fought back in some places, but it was too weak at this point in the war to defeat the Allied troops moving into the country. In late April, the Soviet army surrounded Berlin. Hitler knew that Germany would be defeated. On April 30, 1945, he committed suicide in the ruins of what had once been his headquarters.

The formal surrender of Germany to the Allied forces occurred at the headquarters of General Dwight Eisenhower in Reims, France, on May 8, 1945. This day was celebrated throughout the world as Victory in Europe Day, or V-E Day. The war in Europe was over.

Victory Over Japan By 1945 the Allies were close enough to Japan to invade. However, military leaders warned that invading Japan would be costly. Such an invasion might leave more than a million Allied troops dead.

Instead, the military suggested a different option to end the war. U.S. scientists had developed an **atomic bomb**, a nuclear weapon with a powerful explosion caused by the splitting of atoms. On August 6, 1945, an American B-29 dropped an atomic bomb on the city of Hiroshima, Japan. The effects of the bomb were devastating. More than 70,000 people were killed instantly. Thousands of buildings were destroyed. But the Japanese still did not surrender. Three days later, the Americans dropped another atomic bomb, this time on Nagasaki. At least 35,000 more people died.

As a result, the Japanese surrendered on August 15, 1945, now known as Victory over Japan Day, or V-J Day. V-J Day marked the end of World War II.

Results of the War World War II was the deadliest conflict in human history. Twenty-two million soldiers died. More than 34 million were injured. More than 30 million civilians also lost their lives. Many of those were victims of the Holocaust.

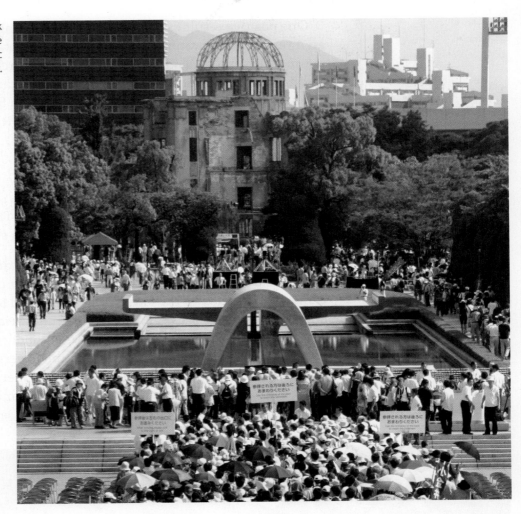

Hiroshima Memorial Park was built to honor the victims of the atomic bomb blast.

Tens of thousands of civilians died in Japan when the atomic bombs were dropped. These nuclear weapons held terrifying possibilities for the future. People feared that another war could wipe out humanity.

The world was greatly changed. The war had weakened the economies and governments of many nations. The United States and the Soviet Union were left as the world's strongest powers. Although they were allies during the war, the two nations now distrusted each other. This distrust led to a period of tense rivalry between the two superpowers.

Costs of World War II	
Military deaths	22,000,000
Military wounded	34,000,000
Civilian deaths	30,000,000
Financial cost to governments	$1,000,000,000,000
Analyze Visuals What does the high number of civilian deaths tell you about where the fighting took place?	

Sources: nationalww2museum.org, time.com, britannica.com

Reading Check
Find Main Ideas
What were the two strongest countries after World War II?

One positive result of the war was the founding of the **United Nations**, an international organization that aims to maintain peace and security around the world. Allied leaders Roosevelt, Churchill, and Stalin agreed to establish the UN at a conference in the Crimean port city of Yalta in February 1945. Fifty countries came together in San Francisco, California, to write the UN charter. The United Nations officially came into being in October 1945.

Postwar Japan

Japan ended the war defeated and destroyed. Its cities, including the capital of Tokyo, had been bombed and burned. There was little industry remaining. The Japanese people suffered from a shortage of food.

War Crimes Trials To deal with those who had carried out the worst atrocities during the war, Allied leaders held war crimes trials. A **war crime** is a violation of the laws of war as defined by international treaties and customs. The Allies conducted war crimes trials of Japanese officials. The trials of 28 Japanese defendants were conducted in English and Japanese. The defendants included military and government leaders who had overseen massacres in China, mistreated prisoners of war, and committed other similar crimes. Twenty-five of the defendants were convicted. Seven were put to death, and the others served prison sentences.

A Japanese officer signs a peace treaty aboard the U.S.S. *Missouri*.
U.S. General Douglas MacArthur looks on.

Causes and Effects of World War II

Causes

- Germany invades neighboring countries in an effort to build a new German empire under Nazi rule.
- Japan invades countries in Asia.

Effects

- More than 50 million people are killed.
- The Jewish population in Europe is almost completely wiped out by the Holocaust.
- The United States and the Soviet Union emerge as the world's strongest powers.
- Japan loses all acquired territory and is occupied by the Allies until 1952.

As the Supreme Commander for Allied Powers in Japan, Douglas MacArthur oversaw the postwar occupation of Japan.

U.S. Occupation of Japan From the end of the war until 1952, the Allies—primarily the United States—occupied Japan. For most of that time, U.S. General **Douglas MacArthur** was the Supreme Commander for Allied Powers in Japan.

The United States wanted to lessen the influence of the military in Japanese life and also bring democracy to the country. U.S. authorities helped Japanese leaders write a new constitution. Emperor Hirohito endorsed the constitution, which was formally adopted in 1947.

The constitution took power away from the emperor and gave power to a national legislature called the Diet. The Diet included two houses, similar to the houses of the U.S. Congress. Both Japanese men and women were given the right to vote. The new constitution also included a bill of rights that guaranteed the rights of Japanese citizens. The military lost the influence it once had in Japan. The Japanese people gained control of the government.

Reading Check
Analyze Effects
What were the effects of World War II on Japan?

Postwar Europe

Just as Japan had been devastated by the war, it had devastated much of Europe. In addition to the loss of human life, many cities had extensive bomb and fire damage. Others were in complete ruins. The fighting had destroyed homes, buildings, bridges, railroad lines, roads, and ports. At least 40 million people had been driven from their homes.

Most countries had very little money to rebuild. Without help, the people of many European countries would have faced extreme difficulty for decades to come. To ensure peace and stability, the United States provided much of the money for rebuilding, especially to the countries of Western Europe.

U.S. aid spurred economic growth in postwar Europe. It also established a friendship between the United States and the countries of Western Europe that continued for decades to come.

Nuremberg Trials The Allies also held a number of war crimes trials of Nazi war criminals at Nuremberg, Germany, after the war. They became known as the **Nuremberg Trials**. Many of the top Nazi leaders, including Adolf Hitler, could not be tried because they were either dead or missing.

In the first set of trials, 24 major Nazi leaders were tried for crimes against humanity and other crimes. All but three were convicted. Some received prison sentences, but 12 were sentenced to death by hanging.

Later, more trials were conducted at Nuremberg and elsewhere in Germany, including trials of doctors, concentration-camp commanders and guards, and other Nazis who had committed crimes against Jews. The trials continued for years in Germany and other countries in an effort to bring the Nazis to justice for their actions during the war.

A Divided Europe One of the most significant consequences of World War II was the division of Europe into East and West. As the war came to a close, the Soviet army had occupied the lands between the Soviet Union and Germany. The Soviets also occupied the eastern part of Germany. In the summer of 1945 at the Potsdam Conference in Germany, Allied leaders discussed the future of Europe. They could not agree on the Soviet Union's future role in the countries it occupied.

The Soviet Union ultimately maintained control over the countries of Eastern Europe for decades. It ensured that all of the countries had communist governments. Germany was also divided into East and West. The Soviet sector became East Germany under Soviet control. The other three sectors became the democratic country of West Germany.

Reading Check
Summarize
What did the United States do for Western Europe after the war?

Summary In this lesson, you learned how World War II ended and about conditions in Europe and Japan after the war.

Lesson 4 Assessment

Review Ideas, Terms, and People

1. a. Recall What was V-E Day?

b. Explain What impact did the atomic bomb have on Hiroshima and Nagasaki?

c. Draw Conclusions Why did nations come together after World War II to found the United Nations?

2. a. Recall What is a war crime?

b. Explain Which of the Allied countries controlled Japan after the war ended?

c. Draw Conclusions How did Japan's new constitution help prevent the country from starting another war?

3. a. Explain What was the condition of Europe at the end of World War II?

b. Recall Who was tried at the Nuremberg Trials?

c. Make Inferences Why did many Eastern European countries become communist after World War II?

Critical Thinking

4. Organize Information In this lesson you learned about how the war affected Europe and Japan. Create a graphic organizer like the one below to rank the three most important effects of World War II, from most important to least important, and explain why you chose that order.

Importance	Why
1.	
2.	
3.	

Social Studies Skills

Construct Timelines

Define the Skill

Timelines are a good way to organize historical information. Timelines clearly show a sequence of historical events over a certain period of time. Many timelines focus on a specific theme within a time period. When you construct a timeline, it often makes the sequence of events easier to follow. Timelines show events in the order they happened and the amount of time between events. Constructing a timeline can therefore help you better understand events' context. For example, organizing events on a timeline can help you determine their causes and effects.

Learn the Skill

When you construct a timeline, you need to make some basic decisions. First, the timeline needs a topic. This topic can be general or specific. One example of a general topic is World War II. A more specific topic might be major European battles of World War II. The timeline should cover a time period that includes the main events related to the topic. For example, it would make sense for a timeline on European battles in World War II to cover the period 1939 to 1945.

The next step in constructing a timeline is gathering information. This includes taking notes on events from the chosen time period related to the topic. It is important to write down the date when each event happened. Putting the events in order before making the timeline is often helpful. If there are too many events, it is a good idea to include only the most important ones.

The first step in actually constructing the timeline is to draw a straight line using a ruler. The next step is to mark even intervals on the timeline. Intervals are dates that divide the timeline into smaller, equal time periods. For example, a timeline of World War II from start to finish might include two-year intervals: 1939, 1941, 1943, and 1945. Then add events in the correct places on the timeline. The beginning and end of the timeline, each interval, and each event should be labeled with dates. The finished timeline should include at least six events. As a final touch, the timeline needs a title. The title tells what the entries in the timeline are about and may include the dates the timeline covers.

Practice the Skill

Follow these instructions to construct a timeline.

1. Using your textbook, choose a topic related to World War II for your timeline. Decide on the dates your timeline will need to cover.

2. Use your textbook to take notes on events to include in your timeline and their dates. Put the events in order.

3. Following the steps described above, construct your timeline. The finished timeline should include clearly labeled dates, at least six events, and a title.

Module 27 Assessment

Review Vocabulary, Terms, and People

Complete each sentence by filling in the blank with the correct term or person.

1. Germany used the tactic of _____ to invade countries at the start of World War II.

2. _____ is a political system that places the interests of the nation above those of the people.

3. Hostility toward Jewish people and discrimination against them is called _____.

4. In 1922, _____ took control of Italy.

5. The _____ was a plan to ship Jews from throughout Europe to killing centers in Poland.

6. The British prime minister who led his country during most of World War II was _____.

7. After the war, Nazis were tried for crimes against humanity at the _____.

8. Adolf Hitler was the leader of the _____.

9. The Supreme Allied Commander in charge of planning for D-Day was General _____.

10. A type of prison camp where political prisoners and other enemies are confined is a _____.

Comprehension and Critical Thinking

Lesson 1

11. a. Describe What is totalitarianism?
    b. Elaborate Why did Hitler expand the army and create an air force for Germany?
    c. Explain What was the policy that Stalin adopted to increase agricultural output, and what did that policy entail?

Lesson 2

12. a. Recall Which country did Germany invade, leading to the start of World War II?
    b. Identify What were the two sides in World War II, and what countries made up each side?
    c. Analyze Why did Stalin urge Roosevelt and Churchill to launch an invasion of Europe from the west?

Lesson 3

13. a. Describe What was the Holocaust?
    b. Recall What was the Final Solution?
    c. Explain By whom were the concentration camps liberated?

Lesson 4

14. a. Analyze Why did the Japanese finally surrender to the Allies?
    b. Make Inferences Why did countries from around the world join the United Nations after World War II?
    c. Explain How was Europe divided after the war was over?

Module 27 Assessment, continued

Review Themes

15. Politics Why did Hitler and the Nazi Party rise to power?

16. Society and Culture The Jews were a minority in German society. Why might this explain how the Nazis got away with their treatment of the Jews?

Reading Skills

Information and Propaganda *Use the Reading Skills taught in the module to answer the question below.*

17. Which of the following is not an example of propaganda?

   a. television announcement sponsored by an interest group

   b. flyer in favor of a new law

   c. poster against a political candidate

   d. set of instructions for a math test

Social Studies Skills

Construct Timelines *Use the Social Studies Skills taught in this module to complete the activity below.*

18. Construct a timeline about the end of World War II, covering the events from late 1944 through 1945.

Focus On Writing

19. Journal Writing Many people throughout history have written in journals to record their personal experiences. Create a journal page (or pages) based on events and people from the time period of World War II. Write your journal as if you were a citizen of Europe, Japan, or the United States during the war.

Memories of
WORLD WAR II

A global conflict, World War II shaped the history of both the United States and the world. Americans contributed to the war effort in numerous ways. Many enlisted in the military and served in Africa, Europe, and the Pacific. Others contributed by working in factories to produce the massive amounts of ships, planes, guns, and other supplies necessary to win the war. In the process, these Americans left behind firsthand accounts of their experiences during the war, both at home and abroad. Explore some of the personal stories and recollections of World War II online. You can find a wealth of information, video clips, primary sources, activities, and more through your online textbook.

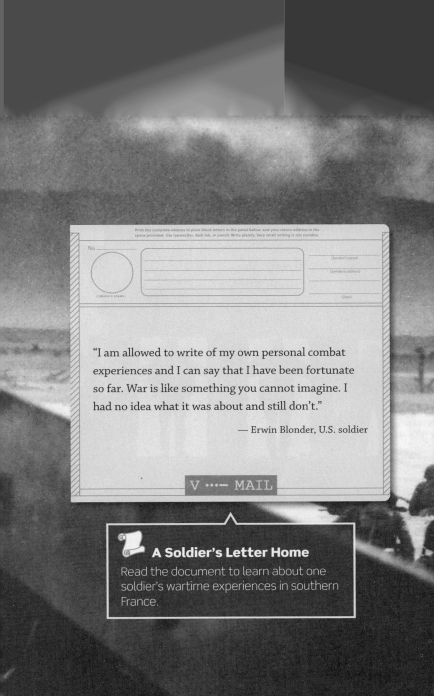

Print the complete address in plain block letters in the panel below, and your return address in the space provided. Use typewriter, dark ink, or pencil. Write plainly. Very small writing is not suitable.

No.

(CENSOR'S STAMP)

(Sender's name)

(Sender's address)

(Date)

"I am allowed to write of my own personal combat experiences and I can say that I have been fortunate so far. War is like something you cannot imagine. I had no idea what it was about and still don't."

— Erwin Blonder, U.S. soldier

V ···— MAIL

A Soldier's Letter Home

Read the document to learn about one soldier's wartime experiences in southern France.

America Mobilizes for War

Watch the video to see how the United States mobilized its citizens for war and how society changed as a result.

Air War Over Germany

Watch the video to see how the P-51 Mustang helped the Allies win the air war over Germany.

The Pacific Islands

Watch the video to hear veterans describe their experiences fighting in the Pacific theater.

Module 28
The Cold War Years

Essential Question
How did the United States and the Soviet Union compete during the Cold War?

About the Photo: Following World War II, communism spread from the Soviet Union into China and Eastern Europe. The Berlin Wall was a symbol of oppression during the Cold War.

▷ *Explore ONLINE!*

HISTORY.

VIDEOS, including...
- Kennedy and the Wall
- The U.S. Becomes a Superpower
- The Arms Race
- Sputnik
- The Marshall Plan
- Cuban Missile Crisis

☑ Document-Based Investigations

☑ Graphic Organizers

☑ Interactive Games

☑ Interactive Table: Rival Nations

☑ Image with Hotspots: The Berlin Wall

☑ Image with Hotspots: The Vietcong Tunnels

In this module you will learn how communism spread in the years following World War II and its eventual collapse in Europe.

What You Will Learn...

Lesson 1: The Cold War Begins. **954**
The Big Idea The opposing economic and political philosophies of the United States and the Soviet Union led to global competition and significant disagreements..

Lesson 2: Cold War Conflicts **961**
The Big Idea The Cold War was not restricted to Europe and flared around the world.

Lesson 3: Changes in Strategy. **969**
The Big Idea From the 1950s until the 1980s the Cold War continued, but there were times when tensions between the Soviets and the United States eased.

Lesson 4: The Breakup of the Soviet Union. **973**
The Big Idea In the 1980s and early 1990s, reform movements in the Soviet Union and Eastern Europe led to the fall of the Iron Curtain.

Timeline of Events 1945–1991 ▶ Explore ONLINE!

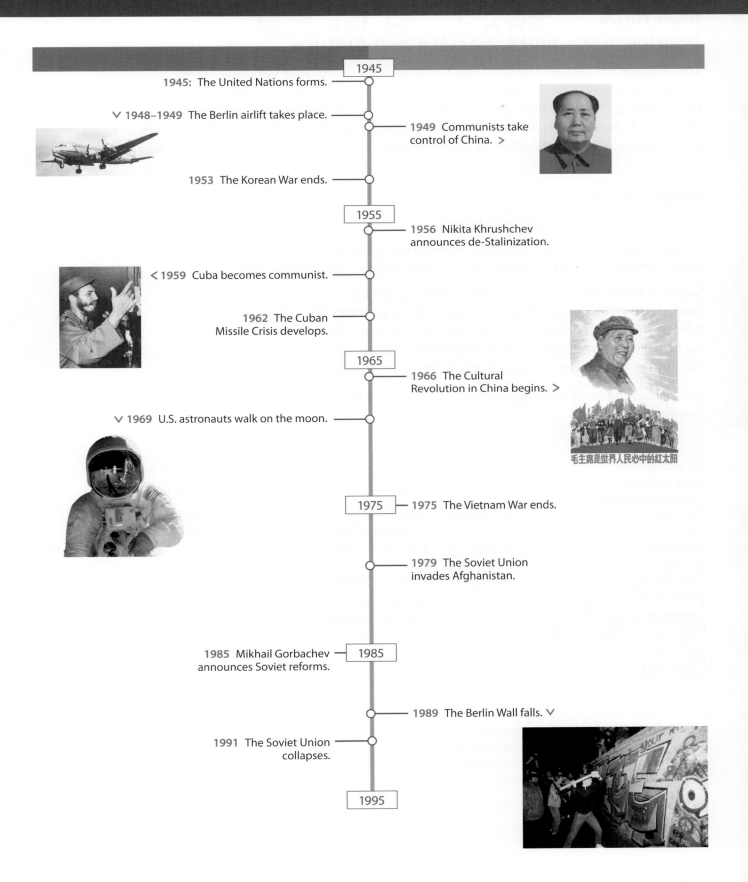

1945

1945: The United Nations forms.

∨ **1948–1949** The Berlin airlift takes place.

1949 Communists take control of China. >

1953 The Korean War ends.

1955

1956 Nikita Khrushchev announces de-Stalinization.

< **1959** Cuba becomes communist.

1962 The Cuban Missile Crisis develops.

1965

1966 The Cultural Revolution in China begins. >

毛主席是世界人民心中的红太阳

∨ **1969** U.S. astronauts walk on the moon.

1975 — **1975** The Vietnam War ends.

1979 The Soviet Union invades Afghanistan.

1985 Mikhail Gorbachev announces Soviet reforms. — 1985

1989 The Berlin Wall falls. ∨

1991 The Soviet Union collapses.

1995

Reading Social Studies

THEME FOCUS:

Politics, Economics, Society and Culture

This module will discuss the Cold War between the United States and the Soviet Union. This war was unlike other wars in that it was mostly political rather than military. The Soviet Union supported communism, an economic system the United States opposed. Communist countries were not democratic, which affected the society and culture of these nations.

READING FOCUS:

Set a Purpose for Reading

Setting a purpose for your reading can help you understand the things that you read. Understanding the author's goal is an important part of this task.

Select a Focus When you open this book to a page you have been assigned to read, there will be clues about what you will be learning. The information in this book is organized under headings that help explain the text. When you read a section like the one below, try to determine how the text explains the heading. Looking at the heading can help you to know what to focus on as you read.

Notice how the headings could help you to determine purpose for reading the passage below.

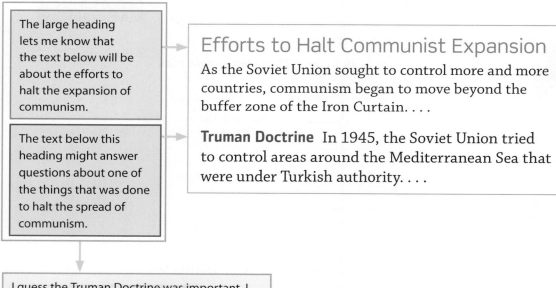

The large heading lets me know that the text below will be about the efforts to halt the expansion of communism.

The text below this heading might answer questions about one of the things that was done to halt the spread of communism.

Efforts to Halt Communist Expansion

As the Soviet Union sought to control more and more countries, communism began to move beyond the buffer zone of the Iron Curtain. . . .

Truman Doctrine In 1945, the Soviet Union tried to control areas around the Mediterranean Sea that were under Turkish authority. . . .

I guess the Truman Doctrine was important. I should read to find out what it was and how it might relate to halting communist expansion.

You Try It!

The following passage is from this module. As you read the passage, look for information in the headings that tells you what to look for.

The Korean War

When World War II ended, Korea was divided in two. . . .

Fighting Begins On June 25, 1950, North Korean troops stormed across the 38th parallel. After the invasion, the United Nations called for a cease-fire. . . .

The War Continues Fierce fighting raged for six weeks before the UN troops turned the tide of the war with a surprise attack. . . .

After you read the passage, answer the following questions.

1. After reading the headings, what do you think this section is going to be about?

2. What are some questions you might ask before reading this section?

3. What information do you think you will learn from this section?

As you read this module, set a purpose before you read each section.

Key Terms and People

Lesson 1
Cold War
containment
Truman Doctrine
Marshall Plan
North Atlantic Treaty Organization
Warsaw Pact
arms race

Lesson 2
Mao Zedong
commune
Ho Chi Minh
domino theory
Vietcong
Fidel Castro
Anwar Sadat

Lesson 3
Nikita Khrushchev
de-Stalinization
Imre Nagy
Alexander Dubček
détente

Lesson 4
Mikhail Gorbachev
glasnost
Ronald Reagan
Margaret Thatcher
perestroika
Václav Havel
European Union

The Cold War Begins

The Big Idea

The opposing economic and political philosophies of the United States and the Soviet Union led to global competition and significant disagreements.

Main Ideas

- After World War II, the Soviet Union and the other Allied powers became enemies.
- Communism expanded as the Soviet Union took control of Eastern European countries.
- The United States took several steps to stop the expansion of communism.
- As the Cold War heated up, tensions between communist and capitalist countries increased.

Key Terms and People

Cold War
containment
Truman Doctrine
Marshall Plan
North Atlantic Treaty
   Organization
Warsaw Pact
arms race

If YOU were there . . .

You live in Vienna, Austria, in Western Europe. After the end of World War II, your city and much of your country lies in ruins. There are no jobs and your parents are out of work. Some of your friends' families are homeless. You hear on the radio that the Soviet Union, which is opposed to democracy and capitalism, is becoming more powerful in Eastern Europe. Then your family finds out the United States is going to lend your country money to help rebuild. The factories and schools will be reopening soon.

How do you feel about living in Western Europe?

Allies Become Enemies

During World War II, the United States and the Soviet Union fought together to defeat Germany and the Axis powers. Despite their alliance, the two nations had many disagreements. The Soviet Union was a communist country that believed centralized control was best. The United States was a democracy and capitalist country. These differences would lead to a conflict called the **Cold War**. This war was "cold" because the Soviets and Americans never fired weapons at each other. However, tensions were high for nearly 50 years.

The Yalta and Potsdam Conferences In 1945, Allied leaders held a series of meetings to discuss the postwar world. The two most important conferences were held in the Soviet town of Yalta and in Potsdam, Germany. At the Yalta Conference, they agreed to divide Germany into four parts that would be occupied by Great Britain, the United States, France, and the Soviet Union.

At the Potsdam Conference, the Allies divided Germany's capital city, Berlin, into four sections as well. They also agreed to put Nazi leaders on trial for war crimes. Germany's

Winston Churchill, Franklin Roosevelt, and Joseph Stalin met at Yalta in 1945.

military would be reduced, and its discriminatory laws would be repealed. However, there were many disagreements between the Soviets and the other Allied powers.

Soviet and American Differences At the end of World War II, the United States and the Soviet Union were the two most powerful nations in the world. However, the war had had a much larger impact on the Soviet Union than on the United States. The Soviet Union had lost tens of millions of people, both soldiers and civilians. Many of its cities were demolished. The United States suffered almost 300,000 deaths, but its cities and factories were not destroyed. As a result, the United States was in much better shape economically.

These differences had an effect on each country's postwar goals. The Soviet Union wanted to protect its borders. Soviet leaders were also committed to spreading communism around the world. The United States remained committed to democracy and capitalism. In 1946, Stalin said communism and capitalism could not exist in the same world. The differences between these two competing ideologies were the underlying issue of the Cold War.

Reading Check
Summarize What happened at the Yalta and Potsdam Conferences?

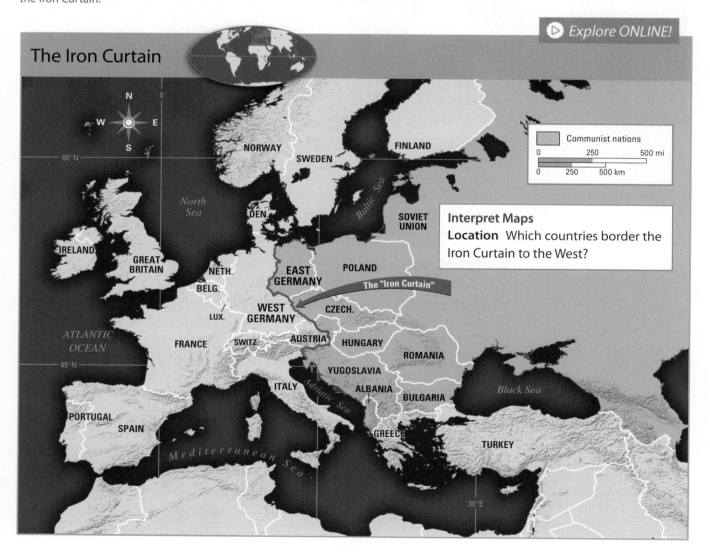

Political cartoons such as this one expressed people's fears and concerns about the Iron Curtain.

Building an Iron Curtain

The Soviet Union wanted to prevent another invasion from the west. Because it lacked natural western borders, Russia had lost many wars. Centuries of history had taught the Soviet leaders to fear invasion.

When World War II ended, Soviet troops occupied the countries along the Soviet Union's western border. Joseph Stalin, the leader of the Soviet Union, regarded these countries as a necessary buffer, or wall of protection. After Stalin established a communist government in Poland, the Soviet Union expanded its control over countries in Eastern Europe, including Hungary and Czechoslovakia. Stalin then did the same in the Balkan countries of Albania, Bulgaria, Romania, and Yugoslavia. In this way, he created "satellite states"—countries under complete Soviet control.

These countries were cut off from contact with the rest of Europe. Travel was restricted, as was migration. In 1946, Winston Churchill

▶ *Explore ONLINE!*

The Iron Curtain

Communist nations

0   250   500 mi
0   250   500 km

Interpret Maps
Location Which countries border the Iron Curtain to the West?

NORWAY • SWEDEN • FINLAND • IRELAND • GREAT BRITAIN • DEN. • SOVIET UNION • NETH. • EAST GERMANY • POLAND • BELG. • WEST GERMANY • The "Iron Curtain" • LUX. • CZECH. • FRANCE • SWITZ. • AUSTRIA • HUNGARY • ROMANIA • YUGOSLAVIA • ITALY • ALBANIA • BULGARIA • GREECE • TURKEY • PORTUGAL • SPAIN

North Sea • *Baltic Sea* • *ATLANTIC OCEAN* • *Adriatic Sea* • *Black Sea* • *Mediterranean Sea*

60°N • 45°N • 30°E • 0°

Reading Check
Analyze Causes
Why did the Soviet Union create satellite states?

described how Soviet control cut these countries off from the Western world. "An iron curtain has descended [fallen] across the [European] Continent," he said. The term *Iron Curtain* came to be used to describe this division. This expansion of communist power and influence was seen as a threat by some in Western Europe and the United States.

Efforts to Halt Communist Expansion

As the Soviet Union sought to control more and more countries, communism began to move beyond the buffer zone of the Iron Curtain. The United States quickly developed a new foreign policy to deal with the Cold War. It was based on the goal of **containment**, or preventing the Soviet Union from expanding its influence around the world.

President Harry Truman led the United States during the beginning of the Cold War.

Truman Doctrine In 1945, the Soviet Union tried to control areas around the Mediterranean Sea that were under Turkish authority. In nearby Greece, Communist rebels threatened to topple the Greek monarchy. At the request of President Harry Truman, Congress passed an aid package worth millions of dollars for Greece and Turkey. Truman explained his thoughts on what the United States should do to stop communism.

"It must be the policy of the United States to support free peoples who are resisting attempted subjugation by armed minorities or by outside pressures. I believe that we must assist free peoples to work out their own destinies in their own way."

—President Harry S. Truman, Speech to Congress, 1947

U.S. aid helped the Greek army defeat the communist rebels and protected Turkey from Soviet expansion. This policy of providing aid to help foreign countries fight communism became known as the **Truman Doctrine**.

The Marshall Plan Meanwhile, the nations of Europe were still devastated from World War II. American secretary of state George C. Marshall saw this as a threat to stability in Europe. Marshall called on European leaders to develop plans for recovery, which the United States would help fund. Under the **Marshall Plan**, Western Europe received more than $13 billion in U.S. loans and grants between 1948 and 1952. This money helped countries rebuild and stabilize their economies. It also made them more sympathetic to U.S. interests. Soviet leaders rejected Marshall Plan aid. They also kept Eastern European nations from participating.

Reading Check
Find Main Ideas
What did the United States do to prevent the Soviet Union from expanding its influence?

Cold War Heats Up

While Europe began rebuilding, the United States and its allies disagreed with the Soviet Union about the future of Germany. The Soviets wanted to keep their former enemy weak and divided. But in 1948, France, Britain, and the United States withdrew their forces from Germany. They allowed their occupation zones to form one nation. The Soviet Union responded by cutting off West Berlin from the rest of Europe.

From June 1948 to May 1949, Allied planes took off and landed every three minutes in West Berlin.

The Berlin Airlift The German capital city of Berlin was located deep within the Soviet occupation zone. It too had been divided. East Berlin was held by the Soviet Union, while the other three Allied powers controlled West Berlin. The Soviet Union wanted the Allied powers to leave Berlin, so they could control the city as part of communist East Germany. They created a blockade that cut off highway, water, and rail traffic into Berlin's western zones. The city faced starvation.

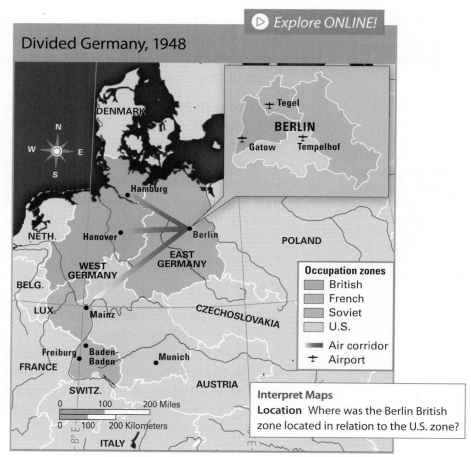

▷ *Explore ONLINE!*

Divided Germany, 1948

BERLIN
+ Tegel
+ Gatow   + Tempelhof

DENMARK

Hamburg

NETH.   Hanover •   • Berlin   POLAND

WEST GERMANY   EAST GERMANY

BELG.

LUX.   • Mainz   CZECHOSLOVAKIA

Freiburg • • Baden-Baden   • Munich
FRANCE

SWITZ.   AUSTRIA

0   100   200 Miles
0   100   200 Kilometers

ITALY

Occupation zones
- British
- French
- Soviet
- U.S.
- ▬ Air corridor
- + Airport

Interpret Maps
Location Where was the Berlin British zone located in relation to the U.S. zone?

At this time, the Soviet Union had a far larger military presence in Germany. Many of the other Allied troops had been sent home at the end of the war. Stalin gambled that the Allies would surrender West Berlin or give up their idea of reunifying Germany. But American and British officials flew food and supplies into West Berlin for nearly 11 months. This was known as the Berlin Airlift. At the height of the effort, planes carrying supplies landed in West Berlin every 45 seconds. In May 1949, the Soviet Union admitted defeat and lifted the blockade.

NATO and the Warsaw Pact The Berlin blockade increased Western Europe's fears of Soviet aggression. As a result, in 1949 ten Western European nations joined with the United States and Canada to form a defensive military alliance. It was called the **North Atlantic Treaty Organization** (NATO). An attack on any NATO member would be met with armed force by all member nations.

The Soviet Union saw NATO as a threat and formed its own alliance in 1955. It was called the **Warsaw Pact** and included Eastern European countries. In 1961, the East Germans built a wall to separate East and West Berlin. The Berlin Wall symbolized a world divided.

Even after World War II ended, there was still tension between West Germany and other Western European countries. To encourage them to get along, a trade association was created. Formed in 1957, it was called the European Economic Community (EEC). It included France, West Germany, Italy, and several other countries. This cooperation stayed strong throughout the Cold War, and became the basis for the current trade and economic agreement in Europe.

The Arms Race and Space Race As these alliances were forming, the Cold War threatened to heat up enough to destroy the world. The United States already had atomic bombs. It had demonstrated their power by using them to end the war with Japan. In 1949, the Soviet Union exploded its own atomic weapon.

President Truman was determined to develop an even more powerful weapon before the Soviet Union did. This resulted in a competition for greater military might called the **arms race**. Truman authorized work on a thermonuclear weapon in 1950. This hydrogen bomb, or H-bomb, would be thousands of times more powerful than the atomic bomb. In 1952, the United States tested the first H-bomb. The Soviets exploded their own in 1953. Over the next four decades, the United States and the Soviet Union made more bombs and built more airplanes. Each side believed that if they had enough weapons, it would stop their enemies from attacking.

Competition between the two countries also extended into space. Both countries wanted to explore and control this new frontier above the Earth. Each government wanted their country to be first. The Soviet Union announced the development of a rocket that could travel great distances. It was called an intercontinental ballistic missile, or ICBM. In 1957, the Soviets used an ICBM to send *Sputnik*, the first unmanned satellite, into orbit. This marked the start of the space race.

Some families built underground bomb shelters to use in case of a nuclear emergency. The shelters were stocked with essentials such as food and water.

Twelve years after *Sputnik*, American astronauts were the first people to walk on the moon.

After *Sputnik*, Americans feared that they had fallen behind in science and technology. Satellites could spy on the world below. And they also worried that rockets that could launch satellites could also be used to send bombs half-way around the world. Thanks to the Cold War and the space race, the U.S. government poured money into science education. New teachers were hired in elementary and high schools, and scholarships were established for students who wanted to study science, math, and engineering. In 1958, the United States launched its own satellite, *Explorer I*. Congress also passed a law creating NASA, the National Aeronautics and Space Administration. Its purpose was to expand human knowledge of space and eventually send astronauts into orbit and beyond. The government hoped NASA would make the United States the winner of the space race.

Summary and Preview After World War II, the United States and the Soviet Union became engaged in a tense, nonviolent conflict. It was called the Cold War. In the next lesson, you will learn how this had an impact on the rest of the world.

Reading Check
Analyze Causes
Why was there an arms race?

Lesson 1 Assessment

Review Ideas, Terms, and People

1. a. Recall Which two World War II allies became enemies in the late 1940s?

   b. Make Inferences Why did world leaders create the United Nations?

   c. Describe How did the impact of World War II on the Soviet Union differ from its impact on the United States?

2. a. Draw Conclusions Why did Winston Churchill use the term *Iron Curtain* to describe the Soviet Union's satellite countries?

   b. Elaborate What does the Soviet expansion tell us about Joseph Stalin?

3. a. Predict What types of problems could the Truman Doctrine have created?

   b. Analyze What was the goal of the Marshall Plan?

4. a. Evaluate Why was the success of the Berlin Airlift so important?

   b. Make Inferences Why were alliances like NATO and the Warsaw Pact helpful to the countries that joined them?

   c. Draw Conclusions Why might the arms race have caused people in the United States and Europe to worry?

Critical Thinking

5. Summarize Draw a diagram like the one here. List three things the United States did to contain the Soviet Union.

Cold War Conflicts

The Big Idea

The Cold War was not restricted to Europe and flared around the world.

Main Ideas

- Following a civil war in China, Communists took control of the country.
- Anti-Communist and pro-Communist forces fought a war in Korea.
- Anti-Communist and pro-Communist forces fought a war in Vietnam.
- Differences led to violent and nonviolent conflicts in Cuba, Africa, and the Middle East.

Key Terms and People

Mao Zedong
commune
Ho Chi Minh
domino theory
Vietcong
Fidel Castro
Anwar Sadat

If YOU were there . . .

You are an American living in Miami, Florida, in 1960. The Soviet Union is strong, and you've heard that they have built up their weapons and missiles, but they are on the other side of an ocean and Europe. Then, you learn that Soviet missiles have been discovered on the island of Cuba, located just 90 miles off the coast of Florida.

How do you react to this news?

Communism in China

In World War II, China fought on the side of the Allies. But the victory proved to be a hollow one for China. During the war, Japan's armies occupied and devastated many of China's cities. Millions of Chinese civilians had been killed. However, conflict did not end with the defeat of the Japanese. In 1945, opposing Chinese armies, who were fighting each other prior to World War II, started fighting again.

Civil War The Chinese Nationalist army outnumbered the Communist army by as much as three to one. However, the Nationalists, who were loyal to the reigning government, did not have popular support. When China's economy collapsed after years of civil war, thousands of Nationalist soldiers switched sides. In the fall of 1949, the Communists took control of the country.

Mao Zedong **Mao Zedong** (MOW ZUH-DOOHNG) was the leader of the Communist army. He became the leader of the new People's Republic of China after the defeat of the Nationalists. Mao wanted to make society more economically equal. Eighty percent of China's people lived in rural areas, but most owned no land. Mao took control of this rural land from the people who owned it. During these takeovers, his forces killed more than a million landlords who resisted giving up their land.

Mao then divided the land among the peasants, and the government forced them to join collective farms. These were large farms where the community all worked under the direction of the state. Mao also changed industry and business. Gradually, private companies were brought under government ownership. In 1953, Mao launched a five-year plan that set high production goals for industry. By 1957, China's output of coal, cement, steel, and electricity had increased dramatically.

The image of communist leader Mao Zedong was often used as symbol of China during the Cold War.

Great Leap Forward To build on the success of the Five-Year Plan, Mao announced the "Great Leap Forward" in early 1958. This plan called for even larger collective farms, or **communes**. In the communes, which were strictly controlled by the government, peasants worked the land together. They ate in communal dining rooms, slept in communal dormitories, and raised children in communal nurseries. They owned nothing. The nation profited from their labor but they did not, so the peasants had no incentive to work hard.

Unfortunately for China, the Great Leap Forward was a giant step backward. Poor planning and inefficient industries slowed growth. The program was ended in 1961 after a famine killed about 20 million people.

The Chinese government used propaganda, or biased information, to rally people behind Mao's programs.

Cultural Revolution The failure of the Great Leap Forward led to changes in how the government controlled the economy. Farm families were allowed to live in their own homes. They could also sell crops they grew on small private plots. Factory workers could compete for wage increases and promotions.

However, Mao thought China's new economic policies were bad for social equality. He wanted to revive the revolution. So in 1966, he urged China's young people to "learn revolution by making revolution." Millions of high school and college students left their classrooms. They formed militia units called Red Guards.

The Red Guards led an uprising known as the Cultural Revolution. Its goal was to establish a society of peasants and workers who were all equal. The new hero was the peasant who worked with his hands. They believed intellectual and artistic activity was useless and dangerous, so the Red Guards shut down colleges and schools. They forced writers,

Reading Check
Summarize How did Mao Zedong try to make Chinese society more economically equal?

teachers, artists, and scholars to "purify" themselves by doing hard labor in remote villages. Thousands of people were executed or imprisoned.

As the chaos grew, it threatened food production and shut down factories. It made daily life more difficult for ordinary people. By 1968, even Mao admitted that the Cultural Revolution had to end. The army was ordered to put a stop to the Red Guards' uprising. Order was restored. However, while China struggled to become stable once more, the Cold War continued.

The Korean War

When World War II ended, Korea was divided in two. Japan had controlled Korea throughout the war. After the war, the Allies divided Korea at the latitude line at 38° North, also known as the 38th parallel. The Soviet Union controlled the northern part of Korea. They wanted it to be a communist country. The United States occupied the south. They wanted Korea to be a capitalist democracy. Neither side recognized the other government as legitimate.

Fighting Begins On June 25, 1950, North Korean troops stormed across the 38th parallel. After the invasion, the United Nations called for a cease-fire. But the North Koreans continued their attack. The United States and the UN decided to join the fight. This was part of the U.S. policy of containment to stop the spread of communism.

American general Douglas MacArthur was put in command of the UN forces, which included troops from the United States and 15 other countries. The majority of the troops were from the United States and South Korea. MacArthur's forces lost early battles and were pushed all the way back to the southern tip of the Korean peninsula.

The War Continues Fierce fighting raged for six weeks before UN troops turned the tide of the war with a surprise attack. Landing at the port city of Inchon, UN forces attacked the North Koreans from behind. About a month later, MacArthur's troops captured Pyongyang, North Korea's capital. They then advanced north to the Yalu River, the border between North Korea and China. MacArthur was so sure that he would win the war and control all of Korea that he told President Truman he would "get the boys home by Christmas."

Then China suddenly sent hundreds of thousands of soldiers across the border to join the North Koreans. They drove UN forces south again, back below the 38th parallel.

By the spring of 1951, UN forces had driven the North Koreans and Chinese back across the 38th parallel. But neither side seemed able to win the war.

Finally in July 1953, the UN forces and North Korea signed a cease-fire agreement. The border between the two Koreas was set near the 38th parallel, almost where it had been before the war. In three years of fighting, 4 million soldiers and civilians had died.

After the War After the war, Korea remained divided. A demilitarized zone, or area where no military personnel or equipment is allowed, separated the two countries. This DMZ still exists today. Communist North Korea established collective farms and built up its military. Today, the country is a totalitarian dictatorship, or ruled under the tight control of a single leader. Famines and significant economic problems have made life in North Korea difficult for ordinary people.

South Korea, however, prospered following the end of the war, due in part to financial aid from the United States and other countries. In the 1960s, South Korea concentrated on developing its industry and expanding foreign trade. In the late 1980s, South Korea became a fully democratic nation.

Political differences have kept the two Koreas apart, even though there have been discussions of reuniting the country. North Korea's possession of nuclear weapons is a major obstacle. The United States still keeps troops in South Korea.

Reading Check
Analyze Effects How did the border between North Korea and South Korea change after the Korean War?

War in Vietnam

After World War II, containment was the main goal of U.S. foreign policy. The United States fought in Korea for this reason. It was also the reason the United States fought in Vietnam.

Domino Theory In the early 1900s, France controlled most of Southeast Asia, including Vietnam. But France faced resistance from nationalist independence movements. A young Vietnamese nationalist,

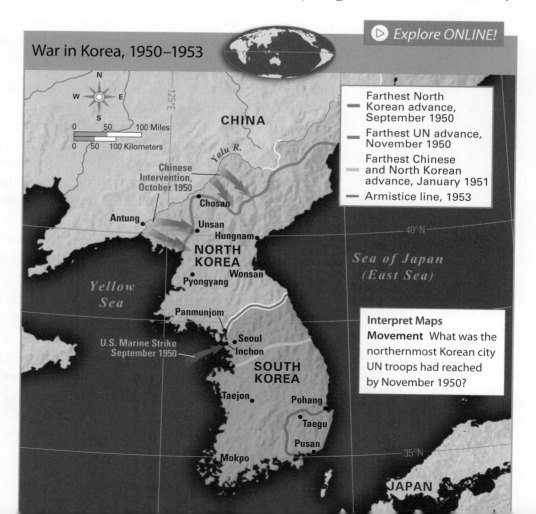

War in Korea, 1950–1953

Explore ONLINE!

Farthest North Korean advance, September 1950

Farthest UN advance, November 1950

Farthest Chinese and North Korean advance, January 1951

Armistice line, 1953

CHINA

Yalu R.

Chinese Intervention, October 1950

Chosan

Antung

Unsan

Hungnam

NORTH KOREA

Wonsan

Pyongyang

Yellow Sea

Panmunjom

Sea of Japan (East Sea)

U.S. Marine Strike September 1950

Seoul

Inchon

SOUTH KOREA

Interpret Maps
Movement What was the northernmost Korean city UN troops had reached by November 1950?

Taejon

Pohang

Taegu

Pusan

Mokpo

JAPAN

Ho Chi Minh (ho chee min), turned to the Communists for help in his struggle against France. During the 1930s, Ho's Communist Party led revolts and strikes. Immediately after World War II, Communist and Nationalist groups joined together to fight against the French. In 1954, the French surrendered to Ho.

The United States had supported France in Vietnam. With the defeat of the French, the United States saw a rising threat to the rest of Asia. President Eisenhower described this threat in terms of the **domino theory**. The Southeast Asian nations were like a row of dominos, he said. If one fell to communism, it would lead to the fall of its neighbors. This theory became a major justification for U.S. foreign policy during the Cold War era.

A Divided Country After France's defeat, Vietnam was divided into two countries. Ho Chi Minh's Communist forces governed North Vietnam. To the south, the United States and France set up an anti-Communist government under the leadership of Ngo Dinh Diem (NOH dihn DYEM).

Diem ruled the south as a dictator. Opposition to his government grew. Communist fighters, called **Vietcong**, began to gain support. The Soviet Union and China sent help and supplies to them as well. Gradually, the Vietcong won control of large areas of the countryside.

Faced with the possibility of a Communist victory in South Vietnam, the United States decided to increase its involvement. They sent soldiers to help fight against the Vietcong. By 1968, more than half a million U.S. soldiers were fighting there.

Because the Soviet Union was helping the Vietcong, The United States viewed the fighting in Vietnam as part of the Cold War. The U.S. army was the best-equipped and most-advanced in the world, but it faced two problems. First, U.S. soldiers were fighting in unfamiliar jungle terrain. Second, their ally, the South Vietnamese government, was becoming unpopular. U.S. forces bombed millions of acres of farmland and forest, trying to destroy enemy forces. However, this bombing only strengthened the people's dislike of the South Vietnamese government.

Back in the United States, the war was becoming more unpopular. Many young people protested and refused to fight if they were drafted into the army. Finally, President Nixon began withdrawing American troops. The last ones left in 1973. The Vietnam War was over, and the United States had lost.

Vietnam After the War The victorious North Vietnamese took harsh measures against the South. Thousands of people were sent to "reeducation camps" to be trained in communist ideas. The government controlled industries and businesses. Communist oppression caused people to flee Vietnam. Most escaped in dangerous, overcrowded ships. Many of these so-called "boat people" died at sea. The survivors then often spent months in refugee camps in Southeast Asia. Some eventually settled in the United States and Canada. Although the government of Vietnam remains officially communist, the country now welcomes foreign investment. The United States resumed normal diplomatic ties with Vietnam in 1995.

Reading Check
Draw Conclusions
Why did the United States withdraw from Vietnam?

Cold War Flares in the Third World

After World War II, the world's nations were grouped politically into three "worlds." The First World was the industrialized capitalist nations, including the United States and its allies. The Second World was the communist nations, led by the Soviet Union. The Third World consisted of developing nations, often newly independent, who were not aligned with either the United States or the Soviet Union. These countries provided yet another arena for competition between the Cold War's so-called superpowers.

Fidel Castro came to power in 1959. Although first seen as a reformer, he eventually imposed harsh controls on the Cuban people.

Cuba's Communist Revolution In 1959, a revolution led by a young lawyer named **Fidel Castro** overthrew an unpopular Cuban dictator. At first, Castro was a nationalist who brought social reforms to Cuba and improved the economy. Yet after he came to power, he also became a dictator. He suspended elections, jailed or executed his opponents, and tightly controlled the press. After President Eisenhower ended trade with Cuba, Castro asked the Soviets for economic and military aid. This led to Cuba becoming a communist country aligned with the Soviet Union during the Cold War.

In July 1962, Soviet leader Nikita Khrushchev secretly began to build missile sites in Cuba. They were discovered by an American spy plane. Since Cuba is only about 90 miles from Florida, President John F. Kennedy demanded the missiles' removal. He also announced a naval blockade of Cuba. This meant the U.S. Navy would not allow any ships to come in or out of Cuba's harbors, stopping all trade with the island. But the Soviets still did not back down.

The Cuban Missile Crisis lasted almost two weeks. People around the world feared nuclear war. After tense negotiations, Khrushchev agreed to remove the missiles if the U.S. would promise not to invade Cuba. This episode was one example of brinkmanship, or pursuing a dangerous policy to the last possible point before stopping. This time, Khrushchev's attempt to use brinkmanship for political gain failed. The Cuban Missile Crisis was ended. Cuba would remain an ally of the Soviet Union for many years to come.

Revolution in Nicaragua The Central American country of Nicaragua had been run by a dictatorship for many decades. In the 1960s, however, people who opposed the dictatorship began to fight back. One group called themselves the Sandinistas, after a resistance hero from Nicaraguan history. This revolution eventually removed the dictator from power in 1979.

However, not everyone was happy. Many Nicaraguans had died during the revolution, and the country was deeply in debt. The United States was worried about the spread of communism in Central America. The new government came under attack by the Contras, forces who were funded and armed by the United States. The Sandinistas in turn asked the Soviet Union and Cuba for support. The government also become more

President Jimmy Carter helped negotiate the peace deal between Egyptian president Anwar Sadat and Israeli prime minister Menachem Begin.

oppressive, in an effort to fight the Contras. Thus the Cold War contributed to a civil war in Nicaragua that lasted nine years and killed 30,000 people.

Egypt Changes Alliances Egypt was one of many Arab nations fighting the neighboring Jewish state of Israel. The Soviet Union was supplying Egypt with military advisors and weapons. The United States did the same for Israel.

However, Egyptian president **Anwar Sadat** was disappointed in his Soviet allies. He felt that they were not providing what they had promised. In 1972, he forced out 20,000 Soviet military advisors and technicians. After more armed conflicts with Israel, Sadat decided that only the United States was strong enough to achieve peace in the Middle East. Egypt became an ally of the United States. With U.S. support, Sadat sought peace with Israel. Despite the disagreements between the nations, he signed a peace treaty with Menachem Begin, the Israeli prime minister, at the White House in 1979. It was one of the few events during the Cold War that at least temporarily ended in peace between two countries.

The Soviet Invasion of Afghanistan For several years after World War II, Afghanistan was an independent country. It was not allied with either the nearby Soviet Union or the United States. In the 1950s, Soviet influence in the country began to grow, and it eventually became a communist country. Even though they were in power, many people did not support the communist government, which was harsh and repressive. By the late 1970s, a revolt threatened to bring down Afghanistan's communist regime. This revolt led to a Soviet invasion in 1979.

The Soviets expected to strengthen the Afghan government and quickly withdraw. Instead, the Soviet military found itself stuck. Like the Vietcong in Vietnam, tribal fighters and Muslim rebel forces called the Mujahideen (mu-ja-hid-EEN) held off a military superpower. The United States believed the Soviet invasion was a threat to Middle Eastern oil supplies, so they supported the Afghan rebels. The United States gave the rebels military and financial support. In the 1980s, the new Soviet leader Mikhail Gorbachev acknowledged the war's devastating costs. He withdrew all troops by 1989.

Changes in Africa After World War II, dozens of European colonies in Africa gained their independence. In some nations, Communist rebels sought to overthrow their colonial rulers. Many nations faced civil war as a result. When South Africa became independent, the government wrote a constitution that gave political power to white South Africans. Black South Africans, the majority of the population, were denied their rights. This was policy was continued by the National Party when it came to power in 1948.

During the 1960s and 1970s, people around the world began to believe that this discrimination was wrong. At the same time, many of South Africa's neighbors had already become communist countries, including Angola and Mozambique. The United States and its allies decided that pursuing the policy of containment against communism was more important than fighting discrimination, so they supported the white government of South Africa during the Cold War.

Reading Check
Analyze Causes
What caused the United States to set up a naval blockade of Cuba?

Summary and Preview The Cold War was not restricted to just Europe. It caused conflicts and tense standoffs around the world. In the next lesson, you will learn more about the impact of Soviet power in Eastern Europe and the eventual thawing of tensions.

Lesson 2 Assessment

Review Ideas, Terms, and People

1. **a. Draw Conclusions** Do you think the United States supported Mao Zedong's Communist government? Why or why not?

   b. Make Inferences Why might Mao think China's economic policies after the Great Leap Forward would weaken the communist goal of social equality?

2. **a. Summarize** Who fought to support the South Koreans in the Korean War?

   b. Draw Conclusions Why did China send troops into Korea when UN forces reached the Chinese border?

   c. Elaborate What do the economic struggles of North Korea tell us about communism?

3. **a. Describe** What was the domino theory?

   b. Analyze Why was the United States unable to win in Vietnam?

4. **a. Explain** Why did Fidel Castro need the economic support of the Soviet Union?

   b. Recall Which country did Anwar Sadat reach a peace deal with?

Critical Thinking

5. **Summarize** Draw a chart like this one. Under each heading, write a sentence that summarizes the relationship between the United States and the country listed.

Korea	Vietnam	Cuba

Changes in Strategy

The Big Idea

From the 1950s until the 1980s the Cold War continued, but there were times when tensions between the Soviets and the United States eased.

Main Ideas

- The Soviet Union maintained firm control over Eastern European communist countries but had disagreements with the Chinese.

- In the 1970s, Cold War tensions eased, but they reemerged by the end of the decade.

Key Terms and People

Nikita Khrushchev
de-Stalinization
Imre Nagy
Alexander Dubček
détente

If YOU were there . . .

You are living in communist Hungary during the 1950s. Conditions have been harsh for a long time. The economy is poor, and you must be very careful about what you say. Many books are banned, and there are strict limits on your freedom to travel. Then, new leaders seem to make the situation better. There are fewer restrictions on speech, and new ideas begin to flow freely. However, troops from the Soviet Union and other Warsaw Pact countries invade. They put an end to the changes.

How do you react to this turn of events?

Policy Changes in the Communist World

After World War II, the Soviet Union tightly controlled its satellite nations in Eastern Europe. Their industries were directed to meet Soviet needs. There were also no free elections, restrictions on freedom of speech, and strict rules to limit travel. These policies negatively affected the region's economic recovery. During the 1950s and 1960s, however, growing protest movements in Eastern Europe threatened Soviet dominance. Increasing tensions with China also diverted Soviet attention and forces.

De-Stalinization After Joseph Stalin died in 1953, more moderate Soviet leaders came to power. They allowed satellite countries more independence, as long as they remained allied with the Soviet Union. The new Communist Party leader **Nikita Khrushchev** (ni-KEE-tuh KROOSH-chef) denounced Stalin for jailing and killing loyal Soviet citizens. This was the start of a policy called **de-Stalinization**, or reforming the country to ease Stalin's repressive policies. To express their relief at the end of Stalin's reign, workers destroyed monuments of the former dictator. Khrushchev also called for "peaceful competition" with capitalist states.

Nikita Khrushchev led the Soviet Union after Joseph Stalin and made reforms to the country.

Hungary This new outlook did little to change life for most people in Soviet satellite countries. Many people took to the streets to protest their lack of freedom and self-rule. In October 1956, the Hungarian army joined protesters to overthrow Hungary's Soviet-controlled government.

A popular Hungarian Communist leader named **Imre Nagy** (IHM-ray NAHJ) formed a new government. Nagy promised free elections and demanded that Soviet troops leave. In response, Soviet tanks and infantry entered the capital city of Budapest. Thousands of Hungarian freedom fighters armed themselves with pistols and bottles. Unfortunately, they were no match for the Soviet forces. A new government that was friendly to the Soviet Union took over.

Czechoslovakia Despite successfully controlling protesters in Hungary, Soviet party leaders were not happy with how Khrushchev had handled the Cuban Missile Crisis. They believed he had acted irresponsibly. In 1964, party leaders voted to remove him from power. His replacement, Leonid Brezhnev, quickly adopted harsh policies. The party enforced laws to limit

Czech protesters and Soviet forces filled the streets of Prague as Prague Spring came to an end in August 1968.

basic human rights, such as freedom of speech and worship. Government censors controlled what writers could publish. Brezhnev punished those who dared to protest his policies.

Brezhnev also punished opposition in Eastern Europe. His policy was put to the test in early 1968. At that time, Czech Communist leader **Alexander Dubček** (DOOB-chehk) loosened controls on censorship, and let writers and newspapers operate more freely. He wanted to offer his country socialism with "a human face." This period of reform, when Czechoslovakia's capital bloomed with new ideas, became known as Prague Spring. However, it did not survive the summer. In August, armed forces from the Warsaw Pact nations invaded Czechoslovakia. Dubček's policies were put to an end.

China While many satellite countries resisted Communist rule, China was committed to communism. In fact, to cement the ties between communist powers, Mao and Stalin had signed a 30-year treaty of friendship in 1950. The Soviet Union assumed that China would follow Soviet leadership in world affairs. However, over time the Chinese communist government resented being in Moscow's shadow. They began to spread their own brand of communism in Africa and other parts of Asia. In 1959, Khrushchev punished the Chinese by refusing to share Soviet nuclear technology. The Soviet-Chinese split grew so wide that fighting broke out along their common border. After repeated incidents, the two neighbors reached a fragile peace as both nations sought stability at home and abroad.

Reading Check
Analyze Causes
What caused the Soviet Union to invade both Hungary and Czechoslovakia?

The United States Seeks Peace

In the 1970s, the United States and the Soviet Union finally backed away from brinkmanship. After the postwar years, both superpowers slowly moved to lower tensions.

End of Brinkmanship and the Beginning of Détente The brinkmanship policy followed by Presidents Eisenhower, Kennedy, and Johnson had led to one terrifying crisis after another. In 1960, a U.S. spy plane was shot down while in Soviet airspace. The Cuban Missile Crisis in 1962 made the superpowers' use of nuclear weapons a real possibility. People around the world were frightened by the prospect of a nuclear war.

Although the Cuban Missile Crisis ended peacefully, tensions remained high. In the 1970s, however, the United States backed away from its policy of direct confrontation with the Soviet Union. **Détente**, a policy of easing Cold War tensions, replaced brinkmanship under President Richard Nixon. Nixon's move toward détente grew out of a philosophy known as *realpolitik*. This term comes from the German word meaning "realistic politics."

In practice, *realpolitik* meant pursuing national interests while still dealing with other nations in a practical way. For example, Nixon visited communist China in 1972. He made this trip because it was more important that the two countries have diplomatic ties than that the United States oppose Chinese communism. While the United States continued to try to contain the spread of communism, the Soviet Union and United States agreed to pursue détente and to reduce tensions.

When Richard Nixon and Leonid Brezhnev signed the SALT I Treaty in 1972, it marked a significant turning point in U.S.-Soviet relations.

One way to reduce tensions was to slow the arms race. In 1972, Nixon visited the Soviet Union. After a series of meetings called the Strategic Arms Limitation Talks (SALT), Nixon and Brezhnev signed the SALT I Treaty. This five-year agreement put limits on the number of missiles each country could have.

End of Détente During the 1970s, the United States improved relations with the Soviet Union. In the late 1970s, however, President Jimmy Carter was concerned about harsh treatment of protesters in the Soviet Union. This threatened to prevent a second round of SALT negotiations. In 1979, Carter and Brezhnev finally signed the SALT II agreement. However, the U.S. Congress refused to ratify SALT II because the Soviets had invaded Afghanistan. World leaders grew concerned as more nations, including China and India, began building nuclear arsenals. When Ronald Reagan was elected President in 1980, he changed to a policy of military readiness to meet the Soviet threat. The arms race was back on, and détente was over.

Reading Check
Analyze Causes
Why do you think both the Soviet Union and United States wanted to sign the SALT I Treaty?

Summary and Preview Communists maintained their grip on power into the 1970s, but leaders from both sides eventually agreed to lower tensions. However, tension once again flared up at the end of the decade. In the next lesson, you will learn about the collapse of the Soviet Union.

Lesson 3 Assessment

Review Ideas, Terms, and People

1. a. **Recall** What did Nikita Khrushchev denounce Stalin for doing?

   b. **Make Inferences** Why do you think the Soviet Union stopped the reform movements in Hungary and Czechoslovakia?

   c. **Summarize** How did the relationship between the Soviet Union and China change over time?

2. a. **Recall** After the terrifying crises of the 1960s, what policy did Richard Nixon adopt?

   b. **Explain** What events in the late 1970s caused tensions between the Soviet Union and the United States to increase?

Critical Thinking

3. **Sequence** Draw a chart like this one. List the series of events that took place between the United States and the Soviet Union in the 1960s and 1970s.

The Breakup of the Soviet Union

The Big Idea

In the 1980s and early 1990s, reform movements in the Soviet Union and Eastern Europe led to the fall of the Iron Curtain.

Main Ideas

- Mikhail Gorbachev's reforms led to the collapse of the Soviet Union.

- The fall of the Berlin Wall marked the beginning of the end of communism in Europe.

Key Terms and People

Mikhail Gorbachev
glasnost
Ronald Reagan
Margaret Thatcher
perestroika
Václav Havel
European Union

Mikhail Gorbachev worked to modernize the Soviet economy.

If YOU were there . . .

You are living in Russia in the 1980s. After years of oppression by the Communist Party, you start to notice changes. You are allowed to speak your mind in public. You can suddenly read books that before had been banned. Your parents have even opened up a small camera shop. Musicians from Western Europe and North America are now allowed to play concerts.

How do you feel about these changes?

Soviet Union Collapses

After taking power in the 1960s, Leonid Brezhnev crushed all political disagreement within the Soviet Union and in the satellite countries behind the Iron Curtain. These policies were carried out with support from the Politburo, the ruling committee of the Communist Party in the Soviet Union.

Mikhail Gorbachev After Brezhnev's death in 1982, the aging leadership of the Soviet Union tried to hold on to power. However, each of Brezhnev's two successors died after only about a year in office. The Politburo then chose **Mikhail Gorbachev** (mih-KYL GAWR-buh-chawf) to be the new leader.

The Soviet people welcomed Gorbachev's election. Gorbachev's supporters praised his youth, energy, and political skills. At 54, he was the youngest Soviet leader since Stalin. Unlike other Soviet leaders, Gorbachev decided to pursue new ideas.

Glasnost and Perestroika Past Soviet leaders had discouraged people from acting on their own or thinking independently. As a result, Soviet society rarely changed, and the Soviet economy didn't grow. Gorbachev realized that needed reforms could not happen without a free flow of ideas and information. In 1985, he announced a policy known as **glasnost** (GLAHS-nuhst), or openness. Glasnost brought remarkable changes. The government allowed churches to reopen. Political prisoners were

Timeline: The Communist Bloc Falls

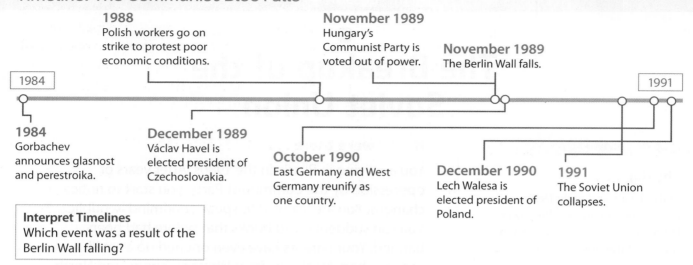

1988
Polish workers go on strike to protest poor economic conditions.

November 1989
Hungary's Communist Party is voted out of power.

November 1989
The Berlin Wall falls.

1984

1991

1984
Gorbachev announces glasnost and perestroika.

December 1989
Václav Havel is elected president of Czechoslovakia.

October 1990
East Germany and West Germany reunify as one country.

December 1990
Lech Walesa is elected president of Poland.

1991
The Soviet Union collapses.

Interpret Timelines
Which event was a result of the Berlin Wall falling?

released from jail. The Communist censors allowed the publication of previously banned books. Reporters were permitted to investigate problems and criticize officials without fear of arrest.

The new openness also allowed Soviet citizens to complain about economic problems. Consumers protested that they had to stand in long lines to buy food and other basics. Shortages of goods were common. Gorbachev blamed these problems on the Soviet Union's system of central planning. Under central planning, party officials told farm and factory managers how much to produce. They also told them what wages to pay and what prices to charge. The system was inefficient, and because individuals could not increase their pay by producing more, they had no reason to be more efficient.

There were also pressures from beyond the borders of the Soviet Union. In 1981, **Ronald Reagan** was elected president of the United States. During his first term, Reagan took a tough stand against the Soviet Union.

When Ronald Reagan became president, he took a hard-line stance against the Soviet Union. His opinion softened after Mikhail Gorbachev put reforms in place. Here, Reagan and Gorbachev talk with each other.

British Prime Minister **Margaret Thatcher** also spoke out strongly against the Soviet Union. She believed the Soviet system of government was dangerous. Her leadership strengthened American resolve to win the Cold War. Reagan quickly expanded the U.S. military. The Soviet Union then tried to match American spending in the arms race. This contributed to desperate economic times in the Soviet Union during the 1980s.

In 1984, Gorbachev introduced the idea of **perestroika** (pehr-ih-STROY-kuh), or economic restructuring. He then made changes to revive the Soviet economy and loosened centralized control. Local managers gained more authority over their farms and factories. People were allowed to open small private businesses. Gorbachev's goal was not to abandon communism. He just wanted to make the economic system more efficient and productive.

Glasnost and perestroika convinced President Reagan of Gorbachev's desire for change. In 1987, the two leaders signed a treaty eliminating all medium-range nuclear weapons in Europe. This reduced Cold War tensions and the global threat of nuclear war.

End of the Soviet Union The success of Gorbachev's new policies led him to support movements for economic and political change. Popular movements for democracy were building in the country, and Gorbachev decided not to oppose reform. Free elections were held across the Soviet Union. People from once-independent Soviet republics began to demand their freedom. Lithuania was the first to declare its independence in 1990. Estonia and Latvia soon followed.

Boris Yeltsin was elected president of the newly named Russian Federation in 1991. At this time, Russia was still part of the Soviet Union under Gorbachev. Yeltsin put even more reforms into place. This upset conservatives who didn't like the changes they saw. In August 1991, these Communist Party officials tried to overthrow Gorbachev and undo his reforms. Their plan failed, and the Communist Party in Russia collapsed. By December, all 15 Soviet republics had declared independence. The Soviet Union was no more.

Reading Check
Summarize What was the impact of glasnost?

Explore ONLINE!

The Breakup of the Soviet Union, 1991

— Border of the Soviet Union

Interpret Maps
Place What were the 15 republics of the former Soviet Union?

Europe After Communism

In the late 1980s, anti-communist reform movements gained strength all across Europe. In Poland, the Communist Party agreed to hold free elections. In nearby Hungary, free-market economic reforms were put into place.

The Berlin Wall Falls While Poland and Hungary were moving toward reform, East German leader Erich Honecker dismissed reforms as unnecessary. Many East Germans were angry that the government would not let them travel to West Germany. Families who had been separated after the war were desperate to see each other again. Also, many East Germans wanted to defect, or escape, to the greater freedoms in the West. Then in 1989, Hungary allowed vacationing East German tourists to cross the border into Austria. From there they could travel to West Germany. Thousands of East Germans took this new escape route. In response, the East German government closed its borders entirely.

By October 1989, huge demonstrations had broken out in cities across East Germany. The protesters demanded the right to travel freely, and later added the demand for free elections. Honecker resigned on October 18.

The new East German leader, Egon Krenz, hoped that he could restore stability by allowing people to leave East Germany. On November 9, 1989, he opened the Berlin Wall. The long-divided city of Berlin celebrated in the streets. People came together and physically tore down the Berlin Wall itself. This was a powerful symbol of the fall of the once-mighty Iron Curtain. However, Krenz's attempt to save communism did not work. By the end of 1989, the East German Communist Party had ceased to exist.

On November 11, 1989, portions of the Berlin Wall were torn down by demonstrators.

Lech Walesa 1943–

When Lech Walesa was 18 months old, his father died. Before he died, he predicted that his wife would be proud of little Lech someday. And he was right—his son grew up to be the president of Poland.

At 24, Walesa began to work at the shipyard in Gdansk, Poland. He took up the struggle for free trade unions after seeing police shoot protestors. During a strike in 1980, Walesa and others locked themselves inside the shipyard. This brought worldwide attention to their demands for a legally recognized union and the right to strike.

The government granted these demands but later outlawed the labor movement, known as Solidarity. They jailed Walesa and other leaders. After his release from jail, he won the Nobel Peace Prize and served as Poland's president from 1990 to 1995.

Identify Cause and Effect
Why might Walesa have been motivated by seeing protestors hurt by police?

After the Fall After the fall of communism in East Germany, Germany became one country again. The newly united Germany faced serious problems. More than 40 years of communist rule had left East Germany in ruins. Its railroads, highways, and telephone system had not been modernized since World War II. East German industries produced goods that could not compete in the global market. Inefficient factories closed, depriving millions of workers of their jobs.

Communist governments continued to fall throughout Europe. After labor unrest and opposition by the Solidarity movement, the communist government of Poland fell in 1989. In Czechoslovakia, protesters gathered to demand democracy and freedom. A playwright named **Václav Havel**, who had been critical of the government, was elected president. The country later peacefully split and became the Czech Republic and Slovakia. Both of these countries are Parliamentary republics. The communist government in Romania also fell after a violent revolution and was replaced with a democracy.

The European Union The end of communism had both good and bad results for the countries of Eastern Europe. Some people saw economic improvement. New reforms created new opportunities. Some people started new businesses. Others could get well-paying jobs in companies and industries that were now privately run instead of state-controlled.

Other people in Eastern Europe fared less well. Earnings did not rise for all workers. Many state-supported factories closed. This caused high unemployment in some areas. These economic problems led many to move to Western Europe, where there were better opportunities. This movement led to problems in some parts of Western Europe. Newcomers competed with longtime residents for jobs and other resources.

The **European Union** (EU) was established in 1992 to build an economic and political union among the nations of Europe. Many Eastern European nations and former Soviet republics joined the EU in the 2000s. These steps created a single economic unit that is large enough to compete with the United States. However, many of the members from former Soviet satellite states were far poorer than the Western European members. As a result, some people in the wealthier nations began to worry that their own economies would suffer.

Summary Reforms were put into place in the Soviet Union and Eastern Europe. These led to the collapse of the Soviet Union and communism in Europe. As a result, Europe changed dramatically.

Reading Check
Draw Conclusions
Why was the fall of the Berlin Wall symbolically important?

Lesson 4 Assessment

Review Ideas, Terms, and People

1. **a. Recall** What was perestroika?

   b. Elaborate How did Ronald Reagan take a strong stance against the Soviet Union?

   c. Summarize What happened after Mikhail Gorbachev chose not to oppose reform?

2. **a. Sequence** What series of events led to the fall of the Berlin Wall?

   b. Analyze What was the effect of the fall of the Berlin Wall on the rest of Europe?

   c. Synthesize What has been the economic impact of the fall of communism in Eastern Europe?

Critical Thinking

3. **Analyze Causes** Draw a graphic organizer like the one shown here. In the boxes to the left and right, identify four causes of the collapse of the Soviet Union.

Use Supporting Evidence

Define the Skill

Writers may collect information and then use that to determine their main idea. Or they may start with an idea or position in mind and then provide information that supports it. This supporting information is called evidence. Writers use evidence to help readers better understand the main idea. Evidence includes facts, examples, and opinions of experts, such as historians. Evidence is used throughout this textbook.

Learn the Skill

Follow these guidelines to learn how to use supporting evidence.

1. Determine what your main idea or position is. Before you do so, you should have a general understanding of the topic.

2. Gather information that helps back up your main idea or position.

3. Decide which information is strongest. In other words, which information does the best job of supporting your main idea or position?

4. Organize the information so that readers will be able to understand what you're saying.

Practice the Skill

The passage below uses evidence to support the main idea "World War II had a much larger impact on the Soviet Union than on the United States." Use the following passage from the module as a source, and then identify and provide the supporting evidence.

> The Soviet Union had lost tens of millions of people, both soldiers and civilians. Many of its cities were demolished. The United States suffered almost 300,000 deaths, but its cities and factories were not destroyed. As a result, the United States was in much better shape economically.

1. In your own words, what is one piece of evidence you could use that supports the main idea?

2. What other evidence not given here could you use?

3. What might be an example of a bad piece of evidence to use?

Module 28 Assessment

Review Vocabulary, Terms, and People

Complete each sentence by filling in the blank with the correct term or person from the module.

1. _____ was the leader of Egypt who sought peace with Israel.

2. The United States sought to prevent the Soviet Union from expanding its influence through _____.

3. The _____ was a defensive military alliance formed by 10 Western European countries, the United States, and Canada.

4. After his Communist forces defeated the Nationalists, _____ became the leader of China.

5. The _____ was the idea that a series of Southeast Asian nations would fall to communism if one became communist.

6. The _____ was a tense, nonviolent conflict between the United States and the Soviet Union.

7. Soviet leader _____ purged the country of Joseph Stalin's memory through de-Stalinization.

8. The _____ was established in 1992 to build an economic and political union in Europe.

9. _____ reformed the Soviet Union's political and economic culture under the programs of glasnost and perestroika.

10. Richard Nixon's policy of _____ replaced brinkmanship with the Soviet Union.

Comprehension and Critical Thinking

Lesson 1

11. **a. Recall** Which two countries were the main countries involved in the Cold War?

    b. Analyze How did the Marshall Plan support the American policy of containment?

    c. Draw Conclusions Do you think the arms race made a violent conflict between the United States and the Soviet Union more likely or less likely?

Lesson 2

12. **a. Describe** What was Mao Zedong's plan for the Chinese economy?

    b. Compare and Contrast How were the Korean War and the Vietnam War similar? How were they different?

    c. Predict What do you think happened to the economy of Cuba after the Soviet Union collapsed?

Lesson 3

13. **a. Describe** How did the Soviet Union and the Warsaw Pact nations respond to uprisings in Hungary and Czechoslovakia?

    b. Analyze Why did Richard Nixon pursue a policy of détente?

Lesson 4

14. **a. Recall** Which British prime minister believed that the Soviet Union's system of government was dangerous?

    b. Analyze Why didn't conservatives in the Soviet Union like the changes Mikhail Gorbachev introduced?

    c. Draw Conclusions Why do you think communist factories produced goods that could not compete on the global market?

Module 28 Assessment, continued

Review Themes

15. Politics One way the Soviet Union kept control over its satellite states was by not allowing a free and open press that could question the government. What do you think could happen in the United States if information were not allowed to flow freely? Why?

16. Economics What economic system is present in the United States? What economic system was present in the Soviet Union during the Cold War years?

17. Society and Culture How do you think the societies and cultures of both East Germany and West Germany changed after Germany was reunited?

Reading Skills

Set a Purpose *Use the Reading Skills taught in this module and the headings below to answer the questions that follow.*

> **Cold War Flares in the Third World**
>
> After World War II, the world's nations were grouped politically into three "worlds". . . . .
>
> **Cuba's Communist Revolution** In 1959, a revolution led by a young lawyer. . . . .
>
> **Revolution in Nicaragua** The Central American country of Nicaragua had been run by a dictatorship. . . . . .

18. After reading the headings, what do you think this section is going to be about?

19. What are some questions you might ask before reading this section?

Social Studies Skills

Use Supporting Evidence *Use the Social Studies Skills taught in this module to answer the question below.*

20. Reflect on what you have learned about the Cold War, communism, and the relationship between the United States and the Soviet Union. Decide to argue in favor of one of these two statements: "The Cold War was a good thing for the world," or "The Cold War had a negative effect on the world." Then review the module and identify three pieces of evidence that you could use to support your position. List the evidence you would use.

Focus on Writing

21. Make an Appeal Imagine that you live in one of the communist countries you read about in this module. Write a letter appealing to your country's leaders asking them to reform laws to cut back on censorship and allow more freedom to travel. Remember to be specific about where you are writing from and what life is like with these restrictions. Describe how life would be better for you and other citizens with the reforms you are suggesting. Use descriptive and emotional language to strengthen your appeal.

OCTOBER FURY:
THE CUBAN MISSILE CRISIS

The Cuban missile crisis was perhaps the most dangerous event of the Cold War period. For several days in October 1962, the United States and the Soviet Union stood on the brink of nuclear war. The crisis began when the Soviet Union sent weapons, including nuclear missiles, to Cuba. It deepened when the United States blockaded Cuba to prevent the Soviets from delivering more missiles. With Soviet ships sailing toward the blockade, a confrontation seemed inevitable. However, at the last moment, the Soviet ships turned back and war was averted.

Explore the development and resolution of the Cuban missile crisis online. You can find a wealth of information, video clips, primary sources, activities, and more through your online textbook.

Prelude to Crisis

Watch the video to learn about the buildup to the Cuban missile crisis.

UNITED KINGDOM

UNITED STATES

Getting Ready for War

Watch the video to see how the missiles in Cuba created tension between the United States and the Soviet Union.

FALLOUT SHELTER IN BASEMENT

Crisis Averted?

Watch the video to see how the Cuban missile crisis brought the United States and the Soviet Union to the brink of nuclear war.

Lessons Learned

Watch the video to learn about the impact of the Cuban missile crisis.

The Postwar World

🌐

Essential Question

How have geography and politics affected Asia, Africa, the Middle East, and Latin America since the end of World War II?

About the Photo: Technological innovations have helped Japan's economy in recent decades. In this photo, workers use robots to assemble a car.

▷ Explore ONLINE!

HISTORY.

VIDEOS, including...
- Tiananmen Square
- Mahatma Gandhi
- The Falklands War

✔ Document-Based Investigations

✔ Graphic Organizers

✔ Interactive Games

✔ Interactive Map: African Independence

✔ Image with Hotspots: Communist China

✔ Image Carousel: Political Change in Africa

In this module, you will learn about the many influences that have shaped the modern politics, economies, and societies in four regions of the world.

What You Will Learn...

Lesson 1: Nationalist Movements in Asia 986
The Big Idea Major political changes in Asia in the early 20th century marked the end of European domination there.

Lesson 2: A New Asia. 993
The Big Idea Since the end of World War II, Asia has experienced major economic, political, and cultural changes.

Lesson 3: Independence Movements in Africa 1000
The Big Idea African colonies began to call for independence after World War II, eventually gaining their freedom.

Lesson 4: Africa Since Independence 1006
The Big Idea The people of Africa have faced both changes and challenges since they won their independence.

Lesson 5: Conflict in the Middle East. 1014
The Big Idea Life in the Middle East since 1900 has been dominated by political change, conflict, and the oil industry.

Lesson 6: Latin America Since 1945 1021
The Big Idea Latin America has seen political, economic, and social challenges in the past several decades.

Timeline of Events 1945–Present

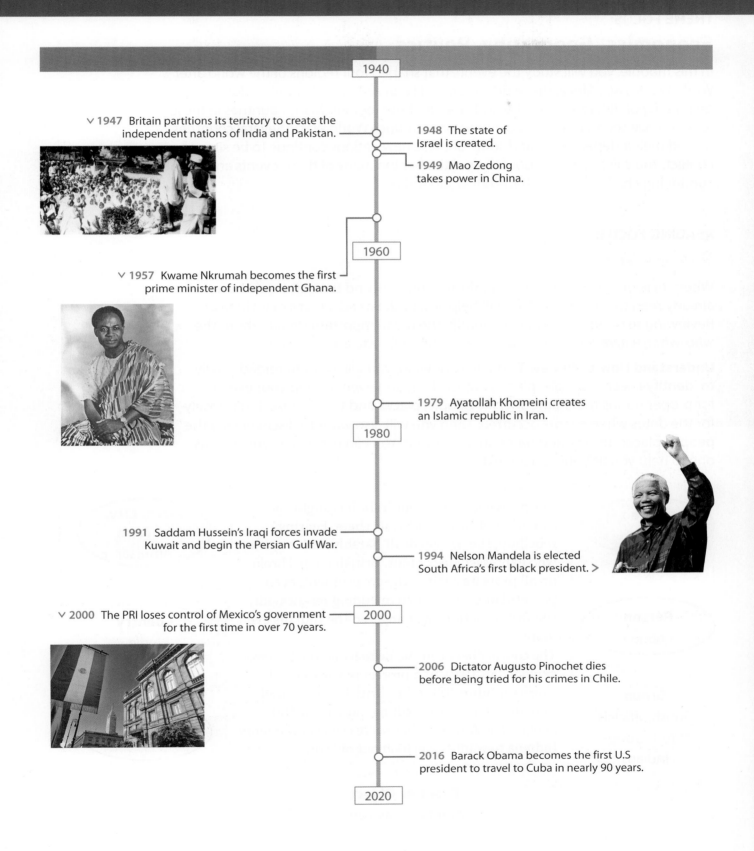

1940

∨ **1947** Britain partitions its territory to create the independent nations of India and Pakistan.

1948 The state of Israel is created.

1949 Mao Zedong takes power in China.

1960

∨ **1957** Kwame Nkrumah becomes the first prime minister of independent Ghana.

1979 Ayatollah Khomeini creates an Islamic republic in Iran.

1980

1991 Saddam Hussein's Iraqi forces invade Kuwait and begin the Persian Gulf War.

1994 Nelson Mandela is elected South Africa's first black president. ❯

∨ **2000** The PRI loses control of Mexico's government for the first time in over 70 years.

2000

2006 Dictator Augusto Pinochet dies before being tried for his crimes in Chile.

2016 Barack Obama becomes the first U.S president to travel to Cuba in nearly 90 years.

2020

Reading Social Studies

THEME FOCUS:

Economics, Geography, Politics

In this module, you will study the events that shaped four regions of the world after World War II: Asia, Africa, the Middle East, and Latin America. You will explore the geography of different countries and areas in these regions. Many countries in these regions have seen significant economic growth since World War II. Several countries gained their independence and some of these new nations continue to be sites of conflict. You will also learn about the politics behind many of these events and the continuing challenges that shape our world today.

READING FOCUS:

Review Texts

When reviewing text, you look for information a second time after you have already read the text once. This will help you understand a text's main ideas. Reviewing text requires that you identify the most important details about the *who, what, where, when, why,* and *how* of the topic you are studying.

Understand How to Review Texts In reviewing, you will want to reread slowly to identify specific people, places, dates, ideas, and events. Keep your eye out for proper nouns that name specific people, places and things. Also, look closely for the dates when events occurred. Then you will also want to discover why the people, places, things, and dates are important. You can use a diagram like this one to help you as your review texts.

Date
1919

Person
none

Group
British officials
British troops
Indians

The growing resentment in India caught the attention of British officials there. Fearing rebellion, the British dealt harshly with anyone who expressed discontent. British troops broke up all protests against the government, even peaceful ones. Rather than ending resentment, the British actions just angered the Indians even more.

The conflict between the British and the Indians exploded in 1919. At a protest in the town of Amritsar (uhm-RIT-suhr), British troops fired into an Indian crowd, killing more than 400 people. The Amritsar Massacre caused even more Indians to want the British out of India.

Place, City, or Town
Amritsar

Country
India

Region
none

Event or Object
Amritsar Massacre

You Try It!

Read the following passage and then answer the questions below.

> Perhaps the best example of a military dictator in Africa was Joseph Mobutu. He rose to power in the Congo in 1965 after the Belgians left. To show his power, he changed the name of the country to Zaire, a traditional African name.

Answer these questions based on the passage you just read.

1. Date?
2. Person?
3. Group?
4. Place, City, or Town?
5. Country?
6. Region?
7. Event or Object?

As you read this module, use dates and proper nouns to help review text so that you understand what happened in each part of the world.

Key Terms and People

Lesson 1
nonviolence
civil disobedience
partition
Pakistan
Diet

Lesson 2
Kashmir
trade surplus
tariff
constitutional monarchies
Tiananmen Square
human rights
Aung San Suu Kyi
Corazon Aquino

Lesson 3
Ghana
Kenya
Mau Mau
Belgian Congo

Lesson 4
apartheid
townships
sanctions
Darfur
Lagos
Kinshasa

Lesson 5
shah
embargo
Taliban
OPEC

Lesson 6
Juan Perón
Augusto Pinochet
immunity
North American Free Trade
   Agreement
informal jobs

Nationalist Movements in Asia

The Big Idea

Major political changes in Asia in the early 20th century marked the end of European domination there.

Main Ideas

- The call for Indian independence was accompanied by nonviolent protests.

- The early 1900s saw the end of China's imperial period and the beginning of communism in the country.

- Changes in Japan's government led to the formation of a new empire.

Key Terms and People

nonviolence
civil disobedience
partition
Pakistan
Diet

If YOU were there . . .

You are a lawyer in India in 1932. One morning two friends approach you with a question. They are unhappy about a new law that the British have passed. One friend wants to take up arms and try to force the British out of the country. The other disagrees. She wants to protest the law, but she does not want to use violence to do it. She does not think violence is necessary and is afraid that people will get hurt. The two ask your opinion on the most effective means of protest.

Whom will you support? Why?

The Call for Indian Independence

By the early 1900s, many Indians resented British interference in their country. Their resentment only increased after World War I. During the war, more than 800,000 Indian soldiers fought for the British. Upon returning home, they hoped that their sacrifices during the war had earned them some respect. Instead, they found that nothing had changed.

Growing Resentment The growing resentment in India caught the attention of British officials there. Fearing rebellion, the British dealt harshly with anyone who expressed discontent. British troops broke up all protests against the government, even peaceful ones. Rather than ending resentment, the British actions just angered the Indians even more.

The conflict between the British and the Indians exploded in 1919. At a protest in the town of Amritsar (uhm-RIT-suhr), British troops fired into an Indian crowd, killing more than 400 people. The Amritsar Massacre caused even more Indians to want the British out of India.

Mohandas Gandhi After the Amritsar Massacre, a new leader arose in the Indian resistance. That leader was Mohandas Gandhi. Gandhi was a lawyer who believed in fair treatment for all people. Resistance and protest were not new to him. For many years Gandhi had lived in South Africa and

Nonviolent Protests

Nonviolent protests in India, like the one in the image on the left, inspired later political activists. Among those inspired were some African Americans who fought for civil rights in the 1960s and staged nonviolent sit-ins like the one in the photo on the right.

Analyze Visuals
What similarities can you see between the two protests shown here?

campaigned against apartheid. He also worked in support of the poor and for women's rights.

Gandhi's protests were based on two key beliefs. The first was **nonviolence**, the avoidance of violent actions. Gandhi did not believe that people should use violence to protest injustice. He believed that peaceful protests were more successful than violent ones. This idea is often found in his writings.

> "It is perfectly true that [the English] used brute force, and that it is possible for us to do likewise, but, by using similar means, we can only get the same thing that they got. . . . [Using violence to gain freedom] is the same as saying we can get a rose through planting a noxious weed."
> –Mohandas Gandhi, *Hind Swaraj, or Indian Home Rule*, 1921

The second of Gandhi's key beliefs was **civil disobedience**, or the refusal to obey laws in order to bring about change. For example, he encouraged people to avoid paying taxes to the British. Gandhi felt that if the Indian people refused to cooperate with British authority, the British would grow frustrated and leave.

Gandhi and his supporters used nonviolent means to protest the British rule of India.

As part of his noncooperation plan, Gandhi encouraged the Indian people to boycott all British products. He stopped wearing British-made clothing and urged others to do the same. Many people began producing homemade cloth to make clothes themselves. As a result, spinning wheels and homemade cloth became symbols of the Indian resistance. Gandhi also encouraged people to stop buying salt from the British and to make their own salt from seawater instead.

Gandhi and his followers were arrested on several occasions. They did not give up, and their persistence convinced more Indians to join them. By the 1930s, millions of people were protesting British rule.

BIOGRAPHY

Mohandas Gandhi 1869–1948

Considered by many to be the father of modern India, Mohandas Gandhi led the struggle for Indian independence. As a leading member of the Indian National Congress, Gandhi led millions in fasts, peaceful protest marches, and boycotts of British goods. He wrote that nonviolence was a more effective means of bringing about change than violence could ever be.

This devotion to nonviolence earned him the name Mahatma, or "Great Soul." Gandhi's efforts proved successful. In 1947, India won its independence from Great Britain.

Draw Conclusions
Why did people call Gandhi "Mahatma"?

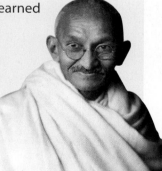

Academic Vocabulary
implications
consequences

Reading Check
Analyze Effects
What was the effect of Gandhi's protesting?

Division and Independence In the end, Gandhi's protests led to change in India. In 1935, the British government gave the Indian people limited self-rule. Not satisfied with this, many people continued their protests. These uprisings showed that Indians had grown tired of British control and expansion in South Asia. Soon the protests against British control would lead to political change throughout the region.

Even as Indians were protesting against the British, tensions between the Hindu and Muslim communities in India caused a crisis. Muslims feared that, even if India became fully independent, they would have little say in the government. Many of them began calling for a separate nation of their own.

To avoid a civil war, Great Britain agreed to the **partition**, or division, of India. In 1947, two independent countries were formed. The British government's decision to divide India had serious **implications**. It led to significant population movements between the new nations. Millions of people rushed to cross these new borders. India now had a majority Hindu population. **Pakistan**, which included the area that is now Bangladesh, now had a majority Muslim population. Many Muslims and Hindus wanted to live in the countries in which they would be part of the majority.

The End of Imperial China

While Indians were calling for freedom from the British, the Chinese were also calling for a change in government. The growing influence of foreign powers in China made many people unhappy with imperial rule. Their unhappiness led to a revolution in China.

Revolution Realizing that the people were unhappy, China's rulers, the Qing dynasty, tried to reform the government. They built new schools and a new army. They even allowed people to elect regional assemblies for the first time.

However, these attempts at reform were too little and too late. Radical activists called for the overthrow of China's government. They wanted China to become a republic.

One of the leaders of these protests was Sun Yixian (SUN yee-SHAHN). Sun wanted to make China a democracy, but he did not think the Chinese people were ready for that yet. He thought it was the government's job to teach the people how to govern themselves.

Inspired by Sun, rebels forced the last Qing emperor—China's last emperor of any dynasty—out of power in 1911. The rebels then formed a republic.

Civil War The creation of a republic did not end the power struggles in China. In the 1920s, two rival groups emerged. One group was the Communists. Opposing them were the Nationalists, led by Jiang Jieshi (jee-AHNG jee-SHEE). For several years the two groups worked together to drive foreign imperialists out of China, but their alliance was always uneasy.

Sun Yixian was instrumental in the overthrow of the Qing Dynasty. He was appointed as provisional president of the Republic of China and later became the leader of the Chinese Nationalist Party.

The alliance broke apart completely in 1929. Afraid that Communist influence in China was growing too strong, Nationalist forces attacked Communists in several cities. This attack began a civil war that lasted 20 years.

For the first years of the civil war, the Nationalists were in control. By the 1930s, though, a new Communist leader had emerged. His name was Mao Zedong (MOW zuh-DOOHNG). By 1949, Mao and the Communists had won. They declared a new Communist government, the People's Republic of China, with Mao as its leader. The surviving Nationalists fled to the island of Taiwan, where they founded the Republic of China.

Communism in China In a communist system, the government owns most businesses and land and controls all areas of life. Therefore, the first action of China's new communist government was taking control of the economy. The government seized all private farms and organized them into large, state-run farms. It also took over all businesses and factories. Those who spoke out against the government were killed or punished.

Communist China

Mao Zedong created the People's Republic of China on October 1, 1949. China celebrates the beginnings of Chinese communism on National Day, October 1. The celebration includes a huge parade in Beijing's Tiananmen Square.

A military parade of soldiers, tanks, and other equipment shows China's power.

The Gate of Heavenly Peace displays Mao Zedong's portrait above the entrance.

The Chinese believe dragon dances bring good fortune to important events.

Beijing

CHINA

PACIFIC OCEAN

Lion dances are performed to spread good blessings to the community.

The parades include couples married on National Day, a popular time to wed.

Analyze Visuals
Why might China's government sponsor such a huge celebration for National Day?

As China's ruler, Mao introduced many changes to Chinese society. He wanted to rid China of its traditional customs and create a new system. His goal was to make China a modern country.

While some of Mao's changes improved life in China, others did not. On one hand, women gained more rights than they had had under the emperors, including the right to work outside the home. On the other hand, the government limited people's freedoms and imprisoned those who criticized it. Hundreds of thousands of people were killed for criticizing the government. In addition, many economic programs were unsuccessful, and some were outright disasters. Poor planning often led to famines that killed millions.

Today, Chinese citizens continue to struggle to gain rights such as freedom of the press and freedom of speech. China's government controls access to the Internet. Social media sites and e-mail can be censored or blocked.

There is no freedom of the press or freedom of speech in modern China. Writers, artists, and reporters struggle to accurately report news or express what they think. Chinese citizens can face harsh penalties if they publicly disagree with government policies. Some have not been allowed to travel outside China. Others have been jailed for several years.

Reading Check
Summarize
How did communism change life in China?

A New Japanese Empire

When the Chinese grew dissatisfied with their government, they overthrew their emperor. When similar feelings took hold in Japan about 50 years earlier, the people there had the opposite reaction. They decided to choose a new emperor to rule their country.

A New Government Japan had officially been ruled by an emperor for several centuries. In truth, however, the emperor had little power. Since the 1100s, real power had been in the hands of military leaders called shoguns.

The arrival of Americans and other Westerners in Japan in the 1800s angered many people. They resented foreign interference in Japan and blamed the shogun. They felt he should have been strong enough to keep the Americans and Europeans out of their country.

In 1868, an alliance of nobles defeated the shogun's army and forced the shogun to step down. By doing so, they restored the power of the emperor. The newly powerful emperor took the name Meiji (MAY-jee), which means "enlightened rule" in Japanese. As a result, the shift back to imperial power in Japan is known as the Meiji Restoration.

Reforms in Japan When Meiji took control of Japan, he made sweeping changes in the government. First, he abolished the old feudal system. Under this system, warriors called samurai had been given land and power in exchange for military service. Meiji took all land away from the samurai and put it under the control of the state.

To replace the feudal system, Meiji sent officials to Europe and the United States to learn about Western government and economics. He then worked to apply in Japan what these officials had learned. For example, he created the **Diet**, the elected legislature that still governs Japan.

Meiji also reformed the Japanese education system. He required all children to attend school. He also encouraged some children to study in other countries to learn more about those countries.

Perhaps most importantly, Meiji worked to industrialize Japan. He built telegraph lines, a postal service, and railroads to improve communication. He also established Japan's first national currency. Japan quickly became a major industrial power in Asia.

Japanese Imperialism Meiji's reforms also led to changes in the country's military. All soldiers were required to swear a personal oath of loyalty to the emperor. The result was a force that would do anything the emperor asked of it.

From 1890 to 1910, Japan launched a series of military strikes against nearby countries. In short order, the Japanese defeated both the Chinese and Russian armies. These victories left Japan the most powerful county in Asia and won Japan the respect of many Western nations.

Respect soon turned to caution, however. In 1910, Japan invaded Korea and made it a colony. At the same time, the government began to expand the Japanese army. Many observers feared the possible consequences of that expansion.

Reading Check
Summarize
Why did some countries become cautious about Japan?

Summary and Preview In this lesson, you learned about political changes in Asia in the 1800s and 1900s. In the next lesson, you will study a conflict between India and Pakistan and learn about the economies and politics of modern Asia.

Lesson 1 Assessment

Review Ideas, Terms, and People

1. **a. Identify** What countries were created from the partition of India?

   b. Form Generalizations How did Gandhi encourage people to oppose the British?

2. **a. Describe** How did China change under the Communist government?

   b. Analyze How do you think most Chinese people felt about Mao's changes in China?

   c. Summarize What examples from the text show that Chinese citizens have struggled to gain rights?

3. **a. Recall** What were the effects of the Meiji Restoration in Japan?

   b. Explain How did Japan's foreign policy change?

Critical Thinking

4. **Summarize** Use your notes to complete the graphic organizer below with a short summary of political changes in each region.

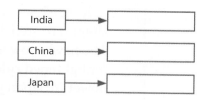

A New Asia

The Big Idea

Since the end of World War II, Asia has experienced major economic, political, and cultural changes.

Main Ideas

- India and Pakistan were in conflict over Kashmir.

- Many Asian countries have found economic success since World War II.

- Political shifts in Asia have led to new governments in many countries.

- Many Asian cultures blend old and new ideas.

Key Terms and People

Kashmir
trade surplus
tariff
constitutional monarchies
Tiananmen Square
human rights
Aung San Suu Kyi
Corazon Aquino

If YOU were there . . .

You are a small business owner living in Taiwan shortly after World War II. Before the war your company made toys by hand. During the war, however, your building and all of your equipment was destroyed. Now that the war is over, a European bank has offered to loan you money to start up your business again. A friend has also told you about a company that sells machines that will make your toys much faster than you could before.

Will you buy the machines? Why or why not?

Conflict in Kashmir

Great Britain finally granted independence for the people of the Indian subcontinent in 1947. Its leaders called for the establishment of a Hindu nation and a Muslim nation. They thought that this action would help make the transition to independence a peaceful one. A mass movement of people on the subcontinent ensured that most Hindus lived in India. Most Muslims now called Pakistan home.

The establishment of an independent India and Pakistan was not enough to bring peace to South Asia, however. After independence in 1947, India and Pakistan began to fight over the region of **Kashmir**. Kashmir is a mountainous area in the north near the Chinese border. The region became the site of armed conflict.

Roots of the Conflict When India was partitioned, Kashmir was ruled by a Hindu prince. Because he was Hindu, he decided to make Kashmir a part of India rather than Pakistan.

This decision angered Kashmir's large Muslim population. The Pakistani government, claiming Kashmir should belong to Pakistan, soon sent troops into Kashmir. India responded by sending in troops of its own. War broke out.

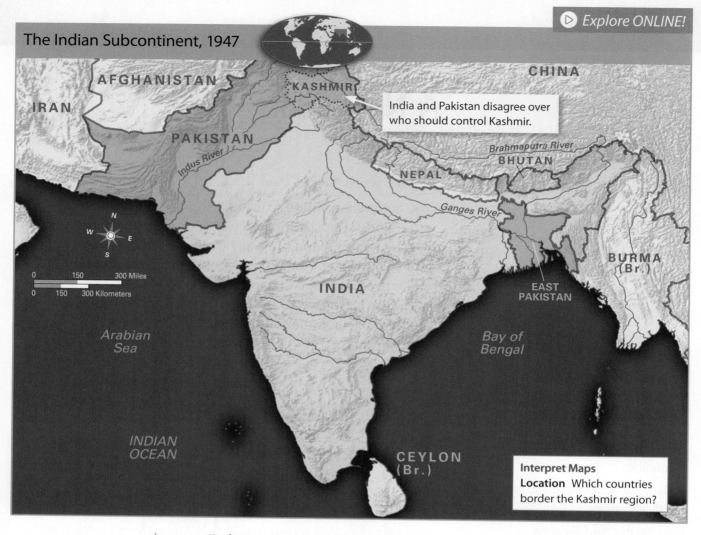

The Indian Subcontinent, 1947

Explore ONLINE!

India and Pakistan disagree over who should control Kashmir.

KASHMIR

AFGHANISTAN

CHINA

IRAN

PAKISTAN

Indus River

Brahmaputra River

BHUTAN

NEPAL

Ganges River

INDIA

EAST PAKISTAN

BURMA (Br.)

Arabian Sea

Bay of Bengal

INDIAN OCEAN

CEYLON (Br.)

Interpret Maps
Location Which countries border the Kashmir region?

Fighting in Kashmir continued for two years. In 1949, the United Nations negotiated a peace treaty. This treaty divided Kashmir in two. India controlled the southern part, and Pakistan the northern part. Later, China also claimed part of Kashmir. Under the treaty, the people of Kashmir were to vote on their future. However, that vote was never held.

Kashmir Today Today, Kashmir is still disputed territory. Conflict continues. Much of the region's Muslim population lives in the Indian-controlled area, and some militants have taken up arms against India. The Indian government claims that these militants are terrorists backed by Pakistan. The Pakistani government, on the other hand, rejects these claims. It says that the militants are simply Kashmir residents who are fighting to break from Indian control.

The disagreement over Kashmir is a constant source of tension between the governments of India and Pakistan. Although full-scale war has not broken out, thousands of people have died in fighting in the region.

Reading Check
Summarize
What led to the conflict in Kashmir?

Economic Success

Conflicts over political and economic differences raged through Asia in the 1940s, 1950s, and 1960s. However, life in Asia also changed in a positive way. The economies of several Asian nations grew during this time.

Before World War II the countries of South and East Asia were not considered economic powerhouses. Few of the countries were heavily industrialized. As a result, they lagged behind the countries of Europe and the Americas.

Since World War II, however, the countries of the region have shifted their focus. Several Asian countries' economies are now ranked among the strongest in the world.

Japan Japan was the Asian country most devastated by World War II. However, it was also the first to recover and prosper. With assistance from Europe and the United States, Japan completely rebuilt its economy. Within a few decades of the war, Japan's economy had grown into one of the strongest in the world.

Link to Economics

Economic Growth in Asia

Although China and Japan have the largest economies in Asia, several smaller countries also found economic success. As you can see in the graph below, the economies of South Korea, Taiwan, and Singapore grew particularly fast in the 1980s to 2000s. Together, they are called the Asian Tigers because of this growth. Their success was made possible by low production costs and a loyal workforce.

Many Asian nations faced hardships during a worldwide economic recession that began in 2007. For the most part, the Asian Tigers were able to quickly recover, and they remain an important part of the global economy today.

Economic Growth in Asia, 1986–2004

GDP (in billions of U.S. dollars) vs. Year

■ South Korea ■ Taiwan ■ Singapore

Sources: The World Bank; International Monetary Fund

Analyze Information
What allowed the Asian Tigers to develop strong economies so quickly?

Academic
Vocabulary
efficient productive
and not wasteful

The most successful area of Japan's economy has been manufacturing. Japanese companies are known for making high-quality products, especially cars and electronics like televisions and DVD players. Clever innovation and **efficient** building have enabled the Japanese to produce excellent products at low costs.

Many Japanese products are intended to be sold outside of the country, especially in China and the United States. In fact, Japan's trade has been so successful that the country has built up a huge trade surplus. A **trade surplus** exists when a country exports more goods than it imports.

Japan is able to export more than it imports in part because of high tariffs. A **tariff** is a fee that a country charges on imports or exports. For many years, Japan's government has placed high tariffs on goods brought into the country. This makes imported goods more expensive, so people buy Japanese goods rather than imported ones.

China When the Communists took over China in the 1940s they established a command economy. A command economy is one in which the government owns all businesses and makes all decisions.

However, the command economy led to major economic problems in China. For example, the production of goods fell drastically. In response, the government closed many state-owned factories and began allowing privately owned businesses. These businesses today produce everything from satellites and chemicals to clothing and toys. In addition, the government has created special economic zones where foreign businesspeople can own companies. This mixed economic approach has helped China's economy boom. Today it has the world's second-largest economy.

India Since India gained its independence, it has become a major industrial power. Its gross domestic product (GDP) places it among the world's top ten industrial countries. However, its per capita GDP is only approximately $1,600. Millions of Indians live in poverty.

The government has taken steps to reduce poverty. For example, it has encouraged farmers to adopt modern farming techniques. It has also attempted to lure new industries to India. It has made the city of Bangalore a center of high-tech industry. In addition, the government has promoted India's film industry. Nicknamed Bollywood, this industry produces more films each year than any other country.

Reading Check
Summarize
How have Asian
economies changed
since World War II?

Political Shifts

South and East Asia have also witnessed major political shifts since World War II. In some countries, democracy has taken root. In others, military rulers have seized control of the governments.

Democracy in Asia Since the end of World War II, several Asian countries have embraced democracy. One such country is Japan. Japan's emperor gave up most of his power at the end of the war and helped create a democratic government there. When India became independent in 1947, it too became a democracy. In fact, India is by population the largest democracy in the world today. Other democratic countries in the region include Bangladesh, Mongolia, and Indonesia.

In addition, some Asian countries have developed **constitutional monarchies**. In this form of democracy, a monarch serves as the head of state, but a legislature makes the laws. Thailand and Malaysia are both constitutional monarchies. Thailand has had the same royal family since the 1780s. In Malaysia, local rulers take turns being the king.

China and Democracy China is not a democracy. Some Chinese people have attempted to bring democracy to their country. However, as you have read, the government harshly punishes people who oppose its policies.

The most famous example of this punishment took place in 1989. In the spring of that year, more than a million Chinese pro-democracy protestors

Tiananmen Square, 1989

More than a million pro-democracy protestors occupied Beijing's Tiananmen Square in the spring of 1989. At first, Chinese leaders tolerated the demonstration, but as the protest grew larger, they decided to crack down. In the evening hours of June 3, the government sent tanks and troops into the square to crush the protestors, killing hundreds.

Day 18
May 30 Near the official portrait of Mao Zedong, students build a large statue that came to be known as the "Goddess of Democracy."

Day 24
June 5 In this famous image from the events at Tiananmen Square, an unarmed man faces down a line of Chinese tanks.

Analyze Visuals
What do these photos suggest about the desire for democracy in China?

gathered in **Tiananmen Square** in Beijing, China's capital. The protestors were demanding more political rights and freedoms. The Chinese government tried to get the protestors to leave the square. When they refused, the government used troops and tanks to make them leave. Hundreds of protestors were killed, and many more were injured or imprisoned.

Military Governments In some cases, political change in Asia was brought about by military leaders. In both Pakistan and Myanmar, for example, military leaders seized power for themselves.

Pakistan has been plagued by unstable governments since it was first created in 1947. Over the years it has suffered from rebellions and the assassination of government leaders. In 2001, General Pervez Musharraf became Pakistan's president after a military coup. One of his main rivals for power was Benazir Bhutto, who in 1988 became the first female prime minister to serve in a Muslim country. Bhutto was assassinated by terrorists in late 2007.

The military seized power in Myanmar, which is also known as Burma, in 1962. For many years, the government has abused people's **human rights**, those rights that all people deserve such as the rights to equality and justice. A Burmese woman, **Aung San Suu Kyi** (AWNG SAHN SOO CHEE), has led a movement for more democracy and rights. She and others have been jailed and harassed for their actions.

Known as "the Lady" in Myanmar, Aung San Suu Kyi rejoined her political party after the government released her from house arrest. This party won a landslide victory in an election held in November 2015. The military is still part of the government, but this election helped bring some democratic ideas to Myanmar. It was the first time in more than 50 years that the Burmese people could choose their leaders.

Martial Law in Asia The Philippines was a territory of the United States until its independence in 1946. It then became a democratic republic. In 1965, however, Ferdinand Marcos was elected president of the Philippines. Marcos ruled as a dictator from 1966 to 1986. Although the constitution limited Marcos to eight years in office, he established martial law—a system of military government in which all other laws become void—from 1972 to 1981. In 1986, **Corazon Aquino** (cor-AH-zohn ah-KEE-no) challenged Marcos in an election. Aquino won, but Marcos refused to acknowledge her victory. When he declared himself the official winner, a public outcry resulted. He was forced into exile in Hawaii, where he later died.

Like the Philippines, Indonesia became independent after World War II. It struggled economically for some 20 years. From 1965 to 1966, members of the military led a coup against the existing government and killed as many as one million Indonesians. A general named Suharto became president in 1967 and turned Indonesia into a police state. He imposed frequent periods of martial law. His government showed little tolerance for religious freedom. Bribery and corruption were common. The economy improved for a while, but the nation suffered a severe financial crisis in 1997 and 1998. Growing unrest over government suppression and the economic crisis forced Suharto to step down in 1998.

Corazon Aquino was the first female president in Asia. Here she is seen leading people to a sit-in to protest the military rule of Ferdinand Marcos.

Reading Check
Synthesize
What forms of government have developed in Asia since World War II?

Asian culture today blends traditional customs with modern influences. New technology shapes life even in traditional Buddhist temples, like this one in Thailand.

Blending Old and New

Asian culture today is a complex blend of old customs and new trends. This blending is evident in architecture. Cities like Shanghai, China, and Kuala Lumpur, Malaysia, have some of the world's tallest and glitziest buildings. Nestled between the modern buildings are tiny ancient temples.

The blending of old and new can also be seen in people's daily lives. Traditional beliefs, such as the Chinese respect for one's ancestors and the Japanese code of honor, remain strong influences in people's lives. At the same time, however, cell phones and the Internet allow people to communicate worldwide. As a result, elements of other cultures, especially those from the West, have seeped into Asian life.

Summary and Preview In this lesson, you learned that Asia's governments, economies, and cultures changed dramatically since World War II. Next, you will learn how African nations gained their independence.

Reading Check
Draw Conclusions
How does the blend of old and new affect life in Asia?

Lesson 2 Assessment

Review Ideas, Terms, and People

1. **Recall** What issue led to fighting in Kashmir?

2. **a. Describe** What are some factors that helped Japan become an economic powerhouse?

   b. Summarize What changes did China make to promote economic growth?

   c. Evaluate Which country do you think has been most successful in rebuilding its economy? Why?

3. **a. Recall** What happened at Tiananmen Square?

   b. Compare How has the government of Myanmar become more like the government of Japan?

   c. Contrast How are the governments of Japan, China, and Myanmar different?

4. **a. Identify** What are two old traditions that remain influential in Asia?

   b. Form Generalizations How has technology led to cultural change in Asia?

Critical Thinking

5. **Sequence** Draw a graphic organizer like this one. Using your notes, fill in the boxes with the steps that led to economic change in Asia.

Independence Movements in Africa

The Big Idea

African colonies began to call for independence after World War II, eventually gaining their freedom.

Main Ideas

- Unhappiness with European rule led to a call for independence in Africa.

- British colonies were some of the first to become free.

- French colonies followed two paths to independence.

- Belgian and Portuguese colonies had to fight for their freedom.

Key Terms and People

Ghana
Kenya
Mau Mau
Belgian Congo

If YOU were there . . .

You are a soldier from the French colony of Morocco. For the last year, you have fought alongside soldiers from France to defeat the German army. Now, the war is over and you are being sent home. You hoped that you would be rewarded for your service, but your commander sent you off without even saying thanks.

How does this lack of gratitude make you feel?

The Call for Independence

Many Africans were understandably unhappy with European control of their homeland. For centuries, they had ruled their own kingdoms and societies. Now, they were forced to accept outsiders as their leaders. After several rebellions against the Europeans were put down, however, people across Africa had resigned themselves to life in European colonies. Their attitudes began to change, though, after the two world wars.

World War I After World War I broke out in Europe in 1914, fighting spread to European colonies as well. Among the areas in which violence broke out was Africa. The Allies, including England and France, attacked German colonies in Africa. They hoped that taking Germany's colonies would weaken the country financially.

Much of the fighting in Africa was done by the people of English and French colonies. Hundreds of thousands of Africans were recruited to assist European armies. Tens of thousands of these recruits died in combat.

When the war ended, the African soldiers returning home thought they would be thanked for their efforts. Instead, they were largely ignored. As a result of this snub, resentment toward Europeans increased in parts of Africa.

Reading Check
Summarize
How did the two world wars lead to calls for independence?

World War II In the late 1930s, war once again broke out in Europe. As before, Africans were called upon to help Europeans fight. Some half a million African troops fought alongside the British, the French, and their allies.

When the war ended, the Africans were once again not suitably thanked for their contributions. Angry leaders began calling for political change in Africa. They wanted their independence.

British Colonies

Among the colonies most loudly calling for independence were those belonging to Great Britain. Their demands only increased in 1947 when Britain granted independence to India. If India could be free, many Africans asked, why couldn't they? Before long, several British colonies in Africa, including Ghana and Kenya, had won their freedom.

Ghana That first British colony to win its freedom was **Ghana**, formerly called the Gold Coast. Its fight was led by Kwame Nkrumah (KWAHM-eh en-KROO-muh). In 1947 Nkrumah organized strikes and demonstrations against the British. The British responded by arresting him.

Even from prison, however, Nkrumah called for independence. Inspired by his courage, many people joined his struggle.

Largely because of Nkrumah's actions, the British granted the Gold Coast its independence in 1957. Nkrumah became the first prime minister. As its leader, he renamed the country Ghana after the ancient empire of West Africa.

DOCUMENT-BASED INVESTIGATION   Historical Source

I Speak of Freedom

The leader of the independence movement in Ghana, Kwame Nkrumah, did not want freedom for only his own people. He wanted all Africans to be free. Nkrumah thought all Africans should band together to achieve their goals.

> *"It is clear that we must find an African solution to our problems, and that this can only be found in African unity. Divided we are weak; united, Africa could become one of the greatest forces for good in the world."*
>
> —Kwame Nkrumah, from *I Speak of Freedom: A Statement of African Ideology*

Analyze Historical Sources
What evidence in the quotation shows that Kwame Nkrumah thought Africa would be better off united than divided?

Kenya Other British colonies did not find the road to independence as smooth as Ghana did. For example, the East African colony of **Kenya** became independent only after a long and violent struggle.

When the British arrived in Kenya, they claimed land that had once been occupied by the Kikuyu people. The British used that land to grow valuable crops, such as coffee, and did not want to give the land back to the Kikuyu. The Kikuyu now wanted independence and their former lands back.

To retake their land, Kikuyu farmers formed a violent movement called the **Mau Mau**. Its goal was to rid Kenya of white settlers. Between 1952 and 1960, the Mau Mau terrorized the British in Kenya. Its members attacked and killed anyone they suspected of opposing their goals. They even attacked Africans who cooperated with the British.

The British responded by arresting and torturing any members of the Mau Mau they could find. Nevertheless, the British eventually realized that they would have to grant Kenya's independence. In 1963, they made Kenya a free country. The colonial era in Kenya was over.

Kenya was now an independent nation. Its first prime minister was Jomo Kenyatta, who had been one of the first people to call for Kenyan freedom. The new country drafted its own constitution. This gave Kenyan citizens more rights and banned many forms of discrimination. Jailed prisoners had to be treated humanely. People had more freedom of speech and were able to freely practice their own religion.

Reading Check
Contrast
How were the paths to independence taken by Ghana and Kenya different?

French Colonies

Like the British, the French began to grant independence to their colonies after World War II. For some colonies, particularly those in West Africa, the transition to independence was smooth. In North Africa, however, the change was rough and violent.

Jomo Kenyatta, Kenya's first prime minister, rides in a parade to celebrate his country's independence in 1963.

West Africa France's attitude toward its colonies in West Africa had always been different from Britain's. While the British saw their colonies as backward societies that needed guidance, the French wanted to make their colonies part of France. After World War II, France's leaders offered Africans more of a role in the colonial government. Largely because they had already been given a role in the government, many African leaders in French colonies did not want to break away from France completely.

In 1958, the French government gave its West African colonies a choice. They could become completely independent, or they could join a new organization called the French Community with political and economic

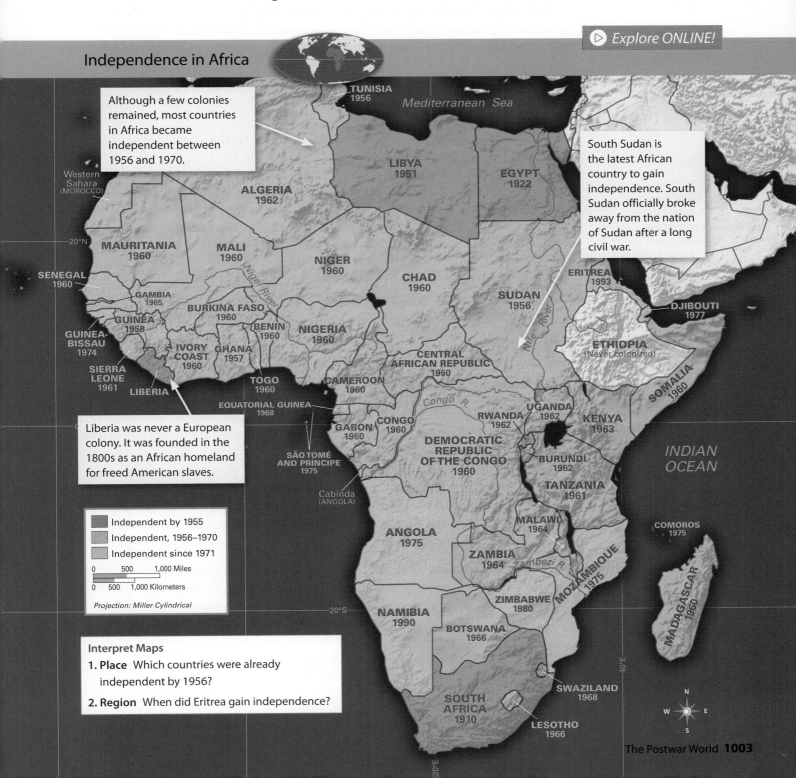

Independence in Africa

Explore ONLINE!

Although a few colonies remained, most countries in Africa became independent between 1956 and 1970.

South Sudan is the latest African country to gain independence. South Sudan officially broke away from the nation of Sudan after a long civil war.

Liberia was never a European colony. It was founded in the 1800s as an African homeland for freed American slaves.

Mediterranean Sea

TUNISIA 1956
LIBYA 1951
EGYPT 1922
Western Sahara (MOROCCO)
ALGERIA 1962
MAURITANIA 1960
MALI 1960
NIGER 1960
CHAD 1960
SUDAN 1956
ERITREA 1993
DJIBOUTI 1977
SENEGAL 1960
GAMBIA 1965
BURKINA FASO 1960
GUINEA 1958
BENIN 1960
NIGERIA 1960
GUINEA-BISSAU 1974
IVORY COAST 1960
GHANA 1957
CENTRAL AFRICAN REPUBLIC 1960
ETHIOPIA (Never colonized)
SIERRA LEONE 1961
LIBERIA
TOGO 1960
CAMEROON 1960
SOMALIA 1960
EQUATORIAL GUINEA 1968
GABON 1960
CONGO 1960
UGANDA 1962
RWANDA 1962
KENYA 1963
SÃO TOMÉ AND PRÍNCIPE 1975
DEMOCRATIC REPUBLIC OF THE CONGO 1960
BURUNDI 1962
INDIAN OCEAN
Cabinda (ANGOLA)
TANZANIA 1961
MALAWI 1964
COMOROS 1975
ANGOLA 1975
ZAMBIA 1964
MOZAMBIQUE 1975
MADAGASCAR 1960
NAMIBIA 1990
ZIMBABWE 1980
BOTSWANA 1966
SWAZILAND 1968
SOUTH AFRICA 1910
LESOTHO 1966

Niger River
Congo R.
Nile River
Zambezi R.

20°N
20°S
40°E
20°E

Independent by 1955
Independent, 1956–1970
Independent since 1971

0   500   1,000 Miles
0 500 1,000 Kilometers

Projection: Miller Cylindrical

Interpret Maps

1. **Place** Which countries were already independent by 1956?

2. **Region** When did Eritrea gain independence?

ties to France. Most chose to become part of the community. A few years later, France granted most of the former colonies full independence anyway.

North Africa Although French colonies in West Africa were willing to work peacefully with the French to gain independence, the colonies of Morocco, Tunisia, and Algeria were not. In all three colonies, protestors calling for independence staged strikes, demonstrations, and attacks. Observers thought that guerrilla wars seemed likely. These political protests were a direct result of French expansion and colonialism in the region.

The French government decided that it could not fight wars in all three colonies. Because Algeria had the largest French population, the French sent their army there. They thought their people would need the army's protection.

With the army in Algeria, the French sent diplomats to Morocco and Tunisia to negotiate. As a result, both countries became independent in 1956.

Meanwhile, violence continued in Algeria. Political groups there attacked French leaders and citizens. In response, the French attacked Algerian Muslims. Finally, France's prime minister suggested a compromise, offering the Algerians some self-government. However, neither the French nor the Algerians were happy with this compromise, and conflict threatened to break out again. Realizing that they could not maintain order in Algeria, the French granted the country its independence in 1962.

Reading Check
Summarize
What steps did France's colonies take to become free?

Belgian and Portuguese Colonies

Not all European countries were willing to set their colonies free. The Belgians and the Portuguese in particular fought to keep their colonies. Neither country willingly gave up its claims in Africa.

The Belgian Congo Belgium controlled only one major colony in Africa—the **Belgian Congo**. After World War II, the Belgians granted some freedoms to the colony's people. Wanting full independence, however, the Congolese people **rebelled**. Various Congolese groups staged riots and even held elections. However, not all of these groups shared the same goals, and conflict between groups was common.

Academic Vocabulary
rebelled to fight against authority

The Belgians refused to recognize the colonists' rights for many years. In 1960, though, they suddenly changed their position. They withdrew from the Congo, and the colony became independent. Shortly afterward, civil war broke out between various groups who wanted to run the newly independent Congo.

Portuguese Colonies Unlike the Belgians, the Portuguese held several colonies in Africa, mostly in the south and east. Even as the other countries of Europe were setting their colonies free, the Portuguese fought to keep theirs.

Reading Check
Analyze Events
Why were the Belgian and Portuguese colonies among the last to become free?

Eventually, however, the people of Portugal's colonies rebelled against them. In Angola, Guinea, and Mozambique, rebels attacked Portuguese troops. These attacks began decades of bloody war.

In 1974, Portugal's military government was overthrown and replaced with a democracy. Shortly afterward, the Portuguese gave up any claim to their colonies and withdrew from Africa completely.

Summary and Preview In this lesson, you learned that by 1970 most colonies in Africa had won their independence. In the next lesson, you will learn how life in Africa changed after independence.

Lesson 3 Assessment

Review Ideas, Terms, and People

1. **a. Recall** What did Africans do in World War I?
   b. Draw Conclusions How did the world wars lead to resentment in Africa?
2. **a. Identify** What was the first British colony to become independent?
   b. Explain Why was the Mau Mau formed?
   c. Analyze How did independence influence human rights in Kenya?
3. **a. Contrast** How was the French attitude toward its West African colonies different from the British?
   b. Elaborate Why do you think many former French colonies wanted to keep ties to France?

4. **a. Describe** What was the struggle for independence in Portuguese colonies like?
   b. Sequence What led to civil war in the Congo?

Critical Thinking

5. **Summarize** Using your notes, complete the chart with one statement that summarizes the path each country's colonies took to win their freedom from the Europeans.

Country	Colonies' Path to Independence
Great Britain	
France	
Belgium	
Portugal	

Africa Since Independence

The Big Idea

The people of Africa have faced both changes and challenges since they won their independence.

Main Ideas

- People in South Africa faced social struggles related to racial equality.
- Many African countries saw political challenges after they became independent.
- The economy and the environment affect life in Africa.
- African culture blends traditional and European elements.

Key Terms and People

apartheid
townships
sanctions
Darfur
Lagos
Kinshasa

If YOU were there . . .

You live in South Africa. One day, you and some friends join a protest against certain unfair government policies. Although the protest is peaceful, a large number of police officers show up and arrest its organizer. As they handcuff him and drag him off to prison, many people are angry.

How do you feel about this event?

Social Struggles in South Africa

Many Africans suffered during the imperial period. They felt their lives would improve once they were free. With independence, many found that their lives were indeed better. At the same time, though, a new set of problems developed.

One example of these new problems could be seen in South Africa. The country gained independence in 1910, much earlier than most African countries. However, racial tensions there led to the creation of an official policy of discrimination.

Apartheid In the early 1900s, South Africa's government was controlled largely by the white descendants of early Dutch, French, and German settlers. Many of these white residents believed that they should have all the power and that black South Africans should have no voice in the government. Understandably, black South Africans opposed this plan. To defend their rights, they formed the African National Congress (ANC) in 1912. The ANC also wrote a constitution. An early version demanded an end to all discrimination. It also called for all adults to have the right to vote. These demands were in response to the absence of rights under South Africa's government.

Despite protests by the ANC, South Africa's government set up a policy of separation of races, or **apartheid** (uh-PAHR-tayt), which means "apartness." This policy divided people into four groups: Whites, Blacks, Coloureds, and Asians. Coloureds were people of mixed ancestry.

Under apartheid, only white South Africans could vote or hold political office. Blacks, who made up nearly 75 percent of the population, were not citizens. They could work only certain jobs and made very little money. They were allowed to live in only certain areas. In cities, black residents had to live in specially designated **townships**, which were often crowded clusters of tiny homes. Only certain types of businesses were allowed in the townships, which ensured that people living there would stay poor. In the 1950s, South Africa's government created "homelands" for various black African tribes. However, these homelands generally did not include good farmland or resources, which were owned by the whites. Coloured and Asian citizens also had restricted rights, though they had more rights than Blacks.

The End of Apartheid By the 1940s, many South Africans, especially members of the ANC, were protesting loudly against apartheid. Among the leaders of these protests was a young lawyer named Nelson Mandela. He urged black South Africans to fight apartheid.

In 1960, the South African government banned the ANC and put Mandela in jail. Even with their leader in jail, however, people continued to protest apartheid. The protests were not limited to South Africa, either. People around the world called for an end to apartheid. Other governments placed **sanctions**—economic or political penalties imposed by one country on another to force a policy change—against South Africa.

Faced with this pressure from inside and outside, the South African government finally began to move away from apartheid in the late 1980s. In 1990, it released Mandela from prison. Soon afterward, South Africans of all races were given the right to vote. In 1994, Mandela was elected South Africa's first black president.

Today all races have equal rights in South Africa. The ANC is now a prominent political party. In the 2014 national elections, it received over 60 percent of the vote. The ANC has amended its constitution to include specific human rights, including the rights of children. It continues to call for a united South African society.

Nelson Mandela 1918–2013

Because he protested against apartheid, Nelson Mandela was imprisoned for 26 years. In 1990, however, South Africa's President de Klerk released Mandela from prison. Mandela and de Klerk shared the Nobel Peace Prize in 1993. One year later, Mandela became South Africa's first black president. He wrote a new constitution and worked to improve the living conditions of all black South Africans.

Summarize
What did Nelson Mandela accomplish when he was South Africa's president?

I Am Prepared to Die

In 1962, Nelson Mandela was arrested for his opposition to the government and apartheid. In 1963, ten other ANC leaders were arrested in a suburb of Johannesburg called Rivonia. At this time the government brought more charges against Mandela. During the opening of the 1964 Rivonia Trial, Mandela made this statement about the injustices in South African society.

Analyze Historical Sources
What do you think was the most important ideal in society for Nelson Mandela?

> *"During my lifetime I have dedicated myself to this struggle of the African people. I have fought against white domination, and I have fought against black domination. I have cherished the ideal of a democratic and free society in which all persons live together in harmony and with equal opportunities. It is an ideal which I hope to live for and to achieve. But if needs be, it is an ideal for which I am prepared to die."*
>
> —from the 1964 speech "I Am Prepared to Die"

Reading Check
Make Inferences
Why did people around the world protest apartheid?

Public schools and universities are open to all people, as are hospitals and transportation. However, full economic equality, which is mentioned in the ANC's constitution as well, has come more slowly. White South Africans are still wealthier than the majority of Blacks. Still, South Africans now have better opportunities for the future.

Political Challenges

South Africa was not the only country to face political challenges after winning independence. Across Africa, people suffered under harsh military dictatorships and long civil wars.

Joseph Mobutu, also known as Mobutu Sese Seko, was president of Zaire (Democratic Republic of the Congo) from 1965–1997.

Military Dictatorships By the late 1960s, most of Africa was independent. In most of the newly free countries, the government was run by military dictators. These dictators kept power by not allowing anyone else to run for office. As a result, the dictator remained in charge. In most countries with military dictatorships, all political organizations that did not support the government were banned.

Perhaps the best example of a military dictator in Africa was Joseph Mobutu. He rose to power in the Congo in 1965 after the Belgians left. To show his power, he changed the name of the country to Zaire, a traditional African name.

As dictator, Mobutu took over foreign-owned industries. He borrowed money from other countries to try to improve the country's industry. However, most farmers suffered during Mobutu's rule. In addition, many government and business leaders were corrupt. While the country's economy collapsed, Mobutu became one of the richest people in the world. Anyone who dared to challenge his authority was met with violence.

Celebrating Mandela's Freedom
South Africans in Soweto warmly welcomed Nelson
Mandela after he was released from prison in 1990.

Ethnic Conflict and Civil War Many Africans were not happy with these military dictators and took steps to replace them. Mobutu, for example, was overthrown after a civil war in 1997. The new government renamed the country the Democratic Republic of the Congo. Similar civil wars were fought in many countries.

Political disagreement has been only one factor leading to violence in Africa. Ethnic conflict is also common. As you recall, when the leaders of Europe divided Africa among themselves, they paid little attention to the people who lived there. As a result, colonies often included people from many ethnic groups. In some cases, these groups did not get along at all.

When colonies became independent years later, these ethnic groups sometimes fought each other for control. Their fighting often led to long, bloody civil wars. In Rwanda, for example, the Hutu and Tutsi ethnic groups went to war in 1994. The government, run by the Hutu, began killing all the Tutsi in the country. About 1 million Tutsi civilians were killed in the conflict. Many more fled the country.

Similar conflict has plagued Sudan for decades. Muslims and Christians have fought each other for years. More recently, a genocide has occurred in the region of **Darfur**. Ethnic conflict there has resulted in tens of thousands of black Sudanese being killed by an Arab militia group. Millions more have fled Darfur. Those who fled are now scattered throughout northern and eastern Africa as refugees.

The countries of Africa underwent many political changes after they became independent. In many countries, those changes led to corrupt governments and violent conflicts. Eventually, most countries formed democratic governments.

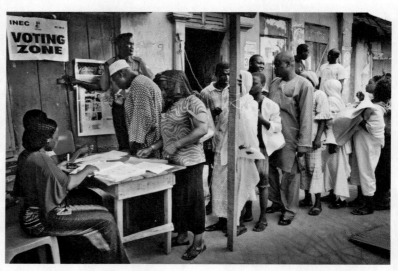

Dictators

Military dictators like Uganda's Idi Amin seized power in many countries.

Democracy

Many African nations today have established democratic governments. The country of Ghana has proved to be a model example of a democracy. Elections are fair, and leaders act in the interests of all citizens.

Civil War and Ethnic Conflict

Ethnic conflict in Darfur, Sudan, has forced millions of people to flee the country as refugees. Some receive food and aid at camps like this one.

Reading Check Synthesize What political challenges have African nations faced?

Democracy in Africa Dictatorships and civil wars were common in Africa through the late 1900s. As the year 2000 approached, however, political changes swept through Africa. People began to demand more democratic forms of government. They wanted to choose their own leaders.

By the early 2000s, more than 30 countries in Africa had abandoned dictatorships and held elections. Although some of these elections were rigged to keep corrupt governments in place, others resulted in true democratic governments coming to power. By 2015, true democracies thrived in such countries as Senegal, Ghana, Tanzania, South Africa, and Botswana.

Economy and Environment

Political challenges were not the only ones faced by Africa's countries. Many countries faced economic challenges as well. At the same time, Africans had to fight environmental issues, including deadly diseases.

Struggling and Booming Economies After they became independent, many African countries had weak economies. Most countries had not industrialized and depended mainly on farming or mining. For example, Ghana earned most of its income from cocoa, and Nigeria from oil.

Since independence, however, many countries have found new economic opportunities. Economies grew strong in the early 2000s but experienced setbacks in the early 2010s. Today, economic success seems likely for a growing number of African countries. Among the countries with Africa's strongest economies are Nigeria, South Africa, Angola, and many countries in North Africa. However, some other countries still have huge debts and little infrastructure and must depend on aid from other countries. Many people in these countries survive by growing just enough crops for their families to survive.

Africa's Largest Cities

Africa's largest cities, such as Kinshasa, offer opportunities and challenges.

Africa's Largest Cities

Source: The World Factbook

Interpret Graphs
What is the approximate population of Lagos? of Kinshasa?

As economies grow in some African countries, so do their cities. These cities often offer more jobs and higher standards of living than rural areas. Each year millions of people move there. As a result, already-large cities like Cairo, Egypt; **Lagos**, Nigeria; and **Kinshasa**, Democratic Republic of the Congo, are growing even larger. Rapid growth has led to crowding and high unemployment in some cities.

Environmental Challenges Economic development in Africa has been slow in part because people have to deal with environmental challenges, including disease. For example, malaria, a disease spread by mosquitoes, is one of the leading causes of death in many parts of Africa. Even more deadly than malaria is AIDS. This disease that weakens the immune system is widespread in Africa. In some countries, such as Swaziland and Botswana, more than one fourth of the entire population is infected with AIDS. Southern Africa is the hardest-hit region of the continent. Almost 6 million people have contracted AIDS in the country of South Africa alone.

Other environmental challenges also make survival difficult. Much of the continent suffered terrible droughts in the 1980s. These droughts left farmers unable to grow crops, and terrible famines swept through Africa. More recently, the people of East Africa faced a devastating dry period in 2011. In 2015 and 2016, a time of drought struck Southern Africa. Desertification, the spread of desertlike conditions, also presents challenges for the continent. In parts of Africa, especially West Africa, farmers must take care to prevent fertile soil from disappearing. Other environment problems African countries currently face include loss of forest, harm to soil, overfishing, and air and water pollution.

Reading Check
Identify Problems
What are two challenges people in Africa have faced?

African Culture

After they became independent, many African countries underwent identity crises. As colonies, they were forced to adopt many elements of European culture. At the same time, however, African peoples had their

African Music

Artists like the Mahotella Queens singing group have brought African culture to a worldwide audience.

own cultures that stretched back through centuries. How would people deal with these mixed cultures?

People reacted in different ways. Many elements of European culture can still be seen in Africa. For example, many people in West Africa still speak French or English in their daily lives.

At the same time, many Africans have rejected European culture and sought to reclaim their own traditional cultures. Writers and musicians draw on traditional themes from African folklore in their works, often written in Swahili or other African languages. Artists create masks, musical instruments, and sculptures from wood and bronze, just as their ancestors did centuries ago.

Reading Check
Analyze Effects
How does African culture reflect African and European ideas?

Summary and Preview In this lesson, you learned how African countries have grown and changed since they became independent. In the next lesson, you will read about society and conflict in a part of the world near Africa, the Middle East.

Lesson 4 Assessment

Review Ideas, Terms, and People

1. **a. Define** What was apartheid?
   b. Elaborate How did international protests help end apartheid?
   c. Identify What issues does the African National Congress (ANC) continue to support today?
2. **a. Describe** What problems did military dictators cause in some African countries?
   b. Explain What led to violence in parts of Africa?
3. **a. Recall** What issues do cities like Lagos and Kinshasa face today?
   b. Analyze How might environmental challenges lead to economic issues?

4. **a. Identify** What is one element of European culture present in Africa today?
   b. Draw Conclusions Why did many Africans want to reclaim their traditional culture?

Critical Thinking

5. **Categorize** Review your notes. Then complete the chart by listing political, economic, and social changes in Africa.

Changes in Africa		
Political	Economic	Social

Conflict in the Middle East

The Big Idea

Life in the Middle East since 1900 has been dominated by political change, conflict, and the oil industry.

Main Ideas

- New governments in the Middle East after World War I brought about major political changes.

- Conflict has challenged many countries in the Middle East.

- The oil industry has been a major influence in the region.

Key Terms

shah
embargo
Taliban
OPEC

If YOU were there . . .

You are a business owner and one of the most influential people in your city. For as long as you can remember, your city has been part of the mighty Ottoman Empire. Now, though, you hear that the empire has lost much of its territory. Your city is now run by the government of Great Britain.

How will this change affect your life?

Political Changes

For centuries most of the Middle East had been dominated by the Muslim Ottoman Empire. During World War I, however, the Ottomans fought on the losing side. When the war ended, they lost most of their territory. Before long, many countries in the region had experienced sweeping political changes.

Turkey Turkey had been the heart of the Ottoman Empire. When the empire collapsed after World War I, military officers took over the government. They were led by a war hero named Mustafa Kemal. He later adopted the name Kemal Atatürk, which means Father of Turks. Atatürk made Turkey a democracy and moved the capital to Ankara. He removed all elements of Islam from the government and closed Islamic schools. He also encouraged people to adopt Western-style clothing and names. Atatürk led a Turkish nationalist movement. He took pride in his country, and he wanted Turkey to be modern and independent.

Egypt Egypt had been a British colony during World War I. It was granted independence shortly afterward. However, the king who ruled the newly independent Egypt maintained close ties with the British. Many Egyptians were unhappy with his rule.

In 1952, a military coup abolished the monarchy and left Egypt in the hands of Gamal Abdel Nasser. To raise money for his government, Nasser tried to take control of the Suez

In the early part of the 1900s, new leaders in the Middle East worked to change their countries. Their goal was to bring the region into the modern world.

Turkish rally to honor Atatürk's policies, 2008

The shah on his throne, 1967

Kemal Atatürk

- took control of Turkey after World War I
- created a democratic government
- removed Islam from the government and closed Islamic schools
- encouraged people to adopt Western customs

Mohammad Reza Pahlavi

- became shah, or king, of Iran in 1941
- became an ally of the United States and Great Britain
- tried to modernize Iran
- angered many Iranians with his programs

Nasser after the British withdrawal from Egypt, 1956

Gamel Abdel Nasser

- seized power in Egypt in 1952
- tried to take control of the Suez Canal
- defied the French and British who owned the canal
- became a hero to many Arabs

Canal from the British and French. Britain and France sent troops into Egypt, but the United States persuaded them to leave. Egypt kept control of the canal. Nasser's defiance of the Europeans made him a hero to many Arabs.

Iran In 1921, an Iranian military officer took power and encouraged change in Iran's government. He claimed the old Persian title of **shah**, or king. In 1941, the shah's son Mohammad Reza Pahlavi took control.

This new shah became an ally of the United States and Great Britain and tried to modernize Iran. However, his programs were unpopular with many Iranians.

Palestine and Israel After World War I the region of Palestine came under British control. The region was inhabited mostly by Muslim Arabs. Since the late 1800s, however, Jews in Europe and other regions had been calling for a Jewish state in their ancient homeland.

In 1947, the United Nations voted to divide Palestine into a Jewish and an Arab state. While Arab countries rejected this plan, the Jews accepted it, and a year later the state of Israel was created.

Reading Check
Find Main Ideas
What political changes took place in the Middle East?

Disagreement and War in the Middle East

In some cases, the political changes that swept through the Middle East led to conflict between or within countries. In some places, cultural and religious differences also led to conflict.

Israel has continued to build settlements in East Jerusalem and the West Bank since capturing these areas during the Six-Day War.

Conflict in Israel Many Arab states were not happy about the founding of Israel. They felt that the United Nations had taken away land that was rightfully theirs. Much of their unhappiness dealt with control of Jerusalem. Now the capital of Israel, Jerusalem has sites that are considered holy by Jews, Christians, and Muslims. Control of the city is a difficult and emotional issue for members of all three religions.

Within a year of the founding of Israel, Arab armies invaded. In a very short war, the Israelis defeated the Arabs. Many Palestinians fled to neighboring Arab countries. Another short war broke out in 1967. During this so-called Six-Day War, Israel captured areas from Jordan and Egypt inhabited by Palestinian Arabs. These captured areas included Gaza, the West Bank, and East Jerusalem.

Since then, about 300,000 Israelis have moved into settlements in the West Bank and East Jerusalem. Israelis and Palestinians dispute the territory. Attempts have been made to divide the land fairly, but this conflict over land as well as terrorist attacks against Israel have caused great tension between Arabs and Israelis.

In the 1990s, Israel agreed to turn over parts of the territories to the Palestinians. In return, the Palestinians agreed to recognize Israel's existence. In 2005, Israel transferred Gaza to the Palestinians. In 2014, Palestinian rocket attacks led Israel to send troops into Gaza.

Some of the world's countries have called for a two-state solution. Israel and an independent Palestine would exist peacefully side by side. With tensions high in the region, however, a peaceful solution seems unlikely in the near future.

Civil War in Lebanon In the 1970s, a civil war broke out in Lebanon between the country's Muslim and Christian populations. Before long, Syria, Israel, and other countries had become involved in the conflict. Many people died, and the capital, Beirut, was badly damaged. Warfare lasted until 1990.

Timeline: Middle Eastern Conflicts

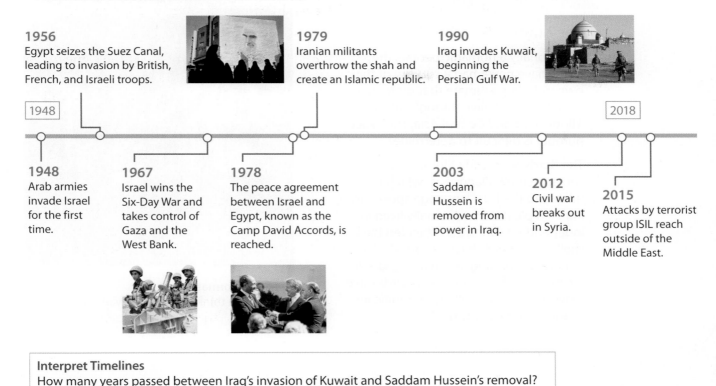

1956
Egypt seizes the Suez Canal, leading to invasion by British, French, and Israeli troops.

1979
Iranian militants overthrow the shah and create an Islamic republic.

1990
Iraq invades Kuwait, beginning the Persian Gulf War.

1948

2018

1948
Arab armies invade Israel for the first time.

1967
Israel wins the Six-Day War and takes control of Gaza and the West Bank.

1978
The peace agreement between Israel and Egypt, known as the Camp David Accords, is reached.

2003
Saddam Hussein is removed from power in Iraq.

2012
Civil war breaks out in Syria.

2015
Attacks by terrorist group ISIL reach outside of the Middle East.

Interpret Timelines
How many years passed between Iraq's invasion of Kuwait and Saddam Hussein's removal?

After 1990, Syria continued to maintain a strong influence in Lebanon. Syrian troops stayed in Lebanon until pressured to leave in 2005. In 2006, cross-border attacks by Lebanese guerrillas against Israel led to fighting between the two countries.

Beginning in 2012 Lebanon has felt the effects of conflict within neighboring Syria. By 2014 more than 1 million Syrian refugees have entered Lebanon. In 2015 Lebanon began to limit the number of Syrians allowed into the country.

The Iranian Revolution Fighting also broke out in Iran in the 1970s. A revolution began in that country in 1978. By 1979, Iranians led by the Ayatollah Khomeini, a religious leader, overthrew the shah and set up an Islamic republic. This type of government follows strict Islamic law.

Soon after Iran's Islamic Revolution began, relations with the United States broke down. A mob of students attacked the U.S. Embassy in Iran's capital, Tehran. With the approval of Iran's government, the students took Americans working at the embassy hostage. More than 50 Americans were held by force for over a year.

Iraqi Aggression In 1968, Saddam Hussein became Iraq's president. Saddam Hussein was a harsh ruler. He controlled Iraq's media, restricted personal freedoms, and killed an unknown number of political enemies.

Under Saddam's leadership, Iraq invaded Iran in 1980. The Iranians fought back, and the Iran-Iraq War dragged on until 1988. Both countries' economies were seriously damaged, and many people died.

The Kurds

Traditionally a nomadic people, the Kurds have never had a country of their own. Scholars estimate that more than 20 million Kurds live throughout the Middle East and Central Asia. The exact number is difficult to determine.

The Kurds are mostly Muslim. They speak their own language, which is related to the Farsi language spoken in Iran. People have traditionally lived in independent tribes, each headed by a sheik. Most Kurds have historically lived as herders, tending sheep and goats. In recent years, however, many Kurds have moved to cities, resulting in significant changes to their way of life.

Analyze Information
Why do you think many Kurds want their own country?

In 1990, Iraq invaded Kuwait, its oil-rich neighbor to the south. This event shocked and worried many world leaders. They were concerned that Iraq might gain control of the region's oil. In addition, they worried about Iraq's supply of weapons of mass destruction, including chemical and biological weapons.

In 1991, an alliance of countries led by the United States forced the Iraqis out of Kuwait. This six-week conflict was called the Persian Gulf War. Saddam remained in power after the war but refused to accept the peace terms recommended by the United Nations (UN). In response, the UN placed an **embargo**, or limit on trade, on Iraq. As a result, Iraq's economy suffered.

Soon after the Persian Gulf War ended, Saddam faced rebellions from Shia Muslims and from Kurds. He brutally put down these uprisings. In response, the UN forced Iraq to end all military activity. The UN also requested that Iraq allow inspectors into the country. They also wanted to make sure that the Iraqi government had destroyed its weapons of mass destruction. Iraq later refused to cooperate completely with the UN.

Afghanistan and the War on Terror In the mid-1990s, a radical Muslim group known as the **Taliban** rose to power in Afghanistan. The Taliban used a strict interpretation of Islamic teachings to rule Afghanistan. It also supported terrorist organizations that shared its strict beliefs. Among those groups was al Qaeda, the network headed by Osama bin Laden, that was responsible for the September 11, 2001, terrorist attacks on New York City and Washington, D.C.

After the attacks, U.S. and British forces attacked Taliban and al Qaeda targets and toppled the Taliban government. Since then, Afghanistan has created a new government headed by an elected president.

The terrorist attacks of September 11 also led to increased tensions between the United States and Iraq. Many U.S. government officials believed that Iraq had aided the terrorists. In March 2003, President George W. Bush ordered U.S. forces to attack Iraqi targets. Within a few weeks the Iraqi army was defeated and Saddam's government was crushed. Saddam went into hiding, but U.S. soldiers later found him in an underground hole in Iraq. Saddam was arrested, tried, and executed for his crimes.

Ethnic Conflict Throughout the twentieth century, political change has also led to ethnic conflict in some parts of the Middle East. As power shifted within countries and new governments were formed, some people felt their rights had been denied. In many cases, these feelings have led to conflict.

Among the groups who have come into conflict with the government are the Kurds. The region in which they live includes parts of eastern Turkey, northern Iraq, and western Iran. This area is unofficially called Kurdistan. For decades, many Kurds have wanted Kurdistan to become an independent country. Some have risen up in rebellion. Both Turkey and Iraq have put down Kurdish revolts, and both governments have treated the Kurds very harshly afterward. The ongoing conflicts with Turkey and Iraq have forced millions of Kurds to leave their homes. Many have migrated to cities in search of economic opportunity.

The skyline of the city of Dubai in the United Arab Emirates is a symbol of the wealth oil has brought to the region.

Reading Check
Form Generalizations
What has led to violence
in the Middle East?

Religious differences can also lead to conflict between ethnic groups. In Iraq, for example, some ethnic groups are mostly Sunni Muslims while others are Shia. Since the collapse of Saddam's government, Sunni and Shia groups have fought each other bitterly for control of the country.

Oil in the Middle East

Other than religion and politics, nothing has shaped life in the Middle East more than the oil industry. The first oil in the region was found in Persia—now Iran—in 1908. Soon afterward, huge reserves were discovered below much of the region.

The production of oil is now the backbone of many Middle Eastern economies. Many countries there are members of the Organization of Petroleum Exporting Countries, or OPEC. Founded in 1960, **OPEC** is an international organization whose members work to influence the price of oil on world markets by controlling the supply. Oil has brought tremendous wealth to the region.

Oil money has allowed Middle Eastern countries to improve their citizens' lives. Some provide free health care and education to all citizens, for example. However, many people worry what will happen to the region's economy when oil supplies finally run dry.

Reading Check
Draw Conclusions
How did oil change life
in the Middle East?

Summary and Preview In this lesson, you learned that new governments and new countries were formed in the Middle East after World War I. Conflicts arose between and within some of these countries. Next, you will learn how the countries of Latin America changed after World War II.

Lesson 5 Assessment

Review Ideas, Terms, and People

1. a. **Identify** Which leader worked to modernize Turkey? Iran?

   b. **Elaborate** What steps did Turkey's leader take to modernize his nation after World War I?

   c. **Explain** Why was Palestine to be divided into two countries?

2. a. **Recall** What led to the Persian Gulf War?

   b. **Summarize** How did Iran change after the Iranian Revolution?

   c. **Identify Problems** How have religious and political differences contributed to conflict in the Middle East?

3. a. **Describe** What is OPEC's purpose?

   b. **Predict Effects** How might life in the Middle East change if the oil supply runs out?

Critical Thinking

4. **Sequence** Using your notes, create a timeline of the major conflicts that have occurred in the Middle East since World War II.

Latin America Since 1945

The Big Idea

Latin America has seen political, economic, and social challenges in the past several decades.

Main Ideas

- Juan Perón and Augusto Pinochet were two Latin American dictators who ruled Argentina and Chile.

- NAFTA influences Latin America because Mexico is part of the agreement.

- Many Latin Americans have informal jobs and are affected by the lack of education in the region.

Key Terms and People

Juan Perón
Augusto Pinochet
immunity
North American Free Trade Agreement
informal jobs

If YOU were there . . .

You are an industrial worker in Argentina. It is 1949, and Juan Perón, the leader of your country, has created a new constitution. He will now be able to remain in power. Perón's government has given your family paid vacations and free medical care. Many people really like his wife, Evita, but you have also heard something upsetting about Perón. You heard he created a new constitution that allows him to stay in power.

Would you be concerned about Juan Perón's actions?

Political Power in Latin America

During the last half of the twentieth century, several Latin American countries came under the control of those who favored only one way to lead. Two oppressive dictators and one powerful political party played major roles in this period of Latin America's history. These nations have now made different political choices, but the effects of the past can still be felt today.

Argentina **Juan Perón** was an army colonel who became president of Argentina in 1946. Perón's government took control of national railroads and utility companies. It increased wages for industrial workers and developed plans to pay for public works projects. People received paid vacations and free medical care. Perón's wife Eva, known as Evita, was quite popular among the people. She helped women in Argentina gain the right to vote.

Despite these positive actions, Perón was a true dictator. He kept firm control of the military. In 1949, Perón even created a new constitution so he could remain in power. However, Perón was removed from power in 1955. He fled Argentina but returned in 1972 at the age of 78. He was briefly president again but died soon after.

Juan Perón and his wife Evita waving to a crowd in 1951.

Argentina faced more challenges after Perón's death. In the late 1970s and early 1980s, military officials ruled the nation. People who protested against the government began to disappear. They were called *desaparecidos* in Spanish, and most were never seen again. Leaders claimed this happened because of civil war, but the United States believed Argentina's government was responsible. President Jimmy Carter stopped sending U.S. aid to the South American nation. This period of Argentine history has come to be known as "the Dirty War." Several former military officials have been convicted of crimes, but many questions still remain about what happened during this time.

⊙ Explore ONLINE!

Modern Latin America

Interpret Maps

1. **Location** What are the capital cities of Argentina and Chile?

2. **Movement** Bolivia and Paraguay are in which direction from Argentina and Chile?

War with Great Britain broke out in 1982. Argentina claimed the Falkland Islands, a small set of islands to the east. Britain sent military resources to the region, and Argentina surrendered. In 2013, the island's residents overwhelmingly voted to remain a British territory.

Chile A military dictator also ruled Chile. His name was General **Augusto Pinochet**. Pinochet came to power during a bloody coup that was supported by the United States. At the time, Chile was led by Salvador Allende, who wanted a socialist government. To keep that from happening, the United States backed Pinochet. Unfortunately, this choice turned out to have brutal consequences for Chile. Pinochet's regime arrested and tortured tens of thousands of people. Several thousand citizens disappeared as they did in Argentina.

In 1988, the military ruler was voted out of office. He stayed in power for another year, but a new leader became president in 1990. However, Pinochet was made a senator for life. This political title was important because it gave him **immunity** in Chile. This meant that he could not be arrested, tried, or punished for any crime. Chilean courts eventually ruled that he could be tried for human rights abuses during his time in power. However, he died in 2006 before any trials could be held.

Since then, Chile has recovered from Pinochet's harsh rule. Chile's first female president, Michele Bachelet, and Sebastián Piñera, who followed her, have helped restore fairness in government.

Mexico For over 70 years, Mexico had a political party that functioned almost like a dictatorship. It caused problems when Mexican citizens tried to exercise an important democratic right—the right to vote in fair elections. This party was the Institutional Revolutionary Party, known as the PRI. The PRI had been around since the late 1920s. Practically every national or local politician belonged to the party. Beginning in the 1970s, people accused the PRI of being violent to protestors and rigging elections.

The PRI candidate, Carlos Salinas de Gortari, was elected as Mexico's president in 1988, but he introduced some election reforms. President

In 1988, candidates from political parties that opposed the PRI won some seats in the Mexican Senate, pictured here. It was the first time that had happened in almost 60 years.

Salinas made it easier for opposition candidates to campaign and compete in state and local elections. The first Mexican governor who was not a PRI candidate was elected in 1989.

Mexican citizens have gained more political rights, but the government continues to be troubled with corruption. The constitution now holds several types of officials responsible for their behavior while they are in office. Reformers want Mexican lawmakers to pass tougher penalties for offenses like taking bribes or writing unethical contracts.

In 2000, Vicente Fox Quesada's election to the presidency ended PRI's long control over Mexico's federal government. The election of Enrique Peña Nieto in 2012 signaled a return of strength for the PRI. Once in office, President Pena Nieto worked to make positive changes, but Mexico still faces many problems.

Reading Check
Analyze Effects
After he was made a senator, how did immunity affect Augusto Pinochet's life in Chile?

The Economics of Oil, Trade, and Tourism

You've read about the oil-producing nations of the Middle East, but did you know Latin America also has one? Tourism and trade bring money to the region as well. A nation that has had limited economic opportunities for years may soon experience more in the future.

Venezuelan Oil Venezuela is one of the founding members of OPEC. Oil and gas make up about 25 percent of what the nation's economy produces. Almost all of the money that Venezuela earns from its exports comes from this natural resource.

The country has plenty of oil, but its economy has experienced challenges in recent years. Venezuela's government, under former leader Hugo Chávez, spent significantly more money than it earned for several years. Money from the sale of oil has proven more difficult to acquire. One reason for this is that Venezuela is not able to access all of its oil. Some of the oil is located where drilling is difficult. Also, oil prices collapsed in 2014. This means Venezuela received less money for the oil it sold.

A Historic Trade Agreement Mexico, the United States, and Canada created a formal trade agreement that went into effect in 1994. This agreement is called the **North American Free Trade Agreement**, or NAFTA. One of its goals is to decrease or eliminate tariffs between the three nations. Supporters believed this would help increase trade and create job opportunities and higher wages for workers. The claims made by NAFTA supporters have come true, but several negative charges have been made against the agreement as well.

Critics believe NAFTA has put some Mexican farmers out of business. Others believe that NAFTA has made it easier to exploit Mexican workers with long hours and low pay. There is also concern that higher levels of pollution in Mexico have occurred in part because of NAFTA. The effects of NAFTA continue to be debated.

Destination Cuba Cuba remains a Communist country, but it has experienced change. Fidel Castro was in poor health, so he made his brother Raúl the new Cuban president in 2008. About five years later, Raúl Castro was

GDP in Latin America

Countries like Brazil, Ecuador, and Peru are also part of Latin America. This graph shows the gross domestic product (GDP) per capita for several countries in the region from 1960 to 2012. GDP is the value of goods and services that a country produces. The term *per capita* means "for the people." So the GDP per capita is determined by dividing that total value by the country's population. A rising GDP means a country's economy is improving.

GDP Per Capita

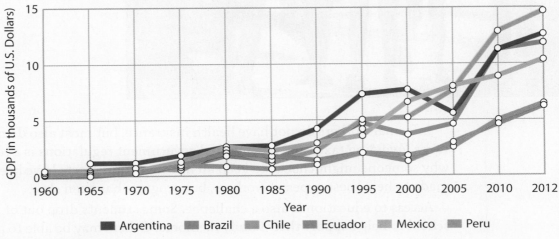

Source: World Development Indicators

Interpret Graphs
What evidence in the graph shows that Chile's economy has improved since 1985?

Reading Check
Identify Problems
What challenges has Venezuela's economy faced in recent years?

photographed shaking hands with President Barack Obama. Many considered this an important moment between the two leaders. Late in 2014, President Obama announced that the United States and Cuba would have diplomatic relations for the first time in decades. President Obama also traveled to Cuba in 2016. An American president had not done that in almost 90 years.

Tourism is a significant source of income for several Latin American countries. There are many vacation resorts throughout the region. Cuba is hoping to take advantage of new opportunities in tourism. It has been a destination for Canadian and European tourists for years. The number of U.S. tourists visiting Cuba is increasing.

Past and Present Social Struggles

Latin America has struggled with social issues since the 1950s. The region's residents frequently feel the strain of two types of inequality. Many face income inequality. In the 1990s, it was estimated that close to half of the region's income went to the richest ten percent of the population.

Job inequality is another issue. Today a large number of Latin Americans have **informal jobs**, such as picking coffee beans or cleaning houses. People who do these jobs often do not earn minimum wages, have regular schedules, or receive retirement benefits when they stop working.

This photo shows Cuban students walking after school. While some students in Latin America can attend good schools, others have limited opportunities to receive a quality education.

Informal workers do not have health insurance, but most also do not pay taxes. Avoiding taxes and complicated government regulations is a reason why someone might choose to keep an informal job. Efforts have been made to help these types of workers, but progress has been slow.

Access to education is also a challenge. Some students drop out of school to help support their family members. Others may be able to go to school, but the education they receive may be poor. These are challenging problems, but Latin American societies are actively looking for solutions.

In the 2010s, Latin America's middle class has grown. Stronger economies have led to lower unemployment. More and more people are speaking out to improve their lives. Still as many 80 million people in the region are considered to live in poverty.

Summary In this lesson, you learned about the politics, economic issues, and social challenges that have existed in Latin America since 1945.

Reading Check
Synthesize
What did estimates show about the income of Latin Americans in the 1990s?

Lesson 6 Assessment

Review Ideas, Terms, and People

1. a. Compare How was life in Argentina and Chile the same during this time period?

   b. Explain How did the PRI function almost like a dictatorship in Mexico?

2. a. Identify Which Latin American country is a founding member of OPEC?

   b. Define What does GDP tell you about a country?

   c. Recall What are the positive and negative claims that have been made about the North American Free Trade Agreement (NAFTA)?

3. Draw Conclusions Why are informal jobs a challenge for some people in Latin America?

Critical Thinking

4. Organize Information In this lesson you learned about the social struggles Latin America has been facing in the past and the present. Fill in a chart similar to the one below by listing the causes and effects of these issues.

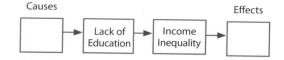

Causes

Lack of Education → Income Inequality →

Effects

Determine the Strength of an Argument

Define the Skill

Studying history often involves learning about different opinions. In order to understand these opinions, it is important to recognize strong arguments. Strong arguments are based on convincing evidence. Examples and points should be true and should make sense in the context of the argument. For example, supporting points should relate to the main idea of the argument. It is also important to consider any evidence against the argument.

Many people in the past have made decisions based on the strength of an argument. Determining the strength of an argument is important for the present as well. Your judgments can help you decide whether or not to support a policy, idea, or candidate.

Learn the Skill

In *I Speak of Freedom,* Kwame Nkrumah explained why political unity would help Africa solve its own problems. Here is part of his argument:

> "It is clear that we must find an African solution to our problems, and that this can only be found in African unity. Divided we are weak; united, Africa could become one of the greatest forces for good in the world."

How strong is his argument? In *I speak of Freedom,* he explains how foreign rulers have only benefited themselves. They have not solved Africa's problems. This evidence makes his argument in the quotation stronger. The evidence he gave in support of his argument was good enough to convince other people to elect him as his nation's leader.

Practice the Skill

Imagine you are a French government official in the early 1960s. You have to decide whether or not to allow Algeria to be independent from French rule. Your decision will depend on the strength of the arguments in favor of independence. Review the module and answer the following questions to help determine the strength of those arguments.

1. What is the evidence for granting Algeria its independence? How strong is this evidence?

2. Is there any evidence to keep Algeria under French rule? How strong is this evidence?

3. Would you grant Algeria independence? Support your answer with specific evidence from the text.

Module 29 Assessment

Review Vocabulary, Terms, and People

For each statement, write T if it is true and F if it is false. If the statement is false, write the correct term that would make the sentence a true statement.

1. India and Pakistan continue to have disputes over <u>Kinshasa</u>, a mountainous area in the north near the Chinese border.

2. The United Nations placed a <u>tolerance</u>, or limit on trade, on Iraq in the 1990s.

3. Iran's rulers took the title <u>shah</u> from the ancient Persian word for king.

4. Gandhi believed in <u>immunity</u>, the avoidance of violent actions.

5. The <u>Mau Mau</u> wanted to rid Kenya of white settlers.

6. <u>Tariffs</u> are forms of democracy in which a monarch serves as the head of state.

7. During apartheid, black South Africans had to live in specially designated clusters of tiny homes called <u>townships</u>.

8. <u>NAFTA</u> is an international organization whose members work to influence the price of oil on world markets.

Comprehension and Critical Thinking

Lesson 1

9. **a. Identify** Who created China's Communist government?

   b. Make Inferences Why do you think Gandhi is widely admired today?

   c. Evaluate Do you think the Meiji Restoration was a positive development in Japan? Why or why not?

Lesson 2

10. **a. Explain** How does modern Asian society reflect a blend of old and new ideas?

    b. Elaborate How did World War II help bring about stronger economies in Asia?

    c. Predict Effects How might life change in Kashmir if India and Pakistan were to sign a peace treaty?

Lesson 3

11. **a. Identify** What were two colonies in which Africans had to fight for their freedom?

    b. Summarize How did Ghana win its freedom?

    c. Evaluate Which new countries do you think had the best relations with Europe? Why?

Lesson 4

12. **a. Identify** Who was Nelson Mandela? For what was he most famous?

    b. Make Inferences Why were many Africans unhappy with military dictatorships?

    c. Predict Effects How do you think African governments will change in the future? Why?

Lesson 5

13. **a. Identify** In which country did the Ayatollah Khomeini lead a revolution?

    b. Explain Why did the creation of the state of Israel lead to conflict in the Middle East?

    c. Elaborate What role does OPEC play in world affairs? How might that affect politics in the Middle East?

Lesson 6

14. **a. Draw Conclusions** What effect would an increase in the price of oil have on Venezuela's economy?

    b. Analyze Why might President Obama's 2016 visit to Cuba be considered an important event?

    c. Recall Which Latin American country is a trading partner in NAFTA?

Module 29 Assessment, continued

Review Themes

15. **Politics** How has the African National Congress (ANC) influenced South Africa since 1994?

16. **Geography** Why is the location of Jerusalem an emotional issue for Jews, Christians, and Muslims?

17. **Economics** What evidence from the text can you find to show some nations in Asia have experienced strong economic growth?

Reading Skills

Review Texts *Use the Reading Skills taught in this module to answer the question about the reading selection below.*

> The most famous example of this punishment took place in 1989. In the spring of that year more than a million Chinese pro-democracy protestors gathered in Tiananmen Square in Beijing, China's capital. The protestors were demanding more political rights and freedoms. The Chinese government tried to get the protestors to leave the square. When they refused, the government used troops and tanks to make them leave. Hundreds of protestors were killed, and many more were injured or imprisoned.

18. Identify the dates and proper nouns in the passage. Remember to list all of the information in the text, including any places, groups, or events.

Social Studies Skills

Determine the Strength of an Argument *Use the Social Studies Skills taught in this module to answer the question about the selection below.*

> When the British arrived in Kenya, they claimed land that had once been occupied by the Kikuyu people. The British used that land to grow valuable crops, such as coffee, and did not want to give the land back to the Kikuyu. The Kikuyu now wanted independence and their former lands back.

19. In your opinion, how strong was the Kikuyu's argument for independence? Support your answer with specific evidence from the text.

Focus On Writing

20. **Create a Website** You have now learned a lot of information about the development of Asia, Africa, the Middle East, and Latin America after World War II. Create a home page and at least two web pages that focus on the geography, politics, and economics in one of these regions. You can write about the topics in paragraph form or in a list of bullet points. You may design the pages either online or on sheets of paper.

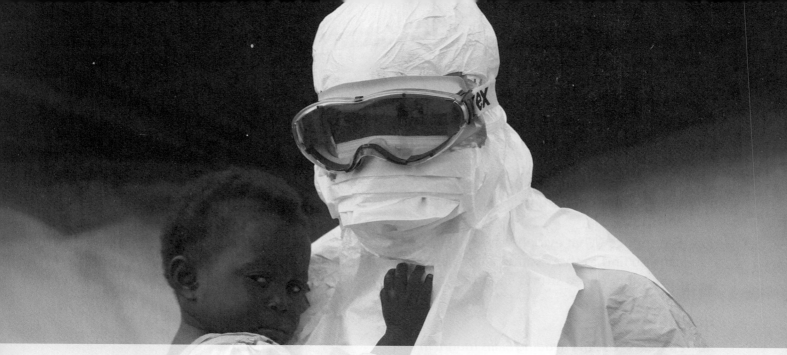

Module 30

Contemporary Issues

Essential Question

What is the most serious problem that the world faces today?

About the Photo: This photo shows a worker helping people during the Ebola pandemic in West Africa. Nongovernmental organizations help people during global health crises as well as in other situations affecting the world's population.

▶ Explore ONLINE!

VIDEOS, including...
- Spaceship Earth
- Observatories: Stonehenge to Space Telescopes
- Microchips and Computers
- The Internet
- Oil Spill
- Climate Change
- Polio Vaccine

☑ Document-Based Investigations

☑ Graphic Organizers

☑ Interactive Games

☑ Image Carousel: The Failed State of Somalia

☑ Image with Hotspots: The International Space Station

☑ Image Carousel: Mars Curiosity Rover

In this module, you will learn about the issues that affect our world. Some of these issues are caused by increasing industrialization and globalization. Other issues are caused by failed governments and war. However, many people today are working to tackle these problems.

What You Will Learn...

Lesson 1: Human Rights **1034**
The Big Idea Governments and other organizations have made progress in protecting individual rights, but human rights abuses still occur in many parts of the world.

Lesson 2: Democracy in the World Today **1044**
The Big Idea Despite many challenges, democracy continues to spread around the world.

Lesson 3: Technology and Globalization **1051**
The Big Idea New technologies have helped to create a global community.

Lesson 4: Protecting the Environment **1059**
The Big Idea Our planet faces a growing population and environmental challenges.

Lesson 5: Global Health **1067**
The Big Idea Technology and scientific advances have improved medical treatment over time, but the world still faces serious health issues.

Lesson 6: Trade and Economic Development **1073**
The Big Idea The economies of the world's nations are tightly linked.

Timeline of Events 2000–Present

▶ Explore ONLINE!

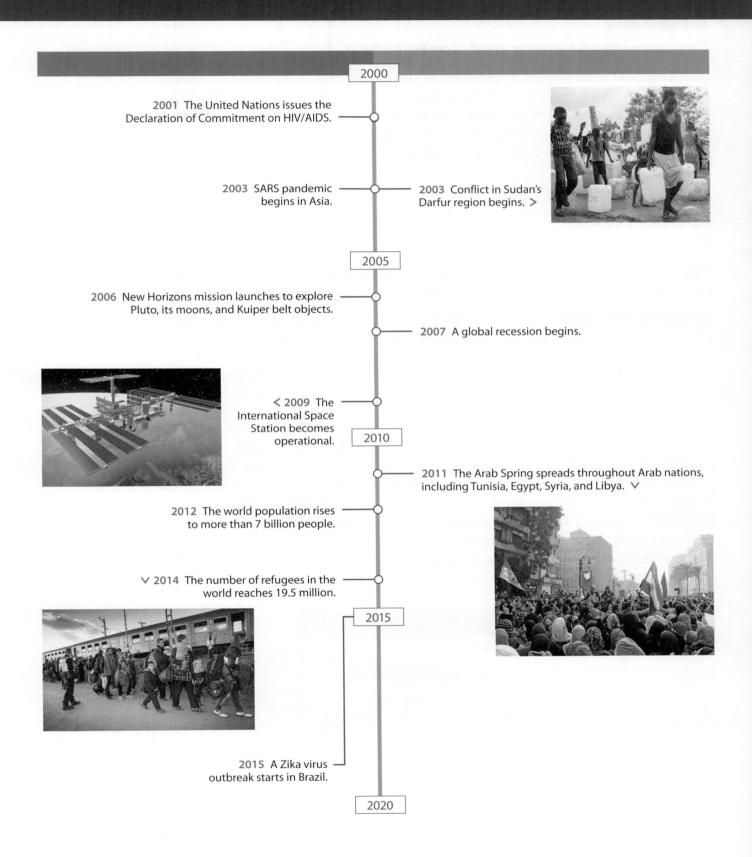

2000

2001 The United Nations issues the Declaration of Commitment on HIV/AIDS.

2003 SARS pandemic begins in Asia.

2003 Conflict in Sudan's Darfur region begins. >

2005

2006 New Horizons mission launches to explore Pluto, its moons, and Kuiper belt objects.

2007 A global recession begins.

< **2009** The International Space Station becomes operational.

2010

2011 The Arab Spring spreads throughout Arab nations, including Tunisia, Egypt, Syria, and Libya. ∨

2012 The world population rises to more than 7 billion people.

∨ **2014** The number of refugees in the world reaches 19.5 million.

2015

2015 A Zika virus outbreak starts in Brazil.

2020

Reading Social Studies

THEME FOCUS:

Economics, Science and Technology

In this module you will learn about many of the problems that the world's people face today. You will also learn about possible solutions to these problems. You will read about recent economic changes. You will also find out about advancements in science and technology. These changes have made the world seem like a smaller place. There are both positive and negative consequences to this development.

READING FOCUS:

Categorize

Categorizing means organizing similar kinds of information into groups. Historians categorize information to help them identify and understand historical patterns.

Categorize Information The following passage describes Earth's population. The chart beneath the passage categorizes information from the passage. As you can see, the chart includes a title and one column for each category. A chart could have more than two categories. Information from the passage has been placed into the chart.

For thousands of years, world population growth was low and relatively steady. About 2,000 years ago, the world had some 300 million people. By 1800, there were almost 1 billion people. Since 1800, better health care and improved food production have supported tremendous population growth. Another reason for this growth is improved living conditions. In 2012, the world's population was greater than 7 billion people. According to research, the world's population will increase to nearly 10 billion by 2050.

Population Figures	Influences on Growth
• AD 1: 300 million	• better health care
• 1800: 1 billion	• improved food production
• 2012: 7 billion	• improved living conditions
• 2050: 10 billion (estimated)	

You Try It!

Read the following passage and then decide which categories you will use to organize the information.

Religious Persecution Governments in many nations, including Egypt, Iran, Pakistan, Saudi Arabia, China, and North Korea, currently limit religious freedom. For example, the Chinese government, which controls Tibet, has persecuted Tibetans for their Buddhist religious beliefs and their desire for political independence. In Egypt, minority Muslim sects, or groups, and members of the Baha'i faith have faced imprisonment, job and education discrimination, and denial of bank accounts, driver's licenses, and birth certificates. The Pakistani government has targeted Christians, Hindus, and Shia Muslims by passing laws that deny religious freedom and inflicting severe punishment on those who break them. The government of North Korea routinely persecutes people who practice any religion.

Answer these questions based on the passage you just read.

1. Make a chart to organize the information in the passage. What categories will you use?
2. Organize the information from the passage in your chart.

As you read this module, think about categorizing the information you learn.

Key Terms and People

Lesson 1
human rights
Universal Declaration of Human Rights
Helsinki Accords
nongovernmental organizations (NGOs)
political dissent
genocide

Lesson 2
secular
Arab Spring
refugees
Petro Poroshenko
failed states
infrastructure

Lesson 3
International Space Station
microchips
Internet
telecommute

Lesson 4
overpopulation
ozone layer
sustainable growth
environmentalism

Lesson 5
genetics
cloning
biotechnology
pharmaceuticals
3D printing
epidemic
pandemic
AIDS

Lesson 6
developed nations
developing nations
gross domestic product (GDP)
standard of living
inflation
recession
free trade
securities
World Bank
International Monetary Fund (IMF)

Human Rights

The Big Idea

Governments and other organizations have made progress in protecting individual rights, but human rights abuses still occur in many parts of the world.

Main Ideas

- Both governmental and nongovernmental organizations protect human rights.

- Human rights abuses affect many groups of people around the world.

- The human rights movement has achieved significant victories.

Key Terms and People

human rights
Universal Declaration of Human Rights
Helsinki Accords
nongovernmental organizations (NGOs)
political dissent
genocide

If YOU were there . . .

You are the president of a powerful nation. One reason you were elected is because you believe in protecting citizens' rights. To address environmental challenges and other global problems, you need to ally yourself with other nations that share your concerns about these issues. However, some possible allies deny citizens their rights.

Do you think you should form an alliance with these countries?

A Changing World

The idea of what it means to be a citizen has changed since it was developed in ancient Greece and then adopted by the Romans. Roman citizens had many privileges, including the right to vote. They had responsibilities, too, such as paying taxes or serving in the Roman army. These responsibilities were eventually granted to people living in conquered territories. Although Roman women were citizens, they had few rights of citizenship.

Today, the rights and responsibilities of a citizen differ from country to country. Many countries allow their citizens to vote. Most nations require their citizens to pay taxes. Some countries, such as Israel, require all citizens to serve in the military. But some nations deny rights to their citizens.

Today, many people believe that everyone has certain rights as a human being. **Human rights** are the basic rights to which all people are entitled. They are not based on a particular economic or political system. Human rights include political rights, such as the right to vote. But they also include social and economic rights. Freedom of expression and equality before the law are examples of human rights.

Groups that Work for Human Rights Many international organizations are committed to guaranteeing human rights for all people. The United Nations (UN) is one such group.

In 1975, 35 nations signed the Helsinki Accords. President Gerald Ford (seated, third from left) signed the agreement for the United States.

The UN works to promote peace and cooperation between nations. It also works to protect the rights of women, children, and other people. Over the years, the UN has passed several declarations setting standards for such rights.

In 1948, the UN adopted the **Universal Declaration of Human Rights**. This declaration outlines human rights goals for the world community. The declaration makes many important points. It states several ideas.

- Everyone is "born free and equal in dignity and rights."
- People "should act towards one another in a spirit of brotherhood."
- "Everyone has a right to take part in the government of his country."

The declaration also calls for free and fair elections and for the guarantee of basic civil liberties. Civil liberties are individual rights that are protected from government violation. These include freedom of speech and religion as well as the right to be treated fairly by one's government.

In 1975, the United States, Canada, and most European countries signed the **Helsinki Accords**, in Helsinki, Finland. Participating nations promised to work together for peace. They also pledged to protect human rights, including freedom of movement and freedom to publish and exchange information. Also, each nation promised to protect "national minorities" within its borders. Nations wanted to make sure that different ethnic groups within a country would not persecute one another.

Neither the declaration nor the accords are binding, so they cannot be legally enforced. If a nation does not follow the terms, it does not suffer any penalty. However, the goals in these documents have inspired many people around the world to continue the fight for human rights.

The Human Rights Movement Besides nations and governments, many **nongovernmental organizations (NGOs)** have made people aware of human rights. An NGO is an organization made up of citizens of a region or the world rather than government officials. Most NGOs are dedicated to solving a specific issue or problem. Many are dedicated "watchdogs" that investigate whether countries are meeting human rights standards.

Much of the modern human rights movement dates back to 1922, when the International Federation for Human Rights was formed in Paris. Initially, this NGO united 10 different human rights groups. Today, it is made up of more than 150 such groups. The main goal of the group is to uphold the UN's Universal Declaration of Human Rights.

The human rights movement grew more visible in the 1960s. During that decade, an NGO called Amnesty International was started. Its main purpose is the freeing of political prisoners. Amnesty International also works to enforce international human rights laws.

In the 1970s, volunteers formed Human Rights Watch. This NGO was created to make sure Eastern European governments followed the Helsinki Accords. Today, Human Rights Watch works to protect human rights in other areas around the world. NGOs perform a valuable service by helping to improve conditions and save lives. They focus world attention on pressing issues. However, protecting human rights remains an uphill battle.

Reading Check
Find Main Ideas
What are two examples of human rights?

Human Rights Abuses

Although the Universal Declaration of Human Rights was adopted in 1948, it remains more of a hopeful dream than a reality. Human rights abuses exist in most parts of the world. Individuals continue to face torture, unfair trials, and restrictions in their freedom of speech. Some groups of people face higher risks of abuse than others. These include women, children, political protestors, and minority racial, ethnic, and religious groups.

Women's Rights Over the centuries, women's rights have improved. However, these gains have not made women equal to men in every major part of their lives or in every country. For example, women often are refused education and not allowed to take part in government. Some

---

— BIOGRAPHY—

Malala Yousafzai (1997–)

Malala Yousafzai grew up in Pakistan. She spoke out after the Taliban invaded the part of Pakistan where she lived. The Taliban is an extremist Muslim political group that enforces strict rules. Taliban members closed schools for girls and limited women's rights. In response, Yousafzai gave an important speech. It was called, "How Dare the Taliban Take Away My Basic Right to Education?" It made Yousafzai famous in Pakistan. She began blogging about life under Taliban rule. Eventually, she appeared on television and became the subject of two documentary films.

In 2012, Yousafzai was shot by a member of the Taliban. She was flown to the United Kingdom for medical treatment. The assassination attempt led to protests and raised awareness of Yousafzai's cause. Pakistan soon passed its first law guaranteeing the right to education. On her sixteenth birthday, Yousafzai addressed the United Nations. In 2014, she won the Nobel Peace Prize. She is the youngest person to receive this award.

Make Inferences
What do you think Yousafzai talked about during her speech at the United Nations?

cannot get proper health care, which results in deaths related to pregnancy and childbirth. In places such as Tanzania, a woman whose husband dies is denied the money or property that belonged to him. Women are often victims of violence in regions of the world that are involved in wars or conflicts. For example, terrorist groups such as the Islamic State of Iraq and the Levant (ISIL) have used force to take some women living in the Kurdish region of Iraq. These women have been enslaved and made to convert to Islam.

In general, women are poorer than men. Some of this is because many women work more than men but are paid less. In places such as sub-Saharan Africa, the Caribbean, Asia, and Latin America, women make up as much as half the workforce. However, many are unpaid.

Beginning in the 1970s, international organizations began to address women's rights. The UN adopted a measure in 1979 to stop discrimination against women. In 2010, a UN body called UN Women was started. The group called on world leaders to establish legal policies to help women achieve justice and to end violence toward them. Because these types of policies are difficult to achieve, efforts to improve women's rights and opportunities worldwide remain uneven.

Children at Risk Children face the highest risk of becoming victims of human rights abuses. These abuses include a lack of food and housing, poor or no access to education, and improper health care. In some countries, such as northern Uganda, fighters have kidnapped thousands of children. These children have been made to fight as soldiers, while others have been enslaved.

Child labor is also a serious problem. Often, children are made to work long hours in dangerous conditions. For example, Iqbal Masih of Pakistan had to work for a local carpet maker to help pay off a family debt. He was

In many countries, children work long hours in dangerous conditions. Here, a child works with bricks in Peru. Brickwork is a difficult, low-paying job.

just four years old. Iqbal worked 12-hour days and often was chained to his workstation. He escaped when he was 10. Then he worked with international organizations to make people aware of abuses against children.

The UN has taken action to try to help protect children. The UN Convention on the Rights of the Child was adopted in 1989. The convention focused on trying to keep children free from hunger, neglect, and abuse. Unfortunately, millions of children worldwide still live in poverty.

Political Dissent In many countries, individuals and groups have been arrested or mistreated for political dissent. **Political dissent** is a difference of opinion over political issues. In China, for example, people who speak out against China's Communist Party have been arrested. Other countries that have persecuted people for their political views include Iran, Pakistan, Cuba, El Salvador, Nigeria, and the former Soviet Union.

In 1966, the UN adopted the International Covenant on Civil and Political Rights. A covenant is an agreement. The covenant called for the protection of all people from political persecution. Today, Amnesty International and Human Rights Watch identify and publicize political persecution.

Ethnic and Racial Conflict In some countries, ethnic or racial differences have led to human rights abuses. For example, in the late 1980s and 1990s ethnic conflict over territory in the former Yugoslavia led to violence

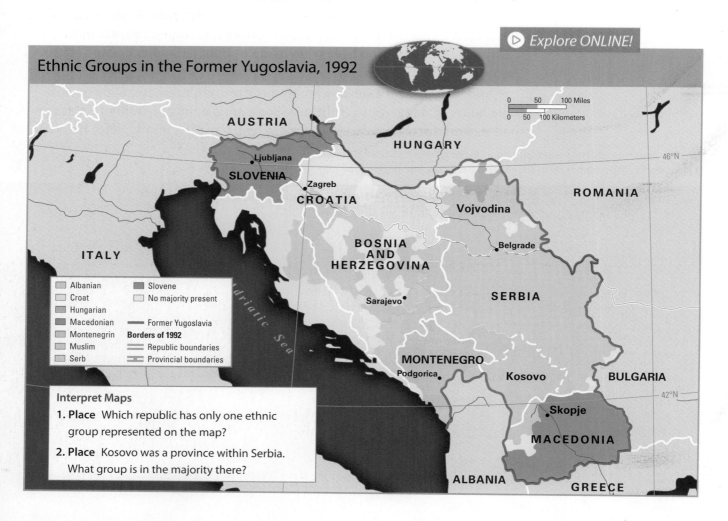

Ethnic Groups in the Former Yugoslavia, 1992

Explore ONLINE!

Legend:
- Albanian
- Croat
- Hungarian
- Macedonian
- Montenegrin
- Muslim
- Serb
- Slovene
- No majority present
- — Former Yugoslavia
- **Borders of 1992**
- Republic boundaries
- Provincial boundaries

Interpret Maps

1. **Place** Which republic has only one ethnic group represented on the map?

2. **Place** Kosovo was a province within Serbia. What group is in the majority there?

and "ethnic cleansing"—an attempt by one ethnic group to eliminate all others from an area. After World War II, Yugoslavia became a federation of six republics. Each republic had a mixed ethnic population, but Serbs dominated Yugoslavia as a whole. In 1991, Slovenia and Croatia declared independence. This led to fighting between Serbs and Croats. In 1992, Macedonia and Bosnia-Herzegovina declared independence.

Although Bosnia's Muslims and Croats backed independence, Bosnian Serbs strongly opposed it. Supported by the Republic of Serbia, the Bosnian Serbs launched a war. Serb military forces used violence against Bosnian Muslims and tried to force them to leave the country. The fighting led to the large-scale killing of people on both sides. In December 1995, leaders involved signed a peace treaty, made possible with help from the UN and the United States.

In 1998, violence erupted in the region again in Kosovo, a province in southern Serbia. Kosovo was made up almost entirely of ethnic Albanians. As an independence movement grew in Kosovo, Serbian military forces invaded the province. Diplomacy failed to bring peace. NATO began a bombing campaign in 1999. Serbian leaders were forced to withdraw their troops from Kosovo.

Africa and Asia have also experienced ethnic conflict and violence. In Rwanda, a civil war broke out between Hutus and Tutsis in 1994. This fighting led to horrible human rights violations and **genocide**—the deliberate destruction of a racial, political, or cultural group of people. Over several months Hutus massacred more than 800,000 Tutsis. The killings ended when a Tutsi rebel group took control of the country.

In response to the genocide, the UN established the International Criminal Tribunal for Rwanda. This international court tried and convicted leaders who were responsible for the genocide. Before it concluded in 2015, the court had sentenced 61 individuals. Within Rwanda's own court system, however, thousands of other people who took part in the genocide were tried.

South Sudan has experienced many years of conflict and violence. Here, South Sudanese children get their daily ration of water.

The Kurds of southwest Asia also have been the victims of ethnic violence. Traditional Kurdish lands cross the borders of Turkey, Iran, Iraq, and Syria. Each country has persecuted the Kurds. For example, the Turks forbade the Kurds to speak their native language. In the late 1980s, the Iraqi government dropped poison gas on the Kurds, killing 5,000. International organizations, including the UN, have made attempts at helping the Kurds become safe from violence in the area.

In the 2000s, conflict intensified in the country of Sudan. A fundamentalist Muslim military regime had taken control of the government after years of conflict between the non-Muslim south and Arab Muslim-dominated north. Southern rebel groups fought the government, and millions were killed in the violence. A peace agreement was signed in 2005, and in 2011, South Sudan declared its independence.

Another part of Sudan, Darfur, faced ethnic cleansing beginning in 2003. Ethnic Arab militia groups began attacking ethnic African groups. Almost 400,000 people were killed, and millions of people were displaced. After these human rights violations became known, the UN started criminal proceedings with the International Criminal Tribunal.

Religious Persecution Human rights violations based on religion have taken place throughout history. Since ancient times, Jews, Christians, Muslims, and others have faced religious and cultural persecution.

Governments in many nations, including Egypt, Iran, Pakistan, Saudi Arabia, China, and North Korea, currently limit religious freedom. For example, the Chinese government, which controls Tibet, has persecuted

North Korea's leaders do not allow religious freedom. Christians and other religious groups face severe treatment, including arrest, torture, execution, or years in a labor camp.

Tibetans for their Buddhist religious beliefs and their desire for political independence. In Egypt, minority Muslim sects, or groups, and members of the Baha'i faith have faced imprisonment, job and education discrimination, and denial of bank accounts, driver's licenses, and birth certificates. The Pakistani government has targeted Christians, Hindus, and Shia Muslims by passing laws that deny religious freedom and inflicting severe punishment on those who break them. The government of North Korea routinely persecutes people who practice any religion other than what has been state-approved.

Reading Check
Make Inferences
Why do you think some governments try to stop people from expressing their political views?

Human Rights Successes

Despite great obstacles, the human rights movement has had many successes. Since the 1980s, the greatest human rights victories have come in the area of political freedoms. In Europe, more countries opened up their political systems and now allow for democratic elections and the free expression of ideas. In 1994, the South African government put an end to the nation's system of racial separation called apartheid and allowed free elections, which brought a multiracial government to power.

Strides in Health Care Along with political freedom, a decent standard of health has been recognized as a basic human right. For much of the world, poor health is the norm. Access to medical or mental-health care is extremely limited for many of the world's people. In Indonesia, for example, it is difficult to gain treatment and medication for mental illness. As a result, more than 18,000 Indonesians with mental illness are kept in chains or confined spaces, without access to medication or treatment for their condition. Under pressure from human rights organizations, the Indonesian minister of health recently committed to providing the country's more than 9,000 health centers with mental-health medication. This could mean better lives for mentally ill Indonesians.

Some groups travel the world to build hospitals or provide care during serious outbreaks of disease. Since 1971, an NGO called Doctors Without Borders has worked to aid the sick and victims of disaster and war. Doctors Without Borders has had many successes worldwide. In 2011, for example, the organization built a hospital in Kunduz, Afghanistan, where its staff provides trauma care to the 250,000 people living in Kunduz. The Doctors Without Borders hospital has an emergency room, two operating rooms, and an intensive care unit. It is the only good hospital in this part of Afghanistan and successfully fills an important hole in the nation's healthcare system.

Many people believe that health care is a basic human right. Here, a Doctors Without Borders medical team leader examines refugees from Libya.

Gains for Women and Children As you read earlier, the rights of women and children are a primary focus of many human rights organizations. USAID work in 2012 helped women victims of torture in the Democratic Republic of the Congo. The group offered medical treatment and social, psychological, legal, and economic help to more than 43,000 survivors. Another NGO, Anti-Slavery International, has met success in helping to end forced child begging in Senegal, in getting a conviction for slavery in Niger, and in uncovering forced labor for migrant workers throughout the Middle East.

A major issue of concern is child marriage, which is common in many countries, including Afghanistan, Bangladesh, Yemen, and Zimbabwe. Research shows that early marriage, which occurs mostly among the poor, prevents girls from being educated and leads to greater domestic violence and illness.

In Zimbabwe, for example, at least one-third of all girls marry before the age of 18. Trying to combat the problem, in March 2016, Zimbabwe's vice president announced that the government was outlawing the practice of monetary payment from a man to a girl's family. By making marriage less profitable for a poor family, the government hopes to make strides toward preventing child marriage altogether. In September of the previous year, the UN made eliminating child marriage a primary goal in its effort to improve the rights of women and children worldwide.

Other Successes There have been other victories as well. For instance, governmental and nongovernmental organizations have raised awareness of the right to housing, protection against religious intolerance, and protecting the rights of indigenous, or native, populations and other minority groups. In 2007, the UN passed the United Nations Declaration on the Rights of Indigenous Peoples. It also created the UN Permanent Forum on Indigenous Issues. The goals of the group are to promote education and better health care for indigenous peoples and to protect their rights to self-government.

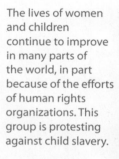

The lives of women and children continue to improve in many parts of the world, in part because of the efforts of human rights organizations. This group is protesting against child slavery.

Other successes have to do with the International Criminal Court, which investigates and tries people accused of crimes that violate international law. The ICC tried participants in the genocides in Yugoslavia and Rwanda. Trials and convictions of leaders who ordered or took part in these acts served as a warning to other leaders taking part in such atrocities. The mission of the ICC is to bring criminals to justice in order to promote long-lasting peace.

Finally, certain trends provide reasons to hope for continued human rights progress. Levels of education are rising. Education provides people with the skills to exercise their political rights. Modern communications networks are also helping. They allow human rights organizations to investigate and report on human rights abuses. In addition, today's mass media can make people instantly aware of abuses.

Summary and Preview Many governments and other groups around the world have abused human rights. Different governmental and non-governmental organizations work to protect human rights. Some have found success in stopping violations. In the next lesson, you will learn about the spread of democracy in today's world.

Reading Check
Analyze Events
What is an example of a success that has taken place in the fight for human rights?

Lesson 1 Assessment

Review Ideas, Terms, and People

1. a. **Define** Write a brief definition of the term *human rights*.

   b. **Recall** What is one important point made by the Universal Declaration of Human Rights?

   c. **Evaluate** Why do volunteers unite for humanitarian reasons?

   d. **Identify** What purpose do nongovernmental organizations (NGOs) serve?

2. a. **Compare** Which issues concerning women's rights are similar in both developing and industrialized nations?

   b. **Describe** From what human rights abuses do children mainly suffer?

   c. **Analyze** Why have so many people from Darfur become refugees?

   d. **Summarize** How have victims of religious persecution been treated?

3. a. **Recall** What progress has been made by the UN related to women's rights?

   b. **Make Inferences** Why do you think some governments continue to practice human rights violations?

Critical Thinking

4. **Evaluate** Draw a graphic organizer like this one. Use it to identify two ways the United Nations has helped protect human rights.

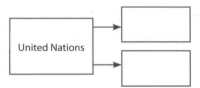

Democracy in the World Today

The Big Idea

Despite many challenges, democracy continues to spread around the world.

Main Ideas

- People around the world seek to have a voice in their government through democracy.

- Democracies face a wide variety of challenges in the twenty-first century.

- Failed states struggle with crumbling infrastructure and violence.

Key Terms and People

secular
Arab Spring
refugees
Petro Poroshenko
failed states
infrastructure

If YOU were there . . .

You are living in a country that has had a dictatorship for many years. Most citizens have few rights and can be imprisoned without a reason. Also, they are denied the right to vote for leaders. Rulers have stayed in power without being elected. People are starting to challenge the lack of democracy. They insist that free elections be held. Many of your fellow citizens fear that they will be imprisoned or killed for challenging the government.

Would you risk your life to support the pro-democracy movement in your country?

Democracy Movements

Now more than ever before, the world's people are aware of how others around the globe live. New technology is largely responsible for this. People see movies made by other cultures, hear breaking news from far away, and communicate electronically over long distances. In doing so, they see similarities and differences in the daily lives of various regions.

These changes have led many to push for more political freedom and for democratic government. At the beginning of World War II, there were fewer than 15 democracies. By 2016, more than 100 countries identified themselves as democracies. The transition to democratic government has not always been easy.

Democracy in South Asia Democracy has taken root in parts of South Asia. In fact, India has the world's largest democracy, and, for the most part, it remains stable. In 2015 India's new prime minister, Narenda Modi, pledged to work to improve the way women, children, and minorities are treated in India. Meanwhile, important developments took place to India's north. Once an absolute monarchy, the nation of Nepal is now a democracy. In 2015, a new constitution created a new republic with a parliament as its lawmaking body. South of India, the island country of Sri Lanka formed a new government that shows signs of giving more freedoms to its people. An addition to its constitution places limits on executive power. Meanwhile, India's neighbor, Pakistan, also has a democratic government, but it remains shaky. For example, the Pakistani prime minister yielded some of his authority to the military in 2015, giving power to unelected officials.

More Freedoms in Southeast Asia Slowly, democratic ideas are reaching more places in Southeast Asia. For many years the military government of Myanmar ruled harshly over citizens of the nation. Protests in 2007 led to the promise of a new representative government. In 2015, the country held free elections. The election process ran fairly smoothly, surprising many. The National League of Democracy political party swept into power. Htin Kyaw became the country's new president. Outspoken activist for democracy Aung San Suu Kyi also gained powerful roles in the government.

At about the same time, Thailand suffered a setback for its democracy. Since 1974, political disagreements have frequently led to military coups that bring an end to the elected government. A coup (KOO) is when an existing government is overturned. After a coup, the military ran the Thai government. In time, new elections were held to choose leaders for a new government. Just such a coup established a period of martial law in 2014. The next year, the interim, or temporary, government promised a new constitution, along with a return to democratic elections.

Historical Source

Medal Recognition for Aung San Suu Kyi

In 2008, the U.S. Congress awarded activist Aung San Suu Kyi a Congressional Gold Medal for her role in fighting for democracy in Burma (Myanmar).

The Congress finds as follows: . . .

(3) On September 24, 1988, the National League for Democracy (NLD) was formed, with Ms. Suu Kyi as the general-secretary, and it was, and remains, dedicated to a policy of non-violence and civil disobedience.

(4) Ms. Suu Kyi was subsequently [later] placed under house arrest, where she remained for the next 6 years—without being charged or put on trial—and has been imprisoned twice more; she currently remains under house arrest. . . .

(7) For her efforts on behalf of the Burmese people, she has been awarded the Sakharov Prize for Freedom of Thought in 1990, the Presidential Medal of Freedom in 2000, and the Nobel Peace Prize in 1991. . . .

(10) Despite an assassination attempt against her life, her prolonged illegal imprisonment, the constant public vilification [extreme criticism] of her character, and her inability to see her children or to see her husband before his death, Ms. Suu Kyi remains committed to peaceful dialogue with her captors, Burma's military regime. . . .

—Congress of the United States, Bill H.R. 4286

Analyze Historical Sources
How did the government of Myanmar punish Aung San Suu Kyi?

Ups and Downs for Democracy in Turkey Located near the Middle East, Turkey stood out from many of its Islamic neighbors. Although the country is mainly Muslim, the government of the republic was **secular**, or free of religious influence. Beginning in 2008, lawmakers began to enact laws meant to strengthen Islam in Turkey. But then, in 2010, lawmakers added 26 amendments that increased democratic principles. Their goal was to gain membership in the European Union.

The Turkish leader Recep Tayyip Erdoğan (reh-JEHP t-eye-YIHP ERR-doh-ahn) has long influenced Turkey in various roles, including three terms as prime minister. Unable to run again for prime minister in 2014, Erdoğan ran instead to become Turkey's president. He won the first election held for the largely ceremonial office. One of his goals is to make the position of president stronger. His actions have led to accusations that he is abusing human rights. After a failed coup attempt in 2016, Erdoğan cracked down harshly on large numbers of citizens he considers to be disloyal. Turkey also continues to deal with other serious issues, including conflict between religious groups, the Syrian refugee crisis, and terrorism.

Reading Check
Find Main Ideas
Which Asian nations experienced setbacks in their move toward democratic government?

Democratic Challenges of the Twenty-First Century

It may surprise you to learn that less than half the world's people live in true democracies. Most of the world's nations say that they are democracies. Yet people have various degrees of freedom and voice in government, depending on where they live.

Keeping Score on Democracy Many human-rights groups rank the quality of democracy in countries around the world. In other words, they give each country's government a grade based on how well it represents its citizens. Among the highest-ranked countries are the United States and Canada, most Western European countries, and Australia. Many countries in Eastern Europe, such as Poland, Lithuania, and the Czech Republic, also receive good grades on democracy. Countries such as China, North Korea, Egypt, Syria, Iran, and Yemen receive very low marks.

Resistance to Democracy in the Middle East With the spread of the Information Age, the people living in Arab countries witnessed first-hand the freedoms held by other people. Their own countries were led by dictators who held all the power. Citizens had little voice in government.

In 2010, citizens of Tunisia in North Africa began to gather together to speak out for freedom. The crowds grew larger and larger. The event appeared in television news broadcasts and on social media sites. Information was also spread from person to person using cell phones. Soon the protests moved to other Arab nations. People across North Africa and the Middle East rose up against their restrictive leaders. The term **Arab Spring** refers to the democratic uprisings that occurred independently in Arab nations in 2011.

The Arab Spring had little success. Although reigning dictators were removed from power in some places, power struggles developed. In Egypt, protests quickly led to the end of the longtime rule of Hosni

Egyptian protestors gather in Cairo's Tahrir Square in 2011 to demand a new government and increased rights.

Mubarak. Egyptians hoped that democracy would take hold, but by mid-2016, the military controlled the government. In Libya, dictator Muammar al-Gaddafi was overthrown, but a civil war broke out in which rival groups fought for power. A UN-supported government took power in 2016 but faced opposition from two other groups also claiming the right to rule.

In Syria, dictator Bashar al-Assad resorted to violence to stop the Arab Spring protestors. In 2011, peaceful protests against the government turned into a full-blown civil war. The Assad government destroyed or occupied homes and used violence, including chemical weapons, to suppress revolts.

Since 2011, more than 470,000 people have been killed in the fighting between troops loyal to Assad and rebel groups. Survivors have lost their homes and access to food, water, and health services. Some 4.5 million Syrians have fled the country. People who leave their country to move to another for safety are called **refugees.** The refugee crisis has caused

Many Syrians have fled their war-torn nation to find safety in other countries.

additional international conflicts over which country will accept the refugees, and how many. Thus far, Turkey, Jordan, and Lebanon have accepted the most Syrian refugees. Some refugees have also fled to Europe.

In addition, the civil war led to the rise of a group called the Islamic State in Iraq and the Levant (ISIL). Its goal is to create a modern-day Islamic state that supports its extreme form of Islam. ISIL has committed acts of terror throughout the world. In November 2015, it bombed several locations throughout Paris, France, killing about 130 people. Other sites of ISIL terrorism include Lebanon, Iraq, Egypt, Tunisia, Ethiopia, Turkey, and Belgium. The world's democracies view ISIL as an immediate threat to their basic beliefs of freedom and fair treatment for all.

The Iraqi government also faces the threat of ISIL, which has taken over large parts of the country. After the U.S. occupation of Iraq ended, Iraqis struggled to form a democracy. The government continues to function and has become more representative but is often charged with corruption and incompetence.

Tunisia, the birthplace of the Arab Spring, has experienced some success with democracy. In 2014 Tunisian leaders wrote a new constitution. The Tunisian government also incorporated more moderate leaders and established greater political and economic freedom. In addition, it supported greater protection of women's rights. As a result of these changes, Tunisia became a target of ISIL. In March 2015 ISIL took responsibility for a terrorist attack on tourists at a museum that killed around 24 people. Many Tunisians also have joined ISIL and other militant groups. Often, it is because they are poor and unemployed and need financial security that the new government cannot provide.

A Rough Road for Ukraine Ukraine's first free elections were held in 1994, indicating that democracy was taking root. However, the country faced deep divisions. The eastern part of the country had more in common culturally and politically with Russia than the western part. Western Ukraine was culturally and politically more similar to Europe. These differences led to armed conflict over which group should control the nation.

Ukrainian president Petro Poroshenko honors Ukrainians who lost their lives speaking out for freedom. Their actions played a role in the removal of Russia-aligned leader Viktor Yanukovych from office.

In 2010, Viktor Yanukovych became president of Ukraine and began to build closer ties between his country and Russia. Ukrainians protested in large numbers when Yanukovych acted to end a planned Ukrainian agreement with the European Union. In time, Yanukovych was removed from office.

Conflict continued over whether Ukraine should have a closer connection with western democracies or with Russia. Russian troops marched into the eastern region of Ukraine known as Crimea. Eventually, Russia annexed Crimea as well as other parts of eastern Ukraine. The Russian government seems intent on claiming more of eastern Ukraine. Elected as Ukraine's president in 2014, **Petro Poroshenko** has stood firm in his determination to keep Ukraine democratic and independent from Russia.

Democracy in Nigeria The people of Nigeria had long sought democracy. Finally, the nation's military government fulfilled its long-awaited promise to hold free elections. In 1999, Nigerians elected their first civilian president in nearly 20 years. Since then, elections have been held regularly. In 2015, Muhammadu Buhari became president. Like past presidents, his government faces challenges from the militant group Boko Haram. Now connected to ISIL, this group continues to fight for control of regions of Nigeria.

Danger of Failed States

Countries whose governments are unable to provide stability to their people and protect their borders are considered **failed states**. The citizens of a failed state do not believe the government is legitimate. The international community does not recognize the governments of failed states, either. These states are also called fragile states.

These countries often experience war and other violent conflict. They have crumbling **infrastructure**, or the basic items a society needs to function, such as roads and bridges. Their schools and hospitals are in poor condition. Failed states often suffer from low literacy rates and high infant mortality. A country's infant mortality rate is the number of babies that die in a country compared to the number of babies born.

The African country of Somalia became a failed state in the 1990s. A dictator who had ruled the country for more than 20 years was overthrown in a violent civil war. Afterward, violent clans continued to battle for control of the country. The clans took control of different regions. The country became unstable, the economy was destroyed, and Somalis were forced to live in terrible conditions.

A new government was established in 2012, but it has only limited control over parts of the country. Many hope that it can eventually restore order to the country.

Failed states can negatively affect both neighboring countries and those far away. Many people living in failed states, such as Somalia, flee to other countries. The countries they flee to must deal with additional strains of caring

Reading Check
Analyze Issues
What has happened in Libya since its dictatorship ended?

Quick Facts

Common Characteristics of Failed States

- Illegitimate government
- Ongoing war or violent conflict
- Crumbling infrastructure
- Low literacy rates
- High infant mortality

A weak government in Somalia has led to increased piracy in the Indian Ocean and the Gulf of Aden. Other nations, such as the United States, help patrol these waters. In this photo, U.S. Navy sailors control a boat suspected of piracy in the Gulf of Aden.

Reading Check
Draw Conclusions
Why is it difficult to repair a failed state?

for a refugee population. Also, without laws, people in a failed state may take illegal actions to survive. For example, modern-day Somali pirates threaten the safety of ships from around the world as well as their cargo and crew. Terrorism also rises in failed states because there is no one to stop the terrorists from organizing to promote violence.

Summary and Preview More nations became democracies in the 21st century. At the same time, democracies have faced many challenges, including terrorism. Failed states have caused problems for their citizens and other countries. In the next lesson, you will learn about how new technology and increased interaction between nations affects the world today.

Lesson 2 Assessment

Review Ideas, Terms, and People

1. a. Identify What is a coup?

   b. Contrast How is Pakistan different from the other countries in South Asia?

   c. Recall How did Myanmar change in 2015?

   d. Summarize How did Turkey once stand out from its Islamic neighbors?

2. a. Identify What are some of the countries that are ranked lowest for their quality of democracy?

   b. Draw Conclusions Why are some people resistant to democracy in the Middle East?

   c. Describe What conflict continues to separate eastern and western Ukraine?

   d. Predict Effects How might the militant group Boko Haram affect Nigeria?

3. a. Summarize What problems exist in failed states?

   b. Make Inferences Why does the new government have limited control in Somalia?

Critical Thinking

4. Categorize Draw a chart like this one. Categorize the countries discussed in this lesson according to those that have made advances toward democracy and those that have experienced setbacks. Be sure you include details in the chart that describe why the country has been placed in the column.

Advances Toward Democracy	Setbacks From Democracy

Technology and Globalization

The Big Idea
New technologies have helped to create a global community.

Main Ideas
- Space exploration has led to international cooperation and technological developments.
- Computers and the Internet have changed how people work and communicate.
- Globalization has led to greater cultural sharing around the world.

Key Terms and People
International Space Station
microchips
Internet
telecommute

If YOU were there . . .

You are an astronaut in a space station orbiting Earth. Your mission is to conduct research for six months. Your fellow astronauts come from several different countries. The team cooperates to complete certain jobs. Together, you observe the blue and green planet Earth beneath you.

How does this experience change your views about life on Earth?

Space Exploration

The United States and the Soviet Union both wanted to be the first nation to reach space. That means the two countries competed to achieve their goals. Although the Soviet Union was first, the United States was not far behind. Eventually, space exploration led to successful cooperation between U.S. and Soviet scientists. Technologies developed for space exploration helped connect other people around the world, too.

Cooperation in Space Even before the end of the Cold War, the U.S. and Soviet space programs worked on a joint project. On July 17, 1975, the United States launched an *Apollo* command module, and the Soviets sent up a *Soyuz* spacecraft. They met in space about 140 miles above Earth and accomplished the first joint docking between nations. This means the two spacecraft joined together. Television viewers around the world watched as the hatch between the space vehicles opened. They saw crews from the two rival countries greet each other in a spirit of international cooperation.

People from other countries worked together to explore space, too. In 1978, the Soviets sent an international crew into space. Their spacecraft, *Soyuz 28,* included a Czech cosmonaut. U.S. space missions also have included astronauts from many countries, including Saudi Arabia, France, Germany, Canada, Italy, Japan, Israel, and Mexico.

Also during the 1970s, the United States and the European Space Research Organization began cooperating on a major project. This project was the launching of the Hubble Space Telescope. It was not until 1990 that the Hubble was put into space. Even today, this orbiting telescope sends back images of objects in distant galaxies. It has helped scientists locate planets outside our solar system.

In 1993, the United States and Russia agreed to combine their space station programs. This led to the development of the **International Space Station** (ISS). The European Space Agency and Japan also joined the program. Beginning in 1998, U.S. and Russian spacecraft carried sections of the ISS into space. These sections were put together in space. Then in May 2009, the first people went to the ISS. During 2015 and 2016, two people spent a year living on the ISS. They were U.S. astronaut Scott Kelly and Russian cosmonaut Mikhail Kornienko. Together, Kelly and Kornienko conducted important studies. These studies included the effects of space travel on the human body. In the future, these investigations may help humans travel safely to Mars.

The Solar System and Beyond The U.S. space shuttle program began in 1981 with the launch of *Columbia*. The other shuttles—*Challenger, Discovery, Atlantis,* and *Endeavour*—continued what *Columbia* had started. Over the next 30 years, these reusable vehicles carried more than 350 people into space. Collectively, the shuttles traveled about half a billion miles on missions that orbited Earth. The space shuttles had human pilots and crews who performed scientific experiments. They also launched satellites and helped build and supply the ISS. The space shuttle program ended on July 21, 2011, with the landing of *Atlantis* at the Kennedy Space Center in Florida. Now, Russian spaceships transport astronauts to the ISS. In addition, private U.S. companies plan to make trips to the ISS. This has allowed NASA to focus on research and building spacecraft and rockets that may take humans to planets such as Mars.

This view of the ISS was taken from the space shuttle *Endeavor*.

Select Unmanned NASA Missions

Unmanned Space Missions	Main Purpose
Voyager 1 (1977)	to observe farthest parts of solar system
Voyager 2 (1977)	to study the four giant planets and where solar wind and the sun's magnetic field dominate space
SOHO (1995)	to watch the sun
Advanced Composition Explorer (1997)	to collect and analyze particles from the solar system
Cassini (1997)	to continue study of Saturn and its rings
Mars Odyssey (2001)	to map the surface of Mars and act as a relay for the Curiosity and Opportunity rovers
New Horizons (2006)	to explore Pluto, its moon, and the Kuiper belt
Dawn (2007)	to explore dwarf planets
Interstellar Boundary Explorer (2008)	to image and map interactions in the outer solar system
Lunar Reconnaissance Orbiter (2009)	to collect data about Earth's moon
Akatsuki (2010)	to study weather patterns on Venus
Juno (2011)	to determine how Jupiter formed and evolved
Mars Science Laboratory/Curiosity (2011)	to look for signs that there was once life on Mars

To prepare for farther space travel, NASA landed two robotic rovers on Mars in 2004. A rover is an unmanned vehicle designed to explore the surface of planets or other bodies in space, such as the moon. The rovers' mission was to study Mars for signs of water or life. The rovers found evidence of water in Mars's past. Then in 2005, NASA launched the Mars Reconnaissance Orbiter, designed to explore Mars from orbit. It has taken photographs of Mars's surface. In 2015, it provided evidence that water occasionally flows on Mars.

More unmanned space missions are taking place throughout the solar system. For example, the New Horizons mission was launched on January 19, 2006. Its goal is to explore Pluto, its moons, and Kuiper belt objects. The Kuiper belt is a region of icy bodies in the outer solar system beyond Neptune's orbit. New Horizons travels about a million miles a day. As it flew by Pluto in 2015, it photographed different features of Pluto, including a mountainous icy region. In years to come, NASA hopes to learn much about this region of the solar system from New Horizons.

The Space Race and Technology Space exploration has had many positive effects, including the development of new technology. For example, artificial satellites, which were originally built to orbit around Earth, now play an important role in worldwide communications. Satellite communications carry television news and entertainment that can be viewed simultaneously around the world. The Global Positioning System (GPS) found on cell phones and in cars is a satellite-based navigation system. Also, GPS technology is used by the military to provide data related to enemy troop movements and missile attacks. Another important benefit from satellites is their use in weather forecasting. Satellites allow meteorologists, scientists who study the weather, to observe global weather patterns. Meteorologists use the information to help them predict weather events such as hurricanes and tornadoes.

Reading Check
Draw Conclusions
Why do you think nations cooperate in space activities?

Other technology benefits that came about because of space exploration include a heart pump for people waiting for heart transplants, improved car tires, video image enhancements for law enforcement, breathing equipment for firefighters, cordless vacuums, and techniques for freeze-drying food.

The Information Age

In the 1940s, computers filled entire rooms. Since then, the circuits that run computers have become smaller. Tiny silicon chips called **microchips** store large amounts of information and are very powerful. Today's smartphones are more powerful than early NASA computers. By today's standards, the computers used to put a person on the moon were simple—no more powerful than a handheld calculator. Computers now carry information at high speeds and have changed information management.

Industries now use computers to produce their products. Cars and trucks have computers that control brakes, engines, entertainment systems, and other parts. Air traffic controllers use computers to keep track of airline traffic.

Link to Today

The Changing World of Cell Phones

The way cell phones look has changed drastically over the past 30 years. The first cell phones were car phones. They were too large for people to carry around. Then, in 1983, the Motorola Company started selling a portable cell phone. Called the DynaTAC 8000x, it was still fairly large. Over time, companies developed smaller cell phones.

The ways in which people use cell phones have also changed over time. At first, cell phones were just used for talking. Then cell phones became "smartphones." This means that they have other functions. These phones can be used to check email, send text messages, and take and store photos and videos. Applications, or "apps," on cell phones also offer different functions. Users can access and update their social media. They can buy and sell products. They can listen to music and watch movies. In fact, there are mobile apps for thousands and thousands of different purposes.

Analyze Visuals
What do the photographs tell you about how cell phones have changed over time?

DynaTAC 8000x

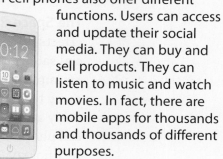

Smartphone

It seems as if computer technology changes every day. People constantly look for new ways to improve equipment and devices. They also create new electronic products. The result is continuous change in the way people work, travel, and communicate.

The Internet In the 1990s, businesses and individuals began using the **Internet**. The Internet is a worldwide network of linked computers. It was started in the late 1960s and mainly used by scientists. It allowed them to share information about research. Once the World Wide Web was developed, the Internet became more popular. The World Wide Web is a system that connects sources of information through the Internet. The Web provides an easy way for people to view content online via websites.

Today, many people use the Internet at home, work, and school. They connect to the Internet using cell phones and other mobile devices. International news is shared instantly. Many businesses and customers take part in e-commerce—the advertising, buying, and selling of goods and services online. Governments also use the Internet to provide citizens with information. People use e-mail and social networking media to communicate. Online social networking also allows people around the world to form online communities. These technologies connect people worldwide.

A New Way of Life The Internet and other technologies have changed where and how many people work. Some people still work in offices, but many workers now **telecommute**—they do their jobs by computer from home. People who buy and sell stocks can conduct business in any stock market in the world from home. Some workers no longer need to live near business offices. Trading, banking, and financial dealings are often done electronically and automatically. Many industries seek out and depend on workers with high-tech skills.

Education has changed because of technology, too. Books were once the main source of learning. However, during the 1990s, classrooms began to use computer technology.

Internet Users in the World by Region, November 2015

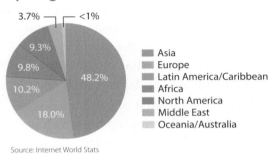

- Asia — 48.2%
- Europe — 18.0%
- Latin America/Caribbean — 10.2%
- Africa — 9.8%
- North America — 9.3%
- Middle East — 3.7%
- Oceania/Australia — <1%

Source: Internet World Stats

Percentage of Population Using the Internet, November 2015

Africa	28.6%
Asia	40.2%
Europe	73.5%
Middle East	52.2%
North America	87.9%
Latin America & the Caribbean	55.9%
Oceania & Australia	73.2%
World Total	46.4%

Interpret Charts
Which world region has a greater percentage of Internet users in its population, Africa, the Middle East, or Latin America and the Caribbean?

Reading Check
Synthesize How do you think the Internet will affect education over the next 50 years?

Today, many classrooms in developed nations have Internet access. Some students use tablets to do their schoolwork. Many students of all ages also take classes online. They are able to interact with other students from their homes.

A Global Community

Once early people began trading with other groups, they began to share parts of their culture. This led to cultural diffusion, or the spread of ideas from one place to another. Today, people share traditional culture and popular, or pop, culture too. Pop culture refers to activities and products enjoyed by many people in a culture. For example, sports, current music, and fashion are parts of pop culture.

However, the spread of culture has changed over time. Technology has made the exchange happen at a faster pace and over greater distances. People from all over the world interact with one another. Also, mass media contributes to cultural sharing. Mass media includes advertising, television, movies, and the Internet. Mass media provides the world's most popular forms of entertainment. But it also shows what different people value and how they live. Mass media spreads pop culture around the globe.

In the United States, most households have at least one television set. The same is true in Western Europe. People in developing nations have less access to television, but this is changing too. The speed at which television can present information creates shared experiences of global events. Military, political, and cultural events in faraway places become part of everyday life.

The Internet also promotes a sense of a global shared experience. Events can be captured on a smartphone and uploaded to an online community. Blogs and social networking sites also send information easily and quickly.

New technologies connect people all over the world, instantly. Even people in remote locations have access to new technology.

Western Influences *Western,* or *the West,* refers to countries in the western part of the world. The West includes countries in North America and Western Europe. The West has a major influence on many cultures today because it dominates worldwide mass media. However, this influence is not new. It may have begun with Western exploration and settlement. It continued in the 19th century with imperialism. Imperialism is the practice of a country extending its power and influence through diplomatic means or military force. These actions have been responsible for spreading Western customs and ideas, including languages.

World's Most Commonly Spoken Languages

Language	Main Countries Where Spoken	Number of Native Speakers
Mandarin Chinese	China, Singapore	897 million
Spanish	Spain, Mexico, most South American countries	427 million
English	United States, United Kingdom, Canada, Australia	339 million
Arabic	Most Southwest Asian countries, North African countries	267 million
Hindi	India, Pakistan	260 million
Portuguese	Portugal, Brazil	202 million
Bengali	Bangladesh	189 million
Russian	Russia, Belarus, Kyrgyzstan, Kazakhstan	171 million
Japanese	Japan	128 million

Over the past 50 years, English has become the main international language. About 340 million people speak English as their first language. Millions more speak it as their second language. Although more people speak Mandarin Chinese than English, English speakers are more widely distributed. English is the most common language used on the Internet and at international conferences. The widespread use of English is partly responsible for our dynamic global culture.

Western influences can be seen in other areas of popular culture. Western television, film, and advertising have influenced fashion. For example, many people in business wear Western-type business suits. Jeans have become the recreational clothing of choice, not just for teens but also for supermodels, farmers, presidents, corporate executives, and stay-at-home parents. People flock to fast-food restaurants worldwide to snack on American-style hamburgers and soft drinks. Western influence also affects the way people see themselves and their overall thinking about the world.

Non-Western Influences Just as Western ideas have spread globally, so, too, have non-Western ideas. Non-Western refers to cultures in Asia, Africa, India, Latin America, and the Middle East. Mass media is also responsible for spreading non-Western ideas, entertainment, fashion, and other information. These offerings now influence people in the Western world. For example, Thai, Japanese, Chinese, and Vietnamese foods are popular in the United States. Many people take classes in martial arts and watch films from Hong Kong and India. Non-Western ideas also have influenced ideas about art, architecture, and religious and moral thinking. Some people in the West have also begun using different kinds of medical treatment from non-Western cultures. Many people follow ancient healing systems from India and China in dealing with pain or illness.

Old Ways Abandoned As mass media spreads new images and ideas, cultures become more similar. This can cause changes in traditional cultures. Old ways may be lost. In some cases, people experience a loss of identity

People around the world share the experience of watching their countries compete in the Olympics every four years. This event connects people globally.

and culture. Or they may find themselves in conflict over competing values. In addition, some observers worry that technology is weakening the old ways of interacting. For example, most people today send e-mails rather than writing and mailing letters.

Sometimes the challenges posed by new ideas and technology can have positive effects. For example, they can stimulate the desire to preserve traditions. Technology may even play a positive role in this process. In the Amazon region of Brazil, for example, some native Brazilians use video cameras to document and preserve traditional ways of life.

Global Interdependence Despite the problems that might come with global interdependence, there are many issues that bring nations closer together. These issues include economic, political, and environmental issues. Nations have begun to recognize that they are dependent on other nations. They are also deeply affected by the actions of others far way. As cultural ideas spread around the world, people share a greater sense of connectedness.

Throughout history, humans have faced challenges to survive and to live better. In the 21st century, the world's people are joined by global interdependence to face the problems together. They have a greater stake in learning to live in harmony. They also have a greater responsibility to the planet.

Reading Check
Draw Conclusions
What effect might a Western ad or commercial have on a non-Western country?

Summary and Preview Space exploration brought about increased cooperation among nations. Advances in technology led to increased globalization. This, in turn, changed the ways people live. In the next lesson, you will learn about environmental issues facing our planet.

Lesson 3 Assessment

Review Ideas, Terms, and People

1. a. Recall What led to the launch of the International Space Station?

   b. Identify Give an example of technology that changed as a result of space exploration.

2. a. Evaluate Why are microchips important?

   b. Describe What impact has the Internet had on society?

   c. Define What does it mean to telecommute?

3. Make Inferences Why do you think some people might fear global interdependence?

Critical Thinking

4. Compare Draw a diagram like this one. Use it to show what factors have helped create global interdependence.

Global Interdependence

Protecting the Environment

The Big Idea

Our planet faces a growing population and environmental challenges.

Main Ideas

- Population growth has put pressure on Earth's resources.

- Technology and industrialization have created environmental challenges that affect the entire world.

- Both government action and new technologies can help solve environmental problems.

Key Terms and People

overpopulation
ozone layer
sustainable growth
environmentalism

If YOU were there . . .

You live in Mexico City. It's one of the largest and most crowded cities in the world. You realize just how crowded it is whenever you ride the subway. You love the excitement of living in a big city. There is always something interesting to do. At the same time, the city has problems. The air is often polluted. Water in the city can be polluted, too.

What do you think causes this pollution?

Population Pressures

Population growth, movement, and distribution can have a major impact on the environment. As the number of people increase in particular locations and in the world as a whole, environments are often harmed. The future of the planet may depend on population decisions.

Population Growth For thousands of years, world population growth was low and relatively steady. About 2,000 years ago, the world had some 300 million people. By 1800, there were almost 1 billion people. Since 1800, better health care and improved food production have led to tremendous population growth. Another reason for this growth is better living conditions. In 2012, the world's population was greater than 7 billion people. According to research, the world's population will increase to nearly 10 billion by 2050.

Two important population trends exist today. The first trend is that the population growth in some developed, or industrialized, nations is slowing. For example, Germany and France have low rates of natural increase. The rate of natural increase is the percentage of population change a country experiences in a given year. It is calculated using birth and death rates.

A second trend is that less-industrialized nations often have high growth rates. These include many countries in Africa and Asia. High population growth rates can cause some challenges. Governments struggle to provide enough jobs for their rapidly growing populations. They also have a difficult time providing education and medical care. Some areas have **overpopulation**. This occurs when there are more people than resources in an area can support. Overpopulation can have many consequences, including migration, or the movement of people from one area to another.

Population Movement The global movement of people has increased dramatically in recent years. This migration has taken place for both negative and positive reasons.

People often move because they feel pushed out of their homelands. Lack of resources, such as food, is an example of a push factor for immigration. A push factor is something that motivates someone to leave his or her home. War, political oppression, and natural disasters are also push factors. In 2014, the number of refugees in the world stood at 19.5 million.

There are also pull factors for migration—conditions that draw people to another place. Most people have strong connections to their homes. They do not leave unless strong positive attractions pull them away. They hope for a better life for themselves and for their children. Therefore,

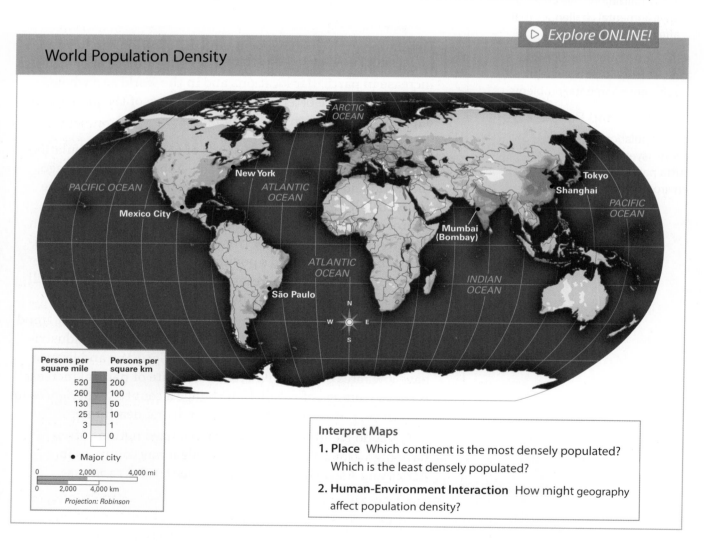

▶ *Explore ONLINE!*

World Population Density

Persons per square mile	Persons per square km
520	200
260	100
130	50
25	10
3	1
0	0

● Major city

0   2,000   4,000 mi
0 2,000 4,000 km
Projection: Robinson

Interpret Maps

1. **Place** Which continent is the most densely populated? Which is the least densely populated?

2. **Human-Environment Interaction** How might geography affect population density?

they migrate to developed nations. For example, hundreds of thousands of people migrate to the United States every year. They come from places such as Africa, Europe, the Middle East, and Latin America.

Population Distribution Growth and migration have changed our planet's population density. Population density is a measure of the number of people living in an area. Currently, about half the world's population lives in rural areas. Yet that percentage is shrinking. More people are moving into cities.

Around the world, cities have certain geographic characteristics in common. Many cities are found in places that allow good transportation, such as along water. Others are found in places with easy access to natural resources. Because of their geographic advantages, cities help the area's economy. They attract businesses and people to work in those businesses. Cultural, educational, or military activities can also attract people to cities.

Some cities have populations of more than a million. Cities with more than 10 million people are called megacities. Both Tokyo and New York City became megacities during the 1950s. By 2014, the number of megacities had grown to 28. These included São Paulo, Brazil, and Shanghai, China.

Such huge cities struggle with overcrowded conditions. Increased demands for resources, such as water, can become major problems in cities. Also, large concentrations of people create more trash and pollution.

Reading Check
Analyze Issues
What are some push and pull factors for population migration?

Environmental Challenges

Technology and industrialization have helped to raise standards of living for many people. But they have also affected the global environment. For two centuries, industrialization has increased the demands for energy and natural resources. In addition, industry and technology have increased the amount of pollution on the planet.

Energy Use and Pollution Various types of human activities create pollution and waste. Many of these activities are connected to the manufacturing of products. Others are connected to the use or transportation of products. These activities require sources of energy.

Around 80 percent of Earth's energy supply now comes from nonrenewable sources. A nonrenewable energy source is one that cannot be replaced once it is used up, such as coal or oil. Using nonrenewable energy sources can cause damage to the environment. When coal and oil are burned, they release carbon dioxide and other gases into the atmosphere. These can pollute the air, water, and land.

Some other sources can cause damage to the environment, too. For example, farmers often spray their crops with pesticides. Pesticides are chemicals used to kill insects and rodents. These materials can get into the ground and contaminate our soil. Eventually, they get into the water and air and harm wildlife.

Manufacturing processes also release chemicals. Some chemicals deplete, or reduce, ozone in Earth's upper atmosphere. The **ozone layer** is a layer of oxygen in Earth's atmosphere. It is our main protection against the sun's damaging ultraviolet rays. These rays can lead to skin cancer. They can also damage populations of plants and plankton, which are the food sources of other species.

Oil spills are another example of energy-related pollution. Every year, serious oil spills take place around the world. They pollute water and shorelines, and kill sea life. Oil companies do take precautions to prevent spills, but they are still frequent.

Climate Change Climates can change over time due to natural processes and the effects of human activity. One important process is caused by the buildup of gases in the atmosphere, such as carbon dioxide and methane. These and other gases are often known as greenhouse gases. They absorb energy radiating from Earth's surface and slow its loss into space. This effect keeps the planet warm enough to sustain life.

Most greenhouse gases occur naturally. But human activities have caused an increase in some greenhouse gases that has led to additional warming. Exhaust from factories, power plants, automobiles, and airplanes releases greenhouse gases into the atmosphere. Agriculture also is a major source of greenhouse gases.

The amount of carbon dioxide in the atmosphere has increased about 35 percent since the Industrial Revolution. Average global temperatures have increased over the same period. Many scientists fear that if global warming trends continue, the results will be disastrous. Changing rain patterns will cause deserts to expand and crops to fail. Wild animals and plants will struggle to survive in their natural environments as climates change. Scientists also predict an increase in extreme weather such as heavy rainfalls. Melting polar ice will raise sea levels. Higher sea levels would flood coastal areas, including many cities.

Water Supplies Besides pollution, another major global concern is the growing strain on natural resources. Industrialization, economic development, and increased population may cause important resources to grow scarce. Clean water is one of the most important natural resources to the world's people.

In the developing world, water pollution and a lack of clean water are serious problems. One-fourth of the world's population has no access to clean water. Many illnesses in developing nations can be traced to inadequate supplies of clean water. Often, these illnesses affect children. To help, the United Nations Children's Emergency Fund has created the WASH program. WASH stands for "water, sanitation, and hygiene." This program provides people with clean water supplies and various health services. It has improved the lives of children in more than 100 nations.

Some nations share water supplies in lakes and rivers. For example, Israel and Jordan share the Jordan River. This is an essential source of water for farming. Any nation that pollutes shared water runs the risk of starting an international conflict. This is also true for any nation that stops water from flowing into another country. Many nations try to cooperate to make sure water supplies remain clean.

Expanding deserts caused by climate change would create less land for growing food.

Deforestation causes problems across the globe, from loss of animal and plant species to water pollution.

In the United States, California has complex water issues. The state's large population and agricultural industry have put major pressure on water sources. Drought has made the problems worse. However, the state is trying to limit drought's effects by developing new ways to conserve water.

Destruction of Forests Another way in which natural resources are lost is through actions that affect the land, or, more specifically, forests. One process, clear cutting, involves cutting down every tree in an area. This is done to create farmland, to build roads, or for other reasons related to economic development. Clear cutting is harmful to forest lands and resources and may lead to soil erosion and desertification. Desertification is the

Deforestation Rates in Brazil

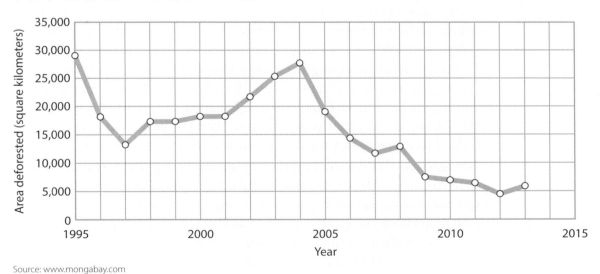

Source: www.mongabay.com

Interpret Graphs
About how many square kilometers were deforested in 2000? About how many were deforested in 2010?

change of fertile land into desert. Both soil erosion and desertification negatively affect the growth of vegetation. This, in turn, can affect animal populations. A second practice, strip mining, is also harmful to the land. Strip mining is the digging for minerals by removing the top layer of land in order to get to the minerals under it. This process destroys forests and can allow harmful minerals to contaminate water sources.

Another critical issue is tropical rainforest destruction in countries such as Malaysia and Brazil. Companies and farmers cut down rainforests for timber or to clear land for farming. By 1990, the world had lost more than half of its rainforests. Between 2000 and 2005, the United Nations estimated deforestation at 50,000 square miles. The loss of rainforests could affect all people on the planet. Rainforests help to maintain water and soil quality. They also recycle rainfall and oxygen into the atmosphere and are home to more than 50 percent of the world's species of plants and animals.

According to the UN, the deforestation rate has slowed since 2005. In addition, some countries have planted new forests. These countries include the United States, India, China, and Vietnam. Still, massive areas of forests are destroyed each year. The battle against deforestation has been limited by the desire of some nations to develop economically. These countries need to achieve **sustainable growth**. Sustainable growth is the process of creating economic growth while preserving the environment.

Preserving Our World

Sustainable growth is just one of the goals of **environmentalism**. Environmentalism is the movement to protect the natural world from destructive human activities.

The Environmental Movement Environmentalism began during the 1800s. People in the United States and Europe began to worry about the effects of the Industrial Revolution. They saw that industrialization was increasing pollution. They also began to discuss preserving natural resources. Many of these people thought that government should get involved and help.

Environmental concern grew more widespread during the 1960s. A book published in the United States called *Silent Spring* had a huge impact. In the book, author Rachel Carson warned against the growing use of pesticides. Carson argued that pesticides poisoned the very food that they were intended to protect. As a result, they killed many birds and fish.

Some NGOs that focused on the environment started during the 1960s and 1970s. For example, the World Wildlife Fund (WWF) stresses the importance of conservation, or protection, of natural resources. Conservation helps keep the environment healthy for both people and animals. Conservation efforts can help provide clean water. Another NGO is Greenpeace, which works to protect endangered animals and to raise awareness of pollution. Greenpeace members sometimes stage protests against governments and companies. Because of this activity, some people view Greenpeace as a radical group.

Reading Check
Summarize Which natural resources may become scarce in the future?

On April 22, 1970, communities around the United States celebrated the first Earth Day. The purpose of this celebration was to spotlight various environmental problems, such as pollution. Concerns over toxic waste and natural resources were also brought to public attention. Earth Day is still celebrated on April 22 each year and remains a popular way to make the public aware of environmental problems. These students are celebrating Earth Day in India.

Governments also began working toward environmental protection during the 1970s. Government agencies set and enforced pollution standards. Governments passed laws protecting endangered animals and regulating auto emissions. In Europe and some Pacific Island nations, "green" parties began forming. These are political parties whose main focus is passing environmental protection laws. Today, many nations have green parties.

Environmentalism Today Governments around the world are trying to combat the problem of global warming. A major step was taken in 2015, when 195 countries negotiated a global climate treaty called the Paris Agreement. The agreement calls upon each country to take action to limit the rise in global average temperatures. However, some critics are skeptical that the agreement will succeed because it does not legally force countries to follow through on their promises.

In recent years, businesses and individual citizens have also worked to protect the environment. Many people have reduced their use of nonrenewable resources. The recycling of glass bottles, newspapers, and other materials is now commonplace. People also purchase "green" products from companies. These are products considered to be environmentally friendly. Often, these products are made from recyclable materials.

Other green products are manufactured in ways that produce less waste. Some automobile manufacturers are producing electric cars. These cars help reduce emission levels of greenhouse gases. Businesses have also developed technologies that transform renewable resources into energy.

Renewable resources are limitless. Renewable resources include wind, water, and solar power. Using renewable resources will help reduce air pollution.

Future environmental progress depends on individuals, groups, and businesses. Cooperation between nations also remains very important. Government action and stronger regulations may provide revolutionary solutions. Problems such as pollution, deforestation, scarcity of clean water, and population growth remain. The nations of the world need to agree on how to achieve sustainable growth.

Reading Check
Draw Conclusions
Why might "green" products be popular among consumers?

Summary and Preview The world's population is growing, and more people are moving to cities. Technology and industrialization have improved the lives of many people. At the same time, they have also negatively affected the global environment. Pollution and the potential shortage of natural resources have prompted change. Individuals, groups, businesses, and governments are looking for ways to better protect our environment. In the next lesson, you will learn about global health issues.

Lesson 4 Assessment

Review Ideas, Terms, and People

1. a. **Define** What is overpopulation?
   b. **Analyze** Why are more people moving from rural areas to cities?
2. a. **Identify** Why is the ozone layer necessary?
   b. **Draw Conclusions** How might countries better conserve water?
3. a. **Recall** When did the modern environmentalist movement begin?
   b. **Explain** How are individuals helping to protect the environment?

Critical Thinking

4. **Categorize** Draw a diagram like this one. Use it to show the causes and effects of the environmental movement.

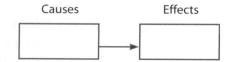

Global Health

The Big Idea

Technology and scientific advances have improved medical treatment over time, but the world still faces serious health issues.

Main Ideas

- Technology has revolutionized modern medicine.

- World health is threatened by a widespread outbreak of diseases.

Key Terms and People

genetics
cloning
biotechnology
pharmaceuticals
3D printing
epidemic
pandemic
AIDS

If YOU were there . . .

You're browsing an online news site. You see a headline that catches your attention: "Scientists Worry About Disease Outbreak." As you read, you learn that the outbreak is occurring in a distant country. Doctors are flying there with medicine to help the sick. They also want to prevent the spread of the disease.

How do you think this outbreak might affect other countries?

Technology Transforms Treatments

Technology plays an important role in communication and the environment. Perhaps even more importantly, technology plays an ever-changing role in health care. Medical technology's innovations have made it safer and faster to diagnose problems, so patients can recover more quickly and live longer and healthier lives.

Before World War II, surgeons rarely performed operations on the eye or brain. Today, surgeons perform some brain surgeries by making small cuts in the eyebrow or eyelid to remove tumors. Doctors correct people's poor vision using laser eye surgery. More advanced imaging, such as CAT scans and MRI techniques, provide data that allow doctors to build three-dimensional images of different organs or body regions.

Genetics, Cloning, and Biotechnology All living things have genes in their cells. These genes are hereditary, which means they are passed down from one's parents. Scientists study genes and how they affect the development of living things. This is called **genetics**. Thousands of diseases in humans, including diabetes and heart disease, have a genetic link. Scientists have learned how to make changes to an organism's genes. This is called genetic engineering. They can take DNA, the substance that carries genetic information in the cells, and place it in another organism. Then they can look for causes of a disease and develop drugs to help treat it. In addition, researchers have made breakthroughs in genetic engineering that are allowing them to change, delete, and replace genes in any animal. Eventually, they hope that the technology will allow them to correct genetic problems and fix genes before people get genetic diseases.

Another part of genetic engineering is **cloning**. This is the creation of identical copies of DNA. Cloning allows scientists to reproduce organisms that are identical to existing ones. In 1996, scientists cloned a sheep from an adult cell. Since then, scientists have cloned other animals, including mice, cows, and goats. While scientists have been able to clone adult stem cells, no one knows whether this technology will be used to clone humans. It is likely to be used to devise therapies to treat certain diseases.

Another area related to genetics is **biotechnology**. This is the use of cells, bacteria, and even plants to make products. It is used in diagnosing or predicting a disease or disabilities. Another use is in making new **pharmaceuticals** (FAR-muh-SOO-ti-kuhls), or manufactured medical drugs. One example is human insulin, which is used to treat diabetes. This small protein is made in genetically engineered bacteria. Other drug therapies are being developed worldwide using knowledge about genes and the proteins they produce. From this, drugs are being made to correct problems that cause certain diseases.

VR and 3D Printing When most people think of virtual reality (VR) technology, they think of gaming and entertainment. VR is an artificial world with computer-generated images and sounds. VR also has applications in medicine. For example, VR is used to help surgeons in training get experience without practicing on a real patient. It is used in robotic

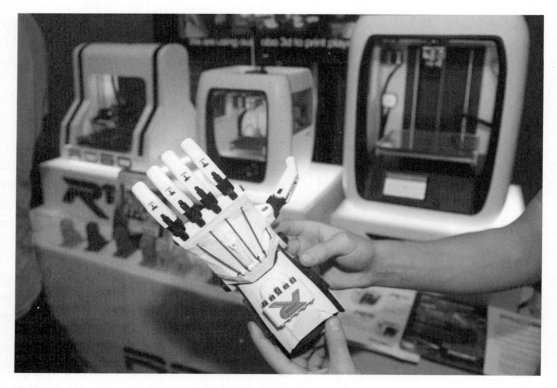

This artificial hand was created using 3D printing technology.

surgery, which is surgery done using a robotic device that is controlled by a human surgeon. Since the robotic device is accurate, there are fewer risks to the patient. Surgeons may also use robotics for remote telesurgery, which means the patient is in one location and the surgeon is in a different location.

In recent years, medicine has adapted another technology, **3D printing**. 3D printing is a way of manufacturing three-dimensional objects. Instead of paper, 3D printers use plastics or other materials. Invented in 1984, this technology has made it possible for doctors to make and customize prosthetic limbs (artificial body parts), hearing aids, and dental appliances for specific patients. 3D printing is also a cost effective way of making these devices. In the future, researchers hope to print tissues for organs to be used in organ replacement. This would save many patients' lives, since there is a long wait time for needed transplant organs. In addition, 3D printing technology is likely to reduce costs for many procedures.

Disease and Treatment

Although recent decades have seen advances in medicine, poor health remains the standard for much of the world. Poor health affects a nation's life expectancy rate. This is a measure of the average length of a person's life in a particular country.

One reason for poor health is that people in developing countries may lack proper health care. It may not be available, or they cannot afford it. Another reason is that many people have little food to eat and unclean water to drink. Some people do not realize they are sick because they have never been educated about symptoms of illnesses. In some places, diseases often spread due to lack of proper sanitation.

Some diseases are noncommunicable. They cannot be spread by direct contact between people. Examples of noncommunicable diseases are diabetes and cancer. Other diseases are infectious, which means that they can be spread from one person to another. Examples of infectious diseases are the flu and chickenpox.

Epidemics and Pandemics An **epidemic** occurs when an infectious disease spreads between many people in a community or region. A **pandemic** occurs when a disease affects many people over a wide area. A disease that affects people in different countries or continents is considered a pandemic.

Pandemics have existed for centuries. The Black Death killed millions of people throughout Europe during the Middle Ages. It led to a collapse in trade, the end of some wars, and a decline in agriculture. The structure of European medieval society changed, too. In the 20th century, a polio pandemic occurred. Polio can lead to paralysis or death. It affected people in Europe, Oceania, and North America. Although polio cannot be cured, a vaccine to prevent it was developed in the 1950s. Another pandemic was reported in 2003 in Asia. It was severe acute respiratory syndrome, or SARS. The virus spread from Asia to North America, South America, and Europe by close person-to-person contact. That means people traveling in

Reading Check
Find Main Ideas
Which medical technology allows surgeons to operate on a patient in another town or city?

Global Health and Security

Diseases affect people in every part of the world. In this passage, Tom Frieden, the director of the U.S. Centers for Disease Control and Prevention, talks about the threat of infectious diseases.

Analyze Historical Sources
Why does Frieden say the entire world needs to fight infectious diseases?

"There may be a misconception [incorrect belief] that infectious diseases are over in the industrialized world. But in fact, infectious diseases continue to be, and will always be, with us. With patterns of global travel and trade, disease can spread nearly anywhere within 24 hours. That's why the ability to detect, fight and prevent these diseases must be developed and strengthened overseas, and not just here in the United States. Global health and national security go hand in hand."

—Dr. Tom Frieden quoted in
"Measles Still Threatens Health Security"

these countries spread the disease to other areas of the world. About 8,000 people were infected with SARS, and 774 died. SARS has been contained for the time being.

Some pandemics continue to affect people across the world. Since 1918, there have been several influenza, or "flu," pandemics. Influenza can be spread through the air by sneezing or coughing. One of the most recent influenza pandemics occurred during 2009–2010. During that period, more than 18,000 people were reported to have died from flu viruses. However, many deaths, particularly in developing nations, go unreported. Some researchers estimate that the total number of deaths might have been as high as 575,000. The world has also been struggling with a tuberculosis pandemic. Like influenza, tuberculosis can be spread through the air by sneezing or coughing. It affects the lungs, is highly contagious, and is deadly. Tuberculosis kills more than one million people each year.

In recent years, two epidemics have alarmed scientists and doctors. Because of increased globalization, these epidemics have threatened to become pandemics. In 2014, an Ebola outbreak occurred in West Africa. A virus causes Ebola. Long-term effects of Ebola may be joint problems and weakness. Many patients die from more severe problems, including organ failures, coma, and bleeding. By March 2016, more than 11,000 people had died from Ebola.

In 2015, another viral disease, called Zika, began affecting people in Brazil and then spread into other parts of South and Central America. Zika is spread through mosquito bites. Zika appears to have the greatest effect on unborn babies. It has led to a birth defect where a baby's head and brain are smaller than expected. Although the virus was first discovered in Africa in 1947, a large-scale outbreak did not occur until 2007, in Micronesia. In 2016, the World Health Organization (WHO) announced that Zika had become a global concern. Many believe that international travelers will spread Zika to more new areas over time.

The AIDS Pandemic Another major global health issue is a disease known as **AIDS**, which stands for acquired immunodeficiency syndrome. It attacks the immune system, leaving sufferers open to deadly infections. It is caused by a virus called human immunodeficiency virus (HIV). AIDS was first detected in the early 1980s. Since that time, it has claimed the lives of nearly 39 million people worldwide. By 2013, there were about 35 million people living with HIV or AIDS. In 2014, about 2 million people became infected with HIV. Although there is no cure for HIV, it can be controlled with medicines. Some of these medicines are expensive, making it difficult for people living in less-developed countries to get them.

AIDS is a worldwide problem, but about 70 percent of all persons infected with HIV live in sub-Saharan Africa. Many people dying of AIDS there are between the ages of 15 and 49. As a result, life expectancy in

Life Expectancy of Selected Countries of the World, 2015	
Country	**Life Expectancy**
Chad (Africa)	49.81
Afghanistan (Asia)	50.87
Namibia (Africa)	51.62
Nigeria (Africa)	53.02
Rwanda (Africa)	59.67
Ethiopia (Africa)	61.48
Haiti (North America)	63.51
Pakistan (Asia)	67.39
Iran (Asia)	71.15
Russia (Europe/Asia)	70.47
Thailand (Asia)	74.43
Turkey (Europe/Asia)	74.57
Colombia (South America)	75.48
China (Asia)	75.41
United States (North America)	79.68
New Zealand (Australia-Oceania)	81.05
Canada (North America)	81.76
Monaco (Europe)	89.52

Interpret Charts
About how much longer is the life expectancy in Colombia than in Afghanistan?

During business classes in Nepal sponsored by the U.S. Agency for International Development, young women learn about AIDS and how to communicate to others in their community that they should be tested for the disease.

these countries is much lower than elsewhere. The tragic loss of so many people of working age has also led to a smaller workforce in the region. In turn, this has caused a slowing of economic growth.

Since the 1990s, the world has made progress in slowing the spread of AIDS. In 2001, the United Nations issued the Declaration of Commitment on HIV/AIDS. This document set targets for halting the spread of AIDS. It also provided guidelines on how countries could pool their efforts. In 2011, there were 700,000 fewer new cases of HIV infection than in 2001. Still, rates of new HIV infection increased during that time in some developing countries. Although an AIDS vaccine doesn't currently exist, scientists remain hopeful that one will be developed in the near future.

Summary and Preview New technology such as genetic engineering and 3D printing has created a wealth of possibilities for improvement in medicine. However, the spread of disease continues. Pandemics can threaten the health of people across the world. In the next lesson, you will learn about the global economy.

Reading Check
Draw Conclusions
Why might a country ban travel during a pandemic?

Lesson 5 Assessment

Review Ideas, Terms, and People

1. a. **Define** What is genetics?

   b. **Explain** What is the connection between biotechnology and pharmaceuticals?

   c. **Predict** How could 3D printing revolutionize medicine in the near future?

2. a. **Draw Conclusions** What might be one way to prevent epidemics from becoming pandemics?

   b. **Identify** What viral disease affects the brains of unborn babies?

   c. **Summarize** How has AIDS affected economic growth in sub-Saharan Africa?

Critical Thinking

3. **Analyze Effects** Draw a graphic organizer like this one. In each of the outer circles, list one medical revolution that has improved the treatment of disease.

Technology Trends in Medicine

Trade and Economic Development

The Big Idea

The economies of the world's nations are tightly linked.

Main Ideas

- Over the past 50 years, the economies of developed and developing nations have changed.

- Globalization has led to increased free trade as well as new political and economic problems worldwide.

- Developing nations face economic challenges and sometimes receive aid from international organizations.

Key Terms and People

developed nations
developing nations
gross domestic product (GDP)
standard of living
inflation
recession
free trade
securities
World Bank
International Monetary Fund (IMF)

If YOU were there . . .

You are attending a family gathering. At one point, a group of your relatives starts talking about politics. This leads to a discussion about a new trade agreement that removes trade barriers between the United States and several other countries. Some of your relatives are in favor of the agreement and say that the cost of certain foreign goods will go down. Other relatives oppose the agreement, claiming that consumers will buy fewer American goods, which will hurt American workers.

Which opinion do you agree with more?

Changing Economies

After World War II, many Western European countries followed the lead of the United States. They built strong free market economies. In a free market economy, individuals and businesses have the freedom to make most economic decisions. The government has little say in what is produced and how it is produced. The countries became economic powerhouses by producing a wide variety of goods and services.

These thriving nations became known as **developed nations**. After all, they had developed all the skills and tools needed to be experts in the production of manufactured goods. Countries that had not become fully industrial became known as **developing nations**. Often, developing nations provided the raw materials developed nations used in manufacturing.

Today, there are many more developing nations than developed nations. Many nations in South America, Africa, and Asia are considered developing nations. So, too, are Eastern European countries that gained independence in the 1990s. At that time, these countries moved to a free market economy from a command economy. A command economy is one in which the government makes all economic decisions.

The Effects of New Economies As time passed, the economies of developed and developing nations changed. Many companies began to move manufacturing jobs from developed nations to developing nations. The movement of manufacturing jobs allowed the companies to keep prices low and stay competitive. Workers in developing nations were willing to work for less money than those in developed countries. Also, many were happy to have a job, even it meant doing the same thing over and over again. The movement of jobs allowed companies to trim manufacturing costs. It also gave them a way to make the best use of their human resources. Human resources are the skills and knowledge of workers.

Workers in developed countries began to shift into other kinds of jobs. Businesses in developed countries created many new types of jobs in information-related industries. These jobs include computer programmers, web developers, and other high-tech positions. These jobs appealed to workers in developed nations because they paid well. As with manufacturing jobs, in recent years some of these jobs have now shifted to developing nations because of lower labor costs.

Gross Domestic Product The shift in where products are made has improved many of the world's economies. The global change has affected the **gross domestic product (GDP)** of nations around the world. GDP is the value of goods and services produced each year by a country. For example, goods and services made in the United States in 2015 were worth $18 trillion, so that figure is its GDP. In contrast, the developing nation of Tanzania in Africa had a GDP of $46 billion. Developed countries have higher GDPs than developing countries. Per capita GDP is the measure of the total GDP divided by the number of people in the country.

There are many reasons why one country may have a larger GDP than another. These include the natural resources available and the number of people available to work, along with the skills they possess.

Economists use GDP as a way to judge how well a nation's economy has performed. They also use a nation's GDP to measure its **standard of living**. Standard of living refers to how well people in a nation can meet their needs and wants. Do they have enough to eat, a safe place to live, and clothing suitable to their environment? Can they afford a luxury item, such as a car, a computer, a television, or a cell phone?

Other factors can be used to measure the economic success of a nation. Experts closely study

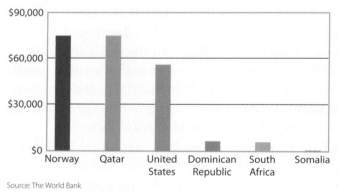

Per Capita GDP for Selected Nations, 2015

Source: The World Bank

Interpret Graphs
What might be the reasons for the difference between per capita GDP of Somalia and Qatar?

Adult Literacy Rates for Select Nations, 2015

Being able to read and write generally increases a person's earning power. Countries with high literacy rates are more likely to be economically successful.

Country	Literacy Rate
Jordan	95.4%
Haiti	60.7%
Russia	99.7%
India	71.2%
Brazil	92.6%
Mali	38.7%

Reading Check
Summarize What factors can measure a nation's economic success?

unemployment rates. They also look at literacy rates, or the percent of people in a country who can read. People who can read usually have higher earning power. In addition, they examine a country's trade balance, or difference between the value of exports and imports. A country that exports much more than it imports is in the best economic shape. That is because it earns more money on items it exports and spends less on items it imports. Experts also look for clues to economic strength by examining infant mortality rate. A low infant mortality rate indicates that a country can properly care for its population.

A nation's GDP increases when its economy is booming. Such a period of growth is called expansion because the economy is growing larger. During a boom period, most people have jobs, and businesses are doing well. However, expansion can also cause economic problems.

Inflation is one problem that often surfaces during good times for an economy. Inflation is a continuing increase in the prices of goods and services. People have more income to spend during good economic times. The demand for goods and services rises because people can afford to buy them. Prices inflate, or rise, as customers compete to buy goods and services. Sometimes, prices rise faster than wages. People have to spend more but do not get more for their money.

Good economic times cannot last forever. Economies can expand only so much before they begin to decline. When this happens, inflation stops and business activity slows down. A severe drop in an economy may become a **recession**, a time of very slow economic activity. During a recession, businesses fail, people lose their jobs, and profits fall. Sometimes, an economy may sink even lower. In that case, a depression may occur. During a depression, unemployment is very high. Unemployed people cannot buy goods or services, so businesses suffer or close. During a recession or a depression, a nation's GDP decreases.

Economic Interdependence and Global Trade

Trade has connected the economies of places around the world for centuries. Today, global trade takes place at a much faster pace than ever before because of improvements in transportation and communication. Cargo ships have grown larger and faster, and specially designed airplanes now move goods at record speeds. Telecommunication, computers, and the Internet have globalized trade and made global buying and selling quick and easy. In addition, large corporations have expanded around the world.

Multinational corporations often locate factories in developing nations, where labor and other costs are lower.

Multinational Corporations Companies that operate in a number of different countries are called multinational corporations. Examples include Nike, Samsung, and Toyota. All these companies sell the products and services they offer to places around the world. They also have manufacturing plants, offices, and stores in many different countries. For their manufacturing plants, they select spots where raw materials or labor are cheapest. They often produce different parts of their products on different continents. The companies then ship the various parts to another location to be assembled. The corporations find that having a presence in a country makes its citizens more likely to buy its products and services.

Many developing nations want multinational corporations to invest in them because they create jobs. Some developing nations offer multinational corporations a promise of low taxes to encourage them to do business there. After all, multinational corporations create jobs and expand the economy of a nation. With additional money coming in because of such globalization, developing countries can improve their infrastructure. In this way, governments are better able to meet the needs of their citizens.

Expanding Free Trade Trading globally helps many countries around the world expand their economies. Therefore, they look for ways to encourage other nations to trade with them. For example, many countries now encourage **free trade**. Free trade is the ending of trade barriers among nations. One type of trade barrier is tariffs. These are taxes on goods imported from another country. As early as 1947, nations began discussing ways to open up trade. The result of these discussions was the General Agreement on Tariffs and Trade (GATT). Over the years, many countries have ended tariffs. As a result, free trade has expanded. Since 1995, the World Trade Organization (WTO) has overseen the GATT. The WTO ensures that trade among nations flows as smoothly and freely as possible.

Regional Trade Blocs In 1951, a group of European nations set up a trade bloc to help strengthen the nations' economies. A trade bloc is an organization to promote free trade among member countries. Six years later, another organization formed. This organization was called the European Economic Community (EEC). Over time, the group has grown and is now known as the European Union (EU).

By 2015, twenty-eight nations were EU members. Membership now includes countries in Eastern Europe, such as Lithuania and Croatia. Many of the EU members have adopted a common European currency called the euro. However, the EU has become controversial in some countries because of its complex rules and concerns about immigration. In 2016, citizens of the United Kingdom voted to leave the EU, 52 percent to 48 percent. More than 30 million people voted in the election.

The success of the EU inspired countries in other regions. They, too, began to make trade agreements. The North American Free Trade Agreement (NAFTA) was put into effect in 1994. This agreement reduced trade restrictions among Canada, the United States, and Mexico. Organizations in Asia, Africa, and elsewhere have also formed regional trade alliances. However, not everyone agrees that free trade is a good idea. Supporters of free trade believe that it encourages trade and grows the economy. Opponents think free trade takes jobs away from local people. Debate over the pros and cons of free trade continues.

Dependence on Oil Because of globalization, worldwide demand for energy and other resources has increased. In addition, interdependence among nations has risen. What happens financially in one country can directly affect the economy of another country. These and other trends have led to political and economic problems.

For the past 50 years, oil has been one of the main sources of energy for the world's nations. Many nations don't have this natural resource and depend on the export of this energy source from oil-rich countries. Decisions made by countries that make up the Organization of Petroleum Exporting Countries (OPEC) can have worldwide effects. A change in oil exports can disrupt economies everywhere. In fact, any interruption in the flow of oil from place to place can cause huge problems.

Prices for oil fluctuated in the early 2000s but, in general, remained fairly high. Then, beginning in 2014, prices took a nosedive because of an oversupply in the market. More countries were providing oil, so there

Many people argue that protected waters should be opened up to offshore oil-drilling platforms like the ones below in order to increase supply and keep prices low. Opponents believe that offshore drilling poses huge environmental dangers.

was much more in the market. At the same time, consumers, such as Chinese manufacturers, were demanding less oil than expected.

Lower prices have both positive and negative effects. Consumers can purchase oil more cheaply. However, oil companies earn less money. This change in the profits gained by oil companies affects economies of nations around the world. Oil prices today rise and fall from day to day based on current events.

A Global Economic Crisis Historically, buying a small piece of a company, a share of its stock, has been a good way to increase wealth. Investments in stocks can earn more money than simply placing money in savings accounts. You may wonder how individuals and companies go about investing in stocks. Today, most of the world's nations have stock exchanges. A stock exchange is a market for buying and selling **securities**. Securities refer to investments in companies or governments. A stock is an example of a security. In some ways, stock exchanges can be considered a mall for buying and selling stocks.

Some stock exchanges have grown extremely large. Two of the largest, the New York Stock Exchange and NASDAQ, are based in the United States. The name NASDAQ stands for the National Association of Securities Dealers Automated Quotations. Other stock exchanges include the Tokyo Stock Exchange and the Financial Times Stock Exchange of London.

People and companies can find economic success from the purchase of stock. When a business does well, people who own stock gain part of its profits. Yet the trade of stock can have negative personal and global effects. One such negative global effect took place in the recent past.

Beginning in 2007, several factors combined to cause a worldwide recession. Housing prices in the United States had skyrocketed. Banks were making housing loans, or mortgages, with few restrictions. The banks then sold the mortgages to other investors. They did not inform the investors of the risks involved in buying the mortgages.

Quick Facts

Arguments for and Against Economic Globalization

For

- promotes peace through trade
- raises the standard of living
- creates jobs in developing countries
- promotes investment in developing nations
- creates a sense of world community

Against

- creates conflict because of an unfair system
- benefits developed nations more than developing nations
- takes jobs from high-paid laborers in developed countries
- may underpay workers in developing nations
- hurts local cultures

As time passed, some people who borrowed too much money for their homes found that they could no longer pay for them. They lost their homes as a result. The demand for homes began to fall, which led to a drop in prices. Investors lost large amounts of money. Many of these investors were banks and other financial institutions. Housing lending slowed down dramatically. Many investors faced bankruptcy. Because the United States plays such a significant role in the global economy, countries around the world began to experience economic crises as well. Millions of people worldwide lost their homes and savings. An overall decline in the global economy resulted, and many people lost their jobs.

Governments took action to deal with the crisis. For example, some countries cut government spending. The world economy remained weak for several years. By 2010, the economies of many countries had rebounded, yet some remained weak. European countries that continued to suffer economically included Greece, Italy, and Spain. Many economists predicted that significant fluctuations in the global economy could be a continuing trend in the years to come.

Reading Check
Analyze Effects
How do trade agreements affect economies in developing and developed countries?

Economic Aid for Developing Nations

Even though developed nations have found ways to strengthen their economies, developing nations still struggle to gain economic stability. They lack the necessary technologies, well-trained workers, and money for investments.

Developed nations have provided aid to developing nations through the work of international organizations. One of these organizations is the **World Bank**. The World Bank provides loans for large projects in countries that need them. These loans could pay for education projects, health care, or infrastructure, such as roads. Another organization is the **International Monetary Fund (IMF)**. The IMF offers emergency loans to countries in financial trouble.

IMF Managing Director Christine Lagarde, right, meets with Cameroon's minister of finance, Alamine Ousmane Mey, in Cameroon.

Although these organizations can play an important role in development, they also have drawbacks. The World Bank, for example, might fund a project that it considers worthy, like the building of a large dam. Yet the project may not help the people of a country. The IMF has been criticized for setting harsh financial conditions for countries receiving loans. For instance, the IMF might require a country to cut its government spending drastically. Nevertheless, developed nations remain interested in helping developing nations. They view developing nations as sources of raw materials and potential markets for goods. Developed nations would like the economies of developing nations to become strong and stable.

Summary The economies of both developed and developing nations have changed in recent years. Reasons for this change include political changes, the creation of multinational corporations, and the establishment of free trade agreements. Global interdependence has led to some problems, such as a global recession. International organizations provide loans to developing nations. These loans can help economies grow stronger and more stable.

Lesson 6 Assessment

Review Ideas, Terms, and People

1. **a. Draw Conclusions** Do you think a nation's gross domestic product (GDP) accurately measures its economic success?

   b. Describe How does inflation affect a nation's economy?

2. **a. Explain** What factors have contributed to globalization in recent decades?

   b. Summarize Why do some people oppose free trade?

   c. Analyze Why was there an oversupply of oil on the market beginning in 2014?

3. **a. Compare** What do the World Bank and the International Monetary Fund (IMF) have in common?

   b. Make Inferences Why do you think loans from international organizations have had varying impacts on countries?

Critical Thinking

4. **Compare and Contrast** Copy the graphic organizer. Use it to compare and contrast the changes that have occurred in the economies of developing and developed nations in recent years.

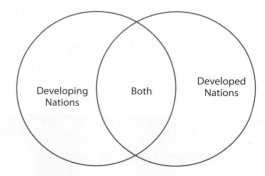

Developing Nations | Both | Developed Nations

Social Studies Skills

Research Current Events

Define the Skill

A *current event* is a newsworthy event occurring in the present. Examples of current events include elections, wars, technological developments, and cultural achievements. Researching current events will help you to better understand the world we live in.

Learn the Skill

One way to research current events is to use the Internet. The Internet connects computers, called servers, around the world. Some servers are maintained by colleges and universities, libraries, and government agencies. Others are maintained by private companies, news networks, and individuals. Each webpage located in a server has its own address. This address is called a universal resource locator, or URL.

You need to be cautious when using the Internet to research current events. For example, some nonprofit websites provide only a certain point of view. The same goes for certain news websites. Also, anyone can write an online article. Even professional writers can be biased about a current event. When researching current events, make sure the websites are valid and the writing is balanced.

Use these tips when researching current events online.

1. Identify the purpose of the website. The part of the URL after http:// is the domain name. The letters after the last period are called the domain extension. The domain extension is helpful in determining a site's purpose. A **.com** extension indicates the website is maintained for profit. An **.edu** extension means the site is maintained by a college or university. A site with a **.gov** extension is maintained by the U.S. government. An **.org** extension indicates a site is maintained by a nonprofit organization.

2. Research the author of the online article. What is the author's background? For example, consider an online article about an election. Is it written by a high school student? Is it written by a politician? Or is it written by a well-known journalist?

3. Think critically about the purpose of the website and the article. Do they present merely factual information? Or are they trying to convince you of a position?

Practice the Skill

Choose one of the nongovernmental organizations mentioned in any of the lessons in this module. Visit its website and use it to answer the questions below.

1. What can you tell about the website based on its domain extension?

2. What is the purpose of the website?

3. Browse through the website. Find one important issue that it discusses, and write a short summary of it.

4. What other websites might you explore to find different opinions on this issue?

Review Vocabulary, Terms, and People

Complete each sentence by filling in the blank with the correct term or person.

1. _____ refers to a general increase in the prices of goods and services.

2. Ukrainian leader _____ was elected as president in 2014 and is determined to keep Ukraine democratic.

3. Today, many workers _____, or do their jobs by computers from home.

4. Many developing nations need to achieve _____ if they want to prevent environmental problems.

5. _____ is the movement to protect the natural world from destructive human activities.

6. Some countries have arrested or mistreated people for expressing _____ .

7. A _____ occurs when a disease affects many people over a wide area, particularly in different countries or continents.

8. A global _____ began in 2007 when people were unable to pay their mortgages.

9. In 1975, several nations signed the _____, which pledged to protect human rights, including freedom of movement.

Comprehension and Critical Thinking

Lesson 1
10. a. **Explain** What is the purpose of the Universal Declaration of Human Rights?

    b. **Describe** What is Amnesty International?

    c. **Recall** In which African nation did genocide occur during 1994?

Lesson 2
11. a. **Analyze** What led to the Arab Spring?

    b. **Explain** What occurred in Syria to stop the Arab Spring?

    c. **Predict Effects** Do you think the number of failed states in the world will decrease or increase over time? Why?

Lesson 3
12. a. **Identify** Which two nations agreed to merge their space-station programs in 1993?

    b. **Contrast** How are the Internet and the World Wide Web different?

    c. **Explain** Why does the West have a huge influence on many different cultures?

Lesson 4
13. a. **Summarize** What is happening to the population growth rate in some developed nations?

    b. **Describe** How does clear-cutting lead to a loss of natural resources?

    c. **Predict Effects** Do you think the Paris Agreement will succeed? Why or why not?

Lesson 5
14. a. **Describe** How is VR used in robotic surgery?

    b. **Contrast** How is an epidemic different from a pandemic?

    c. **Explain** What happened to the rate of new cases of HIV infection between 2001 and 2011?

Lesson 6
15. a. **Describe** What types of industries have multiplied in developed nations?

    b. **Identify** What areas do multinational corporations select for manufacturing plants?

    c. **Evaluate** Do you think the pros of free trade outweigh the cons? Explain.

Review Themes

16. **Economics** Do you think free trade will increase or decrease over the next few decades? Why?

17. **Science and Technology** Why might more nations pursue space travel and exploration in the future?

Reading Skills (21ST CENTURY)

Categorize Use the Reading Skills taught in this module to answer the questions about the passage below.

> "So first, we'll do more to prevent threats and outbreaks. We're going to partner with countries to help boost immunization rates to stop the spread of preventable diseases. We'll work together to improve biological security so nations can store, transport, and work with dangerous pathogens safely. Here in the United States, we're working with our partners to find new ways to stop animal diseases from crossing over into people—which, of course, is how Ebola started. . . . Second, we'll do more to detect incidents and outbreaks. We'll help hospitals and health workers find ways to share information more quickly as outbreaks occur. We want to help countries improve their monitoring systems so they can track progress in real time. And we'll intensify our efforts to diagnose diseases faster. . . . "
>
> —Remarks by President Barack Obama at the Global Health Security Agenda Summit, September 26, 2014

18. What are two possible categories into which you could place information from the passage?

19. List one detail that could go in the first possible category. Then list one detail that could go in the second possible category.

Social Studies Skills

Research Current Events Use the Social Studies Skills taught in this module to answer *the questions about conducting Internet research on current events.*

20. *How might a government website show bias about a political event?*

21. *Imagine that a major international dispute occurs between Russia and the United States. You find two online articles about the dispute. One is written by a Russian reporter. One is written by an American reporter. Which online article would you trust more? Why?*

Focus On Writing

22. **Write an Editorial** Review the problems discussed in this module. Choose one problem you would like to learn more about. Use the Internet to conduct further research on the issue. Then write an editorial about how to solve the problem. Your editorial should provide both your opinion and as many facts as possible.

References

Atlas R2

Writing Workshops R14

English and Spanish Glossary R36

Index R62

Credits and Acknowledgments R92

Available Online:

- Reading Like a Historian
- Biographical Dictionary
- Close-Read Screencasts
- Economics Handbook
- Geography and Map Skills Handbook
- Skillbuilder Handbook

To understand the relative locations of Alaska and Hawaii, as well as the vast distances separating them from the rest of the United States, see the world map.

CANADA

MINNESOTA

Grand Forks
Fargo
Red River

Lake Superior

Duluth
Superior
Marquette
Sault Ste. Marie

MICHIGAN

MAINE

Augusta

Lake Champlain
Burlington
Montpelier
Portland

VT
NH
Concord
Manchester

WISCONSIN

Green Bay

Lake Michigan

Lake Huron

Hudson R.

Boston
Worcester
Providence

Sioux Falls

Minneapolis
St. Paul

Madison
Milwaukee

Grand Rapids
Saginaw
Lansing
Detroit

Rochester
Syracuse
Albany
Springfield
Hartford
CT RI

MA

Cape Cod

Minnesota River
Mississippi River

Buffalo
NEW YORK

Bridgeport
New Haven
Long Island Sound

Sioux City

IOWA

Cedar Rapids
Rockford
Chicago
Gary
South Bend
Fort Wayne

Ann Arbor
Toledo
Cleveland
Youngstown
Akron

Lake Erie

PENNSYLVANIA

Allentown
Harrisburg

Jersey City
Newark
Yonkers
New York City
Trenton

Long Island
40°N

Omaha
Lincoln

Davenport
Des Moines

Illinois River

Peoria

OHIO
Columbus

Susquehanna River

Pittsburgh
Philadelphia
Camden

NJ
Atlantic City

70°W

MISSOURI

Kansas City
Topeka
Kansas City

St. Louis
Springfield

East St. Louis

INDIANA
Indianapolis

ILLINOIS

Dayton
Cincinnati

WEST VIRGINIA

Baltimore
MD
Washington, D.C.
Annapolis

DE
Dover

Delaware Bay

ATLANTIC OCEAN

Wichita

Jefferson City

Lake of the Ozarks

Louisville
Evansville

Frankfort
Lexington

Charleston

VIRGINIA
Richmond

Chesapeake Bay

Springfield

Missouri River

Ohio River

KENTUCKY

Newport News
Norfolk
Virginia Beach

35°N

Keystone Lake

Tulsa
Fayetteville

Lake Barkley

Kentucky Lake

Nashville
Knoxville

Greensboro
Durham
Raleigh

Cape Hatteras

Winston-Salem

Asheville
Charlotte

NORTH CAROLINA

Eufaula Lake

ARKANSAS
Little Rock
Pine Bluff

Memphis

TENNESSEE
Chattanooga

Greenville

SOUTH CAROLINA
Columbia

Lake Texoma

Huntsville

Atlanta

Charleston

Dallas
Waco

MISSISSIPPI

Vicksburg
Jackson

Birmingham

ALABAMA

Meridian
Montgomery

GEORGIA
Macon
Columbus

Savannah

Savannah River
Sea Islands

Shreveport

Red River

Chattahoochee R.

Toledo Bend Reservoir

LOUISIANA

Baton Rouge

Mobile
Pensacola

Tallahassee

Jacksonville

Beaumont
Houston
Galveston

New Orleans
Biloxi
Chandeleur Islands

Gainesville

FLORIDA

Cape Canaveral

Orlando
Tampa

W N E S

St. Petersburg

Lake Okeechobee

BAHAMAS

25°N

Fort Myers

Fort Lauderdale
Miami

Gulf of Mexico

Cape Sable
Florida Keys

Straits of Florida

75°W

85°W
90°W
95°W
80°W

⊕ National capital
★ State capitals
• Other cities

0   100   200 Miles
0   100   200 Kilometers

Projection: Albers Equal Area

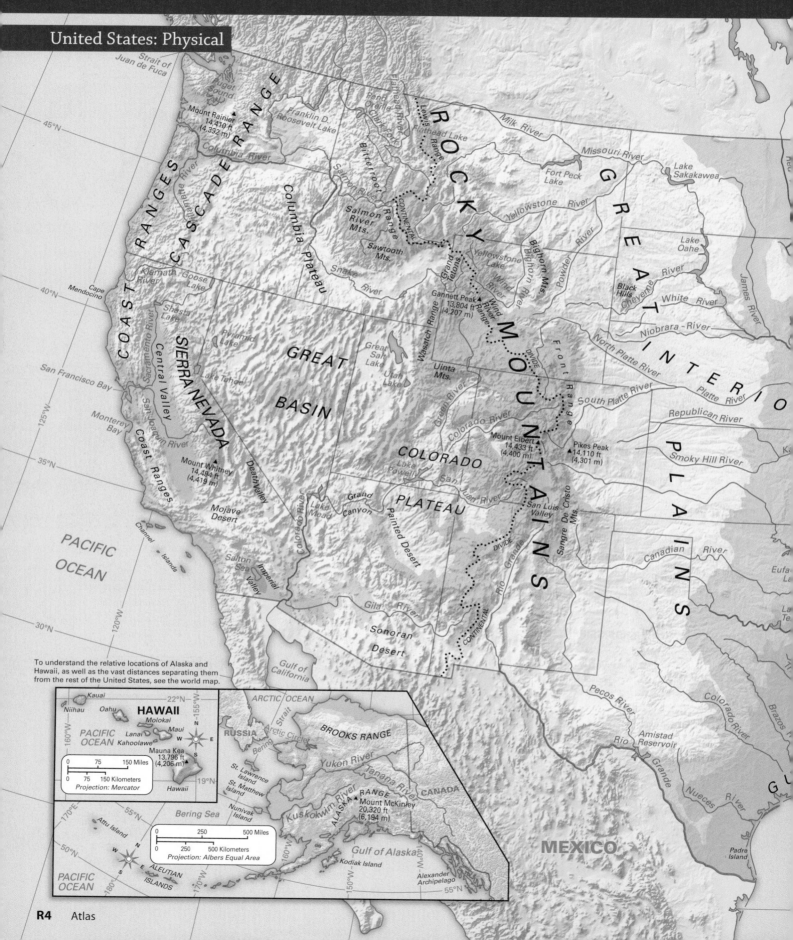

To understand the relative locations of Alaska and Hawaii, as well as the vast distances separating them from the rest of the United States, see the world map.

CANADA

Mesabi Range

Isle
Royale

Lake Superior

St. John River

St. Lawrence Seaway

St. Lawrence River

Longfellow Mts.

Penobscot River

Minnesota River

Wisconsin River

Lake
Huron

Lake Michigan

Lake
Champlain

Adirondack
Mts.

Hudson R.

Green
Mts.

White
Mts.

Connecticut River

Mississippi River

Des Moines River

Missouri River

Lake Ontario

Lake Erie

Cape Cod

Long Island Sound

Long Island

ALLEGHENY

PLATEAU

Allegheny R.

Catskill
Mts.

Susquehanna
River

APPALACHIAN MOUNTAINS

Delaware River

40°N

ansas R.

PLAINS

Illinois River

Scioto River

Wabash River

Ohio
River

Monongahela R.

Potomac River

Delaware
Bay

70°W

ATLANTIC
OCEAN

Lake of the
Ozarks

Kentucky
Lake

Lake
Barkley

Cumberland River

Kanawha River

James River

Chesapeake
Bay

Keystone
Lake

OZARK PLATEAU

White River

Cumberland Plateau

BLUE RIDGE MOUNTAINS

Roanoke River

Pamlico
Sound

35°N

aula
Lake

Arkansas River

Great Smoky
Mts.

Cape Hatteras

Lake
Texoma

Ouachita
Mts.

Tennessee River

Oconee River

Savannah River

ELEVATION

Feet   Meters

Red River

Saline River

Tombigbee River

Coosa River

PIEDMONT

Altamaha River

Sea Islands

13,120   4,000
6,560   2,000
1,640   500
656   200
(Sea level) 0   0 (Sea level)
Below   Below
sea level   sea level

Trinity River

Alabama R.

Chattahoochee River

COASTAL   PLAIN

Okefenokee
Swamp

0   100   200 Miles
0   100   200 Kilometers

Projection: Albers Equal Area

Toledo
Bend
Reservoir

Pearl River

Chandeleur
Islands

Mississippi
Delta

FLORIDA

Cape
Canaveral

80°W

s River

GULF

W   N   E
      S

25°N

Gulf of Mexico

FLORIDA PENINSULA

Lake
Okeechobee

BAHAMAS

95°W

90°W

85°W

The
Everglades

Cape Sable

Florida Keys

Straits of Florida

75°W

World: Political

Legend:

- ✪ National capital
- ● Other city

0 500 1,000 Miles
0 500 1,000 Kilometers

Projection: Mollweide

0 200 400 Miles
0 200 400 Kilometers

Projection: Mercator

	COUNTRY	CAPITAL
1	Antigua and Barbuda	St. Johns
2	St. Kitts and Nevis	Basseterre
3	Dominica	Roseau
4	St. Lucia	Castries
5	St. Vincent and the Grenadines	Kingstown
6	Barbados	Bridgetown
7	Grenada	St. George's

ARCTIC OCEAN
Greenland (DENMARK)
ALASKA (U.S.)
Arctic
ICELAND
60°N
CANADA
Nuuk
Aleutian Islands
Vancouver
Winnipeg
NORTH AMERICA
Ottawa Montreal
Chicago Toronto
40°N UNITED STATES New York City
Washington, D.C.
ATLANTIC OCEAN
Rabat
Los Angeles Casablanca
MOROCCO
Houston
Bermuda (U.K.)
Western Sahara (Claimed by Morocco)
MEXICO
Tropic of Cancer
20°N
MAURITANIA MALI
Mexico City
Nouakchott
HAWAII (U.S.)
CABO VERDE SENEGAL
Dakar BURKINA FASO
GAMBIA Bamako
GUINEA-BISSAU GUINEA GHANA
Caracas SIERRA CÔTE D'IVOIRE
PACIFIC OCEAN LEONE
VENEZUELA GUYANA LIBERIA
Bogotá Georgetown SURINAME
COLOMBIA Paramaribo French Guiana (FRANCE)
0° Equator
Quito
KIRIBATI ECUADOR
Galápagos Islands (ECUADOR)
PERU SOUTH AMERICA
BRAZIL
SAMOA American Samoa
Lima Brasília
BOLIVIA
La Paz
20°S Sucre
TONGA Rio de Janeiro
Tropic of Capricorn PARAGUAY
Asunción São Paulo
CHILE
ATLANTIC OCEAN
URUGUAY
Santiago Buenos Aires
ARGENTINA Montevideo
Falkland Islands (U.K.)
South Georgia (U.K.)
South Sandwich Islands
60°S
160°W 140°W 120°W SOUTHERN OCEAN
Antarctic Circle

Inset map:

90°W 80°W
FLORIDA (U.S.)
Nassau
BAHAMAS
70°W
Havana Tropic of Cancer
Gulf of Mexico
CUBA Turks and Caicos Is. (U.K.)
60°W
ATLANTIC OCEAN
20°N
Cayman Is. (U.K.) HAITI DOMINICAN REPUBLIC Virgin Islands (U.S. and U.K.)
JAMAICA Port-au-Prince
MEXICO Kingston Santo Domingo Puerto Rico (U.S.)
BELIZE Belmopan
GUATEMALA Caribbean Sea Guadeloupe (FRANCE)
Guatemala City HONDURAS Netherlands Antilles (NETHERLANDS) Martinique (FRANCE)
San Salvador Tegucigalpa
EL SALVADOR NICARAGUA Aruba (NETHERLANDS)
Managua Port-of-Spain
COSTA RICA Panama City TRINIDAD AND TOBAGO
San José 10°N
PANAMA VENEZUELA
PACIFIC OCEAN COLOMBIA GUYANA

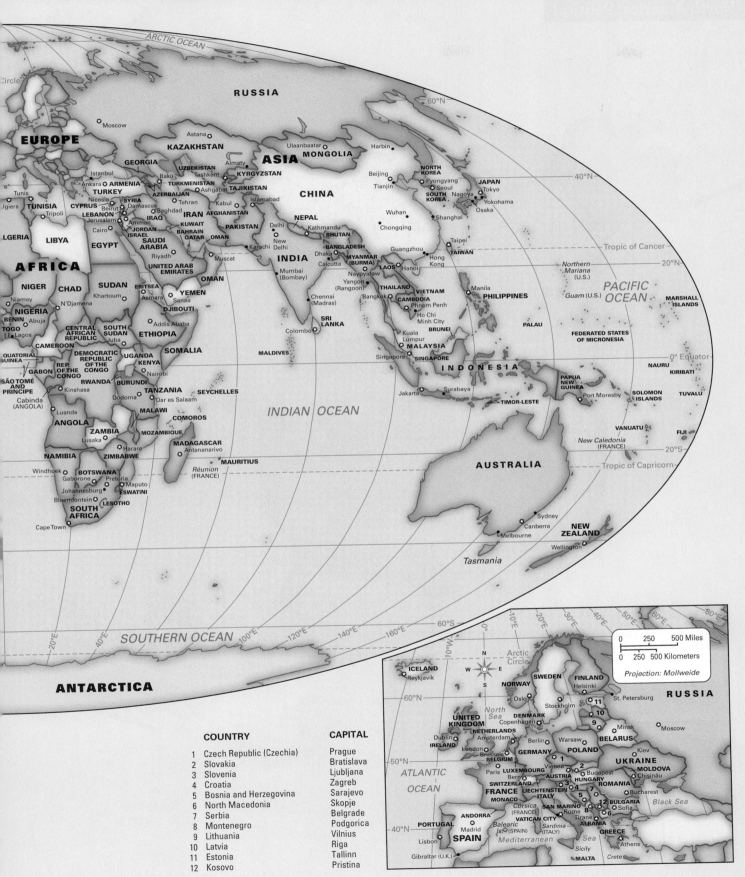

COUNTRY

1	Czech Republic (Czechia)
2	Slovakia
3	Slovenia
4	Croatia
5	Bosnia and Herzegovina
6	North Macedonia
7	Serbia
8	Montenegro
9	Lithuania
10	Latvia
11	Estonia
12	Kosovo

CAPITAL

Prague
Bratislava
Ljubljana
Zagreb
Sarajevo
Skopje
Belgrade
Podgorica
Vilnius
Riga
Tallinn
Pristina

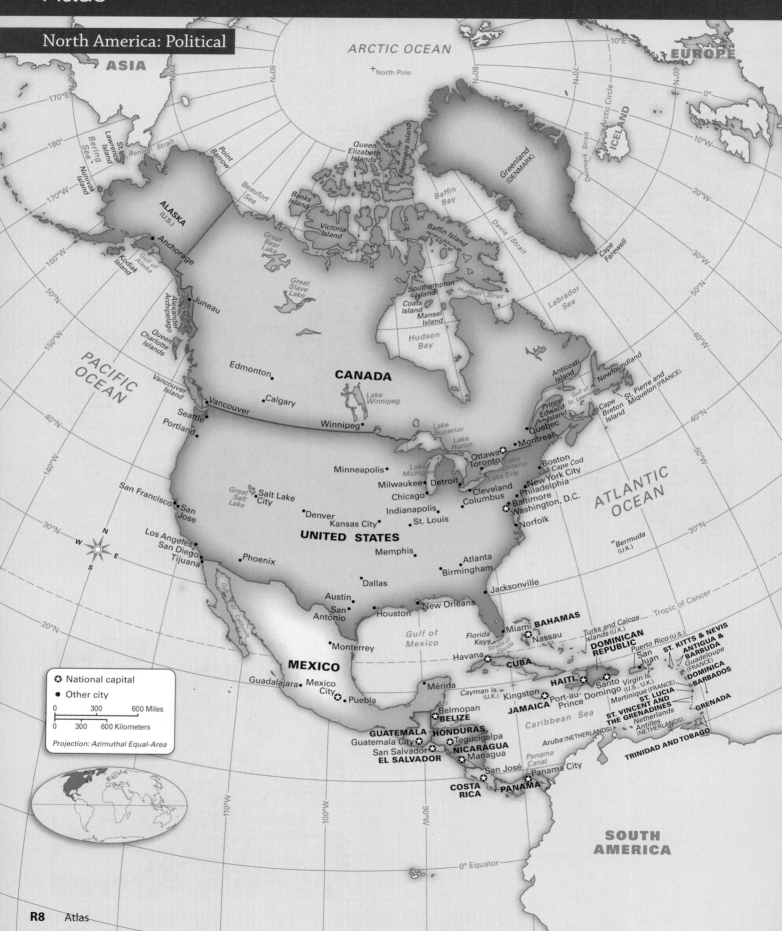

ASIA

ARCTIC OCEAN

EUROPE

North Pole

ICELAND

Greenland (DENMARK)

Queen Elizabeth Islands

Ellesmere Island

Baffin Bay

Banks Island

Beaufort Sea

Victoria Island

Baffin Island

Davis Strait

Cape Farewell

ALASKA (U.S.)

Anchorage

Great Bear Lake

Kodiak Island

Gulf of Alaska

Juneau

Great Slave Lake

Southampton Island

Hudson Strait

Labrador Sea

Alexander Archipelago

Coats Island

Mansel Island

Queen Charlotte Islands

Edmonton

CANADA

Hudson Bay

Anticosti Island

Newfoundland

PACIFIC OCEAN

Vancouver Island

Calgary

Lake Winnipeg

St. Pierre and Miquelon (FRANCE)

Vancouver

Prince Edward Island

Gulf of St. Lawrence

Seattle

Winnipeg

Quebec

Cape Breton Island

Portland

Lake Superior

Montreal

Minneapolis

Lake Michigan

Lake Huron

Ottawa

Toronto

Lake Ontario

Boston

Cape Cod

San Francisco

Milwaukee

Detroit

Lake Erie

New York City

ATLANTIC OCEAN

San Jose

Salt Lake City

Chicago

Cleveland

Philadelphia

Great Salt Lake

Denver

Indianapolis

Columbus

Baltimore

Washington, D.C.

UNITED STATES

Kansas City

St. Louis

Norfolk

Los Angeles

San Diego

Tijuana

Phoenix

Memphis

Bermuda (U.K.)

Dallas

Atlanta

Birmingham

Austin

San Antonio

Houston

New Orleans

Jacksonville

Tropic of Cancer

Monterrey

Gulf of Mexico

Florida Keys

Miami

BAHAMAS

Turks and Caicos Islands (U.K.)

Nassau

DOMINICAN REPUBLIC

Puerto Rico (U.S.)

ST. KITTS & NEVIS

ANTIGUA & BARBUDA

MEXICO

Havana

CUBA

Straits of Florida

HAITI

San Juan

Guadeloupe (FRANCE)

DOMINICA

Guadalajara

Mexico City

Mérida

Cayman Is. (U.K.)

Kingston

Santo Domingo

Virgin Is. (U.S., U.K.)

Martinique (FRANCE)

BARBADOS

Puebla

JAMAICA

Port-au-Prince

ST. LUCIA

ST. VINCENT AND THE GRENADINES

GRENADA

Belmopan

BELIZE

Caribbean Sea

Netherlands Antilles (NETHERLANDS)

GUATEMALA

HONDURAS

Tegucigalpa

Aruba (NETHERLANDS)

TRINIDAD AND TOBAGO

Guatemala City

NICARAGUA

Managua

Panama Canal

San Salvador

EL SALVADOR

San José

Panama City

SOUTH AMERICA

COSTA RICA

PANAMA

Equator

National capital

Other city

0   300   600 Miles

0   300   600 Kilometers

Projection: Azimuthal Equal-Area

South America: Political

Atlas **R9**

Europe: Political

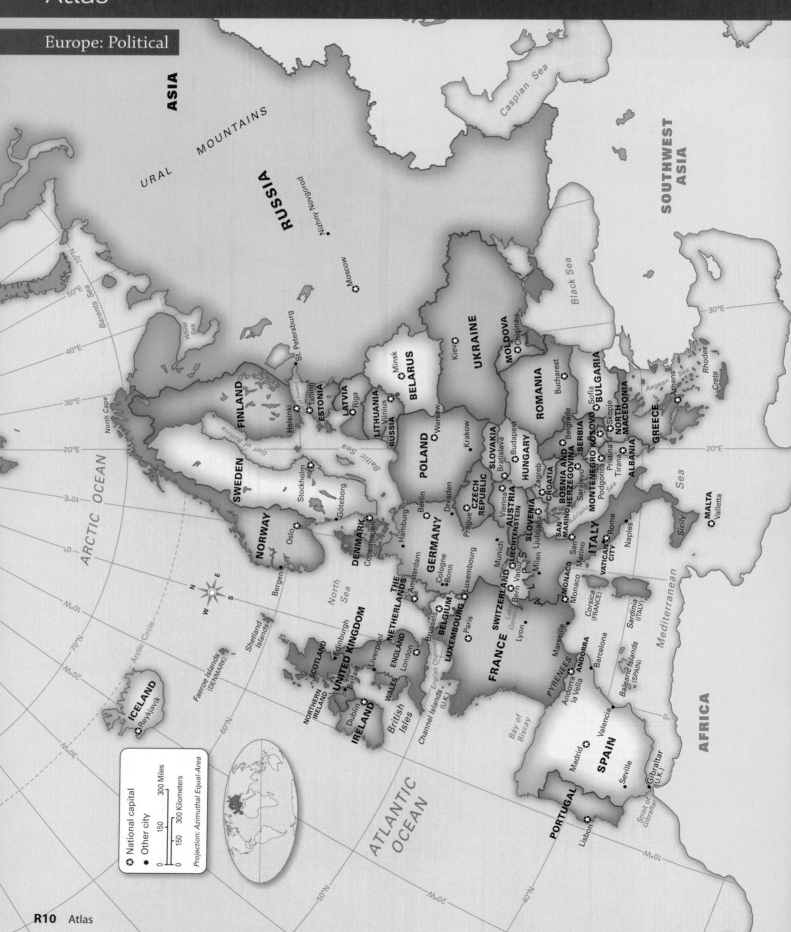

ASIA

URAL MOUNTAINS

RUSSIA

Nizhniy Novgorod

Moscow

Caspian Sea

SOUTHWEST ASIA

Black Sea

Barents Sea

White Sea

St. Petersburg

Gulf of Finland

Helsinki

FINLAND

Tallinn
ESTONIA

Riga
LATVIA

Vilnius
LITHUANIA

Minsk
BELARUS

Kiev

UKRAINE

MOLDOVA
Chişinău

ROMANIA
Bucharest

BULGARIA
Sofia

Aegean Sea

Rhodes

Crete

30°E

North Cape

ARCTIC OCEAN

SWEDEN

Stockholm

Göteborg

Gulf of Bothnia

Baltic Sea

RUSSIA

Warsaw

POLAND

Kraków

SLOVAKIA
Bratislava

HUNGARY
Budapest

Zagreb
CROATIA

Belgrade
SERBIA

SAN MARINO

BOSNIA AND
HERZEGOVINA
Sarajevo

MONTENEGRO
Podgorica

KOSOVO
Pristina

Skopje
NORTH
MACEDONIA

Tirana
ALBANIA

GREECE
Athens

MALTA
Valletta

Sicily

NORWAY

Oslo

Bergen

DENMARK
Copenhagen

Hamburg

Berlin

Dresden

GERMANY

Cologne
Bonn

CZECH
REPUBLIC
Prague

Vienna
AUSTRIA

SLOVENIA
Ljubljana

Milan

Zagreb

San Marino

ITALY
Rome

VATICAN
CITY

Naples

Sardinia
(ITALY)

Mediterranean Sea

North Sea

Shetland Islands

Faeroe Islands
(DENMARK)

ICELAND
Reykjavík

SCOTLAND
Edinburgh

NORTHERN
IRELAND
Belfast

IRELAND
Dublin

British Isles

Liverpool

WALES

ENGLAND
London

UNITED KINGDOM

NETHERLANDS
Amsterdam

Brussels
BELGIUM

Luxembourg
LUXEMBOURG

Paris

FRANCE

Lyon

Marseille

SWITZERLAND
Bern

Geneva
Lake
Geneva

LIECHTENSTEIN
Vaduz

Munich

ALPS

MONACO
Monaco

Corsica
(FRANCE)

English Channel

Channel Islands
(U.K.)

Bay of Biscay

ANDORRA
Andorra
la Vella

PYRENEES

Barcelona

Balearic Islands
(SPAIN)

Valencia

Madrid

SPAIN

Seville

Gibraltar
(U.K.)

Strait of Gibraltar

PORTUGAL
Lisbon

AFRICA

ATLANTIC OCEAN

Arctic Circle

70°N

60°N

50°N

40°N

30°N

10°W

20°W

30°W

40°E

50°E

30°E

20°E

10°E

0°

10°W

0°

N
W E
S

National capital
Other city

150   300 Miles
0   150   300 Kilometers

Projection: Azimuthal Equal-Area

Atlas

Asia: Political

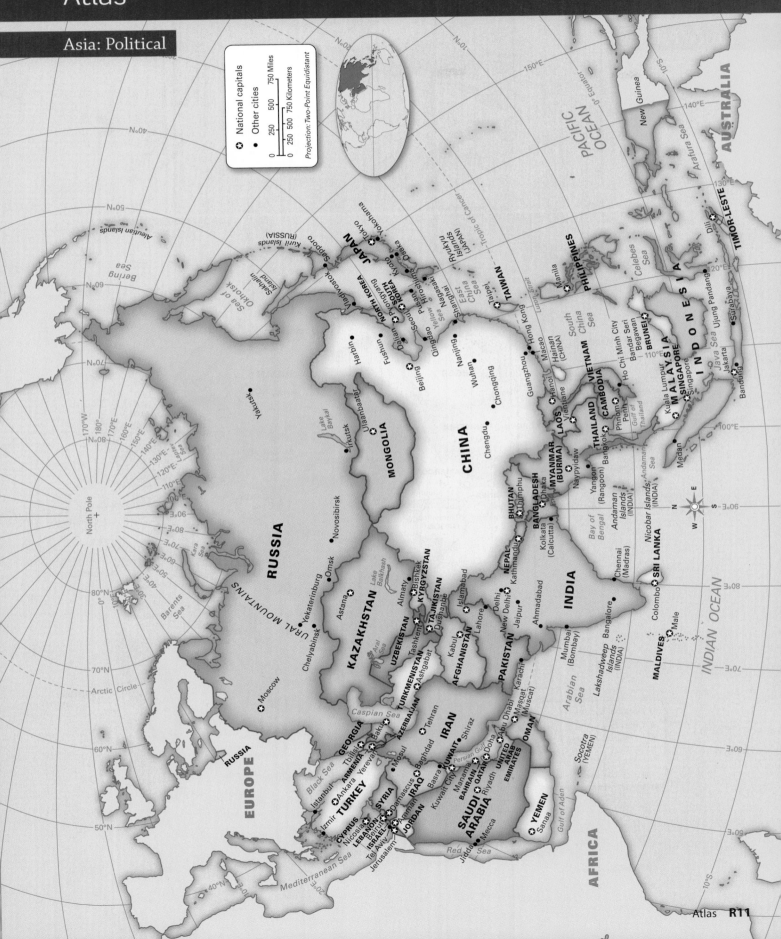

National capitals ✪
Other cities •

750 Miles
500
250

750 Kilometers
500
250

Projection: Two-Point Equidistant

PACIFIC OCEAN

New Guinea

AUSTRALIA

TIMOR-LESTE

Dili

PHILIPPINES

Manila

Celebes Sea

INDONESIA

Kuala Lumpur

MALAYSIA

SINGAPORE

Singapore

BRUNEI

Bandar Seri Begawan

Java Sea Ujung Pandang

Jakarta

Bandung

Surabaya

JAPAN

Tokyo

Yokohama

Sapporo

Kuril Islands (RUSSIA)

Sakhalin Island (RUSSIA)

Sea of Okhotsk

Bering Sea

Aleutian Islands

Osaka

Kyoto

Hiroshima

Nagasaki

Ryukyu Islands (JAPAN)

NORTH KOREA

Pyongyang

SOUTH KOREA

Seoul

Pusan

Vladivostok

TAIWAN

Taipei

East China Sea

Tropic of Cancer

Hong Kong

Macao

Hainan (CHINA)

South China Sea

VIETNAM

Ho Chi Minh City

Hanoi

Vientiane

LAOS

CAMBODIA

Phnom Penh

THAILAND

Bangkok

Gulf of Thailand

MYANMAR (BURMA)

Naypyidaw

Yangon (Rangoon)

Bay of Bengal

Andaman Islands (INDIA)

Andaman Sea

Nicobar Islands (INDIA)

Medan

Harbin

Fushun

Dalian

Qingdao

Yellow Sea

Shanghai

Nanjing

Beijing

Wuhan

Chongqing

Chengdu

Guangzhou

CHINA

MONGOLIA

Ulaanbaatar

Lake Baykal

Irkutsk

Yakutsk

RUSSIA

North Pole

Novosibirsk

Omsk

URAL MOUNTAINS

Yekaterinburg

Chelyabinsk

Astana

KAZAKHSTAN

Aral Sea

Lake Balkhash

Almaty

Bishkek

KYRGYZSTAN

Tashkent

UZBEKISTAN

TAJIKISTAN

Dushanbe

Ashgabat

TURKMENISTAN

Kabul

AFGHANISTAN

Islamabad

Lahore

PAKISTAN

Karachi

NEPAL

Kathmandu

BHUTAN

Thimphu

BANGLADESH

Dhaka

Kolkata (Calcutta)

Delhi

New Delhi

Jaipur

Ahmadabad

Mumbai (Bombay)

Bangalore

Chennai (Madras)

INDIA

SRI LANKA

Colombo

Lakshadweep Islands (INDIA)

MALDIVES

Male

INDIAN OCEAN

Arabian Sea

Socotra (YEMEN)

Gulf of Aden

YEMEN

Sanaa

AFRICA

Red Sea

Jidda

Mecca

SAUDI ARABIA

Riyadh

BAHRAIN

Manama

QATAR

Doha

UNITED ARAB EMIRATES

Abu Dhabi

OMAN

Masqat (Muscat)

Persian Gulf

KUWAIT

Kuwait City

Basra

IRAQ

Baghdad

Mosul

IRAN

Tehran

Shiraz

Caspian Sea

AZERBAIJAN

Baku

GEORGIA

Tbilisi

ARMENIA

Yerevan

Ankara

TURKEY

Istanbul

Izmir

CYPRUS

Nicosia

LEBANON

Beirut

SYRIA

Damascus

ISRAEL

Tel Aviv

Jerusalem

JORDAN

Amman

Mediterranean Sea

Black Sea

Barents Sea

Kara Sea

Laptev Sea

EUROPE

RUSSIA

Moscow

Arctic Circle

Aleutian Islands

Africa: Political

EUROPE

SOUTHWEST ASIA

Strait of Gibraltar

Azores (PORTUGAL)

Madeira (PORTUGAL)

Casablanca • Rabat

Algiers ✪ Tunis ✪

Mediterranean Sea

TUNISIA

✪ Tripoli

MOROCCO

Canary Islands (SPAIN)

El Aaiún

ALGERIA

LIBYA

EGYPT

Alexandria

Giza ✪ Cairo

WESTERN SAHARA (Claimed by Morocco)

Tropic of Cancer

MAURITANIA

✪ Nouakchott

MALI

NIGER

CHAD

SUDAN

ERITREA

Red Sea

Gulf of Aden

CABO VERDE

✪ Praia

SENEGAL

Dakar ✪

GAMBIA

Banjul ✪

Bamako ✪

BURKINA FASO

Niamey ✪

Lake Chad

N'Djamena ✪

Khartoum ✪

Asmara ✪

DJIBOUTI

Djibouti ✪

Bissau ✪

GUINEA-BISSAU

GUINEA

Conakry ✪

Freetown ✪

SIERRA LEONE

Ouagadougou ✪

BENIN

TOGO

GHANA

NIGERIA

✪ Abuja

CENTRAL AFRICAN REPUBLIC

SOUTH SUDAN

ETHIOPIA

Addis Ababa ✪

SOMALIA

CÔTE D'IVOIRE

Yamoussoukro ✪

Monrovia ✪

LIBERIA

Abidjan

Accra ✪

Lomé ✪

Lagos

Porto-Novo

Gulf of Guinea

Malabo ✪

CAMEROON

Yaoundé ✪

Bangui ✪

Juba ✪

Mogadishu ✪

EQUATORIAL GUINEA

SÃO TOMÉ AND PRÍNCIPE

São Tomé ✪

Libreville ✪

GABON

REPUBLIC OF THE CONGO

UGANDA

Kampala ✪

Kisangani •

KENYA

Nairobi •

Lake Victoria

RWANDA

Kigali ✪

Mombasa •

Pemba

Victoria ✪

SEYCHELLES

0° Equator

ATLANTIC OCEAN

N W E S

Brazzaville ✪

Kinshasa

CABINDA (ANGOLA)

DEMOCRATIC REPUBLIC OF THE CONGO

Bujumbura ✪

BURUNDI

TANZANIA

Dodoma ✪

Lake Tanganyika

Zanzibar

Dar es Salaam •

INDIAN OCEAN

St. Helena (U.K.)

Luanda ✪

Lake Malawi (Nyasa)

COMOROS

Moroni ✪

ANGOLA

Lubumbashi •

ZAMBIA

Lusaka ✪

MALAWI

Lilongwe ✪

Harare ✪

MOZAMBIQUE

Antananarivo ✪

MAURITIUS

Port Louis ✪

Tropic of Capricorn

NAMIBIA

Windhoek ✪

BOTSWANA

Gaborone ✪

ZIMBABWE

Bulawayo •

MADAGASCAR

Réunion (FRANCE)

Johannesburg •

Pretoria ✪

Bloemfontein •

Maputo ✪

Mbabane ✪

Maseru ✪

ESWATINI

LESOTHO

SOUTH AFRICA

Cape Town •

✪ National capital
• Other city

0   250   500 Miles

0   250   500 Kilometers

Projection: Azimuthal Equal-Area

The Pacific: Political

NORTH AMERICA

ASIA

NORTH PACIFIC OCEAN

SOUTH PACIFIC OCEAN

Tropic of Cancer

Equator

Tropic of Capricorn

International Date Line

Hawaiian Islands

Hawaii (U.S.)

Midway Island (U.S.)

Johnston Island (U.S.)

Kingman Reef (U.S.)

Palmyra Island (U.S.)

Washington Island

Fanning Island

Jarvis I. (U.S.)

Howland I. (U.S.)

Baker I. (U.S.)

McKean I.

Gardner

Phoenix Islands

KIRIBATI

Starbuck Island

POLYNESIA

Marquesas Islands (FRANCE)

Tuamotu Archipelago (FRANCE)

Rapa Island (FRANCE)

French Polynesia

Society Islands (FRANCE)

Tahiti (FRANCE)

Papeete

Tūbuai Islands (FRANCE)

Pitcairn (U.K.)

Pitcairn Island

Ducie Island

Easter Island (CHILE)

Manihiki Island

Cook Islands (NEW ZEALAND)

Rarotonga Island

Tokelau (N.Z.)

SAMOA

Apia

American Samoa

Pago Pago

Niue (N.Z.)

TONGA

Nuku'alofa

Wallis & Futuna (FR.)

FIJI

Suva

Kermadec Islands (N.Z.)

Chatham Islands (N.Z.)

Auckland

North Island

Wellington

Christchurch

South Island

NEW ZEALAND

Bounty Islands (N.Z.)

Auckland Islands (NEW ZEALAND)

TUVALU

Funafuti

MARSHALL ISLANDS

Eniwetok I.

Kwajalein Island

Majuro

Tarawa

Gilbert Islands

Wake Island (U.S.)

MICRONESIA

NAURU

Palikir

SOLOMON ISLANDS

Honiara

Guadalcanal I.

MELANESIA

Espíritu Santo I.

VANUATU

Malekula I.

Port-Vila

New Caledonia (FRANCE)

Loyalty Islands (FRANCE)

Noumea

Norfolk Island (AUSTRALIA)

Northern Marianas (U.S.)

Bonin Islands (JAPAN)

Volcano Islands (JAPAN)

Guam (U.S.)

Agana

FEDERATED STATES OF MICRONESIA

Truk Is.

Bismarck Archipelago

PAPUA NEW GUINEA

Port Moresby

New Guinea

Ngerulmud

PALAU

Coral Sea

Philippine Sea

South China Sea

Christmas Island (AUSTRALIA)

Arafura Sea

Timor Sea

Darwin

Perth

Adelaide

Melbourne

Hobart

Tasman Sea

Sydney

Canberra

Brisbane

AUSTRALIA

INDIAN OCEAN

Legend:
- ✪ National capital
- ● Other city

1,000 Miles

1,000 Kilometers

500

Projection: Azimuthal Equal-Area

N E W S

Comparing and Contrasting Societies

ASSIGNMENT
Write a paper comparing and contrasting two early human societies.

TIP: USE A GRAPHIC ORGANIZER
A Venn diagram can help you see ways that the two societies are similar and different.

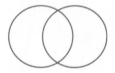

Comparing means finding likenesses between or among things. Contrasting means finding differences. You often compare and contrast things to understand them better and see how they are related.

1. Prewrite

Getting Started Unlike most essays, a compare-and-contrast paper has two subjects. However, it still has only one big idea, or thesis. For example, your idea may be to show how two societies dealt with the same problem or to show how two societies changed over time.

Begin by choosing two subjects. Then identify specific points of similarities and differences between the two. Support each point with historical facts, examples, and details.

Organizing Your Information Choose one of these two ways to organize your points of comparison.

- Present all the points about the first subject and then all the points about the second subject: AAABBB, or block style.
- Alternate back and forth between the first subject and the second subject: ABABAB, or point-by-point style.

2. Write

This framework will help you use your notes to write a first draft.

A WRITER'S FRAMEWORK

Introduction
- Clearly identify your two societies.
- Give background information readers will need in order to understand your points of comparison between the societies.
- State your big idea, or main purpose in comparing and contrasting these two societies.

Body
- Present your points of comparison in block style or point-by-point style.
- Compare the two societies in at least two ways, and contrast them in at least two ways.
- Use specific historical facts, details, and examples to support each of your points.

Conclusion
- Restate your big idea.
- Summarize the points you have made in your paper.
- Expand on your big idea, perhaps by relating it to your own life, to other societies, or to later historical events.

3. Evaluate and Revise

Evaluate Use the following questions to discover ways to improve your paper.

EVALUATION QUESTIONS FOR A COMPARE-AND-CONTRAST PAPER

- Do you introduce both of the societies in your first paragraph?
- Do you state your big idea, or thesis, at the end of your introduction?
- Do you present two or more similarities and two or more differences between the two societies?

- Do you use either the block style or point-by-point style of organization?
- Do you support your points of comparison with enough historical facts, details, and examples?
- Does your conclusion restate your big idea and summarize your main points?

Revise When you are revising your paper, you may need to add compare-and-contrast clue words. They will help your readers see the connections between ideas.

Clue Words for Similarities	Clue Words for Differences
also, another, both, in addition, just as, like, similarly, too	although, but, however, in contrast, instead, on the other hand, unlike

4. Proofread and Publish

Proofread Before sharing your paper, you will want to polish it by correcting any remaining errors. Look closely for mistakes in grammar, spelling, capitalization, and punctuation. To avoid two common grammar errors, make sure that you have used the correct form of *–er* or *more* and *–est* or *most* with adjectives and adverbs when making comparisons.

Publish One good way to share your paper is to exchange it with one or more classmates. After reading each other's papers, you can compare and contrast them. How are your papers similar? How do they differ? If possible, share papers with someone whose big idea is similar to yours.

5. Practice and Apply

Use the steps and strategies outlined in this workshop to write your compare-and-contrast paper.

A Description of a Historical Place

TIP: ORGANIZE DETAILS
Organize the details you gather in one of these ways.

- **Spatial Order** Arrange details according to where they are. You can describe things from right to left, top to bottom, or faraway to close up.
- **Chronological Order** Arrange details in the order they occurred or in the order that you experienced them.
- **Order of Importance** Arrange details from the most to least important or vice versa.

If a picture is worth a thousand words, then a thousand words could add up to a good description. Writers turn to description when they want to explain what a place is like—what you would see if you were there, or what you might hear, smell, or touch.

1. Prewrite

Pick a Subject and a Main Idea Think about the civilizations of ancient Mesopotamia, Egypt, and India. Which civilization seems most interesting to you? What villages, cities, or buildings seem interesting? Select one place and use this textbook, the Internet, or sources in your library to find out more about it.

You also need to decide on your point of view about your subject. For example, was this place scary, exciting, or overwhelming?

Choose Details As you conduct your research, look for details to show your readers what it would have been like to actually be in that place.

- **Sensory Details** What color(s) do you associate with your subject? What shape or shapes do you see? What sounds would you hear if you were there? What could you touch—rough walls, dry grass, a smooth, polished stone?
- **Factual Details** How big was this place? Where was it located? When did it exist? If people were there, what were they doing?

When you choose the details to use in your description, think about your point of view about this place. If it was an exciting place, choose details that will help you show that.

2. Write

This framework will help you use your notes to write a first draft.

A WRITER'S FRAMEWORK

Introduction
- Identify your subject and your point of view about it.
- Give your readers any background information that they might need.

Body
- Describe your subject, using sensory and factual details.
- Follow a consistent and logical order.

Conclusion
- Briefly summarize the most important details about the place.
- Reveal your point of view about the place.

3. Evaluate and Revise

Evaluate Use the following questions to discover ways to improve your paper.

> **EVALUATION QUESTIONS FOR A DESCRIPTION OF A PLACE**
>
> - Do you immediately catch the reader's interest?
> - Do you use sensory and factual details that work together to create a vivid picture of your subject?
> - Do you clearly state your point of view or most important idea?
> - Is the information organized clearly?
> - Do you end the description by summarizing the most important details?

Revise We often help others understand or imagine something by making a comparison. Sometimes we compare two things that are really very much alike. For example, "The city grew like San Diego did. It spread along a protected harbor." At other times we compare two things that are not alike. These comparisons are called figures of speech, and they can help your readers see something in an interesting way.

- Similes compare two unlike things by using words such as *like* or *so*.

  Example *The city center curved around the harbor like a crescent moon.*

- Metaphors compare two unlike things by saying one is the other.

  Example *The city was the queen of the region.*

When you evaluate and revise your description, look for ways you can make your subject clearer by comparing it to something else.

4. Proofread and Publish

- Make sure you use commas correctly with a list of details.

  Example *The temple was 67 feet high, 35 feet wide, and 40 feet deep.*

- Find or create a picture of the place you have described. Ask a classmate or a family member to read your description and compare it to the picture.

5. Practice and Apply

Use the steps and strategies outlined in this workshop to write your description of an ancient place.

TIP: SHOW LOCATION

When describing the physical appearance of something, make sure you use precise words and phrases to explain where a feature is located. Some useful words and phrases for explaining location are *below, beside, down, on top, over, next to, to the right,* and *to the left.*

Why Things Happen

ASSIGNMENT
Write an expository essay explaining one of these topics.

- Why the Aryans developed the caste system

- Why Confucius is considered the most influential teacher in Chinese history

TIP: ORGANIZE INFORMATION
Essays that explain *why* should be written in a logical order. Consider using one of these ways.

- **Chronological order,** the order in which things happened

- **Order of importance,** the order of the least important reason to the most important, or vice versa.

Why do civilizations so often develop in river valleys? Why did early people migrate across continents? You learn about the forces that drive history when you ask why things happened. Then you can share what you learned by writing an expository essay, explaining why events turned out as they did.

1. Prewrite

Consider Topic and Audience Choose one of the two topics in the assignment, and then start to think about your big idea. Your big-idea statement might start out like this.

- The Aryans developed the caste system to . . .
- Confucius is considered the most influential teacher in Chinese history because he . . .

Collect and Organize Information You will need to collect information that answers the question *Why*. To begin, review the information on the topic in the textbook. You can find more information on your topic in the library or on the Internet.

You should not stop searching for information until you have at least two or three answers to the question *Why*. These answers will form the points to support your big idea. Then take another look at your big idea. You may need to revise it or add to it to reflect the information you have gathered.

2. Write

Here is a framework that can help you write your first draft.

A WRITER'S FRAMEWORK

Introduction

- Start with an interesting fact or question.
- Identify your big idea.
- Include any important background information.

Body

- Include at least one paragraph for each point supporting your big idea.
- Include facts and details to explain and illustrate each point.
- Use chronological order or order of importance.

Conclusion

- Summarize your main points.
- Using different words, restate your big idea.

3. Evaluate and Revise

Evaluate Effective explanations require clear, straightforward language. Use the following questions to discover ways to improve your draft.

EVALUATION QUESTIONS FOR AN EXPOSITORY ESSAY

- Does your essay begin with an interesting fact or question?
- Does the introduction identify your big idea?
- Have you developed at least one paragraph to explain each point?
- Is each point supported with facts and details?

- Have you organized your points clearly and logically?
- Did you explain any unusual words?
- Does the conclusion summarize your main points?
- Does the conclusion restate your big idea in different words?

Revise Reread your draft. See whether each point is connected logically to the main idea and the other points you are making. If needed, add transitions—words and phrases that show how ideas fit together.

To connect points and information in time, use words such as *after, before, first, later, soon, eventually, over time, as time passed,* and *then.* To show order of importance, use transitional words and phrases such as *first, last, mainly, to begin with,* and *more important.*

4. Proofread and Publish

Proofread If you create a bulleted or numbered list, be sure to capitalize and punctuate the list correctly.

- **Capitalization:** It is always acceptable to capitalize the first word of each item in the list.

- **Punctuation:** (1) If the items are sentences, put a period at the end of each. (See the list in the tip above.) (2) If the items are not complete sentences, you usually do not need any end punctuation.

Publish Share your explanation with students from another class. After they read it, ask them to summarize your explanation. How well did they understand the points you wanted to make?

5. Practice and Apply

Use the steps and strategies in this workshop to write your explanation.

A Social Studies Report

ASSIGNMENT
Collect information and write an informative report on a topic related to the Hebrews or the ancient Greeks.

TIP: NARROW THE TASK

Broad: Sparta

Less Broad: Women and Girls in Sparta

Focus Question: What was life like for women and girls in Sparta?

The purpose of a social studies report is to share information. Often, this information comes from research. You begin your research by asking questions about a subject.

1. Prewrite

Choose a Subject You could ask many questions about the topic you have just studied.

- Why was Ruth an important person in the history of the Jewish religion?
- What was the role of mythology in the lives of the ancient Greeks?
- What were the most important accomplishments of Pericles?

Jot down some topics that interested you. Then, brainstorm a list of questions about one or more of these topics. Make sure your questions are narrow and focused. Choose the question that seems most interesting.

Find Historical Information Use at least three sources besides your textbook to find information on your topic. Good sources include

- books, maps, magazines, newspapers
- television programs, movies, videos
- Internet sites, CD-ROMs, DVDs

Keep track of your sources of information by writing them in a notebook or on cards. Give each source a number as shown below.

Encyclopedia article
① Littleton, C. Scott. "Mythology." World Book Encyclopedia. 2000.
Book
② Hamilton, Edith. Mythology. Boston: Little, Brown and Company, 1998.
Internet site
③ Lindemans, Micha F. "Greek Mythology: Persephone." Encyclopedia Mythica. 27 April 2004. http://www.pantheon.org.

Take Notes Take notes on important facts and details from your sources. Carefully record all names, dates, and other information from sources. Copy any direct quotation word for word and enclose the words in quotation marks. Along with each note, include the number of its source and its page number.

TIP: STATEMENT OR QUESTION
Your big idea statement can be a statement of the point you want to make in your paper.

- The ancient Greeks used mythology to explain nature.

It can also be a question, similar to your original research question.

- How did the ancient Greeks use mythology to explain their lives?

TIP: MAKE THE MOST OF YOUR OUTLINE
If you write each of your topics and subtopics as a complete sentence, you can use those sentences to create your first draft.

State the Big Idea of Your Report You can easily turn your original question into the big idea for your report. If your question changes a bit as you do your research, rewrite it before turning it into a statement. The big idea of a report is often, but not always, stated in the first paragraph.

Organize Your Ideas and Information Sort your notes into topics and subtopics. Put them in an order that is logical, that will make sense to your reader. We often use one of these ways to organize information.

- placing events and details in the order they happened
- grouping causes with their effects
- grouping information by category, usually in the order of least-to-most important

Here is a partial outline for a paper on Greek mythology.

Big Idea: The ancient Greeks told myths to explain the world.

I. Purpose of mythology in ancient Greece
   A. Greeks' questions about the world around them
   B. Greeks' use of myths for answers
II. Myths about everyday events in the Greeks' lives
   A. The myth of Hestia, goddess of the family
   B. The myth of Hephaestus, god of metallurgy and fire
III. Myths about the natural world of the Greeks
   A. The myth of Apollo, god of the sun
   B. The myth of Persephone, goddess of the seasons

2. Write

It is good to write a first draft fairly quickly, but it's also helpful to organize it as you go. Use the following framework as a guide.

A WRITER'S FRAMEWORK

Introduction

- Start with a quotation or an interesting historical detail.
- State the big idea of your report.
- Provide any historical background readers need in order to understand your big idea.

Body

- Present your information under at least three main ideas.
- Write at least one paragraph for each of these main ideas.
- Add supporting details, facts, or examples to each paragraph.

Conclusion

- Restate your main idea, using slightly different words.
- Close with a general comment about your topic, or tell how the historical information in your report relates to later historical events.

Study a Model Here is a model of a social studies report. Study it to see how one student developed a social studies paper. The first and the concluding paragraphs are shown in full. The paragraphs in the body of the paper are summarized.

INTRODUCTORY PARAGRAPH

Attention grabber

Statement of Big Idea

> The ancient Greeks faced many mysteries in their lives. How and why did people fall in love? What made rain fall and crops grow? What are the planets and stars, and where did they come from? Through the myths they told about their heroes, gods, and goddesses, the Greeks answered these questions. They used mythology to explain all things, from everyday events to forces of nature to the creation of the universe.

BODY PARAGRAPHS

The first body paragraph opens with a statement about how the Greeks used myths to explain their daily lives. Then two examples of those kinds of myths are given. The student summarizes myths about Aphrodite, goddess of love, and Hephaestus, god of metallurgy and fire.

In the next paragraph, the student shows how the Greeks used myths to explain the natural world. The example of such a story is Persephone and her relationship to the seasons.

The last paragraph in the body contains the student's final point, which is about creation myths. The two examples given for these myths are stories about Apollo, god of the sun, and Artemis, goddess of the moon.

CONCLUDING PARAGRAPH

The first two sentences restate the thesis.

The last three sentences make a general comment about the topic, Greek myths.

> The Greeks had a huge number of myths. They needed that many to explain all of the things that they did and saw. Besides explaining things, myths also gave the Greeks a feeling of power. By praying and sacrificing to the gods, they believed they could affect the world around them. All people want to have some control over their lives, and the Greeks' mythology gave them that feeling of control.

Notice that each paragraph is organized in the same way as the entire paper. Each paragraph expresses a main idea and includes information to support that main idea. One big difference is that not every paragraph requires a conclusion. Only the last paragraph needs to end with a concluding statement.

3. Evaluate and Revise

It is important to evaluate your first draft before you begin to revise it. Follow the steps below to evaluate and revise your draft.

EVALUATING AND REVISING AN INFORMATIVE REPORT

- Does the introduction grab the readers' interest and state the big idea of your report?
- Does the body of your report have at least three paragraphs that develop your big idea? Is the main idea in each paragraph clearly stated?
- Have you included enough information to support each of your main ideas? Are all facts, details, and examples accurate? Are all of them clearly related to the main ideas they support?

- Is the report clearly organized? Does it use chronological order, order of importance, or cause and effect?
- Does the conclusion restate the big idea of your report? Does it end with a general comment about your topic?
- Have you included at least three sources in your bibliography? Have you included all the sources you used and not any you did not use?

4. Proofread and Publish

Proofread To correct your report before sharing it, check the following.

- the spelling and capitalization of all proper names for specific people, places, things, and events
- punctuation marks around any direct quotation
- punctuation and capitalization in your bibliography

Publish Choose one or more of these ideas to share your report.

- Create a map to accompany your report. Use a specific color to highlight places and routes that are important in your report.
- File a copy of your report in your school's library for other students' reference. Include illustrations to go with the report.
- If your school has an Internet site, you might post your report there. See if you can link to other sources on your topic.

5. Practice and Apply

Use the steps and strategies outlined in this workshop to research and write an informative social studies report.

TIP: BIBLIOGRAPHY

- Underline the titles of all books, television programs, and Web sites.
- Use quotation marks around titles of articles and stories.

Historical Problem and Solution

ASSIGNMENT
Write about a problem the Romans faced and what their solution was or what you think would have been a better solution.

History is the story of how individuals have solved political, economic, and social problems. Learning to write an effective problem-solution paper will be useful in school and in many other situations.

1. Prewrite

Identify a Problem Think of a problem the Romans faced. Look at the problem closely. What caused it? What were its effects? Here is an example.

Problem: The Goths overran Rome.

Solution A: Pay the Goths a huge ransom to leave Rome. [Caused other groups to attack in the hope of getting similar ransoms]

Solution B: Attack other groups. [Could cause other groups to stop attacking Rome, allowing Rome to gain power]

Find a Solution and Proof Compare the Roman solution to the problem (A) to one they didn't try (B). Choose either the Roman solution or your own solution to write about. Your explanation should answer these questions.

- How does the solution address the cause of the problem?
- How does the solution fix the effects of the problem?

Use historical evidence to support what you say about the problem.

- facts, examples, or quotations
- comparisons with similar problems your readers know about

2. Write

This framework can help you clearly explain the problem and its solution.

A WRITER'S FRAMEWORK

Introduction
- Tell your reader what problem the Romans faced.
- Explain the causes and effects of the problem.
- State your purpose in presenting this problem and its solution.

Body
- Explain the solution.
- Connect the solution directly to the problem.
- Give supporting historical evidence and details that show how the solution deals with the problem.

Conclusion
- Summarize the problem and the solution.
- Discuss how well the solution deals with the problem.

3. Evaluate and Revise

Evaluate Now you'll want to evaluate your draft to see where you can improve your paper. Try using the following questions to decide what to revise.

EVALUATION QUESTIONS FOR A HISTORICAL PROBLEM AND SOLUTION

- Does your introduction state the problem clearly and describe it fully?
- Does the introduction give causes and effects of the problem?
- Do you clearly explain how the solution relates to the problem?

- Do you give supporting historical evidence showing how the solution deals with the problem?
- Do you conclude by summarizing the problem and the solution?

Revise Revise your draft to make what you say clear and convincing. You may need to

- add historical facts, examples, quotations and other evidence to give your readers all the information they need to understand the problem and solution
- reorganize paragraphs to present information in a clear, logical order

4. Proofread and Publish

Proofread To improve your paper before sharing it, check the following.

- spelling of all names, places, and other historical information, especially Latin words, because they can be tricky
- punctuation around linking words such as *so, thus,* and *in addition* that you use to connect causes with effects and solutions with problems

Publish Choose one or more of these ideas to share your report.

- Create a poster that Roman leaders might put up to announce how they will solve the problem.
- Hold a debate between teams of classmates who have chosen similar problems but different solutions. Have the rest of the class vote on whose solutions are best.

5. Practice and Apply

Use the steps and strategies outlined in this workshop to write a problem-solution paper.

TIP: PROBLEM-SOLUTION CLUE WORDS

It's not enough simply to tell your reader what the problem and solution are. You need to show how they are related. Here is a list of words and phrases that will help you do so: *as a result, therefore, consequently, this led to, nevertheless,* and *thus.*

TIP: SEE YOUR PAPER AS OTHERS SEE IT.

To you, your paper makes perfect sense. To others, it may not. Whenever possible, ask someone else to read your paper. Others can see flaws and errors that you will never see. Listen closely to questions and suggestions. Do your best to see the other person's point before defending what you have written.

A Summary of a History Lesson

Write a summary of one lesson in a module you have read.

TIP: HOW LONG IS A SUMMARY?
Here are some guidelines you can use to plan how much to write in a summary. If you are summarizing

- only a few paragraphs, your summary should be about one third as long as the original.
- longer selections such as an article or textbook module, write one sentence for each paragraph or heading in the original.

After you read something, do you have trouble recalling what it was about? Many people do. Writing a summary briefly restating the main ideas and details of something you have read can help you remember it.

1. Prewrite

Read to Understand The first thing you need to do is to read the lesson at least twice.

- **Read** it straight through the first time to see what it is about.
- **Reread** it as many times as necessary to be sure you understand the main idea of the whole lesson.

Identify the Lesson's Main Idea Next, identify the main idea in each paragraph or for each heading in the lesson. Look back at the facts, examples, quotations, and other information in each of them. Ask yourself, *What is the main idea that they all support, or refer to?* State this idea in your own words.

Note Details Note the information that directly and best supports each main idea. Often, several details and examples are given to support a single idea. Choose only those that are most important and provide the strongest support.

2. Write

As you write your summary, refer to the framework below to help you keep on track.

A WRITER'S FRAMEWORK

Introduction

- Give the lesson number and title.
- State the main idea of the lesson.
- Introduce the first main heading in the lesson and begin your summary by identifying the main idea and supporting information under it.

Body

- Give the main idea, along with its most significant supporting details, for each heading in the lesson.
- Use words and phrases that show connections between ideas.
- Use your own words as much as you can, and limit quotations in number and length.

Conclusion

- Restate the main idea of the lesson.
- Comment on maps, charts, other visual content, or other features that were especially important or useful.

3. Evaluate and Revise

Now you need to evaluate your summary to make sure that it is complete and accurate. The following questions can help you decide what to change.

4. Proofread and Publish

Proofread Be sure to enclose all quotations in quotation marks and to place other marks of punctuation correctly before or after closing quotation marks.

- **Commas** and **periods** go **inside** closing quotation marks.
- **Semicolons** and **dashes** go **outside** closing quotation marks.
- **Question marks** and **exclamation points** go **inside** closing quotation marks **when they are part of the quotation** and **outside when they are not**.

Publish Team up with classmates who have written summaries on different lessons of the same module you have. Review one another's summaries. Make sure the summaries include all the main ideas and most significant details in each lesson.

Collect all the summaries to create a module study guide for your team. If possible, make copies for everyone on the team. You may also want to make extra copies so that you can trade study guides with teams that worked on other modules.

5. Practice and Apply

Use the steps and strategies outlined in this workshop to write a summary of one lesson of a module in the textbook.

TIP: FIND MAIN IDEAS IN A HISTORY MODULE
Boldfaced headings in textbooks usually tell what subject is discussed under those headings. The first and last sentences of paragraphs under headings can also be a quick guide to what is said about a subject.

TIP: USE SPECIAL HISTORICAL FEATURES
Don't forget to look at maps, charts, timelines, pictures, historical documents, and even study questions and assignments. They often contain important ideas and information.

Persuasion and Historical Issues

ASSIGNMENT
Write an essay stating your opinion on this topic or another historical topic of your choice:
All great empires are likely to end in the same way the Maya and Aztec empires did.

TIP: FACT VS. OPINION
A fact is a statement that can be proved true. Facts include

- measurements
- dates
- locations
- definitions

An opinion is a statement of a personal belief. Opinions often include judgmental words and phrases such as *better, should,* and *think.*

The study of history raises questions, or issues, that can be argued from both sides. Effective persuasive writing supports a point of view with evidence.

1. Prewrite

Take a Position Do you think all great empires will follow the same course as the Maya and Aztecs, or could an empire take a different course? Write a sentence that states your position, or opinion about, this topic or another topic.

Support Your Position To persuade your audience to agree with your position, you will need reasons and evidence. **Reasons** tell *why* a writer has a particular point of view. **Evidence** backs up, or helps prove, the reasons. Evidence includes facts, examples, and opinions of experts, such as historians. You can find this evidence in this textbook or other books recommended by your teacher.

Organize Reasons and Evidence Try to present your reasons and evidence in order of importance, so that you can end with your most persuasive points. Use transition words such as *mainly, last,* and *most important* to emphasize ideas.

2. Write

This framework can help you state your position clearly and present persuasive reasons and evidence.

A WRITER'S FRAMEWORK

Introduction

- Introduce the topic by using a surprising fact, quotation, or comparison to get your reader's attention.
- Identify at least two differing positions on this topic.
- State your own position on the topic.

Body

- Present at least two reasons to support your position.
- Support each reason with evidence (facts, examples, expert opinions).
- Organize your reasons and evidence in order of importance, with your most persuasive reason last.

Conclusion

- Restate your position.
- Summarize your supporting reasons and evidence.
- Project your position into history by using it to predict the course of current and future events.

3. Evaluate and Revise

Evaluate Use the following questions to evaluate your draft and find ways to make your paper more persuasive.

EVALUATION QUESTIONS FOR A PERSUASIVE ESSAY

- Does your introduction include an opinion statement that clearly states your position?
- Have you given at least two reasons to support your position?
- Do you provide persuasive evidence to back up your reasons?
- Are your reasons and evidence organized by order of importance, ending with the most important?
- Does your conclusion restate your position and summarize your reasons and evidence? Do you apply your opinion to current and future events?

Revise Strengthen your argument with loaded words. Loaded words are words with strong positive or negative connotations.

- Positive: *leader*
- Negative: *tyrant, despot*
- Neutral: *ruler, emperor*

Loaded words can add powerful emotional appeals to your reader's feelings and help persuade them to agree with your opinion.

4. Proofread and Publish

Proofread Keep the following guidelines in mind as you reread your paper.

- Wherever you have added, deleted, or changed anything, make sure your revision fits in smoothly and does not introduce any errors.
- Double-check names, dates, and other factual information.

Publish Team up with one of your classmates who has taken the same position you have. Combine your evidence to create the most powerful argument you can. Challenge a team that has taken an opposing position to a debate. Ask the rest of the class for feedback. *Which argument was more persuasive? What were the strengths and weaknesses of each position?*

5. Practice and Apply

Use the steps and strategies outlined in this workshop to write a persuasive paper.

TIP: USE A COMPUTER TO CHECK SPELLING IN HISTORY PAPERS
Whenever you can, use a spell-checker program to help you catch careless errors. However, keep in mind that it will not solve all your spelling problems.

- It will not catch misspellings that correctly spell other words, such as *their, they're,* and *there,* or *an* instead of *and.*
- It will highlight but not give the preferred spelling for many proper names.
- It cannot be relied upon for correct capitalization.

A Historical Narrative

TIP: ADD DETAILS
Help your audience get a feel for the setting by using sensory details. As you think about everyday life in the Middle Ages, make note of details that describe how things might have looked, felt, sounded, smelled, or tasted.

What was life like in Europe in the Middle Ages? Where did people live? How did they spend their days? You can learn more about history by researching and writing a narrative that is set in a different time and place.

1. Prewrite

Plan Character and Setting You should write your narrative from the point of view of someone who lived during that time.

- **The Narrator** Is the person telling your story a knight, a peasant, or a priest? A lady or a lady's maid?
- **The Event** What event or incident will your narrator experience? A jousting tournament? A Viking invasion? A religious pilgrimage? A famine or fire in the village?
- **The Setting** How will the time, between about AD 500 and 1500, and place, somewhere in Europe, affect this person? What will he or she want out of life or would fear or admire?

Develop a Plot Select an event or incident, and then ask yourself these questions.

- How would the event have unfolded? In other words, what would have happened first, second, third, and so on?
- What problem might your narrator face during this event? How could your narrator solve this problem?

2. Write

Have your narrator tell what happened in the first person, using the first-person pronouns *I, me, we,* and *us.* For example, *I woke up early. We stopped by a stream.* Then use the framework below to help you write your first draft.

A WRITER'S FRAMEWORK

Introduction	Body	Conclusion
• Grab the reader's attention.	• Start with the beginning of the incident or event, and present the actions in the order they happen.	• Show how the narrator solves his or her problem.
• Offer needed background information about the place and the people involved in the event.	• Build to a suspenseful moment when the outcome is uncertain.	• Explain how the narrator changes or how his or her life changes.

3. Evaluate and Revise

Evaluate Read through the first draft of your narrative. Then use the guidelines below to consider its content and organization.

EVALUATION QUESTIONS FOR A FICTIONAL HISTORICAL NARRATIVE

- Do you grab the reader's attention at the very beginning?
- Do you include background information to explain the time, place, and people involved in the event?
- Do you use first-person pronouns to show that your narrator is the central person in the event?

- Do you tell the actions in the order they happen?
- Do you show how the narrator solves the problem or how it is solved for him or her?
- Do you explain how the narrator changes as a result of the event?

Revise Before you share your narrative with others, have a classmate read it and retell the narrative to you. Add details at any point where his or her retelling seems uncertain or dull. Add transition words to show how events are connected in time.

4. Proofread and Publish

Proofread Weak word choice can drain the life from your narrative. Vague nouns and adjectives do little to spark the interest and imagination of readers. In contrast, precise words make your story come alive. They tell readers exactly what the characters and setting are like.

- **Vague Nouns or Pronouns** Words such as *man* and *it* tell your readers little. Replace them with precise words, such as *peasant* and *cottage*.
- **Vague adjectives** Would you prefer an experience that is *nice* or *fun*, or one that is *thrilling, exhilarating,* or *stirring*?

Publish You can publish your historical narrative by reading it aloud in class or by posting it on a class authors' wall. You may also publish all the narratives in your class as an Internet page or in a photocopied literary magazine.

5. Practice and Apply

Use the steps and strategies outlined in this workshop to write your historical narrative.

TIP: DESCRIBE ACTIONS
We communicate not only with our words but also with our actions. By describing specific actions—movements, gestures, and facial expressions—you can make people in your narrative live and breathe.

TIP: CONNECT EVENTS
To improve your narrative, use transition words such as *next, later,* and *finally* to show the order in which the events and actions happen.

Cause and Effect in History

Why did it happen? What happened as a result? Historians ask questions like these in order to study the causes and effects of historical events. In this way, they learn more about historical events and the links that form the chain between them.

1. Prewrite

Identify Causes and Effects A **cause** is an action or event that produces an effect, a result, or a condition. An **effect** is what happens as a result of an event or situation. To understand historical events, we sometimes look at causes, sometimes look at effects, and sometimes look at both. For example, we could look at the causes behind Columbus's discovery of a new land, but we could also limit our discussion to the effects.

Collect and Organize Information After choosing the topic you want to write about, gather information from this textbook, an encyclopedia, or another library source. You can use graphic organizers like the ones below to organize your information.

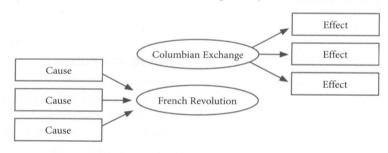

2. Write

You can use this framework to help you write your first draft.

A WRITER'S FRAMEWORK

Introduction

- Briefly identify the event that you will discuss (Columbian Exchange or French Revolution).

- Identify at least three causes or effects you will discuss.

Body

- Explain the causes or effects one at a time, providing supporting facts and examples for each.

- Present the causes or effects in order of importance, placing the most important last.

Conclusion

- Summarize your ideas about the causes or effects of the event.

3. Evaluate and Revise

Evaluate Use the following questions to discover ways to improve your draft.

Revise Keep a sharp eye out for false cause-and-effect relationships. The fact that one event happened after another does not mean that the first event caused the second.

> **Historical events:** *Columbus sailed to America in 1492. John Cabot sailed to Canada in 1497.*

> **False cause-and-effect relationship:** *Because Columbus sailed to America in 1492, John Cabot sailed to Canada in 1497. [Although Columbus's voyage happened before Cabot's discovery, the first event was not a cause.]*

4. Proofread and Publish

Proofread As you proofread your paper, check to see whether you have unclear pronoun references. They occur when you have two different nouns or phrases the pronoun might refer to.

> **Unclear** *After the explorers conquered the native peoples, many of them died. [Does them refer to the explorers or the native peoples?]*

> **Clear** *After the explorers conquered the native peoples, many of the native peoples died.*

Publish With classmates who wrote about the same topic, create a booklet of essays to display in your classroom or in the school library.

5. Practice and Apply

Use the steps and strategies outlined in this workshop to write an explanation of causes or effects.

TIP: SAVE THE BEST FOR THE LAST

Why would you place the most important cause or effect at the end of your paper rather than at the beginning? Think about your own experience. When you read something, what part do you remember best—the first or the last? When you hear a speech or your teacher presents a lesson, what sticks in your mind?

Most of the time, we remember what we heard or read last. That is why it is often a good idea to save the best for last.

TIP: SIGNAL CAUSES AND EFFECTS

Signal that you are about to discuss a cause or an effect with words and phrases like these.

- **Words and phrases that signal causes:** *because, due to, given that, since*
- **Words and phrases that signal effects:** *therefore, thus, consequently, so, as a result, for that reason*

A Biographical Narrative

ASSIGNMENT
Write a biographical narrative about a significant event in the life of a historical figure discussed in the textbook.

People have shaped the world. How does a single person, working alone or with others, change the course of history? What were the critical events in his or her life? How did living in a specific time and place affect those events? These are questions we ask as we try to understand our world.

1. Prewrite

TIP: ORGANIZE INFORMATION
Think about the historical forces that shaped the experiences and actions of the person you choose. Then select an important event in that person's life to show how he or she contributed to history. Arrange details about the event from most to least important.

- **Choose** a person who has, in some way, affected the history of the world since 1750.
- **Choose** a specific event or incident in the person's life. For example, you might choose to discuss Simon Bolívar's role in driving the Spanish out of Bolivia.

Collect and Organize Information

- **Look** for information about your topic in the library or on the Internet. Book-length biographies about the person you choose are a good source.
- **Identify** the parts of the event. Organize them in chronological, or time, order. Note specific details about the people, actions, and places important to the event.

2. Write

As you write your biographical narrative, refer to the framework below to help you keep on track.

A WRITER'S FRAMEWORK

Introduction
- Introduce the person and the event.
- Identify the importance of the event.

Body
- Write at least one paragraph for each major part of the event. Include specific details.
- Use chronological order to organize the parts of the event.

Conclusion
- Restate the importance of the event.
- Summarize the contributions of the person in a final paragraph.

3. Evaluate and Revise

Now you need to evaluate your biographical narrative and make sure that is complete and accurate. The following questions can help you decide what to change.

EVALUATION QUESTIONS FOR A BIOGRAPHICAL NARRATIVE

- Does your introduction identify the person and event and describe the importance of each?
- Do you have one paragraph for each major part of the event?
- Do you include specific details about people, actions, and places?

- Do you use chronological order (time order) to organize the parts of the event?
- Does your conclusion summarize the importance of the person and the event?

4. Proofread and Publish

Proofread Keep the following guidelines in mind as you proofread your paper.

- Make sure your transition words—such as *then*, *next*, *later*, and *finally*—help clarify the order of the actions that took place.
- Make sure you capitalized all proper names.

Publish Team up with classmates who have written biographical narratives on different people. Review one another's essays. Make sure that each biographical narrative clearly describes the contributions of a historical figure and an event from that person's life.

You can share your biographical narrative by creating a biographical dictionary. Collect all biographical narratives to create a class biographical dictionary for the textbook. If possible, make copies for everyone to use as a study tool.

5. Practice and Apply

Use the steps and strategies outlined in this workshop to write a biographical narrative of a historical figure from the textbook.

English and Spanish Glossary

Phonetic Respelling and Pronunciation Guide

Many of the key terms in this textbook have been respelled to help you pronounce them. The letter combinations used in the respelling throughout the narrative are explained in the following phonetic respelling and pronunciation guide. The guide is adapted from *Merriam-Webster's Collegiate Dictionary, 11th Edition; Merriam-Webster's Geographical Dictionary;* and *Merriam-Webster's Biographical Dictionary.*

MARK	AS IN	RESPELLING	EXAMPLE
a	alphabet	a	*AL-fuh-bet
ā	Asia	ay	AY-zhuh
ä	cart, top	ah	KAHRT, TAHP
e	let, ten	e	LET, TEN
ē	even, leaf	ee	EE-vuhn, LEEF
i	it, tip, British	i	IT, TIP, BRIT-ish
ī	site, buy, Ohio	y	SYT, BY, oh-HY-oh
	iris	eye	EYE-ris
k	card	k	KAHRD
ō	over, rainbow	oh	OH-vuhr, RAYN-boh
ů	book, wood	ooh	BOOHK, WOOHD
ò	all, orchid	aw	AWL, AWR-kid
òi	foil, coin	oy	FOYL, KOYN
aů	out	ow	OWT
ə	cup, butter	uh	KUHP, BUHT-uhr
ü	rule, food	oo	ROOL, FOOD
yü	few	yoo	FYOO
zh	vision	zh	VIZH-uhn

*A syllable printed in small capital letters receives heavier emphasis than the other syllable(s) in a word.

A

3D printing *n.* a way of manufacturing three-dimensional objects (p. 1069)
impresión 3D *s.* la fabricación de objetos tridimensionales; en lugar de papel, las impresoras 3D utilizan plásticos u otros materiales

Aborigines *n.* the native people of Australia (p. 874)
Aborígenes *s.* los pueblos originarios de Australia, que son también la cultura más antigua del mundo

acropolis (uh-KRAH-puh-luhs) *n.* a high hill upon which a Greek fortress was built (pp. 260, 301)
acrópolis *s.* colina elevada sobre la que se construyó una fortaleza griega

acupuncture (AK-yoo-punk-cher) *n.* the Chinese practice of inserting fine needles through the skin at specific points to cure disease or relieve pain (p. 211)
acupuntura *s.* práctica china que consisteen insertar pequeñas agujas en la piel en puntos específicos para curar enfermedades o aliviar el dolor

adobe *n.* a type of clay found in the southwestern United States (p. 651)
adobe *s.* un tipo de arcilla

afterlife *n.* life after death; much of Egyptian religion focused on the afterlife (p. 113)
la otra vida *s.* vida después de la muerte

agriculture *n.* farming (p. 56)
agricultura *s.* cultivo de la tierra

AIDS *n.* stands for acquired immunodeficiency syndrome; a disease that attacks the immune system, leaving sufferers open to deadly infections, such as tuberculosis (p. 1071)
SIDA (síndrome de inmunodeficiencia adquirido) *s.* enfermedad que ataca el sistema inmune, dejando expuestos los enfermos a las infecciones mortales, como la tuberculosis

Aksum *n.* a kingdom located along the Red Sea in what is today Ethiopia and Eritrea (p. 135)
Aksum *s.* un reino situado a lo largo del mar Rojo en lo que hoy es Etiopía y Eritrea

alchemy *n.* forerunner of chemistry (p. 775)
alquimia *s.* precursora de la química

alliance *n.* an agreement to work together (p. 277)
alianza *s.* acuerdo de colaboración

Allied Powers *n.* the name for the alliance formed by Great Britain, France, the Soviet Union, and the United States during World War II (p. 924)
Potencias aliadas *s.* el nombre de la alianza formada por Gran Bretaña, Francia, la Unión Soviética y los Estados Unidos durante la Segunda Guerra Mundial

alloy *n.* a mixture of two or more metals (p. 174)
aleación *s.* mezcla de dos o más metales

alphabet *n.* a set of letters that can be combined to form words (p. 90)
alfabeto *s.* conjunto de letras que pueden combinarse para formar palabras

ancestor *n.* a relative who lived in the past (p. 43)
antepasado *s.* pariente que vivió hace muchos años

animism *n.* the belief that bodies of water, animals, trees, and other natural objects have spirits (p. 476)
animismo *s.* creencia de que las masas de agua,los animales, los árboles y otros elementos naturales tienen espíritu

Anti-Imperialist League *n.* group that opposed a peace treaty between the United States and Spain and the creation of an American colonial empire (p. 879)
Liga antiimperialista *s.* grupo estadounidense que se opuso al tratado de paz de 1899 entre España y los Estados Unidos y a la creación de un imperio colonial americano

anti-Semitism *n.* hostility toward and discrimination against Jews (p. 934)
antisemitismo *s.* hostilidad y discriminación contra los judíos

apartheid *n.* policy of separation of races; it means "apartness" (p. 1006)
apartheid *s.* política de separación de razas establecida por el gobierno de Sudáfrica

Apostles (uh-PAHS-uhls) *n.* the 12 chosen disciples of Jesus who spread his teachings (p. 391)
apóstoles *s.* los 12 discípulos elegidos por Jesucristo que difundieron sus enseñanzas

aqueduct (A-kwuh-duhkt) *n.* a human-made raised channel that carries water from distant places (p. 372)
acueducto *s.* canal hecho por el ser humanoque transporta agua desde lugares alejados

Arab Spring *n.* democratic uprisings that occurred independently in Arab nations in 2011 (p. 1046)
Primavera árabe *s.* levantamientos democráticos que se produjeron de forma independiente en los países árabes en 2011

archaeology (ar-kee-AH-luh-jee) *n.* the study of the past based on what people left behind (p. 7)
arqueología *s.* estudio del pasado a través delos objetos que dejaron las personas tras desaparecer

architecture *n.* the science of building (p. 77)
arquitectura *s.* ciencia de la construcción

aristocracy (ar-i-STAHK-ruh-see) *n.* government that is made up of a small group of people from the highest social class in a society (p. 265)
aristocracia *s.* gobierno que se compone de un pequeño grupo de personas de la clase social más alta en una sociedad

aristocrat (uh-RIS-tuh-krat) *n.* a rich landowner or noble (p. 264)
aristócrata *s.* propietario de tierras o noble rico

arms race *n.* the competition between the United States and Soviet Union to build a stronger military (p. 959)
carrera armamentista *s.* la competencia para una mayor potencia militar

English and Spanish Glossary

artifact *n.* an object created and used by humans (p. 10)
artefacto *s.* objeto creado y usado por los humanos

astronomy *n.* the study of stars and planets (p. 176)
astronomía *s.* estudio de las estrellas y los planetas

atlas *n.* a collection of maps (p. 814)
atlas *s.* colección de mapas

atomic bomb *n.* nuclear weapon with a powerful explosion caused by the splitting of atoms (p. 942)
bomba atómica *s.* arma nuclear con una potente explosión causada por la división de átomos

Axis Powers *n.* the name for the alliance formed by Germany, Italy, and Japan during World War II (p. 924)
Potencias del Eje *s.* Alianza que formaron Alemania, Italia y Japón durante la Segunda Guerra Mundial

B

balance of trade *n.* the relationship of goods imported to goods exported (p. 812)
balanza comercial *s.* la relación de los bienes importados con los bienes exportados

Balkan Peninsula *n.* one of the largest peninsulas in Europe; it extends south into the Mediterranean Sea (p. 412)
península balcánica *s.* una de las grandes penínsulas de Europa; que se extiende hacia el sur en el mar Mediterráneo

Bantu *n.* word used by historians to describe the 400 different ethnic groups from the eastern, central, and southern regions of Africa (p. 507)
bantú *s.* palabra usada por los historiadores para describir los 400 grupos étnicos diferentes de las regiones del este, centro y sur de África

barometer *n.* a scientific instrument that measures air pressure (p. 781)
barómetro *s.* un instrumento científico que mide la presión del aire

Belgian Congo *n.* Belgian colony in Central Africa (p. 1004)
Congo Belga *s.* la única gran colonia africana controlada por Bélgica

Berlin Conference *n.* a meeting of European leaders at which a plan to divide Africa was made (p. 867)
Conferencia de Berlín *s.* reunión de líderes europeos, que se inició en 1884, la que llevó a la división de África entre las diversas potencias europeas

Bible *n.* the holy book of Christianity (p. 388)
Biblia *s.* el libro sagrado del cristianismo

biotechnology *n.* the use of cells, bacteria, and even plants to make products (p. 1068)
biotecnología *s.* el uso de células, bacterias e incluso las plantas para fabricar productos

bishop *n.* local Christian leader (p. 400)
obispo *s.* líderes cristianos locales

Black Death *n.* a deadly plague that swept through Europe between 1347 and 1351 (p. 701)
Peste Negra *s.* plaga mortal que azotó Europa entre 1347 y 1351

blitzkrieg *n.* the strategy of moving armies quickly; also called lightning war (p. 925)
blitzkrieg *s.* táctica alemana conocida como la guerra relámpago

Boers *n.* Dutch farmers who settled in South Africa in the 1600s (p. 867)
Boers *s.* agricultores holandeses que llegaron a Sudáfrica en la década de 1600

Boxer Rebellion *n.* an attempt to drive all the Westerners out of China (p. 873)
Levantamiento de los bóxers *s.* un intento, iniciado en 1899, para sacar a todos los occidentales fuera de China

British East India Company *n.* company created to control trade between Britain, India, and East Asia (p. 870)
Compañía Británica de las Indias Orientales *s.* empresa creada para controlar el comercio entre Gran Bretaña, India y Asia Oriental

Buddhism *n.* a religion based on the teachings of the Buddha that developed in India in the 500s BC (p. 162)
budismo *s.* religión basada en las enseñanzas de Buda, originada en la India en el siglo VI a. C.

bureaucracy *n.* a body of unelected government officials (p. 532)
burocracia *s.* cuerpo de empleados no electos del gobierno

Bushido (BOOH-shi-doh) *n.* the code of honor followed by the samurai in Japan (p. 574)
Bushido *s.* código de honor por el que se regían los samuráis en Japón

Byzantine Empire *n.* the society that developed in the eastern Roman Empire after the fall of the western Roman Empire (p. 417)
Imperio bizantino *s.* sociedad que surgió en elImperio romano de oriente tras la caída delImperio rhomano de occidente

C

caliph (KAY-luhf) *n.* a title that Muslims use for the highest leader of Islam (p. 448)
califa *s.* título que los musulmanes le dan al líder supremo del Islam

calligraphy *n.* decorative writing (p. 462)
caligrafía *s.* escritura decorativa

canal *n.* a human-made waterway (p. 68)
canal *s.* vía de agua hecha por el ser humano

capitalism *n.* an economic system in which individuals and private businesses run most industries (p. 816)
capitalismo *s.* sistema económico en el quelos individuos y las empresas privadas controlan la mayoría de las industrias

caravan *n.* a group of traders that travel together (p. 434)
caravana *s.* grupo de comerciantes que viajan juntos

Carpathians *n.* rugged mountains that are an extension of the Alps of west-central Europe (p. 411)
Cárpatos *s.* extensión de los Alpes en el área central oeste de Europa

caste system *n.* the division of Indian society into groups based on rank, wealth, or occupation (p. 152)
sistema de castas *s.* división de la sociedadindia en grupos basados en la clase social, el nivel económico o la profesión

cataracts *n.* rapids along a river, such as those along the Nile in Egypt (p. 104)
rápidos *s.* fuertes corrientes a lo largo de un río, como las del Nilo en Egipto

Catholic Reformation *n.* the effort of the late 1500s and 1600s to reform the Catholic Church from within; also called the Counter-Reformation (p. 755)
Reforma católica *s.* iniciativa para reformar laIglesia católica desde dentro que tuvo lugar a finales del siglo XVI y en el XVII; también conocida como Contrarreforma

causeway *n.* a raised road across water or wet ground (p. 631)
carretera elevada *s.* carretera construida sobre agua o terreno pantanoso

cavalry *n.* a unit of soldiers who ride horses (p. 92)
caballería *s.* grupo de soldados a caballo

celadon *n.* a ceramic glaze that appears green; it originated in China (p. 527)
celadón *s.* un esmalte de color verde pálido

chariot *n.* a wheeled, horse-drawn cart used in battle (p. 84)
cuadriga *s.* carro tirado por caballos usado en las batallas

checks and balances *n.* a system that balances the distribution of power in a government (p. 339)
pesos y contrapesos *s.* sistema creado para equilibrar la distribución del poder en un gobierno

Christian humanism *n.* the combination of humanist and religious ideas (p. 734)
humanismo cristiano *s.* combinación de ideas humanistas y religiosas

Christianity *n.* a religion based on the teachings of Jesus of Nazareth that developed in Judea at the beginning of the first century AD (p. 386)
cristianismo *s.* religión basada en las enseñan-zas de Jesús de Nazaret que se desarrolló en Judea a comienzos del siglo I d. C.

circumnavigate *v.* to go all the way around (p. 799)
circunnavegar *v.* rodear por completo

citizen *n.* a person who has the right to participate in government (p. 265)
ciudadano *s.* persona que tiene el derecho de participar en el gobierno

English and Spanish Glossary

city-state *n.* a political unit consisting of a city and its surrounding countryside (p. 72)
ciudad estado *s.* unidad política formada poruna ciudad y los campos que la rodean

civics *n.* study of citizenship and government (p. 30)
Educación Cívica *s.* estudio de la ciudadanía y el gobierno

civil disobedience *n.* the refusal to obey laws in order to bring about change (p. 987)
desobediencia civil *s.* la oposición de obedecer las leyes con el fin de lograr cambios

civil law *n.* a legal system based on a written code of laws (p. 375)
derecho civil *s.* sistema jurídico basado en un código de leyes escritas

civil service *n.* service as a government official (p. 532)
administración pública *s.* servicio como empleado del gobierno

civilization *n.* an organized society that functions within established geographic boundaries (p. 67)
civilización s. una sociedad organizada que funciona dentro de los límites geográficos establecidos

clan *n.* an extended family (p. 561)
clan *s.* familia extensa

clergy *n.* church officials (p. 691)
clero *s.* funcionarios de la Iglesia

climate *n.* the average weather conditions in a certain area over a long period of time (p. 12)
clima *s.* condiciones del tiempo mediasde una zona específica durante un largo período de tiempo

cloning *n.* the creation of identical copies of DNA (p. 1068)
clonación *s.* la creación de copias idénticas de ADN

codex *n.* an ancient book made of separate pages (p. 637)
códice *s.* libros antiguos hechos de páginas separadas que se usaban para mantener los registros históricos escritos

Cold War *n.* a period of distrust between the United States and Soviet Union after World War II, when there was a tense rivalry between the two superpowers but no direct fighting (p. 954)

Guerra fría *s.* período de desconfianza entre Estados Unidos y la Unión Soviética que siguió a la Segunda Guerra Mundial; existía una rivalidad tensa entre las dos superpotencias, pero no se llegó a la lucha real

collectivization *n.* policy established by Stalin that forced peasants to give up their private farms and become part of large, group-based farms (p. 922)
colectivización *s.* política establecida por Stalin que obligó a los campesinos a entregar sus granjas privadas y formar parte de granjas grupales grandes

Columbian Exchange *n.* the exchange of plants, animals, and ideas between the New World (the Americas) and the Old World (Europe) (p. 806)
Intercambio colombino *s.* El intercambio de plantas, animales e ideas entre el Nuevo Mundo (América) y el Viejo Mundo (Europa)

communes *n.* large collective farms (p. 962)
comuna *s.* establecimientos colectivos grandes

communism *n.* economic and political system in which the government owns all businesses and controls the economy (p. 903)
comunismo *s.* sistema económico y políticoen el que el gobierno es propietario de todos los medios de producción y controla la economía

compass *n.* an instrument that uses the earth's magnetic field to indicate direction (p. 528)
brújula *s.* instrumento que utiliza el campo magnético de la Tierra para indicar la dirección

concentration camp *n.* a type of prison camp where political prisoners and other enemies of the state are confined (p. 936)
campo de concentración *s.* un tipo de campo de prisioneros donde están confinados los presos políticos y otros enemigos del estado

Confucianism *n.* a philosophy based on the ideas of Confucius that focuses on morality, family order, social harmony, and government (p. 195)
confucianismo *s.* filosofía basada en las ideasde Confucio que se basa en la moralidad, el orden familiar, la armonía social y el gobierno

congregation *n.* church assembly (p. 763)
congregación *s.* assamblea de la iglesia

conquistador (kahn-kees-tuh-DOHR) *n.* Spanish soldier (p. 637)
conquistador *s.* soldado españoles

conservatism *n.* a movement that arose to preserve the old social order and governments in an effort to return Europe to the way it was before the French Revolution (p. 847)
conservadurismo *s.* movimiento surgido conel fin de preservar los antiguos gobiernos y orden social en un esfuerzo por que Europa volviese a la situación en la que se encontraba antes de la Revolución francesa

constitution *n.* written plan of government (p. 31)
constitución *s.* plan escrito del gobierno

constitutional monarchy *n.* a form of democracy in which a monarch serves as the head of state but a legislature makes the laws (p. 997)
monarquía constitucional *s.* democracia en la que un monarca es el jefe de estado, pero un cuerpo legislativo hace las leyes

consuls (KAHN-suhlz) *n.* the two most powerful officials in Rome (p. 336)
cónsules *s.* los dos funcionarios más poderosos en Roma

containment *n.* the effort during the Cold War to prevent the Soviet Union from expanding its influence around the world (p. 957)
contención *s.* impedir la expansión de la influencia

Coptic Christianity *n.* local African customs blended with Christian teachings (p. 506)
cristianismo copto *s.* costumbres locales africanas mezcladas con las enseñanzas cristianas

corruption *n.* the decay of people's values (p. 369)
corrupción *s.* decadencia de los valores de las personas

cottage industry *n.* a system in which family members worked in their homes to make part of a product (p. 813)
Industria artesanal *s.* un sistema en el cual los miembros de la familia trabajaban en sus casas para hacer parte de un producto

coup d'état (KOO DAY-tah) *n.* the forceful overthrow of a government (p. 844)
golpe de estado *s.* derrocamiento forzoso de un gobierno

court *n.* a group of nobles who live near and serve or advise a ruler (p. 566)
corte *s.* grupo de nobles que viven cerca de un gobernante y lo sirven o aconsejan

crucifixion (kroo-suh-FIK-shuhn) *n.* a type of execution in which a person was nailed to a cross (p. 389)
crucifixión *s.* tipo de ejecución en la que se clavaba a una persona en una cruz

Crusades *n.* a long series of wars between Christians and Muslims in Southwest Asia; they fought for control of the Holy Land from 1096 to 1291 (p. 685)
cruzadas *s.* larga sucesión de guerras entre cristianos y musulmanes en el sudoeste de Asia para conseguir el control de la Tierra Santa; tuvieron lugar entre el año 1096 y el año 1291

cultural diffusion *n.* the spread of cultural traits from one region to another (p. 544)
difusión cultural *s.* la difusión de los rasgos culturales de una región a otra

culture *n.* the knowledge, beliefs, customs, and values of a group of people (p. 6)
cultura *s.* el conocimiento, las creencias, las costumbres y los valores de un grupo de personas

cuneiform (kyoo-NEE-uh-fohrm) *n.* the world's first system of writing; developed in Sumer (p. 75)
cuneiforme *s.* primer sistema de escrituradel mundo; desarrollado en Sumeria

currency *n.* money (p. 358)
moneda *s.* dinero

czar *n.* the title of Russian emperors (p. 421)
zar *s.* el título de emperadores rusos

D

daimyo (DY-mee-oh) *n.* large landowners of feudal Japan (p. 572)
daimyo *s.* grandes propietarios de tierras del Japón feudal

Danube *n.* river that begins in Germany, flows east across the Great Hungarian Plain, and finally empties into the Black Sea (p. 412)
Danubio *s.* río que comienza en Alemania, fluye hacia el este a través de la gran llanura húngara, y finalmente desemboca en el mar Negro

English and Spanish Glossary

Daoism (DOW-ih-zum) *n.* a philosophy that developed in China and stressed the belief that one should live in harmony with the Dao, the guiding force of all reality (p. 197)
taoism *s.* filosofía que se desarrolló en Chinay que enfatizaba la creencia de que se debe vivir en armonía con el Tao, la fuerza que guía toda la realidad

Darfur *n.* a region in western Sudan (p. 1009)
Darfur *s.* área en Sudán plagado de genocidio debido al conflicto étnico

de-Stalinization *n.* the Soviet policy of easing Joseph Stalin's repressive policies (p. 969)
desestalinización *s.* política de reformar el país para aliviar la represión estalinista

Dead Sea Scrolls *n.* writings about Jewish beliefs, created about 2,000 years ago (p. 239)
manuscritos del mar Muerto *s.* escritos sobrelas creencias judías, redactados hace unos 2,000 años

Declaration of Independence *n.* a document written in 1776 that declared the American colonies' independence from British rule (p. 838)
Declaración de Independencia *s.* documento redactado en 1776 que declaró la independencia de las colonias de Norteamérica del dominio británico

Declaration of the Rights of Man and of the Citizen *n.* a document written in France in 1789 that guaranteed specific freedoms for French citizens (p. 842)
Declaración de los Derechos del Hombre y del Ciudadano *s.* documento redactado en Francia en 1789 que garantizaba libertades específicas para los ciudadanos franceses

delta *n.* a triangle-shaped area of land made from soil deposited by a river (p. 105)
delta *s.* zona de tierra de forma triangular creada a partir de los sedimentos que deposita un río

democracy *n.* a type of government in which people rule themselves (pp. 31, 264)
democracia *s.* tipo de gobierno en el que el pueblo se gobierna a sí mismo

détente *n.* the policy of easing Cold War tensions (p. 971)
Détente *s.* política de aliviar las tensiones de la Guerra Fría

developed nations *n.* countries that have become fully industrial (p. 1073)
países desarrolladas *s.* naciones prósperas que han desarrollado todas las habilidades y herramientas necesarias para ser expertos en la producción de bienes manufacturados

developing nations *n.* countries that have not become fully industrial (p. 1073)
países en desarrollo *s.* países que no se han vuelto totalmente industrial

Diaspora (dy-AS-puhr-uh) *n.* the dispersal of the Jews outside of Judah after the Babylonian Captivity (p. 234)
diáspora *s.* la dispersión de los judíos desde Judá tras el cautiverio en Babilonia

dictator *n.* a ruler who has almost absolute power (p. 331)
dictador *s.* gobernante que tiene poder casi absoluto

Diet *n.* the elected legislature that still governs Japan (p. 992)
Dieta *s.* la legistatura elegida que aún gobierna a Japón

diffusion *n.* the spread of ideas, goods, and technology from one culture to another (p. 213)
difusión *s.* la propagación de ideas, bienes y tecnología de una cultura a otra

disciple *n.* follower (p. 389)
discípulo *s.* seguidor

division of labor *n.* an arrangement in which each worker specializes in a particular task or job (p. 69)
división del trabajo *s.* organización mediantela que cada trabajador se especializa en un trabajo o tarea en particular

domestication *n.* the process of changing plants or animals to make them more useful to humans (p. 55)
domesticación *s.* proceso en el que se modifican los animales o las plantas para que sean más útiles para los humanos

domino theory *n.* the Cold War idea that if one country in Southeast Asia fell to communism, nearby nations would also fall (p. 965)
Teoría del dominó *s.* La nación del sudeste asiático se describía como una "fila de fichas de dominó"; si uno cayó al comunismo, daría lugar a la caída de sus vecinos

dynasty *n.* a series of rulers from the same family (p. 105)
dinastía *s.* serie de gobernantes pertenecientes a la misma familia

E

economy *n.* system of producing, selling, and buying goods and services (p. 22)
economía *s.* sistema de producir, vender y comprar bienes y servicios

Edict of Nantes *n.* law passed in 1598 granting religious freedom in France (p. 762)
Edicto de Nantes *s.* emitido en 1598 por el rey Enrique IV; concede la libertad religiosa en la mayor parte de Francia

elite (ay-LEET) *n.* people of wealth and power (p. 114)
élite *s.* personas ricas y poderosas

embargo *n.* a limit on trade (p. 1018)
embargo *s.* límite en el comercio

empire *n.* land with different territories and peoples under a single rule (p. 73)
imperio *s.* zona que reúne varios territorios y pueblos bajo un mismo gobierno

engineering *n.* the application of scientific knowledge for practical purposes (p. 115)
ingeniería *s.* aplicación del conocimiento científico para fines prácticos

English Bill of Rights *n.* a document approved in 1689 that listed rights for Parliament and the English people and drew on the principles of Magna Carta (p. 838)
Declaración de Derechos inglesa *s.* documento aprobado en 1689 que enumeraba los derechos del Parlamento y del pueblo de Inglaterra, inspirada en los principios de la Carta Magna

Enlightenment n. a period during the 1600s and 1700s when reason was used to guide people's thoughts about society, politics, and philosophy (p. 826)
Ilustración *s.* período durante los siglos XVII y XVIII en el que la razón guiaba la opinión de las personas acerca de la sociedad, la política y la filosofía

entrepreneur *n.* a person who organizes, manages, and assumes the risk of a business (p. 25, 864)
empresario *s.* una persona que organiza, administra y asume el riesgo de una empresa

environment *n.* all the living and nonliving things that affect life in an area (p. 13)
medio ambiente *s.* todos los seres vivos y elementos inertes que afectan la vida de un área

environmentalism *n.* the movement to protect the natural world from destructive human activities (p. 1064)
ecologismo *s.* el movimiento para proteger el mundo natural de las actividades humanas destructivas

epic *n.* long poem that tells the story of a hero (p. 76)
poema épico *s.* poema largos que narran hazaña de héroe

epidemic *n.* when an infectious disease spreads between many people in a community or region (p. 1069)
epidemia *s.* cuando una enfermedad infecciosa se transmite entre muchas personas en una comunidad o región

ethics *n.* moral values (p. 195)
ética *s.* valores morales

Ethiopia *n.* kingdom formed by the descendants of the people of Aksum (p. 506)
Etiopía *s.* reino formado por los descendientes del pueblo de Aksum

Eucharist *n.* central ceremony of the Christian Church (p. 400)
Eucaristía *s.* acto de la Iglesia Cristiana

Eurasia *n.* a large landmass that includes both Europe and Asia (p. 664)
Eurasia *s.* la gran masa de tierra que incluye Europa y Asia

European Union *n.* established in 1992 to build an economic and political union among the nations of Europe (p. 977)
Unión Europea *s.* establecida en 1992 para construir una unión económica y política entre las naciones de Europa

excommunicate *v.* to cast out from the church (p. 680)
excomulgar *v.* expulsar de la Iglesia

English and Spanish Glossary

Exodus *n.* the journey of the Israelites, led by Moses, from Egypt to Canaan after they were freed from slavery (p. 229)
Éxodo *s.* sviaje de los Israelita, guiados por Moisés, desde Egipto hasta Canaán después de su liberación de la esclavitud

exports *n.* items sent to other regions for trade (p. 133)
exportaciones *s.* productos enviados a otras regiones para el intercambio commercial

extended family *n.* a family group that includes the father, mother, children, and close relatives (p. 474)
familia extensa *s.* grupo familiar que incluyeal padre, la madre, los hijos y los parientes cercanos

F

fable *n.* a short story that teaches a lesson about life or gives advice on how to live (p. 285)
fábula *s.* relato breve que presenta una enseñanza u ofrece algún consejo sobre la vida

factory system *n.* a system in which machines rapidly manufacture large quantities of items (p. 859)
sistema de fábrica *s.* un sistema en el que sefabrican grandes cantidades de artículoscon gran rapidez mediante el uso de máquinas

failed state *n.* a country whose government is unable to provide stability to its people and protect its borders (p. 1049)
estado fallido *s.* un país cuyo gobierno no es capaz de proporcionar estabilidad a su gente y proteger sus fronteras

fascism (FASH-iz-uhm) *n.* a political system based on nationalism and strong government; Adolf Hitler in Germany and Benito Mussolini in Italy were the first fascist leaders (p. 918)
fascismo *s.* sistema político basado en el nacionalismo y en un gobierno fuerte; los primeros líderes fascistas fueron Adolf Hitler en Alemania y Benito Mussolini en Italia

fasting *n.* going without food for a period of time (p. 161)
ayunar *s.* dejar de comer durante un período de tiempo

federalism *n.* the sharing of power between local governments and a strong central government (p. 764)
federalismo *s.* sistema de distribución delpoder entre los gobiernos locales y un gobierno central fuerte

Fertile Crescent *n.* an area of rich farmland in Southwest Asia where the first civilizations began (p. 66)
Media Luna de las tierras fértiles *s.* zona de ricastierras de cultivo situada en el sudoeste de Asia, en la que comenzaron las primeras civilizaciones

feudalism (FYOO-duh-lih-zuhm) *n.* the system of obligations that governed the relationships between lords and vassals in medieval Europe (p. 674)
feudalismo *s.* sistema de obligaciones quegobernaba las relaciones entre los señores feudales y los vasallos en la Europa medieval

figurehead *n.* a person who appears to rule even though real power rests with someone else (p. 573)
títere *s.* persona que aparentemente gobiernaaunque el poder real lo ostenta otra persona

Final Solution *n.* plan thought up by Nazi leaders in 1942 that consisted of shipping Jews from throughout Europe to killing centers in Poland (p. 937)
Solución final *s.* el plan ideado por los líderes nazis en 1942, que consistía en el envío de los Judios de toda Europa a los centros de exterminio en Polonia

Five Pillars of Islam *n.* five religious practices required of all Muslims (p. 442)
los cinco pilares del Islam *s.* cinco prácticas religiosas que los musulmanes tienen que observar

Forum *n.* a Roman public meeting place (p. 339)
foro *s.* lugar público de reuniones en Roma

fossil *n.* a part or imprint of something that was once alive (p. 10)
fósil *s.* parte o huella de un ser vivo ya desaparecido

free trade *n.* the ending of trade barriers among nations (p. 1076)
libre cambio *s.* el final de las barreras comerciales entre las naciones

friar *n.* a member of a religious order who lived and worked among the public (p. 694)
fraile *s.* miembro de una orden religiosaque vivía y trabajaba entre la gente

G

genetics *n.* the study of how genes affect the development of living things (p. 1067)
genética *s.* el estudio de los genes y cómo afectan el desarrollo de los seres vivos

genocide *n.* the deliberate destruction of a racial, political, or cultural group of people (pp. 894, 934, 1039)
genocidio *s.* la destrucción deliberada de un grupo racial, político o cultural de personas

geography *n.* the study of Earth's physical and cultural features (p. 12)
geografía *s.* estudio de las características físicas y culturales de la Tierra

Gestapo *n.* a political secret police created by Adolf Hitler to investigate and put down any political opposition (p. 920)
Gestapo *s.* una policía secreta política creada por Adolf Hitler para investigar y reprimir cualquier oposición política

Ghana *n.* West African nation; formerly a British colony called the Gold Coast (p. 1001)
Ghana *s.* antes llamado la Costa de Oro, fue la primera colonia británica en ganar su libertad

ghetto *n.* a district where Jews were isolated (p. 936)
gueto *s.* distrito en el que se aislaron Judíos; normalmente cerrado por paredes, cercas y puertas

glasnost *n.* the Soviet policy of openness (p. 973)
glásnost *s.* política de apertura anunciada por Gorbachov en 1985

government *n.* the organizations and individuals who have the right to rule over a group of people (p. 30)
gobierno *s.* las organizaciones e individuos que tienen el derecho a gobernar sobre un grupo de personas

Grand Canal *n.* a canal linking northern and southern China (p. 518)
canal grande *s.* un canal que conecta el norte con el sur de China

Great Depression *n.* an economic collapse that occurred in the late 1920s and continued well into the 1930s (p. 905)
Gran Depresión *s.* un colapso económico que se produjo a finales de 1920 y continuó hasta la década de 1930

Great Wall *n.* a barrier made of walls across China's northern frontier (p. 203)
Gran Muralla *s.* barrera formada por muros situada a lo largo de la frontera norte de China

Great Zimbabwe *n.* Bantu kingdom founded in about 1000 (p. 508)
Gran Zimbabue *s.* reino bantú fundado cerca de 1000

griot *n.* a West African storyteller (p. 498)
griot *s.* narrador de relatos de África occidental

gross domestic product (GDP) *n.* the value of goods and services produced each year by a country (p. 1074)
producto interno bruto (PIB) *s.* el valor de los bienes y servicios producidos por un país

Guangzhou (GWANG-JOH) *n.* city in China in which European traders were allowed to live; known to the British as the city of Canton (p. 872)
Guangzhou *s.* la única ciudad que los gobernantes chinos permitieron que los comerciantes europeos habitaran; los británicos la conocían como Cantón

gunpowder *n.* a mixture of powders used in guns and explosives (p. 528)
pólvora *s.* mezcla de polvos utilizada en armas de fuego y explosivos

gurdwara *n.* a Sikh place of worship (p. 596)
gurdwara *s.* lugar de culto en la sociedad sij

H

Hammurabi's Code *n.* a set of 282 laws governing daily life in Babylon; the earliest known collection of written laws (p. 83)
Código de Hammurabi *s.* conjunto de 282 leyes que regían la vida cotidiana en Babilonia; la primera colección de leyes escritas conocida

harem *n.* a separate area of a household where women lived away from men (p. 588)
harén *s.* área de un hogar otomano, donde las mujeres vivían para mantenerlas separadas de los hombres

Hellenistic *adj.* Greeklike; heavily influenced by Greek ideas (p. 310)
   helenístico *adj.* al estilo griego; muy influido por las ideas de la Grecia clásica

Helsinki Accords *n.* an international peace agreement signed by diplomats in Helsinki, Finland (p. 1035)
   Conferencia de Helsinki *s.* un compromiso para trabajar juntos por la paz y para proteger los derechos humanos firmado en 1975 por los Estados Unidos, Canadá y la mayoría de los países europeos

heresy (HER-uh-see) *n.* religious ideas that oppose accepted church teachings (p. 702)
   herejía *s.* ideas religiosas que se oponen a la doctrina oficial de la Iglesia

hieroglyphics (hy-ruh-GLIH-fiks) *n.* the ancient Egyptian writing system that used picture symbols (p. 123)
   jeroglíficos sistema *s.* de escritura del antiguo Egipto, en el cual se usaban símbolos ilustrados

High Holy Days *n.* the two most sacred of all Jewish holidays—Rosh Hashanah and Yom Kippur (p. 247)
   Supremos Días Santos *s.* los dos días más sagra-dos de las festividades judías, Rosh Hashanah y Yom Kippur

Hindu-Arabic numerals *n.* the number system we use today; it was created by Indian scholars during the Gupta dynasty (p. 175)
   numerales indoarábigos *s.* sistema numéricoque usamos hoy en día; fue creado por estudiosos de la India durante la dinastía Gupta

Hinduism *n.* the main religion of India; it teaches that everything is part of a universal spirit called Brahman (p. 155)
   hinduismo *s.* religión principal de la India;sus enseñanzas dicen que todo forma parte de un espíritu universal llamado Brahman

history *n.* the study of the past (p. 7)
   historia *s.* el estudio del pasado

Holocaust *n.* the Nazis' effort to wipe out the Jewish people in World War II, when 6 million Jews throughout Europe were killed (p. 934)

   Holocausto *s.* intento de los Nazis de eliminaral pueblo judío; hecho acaecido durante la Segunda Guerra Mundial en el que se asesinó a 6 millones de judíos en toda Europa

Holy Land *n.* the region on the eastern shore of the Mediterranean Sea where Jesus lived, preached, and died (p. 685)
   Tierra Santa *s.* región de la costa este del marMediterráneo en la que Jesús vivió, predicó y murió

hominid *n.* an early ancestor of humans (p. 42)
   homínido *s.* antepasado primitivo de los humanos

Huguenots *n.* French Protestants (p. 762)
   hugonotes *s.* protestantes franceses

human rights *n.* rights that all people deserve, such as the rights to equality and justice (p. 1034)
   derechos humanos *s.* aquellos derechos que todas las personas merecen, como los derechos a la igualdad y la justicia

humanism *n.* the study of history, literature, public speaking, and art that led to a new way of thinking in Europe in the late 1300s (p. 722)
   humanismo *s.* estudio de la historia, la literatura, la oratoria y el arte que produjo una nueva forma de pensar en Europa a finales del siglo XIV

Hundred Years' War *n.* a long conflict between England and France that lasted from 1337 to 1453 (p. 700)
   Guerra de los Cien Años *s.* largo conflicto entreInglaterra y Francia que tuvo lugar entre 1337 y 1453

hunter-gatherers *n.* people who hunt animals and gather wild plants, seeds, fruits, and nuts to survive (p. 48)
   cazadores y recolectores *s.* personas que cazananimales y recolectan plantas, semillas, frutas y nueces para sobrevivir

hypothesis *n.* a solution that a scientist proposes to solve or explain a scientific problem (p. 784)
   hipótesis *s.* una solución que un científico propone resolver o explicar un problema científico

I

ice ages *n.* long periods of freezing weather (p. 50)
eras glaciales *s.* largos períodos de clima helado

icons *n.* religious images painted on wood (p. 423)
iconos *s.* imágenes religiosas pintadas sobre madera

immunity *n.* protection from being arrested, tried, or punished for any crime (p. 1023)
inmunidad *s.* protección contra la detención, juicio o castigo por un crimen

imperialism *n.* the control of a region or country by another country (p. 864)
imperialismo *s.* el control de una región o país por parte de otro país

imports *n.* goods brought in from other regions (p. 133)
importaciones *s.* bienes que se introducen en un país procedentes de otras regiones

income *n.* money gained from collecting taxes and tributes and trading gold (p. 485)
ingreso *s.* dinero obtenido de la recaudación de impuestos y tributos y el comercio de oro

indulgence *n.* a relaxation of penalties for sins people had committed (p. 749)
indulgencia *s.* la relajación de las penas por los pecados que la gente cometió

inflation *n.* a continuing increase in the prices of goods and services (p. 1075)
inflación *s.* un aumento continuo de los precios de los bienes y servicios

informal jobs *n.* jobs that do not provide minimum wages, regular schedules, or retirement benefits (p. 1025)
trabajos informales *s.* puestos de trabajo en el que la gente a menudo no ganan el salario mínimo, no tienen horarios regulares y no reciben beneficios de retiro cuando dejan de trabajar

infrastructure *n.* the basic items a society needs to function, such as roads and bridges (p. 1049)
infraestructura *s.* los edificios, carreteras y medios de crear energía necesaria para el funcionamiento eficaz de una sociedad

inoculation (i-nah-kyuh-LAY-shuhn) *n.* injecting a person with a small dose of a virus to help build up defenses against a disease (p. 176)
inoculación *s.* acto de inyectar una pequeña dosis de un virus a una persona para ayudarla a crear defensas contra una enfermedad

interest *n.* a fee that borrowers pay for the use of someone else's money, usually a certain percentage of the loan (p. 720)
interés *s.* una cuota que los prestatarios pagan por el uso del dinero de otra persona

International Monetary Fund (IMF) *n.* organization that offers emergency loans to countries in financial trouble (p. 1079)
Fondo Monetario Internacional *s.* organización internacional que ofrece préstamos de emergencia a los países con problemas financieros

International Space Station (ISS) *n.* a space station assembled by the United States, Russia, the European Space Agency, and Japan (p. 1052)
Estacion Espacial Internacional *s.* desarrollado cuando los Estados Unidos y Rusia acordaron combinar sus programas espaciales en 1993; la Agencia Espacial Europea y Japón también se unieron al programa

Internet *n.* a worldwide network of linked computers (p. 1055)
internet *s.* una red mundial de computadoras conectadas

Iroquois Confederacy *n.* an alliance of five northeastern Native American peoples (p. 655)
Confederación Iroquesa *s.* alianza formada por las tribus cayuga, mohawk, oneida, onondaga y seneca

irrigation *n.* a way of supplying water to an area of land (p. 68)
irrigación *s.* método para suministrar agua a un terreno

Islam *n.* a religion based on the messages Muhammad is believed to have received from God (p. 438)
Islam *s.* religión basada en los mensajesque se cree que Mahoma recibió de Dios

English and Spanish Glossary   **R47**

English and Spanish Glossary

isolationism *n.* a policy of avoiding contact with other countries (p. 540)
aislacionismo *s.* política de evitar el contacto con otros países

J

jade *n.* a hard gemstone often used in jewelry (p. 188)
jade *s.* piedra preciosa de gran dureza que se suele utilizar en joyería

Jainism *n.* an Indian religion, based on the teachings of Mahavira, that teaches all life is sacred (p. 157)
jainismo *s.* religión de la India, basada en lasenseñanzas de Mahavira, que proclamaque toda forma de vida es sagrada

Janissary *n.* an Ottoman slave soldier (p. 586)
jenízaro *s.* soldado esclavo otomano

Jesuits *n.* members of a Catholic religious order created to serve the pope and the church (p. 756)
jesuitas *s.* miembros de una orden religiosacatólica creada para servir al Papa y a laIglesia

jihad (ji-HAHD) *v.* to make an effort or to struggle; has also been interpreted to mean "holy war" (p. 442)
yihad *v.* esforzarse o luchar; se ha interpretado también con el significado de "guerra santa"

Judaism (JOO-dee-i-zuhm) *n.* the religion of the Hebrews (practiced by Jews today); it is the world's oldest monotheistic religion (p. 228)
judaísmo *s.* religión de los hebreos (practicada por los judíos hoy en día); es la religión monoteísta más antigua del mundo

K

karma *n.* in Buddhism and Hinduism, the effects that good or bad actions have on a person's soul (p. 156)
karma *s.* en el budismo y el hinduismo, losefectos que las buenas o malas acciones producen en el alma de una persona

Kashmir *n.* a mountainous area in the northern part of South Asia, near the Chinese border (p. 993)
Cachemira *s.* zona montañosa en el norte, cerca de la frontera con China

kente *n.* a handwoven, brightly colored West African fabric (p. 502)
kente *s.* tela muy colorida, tejida a mano, característica de África occidental

Kenya *n.* East African nation; formerly a British colony (p. 1002)
Kenia *s.* colonia del África Oriental que se convirtió en independiente sólo después de una lucha larga y violenta

Kinshasa *n.* capital of the Democratic Republic of the Congo (p. 1012)
Kinshasa *s.* ciudad grande en la República Democrática del Congo

kinship system *n.* a system of social organization based on family ties (p. 473)
sistema de parentesco *s.* un sistema de organización social basado en los lazos familiares

knight *n.* a warrior in medieval Europe who fought on horseback (p. 673)
caballero *s.* guerrero de la Europa medieval que luchaba a caballo

Kristallnacht *n.* the night of November 9, 1938, when the Nazis carried out attacks on Jewish businesses, homes, and synagogues (p. 935)
Kristallnacht *s.* 9 de noviembre de 1938; una ola de violencia conocida como la "Noche de los cristales rotos" debido a las muchas ventanas rotas de empresas judías, hogares y sinagogas

L

Lagos *n.* Nigeria's largest city and former capital (p. 1012)
Lagos *s.* ciudad grande en Nigeria

laissez-faire (leh-say-FAYR) *n.* a "let things be" attitude on the part of government toward industry (p. 860)
laissez-faire *s.* actitud de los gobiernos de"dejar hacer" a las industrias

land bridge *n.* a strip of land connecting two continents (p. 50)
puente de tierra *s.* franja de tierra que conecta dos continentes

landforms *n.* the natural features of the land's surface (p. 12)

accidentes geográficos *s.* características naturales de la superficie terrestre

langar *n.* kitchen where food is served without charge (p. 596)

langar *s.* cocina

Latin *n.* the language of the Romans (p. 338)

latín *s.* idioma de los romanos

League of Nations *n.* an organization in which countries would try to solve their problems peacefully (p. 897)

Sociedad de las Naciones *s.* una organización en la que los países tratarían de resolver sus problemas de forma pacífica

Legalism *n.* the Chinese belief that people were bad by nature and needed to be controlled (p. 198)

legalismo *s.* creencia china de que las personas eran malas por naturaleza y debían ser controladas

legion (LEE-juhn) *n.* a group of up to 6,000 Roman soldiers (p. 343)

legión *s.* grupo que podía incluir hasta 6,000 soldados romanos

liberalism *n.* a movement for individual rights and liberties (p. 847)

liberalismo *s.* movimiento a favor de los derechos del individuo y las libertades

limited government *n.* a government that is not all-powerful and is checked by laws and institutions representing the will of the people (p. 830)

gobierno limitado *s.* gobierno que no es omnipotente, pero está marcado por las leyes y las instituciones que representan la voluntad del pueblo

llamas *n.* animals that are related to camels but native to South America (p. 642)

llamas *s.* animales que están relacionados con los camellos, pero nativas de América del Sur

lord *n.* a person of high rank who owned land but owed loyalty to his king (p. 193)

señor feudal *s.* persona de alto nivel social que poseía tierras y debía lealtad al rey

M

magistrate (MA-juh-strayt) *n.* an elected official in Rome (p. 336)

magistrado *s.* funcionario electo en Roma

Magna Carta *n.* a document signed in 1215 by King John of England that required the king to honor certain rights (p. 698)

Carta Magna *s.* documento firmado por elrey Juan de Inglaterra en 1215 que exigía que el rey respetara ciertos derechos

maize (MAYZ) *n.* corn (p. 615)

maíz *s.* cereal también conocido como elote o choclo

majority rule *n.* a system in which the ideas and decisions supported by the most people are followed (pp. 338, 832)

gobierno de la mayoría *s.* un sistema donde las ideas y decisiones apoyadas por la mayoría de las personas se siguen

manor *n.* a large estate owned by a knight or lord (p. 675)

señorío *s.* gran finca perteneciente a un caballero o señor feudal

Maori *n.* the original settlers of New Zealand (p. 875)

Maorí *s.* los nativos que se asentaron en Nueva Zelanda cerca de 950 y 1300 d. C.

market economy *n.* an economic system in which individuals decide what goods and services they will buy (p. 816)

economía de mercado *s.* sistema económicoen el que los individuos deciden qué tipo de bienes y servicios desean comprar

Marshall Plan *n.* plan under which Western Europe received more than $13 billion in U.S. loans and grants between 1948 and 1952 (p. 957)

Plan Marshall *s.* Plan bajo el cual Europa Occidental recibió más de $13 mil millones en préstamos y donaciones de Estados Unidos entre 1948 y 1952

martyrs *n.* people who suffer death for their religious beliefs (p. 398)

mártires *s.* personas que sufren la muerte por sus creencias religiosas

English and Spanish Glossary

Marxism *n.* the belief that the struggle of oppressed workers is the basis for social change (p. 903)
Marxismo *s.* las ideas de Karl Marx

matrilineal *adj.* society in which, even though men still serve as leaders, leadership passes down through the mother's family (p. 475)
sociedad matrilineal *adj.* en la que, a pesar de que los hombres todavía sirven como líderes, el liderazgo pasa a través de la familia de la madre

Mau Mau *n.* violent movement with a goal to rid Kenya of white settlers (p. 1002)
Mau Mau *s.* movimiento violento con el objetivo de liberar a Kenia de colonos blancos

medieval (mee-DEE-vuhl) *adj.* referring to the Middle Ages (p. 667)
medieval *adj.* relativo a la Edad Media

meditation *n.* deep, continued thought that focuses the mind on spiritual ideas (p. 161)
meditación *s.* reflexión profunda y continua, durante la cual la persona se concentra en ideas espirituales

megalith *n.* huge stone monument (p. 57)
megalito *s.* enorme monumento de piedra

mercantilism *n.* a system in which a government controls all economic activity in a country and its colonies to make the government stronger and richer (p. 812)
mercantilismo *s.* sistema en el que el gobiernocontrola toda la actividad económica de un país y sus colonias con el fin de hacerse más fuerte y más rico

merchant *n.* a trader (p. 133)
mercader *s.* comerciante

Mesoamerica *n.* a region that includes the southern part of what is now Mexico and parts of the northern countries of Central America (p. 612)
Mesoamérica *s.* incluye la parte sur de lo que hoy es México y partes de los países del norte de América Central

Mesolithic Era *n.* the middle part of the Stone Age; marked by the creation of smaller and more complex tools (p. 53)
Mesolítico *s.* período central de la Edad dePiedra, caracterizado por la creación de herramientas más pequeñas y complejas

Messiah (muh-SY-uh) *n.* in Judaism, a new leader that would appear among the Jews and restore the greatness of ancient Israel (p. 387)
Mesías *s.* en el judaísmo, nuevo líder que aparecería entre los judíos y restablecería la grandeza del antiguo Israel

metallurgy (MET-uhl-uhr-jee) *n.* the science of working with metals (p. 174)
metalurgia *s.* ciencia de trabajar los metales

microchip *n.* tiny silicon chip used in computers (p. 1054)
microchip *s.* chip miniaturizado de silicio utilizado en las computadoras

Middle Ages *n.* a period that lasted from about 500 to 1500 in Europe (p. 667)
Edad Media *s.* nombre con el que se denomina el período que abarca aproximadamente desde el año 500 hasta el 1500 en Europa

Middle Kingdom *n.* the period of Egyptian history from about 2050 to 1750 BC and marked by order and stability (p. 117)
Reino Medio *s.* período de la historia de Egiptoque abarca aproximadamente del 2050 al1750 a. C. y que se caracterizó por el orden y la estabilidad

migrate *v.* to move to a new place (p. 50)
migrar *v.* desplazarse a otro lugar

militarism *n.* the idea that a country should use a strong military to defend its interests (p. 891)
militarismo *s.* la idea de que un país debe usar un fuerte militar para defender sus intereses

minaret *n.* a narrow tower from which Muslims are called to prayer (p. 461)
minarete *s.* torre fina desde la que se llama a la oración a los musulmanes

missionary *n.* someone who works to spread religious beliefs (p. 165)
misionero *s.* alguien que trabaja para difundir sus creencias religiosas

monarch (MAH-nark) *n.* a ruler of a kingdom or empire (p. 82)
monarca *s.* gobernante de un reino o imperio

mixed economy *n.* a market economy with features of traditional and command systems (p. 25)
economía mixta *s.* una economía de mercado con características de sistemas tradicionales y dirigidas

monastery *n.* a community of monks (p. 668)
monasterio *s.* comunidad de monjes

monk *n.* a religious man who lived apart from society in an isolated community (p. 668)
monje *s.* religioso que vivía apartado de la sociedad en una comunidad aislada

monotheism *n.* the belief in only one God (pp. 236, 397)
monoteísmo *s.* creencia en un solo Dios

monsoon *n.* a seasonal wind pattern that causes wet and dry seasons (p. 145)
monzón *s.* viento estacional cíclico que causa estaciones húmedas y secas

mosaics *n.* pictures made with pieces of colored stone or glass (p. 419)
mosaicos *s.* obras pictóricas elaboradas con piezas de piedra o vidrio de varios colores

mosque (MAHSK) *n.* a building for Muslim prayer (p. 441)
mezquita *s.* edificio musulmán para la oración

mummy *n.* a specially treated body wrapped in cloth for preservation (p. 114)
momia *s.* cadáver especialmente tratado y envuelto en tela para su conservación

Muslim *n.* a follower of Islam (p. 438)
musulmán *s.* seguidor del Islam

mythology *n.* stories about gods and heroes that try to explain how the world works (p. 280)
mitología *s.* relatos sobre dioses y héroes que tratan de explicar cómo funciona el mundo

N

nation-states *n.* self-governing countries made up of people with a common cultural background (p. 888)
naciones-estado *s.* países con gobierno independiente formados por personas con un origen cultural común

nationalism *n.* a devotion and loyalty to one's country; develops among people with a common language, religion, or history (p. 888)
nacionalismo *s.* sentimiento de lealtad a unpaís; se desarrolla entre personas con un idioma, religión o historia en común

natural law *n.* a law that people believed God had created to govern how the world operated (p. 696)
ley natural *s.* ley que las personas pensabanque Dios había creado para controlar el funcionamiento del mundo

natural rights *n.* the belief that developed during the Enlightenment that people had certain rights, such as the right to life, liberty, and property (p. 832)
derechos naturales *s.* creencia que se desarrollódurante la Ilustración de que las personas tenían ciertos derechos, como el derecho a la vida, a la libertad y a la propiedad

Nazi Party *n.* a German political party, which Adolf Hitler joined in 1919 and renamed (p. 919)
Partido Nazi *s.* un partido político alemán al que Adolf Hitler se unió en 1919 y luego fue renombrado

Neolithic Era *n.* the New Stone Age; when people learned to make fire and tools like saws and drills (p. 55)
Neolítico *s.* Nueva Edad de Piedra; el serhumano aprendió a producir fuego y a fabricar herramientas como sierras y taladros manuales

New Deal *n.* the federal government's efforts to reform business practices and to stimulate the economy (p. 908)
Nuevo Trato *s.* los esfuerzos del gobierno federal para reformar las prácticas de negocios y para estimular la economía después de la Gran Depresión

New Kingdom *n.* the period from about 1550 to 1050 BC in Egyptian history, when Egypt reached the height of its power and glory (p. 118)
Reino Nuevo *s.* período de la historia egipciaque abarca aproximadamente desde el 1550 hasta el 1050 a. C., en el que Egipto alcanzó la cima de su poder y su gloria

nirvana *n.* in Buddhism, a state of perfect peace (p. 162)
nirvana *s.* en el budismo, estado de paz perfecta

noble *n.* a rich and powerful person (p. 111)
noble *s.* persona rica y poderosa

English and Spanish Glossary

nongovernmental organization (NGO) *n.* an organization made up of volunteers dedicated to solving a specific issue or problem (p. 1035)
Organización no gubernamental *s.* organizaciones no gubernamentales formadas por voluntarios

nonviolence *n.* the avoidance of violent actions (pp. 158, 987)
no violencia *s.* rechazo de las acciones violentas

North American Free Trade Agreement (NAFTA) *n.* a formal trade agreement signed by Mexico, the United States, and Canada; it went into effect in 1994 (p. 1024)
Tratado de Libre Comercio de América del Norte (TLCAN) *s.* acuerdo comercial formal, puesto en vigor en 1994, destinado a reducir o eliminar los aranceles entre México, Estados Unidos y Canadá

North Atlantic Treaty Organization (NATO) *n.* a defensive military alliance formed by the United States, Canada, and ten Western European countries to protect themselves from Soviet aggression (p. 959)
Organización del Tratado del Atlántico Norte (OTAN) *s.* alianza militar defensiva formada en 1949 por diez países de Europa occidental que se unió con los Estados Unidos y Canadá

Nuremberg Trials *n.* a number of trials of Nazi war criminals held at Nuremberg, Germany, after World War II (p. 946)
Juicios de Núremberg *s.* una serie de juicios de criminales de guerra nazis que se llevó a cabo en Núremberg, Alemania, después de la Segunda Guerra Mundial

O

oasis *n.* a wet, fertile area within a desert (p. 433)
oasis *s.* zona húmeda y fértil en un desierto

obelisk (AH-buh-lisk) *n.* a tall, pointed, four-sided pillar typical of ancient Egypt (p. 126)
obelisco *s.* pilar alto, de cuatro caras y acabado en punta, propio del antiguo Egipto

observatories *n.* buildings used to study astronomy; Mayan priests watched the stars from these buildings (p. 625)
observatorios *s.* edificios que sirven paraestudiar la astronomía; los sacerdotes mayas observaban las estrellas desde estos edificios

obsidian *n.* a sharp, glasslike volcanic rock that came from different parts of Mesoamerica (p. 691)
obsidiana *s.* roca volcánica afilada semejante al vidrio

Old Kingdom *n.* the period from about 2700 to 2200 BC in Egyptian history that began shortly after Egypt was unified (p. 110)
Reino Antiguo *s.* período de la historia egipcia que abarca aproximadamente del 2700 hasta el 2200 a. C. y comenzó poco después de la unificación de Egipto

oligarchy (AH-luh-gar-kee) *n.* a government in which only a few people have power (p. 264)
oligarquía *s.* gobierno en el que sólo unas pocas personas tienen el poder

OPEC *n.* an international organization whose members work to influence the price of oil on world markets by controlling the supply; founded in 1960 (p. 1020)
OPEP *s.* una organización internacional cuyos miembros trabajan para influir en el precio del petróleo en los mercados mundiales mediante el control de la oferta; fundada en 1960

oracle *n.* a prediction by a wise person, or a person who makes a prediction (p. 190)
oráculo *s.* predicción de un sabio o de alguien que hace profecías

oral history *n.* a spoken record of past events (p. 498)
historia oral registro *s.* hablado de hechos ocurridos en el pasado

orator *n.* public speaker (p. 348)
orador *s.* persona que habla en público

overpopulation *n.* when there are more people than resources in an area can support (p. 1060)
superpoblación *s.* ocurre cuando hay más gente que recursos en un área

ozone layer *n.* a layer of oxygen in Earth's atmosphere (p. 1061)
Capa de ozono *s.* capa de oxígeno en la atmósfera de la Tierra; también es nuestra principal protección contra los rayos ultravioletas dañinos del sol

P

Pakistan *n.* a nation formed in 1947; it originally included the area that is now Bangladesh (p. 989)
Pakistán *s.* incluye el área que actualmente es Bangladesh

Paleolithic Era (pay-lee-uh-LI-thik) *n.* the first part of the Stone Age; when people first used stone tools (p. 45)
Paleolítico *s.* primera parte de la Edad dePiedra; cuando el ser humano usó herramientas de piedra por primera vez

pandemic *n.* when a disease affects many people over a wide area, such as in different countries or continents (p. 1069)
pandemia *s.* enfermedad que afecta a personas de diferentes países o continentes

papyrus (puh-PY-ruhs) *n.* a long-lasting, paperlike material, made from reeds, that the ancient Egyptians used to write on (p. 123)
papiro *s.* material duradero hecho de juncos, similar al papel, que los antiguos egipcios utilizaban para escribir

Parliament (PAHR-luh-muhnt) *n.* the lawmaking body that governs England (p. 699)
Parlamento *s.* órgano legislador que gobierna Inglaterra

partition *n.* division (p. 989)
partición *s.* división

Passover *n.* a holiday in which Jews remember the Exodus (p. 247)
Pascua judía *s.* festividad en la que los judíos recuerdan el Éxodo

patricians (puh-TRI-shuhnz) *n.* the nobility in Roman society (p. 333)
patricios *s.* nobles de la sociedad romana

patrilineal *adj.* describes a society in which leadership passes from fathers or grandfathers to sons, grandsons, or nephews (p. 474)
sociedad patrilineal *adj.* en la cual el liderazgo pasa de los padres o abuelos a hijos, nietos, o sobrinos

patron *n.* a sponsor (p. 461)
mecenas *s.* patrocinador

Pax Romana *n.* Roman Peace; a period of general peace and prosperity in the Roman Empire that lasted from 27 BC to AD 180 (p. 358)

Pax Romana *s.* Paz Romana; período de paz y prosperidad generales en el Imperio romano que duró del 27 a. C. al 180 d. C.

peasant *n.* a farmer with a small farm (p. 193)
campesino *s.* agricultor dueño de una pequeña granja

Peloponnesian War *n.* a war between Athens and Sparta in the 400s BC (p. 277)
guerra del Peloponeso *s.* guerra entre Atenas y Esparta en el siglo V a. C.

perestroika *n.* the Soviet policy of economic restructuring (p. 975)
perestroika *s.* la política soviética de la reestructuración económica

Period of Disunion *n.* the time of disorder following the collapse of the Han dynasty (p. 518)
período de desunión *s.* la época de desorden que siguió el derrumbe de la dinastía Han

Persian Wars *n.* a series of wars between Persia and Greece in the 400s BC (p. 94)
guerras persas *s.* serie de guerras entre Persia y Grecia en el siglo V a. C.

persecution *n.* punishment of a group because of its beliefs or differences (p. 398)
persecución *s.* el castigo de un grupo debido a sus creencias o diferencias

perspective *n.* a method of showing a three-dimensional scene on a flat surface so that it looks real (p. 725)
perspectiva *s.* un método de mostrar una escena tridimensional sobre una superficie plana para que se vea real

phalanx (FAY-langks) *n.* a group of Greek warriors who stood close together in a square formation (p. 306)
falange *s.* grupo de guerreros griegos que semantenían unidos en formación compacta y cuadrada

pharaoh (FEHR-oh) *n.* the title used by the rulers of Egypt (p. 105)
faraón *s.* título usado por los gobernantes de Egipto

pharmaceuticals *n.* manufactured medical drugs (p. 1068)
fármacos *s.* drogas medicinales manufacturadas

English and Spanish Glossary

pictograph *n.* a picture symbol (p. 75)
pictograma *s.* símbolo ilustrado

pilgrimage *n.* a journey to a sacred place (p. 439)
peregrinación *s.* viaje a un lugar sagrado

plantation *n.* a large farm (p. 809)
plantación *s.* hacienda de grandes dimensiones

Platt Amendment *n.* amendment to Cuba's constitution that limited Cuba's right to make treaties and allowed the United States to intervene in Cuban affairs (p. 879)
Enmienda Platt *s.* documento que limitó el derecho de Cuba a hacer tratados, y permitió a los Estados Unidos intervenir en los asuntos cubanos

plebeians (pli-BEE-uhnz) *n.* the common people of ancient Rome (p. 333)
plebeyos *s.* gente común de la antigua Roma

polis (PAH-luhs) *n.* the Greek word for a city-state (p. 260)
polis *s.* palabra griega para designar una ciudad estado

political dissent *n.* a difference of opinion over political issues (p. 1038)
desacuerdo político *s.* diferencia de opinión sobre temas políticos

polytheism *n.* the worship of many gods (p. 74)
politeísmo *s.* culto a varios dioses

pope *n.* bishop of Rome (p. 400)
Papa *s.* obispo de Roma

Popol Vuh *n.* a book of Maya legends and history (p. 626)
Popol Vuh *s.* libro que contiene las leyendas mayas y la historia; fue escrito después de la llegada de los españoles

popular sovereignty *n.* the Enlightenment idea that governments should express the will of the people (p. 833)
soberanía popular *s.* idea de la Ilustraciónque consiste en que los gobiernos deben expresar la voluntad del pueblo

porcelain *n.* a thin, beautiful pottery invented in China (p. 526)
porcelana *s.* cerámica bella y delicada creada en China

potlatch *n.* an event where a host prepared a feast and gave valuable gifts (p. 653)
potlach *s.* evento utilizado para el comercio, la socialización y la mejora de las relaciones dentro de la comunidad o con una comunidad de vecinos

prehistory *n.* the time before there was writing (p. 42)
prehistoria *s.* período anterior a la existencia de la escritura

priest *n.* a person who performs religious ceremonies (p. 74)
sacerdote *s.* persona que lleva a cabo ceremonias religiosas

primary source *n.* an account of an event by someone who took part in or witnessed the event (p. 10)
fuente primaria *s.* relato de un hecho porparte de alguien que participó o presenció el hecho

principalities *n.* small states ruled by princes (p. 422)
principados *s.* pequeños estados gobernados por príncipes

profit *n.* the money an individual or business has left after paying expenses (p. 23)
ganancia *s.* el dinero que le queda a un individuo o negocio después de pagar los gastos

prophet *n.* someone who is said to receive messages from God to be taught to others (p. 238)
profeta *s.* alguien del que se cree que recibemensajes de Dios para transmitírselos a los demás

Protestant *n.* a Christian who protested against the Catholic Church (p. 751)
protestante *s.* cristiano que protestaba en contra de la Iglesia católica

proverb *n.* a short saying of wisdom or truth (p. 499)
proverbio *s.* refrán breve que expresa sabiduría o una verdad

province *n.* territory (p. 357)
provincia *s.* territorio

Punic Wars *n.* a series of wars between Rome and Carthage in the 200s and 100s BC (p. 344)
guerras púnicas *s.* sucesión de guerras entreRoma y Cartago en los siglos III y II a. C.

purgatory *n.* in Catholic teachings, a place where souls went before they went to heaven (p. 749)
purgatorio *s.* un lugar donde las almas fueron castigadas por los pecados que cometieron en la vida antes de que pudieran pasar al cielo

pyramid *n.* a huge triangular tomb built by the Egyptians and other peoples (p. 115)
pirámide *s.* tumba triangular y gigantesca construida por los egipcios y otros pueblos

Q

Quechua (KE-chuh-wuh) *n.* the language of the Inca (p. 642)
quechua *s.* idioma de los incas

Qur'an (kuh-RAN) *n.* the holy book of Islam (p. 438)
Corán *s.* libro sagrado del Islam

R

rabbi (RAB-eye) *n.* a Jewish religious leader and teacher (p. 244)
rabino *s.* líder y maestro religioso judío

racism *n.* the belief that some people are better than others because of racial traits, such as skin color (p. 811)
racismo *s.* la creencia de que algunas personas son mejores que otras debido a las características raciales, como el color de la piel

rain forest *n.* a moist, densely wooded area that contains many different plants and animals (p. 472)
selva tropical *s.* zona húmeda y con muchosárboles que contiene muchas variedades de plantas y animales

Raj *n.* the period when the British controlled India (p. 871)
Raj *s.* el período de control británico en la India

rationalist *n.* person who looks at the world in a reasonable and logical way (p. 774)

racionalista *s.* persona que vio al mundo de una manera racional o razonable y lógica

reason *n.* clear and ordered thinking (p. 296)
razón *s.* pensamiento claro y ordenado

recession *n.* a time of very slow economic activity (p. 1075)
recesión *s.* una época de actividad económica muy lenta

Reconquista (re-kahn-KEES-tuh) *n.* the effort of Christian kingdoms in northern Spain to retake land from the Moors during the Middle Ages (p. 703)
Reconquista *s.* esfuerzo de los reinos cristianosdel norte de España por recuperar los territorios en posesión de los moros durante la Edad Media

Reformation (re-fuhr-MAY-shuhn) *n.* a reform movement against the Roman Catholic Church that began in 1517; it resulted in the creation of Protestant churches (p. 748)
Reforma *s.* movimiento de reforma contra la Iglesia católica romana que comenzó en 1517; resultó en la creación de las iglesias protestantes

refugees *n.* people who leave their country to move to another for safety (p. 1047)
refugiados *s.* personas que salen de su país para pasar a otro por la seguridad

regent *n.* a person who rules a country for someone who is unable to rule alone (p. 562)
regente *s.* persona que gobierna un país en lugar de alguien que no puede hacerlo por su cuenta

region *n.* an area with one or more features that make it different from surrounding areas (p. 14)
región *s.* zona con una o varias características que la diferencian de las zonas que la rodean

reincarnation *n.* a Hindu and Buddhist belief that souls are born and reborn many times, each time into a new body (p. 156)
reencarnación *s.* creencia hindú y budista deque las almas nacen y renacen muchas veces, siempre en un cuerpo nuevo

religious order *n.* a group of people who dedicate their lives to religion and follow common rules (p. 692)
orden religiosa *s.* grupo de personas quededican su vida a la religión y respetan una serie de normas comunes

English and Spanish Glossary

Renaissance (re-nuh-SAHNS) *n.* the period of "rebirth" and creativity that followed Europe's Middle Ages (p. 721)
Renacimiento *s.* período de "volver a nacer" y creatividad posterior a la Edad Media en Europa

reparations *n.* payments for war damage (p. 899)
república *s.* sistema de gobierno en el que las personas consienten ser gobernadas por sus líderes electos

republic *n.* a political system in which people elect leaders to govern them (pp. 33, 331)
república *s.* sistema político en el que el pueblo elige a los líderes que lo gobernarán

resources *n.* the materials found on the earth that people need and value (p. 17)
recursos *s.* materiales de la Tierra que las personas necesitan y valoran

Resurrection *n.* in Christianity, Jesus' rise from the dead (p. 389)
Resurrección *s.* en el cristianismo, la vuelta a la vida de Jesús

rift *n.* a long, deep valley formed by the movement of the earth's crust (p. 470)
fisura *s.* valle largo y profundo formado por el movimiento de la corteza terrestre

Roman Senate *n.* a council of wealthy and powerful citizens who advised Rome's leaders (p. 337)
Senado romano *s.* consejo de ciudadanos ricosy poderosos que aconsejaba a los gobernantes de Roma

Romance languages *n.* languages that developed from Latin, including Italian, French, Spanish, Portuguese, and Romanian (p. 375)
lenguas romances *s.* lenguas que surgieron dellatín, como el italiano, el francés, el español, el portugués y el rumano

Rosetta Stone *n.* a huge stone slab inscribed with hieroglyphics, Greek, and a later form of Egyptian that allowed historians to understand Egyptian writing (p. 124)
piedra Roseta *s.* gran losa de piedra en laque aparecen inscripciones en jeroglíficos, en griego y en una forma tardía delidioma egipcio que permitió a los historiadores descifrar la escritura egipcia

rule of law *n.* the idea that everybody must follow the laws of the land (p. 838)
imperio de la ley *s.* principio que establece que los monarcas, como todo el mundo, estaban sujetos a las leyes de la tierra

rural *adj.* referring to a countryside area (p. 72)
rural *adj.* zona del campo

Rus *n.* Vikings from Scandinavia who likely traded with the Slavs (p. 414)
Rus *s.* vikingos de Escandinavia que probablemente negociaron con los eslavos

S

Sahel (sah-HEL) *n.* a semiarid region in Africa, just south of the Sahara, that separates the desert from wetter areas (p. 472)
Sahel *s.* región semiárida de África, situadaal sur del Sahara, que separa el desierto de otras zonas más húmedas

saint *n.* a person known and admired for his or her holiness (p. 396)
santo *s.* una persona conocida y admirada por su santidad

salon *n.* a social gathering held to discuss ideas during the Enlightenment (p. 829)
tertulia *s.* reunión social para debatir ideas; se acostumbraban celebrar durante la Ilustración

samskaras *n.* rites of passage to prepare a person for a certain event or for their next stage in life (p. 157)
samskaras *s.* ritos de paso para preparar a una persona para un determinado evento o para su próxima etapa de la vida

samurai (SA-muh-rye) *n.* a trained professional warrior in feudal Japan (p. 572)
samurai *s.* guerrero profesional del Japón feudal

sanctions *n.* economic or political penalties imposed by one country on another to force a policy change (p. 1007)
sanciones *s.* penalizaciones económicas o políticas impuestas por un país a otro para forzar un cambio de política

sand dunes *n.* hills of sand shaped by the wind (p. 432)
dunas de arena *s.* colinas de arena formadas por el viento

Sanskrit *n.* the most important language of ancient India (p. 151)

sánscrito *s.* el idioma más importante de la antigua India

satire *n.* style of writing that pokes fun at people or society (p. 375)

sátira *s.* estilo de escritura que se burla de las personas o de la sociedad

savannah *n.* an open grassland with scattered trees (p. 472)

sabana *s.* pradera abierta con árboles dispersos

scarcity *n.* when there are not enough resources to meet people's wants (p. 22)

escasez *s.* cuando no hay suficientes recursos para satisfacer las necesidades de las personas

scholar-official *n.* an educated member of the government (p. 532)

funcionario erudito *s.* miembro culto del gobierno

science *n.* a particular way of gaining knowledge about the world (p. 772)

ciencia *s.* manera específica de adquirir conocimientos sobre el mundo

scientific method *n.* a step-by-step method for performing experiments and other scientific research (p. 783)

método científico *s.* método detallado pararealizar experimentos y otros tipos de investigaciones científicas

Scientific Revolution *n.* a series of events that led to the birth of modern science; it lasted from about 1540 to 1700 (p. 772)

Revolución científica *s.* serie de acontecimientos que condujeron al nacimiento de la ciencia moderna; se extendió desde alrededor del 1540 hasta el 1700

scribe *n.* a writer (p. 75)

escriba *s.* escritor

seals *n.* stamped images (p. 146)

sellos *s.* imágenes estampadas

secondary source *n. i*nformation gathered by someone who did not take part in or witness an event (p. 11)

fuente secundaria *s.* información recopiladapor alguien que no participó ni presenció un hecho

securities *n.* investments in companies or governments, such as stock (p. 1078)

valores *s.* inversiones en empresas o gobiernos

sedentary *adj.* settled (p. 434)

sedentario *adj.* establecido

seismograph *n.* a device that measures the strength of an earthquake (p. 211)

sismógrafo *s.* aparato que mide la fuerza deun terremoto

serf *n.* a worker in medieval Europe who was tied to the land on which he or she lived (p. 676)

siervo *s.* trabajador de la Europa medievalque estaba atado al territorio en el que vivía

shah *n.* title for a Persian king (p. 1015)

Shah *s.* el Rey Persa

Shia (SHEE-ah) *n.* a member of the second-largest branch of Islam (p. 591)

shia *s.* miembro de la segunda rama más importante del Islam

Shinto *n.* the traditional religion of Japan (p. 561)

sintoísmo *s.* religión tradicional de Japón

shogun *n.* a general who ruled Japan in the emperor's name (p. 573)

shogun *s.* general que gobernaba Japón en nombre del emperador

shrine *n.* a place at which people worship a saint or a god (p. 439)

santuario *s.* un lugar en el que la gente adora a un santo o un dios

Sikhism *n.* a monotheistic religion that developed in India in the 1400s (p. 158)

sijismo *s.* una religion monoteísta que se desarrolló en la India en el siglo XV

silent barter *n.* a process in which people exchange goods without contacting each other directly (p. 482)

trueque silencioso *s.* proceso mediante el quelas personas intercambian bienes sin entrar en contacto directo

silk *n.* a soft, light, and highly valued fabric developed in China (p. 212)

seda *s.* tejido suave, ligero y muy apreciado que se originó en China

English and Spanish Glossary

Silk Road *n.* a network of trade routes that stretched across Asia from China to the Mediterranean Sea (p. 217)
Ruta de la Seda *s.* red de rutas comercialesque se extendían a lo largo de Asia desdeChina hasta el mar Mediterráneo

silt *n.* a mixture of fertile soil and tiny rocks that can make land ideal for farming (p. 67)
cieno *s.* mezcla de tierra fértil y piedrecitasque pueden crear un terreno ideal para el cultivo

social hierarchy *n.* the division of society by rank or class (p. 75)
jerarquía social *s.* división de la sociedad en clases o niveles

socialism *n.* a political and economic system in which the government owns the means of production (p. 861)
socialismo *s.* sistema social en el que losmedios de producción pertenecen a los trabajadores o están controlados por el gobierno

society *n.* a community of people who share a common culture (p. 47)
sociedad *s.* comunidad de personas que comparten la misma cultura

souk *n.* a market or bazaar (p. 434)
zoco *s.* un mercado o bazar

Spanish Armada *n.* a large fleet of Spanish ships that was defeated by England in 1588 (p. 802)
Armada española *s.* gran flota de barcos españoles que fue derrotada por Inglaterra en 1588

Spanish Inquisition *n.* an organization of priests in Spain that looked for and punished people suspected of secretly practicing their old religion (p. 704)
Inquisición española *s.* organización desacerdotes que perseguía y castigaba a las personas que no eran cristianas en España

spheres of influence *n.* areas in China over which other countries had economic power (p. 872)
esferas de influencia *s.* áreas sobre las cuales los países tienen el poder económico

sphinx (sfinks) *n.* an imaginary creature with a human head and the body of a lion that was often shown on Egyptian statues (p. 126)

esfinge *s.* criatura imaginaria con cabeza humana y cuerpo de león que aparecía re-presentada a menudo en las estatuas egipcias

standard of living *n.* how well people in a nation can meet their needs and wants (p. 1074)
nivel de vida *s.* qué tan bien la gente en una nación puede satisfacer sus necesidades y deseos

stocks *n.* pieces of a company (p. 906)
acciones *s.* representa partes de una empresa

sub-Saharan Africa *n.* Africa south of the Sahara (p. 470)
África subsahariana *s.* parte de África que queda al sur del Sahara

subcontinent *n.* a large landmass that is smaller than a continent, such as India (p. 144)
subcontinente *s.* gran masa de tierra menor que un continente, como la India

Suez Canal *n.* a waterway built in Egypt in the 1860s to connect the Mediterranean and Red Seas (p. 866)
Canal del Suez *s.* una vía de agua construida en Egipto en la década de 1860 para conectar los mares Mediterráneo y Rojo

Sufism (SOO-fi-zuhm) *n.* a movement in Islam that taught people they can find God's love by having a personal relationship with God (p. 459)
sufismo *s.* movimiento perteneciente al Islamque enseñaba a las personas que pueden hallar el amor de Dios si establecen una relación personal con Él

sultan *n.* Ottoman ruler (p. 587)
sultán *s.* gobernante otomano

sundial *n.* a device that uses the position of shadows cast by the sun to tell the time of day (p. 211)
reloj de sol *s.* dispositivo que utiliza laposición de las sombras que proyecta el sol para indicar las horas del día

Sunnah (SOOH-nuh) *n.* a collection of writings about the way Muhammad lived that provides a model for Muslims to follow (p. 442)
Sunna *s.* conjunto de escritos sobre la vidade Mahoma que proporciona un modelo de comportamiento para los musulmanes

Sunni *n.* a member of the largest branch of Islam (p. 591)
  suní *s.* miembro de la rama más importante del Islam

surplus *n.* more of something than is needed (p. 68)
  excedente *s.* cantidad que supera lo que se necesita

sustainable growth *n.* the process of creating economic growth while preserving the environment (p. 1064)
  desarrollo sostenible *s.* el proceso de crear crecimiento económico, preservando el medio ambiente

Swahili *n.* blended African-Arab culture (p. 509)
  suajili *s.* mezcla de la cultura africana y árabe

synagogue (SI-nuh-gawg) *n.* a Jewish house of worship (p. 238)
  sinagoga *s.* lugar de culto judío

T

taiga *n.* vast forest of evergreens, which covers about half of Russia (p. 413)
  taiga *s.* extenso bosque de árboles de hoja perenne, que ocupa la mitad de Rusia

Taliban *n.* a radical Muslim group in Afghanistan (p. 1018)
  Talibán *s.* grupo musulmán radical que llegó al poder en Afganistán en la década de 1990

Talmud (TAHL-moohd) *n.* a set of commentaries and lessons for everyday life in Judaism (p. 239)
  Talmud *s.* Conjunto de comentarios y lecciones para la vida diaria en el judaísmo

tariff *n.* a fee that a country charges on imports or exports (p. 996)
  arancel *s.* una tarifa que cobra un país de importación o exportación

tax *n.* a charge people pay to a government (p. 33)
  impuesto *s.* un cargo que las personas pagan a un gobierno

telecommute *v.* to perform jobs by computer from home (p. 1055)
  teletrabajo *v.* trabajar desde casa

Ten Commandments *n.* in the Bible, a code of moral laws given to Moses by God (p. 230)
  los Diez Mandamientos *s.* en la Biblia, códigode leyes morales que Dios le entregó a Moisés

theocracy *n.* a government ruled by religious authorities (p. 110)
  teocracia *s.* un gobierno regido por las autoridades religiosas

theory *n.* an explanation a scientist develops based on facts (p. 772)
  teoría *s.* explicación que desarrolla un científico basándose en hechos

Thirty Years' War *n.* a long series of wars, mostly between Catholics and Protestants, that involved several countries in Europe, especially in the Holy Roman Empire (p. 762)
  Guerra de los Treinta Años *s.* una serie larga de guerras, sobre todo entre católicos y protestantes, que involucró a varios países de Europa, especialmente en el Sacro Imperio Romano

Tiananmen Square *n.* a public area in Beijing, the capital of China (p. 998)
  Plaza de Tiananmén *s.* ubicación de una protesta en Beijing, China en 1989, que resultó en la muerte de cientos de manifestantes a manos de las tropas del gobierno y tanques

tolerance *n.* acceptance (p. 451)
  tolerancia *s.* aceptación

tool *n.* an object that has been modified to help a person accomplish a task (p. 45)
  herramienta *s.* objeto que ha sido modificado para ayudar a una persona a realizar una tarea

Torah *n.* the first five books of the Hebrew Bible and the most sacred text of Judaism (p. 238)
  Torá *s.* los primeros cinco libros de la biblia hebrea y el texto más sagrado

totalitarianism *n.* a system in which the government controls all aspects of people's lives (p. 920)
  totalitarismo *s.* un sistema en el que el gobierno controla todos los aspectos de la vida de las personas

townships *n.* crowded clusters of tiny homes (p. 1007)
  municipios *s.* zonas especialmente designadas para los residentes negros en las ciudades de África del Sur, con grupos abarrotados de pequeñas casas

English and Spanish Glossary

trade *n.* exchanging goods and services (p. 26)
comercio *s.* intercambio de bienes y servicios

trade network *n.* a system of people in different lands who trade goods back and forth (p. 133)
red comercial *s.* sistema de personas en dife rentes lugares que comercian productos entre sí

trade route *n.* a path followed by traders (p. 119)
ruta comercial *s.* itinerario seguido por los comerciantes

trade surplus *n.* when a country exports more goods than it imports (p. 996)
superávit comercial *s.* cuando un país exporta más bienes de los que importa

Treaty of Versailles *n.* the peace treaty that ended World War I; signed in Versailles, France, on June 28, 1919 (p. 897)
Tratado de Versalles *s.* tratado de paz firmado por los líderes aliados en Versalles después de la Primera Guerra Mundial

Truman Doctrine *n.* policy of providing aid to help foreign countries fight communism (p. 957)
Doctrina Truman *s.* política de proporcionar ayuda a los países extranjeros que luchan contra el comunismo

tyrant *n.* an ancient Greek leader who held power through the use of force (p. 265)
tirano *s.* gobernante de la antigua Grecia que mantenía el poder mediante el uso de la fuerza

U

United Nations (UN) *n.* international organization that aims to maintain peace and security around the world (p. 944)
Naciones Unidas (ONU) *s.* organización internacional que tiene como objetivo mantener la paz y la seguridad en todo el mundo

Universal Declaration of Human Rights *n.* a UN declaration that defines human rights goals for the world community (pp. 998, 1035)
Declaración Universal de los Derechos Humanos *s.* adoptada en 1948, esta declaración define los objetivos de los derechos humanos para la comunidad mundial

unlimited government *n.* a government in which one person or group of people holds all power with no restrictions (p. 830)
gobierno ilimitado *s.* gobierno en el que una persona o grupo de personas tienen todo el poder sin restricciones

Ural Mountains *n.* Russian mountain range (p. 410)
montes Urales *s.* cordillera en Rusia

urban *adj.* referring to a city area (p. 72)
urbano *adj.* zona de ciudad

V

vassal *n.* a knight who promised to support a lord in exchange for land in medieval Europe (p. 674)
vasallo *s.* caballero de la Europa medieval que prometía apoyar a un señor feudal a cambio de tierras

veto (VEE-toh) *v.* to reject or prohibit actions and laws of other government officials (p. 338)
vetar *v.* rechazar o prohibir acciones y leyesde otros funcionarios del gobierno

Vietcong *n.* South Vietnamese fighters who supported the Communist government of North Vietnam (p. 965)
Vietcong *s.* combatientes de Vietnam del Sur que apoyaron el gobierno comunista de Vietnam del Norte

Volga *n.* the longest river in Europe; it flows south through western Russia to the Caspian Sea (p. 412)
Volga *s.* el río más largo de Europa; que fluye hacia el sur a través del oeste de Rusia hasta el mar Caspio

W

wampum *n.* strings of beads (p. 654)
wampum *s.* collares de cuentas

war crime *n.* violation of the laws of war as defined by international treaties and customs (p. 945)
crimen de guerra *s.* violación de las leyes de la guerra tal como se definen en los tratados y costumbres internacionales

Warsaw Pact *n.* an alliance formed by the Soviet Union and Eastern European countries to protect themselves from the threat they believed NATO posed (p. 959)
Pacto de varsovia *s.* una alianza formada por los países de Europa del Este y la Unión Soviética para protegerse de la amenaza que representaba la OTAN

wealth *n.* the value of all possessions that a person or country has (p. 28)
riqueza *s.* el valor de todas las cosas que una persona o un país tiene

woodblock printing *n.* a form of printing in which an entire page is carved into a block of wood, covered with ink, and pressed to a piece of paper to create a printed page (p. 527)
xilografia *s.* forma de impresión en la que una página completa se talla en una planchade madera, se cubre de tinta y se presiona sobre un papel para crear la página impresa

World Bank *n.* organization that provides loans for large projects in countries that need them (p. 1079)
Banco Mundial *s.* organización internacional que proporciona préstamos para proyectos de desarrollo a gran escala

Y

yellow journalism *n.* a type of journalism in which stories are exaggerated in order to attract readers (p. 877)
prensa amarilla *s.* técnica usada por los periódicos de Estados Unidos para atraer a los lectores; la impresión de las noticias sensacionales, con hechos a menudo exagerados

Z

Zealots (ZE-luhts) *n.* radical Jews who supported rebellion against the Romans (p. 242)
zelotes *s.* judíos radicales que apoyaron la rebelión contra los romanos

Zen *n.* a form of Buddhism that emphasizes meditation (p. 569)
zen *s.* forma del budismo que se basa en la meditación

ziggurat *n.* a pyramid-shaped temple in Sumer (p. 77)
zigurat *s.* templo sumerio en forma de pirámide

Index

KEY TO INDEX

c = chart	*p* = photo
f = feature	*R* = Reference
m = map	*t* = table

A

'Abbas, 592, 594

Abbasids, 450

abolition, 862

Aborigines, 874, 875

Abraham, *225t*, 228, *229m*, *232t*; and Kaaba, 441; and Muhammad, 439

absolute dating, 8

absolute location, 15–16

absolute monarchy, *32c*, 33; in China, 200, 201

Abu Bakr, 448

Abu Ubayd al-Bakri, 500

accept social responsibility, 851

acropolis, 260

Acropolis, the, 293, 301 MC1–301 MC2

Actium, Battle of, 352, *352f*

acupuncture, *210f*, 211

adobe, 651

Adwa, Battle of, *868f*, 869

Aeneas, 330, *330f*, 334–335

Aeneid, The, 330, *330f*, 334–335, 375

Aeschylus, 287

Aesop, 285, *285f*

Afghanistan: and Doctors without Borders, 1041; invaded by Soviet Union, *951t*, 967–968; Taliban, 1018

Africa: during the Age of Exploration, 798; Aksum, 135, 506; Bantu migration, 507–508; Berbers, 449; Berlin Conference, 867; Boer War, *855t*, 867–868; cities in, *1011f*, 1012; and Columbian Exchange, 807; communist countries in, 968; culture today, 1012–1013; democracy in, 1010, *1010f*; East, 506–510; economies in, 1011; environmental challenges,

1012; European imperialism in, 864–865, *866m*, 867, 1000, 1001, *1003m*; family life in, 473–475, *475f*, 507; French Community, 1003–1004, *1003m*; geography of, 470–472, *471m*; hominids in, *46c*; infrastructure, 1011; Kush, *101t*, 118, 129–135, *130m*; and migration, 50, 51, *51m*; Nile River, 104–106, 129; Nubia, 129; religion in, 476; resistance to colonization, 868–869, *868f*; resources, 472, 863–864, *864p*, *865f*; and slave trade, 814; Suez Canal, *855t*, 866–867, 1014–1015, *1017t*; trade with Muslims, 450; sub-Saharan, 470; West, 470–477; and World War I, *885t*, 1000; World War II, 928, 1001; Zulu, 868, 869. *See also individual countries*

African National Congress (ANC), 1006–1007

Africanus, Leo, 501

afterlife, 113, *114p*, 116, art for the, 126

Age of Reason, 826–829, *827f*, *828p*

age-sets, 474, 475

agora, 260

agriculture: beginnings of, *39t*, 55–56; in China, 523–524; Harrapan, 146; Hellenistic, *314f*; maize, 617–618; in Mesopotamia, *63t*, 67–68, 69; in Mesoamerica, 612, 615, 617–618; in Nubia, 129; and river valley civilizations, 70; in Roman Republic, 343

Aguinaldo, Emilio, 876, 878, 880

Ahmose, 117

AIDS (acquired immunodeficiency syndrome): 1012, 1071–1072, *1071c*

Ainu culture, 560

air: one of the four elements, 57

Ajanta, 172

Akbar, 600

Akkadian Empire, 73–74, *73m*, *74f*

Akrotiri, 262–263, 293

Aksum, *101t*, 135, 506

alchemy, 775

Alexander the Great, *141t*, *303t*, 307, *319t*, *325t*; blending cultures, 310, 316; death of, 308; empire of, 307–308, *309m*, *314f*; and his horse, *308f*, *308p*; and the Persians, 307, 308

Alexandria (Egypt), *297f*, 313, 316–317, *317i*

Ali, *439f*, 449

al-Idrisi, *452f*, 457–458

algebra, 458

Algeria, 1004

Alighieri, Dante, *713t*, 724

alliance, 277; during World War I, *892m*, 892; during World War II, 924, 927, *927f*; and European nationalism, 892, *892m*

Allied Powers, 924; D-Day invasion, *915t*, 928–929, *928f*, *929m*; leaders of, *927f*; occupation of Japan, 944–945; in Pacific theater, 930–931, *930m*, 949 MC2; V-E Day, 941; V-J Day, 942

Allies (WWI), *885t*, *892m*, 893, *895c*; redrawing European boundaries, 898, *898m*; and Russia's revolution, 904

alloys, 174

al-Masudi, 500

Almoravids, 486

alphabets: Greek, 286; Phoenician, 90

American Indians: Eastern cultures, 654–656, *652m*, *654t*; the Haida, *652m*, 653; the Inuit, *652m*, 653, *653p*; mound builders, 651, 653, *653p*; Northwestern cultures, *652m*, 653; Plains cultures, 654, *652m*; and plantations, 810; Southwestern cultures, 650–651, *650p*, *652m*, *654t*

Index

American Revolution, *823t*; 838–839, 853 MC1-853 MC2, *855t*

Americas: *661t*; first civilizations, 615–618, *617m*; and Columbian Exchange, 806–811, *807m, 808f, 809f*; and the Enlightenment, 833–834, 835–836; geography of, 612, *613m*, 614; migration to, 614–615, *614m*; missionaries to, 759, *759f*, 808; religious divisions, 760–761. *See also* Mesoamerica; North America; South America

Amritsar massacre, 986

Analects, The, 195f, 196. *See also* Confucius

analyze costs and benefits, 299

analyze tables, 789

Anasazi, *650p*, 651

ancestors: in Bantu society, 508; hominids as, 42; and storytellers, 498; in West Africa, 476, 498; worshipped, 58, 189

Anglican Church, 754

Angola, 1005

animals: and Columbian Exchange, 806, 807, *807m*; domestication of, 56, 76

animism, 476, 491

Annam, 548

anthropologists, 42; Donald Johanson, 43–44, *44p*; Tim White, 44

Antigonus, 311–312

Anti-Imperialist League, 879

Antioch, 312

anti-Semitism, 934

Antony, Marc, *313f*, 352

Anubis, 113, *113f, 114p*

apartheid, 1006–1008

Apostles, 391–392, *391p*, 400

aqueduct, 372, *372p*, 631

Aquinas, Thomas, 695–696, *695f*, 775; and the Enlightenment, 827

Aquino, Corazon, 998

Arabia: geography of, 432–433, *433m*; government of, 450; life in, 434; trade centers,

434, *435f*, 436, *436f*; trade routes through, *429t*, 432, 436; Umayyad family, 449; united, *429t*, 448

Arabic numerals, 458, *459f*

Arab Spring, *1031t*, 1046–1047, 1048

archaeologists, *7p*, 7–8, 10, 42; Mary Leakey, 42, *42p*; Louis Leakey, 42, 44

archaeology, 7–8; sites in the Americas, 614–615

Archimedes, 298, 320

architects: in Egypt, 121

architecture: Aztec, 636; Christian, 696, *696f*; Ethiopian, *507p*; Greek, 293; Japanese, 568; Mayan, 625; and the Medici family, 720; of Mughal Empire, 604; Muslim, 461, *461f*; of Ottoman Empire, 589–590, *589p*; Persian, 93; Renaissance, 730; Russian, 423; Safavid, 592, *592p*; Sumerian, 77, *78p*

Argentina, 1021–1022; Falkland Islands, 1023

argument: determine the strength of an, 1027

Aristarchus, 320

aristocracy, 33, 265

aristocrats: in Athens, 264–265

Aristophanes, 288

Aristotle, 269, *269f*, 296, *296i*; and the Enlightenment, 826–827; and the Scientific Revolution, *773f*, 774

Armenia: genocide, 894

arms race, 959, 974; SALT talks, 972

arquebus, 496

art: Aztec, 636, *636f*; cave paintings, 49, *49p*; Chinese, 210–211, *210f*, 522; Christian, 697; Egyptian, 126, 128; Greek, 292–293, Harappan, *147p*; Incan, 646; in India, 170; in the Industrial Revolution, *861f*, 862; Italian, 725; Korean, 547, *547f*; of Muslim Empire, 461–462; Northern Renaissance, 734–736, *735f*;

Persian, 93; perspective in, 725, *726p*; Renaissance, 721, 723, 725, *726p*; Safavid, 593; and the Silk Road, 218; Stone Age, 48–49, *49p*; Sumerian, 78–79; West African, 501–502

Articles of Confederation, 839–840

artifacts, 10

artillery, 701

artisans: Aztec, 634, *634i*; in Chinese, 189; Egyptian, 120

artists: Albrecht Dürer, 735, *735f*, Egyptian, 121; Hans Holbein, 736; Jan van Eyck, 736; and the Medici family, 720; Pieter Brueghel, 735, *735f*; Renaissance, 725

Aryans, *141t*, 149, *150m*, *181t*; caste system of, 152–154, *153f*; government of, 149–150; religion of, 151–152; society of, 150–151

Ascanius, 330

ask questions: to make predictions, 584

assembly: Greek, 267–268, *267f*, Roman, *337f*, 338

Ashkenazim, 245, *246f*. *See also* Jews

Asia: and Columbian Exchange, 807; culture, 999; democracy, 996; economic growth in, 994–995, *995f*; migration to, 50, 51, *51m*; SARS pandemic, *1031t*, 1069–1070; trade with Europe, 718

Askia the Great, 495–496, *495i*, *793t*

Asoka, 164–165, 168–169

Assad, Bashar al-, 1047–1048

assess sources, 662

Assyrian empire, *84m*, 85, *85p*, 118; and Israel, 233, *325t*; and Kush, 133

astrolabe, 456, *457f*, 797

astronauts, *951t*

astronomy: and Aztecs, 636, *636f*; in Babylon, 86; Tyco Brahe, 778; in China, 211;

Copernicus, 776–778, *777p*, *777f*; Galileo, 778–779, *778i*, *779f*; in Hellenistic kingdoms, 320; in India, *175f*, 176; Johannes Kepler, 778, *778i*, *779f*; and Mayans, 625; in Mughal Empire, 603; in Muslim Empire, 456–457, *457f*; and navigation, 90; in Ottoman Empire, 588–589; during Renaissance, 730

Aswan High Dam, 106

Atahualpa, 646–647, *646p*

Atatürk, Kemal, *915t*, 1014, *1015f*

Athens, 32, 94, 95; acropolis, 260; the Acropolis, 293, 301 MC1–301 MC2; alliance, 277; democracy in, *253t*, 264, 267–270, *267f*, *270f*, *609t*; drama in, 287–288; and Macedonia, 306; men in, 275–276; the Parthenon, 293, *294f*; in the Peloponnesian War, 277–278, *278m*; in the Persian Wars, 277; slaves in, 277; society in, *274f*, 275–277, *275f*, *276f*; women in, 276. *See also* Greece

atlas, 814

atman, 151, 156, *157f*

atomic bomb, *915t*, 942, 943

Attila, 368–369, *407t*

Augustine of Hippo, 401

Aung San Suu Kyi, *753f*, 998, 1045, *1045f*

Aurangzeb, 601, 603

Auschwitz-Birkenau, 937, *937f*, *937f*, 939

Australia: Aborigines, 874, 875; and Britain, *855t*, 874–875; migration to, 51, *51m*

Australopithecus, *39t*, 43, *46c*

Austria: *Kristallnacht*, 935; and World War II, 924

Austria-Hungary: as a Central Power, 893; and start of World War I, 892–893; after World War I, 898, *898m*

authoritarian state, 830–831

Avicenna, 458, 730

Avignon papacy, 748

Axis Powers, 924, *927f*

Ayatollah Khomeini, *983t*

Aztec Empire, *467t*, 630, *631m*, *643c*; architecture of, 636; art of, 636, *636f*; and Cortés, *583t*, 637–638, *638i*, 799–800; economy and trade of, 630–631; geography of, 630, 631, *631m*; and Moctezuma II, *609t*, 637, *637f*; oral history of, 637; religion of, 634–635, *635f*; science of, 635–636, *636f*; society of, 632–634; stories of, 637; Tenochtitlán, 631, 632, *632i*, 636, 638, 639; and war, 630

B

Babur, 600

Babylon, 82; under the Chaldeans, 86; conquered by Persians, 91, 118; empire of, *84m*; and Hammurabi, 82–83; Jews enslaved in, *225t*, 233, 238, 245; Seleucus, *303t*

Babylonian Captivity, *225t*, 233, 238, 245

Bacon, Francis, 782, *784f*, 787–788

Baghdad, 452–453

Bahadur Shah II, 603

balance of trade, 812–813

Balboa, Vasco Núñez de, 801

Balkan Peninsula, 412

Balts, 413

banking: and factories, 860; in Florence, 720; Roman, *342f*

Bantu: 507, Great Zimbabwe, *467t*, 508–509; and Islam, 509–510; migration, 507–508, *508m*; society, 508

baptism, 392

barometer, 781

barter system, 27, 57; silent, 482–483

Bastille, 842

Beijing: Forbidden City, 539–540, *539f*

Belgian Congo, 1004, becomes Zaire, 1008, 1009

Belgium: Battle of the Bulge, 930; and the Congo, 1004

Benedict, 668–669

benefits: analyze, 299

ben Zaccai, Yohanan, 244

Berbers, 449, 480

Berlin airlift, 958–959, *958m*

Berlin Conference, 867

Berlin Wall, *951t*, 959

Bessemer, Henry, *855t*, 858, *859f*

Bhagavad Gita, 174

Bhutto, Benazir, 998

bias: identify, 408

Bible: Christian, 228, 388, *438f*; first printed book, 733; Hebrew, 228, 235; *Sermon on the Mount*, 394–395; translated, 752

Bill of Rights: English, 838, *840f*, *841f*; U.S., 840

biotechnology, 1068

bishops, 400, and the Reformation, 748, 749; in Byzantine Empire, 418; and Constantine, 402; and Great Schism, 682

Bismark, Otto von, 889–890, *890p*

Black Death, *515t*, *661t*, 701–702, *701f*, 708–709, 716

Black Tuesday, 906

blitzkrieg, 925, 932

Block, Adriaen, 801

Blue Mosque, *461f*

Boers, 867

Boer War, *855t*, 867–868

Bolívar, Simon, 848, *848f*

Bolivia: declares independence, *823t*, *848f*, *849m*

Bolsheviks, 903, 904

Bonaparte, Napoleon: as emperor, 844–845, *845p*; defeat, 845–846

Book of Golden Meadows, 460

Book of the Dead, *124p*, 125

Bosnia-Herzegovina: ethnic conflict, 1039

Botswana, 1010

Botticelli, Sandro, 725

Boudicca, *325t*

Boxer Rebellion, 873

Brahma, 155, *156f*

Index

brahman, 151, 155

Brahe, Tycho, 778

Brahmins, 151, 152, *153f;* and the Buddha, 162

Brazil: rain forest, *1063c,* 1064; Zika virus, *1031t,* 1070

Brezhnev, Leonid, 970–971, 972, 973

Britain, Battle of, 926

British East India Company, 870–871

British Empire: and India, 598; and Mughal Empire, 603. *See also* England; Great Britain

Bronze Age, 77; in China, *194f*

Brueghel, Pieter, 735, *735f*

Brunelleschi, Filippo, 730

Brutus, 351, 352

bubonic plague, *701f. See also* black death

Buddha, 140, 173, *213p;* Siddhartha Gautama, 160–162; teachings of, 162–163, *163f, 225t*

Buddhism, *101t,* 164–165, *164m;* and Asoka, 168–169; beginnings of, 160–162; challenging Hinduism, 162–163; in China, 169, 212–213, 218, *381t,* 520–522, *521m, 521f,* 531; Eightfold Path, 162, *163f;* Four Noble Truths, 162; and the Gupta dynasty, 170; in Japan, 545, *555t, 562f,* 563–564, *563p, 564p,* 569, *569c;* in Korea, 546; temples, 170, 172, 173, *181t, 563p;* and trade routes, 27; traditions of, 165–166; in Vietnam, *548p,* 549; Zen, 569, *569c,* 575

Bulge, Battle of the, 930

bureaucracy, 532

Burma, 998, 1045

Bush, George W., 1019

Bushido, 574–575, 576

Byzantine Empire, *407t, 417m, 418f;* and Christianity, 418–419, conquered by Muslim Empire, 448, 586–587; and the Crusades, 686; government of, 418

Byzantium, 415

C

Cabot, John, *793t, 800m,* 801

Cabral, Pedro, 799, *800m*

Caesar, Augustus, *225t, 325t,* 352, 354

Caesar, Julius, *313f, 325t;* 348–351; *349p, 351f,* 379 MC2; death of, 351, *350p,* 352, *467t*

Cahokia, *609t*

Calakmul, *429t,* 622

calendar: Aztec, 636, *636f;* Chinese, 190; Egyptian, 125; Mayan, 625, *625f*

Caligula, 354

caliphs, 448; and Muslim conflict, 591; stories about, 460; Umayyad family, 449

calligraphy, *461f,* 462, 568

Callimachus, 310

calpullis, 632

Calvin, John, 753–754, *753f*

Cambyses, 92

camels: and trade, *467t,* 478, 480. *See also* caravans

Canaan, 228, 231

Canada: and exploration, 801; the Haida, *652m,* 653; the Inuit, *652m,* 653, *653p;* part of NAFTA, 1024, 1077

canals, 68, *68f,* 106; in China, 203, 519, 525, *525f,* 536; Panama Canal, 880; Suez Canal, *855t,* 866–867; and the Volga, 412

Candra Gupta I, *141t,* 170

Candra Gupta II, 170

capital, 24

capitalism, 816, *835f,* 860

caravans, 434, 436, 437, *458f,* 478, 480, *492f*

caravels, 797–798, *797f*

Caribbean Islands: explorers, 821 MC1, 821 MC2

Carpathians, 411–412

Carter, Jimmy, *967p,* 972

Carthage: in Punic Wars, *325t,* 344, *344f, 345m;* trade with Phoenicia, 88

Cartier, Jacques, *800m,* 801

cartography: during Renaissance, 730. *See also* maps

Casas, Bartolomé de las, 810

caste system, 152–154, *153f;* and the Buddha, 163; and dharma, 156; in Gupta dynasty, 171; and karma, 156; in Mauryan society, 167

Castro, Fidel, 966, *966p*

Çatal Hüyük, *39t, 56i,* 57, 58

cataracts, 104, 107, *130p*

categorize information, 1032

Cathedral of Saint Sophia, *407t,* 423, *423p*

cathedrals, *696f*

Catherine the Great, 831–832, *831p*

Catholic Church (Roman): Avignon papacy, 682–683; conflict with science, 786–788, *787p;* after Council of Trent, 758; in Europe, *761m;* Great Schism, 682; and Martin Luther, *745t;* missionaries, 758–759, *759f;* and medieval politics, 692; popes, 680–681, 682, *683f;* and the Reformation, 748–750, 763; scholars, 774–775, *774f;* spread of, 759, *759f;* wars with Protestants, 761–763; wealth of, 749. *See also* Christianity; Eastern Orthodox Church

Catholic Reformation, 755, 756–758, *757f;* and missionaries, 758–759, *759f*

cause-and-effect connections: identify, 249

causeways, 631, 638

cavalry, 92

cave paintings, 49, *49p*

Cavour, Camillo di, 889

celadon, 547, *547f*

censors: in Ming dynasty, 540

central issues: identify, 59

Central Powers, 892, *895c*

centuries (army), 343

ceremonies: religious, 74. *See also individual religions*

Cervantes, Miguel de, 737

Cetshwayo, *869p*

Chaldeans, the, 86; and Judah, 233

Index

Champollion, Jean-François, 124

chance, error, and oversight in history, 425

Chang'an, 524

Chang Jiang, 186, 187

chariots, 84, 85, 117, 120, 167; racing, 359, *359p*

charity, 241

Charlemagne, *407t, 555t, 661t,* 669–671, *669f, 670p, 670m*

Charles I, king of England, 837

Charles II, king of England, 837

charts: interpret, 321

Chavez, Cesar, *158f, 753f*

Chavin culture, 617, *617m,* 640

checks and balances: in Roman Republic, 339; in United States, *338f*

chemical warfare, 893

chiefs: Bantu, 508; Japanese, 561; West African, 474, *475f*

children: and clean water, 1062; in Egypt, 122; in medieval Europe, 676; in Incan Empire, 644; Muslim, *444p;* in Nazi Germany, *920p;* rights abuses against, 1037–1038, *1038p,* 1042; in Roman Republic, 340–341; in West Africa, 476. *See also* family; human rights

Chile, *983t,* 1023

Chimu culture, 640

China: absolute monarchy, 200, 201; acupuncture, *210f,* 211; agriculture in, 187, 523–524; art of, 526–257, *527f;* and Buddhism, 212–213, 218, *381t,* 520–522, *521m, 521f,* 531; cities, 524–525; civil service exams, 532–533, *532f,* 540; as a classical civilization, 206; civil war in, 961, 989–990; becomes communist, *951t,* 961, 990–991, *990f;* and Confucianism, 195, 196–197, *196f,* 207, 208, 530–531, *531p;* Cultural Revolution, *951t,* 962–963; early civilization in, 187–188;
economy, 996; Empress Wu, 520, *520f;* family life in, 208–209, *209p,* 531; Forbidden City, 539–540, *539f;* geography of, 184–186, *185m;* Grand Canal, 519, 525, *525p,* 536; Great Wall, 223 MC1–223 MC2, 540, 542–543; growing rice, 523, *524f, 525f;* Han dynasty, *181t, 207t, 207m,* 206–213, *303t, 325t, 368c,* 530–531, 546, *602c;* invaded by Japan, *922p,* 923, 961; inventions in, 527–528, *527f;* isolationism of, 540–541; and Korea, 544, 546–548, *546p, 546f, 548t;* and Kublai Khan, *467t,* 537, 576–577, *576m;* literature of, 214–215, *515t,* 520, 526–527; Long March, *915t;* Mao Zedong, *915t,* 961–963, *962p, 983t;* Marco Polo, *713t;* Ming dynasty, *515t, 528f,* 538, 539–541, *713t;* money system for, 202; Mongols take over, 534–535, *555t;* National Day celebration, *990f;* Period of Disunion, 518, 520; political dissent, 1038; pottery in, *3t;* pro-democracy protestors, 997–998, *997f;* Qin dynasty, *181t, 201t,* 200–203, *201m,* 205, *325t,* 530; Qing dynasty, 989; religious persecution in, 1040; Shang dynasty, *63t, 141t, 181t, 188m,* 189–191; silk production in, 525–526; and the Silk Road, 27, *181t,* 216–218, *217m,* 220–221, *303t;* social hierarchy in, 208; Song dynasty, *519m,* 520, 523, 524, *526m,* 531; and Soviet Union, 971; standardized written language for, 202; Sui dynasty, *515t,* 519, *519m,* 525, 544; Taizong, 520; Tang dynasty, *429t, 515t,* 519–520, *519m,* 524, 525, *526m,* 526–529, *527f,* 531, 546, *548t;* Tiananmen
Square protest, *997f,* 998; trade, 315, 525–526, 529, 536; unified, 202–203, 205; and Vietnam, 548–549, *548p, 548t, 549p;* and Westerners, 872–873, *873m;* during World War II, 961; Xia dynasty, 188–189; Xuanzong, 520; Yuan dynasty, *515t,* 536–537; Zheng He, 538–539, *538f,* 540, *661t;* Zhou dynasty, *101t, 181t,* 192–199, *193t, 193m;* Zhu Yuanzhang, 537–538

Chosun kingdom, 546

Christian humanism, 734

Christianity, 386–387, 389, *399t, 438f;* the Apostles, 391–393, 400; and architecture, 696–697, *696f;* and art, 697; the Bible, 388, 394–395, *438f;* church leaders, 400; the Crusades, 685–689, *688m, 689f;* 711 MC1-711 MC2; Cyril, 422; and the Enlightenment, 827; in Ethiopia, 507; the Eucharist, 400; in Europe, 418–419, 422, 682, 667–671, *667m;* holidays of, *390f;* and Judaism, 241; Methodius, 422; in the Middle Ages, 667–671, *667m,* 680–681, *681m,* 691–692; missionaries, *429t,* 667, 668, 808; monks, 667, 668–669, 692, *693f;* in Muslim countries, 451; Paul, 391, 396–397, *397f, 398m;* in Ottoman Empire, 588; persecution of Christians, 398–399; Peter, 392; and philosophy, 401; prayer, 393; religious orders, 693–694; in Roman Empire, *381t, 399t;* Rome, *680p;* in Russia, 422, 423; scholars, 774–775; *Sermon on the Mount,* 394–395; spread of, 397–398, 400–401, *401m;* and trade routes, 27, 135; universities, 694–695. *See also* Catholic Church; Eastern Orthodox Church; Jesus of Nazareth; Reformation

Christmas, *390f*
chronological order, 40–41
Churchill, Winston: 925, *925f, 927f,* 928, 956–947; Yalta Conference, 944, 954, *955p*
Church of England, 754
Cicero, 348
Cincinnatus, 332, *332f*
circumnavigate, 799
cities, 69; in Africa, *1011f,* 1012; in China, 524–525; and civilization, 69; during Industrial Revolution, 860–861; early South American, 640–641; Harappan, *146f,* 147; Mayan, 621, *621f,* 622; megacities, 1061; in Roman Empire, 358–359; as urban, 72. *See also* city-state
citizens, 30, in Athens, 265, 267–268, 269; human rights, 1034–1036; rights and responsibilities, 1034
citizenship: in Roman Republic, 338–339
city-states, 32; Delian League, 277; Greek, *253t,* 259–261, *260m,* 264; Peloponnesian League, 277; Phoenician, 87; Spartan, 279; Sumerian, 72–73, 74
civic duty: in Roman Republic, 338–339; in United States, *338f*
civics, 30
civil disobedience, 987
civilizations: classical, 93; in early China, 187–188; in Egypt, 106–107, *112c;* empire of first, 72–79; first in Americas, *101t;* and irrigation, *68f;* in Mesopotamia, 66–69, *112c*
civil law, 375–376
civil service, 532–533, 540; exams, *532f,* 540
clans: African, 474–475, *475f;* Aryan, 150; in Japan, 561, 573
classical civilizations, 93; Han dynasty, 206
classical culture: and humanism, 723

Cleisthenes, 267
Clement VII, Pope, 683
Cleopatra VII, *303t,* 313, *313f,* 314, *319t, 325t;* and Roman Republic, 350, 352, *352f*
clergy, 691; call for reform of, 750; corruption and problems, 702, 734; at Council of Trent, 757–758, *758f;* in the First Estate, 841; teaching at universities, 694
Cleveland, Grover, 877
climate, 12–13; and migration, 50, 51
climate change, 1062; Paris Agreement, 1065
cloning, 1068
clothing, 52
Clovis, 368, 669
codex, 637
Cold War, 954, 955; arms race, 959, 974; Berlin airlift, 958–959, *958m;* containment policy, 957; Cuban Missile Crisis, *951t,* 981 MC1–981 MC2; end to, 975, *975m;* satellite states, 956–957, *956m;* space race, 960, *960p*
collective farms: in China, 962
collectivization: in Soviet Union, 922
Colosseum, the, *373f,* 379 MC2
Columbian Exchange, 806–809, *807m, 808f, 809f, 810f*
Columbus, Christopher, *407t, 661t, 704f,* 776, *793t,* 798–799, *799f, 800m*
command economy, 25, 33, 1073; in China, 996
Commentaries, 239, *239f*
commune: in China, 962
communication: Industrial Revolution advances, 859
communism, 903; in Afghanistan, 967–968; in Africa, 968; in China, *951t,* 961–963, 990–991, *990f;* and Cold War, 955; containment policy, 957, 966–967, 968; in Cuba, 966; domino

theory, 965; in Eastern Europe, 946; in Korea, 963–964, *964m;* in Vietnam, 964–965
comparative advantage, 27
compare: and contrast historical facts, 304, 770; historical texts, 856
compass, 528, 797
compass rose, 35, *35m*
competition: 816; and international trade, 27
concentration camp, 936, 937, *937f,* 939, *939p*
conclusions: draw, 516
conduct Internet research, 219, 746
congregation, 763–764, *763p*
Congress of Vienna, 846–847, *846m*
Confucianism, 195, 196–197, *196f,* 530–531, *531p;* and Buddhism, 522; civil service exams, 532–533, *532f;* and Daoism, 197; in the Han dynasty, 207, 208; in Japan, 562–563, *562f;* Neo-, 531
Confucius: birth of, *63t, 181t, 193t, 196f; The Analects, 195f,* 196; and Zhou society, 195–196. *See also* Confucianism
conquistadors: and the Aztecs, 637, 638; and the Incas, *745t*
Conservative Jews, 238
conservatism, 847
Constantine, 366, *381t;* and Christianity, 401–402
Constantinople, *101t, 407t,* 415; and the Crusades, 686; under Justinian, 416–417; and the Ottomans, *583t,* 586, *609t, 713t;* and trade, 415, 418
constitution, 31, *840f;* Greek, 269; U.S., 840
constitutional monarchy, *32c,* 33; in Asia, 997
construct timelines, 947
consuls, 336–337, *337f*
containment, 957
context, determine, 551

continents, 12; and migration, 51, *51m*

continuity and change in history, 403

contrast: and compare historical facts, 304, 770

Coolidge, Calvin, *915t*

Copernicus, Nicolaus, *769t*, 776–778, *777p*, *777f*, 787

Copper Age, 69

Coptic Christianity, 506

Coral Sea, Battle of the, 931

Córdoba, *429t*, *452f*, 453

Corinth, 266

corporations, 1075–1076, *1076p*

corruption: in clergy, 702, 734; in Roman Empire, 369, *368f*

Cortés, Hernán, *583t*, 637, *638i*, 800

costs: analyze, 299

cottage industry, 813

Council of Trent, 757–758, *758f*

Counter-Reformation, 755, 756–758, *757f*

coup d'état, 1045

court (imperial), *515t*, 566

court cases: juries, 269

Crassus, 349

create and interpret databases, 881

creation myths, 113; Hindu, 155–156

Crete, *253t*, 258, *259m*, 262–263

Croatia: ethnic conflict, 1039

Cromwell, Oliver, 837

crucifixion, 389, *399t*

Crusades, *661t*, 685–689, *688m*, *689f*, 711 MC1–711 MC2

cry of Dolores, 848

Cuba, 876–877, 878, 879, *879m*, *951t*; Barack Obama, *983t*, 1025; communism, 966; Fidel Castro, 966, *966p*; missile crisis, *951t*, 966, 981 MC1–981 MC2; and Soviet Union, 966; tourism, 1024–1025

Cuban Missile Crisis, *951t*, 966, 981 MC1–981 MC2

cultural diffusion, 544, 1056

cultural landscapes, 7

Cultural Revolution, *951t*, 962–963

culture, 6; and geography, 17

culture maps, interpret, 657

cuneiform, 75–76, *76c*

Curie, Marie and Pierre, 860

currency, 28, *28c*; Alexanders, 309, 314; in Athens, 266; in China, 526, 529; in Mauryan Empire, 167; Mayan, 621; paper money, 526, *527f*, 529, 717; in Persia, 93; salt as, 482; in Shang dynasty, 189; wampum, 654; yen, *28c*

current events: research, 1081

Cuzco, 641, 645

cylinder seal, *78p*, 79

Cyril, 422, 424

Cyrillic alphabet, 424

Cyrus the Great, *63t*, 91–92

czars, 421

Czechoslovakia: *Kristallnacht*, *915t*, 935; Prague Spring, *970p*, 971; Vaclav Havel, 977; World War II, 924

D

Dachau, 936

daimyo, 572, *573f*, 577

Dai Viet, 549

dance, 503

Daniel, 238

Dante, *713t*, 724

Danube, 412

Dao, 197

Daoism, 197–198, *197f*, *198f*, and Buddhism, 522; and Confucianism, 197; and Legalism, 198

da Palestrina, Giovanni, 726

Darfur: ethnic conflict, *1031t*, 1009, *1039p*, 1040

Darius I, 91, 93–96, *93p*

Dark Age (Greek), 259

databases: create and interpret, 881

dating (historical objects), 8

Dausi, 499–500

David, *225t*, 232, *232p*, *232t*, 233, 387; Book of Psalms, 238

da Vinci, Leonardo, 728, *729f*

D-Day invasion, *915t*, 928–929, *928f*, *929m*

Dead Sea Scrolls, 239–240, *240f*

De Beers, *865f*

decisions: make, 511

Declaration of Commitment on HIV/AIDS, *1031t*, 1072

Declaration of Independence, 838–839, *839p*, *841f*, 853 MC1, 853 MC2

Declaration of the Rights of Man and of the Citizen, *841f*, 842, *842p*

deforestation, 1063–1064, *1063p*, *1063c*

de Gama, Vasco, 798, *800m*

degree, 15

Delian League, 277

delta, 105

Delphi, 282, 293

demand, 23, *23c*

Demeter, 281

demilitarized zone (DMZ), 964

democracy, 31, 32–33, *32c*, *253t*, 1044; in Africa, 1010, *1010f*, 1049; in Asia, 996, 1044–1046, *1045f*; direct, 270, *270f*; documents of, *841f*; father of, 267; in Greece, 264, 267–270, *267f*, *609t*; ideals of, 832–833, *834f*; resistance to in Middle East, 1046–1048; and rationalism, 785–786, *785f*; representative, 271, *270f*; Ukraine, 1048–1049

Democratic Republic of the Congo: Kinshasa, *1011f*, 1012. See also Belgian Congo

demographics, 12

Descartes, René, 783, *784f*

descriptive words, 430

desertification, 1063–1064

deserts: in Africa, 472, *473m*; in Arabia, 432–433, *433m*, *434p*

Index

despotism: in European monarchies, 831
de-Stalinization, *951t*, 969
détente, 971, 972
determine the context of statements, 551
determine the strength of an argument, 1027
developed nations, 966, 1073
develop graphs, 765
developing nations, 966, 1073; and clean water, 1062; economic aid for, 1079–1080; multinational corporations, 1076, *1076p*
develop models, 707
dharma, 156–157
diagrams: interpret, 177
diamonds, 865, *865f*
Dias, Bartolomeu, *793t*, 798, *800m*
Diaspora, 234, 245–246, *245m*
dictators, 309; Roman, 331–332, 350
dictatorship, 32, *32c*; economies of, 33
Diderot, Denis, 829
Diet, 945, 992
diffusion, 213
Diocletian, *325t*, 365, *365t*, 415
direct democracy, 32, *32c*, 270, *270f*
disease, 1069; Aborigines and Maori, 875; AIDS, 1071–1072, *1071c*; and Columbian Exchange, 806; and defeat of the Aztecs, 639, 800; and the New World, 800; protection from, 176; spread of, 27, 29. *See also* health care; medicine
disciples, 389; Apostles, 391–392; Gospels, 391, 392–393, 398
discussion: use vocabulary in, 739
division of labor, *68f*, 69
Djenné, 490, 495
DNA, 44
Doctors without Borders, 1041, *1041p*
dollar, 27, *28c*

Domesday Book, 675
domestication, 55–56, 76
Dominican Republic, 799
domino theory, 965
Don Quixote, *736f*, 737
Draco, 265
Drake, Francis, *745t*, *800m*, 801; as a pirate, 801
drama, 287–288, 375; Aeschylus, 287; Noh, 568; *Romeo and Juliet,* *713t*, 740–741
draw conclusions, 516
drought: as a cause of migration, 52; and control of water, 67–68
Dubcek, Alexander, 971
Du Fu, *515t*, 526
Dürer, Albrecht, 735, *735f*
Dutch East India Company, *793t*

E

Earhart, Amelia, *915t*
earth: map of, 15
earth (one of the four elements), 57
Earth Day, *1065p*
Easter, *390f*
eastern cultures, *652m*, 654–656
Eastern Europe: after fall of communism, 977–978; following World War II, 946; geography of, 410–414, *411m*; and Great Schism, 682; Jews in, 245, *245m*; Orthodox Church, 682–683; peoples of, 413–414; and Soviet Union, 946; trade, 412
Eastern Orthodox Church, 419, 422, 682–683, 689
Ebola, 1070
economic growth, 29
economics: fundamentals of, 22–25; importance of, 28–29
economy: and Adam Smith, 829, *835f*; after World War II, 943; in Africa, 1011; in Asia, 994–995, *995f*; banking, 814–815; capitalism, 816, *835f*, 860; Chinese, 996;

and Columbian Exchange, 809–810; developing nations, 1073, 1079–1080; early, 57; European, 716; free trade, 1076, 1077; global, 1058, *1078f*; global recession, *1031t*, 1078–1079; Indian, 996; Japanese, 996; laissez-faire, 860; market, 815–816, *815f*; mercantilism, 812–814; role of government in, 33–34, 67; study of, 22–25, 28–29; and trade, 26–28; types of, 25
ecosystem, 14
Edict of Nantes, 762
Edison, Thomas, 29
education: in Athens, 275, *275f*, 276, *276f*; and Homer's poetry, 275, 284; in Jewish society, 236, 244; during the Renaissance, 721, 730–731, 733; Roman Catholic, 757; in Sparta, 273, *273f*, *275f*; and technology, 1055–1056; universities, 733
Egypt, *253t*; agriculture in, *101t*; Ahmose, 117–118; and Alexander the Great, 307, 308; ancient civilization, 106–107, 108, *112c*; Anwar Sadat, 967, *967p*; Arab Spring, *1031t*, 1046–1047, *1047p*; belief in the afterlife, 113, *114p*, 116, 126; city of Alexandria, *297f*, 313, 316–317, *317i*; Cleopatra VII, *303t*, 313, *313f*; conquered by Persians, 92; controlling trade routes, 796; First Dynasty, 108–109; Gamal Abdel Nasser, 1014, *1015f*; geography of, 104–106, *105m*; gods of, 113; and the Israelites, 228–229, 244, 247, *247f*; King Tutankhamen, *127f*, 128; and Kush, 130–131; Lower, 104, 105, *105m*, 107; Kushite Dynasty, 132–135; Hellenistic Age, *303t*, *312m*, 313, 314, 316–317, 318–319; hieroglyphics, *609t*; Menes, *63t*, *101t*, 108–109, *108i*;

Middle Kingdom, 117, *118t*; and modern-day Israel, 967, *967p*, *1017t*; New Kingdom, 118–120, *118t*; Old Kingdom, 110–116, *118c*; and Phoenicia, 87; Ptolemy, 313, *313f*, 316, 319; pyramids of, *101t*, 115–116; Queen Hatshepsut, 118–119, *118f*, *181t*; Ramses the Great, *101t*, 120, *120f*, 126, *225t*; religion of, 112–114; religious persecution in, 1040; and Rome, *303t*; society in, 111, *111c*; Suez Canal, *1017t*; trade, 111–112, 118, *119m*; unifying, 108; Upper, 104, *105m*, 107; writing in, 123–125, *124p*, *125c*, *125p*

Eightfold Path, 162, *163f*

Eisenhower, Dwight D., 928

elders, in West Africa, 474, 475–476, *475f*

Eleanor of Aquitaine, 677, *677f*

elephants: war, 167, 597

electricity: and productivity, 29

elite, 114

Elizabeth I: and Francis Drake, 801

Elizabethan Age, 802

embargo, 1018

empire, 73, 82

Encyclopedia, 829

energy use, 1061–1062

Engels, Friedrich, *855t*

engineering, 115; in Greece, 298

England: civil war, *823t*, 837–838, defeats Spanish armada, *555t*, *583t*, 802, *802f*; established Jamestown, *793t*, 801; first missionaries, *429t*; government in, 33, *700t*; Hadrian's Wall, *325t*, 356; Hundred Years' War, *609t*, 700–701; invaded by Caesar, 348; invaded by Hadrian, 356; invasions, 368; Magna Carta, 698–699, *699f*, *700t*, *841f*; and new trade routes, 814; Norman invasion, 675; Parliament, 699, *700t*, 837–838; William the Conqueror, *467t*, *555t*, 675. *See also* Great Britain

English (language), 1057, *1057c*

English Bill of Rights, 838, *840f*, *841f*

Enheduanna, 75

enlightened despots, 831–832

Enlightenment, 826–829, *827f*, *828p*

entrepreneurs, 25, 815–816; in Africa, 864

environment, 13, 14; challenges, 1061–1064; Earth Day, *1065p*; global interdependence, 1058; humans adapting to, 52–54; and people, 19; population growth, 1059–1061, *1060m*; of river valleys, 70; Roman adaptations, 372; sustainable growth, 1064, 1066; protecting, 1064–1066

environmentalism, 1064–1066

epic poetry, 76; Gilgamesh, 76, 80–81; Homer, 283, *283f*; the *Iliad*, 283, *283f*, 290; Indian, 174; the *Odyssey*, 283, *283f*, *284p*, 291

epidemic, 1069

equator, 15

Erasmus, Desiderius, 734, *734f*, 750

Erdoğan, Recep Tayyip, 1046

erosion, 13

Esfahan, 592

Esma'il, 591–592, 593

essential information: identify, 610

estates, 841–842

ethics: and Confucianism, 195, 530

Ethiopia, *467t*, invaded by Italy, 919; kingdom, 506–507, *507p*; resistance, 867, 868, *868f*, 869

ethnic conflict: 1010f; in Darfur, 1009, *1039p*, 1040; as human rights abuse, 1038–1039; in Kosovo, 1039; in Middle East; in Rwanda, 1009, 1039–1040, 1043; in Yugoslavia, 1038–1039, *1038m*, 1042

Etruscans, 331

Eucharist, 400

Euclid, 297, *297f*, 320

Euphrates River, 66–67, *70f*

Eurasia, 664

Euripides, 287, 288

euro, 27, *28c*

Europe: banking, 814–815; economy, 716; effects of Crusades, 689, *689f*; and Charlemagne, 669–671, *669f*, *670p*, *670m*; and Christianity, 667–669, *667m*, *681m*; and Columbian Exchange, 806–811; divided following World War II, 946; geography, 664–666, *665m*, *666f*; invasions, 666, 671–672; market economy, 815–816, *815f*; and mercantilism, 812–814; in Middle Ages, 667–672; middle class, 815; migration to, 50, 51, *51m*; monarchies of, *831m*; post–World War II, 945–946; religious divisions, 760, *761m*; and rivers, 666, *666f*; trade with Asia, 718; using copper tools, *101t*; World War I, *885t*

European Union, 978, 1076

evaluate websites, 746

evidence: use supporting, 979

excommunicate: and Martin Luther, 750–751

Exodus, 229, *229m*; Passover, 247, *247f*

exploration: to Africa, 798; map, *800m*; to the New World, 798–799; reasons for, 796; and the Scientific Revolution, *774f*; and technological advances, 797, *797f*

explorers: Christopher Columbus, *407t*; compass, 528; conquering the Aztec Empire, *467t*; Ferdinand Magellan, *793t*, 799, *800m*; Francis Drake, *745t*, *800m*, 801; Jacques Cartier, *800m*, 801; John Cabot, *793t*, *800m*, 801; Pedro Cabral, 799, *800m*; Ponce de Leon, 821 MC1–821 MC2; Vasco de Gama, 798, *800m*; Vasco Núñez de Balboa, 801

exports, 27, 133

extended family, 474, *475f*

Ezana, King of Egypt, 135

Index

F

fables, 285, *285f*
factors of production, 24
factory system, 859
facts: compare and contrast, 304, 770; identify, 226–227
failed states, 1049–1050, *1049f*
Falkland Islands, 1023
family: Bantu, 507; extended, 474, *475f*; forms of government, 32, *32c*; in Han dynasty, 208–209; in Japan, 563; kinship system, 473–475, 507; in Egypt, 122; and Neo–Confucianism, 531; in Shang dynasty, 189; in West Africa, 473–475, *475f*; in Zhou dynasty, 193–195
farmers: Aztec, 634, *634i*; become leaders, 130; in Egypt, *111c*, 112, 121–122; in Shang dynasty, 189. *See also* peasants
farming: in ancient Egypt, 106, *107p*; in early China, 187
fascism, 918; in Germany, 919–921; in Italy, 918–919
fashion: Japanese, 566
fasting, 161
Fatima, *439f*, 440, 449
federalism, 764
Ferdinand, Francis, archduke of Austria-Hungary, *892p*, 893
Ferdinand, king of Spain, 704, 798
Fertile Crescent: 66–69, *67m*
feudalism, *661t*; 674–675, *674f*; decline of, 678; the manor system, 675–676
fief, 673; the manor system, 675–676, *676f*
figurehead, 573, *573f*
Final Solution, 937, *937f*
fire: controlling, 44, making, 55; one of the four elements, 57
First Continental Congress, 838
First Sermon, 161
Five Dynasties and Ten Kingdoms, 520

Five Pillars of Islam, 443–444, *443f*; the hajj, *443f*, 444, 454–455. *See also* Islam; Muslims
Five Year Plans, 921–922
Flavius Josephus, 231, 243
flooding: and Aswan High Dam, 106; and building, 147; controlling, 68; in the Fertile Crescent, 66–67; of Huang He (Yellow River), 186, 188; of Indus River, 144, 146; of the Nile, 105–106
Florence (Italy), 718, 719, *719f*, 720–721, *720f*
Florida: Ponce de Leon, 821 MC1, 821 MC2
food: kosher, 238; storage, 57; surplus of, 57
Ford, Gerald, *1035p*
formal region, 16
Forum, 339, 341–342, *342f*
fossils, 10, in the Gobi Desert, 21
Fountain of Youth: Ponce de Leon, 821 MC1–821 MC2
four elements, 57
Four Noble Truths, the, 162
France: African colonies, 1002–1004, *1003m*; an Allied Power, 924; Allies, 892; Catholic and Protestant conflict, 762, *762p*; after Congress of Vienna, *846m*, 847; French Revolution, *823t*, 840–843, *842p*, *843f*; Hundred Years' War, *467t*, *609t*, 700–701; King Louis XVI, 830–831, 841; Napoleon as emperor, *823t*, 844–845; and the New World, 801; philosophy of, 828–829; Vietnam, 965; World War II, 925, 928–929
Francis of Assisi, 694, *694f*
Franco, Francisco, *915t*
Frank, Anne, 938, *938f*
Franklin, Benjamin, 835, *836t*
Franks, 368, 669–670; Charlemagne, *407t*, *555t*, *661t*, 669–671, *669f*, *670p*, *670m*; feudalism, 673–675

Frederick II (of Prussia), 831
freedoms, 31
free market, 25
free trade, 1076, 1077
French Revolution, *823t*, 840–843, *842p*, *843f*
fresco, 374, *374p*
friars, 694; looking for heretics, 702
Friedland, Battle of, *845p*
functional region, 16

G

Gaea, 281
Galen, 371
Galilei, Galileo, *583t*, *745t*, *769t*, 778–779, *778i*, *779f*; 781; and the Church, 786–787, *787p*
Gallipoli, 894
Gandhi, Mohandas, *158f*, *915t*, 986–988, *988p*, *988f*, 989
Ganges River, 145
Gao, 490, 493
Garibaldi, Giuseppe, 889
Gaul: and Caesar, 348, *349p*; and the Franks, 368, 669–670; and Roman Republic, 343
Gautama, Siddhartha, 160–161, *161p*
Gemmi, Empress of Japan, 564
General Agreement on Tariffs and Trade (GATT), 1076
geneticist, 44
genetics, 1067–1068
Genghis Khan, 534
Genoa, 718, *719f*
genocide, 894; in Armenia, 894; in Darfur, 1009, 1040; the Holocaust, 934–935, *935p*, 936–937; in Rwanda, 1039–1040
geographic information system (GIS), 16
geographer, 44; Strabo, 310
geography, 12, *17f*; essential elements of, 14; and history, 17, 19; human, *13f*, 14; location, 14–15; maps and tools for, 15–16, *15m*, *18m*; and

Muslim Empire, 457–458, *457f*; natural disasters, 262–263; natural wonders, 20–21; physical, 12–13; problems of, 19; river valley civilizations, 70–71; Roman roads, 362–363; the Silk Road, 220–221; shaping culture, 17; types of regions, 16

geology, 8

geometry, 297, *297f*

George II, King of England, *834p*

Germany, Adolf Hitler, *885t, 915t,* 919–921, *920f,* 924, *927f,* 941; became independent, 763; Berlin Wall, *951t,* 959, 976, *976p*; blitzkrieg, 925, 932; Central Powers, 892; East Germany, 976–977; fascist government, 919–921; Great Depression, 910, 919, 920; *Kristallnacht, 915t,* 935; and militarism, 891; Nazi Party, 919–920; Nuremberg Trials, 946; reparations, 899–900, 910, 919; submarines, 894; Treaty of Versailles, *899f*; unified, *885t,* 889–890, *889m*; World War I, *885t,* 893–895; after World War I, 898, *898m, 899f,* 919; World War II, *915t,* 924–926, 927–928, *927f*; 932–933, 941

Gestapo, 920

Ghana: economy, 1011; *Dausi,* 499–500; decline of empire, 486–487, *661t*; democracy, 1010, *1010f*; empire of, *467t,* 481, *481m,* 482, 484–485, *496t, 515t*; independent, *983t*; Islamic influence, 483–484; trade, 482–483, *484p. See also* West Africa

ghetto: during World War II, 936; resistance, 938

Gibbons, Edward, 3

Gilgamesh, 73, 80–81

Girl with a Pearl Earring, 817–818

glasnost, 973–974, 975, *974t*

Global Positioning System (GPS), 16, 1053

global society: cultural diffusion, 1056; economy, 1058; health, 1069–1072, *1070f, 1071c*; interdependence, 1058; loss of traditional cultures, 1057–1058; water, 1062; Western influence, 1056–1057

globes: interpreting, 377; using, 15, *15m*

Gobi Desert, 21, *21m,* 184, *185m*

gold: in African trade, 472, 478, 482, *483p*

Golden Temple, *583t, 597p,* 598

goods, 22; and the Internet, 26; and taxes, 34; and trade, 26–27

Gorbachev, Mikhail, *951t*; and Afghanistan, 968

Gospels, 391, 392–393, 398

Goths: sacking Rome, *325t, 365t, 366p,* 368

government: in a civilization, 67, 69; and civil service, 532–533; and Confucianism, 195, 532; constitutions, 269; and Daoism, 197; economic role of, 33–34; failed states, 1050; forms of, 31–33, *32c*; Harappan, 146; and Legalism, 198–199; limited, 339, 830; in Neolithic Era, 58; protecting environment, 1065; providing laws, 31; providing services, 30–31, 34; Roman, 331–332, 336–339; and Scientific Revolution, 785; signoria, 720; study of, 30; theocracy, 32, *32c,* 33, 110–111, 231; unlimited, 830–831

Gracchus, Gaius, 346

Gracchus, Tiberius, 346

Grama, 150

Grand Canal, 519, 525, *525f,* 536

Grand Mosque: the hajj, 454

graphs: develop, 765

Great Britain: Boer War, *855t,* 867–868; an Allied Power, 924; as Allies, 892; and American colonies, 834–835; and American Revolution, 838–839; 853 MC1–853 MC2, *855t*; barbarian invasions, 368; defeats Armada, *555t, 583t*; and Australia, *855t,* 874–875; and China, 872, 873, *873m*; defeats Napoleon, 845; early government in, 33; Falkland Islands, 1023; first missionaries, *429t*; Great Depression, 909–910, *909c*; Hadrian's Wall, *325t,* 356; Hundred Years' War, *609t*; in India, 870–872, *871m, 983t,* 986–989; invaded by Caesar, 348; invaded by Hadrian, 356; Neville Chamberlain, 924; and New Zealand, 875; War of 1812, *823t, 855t*; William the Conqueror, *467t, 555t*; Winston Churchill, 925, *925f, 927f,* 928, 944, *955p,* 856–957; writers, 829

Great Departure, *161p*

Great Depression: causes of, 905–906; effects of, 907–908, *907p*; in Germany, 910; Great Britain's response, 909–910, *909c*; New Deal, 908–909, *908p*; start of, *885t*

Great Leap Forward, 962

Great Mosque, *452f*

Great Schism, 682, 748

Great Wall, 203, *203p,* 205, 223 MC1–223 MC2, 540, 542–543; and trade routes, 216

Great War, 893. *See also* World War I

Great Zimbabwe, 508–509

Greece: ancient, 32, 301 MC1–301 MC2; architecture, 293; art, 292–293, 374; city-states, *253t,* 259–260, *260m,* 264; colonies, 261;

Index

compared to other empires, *602c*; Crete, *253t*, 262–263; democracy, 264, 267–270, *267f*; drama in, 287; early settlements, 257; in Eastern Europe, 414; engineering, 298; fables, 285, *285f*; geography of, 256–257, *257m*; gods, 281–282, *281i*; and humanism, 722–723; and Macedonia, 306; mathematics, 297; mythology, 280–282, *287f*; Olympic Games, *282f*; Peloponnesian War, 288; and Persia, *325t*; Persian Wars, *63t*, 94–96, 288, 301 MC2; philosophy, 293, 295–296; poetry, 283–285; spread of culture, 309; trade, 257, 258, *258f*, 259, 260, 261; Trojan War, *253t*; won independence, 888; writers, 287–288. *See also* Hellenistic Age

Greek philosophers, and the Enlightenment, 826–827; and Scientific Revolution, 773–774, *773f*, *774f*

Greek roots, 714

greenhouse gases, 1062

Greenpeace, 1064

Gregory VII, Pope, 683–684, *683f*

grid, 15

griots, 498–499, *499p*, *501f*

gross domestic product (GDP): in India, 996; in Latin America, *1025c*

Guam, 879

Guangzhou, 872

Gulag, 921, *921p*

guilds, 678–679

Guinea, 1005

gunpowder, *527f*, 528, *661t*; and large weapons, 701; used by Ottoman cannons, 586

guns: in Japan, 577, 578

Gupta, Samudra, 170

Gupta Empire, *141t*, 169–171, *169m*, *325t*, *368c*, *381t*; art in, 172–173; literature in, 174; sciences in, 174–176; *175f*

gurdwara, 596, 598

Guru Granth Sahib, 595

Guru Nanak, 158–159, 595

Gutenberg, Johann, *713t*, 732, *733t*

H

habeas corpus, 698

hadith, 442

Hadrian, 356; and the Jews, 386

Hadrian's Wall, *325t*, 356

Haggadah, *247f*

Hagia Sophia, 418, 419, 586, 589

Haida, *652m*, 653

Haiti, 847

hajj, *443f*, 444, 454–455; of Askia the Great, 495, *793t*; of Mansa Musa, 490

Hammurabi, *63t*, 82, *225t*

Hammurabi's Code, 83, *83f*, *225t*

Han dynasty, *181t*, *207t*, *207m*, *303t*, *325t*, *368c*; art, 210–211, *210f*; Buddhism, 212–213; compared to other empires, *602c*; and Confucianism, 208, 209; Emperor Wudi, 206–207; life and family, 208–209; literature, 211; Liu Bang, 206; manufacturing and farming, 211–212; science and medicine, *210f*, 211; and trade, 216–218. *See also* China

Han Fei Zi, 199

Hanging Gardens, 86

Hannibal, 344, *344f*, *345m*

Hanukkah, 247

Harappan civilization, *63t*, *140t*, 146–148, *146f*

harem, 588

Harvey, William, 786

Hastings, Battle of, 675

Havel, Václav, 977

headings: previewing text, 254–255

health care: AIDS, 1012, 1071–1072, *1071c*; Doctors without Borders, 1041, *1041p*; and human rights, 1040–1042; malaria, 1012. *See also* medicine

Hebrew Bible, 228, 235, 238, *239f*

Hebrews, *232t*; with Abraham, 228–229, *229m*; Babylonian Captivity, 233; Diaspora, 234; the Maccabees, 234; with Moses, 229–230, *229m*; religion, 230–231; in Canaan, 228, 231, *232t*; two kingdoms, *231m*, 233; united by kings, 232–233; women, 235

hegira, 440–441

Heian, 566, *661t*

Hellenistic Age, 310, 316, *312m*, *319t*; architecture, 317, *317i*; art, 318, *318f*; economy, *314f*; in Egypt, 313, 316–317, 318; government, 314; literature, 310; in Macedonia, 311–312; philosophy, 319, *319c*; science, 319–320; in Syria, 312; trade, 314–315; women in, 317

helots, 274

Helsinki Accords, 1035, *1035p*

Henry, Patrick, 853 MC2

Henry IV, emperor of Holy Roman Empire, 683–684, *683f*

Henry IV king of France, 762

Henry VIII, king of England, 754, *754i*

Henry the Navigator, *793t*, 798

Hephaestus, 281

Hercules, 282, 289

heresy, 702

Herodotus, 94, 104, 288

heroes, 282

Hidalgo, Father Miguel, 848

hieroglyphics, 123, *123p*, 124, *125p*, *609t*

High Holy Days, 247
Himalayas, 20, *20m,* 144, *145m,* 184, *185m*
Hinduism, *141t,* 151, 157; and beginnings of Buddhism, 160, 162–163; beliefs, 155–156, *157f;* customs, 157; gods, 155, *156f, 157f;* in Gupta dynasty, 169, 170; sacred texts, 155; temples, 170, 172, 173, *173p*
Hindu-Arabic numerals, 175
Hindu Kush, 144
Hippocrates, 297–298
Hirohito, emperor of Japan, 922, 923, 945
Hiroshima, *915t,* 933, 942, *943p*
historians, 6–7, 9; Flavius Josephus, 231, 243; and geography, 12; Greek, 288; Herodotus,104, 288; Polybius, 310; and the Rosetta Stone, 124; Thucydides, 288; using sources, 10, 11
historical facts: compare and contrast, 304, 770
historical inquiry, 7
historical sources, 10–11
historical statements: determine context of, 551
historical texts: compare, 856; identify points of view, 824; summarize, 182
history, 6; chance, error, and oversight in, 425; continuity and change in, 403; and economics, 28–29; and geography, 17, 19; identify facts and opinions, 226–227; make inferences about, 142–143; oral, 498–500; recorded Mayan, 625, *626f;* specialized vocabulary of, 4–5, studying public documents, 886; understanding through, 8–9; write about, 288, 375
Hitler, Adolf, *885t,* 910, *915t,* 918–921, *920f,* 941; and the Jews, 934; and Soviet Union, 921, 924, 926. *See also* Germany; Nazi Party; World War II

Hittites, 84, 87, 118, 120
Ho Chi Minh, 965
Hohokam culture, *609t*
Holbein, Hans, 736
holidays: Buddhist, 166; Christian, *390f*
Holocaust, 934, 942; aftermath, 939; concentration camps, 936, 937, 939; death marches, 939; Final Solution, 937; ghettos, 936; *Kristallnacht,* 935; Nuremberg Laws, 935; resistance, 938–939. *See also* Jews; Nazi Party; World War II
Holy Land: Crusades, *661t,* 685–689, *688m;* 711 MC1–711 MC2
Holy Roman Empire, *407t,* *681m,* 682, *682p;* Thirty Years' War, 762–763; and Treaty of Westphalia, 763
Homer, 283, *283f;* poetry of, 284, 290–291
hominids, *39t,* 42–45; early, *46c;* migration of, 50–51; sites, *43m*
Homo erectus, 44, *46c. See also* hominids
Homo habilis, 44, *46c. See also* hominids
Homo sapiens, 45, *46c. See also* hominids
Hongshan people, 187
Hopewell culture, *609t,* 651, 653, *654t*
Hopi, 651, *652m*
hourly wage, 25
Huang He, 186, *186p,* 187
Huáscar, 646
Hudson, Henry, 801
Huguenots, 762
Huitzilopochtli, 635, *635f*
human geography, 14
HIV (human immunodeficiency virus), 1071
humanism, 722–723; Christian, 734; leads to the Enlightenment, 827; and the Scientific Revolution, *774f,* 775; and universities, 733

human rights: 1034, abuses, 998, 1036–1041; NGOs, 1035–1036, 1064; successes, 1041–1043; and United Nations, 1034–1035, 1036
Human Rights Watch, 1036
humans: adapting to environments, 52–54; early migration of, 51–52, *51m, 53f;* modern, *39t,* 45; suffering of, 161
Human Systems, 14
humanities, 722–723; and education, 731
Hundred Years' War, *467t, 609t*
Hungary, *407t,* 412, 414, 976; Nagy, 970
Huns, 171, *366p,* 367–369, *367m, 407t*
hunter-gatherers, 47–49; settling in Egypt, 106; settling in Mesopotamia, 66
Hussein, Saddam, *983t, 1017t,* 1017–1018, 1019
Hykos, 117, 118
Hypatia, 297
hypothesis, 7, *783f,* 784

I

Ibn Battutah, 457, *448f,* 500, *500f, 535f, 583t,*
Ibn-Sina, 458
Ice ages, *39t,* 50
icon, 423, *424p*
identify central issues, 59
identify facts and opinions, 226–227
identify points of view, 824
identify print research sources, 819
identify relevant information, 610
identify short- and long-term effects, 249
identify stereotypes and bias, 408
Ides of March, 351
Ignatius of Loyola, 757, *757f*
Iliad, the, 283, 284, 290
immigrants: during Industrial Revolution, 860

Immortals, 92

immunity, 1023

imperialism: in Africa, 864–865, *866m,* 867, 1000, 1001, *1003m;* in Australia, 874–875; causing European tensions, 891; in China, 872–873, *873m;* in Japan, 873–874, *874f;* Japanese, 992; in New Zealand, 875

imports, 27, 133

Inca Empire, *641m, 643c;* art, 646; Atahualpa, 646–647; building, *644p,* 645; conquistadors, *745t,* 799–800; Cuzco, 641, 645; economy, 642; fall of, 647; geography, 641–642; government, 642; oral history, 646; Pachacuti, *609t,* 641; Pizarro, 646–647, *769t;* pre-Incas, 640–641; Quechua, 642; religion, 644; roads, 648–649; society, 643–644; taxes of, 33

incentives, 23

income, 25; in Ghana Empire, 485

India: Amritsar massacre, 986; art in, 172–173; Aryans migrate to, *141t, 181t;* British control of, 870–872, *871m,* 986; Buddhism in, *101t,* 160–166, *181t;* democracy, 996, 1044; economy, 996; geography, 144–145, *145m;* Gupta Empire, *325t, 368c, 381t;* Hinduism in, *141t,* 155–157; Kashmir conflict, 993–994, *994m;* literature in, 174; Mauryan Empire, *303t;* missionaries to, 759, *759f;* Mohandas Gandhi, *915t,* 986–988, *988p, 988f;* partitioned, *983t,* 989; resources in, 872; Salt March, *915t;* sciences in, 174–176, *175f,* Sikhism, 157, 158–159, *583t,* 595–599, *596p, 597c;* trade with Hellenistic kingdoms, 315

indigenous populations: rights of, 1042

Indonesia: and Muslim traders, 450; Suharto, 998

indulgences, 749, 750

Indus River Valley, 144, 146, 149

Industrial Revolution: and art, *861f,* 862; and environment, 1062, 1064; factory system, 859; inventions, 858, *859f;* reforms, 862; society, 860–861, 862; workers, 860–861, 862

inference, 142–143

inflation, 1075

influenza, 1070

informal jobs, 1025–1026

information: categorize, 1032; identify relevant, 610

Information Age: and global society, 1054–1055, 1056, *1056p;* technology of, 1054–1055, *1054f, 1055c*

infrastructure: and African economies, 1011; in failed states, 1049

Innocent III, Pope, 702

inoculation, 176

interdependence: global, 1058

interest, 720

International Covenant on Civil and Political Rights, 1038

International Criminal Court, 1043

International Monetary Fund (IMF), 1079–1080, *1079p*

International Space Station, *1031t,* 1052, *1052p*

Internet, 1055, *1055c*

Internet research: conduct, 219

interchangeable parts, 858–859

interpret and create databases, 881

interpret charts, 321

interpret culture maps, 657

interpret diagrams, 177

interpret globes, 377

interpret models, 707

interpret physical maps, 97

Inuit, *652m,* 653

inventions: of the Industrial Revolution, 858, *859f*

investing, 28

Iran, *983t,* 1015–1016, *1015f;* Islamic Revolution, 1017, *1017t*

Iraq: Saddam Hussein, *983t,* 1017–1018, *1017t;* struggle for democracy, 1048; and United States, 1019

Iron Age: in China, *194f*

Iron Curtain, *956i, 956m,* 957; satellite states, 957, 969–971

Iron Pillar, 175

ironwork: in China, 212; in Africa, *467t,* 477, 509

Iroquois Confederacy, *652m, 654t,* 655–656, *655i*

irrigation, 68, *68f,* 70, 106; in China, 203, 523; in early Americas, 640, 642, 651; and the Silk Road, 218

Islam: *440t;* Abu Bakr, 448; beliefs, 442; behavior, 442–443; and the Crusades, 711 MC1–711 MC2; cultural blending, 451; Fatima, *439f,* 440; Five Pillars, 442–444, *443f;* in Ghana Empire, 483–484; hajj, 444, 454–455; and Judaism, 241; Kaaba, 439, 440, 441, 444; Mecca, 439, 441, 454–455; Muhammad, *407t,* 438, *438f,* 439–440, 442, *515t, 661t;* Qur'an, 442, *443f,* 448; sacred texts, *443f;* Shariah, *443f,* 445; spread of, 440–441, *441m,* 450; in sub-Saharan Africa, 509–510; Sunnah, 442–443, *443f,* 444; Sunni and Shia, *439f,* 591; tolerance, 451; in West Africa, 490, 491

Islamic State of Iraq and the Levant (ISIL), *1017t,* 1048

isolationism, in Japan, 577–578; in Ming dynasty, 540–541; United States, 926

Index

Israel, *231m, 232t*; Assyrians, *325t*; Camp David Peace Accords, *1017t*; David, *225t*, 232–233, *232t*; Jerusalem, 233; Menachem Begin, 967, *967p*; modern state of, 940; *983t*, 1016, *1017t*; and Palestine, 1016; re-creating the kingdom of, 242; Six-Day War, 1016, *1017t*; Solomon, *63t, 232t*, 233; split, 233; Temple to God, 233

Israelites, *232t*; with Abraham, 228–229, *229m*; in Canaan, 228, 231, *232t*; Diaspora, 233–234; the Maccabees, 234; with Moses, 229–230, *229m*; religion, 230–231; two kingdoms, *231m*, 233; united by kings, 232–233; women, 235

Istanbul: 586–587, 588; Blue Mosque, *461f*

Italy: art, 725, *726p*; controlling trade routes, 796; fascist government, 918–919; geography, 328–329, *329m*; government, 720; independent states, 719–720; invading Ethiopia, 919; music, 725–726; Mussolini, *915t*, 918–919, *919p*; poets, 725; trade cities, 718–720, *719f, 720f*; unified, *885t*, 888–889, *889m*; writers of, *713t*, 724–725. *See also* Roman Empire; Roman Republic; Rome

Ivan I, *407t*

Ivan III, 421, 422

Iwo Jima, 931

J

jade, *620p*, 621

Jainism, 157, 158, *158f*; and Candragupta Maurya, 167; and the Gupta dynasty, 169

James II, 837–838

Janissaries, 586

Janssen, Zacharias, *769t*, 780

Japan: aggression, 922–923; Ainu culture, 560; architecture, 568; art, 566, *566p*, 568; Buddhism, 545, *555t, 562f*, 563–564, *563p, 564p*, 569, *569c, 569p*; and China, 545, *555t*, 561, *562f, 922p*, 923; and Commodore Perry, *855t*, 874, *874f*; Confucianism, 562–563; court, *515t*, 566; democracy, 996; Diet, 945, 992; drama in, 568; economic growth, 995–996; Emperor Hirohito, 922, 923, 945; Empress Gemmi, 564; family in, 563; fashion in, 566; first Japanese, 561; geography, 558–559, *559m*; Heian, 566, *661t*; imperialism of, 992; isolationism, 577–578; and Korea, 561, 562, *562f*, 922; literature, *555t*, 567–568, 570–571; Manchuria, *885t*, 922; Meiji, 991–992; missionaries to, 759, *759f*; the Mongols, *467t*, 537, 576–577, *576m, 713t*; Nara Period, 564; new constitution, 945; nobles, 566, 567–568, 572, 577; attack on Pearl Harbor, *926f*, 926–927; post–World War II, *943p*, 944–945; Prince Shotoku, *429t, 548t, 555t*, 562, 563–564, *563f, 563p*; and Russia, 901; Russo-Japanese War, 922; samurai, 572–573, *573f*, 574–575, *574f, 575f*, 581 MC1–581 MC2; Shinto, *560p*, 561, 563, *569c*; shogun rule, *555t*, 573, *573f*, 576, 577; *Tale of Genji*, 567, *567p*; Tokugawa, *555t*, 577–578, *745t, 793t*; trade, 562; warriors, 569; and the West, 873–874, *874f*; in World War I, *885t*; in World War II, *915t*, 926–927, *927f*, 930–931, *930m*, 933; Yamato rulers, 561, 564

Jason, 282

Jefferson, Thomas, 835–836, *836t*, 838

Jenner, Edward, 860

Jericho, 57, 58

Jerusalem: capital of Israel, 233, 234; and Constantine, 402; the Crusades, 711 MC1–711 MC2; and the Romans, *225t*, 234, 242–244, *243f*, 386, *386p*

Jesuits, 757, *757f*; missionaries, 759, *759f*

Jesus of Nazareth, *381t*, 386, 388, *389m*; followers of, 391–393; life, 388–389; miracles by, 390; and Muslims, 439; teachings of, 390, 391; *Sermon on the Mount*, 394–395

Jews, *232t*; with Abraham, 228–229, *229m*; Anne Frank, 938, *938f*; and banking, 814–815; Babylonian Captivity, *225t*, 233, 238, 245; Beta Israel, 507; in Canaan, 228, 231, *232t*; in Córdoba, 453, *661t*; after Crusades, 686, 689; culture of, 236–240; Diaspora, 233–234, 245–246, *245m*; discriminated against, 705–706; the Holocaust, 934–937, 942; influence on Western culture, 240–241; and Jerusalem, 233, 234; leaving Spain, 755–756; the Maccabees, 234; and the Messiah, 387, 388; and modern state of Israel, 940, *983t*; with Moses, 229–230, *229m*; and Muslims, 451; and the Nazi Party, 919–920, 934; in Nazi resistance, 938; in Ottoman Empire, 588; and prophets, 386–387; religion of, 230–231, 242; and the Romans, *225t*, 234, 242–244, *243f*, 385–386, *385p, 386p*; scholars, 775–775, *774f*; scribes, 228; traditions, 246–248; two kingdoms, *231m*, 233; united by kings, 232–233; women, 235

Jiang Jieshi, 989

jihad, 442

Joan of Arc, 700–701, *700p*
jobs: telecommute to, 1055
Johanson, Donald, 43–44, *44p*
John the Baptist, 387
Judah, *231m*, *232t*, 233
Judaism, 228, *438f*; charity, 241; Dead Sea Scrolls, 239–240, 240f; influence on Western culture, 240–241; and Jewish society, 236–240, 242; and the Romans, 385–386, *385p*, *386p*; sacred texts, 238–240, *239f*, 240f. *See also* Jews
jury: in Athens, 269
justice: in Jewish society, 237
Justinian, *407t*, 416–417

K

ka, 113, 114
Kaaba, 439, 440, 441, 444
Kalidasa, 174
kami, 561
kamikaze, 577, *713t*
karma, 156, *157f*, 596
Kashmir, 993–994, *994m*
Kassites, 84
kente, 502
Kenya, 1002, *1002p*
Kepler, Johannes, 778, *778f*
Khayyám, Omar, 460
Khufu, 111, 115
Khwarizmi, 458
King, Martin Luther, Jr., *158f*, 753f
kings: in feudal society, *674f*
Kinshasa, *1011f,* 1012
kinship system, 32, 473–475; Bantu, 508
knights, 673–674, *674f*, 678; manor system, 675–676, *676f*
Korea, 544, 546–548, *546p*, *546f*, *548t*; and Japan, 562; War, 963–964, *964m*; writing established, *793t*
Korean War, 963–964, *964m*
Koryo dynasty, 546–548. *See also* Korea
kosher, 238
Kosovo: ethnic conflict, 1039
Kristallnacht, *915t*, 935

Khrushchev, Nikita, *951t*, 966, 969, 970
Kshatriyas, 152, *153f*; and Siddhartha Gautama, 160
Kublai Khan, 535–536, *535f*, *536p*; invading Japan, 576–577, *576m*; and Marco Polo, 717
Kurds, 1018, *1018f*, 1019; ethnic conflict, 1037, 1039
Kush, *101t*, 118, 130, *130m*; culture, 133–135; decline of, 135; and Egypt, 130–131; Kushite Dynasty, 132–135; trade, 133, *134m*; written language, 134
Kuwait: invaded by Iraq, *983t*, 1018

L

labor, 25; division of, 69; educated workers, 29
Ladino, 246
Lagos, *1011f,* 1012
laissez-faire, 860
Lalibela, king of Ethiopia, 506
land, 24; as wealth, 28
land bridge, 50
landforms, 12, 13
langar, 596
languages, 48; in global society, 1057, *1057c*; Greek influence, 286; Romance, 375
Laozi, 198, *198f*
Lares, 360
Last Supper, 728
Latin (language), 338, 375; roots, 714
Latin America, *1022m*; economy, 1024–1025, *1025c*; modern political changes, 1021–1024; social struggles, 1025–1026. *See also* Americas; South America
Latins (people), 330
latitude, 15, 16
law: rule of, 339–340, *340f*
law of demand, 23
law of gravity, 779, *780f*
law of supply, 23
Law of the Twelve Tables, 339–340, *340f*, 341

laws, 31; and the assembly in Athens, 267–268, *267f*; civil, 375–376; Draco's, 265; Hammurabi's Code, *63t*, 83, *83f*; in Hellenistic kingdoms, 317; Jewish, 237–238; in Mesopotamia, 69; Roman, 339–340, *340f*, 341, 375
laws of motion, 780
League of Nations, 897–898; and invasion of Ethiopia, 919
Leakey, Louis, 42, 44
Leakey, Mary, 42, *42p*
Lebanon: and Syria, 1016–1017
Leeuwenhoek, Antoni van, 781, 786
Legalism, 198–199; and Shi Huangdi, 200
legend (map), 35, *35m*
legions, 343; standards, *351p*
Lenin, Vladimir, *885t*, 903, *903p*, 904, 921
Leo IX, Pope, 682
Leyte Gulf, Battle of, 931
liberalism, 847
Li Bo, *515t*; 526
Libya: Arab Spring, *1031t*
limited government: 830; in medieval Europe, 673; in Roman Republic, 339
limited monarchy, *32c*, 33
linguists, 44
Li Qingzao, 527
literature: *The Aeneid,* 330, *330f*, 334–335, 375; Chinese, 211, 522; *Divine Comedy, 713t*, 724; *Don Quixote,* 736f, 737; Epic of Gilgamesh, 80–81; Greek, 288–289; *The Iliad,* 290; in Japan, *555t*, 570–571; Muslim, 459–460, *460f*, 462; *The Odyssey,* 290; Ottoman, 590; Persian, 93; Popol Vuh, 628–629; *The Prince,* 724–725, *724f*; Qur'an, 446–447; Renaissance; 737–738; Roman, 375; *Romeo and Juliet, 713t*, 740–741; Sanskrit, 174; *Sermon on the Mount,* 394–395; *The Shiji,* 214–215; *Sundiata,* 500, 504–505; *Tale of Genji, 555t*, 567, *567p*, 568, 570–571. *See also* drama; poetry

Liu Bang, 206
Livy, 376
llamas, 642, 644
location: absolute, 15–16; essential element of geography, 14; studying, 14–15
Locke, John, 33, *769t, 823t*; 832, *834f,* 835, *835f, 836t,* and U.S. government, 839, 840
London: *381t*; Boudicca, *325t*
longitude, 15, 16
Long March, *915t*
long-term effects: identify, 249
Longus, 310
Lord's Prayer, 393
lords, 193, *194f*; feudal, 673, 674–675, *674f*; Qin dynasty, 201
Louis XIV, king of France, 830–831
Louis XVI, king of France, 841, 842
Louis XVIII, king of France, 847
L'Ouverture, Toussaint, 847
Lower Egypt, 104, 105, *105m,* 132
Lucy, 44
Lusitania, 894
Luther, Martin, *745t,* 750–752, *750p, 752f*; and the Enlightenment, 827; Ninety-Five Theses, 750, *751f*; translating the Bible, 752
Lycurgus, 272
Ly Dai Hanh, *549p*
Ly dynasty, 549–550. *See also* China
Lyric poetry, 284–285

M

MacArthur, Douglas, 945
Maccabees, 234, *303t*
Macedonia: Alexander the Great, 307–308; and Athens, 270, 306; Hellenistic, 311–312, *312m,* 314, *319t*; ethnic conflict, 1039; Philip II, 306–307; and Thebes, 306, 307

Machiavelli, Niccolo, *3t,* 724–725, *724f*
Machu Picchu, 644, *644i*
Madison, James, 840
Magellan, Ferdinand, *793t,* 799, *800m*
magistrates, 336–337, *337f*
Magna Carta, 33, 698–699; *698i, 699f, 700t,* 838, *838p*
Magyars, *407t,* 414, 671, *671m*
Mahabharata, the, 174
Mahan, Alfred Thayer, 877
maharaja, 597
Mahavira, 158
Mahayana, 165
Maimonides, 775
main idea: identify, 64–65; understand support of, 556
maize, *609t,* 615, *615p,* 617–618; and Maya, 619
majority rule, 338, 832
make decisions, 511
make predictions: ask questions to, 584
malaria: in Africa, 1012
Malaysia: constitutional monarchy, 997; rain forest, 1064; and Muslim traders, 450
Mali Empire, *467t, 489m, 496t*; decline of, 493; description of, 500; invaders, 493; Mansa Musa, 490–491, *490i, 491m*; Sundiata, 488–490, 500
Malintzin, 638, *638f, 638i*
mammoth house, *53f*
Manchuria, *885t,* 922
Mandela, Nelson, *983t,* 1007, *1007f, 1008f, 1009p*
manor, 675–676, *676f*; and black death, 702
Mansa Musa, *490i,* hajj, *467t,* 490; ruler of Mali, 490–491, *491m*
manufacturing: in mercantilism, 813
Maori, 875
Mao Zedong, *915t, 983t,* 990–991, *990f*

maps, 15; Americas on, *3t,* 804–805; atlas, 814; compare, *18m*; culture, 657; and exploration, 797, 803, 804–805; make, 15–16, 35; physical, 97; Renaissance cartography, 730; as secondary sources, 11
Marathon, Battle of, 94, *95c*
Marcos, Ferdinand, 998
Marie Antoinette, 841
Marius, Gaius, 347–348, *347f*
market economy, 25, 33, 816
marketplace: Greek, 260
Marne, Battle of, 893
Marshall Plan, 957
Martí, José, 876–877, *877i*
martyrs, 398
Marx, Karl, *855t,* 861, 903, *903p*
Marxism, 903
Mary (Mother of Jesus), 388
Masada, 243–244, *385p*
Masih, Iqbal, 1037–1038
masks: in contemporary Africa, 1013; in West Africa, 502
Masoudi, 460
mathematics: algebra, 458; Arabic numerals, 458, *458f*; calculus, 780; in China, 211; geometry, 297; *297f*; in Greece, 297; in India, 175, *175f*; in Mesopotamia, 77; in Muslim world, 458, *458f*
matrilineal, 475
Mau Mau, 1002
Maurya, Candragupta, 167, 168
Mauryan Empire, 167–168, *168m, 303t*; art, 172–173; literature in, 174; sciences in, 174–176, *175f*
Maya, *381t,* 619, *620m, 643c*; architecture, 625; art of, 625; calendar, 625, *625f*; cities, *609t,* 621, *621f*; decline of, 626–627; fighting among, *429t*; 622 659 MC1–659 MC2; Popol Vuh, 626, 628–629; recording history, 626, *626f*; religion, 624; science of, *624p,* 625; society, 622–624, *623f*; trade, 619–621, *620m*; writing, 626

Mayflower, 769t
McKinley, William, 877, 879
Mecca, 435f, 437, 440t, 441m; and the astrolabe, 456; the hajj, 443f, 444, 454, 455m; and a mosque, 461f; during Ottoman Empire, 587; and prayer, 441
mechanics, 778–779
Medes, 91
Medici, Cosimo de', 720–721
medicine: acupuncture, 210f, 211; advances in, 77; anatomy, 728, 729f; Aztec, 636; in China, 210f, 211; in Greece, 297–298; in India, 175f, 176; during Renaissance, 728, 730; and scientific method, 786; in Songhai Empire, 495; and new technology, 1067–1068; in Muslim world, 458–459, 458f; during World War II, 929
medieval, 667–671; towns, 677–678
Medina, 440, 440t, 441, 441m; during Ottoman Empire, 587
meditation, 161
megacities, 1061
megaliths, 57
Mehmed II, 586–587, 587f
Meiji, 874, 991–992
Memphis (Egypt), 108
men: in Athens, 275, 275f, 276f; in Bantu society, 508; in hunter-gatherer society, 48; Mayan, 623; Spartan, 272–273, 273f; Sumerian, 75; in West African society, 474, 475
Menelik II, Emperor of Ethiopia, 869
Menes, 63t, 101t, 108–109, 108i
mercantilism, 812–814, 835f
merchants, 121, 133; Harappan, 146f; Italian, 718; as spies, 631
Merici, Angela, 757, 757f
Meröe, 101t, 133, 134m, 135
Meroitic, 134

Mesoamerica, 609t; Chavin culture, 617, 617m, 640; geography, 612, 613m, 614; Maya, 619–627, 620m; migration to, 614–615, 614m; Olmecs, 615–616, 616f, 617m, 643c
Mesolithic Era, 53–54
Mesopotamia, 66, agriculture in, 63; Assyrians, 85; and Babylonians, 82; and Chaldeans, 86; civilization of, 68, 70–71, 112c; and flooding, 68f; and Hittites, 84; and Kassites, 84; Sargon, 63; Sumerians, 72–79
messenger system: in Persia, 94
Messiah, 387, 388, 389
metallurgy, 174–175, 175f
metalworking, 174–175, 175f; in China, 194f
Metamorphoses, 375
Methodius, 422, 424
Metternich, Klemens von, 846, 847
Mexico: Carlos Salinas de Gortari, 1023–1024; independence, 848, 849m; Mayans, 381t; NAFTA, 1024, 1077; PRI, 983t, 1023–1024
Michelangelo, 713t, 726–728, 727p, 727i
microchip, 1054
microscope, 780–781, 780p, 786
Middle Ages, 667–671; towns in, 677–678
middle class, 815, 862
Middle East: conflicts, 1016–1020, 1017t; oil wealth, 1019f, 1020; OPEC, 1020, 1077; post–World War II, 1014–1015, 1015f
Middle Kingdom, 117
Middle Stone Age, 53–54
Midway, Battle of, 931, 933
migration: to Americas, 614–615, 614m; early human, 44, 50–52, 51m, 53f; and population density, 1060, 1060m; pull factors, 1060–1061
Milan, 718, 719, 719f

militarism, 891–892; and fascism, 918
military dictatorship, 1010f; Zaire, 1008;
millet, 588
Minamoto clan, 573
minaret, 461, 461f
Ming dynasty, 515t, 528f, 538, 539–541, 713t. *See also* China
Minoan civilization, 253t, 258, 258f, 259, 259m, 262–263
minute, 15
mihrab, 461f
miracles, 390
missionaries: Buddhist, 165; Catholic, 668, 758–759, 759f, 808; Spanish, 823t
Mississippian culture, 653
mita **system,** 34, 642
mixed economy, 25, 33
Mobutu, Joseph, 1008, 1009
Moctezuma II, 609t, 637, 637f
models: develop and interpret, 707
Mohenjo Daro, 146f
Mona Lisa, 728, 729f
monarchs, 82; and Tyrian purple, 89f
monarchy, 32c, 33; in China, 200; economies, 33; in Europe, 831m, 847; Sumerian, 75
monasteries, 668–669; Cluny, 693
money, 27–28
Mongols, 422; Genghis Khan, 534, 535m; and Japan, 467t, 537, 576–577, 576m, 713t; and Korea, 548; Kublai Khan, 535–536, 535m, 535f, 536p; Yuan dynasty, 515t, 535–537, 555t
monks, 668–669, 668f; of Cluny, 692, 693f; copying texts, 733t, 733i
monotheism, 236, 397, 439
monsoons, 145, 186
Montesquieu, Charles-Louis, 832–833, 833f, 834f, 835f, 836t; and U.S. Constitution, 840

moon walk, *951t*

Moors, 450; forced out of Spain, 702–704, *705m*, 755–756, *756p*

Morocco: independence, 1004; invasion of Songhai Empire, *467t*, *496t*

Mosaic law, 237–238

mosaics, 419

Moses, 229, *229m*, 230, *230p*, *232t*, 236, *237p*; Mosaic law, 237–238; and Muhammad, 439

mosque, 441, 461; in Mali, 491; Blue Mosque, *461f*; Grand Mosque, 454; Great Mosque, *452f*; Safavid Empire, 592, *592p*

Mosque of Suleyman, 589, *589p*

mound builders, 651, 653

Mount Fuji, *558p*

Mount Vesuvius, 358

movable type, 528–529, 732, *732i*, *733t*

Mozambique, 1005

Mughal Empire, *583t*, 600–601, *601m*; Akbar, 600; architecture, 604; Aurangzeb, 601, 603; Babur, 600; compared to other empires, *602c*; cultures, 603–604; decline of, 603, *823t*, 871; religion in, 600, 601; and Sikhs, 597

Muhammad, *407t*, *429t*, *515t*, *661t*; daughter of, *439f*, 440; life of, 437–438; as prophet, 438, *441m*, 442; teachings of, 439–440

Mujahideen, 968

multinational corporations, 1076, *1076p*

mummies, *113f*, 114; Incan, 644

mummified man, *3t*, 44

Muscovy, *407t*

music: Renaissance, 725–726; Russian, 424; Sumerian, 79; in United States, *501f*; West African, 501, 503

Muslim Empire, 438, 448–450, *449m*; architecture of, 460–461, *461f*; art of, 461–462; astronomy, 456–457, *457f*;

invading Spain, 450; literature of, 459–460, 462; philosophy, *459f*, 459; tolerance, 451; traders, 450, *451m*; Umayyad family, 449

Muslims, 438, children, *444p*; and the Crusades, *661t*, 685–689, *688m*, 711 MC1–711 MC2; hajj, *443f*, 444, 454–455; invading medieval Europe, 671, *671m*; forced to leave Spain, 702–704, *703m*, 755–756, *756p*; and religious persecution, 1040; Safavid conflict, 591; Saladin, 687–688, *687f*; Shia, 591; and the Sunnah, 442–444, *443f*; Sunni, 591; traders, 718; women, 442

Mussolini, Benito, *915t*, 918–919, *919p*, 927f

Mutsuhito, 874

Myanmar, 998, *1045f*

Mycenaean civilization, 258, *258f*, 259, *259m*, 283

mythology: Greek, 280–282, 286–287, *286p*, *287f*, 288–289; Roman, 375, 360, 361

myths: creation, 113. *See also* mythology

N

Nagasaki, *915t*, 933, 942

Nagy, Imre, 970

Napoleonic Code, 845

Nara Period, 564–565

Nasser, Gamal Abdel, 1014, *1015f*

National Assembly, French, 842

nationalism, 888; causing tension, 891; and fascism, 918

Nationalists, 989–990

nation-state, 704, 888

natural disasters, 262–263

natural law, 696; and the Enlightenment, 828

natural resources, 17, 22, 24, 27; forests, 1063–1064, *1063p*, *1063c*; as a reason for exploration, 796; nonrenewable, 1061, 1065; renewable, 1065; water, 1062–1063

natural rights, 832, *834f*, 839

natural wonders, 20–21, *20–21m*

naval warfare, World War I, 894

navigation, 90

Nazca, 640

Nazi Party, 910, 919–920; resistance, 938

Nebuchadnezzar, 86

needs, 26

Nekhen, 107

Nepal: and democracy, 1044–1045

Neo-Confucianism, 531

Neolithic Era, 55; communities in, 57–58

Neolithic Revolution, 55, 56

Nero, 354–355

Netherlands: and banking, 814–815; Dutch East India Company, *793t*; in historical fiction, 817–818; and the New World, 801

Nevsky, Alexander, 422

New Deal, 908–909, *908p*

New Horizons mission, *1031t*, 1053, *1053c*

New Kingdom, 118–120, *118c*

New Stone Age, 55

Newton, Sir Isaac, *769t*, 779–780, *780f* 787

New World, 798–799. *See also* Americas; North America; South America

New Zealand, 875

Nicaragua, 966–967

Nicholas II, Czar of Russia, *885t*, 902, *902p*, 903

Niger River: Ghana Empire, 481; Mali Empire, 488, *492f*; Songhai Empire, *495p*

Nigeria: democracy, 1049; economy, 1011; Lagos, *1011f*, 1012

Nile River, 104–106; and Kush, 129

Ninety-Five Theses, *745t*, 750, *750p*, *751f*

Ninevah, 85

nirvana, 162, 163, 165

Nixon, Richard, 971, 972, *972p*

Nkrumah, Kwame, *983t*, 1001, *1001f*

nobles, 111, *111c*; Aztec, 632–633; and feudalism, 673–675, *674f*; Japanese, 566; Qin dynasty, 201; in the Second Estate, 841
Noh, 568
Nok culture, *467t*, 477
nomads: in Arabia, 434, *435f*; in China, 518; Tuareg, 493
nongovernmental organization (NGO): and environment, 1064; and health, 1070; and human rights, 1035–1036, 1046
nonprofit organizations, 26
nonrenewable resources, 1061, 1065
nonviolence, 158, *158f*, 987, *987f*, *988p*, *988f*
Norman invasion, 675
North Africa: French colonies, 1004
North America: colonies declare independence, *855t*; early cultures, 650–656; and the Enlightenment, 833–834, 835–836; European discovery of, 776; Jamestown established, *793t*; migration to, 51, *51m*, *609t*
North American Free Trade Agreement (NAFTA), 1024, 1077
North Atlantic Treaty Organization (NATO), 959; Kosovo, 1039
North Korea, 963–964, *964m* religious persecution, *1040p*, 1040
Northwestern cultures, *652m*, 653
Novgorod, *407t*, 414, 420, *421m*, 423, *423p*
Nubia, 129. *See also* Africa; Aksum; Kush
Nuremberg Laws, 935
Nuremberg Trials, 946

O

oasis, 433
Obama, Barak, *983t*, 1025
obelisk, 126
observatories: in Mayan Empire, *624p*, 625; in Ottoman Empire, 588, *588i*, 603
obsidian, 619, *619p*, 621
occupations, 69; and caste system, 152–154, *153f. See also individual occupations*
Octavian, 352, *352f*
Oda Nobunaga, 577
Odyssey, the, 283, *283f*, 284, *284p*, 291
oil: dependence on, 1077; in Middle East, *1019f*, 1020; spills, 1062; in Venezuela, 1024
Old Kingdom, 110–116, *118c*, *141t*
Old Stone Age, 45, 50
oligarchy, 32, in Athens, 264–265
Olmecs, *101t*, *253t*, *609t*, 615–616, *616f*, *617m*, *643c*
Olympic Games, *282f*
online research, 746
OPEC (Organization of Petroleum Exporting Countries), 1020, 1077
Open Door Policy, 873
opinions: identify, 226–227
opportunity cost, 23
oracle, 190, 282–283
oral history, 498–500, *499p*; Aztec, 637; Inca, 646; Maya, 626; the *Sundiata,* 499, 504–505
orator, 348
organization: patterns of, 468
Orthodox Jews, 238
Osiris, 113, *114p*
Ottoman Empire, *407t*, 417; architecture, 589–590, *588p*; army, 586; Blue Mosque, *461f*, conquers Constantinople, *583t*, 586, *609t*, *713t*; expansion, 586–587, *587m*;

government, 588; literature in, 590; Mehmed II, 586–587; science in, 588–589; society in, 588; Suleyman I, 588; in World War I, 894; after World War I, 898, *898m*
Ötzi, *3t*, 44
outlining, 326
overgrazing, 486, *486p*
overpopulation, 1060, *1060m*; megacities, 1061
oversight: in history, 425
Ovid, 375
ozone layer, 1061–1062

P

Pacal, 621
Pachacuti, *609t*, 641
Pacific theater, 930–931, *930m*, 949 MC2
Pact of Umar, 449
Pakistan, *983t*, 989, 998; Kashmir conflict, 993–994, *994m*; rights abuses, *1036f*, 1037, 1040
Palenque, 621, *621f*
Paleolithic Era, 45
Palestine: and the Crusades, 685–689, *685p*, *688m*, *689f*; and modern state of Israel, 940, 1016
Panama, 880
Panama Canal, 880
pandemic, 1069–1070; AIDS, 1071–1072, *1071c*
Pan Gu, 197
Pantheon, *384p*
papermaking, 211, 732, *733t*
papyrus, 124, *124p*, 126
parables, 390
Parliament, 699, *700t*; and English civil war, 837–838
Parthenon, 293, *294f*, 301 MC2
partition, of India, *983t*, 989, 993; Kashmir conflict, 993–994, *994m*
Passover, 247, *247f*

past: study the, 6–8, 10–11, understand the, 8–9

Pasteur, Louis, 860

patricians: in government, 336–338, 339, *340f*; in Roman society, 333, *333f*

Patrick, 668, *668f*

patrilineal, 474

patrons: in Muslim Empire, 461

Paul, 391, 396–397, *397f, 398m*

Pax Romana, 358

Pe, 107

Pearl Harbor, *915t*, 926–927, *926f*

peasants, 193, *194f*; in feudal society, *674f*, 678

Peloponnesian League, 277

Peloponnesian War, *253t*, 277–278, *278m*, 288

penates, 360

people: and geography, 19; study of, 14

perceived region, 16

perestroika, 975

Pericles, *268f*, 269, 293

Period of Disunion, 518, 520, 531

periods of time: terms for, 4–5

permanent settlements, 56–58

Perón, Juan, 1021

Perry, Matthew, *855t*, 874, *874f*

persecution, 398; of Christians, 398–399, *399t*; in Mughal Empire, 601; religious, 1040

Persepolis, 93

Persia: and Alexander the Great, 307, 308; army, 92; conquered by Muslim Empire, 448; and Safavids, *583t*, 591–594, *745t*

Persian empire, *63t*, 87, 91, *92m*; architecture in, 93; art in, 93; Cyrus the Great, 91–92; Darius I, 93–96; conquering Chaldeans, 234; invading Greece, *325t*, 94–96, *95m*; literature of, 93; society, 93–94; trade in, 93–94; and Zoroastrianism, 93

Persian Gulf War, *983t, 1017t*; 1018

Persian Wars, 94–96, *95m*, 288, 301 MC2

Persistratus, 265, *265p*

perspective: artistic, 725, *726p*; historical, 9

peso, 27, *28c*

Peter, 392, 400

Petrarch, 725, 731

phalanx, 306, *307i*

pharaohs, 108; Alexander the Great, 307; Khufu, 111; King Ezana, 135; King Tutankhamen, *127f*, 128; King Unas, 116; Kushite Dynasty, 132, 133; Menes, *63t, 101t*, 108–109, *108i*; and the Israelites, 229; in Old Kingdom, 110–111; Ptolemy, 313, *313f*; and pyramids, 116; in society, *111c*; Thutmose I, 131

pharmaceuticals, 1068

Pharos, 316, *317i, 319t*

Philip II, 306–307

Philippines, 876, 877, 878, *878m*, 879, 880; Corazon Aquino, 998

Philistines, 232, 233

philosophers: Aristotle, 269, *269f*, 296, *296i*; Cicero, 348; Denis Diderot, 829; Francis Bacon, 782, 783, *784f*, 787–788; Karl Marx, 861; Plato, 295–296, *295f, 296i*; René Descartes, 783, *784f*; Socrates, 295, *295f, 296i*; Voltaire, 828–829, *828f*

philosophy: and Christianity, 401; Confucianism, 530–531, *531p*; French, 828–829; Greek, 293, 295–296; Hellenistic, 319, *319c*; and Scientific Revolution, 785; Sufism, *459f*, 459

Phoenicia, 87–88; culture of, 90; Punic Wars, 344, *344f*; and trade, 88–89, 90, *253t*; and Tyrian purple, *89f*

physical geography, 12, *13f*

physical maps, 16; interpret, 97

physical processes, 13

Piankhi, 132, *132f*

pictographs, 75, *76c, 190f*

pilgrimage, 439; for Christians, 691; hajj, *443f*, 444, 454–455

Pinochet, Augusto, *983t*, 1023

pit house, 52

Pizarro, Francisco, 646–647, *646p, 769t*, 800

Plains cultures, *652m*, 654, *654i*

plantations, 809, 810, *810f*, 811

plants: and the Columbian Exchange, 806, 807, *807m*; domestication of, 55, 56

Platea, Battle of, 96

Plato, 295–296, *295f, 296i*; and Christianity, 401

Platt Amendment, 879

plebeians: in government, 336–338; in Roman society, 333, *333f*

poetry: Chinese, *515t*, 520, 526–527; Du Fu, *515t*, 526; epic, 76, 80–81, 283–284, *283f*, 290–291, 499–500; Hellenistic, 310; of Japanese nobles, 567–568; Li Bo, *515t*, 526; Li Qingzao, 527; lyric, 284–285; Omar Khayyám, 460; in Ottoman Empire, 590; Petrarch, 725; Safavid, 593; Roman, 375; Yunus Emre, 590

points of view: identify, 824

Poland: Auschwitz, 937, *937f, 938f*, 939; and blitzkrieg, 925, *925p*; concentration camps, 936, 937; death marches, 939; fall of communism, 977, *977f*; ghettos, 936–937, *936p*; liberation of, 930

polis, 260, 261

political dissent, 1038

political map, 16

politics: global interdependence, 1058

pollution, 14, 1061–1062

Polo, Marco, *535f*, 536–537, *537f, 713t*, 717–718, *717i, 717m, 718f*; spurring more exploration, 796

Polybius, 310

polytheism, 74; in Arabia, 439; in Egypt, 112–113

Pompeii, 358, *358i*, 359

Pompey, 349–350

Ponce de Leon, Juan, 821 MC1–821 MC2

pope, 400; in Byzantine Empire, 418; Great Schism, 748; and Henry VIII, 754; sending missionaries, 668

Popol Vuh, 626, 628–629

popular sovereignty, 833

population growth: *1031t*, 1059–1061, *1061m*; over-, 1060–1061

porcelain, 526, 527, *527f*

Poroshenko, Petro, *1048p*, 1049

potlatch, 653

Potsdam Conference, 946, 954–955

pottery: in China, *3t*

Portugal: African colonies, 1004–1005; caravels, 797–798, *797f*; and mercantilism, 814; and South America, 848

Praise of Folly, The 734f, 750

prayer: Christian, 393; Muslim, 441, 443, *443f*

predictions: ask questions to make, 584

prehistory, 42

preview text, 254–255

price, 22; and supply and demand, 23

priests: Aryan, 149, 151, 152, *153f*; Aztec, 633, 635; behavior leading to Reformation, 748, 749; Brahmins, 151, 152, *153f*, 162; in Egypt, 110; Incan, 644; looking for heretics, 702; Mayan, 622; Sumerian, 74, 75; Zoroastrian, 93

priestesses: Egyptian, 122; Sumerian, 75

primary source, 10; assess, 137, 662

prime meridian, 15

princeps, 352

Principia Mathematica, 769t, 779–780

Prince Shotoku, *429t, 548t, 555t*, 562, 563–564, *563f, 563p*

principalities, in Russia, 422

printing: 3D, 1068–1069, *1068p*

printing press, 732, *733t*; helping the Reformation, 750

print research sources: identify, 819

problem solving, 579

production: factors of, 24

profit, 23; and stocks, 28

propaganda, recognize, 916

prophets, 238, Jewish, 386–387; Muhammad, 438, 442, 443, *443f, 515t*; Muslim, 439

protective tariff, 34; GATT, 1076

Protestants: after Council of Trent, 758; in Europe, *761m*; Huguenots, 762; and Spanish Inquisition, 756; split from Catholic Church, 751; St. Bartholomew's Day massacre, *745t*; wars with Catholic Church, 761–763

proverbs, 499

Proverbs, Book of, 238

provinces: Roman, 357, 359

Psalms, 238

Ptolemy (of Greece), 774, 776

Ptolemy (of Macedonia), 313, *313f*, 314, 319

public documents, 886

public education, 862

Pueblo, 651, *652m*

pueblos (buildings), *650p, 654t*

Puerto Rico, 880

Punic Wars, *325t*, 344, *344f, 345m, 365t*

Punjab: and Sikhs, 597–598, *598m*

Pure Land Buddhism, 569

purgatory, 749

pyramids, 115–116, *115p*; Kushite, *131p*, 133

Pyramid Texts, 116

Pythagoras, 297

Q

Qin dynasty, *181t, 201t, 201m, 325t*; and Confucianism, 530; Shi Huangdi, 200–203, 205. *See also* China

Qing dynasty, 989. *See also* China

Qinling Shandi, 184, *185m*

Quechua, 642

Hatshepsut, queen of Egypt, 119–120, *118f, 181t*

Isabella, queen of Spain, 704, *704f*, 798

queens: in feudal society, *674f*

Shanakhdakheto, queen of Kush, 135

Quetzalcoatl, 637

quipus, 642

Qur'an, 438, *438f*, 442, *443f, 444p*, 446–447, 448; and slavery, 484

R

rabbis, 244

Rabelais, François, 737

racism, 811; apartheid, 1006–1008

rain forests: in Africa, 472, *473m*; destruction of, *1063c*, 1064

Raj, 871

rajas, 150

Ramadan, *443f*, 443–444

Ramayana, the, 174

Ramses the Great, *101t*, 120, *120f*, 126, *225t*

Raphael, 725

rationalism: and democracy, 785–786, *785f*

rationalists, 774

Reagan, Ronald, 972, 974, *974p*, 975

real, *28c*

realism: in art, 734, *861f*, 862

reason, 296, 785; Age of, 826–829

recession: global, *1031t*

recognizing propaganda, 916

Reconquista, 703–704, *703m*

reform: during Industrial Revolution, 862

Reformation, 748–750; Catholic, 755, 756–758, *757f*; German woodcuts, *749f*; John Calvin, 753–754, *753f*; and the Enlightenment, 827; results of, 763, *763p, 764f*; William Tyndale, 752

Reform Jews, 238

refugees, *1031t,* 1047; and failed states, 1050; Syrian, 1047–1048, *1047p*

regent, 562; Empress Gemmi, 564; Prince Shotoku, 562

region, 16; and culture, 17

Reign of Terror, 843

reincarnation, 156, *157f;* and the Buddha, 162–163; and Sikhism, 596

relative dating, 8

relative location, 16

relevant information: identify, 610

religion: *438f;* animism, 476; Aztec, 634–635, *635f;* Buddhism, *101t,* 160–166; Aryan, 151; Christianity, 386–387, 389, *438f;* and Columbian Exchange, 808; of early peoples, 49; as government, 32; Harappan, 146; Hinduism, *141t,* 155–157; Incan, 644; Islam, *438f;* Mayan, 624; in Persia, 93; in Phoenicia, 90; Jainism, 157, 158; Judaism, 228, 236–240, 240–241, *438f;* polytheism, 74; as reason for exploration, 796; in Roman Empire, *365t, 399t;* science, 786–788, *787p;* scholars, 774–775, *774f;* Sikhism, 157, 158–159, 583t, 595–599, *596p, 597c;* in Sumerian society, 74; Ten Commandments, 230–231; theocracy, 32, *32c,* 33, 110–111, 231; and trade routes, 27, 218; Zoroastrianism, 93. *See also* Buddhism; Christianity; Hinduism; Islam; Judaism

religious orders: Dominicans, 694; Franciscans, 694; Jesuits, 756–757, *757f;* monks of Cluny, 692, *693f;* Ursulines, 757, *757f. See also* monks

religious practices: in Neolithic Era, 57–58

Remus, 330–331, *330f*

Renaissance, 721; architecture, 730; art, *723f,* 725, *726p;* astronomy, 730; cartography, 730; and classical culture, 723, 774; and education, 730–731; and humanism, 722–723; leads to the Enlightenment 827; and Leonardo da Vinci, 728, *729f;* literature of, 723, 740–741; medicine in, 730; and Michelangelo, 726–728, *727p, 727i*

renewable resources, 1065

reparations, 899–900; and the Great Depression, 910

representative democracy, 33, *270f,* 271

republic, 33, *32c*

research: current events, 1081; Internet, 219, 746; print sources, 819

resources, 17, 22, 24, 27; and balance of trade, 812–813; as a reason for exploration, 796; nonrenewable resources, 1061, 1065; water, 1062–1063; as wealth, 28

Resurrection, 389, *390f*

retrenchment, 909

review texts, 984

Revolutionary War (American), *823t;* 838–839, 853 MC1–853 MC2

Rhodes, Cecil, 865, *865f*

rice: growing, 523, *524f*

Richard I, king of England, 687, *687f*

rifts, 470

righteousness: in Jewish society, 237

river valley civilizations, 70–71; Mesopotamia, 66–69

roads: Inca, 645, 648–649; in Persia, 94; in Rome, 362–363; in Safavid Empire, 594

Robespierre, Maximilian, 843

Roman Catholic Church: and Martin Luther, *745t;* problems leading to the Reformation, 748–750; split into Catholics and Protestants, 751; wealth, 749

Romance languages, 375

Roman Empire, *365t;* architecture, 373–374, *373f;* art, 374, *374p;* Augustus Caesar, *225t,* *325t,* 352, 354; barbarian invasions, 366–369, *407t;* Caligula, 354; Christianity in, 397–399; cities, 358–359; citizenship, 355; compared to other empires, *602c;* Constantine, 366; Constantinople, *101t,* 366, 415–417, *415m;* country life, 360; decline of, 364–365, *368c,* 369, *369f, 609t;* Diocletian, *325t,* 365, *365m,* 415; division of, *325t,* 365–366, *365m,* 414, 415; in eastern Europe, 414; and Egypt, *303t,* 313; engineering, 371–372, 373, 379 MC1–379 MC2; entertainment, 359, *359p;* Goths, *325t;* government, 356; growth of, 355–356, *356m,* 379 MC2; historians, 375, 376; and Jerusalem, *225t,* 234, 242–244, *243f;* and Judaism, 385–386; Justinian, 416–417; laws, 339–340, *340f,* 341, 375, 416; literature in, 330, *330f,* 334–335, 375; conquering Macedonia, 313, *319t;* military, 355; mythology of, 360, 361, 375; Nero, 354; Paul's letter to, *397f;* Pax Romana, 357, 358; philosophy, 376; religions in, *141t,* 360–361, *381t,* 384–386; science and medicine, 371; and the Silk Road, 27, 220–221, 357; temples, 384, *384p;* Tiberius, 354; trade, 357, *357m,* 366, *467t. See also* Roman Republic; Rome

Roman Republic, *325t,* 331, *332m, 365t;* banking, *342f;* Julius Caesar, 348–351; crises, 346–348; dictators, 331–332; the Forum, 339, 341–342, *341f;* growth of, 342–343, *343m,* 344–345;

Marc Antony, 352; Marius, 347–348; Octavian, 352; Punic Wars, *325t*, 344, *344f*, *345m*, *365t*; slave rebellion, 348; society in, 333, *333f*; Sulla, 347–348; trade, 342, 343; tripartite government, 336–338, *337f*; wars, 331–332. *See also* Roman Empire; Rome

Roman roads, 362–363

Roman Senate, 337, *337f*; Caesar against, 350

romanticism, *861f*, 862

Roman philosophy: and humanism, 722–723

Rome: ancient, 33; Etruscans, 331; founding of, *253t*, *325t*, 330–331, 360; geography of, 328–329, *329m*; roads, 362–363. *See also* Roman Empire; Roman Republic

Romeo and Juliet, *713t*, 740–741

Romulus, 330–331, *330f*

roots: Latin and Greek, 714

Rosetta Stone, *3t*, 124

Rosh Hashanah, 247

Roosevelt, Franklin Delano, *915t*; and New Deal, 908–909, *908p*; Pearl Harbor, *926f*, 927; World War II, *927f*, 928; Yalta Conference, 944, 954, *955p*

Rousseau, Jean–Jacques, 833, *834f*, *836t*, 839

Royal Road, 94

Rubaiyat, The, 460

Rub' al-Khali, 433

rule of law, 339–340, *340f*, 699, 838

rupee, *28c*

rural, 72

Rurik, *407t*, 414

Rus, 414, 420

Russia: 1917 Revolution, 903–904; architecture, 423, *423p*; art, 423–424; becomes Soviet Union, *885t*, 904; Catherine the Great, 831–832, *831p*; Christianity, 422, 423; conflict with Ukraine, 1048–1049; Czar

Nicholas II, *885t*, 902, *902p*, 903; daily life, 422; early, 420, *421m*; food shortages, 901; government, 422; and Japan, *885t*, 901; joins Allies, 893; music, 424; and Napoleon Bonaparte, 845, *845p*; Russo-Japanese War, 922; in World War I, 893, 895, 904; after World War I, 898, *898m*

Rwanda: ethnic conflict, 1009, 1039, 1043

S

sacred texts: Jewish, 238–240, *239f*, *240f*

sacrifice, Aztec, 634; Incan, 644; Mayan, 622, 624

Sadat, Anwar, 967, *967p*

Safavid Empire, *583t*, *745t*; conflict with other Muslims, 591; culture, 592–593, *593p*; economy, 594; expansion, 591–592, *593m*; trade, 594

Sahara, 472, *473m*, 478–479; and salt, 472

Sahel, 472, *473m*

saint, 396, 398

Saint Bartholomew's Day massacre, *745t*, 762, *762p*

Saladin, 687, *687f*

Salamis, Battle of, *96c*, 95–96

salary, 25

salon, 829

salt: in African trade, 472, 478, 482, *483p*; and Moroccan invasion, 496

Salt March, *915t*

samskaras, 157

samurai, 572–573, *573f*, 574–575, *574f*, *575f*, 581 MC1–581 MC2; and the Meiji, 991

sanctions, 1007

sand dunes, 432–433

Sandinistas, 966

San Martín, José de, 848

Sanskrit, 151; literature, 174

Sanxingdui people, 187

Sappho, 285

Sargon, *63t*, 73–74, *74m*; daughter of, 75

satellite, 16

satellite states, 956–957, *956m*, 969–971

satire, 375

satraps, 93

Saul, 232, *232p*, *232t*

savannah, 472, *473m*

scale (map), 35, *35m*

scarcity, 22, 26

schools: educating workers, 29

Schutzstaffel (SS), 936

science: in Aztec Empire, 635–636; birth of modern, 772–775; in Han dynasty, *210f*, 211; Industrial Revolution advances, 860; and Latin, 375; in Mesopotamia, 77; and religion, 786–788, *787p*; scientific method, 783–784, *783f*; and the Silk Road, 218

scientific method, 783–784, *783f*; and medicine, 786

Scientific Revolution, 772–775, 782, 788; Copernicus, 776–778, *777p*, *777f*; doubts lead to, 776; and the Enlightenment, 828; inventions of, 780–781

scholar-official, 532–533

scholars: and the humanities, 722–723; and Renaissance science, 728–729; and Scientific Revolution, 774–775, *774f*

scribe, 75–76; in Egypt, *111c*, 121; Jewish, 228

Sea Peoples, 120

seal, 146, 147, *147p*

secondary source, 11; assessing, 137, 662

Second Temple, 234, 242. *See also* Temple to God

secular, 1046

securities, 1078

Securities and Exchange Commission (SEC), 909

sedentary, 434

seder, 247, *247f*

seismograph, *210f*, 211

Seleucus, *303t*, 312, *312i*, *319t*

Index

self-government: and congregations, 763–764

Senegal, 1010

separation of power, 832, *833f, 834f;* in U.S. Constitution, 840

Sephardim, 246, *246f. See also* Jews

sepoys, 871

sequence chain, 40–41

Serbia: ethnic conflict, 1039; and start to WWI, *829m,* 893

serfs, 676, 678

Sermon on the Mount, 394–395

services, 22; government, 30–31; and the Internet, 26; and taxes, 34; and trade, 26–27

sextant, 16, 797

shah, 591, 1015

Shah Jahan, *583t,* 604, *603p*

Shaka, 869

Shakespeare, William, *713t, 737–738, 737f; Romeo and Juliet,* 740–741

Shang dynasty, *63t, 141t, 181t; 188m;* culture, 189–190; decline of, 191; government and society, 189. *See also* China

Shantytowns, 907

Shariah, *443f,* 445; in Ottoman Empire, 588

shelter, 52; mammoth house, *53f;* pit house, 52

Shia Muslims, *439f,* 449, 591, 592; ethnic conflict, 1020; in Iraq, 1018

Shi Huangdi, 200–203, *201t, 202f,* 205; tomb of, *204f*

Shiji, The, 214–215

Shikibu, Lady Murasaki, *555t,* 567, *567p,* 568, 570–571

Shinto, *560p,* 561, 563

shogun, *555t,* 573, *573f*

short-term effects: identify, 249

shrine, 439; Kaaba, 439, 441

signoria, 720

Sikhism, 157, 158–159, *583t,* 595, *596p;* beliefs and practices, 595–596, *597c;* history, 597–598, *598m;* migration, 598–599

silent barter, 482–483

silk, 212, *212f,* 525–526

Silk Road, 27, *181t,* 216–218, *217m,* 220–221, *303t;* and Buddhism, 165; and Constantinople, 416; reopens, 716–717; and Saharan trade, 479

Silla kingdom, 546, *547f, 548t,*

silt, 67, 70, 106, 144, 186, 187

Sima Qian, 211

Singapore, *995f* Singh, Ranjit, 597–598

Sistine Chapel, *713t*

Six-Day War, 1016, *1017t*

slavery: abolition, 862; in Mauryan society, 167; in Mesopotamia, 75; and plantations, 810–811, *810f;* in Qur'an, 484; and trade routes, 29, 484 in United States, 229, *501f*

slaves: Aztec, 634; in Egypt, *111c,* 122, 130–131, 229; in Ottoman army, 586; in Roman Republic, 341, 343, 348; in Sparta, 272, 274; Spartacus, 348

slave trade, 814

Slavs, 413–414

Slovenia: ethnic conflict, 1039

Smith, Adam, *3t,* 829, *835f*

social contract, 833, *834f, 835f,* 840

social hierarchy: Sumerian, 75

Social Studies Skills: accept social responsibility, 851; analyze costs and benefits, 299; analyze tables, 789; assess primary and secondary sources, 137, 662; chance, error, and oversight in history, 425; conduct Internet research, 219; construct timelines, 947; continuity and change in history, 403; create and interpret databases, 881; determine the context of statements, 551; determine the strength of an argument, 1027; develop and interpret models, 707; develop graphs, 765; identify central issues, 59; identify print research sources, 819; identify short- and long-term effects, 249; interpret charts, 321; interpret culture maps, 657; interpret diagrams, 177; interpret globes, 377; interpret physical maps, 97; make decisions, 511; make maps, 35; research current events, 1081; solve problems, 579; use timelines, 463; use supporting evidence, 979; use visual resources, 911; use vocabulary in a social studies discussion, 739; visualize social studies texts, 605

socialism, 861

society, 47; complex, 69, 120, 152; hunter-gatherer, 47–49

Society of Jesus, 756–757, *757f*

Socrates, 295, *295f, 296i*

soldiers: in Egypt, 121; in Sparta, 272–273, *273f. See also* warriors

Solomon, *63t, 181t, 232t,* 233, *233p;* Book of Proverbs, 238; Temple to God, 233, 234, *234f*

Solon, 265

solve problems, 579

Somalia: as failed state, 1049

Song dynasty, *519m,* 520, 523, 524, *526m,* 531; and civil service, 532–533; inventions, 528–529. *See also* China

Songhai Empire, 493, *494m, 496t, 713t;* Askia the Great, 495–496, *495i, 793t;* government, 496; Morrocan invasion, *467t,* 496–497; Niger River, *495p;* Sunni Ali, 493–494, *713t;* Sunni Baru, 494–495; trade, 496

Sophocles, 287, 288

souk, 434, *436f*

sources: assess, 662; historical, 10–11; primary, 10, 137; secondary, 11, 137

South Africa: ANC, 1006–1007; apartheid, 1006–1008, *1008f*; Boer War, *855t*, 867–868; and containment, 968; democracy, 1010; diamonds, 865, *865f*; Nelson Mandela, *983t*, 1007, *1007f*, *1008f*; sanctions, 1007; townships, 1007

South America: constitutions, 849; European discovery of, 799; independence, *849m*; migration to, 51, *51m*; new government, 849–850; revolutions, 847–848

South Korea, 963–964, *964m*, *995f*

Soviet Union, *885t*, 904; and Afghanistan, *951t*, 967–968; arms race, 959; Berlin airlift, 958–959, *958p*, *958m*; Boris Yeltsin, 975; break up of, 975, *975m*; and China, 971; Cold War, 955; collapse, *951t*, 973–975; collectivization, 922; Cuban Missile Crisis, *951t*, 966, 981 MC1–981 MC2; de-Stalinization, 969; and Eastern Europe, 946; and Germany, 924; Joseph Stalin, *915t*, 921–922, 924, 944, 955, *955p*; Leonid Brezhnev, 970–971, 972, 973; Mikhail Gorbachev, *951t*, 973–975, *974t*, *974p*; Nikita Krushchev, *951t*, 966, 969; satellite states, 956–957, *956m*, 969–971; space exploration, 1051–1052; space race, 960, *960p*; Vladimir Lenin, 903–904, 921; World War II, 926, 927–928, 930, 943

space exploration: cooperation, 1051–1052; International Space Station, 1052, *1052*; shuttle program, 1052; technology, 1053–1054; unmanned missions, 1052–1053, *1053c*

space race, 959–960, *960p*

Spain: conquistadors, 637–638, *745t*, 799–800; civil war, *915t*; Córdoba, *429t*, *452f*, 453; and Cuba, 876–877, 878, *879m*; England defeats Armada, *555t*, *583t*, 802, *802f*; forcing Jews and Muslims out, 702–704, *705m*, 755–756, *756p*; Francisco Franco, *915t*; Golden Age, 755; Inquisition, *745t*, 704–705, *705p*, 756; invaded by Muslim Empire, 449; and Jews, *661t*; and mercantilism, 814; missionaries, *823t*; as a nation-state, 704; and the Philippines, 876, 878, *878m*; ruled by the Moors, 450; and South America, 847–848; Spanish-American War, *855t*, *885t*, 877–878, *878m*, *879m*

Spanish-American War, *855t*, 877–878, *878m*, *879m*

Spanish Civil War, *915t*

Spanish Inquisition, *745t*, 705, *705p*, 756

Sparta, 279; alliance, 277; men, 272–273, *273f*; Persian Wars, 277; Peloponnesian War, 277–278, *278m*; slaves, 272, 274; society, 272–274; women, 274

Spartacus, 348

special-purpose map, 16

specialized vocabulary, 4–5

spheres of influence, 872

sphinxes, 115, *115p*, 126

spy merchants, 631

Sri Lanka, 1045

Stalin, Joseph, *915t*, 921–922, *927f*, 969; Yalta Conference, 944, 954, *955p*

Stalingrad, Battle of, 927–928

Stamp Act, 834

standard of living, 1074

standards, *351p*

steam engine, *855t*, 858

steel, *855t*, 858

steppe, 413

stereotypes: identify, 408

stock market crash, *885t*, 905–906, *915t*

stocks, 28

Stone Age Era: culture, 48–49; Middle, 53; New, 55; Old, 45, 50; tools of, 45, *46c*, 47

Stone Age man, *3t*, 44

Stonehenge, *253t*

storytellers: griots, 498–499, *499p*, *501f*

Strabo, 310

Strategic Arms Limitation Talks (SALT), 972

strength of an argument, 1027

structural patterns, 468–469

stupa, 172

subcontinent, 144

subheadings: previewing text, 254–255

sub-Saharan Africa, 470

Sudan: ethnic conflict, *1031t*, 1009, *1039p*, 1040

Sudetenland, 924

Sudras, 152, *153f*

Suez Canal, *855t*, 866–867, 1014–1015, *1017t*

suffrage: for women, 862

Sufism, *459f*, 459; and poetry, 460

Sui dynasty, *515t*, 519, *519m*, 525, 531, 544. *See also* China

Suleyman I, 588

Sulla, Lucius Cornelius, 347–348, *347f*,

sultan, 587

Sumer, 72; army, 72; art of, 77–79, *78f*; city-states of, 72–73, 74; cultural advances of, 75–76, *101t*; invaders of, 73–74; literature of, 76; religion in, 74; society of, 74–75; technological advances of, 76–77

summarize historical texts, 182–183

Sun Yixian, 989

sundial, 211

Sundiata: ruling Mali, 488–490; the *Sundiata*, 500, 504–505

Sundiata, the, 499, 500, 504–505

Sunnah, 442–444, *443f*

Sunni Ali, *407t*, *467t*, *713t*, 493–494

Sunni Baru, 494–495
Sunni Muslims, *439f*, 449, 591, 592, 1020
supporting evidence, use, 979
supply, 23, *23c*
supply and demand, 23, *23c*, 815–816, *815f*
support of main ideas: understand, 556
surplus, 68, *68f*
sustainable growth, 1064, 1066
sutras, 153–154
Swahili, 509, 510, 1013
symbols: Christian, 399; map, 16
synagogue, 238, 244
Syria: Arab Spring, *1031t*; civil war, *1017t*; Hellenistic, 312–313, *312m*; and Lebanon, 1016–1017; Pact of Umar, 449; refugees, 1047–1048, *1047p*

T

tables: analyze, 789
Tacitus, *3t*
taiga, 413
taiji, 196
Taiwan, *995f*
Taizong, 520
Taj Mahal, *583t, 603p, 604p, 769t, 793t, 823t*
Takrur, 493
Tale of Genji, 555t, 567, *567p,* 568, 570–571
Taliban, 1018
Tallis, Thomas, 726
Talmud, 239, *239f*
Tang dynasty, *429t, 515t,* 519–520, *519m, 526m, 548t;* art and poetry, 526–527, *527f;* city life, 524; inventions, 527–529; Neo-Confucianism, 531; trade, 525. *See also* China
Tanzania: democracy, 1010; first tools found in, 45
Taqi al-Din, 588–589, *588i*
tariff, 34, 996; and GATT, 1076; and NAFTA, 1024, 1077

tax, 33–34; in Ghana Empire, 484–485
technology: 3D printing, 1068–1069, *1068p;* and Columbian Exchange, 808–809, *809f, 810f;* and education, 1055–1056; and the environment, 1061; and exploration, 797, *797f;* and global society, 1056; creating Information Age, 1054–1055; medical, 1067–1068; in Mesolithic Era, 54; in Mesopotamia, 69, 76–77; from space program, 1053–1054; and trade, 27, 218; in World War I, 895
Tehenu, 120
telecommute, 1055
telescope, 781; and Galileo, 778; and Newton, *780f*
temperance, 862
Temple of Apollo, 293
Temple of Karnak, 126
temples: Egyptian, 112, 126, 131; Greek, 281, 293; Indian, 172, *173p*
Temple to God, 233, 234, *234f;* Second, 234, 242–243, *243f*
Ten Commandments, 230–231, 237, 241
Tennessee Valley Authority (TVA), 909
Tenochtitlán, 631, *631m,* 632, *632i,* 636, 638, 639
terra cotta army, *202f, 204f*
terrorism: in failed states, 1050
Thailand: constitutional monarchy, 997
Thales, 297
Thatcher, Margaret, 974
Thebes, 306, 307
theocracy, 32, *32c;* in Arabia, 450; in ancient Egypt, 110–111; economy in a, 33; and the Israelites, 231
Theodora, 417
Theodosius I, *381t, 399t,* 402
theories, 773
Theravada, 165
thermometer, 781
Thermopylae, 95

Theseus, 282, *283f*
Third Estate, 841–842
Thirty Years' War, *745t,* 762–763, *763p*
Thousand and One Nights, The, 460
Thucydides, *3t*
Thutmose I, 131
Tiananmen Square: National Day celebration, *990f;* protest, *997f,* 998
Tiberius, 354
Tiberius Gracchus, 346
Tigris River, 66–67
Tikal, *429t,* 622
Timbuktu, *407t, 467t,* 490, *492f,* 493, *494m;* under Askia the Great, 495–496, *793t*
timeline, 11; interpret, 463
time periods: terms identifying, 4
Titans, 281
Titian, 725
Tlaloc, 635, *635f*
Tojo, Hideki, *927f*
Tokugawa shogun, *555t, 745t, 793t,* 577
tolerance: Muslims, 451
tools: copper, *101t;* geographic, 16; iron, 477; maps, 35; in Mesolithic Era, 53; in Mesopotamia, 69, 77; metal, 69, 77; in Neolithic Era, 55, 57; stone, *39t,* 45, *45p, 46c,* 47, *48f;* timelines, 11
Torah, 238, *239f,* 244, *438f*
torii, *560p*
Torricelli, Evangelista, 781
totalitarianism, 920–921
totalitarian state: Louis XVI's rule, 830
townships, 1007
trade, 26–27; alliance, 277; in Arabia, 434, *435f,* 436, *436f,* 449; between Asia and Europe, 718; Aztec, 630–631; British East India Company, 870–871; in China, 216–218, 220–221, 315, 525–526, 529, 536, 539; and Constantinople, 415, 418; and Columbian Exchange,

806–809; Dutch East India Company, *793t*; in early communities, 57; in Eastern Europe, 412; in Egypt, 112; and Great Zimbabwe, 508, 509; Greek, 257, 258, *258f*, 259, 260, 261; in Harappan society, 148; in Israel, 233; Italian trade cities, 718–720, *719f*; Mayan, 619–621, *620m*; medieval, 678, *678p*; Minoan and Mycenaean, 258, *258f*, 259, *259m*; Olmec, 616; and paper money, 526, 529; in Persia, 93–94; by Phoenicians, *63t*, 88–89; and river travel, 70; role of government in, 34; role of money in, 27–28; in Rome, 357, *357m*, *467t*, in Russia, 422; in Safavid Empire, 594; in Sahara, *467t*, 478–479, *478–479m*; silent barter, 482–483; sub-Saharan; 509; in Sumer, 73, 75; in West Africa, 472, 480, 482–483, *484p*, *492f*, 496

trade agreement, 34; European Union, 1076; NAFTA, 1024, 1077

trade barrier, 34

trade network, 133; of Kushite Dynasty, 133–134, *134m*, 135

trade routes, 27; for Aksum, 135; through Arabia, *429t*, 432, 436; and Buddhism, 165; and Christianity, 27, 135; after the Crusades, 689; drawbacks to, 29; Egyptian, 119, *119m*; Hellenistic kingdoms, 315; Mughal Empire, 601; and exploration, 796, 803, 813–814, *813m*; set by Phoenicia, 89, *253t*; and Renaissance ideas, 718; Silk Road, 27, *181t*, 216–218, *217m*, 220–221, *303t*, 357, 416, 716–717

trade surplus, 996

traditional economy, 25; in early communities, 57

traditions: Jewish, 246–248

Trafalgar, Battle of, 845

Tran dynasty, 550. *See also* Vietnam

transportation: Industrial Revolution advances, 859, *859f*; on water, 77, 797–798, *797f*; and the wheel, 76

Treaty of Versailles, *885t*, 897, 898, *899p*, *899f*

Treaty of Westphalia, 763

Tree of Wisdom, 161

trench warfare, 893, *893f*

triangular trade, 814

tribunes, *337f*, 337–338; Tiberius and Gaius Gracchus, 346

tribute, 190, 623, 630

tripartite government, 336–338, *338f*

Triple Alliance, 892, *892m*. *See also* Central Powers

Triple Entente, 892, *892m*. *See also* Allies

Trojans, *253t*

Trojan War, *253t*, 259; the *Aeneid*, 330; after, 330, *330f*; the *Iliad* and the *Odyssey*, 283, *283f*, 284, 290–291

Truman, Harry S., *915t*

Truman Doctrine, 957

Trung sisters, 549

Tuareg, 493

Tuchman, Barbara, *3t*

tundra, 413

Tunisia: Arab Spring, *1031t*, 1048, independence, 1004

Tunka Manin, 485

Turkey: Çatal Hüyük, *39t*, *56i*, 57, *57i*, 58; and democracy, 1046; Kemal Atatürk, *915t*, 1014, *1015f*

Tutankhamen, King of Egypt, *127f*, 128

Tyndale, William, 752

tyrant, 265–266, *265p*

Tyrian purple, *89f*

U

Ukraine: conflict with Russia, 1048–1049

Umayyad family, 449

Unas, King of Egypt, 116

UN Convention on the Rights of the Child, 1038

understand structural patterns, 468–469

understand support of main ideas, 556

Union of Soviet Socialist Republics, *885t*, 904. *See also* Soviet Union

United Nations, *951t*, 944; and clean water, 1062; Convention on the Rights of the Child, 1038; Covenant on Civil and Political Rights, 1038; Declaration of Commitment on HIV/AIDS, *1031t*, 1072; Declaration of the Rights of Indigenous Peoples, 1042; establishes modern state of Israel, 1016; tribunals, 1040; UN Women, 1037

United States: and abolition, 862; an Allied Power, 927; arms race, 959; Barack Obama, *983t*; Berlin airlift, 958, *958m*; and China, 873, 971; and Cold War, 955, 957, and Cuba, 877, 878, 879, *879m*, 1025; Cuban Missile Crisis, *951t*, 966, 981 MC1–981 MC2; drops atomic bombs on Japan, *915t*, 933, 942, 943; détente, 971; and Enlightenment ideals, 832–836, *833f*, *834f*; government, *270f*, 271, *338f*, 839–840; Great Depression, *885t*, 905–909; and Iran, 1017; and Iraq, 1019; isolationism, 926; and Japan, 874, *874f*; and League of Nations, 897; music of, *501f*; and NAFTA, 1024, 1077; Native American cultures, 650–656; and Panama Canal, 880; Pearl Harbor, *915t*, 926–927, *926f*; and the Philippines, 878,

Index

878m, 880; and philosophy of John Locke, 33; revolutionary war, *823t*, 838–839; 853 MC1–853 MC2, *855t*; and slavery, 229, 862, *501f*; space exploration, 1051–1053, *1053c*; space race, 959–960, *960p*; Spanish-American War, *855t*, *885t*, 877–878, *878m*, *879m*; stock market crash, *885t*, 905–906, *915t*; territories, 879–880; War of 1812, *823t*, *855t*; in World War I, 894, 895, *895c*, 913 MC1–913 MC2; in World War II, *915t*, 926–927, 933, 943, 949 MC1–949 MC2

Universal Declaration of Human Rights, 1035, 1036

universities, 694–696, *695f*; 733

unlimited government, 830–831

untouchables, 153

Upanishads, 151, 156

Upper Egypt, 104, *105m*, 132. *See also* Egypt

Ur, 73, *73m*, 74, 82

Ural Mountains, 410, 414

Uranus, 281

urban, 72; in Harrapan civilization, 146, *146f*

Urban II, Pope, 686

Urban VI, Pope, 682

Ursulines, 757, *757f*

Uses of Geography, 14

use supporting evidence, 979

use timelines, 463

use visual resources, 911

use vocabulary in a social studies discussion, 739

USS *Maine*, *855t*, 877, *877p*

Uzbeks: and Safavids, 592

V

Vaisyas, 152, *153f*

Vandals, 368

van Eyck, Jan, 736

Varnas, 152, *153f*, 163. *See also* caste system

vassal, 674, *674f*, 675

Vedas, 151, 152, 155

Vedic texts, 151, 155; and Buddhism, 162

Venezuela, 1024

Venice, 718, 719, *719f*

veto, 338

Victoria Falls, 20, *20m*

Victory in Europe Day (V-E Day), 941

Victory in Japan Day (V-J Day), 942

Vietcong, 965

Vietnam, 548–550, *548p*, *548t*, *549p*, *951t*; war, 964–965

Vikings: raids by, *429t*, *515t*, *661t*, 671–672, *671m*

Virgil: *The Aeneid*, 330, *330f*, 334–335, 375; in *The Divine Comedy*, 724

Vishnu, 155, *156f*, *173p*

visualize social studies texts, 605

visual resources: use, 911

vocabulary: specialized, 4–5; use in a discussion, 739

volcanoes: on Crete, 258, 262–263; in Greek myth, 282; in Mesoamerica, 612; Mount Fuji, *558p*; Mount Vesuvius, *358p*

Volga River, 412; and trade, 422

Volta, Alessandro, *828p*

Voltaire, 828–829, *828f*

voting: in Athens, 267–268, *267f*; in Roman Republic, 338

W

Walesa, Lech, *977f*

wampum, 654

wants, 26

war crime: of World War II, 944, 946

War of 1812, *823t*, *855t*

Warring States period, *193t*, 194, *194f*, 200

warriors: Aztec, 633, *633i*; the Immortals, 92; knights, 673–674, *674f*, 675–676, *676f*; samurai, 572–573, *573f*, 574–575, *574f*, *575f*, 581 MC1–581 MC2; Zhou dynasty, *194f*

Warsaw ghetto, 936–937; uprising, 938

Warsaw Pact, 959

water: one of the four elements, 57; controlling flow of, 68, *68f*; need for clean, 1062–1063; transportation on, 77. *See also* canals, irrigation

Waterloo, Battle of, 845

Watts, James, *855t*; 858

weather, 13; forecasting technology, 1053–1054

weathering, 13

websites: evaluate, 746–747

West Africa, 470; climate, 472, *473m*; daily life, 475–476; family life in, 473–475, *475f*; French colonies, 1003–1004, *1003m*; Ghana Empire, 481–487, *481m*; iron tools, 477, 481; Niger River, 470–471, *471m*, 481; religion, 476; resources, 472; Songhai Empire, *713t*; trade, 472, 480. *See also* Africa

Western culture: global influence, 1056–1057; influenced by Jewish culture, 240–241

Western Europe: following World War II, 946

White, Tim, 44
Wilhelm, King of Prussia, 890
William of Orange, 838
William the Conqueror, *467t,* *555t,* 675
Wilson, Woodrow, 897, *897p*
Wollstonecraft, Mary, *823t,* 829
women: in Aryan society, 153; in Athens, 276, *276f;* in Bantu society, 508; in Çatal Hüyük, 58; in Egypt, 122; during the Enlightenment, 829; in hunter-gatherer societies, 48; in Hellenistic kingdoms, 317; in Inca Empire, 643; in Israel, 235; in Kush, 135; in Mayan Empire, 623; in medieval Europe, 676, 677; Muslim, 442; in Ottoman Empire, 588; and Renaissance education, 733; in Roman Republic, 338, 340; in samurai families, 574; in Sparta, 274; suffrage for, 862; in Sumer, 75; in West Africa, 474, 475
women's rights, 1036–1037, *1036f,* 1042. *See also* human rights
woodblock printing, 527–528, *527f*
word roots, 714
World Bank, 1079–1080
World Health Organization (WHO), 1070
World Trade Organization (WTO), 1076
World War I, *885t;* alliances, 892, *892m;* Allies victory, 894–896; letters from, 913 MC1–913 MC2; results of, 897–900, *898m;* and Russia's revolution, 904; Treaty of Versailles, *885t,* 897, 898, *899p, 899f;* underlying causes of, 891–893; warfare, 893–896, *893f*

World War II, *915t,* 949 MC1– 949 MC2; Allied Powers, 924, 927, *927f;* Axis Powers, 924, *927f;* battles, 926, 927, 930, 932–933; blitzkrieg, 925; causes of, *945f;* D-Day, 928–929, *928f;* effects of, *945f;* Germany, 924–926; *927f,* 927–928; Great Britain, 925–926, 928; the Holo- caust, 934–939; Italy, 928; Japan, 926; Pacific theater, 930–931, *930m,* 949 MC2; Pearl Harbor, 926–927; Soviet Union, 927–928, *927f;* start of, 924; United States, 926–927, *926f*
World Wide Web, 1055, *1055c*
World Wildlife Fund, 1064
W **questions,** 382
writers: first female, 75; British, 829; Italian, 724–725; Renaissance, 723, 724–725; scribe, 75–76
writing, 42; in China, 189–190, *190f,* 202; codex, 637; devel- opment of, *76c;* in Egypt, 123–125, *123p, 125c, 125p;* Harappan, 148; invention of, 75, *101t;* new forms of, 287–288; Olmec, *616f. See also* drama; fables; literature; poetry
Wu, empress of China, 520, *520f*
Wu Daozi, 526
Wudi, Emperor, 206–207, *207t;* and trade, 216

X

Xavier, Francis, 759
Xenophon, *274f*
Xerxes I, *63t,* 94–96
Xia dynasty, 188–189. *See also* China
Xuanzong, 520

Y

Yalta Conference, 944, 954, *955p*
yang, 196
Yangzi River, 186, 187
Yanukovych, Viktor, 1049
yellow journalism, 877
Yellow River, 186, *186p,* 187
Yeltsin, Boris, 975
yen, *28c*
Yiddish, 246
yin, 196
Yom Kippur, 248
Yousafzai, Malala, *1036f*
yuan, *28c*
Yuan dynasty, *515t, 535f,* 535–537. *See also* China; Kublai Khan; Mongols
Yugoslavia, 1038–1039, *1038m,* 1043
Yunus Emre, 590
Yu the Great, 188

Z

Zaire, 1008, 1009
Zealots, 242, 243–244, *243f*
Zen Buddhism, 569, *569p, 569c;* and samurai, 575
Zhang Heng, 211
Zhang Qian, 216
Zheng He, 538–539, *538f,* 540, *661t*
Zhou dynasty, *101t, 181t, 193t, 193m;* and Confucianism, 195–197; and Daoism, 197–198; decline of, 194; family life in, 193–195; government of, 192–193; and Legalism, 198–199; social order in, 193, *194f. See also* China
Zhu Yuanzhang, 537–538
ziggurat, 77, *78p*
Zika virus, *1031t,* 1070
Zimmermann note, 894–895
Zoroastrianism, 93
Zulu, 868, 869

Credits and Acknowledgments

Text Credits

Excerpt from *The Aeneid* by Virgil, translated by Robert Fitzgerald. Translation copyright © 1980, 1982, 1983 by Robert Fitzgerald. Reprinted by permission of Penelope Fitzgerald for the Estate of Robert Fitzgerald.

Excerpt from "Analects 2:3" from *Chinese Civilization: A Sourcebook*, 2nd Edition. Text copyright © 1993 by Patricia Buckley Ebrey. Reprinted by permission of Simon & Schuster, Inc.

Excerpt from *The Aztecs: A History* by Nigel Davies. Text copyright © 1973 by Nigel Davies. Reprinted by permission of Macmillan Publishers Ltd.

Excerpt from *The Book of the People: Popol Vuh, The National Book of the Ancient Quiché Maya* by Delia Goetz and Sylvanus Griswold Morley. Originally published in Spanish by Adrián Recinos. Text copyright 1954 by University of Oklahoma Press. Reprinted by permission of University of Oklahoma Press.

Excerpt from "Cai Yan and the Poems Attributed to Her" from *Chinese Literature: Essays, Articles, Reviews (CLEAR)* Vol. 5, No. 1/2. Text copyright © 1983 by *Chinese Literature: Essays, Articles, Reviews (CLEAR)*. Reprinted by permission of *Chinese Literature: Essays, Articles, Reviews (CLEAR)*

Excerpt from "Clots of Blood" from *The Koran,* translated with notes by N. J. Dawood. Text copyright © 1956, 1959, 1966, 1968, 1974, 1990, 1993, 1997, 1999 by N. J. Dawood. Reprinted by permission of Penguin Books, Ltd.

Costs of World War II" (retitled from "World-Wide Casualties") by the National World War II Museum (www.nationalww-2museum.org). Copyright © the National World War II Museum. Adapted and reprinted by permission of the National World War II Museum.

Excerpt from *The Epic of Gilgamesh: An English Version with an Introduction by N. K. Sandars*. Text copyright © 1960, 1964, 1972 by N. K. Sandars. Reprinted by permission of Penguin Books Ltd.

"Exodus 20:2–14" from *Tanakh: A New Translation of the Holy Scriptures According to the Traditional Hebrew Text*. Copyright © 1985 by the Jewish Publication Society. Reprinted by permission of the Jewish Publication Society.

Excerpt from "The Festival of the Red Leaves" from *The Tale of Genji* by Lady Murasaki, translated by Arthur Waley. Text copyright © 2000 by Dover Publications Inc. Reprinted by permission of Dover Publications Inc.

Excerpt from *Girl with a Pearl Earring* by Tracy Chevalier. Text copyright © 1999 by Tracy Chevalier. Reprinted by permission of Plume, an imprint of Penguin Group (USA) Inc.

Excerpt from *The Iliad* by Homer, translated by Robert Fitzgerald. Text copyright © 1961, 1963 by Robert Fitzgerald; text copyright renewed © 1989 by Benedict R. C. Fitzgerald, on behalf of the Fitzgerald Children. Reprinted by permission of Ughetta Fitzgerald Lubin for the Fitzgerald Children.

Internet Users in the World by Region, November 2015" by Internet World Stats (www.internetwebstats.com). Copyright © 2001–2016 by Miniwatts Marketing Group. Adapted and reprinted by permission of Miniwatts Marketing Group.

Excerpt from "Heinrich von Treitschke" from *Introduction to Contemporary Civilization in the West* by the staff of Columbia University College. Text copyright © 1946, 1954, 1960 by Columbia University Press. Reprinted by permission of Columbia University Press.

Excerpt from "Isaiah 16–19" from the *Complete Jewish Bible,* translated by David H. Stern. Text copyright © 1998 by David H. Stern. Published by Jewish New Testament Publications, an imprint of Messianic Jewish Publishers. Reprinted by permission of Messianic Jewish Publishers.

Excerpt from "Krina" from *Sundiata: An Epic of Old Mali* by D. T. Niane. Originally published in French by Présence Africaine as *Soundjata, ou L'Epopée Mandingue.* Translated by G. D. Pickett. Text copyright © 2006 by Pearson Education Ltd. Reprinted by permission of Pearson Education Ltd.

Life Expectancy of Selected Countries of the World, 2015" (retitled from "AIDS is Slashing Years off Life Expectancy") by Carl Haub. Copyright © 2001 by the Population Reference Bureau (www.prb.org). Adapted and reprinted by permission of the Population Reference Bureau.

Excerpt from *A Literary History of Persia,* Vol. 4, by Edward G. Browne. Text copyright © 1924, 1959 by Cambridge University Press. Reprinted by permission of Cambridge University Press.

Excerpt from "Luke 10:29–37" from the *New Revised Standard Version of the Bible.* Copyright © 1989 by the Division of Christian Education of the National Council of the Churches of Christ in the USA. All rights reserved. Reprinted by permission of National Council of the Churches of Christ in the USA.

Excerpt from Matthew 5:1–16 from *The New Revised Standard Version of the Bible.* Copyright © 1989 by the Division of Christian Education of the National Council of the Churches of Christ in the USA. Reprinted by permission of National Council of the Churches of Christ in the USA. All rights reserved.

Excerpt from "The Merciful" from *The Koran,* translated with notes by N. J. Dawood (Penguin Books, 1990). Text copyright © 1956, 1959, 1966, 1968, 1974, 1990 by N. J. Dawood. Reprinted by permission of Penguin Books, Ltd.

Excerpt from "Mexico Find Spurs Debate on Earliest 'Writing'" (Mary Pohl quote) by Guy Gugliotta from www.washingtonpost.com, 12/09/2002. Text copyright © 2002 by *The Washington Post.* Reprinted by permission of Pars International Corp.

Excerpt from *The Odyssey* by Homer, translated by Robert Fitzgerald. Text copyright © 1961, 1963 by Robert Fitzgerald; text copyright renewed © 1989 by Benedict R. C. Fitzgerald, on behalf of the Fitzgerald Children. Reprinted by permission of Ughetta Fitzgerald Lubin for the Fitzgerald Children.

Excerpt from "Oldest American Writing Found in Dump" by John Whitfield from www.nature.com, December 6, 2002. Text copyright © 2016 by Macmillan Publishers Ltd. Reprinted by permission of Macmillan Publishers Ltd.

Per Capita GDP for Selected Nations, 2015" (retitled from "World DataBank: World Development Indicators: GDP growth (annual %)") by the World Bank Group (www.worldbank.org). Text copyright © 2016 The World Bank Group. Adapted and reprinted by permission of The World Bank Group.

"Percentage of Population Using the Internet, November 2015" (retitled from "World Internet Usage and Population Statistics") by Internet World Stats (www.internetwebstats.com). Copyright © 2001–2016 by Miniwatts Marketing Group. Adapted and reprinted by permission of Miniwatts Marketing Group.

Excerpt from *Polybius 6.11–18: The Constitution of the Roman Republic.* Translated by John Porter. Text copyright © 1995 by John Porter, University of Saskatchewan. Reprinted by permission of John Porter.

Excerpt from "Proclamation at La Coruña 1808 before the Napoleonic Invasion of Spain." Originally published in Spanish by The Royal Green Jackets as *"Proclama de La Coruña de 1808, ante la invasión Napoleónica en España."* Translated by Caroline Miley. Text copyright by Caroline Miley. Reprinted by permission of Caroline Miley.

"Psalms 23:1–3" from *Tanakh: A New Translation of the Holy Scriptures According to the Traditional Hebrew Text.* Copyright © 1985 by the Jewish Publication Society. Reprinted by permission of the Jewish Publication Society.

"Romans 12:9–18" from *The New Revised Standard Version of the Bible.* Copyright © 1989 by the Division of Christian Education of the National Council of the Churches of Christ in the USA. Reprinted by permission of the National Council of the Churches of Christ in the USA. All rights reserved.

Excerpt from "Search for the First Americans" from *National Geographic*, Vol. 156, No. 3. Text copyright © 1979 by National Geographic Society. Reprinted by permission of National Geographic Society.

Excerpt from "The Shiji" from *Records of the Grand Historian of China, Vol. II: The Age of Emperor Wu*, translated by Burton Watson. Text copyright ©1961 by Columbia University Press. Reprinted by permission of Columbia University Press and by the Research Centre for Translation, The Chinese University of Hong Kong.

Excerpt from "The Sinews of Peace" ("Iron Curtain" speech), March 5, 1946, by Winston Churchill. Text copyright © 1996 by The Churchill Centre. Reprinted by permission of Curtis Brown Group Ltd.

Excerpt from *Survival in Auschwitz* by Primo Levi. Originally published in Italian by The Orion Press as *Se questo è un uomo*. Translated by Stuart Woolf. Text copyright © 1996 by Touchtone Books. Reprinted by permission of Touchtone Books, an imprint of Simon & Schuster Inc.

Excerpt from "We Shall Fight on the Beaches, June 4, 1940" by Winston Churchill. Text copyright © 2016 by Churchill Centre. Reprinted by permission of Curtis Brown Group Ltd.

Excerpt from "Women in Ancient Christianity: The New Discoveries" by Karen L. King from Frontline/PBS Web site: "From Jesus to Christ: The First Christians" at http://www.pbs.org/wgbh/frontline/shows/religion//. New content copyright © 1998 by PBS and WGBH/FRONTLINE. Reprinted by permission of Karen L. King.

Art and Photography Credits

Table of Contents

Ramses II tomb ©Richard Passmore/Stone/Getty Images; *terra-cotta warriors* ©Zhao jian kang/Shutterstock; *camels in desert* ©Getty Images; *Mount Fuji* ©David Ball/Alamy; *Tikal temple* ©craig chiasson/iStockphoto.com/Getty Images; *Mayan carving* ©Trustees of the British Museum, London; *Io, moon of Jupiter* ©Stocktrek/Corbis; *DeWitt Clinton locomotive* Omikron/Getty Images; *Woodrow Wilson* Library of Congress Prints & Photographs Division, Washington, D.C. [LC-USZC2-6247]; *Red Cross poster* Library of Congress Prints & Photographs Division, Washington, D.C. [LC-USZC4-10137]; *Winston Churchill* ©Bettmann/Corbis; *auto assembly line* Photo by Robert Gilhooly/Bloomberg via Getty Images.

Module 1

Clay warriors ©O. Louis Mazzatenta/National Geographic Creative; *Spartan soldier* ©Rolf Richardson/Alamy;

Roman Forum columns ©Christopher Groenhout/Lonely Planet Images/Getty Images; *Napoleon I* Réunion des Musées Nationaux/Art Resource, NY; *Otzi mummy* ©Vienna Report Agency/Sygma/Corbis; *archaeologist* ©STR/Reuters/Corbis; *Aztec bat god* ©Gianni Dagli Orti/Shutterstock; *Chinatown* ©Garry Gay/Alamy; *Big Sur coastline* ©Anne Rippy/Image Bank/Getty Images; *Tanzanian children* ©Corbis; *Victoria Falls* ©Onkelchen/Fotolia; *Himalayas* ©Marta/Fotolia; *Gobi Desert* ©HelloRF Zcool/Shutterstock; *dump truck* Vince Streano/Getty Images; *farmer on tractor* ©Getty Images; *factory worker team* ©Andersen Ross/Getty Images; *woman and bakery* ©Monkey Business Images/Shutterstock; *U.S. dollar* ©Houghton Mifflin Harcourt; *peso* ©Alamy; *euro* ©Alamy; *rupee* ©Shutterstock; *yuan* ©Shutterstock; *yen* ©Shutterstock; *real* ©Shutterstock; *firefighters* ©Getty Images.

Module 2

Lascaux cave painting ©Pierre Vauthey/Sygma/Sygma via Getty Images/Getty Images; *Australopithecus skull* ©Pascal Goetgheluck/Science Source; *wheat* ©Siede Preis/Getty Images; *female head* ©RMN-Grand Palais/Art Resource, NY; *Stone Age tool* ©CM Dixon/Heritage Images/The Print Collector/Alamy; *Homo sapiens skull* ©Pascal Goetgheluck/Science Source; *Mary Leakey* ©Robert I. M. Campbell/National Geographic Society/Image Collection; *Donald Johanson* ©Ferorelli Enterprises, Inc.; *arrowheads* ©DEA/A. Dagli Orti/Getty Images; *Homo erectus skull* ©Pascal Goetgheluck/Science Source; *hand ax* ©John Reader/Science Source; *flint knife* ©Erich Lessing/Art Resource, NY; *surgeons* ©Getty Images; *obsidian arrowhead* ©David R. Frazier Photolibrary, Inc./Alamy; *African cave painting* ©Pierre Vauthey/Sygma/Corbis; *Svaneti Mestia, Georgia* ©Esin Deniz/Shutterstock; *Stonehenge* ©John Nakata/Corbis.

Module 3

Persian palace ruins ©Ramillah/Shutterstock; *Sumerian woman statue* ©Scala/Art Resource, NY; *gold helmet* ©akg-images; *Phoenician vessels* ©DEA/A. DAGLI ORTI/Getty Images; *Harappan seal* ©Borromeo/Art Resource, NY; *Solomon portrait* ©Erich Lessing/Art Resource, NY; *Confucius statue* ©VanniArchive/Art Resource, NY; *pyramid* ©Carmen Redondo/Corbis; *river travel* ©Nik Wheeler/Corbis; *man designing tiles* ©Corbis; *woman working in field* ©Lowell Georgia/Corbis; *cuneiform tablet* ©DEA/Gianni Dagli Orti/Getty Images; *Sumerian plow* ©Dorling Kindersley/Getty Images; *cylinder seals* ©Mesopotamian/The Art Gallery Collection/Alamy; *silver lyre* ©Erich Lessing/Art Resource, NY; *Sumerian bull head* ©DEA Picture Library/De Agostini/Getty Images; *gold dagger* ©The Print Collector/Heritage Images/

Alamy; *Gilgamesh statue* ©Erich Lessing/Art Resource, NY; *Assyrian army relief* ©Gianni Dagli Orti/The Picture Desk Limited/Corbis; *Byzantine mosaic* ©World History Archive/Alamy; *Darius* ©SEF/Art Resource, NY; *Greek vase with battle scene* ©Erich Lessing/Art Resource, NY.

Module 4

Ramses II tomb ©Richard Passmore/Stone/Getty Images; *Egyptian wooden boat model* ©Bridgeman Images; *Sumerian tablet* ©Erich Lessing/Art Resource, NY; *jadeite Olmec god* ©Erich Lessing/Art Resource, NY; *Ramses II* DEA PICTURE LIBRARY/Getty Images; *agriculture along Nile* ©Reza/Webistan/Corbis; *tomb painting* ©Erich Lessing/Art Resource, NY; *farmer plowing field* ©Josef Polleross/The Image Works; *Anubis* The Bridgeman Art Library International; *canopic jars* ©The Trustees of The British Museum/Art Resource, NY; *mummy* ©British Museum, London, UK/The Bridgeman Art Library; *afterlife in ancient Egypt* ©Musee du Louvre, Paris/SuperStock; *Great Sphinx and Great Pyramid of Giza* ©LouieLea/Shutterstock; *perfume oil base* ©Gianni Dagli Orti/Corbis; *Egyptian model* ©Gianni Dagli Orti/Shutterstock; *hieroglyphics* ©DEA/G. DAGLI ORTI/De Agostini/Getty Images; *Book of the Dead* ©The Trustees of the British Museum/Art Resource, NY; *Tutankhamun chair engraving* ©Robert Harding Picture Library; *Tutankhamen tomb interior* ©Scala/Art Resource, NY; *Howard Carter* ©Time Life Pictures/Getty Images; *throne of Tutankhamen* ©Reed Kaestner/Corbis; *King Tut mask* ©Egyptian National Museum, Cairo, Egypt/SuperStock; *Nile River* ©De Agostini/C. Sappa/Getty Images; *Kush pyramids* ©Cavan Images.

Module 5

Swaminarayan Akshardham temple, New Delhi ©Dinodia Photos/Getty Images; *Shiva* ©The Trustees of the British Museum/Art Resource, NY; *bronze tigress* DEA/G. DAGLI ORTI/Getty Images; *Gupta sculpture* ©Réunion des Musées Nationaux/Art Resource, NY; *Alexander the Great* ©Archivo Iconografico, S.A./Corbis; *burial urn* ©Anders Blomqvist/Alamy; *animal seal* ©Borromeo/Art Resource, NY; *Brahma* ©Burstein Collection/Corbis; *Shiva* ©Borromeo/Art Resource, NY; *Vishnu* ©V&A Images, London/Art Resource, NY; *Hindu ceremony* ©Ajit Solanki/AP Images; *Mohandas Gandhi* ©Bettmann/Corbis; *Martin Luther King Jr.* ©Flip Schulke/Corbis; *Cesar Chavez* ©Najlah Feanny Hicks; *Prince Siddhartha painting* ©Gilles Mermet/akg-images; *Siddhartha* ©Godong/Alamy; *Great Buddha statue* ©Luciano Mortula/Shutterstock; *Buddhist students in Sri Lanka* Sena Vidanagama/AFP/Getty Images; *Gupta painting* ©SEF/Art Resource, NY; *Kesava Temple engraving (inset)* ©Lindsay Hebberd/Corbis; *Kesava Temple* ©Sheldan Collins/Corbis; *Gupta*

Module 11

Vatican City ©Vittoriano Rastelli/Getty Images; *Jesus Christ icon* ©Gianni Dagli Orti/The Art Archive at Art Resource, NY; *Buddha statue* Photo ©Juergen Liepe. Museum fuer Asiatische Kunst/Staatliche Museen zu Berlin/Art Resource, NY; *Christians fighting lions* ©akg-images; *Mayan artifact* ©Erich Lessing/Art Resource, NY; *Constantine bust* ©Scala/Art Resource, NY; *Pantheon* ©James L. Stanfield/National Geographic Image Collection; *Fortress of Masada* ©Nathan Benn; *Arch of Titus* The Sack of Jerusalem in AD 70, detail from the Arch of Titus, c. AD 81 (carved stone) (detail of: 84299)/Forum, Rome, Italy/Index/Bridgeman Images; *Adoration of the Magi* ©Alfredo Dagli Orti/Shutterstock; *Nativity* ©Howie McCormick, The Ironton Tribune/AP Images; *The Last Supper* ©Alinari/Art Resource, NY; *Duccio (Jesus with followers)* ©Scala/Art Resource, NY; *St. Paul* ©Johnny van Haeften Gallery, London, UK/The Bridgeman Art Library; *statue of Jesus carrying cross* ©Elio Ciol; *persecution of Christians by Romans* ©Phillips, The International Fine Art Auctioneers; *Theodosius* ©Werner Forman/Universal Images Group/Getty Images.

Module 12

Hagia Sophia ©swisshippo/Fotolia; *Qur'an with ornate cover* ©Gyuszko-Photo/Shutterstock; *St. Sophia Cathedral* ©Kirill Volkov/Shutterstock; *Tomb of Askia* ©Werner Forman/Art Resource, NY; *Carpathian Mountains* ©George Dolgikh/Shutterstock; *Vistula River* ©Pawel Kielpinski/Shutterstock; *Mount Kazbek* Artur Synenko/Fotolia; *Byzantine church* Olga Lipatova/Cutcaster; *Russian chalice* ©Fine Art/Corbis Historical/Getty Images; *St. Sophia Cathedral interior* ©RIA Novosti/Alamy Images; *Russian icon* ©Artem Efimov/Shutterstock.

Module 13

Great Mosque of Mecca ©Mike Nelson/EPA/Shutterstock; *Arab merchants* Scala/Art Resource, NY; *mosques at Medina and Mecca* ©Fitzwilliam Museum, University of Cambridge, UK/The Bridgeman Art Library; *Prince Shotoku* ©Bettmann/Corbis; *Tang dynasty sculpture* ©RMN-Grand Palais/Art Resource, NY; *camels in desert* ©Getty Images; *souk* ©Globe Stock/Alamy; *Hebrew scroll* Topham/The Image Works, Inc.; *Bible* ©akg-images; *Qur'an* ©Gyuszko-Photo/Shutterstock; *door with Fatimah's hand* ©John and Lisa Merrill/Getty Images; *Muslim children* ©AFP/Getty Images; *Qur'anic verse* ©Gianni Dagli Orti/Shutterstock; *Arab trade* Mary Evans Picture Library; *Mosque of Córdoba* ©Vanni Archive/Corbis; *Islamic map* The Granger Collection, New York; *Great Mosque interior* ©Ian Dagnall/Alamy; *Muslim women pilgrims praying* ©Mike Nelson/EPA/Shutterstock; *man in wheelchair on hajj* ©Kamran Jebrelli/AP Images; *Indonesian women on hajj* ©Vahed Salemi/AP Images; *two Saudi Arabian men* AFP/Getty Images; *astrolabe* ©Bibliotheque Nationale de Cartes et Plans, Paris, France/The Bridgeman Art Library; *Jantar Mantar* ©Huw Jones/Getty Images; *Dioscorides Materia* ©Werner Forman/Getty Images; *whirling dervishes* Ritual of the whirling dervishes at Konya (vellum), Ottoman School (17th century) Private Collection/©Bridgeman Images; Blue Mosque interior 1Apix/Alamy; *man reading Qur'an* ©Images & Stories/Alamy; *Blue Mosque detail tiles* ©David Coleman/Alamy.

Module 14

Women in front of mosque ©Glen Allison/PhotoDisc/Getty Images; *Nok terra-cotta head* ©Werner Forman/Art Resource, NY; *camel* G K & Vikki Hart/Image Bank/Getty Images; *ship relief* ©Erich Lessing/Art Resource, NY; *Kublai Khan* ©The Art Archive at Art Resource, NY; *Qur'an manuscript* Erich Lessing/Art Resource, NY; *Tomb of Askia* ©Werner Forman/Art Resource, NY; *double-headed serpent artifact* ©The Trustees of the British Museum/Art Resource, NY; *Sahara* ©Frans Lemmens/Corbis Unreleased/Getty Images; *savannah* ©Nicholas Parfitt/Stone/Getty Images; *rain forest* ©Gary Cook/Alamy; *Nigerian village* Rossi Xavier/Gamma Press, Inc.; *Nigerois women* ©Daniel Berehulak/Getty Images; *Nok terra-cotta sculpture* Photo by DeAgostini/Getty Images; *rock salt market* ©Nik Wheeler/Corbis; *sun pendant* ©Alfredo Dagli Orti/Shutterstock; *objects from Akan* ©Aldo Tutino/Art Resource, NY; *ivory pendant* ©Alfredo Dagli Orti/Shutterstock; *embroidery panel* HIP/Scala/Art Resource, NY; *spices* ©Reza/Webistan/Corbis; *human-snake head statuette* Dr. Roderick McIntosh; *rock salt market* ©John Elk III/Alamy; *Adowa dancer* ©Robert Estall photo agency/Alamy; *African market* ©oversnap/iStock Unreleased/Getty Images; *cattle* Steve McCurry/Magnum Photos; *horse and rider* Djenné, Mali (terra-cotta), African School/Private Collection/Photo ©Heini Schneebeli/Bridgeman Images; *Mansa Musa atlas* ©Sarin Images/Granger, NYC; *Moroccan coin* ©bpk Bildagentur/Musee du Quai Branly/Jacques Chirac/Art Resource, NY; *Niger River* ©Sandro Vannini/Corbis; *storyteller* ©Cavan Images; *West African musician* ©AFP/Getty Images; *women weaving baskets* ©Penny Tweedie/Corbis; *blanket* The Newark Museum/Art Resource, NY; *Christian church at Lalibela* ©Dave Bartruff/Getty Images; *ruins of Great Zimbabwe* ©Jupiterimages/Getty Images.

Module 15

Forbidden City ©Free Agents Limited/Corbis; *Qur'an* itani Images/Alamy; *bronze dragon* ©Corbis; *Tale of Genji* ©The Trustees of the Chester Beatty Library, Dublin/The Bridgeman Art Library; *Genghis Khan painting* ©The Gallery Collection/Corbis; *rat* ©GK Hart/Vikki Hart/PhotoDisc/Getty Images;) *lion sculpture* Freelance Consulting Services Pty Ltd/Corbis; *Grand Buddha statue* JoeyPhoto/Shutterstock; *rice field* ©China Span/Keren Su/Alamy; *rice harvest* Keren Su/Corbis; *Grand Canal barges* ©Carl & Ann Purcell/Corbis; *porcelain jar* ©Paul Freeman/Private Collection/The Bridgeman Art Library; *dragon with fireworks* ©China Photo/Reuters/Corbis; *ancient compass* ©Yi Lu/Corbis; *paying for gas* ©Tom Stewart/Corbis; *Khan bank note (inset)* ©Private Collection/The Bridgeman Art Library; *painting showing Confucian education* Traditionally attributed to: Yan Liben, Chinese, died in 673. Denman Waldo Ross Collection. 31.123/Museum of Fine Arts, Boston; *civil service exam art* Snark/Art Resource, NY; *Kublai Khan on horseback* National Palace Museum, Taipei, Taiwan/Bridgeman Art Library; *Great Wall of China* ©Keren Su/Corbis/NX/Getty Images; *Changdeokgung Palace* ©Photo courtesy of Andrew Miles; *Buddha statue* ©Photo Courtesy of Andrew Miles; *celadon porcelain* ©Topic Photo Agency/Corbis; *gold crown* ©De Agostini/Getty Images; *bronze bell* ©Werner Forman/Universal Images Group/Getty Images; *Buddhist scriptures* ©H Kim/National Geographic/Getty Images; *Vietnam* ©Body Philippe/hemis.fr/Getty Images; *Ly Dai Hanh statue* ©David South/Alamy Images.

Module 16

Mount Fuji ©David Ball/Alamy; *Buddha of Kamakura* ©Corbis; *Prince Shotoku* ©Bettmann/Corbis; *Murasaki Shikibu* ©Art Archive; *Mongol on horseback* (Detail) Bibliotheque Nationale, Paris, France/Bridgeman Art Library; *Yoritomo* National Museum, Tokyo/A.K.G., Berlin/SuperStock; *sea battle* ©Erich Lessing/Art Resource, NY; *Mount Fuji* Spectrum Colour Library; *Japanese screen* Erich Lessing/Art Resource, NY; *early Japanese writing* ©The Picture Art Collection/Alamy; *Confucius* The Granger Collection, NYC; *Buddha* ©Corbis; *Horyuji Temple* ©Kenneth Hamm/Photo Japan; *Buddha in Horyuji Temple* ©J Marshall/Tribaleye Images/Alamy; *fan* ©Burstein Collection/Corbis; *The Tale of Genji* The Tale of Genji, c12th (drawing), Takayoshi, Fujiwara (c. 1127–1179)/Tokugawa Reimeikai Foundation, Tokyo, Japan/Photo ©AISA/The Bridgeman Art Library; *wooden Buddha statue* ©Sakamoto Photo Research Laboratory/Corbis; *Zen garden* ©Catherine Karnow/Corbis; *Heian Court* Sekai Bunka Photo/Ancient Art & Architecture Collection, Ltd.; *Legend of Huge Hoju no Tama* ©Roger Viollet/Getty Images; *samurai writing on tree* ©Fitzwilliam Museum, University of Cambridge, UK/The Bridgeman Art Library; *woodcut of Kabuki actor* Werner Forman/Art Resource, NY; *Kendo class* Kenneth Hamm/Photo Japan;

Bacon ©Sotheby's/akg-images; *Rene Descartes* Erich Lessing/Art Resource, NY; *Galileo on trial* ©RMN-Grand Palais/Art Resource, NY; *Italian scientist* Scala/Art Resource, NY.

Module 23

Columbus's ship replica Image courtesy of NASA/Kennedy Space Center; *compass* ©National Maritime Museum, London, UK/The Bridgeman Art Library; *Tomb of Askia* ©Werner Forman/Art Resource, NY; *Magellan* Réunion des Musées Nationaux/Art Resource, NY; *Taj Mahal* Dave Jacobs/Getty Images; *Christopher Columbus* SuperStock; *constellation* Cetus the Whale, from *Atlas Coelestis* by John Flamsteed (1646–1719), pub. in 1729 (hand-colored engraving), Thornhill, James (1675–1734) (after)/Private Collection/The Stapleton Collection/Bridgeman Images; *world map of Atlantic coastlines* ©Royalty Free/Corbis; *1650 map of North America* ©Corbis; *1820 map of United States* ©The Granger Collection, NYC; *hamburger* Victoria Smith/HMH; *Girl with Pearl Earring* ©Scala/Art Resource, NY; *Ponce de León* ©Cummer Museum of Art & Gardens/SuperStock; *Caribbean Island Encounters, Claiming Florida for Spain, Ponce de León's 1513 Route* ©2010 A&E Television Networks, LLC. All rights reserved.

Module 24

Revolutionary War reenactment Photo by Rich Lipski/The Washington Post/Getty Images; *John Locke* Portrait of John Locke (1632–1704), Kneller, Godfrey (1646–1723) (after)/Private Collection/Photo ©Philip Mould Ltd, London/Bridgeman Images; *royal procession with elephants* Burstein Collection/Corbis; *Mary Wollstonecraft* ©Tate Gallery, London/Art Resource, NY; *capture of the Bastille* ©Active Museum/Le Pictorium/Alamy; *Santa Barbara monastery* ©Cedric Weber/Shutterstock; *Charlemagne crown* Réunion des Musées Nationaux/Art Resource, NY; *Volta's experiment* Scala/Art Resource, NY; *King Louis XIV* Library of Congress Prints & Photographs Division, Washington, D.C. [LC-USZ62-124397]; *Catherine the Great* ©Erich Lessing/Art Resource, NY; *Locke* The Granger Collection, New York; *Montesquieu* ©Stefano Bianchetti/Corbis; *Rousseau* Réunion des Musées Nationaux/Art Resource, NY; *King George III* ©Christopher Hurst/NTPL/Alamy; *signing Magna Carta* ©Bettmann/Corbis; *Washington on the Delaware* ©The Metropolitan Museum of Art/Bridgeman Art Library; *signing the Declaration of Independence* ©Bettmann/Getty Images; *Parliament* ©The Granger Collection, NYC; *Magna Carta* Magna Carta, the final version issued in 1225 by Henry III (vellum), English School (13th century)/National Archives, UK/Bridgeman Images; *English Bill of Rights* ©ART Collection/Alamy; *Declaration of Independence* ©Joseph Sohm/Visions of America/Corbis; *French Declaration* ©Centre historique des Archives nationales; *women marching on Versailles 1789* ©Stock Montage, Inc/

Alamy; *Oath of the Tennis Court* ©RMN-Grand Palais/Art Resource, NY; *Napoleon I* Réunion des Musées Nationaux/Art Resource, NY; *Revolutionary War troops* ©Ted Spiegel/Corbis; *Seeds of Revolution, Independence!, Victory!* ©2010 A&E Television Networks, LLC. All rights reserved.

Module 25

DeWitt Clinton locomotive Omikron/Getty Images; *steam engine* Hulton-Deutsch Collection/Corbis; *Matthew Perry in Tokyo harbor* ©The British Museum, London, UK/The Bridgeman Art Library; *Bessemer furnace* The Granger Collection, New York; *USS Maine explosion* Bettmann/Getty Images; *flying shuttle loom* The Granger Collection, New York; *spinning jenny* ©Bettmann/Corbis; *cotton gin* ©Bettmann/Getty Images; *Hay Wain* The Art Archive/National Gallery, London/John Webb; *barrels in street* Snark/Art Resource, NY; *ivory trade, Zanzibar* ©Bojan Brecelj/Corbis Historical/Getty Images; *diamond mining* ©Mary Evans Picture Library/The Image Works; *examining diamonds* ©James P. Blair/National Geographic Image Collection; *Battle of Adwa* The Abyssinians routing the Italian troops, scene from the Italian invasion of Abyssinia in 1896 (gouache on paper), Ethiopian School (20th century)/Private Collection/Archives Charmet/Bridgeman Images; *Zulu king* "King Cetshwayo, (Cetewayo) King of the Zulus," by Carl Rudolph Sohn, 1882; *Edward, Prince of Wales* Roy Miles Fine Paintings/Bridgeman Art Library; *José Martí* ©Bettmann/Getty Images; *William McKinley* White House Historical Association.

Module 26

Soldiers in trench Photo by adoc-photos/Corbis via Getty Images; *German victory statue* ©David Bartruff/Corbis; *French newspaper* ©Archive for Art and History, Berlin/A.K.G., Berlin/SuperStock; *Lenin statue* ©Smalik/Fotolia; *Adolf Hitler* ©Bettmann/Getty Images; *Otto von Bismarck* ©Everett Historical/Shutterstock; *assassination of Archduke Franz Ferdinand* The Art Archive/Bibliothèque des Arts Décoratifs Paris/Marc Charmet/The Art Archive; *propaganda poster* Library of Congress Prints & Photographs Division, Washington, D.C. [LC-USZC4-1502]; *Woodrow Wilson* Library of Congress Prints & Photographs Division, Washington, D.C. [LC-USZC2-6247]; *Treaty of Versailles* ©Everett Historical/Shutterstock; *Czar Nicholas II and family* Library of Congress Prints & Photographs Division, Washington, D.C. [LC-DIG-ggbain-14545]; *Karl Marx* Georgios Kollidas/Fotolia; *Lenin stamp* Svetlana T/Shutterstock; *soup kitchen* ©Everett Historical/Shutterstock; *steam shovel* ©Everett Historical/Shutterstock; *canned goods poster* Library of Congress Prints & Photographs Division, Washington, D.C. [LC-USZC4-10671]; *Red Cross poster* Library of Congress Prints &

Photographs Division, Washington, D.C. [LC-USZC4-10137]; *Teamwork Wins poster* Library of Congress Prints & Photographs Division, Washington, D.C. [LC-USZC4-9879]; *soldier in trench* ©Bettmann/Corbis; *Over There, War on the Western Front, Surrender!* ©2010 A&E Television Networks, LLC. All rights reserved.

Module 27

Iwo Jima flag raising National Archives at College Park, Still Pictures (RDSS); *Mussolini* ©Bettmann/Getty Images; *Gandhi portrait* ©Mahatma Gandhi (b/w photo), Indian Photographer, (20th century)/Private Collection/Dinodia/Bridgeman Images; *Adolf Hitler* Bettmann/Getty Images; *Mao Zedong* ©Hung Chung Chih/Shutterstock; *mushroom cloud* ©Bettmann/Getty Images; *War Bonds poster* Library of Congress Prints & Photographs Division, Washington, D.C. [LC-DIG-ppmsca-43383]; *Mussolini speech* Photo12/UIG via Getty Images; *Hitler Youth* ©Photos.com/Getty Images Plus/Getty Images; *deported peasants* ©Sovfoto/UIG via Getty Images; *Japanese invasion of Nanking* ©Everett Historical/Shutterstock; *German troops invade Poland* ©Everett Historical/Shutterstock; *Winston Churchill* Library of Congress Prints & Photographs Division, Washington, D.C. [LC-USZ62-64419]; *Pearl Harbor* The Art Archive/National Archives, Washington, D.C.; *Winston Churchill* ©Bettmann/Corbis; *Franklin D. Roosevelt* ©Bettmann/Corbis; *Joseph Stalin* ©Bettmann/Getty Images; *Hideki Tojo* ©Corbis; *Omaha Beach* ©Everett Historical/Shutterstock; *tank* Photos12.com, Collection Bernard Crochet; *battleships* ©AP Images; *background (sky), fighter jets* U.S. Air Force/AP/Wide World Photos; *German Jewish families* United States Holocaust Memorial Museum, Washington, D.C.; *Dachau* United States Holocaust Memorial Museum, Washington, D.C.; *Jewish men in Warsaw ghetto* Universal History Archive/UIG via Getty Images; *Anne Frank* ©akg-images; *concentration camp survivors* Photo by Margaret Bourke-White/The LIFE Picture Collection/Getty Images; *V-E Day* Universal History Archive/UIG via Getty Images; *Hiroshima Memorial Park* ©Eriko Sugita/Reuters; *Japanese surrender* Popperfoto/Getty Images; *Douglas MacArthur* Library of Congress Prints & Photographs Division, Washington, D.C. [LC-USZ62-21027]; *amphibious landing* Library of Congress Prints & Photographs Division, Washington, D.C. [LC-USZC4-4731]; *America Mobilizes for War, Air War Over Germany, The Pacific Islands* ©2010 A&E Television Networks, LLC. All rights reserved.

Module 28

Fall of Berlin Wall Thomas Kienzle/AP/Wide World Photos; *Berlin airlift* Photo12/UIG via Getty Images; *Mao Zedong* ©Hung Chung Chih/Shutterstock; *Fidel Castro* Hulton Archive/Getty Images; *Chinese Cultural Revolution poster* The Advertising Archives/Alamy Stock Photo;